Rick Steves®

SCANDINAVIAN & NORTHERN EUROPEAN CRUISE PORTS

Rick Steves with Cameron Hewitt

CONTENTS

Northern Europe

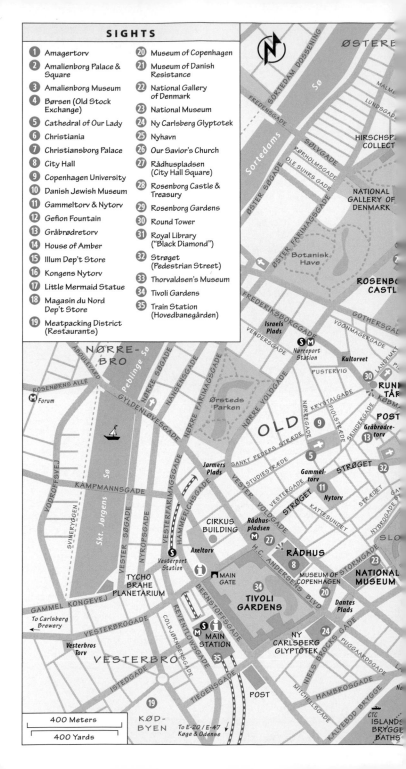

SIGHTS

1. Amagertorv
2. Amalienborg Palace & Square
3. Amalienborg Museum
4. Børsen (Old Stock Exchange)
5. Cathedral of Our Lady
6. Christiania
7. Christiansborg Palace
8. City Hall
9. Copenhagen University
10. Danish Jewish Museum
11. Gammeltorv & Nytorv
12. Gefion Fountain
13. Gråbrødretorv
14. House of Amber
15. Illum Dep't Store
16. Kongens Nytorv
17. Little Mermaid Statue
18. Magasin du Nord Dep't Store
19. Meatpacking District (Restaurants)
20. Museum of Copenhagen
21. Museum of Danish Resistance
22. National Gallery of Denmark
23. National Museum
24. Ny Carlsberg Glyptotek
25. Nyhavn
26. Our Savior's Church
27. Rådhuspladsen (City Hall Square)
28. Rosenborg Castle & Treasury
29. Rosenborg Gardens
30. Round Tower
31. Royal Library ("Black Diamond")
32. Strøget (Pedestrian Street)
33. Thorvaldsen's Museum
34. Tivoli Gardens
35. Train Station (Hovedbanegården)

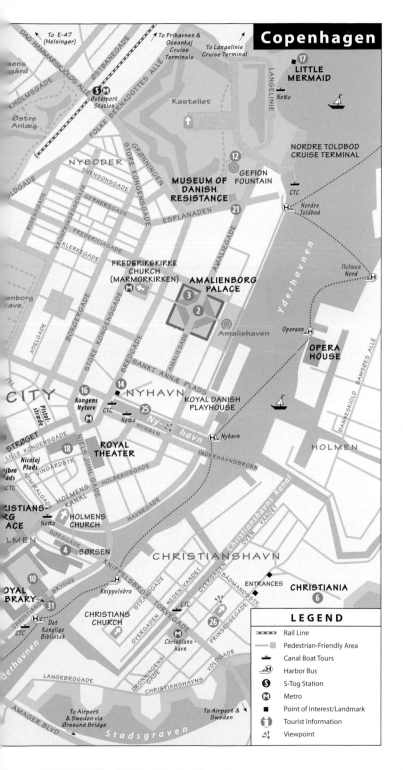

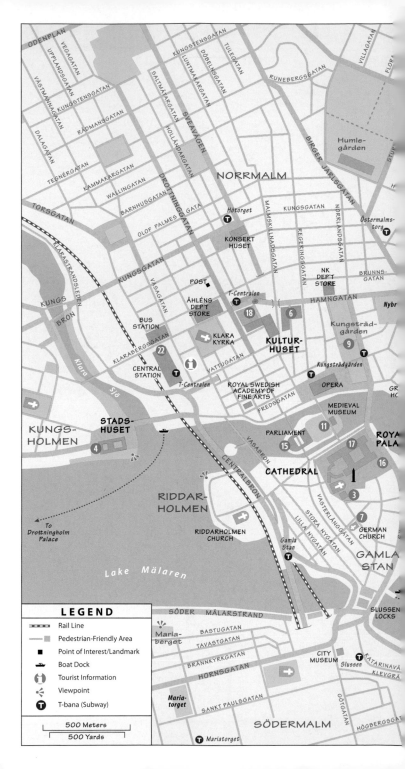

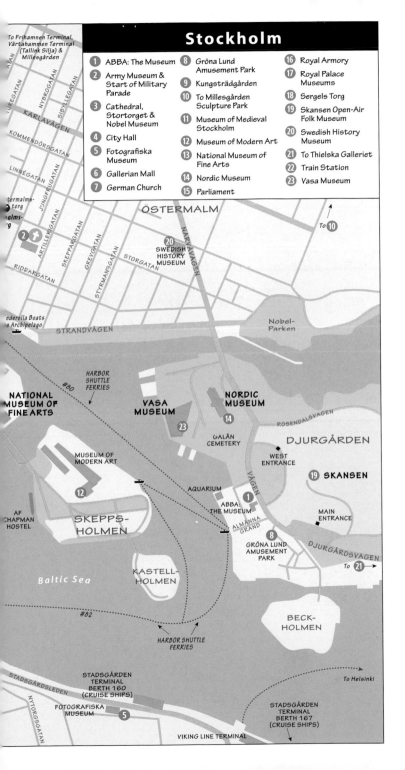

Stockholm

1. ABBA: The Museum
2. Army Museum & Start of Military Parade
3. Cathedral, Stortorget & Nobel Museum
4. City Hall
5. Fotografiska Museum
6. Gallerian Mall
7. German Church
8. Gröna Lund Amusement Park
9. Kungsträdgården
10. To Millesgården Sculpture Park
11. Museum of Medieval Stockholm
12. Museum of Modern Art
13. National Museum of Fine Arts
14. Nordic Museum
15. Parliament
16. Royal Armory
17. Royal Palace Museums
18. Sergels Torg
19. Skansen Open-Air Folk Museum
20. Swedish History Museum
21. To Thielska Galleriet
22. Train Station
23. Vasa Museum

To Frihamnen Terminal, Värtahammen Terminal (Tallink Silja) & Millesgården

ÖSTERMALM

To 10

SWEDISH HISTORY MUSEUM

Nobel-Parken

nderella Boats o Archipelago

STRANDVÄGEN

HARBOR SHUTTLE FERRIES

NATIONAL MUSEUM OF FINE ARTS

VASA MUSEUM

NORDIC MUSEUM

ROSENDALSVÄGEN

GALÄN CEMETERY

DJURGÅRDEN

WEST ENTRANCE

SKANSEN

AQUARIUM

MUSEUM OF MODERN ART

ABBA: THE MUSEUM

MAIN ENTRANCE

AF CHAPMAN HOSTEL

SKEPPS-HOLMEN

ALMÄNNA GRAND

GRÖNA LUND AMUSEMENT PARK

DJURGÅRDSVÄGEN

To 21

Baltic Sea

KASTELL-HOLMEN

BECK-HOLMEN

#82

HARBOR SHUTTLE FERRIES

To Helsinki

STADSGÅRDSLEDEN

STADSGÅRDEN TERMINAL BERTH 160 (CRUISE SHIPS)

FOTOGRAFISKA MUSEUM

STADSGÅRDEN TERMINAL BERTH 167 (CRUISE SHIPS)

VIKING LINE TERMINAL

Street names on map: KARLAVÄGEN, NYBROGATAN, SIBYLLEGATAN, KOMMENDÖRSGATAN, LINNÉGATAN, ARTILLERIGATAN, SKEPPARGATAN, GREVGATAN, STYRMANSGATAN, STORGATAN, RIDDARGATAN, NARVAVÄGEN, termalms-torg, alms-g, NYTORGSGATAN

Helsinki

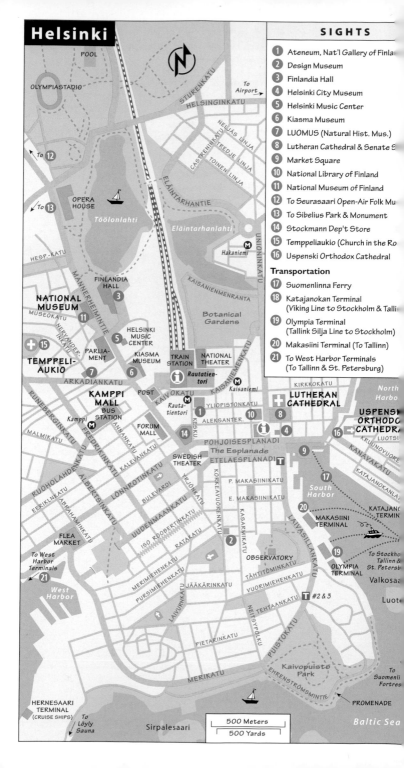

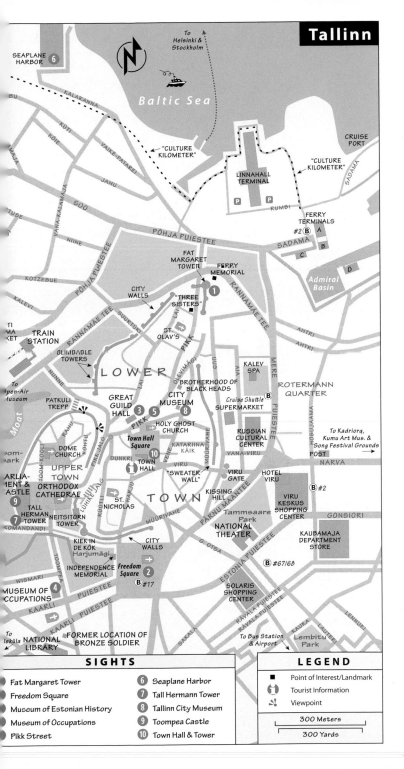

Tallinn

To Helsinki & Stockholm

Baltic Sea

"CULTURE KILOMETER"

"CULTURE KILOMETER"

CRUISE PORT

LINNAHALL TERMINAL

FERRY TERMINALS
#2 Ⓑ   A
B
C
D

Admiral Basin

SADAMA

PÕHJA PUIESTEE

FAT MARGARET TOWER

FERRY MEMORIAL ❶

RANNAMÄE TEE

CITY WALLS

"THREE SISTERS"

ST. OLAV'S

KALEV SPA

ROTERMANN QUARTER

OLEVIMÄGI

BROTHERHOOD OF BLACK HEADS

CITY MUSEUM

Cruise Shuttle Ⓑ
SUPERMARKET

RUSSIAN CULTURAL CENTER

TRAIN STATION

OLÜMPIADE TOWERS

LOWER

To Open-Air Museum

PATKULI TREPP

GREAT GUILD HALL

❸ ❺

PIKK

HOLY GHOST CHURCH

❽

KATARIINA KÄIK

Town Hall Square

❿

TOWN HALL ❶

"SWEATER WALL"

VIRU GATE

HOTEL VIRU

KISSING HILL

VIRU KESKUS SHOPPING CENTER

GONSIORI

KAUBAMAJA DEPARTMENT STORE

To Kadriorg, Kumu Art Mus. & Song Festival Grounds

POST

NARVA

Ⓑ #2

DOME CHURCH

PARLIA-MENT & CASTLE

❾

ORTHODOX CATHEDRAL

UPPER TOWN

TALL HERMAN TOWER ❼

NEITSITORN TOWER

KOMANDANDI

ST. NICHOLAS

TOWN

Tammsaare Park

NATIONAL THEATER

KIEK IN DE KÖK Harjumägi

INDEPENDENCE MEMORIAL

Freedom Square ❷

Ⓑ #17

CITY WALLS

WISMARI

MUSEUM OF OCCUPATIONS ❹

KAARLI

KAARLI PUIESTEE

To Ieküla NATIONAL LIBRARY

FORMER LOCATION OF BRONZE SOLDIER

Ⓑ #67/68

SOLARIS SHOPPING CENTER

To Bus Station & Airport

Lembitu Park

RAVALA PUIESTEE

SIGHTS

❶ Fat Margaret Tower		❻ Seaplane Harbor	
❷ Freedom Square		❼ Tall Hermann Tower	
❸ Museum of Estonian History		❽ Tallinn City Museum	
❹ Museum of Occupations		❾ Toompea Castle	
❺ Pikk Street		❿ Town Hall & Tower	

LEGEND

- ■ Point of Interest/Landmark
- ✚ Tourist Information
- ⚐ Viewpoint

300 Meters

300 Yards

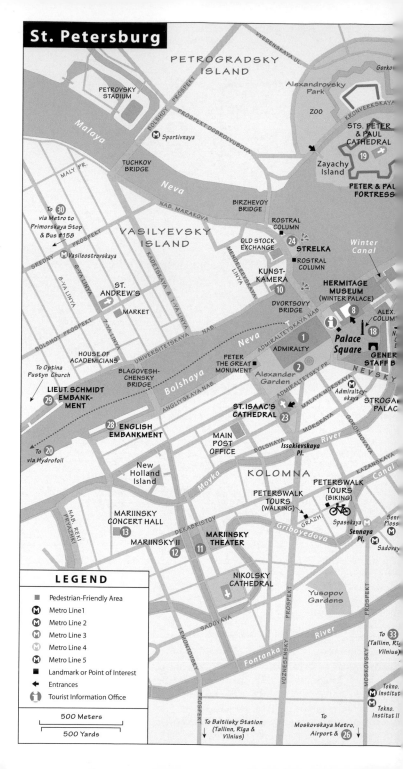

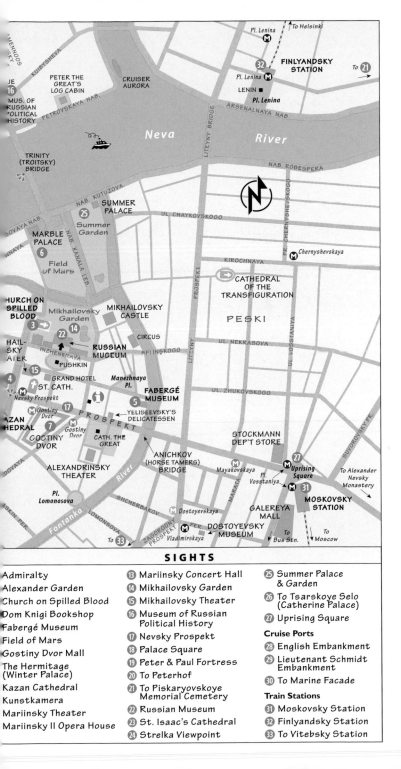

SIGHTS

Admiralty

Alexander Garden

Church on Spilled Blood

Dom Knigi Bookshop

Fabergé Museum

Field of Mars

Gostiny Dvor Mall

The Hermitage (Winter Palace)

Kazan Cathedral

Kunstkamera

Mariinsky Theater

Mariinsky II Opera House

13 Mariinsky Concert Hall

14 Mikhailovsky Garden

15 Mikhailovsky Theater

16 Museum of Russian Political History

17 Nevsky Prospekt

18 Palace Square

19 Peter & Paul Fortress

20 To Peterhof

21 To Piskaryovskoye Memorial Cemetery

22 Russian Museum

23 St. Isaac's Cathedral

24 Strelka Viewpoint

25 Summer Palace & Garden

26 To Tsarskoye Selo (Catherine Palace)

27 Uprising Square

Cruise Ports

28 English Embankment

29 Lieutenant Schmidt Embankment

30 To Marine Facade

Train Stations

31 Moskovsky Station

32 Finlyandsky Station

33 To Vitebsky Station

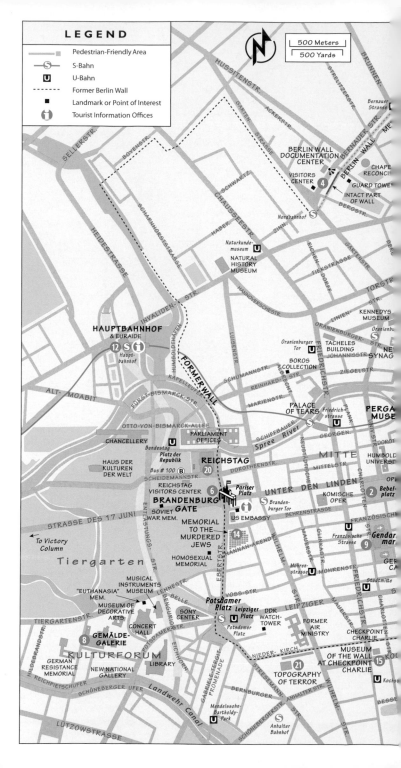

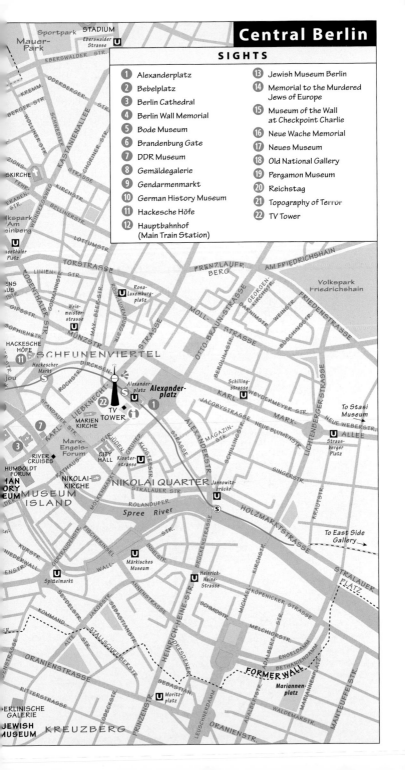

Central Berlin

SIGHTS

1. Alexanderplatz
2. Bebelplatz
3. Berlin Cathedral
4. Berlin Wall Memorial
5. Bode Museum
6. Brandenburg Gate
7. DDR Museum
8. Gemäldegalerie
9. Gendarmenmarkt
10. German History Museum
11. Hackesche Höfe
12. Hauptbahnhof (Main Train Station)
13. Jewish Museum Berlin
14. Memorial to the Murdered Jews of Europe
15. Museum of the Wall at Checkpoint Charlie
16. Neue Wache Memorial
17. Neues Museum
18. Old National Gallery
19. Pergamon Museum
20. Reichstag
21. Topography of Terror
22. TV Tower

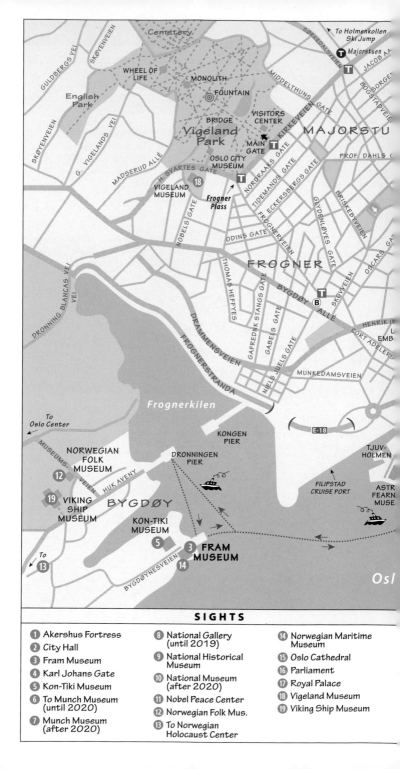

SIGHTS

1. Akershus Fortress
2. City Hall
3. Fram Museum
4. Karl Johans Gate
5. Kon-Tiki Museum
6. To Munch Museum (until 2020)
7. Munch Museum (after 2020)
8. National Gallery (until 2019)
9. National Historical Museum
10. National Museum (after 2020)
11. Nobel Peace Center
12. Norwegian Folk Mus.
13. To Norwegian Holocaust Center
14. Norwegian Maritime Museum
15. Oslo Cathedral
16. Parliament
17. Royal Palace
18. Vigeland Museum
19. Viking Ship Museum

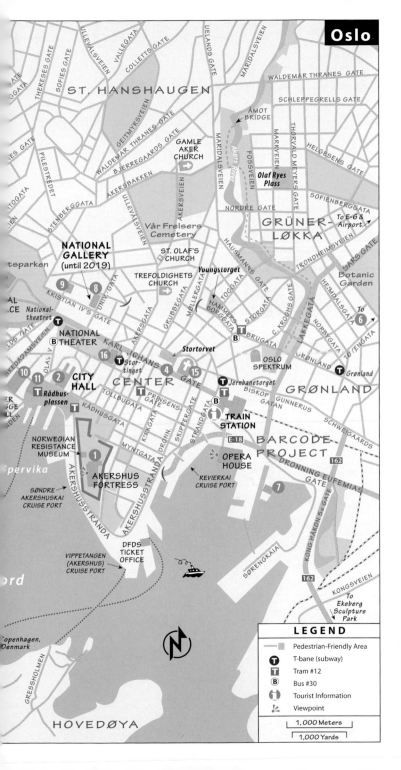

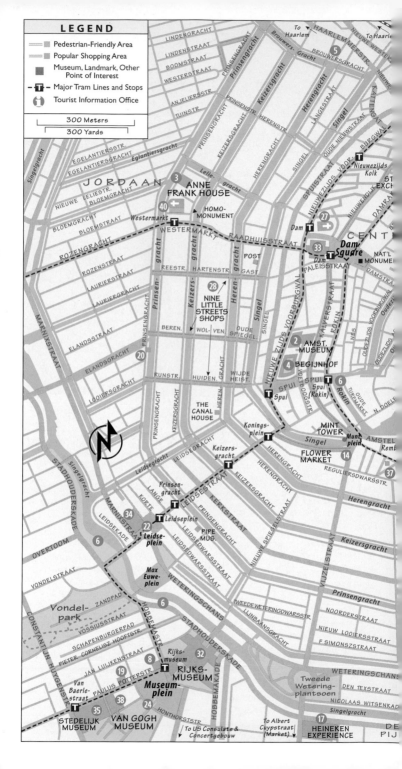

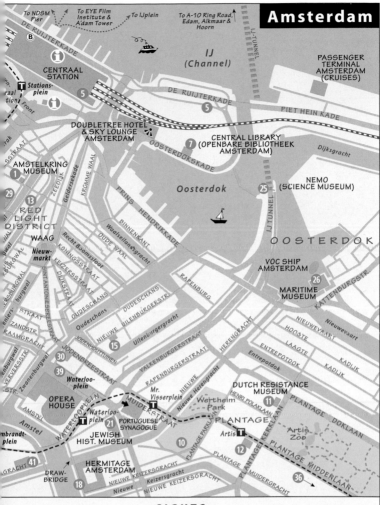

Amsterdam

To NDSM Pier
To EYE Film Institute & Adam Tower
To IJplein
To A-10 Ring Road, Edam, Alkmaar & Hoorn

DE RUIJTERKADE

B

IJ (Channel)

PASSENGER TERMINAL AMSTERDAM (CRUISES)

CENTRAAL STATION

Stations-plein

DE RUIJTERKADE

PIET HEIN KADE

DOUBLETREE HOTEL & SKY LOUNGE AMSTERDAM

OOSTERDOKSKADE

CENTRAL LIBRARY (OPENBARE BIBLIOTHEEK AMSTERDAM) **7**

Dijksgracht

NEMO (SCIENCE MUSEUM)

AMSTELKRING MUSEUM **1**

29

Oosterdok

25

13

RED LIGHT DISTRICT

WAAG

Nieuw-markt

KROMME WAAL

GELDERSEKADE

ZEEDIJK

KONINGSSTRAAT

PRINS HENDRIKKADE

Recht Boomssloot

Waalseilandsgracht

BINNENKANT

OUDE WAAL

RAPENBURG

OOSTERDOK

VOC SHIP AMSTERDAM

26

MARITIME MUSEUM

KATTENBURGSTR.

KEIZERSSTRAAT

DIJKSTRAAT

BINNEN ANTONIESBREESTRAAT

ZANDSTR.

RAAMGRACHT

OUDESCHANS

NIEUWE UILENBURGERSTR.

Uilenburgergracht

Oudeschans

HERENGRACHT

NIEUWEVAART

Nieuwevaart

HOOGTE

LAAGTE

ENTREPOTDOK

Entrepotdok

KADIJK

KADIJK

15

JODENBREESTRAAT

VALKENBURGERSTRAAT

30

39

Waterloo-plein

Zwanenburgwal

Mr. Visserplein

RAPENBURGERSTRAAT

NIEUWE

PLANTAGE PARKLAAN

HENRI POLAKLAAN

DUTCH RESISTANCE MUSEUM

11

PLANTAGE KERKLAAN

PLANTAGE DOKLAAN

OPERA HOUSE

T

Waterloo-plein

T

21

PORTUGESE SYNAGOGUE

MUIDERSTRAAT

Nieuwe Herengracht

Wertheim Park

PLANTAGE

Artis **T**

12

Artis Zoo

PLANTAGE MIDDENLAAN

AMSTEL

Rembrandt-plein

JEWISH HIST. MUSEUM

10

PLANTAGE

36

41

DRAW-BRIDGE

HERMITAGE AMSTERDAM

18

NIEUWE KEIZERSGRACHT

Keizersgracht

NIEUWE KEIZERSGRACHT

PLANTAGE MUIDERGRACHT

SIGHTS

Amstelkring Museum
Amsterdam Museum
Anne Frank House
Begijnhof
Bike Rentals (3)
Canal-Boat Tours (4)
Central Library
Coster Diamonds & Museum
Damrak Sex Museum
De Hortus Botanical Garden
Dutch Resistance Museum
Dutch Theater Memorial
Erotic Museum
Flower Market
Gassan Diamonds

16 Hash, Marijuana & Hemp Museum
17 Heineken Experience
18 Hermitage Amsterdam
19 House of Bols
20 Houseboat Museum
21 Jewish Hist. Museum & Portuguese Synagogue
22 Leidseplein
23 Museum of Bags & Purses
24 Museumplein
25 NEMO (Science Museum)
26 Netherlands Maritime Museum
27 New Church
28 Nine Little Streets Shopping District

29 Old Church
30 Rembrandt's House
31 Rembrandtplein
32 Rijksmuseum
33 Royal Palace
34 Stadsschouwburg Theater
35 Stedelijk Museum
36 To Tropical Museum
37 Tuschinski Theater
38 Van Gogh Museum
39 Waterlooplein Flea Market
40 Westerkerk
41 Willet-Holthuysen Museum

Rick Steves ®

SCANDINAVIAN & NORTHERN EUROPEAN CRUISE PORTS

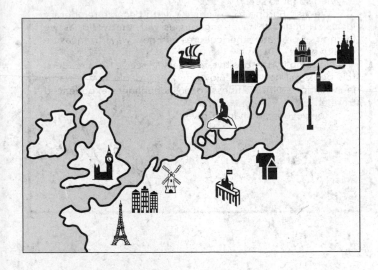

Welcome to Rick Steves' Europe

Travel is intensified living—maximum thrills per minute and one of the last great sources of legal adventure. Travel is freedom. It's recess, and we need it.

I discovered a passion for European travel as a teen and have been sharing it ever since—through my tours, public television and radio shows, and travel guidebooks. Over the years, I've taught thousands of travelers how to best enjoy Europe's blockbuster sights—and experience "Back Door" discoveries that most tourists miss.

For each major destination, this book offers a balanced, comfortable mix of the predictable biggies and a healthy dose of intimacy. Along with marveling at masterpieces in the Louvre, Hermitage, and Rijksmuseum, you can sip a pint in a trendy London pub and sweat with the Finns in a working-class sauna.

I advocate traveling simply and smartly. Take advantage of my money- and time-saving tips on sightseeing, transportation, and more. Try local, characteristic alternatives to expensive hotels and restaurants. In many ways, spending more money only builds a thicker wall between you and what you traveled so far to see.

We visit Europe to experience it—to become temporary locals. Thoughtful travel engages us with the world, as we learn to appreciate other cultures and new ways to measure quality of life.

Judging by the positive feedback I receive from readers, this book will help you enjoy a fun, affordable, and rewarding vacation—with the finesse of an independent, experienced traveler.

Bon voyage and happy travels!

Rick Steves

INTRODUCTION

Imagine yourself lazing on the deck of a floating city as you glide past the spiny skylines of Tallinn, Copenhagen, or St. Petersburg; the jagged fjords of Norway's west coast; or the thousands of picture-perfect islands topped by quaint red vacation cottages in the archipelago between Stockholm and Helsinki. Each day, stepping off the gangway, you're immersed in the vivid life of a different European city. Tour some of the world's top museums, take a Scandinavian-style coffee break while you people-watch from a prime sidewalk café, bask on a surprisingly sunny and sandy Baltic beach, and enjoy some of Europe's most expensive cities on the cheap. After a busy day in port, you can head back to the same cozy bedroom each night, without ever having to pack a suitcase or catch a train. As the sun sets and the ship pulls out of port, you have your choice of dining options—from a tuxedo-and-evening-gown affair to a poolside burger—followed by a world of nightlife. Plying the Baltic and North Sea waters through the night, you wake up refreshed in a whole new city—ready to do it all again.

Cruising in Europe is more popular today than ever before. And for good reason. Taking a cruise can be a fun, affordable way to experience Europe—*if* you choose the right cruise, keep your extra expenses to a minimum...and use this book to make the absolute most of your time in port.

Unlike most cruising guidebooks, which dote on details about this ship's restaurants or that ship's staterooms, *Rick Steves Scandinavian & Northern European Cruise Ports* focuses on the main attraction: some of the grandest cities in Europe. Even if you have just eight hours in port, you can still ride a red double-decker bus through London, paddle a kayak on a Norwegian fjord, stroll Berlin's Unter den Linden or Copenhagen's Strøget, and walk in Lech Wałęsa's footsteps at the Solidarity shipyards in Gdańsk.

Yes, you could spend a lifetime in any of these places. But you've got a few hours...and I have a plan for you. Each of this book's destination chapters is designed as a minivacation of its own, with advice about what to do and detailed sightseeing information for each port. And, to enable you to do it all on your own, I've included detailed instructions for getting into town from the cruise terminal.

In each port, you'll get all the specifics and opinions necessary to wring the maximum value out of your limited time and money. The best options in each port are, of course, only my opinion. But after spending much of my life researching Europe, I've developed a sixth sense for what travelers enjoy.

ABOUT THIS BOOK

The book is divided into three parts: First, I'll suggest strategies for choosing which cruise to take, including a rundown of the major cruise lines, and explain the procedure for booking a cruise. Next, I'll give you a "Cruising 101"-type travel-skills briefing, with advice about what you should know before you go, and strategies for making the most of your time both on and off the ship. And finally, the majority of this book is dedicated to the European ports you'll visit, with complete plans for packing each day full of unforgettable experiences.

I haven't skimped on my coverage of the sights in this book—which is why it's a bricklike tome. To get the most out of the book, please don't hesitate to tear out just the pages you need for each day in port (see sidebar).

IS A EUROPEAN CRUISE RIGHT FOR YOU?

I'm not going to try to convince you to cruise or not to cruise. If you're holding this book, I assume you've already made that decision. But if you're a cruise skeptic—or even a cruise cynic—and you're trying to decide whether cruising suits your approach to experiencing Europe, I'll let you in on my own process for weighing the pros and cons of cruising.

I believe this is the first and only cruising guidebook written by someone with a healthy skepticism about cruises. When

Please Tear Up This Book!

There's no point in hauling around a chapter on Copenhagen for a day in Oslo. That's why I've designed this book to be ripped apart. Before your cruise, attack this book with a utility knife to create an army of pocket-sized mini guidebooks—one for each port of call.

I love the ritual of trimming down the size of guidebooks I'll be using: Fold the pages back until you break the spine, neatly slice apart the sections you want with a utility knife, then pull them out with the gummy edge intact. If you want, finish each one off with some clear, heavy-duty packing tape to smooth and reinforce the spine, or use a heavy-duty stapler along the edge to prevent the first and last pages from coming loose.

To make things even easier, I've created a line of laminated covers with slide-on binders. Every evening, you can make a ritual of swapping out today's pages for tomorrow's. (For more on these binders, see www.ricksteves.com.)

As I travel in Europe, I meet lots of people with even more clever book treatments. This couple was proud of the job they did in the name of packing light: cutting out only the pages they'd be using and putting them into a spiral binding.

While you may be tempted to keep this book intact as a souvenir of your travels, you'll appreciate even more the footloose freedom of traveling light while you're in port.

I was growing up, cruising was a rich person's hobby. I used to joke that for many American cruisers, the goal was not travel but hedonism. (How many meals can you eat in a day and still snorkel when you get into port?)

But now I understand that cruising can be both an efficient and cost-effective way to travel if done smartly. After many years of exploring and writing about Europe, I haven't found a more affordable way to see certain parts of the continent than cruising (short of sleeping on a park bench).

For a weeklong European cruise that includes room, board,

transportation, tips, and port fees, a couple can pay as little as $100 per night—that's what you'd pay for a simple hotel room alone in many cities. To link all the places on an exciting one-week European cruise on your own, the hotels, rail passes, boat tickets, taxi transfers, restaurants, and so on would add up fast. The per-day base cost for mainstream cruises beats independent travel by a mile—particularly in northern Europe, which has one of the highest costs of living in the world. (While a cruise saves money on a trip to Greece or Spain, it's an even better deal in Norway or London—where hotel costs can be more than double.) And there's no denying the convenience and efficiency of sleeping while you travel to your next destination—touring six dynamically different destinations in a single week without wasting valuable daylight hours packing, hauling your bags to the station, and sitting on a train.

And yet, I still have reservations. Just as someone trying to learn a language will do better by immersing themselves in that culture than by sitting in a classroom for a few hours, I believe that travelers in search of engaging, broadening experiences should eat, sleep, and live Europe. Good or bad, cruising insulates you from Europe. If the Russian babushkas selling nesting dolls in St. Petersburg are getting a little too pushy, you can simply retreat to the comfort of 24-hour room service, tall glasses of ice water, American sports on TV, and a boatload of people who speak English as a first language (except, perhaps, your crew). It's fun—but is it Europe?

For many, it's "Europe enough." For travelers who prefer to tiptoe into Europe—rather than dive right in—this approach can be a good way to get your feet wet. Cruising works well as an enticing sampler for Europe, helping you decide where you'd like to return and explore deeper.

People take cruises for different reasons. Some travelers cruise as a means to an end: experiencing the ports of call. They appreciate the convenience of traveling while they sleep, waking up in an interesting new destination each morning, and making the most of every second they're in port. This is the "first off, last on" crowd that attacks each port like a footrace. You can practically hear their mental starter's pistol go off when the gangway opens.

Other cruisers are there to enjoy the cruise experience itself.

They enjoy lying by the pool, taking advantage of onboard activities, dropping some cash at the casino, ringing up a huge bar tab, napping, reading, and watching ESPN on their stateroom TVs. If the *Mona Lisa* floated past, they might crane their necks, but wouldn't strain to get out of their deck chairs.

With all due respect to the latter group, I've written this book primarily for the former. But if you really want to be on vacation, aim for somewhere in the middle: Be sure to experience the ports that really tickle your wanderlust, but give yourself a "day off" every now and again in the less-enticing ports to sleep in or hit the beach.

Another advantage of cruising is that it can accommodate a family or group of people with vastly different travel philosophies. It's possible for Mom to go to the museum, Dad to lie by the pool, Sally to go for a bike ride, Bobby to go shopping, Grandma and Grandpa to take in a show...and then they can all have dinner together and swap stories about their perfect days. (Or, if they're really getting on each other's nerves, there's plenty of room on a big ship to spread out.)

Cruising is especially popular among retirees, particularly those with limited mobility. Cruising rescues you from packing up your bags and huffing to the train station every other day. Once on land, accessibility for wheelchairs and walkers can vary dramatically—though some cruise lines offer excursions specifically designed for those with mobility issues. A cruise aficionado who had done the math once told me that, if you know how to find the deals, it's theoretically cheaper to cruise indefinitely than to pay for a retirement home.

On the other hand, the independent, free-spirited traveler may not appreciate the constraints of cruising. For some, seven or eight hours in port is a tantalizing tease of a place where they'd love to linger for the evening—and the obligation to return to the ship every night is frustrating. Cruisers visiting Paris will never experience the City of Light after dark. If you're antsy, energetic, and want to stroll the cobbles of Europe at all hours, cruising may not be for you. However, even some seasoned globetrotters find that cruising is a good way to travel in Europe on a shoestring budget, yet still in comfort.

One cruise-activities coordinator told me that cruisers can be divided into two groups: Those who stay in their rooms, refuse to try the dozens of activities offered to them each day, and complain about everything; and those who get out and try to get to know their fellow passengers, make the most of being at sea, and have

Top Destinations

200 Kilometers
200 Miles

Atlantic Ocean

SCOTLAND

NORTHERN IRELAND

IRELAND

ENGLAND

WALES

North Sea

NORWEGIAN FJORDS

NORWAY

GEIRAN- FLÅM
GER

BERGEN

STAVANGER

DENMARK

LONDON & PORTS OF SOUTHAMPTON & DOVER

AMSTERDAM

NETH.

BRUGES, BRUSSELS & PORT OF ZEEBRUGGE

PARIS, NORMANDY & PORT OF LE HAVRE

FRANCE

the time of their lives. Guess which type (according to him) enjoys the experience more?

Let's face it: Americans get the least paid vacation in the rich world. Some people choose to dedicate their valuable time off to an all-inclusive, resort-style vacation in Florida, Hawaii, or Mexico: swimming pools, song-and-dance shows, shopping, and all-you-can-eat buffets. Cruising gives you much the same hedonistic experience, all while you learn a lot about Europe—provided you use your time on shore constructively. It can be the best of both worlds.

UNDERSTANDING THE CRUISE INDUSTRY

Cruising is a $37 billion-a-year business. Approximately one out of every five Americans has taken a cruise, and each year about 17 million people take one. In adjusted dollars, cruise prices haven't

risen in decades. This, partly, has sparked a huge growth in the cruise industry in recent years. The aging baby boomer population has also boosted sales, as older travelers discover that a cruise is an easy way to see the world. While the biggest growth has come from the North American market, cruise lines have also started marketing more internationally.

The industry has changed dramatically over the last generation. For decades, cruise lines catered exclusively to the upper crust—people who expected top-tier luxury. But with the popularity of *The Love Boat* television series in the 1970s and 1980s, then the one-upmanship of increasingly bigger megaships in the early 1990s, cruising went mainstream. Somebody had to fill all the berths on those gargantuan vessels, and cruise lines lowered their prices to attract middle-class customers. The "newlyweds and nearly deads" stereotype about cruise clientele is now outmoded. The industry has made bold efforts to appeal to an ever-broader customer base, representing a wide spectrum of ages, interests, and income levels.

In order to compete for passengers and fill megaships, cruise lines offer fares that can be astonishingly low. In fact, they make little or no money on ticket sales—and some "loss-leader" sailings actually lose money on the initial fare. Instead, the cruise lines' main income comes from three sources: alcohol sales, gambling (onboard casinos), and sightseeing "excursions." So while cruise lines are in the business of creating an unforgettable  vacation for you, they're also in the business of separating you from your money (once on the ship) to make up for their underpriced fares.

Just as airlines have attempted to bolster their bottom lines by "unbundling" their fares and charging more "pay as you go" fees (for food, checking a bag, extra legroom, and so on), cruise lines are now charging for things they used to include (such as "specialty restaurants"). The cruise industry is constantly experimenting with the balance between all-inclusive luxury and nickel-and-dime, à la carte, mass-market travel. (For tips on maximizing your experience while minimizing your expenses, see the sidebar on page 74.)

It's also worth noting that cruise lines are able to remain profitable largely on the backs of their low-paid crew, who mostly hail from the developing world. Working 10 to 14 hours a day, seven days a week—almost entirely for tips—the tireless crew are the gears that keep cruises spinning.

Understanding how the cruise industry works can help you take advantage of your cruise experience...and not the other way around. Equipped with knowledge, you can be the smart consumer who has a fantastic time on board and in port without paying a premium. That's what this book is all about.

CHOOSING & BOOKING A CRUISE

CHOOSING A CRUISE

Each cruise line has its own distinct personality, quirks, strengths, and weaknesses. Selecting a cruise that matches your travel style and philosophy can be critical for the enjoyment of your trip. On the other hand, some cruisers care only about the price, go on any line that offers a deal, and have a great time.

Still, the more your idea of "good travel" meshes with your cruise line's, the more likely you are to enjoy both your trip and your fellow passengers. For information on booking a cruise, see the next chapter.

GATHERING INFORMATION

Comparison-shopping can be a fun part of the cruise experience. Read the cruise-line descriptions in this chapter, then browse the websites of the ones that interest you. Ask your friends who've cruised, and who share your interests, about the lines they've used, and what they thought of each one. Examine the cruise lines' brochures or websites—how the line markets itself says a lot about what sort of clientele it attracts. Photos of individual ships' staterooms and amenities can be worth a thousand words in getting a sense of the vibe of each vessel.

Once you've narrowed down the choices, read some impartial reviews. The most popular site, www.cruisecritic.com, has reviews of cruise lines, specific ships, tips for visiting each port, and more. Other well-respected websites are www.cruisediva.com, www.cruisemates.com, and www.avidcruiser.com. If you feel that cruising is all about the ship, check www.shipparade.com, which delves into details about each vessel.

Many travel agencies that sell cruises have surprisingly informative websites. One of the best, www.vacationstogo.com, not only

Cruising the Internet

While there are many cruise-related websites, Cruise Critic (www.cruisecritic.com) dominates cyberspace. Not only are its forums crammed with reviews about ships, excursions, local guides, and ports of call, but it's also a nifty networking tool. By signing up on its Roll Call page for your cruise, you can introduce yourself to others on the same ship and look for partners to share taxis or local guides. Some cruise lines—such as Azamara, Celebrity, Crystal, and Royal Caribbean—even sponsor a social gathering of Cruise Critic members early in the cruise, often with complimentary food and drinks.

sorts different cruise options by price and destination, but also has useful facts, figures, and photos for each ship and port.

Most cruising guidebooks devote more coverage to detailed reviews of specific ships and their amenities than to the destinations—which make them the perfect complement to this book. Look for *The Unofficial Guide to Cruises, Fodor's Complete Guide to European Cruises,* and others. (For destination-specific guidebooks, see the list on page 1067.)

As you compare cruises, decide which of the factors in the following section matter the most to you, then find a cruise line that best matches what you're looking for.

Cruise Considerations

You have several considerations, both big and small, when selecting a cruise. Of these, the three main factors—which should be weighted about equally—are **price, itinerary** (length, destinations, and time spent in each port), and **cruise line** (personality and amenities).

If you've cruised in the Caribbean but not Europe, be aware that there are some important differences. In general, European cruises are more focused on the destinations, while Caribbean cruises tend to be more focused on the ship (passengers spend more time on the ship, and therefore the shipboard amenities are more important). People choosing among European cruises usually base their decision on the places they'll be visiting: Which cities—St. Petersburg, London, Oslo, Copenhagen—appeal? Is the focus more on urban sights or on natural wonders (such as fjords and islands)? In contrast, on a Caribbean cruise the priority is simply hedonistic fun in the sun.

CRUISE LINE

This chapter will give you a quick overview of some of the major lines to help you find a good match. For example, some cruise lines embrace cruising's nautical heritage, with decor and crew uniforms that really let you know you're on a ship. Others are more like Las Vegas casinos at sea. An armchair historian will be disappointed on a hedonistic pleasure boat, and a young person who's in a mood to party will be miserable on the S.S. *Septuagenarian.* Do you want a wide range of dining options on the ship, or do you view mealtime as a pragmatic way to fill the tank? After dinner, do you want to get to bed early, or dance in a disco until dawn?

American vs. European: While most US travelers opt for an American cruise line, doing so definitely Americanizes your travel experience. When you're on board, it feels almost as if you'd never left the good old U. S. of A.—with American shows on the TV, Heinz ketchup in the buffet line, and fellow Yanks all around you. If you'd rather leave North America behind, going with a European-flavored cruise line can be an interesting cultural experience in itself. While Europeans are likely to be among the passengers on any cruise line, they represent a larger proportion on European-owned or -operated boats. Surrounded by Germans who enthusiastically burp after a good meal, Italians who nudge ahead of you in line, and French people who enjoy sunbathing topless—and listening to every announcement translated into six different languages—you'll definitely know you're in Europe. Once I cruised for a week in Norway as one of just 13 Americans on a budget ship with more than 2,000 passengers. I never saw another Yank, spent my time on board and in port with working-class Italians and Spaniards from towns no tourist has ever heard of, and had what was quite possibly the most truly "European" experience of my life.

Environmental Impact: Most forms of travel come with a toll on the environment. And cruise ships are no exception—they gulp fuel as they ply scenic seas, struggling to find waste-disposal methods that are as convenient as possible while still being legal. Some cruise lines are more conscientious about these issues than others. If environmental impact is a major concern, you can compare the records for all the major cruise lines at www.foe.org/cruise-report-card.

TIMING

European cruises can range from a few days to a few weeks. The typical cruiser sails for seven days, but some travelers enjoy taking a 10-, 12-, or 14-day cruise, then adding a few days on land at either end to stretch their trip to two weeks or more. A cruise of seven days or shorter tends to focus on one "zone" of northern Europe

(Norwegian fjords, Baltic highlights); a longer cruise is more likely to provide you with a sampler of the whole area.

Due to the chilly weather at these latitudes, the tourist season in northern Europe is extremely brief: June, July, and August. While a few straggler cruises may be offered outside that window, I'd think twice before heading to Oslo, Helsinki, or St. Petersburg in other months (and if you do, be prepared for rainy and cold weather). For a month-by-month climate chart that includes various ports, see the appendix.

Fortunately, even though tourists bombard the region during those key months, northern European destinations are still typically less crowded than Mediterranean hot spots like Venice or Barcelona. (There are exceptions: Any day during cruise season, the crowds inside St. Petersburg's Hermitage museum are next to unbearable.)

PRICE

From the Mass-Market to the Ultra-Luxury categories, the per-person price can range from $100 to $700+ per day. Sales can lower those prices. (For more on cruise pricing, see the next chapter).

While going with the cheapest option is tempting, it may be worth paying a little extra for an experience that better matches your idea of a dream cruise. If you're hoping for glitzy public spaces and sparkling nightly revues, you'll kick yourself later if you saved $40 a day—but ended up on a musty ship with stale shows. If you want to maximize time exploring European destinations, it can be worth paying an extra $20 a day for an itinerary with two more hours at each port—that translates to just 10 bucks an hour, a veritable steal considering the extra experiences it'll allow you to cram in. Don't be penny-wise and pound-foolish in this regard.

On the other hand, I've noticed that sometimes, the more people pay for a cruise, the higher their expectations—and, therefore, the more prone they are to disappointment. I've cruised on lines ranging from bargain-basement to top-end, and I've noticed an almost perfect correlation between how much someone pays and how much they enjoy complaining. In my experience, folks who pay less are simply more fun to cruise with. When considering the people I'll wind up dining and going on shore excursions with, price tag aside, I'd rather go with a midrange cruise line than a top-end one.

When evaluating prices and making a budget, take into account all of the "extras" you might wind up buying from the cruise line: alcoholic drinks, meals at specialty restaurants, the semimandatory "auto-tip" (about $10-12 per day per person), shore excursions, and your gambling tab from the casino, just to name a few. (For more details on these hidden costs, see page 74.)

SHIP SIZE AND AMENITIES

When it comes to cruise ships, bigger is not necessarily better... although it can be, depending on your interests.

The biggest ships offer a wide variety of restaurants, activities, entertainment, and other amenities (such as resources for kids). The main disadvantage of a big ship is the feeling that you're being herded along with thousands of other passengers—3,000 tourists piling off a ship into a small port town definitely changes the character of the place.

Smaller ships enjoy fewer crowds, access to out-of-the-way ports, and less hassle when disembarking (especially when tendering—see page 109). If you're focusing your time and energy on the destinations anyway, a smaller ship can be more relaxing to "come home" to. On the other hand, for all of the above reasons, cruises on the smallest ships are typically much more expensive. Small ships also physically can't offer the wide range of eateries and activities as the big vessels; intimate, yacht-like vessels have no room for a climbing wall or an ice rink. And on a small ship, you may feel the motion of the sea more than on a big ship (though stabilizers used by small ships help dampen this effect).

Weigh which amenities are important to you, and find a cruise line that offers those things. Considerations include:

Food, both in terms of quality and variety (some cruise lines offer a wide range of specialty restaurants—explained on page 93; generally speaking, the bigger the ship, the more options);

Entertainment, such as a wide range of performers (musicians, dancers, and so on) in venues both big and small;

Athletic facilities, ranging from a running track around the deck, to a gym with equipment and classes, to swimming pools and hot tubs, to a simulated surf pool and bowling alley, to a spa with massage and other treatments;

Children's resources, with activities and spaces designed for teens and younger kids, and a babysitting service (for more on cruising with kids, see page 87).

Other features, such as a good library, lecturers, special events, a large casino, wheelchair accessibility, and so on.

Some first-time cruisers worry they'll get bored while they're on board. Don't count on it. You'll be bombarded with entertainment options and a wide range of activities—particularly on a big ship.

DESTINATIONS AND TIME IN PORT

If you have a wish list of ports, use it as a starting point when shopping for a cruise. It's unlikely you'll find a cruise that visits every one of your desired destinations, but you can usually find one that comes close.

Most itineraries of a week or more include a day "at sea": no stops at ports—just you and the open sea. These are usually included for practical reasons. Most often a day at sea is needed to connect far-flung destinations with no worthwhile stop in between... but cruise lines also don't mind keeping passengers on board, hoping they'll spend more money. Because cruise ships generally travel at around 20 knots—that's only about 23 land miles per hour—they take a long time to cover big distances. For some cruise aficionados, days at sea are the highlight of the trip; for other passengers, they're a boring waste of time. If you enjoy time on the ship, try to maximize days at sea; if you're cruising mainly to sightsee on land, try to minimize them.

If exploring European destinations is your priority, look carefully at how much time the ship spends in each port. Specific itinerary rundowns on cruise-line websites usually show the scheduled times of arrival and departure. Typical stops can range anywhere from 6 to 12 hours, with an average of around 8 or 9 hours. At the same port—or even on the same cruise line—the difference in port time from one cruise ship to another can vary by hours. I was once on one of two ships pulling into Stavanger, Norway, at about the same time. Five hours later, I trudged back to my ship, noticing that the other ship had three more hours before embarkment...giving those passengers just enough time for a visit to the Lysefjord's renowned Pulpit Rock.

Most cruise lines want you on the ship as long as possible (to spend money there—they aren't permitted to open their lucrative casinos and duty-free shops until they're at sea).

In general, the more expensive Luxury- and Ultra-Luxury-class lines offer longer stays in port. However, even if you compare cheaper lines that are similar in price, times can vary. For example, Norwegian, Costa, and MSC tend to have shorter times in port, while Royal Caribbean lingers longer.

REPOSITIONING CRUISES

Ships that cruise in Europe are usually based in the Caribbean during the winter, so they need to cross the Atlantic Ocean each spring and fall. This journey, called a "repositioning cruise," includes a lengthy (5-7 days) stretch where the ship is entirely at sea. Also called a "crossing" or a "transatlantic crossing," these are most common in early April (to Europe), or late October and November (from Europe).

If you really want to escape from it all, and just can't get enough of all the shipboard activities, these long trips can be a dream come true; if you're a fidgety manic sightseer, they're a nightmare. Before committing to a repositioning cruise, consider taking a cruise with a day or two at sea just to be sure you really do enjoy being on a ship that much. Several notes of warning: The seas can be rougher on transatlantic crossings than in the relatively protected waters closer to land; the weather will probably be cooler; and there are a couple of days in the middle of the voyage where some ships lose all satellite communication—no shipboard phones, Wi-Fi, or cable channels. While the officers are in touch with land in the event of emergencies, your own day-to-day contact with the outside world might disappear.

If you're considering a repositioning cruise, don't be misled by the sometimes astonishingly low sticker price. (These typically don't sell as well as the more destination-oriented cruises, so they're perennially on the push list.) You'll only need a one-way plane ticket between the US and Europe—but that may exceed the cost of a round-trip ticket (don't expect to simply pay half the round-trip price).

Cruise Lines

I don't pretend to be an expert on all the different cruise lines—the focus of this book is on the destinations rather than the ships. But this section is designed to give you an overview of options to get you started. (To dig deeper, consider some of the sources listed under "Gathering Information," at the beginning of this chapter.)

While nobody in the cruise industry formally recognizes different "classes" of companies, just about everybody acknowledges that cruise lines fall into four basic categories, loosely based on the price range (estimated per-person prices given here are based on double occupancy in the cheapest cabin, and don't include taxes, port fees, or additional expenses): **Mass-Market** ($100-200/day), **Premium** ($200-350/day), **Luxury** (sometimes called **"Upper Premium"**; $350-700/day), and **Ultra-Luxury** ($700 or more/day). Of course, a few exceptions straddle these classifications and buck the trends, and some cruise lines are highly specialized—such as Disney Cruise Line (very kid-friendly and experience-focused).

Most cruise lines are owned by the same handful of companies. For example, Carnival Corporation owns Carnival, Costa, Cunard, Holland America, Princess, Seabourn, and four other lines (representing about half of the worldwide cruise market). Royal Caribbean owns Celebrity and Azamara Club Cruises. Within these groups, each individual line may be, to varying degrees, operated by a different leadership, but they do fall under the same umbrella and tend to have similar philosophies and policies.

The average hours in port listed below are based on a selection of each line's European itineraries; your cruise could be different, so check carefully.

MASS-MARKET LINES

The cheapest cruise lines, these huge ships have a "resort-hotel-at-sea" ambience. Prices are enticingly low, but operators try to make up the difference with a lot of upselling on board (specialty restaurants, borderline-aggressive photographers, constant pressure to shop, and so on). The clientele is wildly diverse (including lots of families and young people) and, generally speaking, not particularly well-traveled; they tend to be more interested in being on vacation and enjoying the ship than in sightseeing. Mass-Market lines provide an affordable way to sample cruising.

Costa

Contact Info: www.costacruise.com, tel. 800-247-7320
Number and Capacity of Ships: 13 ships, ranging from 1,700 to 4,947 passengers
Average Hours in Port: 7-8 hours

With frequent sales that can drive its prices lower, Costa is one of the cheapest lines for European cruises. It also has the most

seven-day cruises in the region. Although owned by the American- and UK-based Carnival Corporation, Costa proudly retains its Italian identity. Most of your fellow passengers will be Europeans, with large contingents of Italians, French, Spanish, and Germans. (Only a small fraction of Costa passengers come from the US or Canada.) North American cruisers find both pros and cons about traveling with a mostly European crowd: While some relish the fact that it's truly European, others grow weary of the time-consuming multilingual announcements, and have reported "rude" behavior from some fellow passengers (some Europeans are not always polite about waiting in line). The ships' over-the-top, wildly colorful decor borders on gaudy—it can be either appealing or appalling, depending on your perspective. Onboard activities also have an Italian pizzazz, such as singing waiters or heated international bocce-ball tournaments. Outrageous ambience aside, the cruising experience itself is quite traditional (there's usually assigned seating in the dining room, and formal nights are taken seriously). Dining options are limited to the main dining room (serving reliably well-executed, if not refined, Italian fare), huge buffets serving disappointing cafeteria fare, and sparse, overpriced, and underwhelming specialty restaurants.

Costa attracts a wide demographic—from twentysomethings to retirees—and you can expect families during the summer and school breaks. While Costa boasts about its Italian cuisine, some American cruisers have found the food disappointing. In addition to visiting the predictable big ports, Costa is more likely to venture to some lesser-known stops, such as Malta, Morocco, and secondary ports on Sicily. The short hours in port draw criticism—and Costa's shore excursion packages are relatively expensive.

MSC Cruises

Contact Info: www.msccruises.com, tel. 877-655-4655
Number and Capacity of Ships: 16 ships, each carrying 1,984-5,429 passengers
Average Hours in Port: 9-10 hours

Italian-owned MSC's tag line sums up its philosophy: the Mediterranean way of life. Even more so than the similar Costa, this low-priced company caters mostly to Europeans—only about 5 percent of the passengers on their European cruises are from the US or Canada. This is a plus if you want to escape America entirely on your vacation, but can come with some language-barrier and culture-shock issues. Since children ride free, summer and school breaks tend to be dominated by families, while at other times passengers are mostly retirees.

The basic price is often a borderline-outrageous bargain (deep discounts are common), but MSC's cheapest option charges for amenities that are free on many other cruise lines—such as basic drinks and room service. In the dining room, you even have to pay for tap water. MSC's shore excursions have a heightened emphasis on shopping. The food and entertainment are average; your choices at the breakfast and lunch buffets are the same for

the entire cruise. Keep your expectations low—as one passenger noted, "It's not really a cruise—just a bus tour that happens on a nice boat."

Norwegian Cruise Line (NCL)

Contact Info: www.ncl.com, tel. 866-234-7350
Number and Capacity of Ships: 16 ships, ranging from 1,936 to 4,248 passengers
Average Hours in Port: 8-9 hours

Norwegian was an industry leader in the now-widespread trend toward flexibility, and is known for its "Freestyle Cruising" approach. "Whatever" is the big word here (as in, "You're free to do...whatever"). For example, their ships typically have no assigned seating for meals (though reservations are encouraged), and offer the widest range of specialty restaurants, which can include French, Italian, Mexican, sushi, steakhouse, Japanese teppanyaki, and more. Norwegian also has a particularly wide range of cabin categories, from very basic inside cabins to top-of-the-line, sprawling suites that rival the Luxury lines' offerings.

Norwegian has a Las Vegas-style glitz. On the newer ships, such as the gigantic, 4,100-passenger *Norwegian Epic*, the entertainment is ramped up, with world-class shows such as Blue Man Group and Cirque du Soleil—requiring advance ticket purchase. Their vessels tend to be brightly decorated—bold murals curl across the prows of their ships, and the public areas are colorful (some might say garish or even tacky). This approach, coupled with relatively low prices, draws a wide range of passengers: singles and families, young and old, American and European, middle-class and wealthy.

Onboard amenities cater to this passenger diversity; along with all of the usual services, some ships have climbing walls and bowling alleys. The crew is also demographically diverse, and the service is acceptable, but not as doting as on some cruise lines, making some passengers feel anonymous. Education and enrichment activities are a low priority—most lectures are designed to sell you something (excursions, artwork, and so on), rather than prepare you for the port.

Royal Caribbean International

Contact Info: www.royalcaribbean.com, tel. 866-562-7625
Number and Capacity of Ships: 25 ships, ranging from 2,020 to 5,400 passengers
Average Hours in Port: 10 hours

Royal Caribbean is the world's second-largest cruise line (after Carnival). Similar to Carnival and Norwegian, but a step up in both cost and (in their mind, at least) amenities, Royal Caribbean edges toward the Premium category.

Offering an all-around quintessential cruising experience, Royal Caribbean attracts first-time cruisers. The majority are from the US and Canada. The line likes to think of itself as catering to a more youthful demographic: couples and singles in their 30s to 50s on shorter cruises; 50 and up on cruises longer than seven nights. With longer hours in port and onboard fitness facilities (every ship has a rock-climbing wall; some have water parks and mini golf), they try to serve more active travelers.

The food on board is American cuisine, and its entertainment style matches other cruise lines in this category—expect Vegas-style shows and passenger-participation games. Even though some of its ships are positively gigantic, Royal Caribbean, which prides itself on service, delivers; most of its passengers feel well-treated.

PREMIUM LINES

A step up from the Mass-Market lines both in price and in elegance, most Premium lines evoke the "luxury cruises" of yore. The ships can be nearly as big as the Mass-Market options, but are designed to feel more intimate. The upselling is still there, but it's more restrained, and the clientele tends to be generally older, better-traveled, and more interested in sightseeing. While the Mass-Market lines can sometimes feel like a cattle call, Premium lines ratchet up the focus on service, going out of their way to pamper their guests.

Celebrity

Contact Info: www.celebritycruises.com, tel. 800-647-2251
Number and Capacity of Ships: 14 ships, ranging from 16 to 3,030 passengers
Average Hours in Port: 10-11 hours

Originally a Greek company, Celebrity was bought by Royal Caribbean in 1997 and operates as its upscale sister cruise line. (The "X" on the smokestack is the Greek letter "chi," which stands for Chandris—the founder's family name.) Celebrity distinguishes itself from the other Premium category lines with bigger ships and a slightly younger demographic. The company likes to point out that its larger ships have more activities and restaurants than the smaller Premium (or even Luxury category) ships. Most of its passengers are from the US or Canada, and it's reportedly popular with baby boomers, seniors, gay cruisers, and honeymooners. Among the Premium lines, Celebrity offers some of the best amenities for kids (aside from Disney, of course).

Celebrity's smallest stateroom is quite spacious compared with those on other lines in this category. On its European cruises, the main dining room cuisine seems more European than American (with some high-end options—a plus for many travelers), but there are plenty of specialty restaurants, ranging from Asian-fusion to a steakhouse. Most ships are decorated with a mod touch—with all the bright lights and offbeat art, you might feel like you're in Miami Beach. Adding to the whimsy, some ships even come with a real grass lawn on the top deck. Celebrity's service consistently gets high marks, and the onboard diversions include the usual spas, enrichment lectures, Broadway revues, cabarets, discos, theme parties, and casinos.

Cunard Line

Contact Info: www.cunard.com, tel. 800-728-6273
Number and Capacity of Ships: *Queen Elizabeth* carries 2,116 passengers, *Queen Mary 2* carries 3,064, and *Queen Victoria* carries 2,014
Average Hours in Port: 8-10 hours

Cunard Line plays to its long, historic tradition and caters to an old-fashioned, well-traveled, and well-to-do clientele in their 50s and older. Passengers on their European itineraries tend to be mostly British, along with some Americans and other Europeans. Although the line is suitable for families (kids' programs are staffed by trained British nannies), it's not seriously family-friendly. This line features large ships and offers a pleasantly elegant experience with a British bent—you can even have afternoon tea or enjoy bangers and mash in a pub.

About a sixth of the passengers book suites and have access to specialty restaurants—a remnant of the traditional class distinctions in jolly olde England. The entertainment and lecture programs tend to be more "distinguished"; there's a good library; and activities include ballroom dancing, croquet, tennis, fencing, and lawn bowling. Each ship has a viewable collection of historic Cunard artifacts. The famously refined Cunard dress code seems to be more of a suggestion these days, as many show up in relatively casual dress at formal dining events. Passengers give mixed reviews—some feel that the experience doesn't quite live up to the line's legacy.

Disney Cruise Line

Contact Info: www.disneycruise.com , tel. 800-951-3532
Number and Capacity of Ships: 4 ships, ranging from 2,713 to 4,000 passengers
Average Hours in Port: 10 hours

Disney is the gold standard for family cruise vacations. Passengers are families and multigenerational—expect a third to be kids. There'll be plenty of Disney flicks, G-rated floor shows, and mouse ears wherever you turn. Like its amusement parks, Disney's ships have high standards for service and cleanliness. The food is kid-friendly, but the ships also have a high end Italian restaurant for parents. While your kids will never be bored, there are a few adult diversions as well (including an adults-only swimming pool)—but no casino. Disney cruises may be the best option if you're taking along your kids or grandkids. Be warned: Parents who think a little Disney goes a long way might overdose on this line.

Holland America Line (HAL)

Contact Info: www.hollandamerica.com, tel. 877-932-4259
Number and Capacity of Ships: 15 ships, ranging from 835 to 2,650 passengers
Average Hours in Port: 9-10 hours

Holland America, with a history dating back to 1873 (it once carried immigrants to the New World), prides itself on tradition. Generally, this line has one of the most elderly clienteles in the business, though they're trying to promote their cruises to a wider demographic (with some success). Cruisers appreciate the line's delicate balance between a luxury and a casual vacation—it's formal, but not *too* formal.

Ship decor emphasizes a connection to the line's nautical past, with lots of wood trim and white railings; you might feel like you're on an oversized yacht at times. That's intentional: When building their biggest ships, Holland America designers planned public spaces to create the illusion that passengers are on a smaller vessel (for example, hallways bend every so often so you can't see all the way to the far end). This line also has high service standards; they operate training academies in Indonesia and the Philippines, where virtually all of their crew hails from. These stewards are trained to be good-natured and to make their guests feel special. Dining options on board tend to be limited; there isn't a wide range of specialty restaurants.

Holland America takes seriously the task of educating their passengers about the ports; most ships have a "Travel Guide" who lectures on each destination and is available for questions, and some excursions—designated "Cruise with Purpose"—are designed to promote a more meaningful, participatory connection with the destinations (though these are relatively rare in Europe).

Princess

Contact Info: www.princess.com, tel. 800-774-6237
Number and Capacity of Ships: 17 ships, ranging from 670 to 3,560 passengers
Average Hours in Port: 9-10 hours

Princess appeals to everyone from solo travelers to families, with most passengers over 50. Because their market reach is so huge, expect many repeat cruisers enjoying their mainstream cruise experience. While Princess has long been considered a Premium-category line, many cruise insiders suggest that the line has been lowering its prices—and, many say, its standards—so these days it effectively straddles the Premium and Mass-Market categories. Still, Princess passengers tend to be very loyal.

Princess got a big boost when the 1970s *Love Boat* TV series featured two Princess ships. Those "love boats" have been retired, and the Princess fleet is one of the most modern in the industry. It's known for introducing innovative features such as a giant video screen above the main swimming pool showing movies and sports all day... and into the night. Still, while the ships are new, the overall experience is traditional compared with some of the bold and brash Mass-Market lines. The line has the usual activities, such as trivia contests, galley tours, art auctions, and middle-of-the-road musical revues—though some passengers report that they found fewer activities and diversions on Princess ships than they expected for vessels of this size. While its service gets raves and the food is fine, there is some repetition in the main dining room—expect the same dessert choices each night.

LUXURY LINES

While some purists (who reserve the "Luxury" label for something really top-class) prefer to call this category "Upper Premium," it's certainly a notch above the lines listed previously. Luxury lines typically use smaller ships, offer better food and service, command higher prices, and have a more exclusive clientele. You get what you pay for—this is a more dignified experience, with longer days in port and less emphasis on selling you extras. In general, while Luxury ships are very comfortable, the cruise is more focused on the destinations than the ship.

Once you're in this price range, you'll find that the various lines are variations on a theme (though there are a few notable exceptions, such as the unique casual-sailboat ambience of Windstar). It can be hard to distinguish among the lines; within the Luxury category, passengers tend to go with a cruise line recommended to them by a friend.

Note: Luxury and Ultra-Luxury lines (described later) generally run smaller ships, which can visit out-of-the-way ports that larger cruise ships can't. However, remember the drawbacks of smaller ships: fewer onboard activities, a narrower range of restaurants, and—for some travelers prone to seasickness—a slightly rougher ride.

Azamara Club Cruises

Contact Info: www.azamaraclubcruises.com, tel. 855-292-6272
Number and Capacity of Ships: *Journey, Quest,* and *Pursuit* each carry 690 passengers
Average Hours in Port: 11-12 hours

Azamara Club Cruises attracts moderately affluent, educated, and active middle-age to retirement-age travelers. Their stated aim is to allow their customers to immerse themselves in each destination. Azamara passengers want value and are interested in more unusual destinations and longer port stays—their itineraries include more frequent overnight stops. The clientele is mainly American and British, along with a few Germans and other nationalities. There are no programs or facilities for children.

The atmosphere is casual, with open seating at meals and a focus on good food and wine; the cuisine is Mediterranean-influenced with other international dishes and healthy options. With a high crew-to-passenger ratio, the service is attentive. Live entertainment is more limited than on larger ships; the types of programs encourage meeting other guests, which contributes to a cozier, more social experience. Cabins and bathrooms  can be small, but are well laid-out. The company's good-value, all-inclusive pricing covers many amenities you'd pay extra for on other lines, such as good house wine, specialty coffees, bottled water and sodas, basic gratuities (for cabin stewards, bar, and dining), self-service laundry, and shuttle buses in some ports.

Oceania Cruises

Contact Info: www.oceaniacruises.com, tel. 855-623-2642
Number and Capacity of Ships: *Marina* and *Riviera* each carry 1,258 passengers; *Insignia, Nautica, Sirena,* and *Regatta* each carry 684
Average Hours in Port: 9-10 hours

Oceania Cruises appeals to well-traveled, well-heeled baby boomers and older retirees who want fine cuisine, excellent service, and a destination-oriented experience—toeing the fine line between upscale and snooty. The atmosphere is casually sophisticated—tastefully understated elegance. Although the line does not discourage children, kids' amenities (and young passengers) are sparse. Oceania's itineraries tend to be on the longer side.

Staterooms are particularly well-equipped, reminiscent of stylish boutique hotels, with a cozy and intimate atmosphere. On the smaller ships, the staterooms and bathrooms are smaller than on most Luxury ships—but with great beds and fine linens. Oceania touts its cuisine; some of their menus were designed by celebrity chef Jacques Pépin, and their ships have a variety of specialty restaurants—French, Italian, steakhouse, and so on—for no extra charge (but reserve ahead). The larger ships have a culinary arts center with hands-on workshops (for a fee).

Oceania is noted for courting experienced crew members and for low crew turnover. The ships offer extensive onboard libraries, but relatively few organized activities, making these cruises best for those who can entertain themselves (or who make the most of time in port). While a few extras (such as specialty coffee drinks) are included, others are still à la carte; these, and Oceania's excursions, are a bit pricier than average.

Windstar Cruises

Contact Info: www.windstarcruises.com, tel. 844-348-3013
Number and Capacity of Ships: *Wind Surf* carries 312 passengers; *Wind Star* and *Wind Spirit* each carry 148; *Star Pride, Star Breeze,* and *Star Legend* each carry 212
Average Hours in Port: 10 hours

Windstar's gimmick is its sails—each of its ships has four big, functional sails that unfurl dramatically each time the ship leaves port.

(While the sails are capable of powering the ship in strong winds, they're more decorative than practical—although they do reduce the amount of fuel used by the engines.) For many, it's an ideal combination—the romance of sails plus the pampering of a Luxury cruise. For this price range, it has a relatively casual atmosphere, with no formal nights.

Windstar passengers are professionals and experienced independent-minded travelers who range in age from 40s to 70s. First-time cruisers, honeymooners, and anniversary celebrants are enticed by Windstar's unique approach. The smaller ships favor more-focused itineraries and smaller ports, with generous time ashore. Passengers are more "travelers" than "cruisers"—they're here to spend as much time as possible exploring the port towns.

The small vessels also mean fewer on-ship activities. The casino and swimming pool are minuscule, the smaller ships have only one specialty restaurant, and nightlife is virtually nonexistent—though the lounge hosts talented musicians. On some days when the ship is tendered, they lower a platform from the stern, allowing passengers to enjoy water-sports activities right off the back of the vessel. The food is high-quality, and there's a barbecue night on the open deck. Windstar also touts its green-ness (thanks to those sails) and its rare open-bridge policy, whereby passengers can visit the bridge during certain times to see the instruments and chat with the captain and officers.

ULTRA-LUXURY

You'll pay top dollar for these cruises, but get an elite experience in return. The basic features of the previously described Luxury cruises apply to this category as well: small ships (with the exception of Crystal), upscale clientele, a classier atmosphere, less emphasis on onboard activities, and a more destination-focused experience. There's less focus on selling you extras—at these prices, you can expect more and more extras to be included (ranging from alcoholic drinks to shore excursions).

Crystal Cruises
Contact Info: www.crystalcruises.com, tel. 888-722-0021
Number and Capacity of Ships: *Serenity* carries 1,070 passengers, *Symphony* carries 922, and *Esprit* carries 62
Average Hours in Port: 10 hours
While most Luxury and Ultra-Luxury lines have smaller ships, Crystal Cruises distinguishes itself by operating larger ships, closer in size to the less-expensive categories. This allows it to offer more big-ship activities and amenities, while still fostering a genteel, upper-crust ambience (which some may consider "stuffy"). Crystal attracts a retired, well-traveled, well-heeled crowd (although there are also a fair number of people under 50). Approximately 75 percent of the travelers are from the US and Canada, and the rest are mainly British. There are basic programs for children (most kids seem to come with multigenerational family groups) that are better than those on most Ultra-Luxury lines.

The food and the service are both well-regarded (and their seafood comes from sustainable and fair-trade sources). Their acclaimed enrichment programs are noted for having a wide range of minicourses in everything from foreign languages to computer skills, and excursions include opportunities for passengers to participate in a local volunteering effort.

Note: Crystal Cruises are sold exclusively through travel agents.

Regent Seven Seas Cruises (RSSC)
Contact Info: www.rssc.com, tel. 844-473-4368
Number and Capacity of Ships: *Voyager* and *Mariner* each carry 700 passengers, *Explorer* carries 750, and *Navigator* carries 490
Average Hours in Port: 10-11 hours

Regent Seven Seas Cruises appeal to well-educated, sophisticated, and affluent travelers—generally from mid-40s to retirees—looking for a destination-oriented experience. Their exclusive, clubby, understatedly elegant atmosphere attracts many repeat cruisers (the *Voyager* seems especially popular). Most passengers are from North America, with the rest from Great Britain, New Zealand, and Australia. The line welcomes families during summer and school breaks, when it offers a children's program; the rest of the year, there's little to occupy kids.

Their "ultra-inclusive" prices are, indeed, among the most inclusive in the industry, covering premium soft drinks, house wines, tips, ground transfers, round-trip airfare from the US, one night's pre-cruise hotel stay, and unlimited excursions. The ships are known for their spacious, elegantly appointed suites (all with verandas). This line has some of the industry's highest space-per-guest and crew member per-guest ratios, and customers report outstanding service. The French-based cuisine has an international flair, and also attempts to mix in local fare from the ships' ports of call. Passengers tend to be independent-minded and enjoy making their own plans, rather than wanting to be entertained by the cruise line (the entertainment is low-key, and notably, there is no onboard photography service). The crew tries to incorporate the ship's destinations into the entertainment, events, and lectures. Excursions include private tours, strenuous walking tours, and some soft-adventure offerings such as kayaking.

Seabourn Cruise Line

Contact Info: www.seabourn.com, tel. 866-755-5619
Number and Capacity of Ships: *Encore* carries 604 passengers, *Ovation* carries 600, and *Odyssey, Sojourn,* and *Quest* each carry 450
Average Hours in Port: 10 hours
Seabourn Cruise Line attracts affluent, well-traveled couples in their late 40s to late 60s and older, who are not necessarily cruise

aficionados but are accustomed to the "best of the best." Deep down, Seabourn passengers want to be on a yacht, but don't mind sharing it with other upper-class travelers—who, as the line brags, are "both interesting and interested." The focus is on exploring more exotic destinations rather than just relaxing on the ship. Most passengers are American, and the onboard atmosphere is classically elegant. Kids are present in summer and during school vacations, usually with multigenerational groups.

These ships feel like private clubs, with pampering as a priority. The extremely high crew member-to-guest ratio is about 1:1, and the crew addresses guests by name. Activities are designed for socializing with other passengers. Most of the ships offer a stern platform for swimming and kayaking right off the back of the ship. The line's all-inclusive pricing includes freebies like a welcome bottle of champagne, an in-suite bar (with full bottles of your pre-selected booze), and nearly all drinks, including decent wines at mealtime (you pay extra only for premium brands). Also included are tips, some excursions, poolside mini massages, and activities such as exercise classes and wine-tasting seminars.

Silversea Cruises
Contact Info: www.silversea.com, tel. 888-978-4070
Number and Capacity of Ships: 9 ships, ranging from 100 to 596 passengers
Average Hours in Port: 8-10 hours
The Italian-owned, Monaco-based Silversea Cruises is popular with well-educated, well-traveled, upper-crust cruisers, generally ranging in age from late 40s to 80s (with many in their 70s). Most passengers are accustomed to the finest and are very discriminating. The ships' Art Deco design lends an elegant 1930s ambience, and the atmosphere on board is clubby. Half of their clientele is from North America, with the other half predominantly from the UK, Europe, and Australia. There are no organized children's programs, and you'll see few children on board.

The cuisine is very good, and the service excellent; the spacious suites even have an assigned butler. Partly as a function of the ships' small size and fewer passengers, the events and entertainment are low-key.

BOOKING A CRUISE

Once you've narrowed down your cruise-line options, it's time to get serious about booking. This chapter covers where, when, and how to book your cruise, including pointers on cruise pricing, cabin assignments, trip insurance, plans for before and after your cruise, and other considerations.

Where to Book

While plane tickets, rental cars, hotels, and most other aspects of travel have gradually migrated to do-it-yourself, cruises are the one form of travel still booked predominantly through a travel agent.

Though it's possible to book a cruise directly with the cruise line, most lines prefer that you go through an intermediary. That's because their customers are rarely just booking a cruise—they're also looking into airfares, trip insurance, and maybe hotels at either end of the cruise. That's beyond the scope of what cruise lines want to sell—their offices mainly do bookings, they don't advise—so they reduce their overhead by letting travel agents do all that hard work (and hand-holding).

It can also be cheaper to book through a travel agent. Some cruise lines discount fares that are sold through their preferred agents; because they've built up relationships with these agents over the years, they don't want to undersell them. In other cases, the travel agency reserves a block of cabins to secure the lowest possible price, then passes the savings on to customers.

There are, generally speaking, two types of cruise-sales agencies: your neighborhood travel agent, where you can get in-person advice; or a giant company that sells most of its inventory online or by phone. Because cruise prices vary based on volume, a big agency can usually undersell a small one. Big agencies are also more likely to offer incentives (such as onboard credit or cabin upgrades) to sweeten the pot. However, some small agencies belong to a consortium that gives them as much collective clout as a big agency. And some travelers figure the intangible value of personal service they get at a small agency is worth the possibility of paying a little extra. (Although most travel agents don't charge a fee, their commission is built into the cruise price.)

The big cruise agencies often have websites where you can shop around for the best price. These include VacationsToGo, CruiseCompete, and CruCon. One site, Cayole, tries to predict when prices for a particular departure may be lowest, giving you advice about how soon you should book.

I use the big websites to do some comparison-shopping. But—call me old-fashioned—when it comes time to book, I prefer to sit down with a travel agent to make my plans in person. Ideally, find a well-regarded travel agent in your community who knows cruising and will give you the personal attention you need to sort through your options. Tell them the deals you've seen online, and ask if they can match or beat them. A good travel agent knows how to look at your whole travel picture (airfare, hotels, and so on), not just the cruise component. And they can advise you about "insider" information, such as how to select the right cabin. Keep in mind that if you do solicit the advice of a travel agent, you should book the cruise through them—that's the only way they'll get their hard-earned commission. Once you've booked your cruise, you can arrange airfare through your travel agent, or you may choose to do that part on your own; for hotels, I always book direct.

When to Book

Most cruise lines post their schedules a year or more in advance. A specific departure is called a "sailing." If you want to cruise in the summertime, and your plans are very specific (for example, you have your heart set on a certain sailing, or a particular cabin setup, such as adjoining staterooms), it's best to begin looking the preceding November. (For cruises in shoulder season—spring and fall—you may have a little more time to shop around.) Because the cruise lines want to fill up their ships as fast as possible, they typically offer early-booking discounts if you buy your cruise well in advance (at least 6-12 months, depending on the company).

Meanwhile, the most popular time of year to book a cruise is during the first few weeks of January. Dubbed "wave season" by industry insiders, this is when one-third of all cruises are booked. If you wait until this time, you'll be competing with other travelers for the deals. The sooner you book, the more likely you are to

Sample Pretrip Timeline

Use this general timeline as a guide—but be sure to confirm specifics with your cruise line.

What to Do	Time Before Departure
Book cruise and pay initial deposit	8-10 months (for best selection)
Buy trip insurance, if desired	At time of booking (if through cruise line); within about 2 weeks of booking (if through a third party)
Full payment due	45-60 days
Online check-in	Between booking and full payment (check with cruise line)
Fly to meet your cruise	1-2 days ahead (remember you lose one day when flying from the US to Europe)

have your choice of sailing and cabin type—and potentially an even better price.

If a cruise still has several cabins available 90 days before departure, they're likely to put them on sale—but don't count on it. People tend to think the longer they wait, the more likely it is they'll find a sale. But this isn't always the case. Last-minute sales aren't as likely for Europe as they are for some other destinations, such as the Caribbean. The European market has a much shorter season and fewer ships, which means fewer beds to fill...and fewer deals to fill them. And even if you do find a last-minute deal, keep in mind that last-minute airfares to Europe can be that much more expensive.

If you're unsure of when to book, consult a travel agent.

How to Book

Once you find the cruise you want, your travel agent may be able to hold it for you for a day or two while you think it over. When you've decided, you'll secure your passage on the cruise by paying a deposit. While this varies by cruise line, it averages about $500 per person (this becomes nonrefundable after a specified date, sometimes immediately—ask when you book). No matter how far ahead you book, you generally won't have to pay the balance until 45-60 days before departure. After this point, cancellation comes at a heftier price; as the departure date approaches, your cruise becomes effectively nonrefundable. Read the fine print.

CRUISE PRICING

Like rental cars or plane tickets, cruises are priced very flexibly. Some cruise lines don't even bother listing prices in their brochures—they just send customers to their website. In general, for a mass-market cruise, you'll rarely pay the list price. Higher-end cruises are less likely to be discounted.

The main factor that determines the actual cost of a cruise is demand (that is, the popularity of the date, destination, and specific ship), but other factors come into play.

Cruise lines and travel agencies use **sales and incentives** to entice new customers. With the proliferation of megaships, there are plenty of cabins to fill, and cruise industry insiders rigidly follow the mantra, "Empty beds are not tolerated!" The obvious approach to filling up a slow-selling cruise is to reduce prices. But they may also offer "onboard credit," which can be applied to your expenses on the ship (such as tips, alcoholic drinks, or excursions). In other cases, they may automatically upgrade your stateroom ("Pay for Category C, and get a Category B cabin for no extra charge!"). To further entice you, they might even throw in a special cocktail reception with the captain, or a night or two at a hotel at either end of your cruise. Your travel agent should be aware of these sales; you can also look online, or—if you're a fan of a particular cruise line—sign up to get their email offers.

Some cruise lines offer **discounts** for seniors (including AARP members), AAA members, firefighters, military, union workers, teachers, those in the travel industry, employees of certain corporations, and so on. It never hurts to ask.

Keep in mind that you'll pay a premium for **novelty.** It usually costs more to go on the cruise line's newest, most loudly advertised vessel. If you go on a ship that's just a few years older—with most of the same amenities—you'll likely pay less.

If you are a **repeat cruiser**—or think you may become one—sign up for the cruise line's "frequent cruiser" program. Like the airlines' mileage-rewards programs, these offer incentives, upgrades, and access to special deals.

It's best to pay with a **credit card** to give yourself a measure of consumer protection. A credit-card company can be a strong ally in resolving disputes.

If the **price drops after you book** your cruise, try asking for a new price. A good time to ask is just before you make the final payment. They don't have all your money yet and tend to be more eager to look for specials that will reduce your bottom line. You may receive a discount or an upgrade.

Taxes, Port Fees, and Other Hidden Charges

The advertised price for your cruise isn't all you'll have to pay. All the miscellaneous taxes, fees, and other expenses that the ship incurs in port are divvied up and passed on to passengers, under the category **"taxes and port fees."** While these can vary dramatically

BOOKING A CRUISE

from port to port, they'll run you a few hundred dollars per person. These amounts are not locked in at the time you book; if a port increases its fees, you'll pay the difference.

Like airlines, cruise lines reserve the right to tack on a **"fuel surcharge"** if the price of oil goes over a certain amount per barrel. This can be added onto your bill even after you book the cruise.

Once you're on the cruise, most lines automatically levy an **"auto-tip"** of around $12/day per person (which you can adjust upward or downward once on board). While this won't be included in your up-front cruise cost, you should budget for it. Many cruisers also choose to give excellent crew members an additional cash tip.

SPECIAL CONSIDERATIONS

Families, singles, groups, people celebrating milestones, and those with limited mobility are all special in my book.

If you're traveling with a family, note that fares for **kids** tend to be more expensive during spring break and summertime, when they're out of school and demand is high; it can be cheaper to bring them off-season. Adjoining staterooms (also called "connecting" rooms) that share an inside door tend to book up early, particularly in the summertime. If those are sold out, consider an inside cabin across from an outside cabin. Some rooms have fold-down bunk beds (or "upper berths"), so a family of three or four can cram into one room (each passenger after the second pays a reduced fare)— but the tight quarters, already cramped for two people, can be challenging for the whole clan. Like connecting staterooms, these triple or quad cabins sell out early. Note that women who are more than six months **pregnant**—and **babies** who are younger than six months—are typically not allowed on a cruise.

Single cabins are rare on cruise ships; almost all staterooms are designed with couples in mind. Therefore, cruise rates are quoted per person, based on double occupancy. If you're traveling solo, you'll usually have to pay a "single supplement." This can range from reasonable (an additional 10 percent of the per-person double rate) to exorbitant ("100 percent" of the double rate—in other words, paying as much as two people would). On average, figure paying about 50 percent above the per-person double rate for your own single cabin. Sometimes it's possible to avoid the single supplement by volunteering to be assigned a random roommate, but this option is increasingly rare.

Groups taking eight or more cabins may be eligible for discounts if they're booked together—ask. The discounts often don't add up to much, but you may wrangle a shipboard credit or a private cocktail party.

If you'll be celebrating a **special occasion**—such as a birthday or anniversary—on board, mention it when you book. You may get a special bonus, such as a fancy dessert or cocktails with the captain.

If you have **limited mobility,** cruising can be a good way to go—but not all cruise lines are created equal. Some ships are wheelchair-accessible, including fully adapted cabins; others (especially small vessels) may not even have an elevator. When shopping for your cruise, ask the cruise line about the features you'll need, and be very specific. Unfortunately, once you reach port, all bets are off. While some cities are impressively accessible, others (especially smaller towns) may have fewer elevators than the ship you arrived on. The creaky and cobbled Old World doesn't accommodate wheelchairs or walkers very well. Taking a shore excursion can be a good way to see a place with minimum effort; cruise lines can typically inform you of the amount of walking and stairs you'll need to tackle for each excursion.

CABIN CLASSES

Each cruise ship has a variety of staterooms. In some cases, the distinction can be pretty narrow ("Category A" and the marginally smaller "Category B"). On other ships, it can be the difference between a "Class 1" suite with a private balcony and a "Class 10" windowless bunk-bed closet below the waterline. On its website, each cruise line explains the specific breakdown of its various categories, along with the amenities in each one. In general, the highest demand is for the top-end and bottom-end cabins. Also, as verandas are increasingly popular, the most affordable rooms with verandas are often the first fares to sell out.

You'll see these terms:

Inside/Interior: An inside cabin has no external windows (though there's often a faux porthole to at least create the illusion of outside light). While these terrify claustrophobes, inside cabins offer a great value that tempts budget travelers. And many cruisers figure that with a giant ship to explore—not to mention Europe at your doorstep each morning—there's not much point hanging out in your room anyway.

Outside: With a window to the sea, an outside cabin costs more—but for some travelers, it's worth the splurge to be able to see the world go by. But be aware that you're rarely able to open those windows (for that, you need a veranda). If your view is blocked (by a lifeboat, for example), it should be classified as "obstructed."

Veranda: Going one better than an outside cabin, a "veranda" is cruise jargon for a small outdoor balcony

attached to your room.
Because windows can't be
opened, one big advantage
of a veranda is that you
can slide open the door
to get some fresh air. The
size and openness of ve-
randas can vary wildly; for
wind-shear reasons, some

verandas can be almost entirely enclosed, with only a big picture
window-sized opening to the sea. Sitting on the veranda while you
cruise sounds appealing, but keep in mind that most of the time
you're sailing, it'll be dark outside.

Suite: A multiroom suite represents the top end of cruise accommodations. These are particularly handy for families, but if you
can't spring for a suite, ask about adjoining staterooms.

Location Within Ship: In general, the upper decks (with better views, and typically bigger windows and more light) are more
desirable—and more expensive—than the lower decks. Cabins in
the middle of the ship (where the "motion of the ocean" is less no-
ticeable) are considered better than those at either end. And cabins
close to the engines (low and to the rear of the ship) can come with
extra noise and vibrations.

Look for the **deck plan** on your cruise line's website. If you
have a chance to select your own cabin (see next section), study the
deck plan carefully to choose a good location. You'd want to avoid
a cabin directly below a deck that has a lot of noisy foot traffic (such
as the late-night disco or stewards dragging pool chairs across the
deck).

Cabin Assignments and Upgrades

Cruise lines handle specific cabin assignments in different ways.
While some cruise lines let you request a specific stateroom when
you book, others don't offer that option; they'll assign your stateroom number at a future date. In other cases, you can request a
"guarantee"—you pay for a particular class and are guaranteed that
class of cabin (or better), but are not yet assigned a specific stateroom. As time passes and the cruise line gets a better sense of the
occupancy on your sailing, there's a possibility that they will upgrade you to a better cabin for no extra charge. There's no way of
predicting when you'll find out your cabin assignment—it can be
months before departure, or days before. (Cabin assignments seem
to favor repeat cruisers, rewarding customers for their loyalty.)

If you need a specific type of stateroom—for instance, you
have limited mobility and need to be close to the elevator, or you're

traveling with a large family and want to be as close together as possible—opt for a specific cabin assignment as early as you can.

If you don't have special needs, you might as well take your chances with a "guarantee"; you're assured of getting the class of cabin that you paid for...and you could wind up with a bonus veranda.

Assigned Dining: Traditionally, cruisers reserved not only their stateroom, but also a seating—a specific table and time for dinner each night. But while it's still mandatory on a few lines, most either make it optional or have done away with it entirely. If your cruise line requires (or you prefer) a specific seating, reserve it when you book your cruise or cabin. (For more on assigned dining, see page 90.)

TRAVEL INSURANCE

Travel insurance can minimize the considerable financial risks of traveling: accidents, illness, cruise cancellations due to bad weather, missed flights, lost baggage, medical expenses, and emergency evacuation. If you anticipate any hiccups that may prevent you from taking your trip, travel insurance can protect your investment.

Trip-cancellation insurance lets you bail out without losing all the money you paid for the cruise, provided you cancel for an acceptable reason, such as illness or a death in the family. This insurance also covers trip interruptions—if you begin a journey but have to cut it short for a covered reason, you'll be reimbursed for the portion of the trip that you didn't complete.

Travel insurance is also handy in the unlikely event that your ship breaks down midtrip. Though the cruise line should reimburse you for the cruise itself, travel insurance provides more surefire protection and can cover unexpected expenses, such as hotels or additional transportation you might need once you've gotten off the ship.

Travel insurance also includes basic medical coverage—up to a certain amount. If you have an accident or come down with a case of the "cruise-ship virus," your policy will cover doctor visits, treatment, and medication (though you'll generally have to pay a deductible). This usually includes medical evacuation—in the event that you become seriously ill and need to be taken to the nearest adequate medical care (that is, a big, modern hospital).

Baggage insurance, included in most comprehensive policies (and in some homeowner or renter insurance policies), reimburses you for luggage that's lost, stolen, or damaged. However, some items aren't covered (ask for details when you buy). When you check a bag on a plane, it's covered by the airline (though, again, there are limits—ask).

Insurance prices vary dramatically, but most packages cost between 5 and 12 percent of the price of your trip. Two factors affect the price: the trip cost and your age at the time of purchase (rates go up dramatically for every decade over 50). For instance, to insure a 70-year-old traveler for a $3,000 cruise, the prices can range from about $150 to $430, depending on the level of coverage. To insure a 40-year-old for that same cruise, the cost can be about $90 to $215. Coverage is generally inexpensive or even free for children 17 and under. To ensure maximum coverage, it's smart to buy your insurance policy within a week of the date you make the first payment on your trip. Research policies carefully; if you wait too long to purchase insurance, you may be denied certain kinds of coverage, such as for preexisting medical conditions.

Cruise lines offer their own travel insurance, but these policies generally aren't as comprehensive as those from third-party insurance companies. For example, a cruise-line policy only covers the cruise itself; if you book your airfare and pre- and post-cruise hotels separately, they will not be covered. And if your cruise line ceases operations, their insurance likely won't cover it. On the other hand, many cruise-line policies are not tied to age—potentially making them attractive to older passengers who find third-party policies prohibitively expensive.

Reputable independent providers include Allianz (www.allianztravelinsurance.com, tel. 866-884-3556), Travelex (www.travelexinsurance.com, tel. 800-228-9792), Travel Guard (www.travelguard.com, tel. 800-826-4919), and Travel Insured International (www.travelinsured.com, tel. 800-243-3174). InsureMyTrip allows you to compare insurance policies and costs among various providers (they also sell insurance; www.insuremytrip.com, tel. 800-487-4722). Betins is a similar comparison site (www.betins.com, tel. 866-552-8834).

Some credit-card companies may offer limited trip-cancellation or interruption coverage for cruises purchased with the card—it's worth checking before you buy a policy. Also, check whether your existing insurance (health, homeowners, or renters) covers you and your possessions overseas. For more tips, see www.ricksteves.com/insurance.

AIRFARE AND PRE- AND POST-CRUISE TRAVEL

When booking your airfare, consider how much time you want before and after your cruise. Remember that most Europe-bound flights from the US travel overnight and arrive the following day. The nearest airport is often far from the cruise port; allow plenty of time to get to your ship. You'll need to check in at least two hours before your cruise departs (confirm with your cruise line; most passengers show up several hours earlier).

If your travel plans are flexible, consider arriving a few days before your cruise and/or departing a few days after it ends—particularly if the embarkation and disembarkation points are places you'd like to explore. Remember, if you arrive just hours before (or depart just hours after) your cruise, you won't actually have any time to see the beginning and ending ports at all. Common starting and ending points include Copenhagen, Stockholm, Amsterdam, and ports near London (Southampton and Dover)—all of which merit plenty of time (and are covered a little more thoroughly in this book for that reason).

Arriving at least a day early makes it less likely that you'll miss the start of your cruise if your flight is delayed. If you miss the ship, you're on your own to catch up with it at its next port. While I've rarely heard of people missing the boat at a port of call, I've heard many horror stories about flight delays causing passengers to miss the first day of the cruise—and often incurring a time-consuming, stressful, and costly overland trip to meet their ship at the next stop.

In the past, most cruises included what they called "free air" (or "air/sea"), but these days your airfare to and from Europe costs extra—and you're usually better off booking it yourself. (Relatively few cruise passengers book airfare through their cruise line.) If you do book your airfare through the cruise line, you'll typically pay more, but in case of a flight delay, the cruise line will help you meet the ship at a later point. However, booking your airfare this way has its disadvantages—the cruise line chooses the airline and the route. They'll select an airline they have a contract with, regardless of whether it's one you want to fly (though it's sometimes possible to pay a "deviation fee" to switch to an airline and routing of your choice).

If you decide to add some days on either end of your trip, it's best to make your own arrangements for hotels and transfers. While most cruise lines offer pre- and post-tour packages (that include the hotel, plus transfers to and from the airport and the cruise port), they tend to be overpriced. For each of the arrival and departure cities in this book, I've recommended a few hotels to consider.

Some embarkation ports are quite distant from town (for example Dover and Southampton are each about 80 miles from London). For these ports, a cruise-line airport transfer—which can save you a complicated journey through a big city's downtown—may be worth considering. You can often book a transfer even if you're reserving your pre- or post-tour hotel on your own—ask.

In some rare circumstances, it's convenient for a cruise passenger to leave the ship before the cruise is completed—for example, you want to get off to have some extra time in Tallinn, rather than spend a day at sea to return to your starting point in Copenhagen. Cruise lines usually permit this, but you'll pay for the full cost of the cruise (including the portion you're not using), and you'll need to get permission in advance.

ONLINE CHECK-IN

At some point between when you book and when your final payment is due, you'll be invited to check in online for your cruise. This takes only a few minutes. You'll register your basic information and sometimes a credit-card number (for onboard purchases—or you can do this in person when you arrive at the ship). Once registered, you'll be able to print out documents (such as your receipt and boarding pass), access information about shipboard life, and learn about and prebook shore excursions.

BOOKING A CRUISE

TRAVEL SKILLS FOR CRUISING

BEFORE YOUR CRUISE

As any sailor knows, prepare well and you'll enjoy a smoother voyage. This chapter covers what you should know before you go (including red tape, money matters, and other practicalities), as well as pointers for packing.

Know Before You Go

RED TAPE

You need a **passport** to travel to the countries covered in this book. You may be denied entry into certain European countries if your passport is due to expire within six months of your ticketed date of return. Renew your passport if you'll be cutting it close. It can take up to six weeks to get or renew a passport (for more on passports, see www.travel.state.gov).

If your itinerary includes **St. Petersburg, Russia,** you'll have to decide if you want a visa: You'll need one to explore the city on your own—but it's pricey and must be arranged well in advance. If you pay for a cruise-line excursion in St. Petersburg, you don't need a visa but must stay with your guide at all times. For details, see page 324.

If you're traveling with **kids,** each minor must possess a passport—even babies. Grandparents or guardians can bring kids on board sans parents only if they have a signed, notarized document from the parent(s) to prove to authorities that they have permission to take the child on a trip. Even a solo parent traveling with children must demonstrate that the other parent has given approval. Specifically, the letter should grant permission for the accompanying adult to travel internationally with the child. Include your name, the name of your child, the dates of your trip, destination countries, and the name, address, and phone number of the

Before-You-Go Checklist

Here are a few things to consider as you prepare for your cruise:

❏ Contact your **credit- and debit-card companies** to tell them you're going abroad and to ask about fees, limits, and more. See next page.

❏ Ask your **health insurance** provider about overseas medical coverage, both on ship and ashore. See page 76.

❏ Consider buying **trip insurance.** See page 36.

❏ For cruises with **assigned dining,** request your preference for seating time and table size when you reserve. See page 90.

❏ Vegetarians, those with food allergies, or anyone with a **special diet** should notify their cruise line at least 60 days before departure. See page 90.

❏ If you want to use your **mobile phone** while traveling, contact your service provider for details. See page 81.

❏ **Know the PIN** for your credit and/or debit cards. You will likely encounter the chip-and-PIN payment system, which is widely used in Europe. See page 122.

❏ If you'll be visiting St. Petersburg, decide whether you want to get a **visa,** which will enable you to sightsee independently in the city. For details, see page 324.

❏ Some major sights in St. Petersburg, Berlin, Amsterdam, and Paris offer or require **reservations,** and some sights sell tickets online. It's a time-saver, allowing you to bypass long ticket-buying lines. For a list of sights to book in advance, see the "Travel Tips" section in this chapter.

❏ If you'll be going to Warnemünde (Germany), check the **train schedules** at Bahn.com for the best connections to and from Berlin, to help you decide whether to take the train or pay for an excursion. See page 523.

❏ If you'll be going to Flåm (Norwegian fjords), check the schedules for the day of your visit (see www.nsb.no and www.kringom.no)—and compare them to your arrival and all-aboard time to be sure you can comfortably manage the **"Norway in a Nutshell"** loop trip (or part of it). See page 708.

❏ If you're prone to **seasickness,** ask your doctor for advice; certain medication requires a prescription. See page 76.

❏ If you're taking a **child** on a cruise without both parents, you'll need a signed, notarized document from the parent(s). See the "Red Tape" section in this chapter.

parent(s) at home. If you have a different last name from your child, it's smart to bring a copy of the birth certificate (with your name on it). For parents of adopted children, it's a good idea to bring their adoption decree as well.

Pack a photocopy or take a photo of your **passport** in case the originals are lost or stolen. It's easier to replace a lost or stolen passport if you have a copy proving that you really had what you lost. A couple of passport-type pictures brought from home can expedite the replacement process.

MONEY

At the start of your cruise, you must register your credit card (either at check-in or on board the ship). All purchases are made using your room number, and you'll be billed for onboard purchases when you disembark. Be aware that the cruise line may put a hold on your credit card during your trip to cover anticipated shipboard expenses; if you have a relatively low limit, you might come uncomfortably close to it. If you're concerned, ask the cruise line what the amount of the hold will be.

For your time on **land,** bring both a credit card and a debit card. You'll use the debit card at ATMs to withdraw local cash for small purchases, and the credit card to pay for larger items. Some travelers carry a third card as a backup. As an emergency reserve, I also bring a few hundred dollars in hard cash.

Cash

Most cruise ships are essentially cashless (though you may want to bring some US cash for tipping). But on land, cash can be the easiest—and sometimes only—way to pay for cheap food, bus fare, taxis, tips, and local guides. Don't bother changing money before you leave home—ATMs in Europe are easy to find and use (for details, see page 122).

Credit and Debit Cards

For purchases, Visa and MasterCard are more commonly accepted than American Express. Before your trip, contact the company that issued your debit or credit cards and ask them a few questions.

Know your cards and PIN. Debit cards from any major US bank will work in any standard European bank's ATM (ideally, use a debit card with a Visa or MasterCard logo).

Most credit and debit cards have chips that authenticate and secure transactions. Europeans insert their chip cards into the payment machine slot, then enter a PIN. With a US card, you provide a signature instead of a PIN to verify your identity.

An American card will work at any European hotel, restaurant, or shop that accepts credit cards. However, for self-service payment machines, you may need to enter your PIN, so make sure you know the numeric, four-digit PIN for both your debit and credit cards. Request a PIN if you don't have one and allow time to receive the information by mail. While I've been inconvenienced a few times by self-service payment machines in Europe that wouldn't accept my card, it's never caused me serious trouble.

Report your travel dates. Let your bank or other card issuer know that you'll be using your debit and credit cards in Europe, and when and where you're headed.

Adjust your ATM withdrawal limit. Find out how much you can take out daily and ask for a higher daily withdrawal limit if you want to get more cash at once. Note that European ATMs will withdraw funds only from checking accounts; you're unlikely to have access to your savings account.

Ask about fees. For any purchase or withdrawal made with a card, you may be charged a currency conversion fee (1-3 percent), a Visa or MasterCard international transaction fee (1 percent), and—for debit cards—a $2-5 transaction fee each time you use a foreign ATM (some US banks partner with European banks, allowing you to use those ATMs with no fees—ask).

If you're getting a bad deal, consider getting a new debit or credit card. Reputable no-fee cards include those from Capital One, as well as Charles Schwab debit cards. Most credit unions and some airline loyalty cards have low-to-no international transaction fees.

TRAVEL TIPS

Time Zones: While Norwegian cruises stay within the same time zone, cruises on the Baltic are prone to crossing time zones with each sailing. Most of Western Europe—from France to Norway, Denmark, Sweden, and Poland—is in the Central European time zone, or CET (generally six/nine hours ahead of the East/West Coasts of the US). Moving farther east, the Baltic States (Estonia, Latvia, Lithuania) and Finland are in the Eastern European time zone—one hour ahead of CET. And St. Petersburg, Russia, is yet another hour ahead (that is, two hours ahead of CET). Britain is one hour earlier than CET, so if your cruise begins in London and stops in Tallinn on its way to St. Petersburg before ending in Copenhagen, you'll change your watch five times. Time changes are noted in the daily program—and your cabin steward will usually leave a reminder on your bed the evening before.

The exceptions are the beginning and end of Daylight Saving Time: Europe "springs forward" the last Sunday in March (two weeks after most of North America), and "falls back" the last Sunday in October (one week before North America). For a handy online time converter, see www.timeanddate.com/worldclock.

⌂ Stick This Guidebook in Your Ear!

My free Rick Steves Audio Europe app makes it easy for you to download my audio tours of many of Europe's top attractions and listen to them offline during your travels. For northern Europe, these include major sights and neighborhoods in Berlin, Amsterdam, London, and Paris. Sights covered by my audio tours are marked in this book with this symbol: ⌂. The app also offers insightful travel interviews from my public radio show with experts from across northern Europe and around the globe. It's all free! You can download Rick Steves Audio Europe via Apple's App Store, Google Play, or the Amazon Appstore. For more info, see www.ricksteves.com/audioeurope.

Watt's Up? Virtually all cruise ships have American-style outlets, so you don't need an adapter or converter to charge your phone or blow-dry your hair. (If you're cruising with a European line, you may want to confirm the outlet type.)

But if you're staying at a hotel before or after the cruise, you'll need to adapt to Europe's electrical system, which is 220 volts, instead of North America's 110 volts. Most newer electronics (such as laptops, battery chargers, and hair dryers) convert automatically, so you won't need a converter, but you will need an adapter plug with three square prongs for Britain or two round prongs for the rest of Europe (sold inexpensively at travel stores in the US). Avoid bringing older appliances that don't automatically convert voltage; instead, buy a cheap replacement appliance in Europe.

Reservations and Advance Tickets for Major Sights: If you plan ahead, you can scoot right into the following sights, avoiding long, boring ticket-buying lines.

In **St. Petersburg,** the famous Hermitage (palace and art museum) lets you purchase tickets on their website (see page 356), as does Tsarskoye Selo, the palace complex on the outskirts of town (see page 395).

In **Berlin,** reservations are required for climbing the Reichstag dome (see page 565) and highly recommended for entering the Pergamon and Neues museums on Museum Island (see page 567).

In **Amsterdam,** several key sights—including the Rijksmuseum, the Van Gogh Museum, and the Anne Frank House—sell tickets online (see page 735).

In **Paris,** it's essential to reserve tickets for the Eiffel Tower (see page 1043).

Discounts: Discounts for sights are generally not listed in this book. However, many sights offer discounts or free admission for youths (up to age 18), students (with proper identification cards, www.isic.org), families, seniors (loosely defined as retirees or those willing to call themselves a senior), and groups of 10 or more. Always ask.

Online Translation Tip: Google's Chrome browser instantly translates websites. You can also paste text or the URL of a foreign website into the translation window at Translate.google.com. The Google Translate app converts spoken English into most European languages (and vice versa) and can also translate text it "reads" with your smartphone's camera.

Cruise App: Cruise Ship Mate lets you track your ship in real time. It also allows you to see your ship's amenities, chat with other passengers, check reviews about rooms and food, and view photos posted by other cruisers. Best of all, some of its features work without an Internet connection (www.shipmateapp.com).

Packing

One of the advantages of cruising is unpacking just once—in your stateroom. But don't underestimate the importance of packing light. Cruise-ship cabins are cramped, and large suitcases consume precious living space. Plus, you'll still need to get to the airport, on and off the plane, and between the airport and the cruise port. The lighter your luggage is, the easier your transitions will be. And when you carry your own luggage, it's less likely to get lost, broken, or stolen.

Consider packing just one carry-on-size bag (9" by 21" by 14"). I know—realistically, you'll be tempted to bring more. But cruising with one bag can be done without adversely impacting your trip. (I've done it, and was happy I did.) No matter how much you'd like to bring along that heavy jacket or extra pair of shoes, be strong and do your best to pack just what you need.

Here's another reason to favor carry-on bags: If the airline loses your checked luggage and doesn't get it to your embarkation port by the time your ship sets sail, the bags are unlikely to catch up to you. If you booked air travel through the cruise line, the company will do what it can to reunite you with your lost bags. But if you arranged your own flights, the airline decides whether and how to help you—and rarely will it fly your bags to your next port of call. (If you purchase travel insurance, it may cover lost luggage—ask when you buy.) For this reason, even if you check a bag, be sure you pack essentials (medications, a change of clothes, travel documents) in your carry-on.

If you're traveling as part of a couple, and the one-piece-per-person idea seems impossible, consider this compromise: Pack one bag each, as if traveling alone, then share a third bag for bulky cruise extras (such as formal wear). If traveling before or after the cruise, you can leave that third, nonessential bag at a friendly hotel or at a baggage storage place, then be footloose and fancy-free for your independent travel time.

Remember, packing light isn't just about the trip over and back—it's about your traveling lifestyle. Too much luggage marks you as a typical tourist. With only one bag, you're mobile and in control. You'll never meet a traveler who, after five trips, brags: "Every year I pack heavier."

BAGGAGE RESTRICTIONS

Baggage restrictions provide a built-in incentive for packing light. Some cruise lines limit you to two bags of up to 50 pounds apiece; others don't enforce limits (or request only that you bring "a reasonable amount" of luggage). But all airlines have restrictions on the number, size, and weight of both checked and carry-on bags. These days, except on intercontinental flights, you'll most likely pay for each piece of luggage you check—and if your bag is overweight, you'll pay even more. Check the specifics on your airline's website (or read the fine print on your airline eticket).

Knives, lighters, and other potentially dangerous items are not allowed in airplane carry-ons or on board your cruise. Large quantities of liquids or gels must be packed away in checked baggage. Because restrictions are always changing, visit the Transportation Security Administration's website (www.tsa.gov) for an up-to-date list of what you can bring on the plane with you...and what you must check.

If you plan to check your bag for your flight, mark it inside and out with your name, address, and emergency phone number. If you have a lock on your bag, you may be asked to remove it to accommodate increased security checks, or it may be cut off so the bag can be inspected (even a TSA-approved lock may be cut by European inspectors). I've never locked my bag, and I haven't had a problem. Still, just in case, I wouldn't pack anything valuable (such as cash, a camera, or jewelry) in my checked luggage.

WHAT TO BRING

How do you fit a whole trip's worth of luggage into one bag? The answer is simple: Bring very little. You don't need to pack for the worst-case scenario. Pack for the best-case scenario and simply buy yourself out of any jams. Bring layers rather than pack a heavy coat. Think in terms of what you can do without—not what might be handy on your trip. When in doubt, leave it out. The shops on your cruise ship (or on shore) are sure to have any personal items you forgot or have run out of.

Use the "Packing Checklist" later in this chapter to organize and make your packing decisions.

Clothing

Most cruisers will want two to three changes of clothes each day: comfortable, casual clothes for sightseeing in port; more formal evening wear for dinners on the ship; and sportswear, whether it's a swimsuit for basking by the pool or athletic gear for hitting the gym. But that doesn't mean you have to bring along 21 separate outfits for a seven-day cruise. Think versatile. Some port wear can double as evening wear. Two pairs of dressy dinner slacks can be worn on alternating nights, indefinitely. As you choose clothes for your trip, a good rule of thumb is: If you're not going to wear an item more than three times, don't pack it. Every piece of clothing you bring should complement every other item or have at least two uses (for example, a scarf doubles as a shoulder wrap; a sweater provides warmth and dresses up a short-sleeve shirt). Accessories, such as a tie or scarf, can break the monotony.

While most cruises do have a few formal nights with a dress code, they're not as stuffy as you might think. And those formal nights are optional—you can always eat somewhere other than the formal dining room. So dress up only as much as you want to (but keep in mind that most cruise lines forbid shorts or jeans in the dining room at dinnertime). For a general idea of what people typically wear on board, read the "Cruise Ship Dress Code" sidebar.

When choosing clothes for days in port, keep a couple of factors in mind: Most northern European cruises set sail during the best-weather months of June, July, and August. While you shouldn't expect scorching Mediterranean temperatures, summer heat waves can hit Oslo and Berlin. But at these northern latitudes, it can get quite chilly—especially after the sun goes down. The key here is versatility: Wear layers, and always carry a lightweight sweater or raincoat in case clouds roll in and temperatures (or rain drops) drop. Also, a few northern European churches (particularly Orthodox ones, such as those in St. Petersburg) enforce a strict "no shorts or bare shoulders" dress code. Pants with zip-off/zip-on legs can be handy in these situations.

Laundry options vary from ship to ship. Most provide 24-hour laundry service (and charge per piece), enabling those without a lot of clothing to manage fine. Self-service launderettes are rare on board—ask your cruise line in advance about available options. Remember that you can still bring fewer clothes and wash as needed in your stateroom sink. It helps to pack items that don't wrinkle, or look good wrinkled. You should have no trouble drying clothing overnight in your cabin (though it might take longer in humid climates).

Cruise Ship Dress Code

First-time cruisers sometimes worry about the need to dress up on their vacation. Relax. Cruise ships aren't as dressy as they used to be. And, while on certain nights you may see your fellow cruisers in tuxes and gowns, there's usually a place to go casual as well. (In general, the more upscale a cruise is, the more formal the overall vibe—though some luxury lines, such as Windstar, have a reputation for relaxed dress codes.)

During the day, cruisers wear shorts, T-shirts, swimsuits with cover-ups, flip-flops, or whatever they're comfortable in. (On pricier cruises, you may see more passengers in khakis or dressy shorts and polo shirts.)

But in the evenings, a stricter dress code emerges. On most nights, dinner is usually "smart casual" in the main dining room and at some (or all) specialty restaurants. People generally aren't too dressed up—though jeans, shorts, and T-shirts are no-nos. For men, slacks and a button-down or polo shirt is the norm; most women wear dresses, or pants or skirts with a nice top. Plan to wear something a little nicer on the first evening; after you get the lay of the land, you can adjust your wardrobe for the rest of the meals.

Most cruises host one or two "formal" nights per week. On these evenings, men are expected to put on jackets (and sometimes ties), while women generally wear cocktail dresses—or pair a dressy skirt or pants with a nice top. Basically, dress as you would for a church wedding or a night at the theater. A few overachievers show up wearing tuxedos or floor-length dresses. Note that formal nights will sometimes extend beyond the dining room into the ship's main theater venue.

For those who don't want to dress up at all, most cruise ships have informal dining venues—the buffet, the poolside grill, and so on. If you never want to put on a collared shirt, you can simply eat at these restaurants for the entire cruise.

To pack light for your cruise, bring multifunctional clothing that allows you to go minimally formal and also feel stylish when you get off the ship. Men can get by with slacks and a sports coat. (I got a lot of good use out of my summery sports coat.) Women can wear a casual dress and accessorize with jewelry or a wrap.

If you want to get decked out without lugging excess clothing on board, ask if your cruise line has a tuxedo-rental program (some cruise lines also offer a rental program for women's formal wear). You may be able to borrow a jacket or rent a tux on the spot, but selection can be limited—so it's better to order in advance. Provide your measurements beforehand, and a tux will be waiting in your cabin when you board.

It can be worth splurging a little to get just the right clothes for your trip. For durable, lightweight travel clothes, consider ExOfficio, TravelSmith, Tilley Endurables, Eddie Bauer, and REI.

Ultimately—as long as you don't wear something that's outrageous or offensive—it's important to dress in a way that makes you comfortable. No matter how carefully you dress, your clothes probably will mark you as an American. And so what? To fit in and be culturally sensitive, I watch my manners, not the cut of my clothes.

Here are a few specific considerations:

Shirts/blouses. Bring short-sleeved or long-sleeved shirts or blouses in a cotton/polyester blend, ideally in a wrinkle- and stain-camouflaging pattern. Synthetic-blend fabrics (such as Coolmax or microfiber) often dry overnight. A sweater or lightweight fleece is good for cool evenings (warm and dark is best—for layering and dressing up). Indoor areas on the cruise ship can be heavily air-conditioned, so you may need a long-sleeved top, a sweater, or a wrap even in the height of summer.

Pants/skirts and shorts. Lightweight pants or skirts work well, particularly if you hit a hot spell (these are also handy for Orthodox churches with modest dress codes). Jeans typically work well in northern Europe—but they can get hot in muggy weather, and many cruise lines don't consider them appropriate "smart casual" wear. Button-down wallet pockets are safest (though still not as thief-proof as a money belt, described later). Shorts are perfectly acceptable aboard your ship, but on land in Europe they're considered beachwear, mostly worn in coastal or lakeside resort towns. No one will be offended if you wear shorts, but you may be on the receiving end of some second glances.

Shoes. Bring one pair of comfortable walking shoes with good traction. Comfort is essential even on board, where you'll sometimes be walking considerable distances just to get to dinner. And getting on and off tenders (small shuttle boats, sometimes used at Norwegian fjord ports) can involve a short hop to a pier—practical shoes are a must for port days. Sandals or flip-flops are good for poolside use or in case your shoes get wet. And don't forget appropriate footwear to go with your dinner clothes (though again, think versatile—for women, a stylish pair of sandals is nearly as good as heels).

Jacket. Bring a light and water-resistant windbreaker with a hood. Or—more versatile—bring a lightweight Gore-Tex raincoat; rain and cold weather are not uncommon, even in summer.

Swimsuit and cover-up. If you plan on doing a lot of swimming, consider bringing a second swimsuit so that you always have a dry one to put on. Most cruise lines forbid swimsuits anywhere beyond the pool area, so cover-ups are a necessity.

Packing Essentials

Money belt (or neck wallet). This flat, hidden, zippered pouch—worn around your waist (or like a necklace) and tucked under your clothes—is essential for the peace of mind it brings. You could lose everything except your money belt, and the trip could still go on. Lightweight and low-profile beige is best. Whenever you're in port, keep your **cash, credit cards, driver's license,** and **passport** secure in your money belt, and carry only a day's spending money in your front pocket.

Toiletries kit. Because sinks in staterooms come with meager countertop space, I prefer a kit that can hang on a hook or a towel bar. For your overseas flight, put all squeeze bottles in sealable plastic baggies, since pressure changes in flight can cause even good bottles to leak. Pack your own bar of soap or small bottle of shampoo if you want to avoid using the ship-provided "it-sy-bitsies" and minimize waste.

Bring any **medication** and vitamins you need (keep medicine in original containers, if possible, with legible prescriptions), along with a basic **first-aid kit.** If you're prone to motion sickness, consider some sort of **seasickness remedy.** For various options, see page 76. There are different schools of thought on **hand sanitizers** in preventing the spread of germs. Some cruise lines embrace them, others shun them—but they can come in handy when soap and water aren't readily available.

If you wear **eyeglasses** or **contact lenses,** bring a copy of your prescription—just in case. A strap for your glasses/sunglasses is handy for water activities or for peering over the edge of the ship in a strong breeze.

Sunscreen and sunglasses. Bring protection for your skin and your eyes. While you may think of northern Europe as a chilly place, it can be bright and sunny in the summer—especially with the sun reflecting off all that water.

Laundry supplies (soap and clothesline). If you plan to wash clothes, bring a plastic squeeze bottle of concentrated, multipurpose, biodegradable liquid soap. For a spot remover, bring a few Shout wipes or a dab of Goop grease remover in a small plastic container. Some cruise-ship bathrooms have built-in clotheslines, but you can bring your own just in case (the twisted-rubber type needs no clothespins).

Packing aides. Packing cubes, clothes-compressor bags, and shirt-folding boards can help keep your clothes tightly packed and looking good.

BEFORE YOUR CRUISE

Sealable plastic bags. Bring a variety of sizes. In addition to holding your carry-on liquids, they're ideal for packing a picnic lunch, storing damp items, and bagging potential leaks before they happen. Some cruisers use plastic bags to organize their materials (cruise-line handouts, maps, ripped-out guidebook chapters, receipts) for each port of call. If you bring them, you'll use them.

Small daypack. A lightweight pack is great for carrying your sweater, camera, guidebook, and picnic goodies when you visit sights on shore. Don't use a fanny pack—they're magnets for pickpockets.

Fold-up tote bag. A large-capacity tote bag that rolls up into a pocket-size pouch can come in handy for bringing purchases home. It's also useful for the first and last days of your cruise, if you check your larger bags to be carried on or off the ship for you. During these times, you'll want to keep a change of clothes, any medications, and valuables with you.

Water bottle. If you bring one from home, make sure it's empty before you go through airport security (fill it at a drinking fountain once you're through). The plastic half-liter mineral water bottles sold throughout Europe are reusable and work great.

Guidebooks and maps. This book will likely be all you need. (But things can change, so for the latest, see www.ricksteves.com/update.) If you want more in-depth coverage of the destinations or information on a place not covered in this book, consider collecting some other sources (for suggestions, see the appendix). I like to rip out appropriate chapters from guidebooks and staple them together, or use a slide-on laminated book cover. When I'm done, I give them away.

Photos of your family. A small collection of show-and-tell pictures is a fun, colorful conversation piece with fellow cruisers, your crew, and Europeans you meet.

Small notepad and pen. A tiny notepad in your back pocket or daypack is a great organizer, reminder, and communication aid.

Journal. An empty book to be filled with the experiences of your trip will be your most treasured souvenir. Attach a photocopied calendar page of your itinerary. Use a hardbound type designed to last a lifetime, rather than a spiral notebook.

Electronics and Entertainment

As you're packing, try to go light with your electronic gear: You want to experience Europe, not interface with it. Of course, some devices are great tools for making your trip easier or better. As the functions of smartphones, tablets, cameras, and GPS devices become more similar, think creatively about how you might pare down the number of gadgets you bring. Note that many of these are big-ticket items; guard them carefully or look into insuring them.

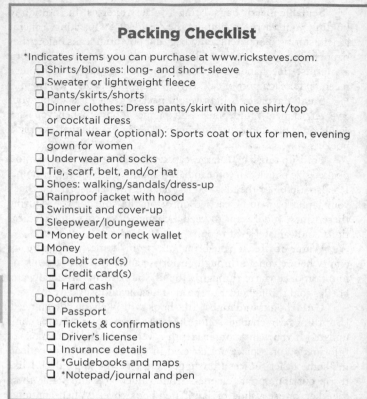

Packing Checklist

*Indicates items you can purchase at www.ricksteves.com.
- ❏ Shirts/blouses: long- and short-sleeve
- ❏ Sweater or lightweight fleece
- ❏ Pants/skirts/shorts
- ❏ Dinner clothes: Dress pants/skirt with nice shirt/top or cocktail dress
- ❏ Formal wear (optional): Sports coat or tux for men, evening gown for women
- ❏ Underwear and socks
- ❏ Tie, scarf, belt, and/or hat
- ❏ Shoes: walking/sandals/dress-up
- ❏ Rainproof jacket with hood
- ❏ Swimsuit and cover-up
- ❏ Sleepwear/loungewear
- ❏ *Money belt or neck wallet
- ❏ Money
  - ❏ Debit card(s)
  - ❏ Credit card(s)
  - ❏ Hard cash
- ❏ Documents
  - ❏ Passport
  - ❏ Tickets & confirmations
  - ❏ Driver's license
  - ❏ Insurance details
  - ❏ *Guidebooks and maps
  - ❏ *Notepad/journal and pen

BEFORE YOUR CRUISE

Note that Wi-Fi aboard cruise ships can be slow and expensive—see "Communicating" in the next chapter.

Consider bringing the following gadgets: **Smartphone/mobile phone** (for details on using a US phone in Europe—or on a cruise ship—see the next chapter); **digital camera** (and associated gear); **other mobile devices** (laptop, tablet); and **headphones/earbuds** (travel partners can bring a Y-jack for two sets of earphones). A small **auxiliary speaker** for your mobile device turns it into a better entertainment center. Bring each device's **charger,** or get a charger capable of charging multiple devices at once. Pack extra **batteries** (you can buy batteries on cruise ships and in Europe, but at a higher price).

Most cruises have limited TV offerings and charge a premium for pay-per-view movies (though you'll find DVD players in some staterooms). If you crave digital distraction, preload your mobile device with a selection of movies or TV shows. Cruise lines generally disable your stateroom TV's input jack, so you can't run a movie from your device on the TV.

- ❏ *Toiletries kit
  - ❏ Basics (soap, shampoo, toothbrush, toothpaste, floss, deodorant, sunscreen)
  - ❏ Medicines & vitamins (seasickness remedies if needed)
  - ❏ *First-aid kit
  - ❏ Hand sanitizer
- ❏ Glasses/contacts/sunglasses (with prescriptions)
- ❏ Earplugs
- ❏ *Laundry soap and *clothesline
- ❏ Sealable plastic bags
- ❏ *Daypack
- ❏ *Fold-up tote bag
- ❏ *Water bottle
- ❏ *Small umbrella
- ❏ Electronics
  - ❏ Mobile phone
  - ❏ Camera & related gear
  - ❏ Tablet
  - ❏ Chargers & batteries
  - ❏ Headphones
  - ❏ *Plug adapters
- ❏ A good book

If you plan to carry on your luggage, note that all liquids must be in 3.4-ounce or smaller containers and fit within a single quart-size sealable bag. For details, see www.tsa.gov.

BEFORE YOUR CRUISE

For long days at sea, bring some leisure reading. Most ships also have free lending libraries and sell US paperbacks at reasonable prices.

Note: Most ships use North American electrical outlets, but if you're staying at a European hotel, you'll need an **adapter** to plug in electronics (for details, see "Watt's Up?" earlier).

Miscellaneous Supplies

The following items are not necessities, but they generally take up little room and can come in handy in a pinch.

Basic **picnic supplies,** such as a Swiss Army-type knife and plastic cutlery, enable you to shop for a very European lunch at a market or neighborhood grocery store (but remember not to pack a knife in your carry-on bag when flying). Munch in port or in your stateroom.

Sticky notes (such as Post-Its) are great for keeping your place in your guidebook. **Duct tape** cures a thousand problems. A **tiny lock** will keep the zippers on your checked baggage shut.

A small **flashlight** is handy for reading under the sheets while your partner snoozes, or for finding your way through an unlit passage (tiny-but-powerful LED flashlights—about the size of your little finger—are extremely bright and compact). **Small binoculars** are great for viewing scenery, sea life, and palace interiors.

Not every stateroom comes with an **alarm clock,** so bring a portable one just in case (or you can use the alarm on your watch or mobile phone). A **wristwatch** is handy for keeping track of important sailing and dinner times, especially if you'll be taking a break from your smartphone.

If night noises bother you, you'll love a good set of expandable foam **earplugs;** if you're sensitive to light, bring an **eye mask.** For snoozing on planes, trains, and automobiles, consider an inflatable **neck pillow.**

A **sewing kit** can help you mend tears and restore lost buttons. Because European restrooms are often not fully equipped, carry some toilet paper or **tissue packets** (sold at all newsstands in Europe).

WHAT NOT TO PACK

Don't bother packing **beach towels,** as these are provided by the cruise line.

Virtually every cruise-ship bathroom comes equipped with a **hair dryer** (though if you need one for before or after your cruise, you may want to check with your hotels). The use of **flat irons, curling irons,** or other hair-care appliances that heat up (and present a potential fire hazard) is discouraged, though most cruise lines tolerate their use.

ON THE SHIP

Now that you've booked your cruise and packed your bags, it's time to set sail. This chapter focuses on helping you get to know your ship and adjust to the seafaring lifestyle.

Initial Embarkation

You've flown across the Atlantic, made your way to the port, and now finally you see your cruise ship along the pier, looming like a skyscraper turned on its side. The anticipation is palpable. But unfortunately, getting checked in and boarding the ship can be the most taxing and tiring part of the entire cruise experience. Instead of waltzing up a gangway, you may spend hours waiting around as hundreds or even thousands of your fellow passengers are also processed. Add the fact that ports are often in ugly and complicated, expensive-to-reach parts of town (not to mention that you're probably jet-lagged), and your trip can begin on a stressful note. Just go with the flow and be patient; once you're on the ship, you're in the clear.

ARRIVAL AT THE AIRPORT

Cruise lines offer hassle-free airport transfers directly to the ship. While expensive, these are convenient and much appreciated if you're jet-lagged or packing heavy. Taxis are always an option for easy door-to-door service but can be needlessly expensive (in many cities, taxis levy additional surcharges for both the airport and the cruise port). Public transportation can be a bit more complicated, and may be a drag with bags, but usually saves you plenty of money. For cities where cruises are likely to begin or end, I've included details on connecting to the airport—either by taxi or by public transit—so you can easily compare the cost and hassle with the transfer options offered by your cruise line. I've also included hotel recommendations.

Don't schedule your arrival in Europe too close to the departure of your cruise, as flights are prone to delays. Arriving on the same day your cruise departs—even with hours to spare—can be risky. And keep in mind that flights departing from the US to Europe generally get in the next calendar day. For more on these topics, see page 37.

Remember: Arriving in Europe a day or more before your cruise gives you the chance to get over jet lag, see your departure city (which is generally not part of your cruise itinerary), and avoid the potential stress of missing your cruise.

CHECKING IN AT THE PORT

Before you leave home, be clear on the exact location of the port for your ship (some cities have more than one port, and large embarkation ports typically have multiple terminals), as well as the schedule for checking in and setting sail. On their initial sailing, most ships depart around 17:00, but cruise lines usually request that passengers be checked in and on board by 15:30 or 16:00. (Like Europe, this book uses the 24-hour clock.) Better yet, arrive at the port at least an hour or two before that to allow ample time to find your way to the ship and get settled in. Most ships are open for check-in around 13:00. You might be able to drop off your bags even earlier—allowing you to explore your embarkation port (or your ship) baggage-free until your stateroom is available. Early check-in also helps you avoid the longest check-in lines of the day, which are typically in the midafternoon.

When you arrive at the terminal, cruise-line representatives will direct you to the right place. There are basically three steps to getting on the ship, each of which might involve some waiting: 1) dropping off bags; 2) check-in; and 3) embarkation (security checkpoint, boarding the ship, and finding your stateroom).

First, you have the option to **drop off your bags**—usually at a separate location from check-in. From here, your bags will be transported to your stateroom. If you're packing light, I recommend skipping the drop-off and carrying your own bags to the cabin, which allows you to dispense with formalities and potential delays (waiting to check the bags, and later, waiting for them to arrive in your cabin). But if you're packing heavy—or just want to be rid of your bags to do a little last-minute sightseeing before boarding—checking your bags typically works fine. Your cruise materials (mailed to you prior to your trip) likely included luggage tags marked with your cabin number; to save time, affix these to your bags before dropping them off (it's handy to bring a small roll of Scotch tape; if you don't have these tags, baggage stewards can give you some on the spot). From here, the crew will deliver your bags to your stateroom. On a big ship, this can take hours; if you'll need anything from your luggage soon after departure—such as a swimsuit, a jacket for dinner, or medication—keep it with you. Don't leave anything fragile in your bags. And be aware that your bags might be sitting in the hallway outside your room for quite some time, where passersby have access to them; while theft is rare, you shouldn't leave irreplaceable documents or other valuables in them. Pack as you would for bags being checked on an airline.

At **check-in,** you'll be photographed (for security purposes) and given a credit-card-like room key that you'll need to show whenever you leave and reboard the ship. Crew members will inspect your passport. They also may ask for your credit-card number to cover any onboard expenses (though some cruise lines ask you to do this after boarding, at the front desk). Remember that they may place a hold on your credit card to cover anticipated charges. If you're accompanying a child on board, see page 42 for the documentation you may need.

As part of check-in, you'll fill out a form asking whether you've had any flu-like symptoms (gastrointestinal or nose/throat) over the last several days, and you may also be asked about recent travel to areas with health epidemics. If you have, the ship's doctor will evaluate you free of charge before you are allowed to board. This is a necessary public-health measure, considering that contagious diseases spread like wildfire on a cruise ship (see the "Health" section, later).

After check-in, you'll be issued a boarding number and asked to wait in a large holding area until your number is called. It could take minutes...or hours.

When your number comes up, you'll have to clear immigration control/customs (usually just a formality—you may not even have to flash your passport) and go through a **security check** to make sure you have no forbidden items, ranging from firearms to alcohol (many cruise lines won't let you BYOB on board, and others limit how much you can bring; for details, see the "Drinks" section, later). Clothes irons and power strips are also typically not allowed; if they are found, they'll be confiscated until the cruise is over.

YOUR FIRST FEW HOURS ON BOARD

Once you're on the ship, head to your **stateroom** and unpack. (For more on your stateroom, see "Settling In," later.) During this time, your cabin steward will likely stop by to greet you. The cabin steward—who is invariably jolly and super-personable—is responsible for cleaning your room (generally twice a day, after breakfast and during dinner) and taking care of any needs you might have.

As soon as you step on board, you'll be very aware that you're

Cruising Terms Glossary

To avoid sounding like a naive landlubber, learn a few nautical terms: It's a "line," not a "rope." It's a "ship," not a "boat."

aft: back of the ship (also called the "stern")

all aboard: time that all passengers must be on board the ship (typically 30 minutes before departure)

astern: toward the stern

beam: width of the ship at its widest point

bearing/course: direction the ship is heading (on a compass, usually presented as a degree)

berth: bed (in a cabin) or dock (at a port)

bow: front of the ship (also called the "fore")

bridge: command center, where the ship is steered from

bulkhead: wall between cabins or compartments

colors: ship's flag (usually the country of registration)

deck: level or "floor" of the ship

deck plan: map of the ship

disembark: leave the ship

draft: distance from the waterline to the deepest point of the ship's keel

embark: board the ship

even keel: the ship is level (keel/mast at 90 degrees)

fathom: unit of nautical depth; 1 fathom = 6 feet

flag: ensign of the country in which a ship is officially registered (and whose laws apply on board)

fore: front of the ship (also called the "bow")

funnel/stack: ship's smokestack

galley: kitchen

gangway: stairway between the ship and shore

gross registered tonnage: unit of a ship's volume; 1 gross registered ton = 100 cubic feet of enclosed space

hatch: covering for a hold

helm: steering device for the ship; place where steering device is located

HMS: His/Her Majesty's Ship (before the vessel name); British-flagged ships only

hold: storage area below decks

hotel manager: officer in charge of accommodations and food operations

hull: the body of the ship

keel: the "fin" of the ship that extends below the hull

knot: unit of nautical speed; 1 knot = 1 nautical mile/hour = 1.15 land miles/hour

league: unit of nautical distance; 1 league = 3 nautical miles = 3.45 land miles

leeward: direction against the wind (that is, into the wind); downwind

lido (lido deck): deck with outdoor swimming pools, athletic area, and other amenities

line: rope

list/listing: tilt to one side

manifest: list of the ship's passengers, crew, and cargo

midship/amidships: spot halfway between the bow and the stern

MS/MSY: motor ship/motorized sailing yacht (used before the vessel name)

muster station: where you go if there's an emergency and you have to board the lifeboats

nautical mile: unit of nautical distance; 1 nautical mile = 1.15 land miles

pilot: local captain who advises the ship's captain, or even steers the ship, on approach to a port

pitch/pitching: rise and fall of the ship's bow as it maneuvers through waves

port: left side of the ship, as you're facing the bow

prow: angled front part of the ship

purser/bursar: officer in charge of finances, sometimes also with managerial responsibilities

quay: dock or pier (pron. "key")

rigging: cables, chains, and lines

roll/rolling: side-to-side movement of a ship

seating: assigned seat and time for dinner in the dining room (often optional)

stabilizer: fin that extends at an angle from the hull of the ship into the water to create a smoother ride

starboard: right side of the ship, as you're facing the bow

stateroom/cabin: "hotel room" on the ship

stem: very front of the prow

stern: back of the ship (also called the "aft")

steward: serving crew, including the cabin steward (housekeeping), dining steward (waiter), or wine steward (sommelier)

superstructure: parts of the ship above the main deck

swell: wave in the open sea

technical call: when the ship docks or anchors, but passengers are not allowed off

tender: small boat that carries passengers between an anchored ship and the shore

tendered: when a ship is anchored (in the open water) rather than docked (at a pier); passengers reach land in tender boats

upper berth: fold-down bed located above another bed

veranda: private balcony off a stateroom

wake: trail of disturbed water that a ship leaves behind it

weigh: raise (for example, "weigh anchor")

windward: in the direction the wind is blowing (with the wind); upwind on a seaborne vessel. You'll quickly remember the old truism about landlubbers having to find their **"sea legs."** At first, you may stagger around like you've had one too many. Hang onto handrails (on stairways and, if it's really rough, in the hallways) and step carefully. You'll eventually get used to it, and you might even discover when you return to shore that you'll need to find your "land legs" all over again. While you may worry that the motion of the ocean will interfere with sleep, many cruisers report exactly the opposite. There's just something soothing about being rocked gently to sleep at night, with the white noise of the engines as your lullaby.

Just before departure, the crew holds an **emergency drill** (or **muster drill**) to brief you on the location of your lifejacket, how to put it on, and where to assemble in the event that the ship is evacuated (called a muster station). After being given a lifeboat number, you must gather at your muster station, along with others assigned to the same lifeboat (though sometimes this drill is held elsewhere on the ship). This is serious business, and all are required to participate. For

more on safety on board—and how to prepare for the worst-case scenario—see the "Cruise-Ship Safety" sidebar.

It's traditional—and fun—for passengers to assemble on the deck while the ship **sets sail,** waving to people on shore and on other ships. On some lines, the ship's loudspeakers play melodramatic music as the ship glides away from land. Sometimes the initial departure comes with live musicians, costumed crew members, and a festive cocktail-party atmosphere.

You'll also get acquainted with the ship's **dining room** or other restaurants. If your ship has traditional "seatings"—an assigned time and seat for dinner each night—this first evening is an important opportunity to get to know the people you'll be dining with. If you have any special requests, you can drop by the dining room a bit before dinnertime to chat with the maître d'.

Memorize your **stateroom number**—you'll be asked for it constantly (when arriving at meals, disembarking, making onboard purchases, and so on). And be aware of not only your cruise line, but the name of your specific ship (e.g., Norwegian *Star*, Royal Caribbean *Serenade of the Seas,* Celebrity *Eclipse,* Holland America *Noordam*)—people in the cruise industry (including those in port) refer to the ship name, not the company.

Various **orientation activities** are scheduled for your first evening; these may include a ship tour or a presentation about the various shore excursions that will be offered during the cruise. While

ON THE SHIP

this presentation is shamelessly promotional, it can help you learn your options.

Life on Board

Your cruise ship is your home away from home for the duration of your trip. This section provides an overview of your ship and covers many of the services and amenities that are offered on board.

SETTLING IN

From tiny staterooms to confusing corridors, it might take a couple of days to adjust to life on board a ship. But before long, you will be an expert at everything from getting to the dining room in the shortest amount of time to showering in tight spaces.

Your Stateroom

While smaller than most hotel rooms, your cabin is plenty big enough if you use it primarily as a place to sleep, spending the majority of your time in port and in the ship's public areas. As you unpack, you'll discover that storage space can be minimal. But—as sailors have done for centuries—cruise-ship designers are experts at cramming little pockets of storage into every nook and cranny. Remember where you tuck things so you can find them when it's time to pack up at the end of your trip.

ON THE SHIP

Unpack thoroughly and thoughtfully right away. Clutter makes a small cabin even smaller. I pack heavier when cruising than when traveling on land, so I make a point to unpack completely, establishing a smart system for keeping my tight little cabin shipshape. Deep-store items you won't need in your suitcase, which you can stow under your bed (or ask your steward to show you any hidden storage areas). Survey all storage areas and make a plan to use them smartly. For example, use one drawer for all things electronic, establish a pantry for food items, and use the safe for some things even if you don't bother locking it. Unclutter the room by clearing out items the cruise line leaves for you (such as promotional materials). I

establish one drawer for all paper material that I think I'm finished with. (The daily handouts will add up, and while it's great to not let paper clutter up your world, you never really know when you might wish you had access to something.) I have a ritual of toggling from shore mode to ship mode by putting my pocket change and money belt (neither of which are of any value on board) in a drawer or the safe when I return to the ship.

Staterooms usually have a safe, minifridge, phone for calling the front desk or other cabins, hair dryer, and television. TV channels include information about the ship, sales pitches for shore excursions and other cruises, various American programming (such as ESPN or CNN), and pay-per-view movies. Some lines even broadcast my TV shows. The beds are usually convertible—if you've got a double bed but prefer twins, your cabin steward can pull them apart and remake them for you (or vice versa). Inside the cabin is a lifejacket for each passenger. Make note of where these are stored, and the best route to your muster station, just as you would the locations of emergency exits on an airplane.

Cabin **bathrooms** are generally tight but big enough to take care of business. First-time cruisers are sometimes surprised at the high water pressure and dramatic suction that powers each flush. Read and heed the warnings not to put any foreign objects down the toilet: Clogged toilets are not uncommon, and on a cruise ship, this can jam up the system for your whole hallway...not a good way to make friends.

Getting to Know Your Ship

After you're settled in your stateroom, start exploring. As you wander, begin to fill in your mental map of the ship with the things

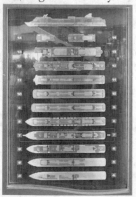

you may want to find later: front desk, restaurants, theater, and so on. Many cruises offer a tour of the ship early on, which can help you get your bearings on a huge, mazelike vessel. Deck plans (maps of the ship) are posted throughout the hallways, and you can pick up a pocket-size plan to carry with you. If your ship has touchscreen activity schedules and deck plans on each floor, use them.

On my first day, I hike the entire ship, deck by deck, inside and out, to see what's where. Ships have peaceful outdoor decks that are rarely visited (perfect for sunsets). They have plenty of bars, cafés, and lounges, some of which may fit your style to a T. Crew members know about their ship's special little places, but many passengers never find them. Discover these on your first day rather than your last. Pop into each of the specialty restaurants for a chat with the

maître d' and to survey the menu, cover charge, and seating.

As you walk down long hallways, it's easy to get turned around and lose track of whether you're headed for the front (fore) or the back (aft) of the ship. For the first couple of days, I carry around my ship deck plan and try to learn landmarks: For example, the restaurants (and my cabin) are near the back of the ship, while entertainment venues (casino, big theater) are at the front. Several banks of elevators are usually spread evenly throughout the ship. Before long, you'll figure out the most direct way between your stateroom and the places you want to go. It can also be tricky to find your room in a very long, anonymous hall with identical doors. Consider marking yours in a low-profile way (for example, tape a small picture below your room number) to help you find it in a hurry.

The double-decker main artery running through the middle of the ship, often called the **promenade deck,** connects several key amenities: theater, main dining room and other eateries, shopping area, library, Internet café, art gallery, photography sales point, and so on. Wrapping around the outside of the promenade deck is the namesake outdoor (but covered) deck, where you can go for a stroll.

At the center of the promenade deck is the main **lobby** (often called the atrium). This area, usually done up with over-the-top decor, has bars, a big screen for occasional presentations, tables of stuff to buy, and not enough seating. If you get lost exploring the ship, just find your way to the lobby and reorient yourself.

The lobby is also where the **guest services desk** is located. Like the reception desk of a hotel, this is your point of contact if you have concerns about your stateroom or other questions. Nearby you'll usually find the excursions desk (where you can get information about and book seats on shore excursions), a "cruise consul-tant" (selling seats on the line's future sailings), and the financial services desk (which handles any monetary issues that the guest services desk can't).

If the lobby is the hub of information, then the **lido deck** is the hub of recreation. Generally the ship's sunny top deck, the lido has

swimming areas, other out-door activities, and usually the buffet restaurant. With a variety of swimming pools (some adults-only, others for kids) and hot tubs; a casual poolside "grill" serving up burgers and hot dogs; ice-cream machines; long rows of sunbathing chairs; and "Margaritaville"-type live music at all hours, the lido deck screams, "Be on vacation!"

INFORMATION

Each evening, the **daily program** for the next day is placed inside your cabin or tucked under your door. These information-packed leaflets offer an hour-by-hour schedule for the day's events, from arrival and all-aboard times to dinner seatings, bingo games, and AA meetings. (They're also peppered with ads touting various spa specials, duty-free sales, and drink discounts.) With a staggering number of options each day, this list is crucial for keeping track of where you want to be and when. I tuck this in my back pocket and refer to it constantly. Bring it with you in port to avoid that moment of terror when you suddenly realize you don't remember what time you have to be back on the ship.

Some cruise lines also give you an **information sheet** about each port of call. These usually include a map and some basic his-torical and sightseeing information. But the dominant feature is a list of the cruise line's "recommended" shops in that port and discounts offered at each one. Essentially, these are the shops that pay the cruise line a commission. These stores can be good places to shop, but they aren't necessarily the best options. (For more details on shopping in port, see page 124.)

The daily program and/or information sheet usually lists your vessel's **port agent** for that day's stop. This is where you'd turn in the unlikely event that you miss your departing ship (for details, see page 130).

Most cruise lines offer **"port talks"**—lectures about upcom-ing destinations. The quality of these can vary dramatically, from educational seminars that will immeasurably deepen your appreciation for the destination, to thinly veiled sales pitches for shore excursions.

Better cruises have a **destination expert** standing by when you get off the ship to answer your questions about that port (usually near the gangway or in the lobby). Again, beware: While some are legitimate experts, and others work for the local tourist board, most are employees of local shops. They can give you some good sightseeing advice, but any shopping pointers they offer should be taken with a grain of salt.

English is generally the first **language** on the ship, though—especially on bigger ships—announcements are repeated in other languages as well (often French, German, Italian, and/or Spanish, depending on the clientele). Most crew members who interact with passengers speak English well—though usually it's their second language.

When passing important landmarks, especially on days at sea, the **captain** may periodically come over the loudspeaker to offer commentary. Or, if the seas are rough, the captain may try to soothe rattled nerves (and stomachs) with an explanation of the weather that's causing the turbulence.

Speaking of **announcements,** cruise lines have varying philosophies about these: Some lines barrage you with announcements every hour or so. On other lines, they're rare. On most ships, in-cabin speakers are only used for emergency announcements. If you can't make out a routine announcement from inside your cabin, crack the door to hear the hallway loudspeakers, or tune your TV to the ship-information channel, which also broadcasts announcements.

YOUR CREW

Your hardworking crew toils for long hours and low pay to make sure you have a great vacation. Whether it's the head waiter who remembers how you like your coffee;

the cabin steward who cleans your room with a smile and shows you pictures of his kids back in Indonesia; or the unseen but equally conscientious workers who prepare your meals, wash your laundry, scrub the deck, or drive the tender boats, the crew is an essential and often unheralded part of your cruise experience.

The all-purpose term for crew members is "steward"—cabin steward (housekeeping), wine steward (sommelier), dining steward (waiter), and so on. Your cabin steward can be very helpful if you have a basic question or request; for something more complicated,

ON THE SHIP

Cruise-Ship Safety

The tragic grounding of the *Costa Concordia* in January 2012 off the coast of Italy had some cruisers asking, "How safe is my cruise ship?" Like any form of travel, cruising comes with risks. But statistically, even taking into account the *Concordia* disaster, cruising remains remarkably safe.

A set of laws called Safety of Life at Sea (SOLAS) has regulated maritime safety since the *Titanic* sank more than a century ago. After the *Concordia* disaster, regulations now require that a safety briefing and muster drill take place before departure. Still, the *Concordia* disaster underscores that cruisers should take responsibility for their own safety. Know where lifejackets are stowed (they're usually in your stateroom, but on very large ships, they may be kept at the muster station). If you are traveling with kids, ask the cruise line for child-size lifejackets to have on hand. Be clear on the location of your muster station, and know how to get there—not only from your stateroom, but also from other parts of the ship. Pack a small flashlight, and keep it handy.

Legally, ships are required to have one lifeboat seat per person on board, plus an additional 25 percent. Aside from the primary lifeboats, large white canisters on the ship's deck contain smaller inflatable lifeboats, which can be launched if the normal lifeboats are disabled. In the event of an evacuation, crew members are responsible for providing instructions and for loading and operating the lifeboats. In theory, a cruise ship's evacuation procedure is designed to safely remove everyone on board within 30 minutes. However, actual full-ship evacuation is almost never practiced. The "women and children first" rule is nautical tradition, but not legally binding. The captain, however, is legally obligated to stay with the ship to oversee the evacuation.

Ultimately, the *Costa Concordia* disaster is a glaring exception to the otherwise sterling safety record of the cruise industry. But it is a cautionary tale that should encourage cruisers to take the initiative to protect themselves, in case the worst-case scenario becomes a reality.

ON THE SHIP

ask the front-desk staff or the concierge. In the dining room, the maître d' assigns tables and manages the dining room, the head waiter takes your order, and the assistant waiters bring your food and bus your dishes.

The ship's cruise director (sometimes called a host or hostess) is a tireless cheerleader, keeping you informed about the various activities and other happenings on board, usually via perky announcements over the ship's loudspeaker several times a day. The cruise director manages a "cruise staff" that leads activities throughout the ship. I have a lot of sympathy for these folks, partly because of my own background as a tour guide—I can't imagine the responsibility of keeping thousands of people informed and entertained 24/7. Experienced cruisers report that the more enthusiastic and energetic the cruise director and staff are, the more likely you are to enjoy your cruise. Gradually you'll come to feel respect, appreciation, and even affection for these people who really, really want you to have a great time on your vacation.

A great bonus for me is to make friends with members of the crew. They are generally hardworking, industrious, young, and fun-loving people who, in spite of their required smiles, genuinely enjoy people. Many are avid travelers, and you'll see them enjoying time on shore (when they are given a break) just like you. While there are strict limits to how crew members can mingle with passengers, you are more than welcome to have real and instructive conversations with them about cruise life, their world back home, or whatever.

Befriending a crew member can also come with a bonus drink. If you see a crew member nursing a drink on their own at a shipboard bar, strike up a conversation. There's a good chance they'll offer to buy you a drink. That's because when drinking alone, they have to pay for their own drinks; but if they're "entertaining" a passenger, both their drink and yours are on the cruise line. It's a win-win.

Crew Wages

ON THE SHIP

Other than the officers and cruise staff, a ship's crew is primarily composed of people from the developing world. With rare exceptions, these crew members are efficient, patient, and friendly (or, at least, always smiling).

It's clear that crew members work hard. But most passengers would be surprised to learn just how long they work—and for how little. Because US labor laws don't apply to sailing vessels, cruise lines can pay astonishingly low wages for very long hours of work. Crew members who receive tips are paid an average base salary (before tips) of about $1 each day. This makes tips an essential part of the crew's income (see "Tipping," later). After tips, the English-speaking service crew who interact with passengers make about $2,000-3,000 per  month, while the anonymous workers toiling at entry-level jobs below decks can make less than $1,000 per month.

These earnings don't seem unreasonable...until you factor in the long hours. Most crew members sign a nine- to ten-month

Running a Cruise Ship

The business of running a ship is divided into three branches, which work together to create a smooth experience: the engine room; the hotel (rooms and food service); and the deck. This last branch includes the physical decks and railings as well as the bridge (the area from which the ship is navigated) and tendering (shore transport). Each department has its leader (chief engineer, hotel manager, and chief officer, respectively), with the captain overseeing the entire operation.

Of course, these days the captain doesn't actually steer the ship while standing at a big wooden wheel. Modern cruise ships are mostly computerized. The "watch"—responsibility for guiding the ship and dealing with any emergencies—rotates among the officers, who usually work four hours on, then eight hours off. The watch continues when the ship is at anchor or

contract, then get two or three months off. While they are under contract, they work seven days a week, at least 10 hours a day; the international legal maximum is 14 hours a day, but according to insiders, some crew members put in up to 16 hours. The hours worked are rarely consecutive—for example, a crew member might work 6 hours, have 2 or 3 hours off, then work 7 more hours. They rarely if ever get a full day off during their entire months-long contract, though they get enough sporadic time off during the day to be able to rest and occasionally enjoy the ports of call. Do the math: If most crew members work an average of 12 hours a day, 30 days a month, that's 360 hours a month—more than double the 160 hours of a 9-to-5 worker.

Cruise lines do cover their crew's accommodations, food, medical care, and transportation (including a flight home once their contract is completed). This means the crew can pocket or send home most of their earnings. While income-tax laws do not apply on the ship, crew members are required to pay taxes in their home countries.

docked, when officers must keep an eye on moorings, make sure the ship is in the correct position, and so on.

The ship is dry-docked (taken out of the water) every two years or so to clean algae, barnacles, and other buildup from the hull and to polish the propeller. A very smooth propeller is crucial for a fluid ride—a dented or porous one can lead to lots of noise and bubbles. Sometimes a crew engineer will put on a wetsuit and dive down to polish the rudder underwater.

As you approach a port (or a challenging-to-navigate passage), a little boat zips out to your cruise ship, and a "pilot"—a

local captain who's knowledgeable about that port—hops off. The pilot advises your ship's captain about the best approach to the dock and sometimes even takes the helm. Once the job is done, another boat might zip out to pick up the pilot.

If you're intrigued by the inner workings of your ship, ask about a behind-the-scenes tour. Many ships offer the opportunity to see the galley (kitchen), food stores, crew areas, and other normally off-limits parts of the ship (usually for a fee).

The Secret Lives of Crew Members

Most cruise lines have somewhere between 1.5 and 2 passengers per crew member. So a 3,000-passenger ship has around 2,000 crew members, who need to be housed and fed—in some ways, they are a vast second set of passengers. The crew's staterooms—the lowest (below the waterline, close to the rumbling engine noise) and smallest on the ship—are far more humble than your own, and usually shared by two to six people. Some cruise staff may have nicer cabins in the passenger areas, but only officers get outside cabins.

While you may see officers eating in the passenger dining room or buffet, most of the crew dines in mess halls with menus that reflect the cuisine of their native lands. Working long hours and far from home, the crew expects to eat familiar comfort food—Southeast Asians want fish and rice; Italians get pasta; and so on. A well-fed crew is a happy crew, which leads to happy passengers—so substantial effort and resources go toward feeding the crew.

The more diverse the crew, the more complicated and expensive it can be to keep everyone satisfied. On some ships, each nationality has its own mess hall and menu that changes day to day. Some cruise lines have found it more efficient to hire employees predominantly from one or two countries. For example, on Holland America, the cabin crew is entirely Indonesian, while the kitchen and dining room crew is Filipino (to recruit employees, the cruise line operates training academies in those two countries).

Many crew members have spouses back home who are raising their children; in port, they buy cheap phone cards or use Skype to keep in touch. In fact, most portside Internet cafés and calling shops target the crew rather than the passengers ("Cheap rates to the Philippines!"). If a café near the port offers free Wi-Fi for customers, you'll invariably see a dozen of your crew huddled over their laptops, deep in conversation.

While many crew members have families to feed, others are living the single life. Workers tend to party together (the crew bar is even more rollicking than the passenger bars), and inter-crew romances are commonplace—though fraternization between members and passengers is strictly forbidden.

Is It Exploitation?

The national and racial stratification of the entire crew evokes the exploitation and indentured servitude of colonial times: The officers and cruise staff are often Americans, Brits, or Europeans, while those in menial roles (kitchen, waitstaff, cleaning crew, engineers) are Indonesian, Filipino, or another developing-world nationality. It's a mark of a socially conscious company when Southeast Asian employees are given opportunities to rise through the ranks and take on roles with greater responsibility.

The cruise lines argue that their employees are making far more money at sea—and in glamorous locations where they get occasional time off to leave the ship and explore the ports—than they would at menial jobs back home. What some see as exploitation, others see as empowerment. Another way to look at it is as "insourcing"—importing cheap labor from the lowest bidder. For better or worse, the natural gregariousness of the crew gives cruisers the impression that they can't be so terribly unhappy with their lives. And the remarkable loyalty of many crew members (working many, many years for the same cruise line) is a testament to the success of the arrangement.

Is it wrong to employ Third World people at low wages to wait on First World, mostly white, generally wealthy vacationers? I don't know. But I do know that your crew members are some of the friendliest people on board. Get to know them. Ask about their families back home. And make sure they know how much you appreciate everything they're doing to make your trip more comfortable.

MONEY MATTERS

Most cruise ships are essentially cashless. Your stateroom key card doubles as a credit card. When buying anything on board, you'll simply present your key card or provide your cabin number, then sign a receipt for the expense. You'll likely need cash on board only for tipping (explained later), paying a crew member to babysit, or playing the casino (most slot machines and table games take cash; you can use your onboard account to finance your gambling, but you'll pay a fee for the privilege). To avoid exorbitant cash-advance fees at the front desk, bring along some US cash for these purposes.

Many cruise lines price everything on board (from drinks to tips to souvenirs) in US dollars, regardless of the countries visited during the trip. Other common currencies are the euro and pound sterling.

Onboard Expenses

First-time cruisers thinking they've paid up front for an "all-inclusive" trip are sometimes surprised by how many add-ons they are offered on board. Your cruise ticket covers accommodations, all the meals you can eat in the ship's main dining room and buffet (with some beverages included), and transportation from port to port. You can have an enjoyable voyage and not spend a penny more (except for expenses in port). But the cruise industry is adept at enticing you with extras that add up quickly. These include shore excursions, casino games, premium drinks (alcohol, soft drinks, and lattes), specialty restaurant surcharges (explained later, under "Eating"), duty-free shopping, fitness classes, spa treatments, photos, and many other goods and services.

It's very easy to get carried away—a round of drinks here, a night of blackjack there, a scuba dive, a castle tour, and more. First-timers—even those who think they're keeping a close eye on their bottom line—can be astonished when they get their final onboard bill, which can easily exceed the original cost of the trip (or so hope the cruise lines).

With a little self-control, you can easily limit your extra expenditures, making your seemingly "cheap" cruise actually cheap. It's a good idea to occasionally check your current balance (and look for mistaken charges) at the front desk or via your cabin TV. You don't have to avoid extras entirely. After all, you're on vacation—go ahead and have that "daily special" cocktail to unwind after a busy day of sightseeing, or stick a $20 bill into a slot machine. But you

Money-Saving Tips

Many people choose cruising because it's extremely affordable. When you consider that you're getting accommodations, food, and transportation for one low price, it's simply a steal. But reckless spending on a cruise can rip through a tight budget like a grenade in a dollhouse. If you're really watching your money, consider these strategies:

Buy as little on board as possible. Everything—drinks, Internet access, knickknacks—is priced at a premium for a captive audience. For most items, you're paying far more than you would off the ship. If you're shopping for jewelry, find a local boutique in port rather than patronize your ship's shop. On the other hand, be aware that some parts of northern Europe can be very expensive. You may find it's cheaper to buy a Coke from your stateroom minibar than at a Norwegian minimart.

Skip the excursions. While cruise-line excursions are easy and efficient, you may be charged $80 to $100 per person for a transfer into town and a walking tour of the old center. But for the cost of a $2 bus ticket, you can get downtown yourself and join a $15 walking tour that covers most of the same sights. This book's destination chapters are designed to help you understand your options.

Stick with the main dining room. If your ship has specialty restaurants that levy a surcharge, skip them in favor of the "free" (included) meals in the main dining room—which are typically good quality.

Save some breakfast for lunch. If you're heading out for a long day in port, help yourself to a big breakfast and bag up the

always have the right to say, "No, thanks." As long as you're aware of these additional expenses and keep your spending under control, a cruise can still be a great value.

Getting Local Cash on Board

While you don't need much cash on board the ship, you will need local money for your time in port, as some European vendors do not accept credit cards and even fewer accept US dollars. It's possible to get local cash on board the ship—but it's expensive. At the front desk, you can exchange cash into the local currency (at bad rates and often with high commissions), or you can get a cash advance on your credit card (at a decent exchange rate but typically with exorbitant fees).

You'll save money if you plan ahead and make use of ATMs near the cruise port. For each destination, I've noted the location of the nearest ATM, which can often be found inside the cruise terminal or close to it (for more on withdrawing money in port, see page 120).

leftovers to keep you going until dinnertime. Some cruise lines will sell you a packed lunch for about $10.

Minimize premium beverage purchases. Because alcohol, soda, and specialty coffee drinks all cost extra, drink tabs can add up fast. Since many cruise lines prohibit or limit bringing your own alcohol on board, you'll pay dearly for wetting your whistle.

Stay out of the casino. With a casino and slots on board, it's easy to fall into a gambling habit. Most cruise lines allow you to use your key card to get cash from your room account for gambling. But read the fine print carefully—you're paying a percentage for this convenience. Also, keep in mind that your odds of winning may be even less than at land-based casinos.

Don't buy onboard photos. Come to think of it, don't even let them take your photo—so you won't be tempted to buy it later.

Minimize use of the ship's mobile phone network and Wi-Fi. Shipboard Internet access and phone rates are very high. To check your email, use a Wi-Fi hotspot in port rather than on board. For details, see "Communicating," later in this chapter.

Take advantage of free services on board. Rather than buy a book, check one out from the ship's library. Instead of ordering a pricey pay-per-view movie in your cabin, enjoy the cruise's free musical performances, classes, and activities. Read your daily program: There's something free going on, somewhere on the ship, virtually every minute of every day.

Don't cheap out at the expense of fun. If you're having a nice dinner, spring for a glass of wine—but keep a mental tally of all these little charges so you're not shocked by the final bill.

ON THE SHIP

Among the destinations in this book, the euro is used in Belgium, Estonia, Finland, France, Germany, Latvia, and the Netherlands. The other destinations have retained their traditional currencies—the Russian ruble, the Norwegian krone, the British pound, and so on. In certain places (as noted in each chapter), it can be tricky to get local funds near your ship. In these cases, it may be worth the added expense to change a small amount of cash on board the ship to finance your trip into town.

Tipping

These days, cruise lines use a standard "auto-tip" system, in which a set gratuity (generally about $12/person per day) is automatically billed to each passenger's account and then divided among the crew. About a third of this tip goes to your cabin steward, a third to the restaurant stewards, and a third to others, including people who worked for you behind the scenes (such as the laundry crew).

Cruise lines explain that, with auto-tipping, additional tipping is "not expected." But it is still most certainly appreciated by the crew. This can cause stress for passengers who are unsure whom, how much, and when to tip. Even more confusing, with all the new alternative dining options, you likely won't be served by the same waiter every night—in fact, you might never eat at the same restaurant twice. In general, the rule of thumb is to give a cash tip at the end of the cruise to those crew members who have provided exceptional service (for specific guidelines, see the "Final Disembarkation" section at the end of this chapter).

At any point, you can increase or decrease your auto-tip amount to reflect your satisfaction with the service you've received. So, if you don't have cash for your final tip, you can simply go to the front desk and increase the auto-tip amount instead (but try to do so before the final night, when accounts are being finalized).

In addition to a monetary tip, crew members appreciate it when you pass along positive feedback. Most cruise lines provide guests with comment cards for this purpose, and they can be taken very seriously when determining promotions. If someone has really gone above and beyond for you, fill out a comment card on their behalf.

HEALTH

Health problems can strike anywhere—even when you're relaxing on a cruise ship in the middle of the sea. Every ship has an onboard doctor (though he or she may not be licensed in the US). If you have to visit the shipboard physician, you will be charged. Before you leave home, ask your health insurance company if the cost is covered or reimbursable; if you buy travel insurance, investigate how it covers onboard medical care.

Fortunately, some of the most common health concerns on cruise ships, while miserable, are temporary and relatively easy to treat.

Seasickness

Naturally, one concern novice cruisers have is whether the motion of the ship will cause them to spend their time at sea with their head in the toilet. And, in fact, a small percentage of people discover (quickly and violently) that they have zero tolerance for life at sea. But the vast majority of cruisers do just fine.

The Baltic is a mostly enclosed sea with very little tide or turbulence; the North Sea can be rougher, but is still calmer than the open ocean. Remember that you're on a gigantic floating city—it takes a lot of agitation to really get the ship moving. Cruise ships are also equipped with stabilizers—wing-like panels that extend below the water's surface and automatically tilt to counteract rolling (side-to-side movement) caused by big swells.

But rough seas can occur, and when they do, waves and winds

may toss your ship around quite noticeably. When this happens, chandeliers and other fixtures begin to jiggle and clink, motion sickness bags discreetly appear in the hallways, and the captain comes over the loudspeaker to comfortingly explain what's being done to smooth out the ride. Lying in bed, being rocked to sleep like a baby, you hear the hangers banging the sides of your closet. Some cruisers actually enjoy this experience; for others, it's pure misery.

If you're prone to motion sickness, visit your doctor before your cruise, and be prepared with a remedy (or several) in case you're laid low. Below are several options that veteran cruisers swear by.

Dramamine (generic name: Dimenhydrinate) is easy to get over the counter but is highly sedating—not ideal unless you are desperate. Some cruisers prefer the less-drowsy formula, which is actually a different drug (called Meclozine, sometimes marketed as **Bonine**). **Marezine** (generic name: Cyclizine) has similar properties and side effects to Dramamine.

Scopolamine patches (sometimes called by the brand name Transderm) are small (dime-sized) and self-adhesive; just stick one on a hairless area behind your ear. They work well for many travelers (the only major side effect is dry mouth), but require a prescription and are expensive (figure $15 for a three-day dose). Some cruisers apply them prophylactically just before first boarding the ship (especially if rough weather is forecast). After removing one of these patches, wash your hands carefully—getting the residue in your eyes can cause dilated pupils and blurry vision.

Acupressure wristbands (such as **Sea-Bands**) have little buds that press on the pressure points on your wrist associated with nausea. You can buy them in any drugstore. They are easy to wear (if a bit goofy-looking—they look like exercise wristbands), and many people prefer them as a cheap and nonmedicinal remedy.

Every cruise aficionado has a favorite homegrown seasickness remedy. Some say that eating green apples or candied ginger can help settle a queasy stomach. Others suggest holding a peeled orange under the nose. Old sea dogs say that if you stay above deck, as close to the middle of the ship as possible, and keep your eyes on the horizon, it will reduce the effects of the motion.

Illness

Like a college dorm or a day-care center, a cruise ship is a veritable incubator for communicable disease. Think about everything that you (and several thousand other passengers) are touching: elevator buttons, railings, serving spoons in the buffet, and on and on. If one person gets sick, it's just a matter of time before others do, too.

The common cold is a risk. But perhaps even more likely are basic gastrointestinal upsets, most often caused by the norovirus

Water, Trash, and Poo: The Inside Scoop

Wondering how cruise ships deal with passengers' basic functions? Here are the answers to some often-asked questions:

Is the water clean and drinkable? Drinking water is usually pumped into the ship at the point of embarkation. Throughout the duration of the cruise, this supply is what comes out of your bathroom tap and is used in restaurant drinks.

Larger ships also have the capacity to desalinize (remove salt from) seawater for use aboard. While perfectly safe to drink, this water doesn't taste good, so it's reserved primarily for cleaning. The water in your stateroom's toilet or shower might be desalinated.

Waste water from the ship is purified on board. While theoretically safe to drink, it's usually deposited into the sea.

Where does the trash go? Trash from shipboard restaurants is carefully sorted into garbage, recyclables, and food waste. Garbage is removed along with other solid waste in port. Cruise lines pay recycling companies to take the recyclables (interestingly, in the US it's the other way around; the companies pay the ship for their recyclables). Food waste is put through a powerful grinder that turns it into a biodegradable puree. This "fish food" is quietly piped out the end of the ship as it sails through the night.

What happens to poo? You may wonder whether shipboard waste is deposited into the sea as you cruise. These things are dictated by local and international law as well as by the policies of individual cruise lines. Most mainstream cruise lines do not dump solid waste into the sea. Instead it is collected, stored, and removed from the ship for proper disposal in port.

(a.k.a. the Norwalk virus)—tellingly nicknamed the "cruise-ship virus." Most often spread through fecally contaminated food or person-to-person contact, the norovirus is your basic nasty stomach bug, resulting in nausea, diarrhea, vomiting, and sometimes fever or cramps. It usually goes away on its own after a day or two.

Because contagious maladies are a huge concern aboard a ship, the cruise industry is compulsive about keeping things clean. Between cruises, ships are thoroughly disinfected with a powerful cleaning agent. When you check in, you'll be quizzed about recent symptoms to be sure you aren't bringing any nasty bugs on board. Some cruise lines won't allow passengers to handle the serving spoons at the buffet for the first two days—the crew serves instead. And, if you develop certain symptoms, the cruise line reserves the right to expel you from the ship at the next port of call (though, in practice, this is rare—more likely, they'll ask you to stay in your stateroom until you're no longer contagious).

Many cruise lines douse their passengers with waterless hand sanitizers at every opportunity. Dispensers are stationed around the

ship, and smiling stewards might squirt your hands from a spray bottle at the entrance to restaurants or as you reboard the ship after a day in port. Whether this works is up for debate. Several studies have demonstrated that using these sanitizers can actually be counterproductive. The US Centers for Disease Control (CDC) recommend them only as an adjunct to, rather than a replacement for, hand washing with soap and warm water. The gels work great against bacteria, but not viruses (such as the norovirus). Following the CDC's lead, some cruise lines have discontinued the use of waterless sanitizers—and

have seen an immediate *decrease* in their rate of outbreaks. The logic is that hand sanitizers actually discourage proper hand-washing behavior. When people apply sanitizers, they assume their hands are clean—and don't bother to wash with soap and water. All the while, that spunky norovirus survives on their hands, gets transferred to the serving spoon at the buffet, and winds up on other people's hands while they're eating dinner.

On your stateroom TV, you might find a channel with instructions on how to wash your hands. Patronizing, yes. But not undeservedly. In a recent international study, Americans were found to be less diligent than other nationalities when it comes to washing their hands after using the bathroom. They then go straight to the buffet, and...you know the rest. It's disgusting but true. If you're a total germophobe, you have two options: Avoid the buffet entirely—or just get over it.

Staying Fit on Board

While it's tempting to head back to the buffet for a second dessert (or even a second dinner) at 11:00 p.m., file away this factoid:

A typical cruise passenger gains about a pound a day. After two weeks at sea, you've put on the "Seafaring 15."

Whether you're a fitness buff or simply want to stave off weight gain, cruise ships offer plenty of opportunities to get your body moving. Most ships have fitness centers with exercise equipment, such as bikes, treadmills, elliptical trainers, and weight machines. Some offer the services of personal trainers, plus classes like boot camp, spinning, Pilates, and yoga (newbies and yoga-heads alike will find it an interesting challenge to hold tree pose on a moving ship). These services usually cost extra, though some classes can be free (usually things like stretching or ab work).

If you're not the gym type, there are other ways to burn calories. Besides swimming pools, many ships have outdoor running tracks that wrap around the deck, complete with fresh air and views. And some ships have more extreme-type sports, such as rock-climbing walls and surfing simulators.

Even if you don't take advantage of sports-related amenities, simply staying active throughout your cruise will help keep those multicourse dinners from going straight to your hips. With multiple levels, your cruise ship is one giant StairMaster. Take the stairs instead of the elevator (which often saves time, too), or run down to the bottom floor and hike back up to the top a couple of times a day. Opt for a walking tour instead of a bus tour when you're in port. Hit the dance floor at night. But just in case, bring along your roomy "Thanksgiving pants."

Smoking

Smoking presents both a public health issue and a fire hazard for cruise lines. While policies are evolving, these days most cruise lines prohibit smoking in nearly all enclosed public spaces and in many outdoor areas, as well as in staterooms or on verandas. You may be able to smoke in certain bars or lounges and in designated outdoor spots. If you're a dedicated smoker or an adamant non-smoker, research the various cruise lines' policies when choosing your vacation.

COMMUNICATING

Because phoning and Internet access are expensive on board—and because the times you'll be in port are likely to coincide with late-night or early-morning hours back home (8:00-17:00 in most of Europe is 2:00-11:00 a.m. on the East Coast and 23:00-8:00 a.m. on the West Coast)—keeping in touch affordably can be tricky. Let the folks at home know not to expect too many calls, or figure out if there are any late evenings in ports when it might be convenient to call home.

Getting Online

It's useful to get online periodically as you travel—to confirm trip plans, get weather forecasts, catch up on email, or post status up- dates and photos. But with high prices and sometimes slower speeds, shipboard In- ternet is not always a good option.

Most cruise ships have Wi-Fi (usually throughout the ship, although it may be slower in your stateroom), and many still have an Inter- net café with a few computer terminals, often in the ship's library. Either way, onboard Internet access can be expensive—typical package deals offer unlimited Wi-Fi for $30-50 a day or $300 for a two-week trip. Other packages charge by "tiered usage": For ex- ample, a package may include social media access for $5-15/day but not email or video streaming; other packages may charge by the amount of data used and/or by the number of devices registered. Check with your cruise line to see if there's any advantage in buy- ing an Internet package before you sail. Others offer promotional deals good only on the day you board.

A few tips: When you're done with an online session, be sure that you properly log out of the shipboard network to avoid running up Internet fees. Also, while using an app such as Skype or Face- Time to make voice or video calls over a Wi-Fi connection is an excellent budget option on land, it's often impractical on the ship, as limited bandwidth means that these services may not work well, or at all. Finally, check if your cruise line has an app—many offer their own branded apps that provide information on deck plans, ac- tivities, shows, menus, and sometimes shipboard-only texting (the latter usually for a fee).

Shipboard Internet access is getting better all the time but can still vary widely in cost and speed by cruise line and even by ship. For the most part, you're often better off waiting until you're in port to get online. If you have a mobile device, find a café on shore where you can sit and download your email or log into Facebook over Wi-Fi while enjoying a cup of coffee—at a fraction of the shipboard cost.

Phoning

If you want to make calls during your trip, you can do it either from land or at sea. It's much cheaper to call home from a mobile phone on a land-based network (explained later). Calling from the middle of the sea is pricey, but if you're in a pinch, you can dial directly from your stateroom telephone or use a mobile phone while roaming on the costly onboard network. For details on how to dial European phone numbers, see the "Staying Connected" section of the appendix.

Stateroom Telephones: Calling **within the ship** (such as to the front desk or another cabin) is free on your stateroom telephone, or from phones hanging at strategic locations around the ship. Some ships provide certain crew members with an on-ship mobile phone and a four-digit phone number. If there's a crew member or service desk you want to contact, just remember their number and dial it toll-free.

Calling **to shore** (over a satellite connection) is usually possible, but expensive—anywhere from $6 to $20 a minute (if you prepay for a large block of calling time, it can be cheaper—for example, $25 for 12 minutes; ask for specifics at the front desk). Note: Similar charges apply if someone calls from shore to your stateroom.

Mobile Phones: US phone service providers offer international service plans that includes calling, messaging, and data. Your normal plan may already include international coverage (T-Mobile's does) through land-based networks. Before your trip, research your provider's international plans and rates. Activate the plan a day or two before you leave, then remember to cancel it when your trip's over.

If you're worried about the added expense, make sure you know how to use your phone cost-effectively. For more on using your phone in Europe, see www.ricksteves.com/phoning. Here are the basics:

1. Disable roaming. To prevent accidentally roaming on the ship-based network, simply disable roaming (or put your phone in "Airplane Mode") as soon as you board the ship. And be warned that receiving a call—even if you don't answer it—costs the same as making a call. You can enable Wi-Fi if you decide to pay the fee onboard your ship or when using Wi-Fi in port.

2. Use land networks. If you are using a mobile phone, it's essential to distinguish between land and sea networks. Because many European cruise itineraries stay fairly close to land, you can often roam on the cheaper land-based networks, even when you're at sea. Your phone will automatically find land-based networks if you're within several miles of shore. The onboard network, which doesn't even turn on until the ship is about 10 miles out, is far more expensive—about $2.50 to $5 per minute (ask your mobile service provider for details about your ship).

Before placing a call or accessing a network from your ship, carefully note which network you're on (this is displayed on your phone's home screen, generally next to the signal bars). You might not recognize the various land-based network names; to be safe, learn the name of the cruise-line network (it's usually something obvious, such as "Phone at Sea")—then avoid making any calls or using data if that name pops up.

3. Turn off data or purchase a data plan. If you plan to use a service like Skype or Facebook Messenger for real-time communication, Wi-Fi is all you need. If you purchase a data plan from your cruise ship or phone service provider, you will need to keep data roaming turned on. In this case, it is recommended to reset your usage stats to monitor how much data you are using during your travels.

ONBOARD ACTIVITIES

Large cruise ships are like resorts at sea. In the hours spent cruising between ports, there's no shortage of diversions: swimming pools,

 hot tubs, and water slides; sports courts, exercise rooms, shuffleboard courts, giant chessboards, and rock-climbing walls; casinos with slots and table games; shopping malls; art galleries with works for sale; children's areas with playground equipment and babysitting services; and spas where you can get a facial, massage, or other treatments. Many activities have an extra charge associated—always ask before you participate.

To avoid crowds, take advantage of shipboard activities and amenities at off times. The gym is quieter late in the evenings, when many cruisers are already in bed. Onboard restaurants are typically less crowded for the later seatings. If you're dying to try out that rock-climbing wall, drop by as soon as you get back on the ship in the afternoon; if you wait an hour or two, the line could get longer. Embarkation day can also work to your advantage: While other passengers are unpacking and exploring the ship, you can have the minigolf course to yourself.

Days at sea are a good time to try all the things you haven't gotten around to on busy port days, but be warned that everyone else on the ship has the same idea. Services such as massages are particularly popular on sea days—book ahead and be prepared to pay full price (if you get a massage on a port day, you might get a discount). Premium restaurants and other activities also tend to fill up far earlier for days at sea, so don't wait around too long to book anything you have your heart set on.

Remember, the schedule and locations for all of these options—classes, social activities, entertainment, and more—are listed in your daily program.

Social Activities

Many ships offer a wide array of activities, ranging from seminars on art history to wine- and beer-tastings to classes on how

to fold towels in the shape of animals (a skill, you'll soon learn, that your cabin steward has mastered). Quite a few of these are sales pitches in disguise, but others are just for fun and a great way to make friends. Bingo, trivia contests, dancing lessons, cooking classes, goofy poolside games, newlywed games, talent shows, nightly mixers for singles, scrapbooking sessions, afternoon tea—there's something for everyone. Note that a few offerings might use code words or abbreviations: "Friends of Bill W" refers to a meeting of Alcoholics Anonymous; "Friends of Dorothy/FOD" or "LGBT" refers to a mixer for gay, bisexual, and transgender people. Ships have a community bulletin board where these and other meetings are posted. You can even post your own.

Entertainment and Nightlife

Most cruise ships have big (up to 1,000-seat) theaters with nightly shows. An in-house troupe of singers and dancers generally puts on

two or three schmaltzy revue-type shows a week (belting out crowd-pleasing hits). On other nights, the stage is taken up by guest performers (comedy acts, Beatles tribute bands, jugglers, hypnotists, and so on). While not necessarily Broadway-quality, these performances are a fun diversion; since they're typically free and have open seating, it's easy to drop by for just a few minutes

(or even stand in the back) to see if you like the show before you commit. On some of the biggest new megaships, the cruise lines are experimenting with charging a fee and assigning seats for more elaborate shows.

Smaller lounges scattered around the ship offer more intimate entertainment with just-as-talented performers—pianists, singers, duos, or groups who attract a faithful following night after night.

ON THE SHIP

Some cruisers enjoy relaxing in their favorite lounge to cap their day.

Cruises often screen second-run or classic movies for passengers. Sometimes there's a dedicated cinema room; otherwise, films play in the main theater at off times.

Eating, always a popular pastime, is encouraged all hours of the day and night. While the main shipboard eateries tend to close by about midnight, large ships have one or two places that remain open 24 hours a day.

And if you enjoy dancing, you have plenty of options ranging from classy ballroom-dance venues to hopping nightclubs that pump dance music until the wee hours.

Shopping

In addition to touting shopping opportunities in port, cruise ships have their own shops on board, selling T-shirts, jewelry, trinkets,

and all manner of gear emblazoned with their logo. At busy times, they might set up tables in the lobby to lure in even more shoppers. In accordance with international maritime law, the ship's casino and duty-free shops can open only once the ship is seven miles offshore.

While shopping on board is convenient and saves on taxes, most items sold on the ship can be found at home or online—for less. If you like to shop, have fun doing it in port, seeking out locally made mementos in European shops. (If you enjoy both sightseeing and shopping, balancing your port time can be a challenge; I'd suggest doing a quick surgical shopping strike in destinations where you have something in particular you'd like to buy, so you won't miss out on the great sights.) You'll find more information on shopping in port on page 124. In the destination chapters, I've given some suggestions about specific local goods to look for.

Casino

Cruise ships offer Vegas-style casinos with all the classic games, including slots, blackjack, poker, roulette, and craps. But unlike Vegas—where casinos clamor for your business with promises of the "loosest slots in town"—cruise ships know they have a captive

Kids' Programs and Activities

Family-friendly cruise lines have "kids clubs" that are open for most of the day. It's a win-win situation for both parents and children. Kids get to hang out with their peers and fill their time with games, story time, arts and crafts, and other fun stuff, while parents get to relax and enjoy the amenities of the ship.

Most kids clubs are for children ages three and older, and require your tots to be potty-trained. Kids are separated by age so that tweens don't have to be subjected to younger children. For older kids, there are teen-only hangouts. If you have kids under three, options are limited: You might find parent/baby classes (no drop-and-go) and, in rare cases, onboard day care.

Rules for kids clubs differ across cruise lines. Some charge for the service, others include it. While kids clubs are generally open throughout the day (about 9:00-22:00), some close at mealtimes, so you'll have to collect your kids for lunch and dinner. Port-day policies vary—some kids clubs require a parent or guardian to stay on board (in case they need to reach you); others are fine with letting you off your parental leash.

There are also plenty of activities outside the kids club. All ships have pools, and some take it to the next level with rock-climbing walls, bowling alleys, and in-line skating. Arcades and movies provide hours of entertainment, and shows are almost always appropriate for all ages. Many scheduled activities are fun for the whole family, such as art classes, ice-carving contests, or afternoon tea.

Babysitting

Because cruise lines want you to explore the ship and have fun (and, of course, spend money at bars and the casino), many have babysitting services. On some ships, you can arrange for a babysitter to come to your stateroom, while others offer late-night group babysitting for a small fee.

To line up babysitting, ask at the front desk or the kids club. Or, if you and your child hit it off with one of the youth counselors at the kids club, you could consider asking her or him for some private babysitting. Oftentimes, crew members have flexible hours and are looking to earn extra money. Some have been separated from their families and even relish the opportunity to play with your kids—let them!

When hiring a babysitter, ask up front about rates; otherwise, offer the standard amount you pay at home. And remember to have cash on hand so you can compensate the babysitter at the end of the evening.

Food

Pizzerias, hamburger grills, ice cream stands...thanks to the diverse dining options on ships, even the pickiest of eaters should be satisfied. Here are some tips for dining with children:

If you prefer to eat with your kids each night, choose the first dinner seating, which has more families and suits kids' earlier eating schedules. If your kids are too squirmy to sit through a multicourse formal dinner every night, choose the buffet or a casual poolside restaurant (described later, under "Eating").

Don't forget about room service. This can be a nice option for breakfast, so you don't have to rush around in the morning. It's also an easy solution if you're cabin-bound with a napping child in the afternoon.

Set ground rules for sweets and soda ahead of time. If your kids have convinced you to let them drink soda (which costs extra on a cruise), buy a soft drink card for the week to save over ordering à la carte.

In Port

If you plan to take your kids off the ship and into town, remember that many European streets and sidewalks are old, cobbled, and uneven—not ideal for a stroller. If your kids can't walk the whole way themselves, consider bringing a backpack carrier rather than a stroller for more mobility.

While excursions are often not worth the expense, they make sense for some ports and activities, especially when you have small kids in tow. You don't have to deal with transportation, nor do you have to worry about missing the ship.

If you do take your small children into port, consider draping a lanyard around their necks with emergency contact information in case you get separated. Include your name and mobile phone number, your ship's name, the cruise line, the itinerary, a copy of the child's passport, and some emergency cash.

ON THE SHIP

Eating

While shipboard dining used to be open-and-shut (one restaurant, same table, same companions, same waitstaff, same time every night), these days you have choices ranging from self-service buffets to truly inspired specialty restaurants. On bigger ships, you could spend a week on board and never eat at the same place twice.

Note that if you have food allergies or a special diet—such as vegetarian, vegan, or kosher—most cruise lines will do their best to accommodate you. Notify them as far ahead as possible (when you book your cruise or 60 days before you depart).

DINING ONBOARD

Most cruise ships have a main dining room, a more casual buffet, a variety of specialty restaurants, and room service.

Main Dining Room

The main restaurant on your ship is the old-fashioned dining room. With genteel decor, formal waiters, and a rotating menu of upscale cuisine, dining here is an integral part of the classic cruise experience.

Traditionally, each passenger was assigned a particular seating time and table for all dinners in the dining room. But over the last decade or so, this **"assigned dining"** policy has been in flux, with various cruise lines taking different approaches. Some lines (including Royal Caribbean, Costa, MSC, Celebrity, and Disney) still have assigned dining. However, some of these lines (notably Celebrity, Costa, and Royal Caribbean) are offering more flexible options, such as plans with increased choice in timing and restaurants, or certain cruises with entirely open dining times. Others companies (such as Holland America, Princess, and Cunard) make seat assignments optional: If you don't want one, just show up and you'll be seated at whichever table is available next. Norwegian Cruise Line, along with several of the smaller luxury lines (Oceania, Silversea, Azamara, Windstar, Star Clippers, Seabourn, and Regent Seven Seas), have no assigned dining—it's first-come, first-served, in any dining venue.

If you choose assigned dining, you'll eat with the same people every night (unless you opt to dine elsewhere on some evenings). Tables for two are rare, so couples will likely wind up seated with others. You'll really get to know your tablemates...whether you like it or not. Some cruisers prefer to be at a table that's as large as pos-

Formal Nights

Many cruises have one or two designated formal nights each week in the main dining room, when passengers get decked out for dinner in suits and cocktail dresses—or even tuxes and

floor-length gowns (for tips on how to pack for formal night, see the sidebar on page 50). In general, on formal nights the whole ambience of the ship is upscale, with people hanging out in the bars, casinos, and other public areas dressed to the nines. And cruises like formal nights because passengers

behave better and spend more money (for example, ordering a nicer bottle of wine or buying the posed photos).

Ships may also have semiformal nights (also one or two per week), which are scaled-down versions of the formal nights—for example, men wear slacks and a tie, but no jacket.

Some passengers relish the opportunity to dress up on formal nights. But if you don't feel like it, it's fine to dress however you choose—as long as you stay out of the dining room. Skip the formal dinners and eat at another restaurant or the buffet, or order room service.

sible—if you are seated with just one other couple, you risk running out of conversation topics sooner than at a table with 10 or 12 people.

Diners are assigned either to an early seating (typically around 18:30) or a late seating (around 20:45). Avid sightseers might prefer the second seating, so they can fully enjoy the port without rushing back to the ship in time to change for dinner (on the other hand, the first seating lets you turn in early to rest up for the next day's port). In general, families and older passengers seem to opt for the first seating, while younger passengers tend to prefer the later one.

If your cruise line has assigned dining (whether mandatory or optional), you can request your seating preferences (time and table size) when you book your cruise. These assignments are first-come, first-served, so the earlier you book and make your request, the better. If you don't get your choice, you can ask to be put on a waiting list.

If you're not happy with your assignment, try dropping by the dining room early on the first night to see if the maître d', who's in charge of assigning tables, can help you. He'll do his best to accommodate you (you won't be the only person requesting a change—

there's always some shuffling around). If the maître d' is able to make a switch, it's appropriate to thank him with a tip.

Some people really enjoy assigned dining. It encourages you to socialize with fellow passengers and make friends. Tablemates sometimes team up and hang out in port together as well. And some cruisers form lasting friendships with people they were, once upon a time, randomly assigned to dine with. If, on the other hand, you're miserable with your dinner companions, ask the maître d' to reseat you. Be aware that the longer you wait to request a change, the more difficult (and potentially awkward) it becomes.

If you get tired of assigned dining, you can always find variety by eating at the buffet or a specialty restaurant, or by ordering room service. And if you have an early seating but decide to skip dinner one night to stay late in port, you can still dine at the other onboard restaurants. Since the various onboard eateries are all included (except for specialty-restaurant surcharges), money is no object. While I enjoy the range of people at my assigned dinner table, I usually end up dining there only about half the nights on a given cruise.

Note that the main dining room is typically also open for breakfast and lunch. At these times, it's generally open seating (no preassigned tables), but you'll likely be seated with others. The majority of travelers prefer to have a quick breakfast and lunch at the buffet (or in port). But some cruisers enjoy eating these meals in the dining room (especially on leisurely sea days) as a more civilized alternative to the mob scene at the buffet; it's also an opportunity to meet fellow passengers who normally sit elsewhere at dinner.

Dress Code: In the main dining room, most cruise lines institute a "smart casual" dress code. This means no jeans, shorts, or T-shirts. Men wear slacks and button-down or polo shirts; women wear dresses or nice separates. On formal nights, the dress code is fancier.

Casual Dining: Buffet and Poolside Restaurants

Besides the main dining room, most ships have at least one additional restaurant, generally a casual buffet. This has much longer

hours than the dining room, and the food is not necessarily a big step down: The buffet often has some of the same options as in the dining room, and it may even have some more unusual items, often themed (Greek, Indian, sushi, and so on). Most ships also have an even more casual "grill" restaurant, usually near the pool, where you can grab a quick burger or hot dog and other snacks. These options are handy if you're in a hurry, or just want a break from the dining room.

When eating at the buffet, keep in mind that this situation—with hundreds of people handling the same serving spoons and tongs, licking their fingers, then handling more spoons and tongs—is nirvana for communicable diseases. Compound that with the fact that some diners don't wash their hands (incorrectly believing that hand sanitizer is protecting them from all illness), and you've got a perfect storm. At the risk of sounding like a germophobe, wash your hands before, during, and after your meal. For more on this cheerful topic, see the "Health" section, earlier.

Dress Code: The buffet and "grill" restaurants have a casual dress code. You'll see plenty of swimsuits and flip-flops, though most cruise lines require a shirt or cover-up in the buffet.

Specialty Restaurants

Most ships (even small ones) have at least one specialty eatery, but some have a dozen or more. If there's just one specialty restau-

rant on board, it serves food (such as steak or seafood) that's a notch above what's available in the dining room. If there are several, they specialize in different foods or cuisines: steakhouse, French, sushi, Italian, Mexican, and so on.

Because specialty restaurants are more in demand than the traditional dining room, it's smart to make reservations if you have your heart set on a particular one. At the beginning of your cruise, scope out the dining room's menu for the week; if one night seems less enticing to you, consider booking a specialty restaurant for that evening. Days at sea are also popular nights in specialty restaurants. I enjoy using the specialty restaurants when I want to dine with people I've met on the ship outside of my usual tablemates. Remember that if you want a window seat with a view, eat early. When darkness settles, the window becomes a pitch-black pane of glass, and that romantic view is entirely gone.

Occasionally these restaurants are included in your cruise price, but more often they require a special cover charge (typically $10-50). In addition to the cover charge, certain entrées incur a supplement ($10-20). A couple ordering specialty items and a bottle of wine can quickly ring up a $100 dinner bill. If you're on a tight budget, remember: Specialty restaurants are optional. You can eat every meal at the included dining room and buffet if you'd rather not spend the extra money. (By the way, if you order a bottle of wine and don't finish it, they can put your name on it and bring it to you in the main dining hall the next night.)

Some routine cruisers allege that the cruise lines are making the food in their dining room intentionally worse in order to steer passengers to the specialty restaurants that charge a cover. But from a dollars-and-cents perspective, this simply doesn't add up. The generally higher-quality ingredients used in specialty restaurants typically cost far more than the cover charge; for example, you might pay $20 to eat a steak that's worth $30. The cover charge is designed not to be a moneymaker, but to limit the number of people who try to dine at the specialty restaurants. It's just expensive enough to keep the place busy every night, but not cheap enough that it's swamped. So if cruise food is getting worse, it's not on purpose.

Dress Code: Specialty restaurants usually follow the same dress code as the main dining room (including on formal nights), though it depends on how upscale the menu is. The steakhouse might be more formal than the main dining room; the sushi bar could be less formal. If you're unsure, ask.

Room Service

Room service is temptingly easy and is generally included in the cruise price (no extra charge). Its menu appears to be much more limited than what you'd get in any of the restaurants, but you can often request items from the dining room menu as well. (If you don't want to dress up on formal night—but still want to enjoy the generally fancier fare on those evenings—ask in advance whether you can get those same meals as room service.) Either way, it's very convenient, especially on mornings when the ship arrives in port early. By eating breakfast in your room (place your order the night before), you can get ready at a more leisurely pace and avoid the crowd at the buffet. You can also arrange for room service to be waiting when you get back on the ship from exploring a port.

It's polite to thank the person who delivers your food with about a $2 tip; sometimes you can put this on your tab and sign for it, but not always, so it's smart to have cash ready.

Dress Code: From tuxes and gowns to your birthday suit, when you order room service, it's up to you.

CRUISE CUISINE

Reviews of the food on cruise ships range wildly, from raves to pans. It's all relative: While food snobs who love locally sourced bistros may turn up their noses at cruise cuisine, fans of chain restaurants are perfectly satisfied on board. True foodies should lower their expectations. High-seas cuisine is not exactly high cuisine.

Cruise food is as good as it can be, considering that thousands

of people are fed at each meal. Most cruise lines replenish their food stores about every two weeks, so everything you eat—including meat, seafood, and produce—may be less than fresh. Except on some of the top-end lines, the shipboard chefs are afforded virtually no room for creativity: The head office creates the recipes, then trains all kitchen crews to prepare each dish. To ensure cooks get it just right, cruise lines hang a photo in the galley (kitchen) of what each dish should look like. This is especially important since most of the cooks and servers come from countries where the cuisine is quite different.

Cruise-ship food is not local cuisine. Today's menu, dreamed up months ago by some executive chef in Miami, bears no resem-blance to the food you saw this af-ternoon in port. It can be frustrat-ing to wander through a Norwegian fjordside market that sells freshly grilled salmon and herb-roasted po-tatoes, then go back to your ship for Caesar salad and prime rib.

On the other hand, cruise menus often feature famous but un-usual dishes that would cost a pretty penny in a top-end restaurant back home. It can be fun to sample a variety of oddball items (such as frog legs, escargot, or foie gras) and higher-end dishes (filet mi-gnon, guinea fowl, lobster, crab) with no expense and no commit-ment. (If you don't like it, don't finish it. Waiters are happy to bring you something else.)

Whether cruise food is good or bad, one thing's for sure: There's plenty of it. A ship with 2,500 passengers and 1,500 crew members might brag that they prepare "17,000 meals a day." Do the math: Someone's going back for seconds.

All things considered, cruise lines do an impressive job of pro-viding variety and quality. But cruise food still pales in comparison to the meals you can get in port, lovingly prepared with fresh in-gredients and local recipes. Some travelers figure there's no point paying for food in port when you can just eat for free on the ship. But after a few days of cruise cuisine, I can't wait to sit down at a real European restaurant or grab some authentic street food...and I can really taste the difference.

ON THE SHIP

DRINKS

In general, tap water, milk, iced tea, coffee and tea, and fruit juices are included. Other drinks cost extra: alcohol of any kind, soft drinks, fresh-squeezed fruit juices, and premium espresso drinks such as lattes and cappuccinos. You'll also pay for any drinks you take from your stateroom's minibar (generally the same price as in the restaurants). Beverages are priced approximately the same as in a restaurant on land (though in the most expensive Scandinavian countries—such as Norway—drink prices in port can exceed what you'll pay on board).

Early in your cruise, ask about special offers for reduced drink prices, such as discount cards or six-for-the-price-of-five beer offers. This also goes for soft drinks—if you guzzle Diet Coke, you can buy an "unlimited drink card" at the start of the cruise and order as many soft drinks as you want without paying more.

Cruise lines want to encourage alcohol sales on board, but without alienating customers. Before you set sail, find out your cruise line's policy on taking alcohol aboard so you can BYOB to save money. Some cruise lines ban it outright; others prohibit only hard liquor but allow wine and sometimes beer. On some ships, you may be able to bring one or two bottles of wine when you first board the ship. Keep in mind that if you bring aboard your own bottle of wine to enjoy with dinner on the ship, you'll most likely face a corkage fee (around $10-20).

To monitor the alcohol situation, cruise lines require you to go through a security checkpoint every time you board the ship. It's OK to purchase a souvenir bottle of booze in port, but you may have to check it for the duration of the cruise. Your purchases will be returned to you on the final night or the morning of your last disembarkation.

If you're a scofflaw who enjoys a nip every now and again, note that various cruising websites abound with strategies for getting around the "no alcohol" rules.

EATING ON PORT DAYS

For some travelers, port days present a tasty opportunity to sample the local cuisine. Others prioritize their port time for sightseeing or shopping rather than sitting at a restaurant waiting for their food to arrive. And still others economize by returning to the ship for lunch (which, to me, seems like a waste of valuable port time). For more tips on eating while in port, see page 127.

To save money, some cruise passengers suggest tucking a few items from the breakfast buffet into a day bag for a light lunch on the go. While this is, to varying degrees, frowned upon by cruise lines, they recognize that many people do it—and, after all, you are paying for the food. If you do this, do so discreetly. Some experi-

ON THE SHIP

enced cruisers suggest ordering room service for breakfast, with enough extra for lunch. Or you can get a room-service sandwich the evening before and tuck it into your minifridge until morning. To make it easier to pack your lunch, bring along sealable plastic bags from home.

Final Disembarkation

When your cruise comes to an end, you'll need to jump through a few hoops before you actually get off the ship. The crew will give you written instructions, and you'll often be able to watch a presentation about the process on your stateroom TV. Many ships even have a "disembarkation talk" on the final day to explain the procedure. I keep it very simple: I review my bill for extra charges, accept the auto-tip, and carry my own bags off the ship any time after breakfast. While the specifics vary from cruise to cruise, most include the following considerations.

On your last full day on the ship, you'll receive an itemized copy of your **bill**. This includes the auto-tip for the crew (explained earlier, under "Tipping"), drinks, excursions, shopping, restaurant surcharges, and any other expenses you've incurred. This amount will automatically be charged to the credit card you registered with the cruise line. If there are any mistaken charges, contest them as soon as you discover them (to avoid long lines just as everyone is disembarking).

If you'd like to give an additional cash **tip** to any crew members (especially those with whom you've personally interacted or who have given you exceptional service), it's best to do so on the final night in case you can't find the tippee in the morning. It's most common to tip cabin stewards and maybe a favorite food server or two. There is no conventional amount or way to calculate tips; simply give what you like, but keep in mind that the crew has extremely low base wages (about $1/day). Some cruise lines provide envelopes (either at the front desk or in your stateroom on the final evening) for you to tuck a cash tip inside and hand it to the crew member.

The night before disembarking, leave any **bags** you don't want to carry off the ship (with luggage tags attached) in the hall outside your room. The stewards will collect these bags during the night, and they'll be waiting for you when you step off the ship. Be sure *not* to pack any items you may need before disembarking the next morning (such as medications, a jacket, or a change of clothes). I prefer to carry off my own bags—that way, I don't have to pack the night before and go without my personal items the last morning. Also, I can leave anytime I want, and I don't have to spend time claiming my bags after I've disembarked.

ON THE SHIP

Before leaving your cabin, check all the drawers, other hidden stowage areas, and the safe—after a week or more at sea, it's easy to forget where you tucked away items when you first unpacked.

In the morning, you'll be assigned a **disembarkation time.** At that time, you'll need to vacate your cabin (so the crew can clean it for the passengers arriving in a few hours) and gather in a designated public area for further instructions on where to leave the ship and claim your luggage.

It's possible to get an **early disembarkation time**—particularly if you're in a hurry to catch a plane or train, or if you just want to get started on your sightseeing. Request early disembarkation near the start of your cruise, as there is a set number of slots, and they can fill up. Another option is to walk off with all your luggage (rather than leaving it in the hall overnight and reclaiming it once off the ship). This opportunity may be limited to a designated number of passengers, so ask about it near the start of your cruise.

If you're hungry, you can have breakfast—your last "free" meal before re-entering the real world. Once you do leave the ship at the appointed time, the bags you left outside your room the night before will be waiting for you in the terminal building.

If you're sightseeing around town and need to **store your bags,** there is often a bag-storage service at or near the cruise terminal (I've listed specifics for certain ports in this book). If you're staying at a hotel after the cruise, you can take your bags straight there when you leave the ship; even if your room is not ready, the hotelier is usually happy to hold your bags until check-in time.

Most cruise lines offer a **transfer** service to take you to your hotel or the airport. Typically you'll do better arranging this on your own (taxis wait at the cruise terminal, and this book's destination chapters include detailed instructions for getting into town or to the airport). But if you book it through the cruise line, they may offer the option to let you pay a little extra to keep your stateroom and enjoy the pool until catching the airport shuttle for your afternoon flight. Some cruise lines also offer excursions at the end of the journey that swing by the city's top sights before ending at your hotel or the airport. This can be a good way to combine a sightseeing excursion with a transfer.

For **customs** regulations on returning to the US, see page 126.

IN PORT

While some people care more about shipboard amenities than the actual destinations, most travelers who take a European cruise see it mainly as a fun way to get to the ports. This is your chance to explore some of Europe's most fascinating cities, characteristic seaside villages, and engaging regions.

Prior to reaching each destination, you'll need to decide whether you want to go on an excursion (booked on board through your cruise line) or see it on your own. This chapter explains the pros and cons of excursions and provides a rundown of which destinations are best by excursion—and which are easy to do independently. It also fills you in on the procedure for getting off and back on the ship, and provides tips on how to make the most of your time on land.

Excursions

In each port, your cruise line offers a variety of shore excursions. While the majority involve bus tours, town walks (led by a local guide hired for the day by the cruise line), and guided visits to museums and archaeological sites, others are more active (biking, kayaking, hiking) or passive (a trip to a beach, spa, or even a luxury-hotel swimming pool for the day). Most also include a shopping component (such as a visit to a Fabergé egg shop in St. Petersburg, a diamond-cutting demonstration in Amsterdam, or a glimpse at glassblowing in Sweden). When shopping is involved, kickbacks are common. Local merchants may pay the cruise line or guide to bring the group to their shops, give them a cut of whatever's bought, or both. In extreme cases, shops even provide buses and drivers for excursions, so there's no risk the shopping stop will be missed. The prices you're charged are likely inflated to cover these payouts.

Excursions aren't cheap. On European cruises, a basic two- to three-hour town walking tour runs about $40-60/person; a half-day bus tour to a nearby sight can be $70-100; and a full-day bus-plus-walking-tour itinerary can be $100-150 or more. Extras (such as a boat ride or a lunch) add to the cost. There seems to be little difference in excursion costs or quality between a mass-market and a luxury line (in fact, excursions can be more expensive on a cheap cruise than on a pricey one).

On the day of your excursion, you'll gather in a large space (often the ship's theater, sometimes with hundreds of others), waiting for your excursion group to be called. You're given a sticker to wear with a number that corresponds to your specific group/bus number. Popular excursion itineraries can have several different busloads. Once called, head down the gangway—or to the tenders (small boats)—to meet your awaiting tour bus and local guide.

EXCURSION OPTIONS

The types of excursions you can book vary greatly, depending on the port. In a typical midsized port city, there might be two different themed walking tours of the city itself (for example, one focusing on the Old Town and art museum, and another on the New Town and architecture); a panoramic drive into the countryside for scenery, sometimes with stops (such as a wine-tasting, a restaurant lunch, or a folk-dancing show); and trips to outlying destinations, such as a neighboring village or an archaeological site.

Some ports have an even wider range of options. For example, if you dock at France's port of Le Havre, you'll be offered various trips into Paris, as well as guided visits to D-Day beaches and Impressionist sights. In these regions, excursions feature destinations bundled in different ways—look for an itinerary that covers just what you're interested in (see the "Excursions" sidebars in each destination chapter to help you sort through your options).

In some cases, there's only one worthy destination, but it takes some effort to reach it. For example, from the German port of Warnemünde, it's a three-hour bus or train ride into Berlin. It's possible—using this book—to get to these places by public transportation. But the cruise line hopes you'll pay them to take you instead.

Most excursions include a guided tour of town, but for those who want more freedom, cruise lines also offer "On Your Own" (a.k.a. "transfer-only" or "transportation-only") excursions: A bus will meet you as you disembark, and you might have a guide who narrates your ride into town. Once you reach the main destination, you're set free and given a time to report back to the bus. While more expensive than public transportation, these transfers cost less than fully guided excursions.

Most cruise lines can also arrange a private driver or guide for you. While this is billed as an "excursion," you're simply paying the cruise line to act as a middleman. It's much more cost-effective to make these arrangements yourself (use one of the guides or drivers I recommend in this book).

BOOKING AN EXCURSION

The cruise lines make it easy to sign up for excursions. There's generally a presentation on excursions in the theater sometime during the first few days of your cruise (or during a day at sea), and a commercial for the different itineraries runs 24/7 on your stateroom TV. You can sign up at the excursions desk, through the concierge, or (on some ships) through the interactive menu on your TV. You can generally cancel from 24 to 48 hours before the excursion leaves (ask when you book); if you cancel with less notice—for any reason—you will probably have to pay for it.

You can also book shore excursions on the cruise line's website prior to your trip. But be warned: It's common to sign up in advance, then realize once on board that your interests have changed. Some cruise lines levy a cancellation fee; most waive that fee if you cancel the first day you're on board, while others will waive it if you upgrade to a more expensive excursion.

If you must cancel because of illness, some cruise lines' excursions desks may be willing to try to sell your tickets to another passenger (and refund your money); if not, they can write you a note to help you recoup the money from your travel insurance.

Cruise lines use the words "limited space" to prod passengers to hurry up and book various extra services—especially excursions. (They're technically correct—if there's not room for every single passenger on board to join the excursion, then space is, strictly speaking, "limited," even if the excursion never sells out.) Sometimes excursions truly do fill up quickly; other times, you can sign up moments before departure. This creates a Chicken Little situation: Since they *always* claim "limited space," it's hard to know whether an excursion truly is filling up fast. If you have your heart set on a particular excursion, book it as far ahead as you can. But if you're on the fence, ask at the excursions desk how many seats are left and how soon they anticipate it filling up. If your choice is already booked when you ask, request to be added to the wait list—

it's not unusual for the cruise line to have last-minute cancellations or to add more departures for popular excursions.

TAKE AN EXCURSION, OR DO IT ON MY OWN?

Excursions are (along with alcohol sales and gambling) the cruise lines' bread and butter. To sell you on them, they'll tell you that you can rest easy, knowing that you're getting a vetted local tour guide on a tried-and-true itinerary that will pack the best experience into your limited time—and you'll be guaranteed not to miss your ship when it leaves that evening.

In practice, some excursions are a great value, whisking you to top-tier and otherwise-hard-to-reach sights with an eloquent guide on a well-planned itinerary. But others can be disappointing time- and money-wasters, carting passengers to meager "sights" that are actually shopping experiences in disguise.

This book is designed not necessarily to discourage you from taking the cruise lines' excursions, but to help you make an informed decision, on a case-by-case basis, about whether a particular excursion is a good value for your interests and budget. In some situations (such as touring the D-Day beaches from Le Havre), I would happily pay a premium for a no-sweat transfer with a hand-picked, top-notch local guide. In other cases (such as the easy walk from Tallinn's cruise port to its atmospheric Old Town), the information in this book will allow you to have at least as good an experience, with more flexibility and freedom, for a fraction of the price.

Pros and Cons of Excursions

Here are some of the benefits of taking an excursion. Evaluate how these selling points fit the way you travel—and whether they are actually perks, or might cramp your style.

Returning to the Ship on Time: Cruise lines gravely remind you that if you're on your own and fail to make it back to the ship on time, it could leave without you. If, however, a cruise-line excursion runs late for some reason, the ship will wait. But in most places, provided that you budget your time conservatively (and barring an unforeseen strike or other crisis), there's no reason you can't have a great day in port on your own and easily make it back on board in time. However, if you don't feel confident about your ability to navigate back to the ship on time, or you have a chronic issue with punctuality, an excursion may be a good option.

Getting Off First: Those going on excursions have priority for getting off the ship. This is especially useful when tendering (riding a small boat from your anchored ship to reach the shore), as tender lines can be long soon after arrival. But if you're organized and get a tender ticket as early as possible, you can make it off the ship almost as fast as excursion passengers.

Optimizing Time in Port: Most excursions are well-planned by the cruise line to efficiently use your limited time in port. Rather than waiting around for a bus or train to your destination, you're whisked dockside-to-destination by the excursion bus. However, when weighing the "time savings" of an excursion, remember to account for how long it takes 50 people (com-

pared to two people) to do everyday tasks: boarding a bus, walking through a castle, even making bathroom stops. If you're on your own and want to check out a particular shop, you can stay as long as you like—or just dip in and out; with a cruise excursion, you're committed to a half-hour, an hour, or however long the shopkeeper is paying your guide to keep you there. Every time your group moves somewhere, you're moving with dozens of other people. In many ports, you may actually reach the city center faster going independently than with an excursion, provided you are ready to hop off the ship as fast as possible, don't waste time getting to the terminal building, and know how, when, and where to grab public transport.

Many cruise lines schedule both morning and afternoon excursions. If you're a 30-minute bus ride from a major destination and select a morning excursion, your guide is instructed to bring you back to the ship (hoping that you'll join an afternoon excursion as well). If you prefer to spend your afternoon in town, it's perfectly acceptable to skip the return bus trip and make your way back to the ship, later, on your own (just be sure your guide knows you're splitting off).

Accessing Out-of-the-Way Sights: In most destinations, there's a relatively straightforward, affordable public-transportation option for getting from the cruise port to the major city or sight. But in a few cases, minor sights (or even the occasional major sight) are challenging, if not impossible, to reach on your own without paying for a pricey taxi or rental car. For example, it's nearly impossible to get from Le Havre to the D-Day beaches by public transportation—so the most reasonable choice is an excur-

Excursion Cheat Sheet

This list will help you answer the question: Should I take a cruise-line excursion? For many ports you can say "no" to the excursion and get around on your own (with this book in hand). For other destinations, an excursion can be your best bet. For details, read the port overview section in each chapter.

Cruise-Line Excursion? No (use this book).

Copenhagen: From all three ports, you can take a cruise-line shuttle bus, a hop-on, hop-off tour bus, or a taxi into town. Copenhagen's two main cruise ports, **Oceankaj** and **Langelinie,** are also served by public buses.

Stockholm: From either port, you can take a hop-on, hop-off tour bus or a cruise-line shuttle bus. From **Stadsgården,** you can take a hop-on, hop-off sightseeing boat to the Old Town (Gamla Stan), or walk there in 15-30 minutes. From **Frihamnen,** you can walk 10 minutes to the bus stop, and ride the public bus into town.

Helsinki: From **West Harbor,** you'll take a bus or tram downtown. From **South Harbor,** you can walk into town in about 15 minutes (or hop on a tram).

Tallinn: It's an easy 15-minute walk from the cruise port into town.

Rīga: It's an easy 10- to 20-minute walk from the cruise port into town.

Gdańsk (Port of Gdynia): From the port at Gydnia, make your way to the train station. It's a 35-minute ride to Gdańsk; once at Gdańsk's train station, it's a brief walk to the heart of town.

Oslo: From the **Søndre Akershus, Vippetangen,** and **Revierkai** berths, it's an easy walk downtown. From **Filipstad,** it's still walkable, but more convenient by cruise-line shuttle bus.

Bergen: From **Skolten,** it's a 10-minute walk into town; from **Jekteviken/Dokken,** ride the free shuttle bus.

Amsterdam: The cruise terminal is a 3-minute tram ride or 15-minute walk from the central train station, with connections to anywhere in the city.

Bruges and Brussels (Port of Zeebrugge): A shuttle bus or tram can take you to the Blankenberge train station, where hourly trains zip to Bruges (15 minutes), Ghent (50 minutes), and Brussels (1.5 hours).

sion. This book is designed to help you determine how easy—or difficult—it is to reach the places you want to see.

Touring with Quality Guides: The guide is the biggest wild card in the success of your tour, but it's also something you have very little control over. You won't know which guide is leading your excursion until he or she shows up to collect you. Most excursions

Cruise-Line Excursion? Maybe.

St. Petersburg: *Without a visa* (expensive, must be arranged in advance—see page 324), you'll be allowed off the ship only if you pay your cruise line for an excursion. On your own *with a visa*, from Marine Facade you can taxi or ride a public-bus-plus-metro connection into town. From Lieutenant Schmidt Embankment or English Embankment it's a 30-minute walk or quick taxi ride.

Berlin (Port of Warnemünde): A transportation-only excursion from your cruise line may be the best way to maximize time in Berlin. On your own, walk 10 minutes to Warnemünde's train station, which has frequent connections to Rostock (20 minutes) and sparse connections to Berlin (3 hours by train—often with change in Rostock, or a cheaper-but-slower bus.

Stavanger: It's an easy walk into downtown (5-15 minutes, depending on where you're docked). Consider an excursion only if you want to side-trip to Pulpit Rock and the Lysefjord.

Sognefjord (Port of Flåm): It's possible to do the best part of the "Norway in a Nutshell" loop trip independently (boat ride, twisty mountain bus, train ride, and another train steeply back down into the fjord). But this requires being organized, double-checking schedules, and getting off the ship quickly. Consider an excursion to skip the hassle.

London (Ports of Southampton or Dover): From **Southampton,** you can walk, take a bus (public or shuttle), or taxi to the train station (depending on your dock). From there, trains go to London (1.5 hours, 2/hour) and Portsmouth (50 minutes, hourly). From **Dover,** ride a shuttle bus or taxi to downtown, then walk to the train station, where trains depart for London (1.5 hours, 2/hour) or Canterbury (30 minutes, 2/hour).

Paris (Port of Le Havre): To see the D-Day beaches (about 1.5 hours west), an excursion works best. To reach Honfleur (30-minute bus), Rouen (1-hour train), or Paris (2.5-hour train), ride a cruise-line shuttle bus or take a taxi from the port to the train/bus station.

Cruise-Line Excursion? Yes.

Geirangerfjord (Geiranger): There's little to see in Geiranger town itself, and public transportation doesn't help you much; it's smart to book a tour to local viewpoints and scenic roads—either through your cruise line or through a local tour operator.

IN PORT

are led by local guides contracted through the cruise line. While all guides have been vetted by the cruise line and are generally high-quality, a few oddball exceptions occasionally sneak through.

An alternative can be to hire a good local guide to show you around on a private tour. For two people, this can cost about as much as buying the excursion, but you get a much more personalized experience, tailored to your interests. And if you can enlist other passengers to join you to split the cost, it's even more of a bargain. I've recommended my favorite guides for most destinations; many are the same ones hired by the cruise lines to lead their excursions. Because local guides tend to book up when a

big cruise ship is in town, it's smart to plan ahead and email these guides well before your trip.

Cruise lines keep track of which guides get good reviews and do their best to use those guides repeatedly. If you do go on an excursion, take the time to give the cruise line feedback, good or bad, about the quality of your guide. They really want to know.

Using Crew Members' Advice

While most cruise lines understand that their passengers won't book an excursion at every port, there is some pressure to get you to sign on. And if you ask crew members for advice on sightseeing (independent of an excursion), they may be less than forthcoming. Take crew members' destination advice with a grain of salt.

Philosophically, most cruise lines don't consider it their responsibility to help you enjoy your port experience—unless you pay them for an excursion. The longer you spend on the ship, the more likely you are to spend more money on board, so there's actually a financial disincentive for crew members to help you get off the ship and find your own way in the port. You're lucky if the best they offer is, "Take a taxi. I have no idea what it costs."

I have actually overheard excursion staff dispense misinformation about the time, expense, and difficulty involved in reaching downtown from a port ("The taxi takes 30 minutes, and I've never seen a bus at the terminal"—when in fact, the taxi takes 10 minutes and there's an easy bus connection). Was the crew being deceptive, or did they not have the facts? Either way, it was misinformation.

The best plan is to do your own sightseeing research. That's why detailed instructions for getting into town from the port are a major feature of this book. To help you out, the local tourist office often sets up a desk or info tent right on the pier, in the terminal, or where shuttle buses drop you. Otherwise, you can usually find a tourist information office (abbreviated **TI** in this book) in the town center.

THE BOTTOM LINE ON EXCURSIONS

Some passengers are on a cruise because they simply don't want to invest the time and energy needed to be independent...they want to be on vacation. Time is money, and you spend 50 weeks a year figuring things out back home; on vacation, you want someone else to do the thinking for you. If that's you, excursions can be a good way to see a place.

But in many destinations, it doesn't take that much additional effort or preparation to have a good experience without paying a premium for an excursion. And cost savings aside, if you have even a middling spirit of adventure, doing it yourself can be a fun experience.

Planning Your Time

Whether you're taking an excursion, sightseeing on your own, or doing a combination of the two, it's important to plan your day on land carefully. Be sure to read this book's sightseeing information and walking tours the night before to make the most of your time, even if you're taking an excursion—many include free time at a sight or neighborhood, or leave you with extra time in port.

First, keep in mind that the advertised amount of time in port can be deceptive. If the itinerary says that the ship is in town from 8:00 to 17:00, mentally subtract an hour or two. It can take a good half-hour to get off a big ship and to the terminal building (or longer, if you're tendering), and from the terminal, you still have to reach the town center. At the end of the day, the all-aboard time is generally a half-hour before the ship departs. Not only do you have to be back on board by 16:30, but you must also build in time to get from downtown to the ship. Your nine-hour visit in port just shrank to seven hours...still plenty of time, but not quite as much time as you expected.

It's essential to realize that if you are late returning to the ship, you cannot expect them to wait for you (unless you're on one of the cruise line's excursions, and it's running late). The cruise line has the right to depart without you...and they will. While this seems harsh, cruise lines pay port fees for every *minute* they are docked, so your half-hour delay could cost them more than your cruise ticket. Also, they have a tight schedule to keep and can't be waiting around for stragglers.

To avoid missing the boat, work backward from the time you must be back on board. Be very conservative, especially if you're going far—for example, riding a train or bus to a neighboring town. Public transportation can be delayed, and traffic can be snarled at rush hour—just when you're heading back to the ship. One strategy is to do the farthest-flung sights first, then gradually work your way back to the ship. Once you know you're within walking distance of the ship, you can slow down.

If you're extremely concerned about missing the ship, just pretend it departs an hour earlier than it actually does. You'll still have several hours to enjoy the destination and be left with an hour to kill back at the cruise port (or on board).

Note that transportation strikes can be a problem in Europe (particularly in France). These can hit at any time, although they are usually publicized in advance. If you're going beyond the immediate area of the port, ask the local TI, "Are there any strikes planned for today that could make it difficult for me to return to my ship?" Even when there is a planned strike, a few trains and buses will still run—ask for the schedule.

If you're an early riser, you'll notice that your ship typically arrives at the port some time before the official disembarkation time. That's because local officials need an hour or more to "clear" the ship (process paperwork, passports, and so on) before passengers are allowed off. Even if you wake up early and find the ship docked, you'll most likely have to wait for the official disembarkation time to get off.

While you should plan your time smartly, don't let anxiety paralyze you: Some travelers—even adventurous ones—get so nervous about missing the boat that they spend all day within view of the cruise port, just in case. Anyone who does that is missing out: In very few cities is the best sightseeing actually concentrated near the port. Cruise excursion directors have told me that entire months go by when they don't leave anyone behind. You have to be pretty sloppy—or incredibly unlucky—to miss your ship (for tips on what to do in the unlikely event this happens to you, see the end of this chapter).

Managing Crowds

Unless you're on a luxury line, you can't go on a cruise and expect to avoid crowds. It's simply a fact of life. So be prepared to visit sights at the busiest possible time—just as your cruise ship funnels a few thousand time-pressed tourists into town (or, worse, when three or four ships simultaneously disgorge).

Keep in mind that my instructions for getting into town might sound easy—but when you're jostling with several hundred others to cram onto a public bus that comes once every 20 minutes, the reality check can be brutal. Be patient...and most important, be prepared. You'll be amazed at how many of your fellow cruisers will step off the ship knowing nothing about their options for seeing the place. By buying and reading this book, and doing just a bit of homework before each destination, you're already way ahead of the game.

Make a point of being the first person down the gangway (or in line for tender tickets) each day, and make a beeline for what you most want to see. While your fellow passengers are lingering over that second cup of coffee or puzzling over the bus schedule, you can be the first person on top of the city wall or on the early train out of town. Yes, you're on vacation, so if you want to take it easy, that's your prerogative. But you can't be lazy and also avoid crowds. Choose one.

Getting Off the Ship

Your ship has arrived at its destination, and it's time to disembark and enjoy Europe. This section explains the procedure for getting off the ship and also provides a rundown of the services you'll typically find at the port.

DOCKING VERSUS TENDERING

There are two basic ways to disembark from the ship: docking or tendering. On most European cruise itineraries, docking is far more common than tendering. (Of the ports covered in this book, the only ones where you may need to tender are on the Norwegian fjords.)

Docking

When a ship docks, it means that the vessel actually ties up to a pier, and you can simply walk off onto dry land. However, cruise piers (like cruise ships) can be massive, so you may have to walk 10-15 minutes from the ship to the terminal building. Sometimes the

port area is so vast, the cruise line will offer a shuttle bus between the ship and the terminal building.

Tendering

If your ship is too big or there's not enough room at the pier, the ship will anchor offshore and send passengers ashore using small boats called tenders. Passengers who have paid for excursions usually go first; then it goes in order of tender ticket (or tender number).

Tender tickets are generally distributed the night before or on the morning of arrival. Show up as early as you can to get your ten-

What Should I Bring to Shore?

Room Key Card: No matter how you leave the ship—tendering or docking, with an excursion or on your own—the crew must account for your absence. Any time you come or go, a security guard will swipe your room key. Your photo will flash onscreen to ensure it's really you. With this punch-in-and-out system, the crew knows exactly who's on board and who's on shore at all times.

Local Cash: After living on a cashless cruise ship, this is easy to forget. If you plan to withdraw local currency at an ATM, be sure to bring your debit card (and a credit card if you plan to make big purchases).

Passport: Whether you take your passport ashore with you is a personal decision. I leave mine in my room (where I feel it's more secure). Many cruise lines recommend you leave it in your room (in the safe, which I have never used), while others recommend bringing your passport along anytime you leave the ship. Many Americans feel safer with their passport with them at all times. If you do carry your passport ashore, have it secured to your body (zipped up or in a money belt—rather than in your day bag, which is the most likely thing you'll lose or have stolen).

　　I find that port vendors that ask for your passport for security or photo ID (such as to rent a scooter) will accept your driver's license instead, but you'd need your passport to travel if you do somehow miss the boat (and some high-security sights require it for entry).

Weather-Appropriate Gear: In chilly or rainy weather, bring a lightweight sweater or raincoat. If it's hot out, that means sunscreen, a hat, sunglasses, lightweight and light-colored clothing, and a water bottle (or buy one in port).

Long Pants: If you plan to visit any Orthodox churches (such as those in St. Petersburg, Helsinki, or Tallinn), you'll encounter a strict "no shorts, no bare shoulders" dress code.

Destination Information Sheet (Daily Program): This is given out by your cruise line. At a minimum, jot down or take a picture of the all-aboard time and—if applicable—the time of the last tender or shuttle bus to the ship, along with contact details for the port agent (see "Port Agents," later in this chapter).

This Guidebook: Tear out just the pages you need for today's port, as explained in the introduction to this book.

IN PORT

der ticket (you may have to wait in line even before the official start time); the sooner you get your ticket, the earlier you can board your tender. Even then, you'll likely have to wait. (Sometimes passengers in more expensive staterooms are given a "VIP tender ticket," allowing them to skip the line whenever they want.)

The tenders themselves are usually the ship's lifeboats, but in

some destinations, the port authority requires the cruise line to hire local tenders. Because tenders are small vessels prone to turbulence, transferring from the ship to the tender and from the tender to shore can be rough. Take your time, be sure of your footing, and let the tender attendants give you a hand—it's their job to prevent you from going for an unplanned swim.

Tendering is, to many passengers, the scourge of cruising, as it can waste a lot of time. Obviously, not everyone on your big ship can fit on those little tenders all at once. Do the math: Your ship carries some 2,000 passengers. There are three or four tenders, which can carry anywhere from 30 to 150 people apiece, and it takes at least 20 minutes round-trip. This can all translate into a lot of waiting around.

There are various strategies for navigating the tender line: Some cruisers report that if you show up at the gangway, ready to go, before your tender ticket number is called, you might be able to slip on early. A crush of people will often jam the main stairwells and elevators to the gangway. Some of these folks might block your passage despite having later tender tickets than yours. If you anticipate crowds while tendering, it's smart to scope out the ship's layout in advance. If you know the layout, you may be able to use a different set of stairs or elevators, then walk through an alternate hallway, to pop out near the gangway rather than get stuck in the logjam on the main stairwell.

Another strategy to avoid the crush of people trying to get off the ship upon arrival is to simply wait an hour or two, when you can waltz onto a tender at will. While you'll miss out on some valuable sightseeing time, some cruisers figure that's a fair trade-off for avoiding the stress of tendering at a prime time.

If there's an advantage to tendering, it's that you're more likely to be taken to an arrival point that's close to the town's main points of interest. When you figure in the time it would take to get from the main cruise port to the city center, tendering might actually save you time—provided you get an early tender ticket. In fact, on smaller ships, it can even be an advantage to tender—there's little to no waiting, and you're deposited in the heart of town.

Crowds are rare on tenders returning to the ship; passengers

you'll usually find a **public bus** stop for getting into town. This is significantly cheaper than a taxi, and often not much slower. Even with an entire cruise ship emptying all at once, waiting in a long line for the bus is relatively rare. These buses usually take local cash only and sometimes require exact change. If you see a kiosk or ticket vending machine near the bus stop, try to purchase a bus ticket there, or at least buy something small to break big bills and get the correct change.

Your cruise line may offer a **shuttle bus** into town; this happens mostly in ports that lack a good public-transit connection (such as Zeebrugge or Dover). If

there is a shuttle, it's often your best option. The shuttle bus typically costs about $4 to $10 round-trip (buses run frequently when the ship arrives, then about every 20 minutes; pay attention to where the bus drops you downtown, as you'll need to find that stop later to return to the ship).

The shuttle bus can get very crowded when the ship first unloads—do your best to get off the ship and onto the bus quickly. At slower times, you might have to wait a little while for the bus to fill up before it departs. Note that the port shuttle sometimes doesn't start running until sometime after your ship actually docks (for example, you disembark at 7:00, but the bus doesn't start running until 8:30). This is a case when it can be worth springing for a taxi to avoid waiting around.

By Excursion: Cruise lines sometimes offer "On Your Own" excursions that include unguided transportation into town, then independent free time. These are worth considering in places where the port is far from the main point of interest (such as the ports of Dover or Southampton for London, the port of Warnemünde for Berlin, or the port of Le Havre for Paris). While more expensive than public transportation—and sometimes even more expensive than a shared cab—this is a low-stress option that allows you freedom to see the sights at your own pace. For details, see "Excursion Options," earlier.

SEEING THE TOWN

If you're touring a port on your own, you have several options for getting around town and visiting the sights (see the destination chapters for specifics).

On a Tour: It's easy to get a guided tour without having to pay excessively for an excursion. And there are plenty of choices, from walking to bus tours. CruiseCritic.com is a great resource for exploring these options.

At or near the terminal, you'll generally find travel agencies offering **package tours.** These tours are similar to the cruise-ship excursions but usually cost far less (half or even a third as much). However, what's offered can change from day to day, so they're not as reliable as the cruise line's offerings. It's possible to reserve these in advance, typically through a third party (such as a travel agency).

A great budget alternative is to join a regularly scheduled **local walking tour** (in English, departing at a specified time every day). Again, these are very similar to the cruise lines' walking tours and often use the same guides. Look for my walking tour recommendations in the destination chapters or ask at the local TI.

In a large city where sights are spread out, it can be convenient to join a **hop-on, hop-off bus tour.** These buses make a circle through town every 30 minutes or so, stopping at key points where passengers can hop on or off at will. While relatively expensive (figure around €25-30 for an all-day ticket), these tours are easier than figuring out public transportation, come with commentary (either recorded or from a live guide), and generally have a stop at or near the cruise port.

Some cruisers hire a **private guide** to meet them at the ship and take them around town (see "Touring with Quality Guides" earlier). Book directly with the guide, using the contact information in this book; if you arrange the guide through a third party—such as a local travel agent or the cruise line—you'll pay a premium.

On Your Own: If you prefer to sightsee independently and are going to London, Paris, Amsterdam, or Berlin, take advantage of my free 🎧 **audio tours,** which guide you through the most interesting neighborhoods and famous sights in each of those cities. Audio tours allow your eyes to enjoy the wonders of the place while your ears learn its story. Before your trip, download the Rick Steves Audio Europe app from Apple's App Store, Google Play, or the Amazon Appstore. For more information, see page 46. These give all the information you'll want, while saving you lots of time and money—perfect for the thoughtful, independent cruiser.

While **renting a car** makes sense for covering a wide rural area (such as the D-Day beaches or the English countryside), I would never rent a car to tour a big city. Public transportation is not only vastly cheaper, but it avoids the headaches of parking, unfamiliar

Taxi Tips

There's no denying that taxis are the fastest way to get from your ship to what you want to see. But you'll pay for that convenience. Regular fares tend to be high, and many cabbies are adept at overcharging tourists—especially cruise passengers—in shameless and creative ways. Here are some tips to avoid getting ripped off by a cabbie.

Finding a Cab: A taxi stand is usually right at the cruise terminal; if not (or if you're already in town), ask a local to direct you. Taxi stands are often listed prominently on city maps; look for the little Ts. Fly-by-night cabbies with a makeshift "Taxi" sign on the rooftop and no company logo or phone number on the door are less likely to be honest.

Establishing a Price: To figure the fare, you can either use the taxi meter or agree on a set price up front. In either case, it's important to know the going rate (the destination chapters include the prevailing rates for the most likely journeys from each port).

In most cities, it's best to use the **taxi meter**—and cabbies are legally required to do so if the passenger requests it. So insist. Cabbies who get feisty and refuse are probably up to no good. If you don't feel comfortable about a situation, get out and find another taxi. Even if I'm using the taxi meter, I still ask for a rough estimate up front, so I know generally what to expect.

Even with the meter, cabbies can still find ways to scam you. For instance, they may try to set it to the pricier weekend tariff, even if it's a weekday—check the list of different meter rates (posted somewhere in the cab, often in English). If you're confused about the tariff your cabbie has selected, ask for an explanation. It's also possible (though obviously illegal) for cab-

traffic patterns, and other problems. In general, given the relatively short time you'll have in port and the high expense of renting a car for the day (figure €40-100/day, depending on the port), this option doesn't make much sense. However, if you're interested, you'll often find car-rental offices or travel agencies at or near the terminal that are accustomed to renting cars for short time periods to cruisers.

In some cities, **renting a bicycle** can be a good option. Northern European cities—especially Copenhagen and Amsterdam—are flat, laced with bike lanes, and very bike-friendly. In these cities, you'll see locals using bikes more routinely than cars...join them.

With Fellow Passengers: The upside of traveling with so many other people is that you have ample opportunities to make friends. On a ship with thousands of people, I guarantee you'll find

bies to tinker with a taxi meter to make it spin like a pinwheel. If you glance away from the meter, then look back and see that it's mysteriously doubled, you've likely been duped. However, some extra fees are on the level (for instance, in most cities, there's a legitimate surcharge for picking you up at the cruise port). Again, these should be listed clearly on the tariff sheet. If you suspect foul play, following the route on your map or conspicuously writing down the cabbie's license information can shame him into being honest.

Agreeing to a **set price** for the ride is another option. While this is usually higher than the fair metered rate would be, sometimes it's the easiest way to go. Just be sure that the rate you agree to is more or less in the ballpark of the rate I've listed in this book. Consider asking a couple of cabbies within a block or two of each other for estimates. You may be surprised at the variation.

Many cabbies hire out for an **hourly rate;** if you want the taxi to take you to a variety of outlying sights and wait for you, this can be a good value. You can also arrange in advance to hire a driver for a few hours or the whole day (for some destinations, I've listed my favorite local drivers).

Settling Up: It's best to pay in small bills. If you use a large bill, state the denomination out loud as you hand it to the cabbie. They can be experts at dropping a €50 note and picking up a €20 one. Count your change. To tip a good cabbie, round up about 5 to 10 percent (to pay a €4.50 fare, give €5; for a €28 fare, give €30). But if you feel like you're being driven in circles or otherwise ripped off, skip the tip.

Ride-Sharing Alternative: Uber is available in a number of European cities, and rides can be cheaper than taxis. Just like at home, you request a car via the Uber app on your mobile device, and the fare automatically gets charged to your credit card.

someone who shares your style of travel. If you and your traveling companion hit it off with others, consider teaming up for your shore time. This "double-dating" can save both money (splitting the cost of an expensive taxi ride) and stress (working together to figure out the best way into town). But be sure you're all interested in the same things before you head ashore.

In-Port Travel Skills

Whether you're taking an excursion or tackling a port on your own, this practical advice will come in handy. This section includes tips on useful services, avoiding theft, using money, sightseeing, shopping, eating, and in general, making the most of your time in port.

TRAVEL SMART

Europe is like a complex play—easier to follow and really appreciate on a second viewing. While no one does the same trip twice to gain that advantage, reading about the places you'll visit before you reach each destination accomplishes much the same thing.

Be your own tour guide: As you travel, get up-to-date info on sights, reserve tickets and tours, and check transit connections. Though you're bound to your ship's schedule, note the best times to visit various sights, and try to hit them as best as you can. Pay attention to holidays, festivals, and days when sights are closed. For example, many museums are closed on Mondays.

Sundays have the same pros and cons as they do for travelers in the US (special events, limited hours, banks and many shops closed, limited public transportation, no rush hour). Saturdays are virtually weekdays with earlier closing times and no rush hour (though transportation connections can be less frequent than on weekdays).

Most important, connect with the culture. Set up your own quest to find the tastiest *kringle* in Denmark or the best *smörgåsbord* in Sweden. Slow down and be open to unexpected experiences. Enjoy the hospitality of the European people. Ask questions—most locals are eager to point you in their idea of the right direction. Wear your money belt, learn the currency, and figure out how to estimate prices in dollars. Those who expect to travel smart, do.

SERVICES

Tourist Information: When in port, visit the local tourist information office (TI). TIs are usually located on the main square, in the City Hall, or at the train station (just look for signs). Many cruise ports also have a temporary TI desk, which answers questions for arriving cruisers. Their job is to make sure your few hours in town are enjoyable, so you'll come back later. At TIs, you can get information on sights and public transit, and pick up a city map and a local entertainment guide. Ask if guided walks, self-guided walking-tour brochures, or audioguides are available. If you need a quick place to eat, ask the TI staff where they go for lunch.

Medical Help: If you get sick or injured while in port—assuming you're not in need of urgent care—do as the Europeans do and go to a pharmacist for advice. European pharmacists diagnose and prescribe remedies for most simple problems. They are usually friendly and speak English, and some medications that are only available by prescription in the US are available over the counter (surprisingly cheaply) in Europe. If necessary, the pharmacist will send you to a doctor or the health clinic. Where possible, I've listed pharmacies close to the cruise port.

Theft or Loss: To replace a **passport,** you'll need to go in person to a US embassy or consulate (neither of which is usually located in a port town) during their business hours, which are generally limited and restricted to weekdays. This can take a day or two. If you lose your passport, contact the port agent or the ship's guest services desk immediately—and be aware that you may not be able to continue your cruise if a replacement passport is not available before the ship sails. Having a photocopy of your passport and a backup form of ID such as your driver's license, as well as an extra passport photo, can speed up getting a replacement.

If your **credit and debit cards** disappear, cancel and replace them (see "Damage Control for Lost Cards," later). File a police report on the spot for any loss (you'll need it to submit an insurance claim). For more info, see www.ricksteves.com/help.

Wi-Fi Access and Phoning: It's easy to find Wi-Fi with your smartphone, tablet, or laptop. There are often hotspots at cafés and

at other businesses. Sometimes Wi-Fi is free; other times you pay by the minute or must buy something in exchange for the network password. Finding an Internet café in Europe can be a challenge; ask at the TI or a crew member.

For details on making calls from your US mobile phone in Europe, see page 82.

OUTSMARTING THIEVES

In Europe, it's rare to encounter violent crime, but petty purse-snatching and pickpocketing are quite common. Thieves target Americans, especially cruise passengers—not because the thieves are mean, but because they're smart. Loaded down with valuables in a strange new environment, we stick out like jeweled thumbs. But being savvy and knowing what to look out for can dramatically reduce your risk of being targeted.

Pickpockets are your primary concern. To avoid them, be aware of your surroundings, don't keep anything valuable in your pockets, and wear a money belt (explained on page 52). In your money belt, carry credit and debit cards, large cash bills, and your passport (if you choose to bring it ashore with you). Keep just a day's spending money in your pocket—if you lose that, it's no big deal.

Many cruise lines hand out cloth bags emblazoned with their

IN PORT

logo. Carrying these around town is like an advertisement for pick-pockets and con artists (not to mention aggressive salesmen). Save them for supermarket runs back home.

Thieves thrive on tourist-packed public-transportation routes—especially buses that cover major sights. When riding the subway or bus, be alert at stops, when thieves can dash on and make off with your day bag. Criminals—often dressed as successful professionals or even as tourists—will often block a bus or subway entry, causing the person behind you to "bump" into you.

Be wary of any unusual contact or commotion in crowded public places (especially touristy spots). For example, while being jostled at a crowded market, you might end up with ketchup or fake pigeon poop on your shirt. The perpetrator then offers profuse apologies while dabbing it up—and pawing your pockets. Treat any disturbance (a scuffle breaking out, a beggar in your face, someone falling down an escalator) as a smokescreen for theft—designed to distract unknowing victims.

Europe also has its share of scam artists, from scruffy babushkas offering you sprigs of rosemary (and expecting money in return) to con artists running street scams, such as the shell game, in which players pay to guess which of the moving shells hides the ball (don't try it—you'll lose every time). Or somebody sells you an item, and turns around to put it in a box while you're getting out your money. Later on the ship, when you open the box, you find only...rocks. Always look inside the box before walking away.

The most rampant scams are more subtle, such as being overcharged by a taxi driver (see the "Taxi Tips" sidebar, earlier). Another common scam is the "slow count": A cashier counts change back with odd pauses, in hopes the rushed tourist will gather up the money quickly without checking that it's all there. Waiters may pad the bill with mysterious charges—carefully scan the itemized bill and account for each item. If paying a small total with a large bill, clearly state the amount you're handing over, and be sure you get the correct change back. Don't be upset about these little scams—treat them as sport.

Nearly all crimes suffered by tourists are nonviolent and avoidable. Be aware of the pitfalls of traveling, but relax and have fun.

MONEY

Whenever you leave the ship, you must use local currency. Many of the countries in this book use the **euro** (Belgium, Estonia, Finland,

France, Germany, Latvia, and the Netherlands); stock up on euros early in your trip, and use them throughout the region.

Other destinations don't officially use the euro (Denmark, Great Britain, Norway, Poland, Russia, and Sweden each have their own currency). In these places, I've occasionally heard cruise-line employees tell passengers, "We're only in the country for a day, and everyone takes euros, so you don't need to change money." That's only partly true: While some merchants in these countries do accept euros, exchange rates are bad, and euros often aren't accepted on public transportation or at major sights and museums. That's why it's best to get local cash, even if you're in town just for a few hours.

Using Cash

Small businesses (mom-and-pop cafés, shops, and so on) may prefer that you pay with cash. In most port cities, ATMs are easy

to find. In some of the more out-of-the-way ports, exchanging a small amount of money for local currency at the cruise ship's front desk can save you time looking for an ATM. If visiting a string of ports that use the same currency, don't waste time in every port tracking down a cash machine—withdraw several days' worth of money, stuff it in your money belt, and see the sights.

When possible, withdraw cash from a bank-run ATM located just outside that bank. Ideally use it during the bank's opening hours; if your card is munched by the machine, you can go inside for help. Avoid "independent" ATMs such as Travelex, Euronet, Moneybox, Cardpoint, and Cashzone. These have high fees, can be less secure than a bank ATM, and may try to trick users with "dynamic currency conversion" (described later). Note that in some Scandinavian and Baltic countries, ATMs are relatively rare; in some ports, there may not be one.

You'll likely wind up with leftover cash. Coins can't be exchanged once you leave the country, so try to spend them while you're in port. But bills are easy to convert to the "new" country's currency. When changing cash, use exchange bureaus rather than banks. Forex desks (easy to find at major train stations) are considered reliable and fair.

Although you can use a credit card to withdraw cash, this only makes sense in an emergency, because it's considered a cash advance (borrowed at a high interest rate) rather than a withdrawal.

IN PORT

Using Credit and Debit Cards

Credit cards are widely accepted and often preferred in this part of the world, even for small transactions. Danes, Swedes, and Norwegians rarely use cash. This can be a relief for cruisers in town who don't want to hassle with ATMs. For purchases, Visa and Master-Card are more commonly accepted than American Express.

I use my credit card to pay for larger items (at hotels before or after a cruise, larger shops and restaurants, travel agencies, car-rental agencies, and so on). I also use my credit card to buy advance tickets for events or sights, and to pay for things near the end of my trip (to avoid another visit to the ATM).

While you can use either a credit or a debit card for most of these purchases, using a credit card offers a greater degree of fraud protection (since debit cards draw funds directly from your bank account).

US cards no longer require a signature for verification, but don't be surprised if a European card reader generates a receipt for you to sign. Some card readers will accept your card as is; others may prompt you to enter your PIN (so it's important to know the code for each of your cards). If a cashier is present, you should have no problems.

At self-service payment machines (transit-ticket kiosks, bike-sharing racks, and so on), results are mixed, as US cards may not work in unattended transactions. If your card won't work, look for a cashier who can process your card manually—or pay in cash.

Dynamic Currency Conversion: If merchants offer to convert your purchase price into dollars (called dynamic currency conversion, or DCC), refuse this "service." You'll pay even more in fees for the expensive convenience of seeing your charge in dollars. Some ATMs also offer DCC, often in confusing or misleading terms. If an ATM offers to "lock in" or "guarantee" your conversion rate, choose "proceed without conversion." Always choose the local currency in these situations.

Damage Control for Lost Cards: If you lose your credit, debit, or ATM card, report the loss immediately to the appropriate global customer-assistance center. Call these 24-hour US numbers collect: Visa (tel. 303/967-1096), MasterCard (tel. 636/722-7111), and American Express (tel. 336/393-1111). European toll-free numbers (listed by country) can be found at the websites for Visa and MasterCard.

You'll need to provide the primary cardholder's identification-verification details (such as birth date, mother's maiden name, or Social Security number). If you report your loss within two days, you typically won't be responsible for any unauthorized transactions on your account, although many banks charge a liability fee of $50. You can generally receive a temporary card within two or three business days in Europe (see www.ricksteves.com/help for more).

SIGHTSEEING

Most cruise passengers are faced with far more to see and do than they have time for. That's why it's helpful to know what you can typically expect when visiting sights.

Entering: Perhaps the biggest challenge is long lines. At sights such as the Hermitage in St. Petersburg, the Eiffel Tower in Paris, the Reichstag in Berlin, and the Anne Frank House in Amsterdam, lines can be a real frustration. Study up, plan ahead, and use the information in this book to minimize time spent in line. For details on making reservations or buying advance tickets at major sights, see page 46.

Some important sights have a security check, where you must open your bag or send it through a metal detector. Some sights require you to check daypacks and coats.

Be warned that you may not be allowed to enter if you arrive 30 to 60 minutes before closing time. And guards start ushering people out well before the actual closing time, so don't save the best for last.

Dress Code: A modest dress code (no bare shoulders, shorts, or above-the-knee skirts) is enforced at Orthodox churches in St. Petersburg, Tallinn, and Helsinki. If you are caught by surprise, you can improvise, using maps to cover your shoulders and a jacket tied around your waist to hide your legs.

Photography: If the museum's photo policy isn't posted, ask a guard. Generally, taking photos without a flash or tripod is allowed. Some sights ban selfie sticks; others ban photos altogether.

Temporary Exhibits: Museums may show special exhibits in addition to their permanent collection. Some exhibits are included in the entry price, while others come at an extra cost (which you may have to pay even if you don't want to see that exhibit).

Expect Changes: Artwork can be on tour, on loan, out sick, or shifted at the whim of the curator. Pick up a floor plan as you enter, and ask museum staff if you can't find a particular item.

Audioguides and Apps: Many sights rent audioguides, which generally offer excellent recorded descriptions in English. If you bring along earbuds, you can enjoy better sound. To save money, bring a Y-jack

IN PORT

and share one audioguide with your travel partner. Museums and sights often offer free apps that you can download to your mobile device (check their websites). And I've produced free downloadable **audio tours** of the major sights and neighborhoods in Amsterdam, Paris, London, and Berlin; look for the 🎧 in this book. For more on my audio tours, see page 46.

Services: Important sights may have a reasonably priced on-site café or cafeteria (handy places to rejuvenate during a long visit). The WCs at sights are free and generally clean.

Before Leaving: Many places sell postcards that highlight their attractions. Before you leave a sight, scan the postcards and thumb through a guidebook to be sure you haven't overlooked something you'd like to see.

Every sight or museum offers more than what's covered in this book. Use the information in this book as an introduction—not the final word.

SHOPPING

Shopping can be a fun part of any traveler's European trip. To have a good experience when you go ashore, be aware of the ins and outs of shopping in port.

At every stop, your cruise line will give you an information sheet that highlights local shopping specialties and where to buy them. Remember that these shops commonly give kickbacks to cruise lines and guides. This doesn't mean that the shop (or what it sells) isn't good quality; it just means you're probably paying top dollar.

Regardless of whether a store is working with the cruise line or not, many places jack up their rates when ships arrive, knowing they're about to get hit with a tidal wave of shoppers. Remember: Northern Europe's cruise season lasts approximately three months—June, July, and August—and many people who live and work in that town must extract a year's worth of earnings from visitors during that period.

Finding Deals

So how can you avoid paying over-the-top, inflated prices for your treasured souvenirs? Go ahead and patronize the obvious tourist shops, but be sure to check out local shopping venues, too. Large department stores often have a souvenir section with standard knickknacks and postcards at prices way below those at cruise-recommended shops. These large stores generally work just like ours,

Clothing Sizes

When shopping for clothing, use these US-to-European comparisons as general guidelines (but note that no conversion is perfect).

Women: For clothing or shoe sizes, add 30 (US shirt size 10 = European size 40; US shoe size 8 = European size 38-39).

Men: For shirts, multiply by 2 and add about 8 (US size 15 = European size 38). For jackets and suits, add 10. For shoes, add 32-34.

Children: Clothing is sized by height—in centimeters (2.5 cm = 1 inch), so a US size 8 roughly equates to 132-140. For shoes up to size 13, add 16-18, and for sizes 1 and up, add 30-32.

and in big cities, most department-store staff are accustomed to wide-eyed foreign shoppers and can speak some English.

If you're adept at bargaining, head over to some of Europe's vibrant outdoor flea markets, where you can find local goods and soft prices. In Russia and at many street markets in some other countries, haggling is the accepted (and expected) method of finding a compromise between the wishful thinking of both the merchant and the tourist.

Bargaining Tips: To be a successful haggler-shopper, first determine the item's value to you. Many tourists think that if they can cut the price by 50 percent they are doing great. So merchants quadruple their prices and the tourist happily pays double the fair value. The best way to deal with crazy prices is to ignore them. Show some interest in an item but say, "It's just too much money." You've put the merchant in a position to make the first offer.

Many merchants will settle for a nickel profit rather than lose a sale entirely. Work the cost down to rock bottom. When it seems to have fallen to a record low, walk away. That last price hollered out as you turn the corner is often the best price you'll get. If the price is right, go back and buy. And don't forget that prices often drop at the end of the day, when flea-market merchants have to think about packing up.

Getting a VAT Refund

Wrapped into the purchase price of your souvenirs is a Value-Added Tax (VAT) of between 18 and 25 percent, depending on the country (for details, see www.ricksteves.com/vat). You're entitled to get most of that tax back if you purchase goods worth more than a certain amount (varies by country) at a store that participates in the VAT-refund scheme. Typically, you must ring up the minimum at a single retailer—you can't add up your purchases from various shops to reach the required amount. (If the store ships the goods to your US home, VAT is not assessed on your purchase.)

Getting your refund is straightforward...and worthwhile if you spend a significant amount on souvenirs.

Get the paperwork. Have the merchant completely fill out the necessary refund document. You'll have to present your passport at the store. Get the paperwork done before you leave the store to ensure you'll have everything you need (including your original sales receipt).

Get your stamp at the border or airport. Process your VAT document at your last stop (for example, at the airport) with the customs agent who deals with VAT refunds. For purchases made in EU countries, process your document when you leave the EU (in this book, that's everywhere but Russia and Norway—and possibly the UK). It doesn't have to be the country where you made your purchases as long as you're still in the EU; if your flight home connects through Paris' Charles de Gaulle airport, you can do it there. For non-EU countries, process your VAT document at your last stop in that country. (VAT refunds for tourists are a recent innovation in Russia; don't be surprised if the system still has a few kinks—or disappears.)

Arrive an additional hour before you need to check in for your flight to allow time to find the local customs office—and to stand in line. It's best to keep your purchases in your carry-on. If they're too large or dangerous to carry on (such as knives), pack them in your checked bags and alert the check-in agent. You'll be sent (with your tagged bag) to a customs desk outside security; someone will examine your bag, stamp your paperwork, and put your bag on the belt. You're not supposed to use your purchased goods before you leave. If you show up at customs wearing your new Norwegian sweater, officials might look the other way—or deny you a refund.

Collect your refund. Many merchants work with services such as Global Blue or Premier Tax Free that have offices at major airports, ports, or border crossings (either before or after security, probably strategically located near a duty-free shop). These services, which extract a 4 percent fee, can refund your money immediately in cash or credit your card (within two billing cycles). Other refund services may require you to mail the documents from home, or more quickly, from your point of departure (using an envelope you've prepared in advance or one that's been provided by the merchant). You'll then have to wait—it can take months.

Customs for American Shoppers

You can take home $800 worth of items per person duty-free, once every 31 days. Many processed and packaged foods are allowed, including vacuum-packed cheeses, dried herbs, jams, baked goods, candy, chocolate, oil, vinegar, mustard, and honey. Fresh fruits and vegetables and most meats are not allowed, with exceptions for some canned items. As for alcohol, you can bring in one liter duty-free (it can be packed securely in your checked luggage, along with any other liquid-containing items).

To bring alcohol (or liquid-packed foods) in your carry-on bag on your flight home, buy it at a duty-free shop at the airport. You'll increase your odds of getting it onto a connecting flight if it's packaged in a "STEB"—a secure, tamper-evident bag. But stay away from liquids in opaque, ceramic, or metallic containers, which usually cannot be successfully screened (STEB or no STEB).

For details on allowable goods, customs rules, and duty rates, visit http://help.cbp.gov.

EATING IN PORT

Eating in Europe is sightseeing for your taste buds. The memories of good meals can satisfy you for years. Even though most of

your meals will be on the ship, you can still experience Europe's amazing cuisine when you're in port. Your options range from grabbing a lunch on the run to lingering over a leisurely meal at a sit-down restaurant. When deciding where to eat, be aware that table service in Europe is slow—sometimes painfully so—by American standards. Don't expect to dine and dash, but you can try explaining to the waitstaff that you're in a hurry.

Lunch on the Go

You can eat quickly and still have a local experience. Every country has its own equivalent of the hot-dog stand, where you can grab a filling bite on the go: Danish *pølse* (sausage) carts and *smørrebrød* (open-face sandwich) shops, French *crêperies*, Berlin's *Currywurst* stands, and Russian *bliny* (potato pancake) shops. Or stop in a heavenly smelling bakery and buy a pastry or sandwich.

Ethnic eateries are usually cheap; eat in, or get your meal to go. Cafeterias, delis, and fast-food chains with salad bars are tourist-friendly and good for a quick meal.

Like businesspeople, cruise travelers have a lot on their daytime agendas and want to eat well but quickly. A good bet is to eat lunch at a place that caters to the local business clientele. You'll find many fine little restaurants advertising fast, two-course business lunches. These are inexpensive and served quickly. Each neighborhood is also likely to have a favorite deli/sandwich place where you'll see a thriving crowd of office workers spilling out onto the curb, eating fine, small meals or gourmet sandwiches—and often sipping a glass of top-end wine with their food.

Lately I've been enjoying Europe's fine market halls—Industrial Age glass-and-steel farmers markets that have been spiced up with great eateries, priced for local shoppers and serving the freshest ingredients. You'll find them in nearly any European city. It's a great way to enjoy lunch and feel the pulse of everyday life.

Picnicking takes a little more time and planning but can be an exciting cultural experience: It's fun to dive into a market and actually get a chance to do business there. Europe's colorful markets overflow with varied cheeses, meats, fresh fruits, vegetables, and still-warm-out-of-the-oven bread. Most markets are not self-service: You point to what you want and let the merchant weigh and bag it for you. The unit of measure throughout the Continent is a kilo, or 2.2 pounds. A kilo has 1,000 grams. One hundred grams is a common unit of sale for cheese or meat—and just the right amount to tuck into a chunk of French bread for a satisfying sandwich.

Keep an eye out for some of my favorite picnic treats: *Wasa* cracker bread (Sport is my favorite; *flatbrød* is ideal for munchies), packaged meat and cheese, brown "goat cheese" *(geitost)*, drinkable yogurt, freshly cooked or smoked fish from markets, fresh fruit and vegetables, lingonberries, and squeeze tubes of mustard and sandwich spreads (shrimp, caviar), which are perfect on rye bread.

Sit-Down Restaurants

For some cruisers, it's unimaginable to waste valuable port time lingering at a sit-down restaurant when they could be cramming their day with sightseeing. For others, a good European restaurant experience beats a cathedral or a museum by a mile.

To find a good restaurant, head away from the tourist center and stroll around until you find a place with a happy crowd of locals. Look for menus handwritten in the native language (usually posted outside) and offering a small selection. This means they're cooking what was fresh in the market that morning for loyal return customers.

Restaurants in Europe usually do not serve meals throughout the day, so don't wait too long to find a place for lunch. Typically restaurants close from mid-afternoon (about 14:00) until the dinner hour.

When entering a restaurant, feel free to seat yourself at any table that isn't marked "reserved." Catch a server's eye and signal to be sure it's OK to sit there. If the place is full, you're likely to simply be turned away: There's no "hostess" standing by to add your name to a carefully managed waiting list.

If no English **menu** is posted, ask to see one. What we call the menu in the US usually goes by some variation on the word "card" in Europe—for instance, *la carte* in French.

Be aware that the word "menu" can mean a fixed-price meal, particularly in France. Many small eateries offer an economical "*menu* of the day" (*plat du jour* in France)—a daily special with a fixed price. The "tourist *menu*" (*menu touristique* in France), popular in restaurants throughout Europe's tourist zones, offers visitors a no-stress, three-course meal for a painless price that usually includes service, bread, and a drink. You normally get a choice of several options for each course. Though locals rarely order this, the tourist *menu* can be a convenient way to sample some regional flavors for a reasonable price. Particularly in Scandinavian countries, many restaurants offer cheap daily lunch specials *(dagens rett)* and buffets, popular with office workers.

In restaurants, Europeans generally drink bottled **water** (for taste, not health), served with or without carbonation. You can normally get free tap water, but you may need to be polite, patient, inventive, and know the correct phrase. There's nothing wrong with ordering tap water, and it is safe to drink in all the countries in this book, except for Russia.

One of the biggest surprises for Americans at Europe's restaurants is the service, which can seem excruciatingly slow when you're eager to get out and sightsee (or in a hurry to get back to your cruise ship). Europeans will spend at least two hours enjoying a good meal, and fast service is considered rude service. If you need to eat and run, make it very clear when you order.

To get the **bill,** you'll have to ask for it. Don't wait until you are in a hurry to leave. Catch the waiter's eye and, with raised hands, scribble with an imaginary pencil on your palm. Dishonest waiters often assume cruise travelers are clueless and easy to rip off. Before your bill comes, make a mental tally of roughly how much your meal should cost. If the total is a surprise, don't be shy. Ask to have it itemized and explained.

Tipping: At European restaurants, a base gratuity is usually included in your bill. Virtually anywhere in Europe, if you're pleased with the service, you can round up a euro or more. In most restaurants, 10 percent is adequate. Please believe me—tipping 15-20 percent in Europe is unnecessary, if not culturally insensitive. Tip only at restaurants with waitstaff; skip the tip if you order food at a counter. Servers prefer to be tipped in cash even if you pay with your credit card; otherwise the tip may never reach them (specifics on tipping are also provided in each country's introduction chapter).

Returning to the Ship

When it's time to head back to your ship, remember that the posted departure time is a bit misleading: The all-aboard time (when you absolutely, positively must be on your ship) is usually a half-hour before departure. And the last shuttle bus or tender back to the ship might leave an hour before departure...trimming your port time even more. If you want to max out on time ashore, research alternative options—such as a taxi or a public bus—that get you back to the ship even closer to the all-aboard time (but, of course, be cautious not to cut it *too* close). Before leaving the ship, make sure you understand when you need to be back on board, and (if applicable) when the last shuttle bus or tender departs.

All of that said, feel free to take every minute of the time you've got. If the last tender leaves at 16:30, don't feel you need to get back to the dock at 16:00.  I make it a point to be the last person back on the ship at every port...usually five minutes or so before all-aboard time. I sometimes get dirty looks from early birds who've been waiting for a few minutes on that last tender, but I didn't waste their time... they did.

WHAT IF I MISS MY SHIP?

You can't count on the ship to wait for you if you get back late. If you're cutting it close, call ahead to the port agent (the phone number is on your ship's port-of-call information sheet and/or daily program) and let them know you're coming. They will notify the ship's crew, so at least they know they didn't miscount the returning passengers. And there's a possibility (though a very slim one) that the ship could wait for you. But if it sets sail, and you're not on it, you're on your own to reach the next port. The cruise line will not cover any of your transportation or accommodations expenses, and you will not be reimbursed for any unused portion of your cruise.

You have approximately 24 hours to reach the ship before it departs from its next destination. Be clear on where the next stop is. If you're lucky, it's an easy two-hour train ride away, giving you bonus time in both destinations. If you're unlucky, it's a 20-hour overland odyssey or an expensive last-minute flight—or worse, the ship is spending the day at sea, meaning you'll miss out on two full cruising days.

First, ask the **port agent** for advice. The agent can typically give you a little help or at least point you in the right direction. Be aware that you'll be steered to the easiest, but not necessarily the most affordable, solution. For example, the agent might suggest hiring a private driver for hundreds of dollars, rather than taking a $50 bus ride. If your ship's policy is to hold passenger passports during the cruise, he'll have it waiting for you.

You can also ask for help from the **TI**, if it's still open. Local **travel agencies** should know most or all of your connection options and can book tickets for you (they'll charge you a small commission). Or **get online** to research your train, flight, and bus options. German Rail's handy, all-Europe train timetables at Bahn.com are a good place to start. Check the website of the nearest airport; these usually show the schedule of upcoming flights in the next day or two. To compare inexpensive flights within Europe, try Skyscanner.com.

Don't delay in making your plans. The sooner you begin investigating your options, the more choices you may have. If you realize you've missed your ship at 20:00, there may be an affordable night train to the next stop departing from the train station across town at 21:00...and if you're not on it, you could pay through the nose for a last-minute flight instead.

Remember, most ships never leave anyone behind over the course of the entire cruise. While the prospect of missing your ship is daunting, don't let it scare you into not enjoying your shore time. As long as you keep a close eye on the time and are conservative in estimating how long it'll take you to get back to the ship, it's easy to enjoy a very full day in port and be the last tired but happy tourist sauntering back aboard

IN PORT

OVERNIGHTING IN PORT

At some major destinations (most often in St. Petersburg), the cruise ship might spend two days and an overnight in port. This allows you to linger in the evening and really feel like you've been to a place—treating your cruise ship like a hotel.

CRUISE PORTS

CRUISE PORTS

The rest of this book focuses on the specific cruise ports where you'll be spending your days. For each one, I've provided detailed instructions for getting from the port into town, and included my suggested self-guided tours and walks for the best one-day plan in that town.

Rick Steves Scandinavian & Northern European Cruise Ports is a personal tour guide in your pocket, organized by destination. Each major destination is a mini-vacation on its own, filled with exciting sights, strollable neighborhoods, and memorable places to eat. You'll find the following sections in most of the destination chapters (although, because cruise port details can vary from place to place, not every destination will include all of these elements):

A **Practicalities** section for each country provides basic facts and figures, along with useful notes (such as the local currency, time zone, phone system, and tipping customs).

Planning Your Time suggests a schedule for how to best use your limited time in port. These plans are what I'd do with my time if I had only a few hours to spend in a particular destination. Be warned—I like to spend the maximum amount of time in port sightseeing, rather than relaxing, shopping, or dining. For each option, I've suggested the minimum amount of time you can reasonably expect to spend to get a good look at the highlights. If you find that my plan packs too much in, or shortchanges something you'd like to focus on, modify the plan by skipping one or two time-consuming options (read the descriptions in the chapters to decide which items interest you).

The **Excursions** sidebars help you make informed, strategic decisions about which cruise-line excursions to outlying destinations best match your interests.

The **Port** sections provide detailed, step-by-step instructions for getting from your cruise ship to wherever you're going (whether it's to the city center, or, in some cases, to a nearby town). Each one begins with a brief "Arrival at a Glance" section to help you get oriented to your options. I've also tracked down helpful services (such as ATMs and pharmacies) at or near each port.

Orientation includes specifics on public transportation, helpful hints, local tour options, easy-to-read maps, and tourist information.

Self-Guided Walks and Tours takes you through interesting neighborhoods and museums.

Sights describes the top attractions and includes their cost and hours. The "At a Glance" sections for bigger cities offer a quick overview of the sights.

Eating serves up a range of options, from inexpensive eateries to fancy restaurants.

Shopping offers advice on the most authentic local souvenirs and where to buy them.

The **What If I Miss My Ship?** section gives you a quick list of options for reaching your next port, in case you get stranded.

Starting or Ending Your Cruise info for the most common embarkation/disembarkation points spells out how to get from the airport to the cruise port, lists a few of my favorite hotels, and adds some nightlife and entertainment options.

RESTAURANT PRICING

I've categorized my recommended eateries based on price, indicated with a dollar-sign rating (see sidebars in the Eating sections of most port chapters). The price ranges suggest the average price of a typical main course—but not necessarily a complete meal. Obviously, expensive items (like steak and seafood), fine wine, appetizers, and dessert can significantly increase your final bill.

The categories also indicate a place's personality: **$ Budget** eateries include street food, takeaway, order-at-the-counter shops, basic cafeterias, and bakeries selling sandwiches. **$$ Moderate** eateries are nice (but not fancy) sit-down restaurants, ideal for a straightforward, fill-the-tank meal. Most of my listings fall into this category—great for a good taste of local cuisine.

$$$ Pricier eateries are a notch up, with more attention paid to the setting, presentation, and cuisine. These are ideal for a memorable meal that doesn't break the bank. This category often includes affordable "destination" or "foodie" restaurants. And **$$$$ Splurge** eateries are dress-up-for-a-special-occasion swanky—typically with an elegant setting, polished service, pricey and intricate cuisine, and an expansive (and expensive) wine list.

I haven't categorized places where you might assemble a picnic, snack, or graze: supermarkets, delis, ice cream-stands, cafés or bars specializing in drinks, chocolate shops, and so on.

HOTEL PRICING

In each of the cities where you're likely to begin or end your trip (Copenhagen, Stockholm, Amsterdam, and London), I list a few of my favorite accommodations. I favor hotels that are handy to your sightseeing activities. Rather than list hotels scattered throughout a city, I choose hotels in my favorite neighborhoods.

I like places that are clean, central, relatively quiet at night, reasonably priced, friendly, small enough to have a hands-on owner or manager and stable staff, and run with a respect for local traditions. I'm more impressed by a convenient location and a fun-loving philosophy than flat-screen TVs and a fancy gym. Most places I recommend fall short of perfection. But if I can find a place with most of these features, it's a keeper.

I've categorized my recommended accommodations based on price, indicated with a dollar-sign rating (specifics given in individual chapters). Room prices can fluctuate significantly with demand and amenities (size, views, room class, and so on), but relative price categories remain constant. Unless otherwise noted, credit cards are accepted, hotel staff speak English, and free Wi-Fi is available.

Comparison-shop by checking prices at several hotels (on each hotel's own website, on a booking site, or by email). For the best deal, it's generally best to book directly with the hotel (that is, not through a booking site). Some accommodations offer a special discount for Rick Steves readers, indicated in this guidebook by the abbreviation **"RS%."** Discounts vary: Ask for details when you reserve. Rick Steves discounts apply to readers with ebooks as well as printed books. Understandably, discounts do not apply to promotional rates.

COPENHAGEN

Denmark

Denmark Practicalities

Denmark (Danmark), between the Baltic and the North Sea, is the smallest of the Scandinavian countries (16,600 square miles—roughly double the size of Massachusetts). But in the 16th century, it was the largest; at one time, Denmark ruled all of Norway and the three southern provinces of Sweden. Today's population is about 5.6 million; 12 percent are immigrants. The predominant religion is Protestant (mostly Evangelical Lutheran). The country consists of the largely flat, extensively cultivated Jutland peninsula, as well as over 400 islands (78 of which are inhabited, including Sjælland/ Zealand, where Copenhagen is located).

Money: 6 Danish kroner (DKK) = about $1. An ATM is called a *pengeautomat*. The local VAT (value-added sales tax) rate is 25 percent; the minimum purchase eligible for a VAT refund is 300 DKK (for details on refunds, see page 125).

Language: The native language is Danish. For useful phrases, see page 207.

Emergencies: Dial 112 for police, medical, or other emergencies. In case of theft or loss, see page 118.

Time Zone: Denmark is on Central European Time (the same as most of the Continent, one hour ahead of Great Britain, and six/nine hours ahead of the East/West Coasts of the US).

Embassies in Copenhagen: The **US embassy** is at Dag Hammarskjölds Allé 24 (tel. 33 41 71 00, after-hours emergency tel. 33 41 74 00, http://dk.usembassy.gov). The **Canadian embassy** is at Kristen Bernikowsgade 1 (tel. 33 48 32 00, www.canada.dk). Call ahead for passport services.

Phoning: With a mobile phone, it's easy to dial: Press and hold zero until you get a + sign, enter the country code (45 for Denmark, 1 for the US/Canada), then the complete phone number (including area code if there is one). When dialing a European phone number, drop an initial zero (except if calling Italy). For more tips, see page 1062.

Tipping: Gratuity is included in the price of sit-down meals, so you don't need to tip further, though it's nice to round up your bill about 5-10 percent for great service. Tip a taxi driver by rounding up the fare a bit (pay 90 DKK on an 85-DKK fare). For more tips on tipping, see page 129.

Tourist Information: www.visitcopenhagen.com

COPENHAGEN

København

Copenhagen, Denmark's capital, is the gateway to Scandinavia. It's an improbable combination of corny Danish clichés, well-dressed executives having a business lunch amid cutting-edge contemporary architecture, and some of the funkiest counterculture in Europe. And yet, it all just works so tidily together. With the Øresund Bridge connecting Sweden and Denmark (creating the region's largest metropolitan area), Copenhagen is energized and ready to dethrone Stockholm as Scandinavia's powerhouse city.

A busy day, choosing some combination of cruising the canals, wandering through the palace, taking an old-town walk, and sampling the Danish good life (including a gooey "Danish" pastry), will make you feel right at home. Live it up in Scandinavia's cheapest and most fun-loving capital.

PLANNING YOUR TIME

Copenhagen is spread out, with lots of sightseeing options. You can't squeeze everything into one day, so be selective. Below I've listed your most likely choices; I'd suggest starting with the first two, then choosing from the remaining list with whatever time you have left. If the weather is dreary, skip the walk and cruise and add more of the later items.

Copenhagen City Walk: This self-guided stroll through town gives you your bearings in about two hours (longer if you tack on the extended route).

Harbor Cruise: On a sunny day, this is well worth the hour it takes, as it gets you out on the water and shows you corners of the city that are otherwise hard to see.

Rosenborg Castle: For a classic Renaissance castle experience right in the city center, plus a peek at the crown jewels, tour this palace. Allow 1.5 hours.

National Museum: Offering an illuminating look at Danish history, this deserves at least 1.5 hours for the quickest visit (ideally longer).

Thorvaldsen's Museum or **Ny Carlsberg Glyptothek:** For fans of Neoclassical sculpture or antiquities and paintings (respectively), each museum deserves an hour or more.

Christiania: You can stroll through this unique hippie squatters' commune in about an hour, though it takes some time to get here.

Tivoli Gardens: This quintessentially Danish amusement park is a delightful way to burn up whatever time you have remaining at the end of your busy Copenhagen day (allow at least an hour for strolling and Dane-watching).

Port of Copenhagen

Arrival at a Glance: From any Copenhagen cruise port, you can take a cruise-ship shuttle bus, a hop-on, hop-off tour bus, or a taxi into town. Copenhagen's two main cruise ports, Oceankaj and Langelinie, are also served by public buses.

Port Overview

As one of the primary cruise ports on the Baltic—and one of the most common places to begin or end a cruise—Copenhagen handles a vast volume of cruise traffic. **Oceankaj,** the city's newest and main cruise port, is the farthest from the city; **Langelinie** and **Nordre Toldbod** are both within walking distance of points of interest. The Frihavnen cruise port, about three miles north of downtown, is used only rarely. If your cruise begins or ends in Copenhagen, odds are it will dock at Oceankaj.

Tourist Information: There's a tiny TI at Oceankaj, but none at the other cruise ports. Signs at each port help you find your way to the nearest bus stop, and you'll also likely find free city maps at displays around port areas. Once in town, you can visit Copenhagen's official TI, near the main train station, but since it's mostly a promotional agency for local businesses, I wouldn't make a big effort to go there.

Excursions from Copenhagen

Most cruise lines offer a variety of bus and/or walking tours of **Copenhagen.** These often include guided tours of sights such as Tivoli Gardens, Rosenborg Castle, Amalienborg Palace, Christiansborg Palace, and Christianshavn. But each of these sights—and my self-guided walk through downtown Copenhagen—are easy to visit on your own and thoroughly covered in this book. Similarly, I wouldn't pay your cruise line for a harbor or canal tour, as these are much easier and cheaper to book direct once you arrive.

Excursions to a few out-of-town sights may be worth considering. Many cruise lines offer a tour combining two of the best castles just outside the city: **Frederiksborg** (with sumptuous rooms and an outstanding museum of Danish history) and **Kronborg** (less engaging inside, but very picturesque and with tentative ties to Hamlet). If you're not interested in Copenhagen itself, an excursion combining these two castles (tricky by public transit) could be a good choice. However, I'd skip the side-trip to the pretty but very touristy fishing village of **Dragør** (the much-touted view of the Øresund Bridge from Dragør is only a bit closer than what you'll see from the deck of your ship).

GETTING INTO TOWN

First I'll cover transportation options that work from all the ports: cruise-line shuttle buses, tours (hop-on, hop-off buses), taxis, and public buses. Then I'll give details specific to each port. To return to your ship, you can generally reverse these directions—I've given suggestions at the end of each section as necessary.

From Any Port

Cruise-Line Shuttle Bus: Many cruise lines run shuttle buses between the port and town, usually stopping at Kongens Nytorv (near Nyhavn) and/or Rådhuspladsen (City Hall Square). If a shuttle is available, consider it first for convenience and saving time. Figure €12 round-trip—not much more than the cost of round-trip public transit tickets.

By Tour: Hop-on, hop-off bus tours are worth considering, as they help you get your bearings in this spread-out city. Cruise passengers arriving at Oceankaj can take a provided shuttle to the *Little Mermaid* statue and pick up a hop-on, hop-off bus there. Those arriving at Langelinie can catch a hop-on, hop-off bus right at the port. For more on these buses, see "Tours in Copenhagen," later.

By Taxi: From Oceankaj, taxis charge about 275 DKK for the ride into town. Taxis also cluster along Langelinie's pier, offering a ride into downtown for about 175 DKK. Head for Rådhuspladsen (City Hall Square) and the start of my city walk.

By Public Bus: Taking a public bus is an economical (but time-consuming) way to get into town. But bear in mind that bus drivers take only Danish kroner, and there are no ATMs at any of the cruise ports. If you plan to take the bus, travelers arriving at Oceankaj have several cashless ticketing options; those arriving at Langelinie should have kroner in their pockets. For details, see the port descriptions below. (For general info on riding the bus, see "Getting Around Copenhagen," later.)

From Oceankaj

The three terminals at this port handle the majority of cruise traffic into Copenhagen. It's also the farthest from the center—roughly 3.5 miles north of downtown. A cruise-line shuttle or a taxi are the easiest options from here, but intrepid travelers can consider the bus option outlined below.

By Public Bus: Riding the bus from Oceankaj into town requires a transfer and can take up to an hour of your time. The #27 bus stop is down the main road leading away from the cruise port—it's just a short walk across the street from Terminal 1; from Terminals 2 or 3, it's a 10- to 15-minute walk. You'll ride bus #27 to a stop near the Østerport train station, transfer to bus #26, and continue to downtown Copenhagen (stops at Nyhavn, Rådhuspladsen, and near Tivoli).

You'll need kroner to buy a ticket on the bus. Ticket kiosks that take credit cards are behind the TI, across from Terminal 1 (single ride-24 DKK, 24-hour pass-80 DKK). If you've preordered a Copenhagen Card (covers all public transportation and admission to three included museums and attractions; see page 145 for details), exchange your voucher for the card at the Oceankaj TI before heading to the bus stop.

From Langelinie

This pier juts out from the north end of Kastellet Park and is within long walking distance of downtown. It has two berths for big ships, but cruises do not typically begin or end here.

By Public Bus: Bus #26 stops near the entrance to Langelinie, but you'll need kroner to pay the driver on board (24 DKK). Without cash, your other option is to buy the 24-hour City Pass online; it will be sent as a text message to your phone (see page 149). To find the bus stop, leaving your ship, go left and walk down the pier (and under a pedestrian overpass) to its entrance at the roundabout, turn right on the street called Indiakaj, and walk a short distance to the bus stop (about 10 minutes from the far end of the pier). Take

Services at the Ports

Expect few services at the piers. You won't find ATMs, but you should be able to use your credit or debit card at public-transit ticket machines (know and use your four-digit PIN). Convenience stores such as 7-Eleven generally sell public-transit tickets and take credit cards.

Here's what you'll find at the two main ports:

At **Oceankaj,** you'll see a bleak cluster of shipping containers across the street, kitty-corner from Terminal 1, offering a TI, WC, and a café (the giant *Hygge* sign—the Danish word for coziness—plopped in the center seems especially ironic). Behind the TI are two transit-ticket kiosks. Oceankaj's three terminals have free Wi-Fi—look for instructions on how to access it.

There's little at **Langelinie,** except a pier-front road with stops for taxis and hop-on, hop-off tour buses, and a row of cruise-oriented shops (duty-free, outlet stores).

bus #26 to Nyhavn, Rådhuspladsen, or the main train station, next to Tivoli.

On Foot: Arriving at Langelinie puts you within walking distance of most of Copenhagen's sights (10 minutes to *The Little Mermaid*, another 15 minutes to Amalienborg Palace, then another 10 minutes to Nyhavn). A good option is to do my self-guided "Copenhagen City Walk" in reverse, starting at *The Little Mermaid* and ending at Rådhuspladsen.

To get to *The Little Mermaid,* turn left from your ship and walk the length of the pier, passing a row of shops on your right. At the entrance end of the pier, continue straight, passing the statue of the decidedly *not*-little mermaid, and cross the footbridge. Keep going straight, bearing uphill, slightly to your right, to walk with the sailboat harbor on your left.

Pass through the park with the angel monument. To reach *The Little Mermaid,* turn left from the park and head along the water to the commotion of tourists. From the *Mermaid,* you can keep walking along the waterfront past Kastellet Park and the Museum of Danish Resistance all the way to Amalienborg Palace. From the palace, it's about another 10-minute walk to the colorful Nyhavn canal, at the edge of the town center.

Returning to Langelinie: Note that not all #26 buses go to Langelinie—be sure to check that the bus reads Søndre Frihavn *Indiakaj* on the front and confirm with the driver that you're on the right one.

You can also return to Langelinie by riding the S-tog train to Østerport Station, where you'll exit the station, turn left, and cross the busy street. Head down into the park, turn left, and walk along the moat of Kastellet Park until you exit from the north end, a short walk from the pier.

From Nordre Toldbod

This modest pier, just south of *The Little Mermaid* and next to Kastellet Park, is used by smaller cruise ships. From here your best options are to walk along the waterfront to Nyhavn (25 minutes) or head a few minutes north to *The Little Mermaid* where you can catch a **hop-on, hop-off bus.**

To walk to Nyhavn, with your back to the water, go left and simply follow the waterfront promenade past Amalienborg Palace to the Nyhavn action.

Returning to Nordre Toldbod: If you don't want to walk back the way you came, you can take the S-tog train to Østerport Station and walk from there. Turn left from the station door, cross the street, and continue straight along the right side of Kastellet Park, following its perimeter until you reach the harbor and Nordre Toldbod.

Copenhagen

Copenhagen is huge (with 1.2 million people), but for most visitors, the walkable core is the diagonal axis formed by the train station, Tivoli Gardens, Rådhuspladsen (City Hall Square), and the Strøget pedestrian street, ending at the colorful old Nyhavn sailors' harbor. Bubbling with street life, colorful pedestrian zones, and most of the city's sightseeing, the Strøget is fun. But also be sure to get off the main drag and explore. By doing things by bike or on foot, you'll stumble upon some charming bits of Copenhagen that many travelers miss. The city feels pretty torn up, as they are deep into a multiyear Metro expansion project, which will add 17 stations to their already impressive system.

Outside of the old city center are two areas of interest to tourists:

To the north are Rosenborg Castle and Amalienborg Palace, with *The Little Mermaid* nearby.

To the east, across the harbor, are Christianshavn (Copenhagen's "Little Amsterdam" district) and the alternative enclave of Christiania.

Most of these sights are walkable from the Strøget, but taking a bike, bus, or taxi is more efficient. In good weather, the city is an absolute delight by bike (see "Getting Around Copenhagen: By Bike," later).

Orientation to Copenhagen

TOURIST INFORMATION

Copenhagen's questionable excuse for a TI, which bills itself as "Wonderful Copenhagen," is actually a blatantly for-profit company. While they can answer basic questions, their two most convenient offices—at the train station (daily 9:00-17:00) and on Vesterbrogade—are worthwhile mostly for their big racks of advertising brochures; you can pick up a free map at many hotels and other places in town (main TI: May-June Mon-Sat 9:00-18:00, Sun until 14:00; July-Aug daily 9:00-19:00; Sept-April Mon-Fri 9:00-17:00, Sat until 16:00, closed Sun, Vesterbrogade 4A, just up the street from the main exit of train station—across from the towering Radisson Blu Royal Hotel, good Lagkagehuset bakery in building; tel. 70 22 24 42, www.visitcopenhagen.com).

Copenhagen Card: This card includes entry to many of the city's sights (including expensive ones, like Tivoli and Rosenborg Castle) and all local transportation in all zones of the greater Copenhagen area. It can save busy sightseers some money and the hassle of choosing the right transportation pass (389 DKK/24 hours, 550 DKK/48 hours, 660 DKK/72 hours, 890 DKK/120 hours—sold at the TI, online, and some hotels; www.copenhagencard.com).

ARRIVAL IN COPENHAGEN

The **main train station** is called Hovedbanegården (HOETH-bahn-gorn; look for *København H* on signs and schedules). It's a temple of travel and a hive of travel-related activity (and 24-hour thievery). Kiosks and fast-food eateries cluster in the middle of the main arrivals hall. Other services include a ticket office, train information kiosk, baggage storage, pay WCs, a post office, and ATMs. The tracks at the back of the station (tracks 9-10 and 11-12) are for the suburban train (S-tog).

Just walk out the front door and you'll run into one of the entrances for Tivoli amusement park; if you go around its left side and up a couple of blocks, you'll be at Rådhuspladsen, where my "Copenhagen City Walk" begins.

HELPFUL HINTS

Pharmacy: Steno Apotek is across from the train station (open 24 hours, Vesterbrogade 6C, tel. 33 14 82 66, see the "Copenhagen" map for location).

Blue Monday: As you plan, remember that most sights close on Monday.

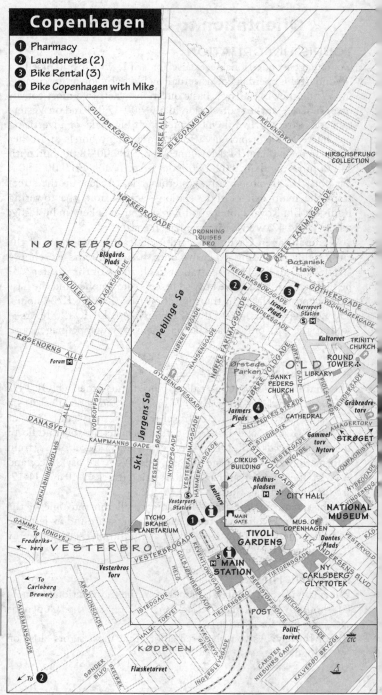

Copenhagen

1. Pharmacy
2. Launderette (2)
3. Bike Rental (3)
4. Bike Copenhagen with Mike

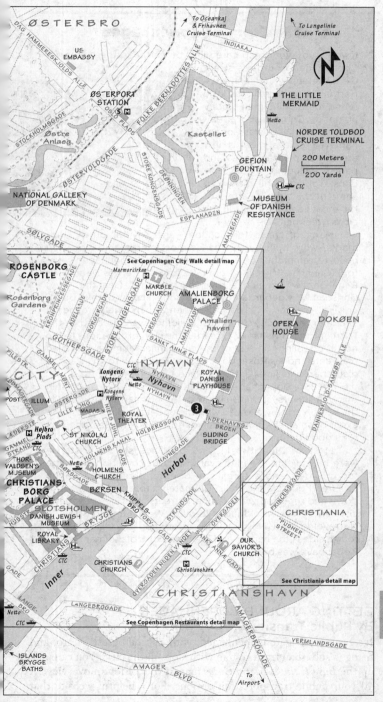

The Story of Copenhagen

If you study your map carefully, you can read the history of Copenhagen in today's street plan. København ("Merchants' Harbor") was born on the little island of Slotsholmen—today home to Christiansborg Palace—in 1167. What was Copenhagen's medieval moat is now a string of pleasant lakes and parks, including Tivoli Gardens. You can still make out some of the zigzag pattern of the moats and ramparts in the city's greenbelt.

Many of these fortifications—and several other landmarks—were built by Denmark's most memorable king. You need to remember only one character in Copenhagen's history: Christian IV. Ruling from 1588 to 1648, he was Denmark's Renaissance king and a royal party animal (see the "King Christian IV" sidebar, later). The personal energy of this "Builder King" sparked a Golden Age when Copenhagen prospered and many of the city's grandest buildings were erected. In the 17th century, Christian IV extended the city fortifications to the north, doubling the size of the city, while adding a grid plan of streets and his Rosenborg Castle. This "new town" was the district around Amalienborg Palace.

In 1850, Copenhagen's 140,000 residents all lived within this defensive system. Building in the no-man's-land outside the walls was only allowed with the understanding that in the event of an attack, you'd burn your dwellings to clear the way for a good defense.

Most of the city's historic buildings still in existence were built within the medieval walls, but conditions became too crowded, and outbreaks of disease forced Copenhagen to spread outside the walls. Ultimately those walls were torn down and replaced with "rampart streets" that define today's city center: Vestervoldgade (literally, "West Rampart Street"), Nørrevoldgade ("North"), and Østervoldgade ("East"). The fourth side is the harbor and the island of Slotsholmen, where København was born.

GETTING AROUND COPENHAGEN
By Public Transit

It's easy to navigate Copenhagen, with its fine buses, Metro, and S-tog (a suburban train system with stops in the city). You can pick up the *Bus, Train & Metro Guide* map at the TI for an overview of all your public transportation options. For a helpful website that covers public transport (nationwide) in English, consult www.rejseplanen.dk.

Tickets: The same tickets are used throughout the system. A 24-DKK, **two-zone ticket** gets you an hour's travel within the center—pay as you board buses, or buy from station ticket offices, convenience stores, or vending machines for the Metro. (Ticket machines should accept American credit cards with a chip, and most machines also take Danish cash; if the machine won't take your credit card, find a cashier.) Assume you'll be within the middle two zones unless traveling to or from the airport, which requires a **three-zone ticket** (36 DKK).

If you're traveling exclusively in central Copenhagen, the **City Pass** is a good value (80 DKK/24 hours, 200 DKK/72 hours, covers travel within zones 1-4, including the airport). You can buy a pass at some train and Metro stations or use www.dinoffentligetransport.dk; it will be sent as a text message to your mobile phone.

Buses: Buses serve all of the major sights in town every five to eight minutes during daytime hours. If you're not riding a bike everywhere, get comfortable with the buses. Bus drivers are patient, have change, and speak English. City maps list bus routes. Locals are usually friendly and helpful. There's also a floating "Harbor Bus" (described later, under "By Boat").

Bus lines that end with "A" (such as #1A) use quiet, eco-friendly, electric buses that are smaller than normal buses, allowing access into the narrower streets of the old town. Designed for tourists, these provide an easy overview to the city center. Among these, the following are particularly useful:

Bus **#1A** loops from the train station up to Kongens Nytorv (near Nyhavn) and then farther north, to Østerport.

Bus **#2A** goes from Christianshavn to the city center, then onward to points west.

Bus **#6A** connects the station to Nørreport, but you'll need to catch it up around the corner on Vesterbrogade.

Other, non-"A" buses, which are bigger and tend to be more direct, can be faster for some trips:

Bus **#5C** connects the station more or less directly to Nørreport.

Bus **#14** runs from Nørreport down to the city center, stopping near the Strøget, and eventually going near the main train station.

Bus **#26** runs a handy route right through the main tourist zone: train station/Tivoli to Slotsholmen Island to Kongens Nytorv (near Nyhavn) to the Amalienborg Palace/*Little Mermaid* area. It continues even farther north to the Langelinie cruise port, but the line splits, so check with the driver to make sure you're on the right bus.

Bus **#66** goes from Nyhavn to Slotsholmen Island to Tivoli.

Metro: Copenhagen's Metro line, while simple, is superfuturistic and growing. For most tourists' purposes, only the airport and three consecutive stops within the city matter: Nørreport (connected every few minutes by the S-tog to the main train station), Kongens Nytorv (near Nyhavn and the Strøget's north end), and Christianshavn. For the latest on the Metro and route maps, see www.m.dk.

S-tog Train: The S-tog is basically a commuter line that links stations on the main train line through Copenhagen; the most important stops are the main train station, Nørreport (where it ties into the Metro system), Østerport (for Langelinie), and Nordhavn (for the little-used Frihavnen port).

By Boat

The hop-on, hop-off "Harbor Bus" (Havnebus) boat stops at the "Black Diamond" library, Christianshavn (near Knippels Bridge),

Nyhavn, the Opera House, and the Nordre Toldbod cruiseship pier, which is a short walk from the *Little Mermaid* site (and a slightly longer walk from the Langelinie cruise port). The boat is part of the city bus system (lines #991 and #992) and covered by the tickets described earlier. Taking a long ride on this boat, from the library to the end of the line, is the "poor man's cruise"—without commentary, of course (runs 6:00-19:00). Or, for a true sightseeing trip, consider a guided harbor cruise (described later, under "Tours in Copenhagen").

By Taxi

Taxis are plentiful, easy to call or flag down, and pricey (35-DKK pickup charge and then about 15 DKK/kilometer—higher on evenings and weekends). For a short ride, four people spend about the same by taxi as by bus. Calling 35 35 35 35 will get you a taxi within minutes...with the meter already well on its way.

By Bike

Cyclists see more, save time and money, and really feel like locals. With a bike, you have Copenhagen at your command. I'd rather have a bike than a car and driver at my disposal. Virtually every street has a dedicated bike lane (complete with bike signal lights). Warning: Police routinely issue hefty tickets to anyone riding on sidewalks or through pedestrian zones. Note also that bikes can't be parked just anywhere. Observe others and park your bike among other bikes. The simple built-in lock that binds the back tire is adequate.

Renting a Bike: Consider one of these rental outfits in or near the city center (see the "Copenhagen" map for locations).

Københavens Cyklebørs, near Nørreport Station, has a good selection of three-gear bikes (Mon-Fri 10:00-17:30, Sat-Sun until 14:00, closed all day Sun in off-season; Gothersgade 157, tel. 33 14 07 17, www.cykelborsen. dk).

Cykelbasen, even closer to Nørreport, rents three- and seven-gear bikes (Mon-Fri 9:00-17:30, Sat until 14:30, closed Sun; Gothersgade 137, tel. 35 12 06 00, www.cykel-basen. dk, select "Info").

Copenhagen Bicycles, at the entrance to Nyhavn by the Inderhavnsbroen pedestrian/bicycle bridge, rents basic three-gear bikes (daily 8:30-17:30, Nyhavn 44, tel. 35 43 01 22, www.

copenhagenbicycles.dk). They also offer guided tours in English and Danish (100 DKK, not including bicycle, April-Sept daily at 11:00, 2.5 hours).

Using City Bikes: The city's public bike-rental program **Bycyklen** lets you ride white, three-gear "smart bikes" (with GPS and an electric motor) for 30 DKK/hour. You'll find them parked in racks near the train station, on either side of City Hall, and at many locations around town. Use the touchscreen on the handlebars to create an account. At their website (http://bycyklen.dk), you can locate docking stations, reserve a bike at a specific station, and create an account in advance. I'd use these bikes for a short hop here or there, but for more than a couple of hours, it's more cost-efficient to rent a regular bicycle.

Tours in Copenhagen

ON FOOT
Copenhagen is an ideal city to get to know by foot. You have several good options:

▲▲Hans Christian Andersen Tours by Richard Karpen
Once upon a time, American Richard Karpen visited Copenhagen and fell in love with the city. Now, dressed as writer Hans Christian Andersen in a 19th-century top hat and long coat, he leads 1.5-hour tours that wander in and out of buildings, courtyards, back streets, and unusual parts of the old town. Along the one-mile route, he gives insightful and humorous background on the history, culture, and contemporary life of Denmark, Copenhagen, and the Danes (140 DKK, kids under 12 free; departs from outside the TI, up the street from the main train station at Vesterbrogade 4A; mid-May-mid-Sept Mon-Sat at 9:30, none on Sun; Richard departs promptly—if you miss him try to catch up with the tour at the next stop at Rådhuspladsen).

Richard also gives one-hour tours of **Rosenborg Castle** while in the role of Hans Christian Andersen (100 DKK, doesn't include castle entry, mid-May-mid-Sept Mon and Thu at 12:00, meet outside castle ticket office). No reservations are needed for any of Richard's scheduled tours—just show up (mobile 91 61 95 02, www.copenhagenwalks.com, copenhagenwalks@yahoo.com).

▲Daily City Walks by Red Badge Guides
Five local female guides work together, giving two-hour English-language city tours. Their walks mix the city's highlights, back lanes, history, art, and contemporary social issues, and finish at Amalienborg Palace around noon for the changing of the guard (100 DKK, daily mid-April-Sept at 10:00, departs from TI at Vesterbrogade 4A, just show up, pay direct, small groups, tel. 20 92 23 87, www.redbadgeguides.dk, redbadgeguides@gmail.com). They also offer private guided tours year-round upon request.

Hans Christian Andersen (1805-1875)

The author of such classic fairy tales as *The Ugly Duckling* was an ugly duckling himself—a misfit who blossomed. Hans Christian Andersen (called H. C., pronounced "hoe see" by the Danes) was born to a poor shoemaker in Odense. As a child he was gangly, high-strung, and effeminate. He avoided school because the kids laughed at him, so he spent his time in a fantasy world of books and plays.

In 1819, at the age of 14, he moved to Copenhagen to pursue an acting career. As rejections piled up for his acting aspirations, Andersen began to shift his theatrical ambitions to playwriting. He won a two-year scholarship to travel around Europe. His experiences abroad were highly formative, providing inspiration for many of his tales. Still in his 20s, he published an obviously autobiographical novel, *The Improvisatore,* about a poor young man who comes into his own while traveling in Italy. The novel launched his writing career, and soon he was hobnobbing with the international crowd—Charles Dickens, Victor Hugo, Franz Liszt, Richard Wagner, Henrik Ibsen, and Edvard Grieg

Though he wrote novels, plays, and travel literature, it was his fairy tales, including *The Ugly Duckling, The Emperor's New Clotnes, The Princess and the Pea, The Little Mermaid, The Snow Queen,* and *The Red Shoes,* that made him Denmark's best-known author, the "Danish Charles Dickens."

▲▲Copenhagen History Tours

Christian Donatzky, a charming Dane with a master's degree in history, runs a walking tour on Saturday mornings. In April and May, the theme is "Old Copenhagen" (covering the period from 1100-1600); in June and July, "King's Copenhagen" (1600-1800); and in August and September, "Hans Christian Andersen's Copenhagen" (1800-present). Those with a serious interest in Danish history will find these tours time well spent (90 DKK, Sat at 10:00, approximately 1.5 hours, small groups of 5-15 people, tours depart from statue of Bishop Absalon on Højbro Plads between the Strøget and Christiansborg Palace, English only, no reservations necessary—just show up, tel. 28 49 44 35, www.historytours.dk, info@historytours.dk).

Copenhagen at a Glance

▲▲▲**Tivoli Gardens** Copenhagen's classic amusement park, with rides, music, food, and other fun. **Hours:** Late March-mid-Sept daily 11:00-23:00, Fri-Sat until 24:00, also open daily 11:00-22:00 for a week in mid-Oct and mid-Nov-New Year's Day. See page 171.

▲▲▲**National Museum** History of Danish civilization, the best of its kind in Scandinavia. **Hours:** Museum—Tue-Sun 10:00-17:00, closed Mon. See page 173.

▲▲▲**Rosenborg Castle and Treasury** Renaissance castle of larger-than-life "warrior king" Christian IV. **Hours:** Mid-June-mid-Sept daily 9:00-17:00; mid-April-mid-June and mid-Sept-Oct daily 10:00-16:00, except closed Mon in April; shorter hours and generally closed Mon rest of year. See page 180.

▲▲▲**Christiania** Colorful counterculture squatters' colony. **Hours:** Guided tours at 13:00 and 15:00 (daily July-Aug, only Sat-Sun rest of year). See page 187.

▲▲**Christiansborg Palace** Royal reception rooms with dazzling tapestries. **Hours:** Reception rooms, castle ruins, kitchen, and stables open daily except closed Mon in Oct-April. Hours vary by sight: Reception rooms 9:00-17:00, Oct-April from 10:00 (may close for royal events); ruins and kitchen 10:00-17:00; stables and carriage museum 13:30-16:00, longer hours possible in July. See page 176.

▲▲**Thorvaldsen's Museum** Works of the Danish Neoclassical sculptor. **Hours:** Tue-Sun 10:00-17:00, closed Mon. See page 177.

BY BOAT
▲Netto-Bådene Canal Boats

For many, the best way to experience the city's canals and harbor is by canal boat. Boats leave at least twice an hour from Nyhavn and Christiansborg Palace, cruise around the palace and Christianshavn area, and then proceed into the wide-open harbor (40 DKK, mid-March-mid-Oct daily 10:00-17:00, runs later in summer, shorter hours in winter, sign at dock shows next departure, generally every 30 minutes, dress warmly—boats are open-top until Sept, tel. 32 54 41 02,

▲**City Hall** Copenhagen's landmark, packed with Danish history and symbolism and topped with a tower. **Hours:** Mon-Fri 9:00-16:00, some Sat 9:30-13:00, closed Sun. See page 172.

▲**Ny Carlsberg Glyptotek** Scandinavia's top art gallery, featuring Egyptians, Greeks, Etruscans, French, and Danes. **Hours:** Tue-Sun 11:00-18:00, Thu until 22:00, closed Mon. See page 172.

▲**Danish Jewish Museum** Exhibit tracing the 400-year history of Danish Jews, in a unique building by American architect Daniel Libeskind. **Hours:** Tue-Sun 10:00-17:00; Sept-May Tue-Fri 13:00-16:00, Sat-Sun 12:00-17:00; closed Mon year-round. See page 178.

▲**Amalienborg Museum** Quick and intimate look at Denmark's royal family. **Hours:** May-Oct daily 10:00-16:00, mid-June-mid-Sept until 17:00; Nov-April Tue-Sun 11:00-16:00, closed Mon. See page 179.

▲**Rosenborg Gardens** Park surrounding Rosenborg Castle, filled with statues and statuesque Danes. See page 186.

▲**National Gallery of Denmark** Good Danish and Modernist collections. **Hours:** Tue-Sun 11:00-17:00, Wed until 20:00, closed Mon. See page 186.

▲**Our Savior's Church** Spiral-spired church with bright Baroque interior. **Hours:** Church—daily 11:00-15:30 but may close for special services; tower—May-Sept Mon-Sat 9:30-19:00, Sun from 10:30; shorter hours off-season, closed mid-Dec-Feb and in bad weather. See page 187.

www.havnerundfart.dk). Best on a sunny day, it's a relaxing way to see *The Little Mermaid* and munch on a lazy picnic during the slow-moving narration. Don't confuse the cheaper Netto and pricier Canal Tours Copenhagen boats: At Nyhavn, the Netto dock is midway down the canal (on the city side); near Christiansborg Palace, the Netto boats leave from Holmen's Bridge in front of the palace.

BY BUS
Hop-On, Hop-Off Bus Tours
Several buses with recorded narration circle the city for a basic 1.25- to 1.5-hour orientation, allowing you to get on and off as you like at the following stops: Tivoli Gardens, Gammel Strand near Christiansborg Palace, *The Little Mermaid*, Rosenborg Castle,

Nyhavn sailors' quarter, and more. Cruise passengers arriving at the Langelinie Pier can catch a hop-on, hop-off bus there; those arriving at the Oceankaj Pier can take a free shuttle to *The Little Mermaid,* where they can pick up a hop-on, hop-off bus.

The same company runs **City Sightseeing**'s red buses and Strömma's green **Hop-On, Hop-Off** buses. Both offer a Mermaid route: City Sightseeing tickets, 195 DKK, are valid 72 hours, and Hop-On, Hop-Off tickets, 175 DKK, are good for 48 hours (pay driver, 2/hour, May-mid-Sept daily 9:30-18:00, shorter hours off-season, buses depart near the TI in front of the Radisson Blu Royal Hotel and at many other stops throughout city, www.citysightseeing.dk or www.stromma.dk). Another operation—called **Red Buses**—does a similar Mermaid route (every 30-40 minutes, shorter hours off-season; 210 DKK/24 hours, www.redbuses.com).

BY BIKE

▲Bike Copenhagen with Mike

Mike Sommerville offers three-hour guided bike tours of the city, offering both historic background and contemporary cultural insights along the way (April-Sept daily at 10:00, second departure Fri-Sat at 14:30, must book all tours in advance; 300 DKK includes bike rental, price same with or without a bike, 50-DKK discount with this book—maximum 2 discounts per book and must have book with you, cash only; participants must have good urban biking skills). All tours are in English and depart from his bike shop at Sankt Peders Straede 47, in the Latin Quarter (see the "Copenhagen" map, earlier, for location). Mike also offers private tours; details at www.bikecopenhagenwithmike.dk.

Copenhagen City Walk

This self-guided walk takes about two hours. It starts at Rådhuspladsen (City Hall Square) and heads along the pedestrian street, the Strøget, through the old city, onto "Castle Island" (home of Christiansborg Palace), along the harbor promenade, and through Nyhavn, the sailors' quarter with the city's iconic canalfront houses. The walk officially ends at Kongens Nytorv ("King's New Square"), though you can continue another 10 minutes to Amalienborg Palace and then another 15 minutes beyond that to *The Little Mermaid.*

❶ Rådhuspladsen

Start from Rådhuspladsen, the bustling heart of Copenhagen, dominated by the tower of the City Hall.

Today this square always seems to be hosting some lively community event, but it was once Copenhagen's fortified west end. For 700 years, Copenhagen was contained within its city walls. By the mid-1800s, 140,000 people were packed inside. The overcrowding led to hygiene problems. (A cholera outbreak killed 5,000.) It was clear: The walls needed to come down...and they did. Those formidable town walls survive today only in echoes—a circular series of roads and the remnants of moats, which are now people-friendly city lakes (see "The Story of Copenhagen" sidebar, earlier).

• *Stand 50 yards in front of City Hall and turn clockwise for a...*

Rådhuspladsen Spin-Tour: The **City Hall,** or Rådhus, is worth a visit (see listing on page 172). Old **Hans Christian Andersen** sits to the right of City Hall, almost begging to be in another photo (as he used to in real life). Climb onto his well-worn knee. (While up there, you might take off your shirt for a racy photo, as many Danes enjoy doing.)

He's looking at ❷ **Tivoli Gardens** (across the street), which he loved and which inspired him when writing some of his stories.

Tivoli Gardens was founded in 1843, when magazine publisher Georg Carstensen convinced the king to let him build a pleasure garden outside the walls of crowded Copenhagen. The king quickly agreed, knowing that happy people care less about fighting for democracy. Tivoli became Europe's first great public amusement park. When the train lines came, the station was placed just beyond Tivoli.

The big, glassy building with the *DI* sign is filled with the offices of Danish Industry—a collection of Danish companies whose logos you can see in the windows (plus the Irma grocery store at street level).

The big, broad boulevard is **Vesterbrogade** ("Western Way"), which led to the western gate of the medieval city (behind you, where the pedestrian boulevard begins). Here, in the traffic hub of this huge city, you'll notice...not many cars. Denmark's 180 percent tax on car purchases makes the bus, Metro, or bike a sweeter option. In fact, the construction messing up this square is part of a huge expansion of the Metro system.

Down Vesterbrogade towers the **Radisson Blu Royal Hotel,** Copenhagen's only skyscraper. Locals say it seems so tall because the clouds hang so low. When it was built in 1960, Copenhageners took one look and decided—that's enough of a skyline. Notice

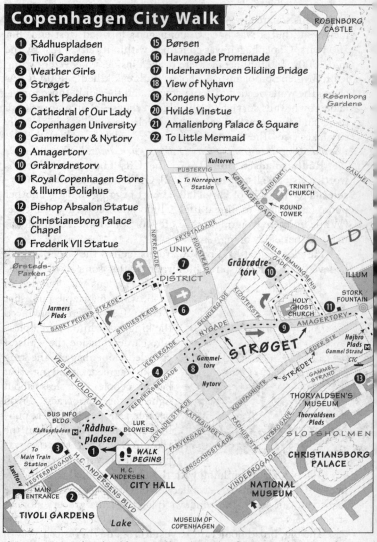

Copenhagen City Walk

1. Rådhuspladsen
2. Tivoli Gardens
3. Weather Girls
4. Strøget
5. Sankt Peders Church
6. Cathedral of Our Lady
7. Copenhagen University
8. Gammeltorv & Nytorv
9. Amagertorv
10. Gråbrødretorv
11. Royal Copenhagen Store & Illums Bolighus
12. Bishop Absalon Statue
13. Christiansborg Palace Chapel
14. Frederik VII Statue
15. Børsen
16. Havnegade Promenade
17. Inderhavnsbroen Sliding Bridge
18. View of Nyhavn
19. Kongens Nytorv
20. Hviids Vinstue
21. Amalienborg Palace & Square
22. To Little Mermaid

there are no other buildings taller than the five-story limit in the old center.

The golden ❸ **weather girls** (on the corner, high above Vesterbrogade) indicate the weather: on a bike (fair weather) or with an umbrella (foul). These two have been called the only women in Copenhagen you can trust, but for years they've been stuck in the almost-sunny mode...with the bike just peeking out. Notice that the red temperature dots max out at 28° Celsius (that's 82° Fahrenheit...a good memory aid: transpose 28 to get 82).

To the right, just down the street, is the Tiger Store (a popular

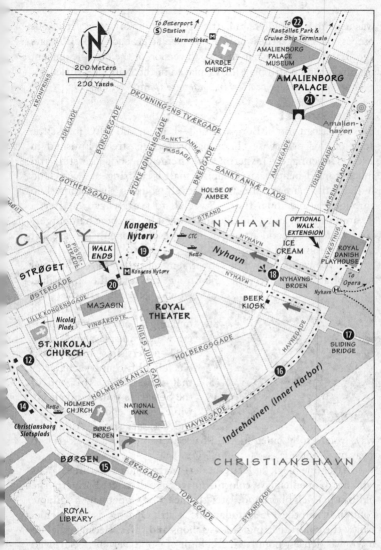

local "dollar store"...nearly everything is super affordable). The next street (once the local Fleet Street, with the big newspapers) still has the offices for *Politiken* (the leading Danish newspaper) and the best bookstore in town, Boghallen.

As you spin farther right, three fast-food joints stand at the entry to the Strøget (STROY-et), Copenhagen's grand pedestrian boulevard—where we're heading next. Just beyond that and the Art Deco-style Palace Hotel (with a tower to serve as a sister to the City Hall) is the ***Lur Blowers* sculpture,** which honors the earliest warrior Danes. The *lur* is a curvy, trombone-sounding horn that was used to call soldiers to battle or to accompany pagan religious processions. The earliest bronze *lur*s date as far back as 3,500 years ago. Later, the Vikings used a wood version of the *lur*. The ancient originals, which still play, are displayed in the National Museum.

• *Now head down the pedestrian boulevard (pickpocket alert).*

❹ The Strøget

The American trio of Burger King, 7-Eleven, and KFC marks the start of this otherwise charming pedestrian street. Finished in 1962, Copenhagen's experimental, tremendously successful, and much-copied pedestrian shopping mall is a string of lively (and individually named) streets and lovely squares that bunny-hop through the old town from City Hall to the Nyhavn quarter, a 20-minute stroll away. Though the Strøget has become hamburger-ized, historic bits and attractive pieces of old Copenhagen are just off this commercial can-can.

As you wander down this street, remember that the commercial focus of a historic street like the Strøget drives up the land value,

which generally trashes the charm and tears down the old buildings. Look above the modern window displays and street-level advertising to discover bits of 19th-century character that still survive. This end of the Strøget is young and cheap, while the far end has the high-end designer shops. Along the way, wonderfully quiet and laid-back areas are just a block or two away on either side.

After one block (at Kattesundet), make a side-trip three blocks left into Copenhagen's colorful **university district.** Formerly the old brothel neighborhood, later the heart of Copenhagen's hippie community in the 1960s, today this "Latin Quarter" is SoHo chic. Enjoy the colorful string of artsy shops and cafés. Because the old town was densely populated and built of wood, very little survived its many fires. After half-timbered and thatched buildings kept burning down, the city finally mandated that new construction be made of stone. But because stone was so expensive, many people built half-timbered structures, then disguised their facades with stucco, which made them look like stone. Exposed half-timbered structures are seen in courtyards and from the back sides. At Sankt Peders Stræde, turn right and walk to the end of the street. Notice the old guild signs (a baker, a key maker, and so on) identifying the original businesses here.

Along the way, look for large mansions that once circled expansive **courtyards.** As the population grew, the city walls constricted Copenhagen's physical size. The courtyards were gradually filled with higgledy-piggledy secondary buildings. Today throughout the old center, you can step off a busy pedestrian mall and back in time in these characteristic, half-timbered, time-warp courtyards. Replace the parked car with a tired horse and the bikes with a line of outhouses, and you're in 19th-century Copenhagen. If you see an open courtyard door, you're welcome to discreetly wander in and look around.

You'll also pass funky shops and the big brick ❺ **Sankt Peders Church**—the old German merchant community's church, which still holds services in German. Its fine 17th-century brick grave chapel (filling a ground-floor building out back due to the boggy nature of the soil) is filled with fancy German tombs.

• *When Sankt Peders Stræde intersects with Nørregade, look right to find the big, Neoclassical...*

❻ Cathedral of Our Lady (Vor Frue Kirche)

The obelisk-like **Reformation Memorial** across the street from the cathedral celebrates Denmark's break from the Roman Catholic Church to become Lutheran in 1536. Walk around and study the reliefs of great Danish reformers protesting from their pulpits. The relief facing the church shows King Christian III presiding over the pivotal town council meeting when they decided to break away from Rome. As a young man, Prince Christian had traveled to Germany, where he was influenced by Martin Luther. He returned to take the Danish throne by force, despite Catholic opposition. Realizing the advantages of being the head of his own state church, Christian confiscated church property and established the state Lutheran Church. King Christian was crowned inside this cathedral. Because of the reforms of 1536, there's no Mary in the Cathedral of Our Lady. The other reliefs show the popular religious uprising, with people taking control of the word of God by translating the Bible from Latin into their own language.

Like much of this part of town, the church burned down in the British bombardment of 1807 and was rebuilt in the Neoclassical style. The cathedral's **facade** looks like a Greek temple. (Two blocks to the right, in the distance, notice more Neoclassicism—the law courts.) You can see why Golden Age Copenhagen (early 1800s) fancied itself a Nordic Athens. Old Testament figures (King David and Moses) flank the cathedral's entryway. Above, John the

Baptist stands where you'd expect to see Greek gods. He invites you in...into the New Testament.

The **interior** is a world of Neoclassical serenity (free, open daily 8:00-17:00). It feels like a pagan temple that now houses Christianity. The nave is lined by the 12 apostles, clad in classical robes—masterpieces by the great Danish sculptor Bertel Thorvaldsen. Each strikes a meditative pose, carrying his identifying symbol: Peter with keys, Andrew with the X-shaped cross of his execution, Matthew and John writing their books, and so on. They

lead to a statue of the *Risen Christ* (see photo), standing where the statue of Zeus would have been: inside a temple-like niche, flanked by columns and topped with a pediment. Rather than wearing a royal robe, Jesus wears his burial shroud, opens his arms wide, and says, "Come to me." (Mormons will recognize this statue—a replica stands in the visitors center at Salt Lake City's Temple Square and is often reproduced in church publications.) The marvelous acoustics are demonstrated in free organ concerts Saturdays in July and August at noon. Notice how, in good Protestant style, only the front half of the pews are "reversible," allowing the congregation to flip around and face the pulpit (in the middle of the church) to better hear the sermon.

• *Head back outside. If you face the church's facade and look to the left (across the square called Frue Plads), you'll see...*

❼ Copenhagen University

Now home to nearly 40,000 students, this university was founded by the king in the 15th century to stop the Danish brain drain to Paris. Today tuition is free (but room, board, and beer are not). Locals say it's easy to get in, but given the wonderful student lifestyle, very hard to get out.

Step up the middle steps of the university's big building;

if the doors are open, enter a colorful lobby, starring Athena and Apollo. The frescoes celebrate high thinking, with themes such as the triumph of wisdom over barbarism. Notice how harmoniously the architecture, sculpture, and painting work together.

Outside, busts honor great minds from the faculty, including (at the end) Niels Bohr, a professor who won the 1922 Nobel Prize for theoretical physics. He evaded the clutches of the Nazi science labs by fleeing to America in 1943, where he helped develop the atomic bomb.

• *Rejoin the Strøget (one block downhill from the Reformation Memorial to the black-and-gold fountain) at the twin squares called...*

❽ Gammeltorv and Nytorv

This was the old town center. In Gammeltorv ("Old Square"), the Fountain of Charity (Caritas) is named for the figure of Charity on top. It has provided drinking water to locals since the early 1600s. Featuring a pregnant woman squirting water from her breasts next to a boy urinating, this was just too much for people of the Victorian Age. They corked both figures and raised the statue to what they hoped would be out of view. The exotic-looking kiosk was one of the city's first community telephone centers from the days before phones were privately owned. Look at the reliefs ringing its top: an airplane with bird wings (c. 1900) and two women talking on a newfangled telephonic device. (It was thought business would popularize the telephone, but actually it was women.)

While Gammeltorv was a place of happiness and merriment, Nytorv ("New Square") was a place of severity and judg-

ment. Walk to the small raised area 20 yards in front of the old ancient-Greek-style former City Hall and courthouse. Do a 360. The square is Neoclassical (built mostly after the 1807 British bombardment). Read the old Danish on the City Hall facade: "With Law Shall Man Build the Land." Look down at the pavement and read the plaque: "Here stood the town's *Kag* (whipping post) until 1780."

• *Now walk down the next stretch of the Strøget—called Nygade—to reach...*

❾ Amagertorv

This is prime real estate for talented street entertainers. Walk to the stately brick Holy Ghost Church (Helligåndskirken). The fine spire is typical of old Danish churches. Under the stepped gable was a medieval hospital run by monks (one of the oldest buildings in town, dating from the 12th century). Today the hospital is an antiques hall. In summer the pleasant courtyard is shared by a group of charities selling light bites and coffee.

Walk behind the church, down Valkendorfsgade—the street just before the church—and through a passage under the reddish-colored building at #32 (if locked, loop back and go down Klosterstræde); here you'll find the leafy and beer-stained ❿ Gråbrødretorv. Surrounded by fine old buildings, this "Grey Friars' Square"—a monastic square until the Reformation made it a people's square—is a popular place for an outdoor meal or drink in the summer. At the end of the square, the street called Niels Hemmingsens Gade returns (past the Copenhagen Jazz House) to the Strøget.

Once back on busy Strøget, turn left and continue down Amagertorv, with its fine inlaid Italian granite stonework, to the next square with the "stork" fountain (actually three herons). The Victorian WCs here (free, steps down from fountain) are a delight.

This square, Amagertorv, is a highlight for shoppers, with the ⓫ **Royal Copenhagen store**—stacked with three floors of porcelain—and **Illums Bolighus**—a fine place to ogle modern Danish design (see "Shopping in Copenhagen," later). A block toward the canal—running parallel to the Strøget—starts Strædet, which is a "second Strøget" featuring cafés and antique shops.

North of Amagertorv, a broad pedestrian mall called **Købmagergade** leads past a fine modern bakery (Holm's) to Christian IV's Round Tower and the Latin Quarter (university district). The recommended Café Norden overlooks the fountain—a good place for a meal or coffee with a view. The second floor offers the best vantage point.

• *Looking downhill from the fountain, about halfway to an imposing palace in the distance, you'll see a great man on a horse. Walk here to view this statue of Copenhagen's founder, ⓬ Bishop Absalon, shown in his Warrior Absalon get-up.*

From the bishop, you'll continue across a bridge toward the palace and the next statue—a king on a horse. As you cross the bridge, look right to see the City Hall tower, where this walk started. (A couple of the city's competing sightseeing boat tours depart from near here—see page 154.)

Christiansborg Palace and the Birthplace of Copenhagen

You're stepping onto the island of Slotsholmen ("Castle Island"), the easy-to-defend birthplace of Copenhagen in the 12th century. It's dominated by the royal palace complex. Christiansborg Palace (with its "three crowns" spire)—the imposing former residence of kings—is now the parliament building.

Ahead of you, the Neoclassical Lutheran church with the low dome is the ❸ **Christiansborg Palace Chapel,** site of 350 years of royal weddings and funerals.

Walk to the next green copper equestrian statue. ❹ **Frederik VII** was crowned in 1848, just months before Denmark got its constitution on June 5, 1849. (Constitution Day is celebrated with typical Danish understatement—stores are closed and workers get the day off.) Frederik, who then ruled as a constitutional monarch, stands in front of **Christiansborg Palace,** which Denmark's royal family now shares with its people's assembly (queen's wing on right, parliament on left; for information on visiting the palace, see page 176). This palace, the seat of Danish government today, is considered the birthplace of Copenhagen. It stands upon the ruins of Absalon's 12th-century castle (literally under your feet). The big stones between the statue and the street were put in for security after the 2011 terror attacks in Norway (in which 77 people were murdered, most of them teens and young adults). While Danes strive to keep government accessible, security measures like this are today's reality.

This is Denmark's power island, with the Folketing (Danish parliament), Supreme Court, Ministry of Finance (to the left), and ❺ **Børsen**—the historic stock exchange (farther to the left, with the fanciful dragon-tail spire; not open to tourists). The eye-catching red-brick stock exchange was inspired by the Dutch Renaissance, like much of 17th-century Copenhagen. Built to promote the mercantile ambitions of Denmark in the 1600s, it was the "World Trade Center" of Scandinavia. The facade reads, "For the profitable use of buyer and seller." The dragon-tail spire with three crowns represents the Danish aspiration to rule a united Scandinavia—or at least be its commercial capital.

Notice Copenhagen's distinctive green copper spires all around you. Beyond the old stock exchange lies the island of **Christianshavn,** with its own distinct spire. It tops the Church of Our Savior and features an external spiral staircase winding to the top for an amazing view. While political power resided here on Slotsholmen, commercial power was in the merchant's district, Christianshavn (neighborhood and church described later, under "Sights in Copenhagen"). The Børsen symbolically connected Christianshavn with the rest of the city, in an age when trade was a very big deal.

• *Walk along the old stock exchange toward Christianshavn, but turn left at the crosswalk with the signal before you reach the end of the building. After crossing the street, go over the canal and turn right to walk along the harborfront promenade, enjoying views of Christianshavn across the water.*

⓰ Havnegade Promenade

The Havnegade promenade to Nyhavn is a delightful people zone with trampolines, harborview benches (a good place to stop, look across the water, and ponder the trendy apartments and old-warehouses-turned-modern-office-blocks), and an ice-cream-licking ambience. Stroll several blocks from here toward the new **⓱ Inderhavnsbroen sliding bridge** for pedestrians and bikes.

This "Kissing Bridge" (it's called that because the two sliding, or retractable, sections "kiss" when they come together) is designed to link the town center with Christianshavn and to make the modern Opera House (ahead on the right, across the water) more accessible to downtown. Walk until you hit the Nyhavn canal.

Across the way, at the end of Nyhavn canal, stands the glassy Royal Danish Theatre's Playhouse. While this walk finishes on Kongens Nytorv, the square at the head of this canal, you could extend it by continuing north along the harbor from the playhouse.

• *For now, turn left and walk to the center of the bridge over the canal for a...*

⓲ View of Nyhavn

Established in the 1670s along with Kongens Nytorv, Nyhavn ("New Harbor") is a recently gentrified sailors' quarter. (Hong Kong is the last of the nasty bars from the rough old days.) With its trendy cafés, jazz clubs, and tattoo shops (pop into Tattoo Ole at #17—fun photos, very traditional), Nyhavn is a wonderful place to hang out. The canal is filled with glamorous old sailboats of all sizes. Historic sloops are welcome to moor here in Copenhagen's ever-changing boat museum. Hans Christian Andersen lived and wrote his first stories here (in the red double-gabled building at #20).

From the bridge, take a few steps left to the cheap **beer kiosk** (on Holbergsgade, open daily until late). At this minimarket, let friendly manager Nagib give you a little lesson in Danish beer, and then buy a bottle or can. Choose from Carlsberg (standard lager, 4.6 percent alcohol), Carlsberg Elephant (strong, 7.2 percent), Tuborg Grøn (standard lager, 4.6 percent), Tuborg Gold (stronger, 5.8 percent), and Tuborg Classic (dark beer, 4.6 percent). The cost? About 15 DKK depending on the alcohol level. Take your beer out to the canal and feel like a local. A note about all the public beer-drinking here: There's no more beer consumption here than in the US; it's just out in public. Many young Danes can't afford to drink in a bar, so they "picnic drink" their beers in squares and along canals, at a quarter of the price for a bottle.

If you crave **ice cream** instead, cross the bridge, where you'll find a popular place with freshly made waffle cones facing the canal (Vaffelbageren).

Now wander the quay, enjoying the frat-party parade of tattoos (hotter weather reveals more tattoos). Celtic and Nordic mythological designs are in (as is bodybuilding, by the looks of things). The place thrives—with the cheap-beer drinkers dockside and the richer and older ones looking on from comfier cafés.

• *Make your way to the head of the canal, where you'll find a minuscule amber museum, above the House of Amber (see "Shopping in Copenhagen," page 191). Just beyond the head of Nyhavn canal sprawls the huge and stately King's New Square. Check it out.*

⓳ Kongens Nytorv

The "King's New Square" is home to the National Theater, French embassy, and venerable Hotel d'Angleterre, where VIPs and pop stars stay. In the mid-1600s the

city expanded, pushing its wall farther east. The equestrian statue in the middle of the square celebrates Christian V, who made this square the city's geographical and cultural center. In 1676, King Christian rode off to reconquer the southern tip of Sweden and reclaim Denmark's dominance. He returned empty-handed and broke. Denmark became a second-rate power, but Copenhagen prospered. In the winter this square becomes a popular ice-skating rink.

Across the square on the left, small glass pyramids mark the Metro. The **Metro** that runs underground here features state-of-the-art technology (automated cars, no driver...sit in front to watch the tracks coming at you). As the cars come and go without drivers, compare this system to the public transit in your town.

Wander into ⓴ **Hviids Vinstue,** the town's oldest wine cellar

COPENHAGEN

(from 1723, just beyond the Metro station, at #19, under a bar) to check out its characteristic dark and woody interior and fascinating old Copenhagen photos. It's a colorful spot for an open-face sandwich and a beer (three sandwiches and a beer for 79 DKK at lunchtime). Their wintertime *gløgg* (hot spiced wine) is legendary. Across the street, towering above the Metro station, is Magasin du Nord, the grandest old department store in town.

• *You've reached the end of this walk. But if you'd like to extend it by heading out to Amalienborg Palace and The Little Mermaid, retrace your steps to the far side of Nyhavn canal.*

Extended Walk: Nyhavn to Amalienborg

Stroll along the canal to the Royal Danish Theatre's Playhouse and follow the harborfront promenade from there left to a large plaza dotted with outdoor cafés and benches, and views across the harbor. You'll then follow a delightful promenade to the modern fountain of Amaliehaven Park, immediately across the harbor from Copenhagen's slick Opera House. The striking Opera House is bigger than it looks—of its 14 floors, five are below sea level. Completed in 2005 by Henning Larsen, it was a $400 million gift to the nation from an oil-shipping magnate.

• *A block inland (behind the fountain) is the orderly...*

㉑ Amalienborg Palace and Square

Queen Margrethe II and her husband live in the mansion to your immediate left as you enter the square from the harborside. (If

the flag's flying, she's home.) The mansion across the street (on the right as you enter) is where her son and heir to the throne, Crown Prince Frederik, lives with his wife, Australian businesswoman Mary Donaldson, and their four children. The royal guesthouse palace is on the far left. And the palace on the far right is the

Amalienborg Museum, which offers an intimate look at royal living (described on page 179).

Though the guards change daily at noon, they do it with royal fanfare only when the queen is in residence. The royal guard often has a police escort when it marches through town on special occasions—leading locals to joke that theirs is "the only army in the world that needs police protection."

The equestrian statue of Frederik V is a reminder that this square was the centerpiece of a planned town he envisioned in 1750. It was named for him—Frederikstaden. During the 18th

The Little Mermaid

"Far out in the ocean, where the water is as blue as a cornflower, as clear as crystal, and very, very deep.." there lived a young mermaid. So begins one of Hans Christian Andersen's best-known stories.

It goes like this: One day, a young mermaid spies a passing ship and falls in love with a handsome human prince. The ship is wrecked in a storm, and she saves the prince's life. To be with the prince, the mermaid asks a sea witch to give her human legs. In exchange, she agrees to give up her voice and the chance of ever returning to the sea. And, the witch tells her, if the prince doesn't marry her, she will immediately die heartbroken and without an immortal soul. The mermaid agrees, and her fish tail becomes a pair of beautiful but painful legs. She woos the prince—who loves her in return—but he eventually marries another. Heartbroken, the mermaid prepares to die. She's given one last chance to save herself: She must kill the prince on his wedding night. She sneaks into the bedchamber with a knife... but can't bear to kill the man she loves. The mermaid throws herself into the sea to die. Suddenly, she's miraculously carried up by the mermaids of the air, who give her an immortal soul as a reward for her long-suffering love.

century, Denmark's population grew and the country thrived (as trade flourished and its neutrality kept it out of the costly wars impoverishing much of Europe). Frederikstaden, with its strong architectural harmony, was designed as a luxury neighborhood for the city's business elite. Nobility and other big shots moved in, but the king came here only after his other palace burned down in a 1794 fire.

Just inland, the striking Frederikskirke—better known as the **Marble Church**—was designed to fit this ritzy new quarter. If it's open, step inside to bask in its vast, serene, Pantheon-esque atmosphere (free, Mon-Thu 10:00-17:00, Fri-Sun from 12:00; dome climb—35 DKK, mid-June-Aug daily at 13:00; off-season Sat-Sun at 13:00).

• *From the square, Amaliegade leads two blocks north to...*

Kastellet Park

In this park, you'll find some worthwhile sightseeing. The 1908 Gefion Fountain illustrates the myth of the goddess who was given one night to carve a hunk out of Sweden to make into Denmark's

main island, Sjælland (or "Zealand" in English), which you're on. Gefion transformed her four sons into oxen to do the job, and the chunk she removed from Sweden is supposedly Vänern, Sweden's largest lake. If you look at a map showing Sweden and Denmark, the island and the lake are, in fact, roughly the same shape. Next to the fountain is an Anglican church built of flint.

• *Climb up the stairs by the fountain and continue along the top of the rampart about five minutes to reach the harborfront site of the overrated, overfondled, and overphotographed symbol of Copenhagen,* Den Lille Havfrue, *or...*

㉑ The Little Mermaid

The Little Mermaid statue was a gift to the city of Copenhagen in 1909 from brewing magnate Carl Jacobsen (whose art collection forms the basis of the Ny Carlsberg Glyptotek). Inspired by a ballet performance of Andersen's story, Jacobsen hired the young sculptor Edvard Eriksen to immortalize the mermaid as a statue. Eriksen used his wife Eline as the model. The statue sat unappreciated for 40 years until Danny Kaye sang "Wonderful Copenhagen" in the movie *Hans Christian Andersen,* and the tourist board decided to use the mermaid as a marketing symbol for the city. For the non-Disneyfied *Little Mermaid* story, see the sidebar.

• *This is the end of our extended wonderful, wonderful "Copenhagen City Walk." From here you can get back downtown on foot, by taxi, on bus #1A from Store Kongensgade on the other side of Kastellet Park, or bus #26 from farther north, along Folke Bernadottes Allé. If your cruise ship is at Langelinie or Nordre Toldbod and you're ready to head back, you're just a short walk away.*

Sights in Copenhagen

NEAR THE TRAIN STATION

Copenhagen's great train station, the Hovedbanegården, is a fascinating mesh of Scandinavian culture and transportation efficiency. From the station, delightful sights fan out into the old city. The following attractions are listed roughly in order from the train station to Slotsholmen Island.

▲▲▲Tivoli Gardens

The world's grand old amusement park—since 1843—is 20 acres, 110,000 lanterns, and countless ice cream cones of fun. You pay one admission price and find yourself lost in a Hans Christian Andersen wonderland of rides, restaurants, games, marching bands, roulette wheels, and funny mirrors. A roller coaster screams through the middle of a tranquil Asian food court, and the Small World-inspired Den Flyvende Kuffert ride floats through Hans Christian Andersen fairy tales. It's a children's fantasyland midday, but it becomes more adult-oriented later. With or without kids, this place is a true magic kingdom.

Cost: 110-120 DKK, free for kids under 8. To go on rides, you must buy ride tickets (from booth at entrance or from machines in the park—machines take credit

card only, 25 DKK/ticket, color-coded rides cost 1-4 tickets apiece); or you can buy a multiride pass for 230 DKK. If you'll be using at least eight tickets, buy the ride pass instead. To leave and come back later, you'll have to buy a 35-DKK re-entry ticket before you exit.

Hours: Late March-mid-Sept daily 11:00-23:00, Fri-Sat until 24:00, shorter hours off-season.

Information: Tel. 33 15 10 01, www.tivoli.dk.

Entertainment at Tivoli: Upon arrival (through main entrance, on left in the service center), pick up a map and look for the events schedule.

Free concerts, pantomime theater, ballet, acrobats, puppets, and other shows pop up all over the park, and a well-organized visitor can enjoy exciting entertainment without spending a single krone beyond the entry fee. The park is particularly romantic at dusk, when the lights go on.

Eating at Tivoli: Inside the park, expect to pay amusement-park prices for amusement-park-quality food. Still, a meal here is part of the fun. **$$ Søcafeen** serves traditional open-face sandwiches and main courses in a fun beer garden with lakeside ambience **$$$ Mazzoli's Caffé & Trattoria,** in a circular building near the lake, serves classic Italian fare and pizza. **$$$ Færgekroen Bryghus** offers a quiet, classy lakeside escape, with traditional dishes washed down by its own microbrew (open-face sandwiches, seafood, pub grub). **$$$ Wagamama** serves healthy noodle dishes (at the far back side of the park, also possible to enter from outside). **$$$ Fru Nimb** offers a large selection of open-face sandwiches in a garden setting. The kid-pleasing **$$$ Piratiriet** lets you dine on a pirate ship. For something more upscale, consider the complex of **Nimb** restaurants, in the big Taj Mahal-like pavilion near the entrance facing the train station. And if these options aren't enough, check out the eateries in the glassy new **Tivoli Food Hall** (facing the train station) that promises "fast gourmet food."

▲City Hall (Rådhus)

This city landmark, between the train station/Tivoli and the Strøget, is free and open to the public (including a public WC).

You can wander throughout the building and into the peaceful garden out back. It also offers private tours and trips up its 345-foot-tall tower.

Cost and Hours: Free to enter building, Mon-Fri 9:00-16:00; you can usually slip in Sat 9:30-13:00 when weddings are going on, or join the Sat tour; closed Sun. Guided English-language tours-50 DKK, 45 minutes, gets you into more private, official rooms; Mon-Fri at 13:00, Sat at 10:00. Tower by escort only-30 DKK, 300 steps for the best aerial view of Copenhagen, Mon-Fri at 11:00 and 14:00, Sat at 12:00, closed Sun. Tel. 33 66 33 66.

▲Ny Carlsberg Glyptotek

Scandinavia's top art gallery is an impressive example of what beer money can do. Brewer Carl Jacobsen (son of J. C. Jacobsen, who

funded the Museum of National History at Frederiksborg Castle) was an avid collector and patron of the arts. (Carl also donated the *Little Mermaid* statue to the city.) His namesake museum has intoxicating artifacts from the ancient world, along with some fine art from our own times. The next time you sip a Carlsberg beer, drink a toast to Carl Jacobsen and his marvelous collection. *Skål!*

Cost and Hours: 95 DKK, free on Tue; open Tue-Sun 11:00-18:00, Thu until 22:00, closed Mon; behind Tivoli at Dantes Plads 7, tel. 33 41 81 41, www.glyptoteket.com. It has a classy **$$$** cafeteria under palms, as well as a rooftop terrace with snacks, drinks, and city views.

Visiting the Museum: Pick up a floor plan as you enter to help navigate the confusing layout. For a chronological swing, start with Egypt (mummy coffins and sarcophagi, a 5,000-year-old hippo statue), Greece (red-and-black painted vases, statues), the Etruscan world (Greek-looking vases), and Rome (grittily realistic statues and portrait busts).

The sober realism of 19th-century Danish Golden Age painting reflects the introspection of a once-powerful nation reduced to second-class status—and ultimately embracing what made it unique. The "French Wing" (just inside the front door) has Rodin statues. A heady, if small, exhibit of 19th-century French paintings (in a modern building within the back courtyard) shows how Realism morphed into Impressionism and Post-Impressionism, and includes a couple of canvases apiece by Géricault, Delacroix, Monet, Manet, Millet, Courbet, Degas, Pissarro, Cézanne, Van Gogh, Picasso, Renoir, and Toulouse-Lautrec. Look for art by Gauguin—from before Tahiti (when he lived in Copenhagen with

his Danish wife and their five children) and after Tahiti. There's also a fine collection of modern (post-Thorvaldsen) Danish sculpture.

Linger with marble gods under the palm leaves and glass dome of the very soothing winter garden. Designers, figuring Danes would be more interested in a lush garden than in classical art, used this wonderful space as leafy bait to cleverly introduce locals to a few Greek and Roman statues. (It works for tourists, too.) One of the original *Thinker* sculptures by Rodin (wondering how to scale the Tivoli fence?) is in the museum's backyard.

▲▲▲National Museum

Focus on this museum's excellent and curiously enjoyable Danish collection, which traces this civilization from its ancient beginnings. Its prehistoric collection is the best of its kind in Scandinavia. Exhibits are laid out chronologically and are eloquently described in English.

Cost and Hours: 75 DKK, Tue-Sun 10:00-17:00, closed Mon, mandatory lockers, enter at Ny Vestergade 10, tel. 33 13 44 11, www.natmus.dk. The **$$** café overlooking the entry hall serves coffee, pastries, and lunch.

Visiting the Museum: Pick up the museum map as you enter, and head for the Danish history exhibit. It fills three floors, from the bottom up: prehistory, the Middle Ages and Renaissance, and modern times (1660-2000).

Danish Prehistory: Start before history did, in the Danish Prehistory exhibit (on the right side of the main entrance hall). Follow the room numbers in order, working counterclockwise around the courtyard and through the millennia.

In the Stone Age section, you'll see primitive tools and still-clothed skeletons of Scandinavia's reindeer hunters. The oak coffins were originally covered by burial mounds (called "barrows"). People put valuable items into the coffins with the dead, such as a folding chair (which, back then, was a real status symbol). In the farming section, ogle the ceremonial axes and amber necklaces.

The Bronze Age brought the sword (several are on display). The "Chariot of the Sun"—a small statue of a horse pulling the sun across the sky—likely had religious significance for early Scandinavians (whose descendants continue to celebrate the solstice with fervor). In the same room are those iconic horned helmets. Contrary to popular belief (and countless tourist shops), these helmets were not worn by the Vikings, but by their predecessors—for ceremonial purposes, centuries earlier. In the next room are huge cases filled with

still-playable *lur* horns (see page 159). Another room shows off a collection of well-translated rune stones proclaiming heroic deeds.

This leads to the Iron Age and an object that's neither Iron nor Danish: the 2,000-year-old Gundestrup Cauldron of art-textbook fame. This 20-pound, soup-kitchen-size bowl made of silver was found in a Danish bog, but its symbolism suggests it was originally from either Thrace (in northeast Greece) or Celtic Ireland. On the sides, hunters slay bulls, and gods cavort with stags, horses, dogs, and dragons. It's both mysterious and fascinating.

Prehistoric Danes were fascinated by bogs. To make iron, you need ore—and Denmark's many bogs provided that critical material in abundance, leading people to believe that the gods dwelled there. These Danes appeased the gods by sacrificing valuable items (and even people) into bogs. Fortunately for modern archaeologists, bogs happen to be an ideal environment for preserving fragile objects. One bog alone—the Nydam bog—has yielded thousands of items, including three whole ships.

Middle Ages and Renaissance: Next, go upstairs and follow signs to Room 101 to start this section. You'll walk through the Middle Ages, where you'll find lots of bits and pieces of old churches, such as golden altars and *aquamaniles,* pitchers used for ritual hand-washing. The Dagmar Cross is the prototype for a popular form of crucifix worn by many Danes (Room 102, small glass display case—with colorful enamel paintings). Another cross in this case (the Roskilde Cross, studded with gemstones) was found inside the wooden head of Christ displayed high on the opposite wall. There are also exhibits on tools and trade, weapons, drinking horns, and fine, wood-carved winged altarpieces. Carry on to find a fascinating room on the Norse settlers of Greenland, material on the Reformation, and an exhibit on everyday town life in the 16th and 17th centuries.

Modern Times: The next floor takes you through the last few centuries, with historic toys and a slice-of-Danish-life (1660-2000)

gallery where you'll see everything from rifles and old bras to early jukeboxes. You'll learn that the Danish Golden Age (which dominates most art museums in Denmark) captured the everyday pastoral beauty of the countryside, celebrated Denmark's smallness and peace-loving nature, and mixed in some Nordic mythology. The collection is capped off by a stall that, until recently, was used for selling marijuana in the squatters' community of Christiania.

ON SLOTSHOLMEN ISLAND

This island, where Copenhagen began in the 12th century, is a short walk from the train station and Tivoli, just across the bridge from the National Museum. It's dominated by Christiansborg Palace and several other royal and governmental buildings. Note that my "Copenhagen City Walk" (earlier) cuts right through Slotsholmen and covers other landmarks on the island.

▲▲Christiansborg Palace

A complex of government buildings stands on the ruins of Copenhagen's original 12th-century fortress: the parliament, Supreme Court, prime minister's office, royal reception rooms, royal library, several museums, and royal stables. Although the current palace dates only from 1928 and the royal family moved out 200 years ago, this building—the sixth to stand here in 800 years—is rich with tradition.

Four palace sights (the reception rooms, old castle ruins, stables, and kitchen) are open to the public, giving us commoners a glimpse of the royal life.

Cost and Hours: Reception rooms-90 DKK, castle ruins, stables, and kitchen-50 DKK each; a combo-ticket for all four-150 DKK. All sights are open daily (except in Oct-April, when they're closed on Mon) but have different hours: reception rooms open 9:00-17:00, Oct-April from 10:00 (may close for royal events); ruins and kitchen open 10:00-17:00; stables and carriage museum open 13:30-16:00—longer hours possible in July.

Information: Tel. 33 92 64 92, www.christiansborg.dk.

Visiting the Palace: From the equestrian statue in front, go through the wooden door; the entrance to the ruins is in the corridor on the right, and the door to the reception rooms is out in the next courtyard, also on the right.

Royal Reception Rooms: While these don't rank among Europe's best palace rooms, they're worth a look. This is still the place where Queen Margrethe II impresses visiting dignitaries. The information-packed, hour-long English tours of the rooms are excellent (included in ticket, daily at 15:00). At other times, you'll wander the rooms on your own in a one-way route, reading the sparse English descriptions. As you slip-slide on protect-the-floor slippers through 22 rooms, you'll gain a good feel for Danish history, royalty, and politics. Here are a few highlights:

After the Queen's Library you'll soon enter the grand Great Hall, lined with boldly colorful (almost gaudy) tapestries. The palace highlight is this dazzling set of modern tapestries—Danish-designed but Gobelin-made in Paris. This gift, given to the queen on her 60th birthday in 2000, celebrates 1,000 years of Danish history, from the Viking age to our chaotic times...and into the future. Borrow the laminated descriptions for blow-by-blow explanations of the whole epic saga. The Velvet Room is where royals privately greet VIP guests before big functions.

In the corner room on the left, don't miss the family portrait of

King Christian IX, which illustrates why he's called the "father-in-law of Europe"—his children eventually became, or married into, royalty in Denmark, Russia, Greece, Britain, France, Germany, and Norway.

In the Throne Room you'll see the balcony where new monarchs are proclaimed (most recently in 1972). And at the end, in the Hall of Giants (where you take off your booties among heroic figures supporting the building), you'll see a striking painting of Queen Margrethe II from 2010 on her 70th birthday. The three playful lions, made of Norwegian silver, once guarded the throne and symbolize absolute power—long gone since 1849, when Denmark embraced the notion of a constitutional monarch.

Castle Ruins: An exhibit in the scant remains of the first fortress built by Bishop Absalon, the 12th-century founder of Copenhagen, lies under the palace. A long passage connects to another set of ruins, from the 14th-century Copenhagen Castle. There's precious little to see, but it is, um, old and well-described. A video covers more recent palace history.

Royal Stables and Carriages Museum: This facility is still home to the horses that pull the queen's carriage on festive days, as well as a collection of historic carriages. While they're down from 250 horses to about a dozen, the royal stables are part of a strong tradition and, as the little video shows, will live on.

Royal Kitchen: Unless you're smitten with old ladles and shiny copper pots and pans, I'd skip this exhibit.

▲▲Thorvaldsen's Museum

This museum, which has some of the best swoon-worthy art you'll see anywhere, tells the story and shows the monumental work of the great Danish Neoclassical sculptor Bertel Thorvaldsen (1770-1844). Considered Canova's equal among Neoclassical sculptors, Thorvaldsen spent 40 years in Rome. He was lured home to Copenhagen with the promise to showcase his work in a fine museum, which opened in the revolutionary year of 1848 as Denmark's first public art gallery. Of the 500 or so sculptures Thorvaldsen completed in his life—including 90 major statues—this museum has most of them, in one form or another (the plaster model used to make the original or a copy done in marble or bronze).

Cost and Hours: 50 DKK, free on Wed, Tue-Sun 10:00-17:00, closed Mon, includes excellent English audioguide on request, located in Neoclassical building with colorful walls next to Christiansborg Palace.

Information: Tel. 33 32 15 32, www.thorvaldsensmuseum.dk.

Visiting the Museum: The ground floor showcases his statues. After buying your ticket, go straight in and ask to borrow a free audioguide at the desk. This provides a wonderful statue-by-statue narration of the museum's key works.

Just before the audioguide desk, turn left into the Great Hall, which was the original entryway of the museum. It's filled with replicas of some of Thorvaldsen's biggest and grandest statues—national heroes who still stand in the prominent squares of their major cities (Munich, Warsaw, the Vatican, and others). Two great equestrian statues stare each other down from across the hall; while they both take the classic, self-assured pose of looking one way while pointing another (think Babe Ruth calling his home run), one of them (Jozef Poniatowski) is modeled after the ancient Roman general Marcus Aurelius, while the other (Bavaria's Maximilian I) wears modern garb.

Then take a spin through the smaller rooms that ring the central courtyard. Each of these is dominated by one big work—most-

ly classical subjects drawn from mythology. At the far end of the building stand the plaster models for the iconic *Risen Christ* and the 12 Apostles (the final marble versions stand in the Cathedral of Our Lady). Peek into the central courtyard to see the planter-box tomb of Thorvaldsen himself. Continue into the next row of rooms: In the far corner room look for Thorvaldsen's (very flattering) self-portrait, leaning buffly against a partially finished sculpture.

Downstairs you'll find a collection of plaster casts (mostly ancient Roman statues that inspired Thorvaldsen) and a video about his career.

Upstairs, get into the mind of the artist by perusing his personal possessions and the private collection of paintings from which he drew inspiration.

▲Danish Jewish Museum (Dansk Jødisk Museum)

In a striking building by American architect Daniel Libeskind, this museum offers a very small but well-exhibited display of 400 years of the life and impact of Jews in Denmark. Be sure to watch the two introductory films about the Jews' migration to Denmark, and about the architect Libeskind (12-minute loop total, English subtitles, plays continuously). As you tour the collection, the uneven floors and asymmetrical walls give you the feeling that what lies around the corner is completely unknown...much like the life and history of Danish Jews. Another interpretation might be that the uneven floors give you the sense of motion, like waves on the sea—a reminder that despite Nazi occupation in 1943, nearly 7,000 Danish Jews were ferried across the waves by fishermen to safety in neutral Sweden.

Cost and Hours: 60 DKK; Tue-Sun 10:00-17:00; Sept-May Tue-Fri 13:00-16:00, Sat-Sun 12:00-17:00; closed Mon year-round; behind "Black Diamond" library at Proviantpassagen 6—enter from the courtyard behind the red-brick, ivy-covered building, tel. 33 11 22 18, www.jewmus.dk.

AMALIENBORG PALACE AND NEARBY

For more information on this palace and nearby attractions, including the famous *Little Mermaid* statue, see the end of my "Copenhagen City Walk," earlier.

▲Amalienborg Museum (Amalienborgmuseet)

While Queen Margrethe II and her husband live quite privately in one of the four mansions that make up the palace complex, another mansion has been open to the public since 1994. It displays the private studies of four kings of the House of Glucksborg, who ruled from 1863-1972 (the immediate predecessors of today's queen). Your visit won't take long—you'll see six to eight rooms on each of two floors—but it affords an intimate and unique peek into Denmark's royal family. On the first floor you'll see the private study of each of the last four kings of Denmark. They feel particularly lived-in—with cluttered pipe collections and bookcases jammed with family pictures—because they were. It's easy to imagine these blue-blooded folks just hanging out here, even today. The earliest study, Frederik VIII's (c. 1869), feels much older and more "royal"—with Renaissance gilded walls, heavy drapes, and a polar bear rug. On the second floor, your visit includes the Gothic library designed for dowager Queen Caroline Amalie, the cheery gala hall (the palace's largest room) with statues by Bertel Thorvaldsen, and a hall gleaming with large gilt-bronze table decorations.

Cost and Hours: 95 DKK, 145-DKK combo-ticket includes Rosenborg Palace—available on the website or at Rosenborg only; May-Oct daily 10:00-16:00, mid-June-mid-Sept until 17:00; Nov-April Tue-Sun 11:00-16:00, closed Mon; with your back to the harbor, entrance is at the far end of the square on the right; tel. 33 15 32 86, www.dkks.dk.

ROSENBORG CASTLE AND NEARBY
▲▲▲Rosenborg Castle (Rosenborg Slot) and Treasury

This finely furnished Dutch Renaissance-style castle was built by King Christian IV in the early 1600s as a summer residence.

Rosenborg was his favorite residence and where he chose to die. Open to the public since 1838, it houses the Danish crown jewels and 500 years of royal knickknacks. While the old palace interior is a bit dark and not as immediately impressive as many of Europe's later Baroque master-pieces, it has a certain lived-in charm. It oozes the personality of the fascinating Christian IV and has one of the finest treasury collections in Europe. For more on Christian, read the sidebar.

Cost and Hours: 110 DKK, 145-DKK combo-ticket includes Amalienborg Museum; mid-June-mid-Sept daily 9:00-17:00; mid-April-mid-June and mid-Sept-Oct daily 10:00-16:00, except closed Mon in April; shorter hours and generally closed Mon rest of the year; mandatory lockers take 20-DKK coin, which will be returned; Metro or S-tog: Nørreport, then 5-minute walk on Østervoldgade and through park.

Information: Tel. 33 15 32 86, www.dkks.dk.

Tours: Richard Karpen leads fascinating one-hour tours in Hans Christian Andersen garb (100 DKK plus entry fee, mid-May-mid-Sept Mon and Thu at 12:00, meet outside castle ticket office—no reservations needed; see listing on page 152). Or take the following self-guided tour that I've woven together from the highlights of Richard's walk. You can also use the palace's free Wi-Fi to follow the "Konge Connect" step-by-step tour through the palace highlights (with audio/video/text explanations for your smartphone or tablet—bring earphones; instructional brochure at ticket desk).

● Self-Guided Tour: Buy your ticket, then head back out and look for the *castle* sign. You'll tour the ground floor room by room, then climb to the third floor for the big throne room. After a quick sweep of the middle floor, finish in the basement (enter from outside) for the jewels.

• *Begin the tour on the palace's ground floor (turn right as you enter), in the Winter Room.*

Ground Floor: Here in the wood-paneled **Winter Room,** all eyes were on King Christian IV. Today, your eyes should be on him, too. Take a close look at his bust by the fireplace (if it's not here,

King Christian IV:
A Lover and a Fighter

King Christian IV (1577-1648) inherited Denmark at the peak of its power, lived his life with the exuberance of the age, and went to his grave with the country in decline. His legacy is ob-

vious to every tourist—Rosenborg Castle, Frederiksborg Palace, the Round Tower, Christianshavn, and on and on. Look for his logo adorning many buildings: the letter "C" with a "4" inside it and a crown on top. Thanks to both his place in history and his passionate personality, Danes today regard Christian IV as one of their greatest monarchs.

During his 50-year reign, Christian IV reformed the government, rebuilt the army, established a trading post in India, and tried to expand Denmark's territory. He took Kalmar from Sweden and captured strategic points in northern Germany. The king was a large man who also lived large. A skilled horseman and avid

hunter, he could drink his companions under the table. He spoke several languages and gained a reputation as outgoing and humorous. His lavish banquets were legendary, and his romantic affairs were numerous.

But Christian's appetite for war proved destructive. In 1626, Denmark again attacked northern Germany, but was beaten back. In late 1643, Sweden launched a sneak attack, and despite Christian's personal bravery (he lost an eye), the war went badly. By the end of his life, Christian was tired and bitter and Denmark was drained.

The heroics of Christian and his sailors live on in the Danish national anthem, "King Christian Stood by the Lofty Mast."

look for it out in the corridor by the ticket taker). Check this guy out—fashionable braid, hard drinker, hard lover, energetic statesman, and warrior king. Christian IV was dynamism in the flesh, wearing a toga: a true Renaissance guy. During his reign, Copenhagen doubled in size. You're surrounded by Dutch paintings (the Dutch had a huge influence on 17th-century Denmark). Note the smaller statue of the 19-year-old king, showing him jousting jauntily on his coronation day. In another case, the golden astronomical clock—with musical works and moving figures—did everything you can imagine. Flanking the fireplace (opposite where you entered), beneath the windows, look for the panels in the tile floor that could be removed to let the music performed by the band in the basement waft in. (Who wants the actual musicians in the dining room?) The audio holes were also used to call servants.

The **study** (or "writing closet," nearest where you entered) was small (and easy to heat). Kings did a lot of corresponding. We know a lot about Christian because 3,000 of his handwritten letters survive. The painting on the right wall shows Christian at age eight. Three years later, his father died, and little Christian technically ascended the throne, though Denmark was actually ruled by a regency until Christian was 19. A portrait of his mother hangs above the boy, and opposite is a portrait of Christian in his prime—having just conquered Sweden—standing alongside the incredible coronation crown you'll see later.

Going back through the Winter Room, head for the door to Christian's **bedroom.** Before entering, notice the little peephole in the door (used by the king to spy on those in this room—well-camouflaged by the painting, and more easily seen from the other side), and the big cabinet doors for Christian's clothes and accessories,

flanking the bedroom door (notice the hinges and keyholes). Heading into the bedroom, you'll see paintings showing the king as an old man...and as a dead man. (Christian died in this room.) In the case are the clothes he wore at his finest hour. During a naval battle against Sweden (1644), Christian stood directing the action when an explosion ripped across the deck, sending him sprawling and riddling him with shrapnel. Unfazed, the 67-year-old monarch bounced right back up and kept going, inspiring his men to carry on the fight. Christian's stubborn determination during this battle is commemorated in Denmark's national anthem. Shrapnel put out Christian's eye. No problem: The warrior king with a knack for heroic publicity stunts had the shrapnel bits removed from his eye and forehead and made into earrings as a gift for his mistress. The earrings hang in the case with his blood-stained clothes (easy to miss, right side). Christian lived to be 70 and fathered 25 children (with two wives and three mistresses). Before moving on, you can peek into Christian's private bathroom—elegantly tiled with Delft porcelain.

Proceed into the **Dark Room.** Here you'll see wax casts of royal figures. This was the way famous and important people were portrayed back then. The chair is a forerunner of the whoopee cushion. When you sat on it, metal cuffs pinned your arms down, allowing the prankster to pour water down the back of the chair (see hole)—making you "wet your pants." When you stood up, the chair made embarrassing tooting sounds.

The **Marble Room** has a particularly impressive inlaid marble floor. Imagine the king meeting emissaries here in the center, with the emblems of Norway (right), Denmark (center), and Sweden (left) behind him.

The end room, called the **King's Chamber,** was used by Christian's first mistress. Notice the ceiling painting, with an orchestra looking down on you as they play.

The long **stone passage** leading to the staircase exhibits an intriguing painting (by the door to the King's Chamber) show-

ing the crowds at the coronation of Christian's son, Frederik III. After Christian's death, a weakened Denmark was invaded, occupied, and humiliated by Sweden (Treaty of Roskilde, 1658). Copenhagen alone held out through the long winter of 1658-1659 (the Siege of Copenhagen), and Sweden eventually had to withdraw from the country. During the siege, Frederik III distinguished himself with his bravery. He seized upon the resulting surge of popularity as his chance to be anointed an absolute, divinely ordained monarch (1660). This painting marks that event—study it closely for slice-of-life details. Next, near the ticket taker, a sprawling family tree makes it perfectly clear that Christian IV comes from good stock. Notice the tree is labeled in German—the second language of the realm.

• *The queen had a hand-pulled elevator, but you'll need to hike up two flights of stairs to the throne room.*

Throne Room (Third Floor): The **Long Hall**—considered one of the best-preserved Baroque rooms in Europe—was great for banquets. The decor trumpets the accomplishments of Denmark's great kings. The four corners of the ceiling feature the four continents known at the time. (America—at the far-right end of the hall as you enter—was

still considered pretty untamed; notice the decapitated head with the arrow sticking out of it.) In the center, of course, is the proud seal of the Danish Royal Family. The tapestries, designed for this room, are from the late 1600s. Effective propaganda, they show the Danes defeating their Swedish rivals on land and at sea. The king's throne—still more propaganda for two centuries of "absolute" monarchs—was made of "unicorn horn" (actually narwhal tusk from Greenland). Believed to bring protection from evil and poison, the horn was the most precious material in its day. The queen's throne is of hammered silver. The 150-pound lions are 300 years old.

The small room to the left holds a delightful **royal porcelain** display with Chinese, French, German, and Danish examples of the "white gold." For five centuries, Europeans couldn't figure out how the Chinese made this stuff. The difficulty in just getting it back to Europe in one piece made it precious. The Danish pieces, called "Flora Danica" (on the left as you enter), are from a huge royal set showing off the herbs and vegetables of the realm.

• *Heading back down, pause at the middle floor, which is worth a look.*

Middle Floor: Circling counterclockwise, you'll see more fine clocks, fancy furniture, and royal portraits. The queen enjoyed her royal lathe (with candleholders for lighting and pedals to spin it hidden away below; in the Christian VI Room). The small mirror room (up the stairs from the main hall) was where the king played Hugh Hefner—using mirrors on the floor to see what was under those hoop skirts. In hidden cupboards, he had a fold-out bed and a handy escape staircase.

• *Back outside, turn right and find the stairs leading down to the...*

Royal Danish Treasury (Castle Basement): The palace was a royal residence for a century and has been the royal vault right up until today. As you enter, first head to the right, into the **wine cellar,** with thousand-liter barrels and some fine treasury items. The first room has a vast army of tiny golden soldiers, and a wall lined with fancy rifles. Heading into the next room, you'll see fine items of amber (petrified tree resin, 30-50 million years old) and ivory. Study the large box made of amber (in a freestanding case, just to the right as you enter)—the tiny figures show a healthy interest in sex.

• *Now head back past the ticket taker and into the main part of the treasury, where you can browse through exquisite royal knickknacks.*

The diamond- and pearl-studded **saddles** were Christian IV's—the first for his coronation, the second for his son's wedding. When his kingdom was nearly bankrupt, Christian had these constructed lavishly—complete with solid-gold spurs—to impress visiting dignitaries and bolster Denmark's credit rating.

Sights in Copenhagen 185

The next case displays **tankards.** Danes were always big drinkers, and to drink in the top style, a king had narwhal steins (#4030). Note the fancy Greenland Inuit (Eskimo) on the lid (#4023). The case is filled with exquisitely carved ivory. On the other side of that case, what's with the mooning snuffbox (#4063)? Also, check out the amorous whistle (#4064).

Drop by the case on the wall in the back-left of the room: The 17th century was the age of **brooches.** Many of these are made of freshwater pearls. Find the fancy combination toothpick and ear spoon (#4140). Look for #4146: A queen was caught having an affair after 22 years of royal marriage. Her king gave her a special present: a golden ring—showing the hand of his promiscuous queen shaking hands with a penis.

Step downstairs, away from all this silliness. Passing through the serious vault door, you come face-to-face with a big, jeweled **sword.** The tall, two-handed, 16th-century coronation sword was drawn by the new king, who cut crosses in the air in four directions, symbolically promising to defend the realm from all attacks. The cases surrounding the sword contain everyday items used by the king (all solid gold, of course). What looks like a trophy case of gold records is actually a collection of dinner plates with amber centers (#5032).

Go down the steps. In the center case is Christian IV's **coronation crown** (from 1596, seven pounds of gold and precious stones, #5124), which some consider to be the finest Renaissance crown in Europe. Its six tallest gables radiate symbolism. Find the symbols of justice (sword and scales), fortitude (a woman on a lion with a sword), and charity (a nursing woman—meaning the king will love God and his people as a mother loves her child). The pelican, which according to medieval legend pecks its own flesh to feed its young, symbolizes God sacrificing his son, just as

the king would make great sacrifices for his people. Climb the footstool to look inside—it's as exquisite as the outside. The shields of various Danish provinces remind the king that he's surrounded by his realms.

Circling the cases along the wall (right to left), notice the fine enameled lady's goblet with traits of a good woman spelled out in Latin (#5128) and above that, an exquisite prayer book (with handwritten favorite prayers, #5134). In the fifth window, the big solid-gold baptismal basin (#5262) hangs above tiny oval silver boxes that contained the royal children's umbilical cords (handy for protection later in life, #5272); two cases over are royal writing sets with wax, seals, pens, and ink (#5320).

Go down a few more steps into the lowest level of the treasury and last room. The two **crowns** in the center cases are more modern (from 1670), lighter, and more practical—just gold and diamonds without all the symbolism. The king's crown is only four pounds, the queen's a mere two.

The cases along the walls show off the **crown jewels**. These were made in 1840 of diamonds, emeralds, rubies, and pearls from earlier royal jewelry. The saber (#5540) shows emblems of the realm's 19 provinces. The sumptuous pendant features a 19-carat diamond cut (like its neighbors) in the 58-facet "brilliant" style for maximum reflection (far-left case, #5560). Imagine these on the dance floor. The painting shows the anointing of King Christian V at the Frederiksborg Castle Chapel in 1671. The crown jewels are still worn by the queen on special occasions several times a year.

▲Rosenborg Gardens

Rosenborg Castle is surrounded by the royal pleasure gardens and, on sunny days, a minefield of sunbathing Danish beauties and picnickers. While "ethnic Danes" grab the shade, the rest of the Danes worship the sun. When the royal family is in residence, there's a daily changing-of-the-guard miniparade from the Royal Guard's barracks adjoining Rosenborg Castle (at 11:30) to Amalienborg Palace (at 12:00). The Queen's Rose Garden (across the moat from the palace) is a royal place for a picnic. The fine statue of Hans Christian Andersen in the park—erected while he was still alive (and approved by him)—is meant to symbolize how his stories had a message even for adults (gardens open daily 7:00-dusk).

▲National Gallery of Denmark (Statens Museum for Kunst)

This museum fills a stately building with Danish and European paintings from the 14th century through today. It's particularly worthwhile for the chance to be immersed in great art by the Danes, and to see its good collection of French Modernists, all well-described in English.

Cost and Hours: 110 DKK, Tue-Sun 11:00-17:00,

Wed until 20:00, closed Mon, Sølvgade 48, tel. 33 74 84 94, www. smk.dk.

CHRISTIANSHAVN

Across the harbor from the old town, Christianshavn—the former merchant's district—is one of the most delightful neighborhoods in town to explore. It offers pleasant canalside walks and trendy restaurants, along with two things to see: Our Savior's Church (with its fanciful tower) and Christiania, a colorful alternative-living community.

Your first look at the island will likely be its main square. Christianshavns Torv has a Metro stop, an early Copenhagen phone kiosk (from 1896), a fine bakery across the street (Lagkagehuset), and three statues celebrating Greenland. A Danish protectorate since 1721, Greenland, with 56,000 people, is represented by two members in the Danish parliament. The square has long been a hangout for Greenlanders, who appreciate the cheap beer and long hours of the big supermarket fronting the square.

▲Our Savior's Church (Vor Frelsers Kirke)

Following a recent restoration, the church gleams inside and out. Its bright Baroque interior (1696) is shaped like a giant cube. The

magnificent pipe organ is supported by elephants (a royal symbol of the prestigious Order of the Elephant). Looking up to the ceiling, notice elephants also sculpted into the stucco of the dome, and a little one hanging from the main chandelier. Best of all, you can climb the unique spiral spire (with an outdoor staircase winding up to its top—398 stairs in all) for great views of the city and of the Christiania commune below.

Cost and Hours: Church interior-free, daily 11:00-15:30 but may close for special services; church tower-40 DKK Mon-Thu, 45 DKK Fri-Sun; May-Sept Mon-Sat 9:30-19:00, Sun from 10:30; shorter hours off-season, closed mid-Dec-Feb and in bad weather; bus #2A, #19, or Metro: Christianshavn, Sankt Annægade 29, tel. 41 66 63 57, www.vorfrelserskirke.dk.

▲▲▲Christiania

In 1971, the original 700 Christianians established squatters' rights in an abandoned military barracks just a 10-minute walk from the Danish parliament building. Two generations later, this "free city" still stands—an ultra-human mishmash of idealists, hippies, potheads, nonmaterialists, and happy children (900 people, 200 cats, 200 dogs, 2 parrots, and 17 horses). There are even a handful of

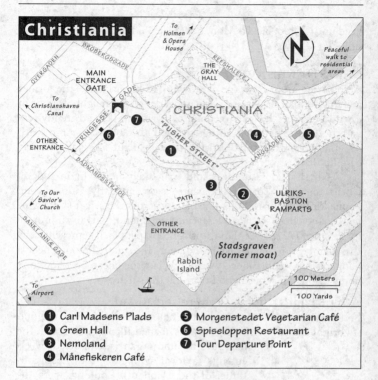

Christiania

To Holmen & Opera House

THE GRAY HALL

Peaceful walk to residential areas

MAIN ENTRANCE GATE

To Christianshavns Canal

CHRISTIANIA

OTHER ENTRANCE

"PUSHER STREET"

ULRIKS-BASTION RAMPARTS

To Our Savior's Church

OTHER ENTRANCE

PATH

Stadsgraven (former moat)

Rabbit Island

To Airport

100 Meters
100 Yards

1 Carl Madsens Plads
2 Green Hall
3 Nemoland
4 Månefiskeren Café
5 Morgenstedet Vegetarian Café
6 Spiseloppen Restaurant
7 Tour Departure Point

Willie Nelson-type seniors among the 180 remaining here from the original takeover. And an amazing thing has happened: The place has become the second-most-visited sight among tourists in Copenhagen, behind Tivoli Gardens. Move over, *Little Mermaid*.

"Pusher Street" (named for the sale of soft drugs here) is Christiania's main drag. Get beyond this touristy side of Christiania, and you'll find a fascinating, ramshackle world of moats and earthen ramparts, alternative housing, cozy tea houses, carpenter shops, hippie villas, children's playgrounds, peaceful lanes, and people who believe that "to be normal is to be in a straitjacket." A local slogan claims, *"Kun døde fisk flyder med strømmen"* ("Only dead fish swim with the current").

Hours and Tours: Christiania is open all the time but quiet (and some restaurants closed) on Mondays, which is its rest day (though "resting" from what, I'm not sure). Guided tours leave from the main entrance (50 DKK, July-Aug daily at 13:00 and 15:00; Sat-Sun only the rest of the year, just show up, 1.5 hours, in English and Danish, info tel. 32 95 65 07, www.rundvisergruppen.dk). You're welcome to snap photos, except on Pusher Street (but ask residents before you photograph them).

The Community: Christiania is broken into 14 administrative

neighborhoods on a former military base. Most of the land, once owned by Denmark's Ministry of Defense, has been purchased by the Christiania community; the rest of it is leased from the state. Locals build their homes but don't own them—individuals can't buy or sell property. When someone moves out, the community decides who will be invited in to replace that person. A third of the adult population works on the outside, a third works on the inside, and a third doesn't work much at all.

There are nine rules: no cars, no hard drugs, no guns, no explosives, and so on. The Christiania flag is red and yellow because when the original hippies took over, they found a lot of red and yellow paint onsite. The three yellow dots in the flag are from the three "i"s in "Christiania" (or, some claim, the "o"s in "Love, Love, Love").

The community pays the city about $1 million a year for utilities and has about $1 million a year more to run its local affairs. A few "luxury hippies" have oil heat, but most use wood or gas. The ground here was poisoned by its days as a military base, so nothing is grown in Christiania. There's little industry within the commune (Christiania Cykler, which builds fine bikes, is an exception—www.pedersen-bike.dk). A phone chain provides a system of communal security (they have had bad experiences calling the police). Each September 26, the day the first squatters took over the barracks in 1971, Christiania has a big birthday bash.

Tourists are entirely welcome here, because they've become a major part of the economy. Visitors react in very different ways to the place. Some see dogs, dirt, and dazed people. Others see a haven of peace, freedom, and no taboos. It's true that this free city isn't always pretty. But watching parents here raise their children with Christiania values makes me a believer in this social experiment. My take: Giving alternative-type people a place to be alternative is a kind of alternative beauty that deserves a place.

Christiania Documentary: For a fascinating, one-hour insight into Christiania, watch the 2011 documentary *Christiania: 40 Years of Occupation*. This film, produced by Seattle production company Bus No. 8, does a wonderful job of chronicling the history of Europe's oldest still existing squatters' community. Today,

COPENHAGEN

this community is closing in on the 50-year mark and is still going strong—but it hasn't been easy. See www.busno8.com for details.

Visiting Christiania: The main entrance is down Prinsessegade, behind the Our Savior's Church spiral tower. Passing under the gate, take Pusher Street directly into the community. The first square—a kind of market square (souvenirs and marijuana-related stuff)—is named Carl Madsens Plads, honoring the lawyer who took the squatters' case to the Danish supreme court in 1976 and won. Beyond that is Nemoland (a food circus, on the right). A huge warehouse called the Green Hall (Den Grønne Hal) is a recycling center and hardware store (where people get most of their building materials) that does triple duty as a night-time concert hall and as a craft center for kids. If you go up the stairs between Nemoland and the Green Hall, you'll climb up to the ramparts that overlook the canal.

On the left beyond the Green Hall, a lane leads to the Måne-fiskeren café, and beyond that, to the Morgenstedet vegetarian

restaurant (the best place for a simple, friendly meal; see "Eating in Christiania," later). Beyond these recommended restaurants, you'll find yourself lost in the totally untouristy, truly local residential parts of Christiania, where kids play in the street and the old folks sit out on the front stoop—just like any other neighborhood. Just as St. Mark's Square isn't the "real Venice," the hippie-druggie scene on Pusher Street isn't the "real Christiania"—you can't say you've experienced Christiania until you've strolled these back streets.

A walk or bike ride through Christiania is a great way to see how this community lives. When you leave, look up—the sign above the gate says, "You are entering the EU."

Smoking Marijuana: Pusher Street was once lined with stalls selling marijuana, joints, and hash. Residents intentionally destroyed the stalls in 2004 to reduce the risk of Christiania being disbanded by the government. (One stall was spared and is on display at the National Museum.) Today, the stalls are back, and you'll likely hear whispered offers of "hash"

during your visit. During my last visit there was a small, pungent stretch of Pusher Street, dubbed the "Green Light District," where pot was being openly sold (signs acknowledged that this activity was still illegal, and announced three rules here: 1. Have fun; 2. No photos; and 3. No running—"because it makes people nervous"). However, purchasing and smoking may buy you more time in Denmark than you'd planned—possession of marijuana remains illegal. Hard drugs are emphatically forbidden in Christiania.

Eating in Christiania: The people of Christiania appreciate good food and count on tourism as a big part of their economy. Consequently, there are plenty of decent eateries. Most of the restaurants are open from lunchtime until late and are closed on Monday (the community's weekly holiday). **Pusher Street** has a few grungy but tasty falafel stands, as well as a popular burger bar. **$ Nemoland** is the hangout zone—a fun collection of stands peddling Thai food, burgers, *shawarma*, and other fast hippie food with great, tented outdoor seating. Its stay-a-while atmosphere comes with backgammon, foosball, bakery goods, and fine views from the ramparts. **$$ Månefiskeren** ("Moonfisher Bar") looks like a modern-day Brueghel painting, with billiards, chess, snacks, and drinks. **$$ Morgenstedet** ("Morning Place") is a good, cheap vegetarian café with a mellow, woody interior and a rustic patio outside. **$$$$ Spiseloppen** is *the* classy, good-enough-for-Republicans restaurant in the community.

Shopping in Copenhagen

Shops are generally open Monday through Friday from 10:00 to 19:00 and Saturday from 9:00 to 16:00 (closed Sun). While big department stores dominate the scene, many locals favor the characteristic, small artisan shops and boutiques.

Uniquely Danish souvenirs to look for include intricate paper cuttings with idyllic motifs of swans, flowers, or Christmas themes; mobiles with everything from bicycles to Viking ships (look for the quality Flensted brand); and the colorful artwork of Danish artist Bo Bendixen (posters, postcards, T-shirts, and more). Jewelry lovers look for amber, known as the "gold of the North." Globs of this petrified sap wash up on the shores of all the Baltic countries.

Where to Shop: For a street's worth of shops selling **"Scantiques,"** wander down Ravnsborggade from Nørrebrogade.

Copenhagen's colorful **flea markets** are small but feisty and surprisingly cheap (May-Nov Sat 8:00-14:00 at Israels Plads; May-Sept Fri and Sat 8:00-17:00 along Gammel Strand and on Kongens Nytorv). For other street markets, ask at the TI.

The city's top **department stores** (Illum at Østergade 52, and Magasin du Nord at Kongens Nytorv 13) offer a good, if expensive,

look at today's Denmark. Both are on the Strøget and have fine caf-
eterias on their top floors. The department stores and the Politiken
Bookstore on Rådhuspladsen have a good selection of maps and
English travel guides.

The section of the Strøget called **Amagertorv** is a highlight
for shoppers. The **Royal Copenhagen** store here sells porcelain on three floors (Mon-Fri 10:00-19:00, Sat 10:00-18:00, Sun
11:00-16:00). The first floor up features figurines and collectibles.
The second floor has a second-quality department for discounts,
proving that "even the best painter can miss a stroke." Next door,
Illums Bolighus shows off three floors of modern Danish design
(Mon-Sat 10:00-19:00, Fri until 20:00, Sun 11:00-18:00).

House of Amber has a shop and a tiny two-room museum
with about 50 examples of prehistoric insects trapped in the amber
(remember *Jurassic Park*?) under magnifying glasses. You'll also see
remarkable items made of amber, from necklaces and chests to Viking ships and chess sets (25 DKK, daily May-Sept 9:00-19:30,
Oct-April 10:00-17:30, at the top of Nyhavn at Kongens Nytorv
2). If you're visiting Rosenborg Castle, you'll see the ultimate examples of amber craftsmanship in its treasury.

Eating in Copenhagen

CHEAP MEALS

For a quick lunch, try a *smørrebrød*, a *pølse*, or a picnic. Finish it off
with a pastry.

Smørrebrød

Denmark's 300-year-old tradition of open-face sandwiches survives. Find a *smørrebrød* takeout shop and choose two or three that
look good (about 35 DKK each). You'll get them wrapped and ready
for a park bench. Add a cold drink, and you have a fine, quick, and
very Danish lunch. Tradition calls for three sandwich courses: herring first, then meat, and then cheese. Downtown, you'll find these
handy local alternatives to Yankee fast-food chains. They range
from splurges to quick stop-offs.

Between Copenhagen University and Rosenborg Castle

My three favorite *smørrebrød* places are particularly handy when
connecting your sightseeing between the downtown Strøget core
and Rosenborg Castle.

$$ Restaurant Schønnemann is a cozy cellar restaurant
crammed with small tables—according to the history on the menu,
people "gather here in intense togetherness." The sand on the floor
evokes a bygone era when passing traders would leave their horses
out on the square while they lunched here. You'll need to reserve

---

Restaurant Code

I've assigned each eatery a price category, based on the average cost of a typical main course. Drinks, desserts, and splurge items (steak and seafood) can raise the price considerably.

$$$$ **Splurge:** Most main courses over 150 DKK
$$$ **Pricier:** 100-150 DKK
$$ **Moderate:** 50-100 DKK
$ **Budget:** Under 50 DKK

In Denmark, a *pølsevogn* or other takeout spot is **$**; a sit-down café is **$$**; a casual but more upscale restaurant is **$$$**; and a swanky splurge is **$$$$**.

---

to get a table, and you'll pay a premium for their *smørrebrød* (two lunch seatings Mon-Sat: 11:30-14:00 & 14:14-17:00, closed Sun, no dinner, Hauser Plads 16, tel. 33 12 07 85, www. restaurantschonnemann.dk).

$$ Café Halvvejen is a small mom-and-pop place serving traditional lunches and open-face sandwiches in a woody and smoke-stained café, lined with portraits of Danish royalty. You can eat inside or at an outside table in good weather (food served Mon-Sat 12:00-15:00, closed Sun, next to public library at Krystalgade 11, tel. 33 11 91 12).

$ Slagteren ved Kultorvet, a few blocks northwest of the university, is a small butcher shop with bowler-hatted clerks selling good, inexpensive sandwiches to go (Mon-Fri 8:00-17:30, Sat until 15:00, closed Sun, sandwiches usually sell out by 13:00; just off Kultorvet square at Frederiksborggade 4, look for gold bull's head hanging outside).

Near Christiansborg Palace

These eateries are good choices when sightseeing on Slotsholmen.

$$ Kanal Caféen, on Frederiksholms Kanal across from Christiansborg Palace, serves lunch only and is a nice place for a traditional open-face sandwich. Inside, you'll rub elbows with locals in what feels like the cozy confines of a low-ceilinged old sailing ship; outside you can dine right above the canal and watch the tour boats go by (Mon-Fri 11:30-17:00, Sat until 15:00, closed Sun, Frederiksholms Kanal 18, tel. 33 11 57 70).

$$ Café Diamanten serves open-face sandwiches, warm dishes, and salads—and pours microbrews from the tap. Take a

Copenhagen Restaurants

- ❶ Restaurant Schønnemann
- ❷ Café Halvvejen
- ❸ Slagteren ved Kultorvet
- ❹ Kanal Caféen
- ❺ Café Diamanten
- ❻ Cock's & Cows
- ❼ Café Nytorv
- ❽ Sorgenfri
- ❾ Kronborg Dansk Rest.
- ❿ Domhusets Smørrebrød
- ⓫ Supermarket (2)
- ⓬ Lagekagehuset Bakeries (4)
- ⓭ Nansens Bakery
- ⓮ Konditori La Glace
- ⓯ Det Lille Apotek
- ⓰ Riz-Raz Steaks & Veggies (2)
- ⓱ Tight
- ⓲ Café Norden
- ⓳ Royal Smushi Café

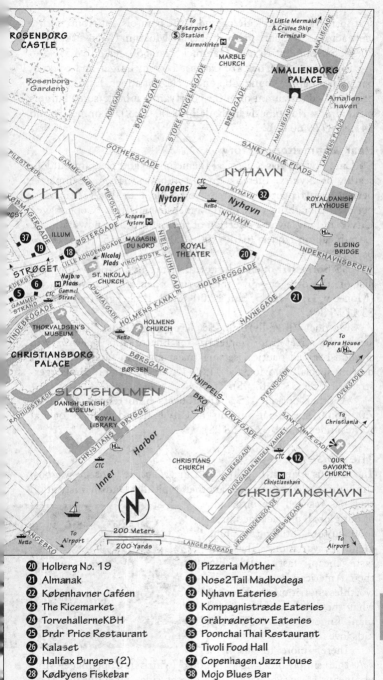

20 Holberg No. 19	30 Pizzeria Mother
21 Almanak	31 Nose2Tail Madbodega
22 Københavner Caféen	32 Nyhavn Eateries
23 The Ricemarket	33 Kompagnistræde Eateries
24 TorvehallerneKBH	34 Gråbrødretorv Eateries
25 Brdr Price Restaurant	35 Poonchai Thai Restaurant
26 Kalaset	36 Tivoli Food Hall
27 Halifax Burgers (2)	37 Copenhagen Jazz House
28 Kødbyens Fiskebar	38 Mojo Blues Bar
29 BioMio & Paté Paté	

seat inside the comfy café or under the parasols out front, with a view across the square to Thorvaldsen's Museum (Mon-Fri 10:00-20:30, Sat-Sun until 19:00, Gammel Strand 50, tel. 33 93 55 45).

Burgers: $$$ Cock's & Cows is a trendy burger-and-cocktail bar with a happy, young vibe on an elegant street. Eat inside the brick-walled restaurant or in the courtyard out back (some burgers piled almost ridiculously high, daily 11:30-21:30, Gammel Strand 34, tel. 69 69 60 00).

Near Gammeltorv/Nytorv

$$ Café Nytorv has a nautical theme inside and pleasant outdoor seating on Nytorv. There's a great deal on a *smørrebrød* sampler—perfect for two people to share (if you smile, they'll serve it for dinner even though it's only on the lunch menu). This "Copenhagen City Plate" gives you a selection of the traditional sandwiches and extra bread on request (daily 9:00-22:00, Nytorv 15, tel. 33 11 77 06).

$$ Sorgenfri offers a local experience in a dark, woody spot just off the Strøget—give the herring open-face sandwich a try (Mon-Sat 11:00-20:45, Sun 12:00-18:00, Brolæggerstræde 8, tel. 33 11 58 80).

Or duck (literally) into **$$ Kronborg Dansk Restaurant,** across the street from Sorgenfri, for finer-quality *smørrebrød* in a wood-beamed nautical setting (meat and fish sandwiches plus herring specialties, Mon-Sat 11:00-17:00, closed Sun, Brolæggerstræde 12, tel. 33 13 07 08).

Another option is **$$ Domhusets Smørrebrød** (Mon-Fri 7:00-15:00, closed Sat-Sun, off the City Hall end of the Strøget at Kattesundet 18, tel. 33 15 98 98).

The *Pølse*

The famous Danish hot dog, sold in *pølsevogne* (sausage wagons) throughout the country, is another typically Danish institution that has resisted the onslaught of our global, prepackaged, fast-food culture. Study the photo menu for variations. These are fast, cheap, tasty, and, like their American cousins, almost worthless nutritionally. Even so, what the locals call the "dead man's finger" is the dog Danish kids love to bite.

There's more to getting a *pølse* than simply ordering a "hot dog" (which in Copenhagen simply means a sausage with a bun on the side, generally the worst bread possible). The best is a *ristet* (or grilled) hot dog *med det hele* (with the works). Employ these other handy phrases: *rød* (red, the basic boiled weenie), *medister* (spicy, better quality), *knæk* (short, stubby, tastier than *rød*), *brød* (a bun, usually smaller than the sausage), *svøb* ("swaddled" in bacon), *Fransk* (French style, buried in a long skinny hole in the bun with sauce). *Sennep* is mustard and *ristet løg* are crispy, fried onions. Wash everything down with a *sodavand* (soda pop).

By hanging around a *pølsevogn*, you can study this institution. Denmark's "cold feet cafés" are a form of social care: People who have difficulty finding jobs are licensed to run these wiener-mobiles. As they gain seniority, they are promoted to work at more central locations. Danes like to gather here for munchies and *pølsesnak*—the local slang for empty chatter (literally, "sausage talk"). And traditionally, after getting drunk, guys stop here for a hot dog and chocolate milk on the way home—that's why the stands stay open until the wee hours.

Picnics

Throughout Copenhagen, small delis *(viktualiehandler)* sell fresh bread, tasty pastries, juice, milk, cheese, and yogurt (drinkable, in tall liter boxes). Two of the largest supermarket chains are **Irma** (in the glassy DI—Danish Industry—building on Vesterbrogade next to Tivoli) and **Super Brugsen. Netto** is a cut-rate outfit with the cheapest prices and a good bakery section (located on Rådhuspladsen at Vestergade). And, of course, there's the ever-present **7-Eleven** chain, with branches seemingly on every corner; while you'll pay a bit more here, there's a reason they're called "convenience" stores—and they also serve pastries and hot dogs.

Pastry

The golden pretzel sign hanging over the door or windows is the Danes' age-old symbol for a bakery. Danish pastries, called *wienerbrød* ("Vienna bread") in Denmark, are named for the Viennese bakers who brought the art of pastry-making to Denmark, where the Danes say they perfected it. Try these bakeries: **Lagkagehuset** (multiple locations around town; the handiest options include one in the train station, another nearby inside the Vesterbrogade TI, one along the Strøget at Frederiksborggade 21, and another on Torvegade just across from the Metro station in Christianshavn) and **Nansens** (on corner of Nansensgade and Ahlefeldtsgade, near Ibsens Hotel). **Emmerys,** a trendy, gluten-free, Starbucks-like organic bakery and café, has more than 20 branches around Copenhagen, and sells good pastries and sandwiches. For a genteel bit of high-class 1870s Copenhagen, pay a lot for a coffee and a fresh Danish at **Konditori La Glace,** just off the Strøget at Skoubogade 3.

RESTAURANTS

I've listed restaurants in the downtown core and near Nørreport, and in the trendy Meatpacking District behind the main train station.

Downtown Core

$$$$ Det Lille Apotek ("The Little Pharmacy") is a candlelit place with seating spread among its four themed "parlours." It's been popular with locals for 200 years, and today it's a hit with tourists, serving open-face sandwiches at lunchtime and traditional dinners in the evening (nightly from 17:30, just off the Strøget, between Frue Church and Round Tower at Store Kannikestræde 15, tel. 33 12 56 06).

$$ Riz-Raz Steaks & Veggies has two locations in Copenhagen: around the corner from the canal boat rides at Kompagnistræde 20 (tel. 33 15 05 75) and across from Det Lille Apotek at Store Kannikestræde 19 (tel. 33 32 33 45). At both places, you'll find a combination of burgers and meat dishes as well as vegetarian, including an all-you-can-eat Middle Eastern/Mediterranean/vegetarian buffet lunch for 90 DKK (great falafel, daily 11:30-16:00) and a bigger dinner buffet for 100 DKK (16:00-24:00). Use lots of plates and return to the buffet as many times as you like.

$$$ Tight resembles a trendy gastropub, serving an eclectic international array of food and drink (Canadian, Aussie, French, and burgers, with Danish microbrews) in a split-level maze of hip rooms that mix old timbers and brick with bright colors (daily 17:00-22:00, just off the Strøget at Hyskenstræde 10, tel. 33 11 09 00).

$$$$ Café Norden, very Danish with modern "world cuisine," seasonal menus, good light meals, and fine pastries, is a big, venerable institution overlooking Amagertorv by the heron fountain. It's family-friendly, with good seats outside on the square, in the busy ground-floor interior, or with more space and better views upstairs (great people-watching from the window seats). Order at the bar—it's the same price upstairs or down (huge splittable portions, daily 9:00-24:00, Østergade 61, tel. 33 11 77 91).

$$$ Royal Smushi Café is a hit with dainty people who like the idea of small, gourmet, open-face sandwiches served on Royal Copenhagen porcelain. You can sit in their modern chandeliered interior or the quiet courtyard (daily 10:00-18:00, next to Royal Copenhagen porcelain store at Amagertorv 6, tel. 33 12 11 22).

$$ Holberg No. 19, a cozy Argentinian-run café with classic ambience, sits just a block off the tourist crush of the Nyhavn canal. With a loose and friendly vibe, it offers more personality and lower prices than the tourist traps along Nyhavn (no real kitchen but reasonably priced salads and sandwiches—some with an international twist, quiche, selection of wines and beers, order at the bar, Mon-Fri 8:00-22:00, Sat 10:00-20:00, Sun 10:00-18:00, Holberg 19, tel. 33 14 01 90).

$$$ Almanak, on the waterfront promenade near the entrance to Nyhavn, dishes artfully prepared (and tasty) open-face sandwiches and main courses in a cool and sleek restaurant and on its outdoor terrace facing the Inner Harbor. Look for the long green building on the promenade with a big sign on the roof that reads *The Standard* (Tue-Sun 12:00-22:00, closed Mon, Havnegade 44, tel. 72 14 88 08).

$$$ København Caféen, cozy and old-fashioned, feels like a ship captain's dining room. The staff is enthusiastically traditional, serving local dishes and elegant open-face sandwiches for a good value. Lunch specials (80-100 DKK) are served until 17:00, when the more expensive dinner menu kicks in (daily, kitchen closes at 22:00, at Badstuestræde 10, tel. 33 32 80 81).

$$$ The Ricemarket, an unpretentious Asian fusion bistro, is buried in a modern cellar between the Strøget and Rosenborg Castle. It's a casual, more affordable side-eatery of a popular local restaurant, and offers a flavorful break from Danish food (seven-dish family-style meal for 285 DKK, daily 12:00-22:00, Hausergade 38 near Kultorvet, tel. 35 35 75 30).

$$ Illum and **Magasin du Nord** department stores serve cheery, reasonable meals in their cafeterias. At Illum, eat outside at tables along the Strøget, or head to the elegant glass-domed top floor (Østergade 52). Magasin du Nord (Kongens Nytorv 13) also has a great grocery and deli in the basement.

Also try **Café Nytorv** at Nytorv 15 or **Sorgenfri** at Brolæggerstræde 8 (both are described under *"Smørrebrød,"* earlier).

Near Nørreport

$$$ TorvehallerneKBH is in a pair of modern, glassy market halls right on Israel Plads. Survey both halls and the stalls on the square before settling in. In addition to produce, fish, and meat stalls, it has several inviting food counters where you can sit to eat a meal, or grab something to go. I can't think of a more enjoyable place in Copenhagen to browse for a meal than this upscale food court (pricey but fun, with quality food; Mon-Thu 10:00-19:00, Fri until 20:00, Sat until 18:00, Sun 11:00-17:00, some places closed Mon; Frederiksborggade 21).

$-$$$$ Brdr. Price Restaurant—an elegant, highly regarded bistro serving creative Danish and international meals just across from Rosenborg Castle—is good for a dressy splurge in their downstairs restaurant, or for classy lighter meals in their upstairs bistro (daily 12:00-22:00, Rosenborggade 15, tel. 38 41 10 20, www.brdr-price.dk).

$$$ Kalaset, in a funky daylight basement with mismatched furniture, bubbles with a youthful energy and is a local favorite. The creative, internationally inspired menu is constantly evolving, and the decent portions are prepared "the way our grandmothers taught us" (daily specials, outdoor seating available, daily 10:00-late, Vendersgade 16, kitty-corner from the recommended Ibsens Hotel, tel. 33 33 00 35).

$$ Halifax, part of a small local chain, serves up "build-your-own" burgers, where you select a patty, a side dish, and a dipping sauce for your fries (Mon-Sat 11:30-22:00, Sun until 21:00, Frederiksborggade 35, tel. 33 32 77 11). They have another location just off the Strøget (at Larsbjørnsstræde 9).

Meatpacking District (Kødbyen)

Literally "Meat Town," Kødbyen is an old warehouse zone huddled up against the train tracks behind the main station. There are three color-coded sectors in the district—brown, gray, and white—and each one is a cluster of old industrial buildings. At the far end is the white zone (Den Hvide Kødby), which has been overtaken by some of the city's most trendy and enjoyable eateries, which mingle with the surviving offices and warehouses of the local meatpacking industry.

The curb appeal of this area is zilch (it looks like, well, a meatpacking district), but inside, these restaurants are bursting with life, creativity, and flavor. These places can fill up, especially on weekend evenings, when it's smart to reserve ahead.

It's a short stroll from the station: If you go south on the bridge called Tietgens Bro, which crosses the tracks just south of the station, and carry on for about 10 minutes, you'll run right into the area. Or you can ride the S-tog to the Dybbølsbro stop.

$$$$ Kødbyens Fiskebar ("Fish Bar") is one of the first restaurants in the Meatpacking District, and still the most acclaimed. Focusing on small, thoughtfully composed plates of modern Nordic seafood, the Fiskebar is extremely popular (reservations are essential). While the prices are high, so is the quality; diners are paying for a taste of the "New Nordic" style of cooking (in summer daily from 17:30, in winter generally closed Sat-Sun; Flæsketorvet 100, tel. 32 15 56 56, http://fiskebaren.dk).

$$$$ BioMio, in the old Bosch building, serves rustic Danish, vegan, and vegetarian dishes, plus meat and fish. It's 100-percent organic, and the young boss, Rune, actually

serves diners (daily 12:00-22:00, Halmtorvet 19, tel. 33 31 20 00, http://biomio.dk).

$$$ Paté Paté, next door to BioMio, is a tight, rollicking bistro in a former pâté factory. While a wine bar at heart—with a good selection of wines by the glass—it has a fun and accessible menu of creative modern dishes and a cozy atmosphere rare in the Meatpacking District (Mon-Sat from 17:30, closed Sun, Slagterboderne 1, tel. 39 69 55 57, www.patepate.dk).

$$$ Pizzeria Mother is named for the way the sourdough for their crust must be "fed" and cared for to flourish. You can taste that care in the pizza, which has a delicious tangy crust. Out front are comfortable picnic benches, while the interior curls around the busy pizza oven with chefs working globs of dough that will soon be the basis for your pizza (daily 11:00-23:00, a block beyond the other restaurants listed here at Høkerboderne 9, tel. 22 27 58 98).

$$ Nose2Tail Madbodega (*mad* means "food") prides itself on locally sourced, sustainable cooking, using the entire animal for your meal (hence the name). You'll climb down some stairs into an unpretentious white-tiled cellar (Mon-Sat 18:00-24:00, closed Sun, Flæsketorvet 13A, tel. 33 93 50 45, http://nose2tail.dk).

Other Central Neighborhoods to Explore

To find a good restaurant, try simply window-shopping in one of these inviting districts.

Nyhavn's harbor canal is lined with a touristy strip of restaurants set alongside its classic sailboats. Here thriving crowds are served mediocre, overpriced food in a great setting. On any sunny day, if you want steak and fries (130 DKK) and a 65-DKK beer, this can be fun. On Friday and Saturday, the strip becomes the longest bar in the world.

Kompagnistræde is home to a changing cast of great little eateries. Running parallel to the Strøget, this street has fewer tourists and lower rent, and encourages places to compete creatively for the patronage of local diners.

Gråbrødretorv ("Grey Friars' Square") is perhaps the most popular square in the old center for a meal. It's like a food court, especially in good weather, with a variety of international dining options outside and in. The French-inspired steakhouse **$$$$ Bøf & Ost** is pricey but good, serving elegant beef and veal dishes—even pigeon—and a wide selection of French and Danish cheeses (daily 11:00-22:00). Across the square, **$$$ Huks Fluks** enjoys a sunny location, dishing up southern European small plates, main courses, and shareable portions, and specializes in ham (daily 11:00-22:00).

Istedgade and the surrounding streets behind the train station (just above the Meatpacking District) are home to an assortment of inexpensive ethnic restaurants. You will find numerous places serving kebabs, pizza, Chinese, and Thai (including tasty meals at **$$ Poonchai Thai Restaurant**—across the street from Hotel Nebo at Istedgade 1).

Starting or Ending Your Cruise in Copenhagen

If your cruise begins or ends in Copenhagen, you'll want some extra time here; for most travelers, at least a full day is a minimum for seeing the city's highlights. For a longer visit here, pick up my *Rick Steves Snapshot Copenhagen & the Best of Denmark* guidebook; for other nearby destinations, see my *Rick Steves Scandinavia* book.

Airport Connections

COPENHAGEN AIRPORT (KASTRUP)

Copenhagen's international airport is a traveler's dream, with a TI, baggage check, bank, ATMs, post office, shopping mall, grocery store, bakery, and more (airport code: CPH, airport tel. 32 31 32 31, www.cph.dk). The three check-in terminals are within walking distance of each other (departures screens tell you which terminal to go to). On arrival, all flights feed into one big lobby in Terminal 3. When you pop out here, a TI kiosk is on your left, taxis are out the door on your right, trains are straight ahead, and shops and eateries fill the atrium above you. You can use dollars or euros at the airport, but you'll get change back in kroner.

Getting Between the Airport and Downtown

Your options include the Metro, trains, and taxis. There are also buses into town, but the train/Metro is generally better.

The **Metro** runs directly from the airport to Christianshavn, Kongens Nytorv (near Nyhavn), and Nørreport, making it the best choice for getting into town if you're staying in any of these areas (36-DKK three-zone ticket, yellow M2 line, direction: Vanløse, 4-10/hour, 11 minutes to Christianshavn). The Metro station is located at the end of Terminal 3 and is covered by the roof of the terminal.

Convenient **trains** also connect the airport with downtown (36-DKK three-zone ticket, covered by rail pass, 4/hour, 12 minutes). Buy your ticket from the ground-level ticket booth (look for *DSB: Tickets for Train, Metro & Bus* signs) before riding the escalator down to the tracks. Track 2 has trains going into the city (track 1 is for trains going east, to Sweden). Trains into town stop at the main train station (signed *København H;* handy if you're sleeping at my recommended hotels behind the train station), as well as the

Nørreport and Østerport stations. At Nørreport, you can connect to the Metro for Kongens Nytorv (near Nyhavn) and Christianshavn.

With the train/Metro trip being so quick, frequent, and cheap, I see no reason to take a taxi. But if you do, **taxis** accept credit cards and charge about 300 DKK for a ride to the town center.

Getting to Oceankaj Port

To reach this port (where nearly all cruises that begin and end in Copenhagen dock) directly from the airport, the easiest choice is to spring for a **taxi** (figure around 400 DKK from the airport or 275 DKK from town). To take a public bus to the port from downtown (cheaper but time-consuming), see the "Port Overview" section at the beginning of this chapter.

Hotels in Copenhagen

$$$$ = **Most rooms over 1,100 DKK; $$$** = 900-1,100 DKK; **$$** = 700-900 DKK; **$** = 500-700 DKK; **¢** = Under 500 DKK

If you need a hotel in Copenhagen before or after your cruise, here are a few to consider.

NEAR NØRREPORT

These hotels are within a 10-minute walk of Nørreport Station (S-tog and Metro). Note that many local trains (including ones from the airport) continue through the main train station to Nørreport Station, saving you a transfer.

$$$$ Ibsens Hotel is a stylish 118-room hotel with helpful staff, located in a charming neighborhood away from the main train station commotion and a short walk from the old center (consider splurging on larger room—smaller rooms can be very tight, great bikes-150 DKK/24 hours, Vendersgade 23, S-tog and Metro: Nørreport—to find Vendersgade after surfacing from the Metro, head for the five-story brown building with the green copper dome, tel. 33 13 19 13, www.ibsenshotel.dk, hotel@ibsenshotel.dk).

$$$ Hotel Jørgensen is a friendly little 30-room hotel in a great location just off Nørreport, kitty-corner from the bustling Torvehallerne KBH food market. With fresh and tidy rooms and a welcoming lounge, it's a fine option, though the halls are a narrow, tangled maze (Rømersgade 11, tel. 33 13 81 86, www.hoteljoergensen.dk, hoteljoergensen@mail.dk). They also rent **¢** dorm beds.

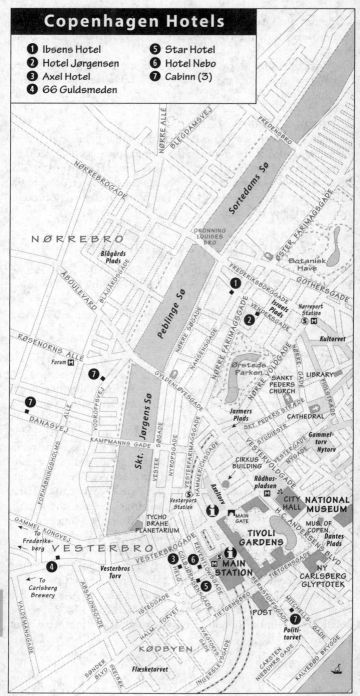

Copenhagen Hotels

1. Ibsens Hotel
2. Hotel Jørgensen
3. Axel Hotel
4. 66 Guldsmeden
5. Star Hotel
6. Hotel Nebo
7. Cabinn (3)

BEHIND THE TRAIN STATION

The area behind the train station mingles elegant old buildings, trendy nightspots, and pockets of modern sleaze. The main drag running away from the station, Istedgade, has long been Copenhagen's red light district; but increasingly, this area is gentrified and feels safe (in spite of the few remaining, harmless sex shops).

$$$$ Axel Hotel and **$$$$ 66 Guldsmeden,** operated by the Guldsmeden ("Dragonfly") company, have more character than most—a restful spa-like ambience decorated with imported Balinese furniture, four-poster beds, and an emphasis on sustainability and organic materials. (**Axel:** breakfast extra, 189 rooms, request a quieter back room overlooking the pleasant garden, restful spa area with sauna and hot tub-295 DKK/person per stay, a block behind the train station at Colbjørnsensgade 14, tel. 33 31 32 66, booking@hotelguldsmeden.com; **66 Guldsmeden:** slightly cheaper than Axel, 64 rooms, Vesterbrogade 66, tel. 33 22 15 00, carlton@hotelguldsmeden.com). Both hotels rent bikes for 150 DKK/day. They share a website: www.hotelguldsmeden.com.

$$$ Star Hotel rents 134 rooms with modern Scandinavian decor and is just a block from the station (breakfast extra, nice courtyard, bike rental-130 DKK/day, Colbjørnsensgade 13, tel. 33 22 11 00, www.copenhagenstar.dk, star@copenhagenstar.dk).

$$$ Hotel Nebo, a secure-feeling refuge with a friendly welcome and 84 comfy if a bit creaky rooms, is just a half-block from the station (cheaper rooms with shared bath, breakfast extra, bike rental-120 DKK/day, Istedgade 6, tel. 33 21 12 17, www.nebo.dk, nebo@nebo.dk).

A DANISH MOTEL 6

$ Cabinn is a radical innovation and a great value, with several locations in Copenhagen: identical, tiny but comfy, with TV, shower, and toilet. Each room has a

single bed that expands into a twin-bedded room with one or two fold-down bunks on the walls. It's tough to argue with this kind of efficiency (family rooms available, breakfast extra, www.cabinn.com). The best of the bunch is **Cabinn City,** with 350 rooms and a great central location (a short walk south of the main train station and Tivoli at Mitchellsgade 14, tel. 33 46 16 16, city@cabinn.com). Two more, nearly identical Cabinns are a 15-minute walk northwest of the station: **Cabinn Copenhagen**

What If I Miss My Ship?

Remember that you can get help from the cruise line's port agent (listed on the destination information sheet distributed on the ship) or the local TI. If the port agent suggests a costly solution (such as a private car with a driver), you may want to consider public transit.

To reach **Oslo,** you could hop on the night boat (DFDS, tel. 33 42 30 10, www.dfdsseaways.us). Otherwise, you can take the train; in addition to Oslo, trains run regularly to **Stockholm, Berlin, Amsterdam,** and **Brussels.** For other points in **Norway,** connect through Oslo; for **Gdańsk,** you'll connect through Berlin. To look up specific connections, use www.bahn.com.

For some destinations, it may be best to take a **plane.** Copenhagen's airport, is easily reached by train from downtown.

Local **travel agents** in Copenhagen can help you sort through your options. For more advice on what to do if you miss the ship, see page 130.

Express (86 rooms, Danasvej 32, tel. 33 21 04 00, express@cabinn. com) and **Cabinn Scandinavia** (201 rooms, family rooms, Vodroffsvej 55, tel. 35 36 11 11, scandinavia@cabinn.com).

Entertainment in Copenhagen

The **Meatpacking District,** behind the main train station, is one of the city's up-and-coming destinations for bars and nightlife. On warm evenings, **Nyhavn** canal becomes a virtual nightclub, with packs of young people hanging out along the water, sipping beers. **Christiania** always seems to have something musical going on after dark. **Tivoli** has evening entertainment daily from mid-April through late September. **Copenhagen Jazz House** is a good bet for live jazz (Niels Hemmingsensgade 10, tel. 33 15 47 00, schedule at www.jazzhouse.dk). For blues, try the **Mojo Blues Bar** (Løngangsstræde 21c, tel. 33 11 64 53, schedule in Danish at www.mojo.dk).

Danish Survival Phrases

The Danes tend to say words quickly and clipped. In fact, many short vowels end in a "glottal stop"—a very brief vocal break immediately following the vowel. While I haven't tried to indicate these in the phonetics, you can listen for them in Denmark...and (try to) imitate.

Three unique Danish vowels are æ (sounds like the *e* in "egg"), ø (sounds like the German *ö*—purse your lips and say "oh"), and å (sounds like the *o* in "bowl"). The letter *r* is not rolled—it's pronounced farther back in the throat, almost like a *w*. A *d* at the end of a word sounds almost like our *th;* for example, *mad* (food) sounds like "math." In the phonetics, ī sounds like the long *i* sound in "light," and bolded syllables are stressed.

English	Danish	Pronunciation
Hello. (formal)	Goddag.	goh-**day**
Hi. / Bye. (informal)	Hej. / Hej-hej.	hī / hī-hī
Do you speak English?	Taler du engelsk?	**tay**-lehr doo **eng**-elsk
Yes. / No.	Ja. / Nej.	yah / nī
Please. (May I?)*	Kan jeg?	kahn yī
Please. (Can you?)*	Kan du?	kahn doo
Please. (Would you?)*	Vil du?	veel doo
Thank you (very much).	(Tusind) tak.	(**too**-sin) tack
You're welcome.	Selv tak.	sehl tack
Can I help (you)?	Kan jeg hjælpe (dig)?	kahn yī **yehl**-peh (dī)
Excuse me. (to pass)	Undskyld mig.	**oon**-skewl mī
Excuse me. (Can you help me?)	Kan du hjælpe mig?	kahn doo **yehl**-peh mī
(Very) good.	(Meget) godt.	(**mī**-ehl) goht
Goodbye.	Farvel.	fah-**vehl**
zero / one / two	nul / en / to	nool / een / toh
three / four	tre / fire	tray / feer
five / six	fem / seks	fehm / sehks
seven / eight	syv / otte	syew / **oh**-deh
nine / ten	ni / ti	nee / tee
hundred	hundred	**hoo**-nuh
thousand	tusind	**too**-sin
How much?	Hvor meget?	vor **mī**-ehl
local currency: (Danish) crown	(Danske) kroner	(**dahn**-skeh) **kroh**-nah
Where is..?	Hvor er...?	vor ehr
...the toilet	...toilettet	toy-**leh**-teht
men	herrer	**hehr**-ah
women	damer	**day**-mah
water / coffee	vand / kaffe	van / **kah**-feh
beer / wine	øl / vin	uhl / veen
Cheers!	Skål!	skohl
Can I have the bill?	Kan jeg få regningen?	kahn yī foh **rī**-ning-ehn

*Because Danish has no single word for "please," they approximate that sentiment by asking "May I?", "Can you?", or "Would you?", depending on the context.

STOCKHOLM

Sweden

Sweden Practicalities

Scandinavia's heartland, Sweden (Sverige) is far bigger than Denmark and far flatter than Norway (174,000 square miles—just larger than California). This family-friendly land is home to Ikea, Volvo, ABBA, and long summer vacations at red-painted, white-trimmed summer cottages. Today's population numbers 9.9 million people. Once the capital of blond, Sweden is now home to a huge mix of immigrants. The majority of ethnic Swedes are nominally Lutheran. A mountain range and several islands separate Sweden's heavily forested landscape from Norway.

Money: 8 Swedish kroner (SEK) = about $1. An ATM is called a *bankomat.* The local VAT (value-added sales tax) rate is 25 percent; the minimum purchase eligible for a VAT refund is 200 kr (for details on refunds, see page 125).

Language: The native language is Swedish. For useful phrases, see page 274.

Emergencies: Dial 112 for police, medical, or other emergencies. In case of theft or loss, see page 118.

Time Zone: Sweden is on Central European Time (the same as most of the Continent, and six/nine hours ahead of the East/West Coasts of the US). That puts Stockholm one hour behind Helsinki, Tallinn, and Rīga; and two hours behind St. Petersburg.

Embassies in Stockholm: The **US embassy** is at Dag Hammarskjölds Väg 31 (tel. 08/783-5375, https://se.usembassy.gov). The **Canadian embassy** is at Klarabergsgatan 23 (tel. 08/453-3000, www.canadainternational.gc.ca/sweden-suede). Call ahead for passport services.

Phoning: With a mobile phone, it's easy to dial: Press and hold zero until you get a + sign, enter the country code (46 for Sweden, 1 for the US/Canada), then the complete phone number (including area code if there is one). When dialing a European phone number, drop an initial zero (except if calling Italy). For more tips, see page 1062.

Tipping: A gratuity is included in the price of sit-down meals, so you don't need to tip further. But for great service, round up your bill—no more than 10 percent. Tip a taxi driver by rounding up the fare a bit (pay 90 kr on an 85-kr fare). For more tips on tipping, see page 129.

Tourist Information: www.visitsweden.com

STOCKHOLM

One-third water, one-third parks, one-third city, on the sea, surrounded by woods, bubbling with energy and history, Sweden's stunning capital is green, clean, and underrated.

The city is built on an archipelago of islands connected by bridges. Its location midway along the Baltic Sea made it a natural port, vital to the economy and security of the Swedish peninsula. In the 1500s, Stockholm became a political center when Gustav Vasa established the monarchy (1523). A century later, the expansionist King Gustavus Adolphus made it an influential European capital. The Industrial Revolution brought factories and a flood of farmers from the countryside. In the 20th century, the fuming smokestacks were replaced with steel-and-glass Modernist buildings housing high-tech workers and an expanding service sector.

Today, with more than two million people in the greater metropolitan area (one in five Swedes), Stockholm is Sweden's largest city, as well as its cultural, educational, and media center. It's also the country's most ethnically diverse city. Despite its size, Stockholm is committed to limiting its environmental footprint. Development is strictly monitored, and pollution-belching cars must pay a toll to enter the city.

For the visitor, Stockholm offers both old and new. Explore Europe's best-preserved old warship and relax on a scenic harbor boat tour. Browse the cobbles and antique shops of the lantern-lit Old Town. Take a trip back in time at Skansen, Europe's first and best open-air folk museum. Marvel at Stockholm's glittering City Hall, slick shopping malls, and art museums.

While progressive and sleek, Stockholm respects its heritage. In summer, military bands parade daily through the heart of town

Excursions from Stockholm

Stockholm, a large and spread-out city, can be challenging to see in a hurry. If your sightseeing is focused, you can do it on your own—but a cruise-line excursion can help you get a good overview. Excursions within Stockholm may include bus or canal-boat trips in town; a walking tour of Gamla Stan (the Old Town); a panoramic visit to Fjällgatan (a scenic viewpoint in Södermalm, just above the cruise port); and/or tours of the Vasa Museum, City Hall, or Royal Palace. Less appealing are visits to the touristy Ice Bar and the Ericsson Globe Arena (a sports arena with "SkyView" observation pods offering distant views of Stockholm). Jewish-themed tours of the city generally include stops in Gamla Stan, the Great Synagogue, and the Holocaust Monument. There's also a "rooftop walk" along the ridgeline of a building on the downtown island of Riddarholmen. Bike tours around Djurgården may entice you, but it's easy to rent your own bike, pick up a free map, and tour the island on your own.

Out-of-town options include the grand **Drottningholm Palace** (impressive but time-consuming to reach—Copenhagen has similar palaces that are easier to see), **Sigtuna** (a historic and touristy small town with traditional architecture), **Lake Mälaren** (the huge lake just west of Stockholm—less beautiful and far less convenient than the archipelago your cruise ship will sail through), and **Haga Park** (another garden-and-palace ensemble, but second-rate after Drottningholm). While some of these—particularly Drottningholm—could be well worth your while on a longer visit, with a short day in port I'd stick to Stockholm proper.

to the Royal Palace, announcing the Changing of the Guard and turning even the most dignified tourist into a scampering kid.

PLANNING YOUR TIME

Stockholm is a spread-out city with a diverse array of sightseeing choices scattered across several islands. Because sailing all the way through the archipelago takes lots of time, most cruises leave Stockholm hours earlier than other ports of call. Your time here will be rushed compared to other ports. On a short, one-day visit, you'll have to be selective. I'd suggest choosing either the Djurgården sights or Gamla Stan, or squeezing in a few items from each. Here are your basic options:

Gamla Stan (Old Town): Follow my self-guided stroll through the historic (if touristy) core of town, allowing about an hour. Add an hour to tour the Nobel Museum (if it hasn't relocated—inquire locally), or 1-2 hours for the Royal Palace (depending on which sights you see, and how long you stay). If your timing is right, you can catch the Changing of the Guard—or even just the parade through town (begins summer Mon-Sat at 11:45, reaches palace at 12:15, one hour later on Sun; not every day off-season).

Djurgården: Stockholm's lush park island has three great sights that could easily gobble up a day: The Vasa Museum, Sweden's single most-visited sight, is tops for the chance to see an astonishingly well-preserved 17th-century warship (allow 1.5-2 hours). The Nordic Museum traces local history (allow 1-2 hours). And Skansen is Europe's original open-air folk museum (allow 2 hours). These are the minimum amounts of time needed for a brief but meaningful visit; if you delve into details, any of these could consume hours. On a nice day, you could also rent a bike for a 1.5-hour spin around the island.

Modern City: My self-guided walk leads you through the hardworking urban core of town in about 1.5 hours. It may not be particularly charming, but this is ground zero for shoppers.

City Hall: Touring Stockholm's City Hall is worthwhile, but its location (on a different island beyond the train station, about a 15-minute walk from either the station or Gamla Stan) makes it tough to squeeze into a tightly scheduled day. Once there, allow an hour for the required tour, plus another hour (including the walk up and down, plus possible waiting time) to climb the tower.

Outlying Sights: If you've already seen Stockholm's biggies or are in town for more than a short port visit (i.e., your cruise begins or ends here), you could visit Drottningholm Palace. Allow about an hour of travel time each way, plus an hour for the guided tour, and at least another hour to explore the grounds—a total of four hours minimum. Another option is the sculpture park at Millesgården (allow about 1.5 hours round-trip travel time, plus at least an hour to see the sculptures—a total of 2.5 hours minimum). Taking a boat trip through Stockholm's archipelago makes little sense, since you'll see much the same scenery as you sail into and/or out of the city.

Tips: When planning your day, think carefully through your transportation options. Public transit is expensive, and taxis are even more so (see "Getting Around Stockholm," later). But there are several different ways to connect any two points: Consider the subway (T-bana), buses, trams, and the often-overlooked boats that shuttle passengers strategically between visit-worthy points (such as the one that connects Djurgården and Gamla Stan). The hop-on, hop-off harbor boat tours can also help you get around efficiently.

Port of Stockholm

Arrival at a Glance: From either port, if your cruise line offers a shuttle bus, consider taking it downtown. From **Stadsgården,** the hop-on, hop-off boat is a handy way to reach both Djurgården and Gamla Stan; otherwise, you can walk to Slussen and across the bridge to Gamla Stan from berth 167 in about 30 minutes; from berth 160, it's an easy 15-minute walk.

From **Frihamnen,** the best plan is to take bus #76 to Djurgården or Gamla Stan.

Port Overview

Stockholm has two main port areas: **Stadsgården** and **Frihamnen.** Close-in Stadsgården is used mainly for ships stopping for the day, while cruises that begin or end in Stockholm typically use the farther-out Frihamnen. A few small ships (or big ships dropping anchor and using tenders) may occasionally dock right along the embankment of **Gamla Stan;** as this is right in the center of the city (and arrivals here are both easy and rare), I haven't described it in detail.

Tourist Information: TI kiosks (with bus tickets and maps) open at both cruise ports when ships arrive, and remain open for about three hours.

GETTING INTO TOWN

First, I'll cover your general transportation options. Then I'll offer specifics on each port. To return to your ship, you can generally reverse these directions—I've given suggestions at the end of each section as necessary.

From Any Port

Cruise-Line Shuttle Buses: Many cruise lines offer shuttle buses into the city (about 120 SEK round-trip). Given the expense of public transit (even a basic one-way bus or subway ride costs 43 SEK—about $5), the shuttle can be a good value, and they're convenient. Shuttles generally drop off along the waterfront side of the Opera House, facing the Royal Palace and Gamla Stan across the harbor. My **"Stockholm's Modern City"** self-guided walk begins from Kungsträdgården, the big park right around the corner from where the shuttle drops you off. From the drop-off point, to reach **Gamla Stan** simply cross the closest bridge, and you'll find yourself directly below the Royal Palace. For **Djurgården** (and the Vasa Museum), ride tram #7—see the "Stockholm" map for the route.

Sightseeing Buses and Other Tours: At either cruise port, you'll be met by hop-on, hop-off tour buses that make a circuit around the city. For details on these buses—as well as local guides for hire, walking tours, and regular bus tours—see "Tours in Stockholm," later.

Taxis: Taxis meet arriving cruise ships, but many overcharge. Before hopping in a cab, check the rates (posted in the back window) and read my advice under "Getting Around Stockholm" to be sure you get a fair fare. Expect to pay these rates: From **Stadsgården** to Gamla Stan-165 SEK; City Hall-200 SEK; Vasa Museum-220 SEK. From **Frihamnen** to Vasa Museum-200 SEK; Gamla Stan or City Hall-300 SEK.

Public Transportation: Stockholm has a handy transit system. I've outlined specific options for using it in the port descriptions below.

From Stadsgården (Slussen)

This embankment stretches along the northern edge of the island called Södermalm, which faces the city center across the water. The two cruise-ship berths here—**160** and **167**—flank the Viking Line Terminal for overnight boats to Helsinki.

Berth 160

From the closer-in berth 160, it's a short 15-minute **walk** to Slussen and Gamla Stan, where you can start exploring the Old Town. **Hop-on, hop-off sightseeing boats** also stop nearby, in front of the Fotografiska photography museum. **Taxis** are plentiful here.

Berth 167

From the more distant berth 167 (on the far side of the Viking Line Terminal), it's a 30-minute **walk** to Gamla Stan, making other transit options worth considering. The best plan depends on where you'd like to go in town—but the hop-on, hop-off sightseeing buses/boats are a tempting offer from this quay.

As you exit berth 167, follow the color-coded lines painted on the pavement. The **red and yellow lines** lead left, to the dock for the **hop-on, hop-off boats** and the private **ferry** *Emelie*, which makes stops at Djurgården and Nybroplan (see "Getting Around Stockholm," later).

By Taxi or Hop-On, Hop-Off Bus: From the berth exit, a **blue line** leads to the right, taking you out the port gate to a small **TI kiosk** (open only when boats arrive; sells bus tickets), **taxi**

stands, and **hop-on, hop-off buses.** Ahead on your right is the huge Viking Line Terminal; a sporadic shuttle runs to the train station from here (55 SEK, see posted schedule or check www. flygbussarna.se).

On Foot or By Public Bus: To reach Slussen/Gamla Stan from here, stay with the trusty **blue line** on the ground until it ends at the traffic light (just past the Viking Line Terminal). From here, you can either turn right to continue on foot, or turn left to catch a public bus.

Walkers should veer right and join the pedestrian path that parallels the busy road. After a few minutes, you'll pass berth 160, the red-brick Fotografiska photography museum, and another stop for the hop-on, hop-off sightseeing boat. From this point, it's another 10 minutes along the waterfront to Slussen.

To catch the **public bus,** turn left at the traffic light to reach the Londonviadukten bus stop (about 50 yards from the intersection), which connects to Slussen and points beyond.

Bus Options: To ride the public bus, buy a ticket at the TI kiosk at the port gate—no tickets are sold on the bus. Or download the easy-to-use SL transit ticket-buying app to your phone (see "Getting Around Stockholm," later). Note that all buses run less frequently on Sundays.

Any bus starting with **#4** (such as #401, departs every few minutes) zips directly to the Slussen stop, under the bridge to the Slussen subway/T-bana stop, with connections throughout the city.

Bus #53 loops up through the fun Södermalm area, then goes past Slussen and along the west side of Gamla Stan to the train station, and finally up to Odenplan (4-5/hour).

Returning to Stadsgården: You can **walk** back to either berth from Gamla Stan—you can see your ship in the distance—though leave yourself plenty of time (figure about 15 minutes to berth 160, 30 minutes to berth 167). The **public bus** will take you back to berth 167, to the Londonviadukten stop (bus #53 from the train station or the embankment on the west side of Gamla Stan; #401 or other #4 series buses from Slussen). From the stop, you'll see the Viking Line Terminal and the port area.

From Frihamnen

This sprawling no-nonsense port is about three miles northeast of the city center. It's used by cruise ships (especially those starting and ending in Stockholm) as well as cargo ships and overnight ferries to St. Petersburg.

Most cruise ships dock at one of three berths: **berths 634** and **638** share one pier; **berth 650** is on a pier across from them. Only berth 638 has a dedicated terminal; otherwise, there's a terminal for overnight ferries.

The cruise terminal building at berth 638, marked Stockholm Cruise Center (a.k.a. Kryssningsterminal) opens when ships are in port. Inside is a user-friendly **TI** (with maps and bus tickets), WCs, Wi-Fi, and a gift shop, but no ATMs (you can use a credit card to buy tickets for any form of transport here). At the base of this pier is the Frihamnsterminalen—the terminal building (WCs but no ATMs inside) for St. Petersburg ferries.

In addition to the TI at berth 638, there's also info available in the little red shed near the bus stop (staffed only when boats arrive—they sell the Stockholm Pass and bus tickets, but even when unstaffed you can pick up a city map here).

By Taxi or Hop-On, Hop-Off Bus: Taxis meet arriving ships, and hop-on, hop-off sightseeing buses stop on the street outside the red-brick ferry terminal.

By Bus: It's easy to reach town on a public bus. There's a stop along the road that skirts the port, near the red TI shed and close to the ferry terminal building. Getting here is simple: From any of the berths, just follow the **blue** line painted on the ground—it's no more than a 10-minute walk.

You can't buy **tickets** on the bus. Get one at the TI inside the berth 638 terminal if you dock there, at the TI shed near the bus stop, or at the machine at the bus stop (credit cards only; follow prompts for buying a single paper ticket). If you'll be using transit even a little, you'll save a lot of hassle by using the system's easy-to-use ticket-buying app (see "Getting Around Stockholm," later).

Bus #76 is the most convenient, passing several major sights in town (4-7/hour Mon-Fri, 3-4/hour Sat-Sun). Stops include Djurgårdsbron (Vasa Museum), Nybroplan, Kungsträdgården (near the Opera House and the start of my "Stockholm's Modern City" self-guided walk), Slottsbacken (by the palace in Gamla Stan), Räntmästartrappan (southern end of Gamla Stan), Slussen, then through Södermalm and back the way it came.

Bus #1 cuts across the top of Östermalm and Norrmalm to the train station (every 5-8 minutes daily).

Returning to Frihamnen by Bus: From several points in town (see list of stops above), you can take public bus #76 or #1. Get off at the Frihamnen stop for berth 650 (riding either #1 or #76); for the other berths, stay on bus #76 one more stop to Frihamnens Färje-terminal, directly in front of the red-brick ferry building.

Stockholm

Greater Stockholm's two million residents live on 14 islands woven together by 54 bridges. Visitors need only concern themselves with these districts, most of which are islands:

Norrmalm is downtown, with hotels and shopping areas, and the combined train and bus station. **Östermalm,** to the east, is more residential.

Kungsholmen, the mostly suburban island across from Norrmalm, is home to City Hall and inviting lakefront eateries.

Gamla Stan is the Old Town island of winding, lantern-lit streets, antique shops, and classy cafés clustered around the Royal Palace. The adjacent **Riddarholmen** is similarly atmospheric, but much sleepier. The locks between Lake Mälaren (to the west) and the Baltic Sea (to the east) are at a junction called **Slussen,** just south of Gamla Stan on the way to Södermalm.

Skeppsholmen is the small, central, traffic-free park/island with the Museum of Modern Art.

Djurgården is the park-island—Stockholm's wonderful green playground, with many of the city's top sights (bike rentals just over bridge as you enter island).

Södermalm, just south of the other districts, is sometimes called "Stockholm's Brooklyn"—it's young and creative. Apart from fine views and some good eateries, this residential island may be of less interest to those on a quick visit.

Orientation to Stockholm

TOURIST INFORMATION

Stockholm's helpful city-run TI is called **Visit Stockholm.** The main office is downtown in the Kulturhuset, facing Sergels Torg (Mon-Fri 9:00-19:00—until 18:00 off-season, Sat until 16:00, Sun 10:00-16:00, Sergels Torg 3, T-bana: T-Centralen, tel. 08/5082-8508, www.visitstockholm.com).

Around town, you'll also see the green *i* logo of **Stockholm Info,** run by a for-profit agency. While less helpful than the official TI, they hand out maps and brochures, and may be able to answer basic questions (locations include the train station's main hall and Gamla Stan). They sell the pricey **City Pass** that covers transportation and a limited number of museums (www.stockholminfo.com).

Stockholm Pass: This pass covers entry to 60 Stockholm sights (including Skansen and the Royal Palace) as well as unlimited City Sightseeing hop-on, hop-off bus/boat tours. It's available in one-day and multiday versions, with an optional Travelcard

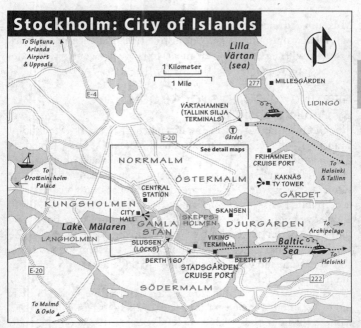

Stockholm: City of Islands

To Sigtuna, Arlanda Airport & Uppsala

Lilla Värtan (sea)

1 Kilometer
1 Mile

E-4

277 · MILLESGÅRDEN

LIDINGÖ

VÄRTAHAMNEN
(TALLINK SILJA
TERMINALS)

E-20

Ⓣ Gärdet

See detail maps

NORRMALM

FRIHAMNEN
CRUISE PORT

To Helsinki & Tallinn

ÖSTERMALM

KAKNÄS
TV TOWER

To Drottningholm Palace

CENTRAL
STATION

GÄRDET

KUNGSHOLMEN

CITY
HALL

SKANSEN

SKEPPS-
HOLMEN

Lake Mälaren

GAMLA
STAN

DJURGÅRDEN

To Archipelago

LÅNGHOLMEN

SLUSSEN
(LOCKS)

VIKING
TERMINAL

Baltic
Sea

To Helsinki

E-20

BERTH 160

BERTH 167

STADSGÅRDEN
CRUISE PORT

222

SÖDERMALM

To Malmö & Oslo

STOCKHOLM

---

transit add-on. Prices range from 600 SEK to 1300 SEK (www. stockholmpass.com).

ARRIVAL IN STOCKHOLM

Stockholm's adjacent stations for trains (Centralstation) and buses (Cityterminalen), at the southwestern edge of Norrmalm, are a hive of services (including an unofficial Stockholm Info "TI"), eateries, shops, exchange desks, and people on the move. From the train station, the bus station is up the escalators from the main hall and through a glassy atrium (lined with sales desks for bus companies and cruise lines). Taxi stands are outside.

HELPFUL HINTS

Theft Alert: Even in Stockholm, when there are crowds, there are pickpockets (such as at the Royal Palace during the Changing of the Guard). Too-young-to-arrest teens—many from other countries—are hard for local police to control.

Pharmacy: The **C. W. Scheele** 24-hour pharmacy is near the train station at Klarabergsgatan 64 (tel. 08/454-8130).

English Bookstore: The aptly named **English Bookshop** sells a variety of reading materials (including Swedish-interest books) in English (Mon-Fri 11:00-18:30, Sat until 16:00, Sun 12:00-16:00, in the Södermalm district at Södermannag 22, tel. 08/790-5510).

Museum Admission: Entry to many of Stockholm's fine state-owned museums swings from free (when left-leaning parties control the reins of government) to fee (when center-right parties are in charge). Ask locally for the latest.

GETTING AROUND STOCKHOLM
By Public Transit

Stockholm's fine but pricey public transport network (Stockholm Transport, officially Storstockholms Lokaltrafik—but signed as *SL*) includes subway (Tunnelbana, called "T-bana") and bus systems, and a single handy tram from the commercial center to the sights at Djurgården. It's a spread-out city, so most visitors will need public transport at some point (transit info tel. 08/600-1000, www.sl.se/english). The subway is easy to figure out, but many sights are better served by bus. The main lines are listed on the back of the official city map. A more detailed system map is available free from subway ticket windows, SL Centers (info desks) in main stations, and TIs.

Tickets: A single ride for subway, tram, or bus costs 43 SEK (up to 1.25 hours, including transfers); a 24-hour pass is 120 SEK, while a 72-hour pass is 240 SEK. Tickets are sold on the tram (with an extra surcharge), but not on buses. All SL ticket-sellers are clearly marked with a blue flag with the *SL* logo.

Locals and savvy tourists carry a blue **SL-Access card,** which you can buy for 20 SEK at ticket agents, subway and commuter rail stations, and SL Centers. You can add value to the card at station machines or with a ticket agent. To use the card, just touch it against the blue pad to enter the T-bana turnstile or when boarding a bus or tram.

It's still possible to buy single-journey **paper tickets** (at Pressbyrån convenience stores inside almost every T-bana station, at self-service machines, and at some transit-ticket offices)—but it's not worth the hassle.

Transit App: SL has an easy-to-use ticketing app (search "SL-Stockholm" in app stores) that you can tie to a bank card (works with US cards). Buy tickets as you need them on your phone, which you'll then hold to a scanner to enter the T-bana turnstile (or show to a bus/tram driver).

By Harbor Shuttle Ferry

In summer, city ferries let you make a fun, practical, and scenic shortcut across the harbor to Djurgården Island. Boat #82 leaves from the southeast end of Gamla Stan, stops near the Museum of Modern Art on Skeppsholmen, then docks near the Gröna Lund amusement park on Djurgården; boat #80 departs from Nybroplan for Djurgården (43 SEK, covered by public-transit passes, 3-4/hour

May-late Sept, 10-minute trip, www.sl.se). The private ferry *Emelie* makes the journey from Nybroplan to Djurgården, landing near the ABBA Museum, then goes on to cruise berth 167 (60 SEK, buy ticket onboard—credit cards only and SL app not valid, hourly, April-Sept roughly Mon-Fri 7:50-18:20, Sat-Sun 9:50-17:50, tel. 08/731-0025, www.ressel.se). While buses and trams run between the same points more frequently, the ferry option gets you out onto the water and can be faster—and certainly more scenic—than overland connections. The hop-on, hop-off boat tour (see "Tours in Stockholm," next) also connects many of these stops.

By Taxi

Stockholm is a good taxi town—provided you find a reputable cab that charges fair rates. Taxis are unregulated, so companies can charge whatever they like. Before hopping in a taxi, look carefully at the big yellow label that should be displayed prominently on the outside of the car (usually in the rear door window). The big number, on the right, shows the "highest unit price" *(högsta järnförpriset)* for a 10-kilometer ride that lasts 15 minutes; this number should be between 290 and 390 SEK—if it's higher, move on. (You're not obligated to take the first cab in line.)

Most cabs charge a drop fee of about 45 SEK. Taxis with inflated rates tend to congregate at touristy places like the Vasa Museum or in Gamla Stan. I've been ripped off enough by cabs here to know: Take only "Taxi Stockholm" cabs with the phone number (08/150-000) printed on the door. (Other reportedly honest companies include Taxi Kurir, tel. 08/300-000, and Taxi 020, tel. 08/850-400 or 020-20-20-20.)

Tours in Stockholm

The sightseeing company **Strömma** has a lock on most city tours, whether by bus, by boat, or on foot. Their website (www.stromma. se) details the entire program, or you can call for more information (08/1200-4000). Tours can be paid for online, or simply as you board.

BY BUS
Hop-On, Hop-Off Bus Tour

Three hop-on, hop-off buses make a 1.5-hour circuit of the city, orienting riders with a recorded commentary and linking all the essential places from Skansen to City Hall; when cruises are in town, they also stop at both cruise ports (Stadsgården and Frihamnen). **Hop-On Hop-Off**'s green buses and **City Sightseeing**'s red buses both cooperate with Strömma (300 SEK/24 hours, ticket covers both buses; May-Sept 2-3/hour daily 10:00-16:00, fewer off-sea-

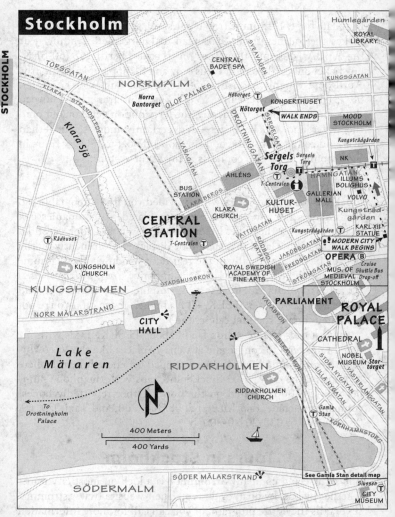

son, none mid-Jan-mid-Feb, www.stromma.se). **Red Buses** offers a similar hop-on, hop-off itinerary in open-top buses for the same price (3/hour, www.redbuses.se). All offer free Wi-Fi.

Quickie Orientation Bus Tour

Several different city bus tours leave from the Royal Opera House on Gustav Adolfs Torg. Strömma's Stockholm Panorama tour provides a good overview—but, as it's the same price as the 24-hour hop-on, hop-off ticket, I'd take this tour only if you want a quick and efficient loop with no unnecessary stops (300 SEK, 4-6/day, fewer Oct-May, 1.25 hours).

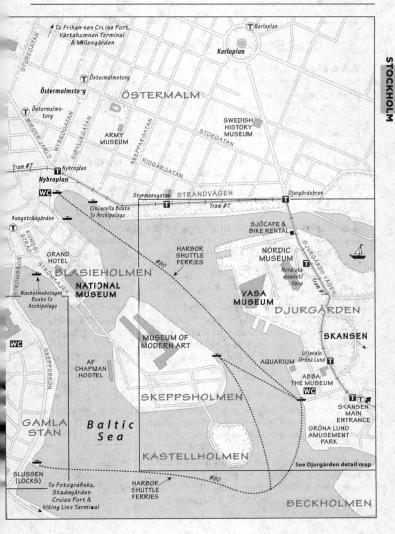

To Frihamnen Cruise Port,
Värtahamnen Terminal
& Millesgården

STUREGATAN

Karlaplan

Karlaplan

Östermalmstorg

Östermalmstorg

ÖSTERMALM

Östermalms-
torg

BIRGER JARLS

NYBOGATAN

SIBYLLEGATAN

SKEPPARGATAN

STORGATAN

SWEDISH
HISTORY
MUSEUM

ARMY
MUSEUM

RIDDARGATAN

Tram #7

Nybroplan

Nybroplan

WC

Styrmansgatan   STRANDVÄGEN   Tram #7   Djurgårdsbron

Cincerella Boats
To Archipelago

SJÖCAFE &
BIKE RENTAL

Kungsträdgården

KUNGS-
TRÄD

STRÖMBRON

GRAND
HOTEL

STRÖMKAJEN

BLASIEHOLMEN

NATIONAL
MUSEUM

HARBOR
SHUTTLE
FERRIES

#80

NORDIC
MUSEUM

Nordiska
museet/
Vasa

DJURGÅRDS VÄGEN

Tram #7

Waxholmsbolaget
Boats To
Archipelago

VASA
MUSEUM

DJURGÅRDEN

WC

SKEPPSBRON

AF
CHAPMAN
HOSTEL

MUSEUM OF
MODERN ART

SKANSEN

Liljevalc
Gröna Lund

AQUARIUM

ABBA:
THE MUSEUM

WC

GAMLA
STAN

Baltic
Sea

SKEPPSHOLMEN

SKANSEN
MAIN
ENTRANCE

GRÖNA LUND
AMUSEMENT
PARK

KASTELLHOLMEN

See Djurgården detail map

SLUSSEN
(LOCKS)

To Fotografiska,
Stadsgården
Cruise Port &
Viking Line Terminal

HARBOR
SHUTTLE
FERRIES

#80

BECKHOLMEN

BY BOAT
▲City Boat Tours

For a good floating look at Stockholm and a nice break, consider a sightseeing cruise. These boat tours are pleasant at the end of the day, when the light is warm and the sights and museums are closed. The handiest are the Strömma/Stockholm Sightseeing boats, which

Stockholm at a Glance

▲▲▲**Skansen** Europe's first and best open-air folk museum, with more than 150 old homes, churches, shops, and schools. **Hours:** Park—opens daily at 10:00, closes at 22:00 late June-Aug and progressively earlier the rest of the year; historical buildings—generally 11:00-17:00, late June-Aug some until 19:00, most closed in winter. See page 247.

▲▲▲**Vasa Museum** Ill-fated 17th-century warship dredged from the sea floor, now the showpiece of an interesting museum. **Hours:** Daily 8:30-18:00; Sept-May 10:00-17:00 except Wed until 20:00. See page 249.

▲▲**Military Parade and Changing of the Guard** Punchy pomp starting near Nybroplan and finishing at Royal Palace outer courtyard. **Hours:** Late April-Aug daily, Sept-late April Wed and Sat-Sun only, start time varies with season but always at midday. See page 240.

▲▲**Royal Armory** A fine collection of ceremonial medieval royal armor, historic and modern royal garments, and carriages, in the Royal Palace (most of museum may be closed for renovation when you visit). **Hours:** Daily May-June 11:00-17:00, July-Aug 10:00-18:00; Sept-April Tue-Sun 11:00-17:00, Thu until 20:00, closed Mon. See page 240.

▲▲**City Hall** Gilt mosaic architectural jewel of Stockholm and site of Nobel Prize banquet, with tower offering the city's best views. **Hours:** Required tours daily generally June-Aug every 30 minutes 9:30-15:30, fewer off-season. See page 242.

▲▲**Swedish History Museum** Collection of artifacts spanning Sweden's entire history, highlighted by fascinating Viking exhibit and Gold Room. **Hours:** Daily 10:00-17:00; Sept-May closed Mon and open Wed until 20:00. See page 245.

leave from Strömkajen, in front of the Grand Hotel, and stop at Nybroplan five minutes later.

Hop-On, Hop-Off Boat Tour

Stockholm is a city surrounded by water, making this boat option enjoyable and practical. Strömma and Red Buses offer the same small loop, stopping at key spots such as Djurgården (Skansen and Vasa Museum), Gamla Stan (near Slussen and again near Royal Palace), the Viking Line dock next to the cruise terminal at Stadsgården, cruise berth 167, and Nybroplan. Use the boat strictly as

▲▲**Drottningholm Palace** Lavish royal residence with nearby Baroque-era theater on Stockholm's outskirts. See page 254.

▲**Nordic Museum** Danish Renaissance palace design and five fascinating centuries of traditional Swedish lifestyles. **Hours:** Daily 9:00-18:00; Sept-May 10:00-17:00 except Wed until 20:00. See page 251.

▲**Nobel Museum** Star-studded tribute to some of the world's most accomplished scientists, artists, economists, and politicians. **Hours:** Daily 9:00-20:00; Sept-May Tue-Fri 11:00-17:00, Tue until 20:00, Sat-Sun 10:00-18:00, closed Mon. See page 238.

▲**Royal Palace Museums** Complex of Swedish royal museums, the two best of which are the Royal Apartments and Royal Treasury. **Hours:** Daily 10:00-17:00, July-Aug from 9:00; Oct-April until 16:00 and closed Mon. See page 241.

▲**Kungsträdgården** Stockholm's lively central square, with life-size chess games, concerts, and perpetual action. See page 234.

▲**Sergels Torg** Modern square with underground mall. See page 236.

▲**ABBA: The Museum** A super-commercial and wildly-popular-with-ABBA-fans experience. **Hours:** Daily 9:00-19:00; Sept-May daily 10:00-18:00 except Wed until 19:00. See page 253.

▲**Millesgården** Dramatic cliffside museum and grounds featuring works of Sweden's greatest sculptor, Carl Milles. **Hours:** Daily 11:00-17:00 except closed Mon Oct-April. See page 254.

▲**Museum of Medieval Stockholm** Underground museum shows off parts of the town wall King Gustav Vasa built in 1530s. **Hours:** Tue-Sun 12:00-17:00, Wed until 19:00, closed Mon. See page 242.

transport from Point A to Point B, or make the whole one-hour loop and enjoy the recorded commentary (180 SEK/24 hours, 2-3/hour May-mid-Sept, pick up map for schedule and locations of boat stops, www.stromma.se or www.redbuses.se).

ON FOOT
Old Town Walk
Strömma offers a 1.25-hour Old Town walk (180 SEK, July-Aug only at 13:30, departs from ticket booth at north end of Gustav Adolfs Torg, www.stromma.se).

Local Guides

Håkan Frändén is an excellent guide who brings Stockholm to life (mobile 070-531-3379, hakan.franden@hotmail.com). **Marita Bergman** is a teacher and a licensed guide who enjoys showing visitors around during her school breaks (1,650 SEK/half-day tour, mobile 073-511-9154, bergman57.mb@gmail.com). You can also hire a private guide through the Association of Qualified Tourist Guides of Stockholm (www.guidestockholm.com). The standard rate is about 1,650 SEK for up to three hours.

BY BIKE

To tour Stockholm on two wheels, you can either use one of the city's shared bikes or rent your own.

Using City Bikes: Stockholm's City Bikes program is a good option for seeing this bike-friendly town. While you'll find similar bike-sharing programs all over Europe, Stockholm's is the most usable and helpful for travelers. It's easy, the bikes are great, and the city lends itself to joyriding.

Purchase a 165-SEK, three-day City Bike card at the TI or at the SL Center (transit info office) at Sergels Torg. The card allows you to grab a bike from one of more than 140 City Bike racks around town. You must return it within three hours (to any rack), but if you want to keep riding, just check out another bike. You can do this over and over for three days (available April-Oct only, www.citybikes.se).

The downside: Unless you have a lock, you can't park your bike as you sightsee. You'll need to return it to a station and get another when you're ready to go—which sounds easy enough, but in practice stations can be full (without an empty port in which to leave a bike) or have no bikes available. To overcome this problem, download City Bike's fun, easy, and free app (search "City Bikes by Clear Channel"), which identifies the nearest racks and bikes.

Renting a Bike: You can also rent bikes (and boats) at the **Sjöcaféet** café, next to Djurgårdsbron bridge near the Vasa Museum. It's ideally situated as a springboard for a pleasant bike ride around the parklike Djurgården island—use their free and excellent bike map/guide. For details, see the Djurgårdsbron section under "Sights in Stockholm," later.

STOCKHOLM

Stockholm Walks

This section includes two different self-guided walks to introduce you to Stockholm, both old (Gamla Stan) and new (the modern city).

▲▲GAMLA STAN WALK

Gamla Stan, Stockholm's historic island old town, is charming, photogenic, and full of antique shops, street lanterns, painted ceilings, and surprises. Until the 1600s, all of Stockholm fit in Gamla Stan. Stockholm traded with other northern ports such as Amsterdam, Lübeck, and Tallinn. German culture influenced art, building styles, and even the language, turning Old Norse into modern Swedish. With its narrow alleys and stairways, Gamla Stan mixes poorly with cars and modern economies. Today, it's been given over to the Royal Palace and to the tourists, who throng Gamla Stan's main drag, Västerlånggatan, seemingly unaware that most of Stockholm's best attractions are elsewhere. While you could just happily wander, this quick walk gives meaning to Stockholm's Old Town.

• *Our walk begins along the harborfront. Start at the base of Slottsbacken (the Palace Hill esplanade) leading up to the...*

Royal Palace: Along the water, check out the ❶ **statue of King Gustav III** gazing at the palace, which was built in the 1700s on the site of Stockholm's first castle (for more about the palace, see the description later in this chapter, under "Sights in Stockholm"). Gustav turned Stockholm from a dowdy Scandinavian port into a sophisticated European capital, modeled on French culture. Gustav loved the arts, and he founded the Royal Dramatic Theater and the Royal Opera in Stockholm. Ironically, he was assassinated by a discontented nobleman, who shot Gustav in the back at a masquerade ball at the Royal Opera House in 1792 (inspiring Verdi's opera *Un Ballo in Maschera*).

Walk up the broad, cobbled boulevard alongside the palace to the crest of the hill. Stop, look back, and scan the harbor. The grand building across the water is the National Museum, which is often mistaken for the palace. Beyond that, in the distance, is the fine row of buildings on Strandvägen street. Until the 1850s, this area was home to peasant shacks, but as Stockholm entered its grand stage, it was cleaned up and replaced by fine apartments, including some of the city's smartest addresses. A

STOCKHOLM

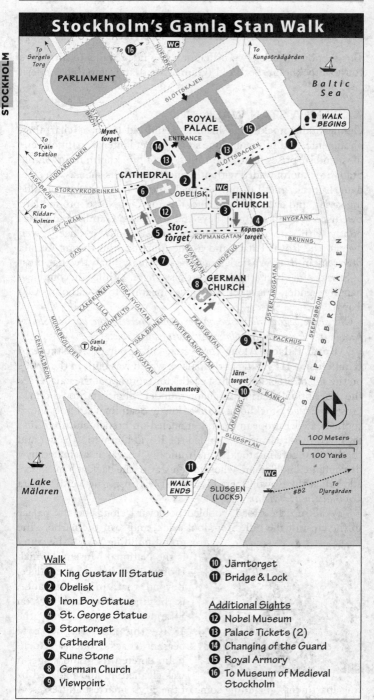

Stockholm's Gamla Stan Walk

Walk
1. King Gustav III Statue
2. Obelisk
3. Iron Boy Statue
4. St. George Statue
5. Stortorget
6. Cathedral
7. Rune Stone
8. German Church
9. Viewpoint
10. Järntorget
11. Bridge & Lock

Additional Sights
12. Nobel Museum
13. Palace Tickets (2)
14. Changing of the Guard
15. Royal Armory
16. To Museum of Medieval Stockholm

blocky gray TV tower stands tall in the distance. Turn to the palace facade on your left (finished in 1754, replacing one that burned in 1697). The niches are filled with Swedish bigwigs (literally) from the mid-18th century.

As you crest the hill, you're facing the ❷ **obelisk** that honors Stockholm's merchant class for its support in a 1788 war against Russia. In front of the obelisk are tour buses (their drivers worried about parking cops) and a pit used for *boules*. The royal family took a liking to the French game during a Mediterranean vacation, and it's quite popular around town today.

Behind the obelisk stands Storkyrkan, Stockholm's cathedral (which we'll visit later on this walk). From this angle you can see its Baroque facade, which was added to better match the newer palace. Opposite the boules court and palace is the Finnish church (Finska Kyrkan, the deep orange building), which originated as the royal tennis hall. When the Protestant Reformation hit in 1527, church services could at last be said in the peoples' languages rather than Latin. Suddenly, each merchant community needed its own church. Finns worshipped here, the Germans built their own church (coming up on this walk), and the Swedes got the cathedral.

Stroll up the lane to the right of the Finnish church into the shady churchyard, where you'll find the fist-sized ❸ *Iron Boy*, the tiniest public statue (out of about 600 statues) in Stockholm. Swedish grannies knit caps for him in the winter. Local legend says the statue honors the orphans who had to transfer cargo from sea ships to lake ships before Stockholm's locks were built. Some people rub his head for good luck (which the orphans didn't have). Others, perhaps needy when it comes to this gift, rub his head for wisdom. The artist says it's simply a self-portrait of himself as a child, sitting on his bed and gazing at the moon.

• *Exit through either of the churchyard gates, turn left onto Trädgårds-gatan, then bear right with the lane until you pop out at...*

Köpmangatan: Take a moment to explore this street from one end to the other. With its cobbles and traditional pastel facades, this is a quintessential Gamla Stan lane—and one of the oldest in town. The mellow yellow houses are predominantly from the 18th century; the reddish facades are mostly 17th century. Once merchants' homes, today these are popular with antique dealers and refined specialty shops. Back when there was comfort living within a city's walls, Gamla Stan streets like this were densely populated.

If you head left, you'll emerge on Köpmantorget square, with the breathtaking ❹ **statue of St. George** slaying the dragon, with a maiden representing Stockholm (about 10 steps to the right) looking on with thanks and admiration. If you go right, you'll reach old Stockholm's main square, our next stop.

❺ **Stortorget:** Colorful old buildings topped with gables line this square—Stockholm's oldest. In 1400, this was the heart of medieval Stockholm (pop. 6,000). Here at the town well, many tangled lanes intersected, making it the natural center for trading. Today Stortorget is home to lots of tourists—including a steady storm of cruise groups following the numbered Ping-Pong paddle of their guides on four-hour blitz tours of the city (300 ships call here between June and September). The square also hosts concerts, occasional demonstrators, and—in winter—Christmas shoppers at an outdoor market.

The grand building on the right is the old stock exchange, now home to the noble **Nobel Museum** (described under "Sights in Stockholm"), although it may move by the time you visit. On the immediate left is the social-services agency **Stockholms Stadsmission** (offering the cheapest and best lunch around at the recommended Grillska Huset). If you peek into the adjacent bakery, you'll get a fine look at the richly decorated ceilings characteristic of Gamla Stan in the 17th century—the exotic flowers and animals implied that the people who lived or worked here were worldly. You'll also spy some tempting marzipan cakes (a local favorite) and *kanelbullar* (cinnamon buns). There's a cheap sandwich counter in the back and lots of picnic benches in the square.

The town well is still a popular meeting point. This square long held the town's pillory. Scan the fine old facades. The site of the **Stockholm Bloodbath** of 1520, this square has a notorious history. During a Danish power grab, many of Stockholm's movers and shakers who had challenged Danish rule—Swedish aristocracy, leading merchants, and priests—were rounded up, brought here, and beheaded. Rivers of blood were said to have flowed through the streets. Legend holds that the 80 or so white stones in the fine

red facade across the square symbolize the victims. (One victim's son escaped, went into hiding, and resurfaced to lead a Swedish revolt against the Danish rulers. Three years later, the Swedes elected that rebel, Gustav Vasa, as their first king. He went on to usher in a great period in the country's history—the Swedish Renaissance.)
• *At the far end of the square (under the finest gables), turn right and follow Trångsund toward the cathedral.*

❻ **Cathedral** (Storkyrkan): Just before the yellow-brick church, you'll see my personal phone booth (Rikstelefon) and the gate to the churchyard—guarded by statues of Caution and Hope. Enter the church—Stockholm's oldest, from the 13th century (60 SEK, daily 9:00-16:00). Signs explain special events, as this church is busy with tours and services in summer.

When buying your ticket, pick up the free, worthwhile English-language flier. Exploring the cathedral's interior, you'll find many styles, ranging from medieval to modern. The front of the nave is paved with centuries-old **tombstones.** The tombstone of the Swedish reformer Olaus Petri is appropriately simple and appropriately located—under the finely carved and gilded pulpit on the left side of the nave. A witness to the Stockholm Bloodbath, Petri was nearly executed himself. He went on to befriend Gustav Vasa and guide him in Lutheranizing Sweden (and turning this cathedral from Catholic to Protestant).

Opposite the pulpit, find the **bronze plaque** in the pillar. It recalls the 1925 Swedish-led ecumenical meeting of Christian leaders that encouraged all churches to renew their efforts on behalf of peace and justice, especially given the horrific toll of World War I.

Next, the best seats in the house: the carved wood **royal boxes,** dating from 1684. This has been a royal wedding church throughout the ages. It was here, in June 2010, that Crown Princess Victoria, heir to the throne, married Daniel Westling (her personal trainer) with much pomp and ceremony.

The fine 17th-century **altar** is made of silver and ebony. Above it, the silver Christ stands like a conquering general evoking the 1650s, an era of Swedish military might.

Next to the altar is a wondrous 1489 statue, carved from oak and elk horn, of **St. George** slaying the dragon (we saw a copy of it outside a few minutes ago). To some, this symbolizes the Swedes overcoming the evil Danes (commemorating a military victory in 1471). In a broader sense, it's an inspiration to take up the struggle against even non-Danish evil. Regardless, it must be the gnarliest dragon's head in all of Europe.

Return to the back of the church to find the exit. Before leaving, just to the left of the door, notice the **painting** that depicts Stockholm in the early 1500s, showing a walled city filling today's Gamla Stan. It's a 1630 copy of the 1535 original. The church, with its black spire, dominated the town back then. The strange sun and sky predicted big changes in Sweden—and as a matter of fact, that's what happened. Gustav Vasa brought on huge reforms in religion and beyond. (The doors just to the left and right of the painting lead to a free WC.)

Heading outside, you'll emerge into the kid-friendly churchyard, which was once the cemetery.

• *With your back to the church's front door, go right. At the next corner, turn left (on Storkyrkobrinken), then left again on...*

Prästgatan: Enjoy a quiet wander down this peaceful 15th-century "Priests' Lane." Västerlånggatan, the touristy drag, parallels this lane one block over. (While we'll skip it now, you can walk back up it from the end point of this walk.) As you stroll Prästgatan, look for bits of its past: hoists poking out horizontally from gables (merchants used these to lift goods into their attics), tie bolts (iron bars necessary to bind the timber beams of tall buildings together), small coal or wood hatches (for fuel delivery back in the good old days), and flaming gold phoenixes under red-crown medallions (telling firefighters which houses paid insurance and could be saved in case of fire—for example, #46).

Like other Scandinavian cities, Stockholm was plagued by fire until it was finally decreed that only stone, stucco, and brick construction (like you see here) would be allowed in the town center.

After a few blocks (at Kåkbrinken), a cannon barrel on the corner (look down) guards a Viking-age ❼ **rune stone.** In case you can't read the old Nordic script, it says: "Torsten and Frogun erected this stone in memory of their son."

• *Continue one block farther down Prästgatan to Tyska Brinken and turn left. Look up to see the powerful brick steeple of the...*

STOCKHOLM

❽ **German Church** (Tyska Kyrkan): The church's carillon has played four times a day since 1666. Think of the days when German merchants worked here. Today, Germans come to Sweden not to run the economy, but to enjoy its pristine nature (which is progressively harder to find in their own crowded homeland). Sweden formally became a Lutheran country even before the northern part of Germany—making this the very first German Lutheran church (free to enter).

• *Wander through the churchyard (past a cute church café) and out the back. Exit right onto Svartmangatan and follow it to the right, ending at an iron railing overlooking Österlånggatan.*

❾ **Viewpoint:** From this perch, survey the street below to the left and right. Notice how it curves. This marks the old shoreline. In medieval times, piers stretched out like fingers into the harbor. Gradually, as land was reclaimed and developed, these piers were extended, becoming lanes leading to piers farther away. Behind you is a cute shop where elves can actually be seen making elves.

• *Walk right to Österlånggatan, and continue on to...*

❿ **Järntorget:** A customs square in medieval times, this was the home of Sweden's first bank back in 1680 (the yellow building with the bars on the windows). The Co-op Nära supermarket on this square offers picnic fixings. From here, Västerlånggatan—the eating, shopping, and commercial pedestrian mall of Gamla Stan—leads back across the island. You'll be there in a minute, but first finish this walk.

• *Continue from the square (opposite where you entered) down Järntorgsgatan until you emerge (suddenly) into traffic hell. For now, things are a bit of a mess because of an enormous redevelopment project that will eventually turn this area into a green people-zone. Let's continue ahead, crossing over the busy street to reach a viewpoint window (cut into the construction wall that lines the bridge).*

⓫ **Bridge Overlooking Slussen:** This area is called Slussen, named for the locks between the salt water of the Baltic Sea (to your left) and the fresh water of the huge **Lake Mälaren** (to your right). In fact, Stockholm exists because this is where Lake Mälaren meets the sea. Traders would sail their goods from far inland to this point, where they'd meet merchants who would ship the goods south to Europe. In the 13th century, the new kingdom of Sweden needed revenue, and began levying duty taxes on all the iron, copper, and furs shipped through here.

From the bridge, you may notice a current in the water, indicating that the weir has been lowered and water is spilling from Lake Mälaren (about two feet above sea level) into the sea. Today, the locks are nicknamed "the divorce lock" because this is where captains and first mates learn to communicate under pressure and in the public eye.

Opposite Gamla Stan is the island of **Södermalm**—bohemian, youthful, artsy, and casual—with its popular Katarina viewing platform. Moored on the saltwater side are cruise ships, which bring thousands of visitors into town each day during the season. Many of these boats are bound for Finland. The towering white syringe is the Gröna Lund amusement park's free-fall ride. The revolving *Djurgården Färjan* sign, along the embankment to your left, marks the ferry that zips from here directly to Gröna Lund and Djurgården.

• *Our walk is finished, but feel free to linger longer in Gamla Stan—day or night, it's a lively place to enjoy.* **Västerlånggatan,** *Gamla Stan's main commercial drag, is a touristy festival of distractions that keeps most visitors from seeing the historic charms of the Old Town—which you just did. Now you're free to window-shop and eat (see "Shopping in Stockholm" and "Eating in Stockholm," later).*

For more sightseeing, consider the other sights in Gamla Stan or at the Royal Palace (all described under "Sights in Stockholm"). Or backtrack to Västerlånggatan (always going straight), to reach the parliament building and cross the water back over onto **Norrmalm** *(where the street becomes Drottninggatan). This pedestrian street leads back into Stockholm's modern town.*

Yet another option is to walk 15 minutes to **Kungsträdgården,** *the starting point of my "Stockholm's Modern City" self-guided walk. Either walk along the embankment and take the diagonal bridge directly across to the square, or walk back through the middle of Gamla Stan, take the stately walkway past the Swedish Parliament building, then turn right when you cross the bridge.*

STOCKHOLM'S MODERN CITY WALK

On this walk, we'll use the park called Kungsträdgården as a springboard to explore the modern center of Stockholm—a commercial zone that puts the focus not on old kings and mementos of superpower days, but on shopping. To trace the route, see the "Stockholm" map, earlier.

• *Find the statue of King Karl XII, facing the waterfront at the harbor end of the park.*

Kungsträdgården: Centuries ago, this "King's Garden" was the private kitchen garden of the king, where he grew his cabbage salad. Today, this downtown people-watching center, worth ▲, is considered Stockholm's living room, symbolizing the Swedes' freedom-loving spirit. While the name implies that the garden is a private royal domain, the giant clump of elm trees just be-

hind the statue reminds locals that it's the people who rule now. In the 1970s, demonstrators chained themselves to these trees to stop the building of an underground train station here. They prevailed, and today, locals enjoy the peaceful, breezy ambience of a teahouse instead.

Farther on, watch for the AstroTurf zone with "latte dads" and their kids, and enjoy a summer concert at the bandstand. There's always something going on. High above is a handy reference point—the revolving NK clock.

Kungsträdgården—surrounded by the harborfront and tour boats, the Royal Opera House, and shopping opportunities (including a welcoming Volvo showroom near the top-left side of the square, showing off the latest in Swedish car design)—is *the* place to feel Stockholm's pulse (but always ask first: *"Kan jag kanna på din puls?"*).

The garden also plays host to huge parties. The Taste of Stockholm festival runs for a week in early June, when restaurateurs show off and bands entertain all day. Beer flows liberally—a rare public spectacle in Sweden.

• *Stroll through Kungsträdgården, past the fountain and the Volvo store, and up to Hamngatan street. From here, we'll turn left and walk the length of the NK department store (across the street) as we wade through...*

Stockholm's Urban Shopping Zone (Hamngatan): In just a couple of blocks, we'll pass some major landmarks of Swedish consumerism. First, anchoring the corner at the top of Kungsträdgården, is the gigantic **Illums Bolighus** design shop. (You can enter from the square and stroll all the way through it, popping out at Hamngatan on the far end.) This is a Danish institution, making its play for Swedish customers with this prime location. Across the street, notice the giant gold *NK* marking the **Nordiska Kompaniet** department store (locals joke that the NK stands for "no kronor left"). It's located in an elegant early-20th-century building that dominates the top end of Kungsträdgården. If it feels like an old-time American department store, that's because its architect was inspired by grand stores he'd seen in the US (circa 1910).

Another block down, on the left, is the sleeker, more modern **Gallerian mall.** Among this two-story world of shops, upstairs you'll find a Clas Ohlson hardware and electronics shop (most Stockholmers have a cabin that's always in need of a little DIY repair). And there are plenty of affordable little lunch bars and classy cafés for your *fika* (Swedish coffee-and-bun break). You may notice that American influence (frozen yogurt and other trendy food chains) is challenging the notion of the traditional *fika*.

• *High-end shoppers should consider heading into the streets behind NK, with exclusive designer boutiques and the chichi Mood Stockholm mall*

Fika: Sweden's Coffee Break

Swedes drink more coffee per capita than just about any other country in the world. The Swedish coffee break—or *fika*—is a ritual. *Fika* is to Sweden what teatime is to Britain. The typical *fika* is a morning or afternoon break in the workday, but can happen any time, any day. It's the perfect opportunity (and excuse) for tourists to take a break as well.

Fika fare is coffee with a snack—something sweet or savory. Your best bet is a *kanel-bulle,* a Swedish cinnamon bun, although some prefer *pariserbulle,* a bun filled with vanilla cream. These can be found nearly everywhere coffee is sold, including just about any café or *konditori* (bakery) in Stockholm. A coffee and a cinnamon bun in a café will cost you about 40 SEK. (Most cafés will give you a coffee refill for free.) But at Pressbyrån, the Swedish convenience stores found all over town, you can satisfy your *fika* fix for 25 SEK by getting a coffee and bun to go. Grab a park bench or waterside perch, relax, and enjoy.

(see *"Shopping in Stockholm,"* later). *Otherwise, just beyond the huge Gallerian mall, you'll emerge into Sergels Torg. (Note that the handy tram #7 goes from here directly to Skansen and the other important sights on Djurgården; departures every few minutes.)*

Sergels Torg and Kulturhuset: Sergels Torg square, worth ▲, dominates the heart of modern Stockholm with its stark 1960s-era functionalist architecture. The glassy tower in the middle of the fountain plaza is ugly in daylight but glows at night, symbolic of Sweden's haunting northern lights.

Kulturhuset, the hulking, low-slung, glassy building overlooking the square, is Stockholm's "culture center"—a public space for everyone in Stockholm. In this lively cultural zone, there are libraries, theater, a space for kids, chessboards, fun shops, fine art cinema, art exhibits, and a music venue (tel. 08/5062-0200, http://kulturhusetstadsteatern.se).

I like to take the elevator to the top of the Kulturhuset and explore each level by riding the escalator back down to the ground floor. On the rooftop, the recommended Cafeteria Panorama has cheap meals and a salad bar with terrific city views.

Back at ground level outside, stand in front of the Kulturhuset (across from the fountain) and survey the expansive square nicknamed "Plattan" (the platter). Everything around you dates from the 1960s and 1970s, when this formerly run-down area was reinvented as an urban "space of the future." In the 1970s, with no nearby residences, the desolate Plattan became the domain of junkies. Now the city is actively revitalizing it, and the Plattan is becoming a people-friendly heart of the commercial town.

DesignTorget (enter from the lower level of Kulturhuset) showcases practical items for everyday use from established and emerging designers. Nearby are the major boutiques and department stores, including, across the way, H&M and Åhléns.

Sergelgatan, a thriving pedestrian and commercial street, leads past the five uniform white towers you see beyond the fountain. These office towers, so modern in the 1960s, have gone from seeming hopelessly out-of-date to being considered "retro," and are now quite popular with young professionals.

• *Walk up Sergelgatan past the towers, enjoying the public art and people-watching, to the market at Hötorget.*

Hötorget: "Hötorget" means "Hay Market," but today its stalls feed people rather than horses. The adjacent indoor market,

Hötorgshallen, is fun and fragrant. It dates from 1914 when, for hygienic reasons, the city forbade selling fish and meat outdoors. Carl Milles' statue of *Orpheus Emerging from the Underworld* (with seven sad Muses) stands in front of the city concert hall (which hosts the annual Nobel Prize award ceremony). The concert house, from 1926, is Swedish Art Deco (a.k.a. "Swedish Grace"). The lobby (open through much of the summer) still evokes Stockholm's Roaring Twenties. If the door's open, you're welcome to look in for free.

Popping into the Hötorget T-bana station provides a fun glimpse at local urban design. Stockholm's subway system was inaugurated in the 1950s, and many stations are modern art installations in themselves.

• *Our walk ends here. For more shopping and an enjoyable pedestrian boulevard leading back into the Old Town, cut down a block to Drottninggatan and turn left. This busy drag leads straight out of the commercial district, passes the parliament, then becomes the main street of Gamla Stan.*

Sights in Stockholm

GAMLA STAN (OLD TOWN)

The best of this island is covered in my "Gamla Stan" self-guided walk, earlier. But here are a few ways to extend your time in the Old Town.

On Stortorget
▲Nobel Museum (Nobelmuseet)

Opened in 2001 for the 100-year anniversary of the Nobel Prize, this wonderful little museum tells the story of the world's most prestigious prize. Pricey but high-tech and eloquent, it fills the grand old stock exchange building that dominates Gamla Stan's main square, Stortorget. By the time you visit, the museum may have relocated to a new building on Blasieholmen—inquire locally.

Cost and Hours: 120 SEK, free Tue after 17:00; daily 9:00-20:00; Sept-May Tue-Fri 11:00-17:00, Tue until 20:00, Sat-Sun 10:00-18:00, closed Mon; audioguide-20 SEK, free 40-minute orientation tours in English—check website for times, tel. 08/5348-1800, www.nobelmuseum.se.

Background: Stockholm-born Alfred Nobel was a great inventor, with more than 300 patents. His most famous invention: dynamite. Living in the late 1800s, Nobel was a man of his age. It was a time of great optimism, wild ideas, and grand projects. His dynamite enabled entire nations to blast their way into the modern age with canals, railroads, and tunnels. It made warfare much more destructive. And it also made Alfred Nobel a very wealthy man. Wanting to leave a legacy that celebrated and supported people with great ideas, Alfred used his fortune to fund the Nobel Prize. Every year since 1901, laureates have been honored in the fields of physics, chemistry, medicine, literature, economic sciences, and peacemaking.

Visiting the Museum: Inside, portraits of all 700-plus prize-winners hang from the ceiling—shuffling around the room like shirts at the dry cleaner's (miss your favorite, and he or she will come around again in six hours). Behind the ticket desk are monitors that represent the six Nobel Prize categories, each honoring the most recent laureate in that category.

Flanking the main hall beyond that—where touchscreens organized by decade invite you to learn more about the laureates of your choice—two rooms run a continuous video montage of quick programs (on one side, films celebrating the creative milieus that encouraged Nobel laureates past and present; on the other side, short films about their various paths to success).

To the right of the ticket desk, find "The Gallery," with a surprisingly captivating collection of items that various laureates have cited as important to their creative process, from scientific equipment to inspirational knickknacks. The randomness of the items offers a fascinating and humanizing insight into the great minds of our time.

Royal Palace Complex (Kungliga Slottet)

Although the royal family beds down at Drottningholm, this complex in Gamla Stan is still the official royal residence. The palace, designed in Italian Baroque style, was completed in 1754 after a fire wiped out the previous palace—a much more characteristic medieval/Renaissance complex. This blocky Baroque replacement, which houses various museums, is big and (frankly) pretty dull. See the "Stockholm's Gamla Stan Walk" map to sort out the various entrances.

Planning Your Time: Visiting the several sights in and near the palace could fill a day, but Stockholm has far better attractions elsewhere. Prioritize.

Visitors in a rush should see the Changing of the Guard, enter the (free) Royal Armory—if it's open when you visit, and skip the rest. Information booths in the semicircular courtyard (at the top, where the guard changes) and just inside the east entry give out a list of the day's guided tours and an explanatory brochure/map that marks the entrances to the different sights. The main entrance to the Royal Palace (including the apartments, chapel, and treasury) faces the long, angled square and obelisk (but you can cut through the palace's interior courtyard to get there).

Tours: In peak season, the main Royal Palace offers a full slate of English tours covering the different sights (included in admission)—allowing you to systematically cover nearly the entire complex. If you're paying the hefty price for a ticket, you might as well join at least one of the tours—otherwise, you'll struggle to appreciate the place. Some tours are infrequent, so be sure to confirm times when you purchase your admission (for more on tours, see the individual listings next).

Expect Changes: Since the palace is used for state functions, it's sometimes closed to tourists. And, as the exterior is undergoing a 20-year renovation, don't be surprised if parts are covered in scaffolding. Most of the Royal Armory is closed for renovation, while the Royal Coin Cabinet has closed and will reopen in a new location in Östermalm in a few years (and is worth visiting when it does)

STOCKHOLM

▲▲Military Parade and Changing of the Guard

Starting from the Army Museum (two blocks from Nybroplan at Riddargatan 13), Stockholm's daily military parade marches over Norrbro bridge, in front of the parliament building, and up to the Royal Palace's outer courtyard, where the band plays and the guard changes. Smaller contingents of guards spiral in from other parts of the palace complex, eventually convening in the same place.

The performance is fresh and spirited, because the soldiers are visiting Stockholm just like you—and it's a chance for young soldiers from all over Sweden in every branch of the service to show their stuff in the big city. Pick your place at the palace courtyard, where the band arrives at about 12:15 (13:15 on Sun). The best spot to stand is along the wall in the inner courtyard, near the palace information and ticket office. There are columns with wide pedestals  for easy perching, as well as benches that people stand on to view the ceremony (arrive early). Generally, after the barking and goose-stepping formalities, the band shows off for an impressive 30-minute marching concert.

Marching Band and Parade: Departs from Army Museum late April-Aug Mon-Sat at 11:45, Sun at 12:45 (11:35 and 12:35, respectively, if departing from Cavalry Barracks); Sept-Oct Wed and Sat at 11:45, Sun at 12:45; off-season departs from Mynttorget Wed and Sat at 12:09, Sun at 13:09. Royal appointments can disrupt the schedule; confirm times at TI. In summer, you might also catch the mounted guards (they don't appear on a regular schedule).

Royal Guards Ceremony at the Palace: Mon-Sat at 12:15, Sun at 13:15, about 40 minutes, in front of the Royal Palace. You can get details at www.forsvarsmakten.se (click on "Activities").

▲▲Royal Armory (Livrustkammaren)

The oldest museum in Sweden is both more and less than an armory. Rather than dusty piles of swords and muskets, it focuses on royal clothing: impressive ceremonial armor (never used in battle) and other fashion through the ages (including a room of kidswear), plus a fine collection of coaches. It's an engaging slice of royal life. Everything is displayed under sturdy brick vaults, beautifully lit, and well-described in English and by a good audioguide. The museum has undertaken a major renovation that closed the main exhibit halls, but the lower level, with a good display of royal coaches, remains open.

Cost and Hours: Free; daily May-June 11:00-17:00, July-Aug 10:00-18:00; Sept-April Tue-Sun 11:00-17:00, Thu until 20:00, closed Mon; audioguide-40 SEK, information sheets in English available in most rooms; entrance at bottom of Slottsbacken at base of palace, tel. 08/402-3010, www.livrustkammaren.se.

▲Royal Palace

The Royal Palace consists of a chapel (free) and four museums. Compared to many grand European palaces, it's underwhelming and flooded with groups who don't realize that Stockholm's best sightseeing is elsewhere.

Cost and Hours: 160-SEK combo-ticket covers all four museums, includes guided tours; daily 10:00-17:00, July-Aug from 9:00; Oct-April until 16:00 and closed Mon; tel. 08/402-6130, www.royalcourt.se.

Royal Apartments: The stately palace exterior encloses 608 rooms (one more than Britain's Buckingham Palace) of glittering 18th-century Baroque and Rococo decor. Guided 45-minute tours in English run twice daily (at 10:30 and 13:30).

Royal Treasury (Skattkammaren): Refreshingly compact compared to the sprawling apartments, the treasury gives you a good, up-close look at Sweden's crown jewels. It's particularly worthwhile with an English guided tour (daily at 11:30) or the included audioguide (which covers basically the same information).

Museum of Three Crowns (Museum Tre Kronor): This museum shows off bits of the palace from before a devastating 1697 fire (guided tours in English offered at 11:30). The models, illustrations, and artifacts are displayed in vaulted medieval cellars that are far more evocative than the run-of-the-mill interior of today's palace. But while the stroll through the cellars is atmospheric, it's basically just more old stuff, interesting only to real history buffs.

Royal Chapel: If you don't want to spring for a ticket, but would like a little taste of palace opulence, climb the stairs inside the main entrance for a peek into the chapel. It's standard-issue royal Baroque: colorful ceiling painting, bubbly altars, and a giant organ.

Gustav III's Museum of Antiquities (Gustav III's Antikmuseum): In the 1700s, Gustav III traveled through Italy and brought home an impressive gallery of classical Roman statues. These are displayed exactly as they were in the 1790s. This was a huge deal for those who had never been out of Sweden.

More Gamla Stan Sights

These sights sit on the Gamla Stan islet of Helgeandsholmen (just north of the Royal Palace).

Parliament (Riksdag)

For a firsthand look at Sweden's government, tour the parliament buildings. Guides enjoy a chance to teach a little Swedish poli-sci along the standard tour of the building and its art. It's also possible to watch the parliament in session.

Cost and Hours: Free one-hour tours go in English late June-mid-Aug, usually 4/day Mon-Fri (when parliament is not in session). The rest of the year tours run 1/day Sat-Sun only; you're also welcome to join Swedish citizens in the viewing gallery (free); enter at Riksgatan 3a, call 08/786-4862 from 9:00 to 11:00 to confirm tour times, www.riksdagen.se..

▲Museum of Medieval Stockholm (Medeltidsmuseet)

This modern, well-presented museum offers a look at medieval Stockholm. When the government was digging a parking garage near the parliament building in the 1970s, workers uncovered a major archaeological find: parts of the town wall that King Gustav Vasa built in the 1530s, as well as a churchyard. This underground museum preserves these discoveries and explains how Stockholm grew from a medieval village to a major city, with a focus on its interactions with fellow Hanseatic League trading cities. Lots of artifacts, models, life-size dioramas, and sound and lighting effects—all displayed in a vast subterranean space—help bring the story to life.

Cost and Hours: Free, Tue-Sun 12:00-17:00, Wed until 19:00, closed Mon; free English guided tours July-Aug Tue-Sun at 14:00, audioguide-20 SEK, enter museum from park in front of parliament—down below as you cross the bridge, tel. 08/5083-1790, www.medeltidsmuseet.stockholm.se.

Nearby: The museum sits in **Strömparterren** park. With its café and Carl Milles statue of the *Sun Singer* greeting the day, it's a pleasant place for a sightseeing break (pay WC in park, free WC in museum).

DOWNTOWN STOCKHOLM

I've organized these sights and activities in the urban core of Stockholm by island and/or neighborhood.

On Kungsholmen, West of Norrmalm

▲▲City Hall (Stadshuset)

The Stadshuset is an impressive mix of eight million red bricks, 19 million chips of gilt mosaic, and lots of Stockholm pride. While churches dominate cities in southern Europe, in Scandinavian capitals, City Halls seem to be the most impressive buildings, celebrating humanism and the ideal of people working together in community. Built in 1923, this is still a functioning City Hall. The members of the city council—101 men and women representing the 850,000 citizens of Stockholm—are hobby legislators with regular day jobs. That's why they meet in the evening once a week. One of Europe's finest public buildings, the site of the annual Nobel Prize banquet, and a favorite spot for weddings (they do two per hour on Saturday afternoons, when some parts of the complex may be closed), City Hall is particularly enjoyable and worthwhile for its entertaining and required 50-minute tour.

Cost and Hours: 110 SEK; English tours offered daily, generally June-Aug every 30 minutes 9:30-15:30, fewer off-season; schedule can change due to special events—call to confirm; 300 yards behind the central train station—about a 15-minute walk from either the station or Gamla Stan, bus #3 or #50, cafeteria open to public at lunch Mon-Fri; tel. 08/5082-9058, www.stockholm.se/stadshuset.

Visiting City Hall: On the tour, you'll see the building's sumptuous National Romantic-style interior (similar to Britain's

Arts and Crafts style), celebrating Swedish architecture and craftwork, and created almost entirely with Swedish materials. Highlights include the so-called Blue Hall (the Italian piazza-inspired, brick-lined courtyard that was originally intended to be painted blue—hence the name—where the 1,300-plate Nobel banquet takes place); the City Council Chamber (with a gorgeously painted wood-beamed ceiling that resembles a Viking longhouse—or maybe an overturned Viking boat); the Gallery of the Prince (lined with frescoes executed by Prince Eugene of Sweden); and the glittering, gilded, Neo-Byzantine-style (and aptly named) Golden Hall, where the Nobel recipients cut a rug after the banquet.

▲City Hall Tower

This 343-foot-tall tower rewards those who make the climb with the classic Stockholm view: The old church spires on the atmospheric islands of Gamla Stan pose together, with the rest of the green and watery city spread-eagle around them.

Cost and Hours: 50 SEK, daily 9:15-17:15, May and Sept until 15:55, closed Oct-April.

Crowd-Beating Tips: Only 30 people at a time are allowed up into the tower, every 40 minutes throughout the day. To ascend, you'll need a timed-entry ticket, available only in person at the tower ticket office on the same day. It can be a long wait for the next available time, and tickets can sell out by mid-afternoon. If you're touring City Hall, come to the tower ticket window first to see when space is available.

Ideally an appointment will coincide with the end of your tour.

▲National Museum of Fine Arts (Nationalmuseum)

Though mediocre by European standards, this 200-year-old museum is small, central, and user-friendly. An extensive renovation may cause it to be closed when you visit—check ahead. Highlights include several canvases by Rembrandt and Rubens, a fine group of Impressionist works, and a sizeable collection of Russian icons. Seek out the exquisite paintings by the Swedish artists Anders Zorn, Ernst Josephson, and Carl Larsson. An excellent audioguide describes the top works.

Cost and Hours: 100 SEK, can be more with special exhibits, audioguide-30 SEK; confirm times on website, likely Wed-Sun 11:00-17:00, until later Tue and Thu, closed Mon; Södra Blasieholmshamnen, T-bana: Kungsträdgården, tel. 08/5195-4310, www.nationalmuseum.se.

On Blasieholmen and Skeppsholmen

The peninsula of Blasieholmen pokes out from downtown Stockholm, and is tethered to the island of Skeppsholmen by a narrow bridge (with great views and adorned with glittering golden crowns). While not connected to the city by T-bana or tram, you can reach this area on bus #65 or the harbor shuttle ferry. Skeppsholmen offers a peaceful break from the bustling city, with glorious views of Gamla Stan on one side and Djurgården on the other.

Museum of Modern Art (Moderna Museet)

This bright, cheery gallery on Skeppsholmen island is as far out as can be. For serious art lovers, it warrants ▲▲. The impressive permanent collection includes modernist all-stars such as Picasso, Braque, Dalí, Matisse, Munch, Kokoschka, and Dix; lots of goofy Dada art (including a copy of Duchamp's urinal); Pollock, Twombly, Bacon, and other postmodernists; and plenty of excellent contemporary stuff as well (don't miss the beloved Rauschenberg *Goat with Tire*). Swedish artists of the 20th and 21st centuries are also featured.

The museum's fine collection of modern and contemporary sculpture is installed on the leafy grounds of Skeppsholmen is-

land—perfect for a stroll even when the museum is closed. The building also houses the Architecture and Design Center, with changing exhibits (www.arkdes.se).

Cost and Hours: Free but sometimes a fee for special exhibits; download the excellent, free audioguide to enhance your visit; open Tue and Fri 10:00-20:00, Wed-Thu and Sat-Sun until 18:00, closed Mon; fine bookstore, good shop, and harborview café; T-bana: Kungsträdgården plus 10-minute walk, or take bus #65; tel. 08/5202-3500, www.modernamuseet.se.

Östermalm

While this ritzy residential area has just one key museum, it makes up for the lack of sights with posh style. Explore its stately streets and explore the delightful, upscale Saluhall food market right on Östermalmstorg (see "Eating in Stockholm," later). Östermalm's harborfront is hemmed in by the pleasant park called Nybroplan; from here, ferries lead to various parts of the city and beyond (as this is the jumping-off point for cruises into Stockholm's archipelago). If connecting to the sights in Djurgården, consider doing Östermalm by foot.

▲▲Swedish History Museum (Historiska Museet)

The displays and artifacts in this excellent museum cover all of Swedish history, but the highlights are its fascinating Viking exhibit and impressive Gold Room. Also worth a look are sections on Scandinavian prehistory, medieval church art, and a well-realized display about the Danish invasion of 1361—the battle of Gotland—in which 1,800 ill-equipped Swedish farmers lost their lives.

Cost and Hours: Free, daily 10:00-17:00; Sept-May closed Mon and open Wed until 20:00; a few blocks north of the Djurgården bridge at Narvavägen 13, bus #67 stops out front, tel. 08/5195-5562, www.historiska.se.

Tours: Audioguide-30 SEK. Daily guided tours are offered in summer (at 12:00 and 13:00), and kids' activities are available in an inner courtyard until 16:00.

Visiting the Museum: The featured exhibit (on the ground floor), titled simply **"Vikings,"** probes the many stories and myths about these people. Were they peaceful traders and farmers—or brutal robbers and pillagers? The focus is on everyday activities, religious beliefs, and family life in the years from 800 to 1050—the Viking Age.

A reconstruction of a Viking village gives a view of early trading communities, but most people lived by farming, hunting, and fishing. Exhibits feature grave goods, combs of horn and bone, gaming pieces, and brooches. A rare find is a wooden chest filled with tools and scrap metal, believed to have belonged to a blacksmith/carpenter.

A fine section of "picture stones" relate the stories of the Norse gods, and amulets shaped like little hammers demonstrate the importance of the god Thor. The small group of Vikings who did venture abroad to trade (and to pillage) returned to Scandinavia with new customs—including Christianity.

The **"Gold Room"** (in the basement) dazzles viewers with about 115 pounds of gold: spiral hair ornaments from 1500 b.c.; gold collars worn by fifth-century aristocrats; hoards of coins from Roman and Arab empires; once-buried treasure troves of jewelry and votive objects; and medieval jewel-encrusted reliquaries.

In all, the museum has about 3,000 finely crafted gold objects—largely thanks to Swedish legislation that has protected antiquities since the 17th century.

DJURGÅRDEN

Four hundred years ago, Djurgården was the king's hunting ground (the name means "Animal Garden"). You'll see the royal gate to the island immediately after the bridge that connects it to the mainland. Now this entire lush island is Stockholm's fun center, protected as a national park. It still has a smattering of animal life among its biking paths, picnicking families, art galleries, various amusements, and museums, which are some of the best in Scandinavia.

Orientation: Of the three great sights on the island, the Vasa and Nordic museums are neighbors, and Skansen is a 10-minute walk away (or hop on any bus or tram—they come every couple of minutes). Several lesser or special-interest attractions (from the ABBA museum to an amusement park) are also nearby.

To get around more easily, consider **renting a bike** as you enter the island. You can get one at Sjöcaféet, a café just over the Djurgårdsbron bridge; they also rent boats (bikes-80 SEK/hour, 275 SEK/day; canoes-150 SEK/hour, kayaks-125 SEK/hour; open daily 9:00-21:00, closed off-season and in bad weather; handy city cycle maps, tel. 08/660-5757, www.sjocafeet.se).

In the concrete building upstairs from the café, you'll find a **Djurgården visitors center,** with free maps, island bike routes,

brochures, and information about the day's events (daily in summer 8:00-20 00, shorter hours off-season).

Getting There: Take tram #7 from Sergels Torg (the stop is right under the highway overpass) or Nybroplan (in front of the gilded theater building) and get off at one of these stops: Nordic Museum (use also for Vasa Museum), Liljevalc Gröna Lund (for ABBA museum), or Skansen. In summer, you can take a city ferry from the southeast end of Gamla Stan or from Nybroplan (see "Getting Around Stockholm," earlier). Walkers enjoy the harborside Strandvägen promenade, which leads from Nybroplan directly to the island.

Museums on Djurgården
▲▲▲Skansen

Founded in 1891, Skansen was the first in what became a Europe-wide movement to preserve traditional architecture in open-air museums. It's a huge park gathering more than 150 historic buildings (homes, churches, shops, and schoolhouses) transplanted from all corners of Sweden. Other languages have borrowed the Swedish term "Skansen" (which originally meant "the Fort") to describe an "open-air museum." Today, tourists enjoy exploring this Swedish-culture-on-a-lazy-Susan, seeing folk crafts in action and wonderfully furnished old interiors. Kids love Skansen, where they can ride a life-size wooden *Dala*-horse and stare down a hedgehog, visit Lill-Skansen (a children's zoo), and take a mini-train or pony ride. This is an enjoyable place to visit on summer days, when it's lively with families and tourists.

Cost and Hours: 180 SEK, kids-60 SEK, less off-season; park opens daily at 10:00, closes at 22:00 late June-Aug and progressively earlier the rest of the year; historical buildings generally open 11:00-17:00, late June-Aug some until 19:00, most closed in winter. Check their excellent online calendar for what's happening during your visit (www.skansen.se) or call 08/442-8000.

Visiting Skansen: Skansen isn't designed as a one-way loop; it's a sprawling network of lanes and buildings, yours to explore. For the full story, invest in the museum guidebook (sold at the info booth just after the entrance). With the book, you'll understand each building you duck into and even learn about the Nordic animals awaiting you in the zoo. While you're at the info booth, check the live crafts  schedule to make a smart Skansen plan (the scale model displayed at the entrance will give you an idea of the park's size—and the need for a plan).

From the entrance, go up the stairs and bear left to find the escalator, and ride it up to **"The Town Quarter"** (Stadskvarteren), where shoemakers, potters, and glassblowers are busy doing their traditional thing (daily 10:00-17:00) in a re-created Old World Stockholm. Continuing deeper into the park—past the bakery, spice shop/grocery, hardware store, and a cute little courtyard café—you'll reach the central square, **Bollnästorget** (signed as "Central Skansen" but labeled on English maps as "Market Street"), with handy food stands. The rest of Sweden spreads out from here. Northern Swedish culture and architecture is in the north (top of park map), and southern Sweden's  in the south (bottom of map). Various homesteads—each clustered protectively around an inner courtyard—are scattered around the complex.

Poke around. Follow signs—or your instincts. It's worth stepping into the old, red-wood Seglora Church (just past Bollnästor-get), which aches with atmosphere under painted beams.

Eating at Skansen: The park has ample eating options to suit every budget. The most memorable—and affordable—meals are at the small folk food court on the main square, **Bollnästorget.** Here, among the duck-filled lakes, frolicking families, and peacenik local toddlers who don't bump on the bumper cars, kiosks dish up "Sami slow food" (smoked reindeer), waffles, hot dogs, and more. There are lots of picnic benches—Skansen encourages **picnicking.** (A small grocery store is tucked away across the street and a bit to the left of the main entrance.)

▲▲▲Vasa Museum (Vasamuseet)

Stockholm turned a titanic flop into one of Europe's great sight-seeing attractions. The glamorous but unseaworthy warship *Vasa*—

top-heavy with an extra cannon deck—sank 40 minutes into her 1628 maiden voyage when a breeze caught the sails and blew her over. After 333 years at the bottom of Stockholm's harbor, she rose again from the deep with the help of marine archae-ologists. Rediscovered in 1956 and raised in 1961, this Edsel of the sea

is today the best-preserved ship of its age anywhere—housed since 1990 in a brilliant museum. The masts perched atop the roof—best seen from a distance—show the actual height of the ship.

Cost and Hours: 130 SEK, includes film and tour; daily 8:30-18:00; Sept-May 10:00-17:00 except Wed until 20:00; WCs on level 3, good café, Galärvarvet, Djurgården, tel. 08/5195-5810, www.vasamuseet.se.

Getting There: The *Vasa* is on the waterfront immediately behind the stately brick Nordic Museum (facing the museum, walk around to the right) and a 10-minute walk from Skansen. From downtown, take tram #7.

Crowd-Beating Tips: There are two lines for tickets: on the right, for machines that take PIN-enabled credit cards; and on the left, for other cards or cash. The museum can have very long lines, but they gener-

ally move quickly—you likely won't wait more than 15-20 minutes. If crowds are a concern, get here either right when it opens, or after about 16:00 (but note that the last tour starts at 16:30).

Tours: The free 25-minute **tour** is worthwhile. Because each guide is given license to cover whatever he or she likes, no two tours are alike—if you're fascinated by the place, consider taking two different tours to pick up new details. In summer, English tours run on the hour and half-hour (last tour at 16:30); off-season (Sept-May) tours go 3/day Mon-Fri, hourly Sat-Sun (last tour at 15:30). Listen for the loudspeaker announcement, or check at the info desk for the next tour. Alternatively, you can access the **audioguide** by logging onto the museum's Wi-Fi (www.vasamuseet.se/audioguide).

Visiting the Museum: For a thorough visit, plan on spending at least an hour and a half—watch the film, take a guided tour, and linger over the exhibits (this works in any order). After buying your ticket, head inside. Sort out your film and tour options at the information desk to your right.

Upon entry, you're prow-to-prow with the great ship. The *Vasa*, while not quite the biggest ship in the world when launched in 1628, had the most firepower, with two fearsome decks of cannons. The 500 carved wooden statues draping the ship—once painted in bright colors—are all symbolic of the king's power. The 10-foot lion on the magnificent prow is a reminder that Europe considered the Swedish King Gustavus Adolphus the "Lion from the North." With this great ship, Sweden was preparing to establish its empire and become more engaged in European power politics. Specifically, the Swedes (who already controlled much of today's Finland and Estonia) wanted to push south to dominate the whole of the Baltic Sea, in order to challenge their powerful rival, Poland.

Designed by a Dutch shipbuilder, the *Vasa* had 72 guns of the same size and type (a rarity on mix-and-match warships of the age), allowing maximum efficiency in reloading—since there was no need to keep track of different ammunition. Unfortunately, the king's unbending demands to build the ship high (172 feet tall) but skinny made it extremely unstable; no amount of ballast could weigh the ship down enough to prevent it from tipping.

Now explore the **exhibits,** which are situated on six levels around the grand hall, circling the ship itself. All displays are well described in English. You'll learn about the ship's rules (bread can't be older than eight years), why it sank (stale bread?), how it's preserved (the ship, not the bread), and so on. Best of all is the chance to do slow laps around the magnificent vessel at different levels.

Now painstakingly restored, 98 percent of the *Vasa*'s wood is original (modern bits are the brighter and smoother planks).

On **level 4** (the entrance level), right next to the ship, you'll see a 1:10 scale model of the *Vasa* in its prime—vividly painted and fully rigged with sails. Farther along, models show how the *Vasa* was salvaged; a colorful children's section re-creates the time period; and a 10-minute multimedia show explains why the *Vasa* sank (alternating between English and Swedish showings). Heading behind the ship, you'll enjoy a great view of the sculpture-slathered stern of the *Vasa*. The facing wall features full-size replicas of the carvings, demonstrating how the ship was originally colorfully painted.

Several engaging displays are on **level 5**. "Life On Board" lets you walk through the gun deck and study cutaway models of the hive of activity that hummed below decks (handy, since you can't enter the actual ship). Artifacts—including fragments of clothing actually worn by the sailors—were salvaged along with the ship. "Battle!" is a small exhibit of cannons and an explanation of naval warfare.

Level 6 features "The Sailing Ship," with models demonstrating how the *Vasa* and similar vessels actually sailed. You'll see the (very scant) remains of some of the *Vasa*'s actual riggings and sails. **Level 7** gives you even higher views over the ship.

Don't miss **level 2**—all the way at the bottom (ride the handy industrial-size elevator)—with some of the most interesting exhibits. "The Ship" explains how this massive and majestic vessel was brought into being using wood from tranquil Swedish forests. Tucked under the ship's prow is a laboratory where today's scientists continue with their preservation efforts. The "Objects" exhibit shows off actual items found in the shipwreck, while "Face to Face" introduces you to some of those who perished when the *Vasa* sunk—with faces that were re-created from skeletal remains. Nearby, you'll see some of the skeletons found in the shipwreck. Those remains have been extensively analyzed, revealing remarkable details about the ages, diets, and general health of the victims.

▲Nordic Museum (Nordiska Museet)

Built to look like a Danish Renaissance palace, this museum offers a fascinating peek at 500 years of traditional Swedish lifestyles. The exhibits insightfully place everyday items into their social/historical context in ways that help you really grasp various chapters of Sweden's past. It's arguably more informative than Skansen. Take time to let the excellent, included audioguide enliven the exhibits.

Cost and Hours: 120 SEK, free Wed Sept-May after 17:00; open daily 9:00-18:00, Sept-May 10:00-17:00 except Wed until

20:00; Djurgårdsvägen 6-16, at Djurgårdsbron, tram #7 from downtown, tel. 08/5195-4770, www.nordiskamuseet.se.

Visiting the Museum: Entering the museum's main hall, you'll be face-to-face with Carl Milles' huge painted-wood statue

of Gustav Vasa, father of modern Sweden. The rest of this floor is usually devoted to temporary exhibits.

Highlights of the permanent collection are on the top two floors. Head up the stairs, or take the elevator just to the left of Gustav. Begin on floor 4 and work your way down.

On **floor 4,** four different exhibits ring the grand atrium. The **"Homes and Interiors"** section displays 400 years of home furnishings, both as individual artifacts and as part of room dioramas. As you travel through this parade of furniture—from dark, heavily draped historical rooms to modern living rooms, and from rustic countryside cottages to aristocratic state bedrooms—you'll learn the subtle meaning behind everyday furniture that we take for granted. For example, the advent of television didn't just change entertainment—it gave people a reason to gather each evening in the living room, which, in turn, became a more-used (and less formal) part of people's homes. You'll learn about the Swedish designers who, in the 1930s, eschewed stiff-backed traditional chairs in favor of sleek perches that merged ergonomics and looks—giving birth to functionalism.

Also on this floor, the **"Folk Art"** section shows off colorfully painted furniture and wood carvings; vibrant traditional costumes; and rustic Bible-story illustrations that adorned the walls of peasants' homes. The **"Sápmi"** exhibit tells the fascinating and often overlooked story of the indigenous Sami people (formerly called "Lapps"), who lived in the northern reaches of Norway, Sweden, Finland, and Russia centuries before Europeans created those modern nations. On display are shoes, ceremonial knives, colorful hats and clothing, and other features of Sami culture.

Floor 3 has several smaller exhibits. The most interesting are **"Table Settings"** (with carefully set tables from the 16th century until about 1950, representing customs and traditions around gathering to share food and drink—from an elegant tea party to a rowdy pub) and **"Traditions"** (showing and describing each old-time celebration of the Swedish year—from Christmas to Midsummer—as well as funerals, confirmations, and other life events).

▲ABBA: The Museum

The Swedish pop group ABBA was, for a time, a bigger business than Volvo. Since bursting on the scene in 1974 by winning the Eurovision Song Contest with "Waterloo," and serenading Sweden's newly minted queen with "Dancing Queen" in 1976, they've sold more than 380 million records, and the musical based on their many hits, *Mamma Mia!*, has been enjoyed by 50 million people. It was only a matter of time before Stockholm opened an ABBA museum, which is conveniently located just across the street from Skansen and next to Gröna Lund amusement park. Like everything ABBA, it is aggressively for-profit and slickly promoted, with the steepest ticket price in town. True to its subject, it's bombastic, glitzy, and highly interactive. If you like ABBA, it's lots of fun; if you love ABBA, it's ▲▲▲ nirvana.

Cost and Hours: 250 SEK—credit cards only, 595 SEK family ticket covers two adults and up to four kids; daily 9:00-19:00, Sept-May 10:00-18:00 except Wed until 19:00, Djurgårdsvägen 68, bus #44 or tram #7 to Liljevalc Gröna Lund stop, tel. 08/1213-2860, www.abbathemuseum.com.

Tours: ABBA aficionados will happily fork over 20 SEK extra for the intimate audioguide, in which Agnetha, Benny, Björn, and Anni-Frid share their memories, in their own words.

Getting In: Only 75 people are let in every 15 minutes with timed-entry tickets. The museum strongly encourages getting tickets in advance from their website or at the TI. In fact, they'll charge you 20 SEK extra per ticket to buy in person (but computer terminals are standing by if you want to "prebook" on the spot). It can be crowded on summer weekends, in which case you may have to wait for a later time.

▲Biking the Garden Island

In all of Stockholm, Djurgården is the most natural place to enjoy a bike ride. There's a good and reasonably priced bike-rental place just over the bridge as you enter the island (Sjöcaféet; see beginning of Djurgården section, earlier), and a world of parklike paths and lanes with harbor vistas to enjoy.

Ask for a free map and route tips when you rent your

bike. Figure about an hour to pedal around Djurgården's waterfront perimeter; it's mostly flat, but with some short, steeper stretches that take you up and over the middle of the island. Those who venture beyond the Skansen park find themselves nearly all alone in the lush and evocative environs.

ON THE OUTSKIRTS

Two worthy sights sit on Stockholm's doorstep: the home and garden of Carl Milles, Sweden's greatest sculptor, and Drottningholm Palace, the summer residence of the Swedish royal family.

▲Millesgården

The villa and garden of Carl Milles is a veritable forest of statues by Sweden's greatest sculptor. Millesgården is dramatically situated on a bluff overlooking the harbor in Stockholm's upper-class suburb of Lidingö. While the art is engaging and enjoyable, even the curators have little to say about it from an interpretive point of view—so your visit is basically without guidance. But in Milles' house, which dates from the 1920s, you can see his north-lit studio and get a sense of his creative genius.

Cost and Hours: 150 SEK; daily 11:00-17:00 except closed Mon Oct-April; English booklet explains the art, restaurant and café, tel. 08/446-7590, www.millesgarden.se.

Getting There: Catch the T-bana to Ropsten, then take bus #207 to within a five-minute walk of the museum; several other #200-series buses get you close enough to walk (allow about 45 minutes total each way).

▲▲Drottningholm Palace (Drottningholms Slott)

The queen's 17th-century summer castle and current royal residence has been called "Sweden's Versailles." It's enjoyable to explore the place where the Swedish royals bunk, and to stroll their expansive gardens. Even more worthwhile is touring the Baroque-era theater on the grounds (itself rated ▲▲), which preserves 18th-century stage sets and rare special-effects machinery.

Cost and Hours: 130 SEK, combo-ticket with Chinese Pavilion-190 SEK; May-Sept daily 10:00-16:30, April until 15:30, rest of year open weekends only—see website for hours, closed last two weeks of Dec; tel. 08/402-6280, www.kungahuset.se.

Tours: You can explore the palace on your own, but with sparse posted explanations and no audioguide, it's worth taking a guided tour (offered daily, usually at 10:00, 12:00, 14:00, and 16:00; fewer tours Oct-May).

Services: The gift shop/café at the entrance to the grounds (near the boat dock and bus stop) acts as a visitors center; Drottningholm's only WCs are in the adjacent building. A handy Pressbyrån convenience store is also nearby (snacks, drinks, and transit tickets), and taxis are usually standing by.

Getting There: Drottingham is an easy boat or subway-plus-bus ride from downtown Stockholm. Consider approaching by water (as the royals traditionally did) and then returning by bus and subway (as a commoner). If your heart is set on touring the palace interior, check the website before you go: It can close unexpectedly for various events.

Boats depart regularly from the Klara Malarstrand pier just across from City Hall for the relaxing hour-long trip (160 SEK one-way, 210 SEK round-trip, on the hour daily, likely additional departures at :30 past the hour on weekends or any day in July-Aug, fewer departures Sept-April, tel. 08/1200-4000, www.stromma. se). The pier is a five-minute walk from the central train station (on Vasagatan, walk toward the water, staying to the right and crossing a plaza under the freeway to reach the pier). It's worth reserving a spot in advance on weekends, or if your day plan requires a particular departure.

It's faster (30-45 minutes total) to take **public transit:** Ride the T-bana about 20 minutes to Brommaplan, where you can catch any #300-series bus for the five-minute ride to Drottningholm (as you leave the Brommaplan station, check monitors to see which bus is leaving next—usually from platform A, E, or F).

Visiting Drottningholm Palace: Ascend the grand staircase (decorated with faux marble and relief-illusion paintings) and buy your ticket on the first floor. Entering the state rooms on the **first floor,** admire the craftsmanship of the walls, with gold leaf shimmering on expertly tooled leather. Then pass through the Green Cabinet and hook right into Hedvig Eleonora's State Bed Chambers. The richly colored Baroque decor here, with gold embellishments, is representative of what the entire interior once looked like. Hedvig Eleonora was a "dowager queen," meaning that she was the widow of a king—her husband, King Karl X, died young at age 24—after they had been married just six years. Looking around the room, you'll see symbolism of this tragic separation. For example, in the ceiling painting, Hedvig Eleonora rides a cloud, with hands joined below her—suggesting that she will be reunited with her beloved in heaven.

This room was also the residence of a later monarch, Gustav III. That's why it looks like (and was) more of a theater than a place for sleeping. In the style of the French monarchs, this is where the ceremonial tucking-in and dressing of the king would take place.

Backtrack into the golden room, then continue down the other hallway. You'll pass through a room of royal portraits with very consistent characteristics: pale skin with red cheeks; a high forehead with gray hair (suggesting wisdom); and big eyes (windows to the soul). At the end of the hall is a grand library, which once held some 7,000 books. The small adjoining room is filled by a large model of a temple in Pompeii; Gustav III—who ordered this built—was fascinated by archaeology, and still today, there's a museum of antiquities named for him at the Royal Palace in Stockholm.

On the **second floor,** as you enter the first room, notice the faux doors, painted on the walls to create symmetry, and the hidden doors for servants (who would scurry—unseen and unheard—through the walls to attend to the royal family). In the Blue Drawing Room is a bust of the then-king's cousin, Catherine the Great. This Russian monarch gave him—in the next room, the Chinese Drawing Room—the (made-in-Russia) faux "Chinese" stove. This dates from a time when exotic imports from China (tea, silk, ivory, Kung Pao chicken) were exciting and new. (Around the same time, in the mid-18th century, the royals built the Chinese Pavilion on Drottningholm's grounds.) The Gobelins tapestries in this room were also a gift, from France's King Louis XVI. In the next room, the darker Oskar Room, are more tapestries—these a gift from England's King Charles I. (Sensing a trend?) You'll pass through Karl XI's Gallery (overlooking the grand staircase)—which is still used for royal functions—and into the largest room on this floor, the Hall of State. The site of royal weddings and receptions, this room boasts life-size paintings of very important Swedes in golden frames and a bombastically painted ceiling.

Drottningholm Court Theater

This 18th-century theater (Drottningholms Slottsteater) has miraculously survived the ages—complete with its instruments, original stage sets, and hand-operated sound-effects machines for wind, thunder, and clouds. The required guided tour is short (30 minutes), entertaining, and informative—I found it more enjoyable than the palace tour.

Cost and Hours: 100 SEK for 30-minute guided tour—buy tickets in the theater shop next door, English tours about hourly May-Aug 11:00-16:30, Sept 12:00-15:30—these are first and last tour times, limited tours possible on weekends in April and Oct-Dec, no tours Jan-March.

Shopping in Stockholm

Sweden offers a world of shopping temptations. Smaller stores are open weekdays 10:00-18:00, Saturdays until 17:00, and Sundays 11:00-16:00. Some of the bigger stores (such as NK, H&M, and Åhléns) are open later on Saturdays and Sundays.

Fun Chain Stores

DesignTorget, dedicated to contemporary Swedish design, receives a commission for selling the unique works of local designers (generally Mon-Fri 10:00-19:00, Sat until 18:00, Sun 11:00-17:00, big branch underneath Sergels Torg—enter from basement level of Kulturhuset, there are other branches around town and at the airport, www.designtorget.se).

Systembolaget is Sweden's state-run liquor store chain. A sample of each bottle of wine or liquor sits in a display case, and a card in front explains how it tastes and suggests menu pairings. Look for the item number and order at the counter. Branches are in Hötorget underneath the movie theater complex, in Norrmalm at Vasagatan 21, and just up from Östermalmstorgat Nybrogatan 47 (Mon-Wed 10:00-18:00, Thu-Fri until 19:00, Sat until 15:00, closed Sun, www.systembolaget.se).

Gudrun Sjödén is named for its fashion-designer founder, whose life's work has been creating cheery, functional clothing for Swedish women. Some might sniff at her sensible but colorful designs (some inspired by her summer garden), but they're free-spirited in a Pippi Longstocking sort of way (think aubergine and sunflower). You'll love it or hate it—all around town (at Regeringsgatan 30, Götgatan 44, and Stora Nygatan 33, daily 10:00-19:00, Sat until 17:00, Sun 12:00-16:00, www.gudrunsjoden.com).

Hamngatan

The main shopping zone between Kungsträdgården and Sergels Torg (described in "Stockholm's Modern City Walk," earlier) has plenty of huge department stores. At the top of Kungsträdgården, **Illums Bolighus** is a Danish design shop. Across the street, **Nordiska Kompaniet** (NK) is elegant and stately; the Swedish design (downstairs) and kitchenware sections are particularly impressive. The classy **Gallerian** mall is just up the street from NK and stretches seductively nearly to Sergels Torg. The **Åhléns** store, kitty-corner across Sergels Torg, is less expensive than NK and has two cafeterias and a supermarket. Affordable clothing chain **H&M** has a store right across the street. Tucked behind Åhléns is **Kartbutiken,** a handy map-and-guidebook shop that covers all of Sweden, Scandinavia, and beyond (daily, at Mäster Samuelsgatan 54).

Mood Stockholm

The city's most exclusive mall is a downtown block filled with big-name Swedish and international designers, plus a pricey food court and restaurants. The upscale decor and mellow music give it a Beverly Hills vibe (Mon-Fri 10:00-20:00, Sat until 18:00, Sun 11:00-17:00, Regeringsgatan 48). The mall anchors a ritzy, pedestrianized shopping zone; for more exclusive shops, browse the nearby streets Jakobsbergsgatan and Biblioteksgatan.

Södermalm

When Swedes want the latest items by local designers, they skip the downtown malls and head for funky Södermalm. **Götgatan,** the main drag that leads from Slussen up to this neighborhood, is a particularly good choice, with shop after shop of mostly Swedish designers. Boutiques along here—some of them one-offs, others belonging to Swedish chains—include Weekday (known for denim), Filippa K (high-end attire), and Tiogruppen (colorful bags and fabrics). More intrepid shoppers will want to explore the area south of **Folkungagatan**—"SoFo," where scores of fun stores feature new and vintage clothing, housewares, and jewelry in the streets surrounding Nytorget.

Nybrogatan

This short and pleasant traffic-free street, which connects Östermalmstorg with the Nybroplan waterfront, is lined with small branches of interesting design shops, including Nordiska Galleriet (eye-catching modern furniture, at #11). It also has shoe and handbag stores, and an enticing cheese shop and bakery.

Flea Markets

For a *smörgåsbord* of Scanjunk, visit the **Loppmarknaden,** northern Europe's biggest flea market, at Vårberg Center (free entry weekdays and Sat-Sun after 15:00, 10-15 ISK on weekends—when it's busiest; Mon-Fri 11:00-18:00; Sat 10:30-16:00, Sun from 11:00; T-bana: Vårberg, tel. 08/710-0060, www.loppmarknaden.se). Hötorget, the produce market, also hosts a Sunday flea market in summer (see "Eating in Stockholm," later).

Eating in Stockholm

At lunch, cafés and restaurants have daily specials called *dagens rätt* (generally Mon-Fri only). Most museums have handy cafés with lunch deals and often with fine views. Convenience stores stock surprisingly fresh takeaway food. As anywhere, department stores and malls are eager to feed shoppers and can be a good, efficient choice. If you want culturally appropriate fast food, stop by a local hot dog stand. Picnics are a great option; there are plenty of park-

---

Restaurant Code

I've assigned each eatery a price category, based on the average cost of a typical main course. Drinks, desserts, and splurge items (steak and seafood) can raise the price considerably.

$$$$	**Splurge:** Most main courses over 200 SEK
$$$	**Pricier:** 150-200 SEK
$$	**Moderate:** 100-150 SEK
$	**Budget:** Under 100 SEK

In Sweden, a hot dog stand or other takeout spot is **$**; a sit-down café is **$$**; a casual but more upscale restaurant is **$$$**; and a swanky splurge is **$$$$**.

---

like, harborside spots to give your cheap picnic some class. I've also listed a few splurges—destination restaurants that offer a good sample of modern Swedish cooking.

IN GAMLA STAN

Most restaurants in Gamla Stan serve a weekday lunch special. Several popular places are right on the main square (Stortorget) and near the cathedral. Järntorget,
at the far end, is another fun tables-in-the-square scene. Touristy places line Västerlånggatan. You'll find more romantic spots hiding on side lanes, such as the stretch of Österlånggatan that hides below Köpmantorget square (where St. George is slaying the dragon). I've listed my favorites below (for locations, see the "Gamla Stan Hotels & Restaurants" map).

$$ Grillska Huset is a cheap and handy cafeteria run by Stockholms Stadsmission, a charitable organization helping the poor. It's grandly situated right on the old square, with indoor and outdoor seating (tranquil garden up the stairs and out back), fine daily specials, a hearty salad bar, and a staff committed to helping others. You can feed the hungry (that's you) and help house the homeless at the same time (daily 10:00-21:00 except Sun-Mon until 20:00, Stortorget 3, tel. 08/787-8605). They also have a fine little bakery *(brödbutik)* with lots of tempting cakes and pastries (closed Sun).

$$$$ Kryp In, a small, cozy restaurant (the name means "hide away") tucked into a peaceful lane, has a stylish hardwood and candlelit interior, great sidewalk seating, and an open kitchen letting you in on Vladimir's artistry. It's gourmet without pre-

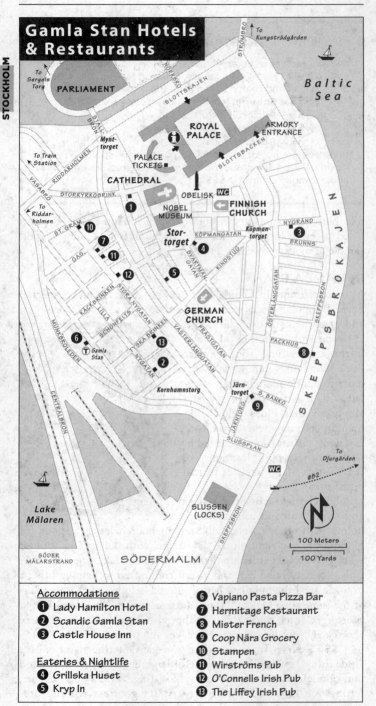

Gamla Stan Hotels & Restaurants

Accommodations
1. Lady Hamilton Hotel
2. Scandic Gamla Stan
3. Castle House Inn

Eateries & Nightlife
4. Grillska Huset
5. Kryp In
6. Vapiano Pasta Pizza Bar
7. Hermitage Restaurant
8. Mister French
9. Coop Nära Grocery
10. Stampen
11. Wirströms Pub
12. O'Connells Irish Pub
13. The Liffey Irish Pub

tense. They serve delicious, modern Swedish cuisine with a 455-SEK three-course dinner. In the good-weather months, they serve weekend lunches, with specials starting at 120 SEK. Reserve ahead for dinner (275-290-SEK plates, daily 17:00-23:00, lunch Sat-Sun 12:00-16:00, a block off Stortorget at Prästgatan 17, tel. 08/208-841, www.restaurangkrypin.se).

$$ Vapiano Pasta Pizza Bar, a bright, high-energy, family-oriented eatery, issues you a smart card as you enter. Circulate to the different stations, ordering up whatever you like as they swipe your card. Portions are huge and easily splittable. As you leave, your card indicates the bill. Add flavor by picking a leaf of basil or rosemary from the potted plant on your table (daily 11:00-24:00, next to entrance to Gamla Stan T-bana station, Munkbrogatan 8, tel. 08/222-940). They also have locations on Östermalm (facing Humlegården park at Sturegatan 12) and Norrmalm (between the train station and Kungsholmen at Kungsbron 15)—for these locations, see the "Stockholm Hotels & Restaurants" map.

$$ Hermitage Restaurant is a faded, hippie-feeling joint that serves a decent vegetarian buffet in a communal dining setting (Mon-Fri 11:00-21:00, Sat-Sun from 12:00, Stora Nygatan 11, tel. 08/411-9500).

Picnic Supplies: The handy and affordable **Coop Nära** mini-market is strategically located on Järntorget, at the Slussen end of Gamla Stan; the **Munkbrohallen** supermarket downstairs in the Gamla Stan T-bana station is also very picnic-friendly (both long hours daily).

DINING ON THE WATER

In Gamla Stan: Sprawling along the harbor embankment, **$$$$ Mister French** faces a gorgeous Stockholm panorama—the main reason to eat here. The entire place opens up to the outdoors in good weather: Choose between the stylish bar (simple bar food), the full restaurant (French cuisine), or—my favorite—the lounge with comfy sofas (daily 11:30-24:00, smart to reserve ahead in good weather, Tullhus 2, tel. 08/202-095, www.mrfrench.se).

In Kungsholmen, Behind City Hall: On a balmy summer's eve, **$$$ Mälarpaviljongen** is a dreamy spot with hundreds of locals enjoying the perfect lakefront scene, as twinkling glasses of rosé shine like convivial lanterns. From City Hall, walk 15 minutes along Lake Mälaren (a treat in itself) to find a hundred casual outdoor tables floating on pontoons and scattered among the trees on shore. When it's cool, they have heaters and blankets (open in good weather April-Sept daily 11:00-late, easy lakeside walk or T-bana to Fridhemsplan plus a 5-minute walk to Nörr Mälarstrand 63, see the "Stockholm Hotels & Restaurants" map for location, no reservations, tel. 08/650-8701).

In Djurgården: Just over the Djurgårdsbron bridge, **$$-$$$ Sjöcaféet** is beautifully situated and greedily soaking up the afternoon sun, filling a woody terrace stretching along the harbor. In summer, this is a fine place for a meal or just a drink before or after your Skansen or *Vasa* visit. They have affordable lunch plates (Mon-Fri 11:00-13:00 only); after 14:00, you'll pay a bit more (order at the bar, daily 8:00-20:00, often later in summer, closed off-season, bike and boat rentals, tel. 08/661-4488). For the location of this and the next restaurant, see the "Stockholm's Djurgården" map, earlier.

$$$$ Oaxen Slip Bistro, a trendy harborfront place 200 yards below the main Skansen gate, serves creative Nordic cuisine with sturdy local ingredients in a sleek interior or on its delightfully woody terrace. Overlooking a canal in what feels like an old shipyard, and filled with in-the-know locals, this place is a real treat. Reservations are smart (daily 12:00-14:00 & 17:00-21:30, Beckholmsvägen 26, tel. 08/5515-3105, www.oaxen.com).

SÖDERMALM STREETS AND EATS

This quickly gentrifying district, just south of Gamla Stan (steeply uphill from Slussen), has some of Stockholm's most enticing food options—especially for beer lovers. It's a bit less swanky, and therefore more affordable, than some of the city's more touristy neighborhoods.

Götgatan and Medborgarplatsen

The neighborhood's liveliest street is Götgatan, which leads from Slussen steeply up into the heart of Södermalm. Here, mixed between the boutiques, you'll find cafés tempting you to join Swedish *fika* (coffee break), plus plenty of other eateries. Even if you don't dine in Södermalm, it's worth a stroll here just for the window-shopping fun.

At the top of the street, you'll pop out into the big square called Medborgarplatsen (you can also ride the T-bana right to this square). This neighborhood hangout is a great scene, with almost no tourists and lots of options—especially for Swedish fast food. Outdoor restaurant and café tables fill the square, which is fronted by a big food hall. The recommended Kvarnen beer hall is just around the corner (see later).

$$ Melanders Fisk, inside the Söderhallarna food hall, offers table service inside or takeaway from their deli counter—but come in good weather and you can enjoy your meal outside on the square. *Skagenröra*, shrimp with mayo on toast or filling a baked potato, is the signature dish—and dear to the Swedish heart. There's also a wine bar that stays open until 22:00 (food served Mon-Sat from

11:00 until at least 15:00, some nights as late as 20:00, Medborgar-platsen 3, tel. 08/644-4040).

Skånegatan and Nytorget

A bit farther south, these cross-streets make another good spot to browse among fun and enticing restaurants, particularly for ethnic cuisine.

$$$ Urban Deli Nytorget is half fancy artisanal delicatessen—with all manner of ingredients—and half white-subway-tile-trendy eatery, with indoor and outdoor tables filled with Stockholmers eating well. If it's busy—as it often is—they'll scrawl your name at the bottom of the long butcher-paper waiting list (no reservations). If it's full, you can grab a place at the bar and eat there—or shop in the attached upscale grocery (lots of creative boxed meals and salads to go) and picnic in the park across the street (daily 7:00-23:00, at the far end of Skånegatan at Nytorget 4, tel. 08/5990-9180). Another branch is near Hörtorget at Sveavägen 44.

Classic Swedish Beer Halls: Two different but equally traditional Södermalm beer halls serve well-executed, hearty Swedish grub in big, high-ceilinged, orange-tiled spaces with rustic wooden tables.

$$$ Kvarnen ("The Mill") is a reliable choice with a 1908 ambience. As it's the home bar for the supporters of a football club, it can be rough. Pick a classic Swedish dish from their fun and easy menu (Mon-Fri 11:00-late, Sat-Sun from 12:00, Tjärhovsgatan 4, tel. 08/643-0380).

$$$$ Pelikan, an old-school beer hall, is less sloppy and has nicer food, including meatballs as big as golf balls. It's a bit deeper into Södermalm (Mon-Thu 16:00-24:00, Fri-Sun from 12:00, Blekingegatan 40, tel. 08/5560-9290).

$$$ Akkurat has a staggering variety of microbrews—both Swedish and international (on tap and bottled)—as well as whisky. It's great if you wish you were in England with a bunch of Swedes (short pub-grub menu, daily 15:00-24:00 except Fri from 11:00 and Sun from 18:00, Hornsgatan 18, tel. 08/644-0015).

IN NORRMALM
At or near the Grand Hotel

$$$S Royal Smörgåsbord: To stuff yourself with all the traditional Swedish specialties (a dozen kinds of herring, salmon, reindeer, meatballs, lingonberries, and shrimp, followed by a fine table of cheeses and desserts) with a super harbor view, consider splurging at the Grand Hotel's dressy **Veranda Restaurant.** While very touristy, this is considered the finest *smörgåsbord* in town. The Grand Hotel, where royal guests and Nobel Prize winners stay, faces the harbor across from the palace. Pick up their English flier

STOCKHOLM

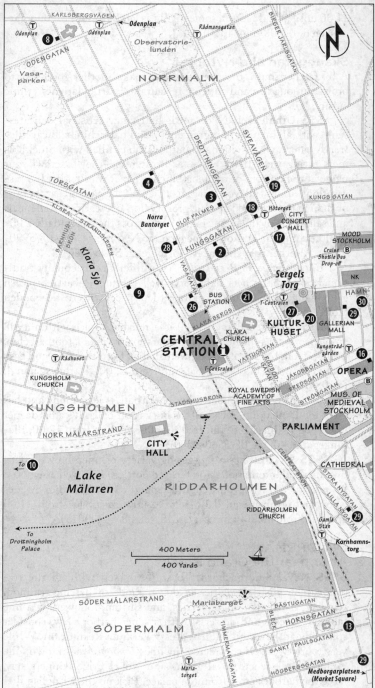

Stockholm Hotels & Restaurants

Accommodations

1 Freys Hotel
2 Scandic No. 53
3 Queen's Hotel
4 Hotel Bema
5 Hotel Wellington
6 Story Hotel Stureplan
7 Hotel Riddargatan
8 Ibis Styles Stockholm Odenplan

Eateries

9 Vapiano Pasta Pizza Bar (2)
10 To Mälarpaviljongen
11 To Södermalm & Skånegatan Eateries; Pelikan Beer Hall
12 Kvarnen Beer Hall
13 Akkurat Beer Hall
14 Veranda Restaurant
15 Restaurang B.A.R.
16 Bakfickan
17 Hötorgshallen, Kajsas Fisk & Systembolaget Liquor Store
18 Kungshallen Food Court
19 Urban Deli
20 Cafeteria Panorama
21 Åhléns Dep't Store & Grocery
22 Saluhall
23 Restaurang Volt
24 Riche
25 Sushi Yama Express
26 Icebar Stockholm

Shopping

27 DesignTorget
28 Systembolaget Liquor Store (2)
29 Gudrun Sjödén (3)
30 Illums Bolighus Design Shop

for a good explanation of the proper way to enjoy this grand buffet. Reservations are often necessary (545 SEK in evening, less at lunch, drinks extra, open nightly 18:00-22:00, also open for lunch Sat-Sun 13:00-16:00 year-round and Mon-Fri 12:00-15:00 in May-Sept, no shorts after 18:00, Södra Blasieholmshamnen 8, tel. 08/679-3586, www.grandhotel.se).

$$$$ Restaurang B.A.R. has a noisy, fun energy, with diners surveying meat and fish at the ice-filled counter, talking things over with the chef, and then choosing a slab or filet. Prices are on the board, and everything's grilled (Mon-Fri 11:30-14:00 & 17:00 until late, Sat 16:00-late, closed Sun, behind the Grand Hotel at Blasieholmsgatan 4, tel. 08/611-5335). They also have a nice (short and lower-priced) takeaway menu.

At the Royal Opera House

The Operakällaren, one of Stockholm's most exclusive restaurants, runs a little "hip pocket" restaurant called **$$$ Bakfickan,** specializing in traditional Swedish quality cooking at reasonable prices. Choose from two different daily specials or order from their regular menu. Sit inside—at tiny private side tables or at the big counter with the locals—or, in good weather, grab a table on the sidewalk, facing a cheery red church (Mon-Thu 11:30-22:00, Fri-Sat until 23:00, Sun 12:00-17:00, on the inland side of Royal Opera House, tel. 08/676-5809).

At or near Hötorget

Hötorget ("Hay Market"), a vibrant outdoor produce market just two blocks from Sergels Torg, is a fun place to picnic-shop. The outdoor market closes at 18:00, and many merchants put their unsold produce on the push list (earlier closing and more desperate merchants on Sat).

Hötorgshallen, next to Hötorget (in the basement under the modern cinema complex), is a colorful indoor food market with an old-fashioned bustle, plenty of exotic and ethnic edibles, and—in the tradition of food markets all over Europe—some great little eateries (Mon-Fri 10:00-18:00, Sat until 16:00, closed Sun). The best is **$$ Kajsas Fisk,** hiding behind the fish stalls. They serve delicious fish soup to little Olivers who can hardly believe they're getting…more. For 110 SEK, you get a big bowl of hearty soup, a simple salad, bread and crackers—plus one soup refill. Their *stekt strömming* (traditional fried herring and potato dish) is a favorite (Mon-Thu 11:00-18:00, Fri until 19:00, Sat until 16:00, closed Sun, Hötorgshallen 3, tel. 08/207-262). There's a great kebab and falafel place a few stalls away.

$ Kungshallen, an 800-seat indoor food court across the square from Hötorget, has more than a dozen basic eateries. What it lacks in ambience it makes up for in variety, quick service, and generally lower prices. The main floor has sit-down places, while the basement is a shopping-mall-style array of fast-food counters (daily 11:00-22:00). Just a few blocks away is a branch of **Urban Deli** (at Sveavägen 44), a good takeaway option described earlier under "Skånegatan and Nytorget."

Near Sergels Torg

Kulturhuset: Handy for a simple meal with great city views, **$$ Cafeteria Panorama** offers cheap eats and a salad bar, inside and outside seating, and jaw-dropping vistas (90-SEK lunch specials with salad bar, Mon-Fri 11:00-19:00, Sat until 18:00, Sun until 17:00).

The many modern shopping malls and department stores around Sergels Torg all have appealing, if pricey, eateries catering to the needs of hungry local shoppers. **Åhléns** department store has a Hemköp supermarket in the basement (daily until 21:00) and two restaurants upstairs with 80-110-SEK daily lunch specials (Mon-Fri 11:00-19:30, Sat until 18:30, Sun until 17:30).

IN ÖSTERMALM

$$$ Saluhall, on Östermalmstorg (near recommended Hotel Wellington), is a great old-time indoor market dating from 1888. While it's nowhere near "cheap," it's one of the most pleasant market halls I've seen, oozing with upscale yet traditional Swedish class. Inside you'll find Middle Eastern fare, sushi, classic Scandinavian open-face sandwiches, seafood salads, healthy wraps, cheese counters, designer chocolates, gourmet coffee stands, and a pair of classic old sit-down eateries (Elmqvist and Tysta Mari). This is your chance to pull up a stool at a lunch counter next to well-heeled Swedes (Mon-Fri 9:30-19:00, Sat until 16:00, closed Sun).

$$$$ Restaurang Volt is a destination restaurant for those looking to splurge on "New Nordic" cooking: fresh, locally sourced ingredients fused into bold new recipes with fundamentally Swedish flavors. Owners Fredrik Johnsson and Peter Andersson fill their minimalist black dining room with just 31 seats, so reservations are essential (no a la carte, choose from 4- or 6-course tasting menus, Tue-Sat 18:00-24:00, closed Sun-Mon, Kommendörsgatan 16, tel. 08/662-3400, www.restaurangvolt.se).

$$$$ Riche, a Parisian-style brasserie just a few steps off Nybroplan at Östermalm's waterfront, is a high-energy place with a youthful sophistication. They serve up pricey but nicely executed Swedish and international dishes in their winter garden, bright dining room, and white-tile-and-wine-glass-chandeliered bar (Mon-Fri 7:30-24:00, Sat-Sun from 11:00, Birger Jarlsgatan 4, tel. 08/5450-3560).

$$ Sushi Yama Express is a quick and tasty option for take-away sushi, sashimi, and rolls (Mon-Fri 10:00-20:00, closed Sat-Sun, at Nybrogatan 18, tel. 08/202-031).

Starting or Ending Your Cruise in Stockholm

If your cruise begins and/or ends in Stockholm, you'll want some extra time here. While you can squeeze the city into a day, two days will let you see more. For a longer visit, pick up my *Rick Steves Snapshot Stockholm* or *Rick Steves Scandinavia* guidebooks.

Airport Connections

ARLANDA AIRPORT
Stockholm's Arlanda Airport is 28 miles north of town (airport code: ARN, tel. 08/797-6000, www.arlanda.se).

Getting Downtown from Arlanda Airport
The **Arlanda Express train** is the fastest way to zip between the airport and the central train station. Traveling most of the way at 125 mph, it gets you downtown in just 20 minutes—but it's not cheap (280 SEK one-way, 540 SEK round-trip, free for kids under 17 with adult, covered by rail pass; generally 4-6/hour; tel. 0771/720-200, www.arlandaexpress.com). Buy your ticket either at the window near the track or from a ticket machine, or pay an extra 100 SEK to buy it on board. It's worth checking the website for advance-purchase discounts and two-for-one weekend specials.

Airport shuttle buses (Flygbussarna) run between the airport and Stockholm's train/bus stations (119 SEK, 6/hour, 45 minutes, may take longer at rush hour; buy tickets online—cheapest, from station kiosks, or from 7-Eleven and Pressbyrån convenience stores at the airport and train/bus station, www.flygbussarna.se).

Taxis between the airport and the city center take 30-40 minutes (about 675 SEK, but look for price posted on side of cab). Establish the price first. Most taxis prefer credit cards.

The **cheapest airport connection** is to take bus #583 from the airport to Märsta, then switch to the *pendeltåg* #36 (suburban train, 4-5/hour), which goes to Stockholm's central train station (86 SEK, 1 hour total journey time).

Getting to Frihamnen Cruise Port

When meeting your cruise at this sprawling port, it helps to know which berth your ship leaves from—berth 650, 634, or 638.

The easiest but most expensive way to reach your cruise ship is by **taxi**—figure about 675 SEK from the airport to Frihamnen, or around 300 SEK from downtown.

Public transportation is workable (and often cheaper), but there's no direct connection from the airport. First make your way downtown using one of the methods outlined above; then catch the bus to the port: Ride bus #1 from the train station, or bus #76 from various points downtown. For more on these buses, see "Port Overview" at the beginning of this chapter.

Arriving at Frihamnen: Near the cruise terminals, there are two stops: Both buses stop at "Frihamnen" (near berth 650), while bus #76 continues one more stop to "Frihamnens Färjeterminal" (closer to berths 634 and 638). A blue line painted on the sidewalk leads to each of the three berths.

If getting off at the "Frihamnen" stop, continue straight ahead along the street to the first intersection, where you'll bear right to reach berth 650 and left to reach berth 634 or 638.

If you get off the bus at "Frihamnens Färjeterminal," proceed straight until you reach the Frihamnsterminalen; turn right just before it and head out the long, wide pier—first passing berth 634, then berth 638.

ALTERNATE AIRPORT

Some discount airlines use Skavsta Airport, about 60 miles south of Stockholm (code: NYO, www.skavsta.se). Flygbussarna shuttle buses connect to the city (159 SEK, cheaper online, 1-2/hour, 80 minutes—but allow extra time for traffic, www.flygbussarna.se).

Hotels in Stockholm

$$$$ = Most rooms over 2,000 SEK; $$$ = 1,500-2,000 SEK; $$ = 1,000-1,500 SEK; $ = 500-1,500 SEK; ¢ = Under 500 SEK

Between business travelers and the tourist trade, occupancy for Stockholm's hotels is healthy but unpredictable, and most hotels' rates vary from day to day with demand.

NEAR THE TRAIN STATION

$$$$ Freys Hotel is a Scan-mod, four-star place, with 127 compact, smartly designed rooms. It's well-situated for train travelers, located on a dead-end pedestrian street across from the central station. While big, it works hard to be friendly and welcoming. Its cool, candlelit breakfast room becomes a bar in the evening, popular for its Belgian microbrews (air-con, Bryggargatan 12, tel. 08/5062-1300, www.freyshotels.com, freys@freyshotels.com).

$$$$ Scandic No. 53 injects modernity into a classic old building a few blocks from the station. The 274 rooms are small and functional (no desk or chair in standard rooms) but comfortable. Everything surrounds a stylish, glassy atrium boasting a lounge/restaurant (live music until 24:00 most weekends), and a peaceful outdoor courtyard (air-con, elevator, Kungsgatan 53, tel. 08/5173-6500, www.scandichotels.com, no53@scandichotels.com).

$$ Queen's Hotel enjoys a great location at the quiet top end of Stockholm's main pedestrian shopping street (about a 10-minute walk from the train station, or 25 minutes from Gamla Stan). The 59 rooms are well worn, but they're generally spacious and have big windows—and it's reasonably priced. Rooms facing the courtyard are quieter (RS%—if booking online enter rate code "RICKS", elevator, Drottninggatan 71A, tel. 08/249-460, www.queenshotel.se, info@queenshotel.se).

$$ Hotel Bema, a bit farther from the center, is a humble place that rents 12 fine rooms for some of the best prices in town (breakfast served at nearby café, reception open Mon-Fri 8:30-17:00, Sat-Sun 9:00-15:00, bus #65 from station to Upplandsgatan 13—near the top of the Drottninggatan pedestrian street, or walk about 15 minutes from the train station—exit toward *Vasagatan* and head straight up that street, tel. 08/232-675, www.hotelbema.se, info@hotelbema.se).

IN ÖSTERMALM

$$$$ Hotel Wellington, two blocks off Östermalmstorg, is in a charming part of town and convenient to the harbor and Djurgården. It's modern and bright, with hardwood floors, 60 rooms, and a friendly welcome. While pricey, it's a cut above in comfort, and its great amenities—such as a very generous buffet breakfast, free coffee all day, and free buffet dinner—add up to a good value (RS%, free sauna, lobby bar, garden terrace, T-bana: Östermalmstorg, exit to Storgatan and walk past big church to Storgatan 6; tel. 08/667-0910, www.wellington.se, cc.wellington@choice.se).

$$$$ Story Hotel Stureplan is a colorful boutique hotel with a creative vibe. Conveniently located near a trendy dining zone between Östermalmstorg and the Nybroplan waterfront, it has 83 rooms above a sprawling, cleverly decorated, affordably priced restaurant. You'll book online, check yourself in at the kiosk, and receive a text message with your door key code (elevator, free minibar drinks, Riddargatan 6, tel. 08/5450-3940, www.storyhotels.com).

$$$ Hotel Riddargatan is well located on the edge of Östermalm—near the restaurants and shops on Nybrogatan and just two blocks from Nybroplan and the harbor. The front-desk staff is friendly, and the 78 rooms, while smallish, are nicely Scan-modern and perfectly functional. This is a hopping neighborhood: Ask for a quiet room when you book (elevator—but you'll climb a few steps to reception, bar/lounge, Riddargatan 14, tel. 08/5557-3000, www.profilhotels.se, hotelriddargatan@profilhotels.se).

$$$ Ibis Styles Stockholm Odenplan rents 76 cookie-cutter rooms on several floors of a late-19th-century apartment building (T-bana: Odenplan, Västmannagatan 61, reservation tel. 08/1209-0000, reception tel. 08/1209-0300, www.ibis.com, odenplan@uniquehotels.se).

IN GAMLA STAN

For locations, see the "Gamla Stan Hotels & Restaurants" map.

$$$$ Lady Hamilton Hotel, classic and romantic, is shoe-horned into Gamla Stan on a quiet street a block below the cathedral and Royal Palace. The centuries-old building has 34 small but plush and colorfully decorated rooms. Each is named for a Swedish flower and is filled with antiques (elevator, Storkyrkobrinken 5, tel. 08/5064-0100, www.ladyhamiltonhotel.se, info@ladyhamiltonhotel.se).

$$$ Scandic Gamla Stan offers Old World elegance in the heart of Gamla Stan (a 5-minute walk from Gamla Stan T-bana station). Its 52 nicely decorated, smallish rooms have cheery wallpaper and hardwood floors (elevator, sauna, Nygatan 25, tel. 08/723-7250, www.scandichotels.com, gamlastan@scandichotels.com).

¢-$$ Castle House Inn is an Ikea-modern hostel/hotel situated in an ancient building that's located in an untrampled part of Gamla Stan, just a few steps off the harbor. The 53 whitewashed rooms are a mix of singles, mixed dorms, standard doubles, and family-friendly quads (breakfast extra, elevator, check-in 15:00-21:30, Brunnsgränd 4, tel. 08/551-5526, www.castlehouse.se, info@castlehouse.se.

Entertainment in Stockholm

Bars and Live Music in Gamla Stan

The street called Stora Nygatan, with several lively bars, has perhaps the most accessible and reliable place for live jazz in town: **Stampen.** It has two venues under one roof: a stone-vaulted cellar below (called Geronimo's FGT) and a fun-loving saloon-like jazz

---

What If I Miss My Ship?

Remember that you can get help from the cruise line's port agent (listed on the destination information sheet distributed on the ship) and the local TI.

Many cruise port cities are accessible by train and bus from Stockholm, including **Oslo** and **Copenhagen.** For points in Norway (such as **Bergen, Stavanger,** or **Flåm**), you'll take the train to Oslo and connect from there. For points south (such as **Warnemünde/Berlin, Amsterdam,** and **Gdańsk**), you'll find it faster (and cheaper) to fly (check www.skyscanner.com). Stockholm's Arlanda Airport is an easy train ride from downtown; for more on the airport, see "Starting or Ending Your Cruise in Stockholm," earlier.

Stockholm is a hub for overnight boats on the Baltic. From here, you can sail overnight to **Helsinki** (two companies: Viking Line, tel. 08/452-4200, www.vikingline.fi; or Tallink Silja, tel. 08/440-5990, www.tallinksilja.com), to **Tallinn** (Tallink Silja), to **Riga** (Tallink Silja), and—in two nights—to **St. Petersburg** (St. Peter Line, www.stpeterline.com). It's faster to reach St. Petersburg by taking the night boat first to Helsinki, then hopping on the express train (www.vr.fi). But you'll need a visa to enter Russia (arranged well in advance of your trip, not possible at the last minute); if you don't have one, you'll likely need to meet your ship at a later port of call, or take the St. Peter Line and do a guided excursion, which allows up to 72 hours in St. Petersburg visa-free.

For more advice on what to do if you miss the boat, see page 130 .

---

and R&B bar upstairs (check out the old instruments and antiques hanging from the ceiling). There's live music every night that Stampen is open (cover Fri-Sat only; Tue-Fri and Sun 17:00-late, Sat from 14:00, closed Mon, Stora Gråmunkegränd 7, tel. 08/205-793, www.stampen.se). Geronimo's, downstairs, is more of a nightclub/concert venue with a menu inspired by the American Southwest (Tue-Sun 17:00 until late, enter at Stora Nygatan 5). For locations, see the "Gamla Stan Hotels & Restaurants" map.

Several other lively spots are within a couple of blocks of Stampen on Stora Nygatan. Your options include **Wirströms Pub** (live blues bands play in crowded cellar Mon-Sat 21:00-24:00, no cover; daily 11:00-late, Stora Nygatan 13, www.wirstromspub.se); **O'Connells Irish Pub** (a lively expat sports bar with music—usually Tue-Sat at 21:00; Mon-Sat 11:00-late, Sun from 12:00, Stora Nygatan 21, www.oconnells.se); and **The Liffey** (classic Irish pub with 150-180-SEK pub grub, live music Wed-Sun from 21:30; daily 12:00-late, Stora Nygatan 40-42, www.theliffey.se).

Icebar Stockholm

If you just want to put on a heavy coat and gloves and drink a fancy vodka in a modern-day igloo, consider the fun, if touristy, Icebar Stockholm. Everything's ice—shipped down from Sweden's far north. The bar, the glasses, even the tip jar are made of ice. You get your choice of vodka drinks and 45 minutes to enjoy the scene (online booking-199 SEK, drop-ins-210 SEK—on weekends

drop-ins only allowed after 21:45, additional drinks-95 SEK, reservations smart; daily 11:15-24:00, Sept-May from 15:00; in the Nordic C Hotel adjacent to the main train station's Arlanda Express platform at Vasaplan 4, tel. 08/5056-3520, www.icebarstockholm.se).

At busy times, people are let in all at once every 45 minutes. That means there's a long line for drinks, and the place goes from being very crowded to almost empty as people gradually melt away.

Swedish Survival Phrases

Swedish pronunciation (especially the vowel sounds) can be tricky for Americans to say, and there's quite a bit of variation across the country; listen closely to locals and imitate, or ask for help. The most difficult Swedish sound is *sj*, which sounds roughly like a guttural "*h*w" (made in your throat); however, like many sounds, this is pronounced differently in various regions—for example, Stockholmers might say it more like "shw."

English	Swedish	Pronunciation
Hello. (formal)	*Goddag!*	goh-**dah**
Hi. / Bye. (informal)	*Hej. / Hej då.*	hey / hey doh
Do you speak English?	*Talar du engelska?*	**tah**-lar doo **eng**-ehl-skah
Yes. / No.	*Ja. / Nej.*	yaw / nay
Please.	*Snälla. / Tack.**	**snehl**-lah / tack
Thank you (very much).	*Tack (så mycket).*	tack (soh **mee**-keh)
You're welcome.	*Ingen orsak.*	**eeng**-ehn **oor**-sahk
Can I help you?	*Kan jag hjälpa dig?*	kahn yaw **jehl**-pah day
Excuse me.	*Ursäkta.*	**oor**-sehk-tah
(Very) good.	*(Mycket) bra.*	(**mee**-keh) brah
Goodbye.	*Adjö.*	ah-**yew**
zero / one / two	*noll / en / två*	nohl / ehn / tvoh
three / four	*tre / fyra*	treh / **fee**-rah
five / six	*fem / sex*	fehm / sehks
seven / eight	*sju / åtta*	*h*woo / **oh**-tah
nine / ten	*nio / tio*	**nee**-oh / **tee**-oh
hundred	*hundra*	**hoon**-drah
thousand	*tusen*	**too**-sehn
How much?	*Hur mycket?*	hewr **mee**-keh
local currency: (Swedish) kronor	*(Svenska) kronor*	(svehn-**skeh**) **kroh**-nor
Where is...?	*Var finns...?*	var feens
...the toilet	*...toaletten*	toh-ah-**leh**-tehn
men	*man*	mahn
women	*kvinna*	**kvee**-nah
water / coffee	*vatten / kaffe*	**vah**-tehn / **kah**-feh
beer / wine	*öl / vin*	url / veen
Cheers!	*Skål!*	skohl
The bill, please.	*Kan jag få notan, tack.*	kahn yaw foh **noh**-tahn tack

*Swedish has various ways to say "please," depending on the context. The simplest is *snälla,* but Swedes sometimes use the word *tack* (thank you) the way we use "please."

HELSINKI

Finland

Finland Practicalities

 We think of Finland (Suomi) as Scandinavian, but it's better to call it Nordic (along with Iceland and Estonia). Finland is bordered by Russia to the east, Sweden and Norway to the north, the Baltic Sea to the west, and Estonia (across the Gulf of Finland) to the south. After gaining independence from Russia in 1917, Finland resisted invasion during World War II—and a low-key but pervasive Finnish pride has percolated here ever since. A mostly flat, forested, lake-filled country of 130,500 square miles (almost twice the size of Washington state), Finland is home to 5.5 million people. Finland's population is more than 72 percent Lutheran, and the vast majority (93 percent) is of Finnish descent.

Money: €1 (euro) = about $1.20. An ATM is called a *pankkiautomaatti;* these are often marked *Otto.* The local VAT (value-added sales tax) rate is 24 percent; the minimum purchase eligible for a VAT refund is €40 (for details on refunds, see page 125).

Language: The native language is Finnish. For useful phrases, see page 318.

Emergencies: Dial 112 for police, medical, or other emergencies. In case of theft or loss, see page 118.

Time Zone: Finland is one hour ahead of Central European Time (seven/ten hours ahead of the East/West Coasts of the US). That puts Helsinki in the same time zone as Tallinn and Rīga; one hour ahead of Stockholm, the rest of Scandinavia, and most other continental cruise ports (including Gdańsk and Warnemünde); and one hour behind St. Petersburg.

Embassies in Helsinki: The **US embassy** is at Itäinen Puistotie 14B (tel. 40/140-5957, emergency tel. 09/616-250, https://fi.usembassy.gov). The **Canadian embassy** is at Pohjoisesplanadi 25B (tel. 09/228-530, www.canadainternational.gc.ca/finland-finlande). Call ahead for passport services.

Phoning: With a mobile phone, it's easy to dial: Press and hold zero until you get a + sign, enter the country code (358 for Finland, 1 for the US/Canada), and then the complete phone number (including area code if there is one). When dialing a European phone number, drop an initial zero (except if calling Italy). For more tips, see page 1062.

Tipping: The bill for a sit-down meal already includes gratuity, so you don't need to add more, though it's nice to round up about 5-10 percent for good service. Round up taxi fares a bit (pay €3 on a €2.85 fare). For more tips on tipping, see page 129.

Tourist Information: www.visitfinland.com.

HELSINKI

Helsinki is the only European capital with no medieval past. Although it was founded in the 16th century by the Swedes in hopes of countering Tallinn as a strategic Baltic port, it never amounted to more than a village until the 18th century. Then, in 1746, Sweden built a huge fortress on an island outside Helsinki's harbor, and the village boomed as it supplied the fortress. After taking over Finland in 1809, the Russians decided to move Finland's capital and university closer to St. Petersburg—from Turku to Helsinki. They hired a young German architect, Carl Ludvig Engel, to design new public buildings for Helsinki and told him to use St. Petersburg as a model. This is why the oldest parts of Helsinki (around Market Square and Senate Square) feel so Russian—stone buildings in yellow and blue pastels with white trim and columns. Hollywood used Helsinki for the films *Gorky Park* and *Dr. Zhivago*, because filming in Russia was not possible during the Cold War.

Though the city was part of the Russian Empire in the 19th century, most of its residents still spoke Swedish, which was the language of business and culture. In the mid-1800s, Finland began to industrialize. The Swedish upper class in Helsinki expanded the city, bringing in the railroad and surrounding the old Russian-inspired core with neighborhoods of four- and five-story apartment buildings, including some Art Nouveau masterpieces. Meanwhile, Finns moved from the countryside to Helsinki to take jobs as industrial laborers. The Finnish language slowly acquired equal status with Swedish, and eventually Finnish speakers became the majority in Helsinki (though Swedish remains a co-official language).

Since downtown Helsinki didn't exist until the 1800s, it was more conscientiously designed and laid out than other European capitals. With its many architectural overleafs and fine Neoclassical and Art Nouveau buildings, Helsinki often turns guests into students of urban design and planning. If you're intrigued by the city's buildings, look for the English-language guide to Helsinki architecture (by Arvi Ilonen) in bookstores.

Despite Helsinki's sometimes severe cityscape and chilly northern latitude, the city bursts with vibrant street life and a joyful creative spirit. In 2012, Helsinki celebrated its stint as a "World Design Capital" and spiffed up the city with exciting projects—including the Helsinki Music Centre concert hall, an extensive underground bike tunnel that cuts efficiently beneath congested downtown streets, and an all-around rededication to its already impressive design. While parts of the city are dark and drab, splashes of creativity and color hide around every corner.

PLANNING YOUR TIME

Helsinki will keep you busy on your day in port. While the downtown core, with most of the big sights, is compact and walkable, several worth-a-detour attractions require a longer walk or bus/tram/taxi ride. Below I've listed the most important sights in town, starting from Market Square and moving outward; while this order makes sense for those arriving at the South Harbor, if you arrive at the West Harbor, it may be more logical to start at the farthest-flung sights, then work your way back toward the town center (and your ship). If you move fast on a longish day in port, you can probably squeeze in all the in-town sights; if you're tight on time, skip the National Museum.

Market Square: This delightful harborfront zone is worth at least a 30-minute browse—more if you shop or grab lunch here.

Helsinki Walk: Starting at Market Square, take this two-part self-guided walk (allow about two hours without stops) for an introduction to the city's sightseeing spine.

Senate Square and Churches: Near Market Square and the start of my self-guided walk, be sure to stroll through Senate Square, visit the **Lutheran Cathedral,** and tour the **Uspenski Orthodox Cathedral** (figure on 30 minutes per church). This part of town won't take you much more than an hour.

Orientation Bus Tour: Early in your visit, consider a 1.75-hour bus tour (or one of the one-hour hop-on, hop-off loops) to conveniently link Helsinki's outlying areas (including the **Sibelius Monument**—which is worth seeing, but not worth the long trip on public transit).

National Museum: For those curious about Finland's story, this pleasant museum tells it well; allow at least an hour (likely more). The landmark Finlandia Hall across the street is also worth a peek (10 minutes).

Temppeliaukio: The dramatic "Church in the Rock" is one of Helsinki's best sights—but also one of its least convenient, burrowed in a residential zone a 10-minute walk behind the National Museum. Allow 30 minutes (plus the time it takes to get there).

Out of Town: Two out-of-town sights are worth the trek for those with a special interest, but will eat up the better part of your time in port. **Suomenlinna Fortress,** the fortified island defending Helsinki's harbor, is reached by a 15-minute boat trip; once there, you'll want at least an hour to explore, plus 30 minutes for the museum and 25 minutes for the entertaining film. **Seurasaari Open-Air Folk Museum** requires a 30-minute bus ride each way from downtown, plus at least 1.5 hours to see the dozens of historic structures.

HELSINKI

Port of Helsinki

Arrival at a Glance: If arriving at the West Harbor or Hernesaari, public transportation is your best bet for getting downtown (bus #14 from Hernesaari quays, tram #9 or #6T from West Harbor Terminals 1 or 2). From the South Harbor (Katajanokan and Olympia terminals), you can walk into town in about 15 minutes (or hop on a tram—#5 from Katajanokan, #2 from Olympia).

Port Overview

Helsinki has several cruise-ship ports: **West Harbor** and **Hernesaari,** southwest of the city, and **South Harbor,** right off Market Square and the Esplanade. West Harbor and South Harbor receive international cruise ships as well as passenger/car ferries that link Helsinki with Tallinn, Stockholm, and St. Petersburg.

Cruise berths at each port are designated by a two- or three-letter code (noted below, along with terminal or quay names in Finnish). See the Helsinki Transit map for locations; for a detailed map, see www.portofhelsinki.fi.

Tourist Information and Services: The quays where the biggest ships dock often lack services. Among the cruise ports, only the Hernesaari quays have a dedicated TI; otherwise, visit the helpful TI in town (near Market Square and the Esplanade). Similarly, you may need to wait to get into downtown Helsinki to find an ATM (where they are abundant, especially along the Esplanade).

GETTING INTO TOWN

First, I'll cover transportation options that work from any port. Then I'll offer specifics on each port. To return to your ship, you can generally reverse these directions—I've given suggestions at the end of each section as necessary.

From Any Port

By Cruise-Line Shuttle Bus: Many cruise lines offer a shuttle bus into downtown (price varies—some are complimentary, others charge a fee). This is especially worth considering if you're arriving at the farther-out Hernesaari quays.

Most cruise shuttles drop off at the head of the Esplanade, just behind the white, round Swedish Theater (at the intersection of Mannerheimintie and Bulevardi), where a pop-up TI is usually open when ships are in town. From here, you can walk to many sights: The Esplanade leads down to Market Square and the beginning of my self-guided Helsinki Walk, and the big, red-brick Stockmann department store is just a block away.

By Tour: Bus tours can be an excellent way to get your bearings in this somewhat spread-out city. You have two options: **orientation bus tours** that do a 1.75-hour circuit around the big sights; or **hop-on, hop-off bus tours** that allow you to get on and off at sights along the route. Neither type of tour serves all the cruise ports (though hop-on, hop-off buses do meet arriving cruisers at the primary Hernesaari quay, and orientation tours leave from near the Katajanokan and Olympia terminals in the morning); in most cases, you'll need to make your way downtown to catch the tour bus. If considering the hop-on, hop-off buses, make sure you understand the schedule and departure point for the bus back to your port.

For more on these and other tour options, see "Tours in Helsinki" on page 287.

By Public Transportation: Helsinki has a great transit system. I've outlined specific options for using it in the port descriptions below (for more, see "Getting Around Helsinki," later).

From West Harbor

West Harbor (Finnish: Länsistama) has two distinct port areas: the quays for big boats on the Hernesaari peninsula, and West Harbor Terminals 1 and 2, which primarily handle passenger and car ferries, although some cruise ships dock nearby.

The Port of Helsinki is in the middle of a years-long project that is gradually centralizing passenger/car ferries at West Harbor Terminals 1 and 2, and big cruise ships at Hernesaari. Expect changes and construction at either of these areas. For the latest, consult www.portofhelsinki.fi.

Hernesaari Quays

Hernesaari is the primary cruise port for Helsinki, with two berths (LHB and LHC). Leaving your ship, you'll run right into a small souvenir store (with Wi-Fi); a parking lot with taxis and shuttle, excursion, and hop-on/hop-off buses; and a handy TI kiosk (open only in the morning when ships are in, it's a good place to pick up a map, get questions answered, and buy an all-day transit pass—see below). A public bus stop is a short walk away. At present, there's no ATM.

Urban Renewal Project: To take advantage of the peninsula's underused waterfront, an ambitious redevelopment project is transforming this area with green spaces, residences, and recreational marinas. A new quay is under construction and a tram line is also slated to go in. You may see some of these improvements when you visit.

By Taxi: Figure on €15-20 for a ride downtown.

By Public Bus: Public bus #14 runs from near the port to the center (runs every 15-20 minutes). To take the bus, buy a €9 all-day transit pass at the TI kiosk (credit card only, no individual tickets sold), or buy a €3.20 single-ride ticket or a day pass from the bus driver (cash only, no large bills). The bus stop is a five-minute walk away: From the port gate and TI, follow the green line through the parking lot to the far end. When you reach the street, turn left and follow it for a short block; the bus stop is down the first street on the right (marked *Pajamäki/Smedjebacka*).

Two stops in town are most useful: Kamppi, a retail complex/transportation hub that's a 10-minute walk from the train station, Stockmann department store, and the Esplanade; and Kauppakorkeakoulut (Handelshögskolorna), for the Church in the Rock.

The Hernesaari quays are very close to the seaside **Löyly sauna** and restaurant. To reach it, ride bus #14 for two stops (to Henry Fordin Katu)—you can't miss the modern wooden building on the right; for details, see page 303.

Returning to Hernesaari by Bus: Ride bus #14 (direction: Hernesaaren laituri) and get off at the last stop (you'll see your ship). The only catch is finding a handy bus stop for the #14 downtown; the most convenient is probably Kamppi, a 10-minute walk from the train station/Finlandia Hall area (see the "Helsinki Walk" map for stop locations).

West Harbor Terminals 1 and 2

Cruise ships use two West Harbor quays (Melkki/LMA and Valtameri/LV7), which are close to the terminals handling passenger and car ferries to Tallinn and St. Petersburg. There are no real services at the quays—but you'll see taxis and buses for cruise excursions. To head into town on your own, proceed to whichever

Helsinki Excursions

Helsinki itself has plenty to fill a day, but many of its sights—including its architectural highlights, the remarkable Church in the Rock, and the Sibelius Monument—are spread far and wide. This, plus the fact that Helsinki is unusually car-friendly (and less pedestrian-oriented), makes an orientation **bus tour** a good way to get your bearings. While your cruise line likely offers this as an excursion, you'll have a similar experience and pay far less if you join a local bus tour when you arrive (see options on page 287). The short, basic Helsinki bus tours generally make three stops: at the Church in the Rock (45 minutes, plus a four-block hike from where the bus parks), the Sibelius Monument (10 minutes), and Senate Square/Market Square (30 minutes)—but you'll likely get more information from this chapter than on one of these excursions.

Cruise lines also offer **walking tours** of downtown Helsinki, including Senate Square and the Esplanade, but you'll do just as well following my self-guided Helsinki Walk (see page 289). Finally, you might combine either a bus ride or a walking tour with a Helsinki **harbor tour,** offering a closer look at the Suomenlinna islands, or, far beyond that, the Archipelago Sea (studded with thousands of little islands, but less scenic than the Stockholm Archipelago).

While gimmicky "ice bar" experiences in other cities are skippable, excursions to Helsinki's "Winter World" facility offers something extra—a complete, snowy indoor world where you can ride a sled, toss a snowball, and hike on a snowy hill. While undoubtedly a tourist trap, this may be worth it on a hot day if you have a limited appetite for Helsinki and prefer snowballs and vodka to sightseeing.

Out-of-town excursions can include the excellent **Seurasaari Open-Air Folk Museum,** offering a look at traditional Finnish culture (and described on page 308); **Porvoo,** the second-oldest town in Finland, with fine wooden architecture; **Sipoo,** a very old and traditional farming area with the stone St. Sigfrid's Church; and **Hvitträsk,** a landmark of Finnish architecture in a pleasant forests-and-lake countryside setting. While any of these might be interesting on a longer visit, with just one day I'd rather explore Helsinki proper (or, if you have a special interest, choose an excursion combining one of these outlying sights with places in town).

terminal building is closest to your berth, the older **West Harbor Terminal 1** (Länsiterminaali 1, used primarily by boats headed to St. Petersburg or Stockholm) or the striking **West Harbor Terminal 2** (Länsiterminaali 2, with service primarily to Tallinn). Each terminal has ATMs, WCs, and limited tourist information. Terminal 1 has luggage lockers.

By Taxi: Figure on €15-20 for a ride downtown.

By Public Tram: Directly in front of each terminal is a stop for **trams #9** and **#6T,** both of which go to the central train station (15-20 minutes, #6T has a more scenic route). Buy tickets at the machine (cash or credit card) by the tram stop, or from the driver (€2.90, cash only, no big bills, €9 for an all-day ticket). Either tram will deliver you to the train station (Rautatieasema/Järnvägssta-tionen stop), right in the middle of my self-guided Helsinki Walk, and within easy walking distance of many top sights. If you ride tram #6T, you can hop out on the appealing, shop-filled Bulevardi street (with the red-brick Hietalahti Market Hall), or stay on to the top end of the Esplanade (Ylioppilastalo stop).

Returning to West Harbor Terminals by Tram: Ride tram #6T or #9 (direction: Länsiterminaali); the easiest place to catch either one downtown is in front of the train station. Note that tram #6T operates only at times when ships are arriving/departing.

From South Harbor

Ringing the scenic South Harbor (Finnish: Eteläsatama) are several terminals and quays for cruise ships and overnight passenger ferries. The South Harbor berths closest to downtown (Kanava and Makasiini) are used mostly by ferries, though occasionally overflow cruise ships may end up here. Your ship is more likely to dock at one of the berths described next.

From any of the South Harbor berths, you can see the green dome marking the Lutheran Cathedral and the city center. If the weather's nice and you're up for a walk, just stroll toward the dome. To return to South Harbor, it's easiest just to walk if you're already near Market Square.

Olympia Terminal (Olympiaterminaali)

This berth (EO) along the harbor's south embankment is used mostly by smaller cruise ships. Ships put in near the Olympia Terminal building (used primarily by Tallink Silja overnight boats to Stockholm), which has ATMs, WCs, and lockers. Out front are hop-on, hop-off buses and the Panorama orientation tour buses. It's an easy 15-minute **walk** along the harbor to Market Square. Or hop on **tram #2,** which departs from the front of the terminal and zips you into town; the third stop is Senate Square (Senaatintori/Senatstorget), and the ninth stop (Sammonkatu) is near Temppeliaukio, the Church in the Rock.

Returning to Olympia Terminal by Tram: Take tram #2 from Sammonkatu (near Temppeliaukio), Senate Square, and City Hall.

Katajanokan Terminal (Katajanokka Terminaali)

Close to town on South Harbor's northern embankment, these quays (ERA and ERB) are an easy walk or quick ride on tram #5 into town. A third berth (EKL) is used more by overnight ferries than cruise ships.

As you exit the port area, turn left and walk to the Viking Line terminal building. Inside, you'll find an ATM, WCs, and lockers; out front are hop-on, hop-off buses and the Panorama orientation tour buses (see page 287).

By Tram: Directly across the street from the terminal is the start-of-the-line stop for **tram #5.** You can ride it straight into town (4-8/hour): the fourth stop, Ritarihuone/Riddarhuset, is the City Hall (near Market Square and TI); the next stop is Senate Square (Senaatintori/Senatstorget); and from there, the tram continues along Aleksanterinkatu, parallel to the Esplanade, to the train station area (Rautatieasema/Järnvägsstationen) stop.

By Foot: Alternatively, you can **walk** to Market Square in about 15 minutes: Simply proceed past the Viking Line terminal and continue straight ahead, with the harbor on your left.

Returning to Katajanokan by Tram: Catch tram #5 near the train station, Senate Square, or the Ritarihuone stop by City Hall.

Helsinki

Helsinki (pop. 616,000) has a compact core. The city's natural gateway is its main harbor (known as the South Harbor). At the top of the harbor is Market Square (Kauppatori), an outdoor food and souvenir bazaar. Nearby are two towering, can't-miss-them landmarks: the white Lutheran Cathedral and the red-brick Orthodox Cathedral.

Helsinki's grand pedestrian boulevard, the Esplanade, begins right at Market Square, heads up past the TI, and ends after a few blocks in the central shopping district. At the top end of the Esplanade, the broad, traffic-filled Mannerheimintie avenue veers north through town past the train and bus stations on its way to many of Helsinki's museums and architectural landmarks. For a do-it-yourself orientation to town along this route, follow my self-guided walk on page 289.

Linguistic Orientation: Finnish is completely different from the Scandinavian languages of Norwegian, Danish, and Swedish. That can make navigating a bit tricky. Place names ending in -*katu* are streets, -*tie* is "road" or "way," and -*tori* or -*aukio* means "square." Complicating matters, Finland's bilingual status means that most street names, tram stops, and map labels appear in both Finnish and Swedish. The two names often look completely different (for example, the South Harbor—where many overnight boats arrive— is called Eteläsatama in Finnish and Södra Hamnen in Swedish; the train station is Rautatieasema in Finnish, Järnvägsstationen in Swedish). The Swedish names can be a little easier to interpret than the Finnish ones. In any event, I've rarely met a Finn who doesn't speak excellent English.

Orientation to Helsinki

TOURIST INFORMATION

The friendly, energetic **main TI,** just off the harbor, offers great service and excellent materials on the city. It's located a half-block inland from Market Square, at the beginning of the Esplanade, at the corner with Unioninkatu (Mon-Sat 9:00-18:00, Sun until 16:00; mid-Sept-mid-May Mon-Fri 9:00-18:00, Sat-Sun 10:00-16:00; tel. 09/3101-3300, www.visithelsinki.fi). Pick up a public-transit map and a detailed pamphlet on the Suomenlinna Fortress. If you want a sightseeing Helsinki Card, you can buy it here (at the on-site Strömma desk; see below).

The tiny **train station TI,** a one-person booth in the main hall, provides many of the same services and publications. There's also a regional tourist information desk at Helsinki airport (open daily year-round).

Strömma/Sightseeing Helsinki: This private service, located within the main TI, sells the Helsinki Card (described next), ferry tickets, and sightseeing tours by bus and boat. They operate the TI branch in the train station and small, summer-only sightseeing kiosks on the Esplanade and by the harbor (all branches open Mon-Sat 9:00-16:30, Sun until 16:00, tel. 09/2288-1600, www.stromma.fi).

Helsinki Card: If you plan to visit a lot of museums in Helsinki, this card can be a good deal. The card includes free entry to nearly 30 museums, fortresses, and other major sights; free use of buses, trams, and the ferry to Suomenlinna; and 24-hour access to a hop-on, hop-off bus (€46/24 hours, multiday passes available; sold online and at all Strömma locations including at main TI and both Viking Line and Tallink Silja ferry terminals, www.helsinkicard.com).

For a cheaper alternative, you could buy a public-transit day ticket (see "Getting Around Helsinki," later), take my self-guided walk, visit the free and low-cost churches (Temppeliaukio Church, Lutheran Cathedral, Uspenski Orthodox Cathedral, and Kamppi Chapel), and stop by the free Helsinki City Museum.

HELSINKI

HELPFUL HINTS

Wi-Fi: Helsinki has free Wi-Fi all along the Esplanade and throughout the city center; look for the "Helsinki City Open" network.

Pharmacy: The **Erottajan pharmacy** *(apteekki)* is conveniently located on the basement level of Stockmann department store (similar hours as store, Mannerheimintie 1, tel. 09/622-9930).

Bike Rental: Helsinki's **HSL** transit company has 140 bike stations throughout the city. To use a bike, buy a pass and register online; you'll then receive an ID and PIN for picking up your bike from any bike station. Passes are sold by the day and the week, and include up to 30 minutes of riding time per bike—but you can keep it and pay more for a longer ride. Convenient bike station locations include Kamppi shopping center, Market Square, the train station, and near the Esplanade (24-hour pass-€5, one-week pass-€10; for bike station maps and more info, see www.hsl.fi/en/citybikes).

Best View: The **Torni Tower's Ateljee Bar** offers a free panorama view. Ride the elevator from the lobby of the venerable Torni Hotel (built in 1931) to the 12th floor, where you can browse around the perch or sit down for a pricey drink (Sun-Thu 14:00-24:00, Fri-Sat from 12:00, Yrjönkatu 26, tel. 020-123-4604).

What's With the Slot Machines? Finns just have a love affair with lotteries and petty gambling. You'll see coin-operated games of chance everywhere, including restaurants, supermarkets, and the train station.

GETTING AROUND HELSINKI

In compact Helsinki, you can get by without using much public transportation, but it can save steps.

By Bus and Tram: With the public-transit route map (available at the TI, also viewable on the Helsinki Region Transport website—www.hsl.fi) and a little mental elbow grease, the buses and trams are easy. The single Metro line is also part of the system, but not useful for most visitors.) and a little mental elbow grease, the buses and trams are easy. The single Metro line is also part of the system, but not useful for most visitors.

Single tickets are good for an hour of travel (€3.20 from driver, €2.90 at ticket machines at a few larger bus and tram stops). A day ticket (€9/24 hours of un-

Helsinki Transit

NATIONAL MUSEUM — Kansallismuseo

Tram #2

Sammonkatu

TEMPPELIAUKIO CHURCH — B #14

ARKADIANKATU

MANNERHEIMINTIE

Tram #5
Tram #4

500 Meters

500 Yards

North Harbor

Tram #2

TRAIN STATION

Tram #3, #6, #6T

Lasipalatsi

Tram #2 & #7

Rautatieasema

Tram #2, #4 & #5

LUTHERAN CATHEDRAL

Senaatintori

USPENSKI ORTHODOX CATHEDRAL

Kamppi Tram, Metro & Bus Stn.

B #14

Ylioppilastalo

ESPLANADE

Tram #2, #4 & #5

Tram #4

Cruise Line Shuttle Bus Stop

B

Tram #3, #6 & #6T

Kauppatori (Market Square) BOATS TO SUOMENLINNA

KANAVA

South Harbor

Tram #5

Kataja-nokka

Tram #7

Ercttaja

HIETALAHTI FLEA MARKET

Tram #6, #6T

Tram #3

Eteläranta

ERA/ERB

KATAJA-NOKAN CRUISES, VIKING LINE TO STOCKHOLM & TALLINN

MAKASIINI LINDA LINE TO TALLINN

Iso Roobertinkatu

#14 B

Tram #2

EO

Olympia-laituri

Luoto

West Harbor

Tram #6T & #9

T-1

WEST/LÄNSI TALLINK SILJA LINE & ECKERÖ LINE TO TALLINN; ST. PETER LINE TO ST. PETERSBURG

Tram #3

OLYMPIA TALLINK SILJA LINE TO STOCKHOLM

To Suomenlinna Fortress

T-2

HERNESAARI (CRUISE SHIPS)

Sirpalesaari

Munkkisaari #14 B

Harakka

Not all Tram & Bus Stops are shown

Tram
Bus
Boat

limited travel, issued on a plastic card you'll touch against the card reader when entering the bus or tram) pays for itself if you take four or more rides. Day tickets can be bought at the ubiquitous yellow-and-blue R-Kiosks (convenience stores), as well as at TIs, the train station, Metro stations, ticket machines at a handful of stops, and on some ferries, but not from drivers. The Helsinki Card also covers public transportation. The HSL mobile ticket app (HSL Mobiililippu) is a convenient way to buy single tickets and day passes on your smartphone (see www.hsl.fi/en).

Tours in Helsinki

The big company Strömma (also called Sightseeing Helsinki) has a near monopoly on city tours, whether by bus, boat, or foot.

▲▲▲Orientation Bus Tours

These 1.75-hour "Helsinki Panorama" bus tours give an ideal city overview with a look at all the important buildings, from the Olympic Stadium to Embassy Row. You stay on the bus the entire

Helsinki at a Glance

▲▲▲**Temppeliaukio Church** Awe-inspiring, copper-topped 1969 "Church in the Rock." **Hours:** June-Sept Mon-Sat 10:00-17:45, Sun 11:45-17:45; closes one hour earlier off-season. See page 305.

▲▲**Uspenski Orthodox Cathedral** Orthodoxy's most prodigious display outside of Eastern Europe. **Hours:** Tue-Fri 9:30-16:00, Sat 10:00-15:00, Sun 12:00-15:00, closed Mon. See page 300.

▲▲**Lutheran Cathedral** Green-domed, 19th-century Neoclassical masterpiece. **Hours:** Daily 9:00-18:00, June-early Aug until 24:00. See page 300.

▲▲**Suomenlinna Fortress** Helsinki's harbor island, sprinkled with picnic spots, museums, and military history. **Hours:** Museum daily 10:00-18:00, Oct-April 10:30-16:30. See page 306.

▲▲**Seurasaari Open-Air Folk Museum** Island museum with 100 historic buildings from Finland's farthest corners. **Hours:** June-Aug daily 11:00-17:00; shorter hours May and Sept, buildings closed rest of the year. See page 308.

▲**Ateneum, The National Gallery of Finland** Largest collection of art in Finland, including local favorites plus works by Cézanne, Chagall, Gauguin, and Van Gogh. **Hours:** Tue and Fri 10:00-18:00, Wed-Thu 9:00-20:00, Sat-Sun 10:00-17:00, closed Mon. See page 302.

▲**National Museum of Finland** The scoop on Finland, featuring folk costumes, an armory, czars, and thrones; the prehistory and 20th-century exhibits are best. **Hours:** Tue-Sun 11:00-18:00, closed Mon. See page 304.

▲**Design Museum** A chronological look at Finland's impressive design pedigree, plus cutting-edge temporary exhibits. **Hours:** Daily 11:00-18:00; Sept-May Wed-Sun 11:00-18:00, Tue until 20:00, closed Mon. See page 301.

time, except for a 10-minute stop or two (when possible, they try to stop at the Sibelius Monument and/or Temppeliaukio Church). You'll learn strange facts, such as how Finns took down the highest steeple in town during World War II so that Soviet bombers flying in from Estonia couldn't see their target. Tours get booked up, so it's wise to reserve in advance online or ask at the TI (€32, free with Helsinki Card, daily May-Aug at 11:00 and 13:30, rest of year at 11:00 with 13:30 departures Fri-Sat only, departs from Espla-

nade—intersection with Fabianinkatu, tel. 09/2288-1600, www.
stromma.fi, sales@stromma.fi).

Bus Tours Departing from South Harbor: Conveniently, the
Helsinki Panorama bus tours pick up cruise-ship passengers from
Katajanokan Terminal at 10:30 (but not during July), and from
Olympia Terminal at 10:45 (tours end at the Esplanade—not back
at the docks).

Hop-On, Hop-Off Bus Tours

If you'd enjoy the tour described above, but want the chance to
hop on and off at will, consider **City Sightseeing Helsinki** (operated by Strömma), with a 1.5-hour loop that connects downtown
Helsinki, several outlying sights—including the Sibelius Monument and Olympic Stadium—as well as the Olympia cruise terminal (on cruise-ship days, the bus generally stops at Hernesaari and
West Harbor's Melkki quay—confirm in advance). Buses run every
30-45 minutes and make 15 stops (€28, €41 combo-ticket also includes harbor tour, all tickets good for 24 hours, May-Sept daily
10:00-16:00, www.stromma.fi). A different company, **Sightseeing
City Tour** (also red buses), offers a similar route for similar prices,
but has fewer departures (www.citytour.fi).

SpåraKoff Pub Tram

In summer, this antique red tram makes a 45-minute loop through
the city while its passengers get looped on the beer for sale on board
(€11 to ride, €6 beer, May-Sept Mon-Sat 14:00-20:00, no trams
Sun, leaves at the top of the hour from the Mikonkatu stop—in
front of the Fennia building, across from train-station tower, www.
koff.fi/sparakoff).

Local Guides

Helsinki Sightseeing can arrange a private guide (book at least
three days in advance, €208/2 hours, tel. 09/2288-1222, sales@
stromma.fi). **Christina Snellman** is a good, licensed guide (mobile
050-527-4741, chrisder@pp.inet.fi). **Archtour** offers local guides
who specialize in Helsinki's architecture (tel. 09/477-7300, www.
archtours.com).

Helsinki Walk

This self-guided walk—worth ▲▲▲—offers a convenient spine for
your Helsinki sightseeing. I've divided the walk into two parts: On
a quick visit, focus on Part 1 (which takes about an hour). To dig
deeper into the city's architectural landmarks—and reach some of
its museums—continue with Part 2 (which adds another 45 minutes). Note that several points of interest on this walk are described
in more detail under "Sights in Helsinki."

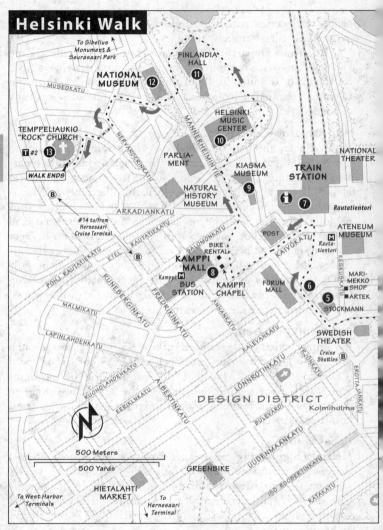

Helsinki Walk

To Sibelius Monument & Seurasaari Park

NATIONAL MUSEUM ⑫

FINLANDIA HALL ⑪

MUSEOKATU

HELSINKI MUSIC CENTER ⑩

TEMPPELIAUKIO "ROCK" CHURCH
T #2 ⑬
WALK ENDS

MANNERHEIMINTIE

PARLIA-MENT

NATIONAL THEATER

KIASMA MUSEUM

TRAIN STATION

Rautatientori

B

#14 to/from Hernesaari Cruise Terminal

NATURAL HISTORY MUSEUM

ARKADIANKATU

⑨

i ⑦

B

RAUTATIEKATU

POHJ. RAUTATIEKATU

ETEL. RAUTATIEKATU

SALOMONKATU

BIKE RENTAL

KAMPPI MALL

Kamppi M

BUS STATION

KAMPPI CHAPEL

⑧

POST

KAIVOKATU

Rauta-tientori

ATENEUM MUSEUM

KESKUSKATU

MARI-MEKKO SHOP
ARTEK

RUNEBERGINKATU

FREDRIKINKATU

ANINANKATU

FORUM MALL

⑥

⑤

STOCKMANN

MALMIKATU

LAPINLAHDENKATU

KALEVANKATU

SWEDISH THEATER

Cruise Shuttles B

EROTAJANKATU

RUOHOLAHDENKATU

EERIKINKATU

ALBERTINKATU

LÖNNROTINKATU

YRJÖNKATU

DESIGN DISTRICT

Kolmikulma

BULEVARDI

UUDENMAANKATU

ISO ROOBERTINKATU

N

500 Meters
500 Yards

GREENBIKE

HIETALAHTI MARKET

To West Harbor Terminals

To Hernesaari Terminal

KATAKATU

PART 1: THE HARBORFRONT, SENATE SQUARE, AND ESPLANADE

• *Start at the obelisk in the center of the harborfront market.*

❶ Market Square (Kauppatori)

This is the **Czarina's Stone,** with its double-headed eagle of imperial Russia. It was the first public monument in Helsinki, designed by Carl Ludwig Engel and erected in 1835 to celebrate the visit by Czar Nicholas I and Czarina Alexandra. Step over the chain and climb to the top step for a clockwise spin-tour:

1. Market Square
2. Senate Square
3. Café Kappeli
4. The Esplanade
5. Artek, Marimekko & Stockmann
6. Three Blacksmiths
7. Central Train Station
8. Kamppi Plaza & Chapel
9. Mannerheim Statue & Kiasma Museum
10. Helsinki Music Center
11. Alvar Aalto's Finlandia Hall
12. National Museum of Finland
13. Temppeliaukio (Church in the Rock)

Begin by facing the **harbor.** The big, red Viking ship and white Silja ship are each floating hotels for those making the 40-hour Stockholm-Helsinki round-trip. Farther back, a giant Ferris wheel spins over the harbor (SkyWheel Helsinki, €12, www.skywheel.fi). Now pan to the right. The brick-and-tan building along the harborfront is the Old Market Hall, with some enticing, more

upscale options than the basic grub at the outdoor market (for a rundown on both options, see "Eating in Helsinki," later). Between here and there, a number of harbor cruise boats vie for your business.

Farther to the right, the trees mark the beginning of Helsinki's grand promenade, the Esplanade. Hiding in the leaves is the venerable iron-and-glass Café Kappeli. The yellow building across from the trees is the TI. From there, a string of Neoclassical buildings lines the harbor. The blue-and-white City Hall was designed by Engel in 1833 as the town's first hotel, built to house the czar and czarina. The Lutheran Cathedral is hidden from view behind this building. Next, after the short peach-colored building, is the Swedish Embassy (flying the blue-and-yellow Swedish flag and designed to look like Stockholm's Royal Palace). Then comes the Supreme Court and, tucked back in the far corner, Finland's Presidential Palace. Finally, standing proud, and reminding Helsinki of the Russian behemoth to its east, is the Uspenski Orthodox Cathedral.

Explore the colorful **outdoor market**—part souvenirs and crafts, part fruit and veggies, part fish and snacks. Sniff the stacks of trivets, made from cross-sections of juniper twigs—an ideal, fragrant, easy-to-pack gift for the folks back home (they smell even nicer when you set something hot on them).

• *Done exploring? Walk to the corner of the square next to City Hall, and turn right up Sofiankatu street (City Hall has huge public WCs in the basement, and free exhibits on Helsinki history). Near the end of the block, you'll pop out right in the middle of...*

❷ Senate Square (Senaatintori)

This was once a simple town square with a church and City Hall—but its original buildings were burned when Russians invaded in 1808. Later, after Finland became a grand duchy of the Russian Empire, the czar sent in architect Carl Ludvig Engel (a German who had lived and worked in St. Petersburg) to give the place some Neo-class. The result: the finest Neoclassical square in Europe. Engel represents the paradox of Helsinki: The city as we know it was built by Russia, but with an imported European architect, in a very intentionally "European" style. So Helsinki is, in a sense, both entirely Russian...and not Russian in the slightest.

The statue in the center of the square honors **Russian Czar Alexander II.** While he wasn't popular in Russia (he was assassinated), he was well-liked by the Finns. That's because he gave Finland more autonomy in 1863 and never pushed the Russification of Finland.

The huge **staircase** leading up to the **Lutheran Cathedral** is a popular meeting (and tanning) spot in Helsinki. Head up those stairs and survey Senate Square from the top. Scan the square from left to right. First, 90 degrees to your left is the yellow **Senate building** (now the prime minister's office). The small, blue-gray stone building with the slanted mansard roof in the far-left corner, from 1757, is one of just two pre-Russian-conquest buildings remaining in Helsinki (it's now the home of the Helsinki City Museum). **Café Engel** (opposite the cathedral at Aleksanterinkatu 26) is a fine place for a light lunch or cake and coffee. The café's winter lighting seems especially designed to boost the spirits of daylight-deprived Northerners.

Facing the Senate directly across the square is its twin, the **University of Helsinki**'s main building (36,000 students, 60 percent female). Symbolically (and physically), the university and government buildings are connected via the cathedral, and both use it as a starting point for grand ceremonies.

Tucked alongside the cathedral, a line of once-grand Russian administration buildings now house the **National Library of Finland.** In czarist times, the National Library received a copy of every book printed in the Russian Empire. With all the chaos Russia suffered throughout the 20th century, a good percentage of its Slavic texts were destroyed. But Helsinki, which enjoyed relative stability, claims to have the finest collection of Slavic books in the world. This purpose-built Neoclassical building, its facade lined with Corinthian columns, is one of Engels' finest and worth a look.

If you'd like to visit the **cathedral interior,** now's your chance; the entrance is tucked around the left side as you face the towering dome (see page 300 for a description).

• *When you're ready, head back down the stairs and angle right through the square, continuing straight down Unioninkatu.*

Along **Unioninkatu,** do a little window-shopping; this is the first of many streets we'll see lined with made-in-Finland shops (though these are more touristy than the norm). In addition to the

jewelry shops and clothes boutiques, look for the Schröder sporting goods store (on the left, at #23), which shows off its famous selection of popular Finnish-made Rapala fishing lures—ideal for the fisher folk on your gift list.

At the end of this street (TI on the right), cross over the tram tracks to reach the fountain called *Havis Amanda.* Designed by Ville Vallgren and unveiled here in 1908, the fountain has become the symbol of Helsinki, the city known as the "Daughter of the Baltic"—graduating students decorate her with a school cap.

The voluptuous figure, modeled after the artist's Parisian mistress, was a bit too racy for the conservative town, and Vallgren had trouble getting paid. But as artists often do, Vallgren had the last laugh: For more than a hundred years now, the city budget office across the street has seen only her backside.

• *Now turn toward the Esplanade's grassy median, with the delightful...*

❸ Café Kappeli

If you've got some time, dip into this old-fashioned, gazebo-like oasis of coffee, pastry, and relaxation (get what you like at the bar inside and sit anywhere). In the 19th century, this was a popular hangout for local intellectuals and artists. Today the café offers romantic tourists waiting for their ship a great cup-of-coffee memory. The bandstand in front hosts nearly daily music and dance performances in summer.

• *Beyond Café Kappeli stretches...*

❹ The Esplanade (Esplanaden)

Helsinki's top shopping boulevard sandwiches a park in the middle (another Engel design from the 1830s). The grandiose street designations—*esplanadi* and *bulevardi*—while fitting today, would have been purely aspirational in rustic little 1830s Helsinki.

The north side (on the right) is interesting for window-shopping, people-watching, and sun-worshipping. In fact, after the first block, shoppers may want to leave the park and cross over to that side of the street to browse (for ideas, see the "Shopping in Helsinki" section, later).

But the rest of you should stay in the park, the green heart of the city. As you stroll, admire the mature linden trees and imagine this elegant promenade in the old days. The Esplanade was laid out in 1826 to connect the old city of the late 18th century—the established power center—with the new parts of town, where impressive new stone houses in a neo-Renaissance style were being built by the 1870s.

Notice the ornately decorated **Hotel Kämp** (on the right at #29). This city landmark is typical of the elegant hotels, shops, and restaurants that began springing up in the late 19th century as the Esplanade become famous as a place to be seen. Today, the street's exclusive air is maintained by enterprises such as **Galleria Esplanad** (entrance at #31), a high-end fashion mall with big-name Finnish and international stores, and the recommended **Strind-**

berg Café, one of many tony spots along the Esplanade to nurse a drink.

At the very top of the Esplanade, the park dead-ends at the **Swedish Theater.** Built under Russian rule to cater to Swedish residents of a Finnish city, this building encapsulates Helsinki's complex cultural mix. (The theater's recommended Teatterin deli and bar are handy for a drink or meal out in the park.)

Right across from the theater, at #39, is the huge **Academic Bookstore** (Akateeminen Kirjakauppa), designed by Modernist architect Alvar Aalto, with an extensive map and travel section, periodicals, English books, and the pricey Café Aalto (with ageless Aalto furniture; see the next stop) on the back mezzanine level.

• *At the end of the Esplanade, on the right, you'll reach a pedestrianized street with several landmarks of Finnish shopping and design...*

❺ Artek, Marimekko, and Stockmann

Around the corner from the Academic Bookstore is **Artek,** founded in 1935 by Alvar Aalto to showcase his practical, modern designs for furniture and housewares. And at the far corner is perhaps Finland's most famous export: **Marimekko,** the fabric designer whose bold and colorful patterns adorn everything from purses to shower curtains (more Marimekko branches are within a block of here). The other side of the street is dominated by Finland's answer to Harrods or Macy's: **Stockmann,** the biggest, best, and oldest department store in town (with a great gourmet supermarket in the basement).

• *Just beyond Stockmann is Helsinki's main intersection, where the Esplanade and Mannerheimintie meet. Turn right on Mannerheimintie. At the far side of Stockmann, you'll see a landmark statue, the...*

❻ Three Blacksmiths

While there's no universally accepted meaning for this statue (from 1932), most say it celebrates human labor and cooperation and shows the solid character of the Finnish people. On the base, note the surviving bullet damage from World War II. The Soviet Union used that war as an opportunity to invade Finland—which it had lost just 20 years prior—to try to reclaim their buffer zone. In a two-part war

(the "Winter War," then the "Continuation War"), Finland held fast and emerged with its freedom—and relatively little damage.

Two Men Who Remade Helsinki

Eliel Saarinen (1873-1950)

At the turn of the 20th century, architect Eliel Saarinen pioneered the Finnish National Romantic style. Inspired by peasant and medieval architectural traditions, his work was fundamental in creating a distinct—and modern—Finnish identity. The château-esque National Museum of Finland, designed by Saarinen and his two partners, was his first major success (see page 304). Two years later, Saarinen won the contract to construct the Helsinki train station (completed in 1919). Its design marks a transition into the Art Nouveau style of the early 1900s.

Alvar Aalto (1898-1976)

Alvar Aalto was a celebrated Finnish architect and designer working in the Modernist tradition; his buildings used abstract forms and innovative materials without sacrificing functionality. Finlandia Hall in Helsinki is undoubtedly Aalto's most famous structure, but that's just the beginning. Aalto concerned himself with nearly every aspect of design, from furniture to light fixtures. Perhaps most notable of these creations was his sinuous Savoy Vase, a masterpiece of simplicity and sophistication. His designs became so popular that in 1935 he and his wife opened Artek, a company that manufactures and sells his furniture, lamps, and textiles to this day (see page 295).

Stockmann's entrance on Aleksanterinkatu, facing the *Three Blacksmiths*, is one of the city's most popular meeting points. Everyone in Finland knows exactly what it means when you say: "Let's meet under the Stockmann's clock." Tram #3 makes a stop around the corner from the clock, on Mannerheimintie. Across the street from the clock, the Old Student Hall is decorated with legendary Finnish heroes.

• *For a shortcut to our next stop, duck through the passage (marked City-Käytävä) directly across the street from Stockmann's clock. This will take you through a bustling commercial zone. You'll enter—and continue straight through—the City Center shopping mall. Emerging on the far side, you're face-to-face with four granite giants guarding the...*

❼ Central Train Station (Rautatieasema)

This Helsinki landmark was designed by Eliel Saarinen (see sidebar). The strange, huge figures on the facade, carrying illuminated globes, seem to have stepped right out of a Nordic myth. Duck into the main hall and the Eliel Restaurant inside to catch the building's early 20th-century ambience.

With your back to the train station, look to the left; diagonally across the square is the **Ateneum**, Finland's national gallery of art.

It faces the **Finnish National Theater** (not visible from here)—founded to promote Finnish-speaking theater in the years Finland was dominated by Russian and Swedish speakers.

• *We've worked our way through the central part of town. Now, if you're ready to explore some more interesting buildings and monuments, continue with...*

PART 2: HELSINKI'S ICONIC ARCHITECTURE

The rest of this walk follows the boulevard called Mannerheimintie, which serves as a showcase for much of Helsinki's signature architecture; this walk also helps you reach some of the city's farther-flung sights. (Details on many of these appear later, under "Sights in Helsinki.")

• *With your back to the station, turn right and follow the tram tracks (along Kaivokatu street) back out to Mannerheimintie. Cross the street and tracks, and continue straight ahead, toward what looks like a giant wooden bowl. You'll pop out in front of the Kamppi shopping mall, at...*

❽ Kamppi Plaza (Narinkkatori) and Kamppi Chapel (Kampin Kappeli)

This plaza is a Helsinki hub—both for transportation (with a Metro stop and bus station nearby) and for shopping (with the towering Kamppi Center shopping mall). Turn your attention to the round, wooden structure at the corner of the plaza nearest the Esplanade. This is one of Helsinki's most surprising bits of architecture: the **Kamppi Chapel.** Enter through the black building just to the right, and enjoy a moment or three of total serenity. (For more on the chapel, see page 302.)

• *Leaving the chapel, cut through the middle of the big plaza, with the shopping mall on your left and the low-lying yellow building on your right. Veer right through the gap at the end of the square, and in a minute you'll see (across the busy street) an equestrian statue. Cross over to it.*

❾ Carl Gustaf Mannerheim and the Kiasma Museum of Contemporary Art (Nykytaiteen Museo Kiasma)

The busy street is named for the Finnish war hero Carl Gustaf Mannerheim, who led anti-Russian forces in the newly independent Finland's 1918 "Civil War." Later, during the "Winter War" of 1939-1940, Mannerheim and his fellow Finns put up a stiff resistance to a massive Soviet invasion. While the Baltic States—across the Gulf of Finland—were quickly "liberated" by the Red Army, dooming them to decades under the Soviet system, the Finns managed to refuse this assistance. Mannerheim became Finland's first postwar president, and thanks to his efforts (and those of countless others), Finland was allowed to chart its own democratic, capitalist course after the war. (Even so, Finland remained officially neutral through the Cold War, providing both East and West a political buffer zone.)

Mannerheim is standing in front of the glassy home of the **Kiasma Museum,** with changing exhibits of contemporary art. A bit farther along and across the street from Kiasma stands the Finnish **Parliament,** with its stoic row of Neoclassical columns.

From Mannerheim and Kiasma, head down into the grassy, sloping park. At the lowest point, watch out—you're crossing a busy **bicycle highway** that cuts right through the middle of the city center. Look left under the tunnel to see how a disused rail line has been turned into a subterranean pedalers' paradise.

• *The glassy building dominating the end of the park is the...*

⑩ Helsinki Music Center (Musiikkitalo)

Completed in 2011, this structure is even bigger than it looks: two-thirds of it is underground, and the entire complex houses seven separate venues. It's decorated, inside and out, with bold art (such as the gigantic pike on tiptoes that stands in the middle of the park). As you approach the bottom of the building, step into the atrium and look up to ogle the shimmering silver sculpture. While you're there, consider stopping by the ticket desk (on the lower floor,  closed Sun) to ask about performances while you're in town (the season is Sept-April). Upstairs is a music store. The interior features a lot of pine and birch accents, which warm up the space and improve the (Japanese-designed) acoustics. It didn't take long for the Music Center to become an integral part of the city's cultural life; in the first season of performances, some 400,000 people attended events here (for English tours of the facility, see "Sights in Helsinki," later).

Back outside, circle around the back side of the Music Center. Follow the straight, flat promenade that runs alongside a grassy park used for special events.

• *Crossing the street, you'll see (on the left) perhaps the most important work of Finnish architecture...*

⓫ Alvar Aalto's Finlandia Hall (Finlandia-talo)

This big, white building can be a bit difficult for casual observers to appreciate. To get the best view of it, walk through the long parking lot all the way to the far end, and look back. The building—entirely designed by Aalto, inside and out—opened in 1971 and immediately became a national icon. Notice how Aalto employs geometric shapes and sweeping lines to create a striking concert hall, seating up to 1,700 guests. Aalto designed

the inclined roof to try to maximize the hall's acoustics—imitating the echo chamber of an old-fashioned church tower—with marginal success. Aalto devotees or newcomers should consider a guided tour to make sense of this distinctive structure (tour-€15, call or visit website for times; hall info point open Mon-Fri 9:00-19:00, closed Sat-Sun; Mannerheimintie 13e, tel. 09/40241, www.finlandiatalo.fi).

The exterior is clad in thin white marble in what appears to be a basket-weave pattern. But this effect (while beautiful) is unintentional: Not long after the hall was finished, the marble panels began bending ever so slightly. So in 1999, they were replaced at great expense—and within 10 years' time they bowed out again. The city is now planning a third renovation, but this time is considering a material that can withstand the freeze/thaw cycles of a Helsinki winter.

Turn to face shimmering **Töölönlahti Bay** (not a lake, but an inlet of the Baltic Sea)—ringed by a popular walking and jogging track. From here, you can see more Helsinki landmarks: across the lake and a bit to the left, the white tower marks the Olympic Stadium that hosted the world in 1952. And to the right are the rides of Helsinki's old-time amusement park, Linnanmäki.

• *If you'd like to extend this walk, join the natives on the waterfront path (which offers even better views of Finlandia Hall). Otherwise, consider...*

More Helsinki Sights

To reach two more major sights, go up the stairs immediately to the right of Finlandia Hall, then continue all the way up to the main road. Directly across the street stands the fine ⓬ **National Museum of Finland,** which tells this country's story with lots of artifacts.

About a 10-minute walk behind the National Museum is the

beautiful "Church in the Rock," ⓭ **Temppeliaukio.** Once inside, sit. Enjoy the music. It's a wonderful place to end this walk.

Sights in Helsinki

NEAR THE SOUTH HARBOR

▲▲Uspenski Orthodox Cathedral (Uspenskin Katedraali)

This house of worship was built for the Russian military in 1868, at a time when Finland belonged to Russia (*Uspenski* is Russian for the Assumption of Mary). It hovers above Market Square and faces the Lutheran Cathedral, just as Russian culture faces Europe.

Cost and Hours: Free; Tue-Fri 9:30-16:00, Sat 10:00-15:00, Sun 12:00-15:00, closed Mon, Pormestarinrinne 1 (about a 10-minute walk beyond the harborfront market).

Visiting the Cathedral: Before heading inside, view the exterior. The uppermost "onion dome" represents the sacred heart of Jesus, while the smaller ones represent his 12 apostles.

The rich imagery of the cathedral's interior is a stark contrast to the sober Lutheran Cathedral. While commonly called the "Russian church," the cathedral is actually Eastern Orthodox, answering to the patriarch in Constantinople (Istanbul). Today, the cathedral is the seat of the archdiocese of Helsinki, to which much of eastern Finland belongs.

The cathedral's Orthodox Mass is beautiful, with a standing congregation, candles, incense, icons in action, priests behind the iconostasis, and timeless vocal music. In the front left corner, find the icon featuring the Madonna and Child, surrounded by rings and jewelry (under glass), given in thanks for prayers answered. Across from the icon, a white marble table holds memorial candles and a dish of wheat seeds, representing new life—the hope of resurrection—for the departed.

▲▲Lutheran Cathedral (Tuomiokirkkoseurakunta)

With its prominent green dome, gleaming white facade, and the 12 apostles overlooking the city and harbor, this church is Carl Ludvig Engel's masterpiece.

Cost and Hours: Free; daily 9:00-18:00, June-early Aug until 24:00, no visits during church services or special events; on Senate Square, www.helsinkicathedral.fi. In summer, free organ concerts are held on Sundays at 20:00.

Visiting the Cathedral: Enter the building around the left side. Finished in 1852, the interior is pure architectural truth.

Open a pew gate and sit, sur-
rounded by the saints of Prot-
estantism to savor Neoclassical
nirvana. Physically, this church
is perfectly Protestant—austere and unadorned—with the
emphasis on preaching (prominent pulpit) and music (huge
organ). Statuary is limited
to the local Reformation big
shots: Martin Luther, Philipp
Melanchthon (Luther's side-
kick), and the leading Finnish
reformer, Mikael Agricola. A follower of Luther at Wittenberg,
Agricola brought the Reformation to Finland. He also translated
the Bible into Finnish and is considered the father of the modern
Finnish language. Agricola's Bible is to Finland what the Luther
Bible is to Germany and the King James Bible is to the English-
speaking world.

Helsinki City Museum

This interesting museum, just off Senate Square in one of the city's
oldest buildings, gives an accessible overview of the city's history
and culture. On the ground floor, visitors use 3-D glasses to view
the many ways the city has changed over the years. Exhibits on
the second floor take you to a typical Helsinki home in the 1950s
and a local bar from the 1970s, complete with vintage soundtracks.
Most visitors won't need to linger, but everyone leaves with a better
understanding of why residents choose to call Helsinki home.

Cost and Hours: Free, Mon-Fri 11:00-19:00, Sat-Sun until
17:00, Aleksanterinkatu 16, www.helsinkicitymuseum.fi.

▲Design Museum

Design is integral to contemporary Finnish culture, and this fine
museum—with a small but insightful permanent collection and
well-presented temporary exhibits—offers a good overview (all in
English). Worth ▲▲▲ to those who came to Finland just for the
design, its interesting and clever installations will appeal to just
about anybody.

Cost and Hours: €10; daily 11:00-18:00; Sept-May Wed-Sun
11:00-13:00, Tue until 20:00, closed Mon; excellent (if pricey) gift
shop, Korkeavuorenkatu 23, www.designmuseum.fi.

Visiting the Museum: From the ticket desk on the ground
floor, turn into the permanent exhibit, called **Utopia Now: The
Story of Finnish Design.** The first gallery considers the process
of design—the steps from inspiration to production—and presents iconic objects from the Golden Age of Finnish design of the

1950s (glass bowls by Alvar Aalto) as well as more recent innovations (the addictive Angry Birds video game; successive generations of Nokia mobile phones).

The "Icons of Design" gallery introduces viewers to the life stories of leading Finnish designers and the functional objects they've created (Aalto's iconic wooden stool, for example—a staple in classrooms around the world). The "Warehouse" collects items from different periods of the museum's collections, with a focus on "better things for everyday life," with everything from brightly colored but practical jerry cans for transporting fuel to a government-issued maternity box (a starter kit for new mothers, including clothes and sheets).

Digital applications throughout the galleries make your visit participatory: You can test how to control a Scorpion harvester (a staple of the Finnish forest industry), or you can animate a Marimekko pattern of your choosing on a wall-sized screen. A virtual headset lets you time travel to Finland's pavilion at the 1900 Paris World's Fair.

Upstairs and downstairs, you'll also find typically excellent **temporary exhibits** that allow individual Finnish designers to take center stage.

BEYOND THE ESPLANADE

These sights are scattered in the zone west of the Esplanade, listed roughly in the order you'll reach them from the city center (and in the order they appear on my self-guided walk, earlier).

▲Ateneum

The Ateneum, Finland's national art gallery, has the country's oldest and largest art collection. Come here to see Finnish artists (mid-18th to 20th century) and a fine international collection, including works by Cézanne, Chagall, Gauguin, and Van Gogh. The museum also hosts good special exhibits of Finnish and international art. To see the cream of the crop, head directly up two flights of the grand entry staircase to Room 13, where classics from Finland's Golden Age of painting occupy every inch of wall space.

Cost and Hours: €15, Tue and Fri 10:00-18:00, Wed-Thu 9:00-20:00, Sat-Sun 10:00-17:00, closed Mon, near train station at Kaivokatu 2, tel. 0294-500-401, www.ateneum.fi.

▲Kamppi Chapel (Kampin Kappeli)

Sitting unassumingly on the busy, commercial plaza in front of the Kamppi shopping mall/bus-station complex, this restful space was

Sauna

Finland's vaporized fountain of youth is the sauna—Scandinavia's answer to support hose and face-lifts. A traditional sauna is a wood-paneled room with wooden benches and a blistering-hot wood-fired stove topped with rocks. Lay your towel on the bench (for hygienic reasons), and sit or lie on it. Ladle water from the bucket onto the rocks to make steam. Choose a higher bench for hotter temperatures. Let yourself work up a sweat, then, just before bursting, go outside to the shower for a Niagara of liquid ice. Suddenly your shower stall becomes a Cape Canaveral launch pad, as your body scatters to every corner of the universe. A moment later you're back together and can re-enter the steam room. Repeat as necessary. The famous birch branches are always available for slapping your skin. Finns claim this enhances circulation while emitting a refreshing birch aroma that opens your sinuses.

Two Helsinki saunas are handy for cruisers: Löyly and Allas. Sophisticated **Löyly** is on the Hernesaari peninsula, with its saunas and a restaurant open to the sea. There are separate dressing rooms and showers for men and women, but the saunas themselves are communal—everyone wears a bathing suit. The attached café/restaurant spills out onto a big view veranda and up to a rooftop terrace (€19/2 hours—includes towel, seat cover, soap, and shampoo; sauna generally open Mon-Wed 16:00-22:00, Thu 13:00-22:00, Fri-Sat 13:00-23:00, Sun 13:00-21:00; **$$** restaurant serves daily 11:00-22:00; Hernesaarenranta 4, tel. 09/6128-6550, www.loylyhelsinki.fi). It's smart to book ahead online.

Allas sits in the middle of the South Harbor action, at the edge of Market Square, with saunas that lead to a huge floating deck with three outdoor pools (fresh and sea water). Inside, there are three saunas: male, female, and mixed (€12, Mon-Fri 6:15-23:00, Sat-Sun from 8:00, café and bistro, Katajanokanlauturi 2a, www.allasseapool.fi).

opened by the city of Helsinki in 2012 to give residents and visitors a place of serenity. The wooden structure, clad in spruce and with an oval footprint, encloses a 38-foot-tall, windowless cylinder of silence. Inside, indirect light seeps in around the edges of the ceiling, bathing the clean, curved, alder-wood paneling in warmth and tranquility. Does it resemble Noah's Ark? The inside of an egg? The architects intentionally left it vague—and open to each visitor's interpretation. Although it's a church, there are no services; it's open to anyone needing a reflective pause. Locals drop by between their shopping chores to sit in a pew and ponder their deity, wrestle with tough issues…or just get a break. In this peaceful spot, secular modern architecture and meditative spirituality converge beautifully.

Cost and Hours: Free, Mon-Fri 8:00-20:00, Sat-Sun 10:00-18:00, Simonkatu 7, enter through adjacent low-profile black building.

▲National Museum of Finland (Kansallismuseo)

This pleasant, easy-to-handle collection is in a grand building designed by three of this country's greatest architects—including Eliel Saarinen—in the early 1900s. The museum is under renovation, with its exhibits gradually being reinstalled in phases. When completed, the galleries will chronologically trace the land of the Finns from prehistory to the 20th century. Highlights include Finland's largest permanent archaeological collection, the 1420 altarpiece dedicated to St. Birgitta (patron saint of Sweden—which owned Finland at the time), and a reconstructed early-1800s "smoke cabin" (sauna). While the renovation is underway, it's best to check the museum's website for current offerings.

Cost and Hours: €10, free on Fri 16:00-18:00; open Tue-Sun 11:00-18:00, closed Mon; Mannerheimintie 34, tel. 09/4050-9552, www.kansallismuseo.fi/en. The museum café has a tranquil outdoor courtyard. It's just a five-minute walk from Temppeliaukio Church (see next listing).

Visiting the Museum: Following the clear English-language descriptions (and perhaps checking with the front desk to hear about the progress of the renovation), visit each of the museum's four parts, in chronological order. First, the **Prehistory of Finland** shows how Stone, Bronze, and Iron Age tribes in this area lived. You'll see lots of early stone tools (ax and arrow heads), pottery, human remains, and—at the end of the exhibit—Iron Age weapons and jewelry.

The Realm picks up the story with the Middle Ages, represented by the 14th-century St. Birgitta, a top saint. You'll pass through dimly lit halls of mostly wood-carved church art—from roughly hewn Catholic altarpieces to brightly painted, post-Reformation, Lutheran pulpits—then learn about Finland's time as part of Sweden (the introduction of the Renaissance). Continuing upstairs, you'll find out about the different social classes in historical Finland—the nobility, the peasants, the clergy, the rulers and monarchs, and the burghers (craftsmen and guild members). Look for a Rococo-period drawing room and—transitioning from Swedish to Russian rule—portraits of Russia's last czars around an impressive throne.

From there, temporary exhibits lead back to the main hall, where you can continue into **A Land and Its People.** In this display of Finnish peasant traditions, you'll see farming and fishing tools, a thought-provoking exhibit about the indigenous Sami people (distributed across the northern reaches of Finland, Sweden, Norway, and Russia), and a particularly fine collection of beautifully decorated tools used for spinning—folk art used to make folk art.

From the folk furniture, find the stairs back down to the ground floor and the **SF-1900** exhibit (that's Suomi/Finland from 1900), starting with the birth of modern Finland in 1917 and its 1918 civil war. A six-minute loop of archival footage shows you early-20th-century Finland. Touchscreen tables help tell the story of the fledgling nation, as do plenty of well-presented artifacts (including clothing, household items, vehicles, and a traditional outhouse).

▲▲▲Temppeliaukio Church

A modern example of great church architecture (from 1969), this "Church in the Rock" was blasted out of solid granite. Architect-brothers Timo and Tuomo Suomalainen won a competition to design the church, which they built within a year's time. Barren of decor except for a couple of simple crosses, the church is capped with a copper-and-skylight dome; it's normally filled with live or recorded music and awe-

struck visitors. Grab a pew. Gawk upward at a 13-mile-long coil of copper ribbon. Look at the bull's-eye and ponder God. Forget your camera. Just sit in the middle, ignore the crowds, and be thankful for peace (under your feet is an air-raid shelter that can accommodate 6,000 people).

The church has excellent acoustics and is a popular concert venue; check at the TI for upcoming programs.

Cost and Hours: €3, generally Mon-Sat 10:00-17:45, Sun from 11:45, closes one hour earlier off-season—but because of frequent events and church services, it's good to confirm open times

HELSINKI

by listening to the recorded message at 09/2340-5940, Lutherinka-tu 3, tel. 09/2340-6320, www.helsinginseurakunnat.fi.

Getting There: The church is at the top of a gentle hill in a residential neighborhood, about a 15-minute walk north of the bus station or a 10-minute walk from the National Museum (or take tram #2 to Sammonkatu stop).

▲Sibelius Monument

Six hundred stainless-steel pipes called "Love of Music"—built on solid rock, as is so much of Finland—shimmer in a park to honor Finland's greatest com-

poser, Jean Sibelius. It's a forest of pipe-organ pipes in a forest of trees. The artist, Eila Hiltunen, was forced to add a bust of the composer's face to silence crit-ics of her otherwise abstract work. City orientation bus tours stop here for 10 minutes—long enough. The monument is a few blocks from the Töölön halli tram stop, and near the bus #24 line that also serves the Seurasaari Open-Air Folk Museum, described below.

OUTER HELSINKI

A weeklong car trip up through the Finnish lakes and forests to Mikkeli and Savonlinna would be relaxing, but you can actually enjoy Finland's green-trees-and-blue-water scenery without leaving Helsinki. Here are two great ways to get out and go for a walk on a sunny summer day if you'd rather skip the city sights.

▲▲Suomenlinna Fortress

The island guarding Helsinki's harbor served as a strategic fortress for three countries: Finland, Sweden, and Russia. It's now a popular

park, with delightful paths, fine views, and a visitors center. On a sunny day, it's a delightful place to stroll among hulking build-ings with recreating Finns. The free Suomenlinna guidebook-let (stocked at the Helsinki TI, ferry terminal, and the visitors center) covers the island thor-oughly. The island has one good museum (the Suomenlinna Museum, at Suomenlinna Centre—described later) and several skippable smaller museums, including a toy museum and several military museums (open summer only).

Getting There: Catch a ferry to Suomenlinna from Market Square. Walk past the high-priced excursion boats to the public HKL ferry (€5 round-trip, covered by day ticket and Helsinki Card, 15-minute trip, May-Aug 2-3/hour—generally at :00, :20, and :40 past the hour, but pick up schedule to confirm; Sept-April every 40–60 minutes). If you'll be taking at least two tram rides within 24 hours of visiting Suomenlinna, it pays to get a day ticket instead of a round-trip ticket. If your goal is the Suomenlinna Centre and the museum, the private JT Line "water bus" gets you closer to them than the public ferry (€7 round-trip, May-Sept 2/hour, departs from Market Square, tel. 09/534-806, www.jt-line.fi).

Visitor Information: The information desk at the Jetty Barracks, at the ferry landing, is open year-round (daily 10:00-18:00, Oct-April until 16:00), tel. 029-533-8410, www.suomenlinna.fi. Pick up the free island map/booklet here.

Tours: The one-hour English-language island tour departs from the Suomenlinna Centre (€11, free with Helsinki Card; June-Aug daily at 11:00, 12:30, and 14:30; Sept-May 1/day Sat-Sun only). The tour is fine if you're a military history buff, but it kind of misses the point of what's now essentially a giant playground for all ages.

Background: The fortress was built by the Swedes with French financial support in the mid-1700s to counter Russia's rise to power. (Russian Czar Peter the Great had built his new capital, St. Petersburg, on the Baltic and was eyeing the West.) Named Sveaborg ("Fortress of Sweden"), the fortress was Sweden's military pride and joy. With five miles of walls and hundreds of cannons, it was the second strongest fort of its kind in Europe after Gibraltar. Helsinki, a small community of 1,500 people before 1750, soon became a boomtown supporting this grand "Gibraltar of the North."

The fort, built by more than 10,000 workers, was a huge investment and stimulated lots of innovation. In the 1760s, it had the world's biggest and most modern dry dock. It served as a key naval base during a brief Russo-Swedish war in 1788-1790. But in 1808, the Russians took the "invincible" fort without a fight—by siege—as a huge and cheap military gift.

Today, Suomenlinna has 800 permanent residents, is home to Finland's Naval Academy, and is most appreciated by locals for its fine scenic strolls. The island is large—actually, it's six islands connected by bridges—and you and your imagination get free run of the fortifications and dungeon-like chambers. When it's time to eat, you'll find a half-dozen cafés and plenty of picnic opportunities.

Visiting Suomenlinna: Start your stroll of the island at the Jetty Barracks near the public ferry landing. A suggested visitors' route, marked with blue signs, runs from north to south across the fortress and will take you to all the key sights. You'll wander on cobbles past dilapidated shiplap cottages that evoke a more robust time for this once-strategic, now-leisurely island. The garrison church on your left doubled as a lighthouse.

A five-minute walk from the ferry brings you to the **Suomenlinna Centre,** which houses the worthwhile Suomenlinna Museum. Inside the (free) lobby, you'll find an information desk, gift shop, café, and giant model of all six islands that make up Suomenlinna—handy for orientation. The exhibits themselves are well-presented but dryly explained: fragments of old walls, cannons, period clothing, model ships, and so on; the upstairs focuses on the site's transition from a fortress to a park. The main attraction is the fascinating 25-minute film that presents the island's complete history (€6.50 for museum and film, runs 2/hour, daily 10:00-18:00, Oct-April 10:30-16:30).

From the Suomenlinna Centre, cross the bridge—noticing the giant, rusted seaplane hall on the right, housing the Regatta Club, with a fun sailboat photo exhibition and shop. On the far side of the hall, peer into the gigantic dry dock.

Back on the main trail, climb five minutes uphill to the right into **Piper Park** (Piperin Puisto). Hike up past its elegant 19th-century café (with rocky view tables), and continue up and over the ramparts to a surreal swimming area. From here, follow the waterline—and the ramparts—to the south. You'll walk above bunkers burrowed underground, like gigantic molehills (or maybe hobbit houses). Periodic ladders let you scramble down onto  the rocks. Imposing cannons, now used as playsets and photo-op props for kids, are still aimed ominously at the Gulf of Finland—in case, I imagine, of Russian invasion...or if they just get fed up with all of those cruise ships. Reaching the southern tip of the island, called King's Gate, peek out through the cannon holes. Then make your walk a loop by circling back to the Suomenlinna Centre and, beyond that, the ferry dock for the ride home.

▲▲Seurasaari Open-Air Folk Museum

Inspired by Stockholm's Skansen, also on a lovely island on the edge of town, this is a collection of 100 historic buildings from every corner of Finland. It's wonderfully furnished and gives rushed visitors an opportunity to sample the far reaches of Finland without leaving the capital city—you can see the highlights here in about an hour (if you're not taking a tour, get the map or the helpful guidebook). But it's easy to stretch out your visit with a picnic

or light lunch (snacks and cakes available in the Antti farmstead at the center of the park). Off-season, when the buildings are closed, the place is empty and not worth the trouble.

Cost and Hours: Free park entry, €9 to enter buildings; June-Aug daily 11:00-17:00; shorter hours May and Sept; buildings closed rest of year; tel. 09/4050-9660, www.seurasaari.fi.

Tours: One-hour English tours are free with entry ticket, offered mid-June-mid-Aug generally at 15:00 (confirm time on website).

Getting There: To reach the museum, ride bus #24 (from the top of the Esplanade, 2/hour, 25 minutes) to the last stop at Seurasaari (note departure times for your return) and walk across the quaint footbridge.

Shopping in Helsinki

Helsinki may be the top shopping town in the Nordic countries. Even in this region of creative design culture, Helsinki is a trendsetter; many Finnish designers are household names worldwide. The easiest place to get a taste of Finnish design is in the shops at the top end of the Esplanade, but with a little more time, it's worth delving into the nearby Design District.

Opening Times: Most shops are open all day Monday through Friday (generally 10:00 or 11:00 until 17:00 or 18:00), and often have shorter hours on Saturday. Most are closed on Sundays. Shops on the Esplanade stay open later and keep Sunday hours.

THE ESPLANADE AND NEARBY

Helsinki's elegant main drag, the Esplanade, is a coffee-sipper's and window-shopper's delight. Practically every big name in Finnish design has a flagship store along or near this people-pleasing strip. Here are some worth dipping into:

Marimekko, the well-known Finnish fashion company, took off on the international stage in the 1960s when Jackie Kennedy bought seven Marimekko dresses (and wore one of them on the cover of *Sports Illustrated*). You'll find the company's colorful, patterned scarves, clothes, purses, and fabrics in locations throughout central Helsinki, including right across from Stockmann department store (at Aleksanterinkatu 50, www.marimekko.com). Other nearby Marimekko branches include one specializing in children's

HELSINKI

items (at Mikonkatu 1), and stores in the Kamppi and Forum shopping centers.

These three shops are strung along the north side of the Esplanade: **Aarikka** (#27, www.aarikka.com) has affordable and casual handmade jewelry, tableware, and home decor, most of it made from colorful spheres of wood. **Iittala** (#23, www.iittala.com) is the flagship store of a longtime Finnish glassmaker. Popping into the shop, you'll see Alvar Aalto's signature wavy-mouthed vases, which haven't gone out of fashion since 1936; Oiva Toikka's iconic "dew drop"-patterned chalices and pedestal bowls from 1964; and an array of other decorative and functional glassware. **Kalevala** (at #25) has been selling finely crafted, handmade-in-Finland jewelry since 1937; some pieces are modern, while others are inspired by old Scandinavian and Sami themes (www.kalevalakoru.com).

Finlayson, on the south side of the Esplanade, is a venerable textile design company that's been around since 1820—but their sheets, towels, rugs, and curtains are fun and modern (#14, www.finlayson.fi).

The Esplanade is capped by the enormous, eight-floor **Stockmann** department store, arguably Scandinavia's most impressive (Mon-Fri 9:00-21:00, Sat until 18:00, Sun 12:00-18:00, great basement supermarket, Aleksanterinkatu 52B, www.stockmann.fi). Bookworms enjoy the impressive **Academic Bookstore** just downhill from Stockmann (#39, same hours as Stockmann). **Artek,** Alvar and Elissa Aalto's flagship store (across from Stockmann at Keskuskatu 1B, www.artek.fi), offers fine furniture and lighting by the leading Finnish design concern.

Fans of Tove Jansson's Moomin children's stories will enjoy the **Moomin Shop,** on the second floor of the Forum shopping mall at Mannerheimintie 20, across the busy tram-lined street from Stockmann (and with the same hours).

THE DESIGN DISTRICT

Helsinki's Design District is a several-block cluster of streets filled with design and antique shops, fashion stores highlighting local designers, and trendy restaurants. Explore this engaging zone to feel the creativity and uniqueness of Finnish design and urban culture. For a handy orientation to the options in this ever-changing area, visit www.designdistrict.fi (with themed walking maps) or pick up the Design District brochure from the TI.

While the Design District sprawls roughly southwest of the Esplanade nearly to the waterfront, the following zones are most worthy of exploration.

Kolmikulma Park and Nearby

Just a block south of the Esplanade's top end (down Erottajankatu), the park called Kolmikulma (Diana Park, with its spear-throwing statue centerpiece) is a handy epicenter of Design District liveliness.

Uudenmaankatu street (west from the park) has the highest concentration of shops, especially fashion boutiques of local designers such as **Ivana Helsinki** (#15, patterned casual dresses). You'll also find **Nounou** (at #2, modern, handmade glass pieces); the recommended **Café Bar No. 9; Astia Taivas** (#13, crammed with secondhand glassware); and, around the corner on Annankatu street, **Momono** (#12, well-selected examples of modern and vintage Finnish design).

Meanwhile, a block south, pedestrianized **Iso Roobertinkatu** has lots of cheap eateries; **Formverk** has fun home decor and kitchenware (on the corner at Annankatu 5).

Fredrikinkatu

This street, which crosses Uudenmaankatu two blocks west of the park, is one of the most engaging streets in town.

Start at the corner with Uudenmaankatu and work your way north to Bulevardi. Besides fashion boutiques, you'll discover **C. Hagelstam Antique Books** (#35, quaint and beautiful shop with vintage prints and books), **Kauniste** (#24, uniquely patterned fabrics and prints) and **Chez Marius** (#26, fun kitchen gadgets and cooking gear). This shop also marks the pleasant intersection with the tree- and tram-lined Bulevardi. **Day,** kitty-corner from the Chez Marius, has funky, quirky home decor and gifts (Bulevardi 11).

Continuing north along Fredrikinkatu, the next block has several home decor shops, including **Casuarina** (#30, with a spare, rustic, reclaimed aesthetic), and **Primavera Interiors** (#41, with a more artistic and funky style).

Browse your way two more blocks up Fredrikinkatu to the cross-street, **Eerikinkatu,** which also has lots of inviting little galleries and boutiques; two are at the same address (at Eerikinkatu 18): **DesiPeli,** with a variety of home decor, including some very cool, Marimekko-type fabrics; and **Napa & Paja,** a collective gallery of three jewelry designers, showcasing their beautiful, unique, delicate designs. They also stock casual handbags and books about Finland.

Near the Design Museum

The Design Museum anchors an appealing area of boutiques—and itself has a good shop with a wide range of Finnish design products (often related to current exhibits). A block south of the museum, on **Korkeavuorenkatu,** you'll find vintage shops, kitchenware, antiques, pop-up stores, fashion boutiques, hair salons, and cafés. Keep an eye out for **Pore Helsinki** (at #3), with casual fashion and accessories; and **Fasaani** (a.k.a. Helsinki Secondhand, at #5)—crammed with affordable pre-owned home-decor items just like those in galleries around town (closed Sun, Korkeavuorenkatu 5, www.fasaani.fi).

OTHER SHOPPING OPTIONS

Market Square: This harborfront square is packed not only with fishmongers and producers, but also with stands selling Finnish souvenirs and more refined crafts (roughly Mon-Fri 6:30-17:00, an hour later in summer, Sat until 16:00, only tourist stalls open on Sun 10:00-16:00).

Modern Shopping Malls: For less glamorous shopping needs, the **Kamppi** mall above and around the bus station is good. The **Forum** shopping center at Mannerheimintie 20 is filled with Euro fashion brands.

Flea Market: The outdoor **Hietalahti Market** is a 15-minute walk from the harbor or a short ride on tram #6 from Mannerheimintie to the Hietalahdentori stop (June-Aug Mon-Fri 9:00-19:00, Sat 8:00-16:00, Sun 10:00-16:00; less action, shorter hours, and closed Sun off-season). The adjacent red-brick indoor Hietalahti Market Hall houses food stands (described later, under "Eating in Helsinki").

Eating in Helsinki

Helsinki's many restaurants are smoke-free and a good value for lunch on weekdays. These low prices evaporate on Saturday and Sunday, when picnics and Middle Eastern kebab restaurants are the only budget options.

FUN HARBORFRONT EATERIES

Stalls on Market Square: Helsinki's delightful and vibrant square is magnetic any time of day...but especially at lunchtime. This really is the most memorable, casual, quick-and-easy lunch place in town. A half-dozen orange tents (erected to shield diners from

---

Restaurant Code

I've assigned each eatery a price category, based on the average cost of a typical main course. Drinks, desserts, and splurge items (steak and seafood) can raise the price considerably.

$$$$ Splurge: Most main courses over €25
$$$ Pricier: €20-25
$$ Moderate: €15-20
$ Budget: Under €15

In Finland, a takeout spot is **$**; a sit-down café is **$$**; a casual but more upscale restaurant is **$$$**; and a swanky splurge is **$$$$**.

---

dive-bombing gulls) serve moose meatballs, smoked reindeer, and creamy salmon soup on paper plates until 18:00. It's not unusual for the Finnish president to stop by here with visiting dignitaries. There's a crêpe place, and at the far end—my favorites—several salmon grills (€11-13 for a good meal). The only real harborside dining in this part of town is picnicking. While these places provide picnic tables, you can also have your food foil-wrapped to go and grab benches right on the water down near Uspenski Orthodox Cathedral.

Old Market Hall (Vanha Kauppahalli): Just beyond the harborside market is a cute, red-brick, indoor market hall. It's beautifully renovated with rich woodwork, and quite tight inside (daily 8:00-18:00, not all stalls open on Sun). Today, along with produce stalls, it's a hit for its fun, inexpensive eateries. You'll find enticing coffee shops with tempting pastries; grilled, smoked, or pickled fish options; mounds of saffron-yellow paella; delectable open-face sandwiches; a handy chance to sample reindeer meat; and an array of ethnic eats, from Middle Eastern and Lebanese meals to Vietnamese banh mi sandwiches. In the market hall, **$ Soppakeittiö** ("Soup Kitchen") serves big bowls of filling, tasty seafood soup.

FINNISH-THEMED DINING

$$$ Zetor mercilessly lampoons Finnish rural culture and cuisine (while celebrating it deep down). Sit next to a cow-crossing sign at a tractor-turned-into-a-table, in a "Finnish Western" atmosphere. Main courses include reindeer, smoked perch pies, grilled liver, and less exotic fare (daily 12:00-24:00, 200 yards north of Stockmann department store, across street from McDonald's at Mannerheimintie 3, tel. 010-766-4450).

$$$$ Lappi Restaurant is a fine place for tasty Lapp (Sami) cuisine, with an entertaining menu (including house-smoked fish, roasted elk, and reindeer shank). The snug, woody atmosphere will have you thinking you've traveled north and lashed your rein-

HELSINKI

Central Helsinki Restaurants

deer to the hitchin' post (Mon-Fri 16:00-22:30, Sat from 13:00, closed Sun, off Bulevardi at Annankatu 22, tel. 09/645-550, www. lappires.com).

VENERABLE ESPLANADE CAFÉS

Restaurants line the sunny north side of the Esplanade—offering creative lunch salads and light meals in their cafés (with fine sidewalk seating), plush sofas for cocktails in their bars, and fancy restaurant dining upstairs.

$$ The **Teatterin Deli** and **Teatterin Bar** are among several interconnected eateries attached to the landmark Swedish Theater. Order a sandwich or salad from the deli counter (facing the Academic Bookstore) to eat in or takeaway. The long cocktail bar that faces the Esplanade is a fun space for a drink and people-watching. Whether you order a meal or a drink, you're welcome to find a seat out on the leafy Esplanade terrace (deli counter open daily until 21:00, at the top of the Esplanade, Pohjoisesplanadi 2, tel. 09/6128-5000). The fancy **$$$$ Grilli** restaurant is also here.

$$$ Strindberg, near the corner of the Esplanade and Mikonkatu, oozes atmosphere and class. Downstairs is an elegant

500 Meters
500 Yards

1. Market Square
2. Old Market Hall Eateries
3. Zetor Restaurant
4. Lappi Restaurant
5. Teatterin Deli, Bar & Grilli
6. Strindberg
7. Spis
8. Juuri
9. Emo Restaurant & Picnic
10. Café Bar No. 9
11. Hietalahti Market Hall
12. Lasipalatsi Café
13. Stockmann Dep't Store
14. S Market Grocery
15. Café Kappeli
16. Café Aalto (in Academic Bookstore)
17. Ateljee Bar (in Torni Tower)

café with outdoor and indoor tables great for people-watching (sandwiches and salads). The upstairs cocktail lounge—with big sofas and bookshelves—has a den-like coziness that attracts an after-work crowd. Also upstairs, the inviting restaurant has huge main dishes with fish, meat, pasta, and vegetarian options; reserve in advance to get a window seat overlooking the Esplanade (restaurant open Mon-Sat 11:00-23:00, closed Sun; café open Mon-Sat 9:00-24:00, Sun 10:00-22:00, Pohjoisesplanadi 33, tel. 09/681-2030).

TRENDY EATERIES IN AND NEAR THE DESIGN DISTRICT

Several creative eateries clustered in the Design District, a short stroll south and west of the Esplanade, offer a fresh take on the cuisine of Finland, featuring seasonal ingredients and modern presentations.

$$$$ Spis is your best Helsinki bet for splurging on Finnish New Nordic. Reserve ahead for one of the prized tables in its tiny, peeling-plaster, rustic-chic dining room (tasting menus only, Tue-

Thu from 18:00, Fri-Sat from 17:30, last seating at 20:30, closed Sun-Mon, Kasarmikatu 26, mobile 045-305-1211, www.spis.fi).

$$$$ Juuri has a casual interior and a few outdoor tables. They serve a variety of "sapas"—small plates highlighting Finland's culinary bounty, such as herring, pike roe, and arctic char (Mon-Fri 11:30-14:30 & 17:00-23:00, Sat 12:00-23:00, Sun 16:00-23:00, Korkeavuorenkatu 27, tel. 09/635-732).

$$$ Emo Restaurant is a pleasantly unpretentious wine bar in a sleepy zone just a block off of the Esplanade. They serve up €10 small plates as well as à la carte choices—cassoulet, rack of pork, rainbow trout (lunch Tue-Fri 11:30-14:30; dinner Mon-Sat 17:00-24:00, closed Sun; Kasarmikatu 44, mobile 010-505-0900, www.emo-ravintola.fi).

Pub Grub: A simpler choice tucked between shops in the heart of the Design District, **$$ Café Bar No. 9** attracts a loyal local following, who enjoy digging into plates of unpretentious pub food (Uudenmaankatu 9, tel. 09/621-4059).

Market Hall: Hiding at the western edge of the Design District, the **$$ Hietalahti Market Hall** is a fun place to browse for a meal. Like the Old Market Hall along the South Harbor, this elegantly renovated (but less touristy) food hall is filled with an enticing array of vendors, with delightful seating upstairs (Mon-Thu 8:00-18:00, Fri-Sat until 22:00, Sun 10:00-16:00, www.hietalahdenkauppahalli.fi).

NEAR THE STATIONS

$$ Lasipalatsi, the renovated, rejuvenated 1930s Glass Palace, is on Mannerheimintie between the train and bus stations. The café—with a youthful terrace on the square out back—offers a self-service buffet (€11 lunch menu available all day); there are always €5 sandwiches and cakes (Mon-Sat 8:30-20:00, closed Sun). Upstairs there's a more expensive **$$$** restaurant that's a Helsinki classic, with bird's-eye city views (Mon-Fri 11:00-24:00, closed Sat-Sun, across from the old post office building at Mannerheimintie 22, tel. 09/612-6700).

PICNICS

In supermarkets, buy the semiflat bread (available dark or light) that Finns love—every slice is a heel. Finnish liquid yogurt is also a treat (sold in liter cartons). Karelian pasties, filled with rice or mashed potatoes, make a good snack. A beautiful, upscale supermarket is in the basement of the **Stockmann** department store—follow the *Delikatessen* signs downstairs (Mon-Fri until 21:00, Sat-Sun until 18:00, Aleksanterinkatu 52B). Two blocks north, **S Market** is a more workaday supermarket under

What If I Miss My Ship?

Remember that you can get help from the cruise line's port agent (listed on the destination information sheet distributed on the ship) and the local TI. If the port agent suggests a costly solution (such as a private car with a driver), you may want to consider public transit.

Two fine and fiercely competitive lines—Viking Line (tel. 0600-41577, www.vikingline.fi) and Tallink Silja (tel. 0600-15700, www.tallinksilja.com)—connect Helsinki to **Stockholm.** Several companies run fast boats to **Tallinn,** including Tallink Silja, Viking Line, Linda Line (www.lindaline.ee), and Eckerö Line (www.eckeroline.fi). To reach points farther west, you could take the night boat to Stockholm, then go by train to **Copenhagen** or **Oslo** (or take the overnight boat from Stockholm to **Rīga**). To research train schedules, see www.bahn.com. But for many of these places, you're probably better off flying (check www.skyscanner.com).

St. Petersburg is well connected to Helsinki, but you'll need a Russian visa (impossible to get last-minute). With a visa, you can take a speedy train (www.vr.fi) or a slower bus. But if you don't have a visa, you're likely better off waiting and meeting your ship at the next stop.

If you need to catch a **plane** to your next destination, you can take a bus to Helsinki's airport, about 10 miles north of the city (www.helsinki-vantaa.fi).

Check with the user-friendly Helsinki Expert desk inside the main TI (see page 285). For more advice on what to do if you miss the ship, see page 130.

the Sokos department store next to the train station (daily until 22:00).

Another option is **$ Picnic,** a casual chain offering fresh, made-to-go sandwiches, salads, and pastries. There's one just south of the midsection of the Esplanade (at Kasarmikatu 42), but you'll see them all around town, including in the Forum and Kamppi shopping centers (www.picnic.fi).

Finnish Survival Phrases

In Finnish, the emphasis always goes on the first syllable. Double vowels (e.g., *ää* or *ii*) sound similar to single vowels, but are held a bit longer. The letter *y* sounds like the German *ü* (purse your lips and say "oh"). In the phonetics, ī sounds like the long *i* in "light," and bolded syllables are stressed.

English	Finnish	Pronunciation
Good morning. (formal)	*Hyvää huomenta.*	**hew**-vaah **hwoh**-mehn-tah
Good day. (formal)	*Hyvää päivää.*	**hew**-vaah **pī**-vaah
Good evening. (formal)	*Hyvää iltaa.*	**hew**-vaah **eel**-taah
Hi. / Bye. (informal)	*Hei. / Hei-hei.*	hey / hey-hey
Do you speak English?	*Puhutko englantia?*	**poo**-hoot-koh **ehn**-glahn-tee-yah
Yes. / No.	*Kyllä. / Ei.*	**kewl**-lah / ay
Please.	*Ole hyvä.*	**oh**-leh **hew**-vah
Thank you (very much).	*Kiitos (paljon).*	**kee**-tohs (**pahl**-yohn)
You're welcome.	*Kiitos. / Ei kestä.*	**kee**-tohs / ay **kehs**-tah
Can I help you?	*Voinko auttaa?*	**voin**-koh **owt**-taah
Excuse me.	*Anteeksi.*	**ahn**-teek-see
(Very) good.	*(Oikein) hyvä.*	(**oy**-kayn) **hew**-vah
Goodbye.	*Näkemiin.*	**nah**-keh-meen
zero / one / two	*nolla / yksi / kaksi*	**noh**-lah / **ewk**-see / **kahk**-see
three / four	*kolme / neljä*	**kohl**-meh / **nehl**-yah
five / six	*viisi / kuusi*	**vee**-see / **koo**-see
seven / eight	*seitsemän / kahdeksan*	**sayt**-seh-mahn / **kah**-dehk-sahn
nine / ten	*yhdeksän / kymmenen*	**ew**-dehk-sahn / **kewm**-meh-nehn
hundred	*sata*	**sah**-tah
thousand	*tuhat*	**too**-haht
How much?	*Paljonko?*	**pahl**-yohn-koh
local currency: euro	*euro*	**ay**-oo-roh
Where is...?	*Missä on...?*	**mee**-sah ohn
...the toilet	*...WC*	**vay**-say
men	*miehet*	**mee**-ay-heht
women	*naiset*	**nī**-seht
water / coffee	*vesi / kahvi*	**veh**-see / **kah**-vee
beer / wine	*olut / viini*	**oh**-luht / **vee**-nee
Cheers!	*Kippis!*	**kip**-pis
The bill, please.	*Saisinko laskun, kiitos.*	**sī**-seen-koh **lahs**-kuhn **kee**-tohs

ST. PETERSBURG

Russia

Russia Practicalities

 Russia (Россия) is a vast, multiethnic country of more than 142 million people. The world's biggest country by area (6.6 million square miles), it is nearly double the size of the US. Though no longer the great military and political power that it was during the Cold War, Russia remains a country of substantial natural resources, including oil. St. Petersburg—Russia's "window on the West"—is the country's northwestern outpost, peering across the Baltic Sea to Europe.

Money: The currency has been in flux, so check the latest rates. As of this writing (in mid-2017), 60 Russian rubles (R, official RUB) = about $1. An ATM is called a bankomat (банкомат). The local value-added sales tax (called ндс/NDS) is 18 percent; the minimum purchase eligible for a VAT refund is 10,000 R (for details on refunds, see page 125). At some sights, you'll see higher "foreigner prices" for non-Russians.

Language: The native language is Russian, which uses the Cyrillic alphabet (see page 410).

Emergencies: Dial 112 for police or other emergencies. Pickpockets and petty theft are a problem in St. Petersburg; for tips, see page 332. In case of theft or loss, see page 118.

Time Zone: St. Petersburg is on Moscow Time (one hour ahead of Helsinki, Tallinn, and Rīga; two hours ahead of Scandinavia and most of the Continent, including Stockholm and Copenhagen; and eight/eleven hours ahead of the East/West Coasts of the US).

Consulate in St. Petersburg: The **US consulate** is at Furshtadtskaya 15 (tel. 331-2600, https://www.usembassy.gov/russia/). There is no **Canadian embassy** in St. Petersburg; instead, contact the Moscow branch (23 Starokonyushenny Pereulok, tel. 495/925-6000, www.russia.gc.ca). Call ahead for passport services.

Phoning: Russia's country code is 7, and St. Petersburg's area code is 812. To call from another country to Russia, dial the international access code (011 from the US/Canada, 00 from Europe, or + from a mobile phone), then 7, followed by the area code and local number. For calls within Russia, dial just the number if you are calling locally; if you're calling long distance, dial 8, then the area code and the number. To call the US or Canada from Russia, dial 8, then dial 10, then 1, then your area code and phone number. For more tips, see page 1062.

Tipping: As service is included at sit-down meals, you don't need to tip further. Tip a taxi driver by rounding up the fare a bit (pay 300 R on a 280-R fare). For more tips on tipping, see page 129.

Tourist Information: www.visit-petersburg.ru

ST. PETERSBURG

Санкт-Петербург

Once a swamp, then an imperial capital, and now a showpiece of vanished aristocratic opulence resurrected from the dingy ruins of communism, St. Petersburg is Russia's most accessible and most tourist-worthy city. During the Soviet era, it was called Leningrad, but in 1991 St. Petersburg reverted to its more fitting historic name, honoring the Romanov czar who willed the city into being. Designed by imported French, Dutch, and Italian architects, this is, arguably, European Russia's least "Russian" city.

Palaces, gardens, statues, and arched bridges over graceful waterways bring back the time of the czars. Neighborhood markets brim with exotic fishes, meats, and produce, and bustle with gregarious vendors offering samples of honey and pickled goodies. Stirring monuments—still adorned with hammers, sickles, and red stars—tower over the masses, evoking Soviet times. Jammed with reverent worshippers, glorious Orthodox churches are heavy with incense, shimmer with icons, and filled with hauntingly beautiful music. Topping things off are two of the world's premier art museums—the Hermitage and the Russian Museum—and one of its most opulent royal houses, the Catherine Palace.

St. Petersburg can challenge its visitors, most of whom have to jump through hoops to get a visa—and then struggle with not enough time, limited English, and an idiosyncratic (and not quite Western) approach to "service" and predictability. But most visitors leave St. Petersburg with vivid memories of a magnificent city, one that lives according to its own rules. While this place can be exasperating, it is worth grappling with. Beyond its brick-and-mortar sights, St. Petersburg gives first-timers a perfect peek into the enigmatic Russian culture.

Save time on a sunny day just to walk. Keep your head up: The upper facades are sun-warmed and untouched by street grime. While Nevsky Prospekt—the city's famous main boulevard—encapsulates all that's wonderful and discouraging about this quixotic burg, get beyond that axis. Explore the back streets along the canals. Stroll through the Summer Garden. Shop for a picnic at a local market hall. Go for a canal boat cruise. Step into a neighborhood church to watch people get intimate with an icon. Take a Metro ride anywhere, just for the experience. Climb St. Isaac's Cathedral for the view. When the Baltic Sea brings clouds and drizzle, plunge into the Hermitage or the Russian Museum.

PLANNING YOUR TIME

St. Petersburg is fantastic and gigantic, with much to see. With two days here, your priorities should include the following:

Hermitage: One of the world's finest palaces, housing one of the world's best art collections. Four hours is just enough for a quick taste (one hour for the staterooms, one hour for Old Masters art, one hour for Modern Masters, and an extra hour just to move around the huge and crowded complex).

Russian Museum: Excellent, manageable, and relatively uncrowded collection of Russian art. Allow two hours.

Nevsky Prospekt: St. Petersburg's bustling main drag, explained by my self-guided walk from Palace Square (behind the Hermitage) to the Fontanka River, and passing several of the biggies listed here. Allow two hours for the walk, not counting sightseeing stops.

Fabergé Museum: One of the world's best collections of Fabergé eggs fills a mansion near the end of my self-guided Nevsky Prospekt walk. An hour gives you a speedy look.

Kazan Cathedral, Church on Spilled Blood, and St. Isaac's: St. Petersburg's three best Orthodox churches—each very different (so they're complementary). Allow about 30 minutes apiece for a quick visit, plus another 30 minutes to climb to the viewpoint atop St. Isaac's.

Peter and Paul Fortress: The city's fortified-island birthplace, with stout ramparts, the burial cathedral of the czars, and a smattering of mildly interesting museums. For a targeted visit (cathedral and quick stroll around the grounds), allow about an hour; an additional hour lets you dip into some of the museums. Either way, budget about 30 minutes each way to get here from the city center (by foot over the Neva, or by Metro from Nevsky Prospekt).

Other Museums: These include the Russian Museum of Ethnography, Kunstkamera (international ethnography and oddities), and Museum of Russian Political History. Allow 30-60 minutes for each one—potentially much more if you're especially interested in their subjects.

Out-of-Town Sights: Those who love opulent palaces can make a pilgrimage to two over-the-top Romanov residences on the city outskirts: **Peterhof** (with gorgeous gardens) or **Tsarskoye Selo** (with the **Catherine Palace** and its sumptuous Amber Room). Given the relative complexity of reaching either palace, most cruisers skip these to focus on the abundant sights in the city center or opt for a cruise-run excursion. On your own, either place can be seen in a half-day targeted tour by taxi or with a hired driver; otherwise, allow a full day.

One-Day Plan

With just one day, you'll have to make some tough decisions. Devout art lovers should tour the Hermitage, then follow my self-guided Nevsky Prospekt walk. For a wider-ranging experience, skip the Hermitage and follow this ambitious plan (if you're not up for it all, omit the Russian Museum):

9:00 Follow my self-guided Nevsky Prospekt walk (about 2 hours), stopping at the Kazan Cathedral (30 minutes), Church on Spilled Blood (30 minutes), and Russian Museum (2 hours). Along the way, grab a quick lunch (30 minutes), shop, and linger (30 minutes).

15:00 Take a canal boat cruise.

16:00 Ride the Metro to the Peter and Paul Fortress, and tour the Romanov tombs at Sts. Peter and Paul Cathedral.

18:00 Walk back across the Neva, pausing at Strelka for a panoramic view.

Evening Attend the ballet (seasonal), a concert, or the circus.

Port of St. Petersburg

Arrival at a Glance: From the **Marine Facade port,** either take a taxi or brave the fun and very cheap bus-plus-Metro option to reach the city's main street, Nevsky Prospekt. If your ship docks along the river in the city, at the **Lieutenant Schmidt** or **English embankments,** it's a longish walk or quick taxi ride to major sights.

Port Overview

St. Petersburg's enormous, U-shaped cruise port is called the **Marine (Morskoy) Facade.** Built on reclaimed land at the western tip of Vasilyevsky Island (facing the Gulf of Finland), its staggering capacity can accommodate seven big ships at once, feeding into four separate terminal buildings (each with roughly the same ser-

Russian Visa Requirements

Note: *The following information was accurate as of 2018, but Russian visa regulations are notoriously changeable. Confirm everything stated here before you make your plans. For the latest requirements, see www.ricksteves.com/russianvisa.*

Do I Need a Visa?

To enter Russia, residents of most countries, including the US and Canada, are required to obtain a visa in advance. The only exception is for travelers arriving by sea (on a cruise ship or passenger ferry), who can be in the country for up to 72 hours without a visa. To explore the city, cruisers without visas must pay for a cruise-line excursion (or book a tour well in advance through a locally based company—for more on this option, see page 342), and remain with your guide or escort the entire time you are on land—you'll have virtually no free time on your own. If you're an adventurous traveler and want to experience the real Russia, consider obtaining a visa and sightseeing on your own.

How to Get a Visa

Getting a Russian visa is not exactly difficult, but it does take a few weeks to accomplish. Before applying for a visa, you must first get an official document called a "visa invitation" (*priglashenie;* sometimes called a "letter of invitation," "visa sponsor," or "tourist support letter") from a Russian organization recognized by the Russian Foreign Ministry. Visa invitations are typically issued either by a hotel or by a tour operator. If you're arriving by cruise, you'll need to arrange an invitation through a third-party agency. These agencies specialize in steering your visa application through the process. They can also help you arrange visa invitations and navigate the confusing application. I've had a good experience with Passport Visa Express (www.passportvisasexpress.com).

In addition to the $123-213 visa price, visa agencies charge a service fee of about $99-160 (plus an additional $50 invitation fee). To ship your passport securely to and from the visa agency costs another $60 or so. Figure at least $350 total per person.

Entering Russia with a Visa: When you enter the country, the immigration officer will ask you to fill out a migration card in duplicate, listing your name, passport number, and other details. The officer will stamp both parts of the card and keep one. Don't lose the other half—it must be presented when you leave the country. (A digital version of this card is being phased in, but you'll still need to carry the hard copy.) While in Russia, you are required to carry your original passport (not just a copy) with you at all times. Police in Russia can stop you at any time and ask to see your documents, though this seldom happens to tourists.

vices; for port information, see www.portspb.ru). If you sail in during muggy weather, keep your veranda door closed; St. Petersburg was built on a swamp, and bugs can swarm here.

Smaller, luxury vessels dock along the Neva River embankment (either the **Lieutenant Schmidt embankment** or the **English embankment**) close to the city center, a long but scenic walk from the Hermitage and other sights.

Tourist Information: There are small TI kiosks at the Marine Facade terminals, but they're not particularly helpful (and often closed). If you happen to see an open one, pick up a map. Otherwise, make your way downtown to find the TI on Palace Square.

ST. PETERSBURG

GETTING INTO TOWN
From Marine Facade

Leaving your ship, you'll go through an **immigration** checkpoint (regardless of whether you have a visa or are with a private guide or excursion). After the immigration checkpoint, you'll enter a sleek terminal building with a crowd of prearranged drivers and tour guides (holding signs with the names of their clients), an **ATM,** a desk for booking a taxi, and gifts shops perfectly positioned to help departing cruisers burn through whatever rubles remain in their pockets.

Given the size of the port, before heading out, be sure you know both your ship's terminal building number and the docking berth number.

By Taxi

Taxis line up in front of the terminal, charging about 1,600 R for a ride downtown (figure 6,000 R one-way to Peterhof or Tsarskoye Selo). If no taxis are standing by, check with the taxi desk inside the terminal.

By Public Transportation

It's easy, cheap, and very local to ride public transportation from the Marine Facade into downtown. The basic plan: Ride a bus to the nearest Metro station, then either whoosh under the city by subway all the way downtown, or get off at the first stop and walk through interesting neighborhoods the rest of the way into the city.

Bus to Metro: At the curb in front of the terminal, look for the stop for **bus #158** (40 R, pay conductor, 2/hour, stops at each terminal). You'll get off in about 15 minutes at the **Primorskaya Metro**

St. Petersburg Overview

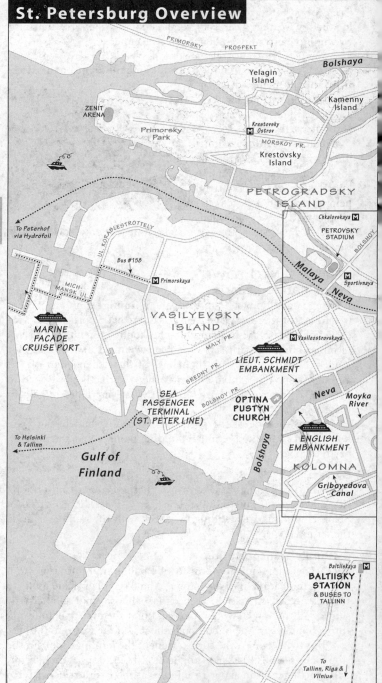

PRIMORSKY PROSPEKT

Bolshaya

Yelagin Island

Kamenny Island

ZENIT ARENA

Primorsky Park

Krestovsky Ostrov Ⓜ

MORSKOY PR.

Krestovsky Island

PETROGRADSKY ISLAND

Chkalovskaya Ⓜ

PETROVSKY STADIUM

BOLSHOY

To Peterhof via Hydrofoil

UL. KORABLESTROTTELY

Bus #158

Ⓜ Primorskaya

MICH-MANSK. UL.

VASILYEVSKY ISLAND

Malaya Neva

Ⓜ Sportivnaya

MARINE FACADE CRUISE PORT

MALY PR.

Ⓜ Vasileostrovskaya

SREDNY PR.

LIEUT. SCHMIDT EMBANKMENT

Neva

Moyka River

SEA PASSENGER TERMINAL (ST. PETER LINE)

BOLSHOY PR.

OPTINA PUSTYN CHURCH

ENGLISH EMBANKMENT

To Helsinki & Tallinn

Gulf of Finland

Bolshaya

KOLOMNA

Griboyedova Canal

Baltiiskaya Ⓜ

BALTIISKY STATION & BUSES TO TALLINN

To Tallinn, Riga & Vilnius

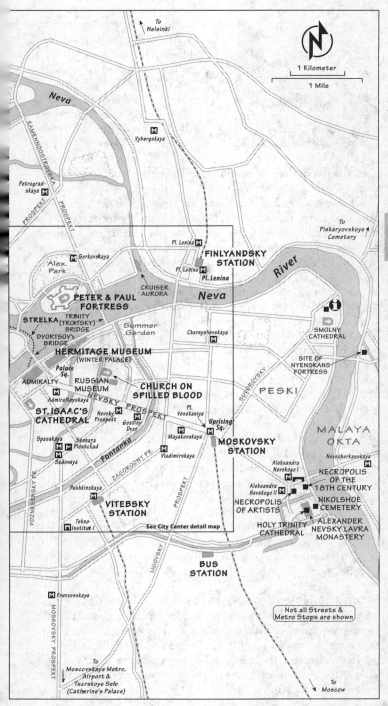

ST. PETERSBURG

station: After leaving the port and driving past apartment blocks, the bus turns left onto a big boulevard with tram tracks, with several shops on the right (look for the *KFC* sign). This is where you hop off (if you're not sure, ask fellow passengers: "Metro?"). From the bus stop, walk straight ahead, between the KFC building and a line of stores. Look for the Metro sign—a bulging *M*.

Head into the Metro station, turn right to find the ticket window, and buy a token (45 R). Use the token to pass through the turnstile, and head down the long escalator. This is the terminus of the green line, so trains run only in the direction of downtown (toward Rybatskoye). For more on St. Petersburg's Metro system, see page 337.

Metro to Downtown: The easiest plan on a tight schedule is to ride the Metro two stops to the **Gostiny Dvor** station. This pops you out onto the city's main avenue, Nevsky Prospekt. From here, it's a 10-minute walk to major sights including the Russian Museum, Church on Spilled Blood, and Kazan Cathedral. To reach the start of Nevsky Prospekt (near Palace Square, behind the Hermitage), ride city bus #3, #7, #24, or #191; or take trolley bus #1, #5, #7, #10, #11, or #22. Of these, trolley buses #5 and #22 continue to St. Isaac's Cathedral. Alternatively, to get to Peter and Paul Fortress, ride the Metro to Gostiny Dvor, then switch to the other Metro line (blue, Nevsky Prospekt stop); ride this line in the direction of Parnas, and get off at the first stop, Gorkovskaya—about a 10-minute walk from the fortress (see directions on page 330).

Returning to Marine Facade by Metro/Bus Combo: From the Gostiny Dvor area downtown (on Nevsky Prospekt), hop on the green Metro line and ride two stops to the end of the line, Primorskaya. Head out front and find bus #158. (From where you got off the bus, cross the busy street and tram tracks to find the "A" stop.) This bus runs about every 30 minutes back to the Marine Facade.

From the Neva Embankment

Smaller ships sometimes put in along either embankment of the Neva River, closer to the city center. Consider yourself lucky if your ship docks here, as it's within (fairly long) walking distance of the big sights. Because there is no ATM at or near the terminal, consider changing some cash on board before you arrive, or be ready to walk into town to find an ATM.

Excursions from St. Petersburg

Most cruisers in St. Petersburg see the city exclusively with excursions, since it's easier than getting a visa for independent sightseeing. But remember that without a visa, you can leave the ship *only* with an excursion or with a private guide. While I prefer getting my own visa, or hiring a guide to sort through the red tape for me (for more on this option, see page 324), the reality is that cruise-line excursions keep it simple. Here's a rundown of the typical choices:

The basic St. Petersburg visit includes a narrated **bus ride** around town, with brief photo-op stops at major landmarks. Many also include a shopping stop and a meal. To add more substance, book a tour that includes in-depth tours of individual sights. The most popular choice is the **Hermitage/Winter Palace.** Excursions usually focus on the main historical rooms and a few select masterpieces from the art collection. Don't expect "free time" to linger or to explore rooms not on the tour. (For example, lovers of Impressionism should be sure to book a tour that explicitly includes this collection—some don't.) If your cruise line offers an after-hours **evening visit of** the Hermitage, it's worth considering—you'll escape the crowds and save valuable daylight time for other priorities.

Also popular are the two sprawling countryside palaces outside town: **Peterhof** (sometimes called the **Summer Palace**) to the west; and **Tsarskoye Selo** (usually billed as the **Catherine Palace** for its grandest structure, sometimes called by its village name, Pushkin), to the south. Seeing both is overkill—choose just one. Peterhof has impressive grounds, while Tsarskoye Selo has opulent interiors. Some tours to the Catherine Palace tack on a quick stop at yet another nearby palace, **Pavlovsk.**

You may also see excursions that include a **river cruise,** which is well worthwhile for the excellent orientation it provides. Other excursions specialize either in **cathedrals and churches** (of which St. Petersburg has many fascinating and lavish examples) or the **Grand Choral Synagogue** (worthwhile only if you have a special interest). Some excursions include a ride on the **Metro,** just for kicks—an enlightening and local-feeling peek at an impressive people-mover.

Evening entertainment includes **folklore shows** and **ballet.** While ballet is a Russian forte, note that great venues such as the Mariinsky and Mikhailovsky Theaters are on hiatus between mid-July and mid-September; carefully read the fine print of any ballet excursion you're offered. Often, it's a crowd-pleasing, made-for-tourists show put on by lower-tier performers in a tired old ballroom.

And, believe it or not, some cruise lines offer one-day excursions all the way to **Moscow** (round-trip by plane).

Lieutenant Schmidt Embankment (North Bank): Named for a naval officer executed for his role in a failed 1905 revolution, the Lieutenant Schmidt (Leytenanta Shmidta) embankment is a scenic 30-minute walk (1.5 miles) from the heart of town. It's right near the beautiful, golden-domed Optina Pustyn church.

To **walk** into town, simply stroll with the river on your right. Cross at the second bridge, Dvortsovy Most, to reach the Hermitage, Palace Square, and Nevsky Prospekt; or turn left just after that bridge to find the Strelka viewpoint and the bridge to Peter and Paul Fortress (about 1.5 miles to either).

You can also reach handy **buses, trolley buses, and trams** from the north embankment—if you have rubles for bus fare (40 R, cash only, pay conductor). Walk to the Optina Pustyn church and turn up the street called "14-ya Liniya/15-ya Liniya" (14-я Линия/15-я Линия). After one long block, you'll hit a main thoroughfare, Bolshoy Prospekt.

If you are heading to the **Hermitage and/or Nevsky Prospekt,** turn left and walk a half-block to the stop for trolley bus #10 or #11 or bus #7, all of which cross Dvortsovy Most to reach Palace Square, then continue up Nevsky Prospekt to Uprising Square (Ploshchad Vosstaniya).

If you're heading to **Peter and Paul Fortress,** walk one very long block beyond the busy Bolshoy Prospekt to Sredny Prospekt; once there, turn right a half-block to the stop for tram #6 or #40. Ride this going to the right; you'll hop out at the first stop after crossing the river—at Zverinskaya street; you can also stay on for three more stops and get off right next to the Gorkovskaya Metro station (it looks like a flying saucer), and walk through the park to the fortress.

English Embankment (South Bank): The nearest berth to the town center, the English (Angliyskaya) embankment is a 20-minute walk from the Hermitage (about a mile away)—head out with the river on your left until you reach the second bridge (Dvortsovy Most). There's no easy, direct public-transit connection.

Returning to Neva Embankment: Both embankment terminals are walkable (and visible) from the city center. If you get turned around, just make your way to the Neva and look downriver for your ship. But leave yourself plenty of time to walk back—it's farther than it looks, and may take as long as 40 minutes from the Hermitage to either terminal. Or consider the tram, bus, and trolley bus connections noted above.

St. Petersburg

St. Petersburg is gigantic and decentralized; plan your time carefully to minimize backtracking. Most of the sights (and the dense urban core) are on the south bank of the Neva River; to the north are the historic Peter and Paul Fortress and the tidy, grid-planned residential zone of Vasilyevsky Island (with the cruise port at its western tip). The city—built over a swamp—is a horizontal one. Foundations for skyscrapers are too challenging.

Orientation to St. Petersburg

Don't go looking for a cutesy, cobbled "old town"; the entire city was deliberately laid out to fit within its three concentric waterways: first the Moyka (Мойка) River, then the Griboyedov Canal (Канал Грибоедова), and finally the Fontanka (Фонтанка) River.

The geographical center of the city is the Admiralty building, with a slender, golden spire that shines like a beacon (next to the river, Hermitage, and Palace Square). From here, bustling avenues (called *prospekty*) radiate out to the distant suburbs. The busiest and most interesting thoroughfare is Nevsky Prospekt (Невский Проспект). Almost everything you'll want to see is either along Nevsky or a few blocks to either side of it. Uprising Square (Ploshchad Vosstaniya, Площадь Восстания)—home to a tall obelisk and the Moskovsky train station—marks the end of the usual tourist zone.

Maps make St. Petersburg appear smaller than it is. What looks like "just a few blocks" can easily translate into a half-hour walk. The two-mile walk along Nevsky from the Admiralty to Uprising Square (Ploshchad Vosstaniya) takes about an hour at a brisk pace. Make things easier on yourself by getting comfortable with the city's cheap and generally well-coordinated public transit. The Metro boasts frequent trains that zip effortlessly below clogged streets. A well-planned network of buses and trolley buses help you bridge the (sometimes long) gaps between sights and Metro stops; while a bit less user-friendly to the uninitiated, buses can save tons of time when mastered.

A few terms you'll see on maps: *ulitsa* is "street," *ploshchad* is "square," *prospekt* is "avenue," and *most* is "bridge." Many street signs are conveniently bilingual. They usually list the house number of the building they're on, as well as the numbers of the buildings to either side (this is convenient, as buildings can be very large).

You may see free maps around town, but if you'll be navigating on your own, buy a good map at one of the bookstores listed later, under "Helpful Hints." Just be sure that the labels on the map are in both English and Cyrillic.

TOURIST INFORMATION

The city TI has several branches. The most convenient branch is in the glass pavilion just to the left of the **Hermitage** (as you face it from Palace Square). The main branch is a few steps off **Nevsky Prospekt** (at Sadovaya 14, across from Gostiny Dvor—watch for the low-profile door and go up one flight of stairs; Mon-Fri 10:00-19:00, closed Sat-Sun, tel. 310-2231, www.visit-petersburg.ru or www.ispb.info). You'll also see TI kiosks in high-tourist areas such as St. Isaac's Cathedral, Peter and Paul Fortress, and on Uprising Square near Moskovsky train station (all generally open daily 9:00-19:00). The city also runs a 24-hour "Tourist Help Line," with English operators, at tel. 303-0555.

Sightseeing Pass: The **St. Petersburg Card** is good for free admission to about 60 museums; hop-on, hop-off buses; and river cruises. Read the fine print, as some museum admissions are restricted (you can get in free to the Catherine Palace, for example—but only from Nov through April). The card can also be topped up and used to pay your fare on the Metro (2-day card-3,500 R; 3-, 5-, and 7- day versions available; cards available online and at TIs and some sights, www.petersburgcard.com).

HELPFUL HINTS

Sightseeing Schedules: Opening times for St. Petersburg's museums and churches can be changeable. When planning your visit, confirm hours online.

Take note of closed days: The Hermitage, Kunstkamera, and Peterhof are closed on Mondays, the Russian Museum and Catherine Palace on Tuesdays, many religious sites (St. Isaac's, Church on Spilled Blood) on Wednesdays, the Museum of Russian Political History on Thursdays, and the Fabergé Museum on Fridays.

Don't Drink the Water: Most locals wash fruit and brush their teeth with tap water, but they don't drink it—and neither should you.

Theft Alert: Russia has hardworking, often unusually aggressive pickpockets who target tourists. Be particularly aware anywhere along Nevsky Prospekt, in crowded shopping areas (such as Gostiny Dvor), and on public transport, particularly when getting on or off a bus at a touristy spot. Assume that any scuffle is a distraction by a team of thieves, and that anyone who approaches you on the street is trying to pull off a scam. Some thieves are well-dressed and even carry guidebooks to fool you. The city's pickpockets are pros: Don't carry anything of value in any pocket, and carry purses and bags in front. Keep anything precious close (wear a money belt for your passport, credit cards, and other valuables, leave the fancy jewelry at home, and don't be careless with cameras and electronics).

Pedestrian Safety: Russian drivers are shockingly forceful, zipping between lanes and around any obstructions. They drive fast, even on small downtown streets. Don't jaywalk: *Always* use crosswalks and look both ways before crossing—especially along Nevsky Prospekt, with its eight lanes of traffic moving at freeway speeds.

Business Hours: Most shops, restaurants, and services are open the same hours seven days a week (the legacy of communism, which tried to do away with weekends). You'll see a surprising number of shops and restaurants open 24/7 (look for *24 Часа*).

"Sightseeing Tax" for Foreigners: The admission price for Russians to various sights can be cheaper than the cost for foreigners. I've listed only the "foreigner" price, but if you happen to have a Russian passport, insist on the lower price.

Words to Know: Don't confuse these two important but similar words: вход means entrance, but выход is an exit.

Tipping: Tipping here is less routine—and much less generous—than in the US. But if you're satisfied with the service, you can round the bill up 5-10 percent (more than that is considered excessive). Tip a taxi driver by rounding up the fare a bit (pay 300 R on an 280-R fare).

Dress Code: In Orthodox churches, modest dress is expected (no shorts or bare shoulders; women are encouraged to cover their heads with a scarf).

Pharmacy: There's a 24-hour pharmacy at Nevsky Prospekt 22, at the intersection with Bolshaya Konyushennaya. The chain called **36.6**—as in the normal Celsius body temperature—can also be handy. There's one at Gorokhovaya 16, near the Admiralteyskaya Metro stop (open long hours daily).

Medical/Dental Services: The (entirely Russian-staffed) **American Medical Clinic** is near St. Isaac's Cathedral on the Moyka embankment (Naberezhnaya reki Moyki 78, tel. 740-2090, www.amclinic.com).

Wi-Fi: Many cafés and restaurants, and even some museums, have free Wi-Fi.

Bookstore: The city's best-known bookstore, **Dom Knigi** ("House of Books," Дом Книги), is in the old Singer sewing machine building at Nevsky Prospekt 28 (across from Kazan Cathedral). It sells English novels and locally produced guidebooks and has a pretty second-floor café with a view over the church (daily 9:00-24:00). **Anglia Bookshop** (Англия), just

ST. PETERSBURG

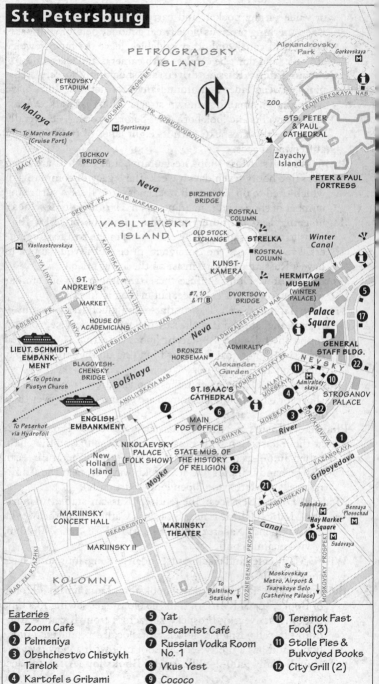

St. Petersburg

PETROGRADSKY ISLAND

Alexandrovsky Park

Gorkovskaya Ⓜ

PETROVSKY STADIUM

ZOO

STS. PETER & PAUL CATHEDRAL

KRONVERKSKAYA NAB.

Malaya

BOLSHOY PROSPEKT

Ⓜ Sportivnaya

PR. DOBROLYUBOVA

Zayachy Island

PETER & PAUL FORTRESS

To Marine Facade (Cruise Port)

TUCHKOV BRIDGE

MALY PR.

SREDNY PR.

Neva

BIRZHEVOY BRIDGE

ROSTRAL COLUMN

NAB. MARAKOVA

VASILYEVSKY ISLAND

OLD STOCK EXCHANGE

STRELKA

ROSTRAL COLUMN

Winter Canal

Ⓜ Vasileostrovskaya

KADETSKAYA & 1 LINYA

KUNST-KAMERA

HERMITAGE MUSEUM (WINTER PALACE)

Ⓢ

ST. ANDREW'S MARKET

BOLSHOY PR.

2 LINYA

#7, 10 & 11 Ⓑ

DVORTSOVY BRIDGE

Palace Square

⑤

⑰

HOUSE OF ACADEMICIANS

UNIVERSITETSKAYA NAB.

Neva

GENERAL STAFF BLDG.

NEVSKY

LIEUT. SCHMIDT EMBANK-MENT

BLAGOVESH-CHENSKY BRIDGE

BRONZE HORSEMAN

ADMIRALTY

Alexander Garden

ADMIRALTEYSKY PR.

⑪

Ⓜ Admiralteyskaya

㉒

⑩

To Optina Pustyn Church

Bolshaya

ANGLIYSKAYA NAB.

ST. ISAAC'S CATHEDRAL

④

STROGANOV PALACE

To Peterhof via Hydrofoil

⑦

⑥

MALAYA MORSKAYA

③

㉒

①

ENGLISH EMBANKMENT

MAIN POST OFFICE

BOLSHAYA MORSKAYA

River

KAZANSKAYA

New Holland Island

NIKOLAEVSKY PALACE (FOLK SHOW)

STATE MUS. OF THE HISTORY OF RELIGION

㉓

Griboyedova

Moyka

MARIINSKY CONCERT HALL

㉑

GRAZHDANSKAYA

Spasskaya Ⓜ

Sennaya Plosschad

PEKABRISTOV

MARIINSKY THEATER

Canal

"Hay Market" Square

⑭

Ⓜ Sadovaya

MARIINSKY II

VOZNESENSKY PROSPEKT

MOSKOVSKY PROSPEKT

NAB. EKI RYUSHKI

KOLOMNA

To Baltisky Station

To Moskovskaya Metro, Airport & Tsarskoye Selo (Catherine Palace)

Eateries

① Zoom Café
② Pelmeniya
③ Obshchestvo Chistykh Tarelok
④ Kartofel s Gribami
⑤ Yat
⑥ Decabrist Café
⑦ Russian Vodka Room No. 1
⑧ Vkus Yest
⑨ Cococo
⑩ Teremok Fast Food (3)
⑪ Stolle Pies & Bukvoyed Books
⑫ City Grill (2)

ST. PETERSBURG

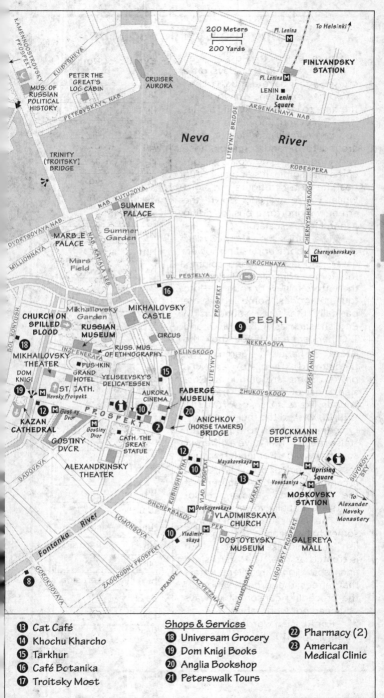

13 Cat Café
14 Khochu Kharcho
15 Tarkhur
16 Café Botanika
17 Troitsky Most

<u>Shops & Services</u>
18 Universam Grocery
19 Dom Knigi Books
20 Anglia Bookshop
21 Peterswalk Tours

22 Pharmacy (2)
23 American
Medical Clinic

Learning the Cyrillic Alphabet

If you're going to Russia—even if just for a couple of days on a cruise—you'll have a much richer, smoother experience if you take the time to learn the Cyrillic alphabet. Once you know the basics, you can (slowly) sound out signs around town, and some of those very long, confusing words will become intelligible. It's actually a fun pastime to try to figure out signs while you're walking down the street, waiting for a bus, or riding a long Metro escalator.

The table shows the Cyrillic alphabet (both upper and lowercase), and in the second column, the Roman equivalent. Notice that the letters fall—very roughly—into four categories: Some letters are basically the same sound as in English, such as А, Е, К, М, О, and Т. Others are easy if you know the Greek alphabet: Г—gamma (g), Д—delta (d), П—pi (p), and Ф—phi (f). Some are unique to Russian; most of these are "fricative" sounds, like *ts, sh, ch,* or *kh* (Ж, З, Ц, Ч, Ш, Щ, Х). And the fourth category seems designed to trip you up: "false friends" that have a different sound than the Roman letter they resemble, such as В, С, Н, Р, Х, and У. It can be helpful to remember that the "backwards" Roman consonants are actually vowels (И, Й, Я).

The letter Ы, which sounds somewhat similar to the *i* in English "ill," looks like two letters but is treated as one. The "hard sign" and "soft sign" are silent letters that affect the pronunciation of the preceding consonant in ways you need not worry about.

For Russian words and phrases, see page 410.

Cyrillic	Roman
Аа	a
Бб	b
Вв	v
Гг	g
Дд	d
Ее	ye, e
Ёё	yō
Жж	zh
Зз	z
Ии	i
Йй	y
Кк	k
Лл	l
Мм	m
Нн	n
Оо	o
Пп	p
Рр	r
Сс	s
Тт	t
Уу	u
Фф	f
Хх	kh
Цц	ts
Чч	ch
Шш	sh
Щщ	shch
Ъъ	hard sign
Ыы	y
Ьь	soft sign
Ээ	e
Юю	yu
Яя	ya

off Nevsky Prospekt facing the Fontanka River (next to the horse statues on the Anichkov Bridge), has a fine selection of English-language books by Russian authors and about Russian history (Mon-Fri 10:00-20:00, Sat-Sun 12:00-19:00, Fontanka 38, tel. 579-8284). You'll also see the **Bukvoyed** (Буквоед) bookstore chain around town, with several handy branches along Nevsky Prospekt (long hours daily).

Currency Fluctuation: The ruble is on a roller-coaster ride. Depending on economic conditions when you travel, you may find higher prices (in rubles) than those quoted here. Because of the currency instability, in some listings I've given prices in US dollars, especially for personal services and smaller vendors (walking tours, private guides, etc.) For current exchange rates, check www.oanda.com.

ATMs: The word for ATM is банкомат *(bankomat)*. They are most commonly inside banks, hotels, restaurants, and other establishments, though you will find a few out on the street. Locals advise using machines inside bank lobbies when possible; you'll also find ATMs in major Metro stations, with conveniently positioned guards usually on duty nearby.

Mail: Mailboxes are blue with "Почта России" in white lettering. The central post office, open 24 hours, is in a historic building a couple of blocks beyond St. Isaac's Cathedral at Pochtamtskaya 9 (look for the archway that crosses the street). The Russian mail service has a reputation for extremely slow delivery, if at all, but for postcards—well, you can risk it.

Convenience Stores: There are small stores in every neighborhood (often down a few steps from street level and open late or even 24 hours) where you can pick up basic necessities. Look for signs saying Продукты ("foodstuffs") or Универсам (Universam, meaning "self-service store"). In the very center, the 24-hour *universam* at Bolshaya Konyushennaya 4 (at the corner of Shvedsky Pereulok) is convenient and decent-sized.

What's With All the Weddings? It's a Russian tradition for bride and groom to visit about 10 different parks and monuments around town on their wedding day and have their photo taken.

GETTING AROUND ST. PETERSBURG

You'll find a subway map and basic info at the official Metro website (www.metro.spb.ru). The best available English-language **journey planner** for St. Petersburg's public transportation is spb.rusavtobus.ru/en. Though not very user-friendly, it covers both the Metro and surface transport.

By Metro: Compared to systems in many other European cities, St. Petersburg's Metro has fewer stations and lines. This means it's a longer walk between stations—but beneath the city you'll

ST. PETERSBURG

St. Petersburg at a Glance

▲▲▲**The Hermitage** One of the world's top art museums with a fabulous collection of European masterworks—housed in the czars' Winter Palace. **Hours:** Tue-Sun 10:30-18:00, Wed and Fri until 21:00, closed Mon. See page 356.

▲▲▲**Russian Museum** Home to the world's largest collection of Russian art, from early Russian sacred art to 21st-century works. **Hours:** Wed and Fri-Mon 10:00-18:00, Thu 13:00-21:00, closed Tue. See page 374.

▲▲▲**Church on Spilled Blood** Onion-domed, exuberantly decorative church built on the site of Czar Alexander II's assassination. **Hours:** Thu-Tue 10:30-18:00, May-Sept also open Thu-Tue 18:00-22:30 (at higher price), closed Wed year-round. See page 385.

▲▲**Fabergé Museum** 14 exquisite Fabergé eggs, including nine imperial Easter eggs, highlight this world's largest collection of works by "jeweler to the czars" Carl Fabergé. **Hours:** Sat-Thu 9:30-20:45, closed Fri. See page 380.

▲▲**Kazan Cathedral** Huge, functioning Russian Orthodox church modeled after St. Peter's Cathedral in Rome. **Hours:** Daily 9:00-20:00, services generally at 10:00 and 18:00. See page 384.

▲▲**Peter and Paul Fortress** The birthplace of St. Petersburg, this fortress has parklike grounds, several museums, and a centerpiece cathedral—the resting place of the czars. **Hours:** Grounds open daily 6:00-22:00; cathedral and prison daily 10:00-19:00 (Sun from 11:00); smaller museums open Thu-Mon 11:00-19:00, Tue 11:00-18:00, closed Wed. See page 390.

▲**Russian Museum of Ethnography** Explore the folk culture of European Russia, Siberia, the Far East, Caucasus, and Crimea. **Hours:** Tue 10:00-21:00, Wed-Sun 10:00-18:00, closed Mon and last Fri of month. See page 379.

▲**St. Isaac's Cathedral** One of the world's largest churches, with a glittering Neoclassical dome reminiscent of the US Capitol building. **Hours:** Thu-Tue 10:30-18:00; May-Sept also open Thu-

move at a shockingly fast pace. The system is clean, efficient, very cheap, and—with a little practice—easy to use. You'll marvel at one of the most impressive people-movers on the planet—at rush hour, it's astonishing to simply stand on the platform and watch the hundreds upon hundreds of commuters pile in and out of each

Tue 18:00-22:00 (at higher price), closed Wed year-round. See page 386.

▲**Kunstkamera** Peter the Great's museum, built for his collection of curiosities, includes anthropological and ethnographic collections from around the globe. **Hours:** Tue-Sun 11:00-18:00, closed Mon and last Tue of month. See page 389.

▲**Museum of Russian Political History** First-rate museum on Russia's communist period, housed in several buildings—including a mansion where Lenin had an office. **Hours:** Sat-Tue 10:00-18:00, Wed and Fri 10:00-20:00, closed Thu and last Mon of month. See page 393.

▲**Peter the Great's Log Cabin** The oldest building in the city, used by Peter as he created St. Petersburg. **Hours:** Wed and Fri-Mon 10:00-18:00, Thu 13:00-21:00, closed Tue. See page 393.

▲**Cruiser *Aurora*** Warship from 1900 that, according to popular history, fired the shot that kicked off the Russian Revolution in 1917. **Hours:** Wed-Sun 11:00-18:00, closed Mon-Tue. See page 394.

Outer St. Petersburg

▲▲▲**Catherine Palace** Opulent imperial palace of Czarina Catherine I, with the vast Great Hall and magnificent Amber Room. **Hours:** Wed-Mon 12:00-16:00 (as late as 20:00 in summer—check online), off-season Wed-Mon 10:00-16:45, closed last Mon of month; closed Tue year-round. See page 396.

▲▲**Catherine Park** Sprawling grounds with gardens and pavilions surrounding Catherine Palace—perfect for wandering. **Hours:** Daily 7:00-21:00 (later in summer). See page 401.

▲▲**Peterhof** Peter the Great's lavish palace is Russia's version of Versailles, with glorious gardens, canals, and Grand Palace museum. **Hours:** Park open daily in summer 9:00-20:00; museum open Tue-Sun 10:30-18:00 (until 19:00 in summer), May-mid-Oct Sat until 21:00, closed Mon year-round. See page 394.

train. It's worth taking the Metro at least once just for the experience.

You enter at a turnstile with a metal token (zheton, жетон), which you can buy for 45 R—either at the ticket windows, or from easy-to-use machines in station entrances (in Russian and English).

A 10-journey pass is sold at ticket windows only (355 R, valid 7 days, cannot be shared). There are no day passes.

Signs in the Metro are fully bilingual, and maps of the system are posted widely. Each of the five lines is numbered and color-coded. It helps to know the end station in the direction you're traveling. Unlike most European subway systems, transfer stations (where two lines meet) have two names, one for each line. Some stations in the center have flood doors along the boarding area that open only when trains arrive. Trains run from about 6:00 in the morning to a little after midnight.

Pickpocket Alert: Metro stations, especially at rush hour, are particularly high-risk for pickpocketing. While any line near a touristy sight is targeted, the busy green line—connecting the cruise port to the city center (Gostiny Dvor)—is particularly plagued.

By Bus and Trolley Bus: Buses and trolley buses are cheap and convenient for getting around the center of town. They're useful for connecting locations not served by the Metro, and let you see the city instead of burying you underground (especially nice when zipping along Nevsky Prospekt). The system takes a little patience to figure out (it helps if you can sound out Cyrillic to decipher posted schedules); ideally, ask a knowledgeable local which bus number to look for.

Along the street, stops are marked by an A (for buses), a flat-topped *M* for trolley buses, and a K for *marshrutki* minibuses (explained later). Signs at bus stops—in Russian only—list the route number, frequency, and sometimes the names of the stops en route. (Tram lines, marked by a T, run only in the city's outer districts.)

All surface transport costs 40 R per ride. Buy a ticket on board: The conductor, who wears a reflective vest, will come find you to collect your fare and hand you a thin paper ticket. Don't try to use anything larger than a 100-R note (the conductor will not have change). There are no transfers, so you pay again if you switch buses.

The buses and trolley buses that run along Nevsky Prospekt (between its start, at Malaya Morskaya, and Uprising Square/Ploshchad Vosstaniya) are useful: buses #3, #7, #24, and #191, and trolley buses #1, #5, #7, #10, #11, and #22. Don't be afraid to make mistakes; if you take the wrong bus and it turns off Nevsky, just hop out at the next stop. Trolley buses #5 and #22 conveniently veer off from the lower end of Nevsky down Malaya Morskaya street to St. Isaac's Cathedral and the Mariinsky Theater.

Marshrutki (Minibuses): These "share taxis"—operated by private companies—travel along set, numbered routes, prefixed with the letter K. You can wave them down anywhere along the way and ask to be dropped off at any point along the route. They're designed more for residents and Russian speakers than for tourists, but can be useful for going to Peterhof, Tsarskoye Selo, or the airport.

By Taxi or Ride-Hailing Service: Tourists can use taxis in St. Petersburg, but should exercise caution. You won't see taxi stands, and there are plenty of sketchy cabs cruising for fares (walk away from cabbies who hail *you* down). Taxis are largely unregulated—each company sets its own rates, and most have a minimum fare, typically 400-500 R (one reliable company is **068**—tel. 068, www.taxi068.ru.) Your best bet is to ask your restaurant, theater, or concert hall to call one for you (few dispatchers or cabbies speak English). Pay the fare on the meter, rounding up a little. Beware that congested city traffic can make a taxi ride slow.

Your **Uber app** will operate in St. Petersburg, too, just like it does in the US, provided you have access to Wi-Fi or a data connection. Some visitors swear by Yandex.Taxi, the Russian version of Uber (there are rumors of a merger, so Yandex may be your best option). Download their app beforehand: https://taxi.yandex.com.

Tours in St. Petersburg

On Foot
Peterswalk has been doing excellent, English-language walking tours of the city since 1996. I like this tour because rather than visiting the crowded, famous sights, you'll simply walk through the city and learn about contemporary life and culture (from 1,300 R/person, 4-plus hours, mobile +7-812-943-1229, www.peterswalk.com, info@peterswalk.com). From April through the end of September, the tour begins every day at 10:30 at the Julia Child Bistro at Grazhdanskaya 27—see map on page 334 for location (tour may run sporadically off-season—check website). Peterswalk also does bike tours, private guided tours, and visa-free tours for cruise travelers (see below).

By Bike
Peterswalk offers 3.5-hour weekend and late-night bike tours (mid-May-Sept Sat-Sun at 11:00, also June-Aug Tue and Thu at 22:30, from 2,000 R/person, starts at the courtyard of the Berthold Centre, at Grazhdanskaya 13—see website for details, www.peterswalk.com).

By Canal Boat

St. Petersburg is a delight to see from the water, making a canal boat tour worth ▲. Low-slung canal boats ply their way through the city, offering a handy orientation to major landmarks. You'll curl through narrow, urban waterways affording close-up views  of aristocratic palaces, and cruise the wide Neva River for a grand panorama of the Hermitage, Admiralty, and Peter and Paul Fortress. It's worth asking the various hawkers around town whether they have an English option, although the cruises are enjoyable without any narration at all. **Neptun** (Нептун), near the Hermitage, offers a multilingual audioguide (1,100-R one-hour cruise; boats go at 13:00, 15:00, 17:00, 19:00, and 21:00; on Moyka embankment at #26, near recommended Troitsky Most restaurant—see map on page 326, tel. 924-4452, www.neptun-boat.ru).

By Hop-On, Hop-Off Bus

CityTour runs red, double-decker, hop-on, hop-off buses that make a circuit of major sights in the center, with recorded commentary. Buses start at Ostrovsky Square (near the statue of Catherine the Great, along Nevsky Prospekt) on the hour from 9:00 to 20:00; the full circle takes two hours (700-R all-day ticket, buy on board or online, mobile +7-961-800-0755, www.citytourspb.ru).

With a Private Guide

Each of the following guide organizations is smart, small, reliable, and committed to helping visitors enjoy and understand their city. I work with them when my tour groups are in town, and they are consistently excellent.

Travelers with a Visa: If you have a visa, you can hire these guides privately for walking or car tours (generally $40/hour for up to 8 people on foot, 4-hour minimum).

Cruisers Without a Visa: If you're coming on a cruise without a visa, book well in advance to allow time for your guide to handle all the red tape (expect to provide your passport details). This can be the ideal way to experience St. Petersburg: It's less hassle than getting a visa but offers a more personalized view of the city than a typical cruise-line excursion. Prices are higher (about $550/person for two full days of sightseeing with a guide and car; less for groups of four or more), but typically include admission fees, and your guide will transport you to and from the cruise terminal.

Natalya German-Tsarkova: Natalya and her team of guides make touring the city easy and meaningful ($40/hour, $300/4 hours, $450/8 hours with car, up to 6 people; mobile +7-921-391-1894, www.tzar-travel.com, natalya.german@gmail.com).

Timofey Kruglikov's "Tailored Tours of St. Petersburg": Tim and his team are passionate about art and history, and they're all Russian scholars ($40/hour, $70/hour with car, 4-hour minimum, mobile +7-921-741-5004, www.tour-petersburg.com, info@tour-petersburg.com).

Peterswalk Private Guides: The most entrepreneurial and "Back Door" of these guide groups, Peterswalk offers daily public walks and bike tours (explained earlier) as well as private tours. Their passion is to be out and about in town, connecting with today's reality ($40/hour for up to 8 people, 4-hour minimum, mobile +7-921-943-1229, www.peterswalk.com, info@peterswalk.com).

ST. PETERSBURG

Nevsky Prospekt Walk

This walk, worth ▲▲▲, offers a fascinating glimpse into the heart of the city. Allow about two hours (not counting sightseeing stops).

Nevsky Prospekt (Нев-ский Проспект)—St. Petersburg's famous main thoroughfare—represents the best and the worst of this beguiling metropolis. Along its two-mile length from the Neva River to Uprising Square (Ploshchad Vosstaniya, Площадь Восстания), this superlative boulevard passes some of the city's most opulent palaces (Hermitage, Stroganov Palace), top museums (Hermitage, Russian Museum), most important churches (Kazan Cathedral, Church on Spilled Blood), finest urban architecture, liveliest shopping zones, verdant parks, and slice upon slice of Russian life.

This walk also gives you a taste of the smog, congestion, and general chaos with which the city perennially grapples. Pickpockets are brazen here, as are drivers—be watchful and use common sense (cross the street only at designated crosswalks or pedestrian underpasses). If it's crowded and you're getting stressed, duck into a serene shopping gallery or café for a break.

As Nevsky Prospekt cuts diagonally through town from the Admiralty building (the bull's eye of this city's layout), it crosses three waterways. We'll focus on the first mile-and-a-quarter stretch to the Fontanka River—though you could carry on all the way to Uprising Square and beyond.

• *Begin your walk on the vast square in front of the Hermitage.*

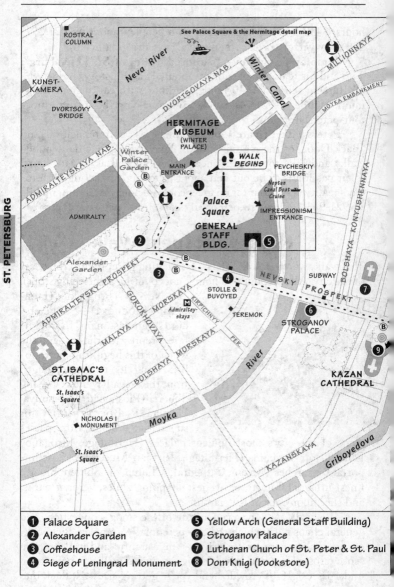

1. Palace Square
2. Alexander Garden
3. Coffeehouse
4. Siege of Leningrad Monument
5. Yellow Arch (General Staff Building)
6. Stroganov Palace
7. Lutheran Church of St. Peter & St. Paul
8. Dom Knigi (bookstore)

Palace Square to the Admiralty

The impressively monumental **❶ Palace Square** (Dvortsovaya Ploshchad)—with the arcing, Neoclassical General Staff Building facing the bulky Baroque Hermitage—lets you know you're in an imperial capital. It oozes blue-blood grandeur.

Take a moment just to let the monumental scale of this space sink in. Like all of St. Petersburg, it was custom-built to impress—

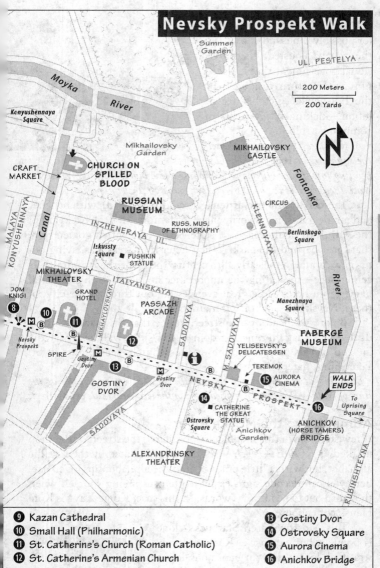

Nevsky Prospekt Walk

Summer
Garden

UL. PESTELYA

Moyka River

Konyushennaya
Square

200 Meters

200 Yards

MIKHAILOVSKY
CASTLE

N

Mikhailovsky
Garden

CRAFT
MARKET

**CHURCH ON
SPILLED
BLOOD**

Fontanka

CIRCUS

ST. PETERSBURG

Canal

**RUSSIAN
MUSEUM**

INZHENERAYA UL.

RUSS. MUS.
OF ETHNOGRAPHY

Berlinskogo
Square

MALAYA KONYUSHENNAYA

Iskussty
Square

PUSHKIN
STATUE

KLENNOVAYA

MIKHAILOVSKY
THEATER

ITALYANSKAYA

GRAND
HOTEL

**PASSAZH
ARCADE**

Manezhnaya
Square

DOM
KNIGI

8

10

MIKHAILOVSKAYA

11

SADOVAYA

**FABERGÉ
MUSEUM**

Nevsky
Prospekt

M
B

B

12

M. SADOVAYA

YELISEEVSKY'S
DELICATESSEN

SPIRE

Gostiny
Dvor

M
B

i

B

TEREMOK

**WALK
ENDS**

GOSTINY
DVOR

13

Gostiny
Dvor

M

NEVSKY

15

AURORA
CINEMA

16

To
Uprising
Square

14

CATHERINE
THE GREAT
STATUE

PROSPEKT

Ostrovsky
Square

Anichkov
Garden

**ANICHKOV
(HORSE
TAMERS)
BRIDGE**

SADOVAYA

**ALEXANDRINSKY
THEATER**

RUBINSHTEYNA

9 Kazan Cathedral
10 Small Hall (Philharmonic)
11 St. Catherine's Church (Roman Catholic)
12 St. Catherine's Armenian Church

13 Gostiny Dvor
14 Ostrovsky Square
15 Aurora Cinema
16 Anichkov Bridge

and intimidate—visiting dignitaries. If your trip also takes you to Estonia, ponder this: The entire Old Town of Tallinn could fit comfortably inside the footprint of this square and palace.

The **Alexander Column** at the center honors Czar Alexander I and celebrates Russia's military victory over Napoleon in 1812. Along with Moscow's Red Square, this is the stage upon which much of early modern Russian history played out. On January 22, 1905, the czar's imperial guard opened fire on peaceful protesters here, massacring hundreds (or possibly thousands). By 1917, the czar was ousted. The provisional government that replaced him was in turn dislodged by the Bolsheviks' October Revolution—kicking off 75 years of communist rule.

• *As you face the Hermitage, exit the square over your left shoulder, heading toward the glittering gold dome a few blocks distant. When you reach the corner of the busy street, look across to the leafy park.*

The ❷ **Alexander Garden** (Alexandrovsky Sad), with benches and jungle gyms, is a favorite place for families. It's the backyard of the **Admiralty** building—the stately structure with a golden spire that's just beyond the park. When Peter the Great was laying out his new capital in the early 18th century, he made the Admiralty its centerpiece—indicating the importance he placed on his imperial navy. From here, three great avenues fan out through the city; of these, Nevsky Prospekt is *the* main drag.

Before we head up the street, notice that **St. Isaac's Cathedral**—with that shimmering dome—is a short walk away (at the far end of this park; for more on this church, see "Sights in St. Petersburg," later).

• *Standing at the corner across from the garden, you're already at the start of Nevsky Prospekt. Let's head down the left (near) side of the street.*

Admiralty to the Moyka River

A few steps down this first block, look across the street for the shop marked ❸ *КОФЕ ХАУЗ*. Visitors are intimidated by the Cyrillic alphabet, but with a little practice (and the alphabet tips given earlier), you can decode signs easily—often surprising yourself when they turn out to be familiar words. In this case, Кофе Хауз is Kofe Haus...coffeehouse.

This Moscow-based Starbucks clone is popular, but expensive. Russia's deeply stratified society has an enormous lower class, a tiny upper class, and virtually no middle class. Trendy shops like this are filled with upwardly mobile urbanites, but poorer locals would never dream of affording a drink here.

Continue down this long block until, about halfway down on the left, you come to the building with *1939* above the gated entryway. On the pillar to the right of the entry, notice the small length of barbed wire and a blue plaque. This is a monument to the WWII ❹ **Siege of Leningrad** (as the city was named from 1924 until 1991). In September 1941, Nazi forces encircled the city—and bombarded it for 872 days, until January 1944. At the outset, the city's population, swollen with refugees, numbered three million. By the siege's end, a million or more people were dead, mostly civilians who succumbed to starvation. The assault claimed more lives than any other siege in world history. St. Petersburg's buildings were ravaged, but not the spirit of those who refused to surrender.

The north side of the street where you're standing was in the direct line of fire from Nazi shells, lobbed in from German positions southwest of the city. The blue sign reads, roughly, "Citizens: During artillery bombardment, this side is more dangerous."

Now face directly across the street and note two handy shops: the recommended **Stolle** (Штолле) restaurant, a chain famous for its savory and sweet pies and, about 30 yards to the left, an outlet of the **Bukvoyed** (Буквоед) bookstore chain, a handy place to pick up a St. Petersburg map.

At the next intersection, look left down Bolshaya Morskaya street to see the magnificent ❺ **yellow arch** of the General Staff Building (which houses the Hermitage's Impressionist collection). The archway opens to Palace Square—where we started this walk. In the other direction, the street leads to a handy branch of the **Teremok** (Теремок) Russian fast-food chain and, beyond that, to the square in front of St. Isaac's Cathedral.

• *Continuing one more block on Nevsky Prospekt brings you to the first of St. Petersburg's concentric waterways, the Moyka River. As you proceed across the bridge, stick to the left side.*

Moyka River to Kazan Cathedral

Crossing the Moyka, you'll likely see many touts selling tickets for **canal boat tours,** which are an excellent way to get your bearings in

St. Petersburg. Most tours offer commentary only in Russian, but the ride is worth it just to soak up the city's sheer grandeur (for details, see "Tours in St. Petersburg," earlier).

The river is lined with fine, mostly 19th-century architecture. The exception is the 18th-century ❻ **Stroganov Palace,** the pink Baroque building with white columns (on your right as you cross the water). The aristocratic family that resided here made their mark all over Russia—commissioning opulent churches,

ST. PETERSBURG

Timeline of Russian History

800s   Spurred by Viking trade along Russia's rivers, states form around the cities of Novgorod and Kiev. ("Russia" comes from a Viking word.)

988   Kiev converts to Christianity and becomes part of the Eastern Orthodox world.

1224-1242   Tatar (Mongol) hordes conquer Russia and exact tribute. But Russia succeeds where the Baltics fail: keeping the Germans out.

1465-1557   The Russian czars consolidate power in Moscow, drive away the Tatars, and form a unified Russian state.

1613   Foundation of the Romanov dynasty, which lasts until 1917. (For a full rundown of the Romanovs, see the "Romanovs 101" sidebar, later.)

1703   Czar Peter the Great founds St. Petersburg as Russia's forward-looking capital and "window on the West." Russia expands southward and eastward under Peter and his successor, Catherine.

1812   Napoleon invades Russia and burns Moscow, but loses an army on the way home.

1855-1861   Russia loses the Crimean War and decides to modernize, including freeing the serfs.

1905   Russia loses a war with the Japanese, contributing to a failed revolution later glorified by the communists as a manifestation of the workers' consciousness.

1917   In March, the Romanov czar is ousted by a provisional government led by Alexander Kerensky; in the October Revolution, the provisional government is ousted by the Bolsheviks (communists), led by Vladimir Lenin. A few months later, the entire Romanov family is executed.

1924   Lenin dies on January 26, and in his honor St. Petersburg is renamed Leningrad (it reverted to St. Petersburg again in 1991).

1924-1939   Josef Stalin purges the government and the army. Forced collectivization causes famine and tens of millions of deaths in Ukraine.

1939-1945   In World War II, Russia loses 20 million people to the Germans (including as many as a million in the Siege of Leningrad), but winds up with control over a sizable chunk of Eastern and Central Europe.

1945-1962   At the peak of the Cold War, Russia acquires the atom bomb, and launches the first satellite and the first manned space mission.

1970s   During a time of stagnation under Leonid Brezhnev, the communist system slowly fails.

1985   Mikhail Gorbachev comes to power and declares the beginning of *glasnost* (openness) and *perestroika* (restructuring) in the Soviet system.

1991   Reactionaries try to topple Gorbachev. They fail to keep power, but so does Gorbachev. Boris Yeltsin takes control of the government and starts reforms.

1993   Reactionaries fail to topple Yeltsin. Weakened, Yeltsin manages to hang on to power until 1999, despite grumbling from the ultranationalist right and the communist left.

1999   On New Year's Eve, Yeltsin suddenly and inexplicably resigns, handing the country over to former KGB officer Vladimir Putin.

2000-2008   Putin serves as president.

2008-2012   The term-limited Putin becomes prime minster, keeping a close watch on the presidency of his handpicked successor, Dmitry Medvedev. (Cynical onlookers dub the arrangement a "tandemocracy.")

2012   Surprise! A convenient change in the law allows Putin to return as president, while Medvedev swaps roles to become prime minster. Russian protesters and international observers grumble about "reforms" that shore up Putin's power.

2014   Sochi, on the Black Sea, hosts the Winter Olympics amid controversy over Putin's laws against "gay propaganda." Ukraine's Crimea region (a traditionally Russian Black Sea peninsula) falls under Russian control, and armed conflict breaks out in eastern Ukraine between pro-Russian and pro-Ukrainian factions. Sanctions and declining oil prices cause the ruble to plummet.

2017   Russia is banned from the 2018 Winter Olympics when the International Olympic Committee finds the nation guilty of conducting a state-backed doping program for its athletes.

2018   Russia hosts the 21st FIFA World Cup.

financing the czars' military agenda, and fostering the fine arts, literature, and theater. (But to most Americans, their lasting legacy is the dish known as beef stroganoff.)

Continue another long block, and watch for another chance to practice your Russian—though the distinctive logo may give it away: САБВЭЙ ("SABVAY" = Subway).

Just beyond Subway, Nevsky Prospekt intersects with the pretty Bolshaya Konyushennaya boulevard, flanked by pastel buildings that were once centers of community life for Dutch and German immigrants. A few steps farther up Nevsky is the German ❼ **Lutheran Church of St. Peter and St. Paul,** set back between two yellow buildings (on the left). Catherine the Great (r. 1762-1796), who—like Peter the Great—loved to promote the multiethnic nature of her empire, encouraged various cultural enclaves to settle into communities like this, with several apartment houses clustered around a church. This

particular church is a reminder that much of St. Petersburg was built by Lutherans: Dutch, Germans, Swedes, and so on. This is only one of the many houses of worship built along this avenue under the auspices of the czars. Later, the aggressively atheistic communist regime repurposed churches all over the city; in this case, the church was turned into a swimming pool.

• *Coming up on the right is the can't-miss-it Kazan Cathedral, with its stately semicircular colonnade and grand dome. We'll take a closer look in a minute, but first head up to the corner, to #28.*

This fine Art Nouveau building is ❽ **Dom Knigi** ("House of Books"). Architecture fans know it as the Singer House (yes, the Russian headquarters of the American sewing machine company—the globe at the top proclaims Singer's worldwide reach). Up close, take a few minutes to examine the facade's fine decorative details in wrought bronze. Inside, the inviting bookshop has a delightfully atmospheric—if pricey—turn-of-the-century café on the second floor (daily 9:00-23:00).

• *Use the crosswalk in front of Dom Knigi to reach the Kazan Cathedral.*

Kazan Cathedral to Griboyedov Canal

Built in the early 1800s and named for a revered Russian icon, ❾ **Kazan Cathedral** was later converted into a "Museum of Atheism" under the communists. It's since been restored to its former glory. It's free to enter and soak in the mystical Orthodox ambience (for details on the interior, see the cathedral listing later, under "Sights in St. Petersburg"). After your visit, pop into the delightful little **grassy park** in front of the church, a good spot to sit, relax, and maybe buy a drink from a vendor.

It's appropriate that Nevsky Prospekt is lined with so many important churches. The street eventually leads to the monastery that holds relics of Alexander Nevsky (1220-1263), an esteemed Russian saint who, as an influential prince, fought off encroaching German and Swedish foes—including in a pivotal 1240 battle on the Neva River, near what would later become St. Petersburg.

• Leaving the park, re-cross Nevsky Prospekt back toward Dom Knigi. While you're waiting for the light, scrutinize the building's distinctive oxidized bronze tower. Notice the unlikely symbol—an American bald eagle, wings spread wide, grasping a laurel wreath in its talons and wearing a stars-and-stripes shield on its breast.

Dom Knigi sits next to the Griboyedov Canal. Walk to the midsection of the bridge over the water (watch out for pickpockets in this highly concentrated tourist zone).

Griboyedov Canal to Gostiny Dvor

Looking down the length of the canal, you can't miss one of Russia's most distinctive buildings: the **Church on Spilled Blood.** Dramatically scenic from here, it gets even prettier as you get closer. To snap some classic photos, work your way to the small bridge partway down the river. If you plan to visit this church, now's a good time (the church is described in more detail later, under "Sights in St. Petersburg"). If you want to do some souvenir shopping, check out the touristy (and overpriced) **crafts market** that lines the right side of the canal. I'll wait right here.

Back already? Let's continue down Nevsky Prospekt (staying on the left side). Just after the river is the ❿ **Small Hall** (Малый Зал)—a performance space of the St. Petersburg Philharmonic—one of the city's great cultural institutions (along with the Mariinsky Theater and the Mikhailovsky Theater). Consider taking in a performance while you're in town; on a short visit, the ballet is a popular choice (for details, see "Entertainment in St. Petersburg," later).

A half-block farther along, tucked between buildings on the left, you'll see the pale yellow facade of the Roman Catholic ⓫ **St. Catherine's Church,** one of several "St. Catherines" along Nevsky Prospekt (many congregations named their churches for

ST. PETERSBURG

the empress who encouraged their construction). This one has a typical starving artists' market out front.

At the next corner, on the left, look up to see the old sign for the **Grand Hotel Europe**—an ultra-fancy five-star hotel that opened in 1875 (the entrance is around the corner if you want a peek inside). Its opulence attracted the likes of Tchaikovsky, Stravinsky, Debussy, and H. G. Wells.

The hotel sits at the corner of Mikhailovskaya street. If you detour one long block down this street, you'll find the main entrance of the **Russian Museum,** with a fantastic collection of works by exclusively Russian artists (described later, under "Sights in St. Petersburg"). Presiding over the park in front of the museum (Ploshchad Iskusstv, "Square of the Arts") is a statue of **Alexander Pushkin** (1799-1837)—Russia's leading poet, considered by many to have raised modern Russian literature to an art form. But let's save your museum visit for later (you'll need about two hours).

Back on Nevsky, capping the red tower across the boulevard from the hotel, notice the black metal skeletal **spire**—like a naked Christmas tree. This was part of an early-19th-century optical telegraph system that stretched more than 800 miles from here to Warsaw (which was then part of the Russian Empire). Each tower in this line-of-sight chain across the empire winked Morse code signals at the next with mirrors.

• *Continue along Nevsky to the middle of the next block.*

In a gap in the buildings on the left, you'll see yet another church—the beautiful robin's-egg-blue home of the local Arme-

nian community. ⓬ **St. Catherine's Church** belongs to the Armenian Apostolic faith, one of the oldest branches of Christianity—founded in A.D. 301, when St. Gregory the Illuminator baptized the Armenian king. In the lane leading to the church, check out the little shop window on the right, which sells breads, jams, and honey imported from Armenia to comfort homesick transplants here.

Now face across the street to confront the gigantic, yellow Gostiny Dvor shopping complex. We'll cross over later to take a

look, but for now, continue past the church. Keep an eye out on the left for #48 (look for the Пассажъ sign above the door; it's before the ramp leading to a pedestrian underpass). Step inside and climb the stairs into the gorgeously restored, glass-roofed **"Passazh" arcade,** an elite haven for high-class shoppers since 1845 (daily 10:00-21:00), making it one of the first shopping malls in the world. The communists converted the Passazh into a supermarket and, later, into a "model store," intended to leave foreigners with a (misleadingly) positive impression of the availability of goods in the USSR. These days it sells designer clothes, perfume, jewels, and decorative glass, giving off a genteel air as mellow music plays in the background.

• *At the end of the block, use the pedestrian underpass (which also leads to a pair of convenient downtown Metro stops—Nevsky Prospekt on the blue line, and Gostiny Dvor on the green line) to cross beneath Nevsky Prospekt: Take the ramp down, turn right, then right again up the next ramp.*

Gostiny Dvor to Fontanka River

You'll pop out of the underpass at ⓭ **Gostiny Dvor** (which means, basically, "merchants' courtyard"—like a Turkish caravanserai).

Built in the 1760s, this marketplace is a giant but hollow structure, with two stories of shops (more than 100 in all) wrapping around a central courtyard. To see an undiscovered corner of Nevsky that most tourists miss, head upstairs: At the corner of the building nearest the underpass, go through the door and up the stairs, then find your way back outside to reach the tranquil, beautifully symmetrical arcades. Standing at the corner, the arches seem to recede in both directions nearly as far as the eye can see.

Looking out, take note of the open plaza in front of Gostiny Dvor. This was recently the site of regular **political protests**—which, in Putin's Russia, are barely tolerated. Article 31 of the Russian constitution guarantees the freedom of assembly—a right that seems always to be in question, especially since any protest must be officially registered. To push the boundaries, once a month, peaceful demonstrators sought government permission to stage a protest here, were denied, then staged the protest anyway—only to be dutifully arrested by riot-gear-clad cops.

• *Go back into the underpass, and this time cross under Sadovaya street, staying on the right side of Nevsky Prospekt for one more block.*

You'll soon reach ⓴ **Ostrovsky Square** (Ploshchad Ostrovskogo), a fine park anchored by a statue of **Catherine the Great.** While Peter the Great gets founding credit for this city, Catherine arguably made it great. A Prussian blue-blood, Catherine married Russia's Czar Peter III, then quickly overthrew him in a palace coup. Throughout her 34-year reign, Catherine never remarried, but she is believed to have cleverly parlayed sexual politics to consolidate her power.

On the plinth below her, Catherine is surrounded by prominent figures from her reign, including **Prince Grigory Potemkin,** one of the statesmen and military leaders with whom she collaborated and consorted. Potemkin is the namesake of the term "Potemkin village" and a fascinating story about how even a great ruler can be fooled. After Potemkin conquered the Crimean peninsula during the Russo-Turkish War, Catherine visited to survey her new domain. To convince her that "Russification" of the Crimea had been a success, Potemkin supposedly created artificially perfect villages, with stage-set houses peopled by "Russian villagers" custom-ordered from Centralsky Cast-

ing. To this day the term "Potemkin village" describes something artificial used to hoodwink a gullible target—a term as applicable to modern Russian and American politics as it was to Catherine's nation-building. In 1972, when President Nixon visited this city, Nevsky Prospekt itself was similarly spruced up to disguise the USSR's economic hardships. (Because Nixon viewed the street from a limo, the authorities only fixed up the bottom two floors of each facade.)

• *From the square, use the crosswalk to head back over Nevsky Prospekt.*

Just across from the park is the pleasantly pedestrianized street called Malaya Sadovaya, with lots of cafés and outdoor eateries. On the corner, **Yeliseevsky's delicatessen** occupies a sumptuously decorated Art Nouveau building (at #56). Once the purveyor of fine food to the Russian aristocracy, Yeliseevsky's was bumped down several pegs when the communists symbolically turned it into

"Grocery Store #1." Now, in another sign of the times, it's been remodeled into an almost laughably over-the-top boutique deli with a small, expensive café—drop in to browse the selection of cheese and chocolates (daily 10:00-23:00, photography strictly prohibited).

Up Nevsky Prospekt a few steps beyond Yeliseevsky's, a passage (at #60, just past the Teremok fast-food joint) leads to the historic ⓯ **Aurora (Аврора) Cinema**—one of the first movie houses in St. Petersburg. Composer Dmitri Shostakovich worked as a pianist here, accompanying silent films. Even with the terrible Siege of Leningrad, the Aurora kept showing films—taking intermissions when German shelling started (eventually conditions became so desperate that the electrical supply was cut and the films stopped). If your Russian is good enough to see a film here, you'll step upon the original tiles in the elegantly decorated main hall.

• *Continue along Nevsky Prospekt for another block and a half, until you hit the Fontanka River.*

Fontanka River to Uprising Square

Of St. Petersburg's many beautiful and interesting bridges, the ⓰ **Anichkov Bridge** is one of the finest. On pillars anchoring each end are statues of a man with a horse. The ensemble, sculpted in 1841 and known collectively as *The Horse Tamers,* expresses humanity's ongoing desire to corral nature. Watch the relationship between horse and man evolve: In one view, it's a struggle, with the man overwhelmed by the wild beast's power; in another, it's a cooperative arrangement, with the man leading the bridled and saddled horse. Looking over the Fontanka River, it's easy to take this as a metaphor for St. Petersburg's relationship with the water. To survive and prosper, the city had to tame the inhospitable, swampy delta on which it was built.

• *You've walked the most interesting stretch of Nevsky Prospekt, but if you'd like to see more of the city center, continue by foot or by bus down Nevsky for a half-mile until you reach* **Uprising Square** *(this intimidatingly huge transit hub is a showcase of Russia's bigger-is-better city-planning aesthetic, with some surviving Soviet touches; for bus numbers, see page 340).*

Otherwise, you have several options. Just to the left along the Fontanka embankment is the exquisite **Fabergé Museum;** *across from the museum is the Anglia Bookshop. To sightsee at the* **Russian Museum,**

Church on Spilled Blood, Kazan Cathedral, or Hermitage, walk back along Nevsky the way you came, or hop on a bus (see page 340 for buses that make the trip; note that a few trolley buses veer off from the end of Nevsky for St. Isaac's Cathedral, saving an extra 10-minute walk).

To easily reach the Peter and Paul Fortress, take the Metro: Backtrack to the underpass in front of Gostiny Dvor, find the Nevsky Prospekt station on the blue line, and ride one stop to Gorkovskaya—a short walk from the fortress.

Sights in St. Petersburg

Most of St. Petersburg's major sights and landmarks are in the central zone that radiates out from the south bank of the Neva River, starting with the city's most famous sight—the Hermitage museum.

▲▲▲THE HERMITAGE (ЭРМИТАЖ)

The museum complex known collectively as the Hermitage contains a staggering three million artworks housed in a series of mostly in-

terconnected imperial buildings on Palace Square. Most prominent is the eggshell blue Winter Palace, built in 1754-62 by Peter the Great's daughter, Elizabeth, as an imperial residence; Catherine the Great added the Small Hermitage next to it in 1762 and filled it with her art collection. When that proved too small to hold everything, Catherine ordered the construction of the adjoining Old and New Hermitages.

The Hermitage's vast collections of just about everything—but especially its European masterworks—make it one of the world's top art museums, ranking with the Louvre and the Prado. Enjoy the Leonardos and Rembrandts while imagining the over-the-top lifestyles of the czars who collected them. Between the canvases, you glide through some of the most opulent ballrooms and throne rooms ever built. While most of the exhibits you'll want to see are in the Winter Palace and its adjoining palaces, the Hermitage's superb collection of Impressionist and Post-Impressionist art is displayed in the General Staff Building, across Palace Square. If you plan to visit the Impressionist galleries, buy your ticket there—it's almost always less crowded.

Cost: 700-R ticket includes Hermitage and General Staff Building exhibits, 300 R for General Staff Building only, $24 two-day ticket sold online only (see later), students free.

Palace Square & the Hermitage

Neva River

HERMITAGE THEATER

OLD HERMITAGE

Winter Canal

NEW HERMITAGE

MILLIONNAYA

To Church on Spilled Blood

DVORTSOVAYA NAB.

SMALL HERMITAGE

Courtyard

ADVANCE TICKET ENTRANCE

MOYKA EMBANKMENT

WINTER PALACE

TICKET MACHINES

PEVCHESKIY BRIDGE

To Dvortsovy Bridge

Neptun Canal Boat Cruise

MAIN ENTRANCE

DVORTSOVAYA PROYEZD

Winter Palace Garden

Palace   Square

ALEXANDER COLUMN

GENERAL STAFF BUILDING (IMPRESSIONISM)

MOYKA EMBANKMENT

Moyka River

ADMIRALTY

START OF NEVSKY PROSPEKT WALK

IMPRESSIONISM ENTRANCE

See detail map

100 Meters

100 Yards

ARCH

Alexander Garden

To Nevsky Prospekt & St. Isaac's Cathedral

ST. PETERSBURG

Hours: Tue-Sun 10:30-18:00, Wed and Fri until 21:00, closed Mon.

Information: Tel. 710-9625 (recorded info) or 710-9079, www.hermitagemuseum.org.

Getting in with a Same-Day Ticket: Individual visitors enter through a courtyard that faces the grand Palace Square with the Alexander Column. Handy machines in the main courtyard sell tickets (available 10:30-17:00—until 20:00 Wed and Fri, clearly explained in English; cash or credit card). To enter the museum, head to the far right end of the courtyard. The long line to the left is for Russians (who qualify for a discounted price unavailable at the machines). With tickets in hand, stay to the right, skipping any lines in the courtyard to head directly into the entry hall. There, wait at the security checkpoint to scan your ticket at the turnstile and enter the museum.

Getting in with an Advance Ticket: It's possible to buy a ticket in advance on the museum website for a slightly inflated price

Romanovs 101

As you tour the many imperial sights in and near St. Petersburg, this cheat sheet will keep you oriented to the Romanov czars and czarinas who built this city and ruled it until the Bolshevik Revolution in the early 20th century. The Romanov dynasty began in 1613 with Mikhail Romanov—but I'll start with his more famous descendant...

Peter I "the Great" (1689-1725): Dynamic and reform-minded, Peter was the founder of modern Russia. He famously moved the capital city from Moscow to St. Petersburg. (For more on Peter, see the sidebar on page 396). When Peter died, his wife Catherine (1684-1727) became empress; at her death, the throne passed to Peter's grandson from a prior marriage...

Peter II (1715-1730): He ruled only two years before dying of an illness. Because the teenaged Peter II lacked an heir, the throne reverted to Peter the Great's half-brother's daughter...

Anna (1693-1740): After a decade as czarina, Anna died of kidney disease. Her infant nephew, Ivan VI, was quickly deposed in a palace coup to install Anna's cousin...

Elizabeth (1709-1762): The overindulged daughter of Peter the Great and Catherine I, Elizabeth was raised in the lap of luxury at the Catherine Palace (which she later bathed in the frilly Elizabethan Baroque style). She never married, so the throne passed to her cousin Anna's son...

Peter III (1728-1762): He ruled just six months before being assassinated in a palace coup to install his wife...

Catherine II "the Great" (1729-1796): A German aristocrat who had married into the Romanov clan, Catherine enjoyed a very successful 34-year reign. She never remarried, but maintained (suspiciously) close relations with a trusted circle of mostly male advisers. The practical Catherine eschewed Baroque excess and popularized a more restrained Neoclassicism. (For more on Catherine, see page 354.) Catherine wasn't fond of her only son, whom she was unable to prevent from succeeding her.

Paul I (1754-1801): Catherine's son ruled only five years before a palace coup assassinated him to install his son...

Alexander I (1777-1825): Alexander's grandmother Cathe-

($18/1 day, $24/2 consecutive days). Print and show your ticket to enter, or show your confirmation code at the Internet ticket desk (at the advance-ticket entrance—see below). Advance tickets are not timed entry or date specific. Note that the two-day ticket is only available online.

Advance-ticket holders can use the main entry on Palace Square, but there's also a **special entry** reserved for them—with far fewer people waiting to get in. It's in the Shuvalovsky passageway between the Small Hermitage and the New Hermitage: To get

rine aspired to make him the czar that she believed her son, Paul, could never be. Alexander enjoyed a long (nearly 25-year) but melancholy reign, while pursuing a more dynamic version of his grandma's Neoclassicism, called the Russian Empire style. When Alexander fell ill and died, he made way for his much younger brother...

Nicholas I (1796-1855): During his 30-year reign, Russia had high points (territorial expansion) and low points (the loss of the Crimean War). Upon his death, the throne passed to his son...

Alexander II (1818-1881): Alexander "the Liberator," who was czar for a quarter-century, boldly freed the serfs in 1861—but also instituted a convoluted land-redemption process that caused peasant uprisings (foreshadowing the eventual fall of the czarist regime). A left-wing terrorist group assassinated Alexander II in St. Petersburg (at the site of the Church on Spilled Blood). The throne passed to his son...

Alexander III (1881-1894): During his uneventful 15 years as czar, Alexander reversed some of his father's reforms and continued the Romanov trends of the 19th century: exuberant imperial decadence coupled with crippling societal ills. The empire was in decline, leaving a mess for Alexander III's son...

Nicholas II (1868-1918): This czar and his family have been much romanticized for their lavish lifestyle and tragic end. Seduced by the trappings of imperial life, and unwilling to grapple with the realities of a changing world, they retreated to Alexander's Palace (in Tsarskoye Selo) and sought solace in the advice of the charismatic and enigmatic mystic, Rasputin. Nicholas oversaw Russia's failed foray into World War I (resulting in millions of Russian deaths) and was ultimately deposed by the February Revolution in 1917, setting the stage for the rise of Vladimir Lenin's Bolsheviks.

On July 17, 1918, Nicholas and his family (including his larger-than-life daughter, Anastasia) were executed by a firing squad—ending more than three centuries of Romanov rule from St. Petersburg.

there, face the main Winter Palace building and go right—you'll see a signboard at the gateway.

Tours: Immediately beyond the security checkpoint is a desk where you can rent an English **audioguide** (500 R, leave ID as deposit; less-crowded audioguide stand at top of main stairway). The audioguide has handy, digestible descriptions of the palace's historical rooms and of major paintings, but isn't worth the high price for a single traveler on a short visit. It's possible to customize your own tour with the museum's **audioguide app** (see the website). **Guided**

tours in English are offered in the entry hall (300 R, times posted in courtyard—usually at 13:30 but call info line to confirm).

Visitor Services: Pick up a free map at the information desk. Down the stairs from the entry hall is an ATM, a cloakroom (remember which of the 14 sections you use), a tiny bookstore (there are better ones later, inside the museum), and a crowded WC (there are more later). In the hall to the right, before you reach the stairway, are more WCs, a mediocre and crowded café, several gift shops, and a large bookstore.

Photography: You'll technically need a photo permit (200 R, sold in entry hall or at the machines)—but this rule is not enforced.

Cruise-Line Evening Visits: If you're visiting St. Petersburg on a cruise, consider taking the evening Hermitage excursion-tour that's offered by many cruise lines. It's a more peaceful museum experience, saves your daylight hours for other activities, and is a good option if you don't mind a shorter look at the collection's highlights.

⊙ Self-Guided Tour

This tour will take you through the Hermitage's highlights, divided into three parts between several buildings: In the **Winter Palace** and its adjacent "Hermitages" are part 1, the historical rooms, and part 2, the Old Masters (Leonardo, Raphael, Rembrandt, etc.). In the **General Staff Building** is part 3, the Modern Masters (Matisse, Chagall, Picasso, etc.).

Very roughly, the first (ground) floor, where you enter, shows ancient art; the second floor has historical rooms plus galleries covering the medieval, Renaissance, and Baroque eras (Old Masters); and the galleries of the General Staff Building are devoted to the 19th and 20th centuries (Modern Masters). Room numbers are posted over the doors to each room, but they're easy to miss in these opulent surroundings.

Length of this Tour: It should take about four hours—including one full hour just to fight the crowds and connect the dots.

Part 1: Historical Rooms

• *At the end of the entry area (the hall with the metal detectors and audioguide stand), head up the...*

Ambassador's Stairs: You are in the Winter Palace, the czar's official city residence, built by Italian architects (notably Francesco Bartolomeo Rastrelli) between 1754 and 1762 in the style called Elizabethan Baroque—named for the czarina who popularized it. At this time, all of St. Petersburg—like this staircase—drew on the talents of artists and artisans imported from Western Europe.

The staircase—and the entire palace—is designed to impress,

astonish, and humble visitors with the power of the Romanov dynasty. The marble stairway gives you a good feeling for the building's sumptuous Baroque style (much of the interior was destroyed in an 1837 fire, then restored). Extravagant gilded decorations cover the walls, alabaster statues of virtues like Justice and Wisdom watch over visitors, and the Greek gods relax in the clouds high above.

• *At the top of the stairs, go through the door and pass through a series of large rooms—Room 192, Room 191 (imagine grand balls of the czar in this room, with inlaid floors and three crystal chandeliers), and Room 190 (with the tomb of Alexander Nevsky, adorned with two tons of silver)—to reach Room 189.*

The Malachite Room: This drawing room, which dates from just after the 1837 fire, is decorated with malachite, a green copper-based mineral found in Russia's Ural Mountains. After the first stage of the Russian Revolution in spring 1917, in which the czar was ousted, a provisional government led by Alexander Kerensky declared Russia a republic. This government took over the Winter Palace and met in the Malachite Room, overlooking the Neva River. Their last meeting was on November 7, 1917. That evening, communist forces, loyal to Vladimir Lenin and the Bolshevik Party, seized power of the city

in a largely bloodless coup. (Although the Bolsheviks took over in November, back then Russia still used the old Julian calendar—so technically it was an "October" Revolution.)

• *At the end of the Malachite Room, turn left into Room 188, then skirt through Room 155 to find the long hallway filled with Romanov portraits (Rooms 153 and 151), which returns you parallel to the way you came. At the end of the hall, turn right, directly into Room 193.*

Field Marshals' Hall: This hall was for portraits of Russia's military generals—perhaps so that the ruling family could keep names and faces straight. After 1917, the paintings were taken down and moved to other museums. But in recent years, the original portraits, dating from 1814 to the 1830s (and evoking the Russian victory over Napoleon and the French), have been returned to their places here.

• *The next, very red room (194) is the...*

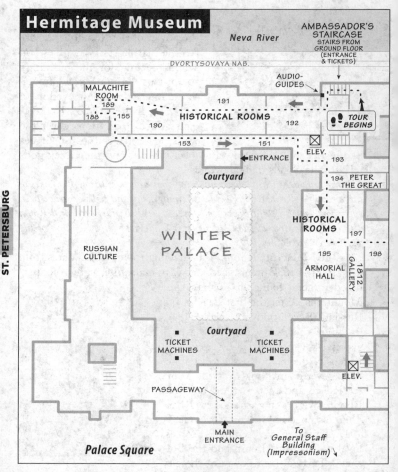

Hermitage Museum

Neva River

AMBASSADOR'S
STAIRCASE
STAIRS FROM
GROUND FLOOR
(ENTRANCE
& TICKETS)

DVORTYSOVAYA NAB.

AUDIO-
GUIDES

MALACHITE
ROOM
189

191

TOUR
BEGINS

188   155

HISTORICAL ROOMS

190   153   151   192

ENTRANCE

ELEV.   193

Courtyard   194 PETER
THE GREAT

RUSSIAN
CULTURE

WINTER
PALACE

HISTORICAL
ROOMS   197

195   198

ARMORIAL
HALL   1812
GALLERY

Courtyard

TICKET
MACHINES

TICKET
MACHINES

ELEV.

PASSAGEWAY

MAIN
ENTRANCE   To
General Staff
Building
(Impressionism)

Palace Square

Peter the Great (Small Throne) Room:
This hall pays homage to Peter the Great, who founded this city a generation before the Winter Palace's construction. You see his portrait (with Minerva, the goddess of wisdom) and a copy of his throne. The walls are emblazoned with the double-headed Romanov eagle. Above, on the wall to either side, are paintings commemorating his decisive victories over Sweden—at Lesnaya in 1708 and Poltava in 1709. (For more on the dynamic Peter, see the "Peter the Great" sidebar on page 396.)

• Continue into the **Armorial Hall** (Room 195), a banquet hall with golden columns and sculptures of knights with

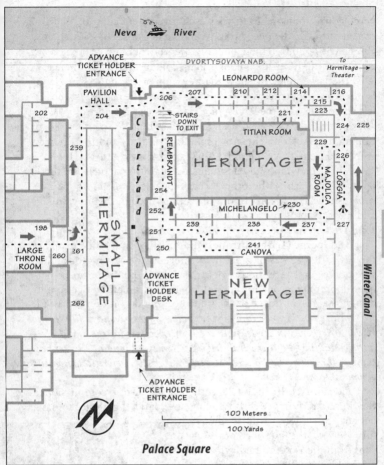

spears in each corner, and take a left into the long, skinny Room 197, known as the....

War Gallery of 1812: Opened in 1826, this hall displays more than 300 portraits of the generals who helped to expel Napoleon from Russia in 1812 and chase him back to France. The Russian and French armies fought to a draw at the battle of Borodino, just west of Moscow, in September. The French troops

were lured into Moscow, but the city was deliberately burned, Russian forces refused to submit to French control, and after some days,

Napoleon's troops realized they were overextended and began to retreat through the deepening winter cold. Napoleon had entered Russia with 400,000 men, but only a tenth would make it back out. This crushing reversal ended his plans for European dominance.

The large portraits show the most important figures in Napoleon's defeat—practice your Cyrillic by reading the names. At the far-left end of the hall, the largest of all is an equestrian portrait of Czar Alexander I (the czar who pushed out the French). To either side of him are the Austrian emperor Franz I (Франц I) and the Prussian emperor Friedrich Wilhelm III (Фридрих-Вильхельм III).

At the end opposite Alexander, one painting depicts the battle of Borodino, while the other (Peter von Hess's *Crossing the Berezina*) shows Napoleon's troops retreating through the snow in rags and disarray, crossing a bridgeless river.

• *Back in the middle of this long hallway, proceed into Room 198.*

St. George (Large Throne) Room: This grand hall, created in the early 1840s, was of great importance as the setting for official ceremonies and receptions in czarist times. The magnificent parquet floor, made from 16 types of wood, is original. Notice that its design is a mirror image of the gilded ceiling decoration overhead.

• *From Room 198, pass through the smaller room beyond it (260) into Room 261 (here you are leaving the Winter Palace for the Small Hermitage building—but the transition is seamless). Hang a left and pass through the looong Room 259 and little Room 203 before stepping into Room 204, the...*

Pavilion Hall: In 1762, Catherine the Great commissioned the Small Hermitage, with two long and parallel galleries to hang her art collection. Admire the fine view of the interior courtyard from the Pavilion Hall windows. Decorated in the French Renaissance style, the room contains the fantastical Peacock Clock (1770s), a timepiece made by British goldsmith James Cox and purchased by Catherine the Great. (The controls are in the large mushroom—a video shows it in action.)

• *You've seen the most important historical rooms in the Hermitage. At this point, it's best to focus on one or two artistic periods from among the Hermitage's vast collections. The basic options are to proceed directly into the **Old Masters** collection in the adjoining rooms (described next, in "Part 2" of this tour); or to skip forward several centuries and head across Palace Square to the General Staff Building and the fine **Modern Masters** collection (described later, in "Part 3").*

Part 2: Old Masters

• *The Italian Renaissance works we'll see are on the same floor as the historic rooms. Just beyond the Pavilion Room and the Peacock Clock, proceed straight, cross the bridge (linking the Small Hermitage and the Old Hermitage), and then pass the top of the stairwell (with the huge, green malachite-and-bronze vase) to enter a long hallway. Here begins the Old Hermitage's collection of Italian art. While there's a lot to see, for now pass through Rooms 207-213 (but pause in Room 209, at the Fra Angelico fresco of Mary and Baby Jesus, and in Room 210, with some fine Della Robbia ceramic works)—until you emerge in the exquisite Room 214.*

Leonardo da Vinci Room

Considering that there are only about 20 paintings in existence by the great Renaissance genius, the two humble Madonnas in the Hermitage are world-class treasures. Leonardo da Vinci (1452-1519) reinvented the art of painting and influenced generations of artists, and these two small works were landmarks in technique, composition, and the portrayal of natural human emotion.

Paintings of mother Mary with Baby Jesus had always been popular in Renaissance Italy. But before Leonardo, large altar-pieces typically showed the Madonna and Child seated formally on a throne, surrounded by saints, angels, elaborate architecture, and complex symbolism. Leonardo reinvented the theme in intimate, small-scale works for private worship. He deleted extraneous characters and focused on the heart of the story—a mother and her child alone in a dark room, sharing a private moment.

• *First up, on the wooden panel straight ahead as you enter the room is the...*

Benois Madonna, 1475-78: A youthful Mary shows Jesus a flower. Jesus inspects this wondrous thing with a curiosity and concentration that's wise beyond his years. It's a tender, intimate moment, but with a serious undertow. The mustard flower—with four petals—symbolizes the cross of Jesus' eventual Crucifixion. This playful moment carries a shadow of grief and death.

This is one of Leonardo's earliest known works. In fact, it may be the first painting he did after quitting the workshop of his teacher, Verrocchio, to strike out on his own. The painting, which was often copied (including by Raphael), was revolutionary. The painstaking detail astonished Leonardo's contemporaries—the folds in Mary's clothes,

Jesus' dimpled flesh, the tiniest wisps of haloes, Mary's brooch. How did he do it? The secret was a new technological advance—oil-based paints. Unlike the more common tempera (egg-based) paint, oils could be made nearly transparent. This allowed Leonardo to apply layer after layer to make the subtlest transitions of color, mimicking real life.

• *Farther along the room is another panel, with the...*

Litta Madonna, 1490-91: Mary nurses Baby Jesus, gazing down proudly. Jesus stays locked onto Mary's breast but turns his

eyes outward absentmindedly—dreamy-eyed with milk—to face the viewer, drawing us into the scene. The highlight of the painting is clearly Mary's radiant face, gracefully tilted down and beaming with tenderness.

Compare the *Litta Madonna* and *Benois Madonna*—each is a slight variation on a popular theme. What they have in common is realistic emotion, and this sets all of Leonardo's Madonnas apart from those of his contemporaries. With a tilt of the head, a shining face, a downturned mouth, the interplay of touching hands and gazes, Leonardo captured an intimacy never before seen in painting. He draws aside a curtain to reveal an unguarded moment, showing mother and child interacting as only they can. These holy people don't need haloes (or only the wispiest) to show that sacred bond.

Before leaving this room, notice the palace architecture itself. The doors are inlaid with ebony, bronze, and tortoiseshell. The scenes decorating the fireplaces are delightful micro-mosaics.

• *The door across from the* Benois Madonna *leads to Room 221, where we'll find...*

Titian Room

Danae, 1553-54: One of art history's most blatantly sexual paintings, this nude has fascinated people for centuries—both for its subject matter and for Titian's bravura technique. The Hermitage's canvas is one of five nearly identical paintings Titian painted of the popular legend.

It shows Danae from Greek mythology, lying naked in her bedchamber. Her father has locked her up to prevent a dreadful prophecy from coming true—that Danae will bear a son who will grow up to kill him. As Danae daydreams, suddenly a storm cloud gathers overhead. In the lightning, a divine face emerges—it's Zeus. He transforms himself into a shower of gold coins. Danae tilts her head and gazes up, transfixed. She goes weak-kneed with desire, and her left leg flops outward. Zeus rains down between Danae's legs, impregnating her. Meanwhile, Danae's maid tries to catch the divine spurt with her apron.

This legend has been depicted since ancient times. Symbolically, it represented how money can buy sexual favors. In medieval times, Danae was portrayed as being as money-hungry as the maid. But Titian clearly wants to contrast Danae and the maid. He divides the canvas, with Danae's warm, golden body on one side and the frigid-gray old maid on the other. Zeus rains straight down, enriching them both, and uniting the composition. *Danae* is a celebration of giving yourself to love.

• *Backtrack through the Leonardo room (214), continue through Rooms 215 and 216 (at the corner, with a love scene by Giulio Romano from Catherine's private erotica collection), and bear right. Pass straight through Room 224 to reach Room 227 and yet another building (the New Hermitage), home to the glorious...*

Raphael Loggia and Majolica Room

This long, narrow hallway—more than 200 feet long, only 13 feet wide, and decorated with colorful paintings—is a replica of one

of the painter Raphael's crowning achievements, the Vatican Loggia in Rome. (The original loggia, in the Vatican Palace, was designed by the architect Bramante—who also authored St. Peter's Basilica in Rome; Raphael and his assistants completed the loggia's fresco decorations in 1518-1519.)

In the 1780s, after admiring color engravings of the Vatican Loggia, Catherine the Great had this exact replica built of Raphael's famous hallway. It's virtually identical to the original, though the paintings here are tempera on canvas. They were copied from the frescoes in Rome (under the direction of Austrian painter Christoph Unterberger) and sent to St. Petersburg along with a scale model of the entire ensemble.

The Loggia exudes the spirit of the Renaissance, melding the Christian world (52 biblical scenes on the ceiling) and the Classical world (fanciful designs on the walls and arches). The complex symbolism, mixing the Christian and pagan, intrigued the educated elite, and the Loggia has come to be called "Raphael's Bible."

• *When you're done in the Loggia, go back to the start of the hallway*

ST. PETERSBURG

(Room 226) and turn left into Room 229, the **Majolica Room.** *Here you'll find two authentic masterpieces by Raphael.*

    Conestabile Madonna, c. 1504: The dinner-plate-size painting in the gilded frame just opposite the entrance is one of Raphael's

first known works, painted when he was still a teenager. Mother Mary multitasks, cradling Baby Jesus while trying to read. Precocious Jesus seems to be reading, too. Though realistic enough, the work shows a geometrically perfect world: Mary's oval face, Jesus' round head, and the perfect oval frame. The influence of Leonardo is clear: in the tilt of Mary's head and position of Jesus' pudgy legs (similar to the *Litta Madonna*) and in the child's beyond-his-years focus on an object (from the *Benois Madonna*). The picture is remarkable for its color harmonies and its perfected forms—characteristics that Raphael would beautifully develop in his later works.

• *At the far end of the Majolica Room, hook right into Room 230.*

Italian Cabinet and Michelangelo

The walls of this gallery are covered with frescoes from an ancient Roman villa. But we're here to see the sculpture in the middle of the room, by Michelangelo.

    Crouching Boy, c. 1530: The nude figure crouches down within the tight "frame" of the block of marble he came from. The statue was likely intended to pose forlornly at the base of a tomb in the Medici Chapel in Florence, possibly to symbolize the vanquished spirit of the deceased's grieving relatives. Though the project (and this statue) were never fully finished, the work possesses Michelangelo's trademark pent-up energy.

• *We'll leave the Italian Renaissance now. Go back one room, turn immediately right, then right again at the blue vase. Head down the skylighted Rooms 237, 238, and 239 (with grand vases). At the last of these rooms (239), watch for the door on the left for the long, pastel-hazy, light-filled Room 241. Slow your pace and stroll through this gorgeous array of Neoclassical sculpture. Just after the doors, look for the...*

Gallery of the History of Ancient Painting and Canova

It's fitting that the works of the great Neoclassical sculptor Antonio Canova are displayed in this gallery devoted to ancient art.

The Three Graces, 1813-16: The great Venetian sculptor shows the three mythological ladies who entertained the Greek gods at dinnertime. They huddle up, hugging and exchanging glances, their heads leaning together. Each pose is different, and the statue is interesting from every angle. But the group is united by their common origin—carved from a single block of marble—and by the sash that joins them. The ladies' velvety soft skin is Canova's signature element. Antonio Canova (1757-1822) combines the cool, minimal lines of Neoclassicism with the warm sentiment of Romanticism.

• *Go back into Room 239, then enter the smaller Room 251. Turn right and go through Room 252 and into the green-hued Room 254, with the best collection of Rembrandts outside the Netherlands.*

Rembrandt Room

The great Dutch painter is beautifully represented at the Hermitage. We'll tune into two works in particular.

• *As you enter the room, look to the left to find...*

Danae, 1636: Compare this large-scale nude of the Greek demi-goddess to Titian's version, which we saw earlier. The scene is similar—a nude woman reclines diagonally on a canopied bed, awaiting her lover (the randy god Zeus), accompanied by her maid (in the dim background). But Rembrandt depicts a more practical, less ecstatic tryst. Where Titian's Danae was helpless with rapture, Rembrandt's is more in control. She's propped upright and focused, and her legs aren't

splayed open. Danae motions to her offstage lover—either welcoming him into her boudoir or warning him to be cautious. Historians note that Danae has the body of Rembrandt's first wife (the original model) and the face of his mistress (painted over a decade later).

Catherine the Great—herself no stranger to bedroom visitors—bought this painting in 1772 as one of the works that grew into the Hermitage collection.

• *At the far end of the room, look for...*

ST. PETERSBURG

The Prodigal Son, c. 1669: In the Bible, Jesus tells this story of the young man who wastes his inheritance on wine, women, and song. He returns home, drops to his knees before his father, and begs forgiveness. Rembrandt recounts the whole story—past, present, and future—in this single moment, frozen in time. The Prodigal Son's tattered clothes and missing shoe hint at the past—how he was once rich and wearing fine clothes, but ended up penniless, alone, bald, and living in a pigsty. His older brother (standing to the right) is the present: He looks down in judgment, ready to remind their dad what a bad son the Prodigal is. But the father's face and gestures foretell the story's outcome, as he bends down to embrace his son with a tenderness that says all will be forgiven. The father's bright-red cloak wraps around the poor Prodigal like loving arms.

The Prodigal Son is one of Rembrandt's last paintings. Some read Rembrandt's own life story into the painting: Rembrandt had been a young prodigy whose God-given talent brought him wealth, fame, and the love of a beautiful woman. Then he lost it all, and was even forced to sell off his possessions to pay his debts. His last years were spent in relative poverty and obscurity.

• *To continue on to Part 3 of this tour, exit the Winter Palace and cross Palace Square to the* **General Staff Building:** *Leave the Rembrandt Room (at the opposite end from where you entered) to find the adjacent staircase and descend one floor. Circle around the staircase and through the next three galleries (130-128)—filled with ancient Greek vases, Pompeiian artifacts, and a giant vase. Just after that huge vase, go right (through ancient Egypt, Room 100) and right again, past a café, to reach the main visitors hall—and* **exit.**

Part 3: Modern Masters in the General Staff Building

The Hermitage has a thoroughly impressive collection of paintings by Impressionist and Post-Impressionist masters. Even if you feel like you've "seen" Impressionism, don't skip these galleries. Many of the paintings hanging here came from the great collections confiscated during the Russian Revolution from two super-wealthy collectors, Sergei Shchukin and Ivan Morozov (both were collecting modern French art well before the French themselves). Another substantial cache of artworks entered the country at the end of World War II, when the Soviets returned home with paintings from German private collections (and literally hid them until the early 1990s).

For this tour, I've highlighted a few paintings that always catch my eye.

• *The **entrance** to the General Staff Building, the yellow building with the arch, is on Palace Square, directly across from the Winter Palace. It is not well signed—look for the wooden doors flanked by freestanding green placards. Inside, you'll pass through security, then head right toward the main visitor hall with ticket windows, bookshop, cloakroom, WCs, and other services. Just beyond that you'll find the main grand staircase, which leads up to elevators. Ride to the fourth floor.*

*Begin your visit in **Room 403**, where there's a sampling of the works collected by Shchukin and Morozov. From there, proceed to Room 404 and continue from room to room: The galleries unfurl in a simple-to-follow circular route.*

Edgar Degas

***Place de la Concorde,** 1876?* (Room 404): Degas apparently painted this rare big canvas for his own pleasure, of his friend Ludovic Lepic with his daughters, casually crossing the Parisian square. Short of cash, Degas persuaded Lepic to buy it. The composition is empty in the middle, with the figures pushed to the edge, and has a helter-skelter feeling: Which way are they going? It's a perfect emblem of the many artistic freedoms the Impressionists would enjoy.

Auguste Renoir

***Boy with a Whip,** 1885* (Room 407): Full of warmth and charm, this portrait of a young boy has the characteristic happy, inviting feeling of Renoir's many canvases of rosy-cheeked women. The artist had no qualms about painting people and things that were "pretty." As Renoir himself said, "There are enough ugly things in life."

***Portrait of the Actress Jeanne Samary,** 1878* (Room 407): One of Renoir's favorite models was Jeanne Samary, an actress with Paris' Comédie-Française. True to the Impressionist credo of painting from life, Renoir set this full-size portrait in a theater foyer, the patterned carpets and wallpaper creating a perfect backdrop for the attractive redhead and her tiered pink dress.

Paul Cézanne

***The Smoker,** 1890-92* (Room 410): Cézanne made a whole series of pictures of smokers and card players, motifs that stretch back to 17th-century Old Masters. Cézanne tossed out the moralizing tone of those old-style paintings, though, and made his subjects the ordinary folks around him at his family's estate near Aix-en-Provence. But Cézanne didn't make portraits, and his smoker doesn't have a particular story to tell. Calm and solid, he remains a "type," a classical figure of the Post-Impressionist age.

Mont Ste-Victoire, 1898-1902 (Room 410): The Impressionists adored landscapes, especially scenes with moving water—a perfect

symbol of the changeability of nature and an ideal vehicle for their flickering, reflective style. Cézanne made many landscapes, but where the Impressionists favored the transitory, Cézanne sought permanence. Here, his brushstrokes follow the form of the mountain, bringing out its stable, steady structure with simple, geometric shapes.

Paul Gauguin

Woman Holding a Fruit, 1893 (Room 411): Gauguin famously left his stockbroker job and family to paint full-time and eventually moved to the South Seas. For him, Tahiti represented the unspoiled, simple way of life he dreamed of—and gave him a complete and welcome break from the conventional mores of Europe. To capture the landscapes and lifestyle of the Tahitians, Gauguin developed his trademark colorful, patterned, and decorative style. The vivid colors and exotic vegetation, the naturalness and the everyday habits of the Tahitians, preoccupied Gauguin for the rest of his life.

Vincent van Gogh

Arena at Arles, 1888 (Room 413): A self-taught phenom who absorbed the Impressionist technique before developing his own unique style, Van Gogh began finding his artistic feet in Arles, in the south of France. Like a spontaneous photograph, this painting captures the bustle of spectators at the town's bullfight ring. Van Gogh was working alongside Paul Gauguin in this period, and he picked up some of Gauguin's flattening of space and patchy use of

color. But Van Gogh's own powerful expressiveness is coming to the fore.

Lilac Bush, 1889 (Room 413): After some bad behavior in Arles (having to do with an ear and a knife), Van Gogh checked into a mental hospital for treatment. But he kept on painting, including this energetic depiction of a lilac bush on the hospital grounds. Van Gogh used the broken brushstrokes of the Impressionists, but his dynamism and expressiveness surpass their efforts. The bush bristles with life, an incubator of energy charged with Van Gogh's strong emotions.

Cottages, 1890 (Room 413): Van Gogh moved to Auvers, north of Paris, in 1890 to be under a doctor's care. This is one of the last paintings he made before his death. The motif of peasant huts had always appealed to him: "The most marvelous of all that I know in the sphere of architecture is huts with their roofs of moss-grown hay." Here, the wavy brushstrokes of the thatched roofs make them seem as organic as the hillside, fields, and sky.

• *There's still more to see. Move ahead to Room 421 and exit to the right. You'll cross a skybridge (and pass WCs) before entering Room 431.*

ST. PETERSBURG

Pablo Picasso

The Absinthe Drinker, 1901 (Room 431): Young Picasso painted this solitary woman, sitting in a grimy café, only a year after he arrived in Paris from his native Spain. The determined newcomer made a probing psychological study of the woman, soothed by a glass of potent alcohol. She leans on a table, deep in thought, with her distorted right arm wrapped around herself protectively. The lines of sight—her unnaturally vertical forearm and the lines on the wall behind her—converge on her face, as if to box in her hopeless loneliness.

Two Sisters, 1902 (Room 431): In his Blue Period (roughly 1901 to 1904), Picasso restricted his palette to blues and blue-greens, and made sorrow and unhappiness his subject. "Art flows from pain and sadness," he said (he would later find plenty of fun in both art and life). This painting started with a sketch Picasso had made of two sisters—one a prostitute and the other a nun. From that specific source, he developed a work of universal despair.

Seated Woman, 1908 (Room 432): This not-quite representational work (and others in this room) shows how Picasso suddenly and radically began creating a new reality in art. The seated woman is nude and big-bodied, her massive limbs shown as blocky, schematic pieces. Picasso was boldly trying out a new pictorial language, which would in time lead him to the geometries and distortions of Cubism.

Henri Matisse

Red Room, 1908 (Room 438): Matisse created this painting, like several of the works in these rooms, for the Russian collector Sergei Shchukin—in this case, for the collector's dining room. At the time, Matisse was down and out in Paris, and Shchukin's support opened the door to a period of vital creativity for the artist. This painting was unlike anything Matisse had made before: big in scale, piercing in color, and unconventional in composition, with the red cloth on the table turning up to merge with the paper on the wall. Matisse turned an ordinary domestic scene into anything but.

Dance and *Music,* 1910 (Room 440): Matisse showed these two big panels of rollicking dancers and meditative musicians to awful

reviews at the Paris Salon, and Sergei Shchukin had second thoughts about buying them, even writing to Matisse that he "hoped to come to like them one day." In the end, Shchukin came to treasure them, and hung them on the staircase of his Moscow mansion. Today, we see them as undeniable masterpieces of color, life, and harmony.

• *Our tour is finished. Make your way back down to the ground floor and plot your escape. Just follow signs with your new favorite word in the Russian language:* ВЫХОД…*"exit."*

MUSEUMS AND GARDENS NEAR NEVSKY PROSPEKT

Two adjacent, related museums—the Russian Museum, with a fine-art collection, and the Russian Museum of Ethnography—sit just beyond the Griboyedov Canal. Behind them is a pair of historic gardens, the Mikhailovsky and Summer Gardens. Farther down Nevsky, near the Fontanka River, is the dazzling Fabergé Museum.

▲▲▲Russian Museum (Русский Музей)

This vast museum houses the largest collection of Russian art in the world, from early Russian sacred art to avant-garde innovators of the early 20th century,

and from Soviet-era Socialist Realism to 21st-century contemporary works. With a few key exceptions, many of the artists shown here are largely unknown in the West, and some of the artworks now on display languished in storerooms during the Soviet era. For visitors, it's a great introduction to the essence of the artistic Russian soul. The artists represented here saw the same rooftops, churches, and street scenes that you do. Their art brings you in touch with the country's turbulent political history and captures the small-town wooden architecture and forest landscapes that you won't see on a visit to this big city.

The museum occupies the Mikhailovsky Palace, built in the 1820s for Grand Duke Mikhail Pavlovich (a grandson of Catherine the Great).

Cost and Hours: 450 R, Wed and Fri-Mon 10:00-18:00, Thu 13:00-21:00, closed Tue, audioguide-350 R.

Information: The museum is at Inzhenernaya 4, two blocks north of Nevsky Prospekt along Griboyedov Canal, near the Church on Spilled Blood. Tel. 595-4248, www.rusmuseum.ru.

Getting In: You'll find the entrance hiding in the far right corner of the museum's main courtyard, down a few stairs at the basement level. Purchase your tickets, pick up a map (listing room numbers), and go through the security checkpoint. On the basement level, you'll find cloakrooms, a bookstore, a post office, WCs, and a small café. For later, notice the back exit, which gives you the option of leaving through the gardens on the north side of the museum (from where you can bear left through the park to reach the Church on Spilled Blood). To reach the exhibits, take the stairs up one flight and scan your ticket at the turnstile. Here, at the base of the grand staircase, you can rent the good audioguide, which interprets 300 of the museum's best works (or, for a quick visit, just use my self-guided tour, below).

Planning Your Time: The museum has 109 numbered rooms (numbers over doorways), but there's no reason to even think of visiting them all. Instead, I've organized this self-guided tour to sample the highlights: Russian icons; historic portraits from the era of Peter the Great; paintings of the 19th-century Wanderers, an important group of breakaway artists; even more groundbreaking examples of early-20th-century abstraction; and a smattering of Socialist Realism, the Soviet-promulgated art style of the early and mid-20th century.

Length of this Tour: Allow about two hours for this huge museum.

◎ Self-Guided Tour

• Be sure to pick up the museum floor plan before you start this tour. Head up the grand staircase and turn into Room 1. We'll take a look at the first five rooms on this floor.

Early Russian Art (Rooms 1-4)

These rooms house an impressive selection of religious icons, the small, elaborate paintings that Orthodox Christians use as tools for prayer. The earliest paintings date back to the 1200s and were collected from the major art centers of Old Russia (including Novgorod and Moscow).

In Room 1, look for **The Angel with Golden Hair** *(Archangel*

ST. PETERSBURG

Gabriel), with the jewel-like colors and flowing lines of the Novgorod style. Dating from around 1200, it's thought to be the oldest surviving icon in Russia. Its Byzantine origins show in the characteristic features of the face: big, almond-shaped eyes, oversized nose, and broad, flat cheeks. Ivan the Terrible himself—the first czar—may have carried the icon from Novgorod, as booty, to Moscow.

Nearby, find a devotional icon of Russia's first saint-martyrs, the prince-brothers **Boris and Gleb.** Presented as warriors of the Church, they wear richly colored robes and hold their usual attributes: crosses and swords. When their father Prince Vladimir of Kiev died, another brother seized the throne—after murdering Gleb and Boris.

In Room 3, spend a few minutes with a pair of monumental icons depicting **Saints Peter and Paul** (c. 1408). They are the work of Andrei Rublev, a Russian master who first broke away from established icon conventions. His saints are graceful and lyrical, their bodies released from the rigid Byzantine style. Just over 10 feet tall, the panels would have been part of the important "deesis" tier of an iconostasis—with Christ at the center, flanked by his archangels and these apostles.

• *We're going to fast-forward to the late 19th century, but before we do, take a peek into Room 5, with a few...*

Historical Portraits Related to Peter the Great (Room 5)

Several interesting portraits in this room are related to Peter the Great, whose urge to Westernize Russia forever changed his court and country.

Comparing a pair of pictures here demonstrates the swiftness with which Peter's reforms swept through the nation. In the late 17th century, an unknown painter made a portrait typical of the time, of one **Yakov Turgenev,** a drinking buddy of Peter's. In the picture in Room 5, Turgenev stands and faces the viewer confidently, a military man of Old Russia, bearded and dressed in fur-trimmed robes, his waist girdled by a traditional sash.

The nearby *Portrait of a Hetman,* made by Peter's court painter Ivan Nikitin some 20 years later, signals the changes Peter wanted. The subject is also a military man, but he is clean-shaven and wears the Westernized uniform of a high-ranking soldier—there's no sign of Slavic style in either the subject or the painting. Peter had sent Nikitin to train in Italy, and it shows in the naturalistic, relaxed pose and the glimmer of real personality in his subject: a battle-worn officer, his eyes red-rimmed with fatigue.

Just a few years later, in 1725, Nikitin would paint his emperor on his deathbed, his body covered with ermine-trimmed bedclothes. Looking at the loosely brushed *Peter the Great on His*

Deathbed, you sense the quickness with which Nikitin must have worked, and feel the immediacy of his grief at the loss of his patron and friend.

• *Backtrack to the landing, head down the grand staircase, and turn right into Room 38 and the adjoining rooms.*

Late-19th-Century Painting: The Wanderers

After Peter the Great's big push to Westernize, Russian artists of the 18th and 19th century by and large followed the aesthetic styles

of secular European art. History painters focused on classical themes (such as Karl Briullov's **Last Day of Pompeii,** 1833, Room 11), and portraits showed bewigged and beribboned aristocrats (see the Frenchified works in Room 10). Truly Russian subjects took a back seat, especially at court.

But in the late 19th century, a "radical" group of painters withdrew from the imperial art academy, called themselves the Wanderers (Peredvizhniki in Russian), and began promoting a Russian artistic agenda that dovetailed with the populist political themes of the day. The Russian subjects adopted by the Wanderers are on display in these rooms (34-38). You'll see Russian girls in fur coats and families promenading across snowy fields, unmistakably Russian landscapes (Viktor Vasnetsov's **North Land,** 1898-99, Room 36), folklorist interpretations of Russian legends (Vasnetsov's **Knight at the Crossroads,** 1882, Room 38), and large-scale historical subjects (Vasily Surkov's **Yermak's Conquest of Siberia,** 1895, Room 36).

Perhaps the most famous of the Wanderers was Ilya Repin. To discover authentically Russian material for his paintings, he trav-

eled throughout the country, observing and sketching everyday people. His **Barge Haulers on the Volga** (1870-73, Room 33) exalts the physical labor of eleven wretched workers, yoked like livestock for the task of pulling a ship against

the current. One of the first works Repin made after leaving the academy, it helped to usher in this new era of realistic genre painting focused, above all, on the Russian spirit.

There's perhaps no writer more associated with that spirit than Leo Tolstoy. Find his portrait, by his good friend Repin, in Room

34 (**Leo Tolstoy Barefoot**, 1901). After achieving great success with his novels, in his later years Tolstoy rejected his literary ambition, dressed as a peasant, and became critical of the czar (his huge popular fame protected him from repercussions).

• *Now we'll jump forward again—to the 20th century. Use your map to reach the top floor of the museum's Benois Wing, housing most of the museum's 20th-century art. Begin in Room 75.*

Russian Abstraction and the Avant-Garde (Rooms 75-77)

At about the same time the Wanderers were pursuing Russian realism, another group of young artists was veering in the opposite direction—toward abstract, nonrepresentational art.

In the early 20th century, Wassily Kandinsky, Kasimir Malevich, Marc Chagall, Vladimir Tatlin, Natalia Goncharova, and Alexander Rodchenko were among the great innovators of abstraction and its spin-offs (Suprematism, Constructivism, Rayonism, Cubo-Futurism, etc.). These artists weren't mere followers of Western art: They were full-fledged collaborators with artists in the West. Their innovations and experiments set much of the direction of modern art in the 20th century.

When you study a work such as Malevich's **Black Square** (1915/1923, Room 76)—a black square on a square canvas against a white background—you might ask: What were these artists trying to do? After centuries of trying to perfect the imitation of nature, the goal now became to liberate painting from representation and to convey instead the "essence" of art. The color and texture of painting became ends in themselves.

Life changed for this talented cadre of artists, as it did for everyone, with the 1917 Revolution. By the early 1930s, the Soviet government had clamped down, and those artists who hadn't already left the country were forced to adopt the style called Socialist Realism.

Socialist Realism (Rooms 78-82)

When Stalin rose to power (after the death of Lenin in 1924), he insisted that Soviet artists practice an optimistic and realistic style to document the communist way of life in the most flattering terms. It was propaganda, pure and simple—art in service to a political ideology. In the canvases in these rooms, you'll see art intended to build the idea of Soviet heroes—in war, in the culture of sport, on collective farms, and among youth groups.

In Room 80, Alexander Samokhvalov's *Militarized Komsomol* (1932-33) conveys the Socialist Realist aesthetic: "realistically" showing everyday people who are, in an idealized way, eagerly participating in the socialist society. In this case, members of a Soviet youth group are gathered on a pastel-green hillside to practice target shooting.

Run (1932-33, Room 81) by Alexander Deineka, celebrates athletic might in a collective portrait of runners on a track. Deineka's subjects hewed to collectivist themes and his artwork is figurative—but there's a sly bit of modernism in his use of large, flattened areas of bright color.

For years, most observers dismissed the art of this era, but many of its practitioners were highly talented artists. In Arkady Plast's *Noon* (1961, Room 82), filled with color and light, a man and woman dip their hands into a well to splash cool water on their sun-reddened faces. Plast's canvas continues in the spirit of the Wanderers, celebrating the harmonious values of the Russian way of life.

The Rest of the Museum

There is much, much more to see in this museum. An entire wing is devoted to crafts and folk art from all over the former Soviet Union, with worthy examples of woodcarving, lace, lacquerwork, embroidery, and folk dresses. To find it, navigate to the Rossi Wing, which you can access from Room 48 on the ground floor.

More Museums

▲Russian Museum of Ethnography
(Российский Этнографический Музей)

This branch of the Russian Museum offers an extensive, if dry, introduction to the various peoples of the European Russia, Siberia, the Far East, Caucasus, and Crimea, reaching from Vilnius to Vladivostok. Fans of folk culture find it worthwhile, and anyone will be impressed by the diversity of one of the planet's biggest and most varied countries. The good, included audioguide (use the free Wi-Fi to download it) tells you more about each culture.

Cost and Hours: 300 R, Tue 10:00-21:00, Wed-Sun until 18:00, closed Mon and last Fri of month, at Inzhenernaya 4—directly to the right as you face the main entrance of the Russian Museum, www.ethnomuseum.ru.

Summer Garden (Летний сад)

The zone behind the Russian Museum is filled with delightful parks and gardens. Directly behind the building, the inviting, tree-filled Mikhailovsky Garden (Михайловский сад) leads (across the canal) into the geometrically regimented Field of Mars (Марсово поле) park, designed to showcase military parades. But best of all (just to the east, across another canal) is the Summer Garden (Летний сад), one of St. Petersburg's most enjoyable public spaces. The oldest garden in the city, it was laid out in 1710 under Peter the Great himself, right where the Fontanka River meets the Neva. It's laced with walking trails, studded with fountains and statues, and generously tree-shaded. Along the Fontanka is Peter's own **Summer Palace** (Летний дворец).

Cost and Hours: Garden free to enter and open in summer daily 10:00-21:00, fountains run Wed-Mon May-Sept only.

▲▲Fabergé Museum (Музей Фаберже)

This sumptuous museum fills the beautifully restored Shuvalov Palace with the world's biggest collection of works by Carl Fabergé, jeweler to the czars and royalty throughout Europe. The undisputed highlight: 14 exquisite Fabergé eggs, including nine imperial Easter eggs. These jeweled fantasies—impossibly lavish, individually created "surprise"-loaded gifts given by the czars to their relatives and friends—represent the pinnacle of Romanov excess. Even those bored by treasury collections are wowed by the chance to get an up-close, 360-degree view of these incredible creations. The sight is a two-fer: Besides ogling the breathtaking treasury of priceless objects, you get to explore the halls of a grand canalside mansion, fueling fantasies of how the czars' aristocratic pals used to live.

Cost and Hours: 450 R, advance tickets available online, audioguide-200 R (plus 1,000-R refundable deposit); Sat-Thu 9:30-20:45, closed Fri; pleasant café, Fontanka 21, tel. 333-2655, www.fabergemuseum.ru.

Getting In: An **advance reservation** must be exchanged for a paper ticket on the day of your visit at the special window for online orders. No advance tickets are sold on-site. Admission to the museum occurs in three time blocks per day: 10:00-14:00, 14:00-18:00, and 18:00-20:45. If you are buying a **same-day ticket,** it makes sense to show up at the start of one of these time blocks, or swing by the museum early in the day to buy tickets for a later time.

Tours: Guided tours run once or twice an hour—but only once or twice a day in English. The English tours fill up; it's best to reserve a tour up to one week in advance online (600 R, includes admission and tour).

Visiting the Museum: After slipping on mandatory shoe covers, you'll ascend the grand staircase, under a gloriously stuccoed dome, to circle the collection counterclockwise. Each room is more amazing than the last. The museum hopes you'll begin in the **Knights' Hall**—filled with precious wine goblets, drinking horns, silver vessels, and military memorabilia—but who are they kidding? Everyone comes here to see those fabulous Fabergé eggs. To begin with them, go straight ahead from the top of the stairs into the **Blue Room.** There you will find 14 magnificent Fabergé Easter eggs. They are displayed in chronological order, illustrating the evolution of their craftsmanship, inventiveness, and extravagance (the cases are numbered; find the first one, with the Hen Egg, through the doorway on the right).

Painstakingly crafted under the direction of court jeweler Peter Carl Fabergé (1846-1920), no two are alike. Each egg required a year's work, which began immediately after Easter so the new egg would be ready for delivery in Holy Week of the next year. The variety of eggs and the surprises they hold are stunning. The first egg (commissioned by Czar Alexander III in 1885 for his wife, Empress Maria Feodorovna) is white enamel; inside it held a golden yolk, which enclosed a golden hen concealing a diamond miniature of the royal crown and a ruby egg.

Later eggs contain increasingly complex mechanisms: A miniature Jesus emerges from a tomb made of agates; a rose-colored egg contains a "bud," whose petals spring open with the press of a button to reveal a diamond crown. The coronation of Nicholas II (the last czar) is celebrated by an egg that reveals an astonishingly detailed miniature coronation carriage—complete with working wheels and suspension. The final imperial egg was given by Nicholas to his mother in 1916. Called the Order of St. George Egg, its relatively simple design, with no elaborate mechanisms or ornate jewels, is a reflection of the times. The dowager empress managed to take this egg with her when she fled Bolshevik Russia in 1919—perhaps for the miniature portraits it contains of her murdered son Nicholas and grandson Alexei.

CHURCHES

Russian Orthodoxy was revived after the end of communism. Duck into any neighborhood church, full of incense, candles, and liturgical chants. It's usually OK to visit discreetly during services,

when the priest opens the doors of the iconostasis, faces the altar, and leads the standing congregation in chant. Smaller churches are usually free to enter (though you can leave a small donation, or buy and light a candle) and full of Russians morning, noon, and night, and will give you more of a feeling for Russian religion than will church-museums

ST. PETERSBURG

The Russian Orthodox Church

The Russian Orthodox Faith

In the 11th century, the Great Schism split the Christian faith into two branches: Roman Catholicism in the west (based in Rome), and Eastern or Byzantine Orthodoxy in the east (based in Constantinople—today's Istanbul).

The Eastern Orthodox Church stayed true to the earliest traditions of the Christian faith, rejecting some theological issues accepted in the West (infallibility of the pope, and the doctrines of Purgatory and the Immaculate Conception, among others). *Orthos* is Greek for "right belief"—and if you believe you've already got it right, you're resistant to change.

The Eastern Orthodox Church is divided into about a dozen branches that are administratively independent even as they share many of the same rituals. Each branch is ruled by a patriarch (similar to a high-ranking bishop). The largest of these—with about half of the world's 300 million Orthodox Christians—is the Russian Orthodox Church.

Under communism, the state religion—atheism—trumped the faith professed by the major-

ity of Russians. The Russian Orthodox Church survived, but many church buildings were seized by the government and repurposed (as museums, municipal buildings, sports facilities, and so on). Many more were destroyed. Soviet citizens who openly belonged to the Church sacrificed any hope of advancement within the communist system. But since the fall of communism, Russians have flocked back to their faith. (Even President Vladimir Putin, a former KGB agent and avowed atheist, revealed that he had secretly been an Orthodox Christian all along.) These days, new churches are being built and destroyed ones are being rebuilt or renovated...and all of them, it seems, are filled with worshippers. Today, three out of every four Russian citizens follows this faith.

Visiting an Orthodox Church

Keep these things in mind as you step inside an Orthodox church.

Before entering an active church, women should cover their heads; women and men both must have their knees covered. (Churches that are tourist attractions may be more flexible.)

Watch worshippers arrive and go through the standard routine: Drop a coin in the wooden box, pick up a candle, say a prayer, light the candle, and place it in the candelabra. Make the sign of the cross and kiss the icon. You're welcome to join in.

Most Orthodox church decorations consist of icons: paintings of saints, packed with intricate symbolism and cast against a shimmering golden background. They are intended to remind viewers of the metaphysical nature of Jesus and the saints, and to inspire the faithful to emulate their virtues. You'll almost never see statues, which, to Orthodox people, feel a little too close to the forbidden worship of graven images.

Most Eastern Orthodox churches have at least one mosaic or painting of Christ in a standard pose—as *Pantocrator,* a Greek word meaning "Ruler of All." The image shows Christ as King of the Universe, facing directly out, with penetrating eyes and a halo-cross behind his head.

The sanctuary is hidden in Orthodox churches. Instead, you'll see an iconostasis: an altar screen covered with curtains and icons. The standard design of the iconostasis calls for four icons flanking the central door. On the right are Jesus and John the Baptist, and on the left are Mary and the Baby Jesus (together in the first panel), and then an  icon featuring the saint or event to which the church is dedicated.

The iconostasis divides the lay community from the priests—the material world from the spiritual one. The spiritual heavy lifting takes place behind the iconostasis, where the priests symbolically turn bread and wine into the body and blood of Christ. Then they open the doors or curtains and serve the Eucharist to their faithful flock.

Notice that there are few (if any) pews. Worshippers stand through the service as a sign of respect (though some older parishioners sit on the seats along the walls). Traditionally, women stand on the left side, and men on the right, equally distant from the altar (because all are equal before God). The Orthodox faith tends to use a Greek cross, with four equal arms (like a plus sign, sometimes inside a circle), which focuses on God's perfection. Many Orthodox churches have Greek-cross floor plans rather than the elongated nave-and-transept designs that are common in Western Europe.

Orthodox services generally involve chanting (a dialogue that goes back and forth between the priest and the congregation), and the church is filled with the evocative aroma of incense, combining to heighten the experience for the worshippers.

such as St. Isaac's or the Church on Spilled Blood. For more on Russian Orthodoxy, see the sidebar.

▲▲Kazan Cathedral (Казанский Собор)

This huge, functioning house of worship, right along Nevsky Prospekt next to the Griboyedov Canal, offers an accessible Orthodox experience, although its interior is not very typical. Reopened as a church after years as a "Museum of Atheism," the building has a sweeping exterior portico patterned after St. Peter's in Rome. Inside you'll find a dim interior, a much-venerated replica of the Icon of Our Lady of Kazan, a monument to the commander who fended off Napoleon's 1812 invasion, and lots of candles and solemn worshippers.

Cost and Hours: Free, daily 9:00-20:00, services generally at 10:00 and 18:00, Nevsky Prospekt 25, www.kazansky-spb.ru.

Visiting the Church: You'll enter through what looks like a side door in the north transept, facing Nevsky Prospekt.

Let your eyes adjust to the low light. Built from 1799 to 1812 and now brilliantly restored, the cathedral seems to rival its model, St. Peter's—typical of this city so determined to be Western... only bigger and better. When Russia tunes into TV for Easter and Christmas services, the broadcast comes from this church. It's often packed with Orthodox visitors from throughout the country.

Appreciate the brilliant silver-arched iconostasis. Worshippers wait in a long line to kiss the church's namesake, the **Icon of Our Lady of Kazan** (left side of the iconostasis). Considered the single most important icon of the Russian Orthodox faith, the original icon was discovered by a young girl (directed by a vision of the Virgin Mary) in a tunnel beneath the city of Kazan in 1579. A monastery was erected on that site, and replicas of the icon were sent to other Russian cities—including St. Petersburg—to be venerated by the faithful. The icon was invoked in many successful military campaigns, including the successful defense of Russia during Napoleon's 1812 invasion. The original icon was stolen from Kazan in 1904 and went missing for nearly 100 years (it resurfaced in the Vatican and was returned to Kazan in 2005, although its authenticity has been questioned). Either way, this is a replica, but still considered holy.

In the left transept, find the statue and tomb of **Field Marshal Mikhail Kutuzov** (1745-1813), who led Russian troops during the Napoleonic conflict. On the pillars flanking the tomb are the keys to the cities that Kutuzov's forces retook from Napoleon as they pushed him back to Paris.

▲▲▲Church on Spilled Blood (Спас на Крови)

This exuberantly decorative church, with its gilded carrot top of onion domes, is a must-see photo op just a short walk off Nevsky

Prospekt. It's built on the place where a revolutionary assassinated Czar Alexander II in 1881—explaining both the evocative name and the structure's out-of-kilter relationship to the surrounding street plan. Ticket windows are on the north side of the church, facing away from Nevsky Prospekt. Go inside to appreciate the dazzling interior, slathered with vivid mosaics.

Cost and Hours: 250 R, Thu-Tue 10:30-18:00, closed Wed; open later May-Sept until 22:30 for 400 R; audioguide-200 R, Kanal Griboyedova 2b, tel. 315-1636, http://eng.cathedral.ru.

Background: Begun just after Alexander's assassination but not finished until 1907, the church is a neo-Russian fantasy, built

to fulfill a romantic image of Russian history and traditions. Psychologically, it seems fitting that the Romanovs, as they fought a rising tide of people power and modernity, would build a church as traditional as their policies and approach to governance.

Alexander II, called "the Great Reformer," freed the serfs in 1861. He gave them land—but expected them to pay for it. The dumbfounded peasants responded by rioting, and the seeds of proletariat discontent were planted. (In this way, Alexander's liberal reforms unwittingly gave rise to the movements that would ultimately decapitate the dynasty.) Memorial plaques around the church exterior (translated in English) list Alexander's many reforms.

Jaw-droppingly beautiful as it was, the church had a short life as a place of worship. The very theme of the church—honoring an assassinated czar—was what the Bolsheviks stood against, so it was looted with gusto during the 1917 Russian Revolution. To add insult to injury, during the communist era, the church was used for storing potatoes, and the streets around it were named for Alexander's assassins. (Out of about 300 churches in the city, only four continued to function during Soviet times.) The Church on Spilled Blood was damaged in World War II, when its crypt did duty as a morgue. Restored in the 1990s, today it serves mostly as a museum.

Interior: Enter the church and look up; Christ gazes down at you from the top of the dome, bathed in light from the windows and ringed by the gold balcony railing. The walls are covered with exquisite mosaics inspired mostly by Byzantium—but some show an idealizing, naturalistic style that celebrates Old Russia (much as late-19th-century Russian painters were doing at the time).

Walk up to the iconostasis (the partition at mid-church). Typically made of wood, this one is of marble, with inlaid doors. In the back of the church, the canopy shows an exposed bit of the cobbled street, marking the spot where Czar Alexander II was mortally wounded—where the czar's blood was spilled. Glass cases to the left show the painstaking restoration work.

▲St. Isaac's Cathedral (Исаакиевский Собор)

The gold dome of St. Isaac's glitters at the end of Malaya Morskaya street, not far from the Admiralty. St. Isaac's was built between 1818 and 1858, and its Neo-classical dome reminds some Americans of the US Capitol building. This is one of the biggest churches in the world, but it's been run as a museum since Soviet times. Nowadays, services are held only in a side chapel, and you'll generally see far more tourists than pilgrims inside.

Cost and Hours: Church interior ("museum")-250 R, Thu-Tue 10:30-18:00, May-Sept also open Thu-Tue 18:00-22:00 for 400 R, closed Wed year-round; roof ("colonnade")-150 R, daily 10:30-18:00, May-Oct also open 18:00-22:00 (300 R), even later during "White Nights"; Isaakievskaya pl. 4, tel. 315-9732, http://eng.cathedral.ru.

Getting Tickets: Bypass the line at the ticket window by using the machines (in English, bills only—no coins). When the main ticket window takes breaks, you can buy tickets at the group window around the corner, or at the machines.

Visiting the Church: Before entering, take a minute to appreciate the **facade.** The granite steps and one-piece granite columns were shipped here from a Finnish quarry 150 miles away. (Massive stonework like this, the grand embankments, and promenades throughout the city date from Catherine the Great's rule.) The enormous building sits upon swampy land, which challenged the French architect and required a huge stone foundation.

The **interior** has a few exhibits, but ultimately it's all about the grand space. Find the case in the nave showing models of the three churches that stood here before this one. Then simply appreciate the massive scale of this church—by some measures, the fourth-largest in Christendom. Notice the grand iconostasis, with its malachite veneer columns. Because the brutal winter weather is tough on paintings, most of what looks like paintings in the church are actually mosaics, which date from the first half of the 19th century. The large mosaic panels at ground level, while made to replace canvas versions on the walls and in the dome, remain parked on the floor. A photo display shows how, during the "Great Patriotic War" (World War II), this church's crypt protected many of the Hermitage treasures.

It's worthwhile to climb the colonnade stairway to the **roof** (262 steps) for the view. Every tenth step (heading up and down) is numbered in a countdown to your goal.

Nearby: Between St. Isaac's Cathedral and the river stands one of the most evocative monuments in the city: the **Bronze Horseman.** This huge statue of Peter the Great on horseback stands atop a massive and symbolic rock inscribed, simply, "From Catherine II to Peter I, 1782." In that year, Catherine the Great—who followed the reforms and approach to ruling of her predecessor—honored Peter with this monument.

SIGHTS NORTH OF THE NEVA RIVER

From the waterfront side of the Hermitage, you can spot several sights across the river that are worth visiting. But you'll have to allow plenty of time; while these places appear close, it takes a while to reach them by foot.

▲▲Strelka Spin-Tour

To reach the Peter and Paul Fortress from the Hermitage, you'll cross the Dvortsovy Bridge and then pass a strategic viewpoint, called Strelka. For a sweeping 360-degree view of St. Petersburg's core, head down to the park that fills the knob of land at water level (between the two pink columns).

You're standing on a corner of the large **Vasilyevsky Island**—one of the many islands that make up St. Petersburg. (A nickname for the town is "City on 101 Islands," although an official count is elusive.)

Literally meaning "Little Arrow," **Strelka** sticks out into the very heart of the Neva River and St. Petersburg. The park filling the point is one of the sites around town where newlyweds are practically obligated to come for wedding pictures. They toast with champagne, then break their glasses against the big granite ball (watch your step).

To begin your spin-tour, face the can't-miss-it **Hermitage,** just across the Neva—the Winter Palace of the czars and today a world-

class art museum. The sprawling complex has several wings: the main green-and-white structure, as well as the yellow and mint-green sections beyond it. No wonder it could take days to fully see the place.

Now spin to the left. The Art Nouveau **Trinity Bridge** (Troitsky Most)—one of St. Petersburg's longest and most beautiful—was completed in 1903, its design having beat out a submission by Gustav Eiffel. It was meant as a symbol of French/Russian cooperation and friendship (a bridge built over Paris' Seine River at about the same time is named for Alexander III).

Before the 1850s, no permanent bridges spanned the Neva; one crossed only on pontoon bridges (in the summer) or a frozen river (in winter). It wasn't unusual for St. Petersburgers to get stranded while waiting for a deep freeze or a thaw. Just beyond the bridge (on its right end), you can faintly see the trees marking the delightful **Summer Garden**—the private garden for Peter the Great's modest Summer Palace, and now a public park and a wonderful place for a warm-weather stroll.

On the left side of the river, you'll see the stoutly walled **Peter and Paul Fortress,** with its slender golden spire (described later in this section). St. Petersburg was born here in 1703, when Peter the Great began building this fortress to secure territory he had won in battle with the Swedes. Are there any sunbathers on the sandy beach out front?

Scanning the waterfront, think for a moment about how strategic this location is, at the mouth of the Neva River. Although very short (only 42 miles), the Neva is an essential link in a vital series of shipping waterways. It connects the Gulf of Finland to Lake Lagoda, which feeds (via a network of canals) into Russia's "mother river," the Volga—Europe's longest river, which cuts north-to-south through the Russian heartland all the way to the Caspian Sea. A series of Soviet-era shipping canals connects the Volga to the Moskva River, the Black Sea, and the Danube. That makes the Neva the outlet for all Russian waterways to all of Europe and beyond. In other words, you could sail from Iran to Volgograd to

Istanbul to Budapest to Moscow to Lisbon—but you would have to go through St. Petersburg.

Turning farther left, you'll spot the first of the two giant, pink **rostral columns** that flank the Strelka viewpoint. Inspired by similar towers built by ancient Greeks and Romans to celebrate naval victories, these columns are decorated with anchors and studded with the symbolic prows of ships defeated in battle. Once topped by gaslights (now electric), the pillars trumpet St. Petersburg's nautical heritage. (A similar column stands in the middle of New York City's Columbus Circle.) Facing Strelka is the white-columned **Old Stock Exchange,** bordered by yellow warehouses.

Just to the left, the turreted pastel-blue building is Peter the Great's **Kunstkamera,** a sort of ethnographical museum built around the czar's original collection. "Kunstkamera" (meaning a cabinet of curiosities) and "Hermitage" (meaning a retreat) are both European words and concepts that Peter the Great imported to class up his new, European-style capital.

Circling a bit farther to the left, the yellow buildings at the end of the bridge (just right of the Hermitage) are the **Admiralty,** the geographical center of St. Petersburg and the headquarters of Peter the Great's imperial navy.

▲Kunstkamera (Кунсткамера)

Peter the Great, who fancied himself a scientist, founded this—the first state public museum in Russia—in 1714. He filled it with his

personal collections, consisting of "fish, reptiles, and insects in bottles," scientific instruments, and books from his library. In the 19th century, Russian travelers returning from the Americas added a rich array of artifacts—and, amazingly, those original collections remain in this same building. The anthropological and ethnographic collections include the best exhibit on northern Native Americans that you'll find on this side of the Atlantic. While many tourists dismiss the Kunstkamera as a "museum of curiosities," locals are proud of its scientific tradition and its impressive collections.

Cost and Hours: 300 R; Tue-Sun 11:00-18:00, closed Mon and last Tue of month, last entry one hour before closing; Universitetskaya Naberezhnaya 3—enter around the left side as you face the steeple from the riverfront; tel. 328-0812, www.kunstkamera.ru.

ST. PETERSBURG

▲▲Peter and Paul Fortress (Петропавловская Крепость)

Founded by Peter the Great in 1703 during the Great Northern War with Sweden, this fortress on an island in the Neva was the birthplace of St. Petersburg. Its gold steeple catches the sunlight, and its blank walls face the Winter Palace across the river. While it's a large complex, the most important parts are easy to see: Wander the grounds, dip into the cathedral to visit the tombs of the Romanovs, and maybe do a little sunbathing on the beach. For those wanting to delve into history, the grounds also host museums about city history, space exploration, and the famous-to-Russians former prison.

Cost: It's free to enter and explore the parklike grounds. The sights inside are covered by individual tickets (cathedral-450 R, other sights-100-200 R each, combo-ticket valid for two days covers cathedral, prison, history museum, and space museum-600 R) and an audioguide (300 R). There are two ticket offices: one in the low, yellow pavilion just to the left of the cathedral, and another just inside the main gate.

Hours: Grounds open daily 6:00-22:00; cathedral and prison daily 10:00-19:00 (Sun from 11:00); smaller museums Thu-Mon 11:00-19:00, Tue 11:00-18:00, closed Wed.

Information: Tel. 230-6431, www.spbmuseum.ru.

Getting There: Footbridges at either end of the fortress's island (Hare Island/Zayachy Ostrov) connect it to the rest of St. Petersburg. Getting there is easy: Just set your sights on the skinny golden spire. The main entrance is through the park from the Gorkovskaya Metro station. The other entrance is at the west end—a scenic, 20-minute walk from Palace Square and the Hermitage. Cross the bridge (Dvortsovy Most) by the Hermitage, angle right past the Strelka viewpoint (worth a quick stop to enjoy the view—described earlier), then cross the next bridge (Birzhevoy Most), turn right, and follow the waterline to a footbridge leading to the fortress' side entrance.

Background: There's been a fortress here as long as there's been a St. Petersburg. When Peter the Great founded the city, in 1703, this was the first thing he built to defend this strategic meeting point of the waterways of Russia and the Baltic. Originally, the center of town was just east of here (near the preserved log cabin where Peter the Great briefly resided).

➋ **Self-Guided Tour:** Pick up a map when you buy your ticket to navigate the sprawling complex. Begin at the cathedral, marked by the golden spire. You'll find pay WCs scattered around the grounds.

Sts. Peter and Paul Cathedral: The centerpiece of the fortress is this cathedral—the first built in St. Petersburg (and, until modern times, the tallest building in the city). This church is the final resting place of the Romanov czars, who ruled Russia from 1613 through 1917.

The early-18th-century cathedral was designed in Baroque style by a Swiss-Italian architect who, like so many other artists

and craftsmen, was imported by Peter the Great to introduce European culture to Russia. Not surprisingly, its interior looks nothing like a typical Russian church. Instead of a Greek-cross plan, it is a hall church, with a nave and side aisles of equal height.

With the Bolshevik Revolution in 1917, mobs of workers and sailors ransacked the place—taking out their anger against the Romanov dynasty, desecrating the tombs, and looting everything they could. It's been a museum since 1922, and was extensively renovated in the last decade. Today, people (Russians included) are understandably caught up in the allure of the glamorous Romanov dynasty: White-marble monuments mark the graves of czars and czarinas, who are buried 10 feet below floor level.

Entering the church, pick up a floor plan identifying each member of the dynasty and their family members. I'll cover just a few highlights.

Start by facing the **main altar,** with its glittering gilded wood-carved iconostasis and its traditional Orthodox imagery in the Russian Baroque style. To the right of the iconostasis are the first **tombs** we'll visit—each marked by a sarcophagus of white marble topped by a gilded bronze cross. It's easy to identify the tombs of the royals who were rulers: They get the double-headed Romanov eagle at each corner of their sarcophagus. On the right, in front, is **Peter the Great** (1672-1725). Marked by his bronze bust, the founder of the city was the first czar to be buried here. He's surrounded by other family and descendants, including **Catherine II the Great** (1729-1796, back left), the wife and usurper of Peter III (Peter the Great's grandson).

In the middle of the church, about a third of the way from the main door to the iconostasis, on the left, is **Maria Fedorovna** (1847-1928). This popular Danish princess (known as Dagmar in her native land) moved from Copenhagen to St. Petersburg, married the second-to-the-last czar (Alexander III, next white tomb),

ST. PETERSBURG

gave birth to the last czar (Nicholas II), and fled the October Revolution to live in exile in Denmark. After her death, she was buried with her fellow Danish royals at Roskilde Cathedral; in 2006, her remains were brought back here to join her adopted clan. Hers is one of the most popular graves in the church.

Now turn to the small chapel at the back of the church (left of the entry door). It contains the tombs of the much romanti-

cized family of the final Romanov czar: **Nicholas II** (1868-1918), his wife, Alexandra, and their four daughters and one son. The czar abdicated in March 1917 and was imprisoned with the rest of his family. The Bolsheviks murdered them all on the night of July 16, 1918. The family was shot at point-blank range with handguns. Because the daughters had diamonds sewn into their dresses, some of the bullets deflected at crazy angles—to be sure they were dead, the assassins bayoneted them. Originally buried in an unmarked grave, the remains of most of the family members were only rediscovered in 1991 and reburied here in 1998 to great fanfare (the event was televised nationally). Today, observant Russians consider the family to have been martyred, and in 2000 the Russian Orthodox Church canonized them.

Persistent legends long surrounded the fate of the Romanov daughter **Anastasia,** who was rumored to have escaped the execution. In the decades since the massacre, different women emerged claiming to be the long-lost Anastasia—most famously Anna Anderson, who turned up in Berlin in the 1920s. But very recent DNA testing has positively identified the remains of the real Anastasia (found only in 2007 and now interred here), while similar tests disproved Anderson's claim.

History Exhibit: Exit through the gift shop (to the left of the main altar), but before leaving, turn right from the shop into a hall with a visual and well-described history of the church and the Romanov dynasty, complete with a family tree and portraits. At the end of this corridor is a collection of tombs of other Romanovs, including late-20th-century family members—grand dukes and grand duchesses—who somewhat controversially have claimed a spot here.

Tower Climb: To climb the spire for a grand view, you must join a guided tour (150 R), offered about four times a day but only sporadically in English. Check times and availability at the desk just inside the cathedral entry.

The Grounds: Strolling the extensive grounds is a pleasant break. From the cathedral, head out through the gateway/tunnel for a peek at the river—as you pass through the tunnel, notice the markers on the right wall indicating the level of devastating flood waters. Until the Neva was contained by a series of dams and locks (completed in 2011), rising water and wet basements were common in the city.

You can also circle around the fortress exterior to find the delightful sandy beach huddled alongside the wall—an understandably popular place for St. Petersburgers to sunbathe on balmy days, and for newlyweds to snap wedding portraits.

To enjoy views from the fortress, join the "Neva Panorama" walking route on top of the wall on the river side of the fortress (250-R ticket). For free views, head to the south end of the island, with a 180-degree panorama of the city, Vasilyevsky Island, and the river (or see the same scenery from a table at the pleasant **$$$$ Koryushka** restaurant, also at the south end under the walls, daily 12:00-24:00, en.ginza.ru).

▲Museum of Russian Political History
(Музея политической истории России)

This is the city's best exhibit about Russia's communist period. Across the moat from the Peter and Paul Fortress, it's partly housed in a mansion where Lenin had an office, and sprawls through several attached buildings. The eclectic collection is best appreciated by someone with a cursory understanding of modern Russian history. The core exhibit—"Man and Power in Russia, 19th-21st Centuries"—is modern and freshly presented, employing historical artifacts, photography, archival footage, sound clips, and touchscreens. Some English information is posted, and you can borrow descriptions in most exhibits, but it's worth investing in an audioguide).

Cost and Hours: 200 R, Sat-Tue 10:00-18:00, Wed and Fri 10:00-20:00, closed Thu and last Mon of month, last entry one hour before closing, audioguide-200 R, Kuybysheva 2 but enter around the corner facing the park at Kronverkskiy Prospekt 1, tel. 233-7052, www.polithistory.ru, nearest Metro: Gorkovskaya.

▲Peter the Great's Log Cabin

The oldest surviving building in St. Petersburg is this log cabin, made of hewn pine on a spot Peter himself chose while overseeing the building of his great city in 1703. Peter was fighting Sweden (then a major European power), and with the foundation of St. Petersburg here, on former Swedish soil, he was making it clear: This was Russia...and Russia now had a gateway to the Baltic Sea, and thus to Europe. Records from Peter's time refer to the cabin as the "initial palace" and the "red mansion," but at only 42 x 19 feet, it is far from palatial (he was only Peter I then, and did not become

"Great" until 1721). But it is undeniably evocative to peer into the czar's sparsely furnished study, dining room, and bedroom. Today, the cabin is preserved within a bigger, brick structure in a tidy riverfront park. Besides the cabin, you see a tiny exhibit on the birth of St. Petersburg and a wooden skiff said to have been built by Peter himself.

Cost and Hours: 200 R, Wed and Fri-Mon 10:00-18:00, Thu 13:00-21:00, closed Tue, Petrovskaya Naberezhnaya 6, www.rusmuseum.ru, nearest Metro: Gorkovskaya.

▲Cruiser *Aurora*

The Soviet Union created a thrilling and inspirational mythology about the revolution that created it. According to popular history, that uprising kicked off with a shot from the battleship *Aurora*, a signal to revolutionaries to storm the Winter Palace in 1917. State-of-the-art when built about 1900, the *Aurora* fought in the Russo-Japanese War (1904-1905). Later, its guns defended Leningrad during the Nazi siege in World War II; when it looked like the Germans might take the city, the Soviets sank the *Aurora* rather than let this relic of the Revolution fall into their hands.

After the war, the much-adored ship was salvaged and substantially rebuilt. It's remained a symbol of the Revolution with an almost religious significance for pilgrims from throughout Russia. This is a first stop for many Russians touring St. Petersburg (and it can get very crowded). Maritime geeks will enjoy the onboard exhibits that tell the history of the cruiser, with a focus on World War I and the October Revolution (be sure to get the audioguide).

Cost and Hours: 600 R, Wed-Sun 11:00-18:00, closed Mon-Tue; audioguide-500 R, Petrogradskaya Naberezhnaya, www.navalmuseum.ru, nearest Metro: Gorkovskaya.

OUTER ST. PETERSBURG

▲▲Peterhof (Петергоф)

Peter the Great's lavish palace at Peterhof (sometimes still called by its communist name, Petrodvorets/Петродворец) sits along the Gulf of Finland west of the city. With glorious gardens, this is Russia's Versailles and the target of many tour groups and travel poster photographers. Promenade along the grand canal, which runs through landscaped grounds from the boat dock up to the terraced fountains in front of the palace. You can visit the museum inside the palace if you want, but it's more fun to stay outdoors.

Children love to run past the trick fountains—sometimes they splash you, sometimes they don't.

Cost and Hours: Park-750 R, open daily in summer 9:00-20:00; Grand Palace museum-700 R, Tue-Sun 10:30-18:00, until 19:00 in summer, May-mid-Oct open Sat until 21:00, last entry at 19:45, closed Mon year-round; audioguide-500 R, www.peterhofmuseum.ru. Consider investing in the good guidebooklet that helps you locate each fountain.

Summertime Palace Visits/Crowd-Beating Tips: Because many tour groups visit the Great Palace in summer, the ticket office is open for individual ticket sales for the palace only during these hours: Tue-Sun 12:00-14:00 & 16:15-17:45 (Sat until 19:45; palace closed Mon). There are no online ticket sales in summer for the palace. Furthermore, individual visitors are combined into groups for entry to the palace. It can take an hour to buy a ticket—and another hour to get into the palace. Once inside, you'll be shuffled through the rooms pretty quickly—that is, if you can get past the tour groups.

If you want to see only the garden and the fountains, visit on a Monday, when the palace is closed and there are far fewer tour groups. You can save time by buying a garden ticket online—print and bring it so you can scan your way through the turnstiles at the lower garden—otherwise you'll have to wait in line to buy the garden ticket.

Getting There: In summer, "Meteor" **hydrofoils,** run by competing companies, leave for Peterhof from docks to either side of the busy Dvortsovy Bridge by the Hermitage, along the Admiralteyskaya embankment (first boat leaves around 10:00 and every 30 minutes thereafter, last boat returns from Peterhof at 19:00 in summer, but confirm return time before you buy your ticket), 30-40-minute trip, 800-R one way, 1,500-R round-trip; hydrofoils stop running in even mildly strong winds). Of the hydrofoil companies, several have English-language websites (www.peterhof-express.com, http://en.citycruises.ru). The hydrofoils can sell out in summer—it may be wise to buy your ticket in advance.

If it's windy, or to save money, you can take **public transportation:** Ride the Metro to the lavishly decorated Avtovo station, cross the street to the right, and find a gang of *marshrutka* minibuses with signs for *Peterhof* (#K224, #K300, or #K424). For variety, consider riding the minibus to the top end of the gardens, enjoying the half-mile stroll downhill through the grounds, and returning via hydrofoil.

Tsarskoye Selo (Царское Село)

About 15 miles south of St. Petersburg is the charming small town of Pushkin. Back when Peter the Great started construction of a

Peter the Great

Every so often, an individual comes along who revolutionizes an entire people. While Russia has had more than its share of those figures, perhaps the most dynamic and influential was Peter the Great.

During the four decades he ruled Russia (1682-1725), Czar Peter I transformed his country into a major European power. Even more self-assured than your average monarch, Peter gave himself the nickname "Peter the Great"—and it stuck. He stood well over six feet tall, and he ruled Russia with a towering power and determination. Full of confidence and charm, Peter mixed easily with all classes of people and at times even dressed cheaply and spoke crudely.

Peter grew up at court in Moscow. In a formative episode, the newly crowned, 10-year-old Peter witnessed a bloody palace coup that sidelined him in a co-rulership for years. But Peter's exile put him in proximity to Moscow's German community, a source of bold new ideas that jolted his worldview. He was particularly taken with the Protestant work ethic, and was fascinated by the idea that humans could conquer nature. He saw this mindset as a refreshing antidote for the fatalistic Russian Orthodox outlook.

Peter came into his own as sole ruler in 1689, and quickly began making up for lost time. He became the first czar in a cen-

summer palace here, it was called Tsarskoye Selo—literally "Czars' Village." The site features a spectacular cluster of over-the-top-opulent Romanov palaces, pavilions, and gardens, built by Peter and his heirs (mostly in the 18th century). The main attraction is the **Catherine Palace,** famous for its breathtaking Amber Room. The adjacent **Catherine Park**—with manicured gardens, fanciful pavilions, tree-lined paths, and other decorative flourishes—surrounds the sprawling Great Pond.

▲▲▲Catherine Palace

Arguably Russia's single most enjoyable palace to tour (and that's saying something), the Catherine Palace lacks the staggering scale of the Hermitage, but gives you much more insight into the dynamic czars and

tury to travel to Europe in peacetime, making an epic journey to Holland and England, great maritime powers from whom Peter wanted to learn everything he could about shipbuilding, technology, navigation, and seamanship. He even went undercover for a stint in an Amsterdam shipyard, sleeping in a humble cupboard bed.

Upon his return, Peter began implementing reforms to give Russia a fresh start. To encourage his subjects to be more enterprising, he created a 14-level "table of ranks," designed to reward hard work rather than heredity. He did away with symbols of the Old World, such as long beards, literally shaving the beards right off of his advisers' faces.

Internationally, Peter the Great refashioned Russia's army to resemble Western models, and he founded the Russian navy. He started the Great Northern War with Sweden to ensure that Russia would have access to the Baltic Sea for trade and strategic purposes. He built an entirely new capital in St. Petersburg and established a shipbuilding industry there. He reorganized the government and introduced new taxes to support his foreign policy.

Although Peter is revered by many Russians today, his reign was not without scandal. A heavy drinker with a short temper, Peter was known to lash out against even his closest advisors. He had his own son killed and exiled his first wife to a convent.

Despite his cruelties, Peter left a positive imprint on Russian history. When Peter took the throne, Russia was a backwater, stuck in the Middle Ages. By the time he died, his country had become a European powerhouse.

czarinas who ruled Russia. (For the Romanov family tree, see the "Romanovs 101" sidebar, earlier.)

Cost and Hours: 1,200 R, 1,500 R if purchased in advance online; open to individual visitors Wed-Mon 12:00-16:00 (stays open as late as 20:00 in summer—check online), off-season open Wed-Mon 10:00-16:45, closed last Mon of month; closed Tue year-round; audioguide-150 R, tel. 466-6669, http://eng.tzar.ru.

Getting There: The palace is most easily reached with a **guide,** who can provide door-to-door service and an efficient, highly focused tour of just the highlights (for private guide services, see page 342).

Crowd-Beating Tips: In peak season (May-Sept), individuals may enter the Catherine Palace only from 12:00 until 16:00, and tickets can sell out. To be sure you'll get in, **reserve a ticket online** up to 30 days in advance (1,500 R, up to 4 tickets per order, includes entry to Catherine Park); you'll receive an email voucher that you'll exchange for a ticket at the booth near the Church Gate (look for onion domes, open Wed-Mon 12:00-16:00; must show ID). Your reservation is for a specific day—not a time. But note that once you exchange your voucher for a ticket, you must enter the palace within one hour.

Background: Peter the Great and his wife, Catherine I, for whom the palace is named, built the original palace at Tsarskoye Selo starting in 1717—when St. Petersburg itself was still in its infancy. In the following decades, the palace was rebuilt and expanded many times, most notably by Peter and Catherine's daughter, Elizabeth, who wanted to make it Russia's answer to Versailles. Most of what you see today was designed by the Italian architect Francesco Bartolomeo Rastrelli in Elizabethan Baroque style. Later, Catherine the Great left her own mark on the palace, expanding and renovating in the more restrained Neoclassical style (with the help of Scottish architect Charles Cameron).

Because the palace had been turned into a museum (and carefully documented) after the Bolshevik Revolution, conservators could authentically restore it from the severe damage it suffered in World War II. As you tour the rooms, keep in mind that some of what you see (like the Great Hall) has been completely rebuilt. Fortunately, conservators had time to remove much of the furniture and furnishings to safety, and they even buried stonework and sculpture on the grounds to protect them.

❂ Self-Guided Tour

This "highlights" tour of the one-way route through the palace introduces you to some of the dynamic figures who shaped Russia, and it's a great way to trace the evolution of imperial aesthetics. To get oriented, make your way to the five shimmering, skinny, golden onion domes that mark the **Palace Church.** The church is attached by a skybridge to the yellow, Neoclassical **Lyceum of Tsarskoye Selo,** a prestigious, Eton-like boarding school for elites. The writer Alexander Pushkin was one of many important Russians who studied here. You'll start the tour from the palace lobby.

• *Once inside, slip on a pair of provided booties (and head up the Grand Staircase, following* Tour's Beginning *signs to our first stop.*

Great Hall: This, the largest room in any Russian palace (more than 9,000 square feet), is multipurpose: Its textbook Elizabethan Baroque interior works as a throne room, a ballroom, or a grand dining hall. The architecture, clearly inspired by the Hall of Mirrors at Versailles (with 300 mirrors, and lit by up to 7,000 candles for big events), exaggerates the spaciousness. It was here that Peter the Great and Catherine hosted extravagant masquerade balls to show off their beautiful daughter, Elizabeth (notice her monogram—"E1"—in the carved, gilded decoration). The lights would dim and a spotlight would be shone on the future czarina for her big entrance.

• *Next you'll pass into a series of...*

Baroque Apartments: This section of the palace represents the peak of Elizabethan Baroque. First, in the **Cavaliers' Dining Room,** ogle the dining table set with precious porcelain decorated with the emblems of the court's cavaliers. Receptions for a smaller number of guests were usually held here. Notice the huge blue-and-white Delft-tiled heater in the corner—you'll see more of these throughout this wing. Fires kept stoked by servants down below provided the heat that radiated from the stoves.

Continue into the **White Dining Room**—set with original Meissen porcelain. The imperial family gathered here for every-day dinners, but in their absence, courtiers ate here, their appetites stimulated by the portraits of game on the walls.

Pass through the crimson and green Pillar Rooms (notice Catherine the Great's chess set on the table in the crimson room), and into the **Portrait Hall.** On the right wall, find Catherine I, the palace's namesake and the first empress of Russia. On the left wall is Catherine's daughter, Elizabeth.

• *Next up is the highlight of the entire palace. Take a deep breath and brace yourself for the crowds of the...*

Amber Room: Wow. Utterly magnificent, this jewel box of a room is slathered with six tons of amber mosaic. Frederick the

Great of Prussia commissioned this work for himself in the early 1700s, but he later sent it to his then-ally Peter the Great (according to legend, in exchange for 55 tall Russian soldiers, a lathe, and an ivory mug made by Peter himself). The panels were first installed in the Winter Palace in St. Petersburg, but in 1755, Elizabeth ordered them sent to Tsarkoye Selo. The architect Rastrelli oversaw their placement here, backing the amber with gold foil and installing mirrored pilasters to magnify its dazzling brightness.

In 1944, the Nazi army completely dismantled the original Amber Room and shipped the pieces to Germany; it's never been seen again. Years later, in 1979, Soviet authorities set about to re-create the original room, relying mostly on black-and-white photographs. This replica is painstakingly accurate—although the exact shades of yellow and brown had to be guessed at. A few decades (and an estimated $350 million) later, Vladimir Putin unveiled the new Amber Room in 2003.

The space is particularly astonishing when you realize how difficult amber is to work with: Its brittleness demanded the highest possible skill to successfully shape each puzzle piece into the exquisite mosaics you see. The four color "paintings" represent the five senses—it was thought that amber was pleasing to the full range of human sensory experience.

• *Linger over the details until you can't take the crowds anymore. Then proceed through...*

More Baroque Apartments: In the **Picture Hall,** almost all the 114 paintings are original (they were squirreled away in Leningrad during the siege). There are no big-name artists or subjects here. Rather, Rastrelli hung the paintings according to the "tapestry" approach: arranged purely according to size, shape, composition, and color scheme, creating a sort of mosaic wallpaper.

Next, in the **Small White Dining Room,** you'll see some paintings of this palace after its expansion in 1757 to (roughly) its current shape.

• *Now we move forward in time to the early 19th century, to see the...*

Private Apartments of Czar Alexander I: You'll begin in the **Drawing Room of Alexander I,** where, on the left wall, you'll see a painting of the room's namesake and Catherine the Great's grandson: Alexander I. Alexander agreed to the palace coup that assassinated his father (Paul I), then went on to rule Russia for the first quarter of the 19th century. He succeeded in expanding Russia's territory (adding Finland and Poland to the realm), and was the czar who turned back Napoleon's forces (but only after the French had burned Moscow in 1812).

• *Soon you'll cross into a section of the palace with an entirely different style.*

Catherine the Great's Neoclassicism: Beginning with the **Green Dining Room,** we leave the Elizabethan Baroque of the mid-1700s and transition into Catherine the Great's Neoclassicism of the late 1700s. The practical empress was unimpressed by overwrought Baroque gaudiness and frilly excess, which give way in the next few rooms to subdued pastels, understated reliefs, and clean, white columns. Catherine imported the Scottish architect Charles Cameron, who had extensively studied the ancient Roman ruins of Pompeii, to remake parts of the palace in the so-called Palladian style in vogue in Italy. Evoking ancient Greek and Roman culture, Neoclassicism eventually evolved into the more beefed-up Russian Empire style of the early 19th century. Another feature that Cameron introduced (from the British Isles) was the open fireplace—notice that throughout this section, you'll see these rather than tall, tiled heaters.

Continue into the **Blue State Drawing Room,** where famous guests gathered to listen to music and discuss the important news of the day. In the **Chinese State Drawing Room,** Cameron combined Neoclassical elements (the gilded frieze around the top of the walls, for example) with a Far Eastern effect, decorating the silk-lined walls with fanciful—and purely imaginary—scenes of Chinese life.

Loop around the end of this wing, passing through a series of smaller, wood-clad rooms that belonged originally to Czar Paul I, and later to his son and successor, Alexander I. The **State Study of Alexander I**—the pink room with Doric columns—shows how this ruler jazzed up Catherine's Neoclassicism to its logical next stage, Russian Empire style.

• *Our palace tour is over. The route out takes you through a hallway lined with photographs that document the damage done to the building in World War II, and the decades-long restoration. From there, head outside and take some time to relax in the...*

▲▲Catherine Park

You could spend hours—or days—exploring the sprawling grounds around the Catherine Palace. Created over the course of two centuries, the grounds are a leafy catalogue of changing imperial taste and landscape traditions. When Catherine the Great inherited the palace, the vast gardens were filled with geometric Baroque beds fanning out from the main building. The empress immediately ordered a makeover, envisioning a garden that combined the latest European styles with pure Russian whimsy. While it's possible to enter some of the garden's landmarks, it's perfectly enjoyable to simply go for a walk in the park.

Cost and Hours: 200-R admission collected May-Oct 9:00-19:00, free at other times; open daily 7:00-21:00 (later in summer).

Shopping in St. Petersburg

With vivid cultural artifacts for sale at reasonable prices, St. Petersburg is an obvious shopping stop for many tourists.

What to Buy: The famous Russian **nesting dolls** called *matryoshka* are one of the most popular items. The classic design shows a ruby-cheeked Russian peasant woman wearing a babushka and traditional dress, but don't miss the entertaining

modern interpretations. You'll see Russian heads of state (Peter the

Great inside Lenin inside Stalin inside Gorbachev inside Putin), as well as every American professional and college sports team you can imagine—each individual player wearing his actual number. Other popular gifts include **amber** pieces and delicately painted **wooden eggs.**

High-quality **porcelain** is sold at numerous outlets of the Imperial Porcelain Factory (Императорский Фарфоровый Завод, sometimes referred to by its Soviet-era name, *Lomonosov*), which made fine tableware for the czars (there's one at Nevsky Prospekt 60, www.imp.ru).

You'll find colorful Russian **textiles,** including shawls and scarves as well as tablecloths and linens at Pavloposadskie Platki (Павлопосадские платки, at Nevsky Prospekt 87 and else-where around town, http://www.platki.ru)—including entertaining themed patterns that memorialize events from Russian history and the lives of favorite saints.

Where to Shop: St. Petersburg's major sights have excellent **museum gift shops,** such as those in the Hermitage and at the Russian Museum.

Big, glitzy **souvenir shops** (like the one facing the Moyka, just off Palace Square) offer a wide variety of items, but the prices are inflated to cover a 30 percent kickback for tour guides—even if you're on your own. Other, similar shops are typically located near major sights—consider popping in to **Galeria Naslediye** (Галерея Наследие) to check out the selection of *matryoshka,* imitation Fabergé eggs, and amber (between the Hermitage and the Church on Spilled Blood on the Moyka embankment at Naberezhnaya reki Moyki 37, www.souvenirboutique.com).

Au Pont Rouge claims to be Russia's first department store (founded in 1907). The imperial family was among its customers, but after the October Revolution the landmark Style Moderne building was converted into a sewing factory. It's now reopened as a fairly glamorous retail space, with a nice mix of Russian gifts and fun fashions (Naberezhnaya reki Moyki 73, www.aupontrouge.ru).

To rub elbows with St. Petersburg's beautiful people, take a stroll down the boulevard called **Bolshaya Konyushennaya** (start at the Nevsky Prospekt end). Big-name shops like Prada are here, but you'll also find a healthy sprinkling of Russian boutiques as well as one big luxury department store, DLT, in a vintage art nouveau building (at #21).

An affordable **outdoor souvenir market** spreads along the canal behind the Church on Spilled Blood. You could check for lower prices among the souvenir shops inside the Gostiny Dvor complex—the section on the ground floor right along Nevsky has some decent souvenir stalls (it's OK to bargain hard here).

Entertainment in St. Petersburg

▲▲Ballet

St. Petersburg is synonymous with classical ballet. Durable masterpieces like "Swan Lake" were first staged at the city's Mariinsky Theater, and many of the world's star dancers, past and present (Anna Pavlova, Rudolf Nureyev, Mikhail Baryshnikov), have trained and performed here.

The best venues in St. Petersburg for ballet are the Mariinsky Theater and the Mikhailovsky Theater. Ballet season at both theaters runs from mid-September to mid-July. Both theaters have storied histories, classic opera-house interiors (the Mariinsky's is a bit more opulent), and well-designed websites that allow you to buy tickets online in advance, in English. Same-day tickets are often available (though not for the most popular ballets).

Although the historic Mariinsky (formerly Kirov) ballet company is the most famous, there are other ballet troupes in town. Some companies stage summer performances especially for tourists (but usually not with their "A-list" dancers).

The **Mikhailovsky Theater** is conveniently located, at Ploshchad Isskustv 1, by the Russian Museum, a block off Nevsky (box office open daily 10:00-21:00, tel. 595-4305, www.mikhailovsky. ru).

The **Mariinsky Theater** (formerly the Kirov Theater) has grown into a complex of buildings southwest of St. Isaac's Cathedral, at Teatralnaya Ploshchad. Two separate but associated buildings face each other across a canal near "Theater Square": The original, traditional Mariinsky Theater; and the sleek, state-of-the-art Mariinsky II opera house. A couple of long blocks to the west, on Pisareva street, is the modern, lower-profile Concert Hall. Be clear on which venue you're attending (box office open daily 11:00-19:00, tel. 326-4141, www.mariinsky.ru). Buses #2, #27, and #50 take you right to Theater Square. Alternatively, you can take the Metro to Sadovaya and walk about 20 minutes.

One of the most opulent performance halls for ballet in town is the Neoclassical **Hermitage Theater**—once the private theater of the czars (Dvortsovaia naberezhnaya 32, tel. 408-1084, https://hermitagetheater.com). A limited repertoire of ballets is performed here, mostly with tourist audiences in mind ("Swan Lake," "The Nutcracker," "Romeo and Juliet," "Sleeping Beauty").

Opera and Classical Music

The Mariinsky and Mikhailovsky theaters (described above) host world-class opera and musical performances—as do other concert halls in the city. For chamber music, check the schedule of the **Small Hall** of the St. Petersburg Philharmonia (box office open daily 11:00-19:00, Nevsky Prospekt 30, tel. 571-8333, www.

philharmonia.spb.ru). The philharmonia itself performs orchestral music at the **Big Hall** (Mikhailovskaya 2, tel. 710-4257, same website and hours as Small Hall). The small, luxurious **St. Petersburg Opera Theater** stages classic and modern pieces in a 19th-century hall (box office open daily 12:00-19:00, Galernaya 33, tel. 702-6101, www.spbopera.ru).

It can be worthwhile to peruse the city's tourist website, which has links to all the theaters in town (www.visit-petersburg.ru). Concert halls typically go dark in August.

Folk Music and Dancing

Every night, a hardworking troupe puts on a pricey, touristy, crowd-pleasing Russian folklore show at the Nikolaevsky Palace (near the Neva embankment, southwest of St. Isaac's Cathedral). The nearly two-hour show kicks off with a men's a cappella quartet, followed by two different dance groups. The experience includes some light snacks and drinks. Popular with big bus groups, it's a rollicking introduction to Russian folk clichés. As seating is first-come, first-served, be sure to arrive early (tickets from 4,900 R, nightly shows at 19:00 and sometimes at 21:00, box office open daily 11:00-21:00, Ploshchad Truda 4, tel. 312-5500, or reserve online at www.folkshow.ru—you can buy the tickets online but you'll need to pick them up from the box office).

▲Circus

The St. Petersburg circus is a revelation: Performed in one intimate ring, it has the typical tigers and lions but also a zany assortment of other irresistible animal acts (ostriches, poodles) as well as aerial acrobats (no nets), impossibly silly clowns, strongmen, and more. Its remarkable performers have been staging their shows since 1877 in the stone "big top" on the edge of the Fontanka River. It's just east of the Russian Museum; some maps label it "Ciniselli Circus" after the Italian circus family that first built the place. The circus season typically runs from September through June (tickets 500-6,000 R, box office open daily 10:00-21:00, tel. 570-5390 or 570-5411, www.circus.spb.ru).

Eating in St. Petersburg

St. Petersburg has a huge selection of eating options, and it's easy to find attractive cafés and restaurants. The listings below are all well-located or good values, and all have English-language menus.

Russians are big on soups and appetizers, and it's perfectly reasonable to order two or three of these at a meal and skip the main dishes. Many cafés offer speedy, convenient meals (sandwiches, light meals, salads, and crêpes—*bliny*). Столовая (Stolovaya) is a

---

Restaurant Code

I've assigned each eatery a price category, based on the average cost of a typical main course. Drinks, desserts, and splurge items (steak and seafood) can raise the price considerably.

$$$$ **Splurge:** Most main courses over 1,200 R

$$$ **Pricier:** 850-1,200 R

$$ **Moderate:** 600-850 R

$ **Budget:** Under 600 R

In Russia, a takeout spot is **$**; a sit-down café is **$$**; a casual but more upscale restaurant is **$$$**; and a swanky splurge is **$$$$**.

---

good word to look for if you're in need of a quick and easy dish—these are inexpensive cafeteria-buffet restaurants (often cash only).

RUSSIAN CUISINE

Cosmopolitan St. Petersburg has international tastes, so you'll see restaurants with eclectic international menus, as in any European metropolis. Restaurants serving traditional Russian cuisine—often in fresh, new interpretations—are popular with both tourists and the local fine-dining crowd.

Russians love soup—popular kinds are beet borscht, fish *ukha*, cabbage *shchi*, and meat *solyanka*. Russians are fond of small dishes that we might think of as appetizers or sides, such as *pelmeni* and *vareniki* (types of dumplings), *kasha* (buckwheat groats) prepared in various ways, *bliny* (crêpes), and high-calorie salads. You'll see beef stroganoff and chicken Kiev on menus at touristy restaurants, but these dishes are rarely served in Russian homes.

In recent years, both local and Western franchise restaurants have sprouted up all over Russia. You'll see Subway, Pizza Hut, KFC, McDonald's, and more. They go toe-to-toe with popular Russian chains such as Teremok and Stolle, which serve more authentic food and can be convenient time-savers during a day of sightseeing.

Russian beer is good. It goes without saying that there are many vodkas to choose from. Russians like to drink inexpensive sparkling wine that's still called *Sovyetskoye shampanskoye* (Soviet champagne). Try *kvas*, a fizzy, fairly sweet, grain-based beverage that is marketed as nonalcoholic (but often has a negligible alcohol content) and *mors* (berry juice). In Russia, always drink bottled water, which is available widely in shops.

Sit-Down Restaurants and Cafés

All of these youthful places (except one) offer a peek at Russian hipster culture and diverse menus with international and Russian dishes.

$$ Zoom Café (Zoom Кафе), its exterior draped in flowers and vines, has a lively atmosphere and fresh menu. Popular and a good value, it's in a pleasant basement-level dining room just off Griboyedov Canal, a bit south of Nevsky Prospekt (by the corner of Gorokhovaya and Kazanskaya at Gorokhovaya 22, Mon-Fri 9:00-24:00, Sat 11:00-24:00, Sun 13:00-24:00, food served until 22:30, tel. 612-1329).

$$ Pelmeniya (Пельмения) is a great place to sample the food for which it's named: delicious filled dumplings. Besides Russian *pelmeni*, choices include *khinkali* (from Georgia, with a thick dough "handle"), *varenyky* (from Ukraine, like Polish pierogi), *manti* (from Turkey and the Caucasus), *gyoza* (from Asia), and even ravioli. The modern interior overlooks the Fontanka River next to the Anichkov Bridge (well-described English-language menu, daily 11:00-23:00, Fontanka 25, tel. 571-8082).

$$$ Obshchestvo Chistykh Tarelok (Общество Чистых Тарелок/"Clean Plates Society") has a great energy, powered by loud music and a lively thirtysomething clientele. Sit at the woody bar or at a table under an oversized Ikea chandelier and enjoy the varied international fare, from burgers to curry to some Russian standbys (daily 12:00-late, Gorokhovaya 13, tel. 934-9764).

$ Kartofel s Gribami (Картофель с Грибами/"Potatoes with Mushrooms") is a fun, jazzy, and central hangout serving unpretentious but thoughtfully crafted Russian "street food"—such as *kapsalon* (a traditional casserole, available with various fillings) and the stuffed-pita sandwich called *shaverma* (daily 12:00-24:00, Gorokhovaya 12, tel. 994-0983).

$$$ Yat (Ять) has a welcoming, country-cottage vibe, just a few steps down from street level, near Palace Square on the Moyka embankment. Their inventive chef gives a fresh twist to the traditional favorites—*pelmeni, vareniki,* cutlets, and borscht, among others (daily 12:00-23:00, Naberezhnaya reki Moyki 16, tel. 957-0023, www.eatinyat.com).

$$ Decabrist Café (Декабрист Кафе), casual and lively, has a rustic but modern interior in a handy location near St. Isaac's Cathedral. They have light meals and soups, burgers, and traditional Russian dishes (daily 8:00-22:00, Yakubovicha 2, tel. 912-1891, www.decabrist.net).

Stuffy, Traditional Russian Cuisine: connected with St. Petersburg's vodka museum, **$$$$ Russian Vodka Room No. 1** is a fancier, more expensive restaurant with classy food and service (and yes, 200 types of vodka) that caters to tourists. You can choose between the elegant, old-time interior or the sidewalk seating, facing the busy boulevard. It's a little beyond St. Isaac's Cathedral—trolley buses #5 and #22 stop conveniently on the same street. The huge building has multiple restaurants—look for the Vodka Room between entrances (подъезд) 5 and 6 (daily 12:00-24:00, Konnogvardeisky Bulvar 4, tel. 570-6420).

Atmospheric Outdoor Dining on Malaya Sadovaya: Pedestrianized Malaya Sadovaya street runs for one block between Nevsky Prospect (at the corner with Yeliseevsky's delicatessen) and Italyanskaya street. It's said to be the city's shortest street, but it's packed with restaurants and cafés—traditional Russian, Spanish, Vietnamese, a tearoom, and more.

"New Russian" Farm-to-Table Eateries

For something a notch above the places listed earlier, foodies dig into these two.

$$$ Vkus Yest (Вкус Есть, "Taste Eat"), with a spare, bare-brick-walls dining room, faces the Bolshoi Drama Theater across the Fontanka River, and there's jazz on the soundtrack. The menu is brief, constantly changing, and adventurous. The name is a pun: Есть means both "to eat" and "there is" (daily 13:00-23:00, Fontanka 23, tel. 983-3376, www.tastetoeat.ru).

$$$ Cococo (Кококо) fills its laid-back, mellow cellar with rustic tables and decor that's a mix of old and new. The fun-to-read menu includes old dishes done a new way, as well as some more innovative alternatives (breakfast served Mon-Fri 7:00-11:00, Sat-Sun until 12:00; lunch and dinner daily 14:00-late, Nekrasova 8, tel. 579-0016, www.kokoko.spb.ru)

Speedy Chain Restaurants

$ Teremok (Теремок) has branches literally all over town. It's quick and convenient for those who don't speak Russian, handy

for families, and lets you share and try lots of different dishes. This is Russian fast food, but it's a perfectly healthy array of Russian standards at very affordable prices. Choose borscht, *ukha* (fish soup), *pelmeni* (dumplings), sweet or savory *bliny* (crêpes), or *kasha* (buckwheat groats) prepared in various ways. If you don't see the English menu brochure, ask for it—or just point to the photos on the posted menu (Bolshaya Morskaya 11, Nevsky Prospekt 60, and Vladimirsky Prospekt 3 are three of many locations; all open daily at least 10:00-23:00).

$ Stolle (Штолле) specializes in crispy pies, both savory and sweet. Their handiest location, near the start of Nevsky Prospekt (at #11), combines order-at-the-counter, point-to-what-you-want efficiency with a refined drawing-room atmosphere. This makes it popular with local tour guides...and with pickpockets. Ask for their English menu. They tend to sell out of many flavors later in the day (daily 9:00-23:00).

$ City Grill (Сити Гриль) keeps it simple, offering freshly grilled burgers and steaks, with beer or soft drinks to wash them down. Their most convenient location is across from the Kazan Cathedral (Naberezhnaya Kanala Griboyedov 20); another branch is just off Nevsky Prospekt at Rubinshteyna 4 (both open daily 10:00-23:00).

GEORGIAN CUISINE

Although any Georgian will tell you it is not "Russian," Georgian cuisine is a much appreciated, flavorful alternative that's popular with Russians and visitors alike. Some classic Georgian dishes are *khachapuri* (хачапури)—hot bread filled with cheese, somewhat like a calzone; *khinkali* (хинкали)—a hearty filled dumpling gathered into a thick, doughy "handle" and dipped into sauces; *pkhali* (пхали)—chopped greens; chicken *satsivi* (сациви)—diced chicken in a spicy yellow sauce; *baklazhan* (баклажан)—eggplant, *lobio* (лобио)—beans, served hot or cold; and plenty of *lavash* (лаваш)—bread. If you want soup, try *kharcho* (харчо), a spicy broth with lots of meat and onions. Main dishes are less special (often grilled meat).

$$ Cat Café (КЭт Кафе)—an institution for expats in St. Petersburg since the end of communism—has a cozy, traditional interior with only eight tables and a friendly vibe (Stremyannaya 22, daily 12:00-23:00, tel. 571-3377, www.cafe-cat.ru).

$$$$ Khochu Kharcho (Хочу Харчо, literally "I want Georgian soup") is a big, boisterous, industrial-strength restaurant facing the busy Sennaya square (where three Metro lines converge). This sprawling mash-up of modern and traditional comes with several seating areas, a busy open kitchen with a wood-fired grill and tandoor oven, and an enticing photo menu that makes ordering easy. While aimed squarely at Russian tourists, it offers a lively and accessible—if pricey—sample of Georgian fare (open daily 24 hours, Sadovaya 39—next to the small footbridge at the southwest corner of the square, tel. 640-1616).

$$$ Tarkhun (Таркун, "Tarragon"), a block off the Fontanka River on a pleasant square near the circus, is a more upscale place to try Georgian dishes (daily 12:00-23:30, Karavannaya 14, tel. 377-6525).

VEGETARIAN FARE

$$ Café Botanika (Кафе Ботаника) is a few blocks beyond the Russian Museum, past the Summer Garden and just over the Fon-

What If I Miss My Ship?

Remember that you can get help from the cruise line's port agent (listed on the destination information sheet distributed on the ship) and the local TI (see page 3324). If the port agent suggests a costly solution (such as a private car with a driver), you may want to consider public transit.

Your biggest concern is a visa. If you've entered St. Petersburg with an excursion (meaning without a visa), chances are your ship won't leave without you, since they are responsible for your presence in Russia. On the off chance that you're left behind, head for the US consulate (https://www. usembassy.gov/russia/) to navigate the red tape—your lack of a visa will make leaving the country next to impossible without soliciting help.

If do you have a visa and missed your ship, you can reach **Helsinki** on the fast train (trains leave from Finland Station/ Finlyandsky Vokzal, Metro: Ploshchad Lenina; train info: www. vr.fi) or a much slower bus. To **Tallinn,** ride the slow bus or the occasional St. Peter Line overnight boat (www.stpeterline. com) To reach **Stockholm** or **Rīga,** you'll probably do best to connect through Tallinn.

If you need to catch a **plane** to your next destination, St. Petersburg's Pulkovo airport is reachable by a Metro-plus-bus combination (via the Moskovskaya Metro stop; www. pulkovoa rport.ru).

Local **travel agents** in St. Petersburg can help you. For more advice on what to do if you miss the boat, see page 130.

tanka River. It's fresh and attractive, with seating both indoors and streetside. The menu includes Russian, Indian, Italian, and Japanese dishes (daily 11:00-24:00, Pestelya 7, tel. 272-7091).

$ Troitsky Most (Троицкий Мост) is an inexpensive vegetarian café near the Hermitage along the Moyka River. Order at the counter (fresh salads on display) and then find a seat. A board, partly translated into English, lists the day's specials (daily 9:00-23:00, Naberezhnaya reki Moyki 30).

Russian Survival Phrases

Russia comes with a more substantial language barrier than most of Europe. In general, young Russians know at least a little halting schoolroom English; hoteliers and museum clerks may speak only a few words; and older people speak none at all.

For help with decoding the Cyrillic alphabet, see the sidebar on page 336.

English	Russian / Transliteration	Pronunciation
Hello. (formal)	Здравствуйте. / Zdravstvuyte.	**zdrah**-stvee-tyeh
Hi. (informal)	Привет. / Privyet.	pree-**vyeht**
Goodbye.	До свидания. / Do svidaniya.	dah svee-**dahn**-yah
Do you speak English?	Вы говорите по-английски? / Vy govoritye po angliyski?	vih gah-vah-**ree**-tyeh pah ahn-**glee**-skee
I (don't) understand.	Я (не) понимаю. / Ya (nye) ponimayu.	yah (nyeh) poh-nee-**mah**-yoo
Yes.	Да. / Da.	dah
No.	Нет. / Nyet.	nyeht
Please.	Пожалуйста. / Pozhaluysta.	pah-**zhahl**-stah
Thank you.	Спасибо. / Spasibo.	spah-**see**-bah
Excuse me.	Извините. / Izvinitye.	eez-vee-**nee**-tyeh
(Very) good.	(Очень) хорошо. / (Ochen) khorosho	(**oh**-cheen) kha-**roh**-show
How much?	Сколько стоит? / Skolko stoit?	**skohl**-kah **stoh**-yeet
one, two	один, два / odin, dva	ah-deen, dvah
three, four	три, четыре / tri, chetyre	tree, cheh-**teer**-yeh
five, six	пять, шесть / pyat, shest	pyaht, shyest
seven, eight	семь, восемь / sem, vosem	syehm, **vwoh**-sehm
nine, ten	девять, десять / devyat, desyat	**dyeh**-veht, **dyeh**-seht
Where is...?	Где...? / Gdye...?	guh-**dyeh**
...the toilet	...туалет / tualet	too-ahl-**yeht**
men	мужчины / muzhchiny	moo-**shee**-neh
women	женщины / zhenshchiny	zhen-**shee**-neh
(to the) right	(на) право / (na) pravo	(nah) **prah**-vah
(to the) left	(на) лево / (na) levo	(nah) **leh**-vah
beer	пиво / pivo	**pee**-vah
vodka	водка / vodka	**vohd**-kah
water	вода / voda	vah-**dah**
coffee	кофе / kofe	**koh**-fyeh
Cheers! (To your health)	На здоровья! / Na zdorovya!	nah zdah-**roh**-veh

TALLINN

Estonia

SAMPO

Estonia Practicalities

Wedged between Latvia and Russia, Estonia borders the Baltic Sea and Gulf of Finland (at 17,500 square miles, it's roughly the size of New Hampshire and Vermont combined). The country also encompasses more than 1,500 islands and islets. Like Finland, Estonia struggled against Swedish and Russian domination throughout its history. After World War I, Estonia achieved independence, but with the next world war, it fell victim to a 50-year communist twilight, from which it's still emerging. Joining the European Union in 2004 has helped bring the country forward. Estonia is home to 1.3 million people, a quarter of whom are of Russian descent. Even two decades after independence, tension still simmers between the ethnic Estonian population and its ethnic Russian population.

Money: €1 (euro) = about $1.20. An ATM is called a *pangaautomaat*, and is sometimes marked *Otto*. The local VAT (value-added sales tax) rate is 20 percent; the minimum purchase eligible for a VAT refund is €38 (for details on refunds, see page 125).

Language: The native language is Estonian. For useful phrases, see page 449.

Emergencies: In case of emergency, dial 112. In case of theft or loss, see page 118.

Time Zone: Estonia is one hour ahead of Central European Time (seven/ten hours ahead of the East/West Coasts of the US). That puts Tallinn in the same time zone as Helsinki and Rīga; one hour ahead of Stockholm, the rest of Scandinavia, and most other continental cruise ports (including Gdańsk and Warnemünde); and one hour behind St. Petersburg.

Embassies in Tallinn: The **US embassy** is at Kentmanni 20 (tel. 668-8100, emergency tel. 509-2129, https://ee.usembassy.gov). The **Canadian embassy** is at Toom-Kooli 13 (tel. 627-3311, www.canada.ee). Call ahead for passport services.

Phoning: With a mobile phone, it's easy to dial: Press and hold zero until you get a + sign, enter the country code (372 for Estonia, 1 for the US/Canada), and then the complete phone number (including area code if there is one). When dialing a European phone number, drop an initial zero (except if calling Italy). For more tips, see page 1062.

Tipping: The bill for a sit-down meal includes gratuity, so you don't need to tip further, though it's nice to round up about 5-10 percent for good service. For taxis, round up the fare a bit (pay €5 on an €4.50 fare) For more tips on tipping, see page 129.

Tourist Information: www.visitestonia.com.

TALLINN

Tallinn is a rising star in the tourism world, thanks to its strategic location (an easy boat ride from Stockholm, Helsinki, and St. Petersburg); its perfectly preserved, atmospheric Old Town, bursting with quaint sightseeing options; and its remarkable economic boom since throwing off Soviet shackles just over two decades ago.

Tallinn's Nordic Lutheran culture and language connect it with Scandinavia, and the country has eagerly reclaimed its unique Nordic identity. While two centuries of czarist Russian rule and 45 years as part of the Soviet Union have left behind some Russian touches, and the city still struggles to effectively incorporate its large Russian minority, Tallinn feels ages away from its Soviet past. Estonian pride is in the air...and it's catching.

Among Nordic medieval cities, there's none nearly as well-preserved as Tallinn. Its mostly intact city wall includes 26 watchtowers, each topped by a pointy red roof. Baroque and choral music ring out from its old Lutheran churches. I'd guess that Tallinn (with about 450,000 people) has more restaurants, cafés, and surprises per capita and square inch than any city in this book—and the fun is comparatively cheap.

As a member of the Hanseatic League, the city was a medieval stronghold of the Baltic trading world. In the 19th and early 20th centuries, Tallinn industrialized and expanded beyond its walls. Architects encircled the Old Town, putting up broad streets of public buildings, low Scandinavian-style apartment buildings, and single-family wooden houses.

After 1945, Soviet planners ringed the city with stands of now-crumbling concrete high-rises where many of Tallinn's Russian immigrants settled. But since the fall of the Soviet Union in 1991, Tallinn has westernized at an astounding rate. New shops, restaurants, and hotels are bursting out of old buildings. The city changes so fast, even locals can't keep up.

Yet the Old World ambience within Tallinn's walled town center has been beautifully preserved. The Old Town is a fascinating package of pleasing towers, ramparts, facades, churches, shops, and people-watching. It's a rewarding detour for those who want to spice their Scandinavian travels with a Baltic twist.

PLANNING YOUR TIME

Tallinn is a snap for cruisers: The port is within walking distance of the Old Town, which contains most of what you'll want to see. On a busy day in port, I'd do the following, in this order:

To hit the ground running, walk 15 minutes to the Fat Margaret Tower and launch into my **self-guided Tallinn Walk,** which leads you past virtually all the best sights (allow 2-3 hours, more if you want to linger).

Spend the afternoon shopping and browsing—or, choose a sight just beyond the center: the **Seaplane Harbor** for boats and planes (allow about 1.5-2 hours, including transit time by foot, taxi, or hop-on, hop-off bus) or **Kadriorg Park** for a stroll through the palace gardens and to tour the delightful Estonian art collection at Kumu (allow about an hour to see the park, including transit time via tram or taxi; add another hour for Kumu).

With more time, you could visit the **Estonian Open-Air Museum** (allow 30 minutes each way to get there, plus a couple of hours to tour the grounds).

While Tallinn's Old Town is understandably popular, sometimes it feels *too* popular; when several cruises are in town, the cobbles can be uncomfortably crammed. To escape the crowds, consider climbing up to the more serene upper town, or focus on outlying sights, such as Kadriorg Park.

Remember to bring a jacket—Tallinn can be chilly even on sunny summer days. And, given that locals call their cobbled streets "a free foot massage," sturdy shoes are smart, too.

Excursions from Tallinn

Tallinn is so walkable, and its Old Town sights so easy to appreciate, that there's no reason to take an excursion here. Most cruise lines offer a walking tour through the **Old Town** with a few brief sightseeing stops (often including quick visits to Town Hall Square, Palace Square, the Russian Orthodox Cathedral, Dome Church, and various viewpoints)—but the self-guided walk in this chapter covers the same ground at your own pace. Other excursions may include a bus tour around the city, sometimes with stops at outlying sights such as the manicured, palatial **Kadriorg Park** and the stirring **Song Festival Grounds**—these are also doable on your own (and affordable by taxi).

Places farther out of town are a bit more challenging to reach on your own on a short port visit. These include the **Estonian Open-Air Museum** at Rocca al Mare (described on page 440); the Pirita beach community; the town of **Rakvere,** about 60 miles east (with its 13th-century castle and "town citizen's museum" of 19th-century life); and the beaches and forests of the **Kakumäe** district, on the western edge of Tallinn. But Tallinn itself is so appealing that these excursions don't merit consideration on a brief visit. Just stick around the city and enjoy the Old World ambience.

Port of Tallinn

Arrival at a Glance: Walking is the obvious way to reach Tallinn's Old Town—it's a quick 15-minute stroll from the cruise port.

Port Overview

The Port of Tallinn (Old Town Harbor) is just northeast of the Old Town. Within this sprawling area, most cruise ships dock at dedicated piers on the northern edge of the harbor (labeled *Kruiisilae-vad* on maps and signs); overflow cruise ships might dock at nearby berths generally used for ferries and catamarans to Helsinki, Stockholm, and St. Petersburg (labeled as *A-Terminal, B-Terminal, C-Terminal,* and *D-Terminal*). Regardless of where you arrive, it's easy to walk into town.

Tourist Information: At the primary cruise dock, passengers will find only basic tourist information (maps and brochures). For more help, head into the Old Town and visit the good TI there (see "Orientation to Tallinn," later).

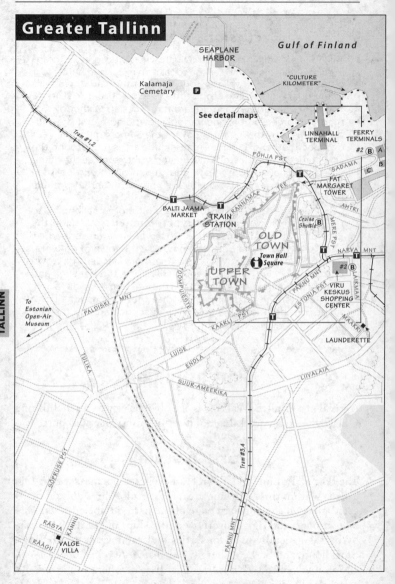

Greater Tallinn

Gulf of Finland

SEAPLANE HARBOR

"CULTURE KILOMETER"

Kalamaja Cemetary

P

See detail maps

LINNAHALL TERMINAL

FAT MARGARET TOWER

FERRY TERMINALS

Tram #1,2

PÕHJA PST

SADAMA

#2

A

B

C

B

BALTI JAAMA MARKET

TRAIN STATION

KANNUMÄE TEE

Cruise Shuttle

B

AHTRI

MERE PST

OLD TOWN

Town Hall Square

UPPER TOWN

NARVA MNT

T

#2

B

To Estonian Open-Air Museum

PALDISKI MNT

TOOMPUIESTE

KAARLI PST

PÄRNU MNT

ESTONIA PST

VIRU KESKUS SHOPPING CENTER

LAIKMAA

MAAKRI

LAUNDERETTE

TULIKA

LUISE

ENDLA

SUUR-AMEERIKA

LIIVALAIA

Tram #3,4

SÕPRUSE PST

RÄSTA

KANNU

RAAGU

VALGE VILLA

PÄRNU MNT

GETTING INTO TOWN

Options that work from any berth are outlined first (shuttle bus, hop-on, hop-off bus, and taxi). Then I'll give details specific to each port area.

From Any Dock

By Cruise Shuttle Bus: Some cruise lines offer shuttles into town

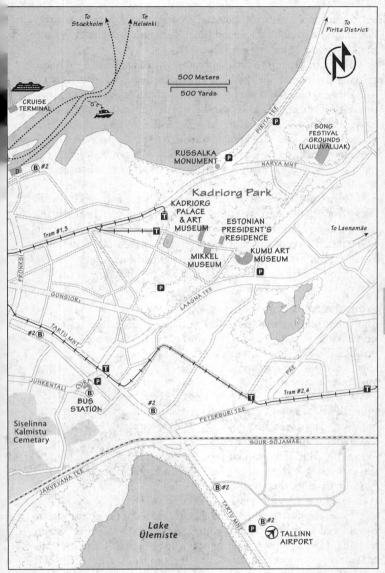

(most drop off along the busy ring road at the south end of the Old Town, near the Viru Turg street market). Because the walk to town is so easy, I'd skip the shuttle unless its free (or for those with limited mobility).

By Tour: Hop-on, hop-off buses meet each arriving ship. Realistically, on a short day in port, you'll likely spend most or all of your day in the walkable Old Town—making a bus trip unnecessary. But to get to outlying sights, these buses can be handy—just be sure to check return times and frequencies (most run hourly). For details on these buses—and other local **tour options** in Tallinn (including local guides)—see page 421.

By Taxi: Taxis meet arriving cruise ships, happy to overcharge arriving passengers for the brief ride into town. A legitimate taxi using the meter should charge €7-10 to anywhere in the Old Town (more to Kadriorg Park). It can be worth the walk to the area in front of A-Terminal, between the main cruise port and the sailboat marina, where you may find a taxi with more reasonable posted rates. Before choosing a taxi, read my tips on page 420. From the main cruise berths or the ferry terminals, you'll be at the town gate within 15 minutes.

Returning to Your Ship: The easiest choice is to simply walk back; from the Old Town, it takes about 15 minutes to reach the main cruise terminal or the lettered terminals (it's a bit longer to D-Terminal). Walk through town on Pikk street, popping out at Fat Margaret Tower, from where you see the ships.

If you catch a taxi (usually waiting around the edges of the Old Town), insist on the meter.

From the Main Cruise Port

The small **main cruise terminal** building contains an unofficial info desk, a souvenir stand, and a currency exchange booth (though no ATMs). Free Wi-Fi is available near the cruise terminal building.

On Foot: To walk to the **Old Town,** exit the terminal building, pass through a gauntlet of shops, and on the far end, follow the blue line painted on the pavement to exit the port gate (bypassing the overpriced taxis and sales reps for hop-on, hop-off bus tours).

From the port gate, proceed directly ahead to the crosswalk (at Rumbi and Logi streets) and go left. At the next big cross street, Sadama, turn right and walk for a few long blocks. Scan ahead to spot a tall, pointy steeple. Keep angling toward it, and you'll soon reach the stout, round, stone Fat Margaret Tower and the gate to the Old Town (and the start of my self-guided walk).

If you'd rather first visit the **Seaplane Harbor,** as you leave the port, look straight ahead for a red-gravel path marked *Kultuuriki-lomeeter,* which takes you to the harbor on a long, scenic, mostly seaside stroll (see map showing the route on page 424).

Services near the Port

You'll find a few services at the port areas; for others, wait until you're downtown.

ATMs: There's no ATM at the main cruise terminal building, but there are several at the nearby A-Terminal. There's also an ATM inside D-Terminal. Once in the Old Town, ATMs are easy to find.

Wi-Fi: The area near the main cruise terminal has free Wi-Fi. Public Wi-Fi is also easy to find in the city center; look for the free "Tallinn WiFi" network.

Pharmacy: The best (and most memorable) choice is in the Old Town—the historic (and still functioning) pharmacy on Old Town Square.

From the A/B and D Terminals

These terminals primarily serve passenger ferries running between Tallinn and Helsinki, Stockholm, or St. Petersburg, but cruise ships may use a berth here.

On Foot: If you arrive at the A/B or D terminals (with ATMs, WCs, and lockers), follow the blue line painted on the pavement to leave the port area. Then follow signs to the city center, always walking toward the tallest pointy tower and the round, fat stone gate at its base (visible from most of the port area), which marks the entrance to the Old Town (and the start of my self-guided walk).

By Local Bus: Local bus #2 stops in front of both the A/B and D-Terminals (2/hour, €2 on board, exact change only). It goes directly to a stop (A. Laikmaa) handy to the Viru Gate at the south end of the Old Town. For more on buses and the Tallinn transit card, see "Orientation to Tallinn," later.

Tallinn

Tallinn's walled Old Town is an easy 15-minute walk from the ferry and cruise terminals, where most visitors land (see "Arrival in Tallinn," later). The Old Town is divided into two parts (historically, two separate towns): the upper town (Toompea) and the lower town (with Town Hall Square). A remarkably intact medieval wall surrounds the two towns, which are themselves separated by another wall.

Town Hall Square (Raekoja Plats) marks the heart of the medieval lower town. The main TI is nearby, as are many sights and eateries. Pickpockets are a problem in the more touristy parts of the Old Town and at the viewpoints in the upper town, so keep valuables carefully stowed. The area around the Viru Keskus mall and Hotel Viru, just east of the Old Town, is useful for everyday shopping (bookstores and supermarkets), practical services (laundry), and public transport.

Orientation to Tallinn

TOURIST INFORMATION

The hardworking and helpful TI is just a block off Town Hall Square (Mon-Fri 9:00-19:00, Sat-Sun until 17:00—stays open an hour later mid-June-Aug and closes an hour earlier Sept-April; Niguliste 2, tel. 645-7777, www.visittallinn.ee).

Tallinn Card: This card—sold at the TIs, airport, train station, travel agencies, ferry ports, and big hotels—gives you free use of public transport and entry to more than 40 museums and major sights (€25/24 hours, €37/48 hours, €45/72 hours, www.tallinncard.ee). A more expensive "Plus" version includes a hop-on, hop-off bus route.

HELPFUL HINTS

Travel Agency: Estravel, at the corner of Suur-Karja and Müürivähe, is handy and sells boat tickets for no extra fee (Mon-Fri 9:00-18:00, closed Sat-Sun, Suur-Karja 15, tel. 626-6233, www.estravel.ee).

Bike Rental: Head for **City Bike,** at the north end of the Old Town (€12/6 hours, €15/24 hours; electric bikes available; daily 10:00-18:00, Vene 33, mobile 511-1819, www.citybike.ee). They also do bike tours (see "Tours in Tallinn," later).

GETTING AROUND TALLINN

By Public Transportation: The Old Town and surrounding areas can be explored on foot, but you'll need to use public transit to reach outlying sights (such as Kadriorg Park, Kumu Art Museum, or the Estonian Open-Air Museum). Tallinn has buses, trams, and trolley buses—avoid mistakes by noting that they reuse the same numbers (bus #2, tram #2, and trolley bus #2 are totally different lines). Maps and schedules are posted at stops, or pick up a transit map at the TI (map also available at www.visittallinn.ee); for an overview of transit stops useful to visitors, see the "Greater Tallinn" map on page 416. As you approach a station, you'll hear the name of the impending stop, followed by the name of the next stop—don't get confused and hop off one stop too early.

You can buy a **single ticket** from the driver for €2 (exact change only). If you'll be taking more than three rides in a day, invest in a **Ühiskaart smartcard.** You can buy one for €2 at any yellow-and-blue R-Kiosk convenience store (found all over town), and then load it up with credit, which is deducted as you travel

(€1.10 for any ride up to 1 hour, €3/24 hours, €5/72 hours, €6/120 hours). The card is shareable by multiple people for single rides, but you'll need separate cards for the multiride options.

Bus #2 (Moigu-Reisisadam) is helpful on arrival and departure, running every 20-30 minutes between the ferry port's A-Terminal and the airport. En route it stops at D-Terminal; at A. Laikmaa, next to the Viru Keskus mall (a short walk south of the Old Town); and at the long-distance bus station.

By Taxi: Taxis in Tallinn are handy, but because rates are not uniform, always confirm a ballpark fare before getting in. The safest way to catch a cab is to order one by phone (or ask a trusted local to call for you)—this is what Estonians usually do.

Tulika is the largest company, with predictable, fair prices (€3.85 drop charge plus €0.69/kilometer, €0.80/kilometer from 23:00-6:00, tel. 612-0001 or 1200, check latest prices at www.tulika.ee). **Tallink Takso** is another reputable option with similar fares (tel. 640-8921 or 1921). Cabbies are required to use the meter and give you a meter-printed receipt. Longer rides around the city (e.g., from the airport to the Old Town) should run around €8-10.

If you must catch a taxi off the street, go to a busy taxi stand where lots of cabs are lined up. Before you get in, take a close look at the yellow price list on the rear passenger-side door; the base fare should be no more than €5.50 and the per-kilometer charge no more than €1.10. If it's not, keep looking. Glance inside—a photo ID license should be attached to the middle of the dashboard. Rates must be posted by law, but are not capped or regulated, so the most common scam—unfortunately widespread and legal—is to list an inflated price on the yellow price sticker, and simply wait for a tourist to hop in without noticing. Singleton cabs lurking in tourist areas are usually fishing for suckers, as are cabbies who flag you down ("Taxi?")—give them a miss.

Tours in Tallinn

Bus and Walking Tour

This enjoyable, narrated 2.5-hour tour of Tallinn comes in two parts: first by bus for an overview of sights outside the Old Town, such as the Song Festival Grounds and Kadriorg Park, then on foot to sights within the Old Town (€30, pay driver, covered by Tallinn Card, in English; daily morning and early afternoon departures from ferry terminals and major hotels in city center; tel. 610-8616, www.traveltoestonia.com).

Local Guides

Mati Rumessen is a top-notch guide, especially for car tours inside or outside town (€35/hour driving or walking tours, price may vary with group size and length of tour, mobile 509-4661, www.

Tallinn at a Glance

Central Tallinn

▲▲▲**Tallinn's Old Town** Well-preserved medieval center with cobblestoned lanes, gabled houses, historic churches, and turreted city walls. See page 423.

▲▲**Russian Orthodox Cathedral** Accessible look at the Russian Orthodox faith, with a lavish interior. **Hours:** Daily 8:00-19:00, icon art in gift shop. See page 431.

▲**Tallinn City Museum** Interesting overview of Tallinn's past, from medieval times into the 20th century. **Hours:** Tue-Sun 10:30-18:00, closes earlier off-season, closed Mon year-round. See page 435.

▲**Museum of Estonian History** High-tech exhibits explain Estonia's engaging national narrative. **Hours:** May-Aug daily 10:00-18:00, same hours off-season except closed Wed. See page 435.

Outside the Core

▲▲**Kumu Art Museum** The best of contemporary Estonian art displayed in a strikingly modern building. **Hours:** May-Sept Tue-Sun 11:00-18:00, Wed until 20:00, closed Mon; same hours off-season except closed Mon-Tue. See page 437.

▲▲**Seaplane Harbor** Impressive museum of boats and planes—including a WWII-era submarine—displayed in a cavernous old hangar along the waterfront. **Hours:** May-Sept daily 10:00-19:00; closes an hour earlier and closed Mon off-season. See page 439.

▲**Kadriorg Park** Vast, strollable oasis with the palace gardens, Kumu Art Museum, and a palace built by Czar Peter the Great. See page 436.

▲**Estonian Open-Air Museum** Authentic farm and village buildings preserved in a forested parkland. **Hours:** Late April-Sept—park open daily 10:00-20:00, buildings open until 18:00; Oct-late April—park open daily 10:00-17:00 but many buildings closed. See page 440.

TALLINN

tourservice.ee, matirumessen@gmail.com). Other fine guides are **Antonio Villacis** (rates negotiable, mobile 5662-9306, antonio. villacis@gmail.com) and **Miina Puusepp** (€20/hour, mobile 551-7028, miinapaul@gmail.com).

Tallinn Traveller Tours
These student-run tours show you the real city without the political and corporate correctness of official tourist agencies. Check www. traveller.ee to confirm details for their ever-changing lineup, and to reserve (or call mobile 5837-4800). They typically offer a two-hour **Old Town Walking Tour** and a **ghost walk** (each €15) and a **food tour** (€20), as well as **bike tours** and **minibus excursions** that get you into the Estonian countryside. All tours start from in front of the main TI.

Hop-On, Hop-Off Bus Tours
Tallinn City Tour offers three different one-hour bus tours—you can take all three (on the same day) for one price. Aside from a stop near Toompea Castle, the routes are entirely outside the Old Town, and the frequency is low (about every 60 minutes). But the tours do get you to outlying sights such as Kadriorg Park and the towering Russalka Monument. You can catch the bus at the port terminals and at Viru Square, near the Viru Turg clothing market (€21/24 hours, free with Tallinn Card, tel. 627-9080, www. citytour.ee). **CitySightseeing Tallinn** also runs three similar routes, with a similarly sparse frequency (€20 for all three lines, www.citysightseeing.ee).

City Bike Tours
City Bike offers a two-hour, nine-mile **Welcome to Tallinn** bike tour that takes you outside the city walls to Tallinn's more distant sights: Kadriorg Park, Song Festival Grounds, the beach at Pirita, and more (€19, 50 percent discount with Tallinn Card, daily at 11:00 year-round, departs from their office at Vene 33 in the Old Town). They can also arrange multiday, self-guided bike tours around Estonia (mobile 511-1819, www.citybike.ee).

Tallinn Walk

This self-guided walk, worth ▲▲▲, explores the "two towns" of Tallinn. The city once consisted of two feuding medieval towns separated by a wall. The upper town—on the hill, called Toompea—was the seat of government for Estonia. The lower town was an autonomous Hanseatic trading center filled with German, Danish, and Swedish merchants who hired Estonians to do their menial labor. Many of the Old Town's buildings are truly old, dating from the boom times of the 15th and 16th centuries. Decrepit

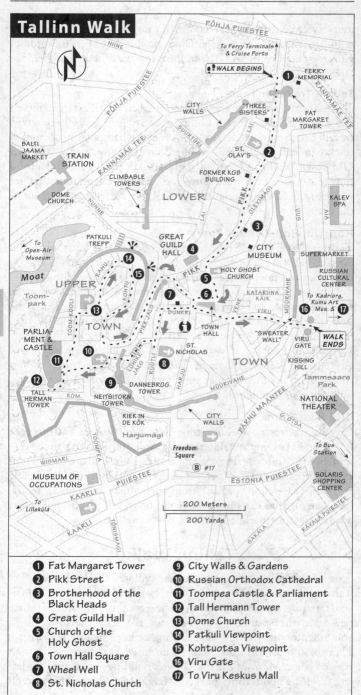

Tallinn Walk

❶ Fat Margaret Tower
❷ Pikk Street
❸ Brotherhood of the Black Heads
❹ Great Guild Hall
❺ Church of the Holy Ghost
❻ Town Hall Square
❼ Wheel Well
❽ St. Nicholas Church
❾ City Walls & Gardens
❿ Russian Orthodox Cathedral
⓫ Toompea Castle & Parliament
⓬ Tall Hermann Tower
⓭ Dome Church
⓮ Patkuli Viewpoint
⓯ Kohtuotsa Viewpoint
⓰ Viru Gate
⓱ To Viru Keskus Mall

before the 1991 fall of the Soviet Union, the Old Town has been entirely revitalized.

Two steep, narrow streets—the "Long Leg" and the "Short Leg"—connect the upper and lower towns. This two-part walk goes up the short leg and down the long leg. Allow about two hours for the entire walk (not counting time to enter museums along the way).

PART 1: THE LOWER TOWN

• The walk starts at Fat Margaret Tower—easy to reach from the port— where cruise ships and ferries from Helsinki arrive (just hike toward

the tall tapering spire, go through a small park, and enter the Old Town through the archway. If you're coming from elsewhere in Tallinn, take tram #1 or #2 to the Linnahall stop, or just walk out to the Fat Margaret Tower from anywhere in the Old Town.

❶ Fat Margaret Tower

Fat Margaret Tower (Paks Margareeta) guarded the entry gate of the town in medieval times (the sea once came much closer than it does today). Besides being a defensive outpost, the tower was made big just to impress anyone (like you) coming to town from the harbor. The relief above the gate dates from the 16th century, during Hanseatic times, when Sweden took Estonia from the German Teutonic Knights. The origin of the tower's name is a bit of a mystery. Some say it was named for a huge cannon, but others think a cook called Margaret worked in the tower long ago.

• Once through the gate, head up Tallinn's main drag...

❷ Pikk Street

Literally "Long Street," the medieval merchants' main drag leads from the harbor up into town. It's lined with interesting and historic buildings. Many were warehouses, complete with cranes on the gables. Strolling here, you'll feel the economic power of those early German trading days.

One short block up the street on the right, the buildings nicknamed **"Three Sisters"** (now a hotel/restaurant) are textbook examples of a merchant home/warehouse/

office from the 15th-century Hanseatic Golden Age. The elaborately carved door near the corner evokes the wealth of Tallinn's merchant class—such detailed decoration would have come with a high price tag.

After another, longer block, you'll pass the Gothic **St. Olav's Church** (Oleviste Kirik, a Baptist church today), notable for what was once the tallest spire in the land. That high spire helped approaching ships set their course—but it was also an effective lightning rod. Unfortunately, lightning strikes caused the church to burn to the ground three times.

If the name didn't tip you off that this was once a Lutheran church, then the stark, whitewashed interior clinches it. Climbing 234 stairs up the tower rewards you with a great view. You can enter both the church and the tower around the back side (church-free entry, daily 10:00-18:00, July-Aug until 20:00; tower-€3, open April-Oct only).

The once-handsome building at **Pikk #59** (the second house after the church, on the right) was, before 1991, the sinister local headquarters of the KGB. "Creative interrogation methods" were used here. Locals well knew that the road of suffering started here, as Tallinn's troublemakers were sent to Siberian gulags.

• *A few short blocks farther up Pikk (after the small park), on the left at #26, is the extremely ornate doorway of the...*

❸ Brotherhood of the Black Heads

Built in 1440, this house was used as a German merchants' club for nearly 500 years (until Hitler invited Estonian Germans back

to their historical fatherland in the 1930s). Before the 19th century, many Estonians lived as serfs on the rural estates of the German nobles who dominated the economy. In Tallinn, the German big shots were part of the Great Guild (which we'll see farther up the street), while the German little shots had to make do with the Brotherhood of the Black Heads. This guild, or business fraternity, was limited to single German men. In Hanseatic towns, when a fire or battle had to be fought, bachelors were deployed first, because they had no family. Because single men were considered unattached to the community, they had no opportunity for power in the Hanseatic social structure. When a Black Head member married a local woman, he automatically gained a vested interest in the town's economy and well-being. He could then join the more prestigious Great Guild, and with that status, a promising economic and political future often opened up.

Today the hall is a concert venue (and, while you can pay to tour its interior, I'd skip it—it's basically an empty shell). Its namesake "black head" is that of St. Maurice, an early Christian soldier-martyr, beheaded in the third century A.D. for his refusal to honor the Roman gods. Reliefs decorating the building recall Tallinn's Hanseatic glory days.

Keep going along Pikk street. Architecture fans enjoy several **fanciful facades** along here, including the boldly Art Nouveau #18 (on the left, reminiscent of the architectural bounty of fellow Baltic capital Rīga; appropriately enough, today this building houses one of Tallinn's cutting-edge architectural firms) and the colorful, eclectic building across the street (with the pointy gable).

On the left, at #16, the famous and recommended **Maiasmokk** ("Sweet Tooth") coffee shop, in business since 1864, remains a fine spot for a coffee-and-pastry break.

• *Just ahead, pause at the big yellow building on the right (at #17).*

❹ Great Guild Hall (Suurgildi Hoone)

With its wide (and therefore highly taxed) front, the Great Guild Hall was the epitome of wealth. Remember, this was the home of the most prestigious of Tallinn's Hanseatic-era guilds. Today it houses the worthwhile **Museum of Estonian History**, offering a concise and engaging survey of this country's story (for details, see "Sights in Tallinn," later).

• *Across Pikk street from the Great Guild Hall is the...*

❺ Church of the Holy Ghost (Pühavaimu Kirik)

Sporting an outdoor clock from 1633, this pretty medieval church is worth a visit. (The plaque on the wall just behind the ticket desk is in Estonian and Russian, but not English; this dates from before 1991, when things were designed for "inner tourism"—within the USSR.) The church retains its 14th-century design. Sometimes flying from the back pillar, the old flag of Tallinn—the same as today's red-and-white Danish flag—recalls 13th-century Danish

TALLINN

rule. (The name "Tallinn" means "Danish Town.") The Danes sold Tallinn to the German Teutonic Knights, who lost it to the Swedes, who lost it to the Russians. The windows are mostly from the 1990s (€1.50, Mon-Sat 9:00-18:00, closes earlier in winter, closed most of Sun to nonworshippers, Pühavaimu 2, tel. 646-4430, www.eelk. ee). The church hosts English-language Lutheran services Sundays at 13:00 (maybe earlier in summer).

• *If you were to go down the street to the left as you face the church, it's a three-minute walk to the* **Tallinn City Museum** *(described later, under "Sights in Tallinn").*

Leading alongside the church, tiny Saiakang lane (meaning "White Bread"—bread, cakes, and pies were long sold here) takes you to...

❻ Town Hall Square (Raekoja Plats)

A marketplace through the centuries, with a cancan of fine old buildings, this is the focal point of the Old Town. The square was

the center of the autonomous lower town, a merchant city of Hanseatic traders. Once, it held criminals chained to pillories for public humiliation and knights showing off in chivalrous tournaments; today it's full of Scandinavians and Russians savoring cheap beer, children singing on the bandstand, and cruise-ship groups following the numbered paddles carried high by their well-scrubbed local guides.

At the passageway where you've entered the square, look left to find the **pharmacy** (Raeapteek) dating from 1422 and claiming to be Europe's oldest. With decor that goes back to medieval times, the still-operating pharmacy welcomes visitors with painted ceiling beams, English descriptions, and long-expired aspirin. Past the functioning counter is a room of display cases with historical exhibits (free entry, Mon-Sat 10:00-18:00, closed Sun).

The **Town Hall** (Raekoda), which opened in 1404 so the city's burgomasters would have a suitable place to meet, dominates the square. Now open to tourists as a museum, it has exhibits on the town's administration and history, along with an interesting bit on the story of limestone. The tower rewards those who climb its 155 steps with a wonderful city view (museum-€5, entrance through cellar, July-Aug Mon-Sat

10:00-16:00, closed Sun and Sept-June; audioguide-€4.75; tower-
€3, June-Aug daily 11:00-18:00, closed Sept-May; tel. 645-7900,
www.tallinn.ee/raekoda).

Town Hall Square is ringed by inviting but touristy eateries.
The TI is a block away (behind Town Hall).

• *Facing the Town Hall, head right up Dunkri street—lined with several more eateries—one long block to the* ❼ *wheel well, named for the
"high-tech" wheel, a marvel that made fetching water easier.*

*Turn left on Rataskaevu street (which soon becomes Rüütli) and
walk two short blocks to...*

❽ St. Nicholas Church (Niguliste Kirik)

This 13th-century Gothic church-turned-art-museum served the
German merchants and knights who lived in this neighborhood

500 years ago. On March 9, 1944,
while Tallinn was in German hands,
Soviet forces bombed the city, and the
church and surrounding area—once a
charming district, dense with medieval
buildings—were burned out; only the
church was rebuilt.

The church's interior houses a fine
collection of mostly Gothic-era ecclesiastical art (€6, Tue-Sun 10:00-17:00,
closed Mon year-round—and Tue off-
season; organ or choir concerts held
most weekends).

Enter the church through the modern cellar, where you can
see photos of the WWII destruction of the building (with its toppled steeple). Then make your way into the vast, open church interior. Front and center is the collection's highlight: a retable (framed
altarpiece) from 1481, by Herman Rode—an exquisite example of
the northern Germanic late-Gothic style. Along with scenes from
the life of St. Nicholas and an array of other saints, the altarpiece
shows the skyline of Lübeck, Germany (Rode's hometown, and—
like Tallinn—a Hanseatic trading city). The intricate symbolism is
explained by a nearby touchscreen. Also look for another work by a
Lübeck master, Bernt Notke's *Danse Macabre* ("Dance of Death").
Once nearly 100 feet long, the surviving fragment shows sinister
skeletons approaching people from all walks of life. This common
medieval theme reminds the viewer that life is fleeting, and no
matter who we are, we'll all wind up in the same place.

• *As you face the church, if you were to turn left and walk downhill on
Rüütli street, you'd soon pass near* **Freedom Square**—*a taste of modern
Tallinn (once a USSR-era parking lot, it's now a glassy plaza that in-
vites locals, and very few tourists, to linger).*

But for now, let's continue our walk into the upper town.

PART 2: THE UPPER TOWN (TOOMPEA)

• *At the corner opposite the church, climb uphill along the steep, cobbled, Lühike Jalg ("Short Leg Lane"), home to a few quality craft shops. At the top of the lane, pause at the arched gateway at #9. Notice the stone tower steps leading to the arched passage and a big oak door. This is one of two gates through the wall separating the two cities. This passage is still the ritual meeting point of the mayor and prime minister whenever there is an important agreement between town and country.*

Now continue through the main gateway and climb up until you emerge into a beautiful view terrace in front of the...

❾ City Walls and Gardens

This view terrace is known as the Danish King's Garden for the ruler who gave the land to the lower town in 1311. Tallinn is famous among Danes as the birthplace of their flag. According to legend, the Danes were losing a battle here, when suddenly, a white cross fell from heaven and landed in a pool of blood. The Danes were inspired and went on to win, and to this day, their flag is a white cross on a red background.

Once you pass through the opening in the wall (to the right), you've officially crossed from the lower to upper town. The imposing city wall once had 46 towers, of which 26 still stand. If you have interest and energy, you can climb some of the towers and ramparts (although we'll be reaching some dramatic viewpoints—overlooking different parts of town—later on this walk).

The easiest ascent is to simply scramble up the extremely steep and tight steps of the nearby **Dannebrog restaurant tower**—but you'll need to order an expensive drink to stay and enjoy the view. To reach a higher vantage point you can pay €3 to enter the **Neitsitorn (Maiden) Tower** (at the far end of the garden terrace). It has a few skippable exhibits, an overpriced café, and great views—particularly from the top floor, where a full glass wall reveals a panoramic townscape (open Tue-Sat 11:00-18:00, closed Sun-Mon, shorter hours Oct-April).

For a genuine tower climb, though, cross into the upper town and follow the gravel path to the left to the **Kiek in de Kök**. This stout, round tower sits farther along the wall (with extremely tight, twisty, steep stone staircases inside). The fun-to-say name "Kiek in de Kök" is Low German for "Peek in the Kitchen"—

so-called because the tower is situated to allow guards to literally peek into townspeople's homes. This tower is bigger than the Neitsitorn Tower, with more impressive exhibits—not a lot of real artifacts, but plenty of cannons, mannequins, model ships, movies, and models of the castle to give you a taste of Tallinn's medieval heyday (€6; extra for tour of tunnels below the tower).

• *When you're finished with the towers and ramparts, head uphill into the upper town to the big, onion-domed church, circling around to the far side (facing the pink palace) to find the entrance.*

⑩ Russian Orthodox Cathedral

The Alexander Nevsky Cathedral—worth ▲▲—is a gorgeous building. But ever since the day it was built (in 1900), it has been a jab in the eye for Estonians. The church went up near the end of the two centuries when Estonia was part of the Russian Empire. And, as throughout Europe in the late 19th century, Tallinn's oppressed ethnic groups—the Estonians and the Germans— were caught up in national revival movements, celebrating

their own culture, language, and history rather than their Russian overlords'. So the Russians flexed their cultural muscle by building this church in this location, facing the traditional Estonian seat of power, and over the supposed grave of a legendary Estonian hero, Kalevipoeg. They also tore down a statue of Martin Luther to make room.

The church has been exquisitely renovated inside and out. Step inside for a sample of Russian Orthodoxy (church free and open daily 8:00-19:00, icon art in gift shop). It's OK to visit discreetly during services (daily at 9:00 and 18:00), when you'll hear priests singing the liturgy in a side chapel. Typical of Russian Orthodox churches, it has glittering icons (the highest concentration fills the big screen—called an iconostasis—that shields the altar from the congregation), no pews (worshippers stand through the service), and air that's heavy with incense. All these features combine to create a mystical, otherworldly worship experience. Notice the many candles, each representing a prayer; if there's a request or a thank-you in your heart, you're welcome to buy one at the desk by the door. Exploring this space, keep in mind that about 40 percent of Tallinn's population is ethnic Russian.

• *Across the street is the...*

⓫ Toompea Castle (Toompea Loss)

The pink palace is an 18th-century Russian addition onto the medieval Toompea Castle. Today, it's the Estonian Parliament (Riigigoku) building, flying the Estonian flag—the flag of both the first (1918-1940) and second (1991-present) Estonian republics. Notice the Estonian seal: three lions for three great battles in Estonian history, and oak leaves for strength and stubbornness. Ancient pagan Estonians, who believed spirits lived in oak trees, would walk through forests of oak to toughen up. (To this day, Estonian cemeteries are in forests. Keeping some of their pagan sensibilities, they believe the spirits of the departed live on in the trees.)

• *Facing the palace, go left through the gate into the park to see the...*

⓬ Tall Hermann Tower (Pikk Hermann)

This tallest tower of the castle wall is a powerful symbol here. For 50 years, while Estonian flags were hidden in cellars, the Soviet flag flew from Tall Hermann. As the USSR was unraveling, Estonians proudly and defiantly replaced the red Soviet flag here with their own black, white, and blue flag.

• *Backtrack to the square in front of the palace, passing the Russian church on your right. Climb Toom-Kooli street to the...*

⓭ Dome Church (Toomkirik)

Estonia is ostensibly Lutheran, but few Tallinners go to church. A recent Gallup Poll showed Estonia to be the least religious country in the European Union—only 14 percent of respondents identified religion as an important part of their daily lives. Most churches double as concert venues or museums, but this one is still used for worship. Officially St. Mary's Church—but popularly called the Dome Church—it's a perfect example of simple Northern European Gothic, built in the 13th century during Danish rule, then rebuilt after a 1684 fire. Once the church of Tallinn's wealthy German-speaking aristocracy, it's littered with more than a hundred coats of arms, carved by local masters as memorials to the deceased and inscribed with German tributes. The earliest dates from the 1600s, the latest from around 1900. For €5, you can climb 140 steps up the tower to enjoy the

view (church entry free, daily 9:00-18:00, organ recitals Sat at 12:00, www.eelk.ee/tallinna.toom).

• *Leaving the church, turn left and hook around the back of the building. You'll pass the big, green, former noblemen's clubhouse on your right (at #1, vacated when many Germans left Estonia in the 1930s). Head down cobbled Rahukohtu lane (to the right of the yellow house with a peaked roof). Strolling the street, notice the embassy signs: Government offices and embassies have moved into these buildings and spruced up the neighborhood. Continue straight under the arch and belly up to the grand...*

⓮ Patkuli Viewpoint

Survey the scene. On the far left, the Neoclassical facade of the executive branch of Estonia's government overlooks a grand view.

Below you, a bit of the old moat remains. The *Group* sign marks Tallinn's tiny train station, and the clutter of stalls behind that is the rustic market. Out on the water, ferries shuttle to and from Helsinki (just 50 miles away). Beyond the lower town's medieval wall and towers stands the green spire of St. Olav's Church, once 98 feet taller and, locals claim, the world's tallest tower in 1492. Far in the distance is the 1,000-foot-tall TV tower, the site of a standoff between Soviet paratroopers and Estonian patriots in 1991.

During Soviet domination, Finnish TV was even more important, as it gave Estonians their only look at Western lifestyles. Imagine: In the 1980s, many locals had never seen a banana or a pineapple—except on TV. People still talk of the day that Finland broadcast the soft-porn movie *Emmanuelle*. A historic migration of Estonians purportedly flocked from the countryside to Tallinn to get within rabbit-ear's distance of Helsinki and see all that flesh onscreen. The refurbished TV tower is now open to visitors.

• *Go back through the arch, turn immediately left down the narrow lane, turn right (onto Toom–Rüütli), take the first left, and pass through the trees to the...*

⓯ Kohtuotsa Viewpoint

Scan the view from left to right. On the far left is St. Olav's Church, then the busy cruise port and the skinny white spire of the Church of the Holy Ghost. The narrow gray spire farther to the right is the 16th-century Town Hall tower. On the far right is the tower of St. Nicholas Church. Below you, visually trace Pikk street, Tallinn's historic main drag, which winds through the Old Town, leading

TALLINN

from Toompea Castle down the hill (from right to left), through the gate tower, past the Church of the Holy Ghost, behind St. Olav's, and out to the harbor. Less picturesque is the clutter of Soviet-era apartment blocks on the distant horizon, but these days they're being crowded out by modern high-rises. The nearest skyscraper (white) is Hotel Viru, in Soviet times the biggest hotel in the Baltics, and infamous as a clunky, dingy slumbermill. Locals joke that Hotel Viru was built from a new Soviet wonder material called "micro-concrete" (60 percent concrete, 40 percent microphones). Underneath the hotel is the modern Viru Keskus, a huge shopping mall and local transit center. To the left of Hotel Viru, between it and the ferry terminals, is the Rotermann Quarter, where old industrial buildings are being revamped into a new commercial zone.

• *From the viewpoint, descend to the lower town. Go out and left down Kohtu, past the Finnish Embassy (on your left). Back at the Dome Church, turn left down Piiskopi ("Bishop's Street"). At the onion domes, turn left again and follow the old wall down Pikk Jalg ("Long Leg Lane") into the lower town (you'll pass a good handcrafts shop on the way). Go under the tower, then straight on Pikk street, and after two doors turn right on Voorimehe, which leads into Town Hall Square.*

⑯ Through Viru Gate

Cross through the square (left of the Town Hall's tower) and go downhill (passing the kitschy medieval Olde Hansa Restaurant, with its bonneted waitresses and merry men). Continue straight down Viru street toward Hotel Viru, the blocky white skyscraper in the distance. Viru street is old Tallinn's busiest and most touristy shopping street. Just past the strange and modern wood/glass/stone mall, Müürivahe street leads left along the old wall, called the "Sweater Wall." This is a colorful and tempting gauntlet of vendors selling knitwear (most is machine-made). Leading left, beyond the sweaters, the picturesque Katariina Käik is a lane with glassblowing, weaving, and pottery shops. Back on Viru street, pass the golden arches and walk through the medieval arches—Viru Gate—that mark the end of old Tallinn. Outside the gates, opposite Viru 23, above the flower stalls, is a small park on a piece of old bastion known as the Kissing Hill (come up here after dark and you'll find out why).

• *Our walk is done. If you want to find the real world, use the crosswalk to your right to reach the* ⑰ *Viru Keskus Mall, with its basement supermarket, ticket service, bookstore, and many bus and tram stops. If you still have energy, you can cross the busy street by the complex and explore the nearby Rotermann Quarter (described later).*

Sights in Tallinn

IN OR NEAR THE OLD TOWN

Central Tallinn has dozens of small museums, most suitable only for specialized tastes. The following are the ones I'd visit first.

▲Museum of Estonian History (Eesti Ajaloomuuseum)

The Great Guild Hall on Pikk street houses this museum with its modern, well-presented exhibits. The museum's "Estonia 101" approach—combining actual artifacts (from prehistory to today) and high-tech interactive exhibits—is geared toward educating first-time visitors about this obscure but endearing little country.

Cost and Hours: €6, daily 10:00-18:00, closed Wed off-season, tel. 696-8690, www.ajaloomuuseum.ee.

▲Tallinn City Museum (Tallinna Linnamuuseum)

This humble but worthwhile museum, filling a 14th-century townhouse, features Tallinn history from 1200 to the 1950s. It's an excellent introduction to Tallinn's past, especially with the help of its good audioguide.

Cost and Hours: €4, includes audioguide, Tue-Sun 10:30-18:00, closes earlier off-season, closed Mon year-round, Vene 17, at corner of Pühavaimu, tel. 615-5180, www.linnamuuseum.ee.

Visiting the Museum: Begin your visit on the first floor, passing through exhibits about Tallinn's medieval past, with an emphasis on its trading days. The Hanseatic League maintained a monopoly in the North Baltic, safeguarding the economic interests of its 100 town-members—of which Tallinn and its Black Heads Guild were major players. You'll see exact replicas of their trading ships and a treasury room filled with precious objects of their merchant wealth. Another display draws attention to the roles Tallinn's townspeople played in support of the merchants and shippers (stonemason, blacksmith, cooper, shoemaker, etc.).

The highlight of the second floor is a model of circa-1825 Tallinn—looking much like it does today. The top floor is devoted to 20th-century life, with re-created rooms from the early 20th century and the Soviet period.

▲Rotermann Quarter (Rotermanni Kvartal)

Sprawling between Hotel Viru and the port, just east of the Old Town, this 19th-century industrial zone is being redeveloped into

shopping, office, and living space. Characteristic old brick shells are being topped with visually striking glass-and-steel additions, and the area's former grain elevators and salt-storage warehouses are being creatively repurposed as restaurants, cafés, boutiques, and offices. To take a look around, start at Hotel Viru, cross busy Narva Maantee and walk down Roseni street (at #7 you'll find the hard-to-resist Kalev chocolate shop), circling around to Stalkeri Käik street, with many restaurants (see "Eating in Tallinn"). In summer, food stalls and craft tables create an open-air market in the neighborhood's central space (Rotermanni Aatrium).

KADRIORG PARK AND THE KUMU MUSEUM
▲Kadriorg Park

This expansive seaside park, home to a summer royal residence and the Kumu Art Museum, is just a five-minute tram ride or a

25-minute walk from Hotel Viru. After Russia took over Tallinn in 1710, Peter the Great built the cute, pint-sized Kadriorg Palace for Czarina Catherine (the palace's name means "Catherine's Valley"). Stately, peaceful, and crisscrossed by leafy paths, the park has a rose garden, duck-filled pond, playground and benches, and old czarist guardhous-

es harkening back to the days of Russian rule. It's a delightful place for a stroll or a picnic. If it's rainy, slip into one of the cafés in the park's art museums (described next).

Getting There: Reach the park on tram #1 or #3 (direction: Kadriorg; catch at any tram stop around the Old Town). Get off at the Kadriorg stop (the end of the line, where trams turn and head back into town), and walk 200 yards straight ahead and up Weizenbergi, the park's main avenue. Peter's summer palace is on the left; behind it, visit the formal garden (free). Across from the palace is the Mikkel Museum, and at the end of the avenue is the Kumu Art Museum, the park's most important sight. A taxi from Hotel Viru to this area should cost €8 or less. If you're returning from here directly to the port to catch your cruise ship, use tram #1—it stops at the Linnahall stop near the main cruise terminal.

Visiting Kadriorg Park: The palace's manicured **gardens** (free to enter) are a pure delight; on weekends, you'll likely see a steady parade of brides and grooms here, posing for wedding pictures. The summer palace itself is home to the **Kadriorg Art Museum** (Kadrioru Kunstimuuseum), with very modest Russian and Western European galleries (€6.50; Tue-Sun 10:00-18:00, Wed until 20:00, closed Mon year-round—off-season also closed Tue; Weizenbergi 37, tel. 606-6400, http://kadriorumuuseum.ekm.ee).

Across the road from the gardens, in the former kitchen building of the palace, is the **Mikkel Museum,** a fine little collection of Meissen porcelain (€5, same hours as Kadriorg Art Museum, http://mikkelimuuseum.ekm.ee).

The fenced-off expanse directly behind the garden is where you'll spot the local "White House" (although it's pink)—home of **Estonia's president.** Walk around to the far side to find its main entrance, with the seal of Estonia above the door, flagpoles flying both the Estonian and the EU flags, and stone-faced guards.

A five-minute walk beyond the presidential palace takes you to the Kumu Art Museum, described next. For a longer walk from here, the rugged park rolls down toward the sea.

▲▲Kumu Art Museum
(Kumu Kunstimuuseum)

This main branch of the Art Museum of Estonia brings the nation's best art together in a striking modern building designed by

an international (well, at least Finnish) architect, Pekka Vapaavuori. The entire collection is accessible, well-presented, and engaging, with a particularly thought-provoking section on art from the Soviet period. The museum is well worth the trip for art lovers, or for anyone intrigued by the unique spirit of this tiny nation.

Cost and Hours: €8; Tue-Sun 11:00-18:00, Wed until 20:00, closed Mon year-round, off-season also closed Tue; audioguide-€4; trendy café, tel. 602-6000, http://kumu.ekm.ee.

Getting There: To reach the museum, follow the instructions for Kadriorg Park, explained above; Kumu is at the far end of the park. To get from the Old Town to Kumu directly (without walking through the park), take bus #67 or #68 (each runs every 10-15 minutes, #68 does not run on Sun); both leave from Teatri Väljak, on the far side of the pastel yellow theater, across from the Solaris shopping mall. Get off at the Kumu stop, then walk up the stairs and across the bridge.

Visiting the Museum: Just off the ticket lobby (on the second floor), the **great hall** has temporary exhibits; however, the permanent collection on the third and fourth floors is Kumu's main draw. While you can rent an audioguide, the laminated gallery guides in most rooms are enough to enjoy the collection. The maze-like layout on each floor presents the art chronologically.

The **third floor** displays classics of Estonian art from the early 18th century until the end of World War II. It starts with idyllic 18th-century portraits of local aristocrats of the Biedermeier era, a time when harmonious family life and clearly defined gender roles took precedence over all else. The exhibit then moves through 19th-century movements, including Romanticism (represented by some nice views of Tallinn, scenes of Estonian nature,  and idealized images of Estonian peasant women in folk costumes). Estonian artists were slow to adopt the art trends of the early 20th century, but in time Modernist styles took hold: Pointillism (linger over the lyrical landscapes of Konrad Mägi and the recently rediscovered works of Herbert Lukk), Cubism, and Expressionism. In the 1930s, the Pallas School provided a more traditional, back-to-nature response to the wilder artistic movements of the time. With the dawn of World War II, a period soon followed by two Soviet and one German occupation, Estonian artists faced extremely difficult and dramatic circumstances. The final canvases on this floor, from the war years, convey an unmistakable melancholy and grim intensity.

The **fourth-floor exhibit,** called "Conflicts and Adaptations," is a fascinating survey of Estonian art from the Soviet era (1940-1991). Soviet officials understood the role of art purely as a means to convey the ideology of the Communist Party. Estonian art, the Soviets insisted, should actively promote the communist struggle, and in the strict canon now called **Socialist Realism.** Art's primary objective was to glorify labor and the state's role in distributing its fruits.

Despite these restrictions, Estonian art in this half-century took a wide range of approaches, from syrupy images of Soviet leadership, to stern portraits of Stalin, to glorifying canvases of miners, protesters, speechifiers, metalworkers, and trac-

tor drivers. Though some Estonian artists flirted with social commentary and the avant-garde, a few ended up in Siberia as a result. But with the condemnation of Stalinism in 1956, artists began to attempt bolder compositions and more contemporary forms of expression. Nonetheless, the social function of art continued to take precedence over personal artistic statements throughout the Soviet era.

The rest of the museum is devoted to temporary exhibits, with contemporary art on the **fifth floor** (where there's a nice view back to the Old Town from the far gallery). Don't forget to admire the **architecture** of the building, which is partly dug into the limestone hill—the facade is limestone, too (for the big picture, look for the model of the building, just inside the main doors).

ALONG THE HARBORFRONT
▲▲Seaplane Harbor (Lennusadam)

One of Tallinn's most ambitious sights, this maritime museum fills a gigantic old hangar along the waterfront north of downtown with everything from tradi-

tional wooden fishing boats to a submarine—all symbolic of the Estonian connection to the Baltic Sea. It has loads of hands-on activities for kids, and thrills anyone interested in the sea.

Cost and Hours: €14; daily 10:00-19:00, Oct-April Tue-Sun 10:00-18:00, closed Mon; last entry one hour before closing, Vesilennuki 6, tel. 620-0550, www.seaplaneharbour.com.

Getting There: It's along the waterfront, about a mile north of the Old Town. Plan on a long but doable **walk,** made more enjoyable if you follow the red-gravel "Culture Kilometer" (Kultuuriki-lomeeter) seaside path from near the cruise terminals (see color map). There's no handy tram or bus to the museum, but a one-way **taxi** from the town center shouldn't cost much more than €6. The **hop-on, hop-off buses** also stop here.

Visiting the Museum: The cavernous old **seaplane hangar** cleverly displays exhibits on three levels: the ground floor features items from below the sea (such as a salvaged 16th-century shipwreck; catwalks halfway up connect exhibits dealing with the sea surface (the impressive boat collection—from buoys to iceboats to the massive *Lembit* sub); and seaplanes are suspended overhead. The star of the show is the 195-foot-long *Lembit* submarine from 1937: Estonian-commissioned and British-built, this vessel saw fighting in World War II and later spent several decades in the service of the USSR's Red Fleet. You can climb down below decks to see how the sailors lived, peek through the periscope, and even stare down the torpedo tubes. A cool café on the top level (above the entrance) overlooks the entire space, which feels endless.

Outside, filling the old harbor, is the maritime museum's collection of **historic ships,** from old-fashioned tall ships to modern-day military boats. The highlight is the steam-powered icebreaker *Suur Tõll,* from 1914.

OUTER TALLINN
▲Estonian Open-Air Museum (Vabaõhumuuseum)

Influenced by their ties with Nordic countries, Estonians are enthusiastic advocates of open-air museums. For this one, they salvaged farm buildings, windmills, and an old church from rural areas and transported them to a parklike setting a few miles west of the Old Town. The goal: to both save and share their heritage. Attendants are posted in many houses, but to really visualize life in the old houses, download the free NUMU app before you visit (or rent an audioguide from ticket office). The park's Kolu Tavern serves traditional dishes. You can rent a bike (€3/hour) for a breezy roll to quiet, faraway spaces in the park.

Cost and Hours: Late April-Sept-€9, park open daily 10:00-20:00, historic buildings until 18:00; Oct-late April-€7, park open daily 10:00-17:00 but many buildings closed; tel. 654-9100, www.evm.ee.

Getting There: Take bus #21 or #21B from the train station or Freedom Square to the Rocca al Mare stop. Because buses back to Tallinn run infrequently, check the departure schedule as soon as you arrive, or ask staff how to find the Zoo stop, with more frequent service, a 15-minute walk away.

Shopping in Tallinn

The Old Town is full of trinkets, but it is possible to find good-quality stuff. Wooden goods, like butter knives and juniper-wood trivets, are a good value. Marvel at the variety of booze in liquor stores, popular with visiting Scandinavians. Tucked into the Old Town are many craft and artisan shops where prices are lower than in Nordic countries.

The **"Sweater Wall"** is a fun place to browse sweaters and woolens, though few are hand-knitted by grandmothers these days. Find the stalls under the wall on Müürivahe street (daily, near the

Estonia's Singing Revolution

When you are a tiny nation lodged between two giants like Russia and Germany, simply surviving is a challenge. Having already endured 200 years of czarist Russian rule and the turmoil of World War I, little Estonia found itself annexed to the Soviet Union at the end of World War II. Their native culture was swept away: Russian replaced Estonian as the language in schools, and Russians and Ukrainians moved in, displacing Estonians. Moscow wouldn't even allow locals to wave their own flag.

But Estonians were determined to maintain their cultural identity. They had no weapons, but they created their own power by banding together and singing. Song has long been a cherished Estonian form of expression. As long ago as 1869 (during another era of Russian subjugation), Estonians gathered in massive choirs to sing and to celebrate their cultural uniqueness.

Finally, as the USSR began to crumble, the Estonians mobilized, using song to demand independence. In 1988, they gathered—300,000 strong, a third of the population—at the Song Festival Grounds outside Tallinn. The next year, the people of Latvia, Lithuania, and Estonia held hands to make the "Baltic Chain," a human chain that stretched 360 miles from Tallinn to Vilnius in Lithuania.

This so-called Singing Revolution, peaceful and nonviolent, persisted for five years, and in the end, Estonians gained their freedom. It was a remarkable achievement: One million singing Estonians succeeded against their Russian occupiers.

And the singing continues: Every five years, the Song Festival Grounds (built in 1959 and resembling an oversized Hollywood Bowl) welcome 25,000 singers and 100,000 spectators. The singers don traditional outfits and march to the festival site from Tallinn's Freedom Square. Overlooking the grounds from the cheap seats is a statue of Gustav Ernesaks, who directed the Estonian National Male Choir for 50 years through the darkest times of Soviet rule. He was a power behind the drive for independence, and lived to see it happen. (To visit the grounds—free and open long hours even in nonfestival years, though there's not much to see—take a City Bike tour, or ride bus #1A, #5, #8, #34A, or #38 to the Lauluväljak stop).

While the Song Festival Grounds host big pop-music acts, too, it's a national monument for the role it played in Estonia's fight for independence. Watch the documentary film *The Singing Revolution* (www.singingrevolution.com) to draw inspiration from Estonia's valiant struggle for freedom.

TALLINN

corner of Viru street, described on page 434). From there, explore the picturesque **Katariina Käik,** a small alley between Müürivahe and Vene streets, which has several handicraft stores and workshops selling pieces that make nice souvenirs.

The cheery **Navitrolla Gallerii** is filled with work by the well-known Estonian artist who goes just by the name Navitrolla. His whimsical, animal-themed prints are vaguely reminiscent of *Where the Wild Things Are* (Mon-Fri 10:00-18:00, Sat until 17:00, Sun until 16:00, Sulevimägi 1, tel. 631-3716, www.navitrolla.ee).

The **Rahva Raamat** bookstore in the Viru Keskus mall (floors 3-4) has English-language literature on the main floor, and a huge wall of travel books upstairs (daily 9:00-21:00).

Estonian handicrafts focus on all kinds of knitted and felted clothing: colorful sweaters, scarves, hats, socks, and mittens. Linen is also widely sold. In the Old Town, you'll find good selections at the **Estonian Handicraft House** (Pikk 27) and **Eesti Käsitöö Kodu** (Vene 12).

Balti Jaama Market, Tallinn's bustling, newly restored market, is behind the train station. It's a great time-warp scene, fragrant with dill, berries, onions, and mushrooms. You'll hear lots of Russian and find vendors selling everything from fresh produce and street food to children's clothes and gadgets. You could easily assemble a rustic picnic here. To find the market from the train station, just walk across the head of the train platforms (following *Jaama Turg* signs) and

keep going (Mon-Sat 9:00-19:00, Sun until 17:00, better early).

For something tamer, the **Viru Turg outdoor market,** a block outside the Old Town's Viru Gate, has a lively, tourist-oriented collection of stalls selling mostly clothing, textiles, and flowers (daily, north of Viru street at Mere Puiestee 1).

Eating in Tallinn

Tallinn's Old Town has a wide selection of mostly tourist-oriented eateries—don't expect bargains here. For a better value (and better food), roam at least a block or two off the main drags. Some restaurants have good-value lunch specials on weekdays (look for the words *päeva praad*). As a mark of quality, watch for restaurants with an *Astu Sisse!* label in the window; this Estonian equivalent of a Michelin star is awarded to just 50 restaurants each year. Tipping is not required, but if you like the service, round your bill up by 5-10 percent when paying. Reserving ahead for dinner is a smart idea.

Authentic Estonian food is easy to find—a hearty mix of meat, potatoes, root vegetables, mushrooms, dill, garlic, bread, and soup. Pea soup is a specialty. You usually get a few slices of bread as a free, automatic side dish. A typical pub snack is Estonian garlic bread *(küüslauguleivad)*—deep-fried strips of dark rye bread smothered in garlic and served with a dipping sauce. Estonia's Saku beer is good, cheap, and on tap at most eateries. Try the nutty, full-bodied Tume variety.

ESTONIAN CUISINE IN THE OLD TOWN

$$ Von Krahli Aed is an elegant, almost gourmet, health-food eatery calling itself "the embassy of pure food." While not vegetarian, it is passionate about serving organic, seasonal, modern Estonian cuisine in a woody, romantic setting. Take your pick from four dining options: under old beams, in the cellar, out front on the sidewalk, or out back on the garden terrace (daily 12:00-23:00, Rataskaevu 8, tel. 626-9088).

$$ Vanaema Juures ("Grandma's Place"), an eight-table cellar restaurant, serves homey, traditional Estonian meals, such as pork roast with sauerkraut and horseradish. This is a fine bet for local cuisine, and dinner reservations are strongly advised (daily 12:00-22:00, Rataskaevu 10, tel. 626-9080, www.vonkrahl.ee/vanaemajuures).

At **$$ Leib** ("Back Bread"), just outside the walls at the seaside end of the Old Town, you enter up steps into a fun garden under the medieval ramparts, and can sit indoors or out. The classy menu—built around a passion for Baltic ingredients (spring cabbage, beets, smoked trout, sturgeon)—changes with the seasons (daily 12:00-15:00 & 18:00-23:00, Uus 31, tel. 611-9026).

TALLINN

Restaurant Code

I've assigned each eatery a price category, based on the average cost of a typical main course. Drinks, desserts, and splurge items (steak and seafood) can raise the price considerably.

$$$$ **Splurge:** Most main courses over €20
$$$ **Pricier:** €15-20
$$ **Moderate:** €10-15
$ **Budget:** Under €10

In Estonia, a takeout spot is **$**; a sit-down café is **$$**; a casual but more upscale restaurant is **$$$**; and a swanky splurge is **$$$$**.

$$$$ Mekk is a small, fresh, upscale place with a name that stands for "modern Estonian cuisine." While their dinner à la carte prices are high, they offer artful weekday lunch specials for just €7 (not available July-Aug), and a €40 four-course chef's menu at dinner (daily 11:00-23:00, Sun until 21:00, Suur-Karja 17, tel. 680-6688, www.mekk.ee).

Modern Cuisine on Freedom Square: The town meeting place since 1937, **$$ Wabadus,** facing the vast and modern square, turns its back on old Tallinn. This sleek, urbane café/restaurant serves coffee, cocktails, and international fare. Enjoy one of the terrace tables on the square if the weather's good (Mon-Thu 9:00-23:00, Fri-Sat 11:00-24:00, Sun 11:00-21:00, Vabaduse Väljak 10, tel. 601-6461).

NEAR ST. NICHOLAS CHURCH

$$$ Pegasus, tucked into three floors of a concrete-and-glass building, is the perfect antidote to the kitsch on Town Hall Square. The decor and the menu are Nordic-inspired, featuring flavorful soups, risottos, fish, and salads (daily 12:00-23:00, Harju 1, tel. 662-3013).

$$$ Grillhaus Daube dishes up grilled ribs, steaks, and fish in the relaxed, light-and-bright dining room of an 18th-century townhouse. Eat in front of the fireplace in bad weather, or out on the terrace in good (daily 12:00-23:00, just inside the walls off Freedom Square, Rüütli 11, tel. 645-5531).

TOURIST TRAPS ON AND NEAR TOWN HALL SQUARE

Tallinn's central square is a whirlpool of tacky tourism, where aggressive restaurant touts (some dressed as medieval wenches or giant *matryoshka* dolls) accost passersby to lure them in for a drink or meal. Surprisingly, some of these restaurants have good (if expensive) food.

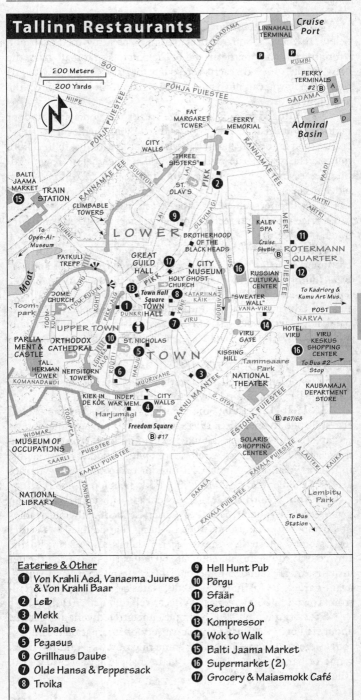

Tallinn Restaurants

Eateries & Other

1. Von Krahli Aed, Vanaema Juures & Von Krahli Baar
2. Leib
3. Mekk
4. Wabadus
5. Pegasus
6. Grillhaus Daube
7. Olde Hansa & Peppersack
8. Troika
9. Hell Hunt Pub
10. Põrgu
11. Sfäär
12. Retoran Ö
13. Kompressor
14. Wok to Walk
15. Balti Jaama Market
16. Supermarket (2)
17. Grocery & Maiasmokk Café

TALLINN

"Medieval" Estonian Cuisine: Two well-run restaurants just below Town Hall Square specialize in re-creating medieval food (from the days before the arrival of the potato and tomato from the New World). They are each grotesquely touristy, complete with gift shops where you can buy your souvenir goblet. Sit inside to feel the atmosphere.

$$$ Olde Hansa, filling three creaky old floors and outdoor tables with tourists, candle wax, and scurrying medieval waitresses, has food far better than it has any right to be (daily 10:00-24:00, musicians circulate Tue-Sun after 18:00, a belch below Town Hall Square at Vana Turg 1, reserve in advance, tel. 627-9020, www.oldehansa.ee).

$$$ Peppersack, across the street, tries to compete in the same price range, and feels marginally less circus-like (Vana Turg 6, tel. 646-6800).

Russian Food: Right on Town Hall Square, with a folkloric-costumed waitstaff, **$$$ Troika** serves *bliny* (pancakes) and *pelmeni* (dumplings), and characteristic main dishes. Sit out on the square (reserve for dinner); in the more casual, Russian-village-themed tavern; or under a fine vault in the atmospheric cellar. A balalaika player usually strums and strolls in the evenings (daily 10:00-23:00, Raekoja Plats 15, tel. 627-6245, www.troika.ee).

PUBS IN THE OLD TOWN

Young Estonians eat well and affordably at pubs. In some pubs, you go to the bar to order and pay before finding a table.

$$ Hell Hunt Pub ("The Gentle Wolf") was the first Western-style pub to open after 1991, and its tasty food and microbrews on tap are still attracting a mixed expat and local crowd. You can make a meal from the great pub snacks plus a salad. Choose a table in its convivial, rustic-industrial interior or on the garden terrace across the street (daily 12:00-24:00, Pikk 39, tel. 681-8333).

$ Von Krahli Baar serves cheap, substantial Estonian grub—such as potato pancakes *(torud)* stuffed with mushrooms or shrimp—in a handsome stone building that doubles as a center for Estonia's alternative theater scene; there's also seating in the tiny courtyard where you enter. It started as the bar of the theater upstairs, then expanded to become a restaurant, so it has a young, avant-garde vibe (daily 10:00-24:00, Rataskaevu 10, a block uphill from Town Hall Square, near Wheel Well, tel. 626-9090).

$$ Põrgu ("Hell"), in a simple, uncluttered cellar, is serious about its beer. They have a wide variety of international and Estonian brews on tap—including some microbrews—and the usual range of bar snacks, salads, and main dishes (daily 12:00-24:00, Rüütli 4, tel. 644-0232).

IN THE ROTERMANN QUARTER

This modern, up-and-coming district (described earlier, under "Sights in Tallin"), is just across the busy road from Tallinn's Old Town and well worth exploring for a jolt of cutting-edge architecture and hipster edginess. It's an antidote to the central area's ye-olde aura. As more and more buildings in this zone are being renovated, this is a fast-changing scene. But these two choices, in a long brick building facing the Old Town, are well-established and a good starting point.

$$$ Sfäär ("Sphere"), which combines an unpretentious bistro with a design shop, is a killing-two-birds look at the Rotermann Quarter. In this lively, cheery place, tables are tucked between locally designed clothes and home decor. The appealing menu features Estonian and international fare (Mon-Fri 8:00-22:00, Sat-Sun from 10:00, shop open Mon-Sat 12:00-21:00—restaurant and shop close Sun at 17:00, Mere Puiestee 6E, mobile 5699-2200).

$$$$ Retoran Ö (Swedish for "Island"), just a few doors down in the same building, is your Rotermann Quarter splurge. The dressy, trendy, retrofitted-warehouse interior feels a sophisticated world away from the Old Town's tourist traps. The seasonal menu highlights an Estonian approach to "New Nordic" cooking—small dishes carefully constructed with local ingredients. Reservations are smart (Mon-Sat 18:00-23:00, closed Sun, Mere Puiestee 6E—enter from the parking lot around back, tel. 661-6150, www.restoran-o.ee).

BUDGET EATERIES

$ Kompressor, a big, open-feeling beer hall, is in all the guidebooks for its cheap, huge, and filling pancakes—savory or sweet (daily 11:00-24:00, Rataskaevu 3, tel. 646-4210).

$ Wok to Walk, a clean and simple spot, offers tasty made-to-order stir-fries (daily 10:00-23:00, just off Viru Square at Vana Viru 14, tel. 444-3320).

Supermarkets: For picnic supplies, try the **Rimi minimart,** just a block off Town Hall Square (daily 8:00-22:00, Pikk 11); there's also a big **Rimi supermarket** just outside the Old Town at Aia 7, near the Viru Gate (daily 8:00-22:00). A larger, more upscale supermarket in the basement of the **Viru Keskus** mall (directly behind Hotel Viru) has inexpensive takeaway meals (daily 9:00-21:00).

BREAKFAST AND PASTRIES

The **$ Maiasmokk** ("Sweet Tooth") café and pastry shop, founded in 1864, is the grande dame of Tallinn cafés—ideal for dessert or breakfast. Even through the Soviet days, this was *the* place for a good pastry or a glass of herby Tallinn schnapps ("Vana Tallinn").

What If I Miss My Ship?

Remember that you can get help from the cruise line's port agent (listed on the destination information sheet distributed on the ship) and the local TI. If the port agent suggests a costly solution (such as a private car with a driver), you may want to consider public transit.

Frequent fast boats connect Tallinn to **Helsinki;** these are operated by Tallink Silja (tel. 631-8320, www.tallinksilja.com), Linda Line (tel. 699-9333, www.lindaline.ee), Eckerö Line (tel. 664-6006, www.eckeroline.fi), and Viking Line (tel. 631-8550, www.vikingline.fi). Tallink Silja boats also go to **Stockholm** overnight. St. Peter Line boats connect to **St. Petersburg,** but you can do this only if you've arranged a visa long in advance (www.stpeterline.com), or if you take one of their excursions. To reach **Rīga,** the bus is easy. For many other destinations—such as **Copenhagen** or **Oslo**—you can take an overnight boat to Stockholm, then connect by train. But for these and other destinations, it may be even better to fly.

If you need to catch a **plane,** you can ride the bus to the convenient Tallinn airport (Tallinna Lennujaam), just three miles southeast of downtown (www.tallinn-airport.ee).

For more advice on what to do if you miss the boat, see page 130.

Point to what you want from the selection of classic local pastries at the counter, and sit down for breakfast or coffee on the other side of the shop. Everything's reasonable (Mon-Fri 8:00-21:00, Sat 9:00-21:00, Sun 9:00-20:00, Pikk 16, across from church with old clock, tel. 646-4079, www.kohvikmaiasmokke.ee). They also have a pricier full-menu café upstairs and a marzipan shop (separate entrance).

Pierre Chocolaterie at Vene 6 has scrumptious fresh pralines, sandwiches, and coffee in a courtyard filled with craft shops (also light meals, daily 8:30-late, tel. 641-8061).

TALLINN

Estonian Survival Phrases

Estonian has a few unusual vowel sounds. The letter *ä* is pronounced "ah" as in "hat," but *a* without the umlaut sounds more like "aw" as in "hot." To make the sound *ö*, purse your lips and say "oh"; the letter *õ* is similar, but with the lips less pursed. Listen to locals and imitate. In the phonetics, ī sounds like the long *i* in "light," and bolded syllables are stressed.

English	Estonian	Pronunciation
Hello. (formal)	Tervist.	**tehr**-veest
Hi. / Bye. (informal)	Tere. / Nägemist.	**teh**-reh / **nah**-geh-meest
Do you speak English?	Kas te räägite inglise keelt?	kahs teh **raah**-gee-teh **een**-glee-seh kehlt
Yes. / No.	Jah. / Ei.	yah / ay
Please. / You're welcome.	Palun.	**pah**-luhn
Thank you (very much).	Tänan (väga).	**tah**-nahn (**vah**-gaw)
Can I help you?	Saan ma teid aidata?	saahn mah tayd ī-dah-tah
Excuse me.	Vabandust.	**vaw**-bahn-doost
(Very) good.	(Väga) hea.	(**vah**-gaw) **hey**-ah
Goodbye.	Hüvasti.	**hew**-vaw-stee
zero / one / two	null / üks / kaks	nuhl / ewks / kawks
three / four	kolm / neli	kohlm / **nay**-lee
five / six	viis / kuus	vees / koos
seven / eight	seitse / kaheksa	**sayt**-seh / **kaw**-hehk-sah
nine / ten	üheksa / kümme	**ew**-hehk-sah / **kew**-meh
hundred	sada	**saw**-daw
thousand	tuhat	**too**-hawt
How much?	Kui palju?	kwee **pawl**-yoo
Where is.. ?	Kus asub...?	koos ah-**soob**
...the toilet	...tualett	**too**-ah-leht
men	mees	mehs
women	naine	**nī**-neh
water / coffee	vesi / kohvi	**vay**-see / **koh**-vee
beer / wine	õlu / vein	**oh**-loo / vayn
Cheers!	Terviseks!	**tehr**-vee-sehks
The bill, please.	Arve, palun.	**ahr**-veh **pah**-luhn

TALLINN

RĪGA
Latvia

Latvia Practicalities

Latvia (Latvija) borders the Baltic Sea, sitting between the other Baltic states: Estonia (to the north) and Lithuania (to the south). The country's population (2.2 million) is made up largely of native Latvians (very roughly two-thirds of the population) and Russians (about a third). Latvia's terrain of generally low plains covers 25,000 square miles, about the size of West Virginia. Latvia's major city and capital is Rīga (at 700,000 residents, the Baltic states' largest city). Roughly half the jobs in Latvia are located in the city. Like its Baltic neighbors, Latvia spent most of its history occupied by foreign powers—Sweden, Russia, Germany, the USSR—but became independent in 1991 (following the breakup of the Soviet Union) and joined both NATO and the European Union in the spring of 2004.

Money: €1 (euro) = about $1.20. An ATM is called a *bankomāti*. The local VAT (value-added sales tax) rate is 21 percent; the minimum purchase eligible for a VAT refund is €44 (for details on refunds, see page 125).

Language: The native language is Latvian.

Emergencies: Dial 112 for police, medical, or other emergencies. (You can also dial 02 for police and 03 for an ambulance.) In case of theft or loss, see page 118.

Time Zone: Latvia is one hour ahead of Central European Time (seven/ten hours ahead of the East/West Coasts of the US). That puts Rīga in the same time zone as Helsinki and Tallinn; one hour ahead of Stockholm, the rest of Scandinavia, and most other continental cruise ports (including Gdańsk and Warnemünde); and one hour behind St. Petersburg.

Embassies in Rīga: The **US embassy** is at 1 Samnera Velsa Iela (tel. 6710-7000, https://lv.usembassy.gov/). The **Canadian embassy** is at 20/22 Baznicas Iela (tel. 6781-3945, http://international.gc.ca/world-monde/latvia-lettonie/). Call ahead for passport services.

Phoning: With a mobile phone, it's easy to dial: Press and hold zero until you get a + sign, enter the country code (371 for Latvia, 1 for the US/Canada), and then the complete phone number (including area code if there is one). When dialing a European phone number, drop an initial zero (except if calling Italy). For more tips, see page 1062.

Tipping: If a gratuity is included in the price of your sit-down meal, you don't need to tip further; otherwise, a tip of roughly 10 percent is customary. Tip a taxi driver by rounding up the fare a bit (pay €3 on a €2.85 fare). For more tips on tipping, see page 129.

Tourist Information: www.latvia.travel

RĪGA

The biggest city of the Baltics is an under-rated gem, with a charming but not cutesy Old Town, a sprawling real-world market, a smattering of good museums, the finest collection of fanciful Art Nouveau buildings in Europe, a palpable civic pride expressed in its luscious parks and stately facades, and fewer cruise passengers clogging its cobbles than most other towns in this book. From a cruiser's perspective, Rīga (pronounced REE-gah) is the sleepy antidote to its Baltic rival, the tourist-crazed Tallinn. Rīga has a bit less Scandinavian-mod style and sugary Old World charm, but it enjoys more big-city realness. And, while Tallinn's ties to the former USSR feel like ancient history, Rīga's Russian connection is more palpable, giving visitors a glimpse into a "half-Russian" society without plunging into the full monty of St. Petersburg.

Centuries before it was Russian (or even Latvian), Rīga was a prominent trading city. Bishop Albert of Bremen, German merchants, and the Teutonic Knights made it the center of Baltic Christianization, commercialization, and colonization when they founded the city in the early 1200s. Rīga came under Polish control for a while during the 16th century; later, in the 17th century, the czars made it the Russian Empire's busiest commercial port. Latvia gained its independence for the first time following World War I in 1918, but that lasted just over two decades; with World War II, it was folded into the USSR's holdings.

Under Soviet rule, Rīga became first an important military center and later, because of its high standard of living, one of the favored places for high-ranking military officers to retire to (to keep them at arm's length from power, they were given a choice of

Excursions from Rīga

Rīga can easily be enjoyed without an excursion. Getting into town is simple, the sights are pleasant but don't require a lot of explanation to enjoy, and the basics are covered in this chapter. Even the outlying sights (such as the Central Market, and the Art Nouveau quarter and museum) are an easy and pleasant walk from downtown. And joining a tour or hiring your own guide in Rīga is easy and affordable (see "Tours in Rīga," later).

Most cruise lines offer walking tours of Rīga's **Old Town,** or a bus-plus-walking-tour option. You can't really see the Old Town core by bus, so if you'd like to get all the stories and legends, a walking tour is best. If you're interested in Rīga's **Art Nouveau** facades, choose a tour that includes some walking, not just a bus ride. A bus tour zips you past several fine examples, but doesn't allow you to linger over the stunning details.

Those with an interest in **Jewish history** may find worthwhile a tour that includes several sites related to Rīga's difficult Holocaust experience: the memorial at the site of the Great Choral Synagogue (burned down by Nazis), the site of the Old Jewish Cemetery (defiled by Nazis), the monument at Rumbula (the site of a mass execution in a forest), and the memorial at Salaspils (the largest Nazi concentration camp in the Baltics).

Cruise lines offer a wide range of excursions to outlying attractions. These include **Jurmala** (Rīga's seaside resort, sometimes combined with a spa visit); **"Middle Ages Rīga"** (including the Gauja River northeast of town, the evocative ruins of Sigulda Medieval Castle, the reconstructed Turaida Castle and nearby church, and the legend-packed Gutmanis cave); and the **Latvian Open-Air Ethnographic Museum** (with 118 traditional buildings relocated here from around the country). Again, as Rīga itself is so easy to enjoy in a relaxed day, I'd skip all of these options.

anywhere in the USSR *except* Moscow, Kiev, and St. Petersburg). The Soviets encouraged Russian immigration, and by the time the USSR fell, Latvians were in the minority in their own capital city. Perceptive travelers will notice that Russian is still widely spoken here. Though Russian-Estonian tensions in neighboring Estonia grab more headlines, Latvia has its own tricky mix to negotiate.

But for visitors, Rīga is a purely enjoyable city, regardless of what language is spoken by the people you'll meet. Stroll the Old Town, browsing the shops (as one of the cheapest destinations in this book, Rīga is a fine place to do a little shopping). Dip into a museum or two; the excellent Museum of the Occupation of Latvia is tops for those intrigued by the Baltics' tumultuous 20th century. For a revealing look at an extremely local-feeling market, linger in the Central Market, which trudges on seemingly oblivious to the cruise passengers just over the berm. Save some time to stroll through some of Rīga's delightful parks, following the meandering river (once a moat) that runs right in front of the towering Freedom Monument. And make a pilgrimage to some of the city's gorgeous Art Nouveau facades, which scream out with fanciful, entertaining details.

PLANNING YOUR TIME

Get your bearings with a stroll through the Old Town. Midmorning, walk to the Central Market for some people-watching and to harvest ingredients for a picnic lunch or snack. For a good picnic alternative, consider lunch at one of the many al fresco cafés downtown. Head to the Museum of the Occupation of Latvia (opens at 11:00) and/or the Art Museum Rīga Bourse. In the early afternoon, see the Freedom Monument, Orthodox Cathedral, and (a few blocks north) the best of Rīga's many Art Nouveau facades, plus the wonderful little Art Nouveau Museum. From the Art Nouveau sights, it's a fairly short walk (mostly through parklands) to the cruise dock.

Port of Rīga

Arrival at a Glance: It's an easy 10- to 20-minute stroll into town—no taxis or buses needed.

Port Overview

One of the simplest, most manageable cruise ports in northern Europe, Rīga is made-to-order for cruise passengers. Ships dock along a river embankment just a 10-minute walk from the edge of the Old Town, or a 20-minute walk from the very heart of town.

To reach Rīga, your ship will pick up a pilot for the journey up the Daugava River. The sailing from the Baltic up the river gives you a revealing glimpse of the grimy, hardworking industry that makes Rīga the Baltics' no-nonsense muscleman. Don't fret—the core of town (where you'll be spending time) is far more pleasant.

Tourist Information: There's no tourist information whatso-

Services near the Port

Stepping off the ship, turn left to find Rīga's passenger port terminal building (marked *Rīga Pasazieru Osta*), with **ATMs,** WCs, a newsstand, and a café. But you might as well turn right and walk into the Old Town, where ATMs abound. The Old Town also has several **pharmacies.**

ever at the port; just walk into town to find TIs on Town Hall Square and just to the north (see "Tourist Information," later).

GETTING INTO TOWN

On Foot: To walk into town, just step off the ship, turn right, and head toward the spires. Here are the details: After turning right to walk along the embankment (with the river on your right), proceed straight and pass under the bridge. At the first crosswalk, turn left and cross the busy highway. Once across, continue straight up Poļu Gāte, alongside the pastel-blue church. At the intersection, turn right onto Pils Iela, which takes you directly to Cathedral Square in the heart of town. If you'd like to visit the TI, you can continue straight all the way to the far end of Cathedral Square (past all the al fresco tables), and turn right down the narrow, café-lined Tirgoņu Iela. The next small square has even more café tables, plus a fun outdoor souvenir market. As you walk through it, watch on your right for a big gap leading to an ugly modern building—this is the Museum of the Occupation of Latvia (though exhibits may be in another location when you visit), which shares Town Hall Square with the TI (in the ornate building in the foreground).

By Taxi: Taxis may meet arriving ships, attempting to drastically overcharge cruisers €4-8 (or even more) for the laughably short ride into town. (The fair, metered rate would be closer to €3-4.) As you'll have trouble getting a fair price, you'll do better taking the easy walk into town.

RETURNING TO YOUR SHIP

Just head north along the river (with the river on your left); you'll run right into your ship. If you're coming from the Art Nouveau district, use a map to navigate your way diagonally through the big Kronvalda Park. When you pop out at the other end, you're just a quick walk from the dock. To cross the highway, it's easiest and safest to use the busy bridge that crosses over both the highway and the river (you can find steps up to the bridge level near the Statoil gas station). Cross partway over, but before reaching the river, look for the stairs down (on your right) to the port gate area.

Rīga

With about 700,000 people, Rīga is the biggest city in the Baltics. But the town core feels small and manageable, and even just a few hours are enough to get a satisfying taste.

Orientation to Rīga

Rīga's Old Town (called Vecrīga) is on the right bank of the wide Daugava River. The cruise port is next to the northernmost of Rīga's bridges. From the river, the main drag—Kaļķu Iela—leads through the Old Town to the Freedom Monument, where it becomes Brīvības Bulvāris and continues out of town. You'll find plenty to keep you busy within the Old Town or a short walk from it.

The Old Town is hemmed in on the east side by a chain of relaxing parks, with the once-genteel urban residential zone stretching beyond. One of Rīga's most worthwhile areas is the cluster of Art Nouveau facades about a 20-minute walk (or €3-4 taxi ride) northeast of the city center. There's no reason to cross the river.

A couple of terms you'll see around town: *Iela* is "street," and *Bulvāris* is "boulevard."

TOURIST INFORMATION

The tourist office is in the ornate brick building attached to the House of Blackheads, right on Town Hall Square (daily May-Sept 9:00-19:00, Oct-April 10:00-18:00, Rātslaukums 6, tel. 6703-7900, www.liveriga.com). A second branch is just a few short blocks away along the main drag, Kaļķu Iela (at #16, tel. 6722-7444).

Tours in Rīga

Since Rīga is best seen by foot, a **walking tour** is probably your best bet. Various local companies offer these, but the main operation is Smile Line, which has a kiosk by the statue of St. Roland in the middle of Town Hall Square, right in front of the TI. Their 1.5-hour introductory walk departs daily at 10:30 (€12). They also have a two-hour departure daily at 13:00 for €15. You could arrange this in advance, or just show up and ask about it on the spot (tel. 2954-2626, www.smileline.lv, info@smileline.lv).

Two companies—Rīga City Tour (www.citytour.lv) and Rīga Sightseeing (www.riga-sightseeing.lv)—run **hop-on, hop-off bus tours** around town, departing about hourly for a one-hour loop (€15-17). But given Rīga's walkability and the tours' measly frequency, this isn't your best option.

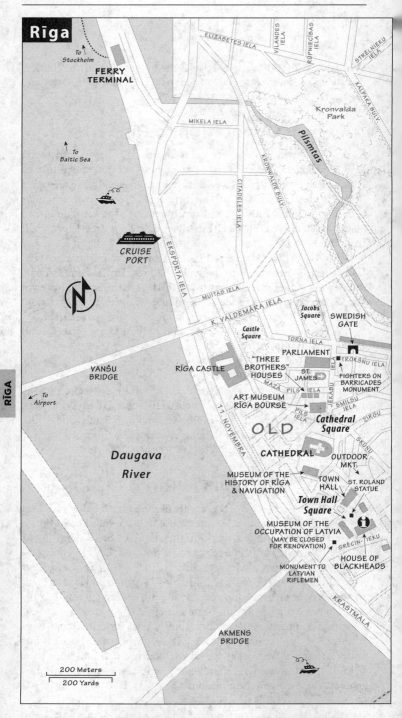

Rīga

To Stockholm

FERRY TERMINAL

ELIZABETES IELA

VILANDES IELA

KUPNIECIBAS IELA

STRELNIEKU IELA

MĪKELA IELA

Kronvalda Park

To Baltic Sea

CITADELES IELA

KRONWALDE BULV.

Pilsmtas

CRUISE PORT

ESPORTA IELA

MUITAS IELA

K. VALDEMĀRA IELA

Jacobs Square

SWEDISH GATE

Castle Square

TORNA IELA

VANŠU BRIDGE

RĪGA CASTLE

PARLIAMENT

"THREE BROTHERS" HOUSES

ST. JAMES

TROKŠNU IELA

FIGHTERS ON BARRICADES MONUMENT

To Airport

11. NOVEMBRA

MAZA PILS IELA

ART MUSEUM RĪGA BOURSE

JEKABU IELA

PILS IELA

SMILŠU IELA

Cathedral Square

ZIRGU

OLD

CATHEDRAL

SKUNU

OUTDOOR MKT.

Daugava River

MUSEUM OF THE HISTORY OF RĪGA & NAVIGATION

TOWN HALL

ST. ROLAND STATUE

Town Hall Square

MUSEUM OF THE OCCUPATION OF LATVIA (MAY BE CLOSED FOR RENOVATION)

GRĒCIN-IEKU

HOUSE OF BLACKHEADS

MONUMENT TO LATVIAN RIFLEMEN

KRASTMALA

AKMENS BRIDGE

200 Meters

200 Yards

RĪGA

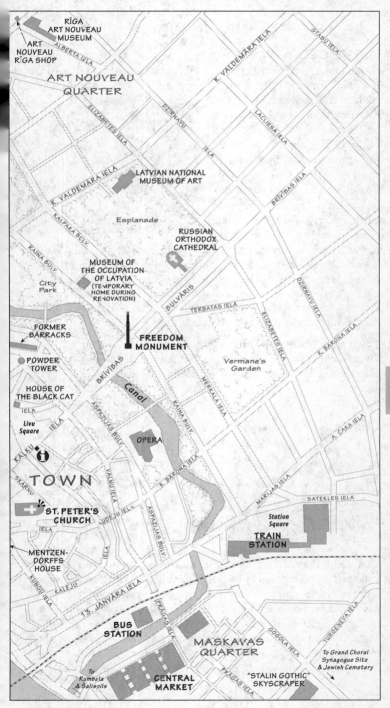

Sights in Rīga

IN THE OLD TOWN

Rīga's Old Town (Vecrīga) isn't as "old" as some; most of its buildings date from the 18th century, when the city boomed as a Russian
trade port. You'll also see several
fine examples of Art Nouveau
buildings from the early 20th
century. The big churches, the
moat, the bastion, fragments of
the city walls, a couple dozen
houses, and the cannonballs embedded in the Powder Tower are
all that survive from the Middle
Ages. Even if the buildings are

newer, Rīga's twisty medieval street plan gives it an Old World
charm. As a cosmopolitan shipping town for much of its history,
Rīga also boasts a wide range of churches: Lutheran, Catholic, Anglican, Orthodox, and more. Enjoyable to explore, the Old Town is
graced with several fine squares; I've listed each below, along with
the landmarks you'll find on or around them.

Town Hall Square (Rātslaukums)

Though not as big or as inviting as Cathedral Square, this space—
closer to the river—is arguably Rīga's "main square." After World

War II, when this area was
devastated, Soviets rebuilt
in an ugly, blocky style
(some of which remains).
But after independence,
the Latvians set about
restoring the square to
its former glory. Its finest
non-Art Nouveau build-
ing, the **House of Blackheads,** is made of vibrant
red brick liberally sprin-

kled with gilded decorations. This was originally the guildhall of
a merchant society that chose as its patron St. Mauritius, a third-
century North African. The nickname came from the guild seal
with disembodied black heads. (Racial sensitivity was clearly not a
medieval forte—and, judging by the fact that the guild seal is still
here, it's not quite a priority these days, either.) See the dates at the
top: Although the guildhall was originally built in 1334, it was
destroyed in World War II and only rebuilt in 1999. The left half of

the building (containing the TI) looks as if it's part of the House of Blackheads, but was built centuries later.

Facing the House of Blackheads is Rīga's stately Town Hall. On the square between them stands a statue of **St. Roland,** Rīga's patron saint. Back then, the tip of Roland's sword was considered the geographical center of the city—the point from which all distances were measured.

A block above Town Hall Square is the towering, almost-onion steeple of **St. Peter's Church** (Petera Baznica), with an austere Lutheran interior and an elevator to an observation deck (€9, closed Mon).

Along the bottom of Town Hall Square is the Soviet-era building that now (with a flourish of poetic justice) houses the Museum of the Occupation of Latvia (exhibits may be in another location when you visit; described below). Around the far side of the building, facing the river, stands the proud **Monument to the Latvian Riflemen.** These soldiers fought on the side of the czar during World War I, but then defected to join Lenin's Bolshevik Revolution. During communist times, the Soviets strategically chose local heroes to venerate in each of its satellites (the heroes conveniently also echoed Soviet ideals).

▲Museum of the Occupation of Latvia (Latvijas Okupācijas Muzejs)

This spunky, thorough exhibit tells Latvia's story during the tumultuous five decades between 1940 and 1991. The museum is undergoing a much-needed overhaul and you may find the exhibits at its temporary home in the former US embassy, just outside the Old Town at Raiņa Bulvāris 7, or possibly back in the main building (double-check with the TI for the current location).

The new collection promises to keep the focus on the periods of Nazi and Soviet oppression—particularly the deportations of Latvians to Siberia. (You can step into a replica of a gulag barrack and see prisoners' letters home written on strips of birch bark.) To get the full story, try to time your visit to join one of the guided tours.

Cost and Hours: Note that these details may change due to ongoing renovations. Free, but donations suggested, daily 11:00-18:00, Raiņa Bulvāris 7 (temporary location) or Strelnieku Laukums 1, tel. 6721-2715, www.occupationmuseum.lv.

Tours: Guided tours are offered in English daily May-Sept at 12:00 and 16:00, or by request; €3/person with a €10 minimum; tel. 6721-1030, ip@omf.lv.

▲▲Cathedral Square (Doma Laukums)

In old Rīga's biggest square, three things jockey for attention: The enormous cathedral, the Art Nouveau facade of the old stock ex-

RĪGA

change museum (now an art museum—described next), and café tables spilling out over the cobbles in every direction.

The **cathedral** (Doma Baznica), with its distinctive copper roof, dates from 1211. Dwarfing everything around it, it's positively huge for the Baltics, where big churches are rare. With additions built over the generations, it's a hodgepodge of architectural styles. During Soviet times, the altars and other religious decorations were taken out and the cathedral was converted into a concert hall. Inside, the inscriptions recall Latvia's German Lutheran heritage, and the crypt holds what's left of Bishop Albert of Bremen, who started it all. It also has a particularly fine and gigantic organ (with more than 6,700 pipes), which is played for brief noontime concerts on certain days during the tourist season (generally Mon, Wed, and Sun at 12:00, www.doms.lv).

Facing the cathedral from across the square is the ornately decorated former stock exchange building, or **Bourse,** which houses the Art Museum Rīga Bourse (described next). The second-story grille hides a carillon, which sweetly chimes the hour.

The far end of the square is the terrain of outdoor café and restaurant tables—a tempting place to sit, nurse a coffee or Latvian beer, and watch the parade of tourists and locals.

From here, you can tour the art museum, wander a couple of streets with fine Art Nouveau houses, or walk along Pils Iela to Rīga Castle (all described later).

Art Museum Rīga Bourse

Rīga's stately old stock exchange building houses temporary exhibits and a modest collection of "foreign art." While the changing collections are generally good, the permanent exhibits (fourth floor—Western European art and painting gallery, third floor—Asian art) take a backseat to the finely restored rooms that house them. The highlights are the airy atrium with beautiful tile floors (viewable for free) and the fourth floor, with gilded chandeliers and other details whose sumptuousness outshines the art.

Cost and Hours: Permanent exhibit-€3,

extra for temporary exhibits or €6 combo-ticket for all; Tue-Sun 10:00-18:00, Fri until 20:00, closed Mon, Doma Laukums 6, tel. 6735-7534, www.rigasbirza.lv.

Rīga Castle

Leave Cathedral Square and walk down Pils Iela to this relatively unimpressive, blocky fortress (a "palace" it ain't) that was the no-nonsense headquarters of the Teutonic Knights who ruled Rīga. Built in the 14th century, the castle stoutly anchored the northern tip of the Old Town as it kept careful watch downriver for potential invaders. The door on the landward side of the castle, with a guard out front, is the office of the Latvian president; nearby is the entrance to the skippable Latvian National History Museum. During Soviet times, the castle was converted into the "Children's Palace"—many older Latvians recall visiting here as youngsters.

Walk to Swedish Gate and Former Barracks

From Rīga Castle, take a stroll through the most historic quarter of the Old Town. With your back to the big, round tower, walk straight ahead up Mazā Pils Iela a block and a half to find (on the right) the **"Three Brothers"**—a trio of the oldest surviving houses in Rīga. The oldest, white house (#17) has minuscule windows—dating from the 15th century, when taxation was based

on window size. Yellow #19 is newer, from 1646, while green and narrow #21 is the baby of the bunch, from the turn of the 18th century.

Continue past the Brothers and turn left up Jēkaba Iela. On the left, you'll pass the corner of Latvia's **parliament.** This is the building where—back when it was the seat of the Latvian Supreme Soviet—independence from the USSR was declared on May 4, 1990. On the nearby corner, look for the little pyramid-shaped monument to the **Fighters on the Barricades,** a brave group of about 15,000 Latvians who, at great personal risk, protected strategic Latvian areas when skirmishes with pro-Soviet forces broke out in January 1991; seven were killed. The Latvians were unsure of whether Soviet leader Mikhail Gorbachev would send the full force of the Red Army to reclaim the Baltics. Although that never happened, Latvians still honor those who were willing to make the ultimate sacrifice for sovereignty.

Near the top of Jēkaba Iela, turn right down the tiny, rocky lane called **Trokšņu Iela.** Watch your step on this ankle-twisting alley, paved with rocks originally carried as ballast on big ships. After a block on this street, you'll pop out at the so-called **Swedish Gate** (built in the 17th century by Swedish soldiers stationed here). Going through it, you'll discover a long row of yellow **barracks** filled with shops and cafés, facing a reconstructed stretch of the former town wall (along Torņa Iela). At the far end is the **Powder Tower,** which once housed the town's supply of gunpowder. The tower defended that cache well over the centuries, as nine Russian cannonballs (from the 17th and 18th centuries) are supposedly embedded in the walls. The Museum of War inside is skippable.

From the Powder Tower, you could turn right and head down Smilšu, for some fun Art Nouveau facades on the way back down to Cathedral Square.

Old Town Art Nouveau

While arguably the best Art Nouveau in Rīga is just outside the historic core (described later), several fine examples from that age line the Old Town streets. The best examples are on or near two streets leading off from Cathedral Square: Smilšu (especially #2 and #8), to the east; and Šķūņu, to the south. Just off of Smilšu, at Meistaru 10, is the famous **House of the Black Cat;** while the building itself is relatively tame, its corner turret is topped with a cat with its back arched defiantly, supposedly placed there as an offensive gesture toward a guild that denied its creator membership.

Other Museums

Rīga's Old Town is packed with small, modest museums that are worth perusing if you have a special interest or it's a rainy day. The **Museum of the History of Rīga and Navigation** (Rīgas Vestures un Kugniecibas Muzejs) gives a fairly good idea of Rīga's early history as a center on the Baltic-Black Sea trade route, explains the Old Town's street plan in terms of a now-silted-up river that used to flow through the center, and shows you everything you wanted to see on interwar Rīga (daily 10:00-17:00, Oct-April Wed-Sun from 11:00, behind the cathedral at Palasta Iela 4, www.rigamuz. lv). The Mentzendorffs House is a meticulously restored 17th-century aristocrat's townhouse (daily 10:00-17:00, Oct-April Wed-Sun from 11:00, Grēcinieku Iela 18, enter on Kungu Iela, www. mencendorfanams.com).

OUTSIDE THE OLD TOWN

While many cruisers stick to the cobbles, some of Rīga's most appealing (and certainly its most local-feeling) attractions are just a short walk beyond the former city walls. The Central Market is just south of the Old Town, while the other places noted here are to the east. I've listed these roughly in order, from nearest to farthest from the Old Town.

▲▲Central Market (Centralais Tirgus)

What do you do when you have five perfectly good zeppelin airship hangars left behind by the Germans after World War I? Latvia's

answer: Move them to the center of the capital city and turn them into extremely spacious market halls. Just beyond the southern edge of the Old Town—only a 15-minute walk from the quaint cobbled squares—is this vast, sprawling market that feels like the outskirts of Moscow. This is not a touristy souvenir market

(though you may find a stall or two), but a real, thriving market where locals buy whatever they need at reasonable prices. If you've been cruising through Scandinavia's more expensive cities, you'll find basic foodstuffs here to be almost scandalously cheap. It's open and bustling every day, though some sections close on certain Mondays (www.rct.lv/en/).

To get to the market, walk to the south end of the Old Town, cross the tram tracks, and find the underpass that runs beneath the big berm. Then explore to your heart's content, wishing you had a full kitchen in your stateroom to cook up all the tempting ingredients. Just past the one hangar that runs sideways, find the colorful and fragrant flower market. Then poke through all five of the zeppelin hangars, each one with a different variety of meats, cheeses, bakery items, dry goods, and (in the final, smelly hall) fish. While nothing here is exactly gourmet—this is not an artisan, organic market—it makes it easy to imagine life for an everyday Rīgan. The old brick warehouses just toward the river from the market zone have been refurbished and now house finer shops.

The Central Market also marks the Maskavas, or **"Little Moscow,"** neighborhood, which contains a huge Russian population. While all the Baltic states have large Russian populations, Rīga became especially Russified during the Soviet period, leaving an awkward tension between its Latvian and Russian groups. As if to mark this territory, looming overhead is a classic "Stalin Gothic" tower (virtually identical in style to similar towers in War-

RĪGA

saw, Moscow, and elsewhere). Originally designed to be a hotel and conference center for collective farmers (who had little use for either hotels or a conference center), it later became, and remains, the Academy of Science.

▲▲Freedom Monument (Brivibas Piemniekelis)

Dedicated in 1935, and located on a traffic island in the middle of Brīvības Bulvāris, this monument features Lady Liberty (here nicknamed "Milda") holding high three stars representing the three regions of Latvia. At the base of the tower, strong and defiant Latvians break free from their chains and march to the future. The Soviets must have decided that removing the monument was either too difficult or too likely to spur protests among Latvians, because they left it standing—but reassigned its major characters: The woman became Mother Russia, and the three stars, the Baltic states. (KGB agents apprehended anyone who tried to come near it.) Now it is again the symbol of independent Latvia, and locals lay flowers between the two soldiers  who stand stoically at the monument's base. The grand building nearby is the Opera House. The bridge near the monument offers beautiful views over Rīga's great parks.

Parks

Rīga's Old Town is hemmed in on its eastern edge by delightful, manicured parks that line up along a picturesque stream that was once the fortified city's moat.

Russian Orthodox Cathedral

Just past the Freedom Monument on Rīga's main drag (Brīvības Bulvāris), sitting at the edge of a park, this striking house of worship dates from the 19th century. During the Soviet period, when the atheistic regime notoriously repurposed houses of worship, the building was used as a planetarium and "house of knowledge." While the interior is far from original—it was gutted by the Soviets—it's serene and otherworldly. Especially if you won't be visiting the Orthodox churches in Tallinn or St. Petersburg, it's worth the short walk out of the Old Town to take a peek.

Latvian National Museum of Art
(Latvijas Valsts Makslas Muzejs)

Housed in a stately old building in the parklands just east of the town center, this fine museum collects works by Latvian and Russian artists. The collection, almost entirely from 1910 to 1940, concentrates all the artistic and political influences that stirred

Latvia then: French Impressionism, German design, and Russian propaganda-poster style on the one hand; European internationalism, Latvian nationalism, rural romanticism, and Communism on the other. The Russian art section is particularly worthwhile if you won't be going to St. Petersburg's superb Russian Museum.

Cost and Hours: Permanent exhibit-€3, Tue-Thu 10:00-18:00, Fri until 20:00, Sat-Sun until 17:00, closed Mon, 1 Janis Rozentāls Square, www.lnmm.lv.

▲▲Art Nouveau Rīga

Worth ▲▲▲ for architecture fans, but interesting even to those who don't know Art Nouveau from Art Garfunkel, Rīga's more

than 800 exuberantly decorated facades from the late 19th and early 20th centuries make it Europe's single best city for the distinctive, eye-pleasing style of Art Nouveau. These are not the flowing, organic curves of Barcelona's Modernista style, but geometrically precise patterns adorned with fanciful details, including an army of highly expressive, gargoyle-like heads.

Art Nouveau Walk: While easy-to-love facades are scattered throughout the city center (including some wonderful examples in the Old Town—see "Old Town Art Nouveau," earlier), it's worth the 20-minute walk northeast of the center to find a particularly impressive batch. It's a pleasant stroll—you can follow the parks most of the way there, and you can tie in visits to the Orthodox Church and (if it's open) the Latvian National Museum of Art.

For the best short stretch of houses, begin at the corner of the park nearest Elizabets Iela, Strēlnieku Iela, and Kaplaka Bulvāris. Head up **Strēlnieku;** on the right, at #4, is a magnificent blue-and-white facade almost *too* cluttered with adornments: stripes, rings, slinky women holding wreaths of victory, and stylized helmeted heads over the windows. (This, like most buildings in this area, was decorated by Mikhail Eisenstein—whose director son Sergei earned a place in every "Intro to Film" college class with his seminal 1925 film, *Battleship Potemkin.*) At the corner, you'll see the yellow turreted building that houses the Art Nouveau Museum, and the fine shop across the street (both described later). If you turn right just before this house, on **Alberta Iela,** you'll find several more grandiose examples: #13 (pale pink, on right; notice the moaning heads at the bases of the turrets), #8 (blue and white, on the left; tree-trunk supports grow and leaf into a lion's head), #4 (beige, on the left; with griffins flanking the ornately framed doorway, three

Medusa heads up top, and lions guarding the towers), and (shabby but still impressive, the next two on the left) #2 and #2a. At the end of Alberta, jog right for a block, then head left down **Elizabets Iela** to find a couple more examples at #10a and #10b (blue and gray, with hoot-owls over the doors). All of these glorious buildings were turned into communal apartments under the communist regime.

Rīga Art Nouveau Museum: When you're done ogling the facades, head back the way you came, to the corner of Alberta and Strēlnieku. Head a few steps up Strēlnieku (to the right) to find the excellent little Rīga Art Nouveau Museum, in the bottom of the yellow castle-like building with the pointy red turret (€6, Tue-Sun 10:00-18:00, closed Mon, audioguide-€2.50, guided tour-€14.50/group—call or email ahead to arrange, Alberta 12, enter on Strēlnieku, tel. 6718-1465, www.jugendstils.riga.lv, jugendstils@riga.lv).

This museum shows what life was like behind those slinky facades back in the early 20th century. Buzz the doorbell to get inside, then peer up the stairwell.

Inside the museum, you're greeted by docents dressed in period costumes, who invite you to don a fancy, feathery hat for your stroll through a finely decorated, circa-1903 apartment, with furniture, clothes, decorative items, rugs, and lots of other details dating from the age.

This was the personal apartment of architect Konstantīns Pēkšēns, whose photo you'll see in the first room. You'll go through several rooms, including a dining room, bedroom, kitchen (with tiny maid's chamber on the side), bathroom (the apartment had hot water and even central heating—cutting-edge at the time), and more. Take your time and savor all the details—the gently seductive curve of the plant stand, the ribbons delicately tied to flower vases on the dining table, the old-school icebox and coffee grinder in the kitchen, and the natural motifs painted high on the walls in each room (based on items found in the Latvian countryside). Very few barriers or cordons separate you from the world of a century ago, making this a particularly appealing and immersive little museum.

Nearby: If you'd like to take some of this Art Nouveau home with you, directly across the street from the museum is the **Art Nouveau Rīga shop,** with piles of souvenirs inspired by this distinctive style (daily 10:00-19:00, Strēlnieku 9, tel. 6733-3030, www.artnouveauriga.lv).

More Art Nouveau: The tiny area described above is just the

What If I Miss My Ship?

Remember that you can get help from the cruise line's port agent (listed on the destination information sheet distributed on the ship) and the local TI.

Buses connect Rīga to **Tallinn.** For **Stockholm,** Tallink Silja offers overnight ferry trips (www.tallinksilja.com). To get to **St. Petersburg** or **Helsinki,** it's probably easier to go to Tallinn or Stockholm and connect from there (but remember that you'll need a visa—arranged weeks in advance—to enter Russia). **Gdańsk** requires a long overland journey; because the route from Latvia to Poland is flanked by Kaliningrad (part of Russia) and Belarus, both of which require transit visas, you'll need to determine a route via the relatively short Lithuanian-Polish border instead—ask the TI for help.

If you need to catch a **plane** to your next destination, you can ride a public bus to Rīga's international airport (www.riga-airport.com). For more advice, see page 130.

beginning of Rīga's Art Nouveau neighborhood. A couple of blocks to the west, just north of the parklands, **Vīlandes Iela** and the parallel **Rūpniecības Iela** have several fine facades. The area just south and east of the Brīvības Bulvāris main drag (such as **Tērbatas Iela** and **Aleksandra Čaka Iela**) also has several examples.

Shopping in Rīga

The souvenirs you'll see most often here are linens (tablecloths, placemats, and scarves) and carved-wood items (such as spoons and trivets). There are a few sparse souvenir stands at the **Central Market,** but that's really designed more for the natives. Souvenir shops are peppered through the Old Town, and an entertaining open-air **souvenir market** pops up in summer in the small square just north of Town Hall Square.

If you're turned on by Rīga's Art Nouveau bounty, another good option is "faux Nouveau"—replica items such as tiles, cards, textiles, jewelry, and so on. The best choices are at the **Art Nouveau Rīga shop,** across the street from the Art Nouveau Museum.

Eating in Rīga

Central Rīga—particularly the area between Cathedral Square and Town Hall Square—is full of tempting open-air cafés and restaurants. Rather than seek out a particular place, I'd simply window-shop to find an appealing cuisine and people-watching vantage point.

RĪGA

GDAŃSK

Poland

Poland Practicalities

Poland (Polska), arguably Europe's most devoutly Catholic country, is sandwiched between Protestant Germany and Eastern Orthodox Russia. Nearly all of the 38.5 million people living in Poland are ethnic Poles. The country is 121,000 square miles (the same as New Mexico) and extremely flat, making it the chosen path of least resistance for many invading countries since its infancy. Poland was dominated by foreigners for the majority of the last two centuries, finally gaining true independence (from the Soviet Union) in 1989. While parts of the country are still cleaning up the industrial mess left by the Soviets, Poland also has some breathtaking medieval cities—such as Gdańsk—that show off its kindhearted people, dynamic history, and unique cultural fabric.

Money: 4 złoty (zł, or PLN) = about $1. An ATM is called a *bankomat.* The local VAT (value-added sales tax) rate is 23 percent; the minimum purchase eligible for a VAT refund is 300 zł (for details on refunds, see page 125).

Language: The native language is Polish. For useful phrases, see page 517.

Emergencies: Dial 112 for police, medical, or other emergencies. In case of theft or loss, see page 118.

Time Zone: Poland is on Central European Time (the same as most of the Continent, one hour ahead of Great Britain, and six/nine hours ahead of the East/West Coasts of the US). That puts Gdańsk one hour behind Rīga, Tallinn, and Helsinki, and two hours behind St. Petersburg.

Embassies in Warsaw: The **US embassy** is at Aleje Ujazdowskie 29; appointments are required for routine services (tel. 022 504 2000, https://pl.usembassy.gov/). The **Canadian embassy** is at Ulica Jana Matejki 1-5 (tel. 022-584-3100, www.poland.gc.ca). Call ahead for passport services.

Phoning: With a mobile phone, it's easy to dial: Press and hold zero until you get a + sign, enter the country code (48 for Poland, 1 for the US/Canada), and then the complete phone number (including area code if there is one). When dialing a European phone number, drop an initial zero (except if calling Italy). For more tips, see page 1062.

Tipping: A gratuity is included at sit-down meals, so you don't need to tip further, though it's nice to round up your bill about 5-10 percent for great service. Tip a taxi driver by rounding up the fare a bit (pay 30 zł on a 27-zł fare). For more tips on tipping, see page 129.

Tourist Information: www.poland.travel

GDAŃSK
& the PORT of GDYNIA

Gdańsk (guh-DAYNSK) is a true find on the Baltic Coast of Poland. You may associate Gdańsk with dreary images of striking dockworkers from the nightly news in the 1980s—but there's so much more to this city than shipyards, Solidarity, and smog. It's surprisingly easy to look past the urban sprawl to find one of northern Europe's most historic and picturesque cities. Gdańsk is second only to Kraków as Poland's most appealing destination.

Exploring Gdańsk is a delight. The gem of a Main Town boasts block after block of red-brick churches and narrow, colorful, ornately decorated Hanseatic burghers' mansions. The riverfront embankment, with its trademark medieval crane, oozes salty maritime charm. Gdańsk's history is also fascinating—from its 17th-century Golden Age to the headlines of our own generation.

Gdańsk is the anchor of the three cities that make up the metropolitan region known as the Tri-City (Trójmiasto). The other two parts are as different as night and day: a once-faded, now-revitalized seaside resort (Sopot) and a practical, nose-to-the-grindstone business center and cruise port (Gdynia). Although your ship arrives at Gdynia (guh-DIN-yah), don't waste your time there—make a beeline to the main attraction, Gdańsk. With extra time, consider a quick visit to Sopot.

PLANNING YOUR TIME

Minimize your time in Gdynia and max out in Gdańsk. The best plan is to spend the morning in Gdańsk's Main Town and along the embankment, and the afternoon at the Solidarity shipyard. (From the shipyard, it's easy to get to the train station; for effi-

Excursions from Gdynia

Gdańsk is clearly the best choice. Most cruise-line excursions include a walking tour through the Main Town; some may include guided visits to the giant, red-brick **St. Mary's Cathedral** or the **European Solidarity Center** museum at the Solidarity shipyard. You'll want to explore the town after your tour, so look for an itinerary that includes some free time—or skip the return bus ride to your ship and head back later on your own (by train, using this book's instructions).

I'd prefer to spend a full day in Gdańsk, but excursions often tack on visits to other locations outside town. These may include (in order of worthiness):

Sopot: A relaxing beach resort, this town's location halfway between Gdynia and Gdańsk makes it an easy add-on.

Malbork Castle: The fearsome Teutonic Knights built this sprawling castle as their headquarters. Though impressive, it's farther from town than other sights, and the expansive complex takes time to fully see.

Stutthof Concentration Camp: This Nazi concentration camp memorial offers a poignant look at this region's troubled 20th century.

Oliwa Cathedral: This red-brick church is far from unique in this region, but its impressive organ (with animated figures that move when it plays) is a crowd-pleaser.

ciency, wrap up your Main Town activities before heading to the Solidarity sights.) When planning your day, be sure to allow plenty of time to make it from your ship in Gdynia to your points of interest in Gdańsk—I'd allow roughly 1.5 hours each way.

Gdańsk Main Town: Follow Part 1 of my Gdańsk Walk, a self-guided walking tour of the picturesque old core and embankment (allow one hour, including a visit to St. Mary's Church interior). If you can, take more time to linger and enjoy the Amber Museum, Uphagen House, Main Town Hall, Artus Court, or National Maritime Museum (allow about 30 minutes apiece for a quick stop).

Solidarity Shipyard: Follow Part 2 of my self-guided Gdańsk Walk to bring meaning to this 30-minute stroll, then allow about 2.5 hours to visit the shipyard and European Solidarity Center.

Sopot: Cruisers see Sopot as a handy, pleasant place to kill time on their way back to their ship in Gdynia. As it's halfway between Gdynia and Gdańsk, right on the train line, this is an easy stopover. If you have time, hop off the train in Sopot and stroll down the manicured main drag to the pleasure pier and beach. Allow at least 15 minutes to walk between Sopot's station and its beachfront, plus up to 15 minutes waiting for the train to Gdynia, plus however much time you want to linger at the beach.

Gdynia/Gdańsk Area

To Karlskrona, Sweden

Władysławowo

20 Kilometers
20 Miles

Jastarnia

To Szczecin
& Berlin   Jurata   Hel Peninsula

Baltijsk   RUSSIA
(Kaliningrad)

Hel

A-194

*Baltic
Sea*

Gdynia

Sopot   Oliwa   WESTERPLATTE

Wiślany Lagoon

TRI-CITY

Gdańsk

To Kaliningrad &
Vilnius, Lithuania

Motława River

Braniewo

Pruszcz
Gdański

POLAND

E-75   *Vistula River*   E-77   Elbląg   Orneta

Tczew

Malbork   Paslęk

To Poznań
& Berlin   E-77

Starogard
Gdański   To Toruń
& Warsaw   To Warsaw

Port of Gdynia

Arrival at a Glance: Ride the shuttle bus 5-10 minutes into Gdynia's town center, then walk 15 minutes to the train station for the 35-minute ride into Gdańsk (the Gdańsk Śródmieście station is a brief walk from the sights).

Port Overview

Because Gdańsk's port is relatively shallow, the biggest cruise ships must put in at the massive harbor at Gdynia, about 22 miles away. Among the northern cruise ports, Gdynia's sprawling dock area is the least user-friendly for arriving passengers. Cruise ships are shuffled among industrial piers with few amenities.

Each of the port's many piers is named for a country or region. Most cruise ships use **French Quay** (Nabrzeże Francuskie), which is surrounded by heavy industry. Smaller ships can use the convenient **Pomeranian Quay** (Nabrzeże Pomorskie, part of the Southern Pier)—which is closer to downtown and located alongside Gdynia's one "fun" pier, with museums and pleasure craft. Port information: www.port.gdynia.pl.

Money Matters: Don't expect to find an ATM or other money-exchange option at the dock. Ride your cruise line's shuttle bus (or, from the Pomeranian Quay, walk) to the downtown's main square, Skwer Kościuszki, where ATMs and banks abound. Taxi drivers generally take euros, though their off-the-cuff exchange rate may not be favorable; Uber is convenient, since you can simply pay by credit card.

Tourist Information: TI representatives meet arriving cruise ships to hand out maps and answer questions. In downtown Gdynia, the TI is on the main drag between the shuttle-bus drop-off and the train station (Mon-Fri 9:00-18:00, Sat-Sun until 16:00, closes one hour earlier and closed Sun off-season, on the right at 24 ulica 10 Lutego, tel. 58-622-3766).

Sights in Gdynia: Gdynia is less historic (and less attractive) than Gdańsk or Sopot, as it was mostly built in the 1920s to be Poland's main harbor after Gdańsk became a "free city" (see "Gdańsk History" sidebar, later). Today, it's primarily a business center. Gdynia's renovated downtown core is becoming known for its top-tier shopping—all the big designers have boutiques here.

The French Quay is home to Gdynia's best sight, the **Emigration Museum.** This modern, comprehensive exhibit tells the story of Poles who left through Gdynia to find a better life in the New World. This is a good place to spend any remaining time before "all aboard"; for those with Polish ancestry—or anyone interested in emigration—it's worth budgeting serious time for this museum (10 zł, Wed-Sun 10:00-18:00, Tue 12:00-20:00, closed Mon, www.polska1.pl).

Aside from that, most of Gdynia's sightseeing is along its waterfront. Directly toward the water from the shuttle-bus drop-off (through the park) is the **Southern Pier** (Molo Południowe). This concrete slab—nowhere near as charming as Sopot's wooden-boardwalk version—features a modern shopping mall and a smattering of sights, including an aquarium and a pair of permanently moored museum boats. More appealing is the broad beach south of the pier—a good place to feel sand between your toes or grab a beer at one of several beachfront cafés.

Alternate Port Near Gdańsk: Some smaller ships dock closer to Gdańsk, at **Westerplatte Quay** (Nabrzeże Obrońców Westerplatte)—at the site of a fortress where the first shots of World War II were fired. The park and its memorial to the "Defenders of Westerplatte" is worth a few minutes to appreciate its historic significance, but there's little else to do here. Unfortunately, there are limited cruise services (no ATMs) and no good public transportation into downtown. If your cruise line offers a shuttle bus into town, take it. An honest taxi should charge about 40-50 zł for the ride into town; you could also summon an Uber.

GDAŃSK

GETTING INTO GDYNIA (AND ON TO GDAŃSK)

These instructions assume you've arrived in Gdynia and plan to head directly to Gdańsk (which you should). While taxis are fast, they're pricey, and the train is cheap and doable. If you're interested in hiring a private guide, see "Tours in Gdańsk," later.

From French Quay to Gdynia Train Station

The easiest option is to take your cruise line's **shuttle bus.** The shuttle drops you off at Skwer Kościuszki, in the heart of downtown Gdynia (5-10-minute trip).

From the shuttle-bus stop at Skwer Kościuszki, it's about a 15-minute **walk** to the train station (Dworzec Główna): Head up the broad, parklike boulevard, going away from the water (if you need cash, you'll spot several ATMs in this part of town). At the top of the square, the street becomes ulica 10 Lutego and continues straight (very gradually uphill)—follow it. A few short blocks later, watch for the Gdynia TI on the right. Just beyond that, the street curves to the right; once you're around the corner, use the crosswalk to reach the train station (marked *Dworzec Podmiejski*).

Infrequent **public buses** (#119, #133, #137, and #147) link the French Quay's "Dworzec Morski—Muzeum Emigracji" stop to Gdynia's train station. If you know you'll be taking the bus, change a little money on the ship so you can buy a bus ticket.

From Pomeranian Quay to Gdynia Train Station

If you're fortunate enough to arrive at the **Pomeranian Quay** (Nabrzeże Pomorskie), simply walk away from the waterfront about 10 minutes to reach Skwer Kościuszki, then follow the walking instructions given above for reaching the train station.

From Gdynia Train Station to Gdańsk

Gdynia's main train station (Gdynia Główna) has an ATM just outside the station's front door; inside are lockers, WCs, and snack stands.

The station is best connected to Gdańsk, Sopot, and other towns by yellow-and-blue regional commuter trains (*kolejka*, operated by SKM). These **SKM trains** go in each direction about every 10-15 minutes, and make several stops en route to Gdańsk (35 minutes, 6.50 zł), including the resort town of Sopot (15 minutes, 4.20 zł).

You can buy a ticket at the ticket office (*kasa biletowa;* stamp your ticket in the easy-to-miss yellow slots at the bottom of the stairs leading up to the tracks) or at the ticket machine marked *SKM Bilety* (near the head of platform 4, with English instructions; these tickets do not need to be validated). Climb the stairs to platform 1; Gdańsk-bound trains leave from the side of the platform facing away from the city center and sea (labeled *tor 502;* look for *Gdańsk* on the list of stops).

Know Your Stop: Each city has multiple stops. In **Gdańsk,** the train stops first at "Gdańsk Główny" (the main station), but the next stop—"Gdańsk Śródmieście"—is closer to the sights (from the station, make your way across the busy street toward the towers of the Main Town, then turn left and walk along the road to the Upland Gate and the start of my self-guided walk). To visit **Sopot,** use the stop called simply "Sopot" (only one word). When returning to **Gdynia,** your stop is "Gdynia Główna" (the main station).

Note that Gdynia's main train station is also served by long-distance **PKP trains.** These are faster but less frequent than SKM commuter trains, and they don't use the handy Gdańsk Śródmieście station. Tickets for one system can't be used on the other.

Returning to Your Ship: To take the train back to Gdynia, return to either the main station (closer to the Solidarity shipyard zone) or the Śródmieście station (closer to the historic center). Before boarding the train, buy tickets at any ticket window (validate ticket in yellow box) or from a machine marked *SKM* (no validation required). Then take any blue-and-yellow SKM train heading for Gdynia. If you have lots of time to spare before your ship leaves, consider hopping out at Sopot for a stroll down to the waterfront.

In Gdynia, get off at the main station, **Gdynia Główna,** and head down toward the water on ulica 10 Lutego to find your cruise shuttle-bus stop in the middle of Skwer Kościuszki.

Getting Around by Taxi

Taxi drivers line up to meet arriving cruise ships. While I've listed the legitimate fare estimates below, many cabbies try to charge far more. Try asking several drivers until you get a quote that resembles my figures, and be sure they use the meter. Taxi drivers generally accept (and give quotes in) euros—though if you have Polish złotys, they'll take those, too.

To Gdynia's train station (*Dworzec,* DVOH-zhets): 20 zł (about €5)

To Gdańsk's Main Town: 125 zł (about €30)

To Sopot: 60-80 zł (about €15-20)

Many taxis that line up at the ship are looking for the long fare into Gdańsk and may not be willing to take you on the shorter trip to the Gdynia train station. If that's the case, walk out the port gate and look for a taxi—but be aware that the outside-the-port cabbies are probably unregulated and are more likely to overcharge.

Note that **Uber** is also active in Poland, and is often cheaper than the official taxi rate.

Gdańsk

With 460,000 residents, Gdańsk is part of the larger urban area known as the Tri-City (Trójmiasto, total population 1 million). But the tourist's Gdańsk is compact, welcoming, and walkable—virtu-

ally anything you'll want to see is within a 20-minute stroll of everything else.

Focus on the Main Town (Główne Miasto), home to most of the sights described, including the spectacular Royal Way main drag, ulica Długa. The Old Town (Stare Miasto) has a handful of old brick buildings

and faded, tall, skinny houses—but the area is mostly drab and residential, and not worth much time. Just beyond the northern end of the Old Town (about a 20-minute walk from the heart of the Main Town) is the entrance to the Gdańsk Shipyard, with the excellent European Solidarity Center and its top-notch museum. From here, shipyards sprawl for miles.

The second language in this part of Poland is German, not English. As this was a predominantly German city until the end of World War II, German tourists flock here in droves. But you'll win no Polish friends if you call the city by its more familiar German name, Danzig.

Orientation to Gdańsk

TOURIST INFORMATION

The regional TI occupies the **Upland Gate,** facing the busy road that hems in the Main Town, at the start of my self-guided walk (May-Sept Mon-Fri 9:00-20:00, Sat-Sun until 18:00; Oct-April daily 9:00-18:00; tel. 58-732-7041, www.pomorskie.travel). The city TI is conveniently located at the bottom end of the main drag, at **Długi Targ 28** (just to the left as you face the river gate; daily 9:00-19:00, Oct-April until 17:00; tel. 58-301-4355, www.gdansk4u.pl), with a satellite TI at the **main train station.** Another handy tourist website is www.visitgdansk.com.

Busy sightseers should consider the **Tourist Card,** which includes entry to several sights in Gdańsk, Gdynia, and Sopot, and discounts at others.

Gdańsk at a Gdlance

▲▲▲**Royal Way/Ulica Długa Walk** Gdańsk's colorful show-piece main drag, cutting a picturesque swath through the heart of the wealthy burghers' neighborhood. See page 485.

▲▲▲**Solidarity Sights and Gdańsk Shipyard** Home to the beginning of the end of Eastern European communism, with a towering monument and excellent museum. **Hours:** Memorial and shipyard gate-always open. European Solidarity Center exhibit-Mon-Fri 10:00-19:00, Sat-Sun until 20:00; Oct-April Mon and Wed-Fri 10:00-17:00, Sat-Sun until 18:00, closed Tue. See page 501.

▲▲**Main Town Hall** Ornate meeting rooms, town artifacts, and tower with sweeping views. **Hours:** Mid-June-mid-Sept Mon-Thu 9:00-16:00, Fri-Sat 10:00-18:00, Sun 10:00-16:00; mid-Sept-mid-June Tue 10:00-13:00, Wed-Sat until 16:00, Thu until 18:00, Sun 11:00-16:00, closed Mon. See page 500.

▲▲**Artus Court** Grand meeting hall for guilds of Golden Age Gdańsk, boasting an over-the-top tiled stove. **Hours:** Same as Main Town Hall. See page 500.

▲▲**St. Mary's Church** Giant red-brick church crammed full of Gdańsk history. **Hours:** Mon-Sat 8:30-18:30, Sun 11:00-12:00 & 13:00-18:30; Oct-April daily until 17:00. See page 492.

▲**Amber Museum** High-tech exhibit of valuable golden globs of petrified tree sap. **Hours:** Same as Main Town Hall, above. See page 498.

▲**Uphagen House** Tourable 18th-century interior, typical of the pretty houses that line ulica Długa. **Hours:** Same as Main Town Hall. See page 499.

▲**National Maritime Museum** Sprawling exhibit on all aspects of the nautical life, housed in several venues connected by a ferry boat. **Hours:** July-Aug daily 10:00-18:00; Sept-June shorter hours and closed Mon. See page 500.

GDAŃSK

GETTING AROUND GDAŃSK

Most of the recommended sights are within easy walking distance. Public transportation is generally unnecessary for sightseers spending their time in town.

One public bus worth knowing about is Gdańsk's **bus #100.** Every 20 minutes, this made-for-tourists minibus (designed to navigate the twisty streets of the town center) makes a loop through the Old Town and Main Town, with stops strategic for sightseeing (covered by regular transit ticket, 3.20 zł, buy at user-friendly machines or pay a little more on board).

Taxis cost about 8 zł to start, then 2-3 zł per kilometer. Find a taxi stand, or call a cab (try Neptun, tel. 19686 or 585-111-555; or Dajan, tel. 58-19628)

Tours in Gdańsk

Private Guides

Hiring a local guide is an exceptional value. **Agnieszka Syroka** — youthful, bubbly, and personable—is a wonderful guide (400 zł for up to 4 hours, more for all day, mobile 502-554-584, www. tourguidegdansk.com, syroka.agnieszka@gmail.com). **Jacek "Jake" Podhorski,** who teaches economics at the local university, guides in the summer. He's been around long enough to have fascinating personal memories of the communist days (400 zł/3 hours, 100 zł extra with his car, mobile 603-170-761, ekojpp@ug.edu.pl).

Gdańsk Walk

In the 16th and 17th centuries, Gdańsk was Poland's wealthiest city, with gorgeous architecture (much of it in the Flemish Mannerist style) rivaling that in the two historic capitals, Kraków and Warsaw. During this Golden Age, Polish kings would visit this city of well-to-do Hanseatic League merchants and gawk along the same route trod by tourists today.

The following self-guided walk (rated ▲▲▲) introduces you to the best of Gdańsk. It bridges the two historic centers (the Main Town and the Old Town), dips into St. Mary's Church (the city's most important church), and ends at the famous shipyards and Solidarity Square (where Poland began what ultimately brought down the USSR). I've divided the walk into two parts (making it easier to split up, if you like): The first half focuses on a loop through the Main Town (with most of the high-profile sights), while the second part carries on northward, through the less touristy Old Town to the shipyards.

GDAŃSK

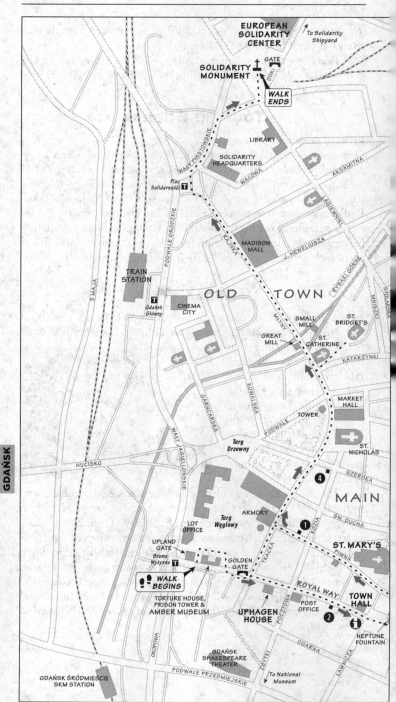

GDAŃSK

Gdańsk

1. Bar pod Rybą Restaurant
2. Bar Mleczny Neptun
3. Pijalnia Wódki i Piwa
4. Bar Turystyczny
5. Baryłka, Kamienica Goldwasser & Sushi 77
6. Lao Thai
7. Targ Rybny/Fishmarkt Restaurant
8. Restauracja Kubicki

MŁODY MIASTO DEVELOPMENT ZONE ("YOUNG CITY")

MUSEUM OF THE SECOND WORLD WAR

KROSNA

OLEJARNA

TANECZNA

STAROMIEJSKIE

Targ Rybny

River

STRAGANIARSKA

GROBLA

SWIETOJAŃSK

DŁUGIE POBRZEZE

MARITIME CULTURAL CENTER

SS SOŁDEK

NATIONAL MARITIME MUSEUM

TOWN

THE CRANE

ARCHAEOLOGICAL MUSEUM

MARIACKA

GOTYK HOUSE

ARTUS COURT

FIVE LITTLE LADIES

EMBANKMENT

Motława

3

Long Market (Długi Targ)

GREEN GATE

HISTORICAL ZONE OF FREE CITY OF GDAŃSK

CHMIELNA

Granary Island

MOTŁAWSKA

SZAFARNIA

200 Meters

200 Yards

To "Blue Lamb" Archaeologica Center & National Museum

STĄGIEWNA

LASTADIA

B Shuttle from Cruise Port

GDAŃSK

PART 1: THE MAIN TOWN

• Begin at the west end of the Main Town, just beyond the last gate at the edge of the busy road (at a road sign that says Sztokholm...a reminder that the car ferry to Sweden leaves from near here).

Upland Gate (Brama Wyżynna)

The Main Town's fortifications were expanded with a Renaissance wall bound by the Upland Gate (built in 1588). "Upland" refers to the hills you see beyond—considered high country in this flat region. Standing with your back to the busy arterial (which traces the old moat), study the gate. Find its three coats of arms (the black eagle for Royal Prussia, the crowned white eagle for Poland, and the two crosses for Gdańsk). Recall that this city has, for almost the entirety of its history before the mid-20th century, been bicultural: German and Polish, coexisting more or less peacefully. Also notice the little wheels that once hoisted a drawbridge.

• It's a straight line from here to the river. Walk through the arch (which houses a TI) to the next arch, just a few steps ahead.

Torture Chamber (Katownia) and Prison Tower (Wieża Więzienna)

The tall, Gothic brick gate before you was part of an earlier protective wall made useless after the Renaissance walls were built in 1588. While today these structures house the Amber Museum (described later), it's free to walk through the evocative passage. Inside, find gargoyles (on the left, a town specialty) and the shackles from which prisoners were hung (on the right). Look up at the inside of the high gable to the headless man, identifying this as the torture chamber. This old jail—with its 15-foot-thick walls—was used as a prison even in modern times, under Nazi occupation.

As you leave the Torture Chamber and Prison Tower, look to your left (100 yards away) to see a long, brick building with four fancy, uniform gables. This is the **armory** *(zbrojownia),* one of the finest examples of Dutch Renaissance architecture anywhere. Though this part of the building appears to have the facades of four separate houses, it's an urban camouflage to hide its real purpose from potential attackers. But there's at least one clue to what the building is really for: Notice the exploding cannonballs at the tops of the turrets. (We'll get a better look at the armory from the other side, later in this walk.)

The round, pointy-topped tower next to the armory is the **Straw Tower** (Baszta Słomiana). Gunpowder was stored here, and the roof was straw—so if it exploded, it could easily blow its top without destroying the walls.

• Straight ahead, the final and fanciest gate between you and the Main Town is the...

Golden Gate (Złota Brama)

While the other gates were defensive, this one's purely ornamental. The four women up top represent virtues that the people of Gdańsk should exhibit toward out-

siders (left to right): Peace, Freedom, Prosperity, and Fame. The gold-lettered inscription, a psalm in medieval German, compares Gdańsk to Jerusalem: famous and important. Directly above the arch is the Gdańsk coat of arms: two white crosses under a crown on a red shield. We'll see this symbol all over town. Photographers love the view of the Main Town framed in this arch. Inside the arch, study the old photos showing the 1945 bomb damage. On the left is the glorious view you just enjoyed...ravaged by war. And on the right is a heartbreaking aerial view of the city in 1945, when 80 percent of its buildings were in ruins.

• *Passing through the Golden Gate, you reach the Main Town's main drag.*

The Royal Way

Before you stretches ulica Długa (cleverly called the "Long Street")—the main promenade of what, 600 years ago, was the biggest and richest city in Poland, thanks to its profitable ties to the Hanseatic League of merchant cities. This promenade is nicknamed the "Royal Way" because (just as in Warsaw and Kraków) the king would follow this route when visiting town.

Walk half a block, and then look back at the Golden Gate. The women on top of this side represent virtues the people of Gdańsk should cultivate in themselves (left to right): Wisdom, Piety, Justice, and Concord (if an arrow's broken, let's take it out of the quiver and fix it). The inscription—sharing a bit of wisdom as apropos today as it was in 1612—reads, "Concord makes small countries develop, and discord makes big countries fall." Gdańsk was cosmopolitan and exceptionally tolerant in the Middle Ages, attracting a wide range of people, including many who were persecuted elsewhere: Jews, Scots, Dutch, Flemish, Italians, Germans, and more. Members of each group brought with them strands of their culture, which they wove into the tapestry of this city—demonstrated by the eclectic homes along this street. Each facade and each gable were different, as nobles and aristocrats wanted to display their wealth. On my last visit, a traveler seeing this street for the first time gasped to me, "It's like stepping into a Fabergé egg."

GDAŃSK

Gdańsk History

Visitors to Gdańsk are surprised at how "un-Polish" the city's history is. In this cultural melting pot of German, Dutch, and Flemish merchants (with a smattering of Italians and Scots), Poles were only a small part of the picture until the city became exclusively Polish after World War II. However, in Gdańsk, cultural backgrounds traditionally took a back seat to the bottom line. Wealthy Gdańsk was always known for its economic pragmatism—no matter who was in charge, merchants here made money.

Gdańsk is Poland's gateway to the waters of Europe, where its main river (the Vistula) meets the Baltic Sea. The town was first mentioned in the 10th century, and was seized in 1308 by the Teutonic Knights (who called it "Danzig"). The Knights encouraged other Germans to settle on the Baltic coast, and gradually turned Gdańsk into a wealthy city. In 1361, Gdańsk joined the Hanseatic League, a trade federation of mostly Germanic merchant towns that provided mutual security. By the 15th century, Gdańsk was a leading member of this mighty network, which virtually dominated trade in northern Europe.

In 1454, the people of Gdańsk rose up against the Teutonic Knights, burning down their castle and forcing them out of the city. Three years later, the Polish king borrowed money from wealthy Gdańsk families to hire Czech mercenaries to take the Teutonic Knights' main castle, Malbork. In exchange, the Gdańsk merchants were granted special privileges, including exclusive export rights. Gdańsk now acted as a middleman for much of the trade passing through Polish lands.

The 16th and 17th centuries were Gdańsk's Golden Age. Now a part of the Polish kingdom, the city had access to an enormous

During Gdańsk's Golden Age, these houses were taxed based on frontage (like the homes lining Amsterdam's canals)—so they were built skinny and deep. The widest houses belonged to the super-elite. Different as they are from the outside, every house had the same general plan inside. Each had three parts, starting with the front and moving back: First was a fancy drawing room, to show off for visitors. Then came a narrow corridor to the back rooms—often along the side of an inner courtyard. Because the houses had only a few windows facing the outer street, this courtyard provided much-needed sunlight to the rest of the house. The residential quarters were in the back, where the family actually lived: bedroom, kitchen, office. To see the interior of one of these homes, pay a visit to the interesting **Uphagen House** (at #12, on the right, a block and a half in front of the Golden Gate; described later).

This lovely street wasn't always so lively and carefree. At the end of World War II, the Royal Way was in ruins. That epic war

hinterland of natural resources to export—yet it maintained a privileged, semi-independent status. Like Amsterdam, Gdańsk became a progressive and booming merchant city. Its mostly Germanic and Dutch burghers imported Dutch, Flemish, and Italian architects to give their homes an appropriately Hanseatic flourish. At a time of religious upheaval in the rest of Europe, Gdańsk became known for its tolerance—a place that opened its doors to all visitors (many Mennonites and Scottish religious refugees emigrated here).

Along with the rest of Poland, Gdańsk declined in the late 18th century and became part of Prussia (today's northern Germany) during the Partitions. But the people of Gdańsk—even those of German heritage—weren't enthusiastic about being ruled from Berlin. After World War I, in a unique compromise to appease its complex ethnic makeup, Gdańsk did not fall under German or Polish control, but once again became an independent city-state: the Free City of Danzig. The city, along with the so-called Polish Corridor connecting it to Polish lands, effectively cut off Germany from its northeastern territory. On September 1, 1939, Adolf Hitler started World War II when he invaded Gdańsk in order to bring it back into the German fold. Later, nearly 80 percent of the city was destroyed when the Soviets "liberated" it from Nazi control.

After World War II, Gdańsk officially became part of Poland, and was painstakingly reconstructed. In 1970, and again in 1980, the shipyard of Gdańsk witnessed strikes and demonstrations that would lead to the fall of European communism. Poland's great anticommunist hero and first postcommunist president, Lech Wałęsa, is Gdańsk's most famous resident.

actually began here, in what was then the "Free City of Danzig." Following World War I, nobody could decide what to do with this influential and multiethnic city. So, rather than assign it to Germany or Poland, it was set apart as its own little autonomous statelet. In 1939, Danzig was 80 percent German-speaking—enough for Hitler to consider it his. And so, on September 1 of that year, the Nazis seized it in one day with relatively minor damage (though the attack on the Polish military garrison on the city's Westerplatte peninsula lasted a week).

But six years later, when the Soviets arrived (March 30, 1945), the city was left devastated. This was the first traditionally German city that the Red Army took on their march toward Berlin. And, while it was easy for the Soviets to seize the almost empty city, the commander then insisted that it be leveled, building by building—in retaliation for all the pain the Nazis had caused in Russia. (Soviets didn't destroy nearby Gdynia, which they considered Polish rather than German.) Soviet officers turned a blind eye as their soldiers raped and brutalized residents. An entire order of horrified nuns committed suicide by throwing themselves into the river.

It was only thanks to detailed drawings and photographs that these buildings could be so carefully reconstructed. Notice the cheap plaster facades done in the 1950s—rough times under communism, in the decade after World War II. (Most of the town's medieval brick was shipped to Warsaw for a communist-sponsored "rebuild the capital first" campaign.) While the fine facades were restored, the buildings behind the facades were completely rebuilt to modern standards.

Just beyond Uphagen House, **Cukiernia Sowa** ("The Owl," on the right at #13) is *the* place for cakes and coffee. Directly across the street, **Grycan** (at #73) has been a favorite for ice cream here for generations.

Just a few doors down, on the left, are some of the most striking **facades** along the Royal Way. The blue-and-white house with the three giant heads is from the 19th century, when the hot style was eclecticism—borrowing bits and pieces from various architectural eras. This was one of the few houses on the street that survived World War II.

At the next corner on the right is the huge, blocky, red **post office,** which doesn't quite fit with the skinny facades lining the rest of the street. Step inside. With doves fluttering under an airy glass atrium, the interior's a class act. Directly across the street, the candy shop **(Ciuciu Cukier Artist)** is often filled with children clamoring to see lollipop-making demos. Step in and inhale a universal whiff of childhood.

A few doors farther down, on the left at #62, pop into the **Millennium Gallery** amber shop (which would love to give you an educational amber polishing demo) to see the fascinating collection of old-timey photos, letting you directly compare Gdańsk's cityscape before and after the WWII destruction.

Above the next door, notice the colorful **scenes.** These are slices of life from 17th-century Gdańsk: drinking, talking, buying, playing music. The ship is a *koga,* a typical symbol of Hanseatic ports like Gdańsk.

Across the street and a few steps down are the fancy facades of three houses belonging to the very influential medieval **Ferber family,** which produced many burghers, mayors, and even a bishop. On the house with the little dog over the door (#29), look for the heads in the circular medallions. These are Caesars of Rome. At the top of the building is Mr. Ferber's answer to the constant question, "Why build such an elaborate house?"—*PRO INVIDIA*, "For the sake of envy."

A few doors down, on the right, is Gdańsk's most scenically situated milk bar, the recommended **Bar Mleczny Neptun.** Back in communist times, these humble cafeterias were subsidized to give workers an affordable place to eat out. To this day, they offer simple and very cheap grub.

Next door (at #35) is the **Russian Culture Center,** with Russian movies and art exhibits. With a complicated history—and many Poles now siding with Ukraine in their stand against Vladimir Putin's incursion into Ukrainian territory—this is a poignant address.

Before you stands the **Main Town Hall** (Ratusz Głównego Miasta) with its mighty brick clock tower. Consider climbing its observation tower and visiting its superb interior, which features ornately decorated meeting rooms for the city council (described later).

• *Just beyond the Main Town Hall, ulica Długa widens and becomes...*

The Long Market (Długi Targ)

Step from the Long Street into the Long Market, and do a slow, 360-degree spin to appreciate the amazing array of proud archi-

tecture here in a city center that rivals the magnificent Grand Place in Brussels. The centerpiece of this square is one of Gdańsk's most important landmarks, the statue of **Neptune**—god of the sea. He's a fitting symbol for a city that dominates the maritime life of Poland. Behind him is another worthwhile museum, the **Artus Court.** Step up to the magnificent door and study the golden relief just above, celebrating the Vistula River (in so many ways the lifeblood of the Polish nation): Lady Vistula is exhausted after her heroic journey, and is finally carried by Neptune to her ultimate destination, the Baltic Sea. (This is just a preview of the ornate art that fills the interior of this fine building—described later.)

Midway down the Long Market (on the right, across from the Hard Rock Café) is a glass case with the **thermometer and barometer of Daniel Fahrenheit.** Although that scientist was born here, he did his groundbreaking work in Amsterdam.

• *At the end of the Long Market is the...*

Green Gate (Zielona Brama)

This huge gate (named for the Green Bridge just beyond) was actually built as a residence for visiting kings...who usually preferred to stay back by Neptune instead (maybe because the river, just on the other side of this gate, stank). It might not have been good enough for kings and queens, but it's plenty fine for a former president: Lech Wałęsa's office is upstairs (see the plaque on the left side, *Biuro Lecha Wałęsy*). His windows, up in the gable, overlook the Long Market. A few steps down the skinny lane to the left is the endearing little **Historical Zone of the Free City of Gdańsk** museum, which explains the interwar period when "Danzig" was an independent and bicultural city-state.

• *Now go through the gate, walk out onto the Green Bridge, anchor yourself in a niche on the left, and look downstream.*

Riverfront Embankment

The Motława River—a side channel of the mighty Vistula—flows into the nearby Baltic Sea. This port was the source of Gdańsk's phenomenal Golden Age wealth. This embankment was jam-packed in its heyday, the 14th and 15th centuries. It was so crowded with boats that you would hardly have been able to see the water, and boats had to pay a time-based moorage fee for tying up to a post.

Look back at the Green Gate and notice that these bricks are much smaller than the locally-made ones we saw earlier on this walk. These bricks are Dutch: Boats from Holland would come here empty of cargo, but with a load of bricks for ballast. Traders filled their ships with goods for the return trip, leaving the bricks behind.

The old-fashioned **galleons** and other tour boats moored nearby depart hourly for a fun cruise to Westerplatte (where on September 1, 1939, Germans fired the first shots of World War II) and back.

Across the river is **Granary Island** (Wyspa Spichrzów), where grain was stored until it could be taken away by ships. Before World War II, there were some 400 granaries here. Today, much of the island is still in ruins while developers make their plans. Recently, the city ringed the island with an inviting boardwalk, which offers a restful escape from the city and fine views across the narrow river to the embankment. In the summer, sometimes they erect a big Ferris wheel here. And someday there will be several more rebuilt granaries in this area (likely mixed with modern buildings) to match the ones you already see on either side of the bridge. The three rebuilt granaries downstream, in the distance on the next island, house exhibits for the National Maritime Museum (described later).

From your perch on the bridge, look down the embankment (about 500 yards, on the left) and find the huge wooden **Crane (Żuraw)** bulging over the water. This monstrous 15th-century crane—a rare example of medieval port technology—was once used for loading and repairing ships...beginning a shipbuilding tradition that continued to the days of Lech Wałęsa. The crane mechanism was operated by several workers scrambling around in giant hamster wheels. Treading away to engage the

gears and pulleys, they could lift 4 tons up 30 feet, or 2 tons up 90 feet.

• *Walk along the embankment about halfway to the Crane, passing the lower embankment, with excursion boats heading to the Westerplatte monument. Pause when you reach the big brick building with green window frames and a tower. This red-brick fort houses the **Archaeological Museum**. Its collection includes the five ancient stones in a small garden just outside its door (on the left). These are the **Prussian Hags**— mysterious sculptures from the second century A.D. (each described in posted plaques).*

Turn left through the gate in the middle of the brick building. You'll find yourself on the most charming lane in town...

Mariacka Street

The calm, atmospheric "Mary's Street" leads from the embankment to St. Mary's Church. Stroll the length of it, enjoying the most romantic lane in Gdańsk. The **porches** extending out into the street, with access to cellars underneath, were a common feature in Gdańsk's Golden Age. For practical reasons, after the war, these were restored only on this street. Notice how the porches are bordered with fine stone relief panels and gargoyles attached to storm drains. If you get stuck there in a hard rainstorm, you'll understand why in Polish these are called "pukers." Enjoy a little amber comparison-shopping. As you stroll up to the towering brick St. Mary's Church, imagine the entire city like this cobbled lane of proud merchants' homes, with street music, delightful facades, and brick church towers high above.

Look up at the church tower viewpoint—filled with people who hiked 409 steps for the view. Our next stop is the church, which you'll enter on the far side under the tower. Walk around the left side of the church, appreciating the handmade 14th-century bricks on the right and the plain post-WWII facades on the left.

(Reconstructing the Royal Way was better funded. Here, the priority was simply getting people housed again.) In the distance is the fancy facade of the armory (where you'll head after visiting the church).

• *But first, go inside...*

St. Mary's Church (Kościół Mariacki)

Of Gdańsk's 13 medieval red-brick churches, St. Mary's (rated ▲▲) is the one you must visit. It's the largest brick church in the world—with a footprint bigger than a football field (350 feet long and 210 feet wide), it can accommodate 20,000 standing worshippers.

Cost and Hours: 4 zł, 6 zł with tower climb—described later; Mon-Sat 8:30-18:30, Sun 11:00-12:00 & 13:00-18:30; Oct-April daily until 17:00; tower closed Dec-late March.

❂ Self-Guided Tour

Inside, sit directly under the fine carved and painted 17th-century Protestant pulpit, midway down the nave, to get oriented.

Overview: Built from 1343 to 1502 by the Teutonic Knights (who wanted a suitable centerpiece for their newly-captured main city), St. Mary's remains an important symbol of Gdańsk. The church started out Catholic, became Lutheran in the mid-1500s, and then became Catholic again after World War II. (Remember, Gdańsk was a Germanic city before World War II and part of the big postwar demographic shove, when Germans were sent west, and Poles from the east relocated here. Desperate, cold, and homeless, the new Polish residents moved into what was left of the German homes.) While the church was originally frescoed from top to bottom, the Lutherans whitewashed the entire place. Today, some of the 16th-century whitewash has been peeled back (behind the high altar—we'll see this area soon), revealing a bit of the original frescoes. The floor is paved with 500 gravestones of merchant families. Many of these were cracked when bombing sent the brick roof crashing down in 1945.

Most Gothic stone churches are built of stone in the basilica style—with a high nave in the middle, shorter aisles on the side, and flying buttresses to support the weight. (Think of Paris' Notre-Dame.) But with no handy source of stone available locally, most Polish churches are built of brick, which won't work with the basilica design. So, like all Gdańsk churches, St. Mary's is a "hall church"—with three naves the same height and no exterior buttresses.

GDAŃSK

Also like other Gdańsk churches, St. Mary's gave refuge to the Polish people after the communist government declared martial law in 1981. When a riot broke out and violence seemed imminent, people flooded into churches, knowing that the ZOMO riot police wouldn't dare follow them inside.

Most of the church decorations are original. A few days before the Soviets arrived to "liberate" the city in 1945, locals—knowing what was in store—hid precious items in the countryside. Take some time now to see a few of the highlights.

• *From this spot, you can see most of what we'll visit in the church: As you face the altar, the astronomical clock is at 10 o'clock, the Ferber family medallion is at 1 o'clock, the Priests' Chapel is at 3 o'clock (under a tall, colorful window), and the magnificent 17th-century organ is directly behind you (it's played at each Mass and during free concerts on Fri in summer).*

Pulpit: For Protestants, the pulpit is important. Designed as an impressive place from which to share the Word of God in the people's language, it's located midnave, so all can hear.

• *Opposite the pulpit is the moving...*

Priests' Chapel: The 1965 statue of Christ weeping commemorates 2,779 Polish chaplains executed by the Nazis because they were priests. See the grainy black-and-white photo of one about to be shot, above on the right.

• *Head up the nave to the...*

High Altar: The main altar, beautifully carved in 1517, is a triptych showing the coronation of Mary. She is surrounded by the Trinity: flanked by God and Jesus, with the dove representing the Holy Spirit overhead. The church's medieval stained glass was destroyed in 1945. Poland's biggest stained-glass window, behind the altar, is from 1980.

• *Start circling around the right side of the altar. Look right to find (high on a pillar) the big, opulent family marker.*

Ferber Family Medallion: The falling baby (under the crown) is Constantine Ferber. As a precocious child, li'l Constantine leaned out his window on the Royal Way to see the king's processional come through town. He slipped and fell, but landed in a salesman's barrel of fish. Constantine grew up to become the mayor of Gdańsk.

• *As you continue around behind the altar, search high above you, on the walls to your right, to spot those restored pre-Reformation frescoes. Directly behind the altar, under the big window, is the...*

Empty Glass Case: This case was designed to hold Hans Memling's *Last Judgment* painting, which used to be in this church, but is currently being held hostage by the National Museum in Gdańsk. To counter the museum's claim that the church wasn't a good environment for such a precious work, the priest had this display case built—but that still wasn't enough to convince the museum to give the painting back. (You'll see a small replica of the painting in the rear of this church.)

• *Now circle back the way you came to the area in front of the main altar, and proceed straight ahead into the transept. High on the wall to your right, look for the...*

Astronomical Clock: This 42-foot-tall clock is supposedly the biggest wooden clock in the world. Below it is an elaborate circular calendar that, like a medieval computer, calculates on which day each saint's festival day falls in different years (see the little guy on the left, with the pointer). Above are zodiac signs and the time (back then, the big hand was all you needed). Way up on top, Adam and Eve are naked and ready to ring the bell. Adam's been swinging his clapper at the top of the hour since 1473...but sadly, the clock is broken.

• *A few steps in front of the clock is a modern chapel with the...*

Memorial to the Polish Victims of the 2010 Plane Crash: The gold-shrouded Black Madonna honors the 96 victims of an air disaster that killed much of Poland's government—including the president and first lady—during a terrible storm over Russia. The main tomb is for Maciej Płażyński, from Gdańsk, who was leader of the parliament. On the left, the jagged statue has bits of the wreckage and lists each victim by name.

• *In a small chapel in the rear corner of the church—on the far right with your back to the high altar—you'll find the...*

Pietà and Memling Replica: The pietà, carved of limestone and painted in 1410, is by the Master of Gdańsk. In the same room is a musty old copy of Memling's *Last Judgment*—the exquisite original once graced this very chapel.

• *Next door are stairs leading to the...*

Church Tower: You can climb 409 steps to burn off some pierogi and earn a grand city view. It's a long hike (and you'll know it—every 10th step is numbered). But because the viewpoint is surrounded by a roof, the views are distant and may not be worth the effort. The first third is up a tight, medieval spiral staircase. Then you'll walk through the eerie, cavernous area between the roof and the ceiling, before huffing up steep concrete steps that surround the square tower (as you spiral up, up, up around the bells). Finally you'll climb a little metal ladder and pop out at the viewpoint.

• *Leaving the church, angle left and continue straight up ulica Piwna ("Beer Street") toward the sprightly facade of the armory.*

Gdańsk Armory (Zbrojownia)

The 1605 armory, which we saw from a distance at the start of this walk, is one of the best examples of Dutch Renaissance architecture in Europe. Athena, the goddess of war and wisdom, stands in the center, amid motifs of war and ornamental pukers.

• *If you want to make your walk a loop, you're just a block away from where we started (to the left). But there's much more to see. Facing the armory, turn right and start the second half of this walk.*

PART 2: THROUGH THE OLD TOWN TO THE SHIPYARDS

• *From here, we'll work our way out of the Main Town and head into the Old Town, toward Solidarity Square and the shipyards. We'll be walking along this street (which changes names a couple of times) nearly all the way. Keep in mind that this part of the walk ends at the European Solidarity Center's fine museum.*

From the armory, head down Kołodziejska, which quickly becomes Węglarska. After two blocks (that is, one block before the big market hall), detour to the right down Świętojańska and use the side door to enter the brick church.

St. Nicholas Church (Kościół Św. Mikołaja)

Near the end of World War II, when the Soviet army reached Gdańsk on its march westward, they were given the order to burn all the churches. Only this one survived—because it happened to be dedicated to Russia's patron saint. As the best-preserved church in town, it has a more impressive interior than the others, with lavish black-and-gold Baroque altars.

• *Backtrack out to the main street and continue along it, passing a row of seniors selling their grown and foraged edibles. Immediately after the church is Gdańsk's...*

Market Hall

Built in 1896 and renovated in 2005, Gdańsk's market hall is fun to explore. Appreciate the delicate steel-and-glass canopy overhead. This is a totally untouristy scene: You'll see everything from skintight *Polska* T-shirts, to wedding gowns, to maternity wear. The meat is downstairs, and the veggies are outside on the adjacent square. As this was once the center of a monastic community, the basement has the graves of medieval Dominican monks, which were exposed when the building was refurbished: Peer over the glass railing, and you'll see some of those scant remains.

Across the street from the Market Hall, a round, red-brick **tower,** part of the city's protective wall back in 1400, marks the end of the Main Town and the beginning of the Old Town.

• *Another block up the street, on the right, is the huge...*

St. Catherine's Church (Kościół Św. Katarzyny)

"Katy," as locals call it, is the oldest church in Gdańsk. In May of 2006, a carelessly discarded cigarette caused the church roof to burst into flames. Local people ran into the church and pulled everything outside, so nothing valuable was damaged; even the carillon bells were saved. However, the roof and wooden frame were totally destroyed. The people of Gdańsk were determined to rebuild this important symbol of the city. Within days of the fire, fundraising concerts were held to scrape together most of the money needed to raise the roof once more. Step inside. On the left side of the gate leading to the nave, photos show bomb damage. Farther in, on the left, are vivid photos of the more recent conflagration. The interior is evocative, with still-bare-brick walls that almost seem intentional—as if they're trying for an industrial-mod look.

• *The church hiding a block behind Katy—named for Catherine's daughter Bridget—has important ties to Solidarity and is worth a visit. Go around the right side of Katy and skirt the parking lot to find the entrance.*

St. Bridget's Church (Kościół Św. Brygidy)

This was the home church of Lech Wałęsa during the tense days of the 1980s. The church and its priest, Henryk Jankowski, were particularly aggressive in supporting the ideals of Solidarity. Jankowski became a mouthpiece for the movement. In gratitude for the church's support, Wałęsa named his youngest daughter Brygida.

Cost and Hours: 2 zł, daily 10:00-18:00.

Visiting the Church: Head inside. For your visit, start at the high altar, then circle clockwise back to the entry.

The enormous, unfinished **high altar** is made entirely of amber—more than a thousand square feet of it. Features that are already in place include the Black Madonna of Częstochowa, a royal Polish eagle, and the Solidarity symbol (tucked below the Black Madonna). The structure, like a scaffold, holds pieces as they are completed and added to the ensemble. The video you may see playing overhead gives you a close-up look at the amber elements.

The wrought-iron gate of the adjacent **Chapel of Fatima** (right of main altar) recalls great battles and events in Polish history from 966 to 1939, with important dates boldly sparkling in gold. Some say the Polish Church is too political. But it was only through a politically-engaged Church that this culture survived the Partitions of Poland over a century and a half, plus the brutal anti-religious policies of the communist period. The national soul of the Polish people—whether religious or not—is tied up in the Catholic faith.

Henryk Jankowski's tomb—a white marble box with red trim—is a bit farther to the right. Jankowski was a key hero during Solidarity times; the tomb proclaims him *Kapelan Solidarności* ("Solidarity Chaplain"). But his public standing took a nosedive near the end of his life—thanks to ego-driven projects like his amber altar, as well as accusations of anti-Semitism and corruption. Forced to retire in 2007, Jankowski died in 2010. (An offering box is next to his tomb, if you'd like to donate to the amber altar project.)

In the rear corner, where a figure lies lifeless on the floor under a wall full of wooden crosses, is the tomb of Solidarity martyr **Jerzy Popiełuszko**. A courageous and famously outspoken Warsaw priest, in 1984 Popiełuszko was kidnapped, beaten, and murdered by the communist secret police. Notice that the figure's hands and feet are bound—as his body was found. The crosses are historic— each one was carried at various strikes against the communist regime. The communists believed they could break the spirit of the Poles with brutality—like the murder of Popiełuszko. But it only made the rebels stronger and more resolved to ultimately win their freedom. (Near the exit, on a monitor, a fascinating 12-minute video shows great moments of this church, with commentary by Lech Wałęsa himself.)

• *Return to the main street, turn right, and continue on. The big brick building ahead on the left, with the many windows, is the Great Mill. Walk past that and look down at the canal that once powered it.*

The Great Mill

This huge brick building dates from the 14th century. Look at the waterfalls and imagine standing here in 1400—with the mill's 18

wheels spinning 24/7, powering grindstones that produced 20 tons of flour a day. Like so much else here, the mill survived until 1945. Until recently it housed a shopping mall, but it may soon become home to one of the city's many museums.

The **park** just beyond the mill is worth a look. In the distance is the Old City Town Hall (Dutch Renaissance style, from 1595). The monument in the middle honors the 17th-century astronomer Jan Haweliusz. He's looking up at a giant, rust-colored wall with a map of the heavens. Haweliusz built the biggest telescopes of his era to better appreciate and understand the cosmos. Behind the mill stands the miller's home—its opulence indicates that, back in the Middle Ages, there was a lot of money in grinding. Just steps into the family-friendly park is a fountain that brings shrieks of joy to children on hot summer days.

• *To get to the **shipyards**, keep heading straight up Rajska. You'll pass the modern Madison shopping mall. After another long block, jog right, passing to the right of the big, ugly, and green 1970s–era skyscraper. On your right, marked by the famous red sign on the roof, is today's **Solidarity headquarters** (which remains the strongest trade union in Poland, with 700,000 members, and is also active in many other countries). Just in front of the Solidarity building, you may see two big chunks of **wall**: a piece of the Berlin Wall and a stretch of the shipyard wall that Lech Wałęsa scaled to get inside and lead the strike. The message: What happened behind one wall eventually led to the fall of the other Wall.*

From here, hike on (about 100 yards) to the finale of this walk.

Solidarity Square and the Shipyards

Three tall crosses mark Solidarity Square and the rust-colored European Solidarity Center (with an excellent museum). For the exciting story of how Polish shipbuilders set in motion events that led to the end of the USSR, turn to page 501.

Sights in Gdańsk

The following sights are all in the Main Town, listed roughly in the order you'll see them on the self-guided walk of the Royal Way (except for the National Maritime Museum, which sits on the riverfront).

Gdańsk Historical Museum

The Gdańsk Historical Museum has four excellent branches: the Amber Museum, Uphagen House, Main Town Hall, and Artus Court. Along with St. Mary's Church (described earlier), these are the four most important interiors in the Main Town. All have the same hours, but you must buy a separate ticket for each.

Cost and Hours: 10 zł for Uphagen House and Artus Court, 12 zł for Amber Museum and Main Town Hall; hours fluctuate, but typically open mid-June-mid-Sept Mon-Thu 9:00-16:00, Fri-Sat 10:00-18:00, Sun 10:00-16:00; mid-Sept-mid-June Tue 10:00-13:00, Wed-Sat until 16:00, Thu until 18:00, Sun 11:00-16:00, closed Mon.

Information: The museums share a phone number and website (central tel. 58-767-9100, www.mhmg.pl).

▲Amber Museum (Muzeum Bursztynu)

Housed in a pair of connected brick towers (the former Prison Tower and Torture Chamber) just outside the Main Town's Golden Gate, this museum has two oddly contradictory parts. One shows

All About Amber

Poland's Baltic seaside is known as the Amber Coast. You can see amber *(bursztyn)* in Gdańsk's Amber Museum, and in shop windows everywhere. This fossilized tree resin originated here on the north coast of Poland 40 million years ago. It comes in as many different colors as Eskimos have words for snow: 300 distinct shades, from yellowish white to yellowish black, from opaque to transparent. (I didn't believe it either, until I toured Gdańsk's museum.) Almost 75 percent of the world's amber is mined in northern Poland, and it often simply washes up on the beaches after a winter storm.

Some Poles believe that, in addition to being good for the economy, amber is good for their health. A traditional cure for arthritis pain is to pour strong vodka over amber, let it set, and then rub it on sore joints. Other remedies call for mixing amber dust with honey or rose oil. It sounds superstitious, but users claim that it works.

off Gdańsk's favorite local resource, amber, while the other focuses on implements of torture. You'll follow the one-way route through four exhibits on amber (with lots of stairs), and then walk the rampart to the Prison Tower and the torture exhibit—with sound effects, scant artifacts, and mannequins helpfully demonstrating the grisly equipment (the 1.5-hour audioguide is overpriced at 25 zł). For a primer before you visit, read the "All About Amber" sidebar.

GDAŃSK

▲Uphagen House (Dom Uphagena)

This interesting place, at ulica Długa 12, is your chance to glimpse what's behind the colorful facades lining this street. It's the only grand Gdańsk mansion rebuilt as it was before 1945. The model near the entry shows the three parts: dolled-up visitors' rooms in front, a corridor along the courtyard, and private rooms in the back. The finely decorated salon was used to show off for guests. Most of this furniture is original (saved from WWII bombs by locals who hid it in the countryside). Passing into the dining room, note the knee-high paintings of hunting and celebrations. Along the passage to the back, each room has a theme: butterflies in the smoking room, then flowers in the next room, then birds in the music room. In the private rooms at the back, the decor is simpler. Downstairs, you'll pass through the kitchen, the pantry, and a room with photos of the house before the war, which were used to reconstruct what you see today.

▲▲Main Town Hall (Ratusz Głównego Miasta)

This landmark building contains remarkable decorations from Gdańsk's Golden Age. Inside, you'll pass through an ornately-carved wooden **door** from the 1600s into the lavish **Red Hall,** where the Gdańsk city council met in the summertime, then into the less-impressive **Winter Hall,** and finally through another room into one with photos of **WWII damage.** Up-stairs are some temporary exhibits and several examples of **Gdańsk-style furniture** (characterized by lots of ornamentation) and a coin collection, from the days when Gdańsk had the elite privilege of minting its own currency. Head upstairs to a fascinating exhibit about Gdańsk's time as a **"free city"** between the World

Wars. Near the end of this room, you have the option to climb 293 concrete steps to the top of the tower for commanding views (5 zł extra, mid-June–mid-Sept only).

▲▲Artus Court (Dwór Artusa)

In the Middle Ages, Gdańsk was home to many brotherhoods and guilds (like businessmen's clubs). For their meetings, the city

provided this elaborately decorated hall, named for King Arthur—a medieval symbol for prestige and power. Just as in King Arthur's Court, this was a place where powerful and important people came together. Of many such halls in Baltic Europe, this is the only original one that survives (skip the dry and too-thorough audioguide; in tall, white, triple-arched building behind Neptune statue at Długi Targ 43).

▲National Maritime Museum
(Narodowe Muzeum Morskie)

Gdańsk's history and livelihood are tied to the sea. This collection, spread among several buildings on either side of the river, examines all aspects of this connection. Nautical types may get a thrill out of the creaky, sprawling museum, but most visitors find it little more

GDAŃSK

than a convenient way to pass some time and enjoy a cruise across the river. The museum's lack of English information is frustrating; fortunately, some exhibits have descriptions you can borrow.

Cost and Hours: Each part of the museum has its own admission (6-8 zł; ask about combo-tickets). It's open July-Aug daily 10:00-18:00; Sept-June shorter hours and closed Mon; ulica Ołowianka 9, tel. 58-301-8611, www.cmm.pl.

SOLIDARITY AND THE GDAŃSK SHIPYARD

Gdańsk's single most memorable experience is exploring the shipyard (Stocznia Gdańska) that witnessed the beginning of the end of communism's stranglehold on Eastern Europe. Taken together, the sights in this area are worth ▲▲▲. Here in the former industrial wasteland that Lech Wałęsa called the "cradle of freedom," this evocative site tells the story of the brave Polish shipyard workers who took on—and ultimately defeated—an Evil Empire. A visit to the Solidarity sights has two main parts: Solidarity Square (with the memorial and gate in front of the shipyard), and the outstanding museum inside the European Solidarity Center.

Getting to the Shipyard: These sights cluster around Solidarity Square (Plac Solidarności), at the north end of the Old Town, about a 20-minute walk from the Royal Way. For the most interesting approach, follow "Part 2" of my self-guided walk (earlier), which ends here.

Background: After the communists took over Eastern Europe at the end of World War II, oppressed peoples throughout the Soviet Bloc rose up in different ways. The most dramatic uprisings—Hungary's 1956 Uprising and Czechoslovakia's 1968 "Prague Spring"—were brutally crushed under the treads of Soviet tanks. The formula for freedom that finally succeeded was a patient, nearly decade-long series of strikes and protests spearheaded by Lech Wałęsa and his trade union, called Solidarność—"Solidarity." (The movement also benefited from good timing, as it coincided with the *perestroika* and *glasnost* policies of Soviet premier Mikhail Gorbachev.) While some American politicians might like to take credit for defeating communism, Wałęsa and his fellow workers were the ones fighting on the front lines, armed with nothing more than guts.

Solidarity Square (Plac Solidarności)

The seeds of August 1980 were sown a decade before. Since becoming part of the Soviet Bloc, the Poles staged frequent strikes, protests, and uprisings to secure their rights, all of which were put down by the regime. But the bloodiest of these took place in December 1970—a tragic event memorialized by the **"Monument**

Lech Wałęsa

In 1980, the world was turned on its ear by a walrus-mustachioed shipyard electrician. Within three years, this seemingly run-of-the-mill Pole had precipitated the collapse of communism, led a massive 10-million-member trade union with enormous political impact, been named *Time* magazine's Man of the Year, and won a Nobel Peace Prize.

Lech Wałęsa was born in Popowo, Poland in 1943. After working as a car mechanic and serving two years in the army, he became an electrician at the Gdańsk Shipyard in 1967. Like many Poles, Wałęsa felt stifled by the communist government, and was infuriated that a system that was supposed to be for the workers clearly wasn't serving them.

When the shipyard massacre took place in December of 1970, Wałęsa was at the forefront of the protests. He was marked as a dissident, and in 1976, he was fired. Wałęsa hopped from job to job and was occasionally unemployed. But he soldiered on, fighting for the creation of a trade union and building up quite a file with the secret police.

In August 1980, Wałęsa heard news of the beginnings of the Gdańsk strike and raced to the shipyard. In an act that has since

of the Fallen Shipyard Workers," whose three crosses tower over what's now called Solidarity Square.

The 1970 strike was prompted by price hikes. The communist government set the prices for all products. As Poland endured drastic food shortages in the 1960s and 1970s, the regime frequently announced what it called "regulation of prices." Invariably, this meant an increase in the cost of essential foodstuffs. (To be able to claim "regulation" rather than "increase," the regime would symbolically lower prices for a few select items—but these were always non-essential luxuries, such as elevators and TV sets, which nobody could afford anyway.) The regime was usually smart enough to raise prices on January 1, when the people were fat and happy after Christmas, and too hungover to complain. But on December 12, 1970, bolstered by an ego-stoking

become the stuff of legend, Wałęsa scaled the shipyard wall to get inside.

Before long, Wałęsa's dynamic personality won him the unofficial role of the workers' leader and spokesman. He negotiated with the regime to hash out the August Agreements, becoming a rock star-type hero during the so-called 16 Months of Hope... until martial law came crashing down in December 1981. Wałęsa was arrested and interned for 11 months. After being released, he continued to struggle underground, becoming a symbol of anticommunist sentiment.

Finally, the dedication of Wałęsa and Solidarity paid off, and Polish communism dissolved—with Wałęsa rising from the ashes as the country's first postcommunist president. But the skills that made Wałęsa a rousing success at leading an uprising didn't translate well to the president's office. Wałęsa proved to be a stubborn, headstrong politician, frequently clashing with the parliament and squabbling with his own party.

Wałęsa was defeated at the polls, by the Poles, in 1995, and when he ran again in 2000, he received a humiliating one percent of the vote. Since leaving office, Wałęsa has kept a lower profile, but still delivers speeches worldwide. Poles say there are two Lech Wałęsas: the young, bombastic, working-class idealist Lech, at the forefront of the Solidarity strikes, who will always have a special place in their hearts; and the failed President Wałęsa, who got in over his head and tarnished his legacy.

visit by West German Chancellor Willy Brandt, Polish premier Władysław Gomułka increased prices. The people of Poland—who cared more about the price of Christmas dinner than relations with Germany—struck back.

A wave of strikes and sit-ins spread along the heavily industrialized north coast of Poland, most notably in Gdańsk, Gdynia, and Szczecin. Thousands of angry demonstrators poured through the gate of this shipyard, marched into town, and set fire to the Communist Party Committee building. In an attempt to quell the riots, the government-run radio implored the people to go back to work. On the morning of December 17, workers showed up at shipyard gates across northern Poland, and were greeted by the army and police. Without provocation, the Polish army opened fire on the workers. While the official death toll for the massacre stands at 44, others say the true number is much higher. The monument, with a trio of 140-foot-tall crosses, honors those lost to the regime that December.

Go to the middle of the **wall** behind the crosses, to the monument of the worker wearing a flimsy plastic work helmet, attempting to shield himself from bullets. Behind him is a list—pockmarked with symbolic bullet holes—of workers murdered on that day. *Lat* means "years old"—many teenagers were among the dead. The quote at the top of the wall is from St. John Paul II, who was elected pope eight years after this tragedy. The pope was known for his clever way with words, and this very carefully phrased quote—which served as an inspiration to the Poles during their darkest hours—skewers the regime in a way subtle enough to still be tolerated: "Let thy spirit descend, and renew the face of the earth—of *this* earth" (that is, Poland). Below that is the dedication: "They gave their lives so you can live decently."

Stretching to the left of this center wall are plaques representing labor unions from around Poland—and around the world (look for the Chinese characters)—expressing solidarity with these workers. To the right is an enormous Bible verse: "May the Lord give strength to his people. May the Lord bless his people with the gift of peace" (Psalms 29:11).

Inspired by the brave sacrifice of their true comrades, shipyard workers rose up here in August 1980, formulating the "21 Points" of a new union called Solidarity. Their demands included the right to strike and form unions, the freeing of political prisoners, and an increase in wages. The 21 Points are listed in Polish on the panel at the far end of the right wall, marked *21 X TAK* ("21 times yes"). An unwritten precondition to any agreement was the right for the workers of 1980 to build a memorial to their comrades slain in 1970. The government agreed, marking the first time a communist regime ever allowed a monument to be built to honor its own victims. Wałęsa called it a harpoon in the heart of the communists. The towering monument, with three crucified anchors on top, was designed, engineered, and built by shipyard workers. The monument was finished just four months after the historic agreement was signed.

• *Now continue to the gate and peer through into the birthplace of Eastern European freedom.*

Gdańsk Shipyard (Stocznia Gdańska) Gate #2

When a Pole named Karol Wojtyła was elected pope in 1978—and visited his homeland in 1979—he inspired his 40 million countrymen to believe that impossible dreams can come true. Prices continued to go up, and the workers continued to rise up. By the summer of 1980, it was clear that the dam was about to break.

In August, Anna Walentynowicz—a Gdańsk crane operator and known dissident—was fired unceremoniously just short of her retirement. This sparked a strike in the Gdańsk Shipyard (then called the Lenin Shipyard) on August 14, 1980. An electrician named Lech Wałęsa had been fired as an agitator years before and wasn't allowed into the yard. But on hearing news of the strike, Wałęsa went to the shipyard and climbed over the wall to get inside. The strike now had a leader.

These were not soldiers, nor were they idealistic flower children. The strike participants were gritty, salt-of-the-earth manual laborers forklift operators, welders, electricians, machinists. Imagine being one of the 16,000 workers who stayed here for 18 days during the strike—hungry, cold, sleeping on sheets of Styrofoam, inspired by the new Polish pope, excited about finally standing up to the regime...and terrified that at any moment you might be

gunned down, like your friends had been a decade before. Workers, afraid to leave the shipyard, communicated with the outside world through this gate—wives and brothers showed up here and asked for a loved one, and those inside spread the word until the striker came forward. Occasionally, a truck pulled up inside the gate, with Lech Wałęsa standing atop its cab with a megaphone. Facing the thousands of people assembled outside the gate, Wałęsa gave progress reports on the negotiations and pleaded for supplies. The people of Gdańsk responded, bringing armfuls of bread and other food to keep the workers going. Solidarity.

During the strike, two items hung on the fence. One of them (which still hangs there today) was a picture of Pope John Paul II—a reminder to believe in your dreams and have faith in God. The other item was a makeshift list of the strikers' 21 Points—demands scrawled in red paint and black pencil on pieces of plywood.

• *Walk around the right end of the gate and enter the former shipyard.*

The shipyard churned out over a thousand ships from 1948 to 1990, employing 16,000 workers. About 60 percent of these ships were exported to the USSR—and so, when the Soviet Bloc broke apart in the 1990s, they lost a huge market. Today the facilities employ closer to 1,200 workers...who now make windmills.

Before entering the museum, take a look around. This part of the shipyard, long abandoned, is being redeveloped into a **"Young City"** (Młode Miasto)—envisioned as a new city center for Gdańsk, with shopping, restaurants, offices, and homes. Rusting shipbuilding equipment has been torn down, and old brick buildings are being converted into gentrified flats. The nearby boulevard called Nowa Wałowa will be the spine connecting this area to the rest of the city. Farther east, the harborfront will also be rejuvenated, creating a glitzy marina and extending the city's delightful waterfront people zone to the north (see www.ycgdansk.com). Fortunately, the shipyard gate, monument, and other important sites from the Solidarity strikes—now considered historical monuments—will remain.

• *The massive, rust-colored European Solidarity Center, which faces Solidarity Square, houses the museum where we'll learn the rest of the story.*

▲▲▲European Solidarity Center (Europejskie Centrum Solidarności)

Europe's single best sight about the end of communism is made even more powerful by its location: in the very heart of the place where those events occurred.

Filling just one small corner of a huge, purpose-built educational facility, the permanent exhibition uses larger-than-life photographs, archival footage, actual artifacts, interactive touchscreens, and a state-of-the-art audioguide to eloquently tell the story of the end of Eastern European communism.

Cost and Hours: 20 zł, includes audioguide, Mon–Fri 10:00–19:00, Sat–Sun until 20:00; Oct–April Mon and Wed–Fri 10:00–17:00, Sat–Sun until 18:00, closed Tue; last entry one hour before closing, Plac Solidarności 1, tel. 506-195-673, www.ecs.gda.pl.

⊙ Self-Guided Tour: First, appreciate the architecture of the **building** itself. From the outside, it's designed to resemble the rusted hull of a giant ship—seemingly gloomy and depressing. But step inside to find an interior flooded with light, which cultivates a surprising variety of life—in the form of lush gardens that make the place feel like a very expensive greenhouse. You can interpret this symbolism a number of ways: Something that seems dull and dreary from the outside (the Soviet Bloc, the shipyards themselves, what have you) can be full of brightness, life, and optimism inside.

In the lobby, buy your ticket and pick up the essential, included audioguide. The exhibit has much to see, and some of it is arranged in a conceptual way that can be tricky to understand without a full grasp of the history. I've outlined the basics in this self-guided tour, but the audioguide can illuminate more details—including translations of films and eyewitness testimony from participants in the history.

• *The permanent exhibit fills seven lettered rooms—each with its own theme—on two floors. From the lush lobby, head up the escalator and into...*

The Birth of Solidarity (Room A): This room picks up right in the middle of the dynamic story we just learned out on the square. It's August 1980, and the shipyard workers are rising up. You step straight into a busy shipyard: punch clocks, workers' lockers, and—up on the ceiling—hundreds of plastic helmets. A big **map** in the middle of the room shows the extent of the shipyard in 1980. Inside the cab of the **crane**, you can watch an interview with spunky Anna Walentynowicz, whose firing led to the first round of strikes. Nearby stands a **truck;** Lech Wałęsa would stand on top of the cab of a truck like this one to address the nervous locals who had amassed outside the shipyard gate, awaiting further news.

In the middle of the room, carefully protected under glass, are those original **plywood panels** onto which the strikers scrawled their 21 demands, then lashed to the gate. Just beyond that, a giant wall of photos and a map illustrate how the strikes that began here spread like a virus across Poland. At the far end of the room, behind the partition, stand **two tables** that were used during the talks to end the strikes (each one with several actual items from that era, under glass).

After 18 days of protests, the communist authorities finally agreed to negotiate. On the afternoon of August 31, 1980, the Governmental Commission and the Inter-Factory Strike Committee (MKS) came together and signed the August Agreements, which legalized Solidarity—the first time any communist government permitted a workers' union. As Lech Wałęsa sat at a big table and signed the agreement, other union reps tape-recorded the proceedings and played them later at their own factories to prove that the unthinkable had happened. Take a moment to linger over the rousing **film** that plays on the far wall, which begins with the strike, carries through with the tense negotiations that a brash young Lech Wałęsa held with the authorities, and ends with the triumphant acceptance of the strikers' demands. Lech Wałęsa rides on the shoulders of well-wishers out to the gate to spread the good news.

• *Back by the original 21 demands, enter the next exhibit...*

The Power of the Powerless (Room B): This section traces the roots of the 1980 strikes, which were preceded by several far less successful protests. It all begins with a kiss: a giant photograph of Russian premier Leonid Brezhnev mouth-kissing the Polish premier Edward Gierek, with the caption **"Brotherly Friendship."** Soviet premiers and their satellite leaders really did greet each other "in the French manner," as a symbolic gesture of their communist brotherhood.

Working your way through the exhibit, you'll see the door to a **prison cell**—a reminder of the intimidation tactics used by the

Soviets in the 1940s and 1950s to deal with their opponents as they exerted their rule over the lands they had liberated from the Nazis.

The typical **communist-era apartment** is painfully humble. After the war, much of Poland had been destroyed, and population shifts led to housing shortages. People had to make do with tiny spaces and ramshackle furnishings. Communist propaganda blares from both the radio and the TV.

A map shows **"red Europe"** (the USSR plus the satellites of Poland, Czechoslovakia, Hungary, and East Germany), and a **timeline** traces some of the smaller Soviet Bloc protests that led up to Solidarity: in East Germany in 1953, in Budapest and Poznań in 1956, the "Prague Spring" of 1968, and other 1968 protests in Poland.

In the wake of these uprisings, the communist authorities cracked down even harder. Peek into the **interrogation room,** with a wall of file cabinets and a lowly stool illuminated by a bright spotlight. (Notice that the white Polish eagle on the seal above the desk is missing its golden crown—during communism, the Poles were allowed to keep the eagle, but its crown was removed.)

The next exhibit presents a day-by-day rundown of the **1970 strikes,** from December 14 to 22, which resulted in the massacre of the workers who are honored by the monument in front of this building. A wall of mug shots gives way to exhibits chronicling the steady rise of dissent groups through the 1970s, culminating in the June 1976 protests in the city of Radom (prompted, like so many other uprisings, by unilateral price hikes).

• *Loop back through Room A, and proceed straight ahead into...*

Solidarity and Hope (Room C): While the government didn't take the August Agreements very seriously, the Poles did...and before long, 10 million of them—one out of every four, or effectively half the nation's workforce—joined Solidarity. So began what's often called the **"16 Months of Hope."** Newly legal, Solidarity continued to stage strikes and make its opposition known. Slick Solidarity posters and children's art convey the childlike enthusiasm with which the Poles seized their hard-won kernels of freedom. The communist authorities' hold on the Polish people began to slip. Support and aid from the outside world poured in, but the rest of the Soviet Bloc looked on nervously, and the Warsaw Pact army assembled at the Polish border and glared at the uprisers. The threat of invasion hung heavy in the air.

• *Exiting this room, head up the staircase and into...*

At War with Society (Room D): You're greeted by a wall of TV screens delivering a stern message. On Sunday morning, December 13, 1981, the Polish head of state, **General Wojciech Jaruzelski**—wearing his trademark dark glasses—appeared on national TV and announced the introduction of **martial law.** Solidarity was outlawed, and its leaders were arrested. Frightened Poles heard the announcement and looked out their windows to see Polish Army tanks rumbling through the snowy streets. (On the opposite wall, see footage of tanks and heavily armed soldiers intimidating their countrymen into compliance.) Jaruzelski claimed that he imposed martial law to prevent the Soviets from invading. Today, many historians question whether martial law was really necessary, though Jaruzelski remained unremorseful through his death in 2014.

Continuing deeper into the exhibit, you come to a **prisoner transport.** Climb up inside to watch chilling scenes of riots, demonstrations, and crackdowns by the ZOMO riot police. In one gruesome scene, a demonstrator is quite intentionally—and practically in slow motion—run over by a truck. From here, pass through a gauntlet of *milicja* riot-gear shields to see the truck crashing through a gate. Overhead are the uniforms of miners from the **Wujek mine** who were massacred on December 16, 1981 (their names are projected on the pile of coal below).

Martial law was a tragic, terrifying, and bleak time for the Polish people. It didn't, however, kill the Solidarity movement, which continued its fight after going underground. Passing prison cells, you'll see a wall plastered with handmade, underground posters and graffiti. Notice how in this era, **Solidarity propaganda** is much more primitive; circle around the other side of the wall to see several presses that were actually used in clandestine Solidarity print shops during this time. The outside world sent messages of support as well as supplies—represented by the big wall of cardboard boxes. This approval also came in the form of a Nobel Peace Prize for Lech Wałęsa in 1983; you'll see video clips of his wife accepting the award on his behalf (Wałęsa feared that if he traveled abroad to claim it, he would not be allowed back into the country).

• *But even in these darkest days, there were glimmers of hope. Enter...*

The Road to Democracy (Room E): By the time the Pope visited his homeland again in 1983, martial law had finally been lifted, and Solidarity—still technically illegal—was gaining momentum, gradually pecking away at the communists. Step into the small inner room with footage of the **Pope's third pilgrimage** to his homeland in 1987, by which time (thanks in no small part to his inspirational role in the ongoing revolution) the tide was turning.

Enter the room with the big, white **roundtable.** With the moral support of the pope and the entire Western world, the brave Poles were the first European country to throw off the shackles of communism when, in the spring of 1989, the "Roundtable Talks" led to the opening up of elections. (If you look through the viewfinders of the TV cameras in the corners, you'll see footage of those meetings.) The government arrogantly called for parliamentary elections, reserving 65 percent of seats for themselves.

In the next room, you can see Solidarity's strategy in those **elections:** On the right wall are posters showing Lech Wałęsa with each candidate. Another popular "get out the vote" measure was the huge poster of Gary Cooper—an icon of America, whom the Poles deeply respected and viewed as their friendly cousin across the Atlantic—except that, instead of a pistol, he's packing a ballot. Rousing reminders like this inspired huge voter turnout. The communists' plan backfired, as virtually every open seat went to Solidarity. It was the first time ever that opposition candidates had taken office in the Soviet Bloc. On the wall straight ahead, flashing a V-for-*wiktoria* sign, is a huge photo of Tadeusz Mazowiecki—an early leader of Solidarity, who became prime minister on June 4, 1989.

• *For the glorious aftermath, head into the final room.*

The Triumph of Freedom (Room F): This room is dominated by a gigantic **map of Eastern Europe.** A countdown clock on the right ticks off the departure of each country from communist clutches, as the Soviet Bloc "decomposes." You'll see how the success of Solidarity in Poland—and the ragtag determination of a scruffy band of shipyard workers right here in Gdańsk—inspired people all over Eastern Europe. By the winter of 1989, the Hungarians had opened their borders, the Berlin Wall had crumbled, and the Czechs and Slovaks had staged their Velvet Revolution. (Small viewing stations that circle the room reveal the detailed story for each country's own road to freedom.) Lech Wałęsa—the shipyard electrician who started it all by jumping over a wall—became the first president of postcommunist Poland. And a year later, in Poland's first true elections since World War II, 29 different parties won seats in the parliament. It was a free-election free-for-all.

In the middle of the room stands a white wall with **inspirational quotes** from St. John Paul II and Václav Havel—the Czech poet-turned-protester-turned-prisoner-turned-president—which are repeated in several languages. On the huge wall, the **Solidarity "graffiti"** is actually made up of thousands of little notes left behind by visitors to the museum. Feel free to grab a piece of paper and a pen and record your own reflections.

• *Finally, head downstairs and find the...*

St. John Paul II Room (Room G): Many visitors find that touring this museum—with vivid reminders of a dramatic and pivotal moment in history that took place in their own lifetimes and was brought about not by armies or presidents, but by everyday people—puts them in an emotional state of mind. Designed for silent reflection, this room overlooks the monument to those workers who were gunned down in 1970.

Shopping in Gdańsk

The big story in Gdańsk is amber *(bursztyn)*, a fossil resin available in all shades, shapes, and sizes (see the "All About Amber" sidebar, earlier). While you'll see amber sold all over town, the best place to browse and buy is along the atmospheric ulica Mariacka (between the Motława River and St. Mary's Church). This pretty street, with old-fashioned balconies and dozens of display cases, is fun to wander even if you're not a shopper. Other good places to buy amber are along the riverfront embankment and on ulica Długa.

To avoid rip-offs—such as amber that's been melted and reshaped—always buy it from a shop, not from someone standing on the street. (But note that most shops also have a display case and salesperson out front, which are perfectly legit.) Prices everywhere are about the same, so instead of seeking out a specific place, just window shop until you see what you want. Styles range from gaudy necklaces with huge globs of amber, to tasteful smaller pendants in silver settings, to cheap trinkets. All shades of amber—from near-white to dark brown—cost about the same, but you'll pay more for inclusions (bugs or other objects stuck in the amber).

Gdańsk also has several modern shopping malls, most of them in the Old Town or near the main train station. The walk between the Main Town and the Solidarity shipyard earlier goes past some of the best malls.

Eating in Gdańsk

In addition to traditional Polish fare, Gdańsk has some excellent Baltic seafood. Herring *(śledź)* is popular here, as is cod *(dorsz)*. Natives brag that their salmon *(łosoś)* is better than Norway's. For a stiff drink, sample *Goldwasser* (similar to Goldschlager). This sweet and strong liqueur, flecked with actual gold, was supposedly invented here in Gdańsk. The following options are all in the Main Town, within three blocks of the Royal Way.

BUDGET RESTAURANTS IN THE CITY CENTER

These places are affordable, tasty, quick, and wonderfully convenient—on or very near the Royal Way (ulica Długa). They're worth considering even if you're not on a tight budget.

$ Bar pod Rybą ("Under the Fish") is nirvana for fans of baked potatoes *(pieczony ziemniak)*. They offer more than 20 varieties, piled high with a wide variety of toppings and sauces, from Mexican beef to herring to Polish cheeses. They also serve fish dishes with salad and potatoes, making this a cheap place to sample local seafood. The tasteful decor—walls lined with old bottles, antique wooden hangers, and old street signs—is squeezed into a

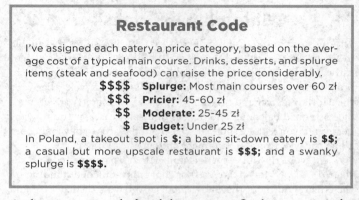

Restaurant Code

I've assigned each eatery a price category, based on the average cost of a typical main course. Drinks, desserts, and splurge items (steak and seafood) can raise the price considerably.

$$$$ **Splurge:** Most main courses over 60 zł
$$$ **Pricier:** 45-60 zł
$$ **Moderate:** 25-45 zł
$ **Budget:** Under 25 zł

In Poland, a takeout spot is **$**; a basic sit-down eatery is **$$**; a casual but more upscale restaurant is **$$$**; and a swanky splurge is **$$$$**.

single cozy room packed with happy eaters. In the summer, order inside, and they'll bring your food to you at an outdoor table (daily 10:00-22:00, ulica Piwna 61, tel. 58-305-1307).

$ Bar Mleczny Neptun is your handiest milk-bar (communist-style budget cafeteria) option in the Main Town. This popular place has outdoor seating along the most scenic stretch of the main drag, and an upstairs dining room overlooking it all. The items on the counter are for display—point to what you want, and they'll dish it up fresh (Mon-Fri 7:30-19:30, Sat-Sun 10:00-19:00, may have shorter hours off-season, ulica Długa 33, tel. 58-301-4988).

$ Pijalnia Wódki i Piwa, part of a popular Polish chain, hides half a block behind the Hard Rock Café (on Kuśnierska). This little vodka-and-herring bar takes you back to the 1970s. Pop in to study the retro decor: ads from the 1970s and photos of the lines that people routinely endured. The place is literally wallpapered with pages from the "Tribune of the Masses" newspaper infamous for its propaganda that passed for news. They play pop hits from the last years of communism. The menu is fun, accessible, and simple: 4 zł for vodka or other drinks, and 8 zł for herring or other bar nibbles (open daily 9:00-late).

$ Bar Turystyczny is misnamed—not just for tourists, it has become beloved by locals as the central area's favorite milk bar. Easy to miss on the way between the Main Town and the Solidarity sights, it's always jammed (Mon-Fri 8:00-18:00, Sat-Sun 9:00-17:00, Szeroka 8, tel. 58/301-6013).

ON THE RIVERFRONT EMBANKMENT

Perhaps the most appealing dining zone in Gdańsk stretches along the riverfront embankment near the Crane. While these restaurants are mostly interchangeable, I've listed a few to consider, in the order you'll reach them as you walk north along the embankment.

$$ Baryłka ("Barrel") is a simpler, more affordable alternative to some of the pricier places along here. While the outdoor seat-

ing is enticing, the elegant
upstairs dining room, with
windows overlooking the
river, is also appealing
(daily 9:00-24:00, Długie
Pobrzeże 24, tel. 58-301-
4938).

**$$$$ Kamienica
Goldwasser** offers high-
quality Polish and inter-
national cuisine. Choose
between cozy, romantic indoor seating on several levels, or scenic
outdoor seating (daily 10:00-24:00, occasional live music, Długie
Pobrzeże 22, tel. 58-301-8878).

$$$ Sushi 77, serving up a wide selection of surprisingly good
sushi right next to the Crane, is a refreshing break from ye olde
Polish food. Choose between the outdoor tables bathed in red light,
or the mod interior (daily 12:00-23:00, Długie Pobrzeże 30, tel.
58-682-1823).

Past the Crane

About 100 yards past the Crane, near the old fish market (Targ
Rybny), cluster several more options.

$$ Lao Thai is a modern space right along the embankment,
selling surprisingly high-quality, yet still affordable, Thai cuisine
(daily 12:00-22:00, ulica Targ Rybny 11, tel. 58/305-2525).

$$$ Targ Rybny/Fischmarkt ("The Fish Market") has less
appealing outdoor seating that overlooks a park and parking lot.
But the warm, mellow-yellow nautical ambience inside is pleasant,
making this a good bad-weather option. It features classy but not
stuffy service, and an emphasis on fish (daily 10:00-23:00, ulica
Targ Rybny 6C, tel. 58-320-9011).

$$ Restauracja Kubicki, along the water just past the Hilton,
has a long history (since 1918), but a recent remodel has kept the
atmosphere—and its food—feeling fresh. This is a good choice for
high-quality Polish and international cuisine in a fun, sophisticat-
ed-but-not-stuffy interior that's a clever mix of old and new (daily
12:00-23:00, Wartka 5, tel. 58-301-0050).

Sopot

Sopot (SOH-poht), dubbed the "Nice of the North," was a celebrated haunt of beautiful people during the 1920s and 1930s, and
it remains a popular beach getaway to this day.

Sopot was created in the early 19th century by Napoleon's
doctor, Jean Georges Haffner, who believed Baltic Sea water to

be therapeutic. By the 1890s, it had become a fashionable seaside resort. This gambling center boasted enough high-roller casinos to garner comparisons to Monte Carlo.

The casinos are gone, but the health resorts remain, and you'll still see more well-dressed people here per capita than just about anywhere else in the country. While it's not quite Cannes, Sopot feels relatively high class, which is unusual in otherwise unpretentious Poland. But even so, a childlike spirit of summer-vacation fun pervades this St-Tropez-on-the-Baltic, making it an all-around enjoyable place.

Orientation to Sopot

The main pedestrian drag, Monte Cassino Heroes street (ulica Bohaterów Monte Cassino), leads to the Molo, the longest pleasure pier in Europe. From the Molo, a broad, sandy beach stretches in each direction. Running parallel to the surf is a tree-lined, people-filled path made for strolling.

Tourist Information: The TI is near the base of the Molo at Plac Zdrojowy 2 (daily 10:00-18:00, mobile 790-280-884, www.sopot.pl).

Arrival in Sopot: From the SKM station, exit to the left and walk down the street. After a block, you'll see the PKP train station on your left. Continue on to the can't-miss-it main drag, ulica Bohaterów Monte Cassino (marked by the big red-brick church steeple). Follow it to the right, down to the seaside.

Sights in Sopot

▲Monte Cassino Heroes Street
(Ulica Bohaterów Monte Cassino)

Nicknamed "Monciak" (MOHN-chak) by locals, this in-love-with-life promenade may well be Poland's most manicured street (and is named in honor of the Polish soldiers who helped the Allies pry Italy's Monte Cassino monastery from Nazi forces during World War II). Especially after all the suburban and industrial dreck you passed through to get here, it's easy to be charmed by this pretty drag. The street is lined with happy tourists, trendy cafés, al fresco restaurants, movie theaters, and late-19th-century facades (known for their wooden balconies).

The most popular building along here (on the left, about halfway down) is the so-called **Crooked House** (Krzywy Domek), a trippy, Gaudí-inspired building that looks like it's melting. Hard-partying Poles prefer to call it the "Drunken House," and say that when it looks straight, it's time to stop drinking.

Molo (Pier)

At more than 1,600 feet long, this is Europe's longest wooden entertainment pier. While you won't find any amusement-park rides, you will be surrounded by vendors, artists, and Poles having the time of their lives. Buy a *gofry* (Belgian waffle topped with whipped cream and fruit) or an oversized cloud of *wata cukrowa* (cotton candy), grab your partner's hand, and stroll with gusto (7.50 zł, free Oct-April, open long hours daily, www.molo.sopot.pl).

Climb to the top of the Art Nouveau lighthouse for a water-front panorama. Scan the horizon for sailboats and tankers. Any pirate ships? For a jarring reality check, look over to Gdańsk. Barely visible from the Molo are two of the most important sites in 20th-century history: the towering monument at Westerplatte, where World War II started, and the cranes rising up from the Gdańsk Shipyard, where Solidarity was born and European communism began its long goodbye.

In spring and fall, the Molo is a favorite venue for pole vaulting—or is that Pole vaulting?

The Beach

Yes, Poland has beaches. Nice ones. When I heard Sopot compared to places like Nice, I'll admit that I scoffed. But when I saw those stretches of inviting sand as far as the eye can see, I wished I'd packed my swim trunks. (You could walk from Gdańsk all the way to Gdynia on beaches like this.) Most of the beach is public, except for a small private stretch in front of the Grand Hotel Sopot. Year-round, it's crammed with locals. At these northern latitudes, the season for bathing is brief and crowded.

Overlooking the beach next to the Molo is the **Grand Hotel Sopot.** It was renovated to top-class status just recently, but its history goes way back. They could charge admission for room #226, a multiroom suite that has hosted the likes of Adolf Hitler, Marlene Dietrich, and Fidel Castro (but not all at the same time). With all the trappings of Sopot's belle époque—dark wood, plush upholstery, antique furniture—this room had me imagining Hitler sitting at the desk, looking out to sea, and plotting the course of World War II.

What If I Miss My Ship?

Remember that you can get help from the cruise line's port agent (listed on the destination information sheet distributed on the ship) and the local TI. If the port agent suggests a costly solution (such as a private car with a driver), you may want to consider public transit.

Most train connections—including **Warnemünde,** Copenhagen, Amsterdam, and beyond—are via Berlin; to research train schedules, see www.bahn.com. Overland connections to **Rīga** and **Tallinn** are time-consuming; for these and other points north and east, flying may be your best choice. Gdańsk's **Lech Wałęsa Airport** is well connected to downtown by train, public bus #210, Uber, or taxi (www.airport.gdansk.pl).

For more advice on what to do if you miss the boat, see page 130.

Polish Survival Phrases

Keep in mind a few Polish pronunciation tips: **w** sounds like "v," **ł** sounds like "w," **ch** is a back-of-your-throat "kh" sound (as in the Scottish "loch"), and **rz** sounds like the "zh" sound in "pleasure." The vowels with a tail (**ą** and **ę**) have a slight nasal "n" sound at the end, similar to French.

English	Polish	Pronunciation
Hello. (formal)	Dzień dobry.	jehn **doh**-brih
Hi. / Bye. (informal)	Cześć.	cheshch
Do you speak English? (asked of a man)	Czy Pan mówi po angielsku?	chih pahn **moo**-vee poh ahn-**gyehl**-skoo
Do you speak English? (asked of a woman)	Czy Pani mówi po angielsku?	chih **pah**-nee **moo**-vee poh ahn-**gyehl**-skoo
Yes. / No.	Tak. / Nie.	tahk / nyeh
I (don't) understand.	(Nie) rozumiem.	(nyeh) roh-**zoo**-myehm
Please. / You're welcome. / Can I help you?	Proszę.	proh-sheh
Thank you (very much).	Dziękuję (bardzo).	jehn-**koo**-yeh (**bard**-zoh)
Excuse me. / I'm sorry.	Przepraszam.	psheh-**prah**-shahm
(No) problem.	(Żaden) problem.	(zhah-dehn) proh-blehm
Good.	Dobrze.	dohb-zheh
Goodbye.	Do widzenia.	doh veed-**zay**-nyah
one / two / three	jeden / dwa / trzy	yeh-dehn / dvah / tzhih
four / five / six	cztery / pięć / sześć	chteh-rih / pyench / sheshch
seven / eight	siedem / osiem	shyeh-dehm / oh-shehm
nine / ten	dziewięć / dziesięć	jeh-vyench / jeh-shench
hundred / thousand	sto / tysiąc	stoh / tih-shants
How much?	Ile?	ee-leh
local currency	złoty (zł)	zwoh-tih
Write it.	Napisz to.	nah-peesh toh
Is it free?	Czy to jest za darmo?	chih toh yehst zah **dar**-moh
Is it included?	Czy jest to wliczone?	chih yehst toh vlee-**choh**-neh
Where can I find / buy...?	Gdzie mogę dostać / kupić...?	guh-**dyeh** moh-geh **doh**-statch / **koo**-peech
I'd like... (said by a man)	Chciałbym...	khchaw-beem
I'd like... (said by a woman)	Chciałabym...	khchah-wah-beem
We'd like...	Chcielibyśmy...	khchehl-ee-bish-mih
...a room.	...pokój.	poh-kooey
...a ticket to ___.	...bilet do ___.	bee-leht doh ___
Is it possible?	Czy jest to możliwe?	chih yehst toh mohzh-**lee**-veh
Where is...?	Gdzie jest...?	guh-**dyeh** yehst
...the train station	...dworzec kolejowy	dvoh-zhehts koh-leh-**yoh**-vih
...the bus station	...dworzec autobusowy	dvoh-zhehts ow-toh-boos-**oh**-vih
...the tourist information office	...informacja turystyczna	een-for-**maht**-syah too-ris-**titch**-nah
...the toilet	...toaleta	toh-ah-**leh**-tah
men / women	męska / damska	mehn-skah / dahm-skah
left / right / straight	lewo / prawo / prosto	leh-voh / **prah**-voh / proh-stoh
At what time...?	O której godzinie...?	oh kuh-**too**-ray gohd-**zhee**-nyeh
...does this open / close	...będzie otwarte / zamknięte	bend-zheh oht-**vahr**-teh / zahm-**knyehn**-teh
Just a moment.	Chwileczkę.	khvee-**letch**-keh
now / soon / later	teraz / niedługo / później	teh-rahz / nyed-**woo**-goh / poozh-nyey
today / tomorrow	dzisiaj / jutro	jee-shigh / **yoo**-troh

BERLIN

Germany

Germany Practicalities

Germany (Deutschland) is energetic, efficient, and organized. It's Europe's muscleman, both economically and wherever people line up (Germans have a reputation for pushing ahead). At 138,000 square miles (about half the size of Texas), Germany is bordered by nine countries. The terrain gradually rises—from the flat lands of the north to the rugged Alps in the south. The European Union's most populous country and biggest economy, Germany is home to 82 million people—one-third Catholic and one-third Protestant. Germany is young compared with most of its European neighbors ("born" in 1871) but was a founding member of the EU. Germany's geographic diversity and cultural richness draw millions of visitors every year. While it's easy to fixate on the eerie Nazi remnants and chilling reminders of the Cold War, don't overlook Germany's lively squares, fine people zones, and many high-powered sights.

Money: 1 euro (€) = about $1.20. An ATM is called a *Geldautomat*. The local VAT (value-added sales tax) rate is 19 percent; the minimum purchase eligible for a VAT refund is €25 (for details on refunds, see page 125).

Language: The native language is German. For useful phrases, see page 588.

Emergencies: Dial 112 for police, medical, or other emergencies. In case of theft or loss, see page 118.

Time Zone: Germany is on Central European Time (the same as most of the Continent, one hour ahead of Great Britain, and six/nine hours ahead of the East/West Coasts of the US).

Embassies in Berlin: The **US embassy** is at Pariser Platz 2, tel. 030/83050; consular services at Clayallee 170 (tel. 030/8305-1200—consular calls answered Mon-Thu 14:00-16:00 only, https://de.usembassy.gov/). The **Canadian embassy** is at Leipziger Platz 17 (tel. 030/203-120, www.germany.gc.ca). Call ahead for passport services.

Phoning: With a mobile phone, it's easy to dial: Press and hold zero until you get a + sign, enter the country code (49 for Germany, 1 for the US/Canada), and then the complete phone number (including area code if there is one). When dialing a European phone number, drop an initial zero (except if calling Italy). For more tips, see page 1062.

Tipping: A gratuity is included in your bill at sit-down meals, so you don't need to tip further, but it's nice to round up your bill about 10 percent for great service. Tip a taxi driver by rounding up the fare a bit (pay €3 on a €2.85 fare). For more tips on tipping, see page 129.

Tourist Information: www.germany.travel

BERLIN
& the PORT of WARNEMÜNDE

Port of Warnemünde • Rostock • Berlin

Berlin—Germany's historic capital—is one of Europe's great cities, and certainly deserves a place on any itinerary. But cruise ships calling at landlocked Berlin actually put in at the port town of Warnemünde (VAHR-neh-mewn-deh)—150 miles north of Berlin. Many cruises allow a generous 12 to 14 hours in port here, but a visit to Berlin means you'll spend almost as much time in transit—six hours round-trip—as you will in the city itself. Berlin decisively wins the prize for "longest journey time from port."

This chapter covers detailed directions for getting from Warnemünde's cruise port to Berlin and offers tips on how to spend your limited time in the city. For those who want to stay closer to port, I've suggested ideas for a day spent in Warnemünde and/or the neighboring city of Rostock.

TO BERLIN OR NOT TO BERLIN?

Your first decision is whether to make the long trip to the German capital. Make no mistake: By train, by bus, or by Porsche on the autobahn, plan on at least three hours of travel time each way between the port of Warnemünde and Berlin—and then add time for making connections and for sightseeing in the city. Fortunately, Warnemünde's train station is a simple 10-minute walk from your ship.

To get a realistic sense of how much time you'll have in Berlin, check train schedules for your day in port at www.bahn.com (traveling between Warnemünde and "Berlin Hbf," Hauptbahnhof, the city's main station). There are some direct connections to Berlin, but most trains from Warnemünde require an easy change in Rostock. When planning your return from Berlin, be very clear on your ship's all-aboard time and work backward—and allow a cushion for possible delays.

You can also look for connections on a low-cost bus, or take a "Berlin On Your Own" cruise excursion. While more expensive than the train or bus, an excursion may suit your schedule better and avoids the stress of making transit connections. For more on all your options, see "From Warnemünde to Berlin," later.

Neither Warnemünde nor Rostock would be worth a special trip if you were putting together a "best of Germany" itinerary by train or car—but for a cruiser who doesn't want to bother with Berlin, I can think of worse places to spend a day. You could also treat this as a "half-day at sea"—enjoy nearby sightseeing for a few hours, then retreat to your ship for whatever onboard activities you haven't gotten around to yet.

PLANNING YOUR TIME
In Berlin

Remember, it takes at least six hours round-trip to get to and from Berlin. That likely leaves you with five or six hours in the city. Don't be too ambitious. You'll have time for my "Berlin City Walk" and possibly one more sight (two if you're quick). The key in Berlin is being selective: Read my descriptions on the train ride in, make your choices, and then hit the ground running.

Berlin City Walk: This self-guided walk links the **Reichstag** and **Brandenburg Gate** with sights along **Unter den Linden** to **Museum Island** and the **Spree River.** From the Hauptbahnhof, ride the U-Bahn or walk about 15 minutes to the Reichstag. Ogle the exterior (or, if you've made reservations, ascend the dome), then see the Brandenburg Gate, pause at the Memorial to the Murdered Jews of Europe, and walk up Unter den Linden (considering a detour partway along to the Checkpoint Charlie Museum). Allow 1.5 hours without stops, or—better—up to 3 hours if you fit in a few sights en route. The pleasant square called Gendarmenmarkt is worth the easy five-minute detour south of Unter den Linden (and is on the way to the 20th-century sights mentioned next).

From this sightseeing spine, these are your top options:

Museum of the Wall at Checkpoint Charlie and **Topography of Terror:** If you're interested in Berlin's turbulent 20th-century history, consider detouring a few blocks south of Unter den Linden to this little pocket of sights. Allow an hour for the Checkpoint Charlie Museum, and another hour-plus for the Topography of Terror—history buffs should budget even more time.

Art Museums: If you're primarily interested in art, consider spending some of your day at Museum Island (especially the Pergamon Museum, for ancient items—allow 1-2 hours; and the Neues Museum, to see the bust of Nefertiti—allow 1 hour), or the Gemäldegalerie, with Old Masters, at the Kulturforum complex—allow 2 hours). These museum zones are in different parts of town—ideally, choose one or the other.

Other Museums on Unter den Linden: You may want to choose additional museums that are on the route of the walk. These include the excellent German History Museum (allow at least 1 hour) or the quirky DDR Museum, for a look at communist-era East Germany (allow 1 hour).

Additional Sights: If you have a special interest, consider the Jewish Museum Berlin (allow 1-2 hours) or the Berlin Wall Memorial (allow 1.5 hours). Be aware that because they're not right along Unter den Linden, they'll eat up more transit time.

In Warnemünde and/or Rostock

If you'd rather not make the trip to Berlin, you can stick around the Warnemünde/Rostock area. Both towns have a Hanseatic flair—tidy street plans, with cutesy half-timbered homes and lots of red brickwork. But both were part of the communist former East Germany (DDR), which also left them with some less-than-charming architecture. Today **Warnemünde** is a cheery, borderline-tacky seafront resort, with a vast sandy beach and a pretty harbor lined with low-impact diversions. And parts of the nearby city of **Rostock** (a 20-minute train ride away) verge on quaint—it has a fine old church, some museums, and a pedestrian core lined with shops and eateries that cater more to locals than to tourists. If the weather is nice, you could head to the beach in Warnemünde right away; otherwise, take the train to Rostock, see that town, then return to Warnemünde for an afternoon at the beach.

Port of Warnemünde

Arrival at a Glance: To reach **Berlin,** walk (10 minutes) to the train station (3 hours one-way), take a cheaper (but slower) bus, or spring for a cruise-line excursion. Or ride the train to **Rostock,** just 20 minutes away. If staying in **Warnemünde,** you can explore the town center and walk to the beach.

Port Overview

Warnemünde is a pleasant former fishing town/seaside resort, situated at the mouth of the Warnow River. Cruise ships put in conveniently at a long pier immediately next to the train station and a short walk from the heart of town.

Tourist Information: The main TI is just past the train station and Alter Strom canal (closed Sun; Am Strom 59, enter around the corner on Kirchenstrasse, free Wi-Fi, WCs nearby, tel. 0381/381-

BERLIN

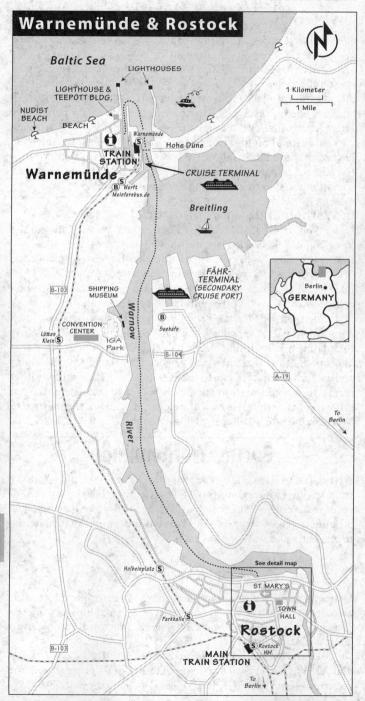

Warnemünde & Rostock

Baltic Sea

LIGHTHOUSES

LIGHTHOUSE &
TEEPOTT BLDG.

NUDIST
BEACH

BEACH

Warnemünde

TRAIN
STATION

Warnemünde

Hohe Düne

CRUISE TERMINAL

Werft
Meinfernbus.de

Breitling

1 Kilometer

1 Mile

FÄHR-
TERMINAL
(SECONDARY
CRUISE PORT)

B-103

SHIPPING
MUSEUM

Warnow

Seehafn

CONVENTION
CENTER

Lütten
Klein

IGA
Park

B-104

A-19

River

To
Berlin

Berlin
GERMANY

See detail map

Holbeinplatz

ST. MARY'S

TOWN
HALL

Parkhalle

Rostock

Rostock
Hbf.

B-103

MAIN
TRAIN STATION

To
Berlin

BERLIN

2222, www.rostock.de). There's also a small TI desk at the Pier 7 restaurant, between the cruise terminal and the station.

GETTING INTO WARNEMÜNDE, ROSTOCK, OR BERLIN

First, I'll cover transportation options for getting from the port to Warnemünde and/or Rostock. Then I'll offer specifics for getting to Berlin. To return to your ship, you can generally reverse these directions—I've given suggestions at the end of each section as necessary.

From the Port of Warnemünde to the Station and Town Center

It's a short stroll to the train station (with connections to Rostock or Berlin), and just a bit farther to Warnemünde's town center, TI, lone museum, and beach.

Go through the terminal building, exit to the right, and walk with the train tracks on your left and the river on your right. You'll pass a hokey gift shop, the Pier 7 restaurant (TI desk inside), a car-ferry dock, and then excursion boats to Rostock. About 50 yards beyond the car-ferry dock, look for signs on the left (*Tourist Information* and *Zentrum/City*) and follow them through the trees and into an underpass beneath the train tracks; you'll emerge on the other side at the **train station** plaza. A departures board is overhead; red-and-white ticket machines are to your left; and the yellow building on your right houses the ticket office *(Reiseagentur)* and Mabuhay store (with Wi-Fi). For specifics on continuing by train to Rostock or Berlin, see below.

To instead proceed to the **town center,** walk directly ahead from where you entered the train station plaza and cross the little bridge over the Alter Strom (old harbor). Continue straight to find the TI, Heimatmuseum (both on the left after one block), and—one block farther—the big Kirchplatz (Church Square, with ATMs and a pharmacy).

From Warnemünde to Rostock

By Taxi: You'll pay about €15-20 for a one-way taxi ride from the ship dock to Rostock.

By Train: Suburban trains (called S-Bahn) depart for Rostock from the Warnemünde station every 10 minutes (about a 20-min-

Excursions from Warnemünde

Most cruisers arriving in Warnemünde head into **Berlin** (3 hours each way by tour bus; some cruise lines charter a train for the journey).

For maximum freedom, consider a **Berlin On Your Own**-type excursion, which is simply a round-trip bus transfer to a central point in the city (often Gendarmenmarkt, just south of Unter den Linden). At around $150-200, this costs more than the round-trip train fare (around $50-130), but saves you the stress of coordinating train schedules to get there and back.

For about double the price ($300-350), most cruise lines offer an **all-day trip** that includes transportation, a narrated bus ride around Berlin, and photo-op stops at major landmarks (such as the Reichstag, Brandenburg Gate, Memorial to the Murdered Jews of Europe, Checkpoint Charlie, Gendarmenmarkt, or Bebelplatz—all of which are well worth seeing). Some tours also include more in-depth sightseeing stops at a sight or two and/or time on your own before returning to the ship. After transit time, if you have roughly six hours in Berlin, a two- to three-hour bus tour combined with about three hours of free time is a good day.

Carefully note which sights are included in your excursion. For example, cruisers interested in antiquities may appreciate a tour of the **Pergamon,** one of Europe's best museums for ancient sculpture. A **boat trip** on the Spree River through downtown Berlin provides a fine orientation to the city center. Some sights, however, should be avoided on a short visit. **Charlottenburg Palace,** while pretty, does not merit your limited time. And, while the distantly located **Allied Museum** tells the fascinating story of the early days of the Cold War here, I'd much rather spend an hour

ute ride). A one-way ticket (€2.10) is good for an hour—including the onward tram ride from Rostock's train station to the main square. Warning: There are multiple stops named Rostock on this line; wait to get off at Rostock Hbf (Hauptbahnhof, the main station).

By Excursion Boat: Boats to Rostock depart at least hourly from near the car-ferry dock (€12 one-way, €18 round-trip, 45 minutes each way).

From Warnemünde to Berlin
By Train

Train departures to Berlin vary with the day of the week. On weekends, a super-fast IC train goes from Warnemünde in just over two hours (departing around 10:59). On weekdays—and for other weekend connections—you'll typically have to take the S-Bahn to Rostock (see above), then transfer to a regional "RE5 Nord" train, with a total journey time to Berlin of just over three hours (leaves

walking the streets where that history happened than reading about it in a museum.

A themed excursion is worth considering. Most cruise lines offer a guided tour to several sites of important **Nazi/WWII/Cold War** history. **Jewish heritage** excursions may visit the outstanding Jewish Museum, the sumptuous New Synagogue, and the poignant Memorial to the Murdered Jews of Europe.

For those who want to stay closer to the ship, or who have already been to Berlin, there are several options—but be aware that cruise lines push these more for their proximity than for their sightseeing worthiness. Most common are guided visits of **Warnemünde** and **Rostock**—either separately or combined. Nearby are **Bad Doberan** (with a red-brick Cistercian convent-turned-minster)—a visit here is often combined with a ride on the Molli narrow-gauge steam train to the seaside resorts of Heiligendamm and/or Kühlungsborn; **Wismar** (colorful Hanseatic port town oozing with red-brick buildings), sometimes combined with the even more striking town of **Lübeck; Güstrow Castle** (housing an art museum); and **Schwerin Castle** (a pretty Loire-style palace overlooking an idyllic lake). The "Worst Possible Value" award goes to the **Rostock On Your Own** "excursion," providing a round-trip bus ride to downtown Rostock and back for $60—more than 10 times the price of the easy train connection.

Other sights to consider include the palaces of Prussian royalty at **Potsdam** (opulent, but not uniquely so) and **Sachsenhausen Concentration Camp** (with a compelling documentation center of Nazi atrocities). Either requires a long bus ride.

Rostock about every two hours—likely at 8:34, 10:34, and so on; occasionally a faster IC connection goes from Rostock to Berlin). Check the return schedule carefully—only a few trains depart for Warnemünde in the afternoon. Allow plenty of time (at least 10 minutes) to walk from the Warnemünde train station to your ship.

Buying Train Tickets: Ticket prices fluctuate dramatically depending on current "saver" deals; a same-day round-trip can be anywhere from €45 to €120. Fortunately, it's easy to research and book your connection in advance: Simply go to www.bahn.com, select English as your language, and search for round-trip connections between "Warnemuende" and "Berlin Hbf" for the date and time of your travel (don't cut it too close when planning your return ride to the ship). You can pay online with a US credit card and have a scannable ticket sent to your phone.

Otherwise, at the Warnemünde station, buy tickets at the desk inside or at the red-and-white ticket machines at the platform (English instructions, accepts euros or credit cards). If you buy a

BERLIN

Services near the Port

There are few services directly at the port, but you'll find what you need a short walk away.

ATMs and Pharmacy: The nearest pharmacy to the port is Detharding Apotheke, on Kirchplatz—the square in front of Warnemünde's church, just past the TI (closed Sun). You'll also find ATMs on the square.

Wi-Fi: The main **TI** and surrounding area has free Wi-Fi. Inside the train station building is **Mabuhay,** a sweet little Tagalog-run shop that caters to crew members with inviting tables, a variety of snacks, free Wi-Fi with purchase, pay Internet terminals, and cheap long-distance calls.

ticket at the machine, validate it in the orange box at the platform before boarding your train.

Returning to Your Ship: In Berlin, use the main east-west S-Bahn line to return to Berlin Hauptbahnhof (main station) from various points in town (including Friedrichstrasse, three blocks north of Unter den Linden; Hackescher Markt, a short walk north of Museum Island; and Alexanderplatz, at the end of Unter den Linden). From these stops, take any S-Bahn going west and hop off at Hauptbahnhof. You'll exit the S-Bahn on the top level of the station; your Rostock/Warnemünde train leaves from the bottom level, five stories below (ride the elevator down). This S-Bahn ride is covered by your ticket to Warnemünde. Alternatively, you could ride the U-Bahn line two stops from the Brandenburger Tor stop (but this ride is *not* covered by your train ticket). If you're in a pinch, hail a taxi and say, "Hauptbahnhof"—though at rush hour, the S-Bahn can be much faster.

You'll likely need to change to a suburban S-Bahn train at Rostock's Hauptbahnhof; they depart for Warnemünde every 10 minutes (about 20 minutes; ride to the end of the line).

Once you're back at the Warnemünde station, go down the stairs between tracks 3 and 4 (labeled *Passagierkai*); walk through the trees, turn right, and follow the water to your awaiting ship (allow at least 10 minutes).

By Bus

A low-cost company called Meinfernbus.de runs direct buses to Berlin from the Warnemünde Werft S-Bahn station—one train stop or a 15-minute walk from the cruise terminal. While it's a little slower (3-4 hours) and more traffic-dependent than the train, it's several times cheaper (as little as €22 round-trip). For the best fares and to guarantee a seat, it's smart to book a few days in advance. When choosing your drop-off point in Berlin, "Berlin Alexanderplatz" is the most central.

Returning to Your Ship: If coming back on the Meinfernbus, you'll get off at the Warnemünde Werft stop, then either ride the S-Bahn one stop to Warnemünde, or walk about 15 minutes.

By Cruise-Line Excursion

In addition to fully guided excursions to Berlin, many cruise lines offer a transportation-only "On Your Own" option. These unguided bus rides from the pier in Warnemünde to Berlin and back generally leave you with five or six hours in the capital. Some cruise lines even charter a train to make this trip. Although pricey (around $150-200 or more), this option is worth serious consideration for the peace of mind it buys. Remember, if you're on a cruise-line bus and there's a traffic jam coming back, the ship will wait for you—but not so if you're returning on your own.

Your cruise excursion will likely drop you off at the delightful square called **Gendarmenmarkt,** in the very center of the Berlin and just south of the street called Unter den Linden, Berlin's main sightseeing spine (for a description of this square and to locate it on a map, see page 552). From Gendarmenmarkt here, you can walk two blocks up Charlottenstrasse and turn left on Unter den Linden to reach Brandenburg Gate and the Reichstag (and the start of my self-guided "Berlin City Walk."

Returning to Your Ship: The shuttle bus will pick you up wherever it dropped you off (likely Gendarmenmarkt). Two different U-Bahn stations (U6: Französische Strasse; U2 or U6: Stadtmitte) are within a block of Gendarmenmarkt, if that's where you'll meet your bus.

By Tour

Several Berlin companies pick up groups at the dock in Warnemünde for all-day tours of the city. Although quite expensive on your own, these tours become affordable when you divide the cost with fellow cruisers. **Ship2shore,** with top-quality guides, offers Berlin day trips tailored to your interests starting at €99 per person (based on a minimum of 15 people, smaller groups also possible, 10 percent cash discount for my readers; tel. 030/243-58058, www.ship2shore.de, info@ship2shore.de). **Original Berlin Walks** also runs Berlin excursions from Warnemünde (contact them for pricing, includes private driver, available for 2-21 people, www.berlinwalks.de).

By Taxi

If you're willing to pay a premium, you can reach Berlin for (at least) €250 one-way.

From Fährterminal Dock to Rostock

When Warnemünde's main cruise port fills up, overflow ships are

BERLIN

sent to an alternate port, across the river and harbor area, at the passenger ferry terminal called Fährterminal. While the location is less convenient, some cruise lines offer a shuttle bus directly to Rostock, and the terminal is served by public transportation.

By Bus: Walk from the terminal to the Seehafen bus stop to catch bus #45 or #49 (run about hourly) under the river to the Lütten Klein train station, about halfway between Rostock and Warnemünde (10 minutes to either town, onward connection covered by bus ticket; Warnemünde-bound trains at track 1, Rostock-bound trains at track 2).

You can also take bus #49 going away from the river—in that direction, it stops near Rostock's Kröpeliner Tor, then continues to the main train station. If headed to Berlin, it makes sense to ride first to Rostock's main train station, and transfer there.

Warnemünde

A pleasant old fishing town, Warnemünde (pop. 8,500) has the feel of an unabashedly fun-loving beachfront resort—like Atlantic City or Brighton...although on a much smaller scale. This town has more than its share of bars, fast-food joints, divey hotels, beachwear boutiques, and Euro-vacationers.

To explore a bit, venture along the lane that runs parallel to the old harbor a block inland, **Alexandrinenstrasse,** lined with uniform, picturesque, half-timbered cottages. It's so quaint, you could swear you're in Denmark rather than Deutschland.

Tours in the Warnemünde Area: If you're sticking close to your ship, consider the **Friends of Dave Tours.** Their 10-hour "Mega Mecklenburg" excursion includes walking tours of Warnemünde and the port town of Wismar, as well as Schwerin Castle, with plenty of history about the Hanseatic League and the local Mecklenburg dynasty. Dave and his colleague, Christian, are endearing personalities (€155/person—includes all transportation, admissions, tips, and lunch; tours run every day a cruise is in town; mobile 0174-333-8363, www.friendsofdavetours.com).

Sights in Warnemünde

Old Harbor (Alter Strom)

Lined with colorful boats and fronted by bars, restaurants, hotels, and shops, this historic canal runs through the middle of Warnemünde. A boat-spotting stroll here is an entertaining way to while away some of your vacation time. From the seaward end of the canal, excursion boats try to lure you in for a one-hour cruise around the harbor and back (around €10, catering mostly to German tourists).

Warnemünde History Museum (Heimatmuseum)

This modest museum, tucked in a cute 18th-century house across from the TI, traces the history of this modest burg from fishing village to seaside resort, and lets visitors walk through furniture-crammed, creaky-floored rooms. While it has not a word of English, it sweetly evokes the town's history.

Cost and Hours: €3; Tue-Sun 10:00-17:00, closed Mon (closed Mon-Tue Nov-March); Alexandrinenstrasse 31, tel. 0381/52667, www.heimatmuseum-warnemuende.de.

Lighthouse (Leuchtturm)

Strategically situated to watch over both the Old Harbor and the beach, Warnemünde's symbol is its 105-foot-tall, tile-clad lighthouse. Completed in 1898, the lighthouse sits next to the distinctively shaped Teepott building. In the summer, you can climb to the tower's top for a view over Warnemünde and its beach.

Cost and Hours: €2, daily 10:00-19:00, closed Nov-March.

Beach (Badestrand)

Those who don't associate Germany with beaches haven't yet laid eyes on its Baltic seafront. Warnemünde has an incredibly broad, long stretch of white sand. While access to the beach is free, German holiday makers enjoy renting charming, almost whimsical, wicker cabana chairs called *Strandkörbe* ("beach baskets") for some shade and comfort (you'll find a big swathe of these at the lighthouse end of the beach). A wide and pleasant promenade stretches the full length of the sand. At the far end, keep your eyes peeled for the letters "FKK"—German code for "nude beach."

Getting There: To reach the beach, turn right just after the bridge into town and walk up the long, harborfront street called Am Strom. When the buildings end and you start to see sand dunes, look left to find Warnemünde's trademark old lighthouse. Going up the stairs past the lighthouse, you'll come to beachfront promenade, with several beach access points.

Rostock

Rostock, a regional capital with sprawling industrial ports and an enjoyable Old Town, clusters along the Warnow River about nine miles inland from the sea (and Warnemünde).

Back in medieval times, Rostock was an important shipping and shipbuilding center. It was a key player in the Hanseatic League, which connected it with trading partners from Scandinavia to Russia. Its university, founded in 1419, earned the city its nickname, "Light of the North." But the town declined in the 17th century after the Thirty Years' War.

Later, the mid-20th century dealt the town a devastating one-two punch: First, because it had several important aircraft factories, it was leveled by WWII bombs. Second, in the postwar era, it fell on the eastern side of the Iron Curtain, and—although it was the DDR's primary industrial port—Rostock's communist caretakers did an architecturally questionable job of rebuilding. A few historic buildings are scattered around town, and it all feels quite well-kept, but on the whole it lacks the charm of many mid-sized German cities.

That said, Rostock does have a smattering of attractions for cruisers who'd like to do some real sightseeing during their day at the port of War-nemünde. Nearly everything worth seeing is in the compact Old Town (Altstadt), which is about a mile due north of the main train station.

PLANNING YOUR TIME

For a quick, targeted visit in the Old Town, head to the main square (Neuer Markt) and tour St. Mary's Church (30 minutes). Then head down the pedestrian shopping drag called Kröpeliner Strasse to reach University Square, the Cultural History Museum, and the Kröpelin Gate (allow about an hour). On the way back to the station, history buffs will want to visit the Stasi Documentation Center and Memorial (allow another hour; it's a five-minute walk south of the Old Town). All told, three or four hours are plenty to get a good taste of Rostock.

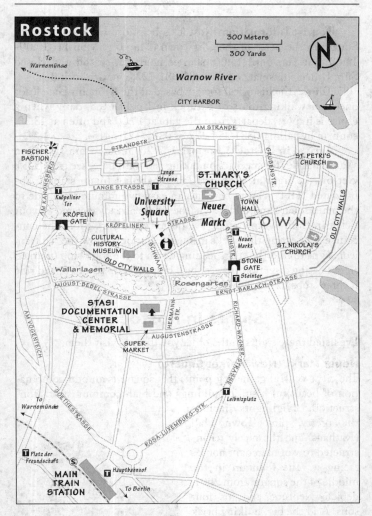

Orientation to Rostock

The hulking St. Mary's Church anchors an Old Town that's not quite old, but is where you'll find most of what there is to see: fragments of the old city walls (including an intact tower), a few museums and churches, and, above all, a workaday urban core where locals seem to go about their business oblivious to the big glitzy cruise ships that put in just down the river. The nondescript zone between the Old Town and train station hides a fascinating site for those interested in the Cold War: a former Stasi (communist secret police) prison block that's been converted into a museum and documentation center.

Tourist Information: Rostock's helpful TI is on University Square in the heart of the Old Town (May-Oct Mon-Fri 10:00-18:00, Sat-Sun until 15:00; shorter hours off-season and closed Sun; Universitätsplatz 6, tel. 0381/381-222, www.rostock.de).

Tours: The historical society based at the Kröpelin Gate leads one-hour walking tours of Rostock in English (€5, daily when a cruise is in port, departs from the gate at 11:00 and often at 13:30, confirm by calling 0381/454-177 or 0381/121-6415).

Arrival in Rostock: Rostock is a 20-minute train ride from Warnemünde (for specifics on taking the train here, see page 525). Get off the train at Rostock's Hauptbahnhof (main station, abbreviated "Hbf"). From here, it's an easy five-minute tram ride to the main square and Old Town (the ride is already covered by your ticket in from Warnemünde—valid for one hour). From the concourse connecting the tracks inside the station, follow the red tram icon signs to find the stairs leading down to the tram stop (marked *A*, indicating direction: city center). Hop on tram #5 or #6, and ride it three stops to Neuer Markt.

Sights in Rostock

I've listed these sights in the order you'll likely visit them.

Neuer Markt (New Market Square)

The city's central gathering point, this square is an odd combination of beautiful historic buildings and blah communist-era construction. Highlights include the pretty, pink Town Hall (Rathaus) and the nicely reconstructed row of merchant houses facing it. The fountain in the middle of the square, from 2001, depicts Neptune and his four sons. And the big, hulking brick building overlooking it all is St. Mary's Church. Open-air food

and craft stands are often set up in the market square; several other easy street food options line the pedestrian streets that branch off from here.

▲St. Mary's Church (Marienkirche)

Dating from the 14th century (with WWII damage finally repaired in the 1990s), this is Rostock's main church. Inside, this Gothic brick church is tall, white, and spacious—classic Lutheran.

Cost and Hours: €1.50 suggested donation; May-Sept Mon-Sat 10:00-18:00, Sun 11:15-17:00, shorter hours off-season.

Visiting the Church: The church has some charming details that are worth lingering over. As you enter, turn right and head to the far wall to find a dramatic **astronomical clock.** Built in 1472, it supposedly still has all of its original working parts. The upper dial tells the time and the sign of the zodiac, while the bottom dial lists the saint's day. At noon, the little door next to Jesus at the very top opens to let the apostles shuffle around their savior.

Just past the clock is a priceless, bronze **baptismal font** dating from 1290. It's loaded with symbolic detail—from the four figures supporting it (representing the four elements) to the bird perched proudly on top (the Holy Spirit, which appeared in the form of a dove at Jesus' own baptism). The base features scenes from Jesus' life.

Circle back around to the transept. On one of the pillars is an elaborately decorated Renaissance **pulpit.** Just past the pulpit is a gorgeous Baroque organ. As you leave the church, look up to see a striking stained-glass **window** from 1904 in the south portal ("Christ as Judge of the World").

Organ Performance: Mondays through Saturdays in summer (May-mid-Oct), a brief prayer service from 12:00 to 12:10 includes organ music. Music lovers who show up a few minutes early can meet the organist and go up into the loft to watch him play. In return, they ask that you make a donation and consider buying a CD.

University Square (Universitätsplatz)

From Neuer Markt, the lively, traffic-free, shop-lined Kröpeliner Strasse leads to this square. (The TI is in the yellow building on the left as you enter the square.) The centerpiece Fountain of Joy, an unusually lighthearted communist-era creation, sits in front of the university headquarters. Along the right side (as you face the fountain) are the so-called Five Gables—brick buildings whose modern flourishes are meant to echo the shape and style of Rostock's historic original houses blown apart by WWII bombs. Around the left side of the fountain, past the mustard-yellow building with columns and through the brick gate, is a charming lane leading to the Cultural History Museum (described next).

When you're done exploring here, you can continue two more short blocks on Kröpeliner Strasse (out the far end of the square) to reach the Kröpelin Gate.

BERLIN

Cultural History Museum (Kulturhistorisches Museum)

This fine collection of historical items relating to Rostock is situated around a pleasant former cloister. There's little English information, but the exhibits are worth a browse on a rainy day. The ground floor has historic portraits of important Rostockers, old wooden chests, ecclesiastical art (altars and statues), and old grave markers. Up on the first floor, you'll find paintings and a model of historic Rostock, a particularly nice collection of old toys, decorative arts (porcelain, glassware, pewterware, clocks), and a fine coin collection. A top-floor room shows off early-20th-century art.

Cost and Hours: Free, Tue-Sun 10:00-18:00, closed Mon, Klosterhof 7, tel. 0381/203-5901.

Kröpelin Gate (Kröpeliner Tor)

One of two surviving watchtowers from the old city wall, this picturesque gate (which strikes a medieval pose at the end of Kröpeliner Strasse) offers a disappointing little history exhibit and a view from the top that's not worth the 100 steps.

Cost and Hours: €3, daily 10:00-18:00.

Nearby: Next to the gate is a surviving stretch of the original **town wall.** This also marks the course of an inviting **park** that hems in the southern end of the Old Town. From the tram stop near the tower, trams #5, #6, or #E will take you back to the station.

▲Stasi Documentation Center and Memorial

Hiding in a humdrum part of town is a building that once held prisoners of the communist state. Today this former prison block

has been converted into a museum and documentation center about the crimes of the former regime—specifically, its secret police, known as the Stasi (see sidebar). Worth ▲▲ for those interested in the Cold War, the museum provides an opportunity to better understand some of Rostock's darkest days.

From 1960 to 1989, this prison held 4,800 people (110 at a time) accused of crimes against the state—ranging from participating in protests to attempting to flee the country to simply telling a joke about the regime. Though this was supposed to be a "pretrial prison," some individuals were held here for up to a year and a half. With the help of borrowable English explanations and a free audioguide, you'll walk through the prison, peering into cells; some contain exhibits about the Stasi, while others are preserved as they were when they held prisoners. Artifacts illustrate the crimes and methods of the Stasi—from hidden microphones to yellow cloths

The Stasi (East German Secret Police)

To keep their subjects in line, the DDR government formed the Ministerium für Staatssicherheit (MfS, "Ministry for State Security")—the Stasi. Modeled after the Soviet Union's secret police, the Stasi actively recruited informants from every walk of life, often intimidating them into cooperating by threatening their employment, their children's education, or worse. The Stasi eventually gathered an army of some 600,000 "unofficial employees" *(inoffizielle Mitarbeiter)*, nearly 200,000 of whom were still active when communism fell in 1989. These "employees" were coerced into reporting on the activities of their coworkers, friends, neighbors, and even their immediate family members.

Preoccupied with keeping track of "nonconformist" behavior, the Stasi collected whatever bits of evidence they could about suspects—including saliva, handwriting, odors, and voice recordings—and wound up with vast records on East Germany's citizens. In late 1989, when the Berlin Wall fell, Stasi officials attempted to destroy their files—but barely made a dent before government officials decreed that all documentation be preserved. These days, German citizens can read the files that were once kept on them. (Locals struggle with the decision: Request a full view of their record—and see which friends and loved ones were reporting on them—or avoid the likely painful truth.) For a film that brilliantly captures the paranoid Stasi culture, see the 2006 Oscar-winner *The Lives of Others*.

impregnated with a suspect's scent (sweat captured during interrogations)...one bizarre example of the many ways the Stasi kept tabs on those they were investigating.

Cost and Hours: Free; Tue-Fri 10:00-18:00 (Nov-Feb until 17:00), Sat 10:00-17:00, closed Sun-Mon; Hermannstrasse 34b, tel. 0381/498-5651, www.bstu.bund.de.

Getting There: The prison is in a residential zone just south of the Old Town. To find it, from University Square, head south on Schwaansche Strasse, pass through the park, and cross the ring road, continuing straight as the street becomes Hermannstrasse. Turn right into the parking lot just before the Penny supermarket (noticing the low-profile brown sign for *ehem. Stasi-U-Haft*)—the museum entrance is at the far end of the lot, on the right.

Berlin

Berlin is a city of leafy boulevards, grand Neoclassical buildings, world-class art, glitzy shopping arcades, and funky graffitied neighborhoods with gourmet street food. It's big and bombastic—the showcase city of kings and kaisers, of the Führer and 21st-century commerce.

Of course, Berlin is still largely defined by its WWII years and the Cold War. The East-West division was set in stone in 1961, when the East German government surrounded West Berlin with the Berlin Wall. Since the fall of the Wall in 1989, Berlin has been a constant construction zone. Standing on ripped-up streets and under a canopy of cranes, visitors have witnessed the city's reunification and rebirth.

In the city's top-notch museums, you can walk through an enormous Babylonian gate amid rough-and-tumble ancient statuary, fondle a chunk of the concrete-and-rebar Berlin Wall, and peruse canvases by Dürer and Rembrandt. A series of thought-provoking memorials confront Germany's difficult past. And some of the best history exhibits anywhere—covering everything from Prussian princes to Nazi atrocities to life under communism—have a knack for turning even those who claim to hate history into armchair experts.

Orientation to Berlin

Berlin is huge and spread out—a series of pleasant neighborhoods, with broad boulevards, long blocks, and low five-story buildings. Berlin's "downtown" alone stretches five miles, following the flow of the Spree River.

Historic Core: Berlin's 1.5-mile sightseeing axis runs west-to-east along Unter den Linden boulevard, with a mix of 19th-century Neoclassical grandeur and 21st-century glitz. At the western edge, you'll find the Reichstag (Germany's domed parliament), the historic Brandenburg Gate, and a scattering of poignant memorials. Unter den Linden passes the grand squares called Gendarmenmarkt and Bebelplatz before it terminates at Museum Island—the birthplace of Berlin and today home to a cluster of top museums showcasing ancient wonders (the Pergamon and Neues museums) and German paintings (Old National Gallery). Also within this core are Berlin's towering Cathedral and the German History and DDR museums.

Northern Berlin: The trendy **Scheunenviertel** ("Barn Quarter") neighborhood, near the Hackescher Markt transit hub, is a short walk north of Unter den Linden; here you'll find eateries and

The History of Berlin

Berlin was a humble, marshy burg until prince electors from the Hohenzollern dynasty made it their capital in the mid-15th century. Gradually their territory spread and strengthened, becoming the powerful Kingdom of Prussia in 1701. As the leading city of Prussia, Berlin dominated the northern Germanic world—both militarily and culturally—long before there was a united "Germany."

Thanks largely to Frederick the Great (1712-1786), the enlightened despot who was both a ruthless military tactician and a cultured lover of the arts, Prussia was well-positioned to lead the German unification movement in the 19th century. And when Germany became a unified modern nation in 1871, Berlin was its natural capital. The city boomed with Germany's industrialization, quadrupling its population over the next 40 years. After Germany's humiliating defeat in World War I, Berlin thrived as an anything-goes cultural capital of the Roaring Twenties. During World War II, the city was Hitler's headquarters—and the place where the Führer drew his final breath.

When the Soviet Army reached Berlin in 1945, the protracted fighting left the city in ruins. Berlin was divided by the victorious Allied powers—the American, British, and French sectors became West Berlin, and the Soviet sector, East Berlin. The city became the main battlefield of the nascent Cold War. In 1948, the Soviets tried to starve the 2.2 million residents of the western half in an almost medieval-style siege, which was broken by the Allies' Berlin Airlift. Later, with the overnight construction of the Berlin Wall in 1961, an Iron (or, at least, concrete) Curtain completely encircled West Berlin—cutting Berlin in half. While East Berliners lived through difficult times, West Berlin became a magnet for artists, punks, squatters, and free spirits.

Finally, on November 9, 1989, the Wall came down. Two cities—and countries—became one at a staggering pace. Today, going on 30 years later, the old East-West divisions are a distant memory. Berlin is a new city—ready to welcome visitors.

BERLIN

Berlin Overview

WEDDING

·········· COURSE OF FORMER WALL

Ⓢ ELEVATED S-BAHN LINE & STATIONS

1 Kilometer

1 Mile

MOABIT

ALT-MOABIT

STROMSTRASSE

CHAUSSEE-STR.

HAUPT-BAHNHOF Ⓢ

Spree River

PARK OFFICES

CHARLOTTENBURG PALACE

Ⓢ Westend

SCHARF-GERSTENBERG MUSEUM

CHARLOTTEN-BURG

Bellevue Ⓢ

REICHSTAG

Tiergarten Ⓢ

STRASSE DES 17 JUNI

VICTORY COLUMN

BRANDENBURG GATE

MEM. TO MURDERED JEWS

Tiergarten

KAISERDAMM

Ernst-Reuter-Platz

Landwehr Canal

GEMÄLDE-GALERIE

SONY CTR.

Central Bus Station (ZOB) Ⓑ

Messe Nord/ICC

HARDENBERG

Zoologischer Garten Ⓢ

KULTURFORUM

Potsdamer Platz

MASURENALLEE

KANTSTRASSE

BERLIN ZOOLOGICAL GARDEN

GERMAN RESISTANCE MEMORIAL

POTSDAMER STR.

Savigny-platz

EUROPA CENTER

Charlotten-burg Ⓢ

Savignyplatz

Wittenberg platz

Westkreuz Ⓢ

KURFÜRSTENDAMM

LIETZEN STR.

KOLLWITZ MUSEUM

MEMORIAL CHURCH

KaDeWe STORE

CITY WEST

KURFÜRSTENSTR.

KLEISTSTRASSE

PAULSBORNER STR.

shopping. Farther out is the even hipper **Prenzlauer Berg** residential area, with restaurants and shopping. Also in this zone are the **Berlin Wall Memorial**—the best place in town to learn more about the Wall—and the Hauptbahnhof (main train station).

Southern Berlin: South of Unter den Linden, **fascism and Cold War sights** dominate, anchored by Checkpoint Charlie (the former border crossing through the Wall) and the Topography of Terror (documenting Nazi atrocities). The Jewish Museum Berlin is also here.

Eastern Berlin: East of Museum Island, Unter den Linden changes its name to Karl-Liebknecht-Strasse and leads to **Alexanderplatz**—formerly the hub of communist East Berlin, still marinated in brutal architecture, and marked by its impossible-to-miss TV Tower.

Western Berlin: Just west of the Brandenburg Gate is the entrance to Berlin's huge central park, **Tiergarten.** South of the park, **Potsdamer Platz** is home to Berlin's 21st-century glitz, with skyscrapers and shopping plazas. Down the street, the **Kulturforum** is a cluster of museums, including the impressive Gemäldegalerie (starring Rembrandt, Dürer, and more).

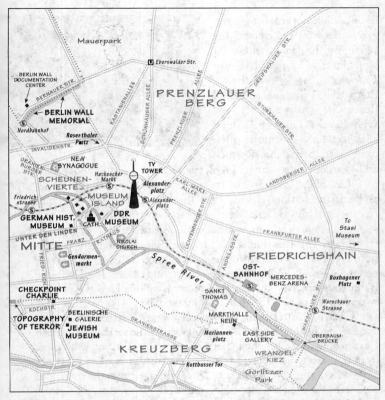

West of the park is **City West**—the former heart of communist-era West Berlin, lined up along the boulevard named Kurfürstendamm ("Ku'damm" for short). Today this modern area feels more like a classy suburb.

TOURIST INFORMATION

Berlin's TIs are for-profit agencies that are only marginally helpful (tel. 030/250-025, www.visitberlin.de). You'll find them at the **Hauptbahnhof** (daily 8:00-22:00, by main entrance on Europaplatz) and at the **Brandenburg Gate** (daily 9:30-19:00, until 18:00 Nov-March).

ARRIVAL IN BERLIN
By Train

Trains from Warnemünde and Rostock arrive at Berlin Hauptbahnhof ("Berlin Hbf" on schedules)—a massive, state-of-the-art temple of railroad travel in the heart of the city. This mostly underground train station is where the national train system meets Berlin's S-Bahn.

Orientation: The gigantic station has five floors, but its open

layout makes it easy to navigate...once you understand the
signage. The main floor, at
street level, is labeled "EG" (for
Erdgeschoss), or level 0. Below
that are UG1 (level -1) and UG2
(level -2), while above it are
OG1 (level +1) and OG2 (level
+2). Tracks 1-8—most often
used by trains to/from Rostock

and Warnemünde—are on UG2; tracks 11-16 and the S-Bahn are
on OG2. Shops and services are on the three middle levels. Enter
and exit the station on level EG: The Washingtonplatz entrance
faces south (toward the Reichstag and downtown, with a taxi
stand). The north entrance is marked *Europaplatz*.

Train Information and Tickets: Before leaving the station, it's smart to reconfirm the schedule for trains back to Warnemünde—and, while you're at it, buy your ticket. The Deutsche
Bahn *Reisezentrum* information center is up one level (OG1), between tracks 12 and 13 (open long hours daily).

Getting into Town: You'll likely want to head straight for
the Reichstag and the Brandenburg Gate, at the start of Unter den
Linden (and my self-guided "Berlin City Walk." You can walk there
from the station in about 15 minutes (use the exit marked *Washingtonplatz*, cut through the plaza to the footbridge, cross the river, and
bear left past the boxy Bundestag building toward the glass dome
of the Reichstag). To save time, ride the subway: The station's sole
U-Bahn line—U55—goes two stops, to the Brandenburger Tor
station.

To reach other points in town (or for a quick return to the station), consider the handy S-Bahn. It's simple: S-Bahn trains are on
tracks 15 and 16 at the top of the station (level OG2). Trains on
track 15 go east, stopping at Friedrichstrasse, Hackescher Markt,
Alexanderplatz, and Ostbahnhof (trains on track 16 go west). Your
train ticket to Berlin covers any connecting S-Bahn ride (but for
the U-Bahn, trams, or buses, you'll need an additional ticket; see
page 543).

HELPFUL HINTS

Closures: The Berlin Wall Memorial Visitors Center and Documentation Center, the Old National Gallery, and the Gemäldegalerie are closed on Monday.

Cold War Terminology: What Americans called "East Germany" was technically the German Democratic Republic—the
 Deutsche Demokratische Republik, or DDR. You'll still see
 those initials around what was once East Germany. The name

for what was "West Germany"—the Federal Republic of Germany (Bundesrepublik Deutschland, or BRD)—is now the name shared by all of Germany.

GETTING AROUND BERLIN
By Public Transit

Berlin's transit system uses the same ticket for its many modes of transportation: buses, trams *(Strassenbahn)*, and trains. There

are two types of trains: The U-Bahn—like a subway, making lots of short hops around town—is run by the local transit authority (BVG); the S-Bahn, a light rail that goes faster and stops only at major stations, is operated by German Railways (Deutsche Bahn).

For all types of transit, there are three lettered zones: A, B, and C. Most of your sightseeing will be in zones A and B (the city proper).

Information: Timetables and prices are available on the helpful BVG website or app (www.bvg.de); on-the-go trip routing with U-Bahn, S-Bahn, and tram connections are on the handy VBB public transit website (www.vbb.de; good free app).

Ticket Options: The €2.80 basic single ticket *(Einzelfahrschein)* covers two hours of travel in one direction. It's easy to make this ticket stretch to cover several rides...as long as they're in the same direction.

The €1.70 **short-ride** ticket *(Kurzstrecke Fahrschein)* covers a single ride of up to six bus/tram stops or three subway stations (one transfer allowed on subway). You can save on short-ride tickets by buying them in groups of four (€5.60).

The €9 **four-trip** ticket *(4-Fahrten-Karte)* is the same as four basic single tickets at a small discount.

The **day pass** *(Tageskarte)* is good until 3:00 the morning after you buy it (€7 for zones AB, €7.40 for zones ABC).

Buying Tickets: You can buy U-Bahn/S-Bahn tickets from machines at stations. Tickets are also sold at BVG pavilions at train stations and at the TI, from machines onboard trams, and on buses from drivers, who'll give change. You'll need coins or paper bills (only German "EC" credit cards are accepted as payment at transit ticket machines or retailers).

As you board the bus or tram or enter the subway, validate your ticket in a clock machine (or risk a €60 fine; with a pass, stamp it only the first time you ride). Tickets are checked periodically,

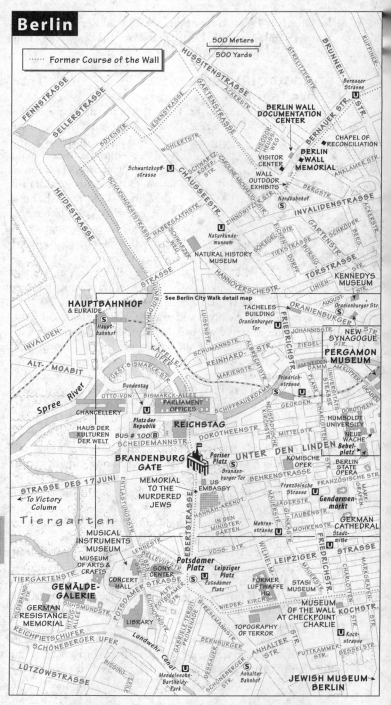

Berlin

..... Former Course of the Wall

500 Meters
500 Yards

FENNSTRASSE

SELLERSTRASSE

HEIDESTRASSE

HUSSITENSTRASSE

GARTENSTRASSE

ACKERSTR.

LIESENSTR.

BRUNNEN-STR.

RUPPINER

STRELITZERSTR.

Bernauer Strasse

BERNAUER STR.

BERLIN WALL DOCUMENTATION CENTER

BÖYENSTR.

WOHLERTSTR.

CAROLINE-MICHAELIS-STR.

THEODOR-HEUSS-WEG

CHAPEL OF RECONCILIATION

VISITOR CENTER

BERLIN WALL MEMORIAL

ANKLAMER STR.

Schwartzkopf-strasse

SCHWARTZ-KOPFF-STR.

CHAUSSEESTR.

WALL OUTDOOR EXHIBITS

BERGSTR.

SCHARNHORSTSTRASSE

HABERSAATHSTR.

SCHWARZER WEG

ZINNOWITZER STR.

Nordbahnhof

INVALIDENSTRASSE

ACKERSTR.

SCHRÖDER

GARTENSTR.

BERG

Naturkunde-museum

SCHLEGELSTR.

TIECKSTRASSE

BORSIG-DORF-

LINIEN

TORSTRASSE

KENNEDYS MUSEUM

NATURAL HISTORY MUSEUM

HANNOVERSCHESTR.

HAUPTBAHNHOF & EURAIDE

STRASSE

HUMBOLDTHAFEN

See Berlin City Walk detail map

LUISENSTR.

TACHELES BUILDING

Oranienburger Tor

ORANIENBURGER

FRIEDRICHSTR.

AUGUST

Oranienburger Str.

NEW SYNAGOGUE STR.

Haupt-bahnhof

KAPELLE-UFER

INVALIDEN-

ALT-MOABIT

FÜRST-BISMARCK-STR.

SCHUMANNSTR.

REINHARD-STR.

ALBRECHTSTR.

JOHANNISSTR.

ZIEGEL

PLANCK

AM WEIDEN-DAMM

UNIVERSITÄTS-STRASSE

PERGAMON MUSEUM

AM KUPFER-GRABEN

Spree River

Bundestag

OTTO-VON-BISMARCK-ALLEE

MARIENSTR.

Friedrich-strasse

GEORGEN-

DOROTHEEN-

CHARLOTTEN-

HUMBOLDT UNIVERSITY

CHANCELLERY

PARLIAMENT OFFICES

SCHIFFBAUERDAMM

NEUSTÄDTISCHE

MITTELSTR.

NEUE WACHE

HAUS DER KULTUREN DER WELT

Platz der Republik

BUS # 100 B

SCHEIDEMANNSTR.

REICHSTAG

DOROTHEENSTR.

KIRCHSTR.

Bebel-platz

UNTER DEN LINDEN

BERLIN STATE OPERA

BRANDENBURG GATE

Pariser Platz

Branden-burger Tor

KOMISCHE OPER

BEHRENSTRASSE

FRANZÖSISCHE STR.

STRASSE DES 17 JUNI

MEMORIAL TO THE MURDERED JEWS

US EMBASSY

EBERTSTRASSE

HANNAH-ARENDT-

Französische Strasse

JÄGERSTR.

GLINKAST.

TAUBENSTR.

Gendarmen-markt

GERMAN CATHEDRAL

Stadt-mitte

Tiergarten

ENTLASTUNGSSTR.

IN DEN MINISTER-GARTEN

Mohren-strasse

MOHRENSTR.

MAUERSTR.

FRIEDRICHSTR.

CHARLOTTEN-STR.

MUSICAL INSTRUMENTS MUSEUM

VOSS-STR.

LEIPZIGER

STRASSE

MARKGRAFEN-

MUSEUM OF ARTS & CRAFTS

LENNÉSTR.

BELLEVUESTR.

SONY CENTER

Potsdamer Platz

Leipziger Platz

WILHELM-

STASI MUSEUM

MAUERSTR.

KOCHSTR.

GEMÄLDE-GALERIE

CONCERT HALL

POTSDAMER STRASSE

Potsdamer Platz

FORMER LUFTWAFFE HQ

MUSEUM OF THE WALL AT CHECKPOINT CHARLIE

TIERGARTENSTR.

GERMAN RESISTANCE MEMORIAL

SIGISMUNDSTR.

HITZIG

LIBRARY

ALTE POTSDAMER STR.

EICHHORNSTR.

NIEDER-KIRCH-

STRESEMANNSTR.

TOPOGRAPHY OF TERROR

BERNBURGER

ANHALTER STR.

Koch-strasse

BESSELSTR.

PUTTKAMER-STR.

REICHPIETSCHUFER

SCHÖNEBERGER UFER

Landwehr Canal

GABRIELE-TERGIT-PROMENADE

DESSAUER STR.

SCHÖNEBERGER STR.

LÜTZOWSTRASSE

BISSING-TEILE

Mendelssohn-Bartholdy-Park

Anhalter Bahnhof

JEWISH MUSEUM → BERLIN

To Victory Column

HAUS DER

BERLIN

LIBRARY

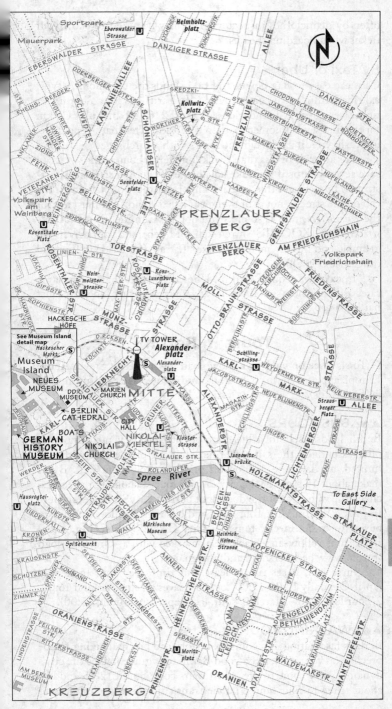

To East Side Gallery

BERLIN

often by plainclothes inspectors. You may be asked to show your ticket when boarding the bus.

By Taxi or Uber

Cabs are easy to flag down, and **taxi** stands are common. A typical ride within town costs around €10. Tariff 1 is for a *Kurzstrecke* ticket (see next). All other rides are tariff 2 (€3.90 drop plus €2/km for the first seven kilometers, then €1.50/km after that). If possible, use cash: Credit card payment comes with a surcharge.

For any ride of less than two kilometers (about a mile), you can save several euros if you take advantage of the *Kurzstrecke* (short-stretch) rate. To get this rate, it's important that you flag down the cab on the street—not at or even near a taxi stand. You must ask for the *Kurzstrecke* rate as soon as you hop in: Confidently say *"Kurzstrecke, bitte"* (KOORTS-shtreh-keh, BIT-teh), and your driver will grumble and flip the meter to a fixed €5 rate (for a ride that would otherwise cost €8).

Local laws require Berlin's **Uber** drivers to charge the same rates as taxis; there's no financial advantage to using Uber over just hailing a cab.

Tours in Berlin

🎧 To sightsee on your own, download my free Rick Steves Audio Europe app and Berlin City Walk **audio tour** (see sidebar on page 46 for details).

▲▲▲BUS TOURS

Berlin lends itself to a bus-tour orientation. Several companies offer essentially the same routine: a circuit of the city with unlimited, all-day hop-on, hop-off privileges for about €20. Buses make about 15 stops at the city's major tourist spots. For specifics, check the websites for the dominant outfits: **CitySightseeing Berlin,** a.k.a. Berlin City Tour, runs red buses and yellow-and-green buses (www.berlin-city-tour.de). **City Circle Sightseeing,** a.k.a. BEX, runs yellow-and-black buses marked with a "Grayline" logo (http://www.berlinerstadtrundfahrten.de).

In season, buses run at least four times per hour (generally April-Oct daily 10:00-18:00, last bus leaves all stops around 16:00, 2-hour loop; Nov-March 2/hour, last departure around 15:00).

▲▲▲WALKING TOURS

Berlin's fascinating and complex history can be challenging to appreciate on your own, but a good Berlin tour guide makes the city's dynamic story come to life. Most tours cost about €12-15 and last about three to four hours; public-transit tickets and entrances to sights are extra. For more details than I've given here—including prices, specific schedules, and other themed tours—see each company's website.

Original Berlin Walks

With a strong commitment to quality guiding, Original Berlin's Discover Berlin walk offers a good overview in four hours (daily at 10:30 except no walks on Tue Nov-March, April-Oct also daily at 14:00). They also offer a Third Reich walking tour (Hitler's Germany), among others. Get a €1 discount per tour with this book. Tours depart from opposite the Hackescher Markt S-Bahn station, outside the Weihenstephaner restaurant (tel. 030/301-9194, www.berlinwalks.de).

Brewer's Berlin Tours

Specializing in in-depth walks led by enthusiastic historians, these city tours are intimate, relaxed, and can flex with your interests. Their Best of Berlin introductory tour, billed at six hours, can last for eight (daily at 10:30). They also do a shorter 3.5-hour tour (free, tip expected, daily at 13:00). All tours depart from Bandy Brooks ice cream shop at the Friedrichstrasse S-Bahn station (tel. 0177-388-1537, www.brewersberlintours.com).

Insider Tour

This well-regarded company runs the full gamut of itineraries: introductory walk (daily), themed and museum tours, and so on. Their tours have two meeting points: in Western Berlin, in front of the McDonald's outside the Zoologischer Garten station; and in the Scheunenviertel neighborhood, outside the AM to PM Bar at the Hackescher Markt S-Bahn station (tel. 030/692-3149, www.insidertour.com).

"Free" Tours

You'll see ads for "free" introductory tours all over town. Popular with students (free is good), it's a business model that has spread across Europe: English-speaking students (often Aussies and Americans) deliver a memorized script before a huge crowd lured in by the promise of a free tour. The catch: Guides expect to be "tipped in paper" (€5/person minimum is encouraged).

Local Guides

Berlin guides are generally independent contractors who work with tour companies (such as those listed here) but can also be hired privately (generally charging around €50-60/hour or €200-300/day, confirm when booking). I've personally worked with and can strongly recommend each of the following guides: Archaeologist **Nick Jackson** (mobile 0171-537-8768, www.jacksonsberlintours.com); **Lee Evans** (makes 20th-century Germany a thriller, mo-

Berlin at a Glance

▲▲▲**Reichstag** Germany's historic parliament building, topped with a striking modern dome you can climb (reservations required). **Hours:** Daily 8:00-24:00. See page 565.

▲▲▲**Brandenburg Gate** One of Berlin's most famous landmarks, a massive columned gateway, at the former border of East and West. See page 554.

▲▲▲**Pergamon Museum** World-class museum of classical antiquities on Museum Island, partially closed through 2025 (including its famous Pergamon Altar). **Hours:** Daily 10:00-18:00, Thu until 20:00. See page 568.

▲▲▲**German History Museum** The ultimate swing through Germany's tumultuous story. **Hours:** Daily 10:00-18:00. See page 571.

▲▲▲**Berlin Wall Memorial** A "docu-center" with videos and displays, several outdoor exhibits, and lone surviving stretch of an intact Wall section. **Hours:** Tue-Sun 10:00-18:00, closed Mon; outdoor areas accessible daily 24 hours. See page 576.

▲▲**Memorial to the Murdered Jews of Europe** Holocaust memorial with almost 3,000 symbolic pillars, plus an exhibition about Hitler's Jewish victims. **Hours:** Memorial always open; information center Tue-Sun 10:00-20:00, Oct-March until 19:00, closed Mon year-round. See page 567.

▲▲**Unter den Linden** Leafy boulevard through the heart of former East Berlin, lined with some of the city's top sights. See page 558.

bile 0177-423-5307, lee.evans@ berlin.de); **Torben Brown** (a walking Berlin encyclopedia, mobile 0176-5004-2572, www.berlinperspectives.com); journalist **Holger Zimmer** (a cultural connoisseur who also guides my groups, mobile 0163-345-4427, explore@ berlin.de); **Carlos Meissner** (a

historian with a professorial earnestness, mobile 0175-266-0575, www.berlinperspectives.com); young British expat **Maisie Hitchcock** (mobile 01763-847-2717, maisiehitchcock@hotmail.com); **Caroline Marburger** (a sharp historian who has lived and stud-

▲▲**Neues Museum** Egyptian antiquities collection and proud home of the exquisite 3,000-year-old bust of Queen Nefertiti. **Hours:** Daily 10:00-18:00, Thu until 20:00. See page 570.

▲▲**Old National Gallery** German paintings, mostly from the Romantic Age. **Hours:** Tue-Sun 10:00-18:00, Thu until 20:00, closed Mon. See page 571.

▲▲**DDR Museum** Quirky collection of communist-era artifacts. **Hours:** Daily 10:00-20:00, Sat until 22:00. See page 572.

▲▲**Topography of Terror** Chilling exhibit documenting the Nazi perpetrators, built on the site of the former Gestapo/SS headquarters. **Hours:** Daily 10:00-20:00. See page 575.

▲▲**Gemäldegalerie** Germany's top collection of 13th- through 18th-century European paintings, featuring Holbein, Dürer, Cranach, Van der Weyden, Rubens, Hals, Rembrandt, Vermeer, Velázquez, Raphael, and more. **Hours:** Tue-Fri 10:00-18:00, Thu until 20:00, Sat-Sun 11:00-18:00, closed Mon. See page 573.

▲**Gendarmenmarkt** Inviting square bounded by twin churches, a chocolate shop, and a concert hall. See page 561.

▲**Museum of the Wall at Checkpoint Charlie** Stories of brave Cold War escapes, near the site of the famous former East-West border checkpoint; the surrounding street scene is almost as interesting. **Hours:** Daily 9:00-22:00. See page 574.

ied abroad, mobile 0176-7677-9920, www.berlinlocals.com); and **Bernhard Schlegelmilch** (the only guide listed here who grew up behind the Wall, mobile 0176-6422-9119, www.steubentoursberlin.com).

Guides can get booked up—especially in the summer—so reserve ahead. Many of these guides belong to a guiding federation called Bündnis Berliner Stadtführer, which is a great source for connecting with even more guides (www.guides-berlin.org).

BERLIN

BIKE AND BOAT TOURS
Fat Tire Bike Tours

Fat Tire offers several different guided bike tours from April through October (most €28, 4-6 hours, 6-10 miles, check schedules at www.fattiretours.com/berlin): City Tour (daily; also available as a more expensive e-bike version), Berlin Wall Tour, Third Reich, Modern Berlin Tour, and private tours for families and small groups. Meet at the TV Tower at Alexanderplatz (reservations smart, tel. 030/2404-7991).

▲▲Spree River Cruises

Several boat companies offer €14 trips up and down the river. In one relaxing hour, you'll listen to excellent English audio-guides, see lots of wonderful  new government-commissioned architecture, and enjoy the lively park action fronting the river. Boats leave from docks clustered near the bridge behind the Berlin Cathedral (just off Unter den Linden, near the DDR Museum). I enjoyed the Historical Sightseeing Cruise from **Stern und Kreisschiffahrt** (mid-March-Nov daily 10:00-19:00, leaves from Nikolaiviertel Dock—cross bridge from Berlin Cathedral toward Alexanderplatz and look right; not all boats have English commentary—ask; tel. 030/536-3600, www.sternundkreis.de).

Berlin City Walk

Trace Germany's turbulent 20th-century history on this roughly 1.5-mile self-guided walk, worth ▲▲▲. We'll start in front of the Reichstag, pass through the Brandenburg Gate, walk down Unter den Linden, and finish on Museum Island near the Spree River. Allow 2-3 hours at a brisk pace, not counting museum visits. By the end, you'll have seen the core of Berlin and its most important sights.

You can download a free ∩ Rick Steves audio version of this walk; see page 46.

THE REICHSTAG TO UNTER DEN LINDEN

• *Start in Platz der Republik and take in your surroundings. Dominating this park is a giant domed building.*

❶ Reichstag

The Reichstag is the heart of Germany's government. It's where the Bundestag—the lower house of parliament—meets to govern the nation (similar to the US House of Representatives).

Think of the history the Reichstag has seen. When the building was inaugurated in 1895, Germany was still a kingdom. Back then, the real center of power was a mile east of here, at the royal

palace. But after the emperor was deposed in World War I, the German Republic was proclaimed right on this spot.

That first democracy proved weak. Meanwhile, the storm of National Socialism was growing—the Nazis. Soon the Reichstag had dozens of duly elected National Socialists, and Adolf Hitler seized power. Then, in 1933, the Reichstag building nearly burned down. Many believe that Hitler planned the fire as an excuse to frame the communists and grab power for himself.

With Hitler as *Führer* and real democracy a thing of the past, the Reichstag was hardly used. But it remained a powerful symbol and therefore was a prime target for Allied bombers. As World War II wound down, and Soviet troops advanced on the city, it was here at the Reichstag that 1,500 German troops made their last stand. After the war, Berlin was divided and the Berlin Wall ran right behind the Reichstag. The building fell into disuse, and the West German capital was moved from Berlin to the remote city of Bonn.

After the Berlin Wall fell, the Reichstag again became the focus of the new nation. It was renovated by British architect Norman Foster, who added the glass dome, or cupola. In 1999, the new Reichstag reopened, and the parliament reconvened. To many Germans, the proud resurrection of their Reichstag symbolizes the end of a terrible chapter in their country's history.

Look now at the Reichstag's modern **dome.** The cupola rises 155 feet above the ground. Inside the dome, a cone of 360 mirrors reflects natural light into the legislative chamber below, and an opening at the top allows air to circulate. Lit from inside after dark, it gives Berlin a memorable nightlight. Entering the Reichstag is free but requires a reservation; once inside, you can climb the spiral ramp all the way to the top of the dome for a grand city view (for details on visiting, see "Sights in Berlin," later).

• *Walk up closer to the Reichstag, turn right, walk nearly to the street, and find a small memorial next to the shipping-container-like entrance buildings. It's a row of slate stones sticking out of the ground—it looks like a bike rack. This is the...*

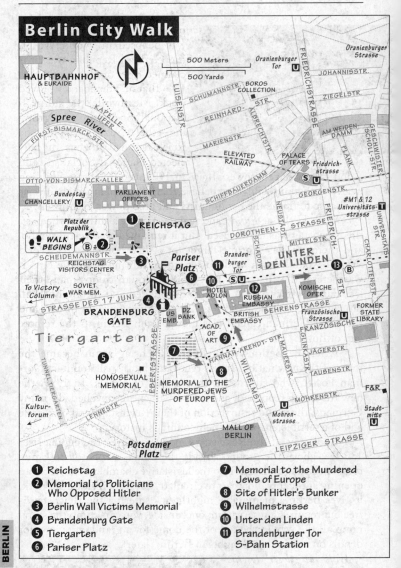

Berlin City Walk

500 Meters

500 Yards

- **1** Reichstag
- **2** Memorial to Politicians Who Opposed Hitler
- **3** Berlin Wall Victims Memorial
- **4** Brandenburg Gate
- **5** Tiergarten
- **6** Pariser Platz
- **7** Memorial to the Murdered Jews of Europe
- **8** Site of Hitler's Bunker
- **9** Wilhelmstrasse
- **10** Unter den Linden
- **11** Brandenburger Tor S-Bahn Station

2 Memorial to Politicians Who Opposed Hitler

These 96 slabs honor the 96 Reichstag members who spoke out against Adolf Hitler and the rising tide of fascism. When Hitler became chancellor, these critics were persecuted and murdered. On each slab, you'll see a name and political party—most are KPD (Communists) and SPD (Social Democrats)—and the date and location of death (*KZ* denotes those who died in concentration camps).

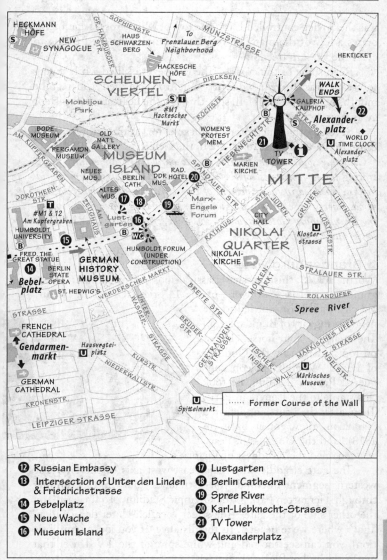

① Russian Embassy

⑬ Intersection of Unter den Linden & Friedrichstrasse

⑭ Bebelplatz

⑮ Neue Wache

⑯ Museum Island

⑰ Lustgarten

⑱ Berlin Cathedral

⑲ Spree River

⑳ Karl-Liebknecht-Strasse

㉑ TV Tower

㉒ Alexanderplatz

BERLIN

• *Walk east, along the right side of the Reichstag, on busy Scheidemannstrasse, toward the rear of the building. When you reach the intersection at the back of the Reichstag, turn right and cross the street. Once across, you'll see a row of white crosses along the sidewalk.*

❸ Berlin Wall Victims Memorial

The Berlin Wall once stood right here, running north-south down what is now busy Ebertstrasse, dividing the city in two. This side (near the crosses) was democratic West Berlin. On the other side was the Soviet-controlled East. The row of white crosses commemorates a few of the many brave East Berliners who died trying to cross the Wall to freedom.

Read some of the crosses. The last person killed while trying to escape was 20-year-old Chris Gueffroy. He died a mere nine months before the Wall fell, shot through the heart just a few steps away from here.

Several other memorials dedicated to various groups (from Sinti/Roma to homosexuals) are in the vicinity.

• *Continue south down Ebertstrasse toward the Brandenburg Gate, tracing the former course of the Berlin Wall. A thin strip of memorial bricks embedded in the pavement of Ebertstrasse indicate where it once stood. Ebertstrasse spills into a busy intersection dominated by the imposing Brandenburg Gate. To take in this scene, cross the Berlin Wall bricks to the piazza in front of the...*

❹ Brandenburg Gate

Worth ▲▲▲, this massive classical-looking monument is the grandest—and last survivor—of the 14 original gates in Berlin's old city wall. (This one led to the neighboring city of Brandenburg.) The majestic four-horse chariot on top is driven by the Goddess of Peace. When Napoleon conquered Prussia in 1806, he took this statue to the Louvre in Paris. Then, after the Prussians defeated Napoleon, they got it back (in 1813)...and the Goddess of Peace was renamed the "Goddess of Victory."

The gate straddles the major east-west axis of the city. The western segment—behind you—stretches four miles, running through Tiergarten Park to the Olympic Stadium. To the east—on the other side of the gate—the street is called Unter den Linden. That's where we're headed. In the distance (if you jockey for position), you can see the red-and-white spire of the TV Tower that marks the end of Berlin's main axis.

Historically, the Brandenburg Gate was just another of this city's many stately Prussian landmarks. But in our lifetime, it became *the* symbol of Berlin—of its Cold War division and its reunification. That's because, from 1961 to 1989, the gate was stranded in the no-man's land between East and West. For an entire generation, scores of German families were divided—some on this side of the Wall, some on the other. This landmark stood tantalizingly close to both East and West...but was completely off-limits to all.

By the 1980s, it was becoming clear that the once-mighty

The Berlin Wall: The Basics

West Berlin was a 185-square-mile island of capitalism surrounded by East Germany. Between establishment of the DDR (East Germany) in 1949 and construction of the Berlin Wall in 1961, an estimated three million East Germans emigrated

(fled) to freedom. To staunch their population loss, the DDR erected the 96-mile-long "Anti-Fascist Protective Rampart" almost overnight, beginning on August 13, 1961.

The Berlin Wall *(Berliner Mauer)* was actually two walls. The outer was a 12-foot-high concrete barrier topped with barbed wire and a rounded, pipe-like surface to discourage grappling hooks. The inner wall was lower-profile. Sandwiched between was a no-man's-land ("death strip") between 30 and 160 feet wide.

There were eight points where you could legally cross between West and East Berlin, the most famous of which were Checkpoint Charlie (see page 574) and the Friedrichstrasse train station. In general, Westerners could temporarily enter the East, but not vice versa.

Even after the Wall went up, people didn't stop trying to escape. During the Wall's 28 years, there were about 5,000 documented successful escapes—and 565 of those were East German guards. An estimated 136 people were killed at the Wall while trying to escape. Meanwhile, living in West Berlin—surrounded by concrete, barbed wire, and enemy soldiers armed to the teeth—was no picnic.

The Berlin Wall came to symbolize the larger Cold War between East and West. President John F. Kennedy gave a speech of solidarity in West Berlin, declaring, *"Ich bin ein Berliner"*—I am a Berliner. A generation later, President Ronald Reagan stood directly in front of the Brandenburg Gate and demanded of his Soviet counterpart, "Mr. Gorbachev, tear down this wall."

Finally, one November night in 1989, the Berlin Wall came down, as suddenly as it went up.

Soviet empire was slowly crumbling from within. Finally, on November 9, 1989, the world rejoiced at the sight of happy Berliners standing atop the Wall. They chipped away at it with hammers, passed beers to their long-lost cousins on the other side, and adorned the Brandenburg Gate with flowers like a parade float. A month and a half later, on December 22, West German Chancellor Helmut Kohl led a triumphant procession through the Brandenburg Gate to shake hands with his (soon-to-be-defunct) East German counterpart—the literal opening of a big gateway that marked the symbolic closing of a heinous era.

• *Turn 180 degrees and take in the vast, green expanse of the park called...*

❺ Tiergarten

This vast, 500-acre park, once a royal hunting ground, is now packed with cycling paths, joggers, and—on hot days—nude sunbathers. Look down the long boulevard (Strasse des 17. Juni) that bisects the park called Tiergarten ("Animal Garden"). The boulevard's name comes from the 17th of June, 1953, when brave East Germans rose up against their communist leaders. The rebellion was crushed, and East Berliners had to wait another 36 years for the kind of freedom you can enjoy next.

In the distance is the 220-foot **Victory Column,** topped with a golden statue that commemorates the three big military victories that established Prussia as a world power in the late 1800s—over France, Denmark, and Austria—and kicked off Berlin's Golden Age.

• *Walk through the Brandenburg Gate, entering what for years was forbidden territory. Just past the gate, there's a small TI on the right, and on the left is the Room of Silence, dedicated to quiet meditation on the cost of freedom. As you emerge on the other side of the gate, you enter a grand square known as...*

❻ Pariser Platz

Pariser Platz marks the start of Unter den Linden, the broad boulevard that stretches before you. "Parisian Square" was so named

after the Prussians defeated France and Napoleon in 1813. The square was once filled with important government buildings, but all were bombed to smithereens in World War II. For decades, it was an unrecognizable, deserted no-man's-land, cut off from both East and West by the Wall. But now it's rebuilt, and the winners of World War II—the US, France, Great Britain, and Russia—continue to enjoy this prime real estate: Their embassies are all on or near this square.

Check out some of the buildings facing the square (on the right as you come through the gate). The **US Embassy** reopened here in its original location on July 4, 2008. To the left of the US Embassy is the **DZ Bank Building,** built as a conference center in 2001 by Canadian-American architect Frank Gehry. Two doors past the bank is the ritzy **Hotel Adlon.** Over the years, this place has hosted celebrities and VIPs from Charlie Chaplin to Albert Einstein. And, yes, this was where pop star Michael Jackson shocked millions by dangling his infant son over the railing (from the second balcony up).

• *The most direct route to our next stop is by passing through the **Academy of Arts** (Academie der Kunst) building—it's between Hotel Adlon and the DZ Bank, at Pariser Platz 4. (If the Academy of Arts is closed, loop to the left, circling around the Hotel Adlon to Behrenstrasse.) As you exit out the back of the building (WC in basement), veer right on Behrenstrasse and cross the street. You'll wind up at our next stop, a sprawling field of stubby concrete pillars.*

❼ Memorial to the Murdered Jews of Europe

This memorial consists of 2,711 coffin-shaped pillars covering an entire city block. It commemorates the six million Jews who

were killed by the Nazis during World War II. Completed in 2005 by the Jewish-American architect Peter Eisenman, this was the first formal, German-government-sponsored Holocaust memorial. Using the word "murdered" in the title was intentional, and a big deal. Germany, as a nation, was admitting to a crime. Please be discreet at this powerful site.

Inside the **information center** (in the far-left corner), exhibits trace the rise of Nazism and how it led to World War II (for details on visiting the memorial, see page 567). Today's Germans—even several generations removed from the atrocities of their ancestors—still live by the ethic: "Never forget."

• *At the far-left corner, a little beyond the information center, you eventually emerge on the street corner. Our next stop is about a block farther. Carefully jaywalk across Hannah-Arendt-Strasse and continue straight (south) down Gertrud-Kolmar-Strasse. On the left side of the street, you'll reach a rough parking lot. At the far end of the lot is an information plaque labeled Führerbunker. This marks the...*

❽ Site of Hitler's Bunker

You're standing atop the buried remains of the *Führerbunker*. In early 1945, as Allied armies advanced on Berlin and Nazi Germany lay in ruins, Hitler and his staff retreated to this bunker complex behind the former Reich Chancellery. He stayed here for two months. It was here, on April 30, 1945—as the Soviet army tightened its noose on the Nazi capital—that Hitler and Eva Braun, his wife of less than 48 hours, committed suicide. A week later, the war

in Europe was over. The information board here explains the
rest of the story. Though the site
of Hitler's Bunker is certainly
thought-provoking, there really isn't much to see here. And
that's on purpose. No one wants
to turn Hitler's final stronghold
into a tourist attraction.

• *Backtrack up Gertrud-Kolmar-
Strasse, and turn right on Hannah-Arendt-Strasse. Then take your first
left (at the traffic light) on...*

❾ Wilhelmstrasse

This street was the traditional center of the German power, beginning back when Germany first became a nation in the 19th century.
It was lined with stately palaces, housing foreign embassies and
government offices. This was the home of the Reich Chancellery,
where the nation's chief executive presided. When the Nazis took
control, this street was where Hitler waved to his adoring fans, and
where Joseph Goebbels had his Ministry of Propaganda.

During World War II, Wilhelmstrasse was the nerve center
of the German war command. From here, Hitler directed the war,
and ordered the Blitz (the air raids that destroyed London). As the
war turned to the Allies' side, Wilhelmstrasse and the neighborhood around it were heavily bombed. Most of the stately palaces
were destroyed, and virtually nothing historic survives today.

• *The pedestrianized part of the street is home to the **British Embassy**.
Wilhelmstrasse spills out onto Berlin's main artery, the tree-lined Unter
den Linden, next to the Hotel Adlon.*

❿ Unter den Linden

This boulevard, worth ▲▲, is the heart of imperial Germany. During Berlin's Golden Age in the late 1800s, this was one of Europe's grand boulevards—the
Champs-Élysées of Berlin, a
city of nearly 2 million people.
It was lined with linden trees,
so as you promenaded down,
you'd be walking "*unter den
Linden.*" The street got its start
in the 15th century as a way
to connect the royal palace (a
half-mile down the road) with

the king's hunting grounds (today's big Tiergarten Park). Over the centuries, aristocrats moved into this area so their palaces could be close to their king's.

Many of the grandest landmarks we'll pass along here are thanks to Frederick the Great, who ruled from 1740 to 1786, and put his kingdom (Prussia) and his capital (Berlin) on the map. We'll also see a few signs of modern times; after World War II, this part of Berlin fell under Soviet influence, and Unter den Linden was the main street of communist East Berlin.

• *Turn your attention to the subway stop in front of the Hotel Adlon (labeled Brandenburger Tor).*

⓫ Brandenburger Tor S-Bahn Station

For a time-travel experience back to DDR days, head down the stairs into this station (no ticket necessary). As you go down the stairs, keep to the right (toward the S-Bahn, not the U-Bahn), to the subway tracks. You can walk along the platform about 200 yards, before popping back up to the surface.

For decades, the Brandenburger Tor S-Bahn station was unused—one of Berlin's "ghost stations." While you're down under,

notice how mid-20th-century the station still looks. There's the original 1930s green tile-work on the walls, and harsh fluorescent lighting. Some old signs (on the central pillars) still have *Unter den Linden* written in old Gothic lettering. During the Cold War, the zigzag line dividing East and West Berlin meant that some existing train lines crossed the border underground. To make a little hard Western cash, the East German government allowed a few trains to cut under East Berlin on their way between Western destinations. The only catch: No one could get on or off while the train was in East Berlin. For 28 years, stations like this were unused, as Western trains slowly passed through, and passengers saw only East German guards...and lots of cobwebs. Then, in 1989, literally within days of the fall of the Wall, these stations were reopened.

• *At the far end of the platform, ascend the escalator, bear right, and head up the stairs to exit. You'll emerge on the right side of Unter den Linden (at #63). Belly up to the bars and look in at the...*

⓬ Russian Embassy

Built from the ashes of World War II, this imposing building—it's Europe's largest embassy—made it clear to East Berliners who was now in charge: the Soviet Union. It was the first big postwar building project in East Berlin, built in the powerful, simplified Neoclassical style that Stalin liked. Standing here, imagine Unter den Linden as a depressing Cold War era cul-de-sac, dead-ending at the walled-off Brandenburg Gate. After the fall of the Soviet Union in 1991, this building became the Russian Embassy, flying the white, blue, and red flag. Find the hammer-and-sickle motif decorating the window frames—a reminder of the days when Russia was part of the USSR.

· *Keep walking down the boulevard for two blocks. Pause when you reach the intersection with...*

⓭ Friedrichstrasse

You're standing at perhaps the most central crossroads in Berlin—named for, you guessed it, Frederick the Great. Before World War II, Friedrichstrasse was the heart of cultural Berlin. In the Roaring Twenties, it was home to anything-goes nightlife and cabarets where entertainers like Marlene Dietrich, Bertolt Brecht, and Josephine Baker performed. And since the fall of the Wall, it's become home to supersized department stores and big-time hotels.

Consider popping into the grand **Galeries Lafayette** department store (two blocks down to your right). Inside, you can ogle a huge glass-domed atrium—a miniature version of the Reichstag cupola. Before moving on, note that there's a WC and a handy designer food court in the basement. (If you were to continue down Friedrichstrasse from here, you'd wind up at **Checkpoint Charlie** in about 10 minutes.)

· *Head down Unter den Linden a few more blocks, past the large equestrian statue of **Frederick the Great**, who ruled as king of Prussia in the mid-1700s. Turn right into Bebelplatz. Head to the center of the square, and find the square of glass window set into the pavement.*

BERLIN

⓮ Bebelplatz: The Square of the Books

Frederick the Great built this square to show off Prussian ideals: education, the arts, improvement of the individual, and a tolerance for different groups—provided they're committed to the betterment of society. This square was the cultural center of Frederick's capital. In many ways, it still is. Spin counterclockwise to take in the cultural sights, some of which date back to Frederick's time.

Start by looking across Unter den Linden. That's **Humboldt University,** one of Europe's greatest. Continue panning left. Fronting Bebelplatz is the **former state library**—which was funded by

Frederick the Great. After the library was damaged in World War II, communist authorities decided to rebuild it in the original style...but only because Lenin studied here during much of his exile from Russia. The square is closed by one of Berlin's swankiest lodgings—**Hotel de Rome,** housed in a historic bank building.

Next, the green-domed structure is **St. Hedwig's Church** (nicknamed the "Upside-Down Teacup"). It stands as a symbol of

Frederick the Great's religious and cultural tolerance. The pragmatic king wanted to encourage the integration of Catholic Silesians into Protestant Prussia. But Frederick's progressivism had its limits: St. Hedwig's is set back from the street, suggesting its inferiority to Protestant churches.

Up next is the **Berlin State Opera** *(Staatsoper)*—originally established in Frederick the Great's time. Frederick believed that the arts were essential to having a well-rounded populace. He moved the opera house from inside the castle to this showcase square.

Now look down through the glass window in the pavement, which gives a glimpse at what appears to be a room of empty bookshelves. This **book-burning memorial** commemorates a notorious event that took place here during the Nazi years. It was on this square in 1933 that staff and students from the university built a bonfire. Into the flames they threw 20,000 newly forbidden books authored by the likes of Einstein, Hemingway, Freud, and T. S. Eliot. Overseeing it all was the Nazi propaganda minister, Joseph Goebbels.

• *Before leaving Bebelplatz, consider detouring one block south to Berlin's finest square,* **Gendarmenmarkt.** *The square, like its name ("Square of the Gens d'Armes," Frederick the Great's French guard), is a hybrid of Prussia and France, bookended by two matching churches, with the Berlin Symphony's Concert Hall in the middle. While the square is more about simply enjoying a genteel space than it is about sightseeing, you can dip into its church/museums or visit a pair of fun chocolate shops nearby.*

Otherwise, to continue this walk, leave Bebelplatz back toward Unter den Linden, cross to the university side, and continue heading east. You'll pass in front of Humboldt University's main gate. Immediately in front of the gate, embedded in the cobbles, notice the row of square, bronze plaques—each one bearing the name of a university student who was executed by the Nazis. You'll see similar **Stolpersteine** *("stumbling stones") all over Berlin. Just beyond the university on the left, head for a building that looks like a Greek temple set in a small park filled with chestnut trees.*

⓯ Neue Wache

The "New Guardhouse" was built in 1816 as just that—a fancy barracks for the bodyguards of the Crown Prince. (The Prince lived across the street in the Neoclassical building just ahead—it's the one with four tall columns marking the doorway.) Over the years, the Neue Wache has been transformed into a memorial for fallen warriors. Check out the pediment over the doorway: The goddess of Victory stands in the center amid the chaos of war, as soldiers fall.

The Neue Wache represents the strong, united, rising Prussian state Frederick created. It was just one of the grand new buildings built to line either side of this stretch of Unter den Linden. The style was Neoclassical—structures that looked like Greek temples, with columns and triangular pediments.

Step inside. In 1993, the interior was fitted with the statue we see today—a replica of *Mother with Her Dead Son*, by Käthe Koll-

witz, a Berlin artist who lived through both world wars. The statue marks the tombs of Germany's unknown soldier and an unknown concentration camp victim. The inscription reads, "To the victims of war and tyranny."

• *Continue down Unter den Linden, passing by the pink-yet-formidable Zeughaus (early 1700s), the oldest building on the boulevard. Built in the Baroque style as the royal arsenal, it later became a military museum, and today houses the excellent* **German History Museum** *(see page 571). When you reach the bridge, cross the Spree and step onto Museum Island.*

⓰ Museum Island

This island, sitting in the middle of the Spree River, is Berlin's historic birthplace. Take in the scene: the lazy river, the statues along the bridge, and the impressive buildings all around you.

Berlin was born on this marshy island around the year 1200. As the city grew, this island remained the site of the ruler's castle and residence— from Brandenburg dukes and Hohenzollern prince-electors, to the kings of Prussia and the kaisers of the German Empire. At its peak under Prussian rulers

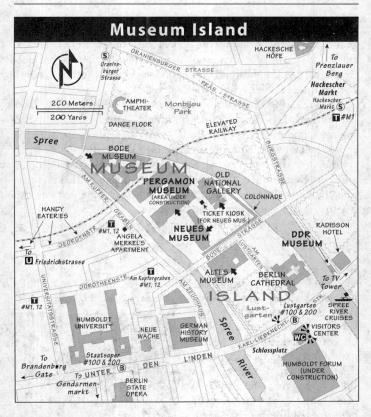

Museum Island

(1701-1918), it was a splendid and sprawling Baroque palace called the Stadtschloss, topped at one end with a dome.

So, uh, where is this palace? It's gone. The palace was gutted in a 1945 air raid in the last days of World War II. Now the site is a major construction zone. Germany is building the **Humboldt Forum**, a huge public venue that will resemble the original Baroque palace, complete with a dome on one end (you can already see it taking shape).

• *Now, turn your attention to the left side of Unter den Linden. There's a spacious garden, bordered on two sides by impressive buildings.*

Museum Island Sights

For 300 years, the ❼ **Lustgarten** has flip-flopped between being a military parade ground and a people-friendly park, depending on the political tenor of the time. In the Nazi era, Hitler enjoyed giving speeches here—from the top of the museum steps overlooking this square. At the far end of the Lustgarten are a cache of grandiose museum buildings that represent the can-do German spirit of the 1800s, when city leaders envisioned the island as an oasis of culture and learning. Today, the island's impressive buildings host **grand museums,** including the **Neues Museum** (with the ethereal Bust of Nefertiti), the **Pergamon Museum** (with classical antiquities), and the **Old National Gallery** (German Romantic painting). For details, see "Sights in Berlin," later.

Dominating the island is the towering, green-domed ❸ **Berlin Cathedral** (Berliner Dom). This is only a century old, built during the reign of Kaiser Wilhelm II—that jingoistic emperor in the spiked helmet who led Europe into World War I. The Wilhelmian style is over-the-top: a garish mix of Neoclassical, Neo-Baroque, and Neo-Renaissance, with rippling stucco and gold-tiled mosaics. The church is at its most impressive from the outside, but you can pay to climb the dome for great views.

• *Continue down Unter den Linden past the cathedral, and pause on the bridge over the Spree.*

❹ Spree River

The Spree River is people-friendly and welcoming. A parklike promenade leads all the way from here to the Hauptbahnhof.

Along it, you'll find impromptu "beachside" beer gardens with imported sand, BBQs in pocket parks, and lots of locals walking their dogs, taking a lazy bike ride, or jogging. Spree River boat tours depart from near here (for details, see page 550). At the end of the bridge, look down on your left to see the **DDR Museum,** where everyday artifacts paint a vivid picture of life in Cold War-era East Germany (for details, see page 572).

• *Our walk is over. From here you could return to Museum Island to see the sights there, or backtrack to the German History Museum.*

But if you're itching to keep walking, just cross the bridge and proceed along ❷⓪ Karl-Liebknecht-Strasse. You'll soon reach the base of the 1,200-foot-tall ❷① TV Tower with its glittering disco ball—a legacy from communist East Germany (you can ride the elevator to the top, www.tv-turm.de). From here, the closest S- and U-Bahn stations are a five-minute walk away at ❷② Alexanderplatz, a kitschy-futuristic space that was the main square of DDR-era East Berlin.

Sights in Berlin

REICHSTAG AND BRANDENBURG GATE AREA

This area is covered in detail in my Berlin City Walk (see earlier; also available as a free 🎧 audio tour).

▲▲▲Reichstag

Germany's historic parliament building—completed in 1894, burned in 1933, sad and lonely in a no-man's-land throughout the

Cold War, and finally rebuilt and topped with a glittering glass cupola in 1999—is a symbol of a proudly reunited nation. Visit here to spiral up the remarkable dome and gaze across Berlin's rooftops, and to watch today's parliament in action. Because of security concerns, you'll need a reservation.

Cost and Hours: Free, reservations required—see next, daily 8:00-24:00, last entry at 22:00, metal detectors, no big luggage allowed, Platz der Republik 1; S- or U-Bahn: Friedrichstrasse, Brandenburger Tor, or Bundestag; tel. 030/2273-2152, www.bundestag.de.

Reservations: You must make a free reservation. It's easy to do online, but book early—spots often book up several days in advance. Go to www.bundestag.de, and from the "Visit the Bundestag" menu, select "Online registration." You have two choices: "Visit to the dome" includes a good audioguide and is plenty for most; the 90-minute guided tour provides more in-depth information. After choosing your preferred date and time, you'll be sent an email link to a website where you'll enter details for each person in your party. A final email will contain your reservation (with a letter you must print out and bring with you).

Without a Reservation: Tickets may be available even when online sales are "sold out"—inquire at the tiny visitors center on the Tiergarten side of Scheidemannstrasse, across from Platz der Republik (open daily 8:00-20:00, until 18:00 Nov-March; bookings from 3 hours to 2 days in advance, go early to avoid lines). When booking, the whole party must be present and ID is required.

Getting In: Report 15 minutes before your appointed time to the temporary-looking entrance facility in front of the Reichstag, and be ready to show ID and your reservation print-out. After passing through a security check, you'll wait with other visitors for a guard to take you to the Reichstag entrance.

Visiting the Reichstag: The open, airy **lobby** towers 100 feet high, with 65-foot-tall colors of the German flag. See-through glass doors show the central legislative chamber. The message: There will be no secrets in this government. Look inside. Spreading his wings behind the podium is a stylized German eagle, the *Bundestagsadler* (affectionately nicknamed the "Fat Hen"), representing the Bundestag (each branch of government has its own symbolic eagle). Notice the doors marked *Ja* (Yes), *Nein* (No), and *Enthalten* (Abstain)...an homage to the Bundestag's traditional "sheep jump" way of counting votes by exiting the chamber through the corresponding door. (For critical votes, however, they vote with electronic cards.)

Germany's Bundestag (comparable to the US House of Representatives) meets here. Its 631 members are elected to four-year terms. They in turn elect the chancellor. Unlike America's two-party system, Germany has a handful of significant parties, so they must form coalitions to govern effectively. Bundestag members have offices in the building to the left of the Reichstag.

Ride the elevator to the base of the **glass dome.** The dome is 80 feet high, 130 feet across, and weighs a quarter of a million pounds. It uses about 33,000 square feet of glass, or nearly enough to cover a football field. You'll pick up your audioguide at the base of the dome.

Study the photos and read the circle of captions (around the base of the central funnel) telling the Reichstag story. Then study the surrounding architecture: a broken collage of new on old, torn between antiquity and modernity, like Germany's history. Notice the dome's giant and unobtrusive sunscreen that moves as necessary with the sun. Peer down through the skylight to look over the shoulders of the elected representatives at work. For Germans, the best view from here is down—keeping a close eye on their government.

Walking up the **ramp,** you'll spiral past 360-degree views of the city, including the Tiergarten, the "green lungs of Berlin"; the Teufelsberg ("Devil's Hill"; famous during the Cold War as a powerful ear of the West—notice the telecommunications tower on top); Potsdamer Platz, Brandenburg Gate; Frank Gehry's curving fish-like roof of the DZ Bank building; the Memorial to the Murdered Jews of Europe; the former East Berlin, with a forest of 300-foot-tall skyscrapers in the works; Berlin's huge main train station; and the blocky, postmodern Chancellery, the federal government's headquarters (the audioguide explains what you're seeing as you walk).

BERLIN

▲▲Memorial to the Murdered Jews of Europe
(Denkmal für die Ermordeten Juden Europas)

This labyrinth of 2,711 irregularly shaped pillars memorializes the six million Jewish people who were executed by the Nazis.

Loaded with symbolism, it's designed to encourage a pensive moment in the heart of a big city. At its information center, you can learn more about the Nazis' crimes and see items belonging to the victims. Six portraits, representing the six million Jewish victims, put a human face on the staggering numbers. You'll see diaries, letters, and final farewells penned by Holocaust victims. And you'll learn about 15 Jewish families from very different backgrounds, who all met the same fate. A continually running soundtrack recites victims' names. To read them all aloud would take more than six and a half years.

Cost and Hours: Memorial-free and always open; information center-free, open Tue-Sun 10:00-20:00, Oct-March until 19:00, closed Mon year-round, last entry 45 minutes before closing, brief security screening at entry, audioguide-€4; S-Bahn: Brandenburger Tor or Potsdamer Platz, tel. 030/2639-4336, www.stiftung-denkmal.de.

ART AND HISTORY MUSEUMS

Several of Berlin's top museums—featuring art and artifacts from around the world—are just a few steps apart on Museum Island. Two more museums lie on either side of the island: the German History Museum (on Unter den Linden), and the DDR Museum (on the Spree riverbank). For locations, see the map on page 563.

Farther from the center, but of special interest, are the Jewish Museum Berlin (south of Unter den Linden) and the Gemäldegalerie (in the Kulturforum complex). See the map on page 544 for locations.

Museum Island (Museumsinsel)

Filling a spit of land in the middle of the Spree River, Museum Island has perhaps Berlin's highest concentration of serious sightseeing. Envisioned as an oasis of culture and learning, the island's imposing Neoclassical buildings host five grand museums (each described next).

Cost and Hours: Each museum has its own admission (€10-12, includes audioguide). If you're visiting at least two museums here, invest in the €18 Museum Island Pass (which covers all 5). The museums are open 10:00-18:00 (until 20:00 on Thu). The Pergamon and Neues museums are open daily; the Old National Gallery, Bode Museum, and Altes Museum are open Tue-Sun, closed Mon.

Information: Tel. 030/266-424-242, www.smb.museum.

Avoiding Crowds: The always-busy Pergamon is most crowded in the morning, on weekends, and when it rains. You can also book a timed-entry ticket (or, if you have a pass, a reservation).

Getting There: The island is a 10-minute walk from the Hackescher Markt or Friedrichstrasse S-Bahn stations. Trams #M1 and #12 connect to Prenzlauer Berg. Buses #100 and #200 run along Unter den Linden, stopping near the museums at the Lustgarten stop.

▲▲▲Pergamon Museum (Pergamonmuseum)

This world-class museum contains Berlin's Collection of Classical Antiquities (Antikensammlung)—in other words, full-sized buildings from the most illustrious civilizations of the ancient world. Its namesake and highlight—the gigantic Pergamon Altar—is under renovation and off-limits to visitors until 2025. In the meantime, there's still plenty to see: the massive Babylonian Processional Way and Ishtar Gate (slath-

ered with glazed blue tiles, from the sixth century B.C.); artifacts from the Assyrians (7th-10th century B.C.); the full-sized market gate from the ancient Roman settlement of Miletus (first century B.C.); and, upstairs, an extensive collection of treasures from the Islamic world.

Visiting the Museum: The superb audioguide (included) helps broaden your experience. From the entry hall, head up to floor 1 and all the way back to 575 B.C. and Mesopotamia.

Processional Way and Ishtar Gate: The ruler Nebuchadnezzar II made sure that all who approached his city got a grand first impression. His massive blue Ishtar Gate stands 46 feet tall and 100 feet wide (counting its jutting facets). This was the grandest of Babylon's gates, one of eight in the 11-mile wall that encompassed this city of 200,000. In its day, the Ishtar Gate was famous—one of the original Seven Wonders of the World. All the pieces in this hall—the Ishtar Gate, Processional Way, and Throne Room panels—are made of decorative brick, glazed and fired in the ancient Egyptian faience technique.

BERLIN

The museum's Babylonian treasures are meticulous reconstructions. After a Berlin archaeologist discovered the ruins in modern-day Iraq in 1900, the Prussian government financed their excavation. What was recovered was little more than piles of shattered shards of brick. It's since been augmented with modern tilework and pieced together like a 2,500-year-old Babylonian jigsaw puzzle. (You might peek into Room 6 to see a model of ancient Babylon).

Assyrian Artifacts: The rooms at the opposite end of the Processional Way are filled with artifacts from the Babylonians' northern cousins, the Assyrians. Look for the Esarhaddon Stele, a ceremonial column marking the passing of the baton between the two great Mesopotamian powers, and the 10-foot-tall statue of the weather god Hadad. Browse through these rooms to get a sense of Assyrian grandeur, then return to the Ishtar Gate.

Market Gate of Miletus: From the Ishtar Gate, you'll pass into a large hall with supersized monuments from ancient Rome. You've flash-forwarded 700 years to the ancient city of Miletus, a wealthy and cosmopolitan Roman-ruled, Greek-speaking city on the southwest coast of Asia Minor (modern Turkey). Dominating this room is the huge Market Gate of Miletus—50 feet tall, 100 feet wide. This served as the entrance to the town's agora, or marketplace. Traders from across the Mediterranean and Middle East passed through the three arched doorways into a football-field-sized courtyard surrounded by arcades, where business was conducted.

The Rest of the Museum: To complete your tour of civilizations, on floor 1 you can see artifacts from several royal palaces of the Assyrian kings (the Babylonians' northern cousins). Then find the stairs in front of the Ishtar Gate and head up to floor 2, which is dedicated to the **Museum of Islamic Art.** It demonstrates how—after Rome fell and Europe was mired in medievalism—the Islamic world carried the torch of civilization. The impressive Aleppo Room is illustrated with motifs from Christian, Arabic, Persian, and Jewish traditions.

What About the Pergamon Altar? The museum's namesake and most famous piece—the Pergamon Altar—is being stored out of view while the hall that houses it is slowly modernized. The altar likely won't be back until around 2025. (The "altar" is actually a temple, a masterpiece of Hellenistic art from the second century B.C.) While the restoration is ongoing, a nearby pavilion (on Am Kupfergraben, directly across from Museum Island) will house a **temporary exhibit** about the altar. See www.smb.museum for updates.

BERLIN

▲▲Neues (New) Museum

This beautifully renovated museum, featuring objects from the prehistoric (i.e., pre-Pergamon) world, contains three collections. Most visitors focus on the Egyptian Collection, with the famous and even-more-stunning-in-person bust of Queen Nefertiti. But it's also worth a walk through the Museum of Prehistory and Early History and the Collection of Classical Antiquities (artifacts from ancient Troy). Everything is well-described in English (fine audioguide included with admission; for more on the museum, see www.neues-museum.de).

Visiting the Museum: The Neues Museum ticket desk is across the courtyard from the entrance. Ticket in hand, enter and pick up the floor plan. The main reason to visit is to enjoy one of the great thrills in art appreciation—gazing into the still young and beautiful face of Queen Nefertiti. If you're in a pinch for time, make a beeline to her (floor 2, far corner of Egyptian Collection in Room 210).

To tour the whole collection, start at the top (floor 3), the **prehistory section.** The entire floor is filled with Stone Age, Ice Age, and Bronze Age items. You'll see early human remains, tools, spearheads, and pottery.

On floor 2, in a room all her own (Room 210) is the 3,000-year-old bust of **Queen Nefertiti,** wife of Akhenaton—the most famous

piece of Egyptian art in Europe. Nefertiti has all the right beauty marks: long slender neck, perfect lips, almond eyes, symmetrical eyebrows, pronounced cheekbones, and a perfect spray-on tan. And yet, despite her seemingly perfect beauty, Nefertiti has a touch of humanity. Notice the fine wrinkles around the eyes—these only enhance her beauty. She has a slight Mona Lisa smile, pursed at the corners.

Downstairs on level 1, make your way to Rooms 103-104. The text panels help explain the craze for antiquities that brought us the Neues Museum. Much of it can be traced to the man featured in these rooms: **Heinrich Schliemann** (1822-1890). Having read Homer's accounts of the Trojan War, Schliemann set out on a quest to find the long-lost ruins of the city of Troy. He (probably) found the capital of the Trojans (in Turkey), as well as the capital of the Greeks (Mycenae, in the Greek Peloponnese). Displays tell the fascinating story of how Schliemann smuggled the treasures out in fruit baskets, then their long journey until they were donated to the German government.

▲▲Old National Gallery (Alte Nationalgalerie)

Of Berlin's many top-notch art collections, this is the best for *German* art—mostly paintings from the 19th century, the era in which

"German culture" first came to mean something. For a concise visit, focus on the Romantic German paintings (top floor), where Caspar David Friedrich's hauntingly beautiful canvases offer an insightful glimpse into German landscapes...and the German psyche.

Bode Museum

This fine building—at the northern tip of the island—contains a hodgepodge of collections: Byzantine art, historic coins, ecclesias-

tical art, sculptures, and medals commemorating the fall of the Berlin Wall and German reunification. While this museum is too deep a dive for casual sightseers, avid museumgoers find plenty exciting here—including the stunning Ravenna Mosaic, transplanted here from the Byzantine world of sixth-century Italy. For a free, quick look at its lavish interior, climb the grand staircase under a sweeping dome to the charming café on the first floor.

Altes (Old) Museum

Of the five Museum Island collections, this is the least exciting—unless you're an enthusiast of obscure Etruscan, Roman, and Greek art and artifacts.

Near Museum Island
▲▲▲German History Museum (Deutsches Historisches Museum)

This impressive museum offers the best look at German history under one roof, anywhere. The permanent collection packs 9,000 artifacts into two huge rectangular floors of the old arsenal building. You'll stroll through insightfully described historical objects, paintings, photographs, and models—all intermingled with multimedia stations. The 20th-century section—on the ground floor—is far better than any of the many price-gouging historical Nazi or

Cold War "museums" all over town. A thoughtful visit here provides valuable context for your explorations of Berlin (and Germany).

Cost and Hours: €8, daily 10:00-18:00, good €3 audioguide, Unter den Linden 2, tel. 030/2030-4751, www.dhm.de.

Getting There: It's at Unter den Linden 2, immediately west of Museum Island (just across the river). Buses #100, #200, and #TXL stop right in front (Staatsoper stop). By tram, the Am Kupfergraben stop (for trams #M1 and #12) is a block behind the museum. The nearest S-Bahn stop  is Friedrichstrasse, a 10-minute walk away; Hackescher Markt S-Bahn station is nearly as close.

Visiting the Museum: The first floor (up the stairs) covers the period starting in 500, up until the early 20th century. The ground floor takes you from World War I through the fall of the Berlin Wall. As you tour the collection, stay on track by locating the museum's information pillars along the way (each marked with a date span), then browse the exhibits nearby. At the top of the stairs, consider taking 45 minutes for the dry but informative film on German history (with English subtitles).

▲▲DDR Museum

While overpriced, crammed with school groups, and frustrating to local historians, the DDR Museum has a knack for helping  ing outsiders understand life in communist East Germany (the *Deutsche Demokratische Republik,* or DDR). Visitors walk through a reconstructed home—peeking into bathroom cabinets and wardrobes—and are encouraged to pick up and handle anything that isn't behind glass. The museum is well-stocked with kitschy everyday items from the DDR period, plus photos, video clips, and concise English explanations.

Cost and Hours: €9.50, daily 10:00-20:00, Sat until 22:00, just across the Spree from Museum Island at Karl-Liebknecht-Strasse 1, tel. 030/847-123-731, www.ddr-museum.de.

South of Unter den Linden
▲Jewish Museum Berlin (Jüdisches Museum Berlin)

Combining a remarkable building with a thoughtful permanent exhibit, this is the most educational Jewish-themed sight in Ber-

lin—easily worth ▲▲ (and the effort to reach it) for those with an interest in Jewish history. The exhibit provides a detailed overview of the rich culture and history of Europe's Jewish community. And the building itself—which enhances the overall experience—is packed with symbolism and offers several spaces designed for pondering what you've learned. To really dig into the place, give yourself at least two hours. English explanations interpret both the exhibits and the building, but the excellent €3 audioguide—with four hours of commentary—is essential to fully appreciate the collection.

Cost and Hours: €8, daily 10:00-20:00, Mon until 22:00, closed on Jewish holidays. Tight security includes bag check and metal detectors. Tel. 030/2599-3300, www.jmberlin.de.

Getting There: Take the U-Bahn to Hallesches Tor, find the exit marked *Jüdisches Museum*, exit straight ahead, then turn right on Franz-Klühs-Strasse. The museum is a five-minute walk ahead on your left, at Lindenstrasse 9. For the location, see the map on page 544.

In the Kulturforum Complex

Berlin's *other* ensemble of museums (after Museum Island) fills a purpose-built facility just beyond Potsdamer Platz. Here you'll find a variety of impressive museums and other cultural institutions, the most significant of which is the collection of exquisite European Masters at the Gemäldegalerie.

▲▲Gemäldegalerie

This "Painting Gallery" is one of Germany's top collections of great works by European masters. The Gemäldegalerie shows off fine works from the 13th through 18th century. While there's no one famous piece of art, you'll get an enticing taste of just about all the big names. In the North Wing are painters from Germany (Albrecht Dürer, Hans Holbein, Lucas Cranach), the Low Countries (Jan van Eyck, Pieter Brueghel, Peter Paul Rubens, Anthony van Dyck, Frans Hals, Johannes Vermeer), Britain (Thomas Gainsborough), France (Antoine Watteau), and an impressive hall of Rem-

BERLIN

brandts. The South Wing is the terrain of Italian greats, including Giotto, Botticelli, Titian, Raphael, and Caravaggio.

Cost and Hours: €10, includes audioguide, Tue-Fri 10:00-18:00, Thu until 20:00, Sat-Sun 11:00-18:00, closed Mon, loaner stools, great salad bar in cafeteria upstairs, Matthäikirchplatz 4, tel. 030/266-424-242, www.smb.museum.

Getting There: Ride the S-Bahn or U-Bahn to Potsdamer Platz, then walk along Potsdamer Platz; you can take bus #200 to Philharmonie (though this can be slow during rush hour). For the location, see the map on page 544.

FASCISM AND COLD WAR SITES
Near Checkpoint Charlie

A variety of fascinating sites relating to Germany's tumultuous 20th century clusters south of Unter den Linden. They are listed roughly north to south (as you'd reach them from Unter den Linden). For locations, see the map on page 544.

▲Checkpoint Charlie

Famous as the place where many visiting Westerners crossed into East Berlin during the Cold War, the original Checkpoint Char-

lie is long gone. But today a reconstructed guard station—with big posters of American and Soviet guards, and a chilling "You are leaving the American sector" sign—attracts curious tourists for a photo op. Nothing here is original (except for the nearby museum—described next), and the whole area feels like a Cold War theme park, with kitschy communist-themed attractions, Trabi rides, hucksters, buskers, and sleazy vendors who charge through the nose for a DDR stamp in your passport. The replica checkpoint is free to view and always open (but you'll pay to take photos with the "guards").

▲Museum of the Wall at Checkpoint Charlie (Mauermuseum Haus am Checkpoint Charlie)

This ragtag but riveting celebration of the many ways desperate East Germans managed to slip through the Wall to freedom has stood here since 1963...taunting DDR authorities. Today East Germany and its Wall are long gone, but the museum is still going strong. Some of the displays have yellowed, the place is cramped and confusing, and the ticket prices are way too high, but the museum retains a special sense of history. Visiting here, you'll learn

about the creation of the Wall and the many escape attempts (including several of the actual items used by clever escapees). Compared to the soberly academic official Berlin Wall Memorial near the Nordbahnhof, this museum has more personality, buoyed by a still-defiant spirit.

Cost and Hours: €12.50, daily 9:00-22:00, last entry one hour before closing, audioguide-€5, U6 to Kochstrasse or U2 to Stadtmitte, Friedrichstrasse 43, tel. 030/253-7250, www.mauermuseum.de.

▲▲Topography of Terror (Topographie des Terrors)

A rare undeveloped patch of land in central Berlin, right next to a surviving stretch of Wall, was once the nerve center for the Gestapo and the SS—the most despicable elements of the Nazi government.

Today this site hosts a modern documentation center, along with an outdoor exhibit in the Gestapo headquarters' excavated foundations. While there isn't much in the way of original artifacts, the exhibit does a good job of telling this powerful story,

in the place where it happened. The information is a bit dense, but WWII historians (even armchair ones) find it fascinating.

Cost and Hours: Free, includes audioguide (ID required), daily 10:00-20:00, outdoor exhibit closes at dusk and closed entirely mid-Oct-mid-April, Niederkirchnerstrasse 8, U-Bahn: Potsdamer Platz or Kochstrasse, S-Bahn: Anhalter Bahnhof or Potsdamer Platz, tel. 030/254-5090, www.topographie.de.

Nearby: Immediately next door is an unusually long surviving stretch of the Berlin Wall. A block beyond that is the looming, very fascist-style Former Air Ministry—built by Hitler to house his Luftwaffe (Nazi air force), later the DDR's "Hall of Ministries," today the German Finance Ministry, still adorned with cheery 1950s communist propaganda. And a short walk away is a surviving DDR Watchtower, which kept careful vigil over the Wall.

Away from the Center
▲▲▲Berlin Wall Memorial (Gedenkstätte Berliner Mauer)

This is Berlin's most substantial and educational sight relating to its gone-but-not-forgotten Wall. As you visit the park, you'll learn about how the Wall went up, the brutal methods used to keep Easterners in, and the brave stories of people who risked everything to be free.

Exhibits line up along several blocks of Bernauer Strasse, stretching more than a mile northeast from the Nordbahnhof S-Bahn station (one of the DDR's "ghost stations") to Schwedter Strasse and the Mauerpark. For a targeted visit, focus on the engaging sights clustered near the Nordbahnhof: two museums (with films, photos, and harrowing personal stories); various open-air exhibits and memorials; original Wall fragments; and observation tower views into the only preserved, complete stretch of the Wall system (with a Cold War-era "death strip").

Cost and Hours: Free; outdoor areas accessible daily 24 hours; Visitors Center and Documentation Center both open Tue-Sun 10:00-18:00, closed Mon, memorial chapel closes at 17:00; on Bernauer Strasse at #119 (Visitors Center) and #111 (Documentation Center), tel. 030/4679-86666, www.berliner-mauer-gedenkstaette.de.

Getting There: Take the S-Bahn (line S1, S2, or S25) to Nordbahnhof. Exit by following signs for *Bernauer Strasse*—you'll pop out across the street from a long chunk of Wall and kitty-corner from the Visitors Center. You can also get there on tram #12 or #M10. For location, see the map on page 544.

Overview: Begin at the Nordbahnhof and pick up an informational pamphlet from the Visitors Center (note that there are different brochures for the four sections—A, B, C, and D—so be sure to take all you'll need). Then head up Bernauer Strasse, visit the exhibits and memorials that interest you, and ride back to the center from the Bernauer Strasse U-Bahn station. For a longer visit, walk several more blocks all the way to the Mauerpark. The entire stretch is lined with informational posts (some with video or audio clips) and larger-than-life images from the Wall, painted on the sides of buildings.

❍ Self-Guided Tour: Start your visit at the Visitors Center, the rust-colored, blocky building located kitty-corner from the Nordbahnhof (at the far west end of the long Memorial park, at Bernauer Strasse 119).

Berlin Wall Memorial

Legend:
- Berlin Wall Memorial
- ⋯⋯ Former Course of the Wall

To Sections C & D,
Ⓤ Bernauer Strasse,
Ⓣ #M10 to Prenzlauer Berg
& Mauerpark

TOUR ENDS

STRELITZER STR.

TUNNEL 57

OPEN-AIR DISPLAY

CHAPEL OF RECONCILIATION

SECTION B

HUSSITENSTRASSE

ACKERSTRASSE

BERNAUER STRASSE

ESCAPE ATTEMPTS

#M10 Ⓣ

DOCUMENTATION CENTER

GUARD TOWER

PRESERVED PART OF WALL

CEMETERY CROSS

WALL OF REMEMBRANCE

WALL FRAGMENTS

Sophien Parish Cemetery

SECTION A

100 Meters
100 Yards

ACKERSTRASSE

TOUR BEGINS

VISITORS CENTER

"DEATH STRIP"

3-D MAP

#M10 Ⓣ

NORDBAHNHOF EXIT

BERGSTRASSE

GARTENSTRASSE

Ⓢ Nordbahnhof

INVALIDENSTRASSE

1. Visitors Center
2. 3-D Map of the Former Neighborhood
3. "Death Strip"
4. Wall of Remembrance
5. The Wall
6. Documentation Center
7. Escapes from Border Strip Buildings
8. Chapel of Reconciliation
9. Tunnel 57

❶ Visitors Center (Bezucherzentrum): Check the next show-times for the two 15-minute introductory films. (If you're in a hurry, don't wait for the English versions—the German ones have subtitles and easy-to-follow graphics.) The film titled *The Berlin Wall* covers the four-decade history of the Wall. The other film, *Walled In!*, uses computer graphics for a 3-D re-creation of the former death strip, helping you visualize what it is you're about to walk through.

• *Exit the Visitors Center, cross Bernauer Strasse, and enter the Memorial park. You're leaving former West Berlin and entering the no-man's-land that stood between East and West Berlin. Once in the park, find the rusty rectangular monument with a 3-D map.*

❷ 3-D Map of the Former Neighborhood: The map shows what this neighborhood looked like back in the Wall's heyday.

The shiny metal dot shows where you are on the map. If you were standing here 50 years ago, you'd be right at the division between East and West Berlin—specifically, in the narrow no-man's-land between two sets of walls.

• *Stroll along the path through this first section of the park ("Section A"). You're walking through the...*

❸ **"Death Strip"** (Section A): Today's grassy park with a pleasant path through it was once the notorious "death strip" *(Todesstreifen)*. If someone were trying to escape from the East, they'd have to scale one wall (a smaller one, to your right), cross this narrow strip of land, and climb the main wall (to your left, along Bernauer Strasse). The death strip was an obstacle course of barbed wire, tire-spike strips to stop cars, and other diabolical devices. It was continually patrolled by East German soldiers leading German Shepherds. Armed guards looked down from watchtowers, with orders to shoot to kill.

• *About midway through this section of the park, find the freestanding rusted-iron* ❹ *Wall of Remembrance, filled with photos. Continue walking through Section A, along the original, preserved asphalt patrol path. Now, walk across the grass and find a place to get a good close-up look at...*

❺ **The Wall:** The Wall here is typical of the whole system: about 12 feet tall, made of concrete and rebar, and capped by a rounded pipe that made it tough for escapees to get a grip. The top would have been further adorned with coils of barbed wire. This was part of a 96-mile-long Wall that encircled West Berlin, making it an island of democracy in communist East Germany.

• *Now, exit the park, turn right along Bernauer Strasse, and make your way across Bernauer Strasse to the modern gray building with a view terrace, located at #119 (labeled Gedenkstätte Berliner Mauer). This is the Berlin Wall Memorial's...*

❻ **Documentation Center** (Dokumentationszentrum Berliner Mauer): This excellent museum is geared to a new generation of Berliners who can hardly imagine their hometown split so brutally in two. The **ground floor** (1961-1988) has photos and displays to explain the logistics of the city's division and its effects. The next floor up gives the historical and political context behind the Wall's construction and eventual destruction. Climb the stairs or take the elevator to the top floor, the **Tower** *(Turm)*. From this high viewpoint, you can look across Bernauer Strasse, and down at Berlin's last preserved stretch of the death strip with the original guard tower.

• *Exit and continue on. Cross Bernauer Strasse (where it intersects with Ackerstrasse) and enter the next section of the Memorial park...*

❼ Escapes from Border Strip Buildings (Section B): Nearby you'll see a group of information panels that tell the story of what happened here: On August 13, 1961, the East German government officially closed the border. People began fleeing to the parts of Berlin controlled by other European powers—like the French, who held the neighborhood on the north side of Bernauer Strasse. Over the next few weeks and months, bit by bit, the border hardened. Ackerstrasse was closed to traffic, as East German soldiers laid down rows of barbed wire. People were suddenly separated from their West Berlin neighbors just across the street.

• *Keep going up the path through Section B, to the round building up ahead.*

❽ The Chapel of Reconciliation (Kapelle der Versöhnung): This modern "Chapel of Reconciliation" stands on the site of the old Church of Reconciliation. Built in 1894, that old Gothic-style church served the neighborhood parish. When the Wall went up, it found itself stranded in the death strip. Border guards used the steeple as a watchtower. The church itself was finally blown up by the East Germans in 1985. After the Wall came down, this chapel was built to remember the troubled past and try to heal the memory.

• *Continue past the chapel into the second portion of Section B.*

Tunnels and More: Walk up the mild incline, then bear left to a large open-air display under a canopy (amid the ruins of a destroyed Bernauer Strasse home). Photos, info boards, and press-the-button audio clips explain what it was like to live here, so close to the front line of the Cold War. Head back up to the main path, turn left, and continue. You'll pass two parallel rows of metal slabs, labeled *Fluchttunnel 1964.* This marks the route of the most famous tunnel of all: **❾ Tunnel 57,** built by a group of grad students in West Berlin to free their friends in the East, and named after the 57 people who escaped through it.

• *To experience more of the Memorial, you could continue through Sections C and D, where you'll find more open-air exhibits. Or, if you're ready to leave the area, the Bernauer Strasse U-Bahn station is just a block further up Bernauer Strasse.*

BERLIN

Shopping in Berlin

Shops all over town stock the typical array of **souvenirs** (T-shirts, posters, bottle openers, etc.) emblazoned with icons of Berlin: Brandenburg Gate, TV Tower, Berlin Wall, bears (the namesake and official mascot of "Bear-lin"), and so on.

One big draw is **communist kitsch.** Gift shops at museums (such as the DDR Museum or the Museum of the Wall at Checkpoint Charlie) sell a variety of "East Berlin" paraphernalia: circa-1968 city maps that mysteriously leave out West Berlin, postcards and posters of DDR propaganda or famous Wall escapes, miniature Trabis, old DDR military armbands and medals, and defunct communist currency.

Maybe *the* top communist kitsch souvenir is something—anything—with the image of the *Ampelmann* (traffic-light man), the DDR-era crossing-guard symbol that's become Berlin's unofficial mascot. The best selection is at the local chain of Ampelmann shops, with locations all over the city. The flagship store—with a hunk of Berlin Wall autographed by David Hasselhoff (no joke)—is along Unter den Linden at #35 (at the corner with Friedrichstrasse).

One communist-era souvenir to avoid is an **"authentic" chunk of the Berlin Wall**—enough of which have been sold since 1989 to encircle all of Germany. Don't trust any vendor who swears they chipped it off the Wall themselves. (And, because the few remaining stretches of Wall are now protected monuments, it's not appropriate to chisel off your own souvenir.)

Berlin's true forte is **design.** In this city of stylish young urbanites, the streets are lined with hipster gift shops that sell ironic T-shirts, clever kitchen or desk gadgets, snarky books and postcards, and so on.

Browsing Areas

Prenzlauer Berg: This is an enjoyable place to window-shop. It's a delight to simply wander colorful Kastanienallee between Eberswalder Strasse (with a U-Bahn station) and Weinbergspark.

The **Kulturbrauerei** brewery-turned-cultural center (Schönhauser Allee 36, www.kulturbrauerei.de) has a smattering of little shops, including Green Living (with environmentally friendly housewares and home decor). The Kollwitzkiez (a few blocks east) is mostly residential, but you'll also find some pleasant shops here. For local products, stop by **Brandenburgerie,** with a variety of mostly edible goods (meat, cheese, chocolate, juices, schnapps) made in the Brandenburg region that surrounds Berlin (closed Mon-Sun, Sredzkistrasse 36).

Rosenthaler Strasse: The street that connects the Hackescher

Markt and Rosenthaler Platz areas (along the handy tram #M1 route) attracts those interested in Berlin's fashion and design scene. Most shops along here are pop-up spaces, giving you a glimpse at what local designers are up to right now. A couple of permanent fixtures are worth checking out: Kauf dich Glücklich, a ramshackle Berlin café famous for its waffles (but which has since moved into fashion (at #17, www.kaufdichgluecklich-shop.de); and Schee, with appealing handmade items, including prints and textiles (at #15, www.schee.net).

Hackesche Höfe: This delightfully restored old series of eight interlocking shopping courtyards sits in the heart of the Scheunenviertel neighborhood. While not cheap, it's a convenient and tempting place to window-shop for everything from locally made porcelain to artisanal local foods to fashion (shops typically open Mon-Sat from 10:00 or 11:00 until 19:00, closed Sun, Rosenthaler Strasse 40, www.hackesche-hoefe.com).

Chocolate Shops on Gendarmenmarkt: The delightful square called Gendarmenmarkt—a short detour south of Unter den Linden—has two very different chocolate shops that are fun to browse: one bourgeois, and the other proletarian. For locations see the map on page 584.

Fassbender & Rausch claims to be Europe's biggest chocolate store. After 150 years of chocolate-making, this family-owned business proudly displays its sweet delights—250 different kinds—on a 55-foot-long buffet. Truffles are sold for about €1 each; it's fun to compose a fancy little eight-piece box of your own. Upstairs is an elegant café with fine views (Mon-Sat 10:00-20:00, Sun from 11:00, corner of Mohrenstrasse at Charlottenstrasse 60—look for green awnings directly behind German Cathedral, tel. 030/757-882-440).

If you're a choco-populist, head to the opposite end of Gendarmenmarkt, near the French Cathedral, for the Volkswagen of candy. **Rittersport Bunte Schokowelt** is home to the flagship store of Rittersport, the famous chocolate company—*"quadratisch, praktisch, gut"* ("square, practical, good"). This is basically Germany's answer to the M&M's store (Mon-Wed 10:00-19:00, Thu-Sat until 20:00, Sun until 18:00, Französische Strasse 24, tel. 030/200-950-810).

Big, Glitzy Department Stores
Central Berlin: Unter den Linden is lined with some high-end shops, but for a wider selection, head a few blocks south. The French department store Galeries Lafayette has a large outpost here with several floors of high-end goods under a glass dome (top-quality basement food court; Mon-Sat 10:00-20:00, closed Sun, Französische Strasse 23).

Several blocks west is the massive Mall of Berlin, with 270 shops surrounding a cavernous glass-covered passageway (Mon-Sat 10:00-21:00, closed Sun, Vossstrasse 35, www.mallofberlin. de). Nearby, Potsdamer Platz and Sony Center have additional shops.

City West: Several swanky shops line Kurfürstendamm, the area's main boulevard. The trendy Bikinihaus shopping center faces Europaplatz on one side and the Berlin Zoo on the other. This "concept mall" has a mix of international chains, artisan boutiques, food stalls, a small Kaiser's supermarket, and "pop-up boxes" highlighting Berlin vendors (plus a free glimpse of the zoo's monkeys; Mon-Sat 10:00-20:00, closed Sun, Buda-pester Strasse 38, www.bikiniberlin.de).

City West's most venerable shopping is a couple of blocks east (near the Wittenbergplatz U-Bahn), at **Kaufhaus des Westens,** better known as **KaDeWe**—one of Europe's fanciest department stores, in business since 1907 and a worthwhile sight in itself. You can get everything from a haircut (third floor) to souvenirs (fourth floor). The sixth floor is a world of gourmet taste treats. Ride the glass elevator to the seventh floor's glass-domed Winter Garden, a self-service cafeteria—fun but pricey (Mon-Thu 10:00-20:00, Fri until 21:00, Sat 9:30-20:00, closed Sun, S-Bahn: Zoologisch-er Garten or U-Bahn: Wittenbergplatz, tel. 030/21210, www.kadewe.de).

Eating in Berlin

Berlin has a world of ever-changing restaurants from which to choose. While the city abounds with traditional German eateries, Berliners consider this cuisine old-school; when they go out to eat, they're not usually looking for traditional local fare. But if you do eat German food in Berlin, popular dishes include *Buletten* and *Königsberger Klopse* (both meatball dishes), plus other meaty plates, such as *Schnitzel Holstein* (veal cutlet with egg), *Eisbein* (boiled ham hock), *Leber Berliner Art* (veal liver), *Kassler* (or *Kasseler;* smoked pork), and *Mett* (or *Hackepeter;* minced pork). Also popular are *Aal grün* (boiled eel), *Rollmops* (pickled herring), and *Senfeier* (hard-boiled eggs with potatoes). As for sweets, *Berliner Pfannkuchen* is the local jelly doughnut, and *Berliner Luft* is a popular dessert.

Berliner Street Food

Sausage stands are everywhere—including the reigning local favorites, Konnopke's Imbiss and Curry 36. You may even see portable human hot-dog stands—two companies, Grillrunner and Grillwalker, outfit their cooks in clever harnesses that let them grill and sell hot dogs from under an umbrella.

Most sausage stands specialize in *Currywurst,* created in Berlin after World War II, when a fast-food cook got her hands on some curry and Worcestershire sauce from British troops stationed here. It's basically a grilled pork sausage smothered with curry sauce. *Currywurst* comes either *mit Darm* (with casing) or *ohne Darm* (without casing). f the casing is left on to grill, it gives the sausage a smokier flavor. (*Berliner Art*—"Berlin-style"—means that the sausage is boiled *ohne Darm,* then grilled.) Either way, the grilled sausage is then chopped into small pieces or cut in half (East Berlin style) and topped with sauce. While some places simply use ketchup and sprinkle on some curry powder, real *Currywurst* joints use a proper *Currysauce:* tomato paste, Worcestershire sauce, and curry. With your wurst comes either a toothpick or small wooden fork; you'll usually get a plate of fries as well, but rarely a roll.

The other big Berlin street food is the kebab—either *döner kebab* (Turkish-style skewered meat slow-roasted and served in pita bread) or the recently trendy, healthier, vegetarian alternative, *Gemüse kebab* (with lots of veggies, and sometimes falafel). Other variations include the *döner teller* (on a plate instead of in bread) and *döner dürüm* (in a thin flatbread wrap, also called *dürüm kebab* or *yufka*). Just as Americans drop by a taco truck for a quick bite, Germans find a kebab stand.

HISTORIC CORE

I've listed places handy for your sightseeing, all a short walk from Unter den Linden. But if your goal is to conserve your time for sightseeing, it's worth considering a quick bite at a sausage stand or kebab shop (see sidebar) instead of a sit-down meal. You'll also find good eateries at many museums, including the German History Museum, the Bode Museum (on Museum Island), the Gemälde-galerie (Kulturforum complex), and the Jewish Museum Berlin.

BERLIN

Near Museum Island

Georgenstrasse, a block behind the Pergamon Museum and under the

Berlin Restaurants

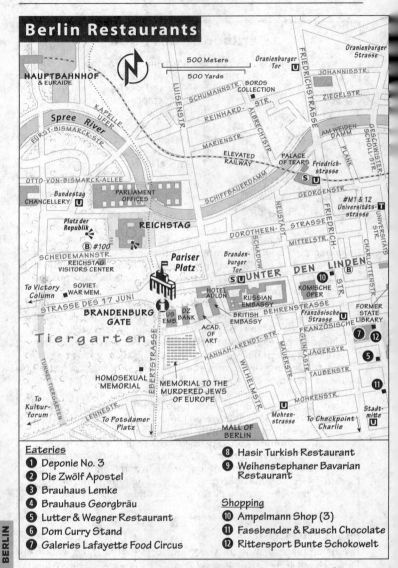

500 Meters
500 Yards

Eateries
1. Deponie No. 3
2. Die Zwölf Apostel
3. Brauhaus Lemke
4. Brauhaus Georgbräu
5. Lutter & Wegner Restaurant
6. Dom Curry Stand
7. Galeries Lafayette Food Circus
8. Hasir Turkish Restaurant
9. Weihenstephaner Bavarian Restaurant

Shopping
10. Ampelmann Shop (3)
11. Fassbender & Rausch Chocolate
12. Rittersport Bunte Schokowelt

S-Bahn tracks, is lined with fun places (bars, sit-down eateries, frozen yogurt, designer coffee, etc.) filling the arcade of the train trestle.

$$ Deponie No. 3 is a reliable, rustic, but sophisticated Berlin *Kneipe* (pub). Garden seating in the back is nice if you don't mind the noise of the S-Bahn passing directly above you. The bar interior is a cozy, wooden wonderland with several inviting spaces. They serve basic salads, traditional Berlin dishes, and hearty daily specials (daily 10:00-24:00, S-Bahn arch #187 at Georgenstrasse 5, tel. 030/2016-5740).

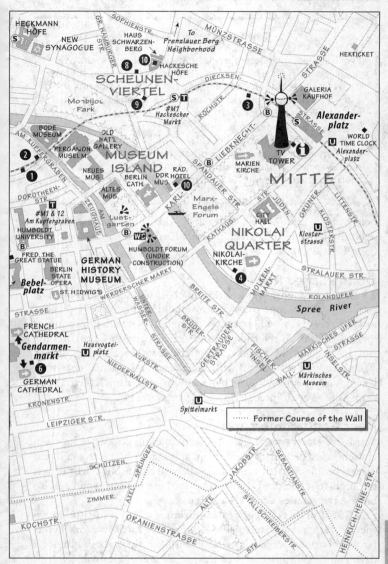

$$ Die Zwölf Apostel ("The Twelve Apostles") serves up Italian dishes in a vast, romantic, dimly lit interior under frescoed arches (daily 11:00-23:00, S-Bahn arch #177 at Georgenstrasse 2, tel. 030/201-0222).

Near the TV Tower

$$ Brauhaus Lemke is a big, modern, lively beer hall that makes its own brews and offers a menu of Berliner specialties and Bavarian dishes. They have decent salads and serve a six-beer sampler

Restaurant Code

I've assigned each eatery a price category, based on the average cost of a typical main course. Drinks, desserts, and splurge items (steak and seafood) can raise the price considerably.

$$$$ **Splurge:** Most main courses over €20
$$$ **Pricier:** €15-20
$$ **Moderate:** €10-15
$ **Budget:** Under €10

In Germany, a wurst stand or other takeout spot is **$**; a beer hall, *Biergarten*, or basic sit-down eatery is **$$**; a casual but more upscale restaurant is **$$$**; and a swanky splurge is **$$$$**.

board (daily 12:00-24:00, across from the TV Tower and tucked a bit back from the street at Karl-Liebknecht-Strasse 13, tel. 030/3087-8989).

On the Spree River

$$ Brauhaus Georgbräu is a thriving beer hall serving homemade suds on a picturesque courtyard overlooking the Spree River. Eat in the lively and woody but mod-feeling, hops-infused interior, or outdoors with fun riverside seating—thriving with German tourists. It's a good place to try one of the few typical Berlin dishes: *Eisbein* (boiled ham hock) with sauerkraut and mashed peas with bacon (daily 12:00-24:00, 2 blocks south of Berlin Cathedral and across the river at Spreeufer 4, tel. 030/242-4244).

Near Gendarmenmarkt

South of Unter den Linden, Gendarmenmarkt, with its twin churches, is a delightful place for an al fresco meal. Here you'll find several business-lunch-type places that are handy but pricey (given the high-rent location). In addition to these options, you can also browse the eateries along Charlottenstrasse.

$$$ Lutter & Wegner Restaurant is a Berlin institution respected for its Austrian cuisine (*Schnitzel* and *Sauerbraten*). Popular with businesspeople, it's dressy, with fun sidewalk seating or a dark and elegant interior. Lunch specials are an affordable way to sample their cooking (daily 11:00-24:00, Charlottenstrasse 56, tel. 030/202-9540, www.l-w-berlin.de).

The **$ Dom Curry** *Currywurst* stand, behind the German Cathedral, works for a quick bite out on the square (daily 11:00-18:00, closed in winter, operated by the nearby Hilton).

$$ Galeries Lafayette Food Circus is a French festival of fun eateries in the basement of the landmark department store—ideal for a quality lunch. You'll find a variety of prices and food, including sandwiches, savory crêpes, quiches, sushi bar, oyster bar, *les*

BERLIN

What If I Miss My Ship?

Remember that you can get help from the cruise line's port agent (listed on the destination information sheet distributed on the ship) and the local TI. If the port agent suggests a costly solution (such as a private car with a driver), you may want to consider public transit.

Rostock has a few long-distance overnight ferry connections to other cities, but these are sporadic and unlikely to reach where you're going. For the most part, you'll need to go by train to Berlin and connect from there to just about any other cruise port: to **Amsterdam** (and onward to **Zeebrugge, Paris/LeHavre,** or **London**); to **Copenhagen** (and onward to **Stockholm, Oslo,** and other Norwegian stops); to **Gdańsk;** and so on

If you need to catch a **plane** to your next destination, you'll find an easy bus connection (bus #TXL) from either Berlin's Hauptbahnhof or Alexanderplatz to Tegel Airport.

For more advice on what to do if you miss the boat, see page 130.

---

macarons, and so on (Mon-Sat 10:00-20:00, closed Sun, Friedrichstrasse 76, U-Bahn: Französische Strasse, tel. 030/209-480).

Hackescher Markt Area

Of Berlin's trendy dining zones, this is the closest to the main sightseeing core (a reasonable walk from Unter den Linden and within a few minutes of the Hackescher Markt S-Bahn station). You'll find an interchangeable line-up of restaurants, cafés, and bars in the square just outside the S-Bahn station. These are just two of many places to consider.

$$$ Hasir Turkish Restaurant is a popular, upscale, somewhat stuffy opportunity to splurge on Anatolian specialties amid candles and hardwood floors. While a bit past its prime and with hit-or-miss service, Hasir remains fairly respected, and enjoys a handy location in a courtyard next to the Hackesche Höfe shopping complex (large and splittable portions, daily 11:00-24:00, a block from the Hackescher Markt S-Bahn station at Oranienburger Strasse 4, tel. 030/2804-1616).

$$ Weihenstephaner Bavarian Restaurant serves upmarket traditional Bavarian food in an atmospheric cellar, on an inner courtyard, or on a busy people-watching terrace facing the delightful Hackescher Markt square; and, of course, it has excellent beer (daily 11:00-24:00, Neue Promenade 5 at Hackescher Markt, tel. 030/8471-0760).

German Survival Phrases

In the phonetics, ī sounds like the long i in "light," and bolded syllables are stressed.

English	German	Pronunciation
Good day.	*Guten Tag.*	**goo**-tehn tahg
Do you speak English?	*Sprechen Sie Englisch?*	**shprehkh**-ehn zee **ehgn**-lish
Yes. / No.	*Ja. / Nein.*	yah / nīn
I (don't) understand.	*Ich verstehe (nicht).*	ikh fehr-**shtay**-heh (nikht)
Please.	*Bitte.*	**bit**-teh
Thank you.	*Danke.*	**dahng**-keh
I'm sorry.	*Es tut mir leid.*	ehs toot meer līt
Excuse me.	*Entschuldigung.*	ehnt-**shool**-dig-oong
(No) problem.	*(Kein) Problem.*	(kīn) proh-**blaym**
(Very) good.	*(Sehr) gut.*	(zehr) goot
Goodbye.	*Auf Wiedersehen.*	owf **vee**-der-zayn
one / two	*eins / zwei*	īns / tsvī
three / four	*drei / vier*	drī / feer
five / six	*fünf / sechs*	fewnf / zehkhs
seven / eight	*sieben / acht*	**zee**-behn / ahkht
nine / ten	*neun / zehn*	noyn / tsayn
How much is it?	*Wieviel kostet das?*	**vee**-feel **kohs**-teht dahs
Write it?	*Schreiben?*	**shrī**-behn
Is it free?	*Ist es umsonst?*	ist ehs oom-**zohnst**
Included?	*Inklusive?*	in-kloo-**zee**-veh
Where can I buy / find...?	*Wo kann ich kaufen / finden...?*	voh kahn ikh **kow**-fehn / **fin**-dehn
I'd like / We'd like...	*Ich hätte gern / Wir hätten gern...*	ikh **heh**-teh gehrn / veer **heh**-tehn gehrn
...a room.	*...ein Zimmer.*	īn **tsim**-mer
...a ticket to ____.	*...eine Fahrkarte nach ____.*	ī-neh **far**-kar-teh nahkh
Is it possible?	*Ist es möglich?*	ist ehs **mur**-glikh
Where is...?	*Wo ist...?*	voh ist
...the train station	*...der Bahnhof*	dehr **bahn**-hohf
...the bus station	*...der Busbahnhof*	dehr **boos**-bahn-hohf
...the tourist information office	*...das Touristen- informations- büro*	dahs too-**ris**-tehn- in-for-maht-see-**ohns**- **bew**-roh
...the toilet	*...die Toilette*	dee toh-**leh**-teh
men	*Herren*	**hehr**-rehn
women	*Damen*	**dah**-mehn
left / right	*links / rechts*	links / **rehkhts**
straight	*geradeaus*	geh-**rah**-deh-ows
What time does this open / close?	*Um wieviel Uhr wird hier geöffnet / geschlossen?*	oom **vee**-feel oor veerd heer geh-**urf**-neht / geh-**shloh**-sehn
At what time?	*Um wieviel Uhr?*	oom **vee**-feel oor
Just a moment.	*Moment.*	moh-**mehnt**
now / soon / later	*jetzt / bald / später*	yehtst / bahld / **shpay**-ter
today / tomorrow	*heute / morgen*	**hoy**-teh / **mor**-gehn

OSLO

Norway

Norway Practicalities

 Norway (Norge) is stacked with superlatives—it's the most mountainous, most scenic, and most prosperous of all the Scandinavian countries. Perhaps above all, Norway is a land of intense natural beauty, its famously steep mountains and deep fjords carved out and shaped by an ancient ice age. Norway (148,700 square miles—just larger than Montana) is on the western side of the Scandinavian Peninsula, with most of the country sharing a border with Sweden to the east. Rich in resources like timber, oil, and fish, Norway has rejected joining the European Union, mainly to protect its fishing rights. Where the country extends north of the Arctic Circle, the sun never sets at the height of summer and never comes up in the deep of winter. The majority of Norway's 5.3 million people consider themselves Lutheran.

Money: 8 Norwegian kroner (kr, officially NOK) = about $1. An ATM is called a *minibank*. The local VAT (value-added sales tax) rate is 25 percent; the minimum purchase eligible for a VAT refund is 315 kr (for details on refunds, see page 125).

Language: The native language is Norwegian (the two official forms are Bokmål and Nynorsk). For useful phrases, see page 645.

Emergencies: Dial 112 for police, medical, or other emergencies. In case of theft or loss, see page 118.

Time Zone: Norway is on Central European Time (the same as most of the Continent, one hour ahead of Great Britain, and six/nine hours ahead of the East/West Coasts of the US).

Embassies in Oslo: The **US embassy** is at Morgedalsvegen 36 (tel. 21 30 85 58, emergency tel. 21 30 85 40, https://no.usembassy.gov) The **Canadian embassy** is at Wergelandsveien 7 (tel. 22 99 53 00, www.canadainternational.gc.ca/norway-norvege). Call ahead for passport services.

Phoning: With a mobile phone, it's easy to dial: Press and hold zero until you get a + sign, enter the country code (47 for Norway, 1 for the US/Canada), and then the complete phone number (including area code if there is one). When dialing a European phone number, drop an initial zero (except if calling Italy). For more tips, see page 1062.

Tipping: Service is included at sit-down meals, but this goes to the owner, so for great service it's nice to round up your bill about 10 percent. Tip a taxi driver by rounding up the fare (pay 90 kr on an 85-kr fare). For more tips on tipping, see page 129.

Tourist Information: www.goscandinavia.com

OSLO

While Oslo is the smallest of the Scandinavian capitals, this brisk little city offers more sightseeing thrills than you might expect. As an added bonus, you'll be inspired by a city that simply has its act together.

Sights of the Viking spirit—past and present—tell an exciting story. Prowl through the remains of ancient Viking ships, and marvel at more peaceful but equally gutsy modern boats (the *Kon-Tiki, Ra, Fram,* and *Gjøa*). Dive into the traditional folk culture at the Norwegian open-air folk museum, and get stirred up by the country's heroic spirit at the Norwegian Resistance Museum.

For a look at modern Oslo, tour the striking City Hall, take a peek at sculptor Gustav Vigeland's people pillars, walk all over the Opera House, and celebrate the world's greatest peacemakers at the Nobel Peace Center.

Situated at the head of a 60-mile-long fjord, surrounded by forests, and populated by more than a half-million people, Oslo is Norway's cultural hub. For 300 years (1624-1924), the city was called Christiania, after Danish King Christian IV. With independence, it reverted to the Old Norse name of Oslo. As an important port facing the Continent, Oslo has been one of Norway's main cities for a thousand years and the de facto capital since around 1300. Still, Oslo has always been small by European standards; in 1800, Oslo had 10,000 people, while cities such as Paris and London had 50 times as many.

Today the city sprawls out from its historic core to encompass nearly a million people in its metropolitan area—about one in five Norwegians. Oslo's port hums with international shipping and a sizeable cruise industry. Its waterfront, once traffic-congested and

slummy, has already undergone
a huge change. The vision: a five-
mile people-friendly and traffic-
free promenade stretching from
east to west the entire length of
its waterfront. Cars and trucks
travel in underground tunnels,
upscale condos and restaurants
are taking over, and the neighborhood has a splashy Opera
House. The metropolis feels as if
it's rushing to prepare for an Olympics-like deadline. But it isn't—
it just wants to be the best city it can be.

You'll see a mix of grand Neoclassical facades and plain 1960s-
style modernism, and a sprouting Nordic Manhattan-type skyline
of skyscrapers nicknamed "the bar code buildings" for their sleek
yet distinct boxiness. But overall, the feel of this major capital is
green and pastoral—spread out, dotted with parks and lakes, and
surrounded by hills and forests. For the visitor, Oslo is an all-you-
can-see *smörgåsbord* of historic sights, trees, art, and Nordic fun.

PLANNING YOUR TIME

Oslo is made-to-order for the cruise traveler who wants to see a lot
in a single day on shore. While the city is spread out, its sightseeing highlights are concentrated in three zones (noted below). On a
short port visit, I'd choose two of these zones to focus on. If you're
nervous about straying too far from your ship, start at the farthest-
flung areas (Bygdøy or Vigeland Park), then work your way back
toward the city-center sights, which cluster near the cruise berths.

City Center: To get a look at today's Oslo, take my self-guided
"Oslo Walk" (allow 45 minutes to sprint, more if you linger). The
two top sights downtown—both within a few steps of the walking
route—are **City Hall** (allow an hour for a guided tour) and the
National Gallery (allow about an hour; note that the gallery will
move to a new location in 2019 or 2020). Lesser, but still worthwhile, sights include the **Nobel Peace Center, Opera House** (with
50-minute guided tours), and **Norwegian Resistance Museum;**
choose what appeals to you, and allow 30-60 minutes each.

Vigeland Park: This delightful people zone, populated by locals, tourists, and Gustav Vigeland's remarkable statues, is worth
the 15-minute tram or bus ride west of downtown; once there,
allow at least an hour to explore.

Bygdøy: This "museum island" is most easily and scenically
reached on a 10- to 15-minute ferry ride from Oslo's main harbor (check return schedule to leave plenty of time to get back to
your ship). Once here, you could spend all day at the many fine

museums, ranging from an open-air folk museum to Viking ships to other Norwegian seafaring vessels (allow at least an hour per museum—and even more time for the spread-out Norwegian Folk Museum).

Sightsee Oslo Fjord from Your Ship: Oslo sits at the end of a long fjord. For many cruise itineraries, the hour approaching and the hour leaving Oslo is one of the most scenic parts of your cruise. Make a point to be on deck to enjoy the ride. About an hour out of town is a very narrow channel at Drøbak. This is famous among Norwegians as the place where they sank a big German warship at the start of World War II.

Excursions from Oslo

Most cruise lines offer activities within **Oslo** itself. As the city is user- and pedestrian-friendly (in most areas, and public transit works fine for others), I wouldn't pay for an excursion here. But if you'd like someone else to do the planning, various walking and bus tours lead you through the city center (Karl Johans Gate and harborfront area, including City Hall, Akershus Fortress, and Norwegian Resistance Museum), while others focus on the sights on Bygdøy (open-air museum—with Gol stave church—as well as Viking ships and other nautical museums). One place I'd avoid is the Magic Ice Bar, a decidedly touristy venture near the National Museum. While it's entertaining, and can be refreshing on the rare hot day in Oslo, it's hardly an authentic look at the city or Norwegian culture.

A few excursions include some out-of-town sights, such a trip out to the **Holmenkollen Ski Jump** and surrounding hills (of interest mostly to avid skiers and Olympics pilgrims). Others offer a boat trip on the **Oslofjord** (which doesn't seem worth it—since you'll cruise in and out of the fjord on your ship anyway—unless you opt for a trip that's on a tall ship or makes stops that appeal to you) and a visit to the charming but super-touristy fjordside village of **Drøbak.** Train enthusiasts might enjoy a trip on the steam-powered **Krøderbanen** heritage railway line, while shoppers enjoy the 250-year-old **Hadeland Glassverk.** All of these less-urban options have their fans, but Oslo has plenty to fill a day.

Port of Oslo

Arrival at a Glance: It's easy to walk downtown from the **Søndre Akershus, Vippetangen,** and **Revierkai** berths. **Filipstad** is farther out—still walkable, but more convenient by cruise-line shuttle bus. I'd avoid taxis, as the hefty $20 minimum makes even a short trip outrageously expensive.

Port Overview

Oslo uses four piers for cruise ships. Right on the harbor below Akershus Fortress are two quays: **Søndre Akershus,** closest to town, and **Vippetangen,** just south of Søndre Akershus. Ships also tie up at **Revierkai,** facing the Opera House (around the east side of the Akershus Fortress peninsula), and at **Filipstad,** west of downtown (around the far side of Aker Brygge from City Hall).

Expect Changes: Oslo's waterfront is undergoing extensive redevelopment. Because much of this work also affects the cruise port areas, don't be surprised if some of the details in this section have changed. The long-term vision is for Filipstad to take more cruise traffic.

Tourist Information: The city's **Visit Oslo** office is in the Øst-banehallen, right next to the train station (handy for those walking in from Revierkai). For more on the TI, see "Tourist Information," later.

GETTING INTO TOWN

First, I'll cover your taxi and tour options. Then I'll offer walking instructions from the ports to the City Hall/Aker Brygge area overlooking the harbor. To return to your ship, you can generally reverse these directions—I've given suggestions at the end of each section as necessary.

From Any Port

By Cruise-Line Shuttle: If your cruise line offers a shuttle bus, it will generally drop off in the City Hall area at the head of the main harbor. This is most worthwhile if your ship berths at Filipstad.

By Taxi: A few taxis meet arriving ships, but they're very pricey and the city is workable without them. The 150-NOK minimum (yes, that's almost $20) will cover your trip into downtown from any of the cruise ports. A taxi to the museums on Bygdøy runs around 300 NOK from downtown. You can negotiate an hourly rate, but I'd skip the big bill and take advantage of Oslo's walkability and fine public transportation. (A taxi can, however, be a good value for a small group that splits the bill; minibus taxis are available.) If you need a taxi but can't find one, call 02323.

By Tour: Open Top Sightseeing's hop-on, hop-off bus tours meet arriving cruise ships at or near all ports and provide a good, affordable way to connect outlying sights, including Vigeland Park and Bygdøy. For details and more tour options, see the "Tours in Oslo" section, later.

From Søndre Akershus and Vippetangen

By far the easiest place in town to arrive, these berths are within pleasant strolling distance of City Hall (10 minutes or less). From the **Søndre Akershus** berth, a bit closer to town, you can see the boxy twin towers of City Hall—just turn left from your ship and head straight for it. The cruise terminal in front of this pier has shops and a duty-free tax refund station (but no ATMs—

for that, you'll need to head into town). **Vippetangen** is a bit farther out, but it's still an easy walk (just 5 minutes longer); as you head into town, just walk with the water on your left.

Returning to Søndre Akershus or Vippetangen: To reach the cruise berths near Akershus, head for City Hall and look for your ship (tram #12 brings you to the Rådhusplassen stop, between City Hall and your ship).

From Revierkai

On the east side of the Akershus peninsula, the Revierkai port faces Oslo's strikingly modern Opera House, with its sloping roof leading right into the waters of the Oslofjord. If arriving here, you have several options: A fun first activity is to go for a stroll on the **Opera House** roof—to get there, simply walk to the end of the harbor and hook around to the right.

To head to the **City Hall** area, several streets leading away from your ship can take you there; the most direct shot is along Rådhusgata, which is just beyond the giant, pink building with the towers. Walk along this street for about 15 minutes: You'll pass the entrance to Akershus Fortress, then pop out at City Hall.

To begin with my self-guided walk—which ends near City Hall and shows you a lot more of downtown Oslo en route—head to the **train station,** which is a five-minute walk straight inland from the Opera House. Circle around to the left to reach the plaza in front of the station, where the walk begins. From your ship to the station, figure about a 15-minute walk.

Returning to Revierkai: Make your way to the train station, exit out the side to cross the busy street to the Opera House, and circle around the harbor to your ship. Or, from the City Hall area, walk 10 minutes up Rådhusgata.

From Filipstad

This farther-out port is located in an industrial area to the west of downtown (around the far side of Aker Brygge from City Hall).

By Cruise-Line Shuttle Bus: Filipstad merits a shuttle bus, and cruises provide one (either free or about $8 each way). The shuttle will generally drop you at the harbor terminal at the Akershus dock or in the City Hall area.

On Foot: If you'd rather walk from Filipstad into town, it'll take you about 20 minutes to get from your ship to City Hall, but the stroll is far from interesting. Your ship's upper deck provides the perfect high-altitude vantage point for scouting your options before disembarking.

Exiting your ship at Filipstad, find your way to the port gate (at the far-left end of the big parking-lot zone at the pier). Continue

---

Services near City Hall and the Train Station

The quays where ships tie up lack services. But once you're in town, resources abound.

ATMs: ATMs are easy to find behind the City Hall and around the train station.

Wi-Fi: The train station has free Wi-Fi.

Pharmacy: An Apotek 1 is between City Hall and Karl Johans Gate. There's a 24-hour pharmacy directly across the street from the train station's main entrance.

---

straight out to the little roundabout and turn right, following the path and the signs to *Sentrum*.

Walking past a bus stop, you'll hit a foot/bike path that runs along a busy highway; turn right and follow this path into town. Soon you'll see City Hall's boxy twin towers ahead; the new National Museum is under construction on the right. When you reach the cross-street called Dokkveien (with the tram tracks), you have a choice: To get to the harbor, turn right and take the road down to Aker Brygge and the Nobel Peace Center. If you'd rather head to the park near Karl Johans Gate in the heart of Oslo, go straight, and you'll pop out at the National Theater.

Returning to Filipstad: Leave yourself plenty of time for the dull hike back, or—ideally—catch the cruise-line shuttle bus from Akershus pier (or wherever it dropped you off).

Oslo

Oslo (pop. 660,000) is easy to manage. Most sights are contained within the monumental, homogenous city center. Much of what you'll want to see clusters in three easy-to-connect zones: the **city center**, around the harbor and the main boulevard, Karl Johans Gate (with the Royal Palace at one end and the train station at the other); in the **Bygdøy** (big-duhy) district, a 10-minute ferry ride across the harbor (see "Oslo" map in the front of the book); and **Vigeland Park** (with Gustav Vigeland's statues), about a mile behind the palace.

Orientation to Oslo

No matter where your ship docks, you'll probably start your Oslo exploration in the **harborfront zone** in front of City Hall—with the Akershus Fortress on one side, and the Nobel Peace Center and Aker Brygge mall complex on the other. To get oriented, you can follow the last parts of my self-guided Oslo walk, starting with City Hall. To reach the busy **city center** from the harborfront, circle around the City Hall building and go up the street directly behind it. You'll run into the inviting park that runs alongside Karl Johans Gate, a short walk from the National Gallery and other sights.

If you'd like to zip to the **train station** area and the start of my self-guided walk, you can take a tram. You'll find two tram stops (serving the same trams) in the zone in front of City Hall: The Aker Brygge stop is in front of the yellow Nobel Peace Center (to the right as you face the harbor), and the Rådhusplassen stop is at the far end of the City Hall complex, near the start of the Akershus Fortress area (look for the grass strip around the tracks, to the left as you face the harbor). From either tram stop, take tram #12 (direction: Disen) and ride it to Jernbanetorget, the square in front of the train station. You can also use tram #12 to reach Vigeland Park.

TOURIST INFORMATION

The big, high-tech Visit Oslo office is in the Østbanehallen—the traditional-looking building next to the central train station. Standing in the square (Jernbanetorget) by the tiger statue and facing the train station, you'll find the TI's entrance in the red-painted section between the station and Østbanehallen. You can also enter the TI from inside the train station (July-Aug Mon-Sat 8:00-19:00, Sun 9:00-18:00; May-June and Sept daily 9:00-18:00; slightly shorter hours Oct-April; tel. 81 53 05 55, www.visitoslo.com).

At the TI, pick up these freebies: an Oslo map (with a helpful public-transit map on the back); the annual *Oslo Guide* (a handy overview of museums, eating, and nightlife); *U.F.O.* (the exhibition guide, listing current museum events); and the *What's On Oslo* monthly (with updated museum prices and hours, and an extensive events listing).

Oslo Pass: Sold at the TI, this pass covers the city's public transit, ferry boats, and entry to nearly every major sight—all described in a useful handbook (395 NOK/24 hours, 595 NOK/48 hours, 745 NOK/72 hours; big discounts for kids ages 4-15 and seniors age 67 and over).

HELPFUL HINTS

Theft Alert: Pickpockets are a problem in Oslo, particularly in crowds on the street and on subways and buses. Oslo's street population loiters around the train station; you may see aggressive panhandlers there and along Karl Johans Gate. While this rough-looking bunch can seem a bit unnerving to some travelers, locals consider them harmless (but keep an eye on your wallet). To call the police, dial 112.

Money: Banks in Norway don't change money. Use ATMs or the Forex exchange office at the train station.

Pharmacy: Jernbanetorgets Vitus Apotek is open 24 hours daily (across from train station on Jernbanetorget, tel. 23 35 81 00).

GETTING AROUND OSLO
By Public Transit

Oslo's excellent transit system is made up of buses, trams, ferries, and a subway (*Tunnelbane,* or T-bane for short; see the "Sightseeing by Public Transit" sidebar). The system is run by Ruter, which has a transit-information center below the tall, skinny, glass tower in front of the central train station (Mon-Fri 7:00-20:00, Sat-Sun 8:00-18:00, tel. 177 or 81 50 01 76, www.ruter.no).

Schedules: To navigate, use the public transit map on the back of the free TI city map, or download the RuterReise app. The system runs like clockwork, with schedules clearly posted and followed. Most stops have handy electronic reader boards showing the time remaining before the next tram arrives (usually less than 10 minutes).

Tickets: A different app—called RuterBillett—lets you buy tickets on your phone (with your credit card) rather than having to buy paper tickets; however, it may not work with American cards, and requires Wi-Fi or data to work. Individual **tickets** work on buses, trams, ferries, and the T-bane for one hour (33 NOK at machines, transit office, Narvesen kiosks, convenience stores such as 7-Eleven or Deli de Luca, or with the RuterBillett app—or a hefty 55 NOK from the driver). Other options include the **24-hour ticket** (90 NOK; buy at machines, transit office, or on RuterBillett app; good for unlimited rides in 24-hour period) and the **Oslo Pass** (gives free run of entire system; described earlier). Validate your ticket by holding it next to the card reader when you board.

By Taxi

Taxis come with a 150-NOK drop charge (yes, that's nearly $20 just to get in the car) that covers you for three or four kilometers—about two miles (more on evenings and weekends). Taxis are a good value only if you're with a group. If you use a minibus taxi, you are welcome to negotiate an hourly rate. To get a taxi, wave one down, find a taxi stand, or call 02323.

OSLO

Sightseeing by Public Transit

With a transit pass or an Oslo Pass, take full advantage of the T-bane and the trams. Just spend five minutes to get a grip on the system, and you'll become amazingly empowered. Here are the T-bane stations you're likely to use:

Jernbanetorget (central station, bus and tram hub, express train to airport)

Stortinget (top of Karl Johans Gate, near Akershus Fortress)

Nationaltheatret (National Theater, also a train station, express train to airport, near City Hall, Aker Brygge, Royal Palace)

Majorstuen (walk to Vigeland Sculpture Park, trendy shops on Bogstadveien)

Trams and buses that matter:

Trams #11 and #12 ring the city (stops at central station, fortress, harborfront, City Hall, Aker Brygge, Vigeland Park, Bogstadveien, National Gallery, and Stortorvet)

Trams #13 and #19, and bus #31 (south and parallel to Karl Johans Gate to central station)

Bus #30 (train station, near Karl Johans Gate, National Theater, and Bygdøy, with stops at each Bygdøy museum)

Tours in Oslo

Oslofjord Cruises

A fascinating world of idyllic islands sprinkled with charming vacation cabins is minutes away from the Oslo harborfront. For locals, the fjord is a handy vacation getaway. Tourists can get a glimpse of this island world by public ferry or tour boat. Cheap ferries regularly connect the nearby islands with downtown (free with Oslo Pass).

Several tour boats leave regularly from pier 3 in front of City Hall. **Båtservice** has a relaxing and scenic 1.5-hour hop-on, hop-off service, with recorded multilingual commentary. It departs from the City Hall dock (215 NOK, daily at 9:45, 11:15, 12:45, and 14:15; departs 30 minutes earlier from the Opera House and 30 minutes later from Bygdøy; tel. 23 35 68 90, www.boatsightseeing. com). They won't scream if you bring something to munch. They also offer two-hour fjord tours with lame live commentary (299 NOK, 3/day late March-mid-Oct, may run on winter weekends).

Guided Walking Tour

Oslo Guideservice offers 1.5-hour historic "Oslo Promenade" walks from mid-May through August (200 NOK, free with Oslo Pass; Mon, Wed, and Fri at 17:30; leaves from harbor side of City

Hall, confirm departures at TI, tel. 22 42 70 20, www.guideservice. no).

Local Guides

You can hire a private guide for around 2,000 NOK for a two- to three-hour tour. I had a good experience with **Oslo Guideservice** (2,000 NOK/2 hours, tel. 22 42 70 20, www.guideservice.no); my guide, Aksel, had a passion for both history and his hometown of Oslo. Or try **Oslo Guidebureau** (tel. 22 42 28 18, www. osloguidebureau.no, info@osloguide.no).

Bike Tours

Viking Biking gives several different guided tours in English, including a three-hour Oslo Highlights Tour that includes Bygdøy beaches and a ride up the Akers River (350 NOK, May-Sept daily at 14:00, Nedre Slottsgate 4, tel. 41 26 64 96, www.vikingbikingoslo. com).

Bus Tours

Båtservice, which runs the harbor cruises, offers four-hour **bus tours** of Oslo, with stops at the Bygdøy museums and Vigeland Park (410 NOK, daily at 10:30, departs from next to City Hall, longer tours available, tel. 23 35 68 90, www.boatsightseeing.com). **HMK** also does daily city bus tours (330 NOK/2.5 hours, 450 NOK/4.5 hours, departs from next to City Hall, tel. 22 78 94 00, www.hmk.no).

Open Top Sightseeing runs **hop-on, hop-off bus tours** (300 NOK/all day, 18 stops, www.city-sightseeing.com; every 30 minutes from City Hall, English headphone commentary, buy ticket from driver). Be aware that you may wait up to an hour at popular stops (such as Vigeland Park) for a chance to hop back on.

Oslo Tram Tour

Tram #12, which becomes tram #11 halfway through its loop (at Majorstuen), circles the city from the train station, lacing together many of Oslo's main sights. Apart from the practical value of being able to hop on and off as you sightsee your way around town (trams come by at least every 10 minutes), this 40-minute trip gives you a fine look at parts of the city you wouldn't otherwise see.

This tour starts at the main train station, at the traffic-island tram stop located immediately in front of the Ruter transit office tower. The route makes almost a complete circle and finishes at Stortorvet (the cathedral square), dropping you off a three-minute walk from where you began the tour.

Starting out, you want tram #12 as it leaves from the second set of tracks, going toward Majorstuen. Confirm with your driver that the particular tram #12 you're boarding becomes tram #11 and finishes at Stortorvet; some turn into tram #19 instead, which

OSLO

Oslo at a Glance

▲▲▲**City Hall** Oslo's artsy 20th-century government building, lined with huge, vibrant, municipal-themed murals, best visited with included tour. **Hours:** Daily 9:00-16:00, until 18:00 June-Aug; 3 tours/day June-Aug. See page 614.

▲▲▲**National Gallery** Norway's cultural and natural essence, captured on canvas. **Hours:** Tue-Fri 10:00-18:00, Thu until 19:00, Sat-Sun 11:00-17:00, closed Mon. See page 621.

▲▲▲**Vigeland Park** Set in sprawling Frogner Park, with tons of statuary by Norway's greatest sculptor, Gustav Vigeland, and the studio where he worked (now a museum). **Hours:** Park-always open; Vigeland Museum-Tue-Sun 10:00-17:00, Sept-April 12:00-16:00, closed Mon year-round. See page 623.

▲▲▲**Fram Museum** Captivating exhibit on the Arctic exploration ships *Fram* and *Gjøa*. **Hours:** Daily June-Aug 9:00-18:00, May and Sept 10:00-17:00, Oct and March-April until 16:00; Nov-Feb Mon-Fri 10:00-15:00, Sat-Sun until 16:00. See page 633.

▲▲**Norwegian Folk Museum** Norway condensed into 150 historic buildings in a large open-air museum. **Hours:** Daily 10:00-18:00—grounds open until 20:00; mid-Sept-mid-May Mon-Fri 11:00-15:00, Sat-Sun until 16:00, but most historical buildings closed. See page 631.

▲▲**Norwegian Resistance Museum** Gripping look at Norway's tumultuous WWII experience. **Hours:** Mon-Sat 10:00-17:00, Sun from 11:00; Sept-May Mon-Fri until 16:00, Sat-Sun from 11:00. See page 622.

▲▲**Viking Ship Museum** An impressive trio of ninth-century Viking ships, with exhibits on the people who built them. **Hours:** Daily 9:00-18:00, Oct-April 10:00-16:00. See page 632.

▲▲**Kon-Tiki Museum** Adventures of primitive *Kon-Tiki* and *Ra II* ships built by Thor Heyerdahl. **Hours:** Daily 9:30-18:00, March-May and Sept-Oct 10:00-17:00, Nov-Feb until 16:00. See page 634.

takes a different route. If yours becomes #19, simply hop out at Majorstuen and wait for the next #11. (If #11 is canceled due to construction, leave #12 at Majorstuen and catch #19 through the center back to the train station, or hop on the T-bane, which zips every few minutes from Majorstuen to the National Theater—closest to the harbor and City Hall—and then to the station). Note that

▲**Oslo Opera House** Stunning performance center that's helping revitalize the harborfront. **Hours:** Foyer and café/restaurant open Mon-Fri 10:00-23:00, Sat from 11:00, Sun 12:00-22:00; Opera House tours-3/day year-round. See page 620.

▲**Akershus Fortress Complex and Tours** Historic military base and fortified old center, with guided tours, a ho-hum castle interior, and the excellent Norwegian Resistance Museum (listed earlier). **Hours:** Park generally open daily 6:00-21:00—until 18:00 in winter; one-hour tour daily July-mid-Aug, weekends only off-season. See page 617.

▲**Norwegian Maritime Museum** A briny voyage through Norway's rich seafaring heritage. **Hours:** Daily 10:00-17:00; Sept-mid-May Tue-Sun until 16:00, closed Mon. See page 635.

▲**Ekeberg Sculpture Park** Hilly, hikeable 63-acre forest park with striking contemporary art and city views. See page 637.

▲**Edvard Munch Museum** Works of Norway's famous Expressionistic painter. **Hours:** Daily 10:00-17:00, early Oct-early May until 16:00. See page 636.

▲**Aker Brygge and Tjuvholmen** Oslo's harborfront promenade, and nearby trendy Tjuvholmen neighborhood with Astrup Fearnley Museum, upscale galleries, shops, and cafés. See page 616.

Norwegian Holocaust Center A high-tech look at the rise of anti-Semitism, the Holocaust in Norway, and racism today. **Hours:** Daily 10:00-18:00; Sept-May Mon-Fri 10:00-16:00, Sat-Sun from 11:00. See page 636.

Nobel Peace Center Exhibit celebrating the ideals of the Nobel Peace Prize and the lives of those who have won it. **Hours:** Daily 10:00-18:00, closed Mon Sept-mid-May. See page 616.

you can also begin this tour at either of the harborfront tram stops in front of City Hall.

Here's what you'll see and places where you might want to hop out:

From the **station,** you'll go through the old grid streets of 16th-century Christiania, King Christian IV's planned Renaissance town. After the city's 17th fire, in 1624, the king finally got fed up. He decreed that only brick and stone buildings would be permitted in the city center, with wide streets to serve as fire breaks.

You'll turn a corner at the **fortress** (Christiania Torv stop; get off here for the fortress and Norwegian Resistance Museum), then head for **City Hall** (Rådhus stop). Next comes the harbor and upscale **Aker Brygge** waterfront neighborhood (jump off at the Aker Brygge stop for the harbor and restaurant row). Passing the harbor, you'll see on the left a few old shipyard buildings that still survive. Then the tram goes uphill, past the **House of Oslo** (a mall of 20 shops highlighting Scandinavian interior design; Vikatorvet stop) and into a district of ugly 1960s buildings (when elegance was replaced by "functionality"). The tram then heads onto the street Norwegians renamed **Henrik Ibsens Gate** in 2006 to commemorate the centenary of Ibsen's death, honoring the man they claim is the greatest playwright since Shakespeare.

After Henrik Ibsens Gate, the tram follows Frognerveien through the chic **Frogner neighborhood.** Behind the fine old facades are fancy shops and spendy condos. Here and there you'll see 19th-century mansions built by aristocratic families who wanted to live near the Royal Palace; today, many of these house foreign embassies. Turning the corner, you roll along the edge of **Frogner Park** (which includes **Vigeland Park,** featuring Gustav Vigeland's sculptures), stopping at its grand gate (hop out at the Vigelandsparken stop).

Ahead on the left, a statue of 1930s ice queen Sonja Henie marks the arena where she learned to skate. Turning onto Bogstadveien, the tram usually becomes #11 at the Majorstuen stop. **Bogstadveien** is lined with trendy shops, restaurants, and cafés—it's a fun place to stroll and window-shop. (You could get out here and walk along this street all the way to the Royal Palace park and the top of Karl Johans Gate.) The tram veers left before the palace, passing the **National Historical Museum** and stopping at the **National Gallery** (Tullinløkka stop). As you trundle along, you may notice that lots of roads are ripped up for construction. It's too cold to fix the streets in winter, so, when possible, the work is done in summer. Jump out at **Stortorvet** (a big square filled with flower stalls and fronted by the cathedral and the big GlasMagasinet department store). From here, you're a three-minute walk from the station, where this tour began.

Oslo Walk

This self-guided stroll, worth ▲▲, covers the heart of Oslo—the zone where most tourists find themselves walking—from the train station, up the main drag, and past City Hall to the harborfront. Allow a brisk 45 minutes without stops.

Train Station: Start at the plaza just outside the main entrance of Oslo's central train station (Oslo Sentralstasjon), near the statue of the **tiger** prowling around out front. This alludes to the town's nickname of Tigerstaden ("Tiger Town"), and commemorates the 1,000th birthday of Oslo's founding, celebrated in the year 2000. In the 1800s, Oslo was considered an urban tiger, leaving its mark on the soul of simple country folk who ventured into the wild and crazy New York City of Norway.

In the middle of the plaza, look for the tall, skinny, glass ❶ **Ruter tower** that marks the public transit office. From here, trams zip to City Hall (harbor, boat to Bygdøy), and the underground subway (T-bane, or *Tunnelbane*—look for the *T* sign to your right) goes to Vigeland Park (statues) and Holmenkollen. Tram #12—featured in the self-guided tram tour described earlier—leaves from directly across the street.

The green building behind the Ruter tower is a shopping mall called **Byporten** (literally, "City Gate," see big sign on rooftop), built to greet those arriving from the airport on the shuttle train. Oslo's 37-floor pointed-glass **skyscraper,** the Radisson Blu Plaza Hotel, pokes up behind that. The hotel's 34th-floor SkyBar welcomes the public with air-conditioned views and pricey drinks. The tower was built with reflective glass so that, from a distance, it almost disappears. The area behind the Radisson—the lively and colorful "Little Karachi," centered along a street called Grønland—is where many of Oslo's immigrants settled. It's become a vibrant nightspot, offering a fun contrast to the predictable Norwegian cuisine and culture.

Oslo allows hard-drug addicts and prostitutes to mix and mingle in the station area. (Signs warn that this is a "monitored area," but victimless crimes proceed while violence is minimized. (Watch your valuables here.)

• *Note that you are near the Opera House if you'd like to side-trip there now (through the park to the right of the station). Otherwise, turn your back to the station. You're now looking (across the street) up Norway's main drag, called...*

Karl Johans Gate: This grand boulevard leads directly from the train station to the Royal Palace. The street is named for the French general Jean Baptiste Bernadotte, who was given a Swedish name, established the current Swedish dynasty, and ruled as

Oslo

To
Vigeland Park

Oslo Walk

1. Ruter Tower
2. Oslo Cathedral
3. Stortorvet (Square)
4. Crest of Karl Johans Gate
5. Freia Sign
6. Grand Hotel & Café
7. Parliament Building
8. Statue of Wergeland
9. National Theater
10. City Hall
11. Harbor View
12. Nobel Peace Center

Shopping & Services

13. Norway Designs
14. Paleet
15. Dale of Norway
16. Heimen Husfliden Shop
17. GlasMagasinet Dep't Store & Husfliden Shop
18. Oslo Sweater Shop
19. Byporten Mall
20. To Bogstadveien Shops & Flea Market
21. Oslo Flaggfabrikk
22. Vinmonopolet (2)
23. To Laundry
24. Bike Rental

a popular king (1818-1844) during the period after Sweden took Norway from Denmark.

Walk three blocks up Karl Johans Gate. This stretch is sometimes called **"Desolation Row"** by locals because it has no soul—just shops greedily devouring tourists' money. If you visit in the snowy winter, you'll walk on bare concrete: Most of downtown Oslo's pedestrian streets are heated.

• Hook right around the curved old brick structure of an old market and walk to the...

❷ **Oslo Cathedral** (Domkirke): This Lutheran church is the third cathedral Oslo has had, built in 1697 after the second one burned down. It's where Norway commemorates its royal marriages and deaths. Seventy-seven deaths were mourned here following

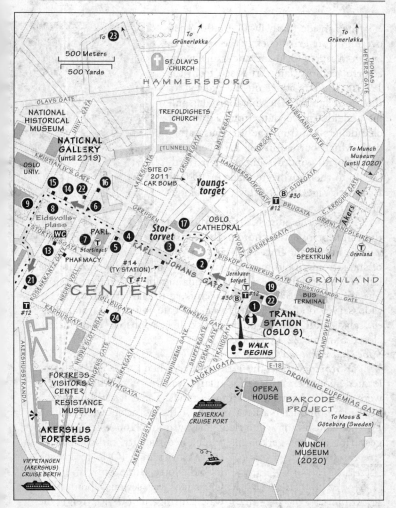

a tragic bombing and mass shooting in July 2011, when an anti-immigration fanatic named Anders Behring Breivik went berserk, setting off a car bomb in Oslo, killing eight, and then traveling to a Labor Party summer camp where he shot and killed 69 young people and counselors. In the grass in front of the cathedral, you may see a plastic heart on a pole—a semipermanent memorial to the victims.

Look for the cathedral's cornerstone (near the base of the steeple), a thousand-year-old carving from Oslo's first and long-gone cathedral showing how the forces of good and evil tug at each of us. Look high up on the tower. The tiny square windows midway up the copper cupola were once the lookout quarters of the fire watchman.

Step inside (daily 10:00-16:00, open overnight on Fri) beneath the red, blue, and gold seal of Oslo and under an equally colorful ceiling (late Art Deco from the 1930s). The box above on the right is for the royal family. The fine Baroque pulpit and altarpiece date from 1700. The chandeliers are from the previous cathedral (which burned in the 17th century). The colorful windows in the choir (leading up to the altar) were made in 1910 by Emanuel Vigeland (Gustav's less famous brother).

Leaving the church, stroll around to the right, behind the church. The **courtyard** is lined by a circa-1850 circular row of stalls from an old market. Rusty meat hooks now decorate the lamps of a peaceful café, which has quaint tables around a fountain. The atmospheric **$$$$ Café Bacchus,** at the far left end of the arcade, serves food outside and in a classy café downstairs (sandwiches, salads, full meals, good cakes, coffee, Mon-Sat 11:30-22:30, closed Sun, tel. 22 33 34 30).

• *The square that faces the cathedral is called...*

❸ **Stortorvet:** In the 17th century, when Oslo's city wall was located about here, this "Big Square" was the point where farmers were allowed to enter and sell their goods. Today it's still lively as a flower and produce market (Mon-Fri). The statue shows Christian IV, the Danish king who ruled Norway around 1600, dramatically gesturing at some geraniums. He named the city, rather immodestly, Christiania. (Oslo took back its old Norse name only in 1925.) Christian was serious about Norway. During his 60-year reign, he visited it 30 times (more than all other royal visits combined during 300 years of Danish rule). The big GlasMagasinet department store is a landmark on this square.

• *Return to Karl Johans Gate, and continue up the boulevard past street performers, cafés, shops, and hordes of people. At the next corner, Kongens Gate leads left, past the 17th-century grid-plan town to Akershus Fortress (described in "Sights in Oslo," later).*

OSLO

But we'll continue hiking straight up to the crest of the hill, enjoying some of the buskers along the way.

Pause at the wide spot in the street just before Akersgata (near the T-bane stop) to appreciate the...

❹ **Crest of Karl Johans Gate** (Egertorget): Look back at the train station. A thousand years ago, the original (pre-1624) Oslo was located at the foot of the wooded hill behind the station. Now look ahead to the **Royal Palace** in the distance, which was built in the 1830s "with nature and God behind it and the people at its feet." If the flag flies atop the palace, the king is in the country. (To tour the palace when it opens to visitors in summer months, book ahead at www.ticketmaster.no, or by calling 81 53 31 33; see www.kongehuset.no for more information.)

Karl Johans Gate, a parade ground laid out in about 1850 from here to the palace, is now the axis of modern Oslo. Each May 17, Norway's Constitution Day, an annual children's parade turns this street into a sea of marching student bands and costumed young flag-wavers, while the royal family watches from the palace balcony. Since 1814, Norway has preferred peace. Rather than celebrating its military on the national holiday, it celebrates its children.

In the middle of the small square, the *T* sign marks a stop of the T-bane (Oslo's subway). W. B. Samson's bakery is a good place for a quick, affordable lunch, with a handy cafeteria line (WC in back)—duck inside and be tempted by the pastries. Two traditional favorites are *kanelboller* (cinnamon rolls) and *skolebrød* ("school bread," with an egg-and-cream filling).

High overhead, the big neon ❺ **Freia sign** (dating from 1911) trumpets another sweet Norwegian treat. Norway's answer to Cadbury, the Norwegian chocolatier Freia is beloved...or it was, until it was bought by an American company. Still, the local factory is partly operational, and nostalgic Norwegians will always think of Freia as "a little piece of Norway."

From here, the street called **Akersgata** (on the right) kicks off a worthwhile stroll past the site of the July 2011 bombing, the national cemetery, and through a parklike river gorge to the Mathallen food hall and the trendy Grünerløkka quarter (an hour-long walk).

Continuing down Karl Johans Gate: People-watching is great along Karl Johans Gate, but remember that if it's summer, half of the city's regular population is gone—vacationing in their cabins or farther away—and the city center is filled mostly with visitors.

Hike two blocks farther down Karl Johans Gate, passing the big brick Parliament building (on the left). On your right, seated in the square, is a bearded, tubby statue of the 19th-century painter Christian Krohg.

Browsing

The pulse of the real, down-to-earth Oslo is best felt by strolling. Three good areas are along and near the central Karl Johans Gate, which runs from the train station to the palace (follow my self-guided "Oslo Walk"); in the trendy harborside Aker Brygge mall, a glass-and-chrome collection of sharp cafés, fine condos, and polished produce stalls (really lively at night, tram #12 from train station); and along Bogstadveien, a bustling shopping street with no-nonsense modern commerce, lots of locals, and no tourists (T-bane to Majorstuen and follow this street back toward the palace and tourist zone).

If you'd like to get a city view (and perhaps some pricey refreshment), enter the glass doors facing the street at #27 (not the bank entrance at the corner) and take the elevator to the eighth-floor rooftop bar, aptly named Eight (cocktails-150 NOK, beers-90 NOK).

A few doors farther down Karl Johans Gate, just past the Freia shop (selling that favorite Norwegian chocolate at only slightly inflated prices), the venerable **Grand Hotel** (Oslo's celebrity hotel—Nobel Peace Prize winners sleep here) overlooks the boulevard.

• *Politely ask the waiter at the Grand Café—part of the Grand Hotel—if you can pop inside for a little sightseeing (he'll generally let you).*

❻ **Grand Café:** This historic café was for many years the meeting place of Oslo's intellectual and creative elite (playwright Henrik Ibsen was a regular here). While it's been renovated, it still has some beautiful old artwork—including (at the far back) a wall-length **mural** showing Norway's literary and artistic clientele—from a century ago—enjoying this fine hangout. On the far left, find Ibsen, coming in as he did every day at 13:00. Edvard Munch is on the right, leaning against the window behind the waiter, looking pretty drugged. Names are on the sill beneath the mural.

• *For a cheap bite with prime boulevard seating, continue past the corner to Deli de Luca, a convenience store with a super selection of takeaway food and a great people-watching perch. Across the street, a little park faces Norway's...*

❼ **Parliament Building** (Stortinget): Norway's parliament meets here (along with anyone participating in a peaceful protest outside). *Stortinget*—from an old Viking word—basically means "Big Gathering." Built in 1866, the building seems to counter the Royal Palace at the other end of Karl Johans Gate. If the flag's flying, parliament's in session. Today the king is a figurehead, and Norway is run by a unicameral parliament and a prime minister. Guided tours of the Stortinget are offered for those interested in Norwegian government (free, 1 hour, typically Sat mornings, may be more frequent in summer—check schedule at www.stortinget.no, enter on Akersgata—on the back side of the building).

• *Cross over into the long median park. On your left, notice the red, white, and blue coin-op public WCs. (Free WCs are inside the Paleet shopping mall, on the right side of the boulevard).*

Enjoying the park, stroll toward the palace, past the fountain. Pause at the...

❽ Statue of Wergeland: The poet Henrik Wergeland helped inspire the national resurgence of Norway during the 19th century. Norway won its independence from Denmark in 1814, but within a year it lost its freedom to Sweden. For nearly a century, until Norway won independence in 1905, Norwegian culture and national spirit was stoked by artistic and literary patriots like Wergeland. In the winter, the pool here is frozen and covered with children happily ice-skating.

Across the street behind Wergeland stands the **❾ National Theater** and statues of Norway's favorite playwrights: Ibsen and Bjørnstjerne Bjørnson. Across Karl Johans Gate, the pale yellow building is the first university building in Norway, dating from 1854. A block behind that is the National Gallery, with Norway's best collection of paintings.

Take a moment here to do a 360-degree spin to notice how quiet and orderly everything is. People seem content—and, according to most surveys, Norwegians are among the happiest people on earth. If you ask them why, their hunch is that it's because they live collectively. The Vikings would famously share one large bowl of mead, passing it around the circle. Nobody—no matter how big, angry, hairy, or smelly—gulped more than his share. They all made sure that everyone got some.

In modern times, Norwegians at the dinner table are still mindful when helping themselves not to take too much: They mentally ration enough for the people who come after them. It's a very considerate—and a very Norwegian—way of thinking. (Similarly, upper-Midwesterners in the US are familiar with the "Minnesota Slice": The Scandinavian-American tendency to carve off a little sliver of the last slice of pie, rather than take the entire thing for themselves.)

• *Facing the theater, turn left and follow Roald Amundsens Gate to the towering brick...*

❿ City Hall (Rådhuset): Built mostly in the 1930s with contributions from Norway's leading artists, City Hall is full of great art and is worth touring (see listing later, under "Sights in Oslo").

The mayor has his office here (at the base of one of the two 200-foot towers), and every December 10, this building is where the Nobel Peace Prize is presented. The semicircular square facing the building, called Fridtjof Nansens Plass, was designed to evoke Il Campo, the main square in Siena, Tuscany. Just like Oslo, Siena's main building (dominating Il Campo) is its City Hall.

For the City Hall's best exterior art, step up into the U-shaped courtyard and circle it clockwise, savoring the colorful woodcuts in the arcade. Each shows a scene from Norwegian mythology, well-explained in English: Thor with his billy-goat chariot, Ask and Embla (a kind of Norse Adam and Eve), Odin on his eight-legged horse guided by ravens, the swan maidens shedding their swan disguises, and so on.

Facing City Hall, circle around its right side (through a lovely garden) until you reach the front. Like all of the statues adorning the building, the **six figures** facing the waterfront—dating from a period of Labor Party rule in Norway—celebrate the nobility of the working class. Norway, a social democracy, believes in giving respect to the workers who built their society and made it what it is, and these laborers are viewed as heroes.

• *Walk to the...*

⓫ Harbor: Over a decade ago, you would have dodged several lanes of busy traffic to reach Oslo's harborfront. Today, the traffic passes beneath your feet in tunnels. In addition, the city has made its town center relatively quiet and pedestrian-friendly by levying a toll on every car entering town. (This system, like a similar one in London, subsidizes public transit and the city's infrastructure.)

Head to the end of the stubby pier (just to the right). This is the ceremonial "enter the city" point for momentous occasions. One such instance was in 1905, when Norway gained its independence from Sweden and a Danish prince sailed in from Copenhagen to become the first modern king of Norway. Another milestone event occurred at the end of World War II, when the king returned to Norway after the country was liberated from the Nazis.

• *Stand on that important pier and give the harbor a sweeping counterclockwise look.*

Harborfront Spin-Tour: Oslofjord is one big playground, with 40 city-owned, parklike islands. Big white cruise ships—a large part of the local tourist economy—dock just under the Akershus Fortress on the left. (The big, boxy building clinging to the top of the fortress—just under the green steeple—is the excellent Norwegian Resistance Museum.) Just this side of the fort's impressive 13th-century ramparts, a **statue of FDR** grabs the shade. He's here in gratitude for the safe refuge the US gave to members of the royal family (including the young prince, Harald, who is now Norway's king) during World War II—while the king and his government-in-exile waged Norway's fight against the Nazis from London.

Panning left, enjoy the grand view of City Hall. The yellow building farther to the left was the old West Train Station; today it houses the ⓬ **Nobel Peace Center,** which celebrates the work of Nobel Peace Prize winners. Just to the left and behind that is the construction site for the new home of the National Museum, including the fine art collection of the National Gallery (slated to open in 2020).

The next pier over is the launchpad for harbor boat tours and the shuttle boat to the Bygdøy museums. At the base of this pier, the glassy box is a new fish market, serving a mix of locals and tourists. You may see a fisherman mooring his boat near here, selling shrimp from the back. Along the right side of the harbor, shipyard buildings (this was the former heart of Norway's once-important shipbuilding industry) have been transformed into **Aker Brygge**—

Oslo's thriving restaurant/shopping/nightclub zone.

Just past the end of Aker Brygge is a new housing development—dubbed Norway's most expensive real estate—called **Tjuvholmen.** It's anchored by the Astrup Fearnley Museum, an international modern art museum complex designed by renowned architect Renzo Piano (most famous for Paris' Pompidou Center).

An ambitious urban renewal project called Fjord City (Fjordbyen)—which kicked off years ago with Aker Brygge, and led to the construction of Oslo's dramatic Opera House—has made remarkable progress in turning the formerly industrial waterfront into a flourishing people zone.

• *From here, you can stroll out Aker Brygge and through Tjuvholmen to a tiny public beach at the far end; tour City Hall; visit the Nobel Peace Center; hike up to Akershus Fortress; take a harbor cruise (see "Tours in Oslo," earlier); or catch a boat across the harbor to the museums on Bygdøy (from pier 3).*

Sights in Oslo

CITY CENTER
Near the Harborfront
▲▲▲City Hall (Rådhuset)

In 1931, Oslo tore down a slum and began constructing its richly decorated City Hall. It was finally finished—after a WWII delay—in 1950 to celebrate the city's 900th birthday. Norway's leading artists all contributed to the building, which was an avant-garde thrill in its day. City halls, rather than churches, are the dominant buildings in Scandinavian capitals. The prominence of this building on the harborfront makes sense in this most humanistic, yet least church-going, northern end of the Continent. Up here, people pay high taxes, have high expectations, and are generally satisfied with what their governments do with their money.

Cost and Hours: Free, daily 9:00-16:00—until 18:00 June-Aug, free and fine WC in the basement, tel. 23 46 12 00.

Tours: Only in the summer months (June-Aug), the City Hall offers 50-minute guided tours daily at 10:00, 12:00, and 14:00.

❍ **Self-Guided Tour:** For descriptions of the building's exterior features and symbolism, see the City Hall section of my "Oslo Walk," earlier. On this tour, we'll focus on the interior.

The visitor entrance is on the Karl Johans Gate side (away from the harbor). You'll step into a cavernous **main hall,** which feels like a temple to good government, with its altar-like murals celebrating "work, play, and civic administration." It's decorated with 20,000 square feet of bold and colorful Socialist Realist murals celebrating a classless society, with everyone—town folk, country folk, and people from all walks of life—working harmoniously for a better society. The huge murals take you on a voyage through the collective psyche of Norway, from its simple rural beginnings through the scar tissue of the Nazi occupation and beyond.

First, turn around and face the mural over the door you came in, which celebrates the **traditional industries** of Norway (from left to right): the yellow-clad fisherman (standing in his boat, glancing nervously at a flock of seagulls), the factory worker (with his heavy apron), the blue-clad sailor (he's playing with exotic beads acquired through distant trade), the farmer (in a striped dress, with a bushel under her arm), and the miner (lower right, lifting a heavy rock). Flanking these figures are portraits of two important Norwegians: On the far right is Bjørnstjerne Bjørnson (1832-1910), a prominent poet and novelist whose works pluck the patriotic heart-strings of Norwegians. And on the far left is Fridtjof Nansen (1861-1930), the famous Arctic explorer (you can learn more about him at the Fram Museum on Bygdøy). Here Nansen is seen shedding the heavy coat of his most famous endeavor—polar exploration—as he embarks on his "second act": Once retired from seafaring, he advocated for the dissolution of Norway's union with Sweden—which took place in 1905, making Norway fully independent.

Now turn 180 degrees and face the hall's main mural, which emphasizes **Oslo's youth** participating in community life—and rebuilding the country after Nazi occupation. Across the bottom, the slum that once cluttered up Oslo's harborfront is being cleared out to make way for this building. Above that, scenes show Norway's pride in its innovative health care and education systems. Left of center, near the top, Mother Norway stands next to a church—reminding viewers that the Lutheran Church of Norway (the official state church) provides a foundation for this society. On the right, four forms represent the arts; they illustrate how creativity springs from children. And in the center, the figure of Charity is surrounded by Culture, Philosophy, and Family.

The **"Mural of the Occupation"** lines the left side of the hall, tucked under the balustrade. Scan it from left to right to see the story of Norway's WWII experience: First, the German blitzkrieg overwhelms the country. Men head for the mountains to organize a resistance movement. Women huddle around the water well, traditionally where news is passed, while Quislings (traitors named after the

Norwegian fascist who ruled the country as a Nazi puppet) listen in. While Germans bomb and occupy Norway, a family gathers in their living room. As a boy clenches his fist (showing determination) and a child holds the beloved Norwegian flag, the Gestapo steps in. Columns are toppled to the ground, symbolizing how Germans shut down the culture by closing newspapers and the university. Two resistance soldiers stand up against a wall—about to be executed by firing squad. A cell of resistance fighters (wearing masks and using nicknames, so if tortured they can't reveal their compatriots' identities) plan a sabotage mission. Finally, prisoners are freed, the war is over, and Norway celebrates its happiest day: May 17, 1945—the first Constitution Day after five years under Nazi control.

OSLO

At the base of the grand marble staircase is a mural of the 11th-century **St. Hallvard,** the patron saint of Oslo. In front of the mural is a **bell** from the ship that brought Norway's royal family back home after World War II—landing at the pier right in front of City Hall.

Now head up the stairs and explore several **ceremonial rooms,** each well-described in English. The wood-paneled Munch Room is dominated by the artist's oil painting *Life*. Circle around the gallery to the City Council Assembly Room, where Oslo's leadership steers the agenda of this impressive city. The city council acts collectively as a virtual "mayor"—a system, originating here in Oslo in 1986, called "parliamentary metropolitan government." Notice how this room evokes the semicircular shape of the square where you entered.

Nearby: Fans of the explorer Fridtjof Nansen might enjoy taking a break for a bite and a coffee or beer across the street at **Fridtjof,** an atmospheric bar filled with memorabilia from Nansen's Arctic explorations. A model of his ship, the *Fram,* hangs from the ceiling, and 1894 photos and his own drawings are upstairs (Mon-Sat 12:00 until late, Sun 14:00-22:00, Nansens Plass 7, tel. 93 25 22 30).

Nobel Peace Center (Nobels Fredssenter)

This museum, housed in the former West Train Station (Vestbanen), poses the question, "What is the opposite of conflict?" It celebrates the 800-some past and present Nobel Peace Prize winners with touchscreen exhibits (with good English explanations).

Cost and Hours: 100 NOK; daily 10:00-18:00, closed Mon Sept-mid-May; includes English guided tours at 14:00 and 15:00—off-season weekends only at 14:00; Brynjulfs Bulls Plass 1, tel. 48 30 10 00, www.nobelpeacecenter.org.

Visiting the Center: The ground floor is dominated by generally good, thought-provoking temporary exhibits. The permanent collection upstairs is modest: First you'll step into "The Nobel Field," a sea of lights and touchscreens profiling various past prizewinners (from Teddy Roosevelt to Mother Theresa). Next, "The Nobel Chamber" has a big virtual book that invites you to learn more about the life and work of Alfred Nobel, the Swedish inventor of dynamite, who initiated the prizes—perhaps to assuage his conscience. While it's a nice museum, unless the temporary exhibits intrigue you, save your time and money for the better Nobel Prize Museum in Stockholm.

▲Aker Brygge and Tjuvholmen

Oslo's harborfront was dominated by the **Aker Brygge** shipyard until it closed in 1986. In the late 2000s, it became the first finished part of a project (called Fjordbyen, or Fjord City) to convert the central stretch of Oslo's harborfront into a people-friendly park and culture zone. Today's Aker Brygge is a stretch of trendy, if over-priced, yacht-club style restaurants facing a fine promenade—just the place to join in on a Nordic paseo on a balmy summer's eve.

The far end of Aker Brygge is marked by a big black anchor from the wreck of the German warship *Blücher,* sunk by Norwegian forces near Drøbak while heading for Oslo during the Nazi invasion on April 9, 1940. From there a bridge crosses over onto **Tjuvholmen** (where they hung thieves back in the 17th century). This is a planned futuristic community, with the trendiest and costliest apartments in town, private moorings for luxury jet boats, boardwalks with built-in seating to catch the sun, elegant shops and cafés, and the striking, wood-clad, glass-roofed **Astrup Fearnley Museum of Modern Art** (good temporary exhibits of contemporary art, closed Mon, www.afmuseet.no). On the harbor side of the museum, find the grassy little knob of land with an appealing sculpture park. This area is well worth a wander—and don't be afraid to explore the back lanes away from the waterfront. As you stroll through Tjuvholmen, admire how, while the entire complex feels cohesive, each building has its own personality.

Eating: Dining here is appealing, but be prepared to pay royally for the privilege. Choose from many restaurants, or—to eat on a budget—take advantage of the generous public benches, lounge chairs, and picnic tables (grocery stores are a block away from the harborfront views).

▲Akershus Fortress Complex

This parklike complex of sights scattered over Oslo's fortified old center is still a military base. (You'll see uniformed members of the Royal Guard keeping watch, because the castle is a royal mausoleum.) But the public is welcome, and as you dodge patrol guards and vans filled with soldiers, you'll see the castle, war memorials, the Norwegian Resistance Museum, and cannon-strewn ramparts affording fine harbor views and picnic perches. There's an unimpressive changing of the guard—that's singular "guard," as in just one—daily at 13:30 (at the parade ground, deep in the castle complex). The park is generally open daily 6:00-21:00 (until 18:00 in winter), but because the military is in charge here, times can change without warning. Expect bumpy cobblestone lanes and steep hills. To get here from the harbor, follow the stairs (which lead past the FDR statue) to the park.

Getting Oriented: It's a sprawling complex. You can hike up the stairs by the FDR statue on the harbor, or (less steeply) from the grid of streets just east of City Hall. As you hike up toward the ramparts, go through the gate smack in the middle of the complex (rather than hooking up around to the right). You'll pop out into an inner courtyard. The visitors center is to the left, and the other sights are through the gate on the right. Heading through this gate, you'll curl up along a tree-lined lane, then pass the Norwegian Resistance Museum on your right (capping the ramparts). The entrance to the castle is dead ahead. There are terrific harbor views (often filled with a giant cruise ship) from the rampart alongside the Resistance Museum.

Fortress Visitors Center: Stop here to pick up the fortress trail and site map, quickly browse through a modest exhibit tracing the story of Oslo's fortifications from medieval times, use the free WCs, and consider catching a tour (daily July-mid-Aug 11:00-17:00, until 16:00 in shoulder season, shorter hours off-season, tel. 23 09 39 17, www.akershusfestning.no).

Fortress Tours: The 60-NOK, hour-long English walking tours of the grounds help you make sense of the most historic piece of real estate in Oslo (July-mid-Aug daily in English at 13:00, weekends only off-season; departs from Fortress Visitors Center, call ahead to confirm tour is running).

▲▲Norwegian Resistance Museum (Norges Hjemmefrontmuseum)

This fascinating museum tells the story of Norway's WWII experience: appeasement, Nazi invasion (they made Akershus one of their headquarters), resistance, liberation, and, finally, the return of the king. With good English descriptions, this is an inspirational look at how the national spirit can endure total occupation by a malevolent force. While the exhibit grows a bit more old-fashioned with each passing year, for those with an appetite for WWII history and the patience to read the displays, it's still both riveting and stirring. Norway had the fiercest resistance movement in Scandinavia, and this museum shows off their (hard-earned) pride.

Cost and Hours: 60 NOK; Mon-Sat 10:00-17:00, Sun from 11:00; Sept-May Mon-Fri 10:00-16:00, Sat-Sun from 11:00; next to castle, overlooking harbor, tel. 23 09 31 38, www.forsvaretsmuseer.no.

Visiting the Museum: It's a one-way, chronological, can't-get-lost route. As you enter the exhibit, you're transported back to 1940, greeted by an angry commotion of rifles aimed at you. A German notice proclaiming "You will submit or die" is bayonetted onto a gun in the middle. A **timeline** on the right wall traces the brief history of skirmishes between Nazi and improvised Norwegian forces following the invasion on April 9, 1940. This ends abruptly on June 10, when the Norwegian government officially capitulates.

On the left, you'll see the German ultimatum to which King Haakon VII gave an emphatic "No." A video screen nearby plays the radio address by Vidkun Quisling, the fascist Nasjonal Samling (National Union Party) politician who declared himself ruler of Norway on the day of the invasion. (Today, Quisling's name remains synonymous with "traitor"—the Norwegian version of Benedict Arnold.)

Head **downstairs** and take some time with the in-depth exhibits. Various displays show secret radios, transmitters, and underground newspapers. The official name for the resistance was Milorg (for "Military Organization")—but Norwegians affectionately referred to the ragtag, guerilla force as simply *gutta på skauen* ("the boys in the forest"). Look for the display case explaining wartime difficulty and austerity in Norway. Red knit caps were worn by civilians to show solidarity with the resistance—until the hats were outlawed by Nazi officials. In the same case, notice the shoes made of fish skin, and the little row of *erstatning* (ersatz, or replacement) products. With the Nazi occupation, Norway lost its trade partners, and had to improvise.

You'll also learn about the military actions against the occupation. British-trained special forces famously blew up a strategic heavy water plant (a key part of the Nazis' atomic bomb program)—still fondly recalled by Norwegians, and immortalized in the not-so-accurate 1965 Kirk Douglas film *The Heroes of Telemark*. Nearby, see the case of crude but effective homemade weapons, and the German machine used to locate clandestine radio stations. Exhibits explain how the country coped with 350,000 occupying troops; how airdrops equipped a home force of 40,000 so they were ready to coordinate with the Allies when liberation was imminent; and the happy day when the resistance army came out of the forest, and peace and freedom returned to Norway. Liberation day was May 8, 1945...but it took a few days to pull together the celebration, which coincided neatly with the 17th of May—Constitution Day. (That's partly why May 17 is still celebrated so fiercely today.)

Back **upstairs,** notice the propaganda posters trying to recruit Norwegians to the Nazi cause and "protect the eastern border" from the Soviets and communism. A more recent addition to the museum (downstairs) considers the many Norwegians who did choose to cooperate with (and profit from) the Nazis.

The museum is particularly poignant because many of the patriots featured inside were executed by the Germans right outside the museum's front door; a **stone memorial** marks the spot. (At war's

end, the traitor Vidkun Quisling was also executed at the fortress, but at a different location.)

Akershus Castle

Although it's one of Oslo's oldest buildings, the castle overlooking the harbor is mediocre by European standards; the big, empty

rooms recall Norway's medieval poverty. The first fortress here was built by Norwegians in 1299. It was rebuilt much stronger by the Danes in 1640 so the Danish king (Christian IV) would have a suitable and safe place to stay during his many visits. When Oslo was rebuilt in the 17th century, many of the stones from the first Oslo cathedral were reused here, in the fortress walls.

Cost and Hours: 100 NOK, includes audioguide; Mon-Sat 10:00-16:00, Sun from 12:00; Sept-April Sat-Sun 12:00-17:00 only, closed Mon-Fri; tel. 23 09 35 53. Note that renovation work may affect these hours or close the castle; check locally.

Visiting the Castle: From the old kitchen, where the ticket desk and gift shop are located, you'll follow a one-way circuit of rooms open to the public. Descend through a secret passage to the dungeon, crypt, and royal tomb. Emerge behind the altar in the chapel, then walk through echoing rooms including the Daredevil's Tower, Hall of Christian IV (with portraits of Danish kings of Norway on the walls), and Hall of Olav V.

On the Waterfront, Near the Train Station
▲Oslo Opera House (Operahuset Oslo)

Opened in 2008, Oslo's striking Opera House was a huge hit. The building angles up from the water on the city's eastern harbor, across the highway from the

train station. Its boxy, low-slung, glass center holds a state-of-the-art 1,400-seat main theater with a 99-piece orchestra "in the pit," which can rise to put the orchestra "on the pedestal." The season is split between opera and ballet.

Cost and Hours: Foyer and café/restaurant open Mon-Fri 10:00-23:00, Sat from 11:00, Sun 12:00-22:00.

Tours: Year-round, you can take a fascinating 50-minute

guided tour of the stage, backstage area, and architecture (100 NOK; usually 3 tours/day in English—generally at 11:00, 12:00, and 14:00; reserve online at www.operaen.no, tel. 21 42 21 00).

Daytime Mini-Concerts: For a few weeks in the summer, the Opera House offers sporadic one-hour daytime "Concerts at the Balcony" (70 NOK, many days in late July at 14:00).

Getting There: You'll find it on Bjørvika, the next harbor over from City Hall and Akershus Fortress—just below the train station.

Visiting the Opera House: Information-packed, 50-minute tours explain what makes this one of the greenest buildings in Europe and why Norwegian taxpayers helped foot the half-billion-dollar cost for this project—to make high culture (ballet and opera) accessible to the younger generation and a stratum of society who normally wouldn't care. You'll see a workshop employing 50 people who hand-make costumes, and learn how the foundation of 700 pylons set 40 or 50 meters deep support the jigsaw puzzle of wood, glass, and 36,000 individual pieces of marble. The construction masterfully integrates land and water, inside and outside, nature and culture.

The jutting white marble planes of the Opera House's roof double as a public plaza. You feel a need to walk all over it. The Opera House is part of a larger harbor-redevelopment plan that includes rerouting traffic into tunnels and turning a once-derelict industrial zone into an urban park. If you hike all the way to the top of the building (watch your footing—it's slippery when wet), you can peek over the back railing to see the high-rise development known as the "Barcode Project." The new Munch Museum (likely opening in 2020) resides in the futuristic Lambda building on the adjacent pier.

Downtown Museums
▲▲▲National Gallery (Nasjonalgalleriet)
While there are many schools of painting and sculpture displayed in Norway's National Gallery, focus on what's uniquely Norwegian.

Paintings come and go in this museum, but you're sure to see plenty that showcase the harsh beauty of Norway's landscape and people. A thoughtful visit here gives those heading into the mountains and fjord country a chance to pack along a little of Norway's cultural soul. Tuck

Edvard Munch (1863-1944)

Edvard Munch (pronounced "moonk") is Norway's most famous and influential painter. His life was rich, complex, and sad. His father was a doctor who had a nervous breakdown. His mother and sister both died of tuberculosis. He knew suffering. And he gave us the enduring symbol of 20th-century pain, *The Scream*.

He was also Norway's most forward-thinking painter, a man who traveled extensively through Europe, soaking up the colors of the Post-Impressionists and the curves of Art Nouveau. He helped pioneer a new style—Expressionism—using lurid colors and wavy lines to "express" inner turmoil and the angst of the modern world.

After a nervous breakdown in late 1908, followed by eight months of rehab in a clinic, Munch emerged less troubled—but a less powerful painter. His late works were as a colorist: big, bright, less tormented...and less noticed.

these images carefully away with your goat cheese—they'll sweeten your explorations.

The gallery also has several Picassos, a noteworthy Impressionist collection, a Van Gogh self-portrait, and some Vigeland statues. Its many raving examples of Edvard Munch's work include one of his famous *Scream* paintings. It has about 50 Munch paintings in its collection, but only about a third are on display. Be prepared for changes, but don't worry—no matter what the curators decide to show, you won't have to scream for Munch's masterpieces.

Cost and Hours: 100 NOK, free on Thu; Tue-Fri 10:00-18:00, Thu until 19:00, Sat-Sun 11:00-17:00, closed Mon; obligatory lockers, Universitets Gata 13, tel. 21 98 20 00, www.nasjonalmuseet. no. Pick up the guidebooklet to help navigate the collection.

Tours: Invest 50 NOK in the evocative audioguide.

Eating: The richly ornamented **$$ French Salon café** offers an elegant break (150-NOK lunches).

Closure and Move: The gallery is scheduled to close in September 2019, when the collection will move to a new purpose-built home in the new National Museum near the harbor, behind the Nobel Peace Center (not far from City Hall, likely opening in 2020). Confirm details locally. As the museum is in flux, you may find even more changes to the collection than usual.

National Historical Museum (Historisk Museum)

Directly behind the National Gallery and just below the palace is a fine Art Nouveau building offering an easy (if underwhelming) peek at Norway's history. It includes the country's top collection of Viking artifacts, displayed in low-tech, old-school exhibits with barely a word of English.

Cost and Hours: 100 NOK, same ticket covers Viking Ship Museum for 48 hours; open Tue-Sun 10:00-17:00, mid-Sept-mid-May 11:00-16:00; closed Mon year-round; Frederiks Gate 2, tel. 22 85 19 00, www.khm.uio.no.

VIGELAND PARK

The sprawling Frogner Park anchors an upscale neighborhood of the same name, 1.5 miles west of the city center. Here you'll find a breathtaking sculpture park and two museums.

▲▲▲Vigeland Park

Within Oslo's vast Frogner Park is Vigeland Park, containing a lifetime of work by Norway's greatest sculptor, Gustav Vigeland (see sidebar). In 1921, he made a deal with the city. In return for a great studio and state support, he'd spend his creative life beautifying Oslo with this sculpture garden. From 1924 until his death in 1943 he worked on-site, designing 192 bronze and granite statue groupings—600 figures in all, each nude and unique. Vigeland even planned the landscaping.

Today the park is loved and respected by the people of Oslo (no police, no fences—and no graffiti). At once majestic, hands-on, entertaining, and deeply moving, why this sculpture park isn't considered one of Europe's top artistic sights, I can only guess. In summer, this is a tempting destination in the late afternoon—after the museums have closed and there's still plenty of daylight to go. (But if you want to visit the nearby Vigeland Museum, be aware that it closes at 17:00.) Vigeland Park is more than great art: It's a city at play. Appreciate its urban Norwegian ambience.

Cost and Hours: The garden is always open and free. The park is safe (cameras monitor for safety).

Getting There: Tram #12—which leaves from the central train station, Rådhusplassen in front of City Hall, Aker Brygge, and other points in town—drops you off right at the park gate

Gustav Vigeland (1869-1943)

Gustav Vigeland's father was a carpenter in the city of Mandal, in southern Norway. Vigeland grew up carving wood, and showed promise. And so, as a young man, he went to Oslo to study sculpture, then supplemented his education with trips abroad to Europe's art capitals. Back home, he carved out a successful, critically acclaimed career feeding newly independent Norway's hunger for homegrown art.

During his youthful trips abroad, Vigeland frequented the studio of Auguste Rodin, admiring Rodin's naked, restless, intertwined statues. Like Rodin, Vigeland explored the yin/yang relationship of men and women. Also like Rodin, Vigeland did not personally carve or cast his statues. Rather, he formed them in clay or plaster, to be executed by a workshop of assistants. Vigeland's sturdy humans capture universal themes of the cycle of life—birth, childhood, romance, struggle, child-rearing, growing old, and death.

(Vigelandsparken stop). Tram #19 (with stops along Karl Johans Gate) takes you to Majorstuen, a 10-minute walk to the gate (or you can change at Majorstuen to tram #12 and ride it one stop to Vigelandsparken).

Information and Services: For an illustrated guide and fine souvenir, consider the 120-NOK book in the **visitors center** (Besøkssenter) on your right as you enter. The modern **$$ cafeteria** has sandwiches and light meals (indoor/outdoor seating, daily 9:00-20:30 in summer, shorter hours off-season), plus books, gifts, and pay WCs.

● **Self-Guided Tour:** The park is huge, but this visit is a snap. Here's a quick, four-stop, straight-line, gate-to-monolith tour.

• *Begin by entering the park through the grand gates, from Kirkeveien (with the tram stop). In front of the visitors center, look at the...*

Gustav Vigeland Statue: Vigeland has his hammer and chisel in hand...and is drenched in pigeon poop. Consider his messed-

up life. He lived with his many models. His marriages failed. His children entangled his artistic agenda. He didn't age gracefully. He didn't name his statues, and refused to explain their meanings. While those who know his life story can read it clearly in the granite and bronze, I'd forget Gustav's troubles and see his art as observations on the bittersweet cycle of life in general—from a man who must have had a passion for living.

• *Now walk 100 yards toward the fountain and the pillar.*

Bridge: The 300-foot-long bridge is bounded by four granite columns: Three show a man fighting a lizard, the fourth shows a woman submitting to the lizard's embrace. Hmmm. (Vigeland was familiar with medieval mythology, where dragons represent man's primal—and sinful—nature.)

But enough lizard love; the 58 bronze statues along the bridge are a general study of the human body. They capture the joys of life (and, on a sunny day, so do the Norwegians and tourists filling the park around you). Many deal with relationships between people. In the middle, on the right, find the circular statue of a man and woman going round and round—perhaps the eternal attraction and love between the sexes. But directly opposite, another circle feels like a prison—man against the world, with no refuge.

On your left, see the famous *Sinnataggen,* the hot-headed little boy and a symbol of the park. (Notice his left hand is worn shiny from too many hand-holdings.) It's said Vigeland gave a boy chocolate and then took it away to get this reaction. Look below the angry toddler, to the lower terrace—with eight bronze infants circling a head-down fetus.

• *Continue through a rose garden to the earliest sculpture unit in the park.*

Fountain: Six giants hold a fountain, symbolically toiling with the burden of life, as water—the source of life—cascades steadily around them. Twenty tree-of-life groups surround the fountain. Four clumps of trees (on each corner) show humanity's relationship to nature and the seasons of life: childhood, young love, adulthood, and winter.

Take a quick swing through life, starting on the right with youth. In the branches you'll see a swarm of children (Vigeland called them "geniuses"): A boy sits in a tree, other boys actively climb while most girls stand by quietly, and a girl glides through the branches wide-eyed and ready for life...and love. Circle clockwise to the next stage: love scenes. In the third corner, life becomes more complicated: a sad woman in an animal-like tree, a lonely child, a couple plummeting downward (perhaps falling out of love), a man desperately clinging to his tree, and finally an angry man driving away babies. The fourth corner completes the cycle, as death melts into the branches of the tree of life and you realize new geniuses will bloom.

The 60 bronze reliefs circling the basin develop the theme further, showing man mixing with nature and geniuses giving the carousel of life yet another spin. Speaking of another spin, circle again and follow these reliefs.

The pattern in the pavers surrounding the basin is a maze—life's long and winding road with twists, dead ends, frustrations, and, ultimately, a way out. If you have about an hour to spare, enter the labyrinth (on the side nearest the park's entrance gate, there's a single break in the black border) and follow the white granite path until (on the monolith side) you finally get out. (Tracing this path occupies older kids, affording parents a peaceful break in the park.)

• *Or you can go straight up the steps to the...*

Monolith: The centerpiece of the park—a teeming monolith of life surrounded by 36 groups of granite statues—continues Vigeland's cycle-of-life motif. The figures are hunched and clearly earthbound, while Vigeland explores a lifetime of human relationships. At the center, 121 figures carved out of a single block of stone rocket skyward. Three stone carvers worked daily for 14 years, cutting Vigeland's full-size plaster model into the final 180-ton, 50-foot-tall erection.

Circle the plaza, once to trace the stages of life in the 36 statue groups, and a second time to enjoy how Norwegian kids relate to the art. The statues—both young and old—seem to speak to children.

Vigeland lived barely long enough to see his monolith raised. Covered with bodies, it seems to pick up speed as it spirals skyward. Some people seem to naturally rise. Others struggle not to fall. Some help others. Although the granite groups around the monolith are easy to understand, Vigeland left the meaning of the monolith itself open. Like life, it can be interpreted many different ways.

From this summit of the park, look a hundred yards farther, where four children and three adults are intertwined and spinning in the Wheel of Life. Now, look back at the entrance. If the main gate is at 12 o'clock, the studio where Vigeland lived and worked—now the Vigeland Museum—is at 2 o'clock (see the green copper tower poking above the trees). His ashes sit in the top of the tower in clear view of the monolith. If you liked the park, visit the Vigeland Museum (described next), a delightful five-minute walk away, for an intimate look at the art and how it was made.

▲▲Vigeland Museum

This palatial city-provided studio was Gustav Vigeland's home and workplace for the last two decades of his life. The high south-facing

windows provided just the right light. Vigeland, who had a deeply religious upbringing, saw his art as an expression of his soul. He once said, "The road between feeling and execution should be as short as possible." Here, immersed in his work, Vigeland supervised his craftsmen like a father, from 1924 until his death in 1943.

Today it's filled with plaster casts and studies of many of the works you'll see in the adjacent park—shedding new light on that masterpiece, and allowing you to see familiar pieces from new angles. It also holds a few additional works, and explains Vigeland's creative (and technical) process. While his upstairs apartment is usually closed to the public, it is open a few times a year—check the website to find out when.

Cost and Hours: 80 NOK; Tue-Sun 10:00-17:00, Sept-April 12:00-16:00, closed Mon year-round; bus #20 or tram #12 to Frogner Plass, Nobels Gate 32, tel. 23 49 37 00, www.vigeland. museum.no.

Visiting the Museum: It's all on one floor, roughly arranged chronologically, which you'll see in an easy clockwise loop. **Rooms I-III** explain Vigeland's development, including his early focus on biblical themes. In *Accused* (1891), Cain flees with his family, including their dog. But gradually, Vigeland grew more interested in the dynamics that dictate relationships in families, and between men and women. In these first rooms, look for two particularly touching sculptures in marble (a medium you won't often see used by Vigeland): *Mother and Child* (1909) and *Young Man and Woman* (1906).

Room IV is a long hall of portrait busts, which Vigeland often created without payment—he considered this task an opportunity to practice. While most of the busts don't depict famous people, you will see King Oscar II and Arctic explorer Fridtjof Nansen.

Room V continues this theme, with a few portraits (mostly full-body) of more recognizable figures: Beethoven, Ibsen, Wergeland, Bjørnson.

Room VI, with a 1942 self-portrait, explains the process by which Vigeland created his statues. See his tools displayed in a case, and read the explanation: Using the "sand casting" method, Vigeland would make a small plaster model, which guided his workers in creating a metal "skeleton." Vigeland would then bring the skeleton to life with soft clay—which he enjoyed using because its pliability allowed him to be spontaneous in his creativity. Once the clay piece was finished, plaster and sand were used to create a plaster cast, used for the final bronze piece. For his stone works, they used a "pointing machine" to painstakingly measure the exact nuances of Vigeland's contours. Examples of using both methods (including five different versions of the famous "angry baby" bronze) are displayed around the room.

Room VII holds temporary exhibits, while **Room VIII** features the full-sized plaster models for the park's bronze fountain. The large **Room IX** has more pieces from the park, including a one-fifth-scale model of the fountain (used to win the Oslo City Council's support for the project) and the four dragon statues that top the bridge's pillars (high up and difficult to see in the park, but fascinating up close).

Room X is the dramatic climax of the museum, with a model of the entire park, and the life-size plaster models for the Monolith—in three pieces, making it easy to scrutinize the details. You'll also see wrought-iron chained dragons—originally designed as a feature for the park gates—and several plaster models for the statues that surround the Monolith. Notice the many little "freckles" on these statues, left behind by the pointer used by craftsmen to replicate Vigeland's work. The museum finishes with more temporary exhibits (in Rooms XI and XII).

BYGDØY NEIGHBORHOOD

This thought-provoking and exciting cluster of sights, worth ▲▲, is on a parklike peninsula just across the harbor from downtown Oslo. It provides a busy and rewarding half-day (at a minimum) of sightseeing.

Here, within a short walk, are six major sights (listed in order of importance): the **Norwegian Folk Museum,** an open-air museum with traditional wooden buildings from all corners of the country, a stave church, and a collection of 20th-century urban buildings; the **Viking Ship Museum,** showing off the best-preserved Viking ships in existence; the **Fram Museum,** showcasing the modern Viking spirit with the *Fram,* the ship of Arctic-exploration fame, and the *Gjøa,* the first ship to sail through the Northwest Passage; the **Kon-Tiki Museum,** starring the *Kon-Tiki* and the

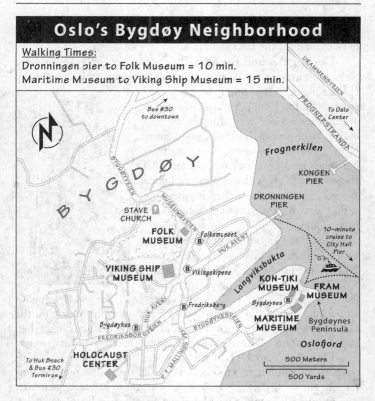

Oslo's Bygdøy Neighborhood

Walking Times:
Dronningen pier to Folk Museum = 10 min.
Maritime Museum to Viking Ship Museum = 15 min.

Ra II, in which Norwegian explorer Thor Heyerdahl proved that early civilizations—with their existing technologies—could have crossed the oceans; the **Norwegian Maritime Museum,** interesting mostly to old salts, has a wonderfully scenic movie of Norway; and the **Norwegian Holocaust Center,** memorializing the Holocaust in Norway.

Getting to Bygdøy: Sailing from downtown to Bygdøy is fun, fast, and gets you in a seafaring mood. Ride the Bygdøy **ferry**—marked *Public Ferry Bygdøy Museums*—from pier 3 in front of City Hall (45 NOK one-way at the ticket desk, 60 NOK on board; 65 NOK round-trip at the ticket desk; covered by Oslo Pass; 3/hour, 10-15-minute trip; runs mid-May-Aug daily 8:55-20:55, fewer sailings spring and fall, doesn't run mid-Oct-mid-March). Boats generally leave from downtown at :05, :25, and :45 past each hour. In summer, avoid the nearby (much more expensive) tour boats.

For a less memorable approach, you can take **bus #30** (from train station, National Theater, or in front of City Hall, direction: Bygdøy; 20-minute trip).

Returning to Oslo: Note that after 17:00, bus and boat departures back to downtown are sparse. If returning by ferry, get to the dock a little early—otherwise the boat is likely to be full, and you'll have to wait for the next sailing.

Getting Around Bygdøy: The Norwegian Folk and Viking Ship museums are a 10-minute walk from the ferry's first stop (Dronningen). The other boating mu-seums (Fram, Kon-Tiki, and Maritime) are at the second ferry stop, in an area called Bygdøynes. The Holocaust Center is off Fredriksborgveien, about halfway between these two museum clusters. All Bygdøy sights are within a pleasant (when sunny) 15-minute walk of each other. The walk gives you a picturesque taste of sub-urban Oslo.

City bus #30 connects the sights four times hourly in this order: Norwegian Folk Museum, Viking Ship Museum, Kon-Tiki Museum, Norwegian Holo-caust Center. (For the Holocaust Center, you'll use the Bygdøyhus stop a long block away; tell the bus driver you want the stop for the "HL-Senteret.") The bus turns around at its final stop (Huk), then passes the sights in reverse order on its way back to the city center.

Planning Your Day: If the weather's good, hit the Folk Museum first (before it gets too hot). If it's ugly out—but may get better—begin with the mostly indoor boat museums at Bygdøynes. The marginally interesting Holocaust Center is a bit of a detour, and skippable if you're short on time. The Bygdøynes museums offer a 10 percent discount if you buy tickets for all three at the same time; decide before you buy your first ticket, and save a few bucks. The major museums all have free lockers, Wi-Fi, and WCs.

Eating on Bygdøy: Each of the museum areas has $ food options. At the boat museum cluster (Bygdøynes), you'll find the **Framheim Café** inside the Fram Museum; the little **Cargo Café** window with hot dogs and ice cream outside the Kon-Tiki Mu-seum; and two more substantial eateries at the Maritime Muse-um: an **indoor café** with sandwiches and soup, and the outdoor **Fjordterrassen Café,** with hot dogs and deep-fried fish and veggie burgers, and tables overlooking the harbor. The Norwegian Folk Museum has a decent **Kafe Arkadia** at its entrance, and a fun little **farmers market** stall across the street (produce, drinks, yogurt—just enough to forage a healthy lunch). The Viking Ship Museum has an outdoor **snack window** selling shrimp and salmon sand-wiches. The Holocaust Center has a small **café** upstairs.

Museums on Bygdøy
▲▲Norwegian Folk Museum (Norsk Folkemuseum)

Brought from all corners of Norway, 150 buildings have been re-assembled here on 35 acres. While Stockholm's Skansen was the first museum of this kind to open to the public, this collection is a bit older, started in 1881 as the king's private collection (and the inspiration for Skansen). The folk museum is most lively (and worth ▲▲▲) June through mid-August, when buildings are open and staffed with attendants in period clothing (who'll happily answer your questions—so ask many). And during peak season you'll also see craftspeople doing their traditional things and barnyard animals roaming about. Otherwise, the indoor museum is fine, but the park is just a pleasant walk past lots of locked-up log cabins.

Cost and Hours: 130 NOK, daily 10:00-18:00—grounds open until 20:00; mid-Sept-mid-May park open Mon-Fri 11:00-15:00, Sat-Sun until 16:00 but most historical buildings closed; Museumsveien 10, bus #30 stops immediately in front, tel. 22 12 37 00, www.norskfolkemuseum.no.

Visiting the Museum: Think of the visit in three parts: the park sprinkled with old buildings, the re-created old town, and the folk-art museum. As you enter, you'll cut through the courtyard with the museum to reach the open-air sections.

Upon arrival, pick up the site map and review the list of the day's activities, concerts, and guided tours (on a video screen near the ticket desk). In summer, there are two guided tours in English per day; the Telemark Farm hosts a small daily fiddle-and-folk-dance show; and a folk music-and-dance show is held each Sunday. If you don't take a tour, invest in a guidebook and ask questions of the informative attendants stationed in buildings throughout the park.

The **park** is loaded with mostly log-built, sod-roofed cabins

from various parts of Norway (arranged roughly geographically). Be sure to go inside the buildings. The evocative Gol stave church, at the top of a hill at the park's edge, is worth the climb. Built in 1212 in Hallingdal and painstakingly reconstructed here, it has a classic design and, inside, beautiful-yet-primitive wood paintings on the apse walls (c. 1452). If you won't make it to a stave church elsewhere on your trip, this is a must.

Back near the entrance building, the **old town** has a variety of

OSLO

homes and shops that focus on urban lifestyles. It's worth exploring the tenement building, in which you can explore intimate, fully furnished apartments from various generations and lifestyles—1905, 1930, 1950, 1979, and even a Norwegian-Pakistani apartment.

In the **museum,** the ground floor beautifully presents woody, colorfully painted, and exactingly carved folk art; traditional Norwegian knitting; and weapons. Upstairs are exquisite-in-a-peasant-kind-of-way folk costumes. I'd skip the sleepy collection of Norwegian church art (in an adjoining building). But don't miss the best Sami culture exhibit I've seen in Scandinavia (across the courtyard in the green building, behind the toy exhibit). Everything is thoughtfully explained in English. A new exhibit showing various slices of Oslo life is scheduled to open in 2019.

▲▲Viking Ship Museum (Vikingskiphuset)

In this impressive museum, you'll gaze with admiration at two finely crafted, majestic oak Viking ships dating from the 9th and 10th centuries, and the scant remains of a third vessel. Along with the two well-preserved ships, you'll see the bones of Vikings buried with these vessels and remarkable artifacts that may cause you to consider these notorious raiders in a different light. Over a thousand years ago, three things drove Vikings on their far-flung raids: hard economic times in

their bleak homeland, the lure of prosperous and vulnerable communities to the south, and a mastery of the sea. There was a time when most frightened Europeans closed every prayer with, "And deliver us from the Vikings, Amen." Gazing up at the prow of one of these sleek, time-stained vessels, you can almost hear the screams and smell the armpits of those redheads on the rampage.

Cost and Hours: 100 NOK, ticket also covers the National Historical Museum in downtown Olso for 48 hours; daily 9:00-18:00, Oct-April 10:00-16:00; Huk Aveny 35, tel. 22 13 52 80, www.khm.uio.no.

Visitor Information: The museum doesn't offer tours, but everything is well-described in English. You can use the free Wi-Fi to download a free, informative audio tour app. You probably don't need the little museum guidebook—it repeats exactly what's already posted on the exhibits.

Visiting the Museum: Focus on the two well-preserved ships, starting with the *Oseberg*, from A.D. 834. With its ornate carving and impressive rudder, it was likely a royal pleasure craft. It seems designed for sailing on calm inland waters during festivals, but not in the open ocean.

The *Gokstad*, from A.D. 950, is a practical working boat, capable of sailing the high seas. A ship like this brought settlers to the west of France (Normandy was named for the Norsemen). And in such a vessel, explorers such as Eric the Red hopscotched from Norway to Iceland to Greenland and on to what they called Vinland—today's Newfoundland in Canada. Imagine 30 men hauling on long oars out at sea for weeks and months at a time. In 1892, a replica of this ship sailed from Norway to America in 44 days to celebrate the 400th anniversary of Columbus *not* discovering America.

You'll also see the ruins of a third vessel, the **Tune Ship** (c. A.D. 910), which saw service only briefly before being used as the tomb for an important chieftain. In this hall, every 20 minutes, the lights dim and a wrap-around film plays on the walls around the ship for five minutes—with dramatic virtual footage of the Vikings and their fleet.

The ships tend to steal the show, but don't miss the hall displaying **jewelry and personal items** excavated along with the ships. The ships and related artifacts survived so well because they were buried in clay as part of a gravesite. Many of the finest items were not actually Viking art, but goodies they brought home after raiding more advanced (but less tough) people. Still, there are lots of actual Viking items, such as metal and leather goods, that give insight into their culture. Highlights are the cart and sleighs, ornately carved with scenes from Viking sagas.

▲▲▲Fram Museum (Frammuseet)

Under its distinctive A-frame roof, this museum holds the 125-foot, steam- and sail-powered ship that took modern-day Vikings  Roald Amundsen and Fridtjof Nansen deep into the Arctic and Antarctic, farther north and south than any vessel had gone before. In an adjacent A-frame is Amundsen's *Gjøa*, the first ship to sail through the Northwest Passage. Together, the exhibit spins a fascinating tale of adventure, scientific exploration, and human determination...all at subzero temperatures.

Cost and Hours: 100 NOK; daily June-Aug 9:00-18:00, May and Sept 10:00-17:00, Oct and March-April until 16:00; Nov-Feb Mon-Fri 10:00-15:00, Sat-Sun until 16:00; Bygdøynesveien 36, tel. 23 23 29 50, www.frammuseum.no.

OSLO

Visiting the Museum: The Fram Museum tells the tale of several great Norwegian explorers. Stepping into the museum, you're immediately bow-to-bow with the 128-foot *Fram*. Before diving in, remember that there are two parts to the museum: The *Fram*, which you're looking at, and to the left through a tunnel, the smaller *Gjøa*. I'd see the *Gjøa* first, because it's a better lead-up to the main event, and because it features a short film that's a fine introduction to the entire museum.

Crossing through the tunnel to the **Gjøa,** you'll learn about the search for the Northwest Passage (that long-sought-after trade route through the Arctic from the Atlantic to the Pacific). Exhibits tell the story of how explorer Roald Amundsen (1872-1928) and a crew of six used this motor- and sail-powered ship to successfully navigate the Northwest Passage (1903-1906). Exhibits describe their ordeal as well as other Arctic adventures, such as Amundsen's 1925 flight to 88 degrees north (they had to build a runway out of ice to take off and return home); and his 1926 airship (zeppelin) expedition from Oslo over the North Pole to Alaska. This section also features a 100-seat cinema showing an excellent 15-minute film about the exploration of the earth's polar regions (shows every 15 minutes).

Now return to the **Fram,** and peruse the exhibits—actual artifacts and profiles of the brave explorers and their crew. The upper floor focuses on another explorer, Fridtjof Nansen (1861-1930), and his voyages to the North Pole on the *Fram*, including an early kayak, a full-size stuffed polar bear, and a model of the ship. Here you can cross a gangway to explore the *Fram*'s claustrophobic but fascinating interior. A simulated "Northern Lights Show," best viewed from the *Fram*'s main deck, is presented every 20 minutes.

Exhibits on the middle floor follow Roald Admundsen (1872-1928), who picked up where Nansen left off and explored the South Pole. You'll see an actual dogsled Admundsen's team used, and a small model of the motorized sled used by the rival Scott expedition. Also featured are a tent like the one Amundsen used, reconstructed shelves from his Arctic kitchen, models of the *Fram*, and a "polar simulator" plunging visitors into a 15° Fahrenheit environment.

▲▲Kon-Tiki Museum (Kon-Tiki Museet)

Next to the *Fram* is a museum housing the *Kon-Tiki* and the *Ra II*, the ships built by the larger-than-life anthropologist, seafarer, and adventurer Thor Heyerdahl (1914-2002). Heyerdahl and his crew used these ships—constructed entirely without modern technology—to undertake tropical voyages many had thought impossible. Both ships are well-displayed and described in English. This museum—more lighthearted than the other boat-focused exhibits—puts you in a castaway mood.

Cost and Hours: 100 NOK, daily 9:30-18:00, March-May and Sept-Oct 10:00-17:00, Nov-Feb until 16:00, Bygdøynesveien 36, tel. 23 08 67 67, www.kon-tiki.no.

Background: Thor Heyerdahl believed that early South Americans could have crossed the pacific to settle Polynesia. To prove his point, in 1947 Heyerdahl and five crewmates constructed the *Kon-Tiki* raft out of balsa wood, using only premodern tools and techniques—and adorned with a giant image of the sun god Kon-Tiki on the sail. They set sail from Peru on the tiny craft, surviving for 101 days on fish, coconuts, and sweet potatoes (which were native to Peru). About 4,300 miles later, they arrived in Polynesia. (While Heyerdahl proved that early South Americans *could* have made this trip, anthropologists doubt they did.) The *Kon-Tiki* story became a best-selling book and award-winning documentary (and helped spawn the "Tiki" culture craze in the US). Funded by the *Kon-Tiki* success, Heyerdahl went on to explore Easter Island (1955), and then turned his attention to another voyage—this time across the Atlantic. In 1970, Heyerdahl's *Ra II* made a similar 3,000-mile journey from Morocco to Barbados—on a vessel made of reeds—to prove that Africans could have populated the Americas.

Visiting the Museum: You'll see both the *Kon-Tiki* and the *Ra II,* and learn about Heyerdahl's other adventures (including Easter Island and the *Ra I,* which sank partway into its journey). Everything's well-described in English and very kid-friendly. In the basement, you'll see the bottom of the vessel with a life-size model of a whale shark (the largest fish on earth) and other marine life that the crew observed at sea. Nearby, a small theater continuously plays a 10-minute documentary about the voyage; every day at 12:00, they show the full-length (67-minute), Oscar-winning 1950 documentary film *Kon-Tiki.*

▲Norwegian Maritime Museum (Norsk Maritimt Museum)

If you're into the sea and seafaring, this museum is a salt lick, providing a wide-ranging look at Norway's maritime heritage through exhibits, art, and a panoramic film soaring over Norway's long and varied coastline.

Cost and Hours: 100 NOK; daily 10:00-17:00; Sept-mid-May Tue-Sun until 16:00, closed Mon; Bygdøynesveien 37, tel. 22 12 37 00, www.marmuseum.no.

Visiting the Museum: On the ground floor, you'll see a collection of small vessels, temporary exhibits, and an exhibit called *At Sea (Til Sjøs),* exploring what life is like on the ocean, from Viking days to the present. If you appreciate maritime art, the collection

OSLO

in the gallery should float your boat. Downstairs is *The Ship (Ski-pet)*, tracing two millennia of maritime development. You'll see a 2,200-year-old dugout boat, heft various materials used to make ships, and pilot model boats in a little lagoon. Nearby, watch the wrap-around, 20-minute movie *The Ocean: A Way of Life* (look for *Supervideografen* signs). Dated but still dramatic—and quite relax-ing—it swoops you scenically over Norway's diverse coast, show-ing off fishing townscapes, shiplap villages, industrial harbors, and breathtaking scenery from here all the way to North Cape in a comfy theater (starts at the top and bottom of the hour). Upstairs, past the library, the *Norway Is the Sea* exhibit considers how tech-nology has transformed the way Norwegians earn their living at sea.

Norwegian Holocaust Center (HL-Senteret)

Located in the stately former home of Nazi collaborator Vidkun Quisling—whose name is synonymous with "complicit in atroci-ties"—this museum and study center offers a high-tech look at the racist ideologies that fueled the Holocaust. It's designed primarily for Norwegians, but you can borrow a tablet with English trans-lations of the exhibits. The ground floor displays historical docu-ments about the rise of anti-Semitism and personal effects from Holocaust victims. The exhibits continue downstairs; near the end of the exhibit, the names of 760 Norwegian Jews killed by the Nazis are listed in a bright, white room. Out front, the *Innocent Questions* glass-and-neon sculpture shows an old-fashioned punch card, re-minding viewers of how the Norwegian puppet government col-lected seemingly innocuous information before deporting its Jews.

Cost and Hours: 70 NOK; daily 10:00-18:00; Sept-May Mon-Fri 10:00-16:00, Sat-Sun from 11:00; Huk Aveny 56—take bus #30 to the Bygdøyhus stop and follow brown *HL-Senteret* signs, tel. 22 84 21 00, www.hlsenteret.no.

EAST OF DOWNTOWN

▲Edvard Munch Museum (Munch Museet)

The only Norwegian painter to have had a serious impact on Eu-ropean art, Munch (pronounced "moonk") is a surprise to many who visit this fine museum—displaying the emotional, disturbing, and powerfully Expressionistic work of this strange and perplex-ing man. You'll see an extensive collection of paintings, drawings, lithographs, and photographs. Remember that you can see an ar-guably better (more concise and thoughtfully arranged) collection of a dozen great Munch paintings, including *The Scream,* at the National Gallery.

Cost and Hours: Likely 100 NOK; daily 10:00-17:00, early

May-early Oct until 16:00; confirm hours and location, tel. 23 49 35 00, www.munchmuseet.no.

Getting There: In 2020, the museum is scheduled to move to a brand-new, state-of-the-art location in the Lambda building, on a little spit in the harbor next to the Opera House; before then, you may find it at its original location a mile east of downtown (Tøyengata 53; ride the T-bane to Tøyen or bus #20 to Munchmuseet).

▲Ekeberg Sculpture Park

In 2013, this piece of wilderness—on a forested hill over town, with grand city views—was transformed into a modern sculpture park. The art collector who financed the park loves women and wanted his creation to be a "celebration of femininity." While that vision was considered a bit ill-advised and was scaled back, the park is plenty feminine and organic.

Getting There: The park, always open and free, is a 10-minute tram ride southeast of the center (at the train station, catch tram #18 from platform E, or #19 from platform C; take either one in the direction of Ljabru). Ride just a few stops to Ekebergparken, right at the park's entrance.

Visiting the Park: A visit here involves lots of climbing on trails through the trees. While some people come for the statues (35 in all, including some by prominent artists such as Dalí, Rodin, Renoir, Vigeland, and Damien Hirst), others simply enjoy a walk in nature...and most agree that the views of Oslo's fast-emerging harbor scene (the Opera House and Barcode Project) may be the highlight. From the tram stop, hike up to the little cluster of buildings (including the visitors center, where you can pick up a map and join a 1.5-hour guided walk in English—see schedule at www.ekebergparken.com). In this area, you can see the first of the sculptures. For views and more art, keep heading up the hill to the restaurant...and beyond. Maps, suggesting various walking routes, are posted throughout the park.

Shopping in Oslo

Shops in Oslo are generally open 10:00-18:00 or 19:00. Many close early on Saturday and all day Sunday. Shopping centers are open Monday through Friday 10:00-21:00, Saturday 9:00-18:00, and are closed Sunday. Remember, when you make a purchase of 315 NOK or more, you can get the 25 percent tax refunded when you leave the country (see page 125). Here are a few favorite shopping opportunities many travelers enjoy, but not on Sunday, when they're all closed.

Norway Designs, just outside the National Theater, shows off the country's sleek, contemporary designs in clothing, kitchenware, glass, textiles, jewelry—and high prices (Stortingsgata 12, T-bane: Nationaltheatret, tel. 23 11 45 10).

Paleet is a mall in the heart of Oslo, with 30 shops on three levels and a food court in the basement (Karl Johans Gate 37, tel. 23 08 08 11).

Dale of Norway, considered Norway's biggest and best maker of traditional and contemporary sweaters, offers its complete collection at their "concept store" in downtown Oslo (Karl Johans Gate 45, tel. 97 48 12 07).

Heimen Husfliden has a superb selection of authentic Norwegian sweaters, *bunads* (national costumes), traditional jewelry, and other Norwegian crafts (top quality at high prices, Rosenkrantz Gate 8, tel. 23 21 42 00).

GlasMagasinet is one of Oslo's oldest and fanciest department stores (top-end, good souvenir shop, near the cathedral at Stortorvet 9, tel. 22 82 23 00).

The Husfliden Shop, in the basement of the GlasMagasinet department store (listed above), is popular for its Norwegian-made sweaters, yarn, and colorful Norwegian folk crafts (tel. 22 42 10 75).

The Oslo Sweater Shop has competitive prices for a wide range of Norwegian-made sweaters, including Dale brand (in Radisson Blu Scandinavia Hotel at Tullinsgate 5, tel. 22 11 29 22).

Byporten, the big, splashy mall adjoining the central train station, is filled with youthful and hip shops, specialty stores, and eateries (Jernbanetorget 6, tel. 23 36 21 60).

The street named **Bogstadveien** is considered to have the city's trendiest boutiques and chic, high-quality shops (stretches from behind the Royal Palace to Majorstuen near Vigeland Park).

Oslo's Flea Market makes Saturday morning a happy day for those who brake for garage sales (at Vestkanttorvet, March-Nov only, two blocks east of Frogner Park at the corner of Professor Dahl's Gate and Neubergsgate).

Oslo Flaggfabrikk sells quality flags of all shapes and sizes, including the long, pennant-shaped *vimpel*, seen fluttering from flagpoles all over Norway (an 11.5-foot *vimpel* dresses up a boat or cabin wonderfully, near City Hall at Hieronymus Heyerdahlsgate 1, entrance on Tordenskioldsgate—on the other side of the block, tel. 22 40 50 60).

Vinmonopolet stores are the only places where you can buy wine and spirits in Norway. The most convenient location is at the central train station. Another location, not far from Stortinget, is at Rosenkrantz Gate 11. The bottles used to be kept behind the counter, but now you can actually touch the merchandise. Locals say it went from being a "jewelry store" to a "grocery store." (Light beer is sold in grocery stores, but strong beer is still limited to Vin-monopolet shops.)

Eating in Oslo

Eating out is expensive in Oslo. How do average Norwegians afford their high-priced restaurants? They don't eat out much. This is one city in which you might want to settle for simple or ethnic meals—you'll save a lot and miss little. Many menus list small and large plates. Because portions tend to be large, choosing a small plate or splitting a large one makes some otherwise pricey options reasonable. You'll notice

many locals just drink free tap water, even in fine restaurants.

Picnic for lunch. Basements of big department stores have huge, first-class supermarkets with lots of alternatives to sandwiches. You'll save by getting takeout food from a restaurant rather than eating inside. (The tax on takeaway food is 12 percent, while restaurant food is 24 percent.) Fast-food restaurants ask if you want to take away or not before they ring up your order on the cash register. Even McDonald's has a two-tiered price list.

Oslo is awash with little budget eateries (modern, ethnic, fast food, pizza, department-store cafeterias, and so on). **Deli de Luca**, a cheery convenience store chain that's notorious for having a store on every key corner in Oslo, is a step up from the similarly ubiquitous 7-Elevens and Narvesens. Most are open 24/7, selling sandwiches, pastries, sushi, and to-go boxes of warm pasta or Asian noodle dishes. You can fill your belly here for about 80 NOK. Some outlets (such as the one at the corner of Karl Johans Gate and Rosenkrantz Gate) have seating on the street or upstairs. Beware: Because this is still a *convenience* store, not everything is well-priced. Convenience stores—while convenient—charge double what supermarkets do.

KARL JOHANS GATE STRIP

Strangely, **Karl Johans Gate**—the most Norwegian of boulevards—is lined with a strip of good-time American chain eateries and sports bars where you can get ribs, burgers, and pizza, including T.G.I. Fridays and the Hard Rock Café. **$$ Egon Restaurant** offers a daily 110-NOK all-you-can-eat pizza deal (available Tue-Sat 11:00-18:00, Sun-Mon all day)—though the rest of their menu

Restaurant Code

I've assigned each eatery a price category, based on the average cost of a typical main course. Drinks, desserts, and splurge
items (steak and seafood) can raise the price considerably.

$$$$ **Splurge:** Most main courses over 175 NOK
$$$ **Pricier:** 125-175 NOK
$$ **Moderate:** 75-125 NOK
$ **Budget:** Under 75 NOK

In Norway, a Deli de Luca or other takeout spot is **$**; a sit-down
café is **$$**; a casual but more upscale restaurant is **$$$**; and a
swanky splurge is **$$$$**.

is overpriced. Each place comes with great sidewalk seating and
essentially the same prices.

$$$$ Grand Café is perhaps the most venerable place in
town, with genteel decor. They have a seasonal menu, with high-
end Nordic, French, and international dishes. Reserve a window,
and if you hit a time when there's no tour group, you're suddenly
a posh Norwegian (Mon-Fri 11:00-23:00, Sat-Sun 12:00-23:00,
Karl Johans Gate 31, tel. 98 18 20 00).

$ Deli de Luca, just across from the Grand Café, offers good-
value food and handy seats on Karl Johans Gate. For a fast meal
with the best people-watching view in town, you may find yourself
dropping by here repeatedly (for 70 NOK you can get a calzone,
or a portion of chicken noodles, beef noodles, or chicken vindaloo
with rice—ask to have it heated up, open 24/7, Karl Johans Gate
33, tel. 22 33 35 22).

$$ Kaffebrenneriet is a good local coffeehouse chain serving
quality coffee drinks and affordable sandwiches, salads, and pas-
tries. Convenient locations include in the park along Karl Johans
Gate at #24, closer to the cathedral and train station at Karl Johans
Gate 7, behind the cathedral at Storgata 2, facing the back of the
Parliament building at Akersgata 16, and next to City Hall at Hi-
eronymus Heyerdahls Gate 1. Most have similar hours (typically
Mon-Fri 7:00-19:00, Sat 9:00-18:00, closed Sun).

$$ United Bakeries, next to the Paleet mall, is a quiet bit
of Norwegian quality among sports bars, appreciated for its 80-
NOK sandwiches, salads, light weekday lunches, and fresh pastries
(seating inside and out, Mon-Fri 7:30-20:00, Sat 9:00-18:00, Sun
11:00-17:00).

$$$ Kaffistova, a block off the main drag, is where my thrifty
Norwegian grandparents always took me. And it remains almost
unchanged since the 1970s. This alcohol-free cafeteria still serves
simple, hearty, and typically Norwegian (read: bland) meals for a

good price (big portions of Norwegian meatballs, Mon-Fri 11:00-21:00, Sat-Sun until 19:00, Rosenkrantz Gate 8, tel. 23 21 41 00).

$$$$ Theatercaféen, since 1900 the place for Norway's illuminati to see and be seen (note the celebrity portraits adorning the walls), is a swanky splurge steeped in Art Nouveau elegance (Mon-Sat 11:00-23:00, Sun 15:00-22:00, in Hotel Continental at Stortingsgata 24, across from National Theater, tel. 22 82 40 50).

NEAR AKERSHUS FORTRESS

$$$$ Café Skansen is a delightful spot for a quality meal—especially in good weather, when its leafy, beer garden-like terrace fills with a convivial, mostly local crowd. Or huddle in the old-time interior, and dig into classic Norwegian dishes. They serve more affordable lunches until 16:00, and good salads anytime (Mon-Fri 11:00-23:00, Sat-Sun 12:00-22:00, Rådhusgata 32, tel. 24 20 13 11).

$$$$ Engebret Café is a classic old restaurant in a 17th-century building in the Christiania section of town below the fortress. Since 1857, it's been serving old-fashioned Norse food (reindeer is always on the menu) in a classic old Norwegian setting. In good weather, you can sit out on the delightful square with a gurgling fountain (Mon-Fri 11:30-23:00, Sat from 17:00, closed Sun and most of July, Bankplassen 1, tel. 22 82 25 25).

$$$$ Solsiden ("Sunny Side"), filling a glassed-in former warehouse on the embankment just under the fortress, is a local favorite for a harborfront splurge. You'll dig into fish and seafood meals in an open, unpretentious, nautical-themed, blue-and-white interior that doesn't distract from the cooking. Think of this as a less posh-feeling alternative to the Aker Brygge scene across the harbor. Reserve ahead, and ask for a table with a view (May-mid-Sept daily 16:30-22:00, Akershusstranda 13, tel. 22 33 36 30, www.solsiden.no).

Top-End Picnic Shopping: Near City Hall, **Fenaknoken** is a characteristic deli specializing in gourmet Norwegian products—from salmon and lefse to moose salami and dried fish. If you value authentic quality products over price, this is the place to assemble a blowout Norwegian picnic to enjoy out along the harbor (Mon-Fri 10:00-17:00, Sat until 13:30, closed Sun, Tordenskioldsgate 12, tel. 22 42 34 57, www.fenaknoken.no).

HARBORSIDE DINING IN AKER BRYGGE

Aker Brygge, the harborfront development near City Hall, is popular with businesspeople and tourists. While it isn't cheap, its inviting cafés and restaurants with outdoor, harborview tables make for a memorable waterfront meal. Before deciding where to eat, walk the entire lane (including the back side), considering both the

OSLO

Oslo Restaurants

1. Egon Restaurant & United Bakeries
2. Grand Café
3. Deli de Luca
4. Kaffebrenneriet
5. Kaffistova
6. Theatercaféen
7. Café Skansen
8. Engebret Café
9. Solsiden
10. Fenaknoken Deli
11. Aker Brygge Eateries
12. Groceries (2)
13. Youngstorget Eateries
14. Illegal Burger Bar
15. Torggata North Eateries
16. Peloton
17. Torggata South Eateries
18. To Lofotstua; Curry & Ketchup Indian

brick-and-mortar places (some with second-floor view seating) and the various floating options. Nearly all are open for lunch.

Budget Tips: If you're on a budget, try a hotdog from a *pølse* stand or get a picnic from a nearby grocery store and grab a bench along the boardwalk.

NEAR YOUNGSTORGET

Central Oslo's most appealing dining zone percolates just a 10-minute stroll north of Karl Johans Gate, around the otherwise nondescript urban square named Youngstorget. This aptly named square feels fresh and trendy, although it's tucked between all-business high-rises and Thon hotels. The square itself has several fine options, but the streets leading off it are also worth a browse—especially Torggata, lined with a couple dozen eclectic options more tempting than anything in the touristy downtown.

First, check out the hipster **food carts** that are often parked in the middle of the square, which can be a great spot for a quick, affordable al fresco bite. If you were to hike up to the old police station and turn right (at the uphill corner of the square), you'd find

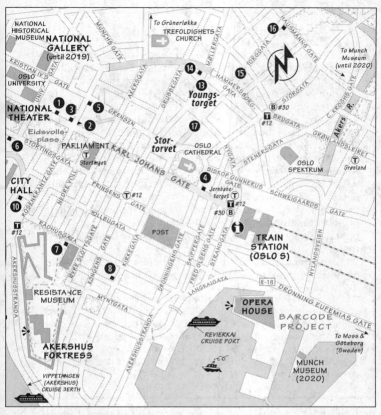

$$$ Illegal Burger Bar—the best-regarded of Oslo's many trendy burger joints, with a long, creative menu of gourmet burgers (daily 14:00–late, Møllergata 23, tel. 22 20 33 02).

For even more options, simply stroll from Youngstorget up **Torggata to the north** and comparison-shop menus, ignoring the American fast-food chains. **$$$ Peloton** is a casual and inviting *sykkelcafe*—a bright, cheery "bicycle café" serving pizza and long list of beers, with a bike shop in the back (Mon 8:00-18:00, Tue-Fri until 24:00, Sat 10:00-24:00, Sun 12:00-23:00, tel. 92 15 61 81).

The stretch of **Torgatta to the south,** where it connects Youngstorget to Karl Johans Gate, feels less residential and more shopping-oriented. But it's also lined with a fun variety of eateries—most of which double as hard-partying nightspots into the wee hours.

DINING NEAR VIGELAND PARK

$$S$ Lofotstua Restaurant feels transplanted from the far northern islands it's named for. Kjell Jenssen and his son, Jan Hugo,

What If I Miss My Ship?

Remember that you can get help from the cruise line's port agent (listed on the destination information sheet distributed on the ship) and the local TI. If the port agent suggests a costly solution (such as a private car with a driver), you may want to consider public transit.

Trains connect Oslo easily to **Bergen** and **Stavanger**. **Flåm** is an easy bus or train ride off the main Oslo-Bergen line. Trains are also likely your best option for **Copenhagen** and **Stockholm;** for other points on the continent (such as **Amsterdam, Warnemünde/Berlin,** or **Zeebrugge/Brussels**), you'll probably connect through Copenhagen (for train connections, see www.bahn.com), but it's cheaper and faster to fly (check www.skyscanner.com). To reach **Tallinn, Helsinki,** or **St. Petersburg** (only if you already have a visa), your best option is likely to train to Stockholm, then take the boat from there.

Another option for reaching **Copenhagen** is the overnight boat operated by DFDS Seaways (Danish tel. 00 45 33 42 30 10, www.dfdsseaways.us).

If you need to catch a **plane** to your next destination, you can ride an express train to Oslo's airport *(lufthavn)*, also called Gardermoen (tel. 91 50 64 00, www.osl.no). Some discount airlines use the smaller Sandefjord Airport Torp (70 miles south of Oslo, tel. 33 42 70 00, www.torp.no).

For more advice on what to do if you miss the boat, see page 130.

proudly serve up fish Lofoten-style. Evangelical about fish, they will patiently explain to you the fine differences between all the local varieties, with the help of a photo-filled chart (Mon-Fri 15:00-21:30, closed Sat-Sun, generally closed in July, 5-minute walk from Vigeland Park's main gate, tram #12, in Majorstuen at Kirkeveien 40, tel. 22 46 93 96). This place is packed daily in winter for their famous lutefisk.

$$$ Curry and Ketchup Indian Restaurant is filled with locals enjoying hearty, decent meals for about 130 NOK. This happening place requires no reservations and feels like an Indian market, offering a flavorful meal near Vigeland's statues (daily 14:00-23:00, a 5-minute walk from Vigeland Park's main gate, tram #12, in Majorstuen at Kirkeveien 51, tel. 22 69 05 22).

Norwegian Survival Phrases

Norwegian can be pronounced quite differently from region to region. These phrases and phonetics match the mainstream Oslo dialect, but you'll notice variations. Vowels can be tricky: *å* sounds like "oh," *æ* sounds like a bright "ah" (as in "apple"), and *u* sounds like the German *ü* (purse your lips and say u). Certain vowels at the ends of words (such as *d* and *t*) are sometimes barely pronounced (or not at all). In some dialects, the letters *sk* are pronounced "sh." In the phonetics, ī sounds like the long i in "light," and bolded syllables are stressed.

English	Norwegian	Pronunciation
Hello. (formal)	*God dag.*	goo dahg
Hi. / Bye. (informal)	*Hei. / Ha det.*	hī / hah deh
Do you speak English?	*Snakker du engelsk?*	**snahk**-kehr dew **eng**-ehlsk
Yes. / No.	*Ja. / Nei.*	yah / nī
Please.	*Vær så snill.*	vayr soh sneel
Thank you (very much).	*(Tusen) takk.*	(**tew**-sehn) tahk
You're welcome.	*Vær så god.*	vayr soh goo
Can I help you?	*Kan jeg hjelpe deg?*	kahn yī **yehl**-peh dī
Excuse me.	*Unnskyld.*	**ewn**-shuld
(Very) good.	*(Veldig) fint.*	(**vehl**-dee) feent
Goodbye.	*Farvel.*	fahr-**vehl**
zero / one / two	*null / en / to*	newl / ayn / toh
three / four	*tre / fire*	treh / **fee**-reh
five / six	*fem / seks*	fehm / sehks
seven / eight	*syv / åtte*	seev / **oh**-teh
nine / ten	*ni / ti*	nee / tee
hundred	*hundre*	**hewn**-dreh
thousand	*tusen*	**tew**-sehn
How much?	*Hvor mye?*	voor **mee**-yeh
local currency: (Norwegian) crown	*(Norske) kroner*	(**norsh**-keh) **kroh**-nehr
Where is...?	*Hvor er...?*	voor ehr
...the toilet	*...toalettet*	toh-ah-**leh**-teh
men	*menn / herrer*	mehn / **hehr**-rehr
women	*damer*	**dah**-mehr
water / coffee	*vann / kaffe*	vahn / **kah**-feh
beer / wine	*øl / vin*	uhl / veen
Cheers!	*Skål!*	skohl
The bill, please.	*Regningen, takk.*	**rī**-ning-ehn tahk

STAVANGER

Norway

Norway Practicalities

Norway (Norge) is stacked with superlatives—it's the most mountainous, most scenic, and most prosperous of all the Scandinavian countries. Perhaps above all, Norway is a land of intense natural beauty, its famously steep mountains and deep fjords carved out and shaped by an ancient ice age. Norway (148,700 square miles—just larger than Montana) is on the western side of the Scandinavian Peninsula, with most of the country sharing a border with Sweden to the east. Rich in resources like timber, oil, and fish, Norway has rejected joining the European Union, mainly to protect its fishing rights. Where the country extends north of the Arctic Circle, the sun never sets at the height of summer and never comes up in the deep of winter. The majority of Norway's 5.3 million people consider themselves Lutheran.

Money: 8 Norwegian kroner (kr, officially NOK) = about $1. An ATM is called a *minibank*. The local VAT (value-added sales tax) rate is 25 percent; the minimum purchase eligible for a VAT refund is 315 kr (for details on refunds, see page 125).

Language: The native language is Norwegian (the two official forms are Bokmål and Nynorsk). For useful phrases, see page 660.

Emergencies: Dial 112 for police, medical, or other emergencies. In case of theft or loss, see page 118.

Time Zone: Norway is on Central European Time (the same as most of the Continent, one hour ahead of Great Britain, and six/nine hours ahead of the East/West Coasts of the US).

Embassies in Oslo: The **US embassy** is at Morgedalsvegen 36 (tel. 21 30 85 58, emergency tel. 21 30 85 40, https://no.usembassy.gov) The **Canadian embassy** is at Wergelandsveien 7 (tel. 22 99 53 00, www.canadainternational.gc.ca/norway-norvege). Call ahead for passport services.

Phoning: With a mobile phone, it's easy to dial: Press and hold zero until you get a + sign, enter the country code (47 for Norway, 1 for the US/Canada), and then the complete phone number (including area code if there is one). When dialing a European phone number, drop an initial zero (except if calling Italy). For more tips, see page 1062.

Tipping: Service is included at sit-down meals, but this goes to the owner, so for great service it's nice to round up your bill about 10 percent. Tip a taxi driver by rounding up the fare (pay 90 kr on an 85-kr fare). For more tips on tipping, see page 129.

Tourist Information: www.goscandinavia.com

STAVANGER

This burg of about 125,000 is a mildly charming (if unspectacular) waterfront city with streets that are lined with unpretentious shiplap cottages that echo its perennial ties to the sea. Stavanger feels more cosmopolitan than most small Norwegian cities, thanks in part to its oil industry—which brings multinational workers (and their money) into the city. Known as Norway's festival city, Stavanger hosts several lively events, including jazz in May (www.maijazz.no), Scandinavia's biggest food festival in July (www.gladmat.no), and chamber music in August (www.icmf.no).

From a sightseeing perspective, Stavanger barely has enough to fill a day: The Norwegian Petroleum Museum is the only big-time sight in town. The city's fine cathedral is worth a peek. But for most visitors, the main reason to come to Stavanger is to use it as a launch pad for side-tripping to Lysefjord and/or the famous, iconic Pulpit Rock: an eerily flat-topped peak thrusting up from the fjord, offering perfect, point-blank views deep into the Lysefjord.

PLANNING YOUR TIME

Stavanger is a small town with enjoyable ambience, but it lacks big sights; you'll probably look for ways to kill time rather than run out of it. The one big exception is a side-trip to the Lysefjord and/or Pulpit Rock, which can eat up the better part of your day in port (but may not be possible, depending on your cruise arrival and departure schedule). If you stick around town, take your pick from these options—noting that some may not open until well after your ship docks.

Cathedral: This is worth a quick look (easy to see in less than 30 minutes).

Excursions from Stavanger

The one cruise-line excursion that's worth considering is to the **Lysefjord,** across the bay, and the iconic **Pulpit Rock** that overlooks it. You can do a similar trip on your own, but your options are limited, and it's tricky to coordinate schedules with your cruise's arrival and departure. If you've always wanted to see Pulpit Rock, and this is your best chance, an excursion may be the right choice.

Otherwise, various excursions cobble together sights in and around Stavanger, including the Petroleum Museum, the Sverd i Fjell monument ("Swords in Rock," honoring a historic A.D. 872 battle), an Iron Age farm, a cheese factory, the charming and well-preserved Utstein Abbey (often with a musical recital), a pile of prehistoric avalanche boulders called Gloppedalsura, and a drive to Byrkjelandsvatnet Lake. Any of these can be interesting, and—as there's little to see in Stavanger itself—they can be a nice way to get out into the countryside. The cruise around Stavanger Archipelago is pointless (offering little to see beyond what you'll see coming and going on your cruise ship).

Norwegian Petroleum Museum: The city's main museum deserves at least an hour, or two hours if you want to watch all the movies (or are traveling with kids who'd enjoy the interactive features).

Other Museums: Stavanger's many small museums can round out your day, but none of them demands more than 30 to 60 minutes.

Strolling Town: Spend whatever time you have left exploring, especially the atmospheric lanes of Gamle Stavanger and Kirkegata, the main drag through town.

With relatively little else to do in Stavanger, many visitors choose to use this day for a side-trip to the **Lysefjord** and/or **Pulpit Rock.** Handy fjord excursion boats leave from the harbor, near where the cruise ships put in. Ideally, do some homework and confirm schedules before you arrive, so you know which company (if any) has a trip that fits with your ship's arrival and departure.

Excursion Alert: Before joining a Lysefjord or Pulpit Rock excursion run by anyone other than your cruise line, be absolutely clear on the return time—and before you book, make sure the guide knows what time you need to be back.

Port of Stavanger

Arrival at a Glance: It's simple: Just walk along the harbor into the town center (5-15 minutes, depending on where you're docked).

Services in Stavanger

Take the short walk into the heart of town, where you'll find the following:

ATMs: The most central options are at the SpareBank and the DnB overlooking the market square, facing the cathedral.

Internet Access: The TI can tell you the password for their free Wi-Fi connection. There's also free Wi-Fi in the lobby of the Maritime Museum, along Strandkaien.

Pharmacy: The handiest is Apotek 1, inside the Arkaden Torgterrassen mall facing the market plaza just below the cathedral (Mon-Fri 9:00-20:00, Sat 10:00-18:00, closed Sun).

Port Overview

Cruise ships dock on either side of Stavanger's central harbor (Vågen), an inlet between Gamle Stavanger (the Old Town) and the city-center peninsu-la. Ships dock along the west embankment, called **Strandkaien;** or along the east side, called **Skagen-kaien.** When more ships are in town, they dock far-ther out along these em-bankments.

Tourist Information:

The TI is located in the yellow Port of Stavanger building just next to the **Strandkaien** embankment (see "Tourist Information," later).

GETTING INTO TOWN

Stavanger is extremely cruiser-friendly. The route into town is so walkable that taxis don't bother meeting cruise ships, and there's no point taking public transportation. To return to your ship, just reverse the walking directions I've given below for each embank-ment.

From Strandkaien

On Foot: Arriving at Strandkaien, you face rows of pointy-topped, white, wooden houses climbing the hill into Gamle Stavanger—to explore, just head up any narrow, cobbled lane.

To reach the town center, turn left and walk along the water-front. On your way, you'll pass the TI (with free Wi-Fi), then the Maritime Museum. Circling around the end of the harbor, head up through the small market plaza to reach the cathedral.

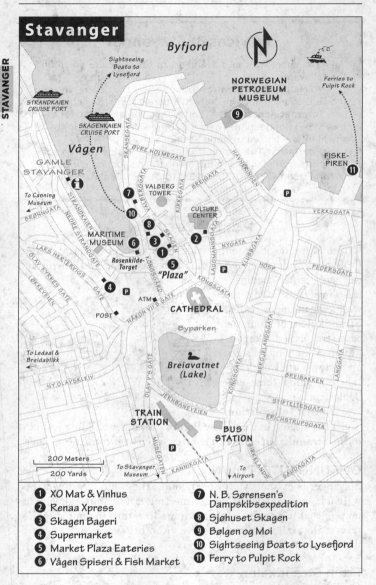

Stavanger

- **1** XO Mat & Vinhus
- **2** Renaa Xpress
- **3** Skagen Bageri
- **4** Supermarket
- **5** Market Plaza Eateries
- **6** Vågen Spiseri & Fish Market
- **7** N. B. Sørensen's Dampskibsexpedition
- **8** Sjøhuset Skagen
- **9** Bølgen og Moi
- **10** Sightseeing Boats to Lysefjord
- **11** Ferry to Pulpit Rock

From Skagenkaien

On Foot: Exiting your ship, turn right and walk along the harborfront, passing the departure point for excursion boats to the Lysefjord. You'll quickly arrive at the end of the harbor; from here, you can angle up through the market square to reach the cathedral or continue around the other side of the harborfront to reach the TI.

Orientation to Stavanger

Stavanger is most interesting around its harbor, where you'll find the Maritime Museum, lots of shops and restaurants (particularly around the market plaza and along Kirkegata, which connects the cathedral to the Petroleum Museum), the indoor fish market, and a produce market (closed Sun). The artificial Lake Breiavatnet—bordered by Kongsgaten on the east and Olav V's Gate on the west—separates the train and bus stations from the harbor.

TOURIST INFORMATION

The centrally located TI can help with day trips, including logistics for reaching Pulpit Rock and other scenic hikes (June-Aug daily 8:00-18:00; Sept-May Mon-Fri 9:00-16:00, Sat until 14:00, closed Sun; free Wi-Fi, Strandkaien 61, tel. 51 85 92 00, www.regionstavanger.com).

Sights in Stavanger

▲Stavanger Cathedral (Domkirke)

While it's hardly the most impressive cathedral in Scandinavia, Stavanger's top church—which overlooks the town center on a small ridge—has a harmonious interior and a few intriguing details worth lingering over. Good English information throughout the church brings meaning to the place.

Cost and Hours: 30 NOK, open daily 11:00-16:00, tel. 51 84 04 00, www.stavangerdomkirke.no.

Visiting the Church: St. Swithun's Cathedral (its official name) was originally built in 1125 in a Norman style, with basket-handle

Romanesque arches. After a fire badly damaged the church in the 13th century, a new chancel was added in the pointy-arched Gothic style. You can't miss where the architecture changes about three-quarters of the way up the aisle. On the left, behind the baptismal font, notice the ivy-lined railing on the stone staircase; this pattern is part of the city's coat of arms. And nearby, appreciate the colorful, richly detailed "gristle Baroque"-style pulpit (from 1658). Notice that the whole thing is resting on Samson's stoic shoulders—even as he faces down a lion.

Stroll the church, perusing its several fine "epitaphs" (tomb markers), which are paintings in ornately decorated frames. Go on a scavenger hunt for two unique features; both are on the second columns from the back of the church. On the right, at the top facing away from the nave, notice the stone carvings of Norse mythological figures: Odin on the left, and a wolf-like beast on the right. Although the medieval Norwegians were Christians, they weren't ready to entirely abandon all of their pagan traditions. On the opposite column, circle around the base and look at ankle level, facing away from the altar. Here you see a grotesque sculpture that looks like a fish head with human hands. Notice that its head has been worn down. One interpretation is that early worshippers would ritualistically put their foot on top of it, as if to push the evil back to the underworld. Mysteriously, both of these features are one-offs—you won't find anything like them on any other column in the church.

▲▲Norwegian Petroleum Museum (Norsk Oljemuseum)

This entertaining, informative museum—dedicated to the discovery of oil in Norway's North Sea in 1969 and the industry built up around it—offers an unapologetic look at the country's biggest moneymaker. With half of Western Europe's oil reserves, the formerly poor agricultural nation of Norway is the Arabia of the North, and a world-class player. It's ranked third among the world's top oil exporters, producing 1.6 million barrels a day.

Cost and Hours: 120 NOK; daily 10:00-19:00; Sept-May Mon-Sat 10:00-16:00, Sun until 18:00; tel. 51 93 93 00, www.norskolje.museum.no. The small museum shop sells various petroleum-based products. The museum's Bølgen og Moi restaurant has an inviting terrace over the water; see "Eating in Stavanger," later.

Visiting the Museum: The exhibit describes how oil was formed, how it's found and produced, and what it's used for. You'll see models of oil rigs, actual drill bits, see-through cylinders that you can rotate to investigate different types of crude, and lots of explanations (in English) about various aspects of oil. Interactive exhibits cover everything from the "History of the Earth" (4.5 billion years displayed on a large overhead globe, showing how our planet has changed—stay for the blast that killed the dinosaurs), to day-to-day life on an offshore platform, to petroleum products in our lives (though the peanut-butter-and-petroleum-jelly sandwich is a bit much). Kids enjoy climbing on the model drilling platform, trying out the emergency escape chute at the platform outside, and playing with many other hands-on exhibits.

Several included movies delve into specific aspects of oil: The main movie, *Oljeunge (Oil Kid)*, stars a fictional character who was born in 1969—the year Norway discovered oil—and shows how that discovery changed Norwegian society over the last 50 years. Other movies (in the cylindrical structures outside) highlight intrepid North Sea divers and the construction of an oil platform. Each film runs in English at least twice hourly.

Even the museum's architecture was designed to echo the foundations of the oil industry—bedrock (the stone building), slate and chalk deposits in the sea (slate floor of the main hall), and the rigs (cylindrical platforms). While the museum has its fair share of propaganda, it also has several good exhibits on the environmental toll of drilling and consuming oil.

Gamle Stavanger

Stavanger's "old town" centers on Øvre Strandgate, on the west side of the harbor. Wander the narrow, winding, cobbled back lanes, with tidy wooden houses, oasis gardens, and flower-bedecked entranceways. Peek into a workshop or gallery to find ceramics, glass, jewelry, and more. Many shops are open roughly daily 10:00-17:00, coinciding with the arrival of cruise ships (which loom ominously right next to this otherwise tranquil zone).

Museum Stavanger (M.U.S.T.)

This "museum" is actually 10 different museums scattered around town (covered by individual tickets or a single combo-ticket, most closed Mon off-season, for details see www.museumstavanger.no). The various branches include the **Stavanger Museum,** featuring the history of the city and a zoological exhibit (Muségate 16); the **Maritime Museum** (Sjøfartsmuseum), near the bottom end of Vågen harbor (Nedre Strandgate 17-19); the **Norwegian Canning Museum** (Norsk Hermetikkmuseum—the *brisling*, or herring, is smoked the first Sunday of every month—Øvre Strandgate 88A); **Ledaal,** a royal residence and manor house (Eiganesveien 45); and **Breidablikk,** a wooden villa from the late 1800s (Eiganesveien 40A).

DAY TRIPS TO LYSEFJORD AND PULPIT ROCK

The nearby Lysefjord is an easy day trip. Those with more time (and strong legs) can hike to the top of 2,000-foot-high Pulpit Rock (Preikestolen). Its dramatic 270-square-foot natural platform gives you a fantastic view of the fjord and surrounding mountains. If you decide to book your own excursion, rather than going through your cruise line, the TI has brochures for several boat tour companies and sells tickets.

Reminder: Timing a Pulpit Rock trip that coincides with your cruise-ship departure is risky business. Be absolutely clear on your trip's return time and your ship's all-aboard time—and don't cut it close, just in case.

Boat Tour of Lysefjord

Rødne Clipper Fjord Sightseeing offers three-hour round-trip excursions from Stavanger to Lysefjord (including a view of Pulpit Rock—but no stops). Conveniently, their boats depart from the main Vågen harbor in the heart of town (east side of the harbor, in front of Skansegata, along Skagenkaien; 490 NOK; May-Sept daily at 10:00 and 14:00, also at 12:00 July-Aug; April and Oct daily at 11:00; Jan-Feb and Nov-Dec Wed-Sun at 11:00; tel. 51 89 52 70, www.rodne.no). A different company, **Norled,** also runs similar trips, as well as slower journeys up the Lysefjord on a "tourist car ferry" (www.norled.no).

Ferry and Bus to Pulpit Rock (Preikestolen)

Hiking up to the top of Pulpit Rock is a popular outing that will take the better part of a day; plan on at least four hours of hiking (two hours up, two hours down), plus time to linger at the top for photos, plus round-trip travel from Stavanger (about an hour each way by a ferry-and-bus combination)—eight hours minimum should do it. The trailhead is easily reached in summer by public transit or tour package.

Two different companies sell ferry-and-bus packages to the trailhead from Stavanger. Ferries leave from the Fiskepiren boat terminal to Tau; buses (labeled *Preikestolen*) meet the incoming ferries and head to the Preikestolen Fjellstue lodge and Preikestolhytta hostel, both near the trailhead. Be sure to time your hike so that you don't miss the last bus leaving the trailhead for the ferry (confirm time when booking your ticket). These trips generally go daily from mid-May through mid-September; weekends only in April, early May, and late September; and not at all from October to March (when the ferry stops running). Confirm schedules with the TI or the individual companies: **Tide Reiser** (320 NOK, best options for an all-day round-trip are weekdays at 8:40 or 9:20 or Sat-Sun at 9:00, return bus from trailhead corresponds with ferry to Stavanger, tel. 55 23 88 87, www.tidereiser.com) and **Boreal** (190

NOK for the bus plus 112 NOK for the ferry round-trip—you'll buy the ferry ticket separately, best options depart at 8:40 or 9:20, last bus from trailhead to ferry leaves at 21:15, tel. 51 74 02 40, www.pulpitrock.no).

Rødne Clipper Fjord Sightseeing (listed earlier) runs a handy trip that begins with a scenic Lysefjord cruise (2.5 hours), then drops you off at Oanes to catch the bus to the Pulpit Rock hut trailhead; from there you can do the four-hour round-trip trek to Pulpit Rock and back; afterwards, you catch the bus to Tau for the ferry return to Stavanger. It's similar to the options described above, but adds a scenic fjord cruise at the start (780 NOK plus 56 NOK for return ferry to Stavanger, May-Sept daily at 10:00, also July-Aug at 12:00, tel. 51 89 52 70, www.rodne.no).

Hiking to Pulpit Rock

At just over 4.5 miles round-trip, with an elevation gain of about 1,100 feet, this hike takes four hours total—longer if the trail is very crowded. The hike is fairly strenuous and includes scrambling over sometimes tricky, rocky terrain. Bring food and plenty of water, pack extra clothes as the weather is changeable, and wear sturdy hiking shoes or boots. Start early or you'll be sharing the trail with dogs on long leashes, toddlers navigating boulders, and the unprepared Bermuda-shorts crowd in flip-flops.

The trail starts by the big sign at the entrance to the main parking lot. From there the path climbs steadily through forest at first and eventually into open, rocky terrain. Along the way, you can thank Nepalese Sherpas—who were hired to improve sections of the route—for their fine stonework on the trail.

The farther and higher you go, the more rocky and spectacular the scenery becomes. Whenever the trail disappears onto bare rock, look for the red T's painted on stones or posts marking the route. As you near Pulpit Rock, the path tiptoes along the cliff's edge with airy views out to the Lysefjord that can only be topped by those from the rock itself.

Before you head back, scramble up the mountainside behind the rock for that iconic, tourist-brochure scene of the people-speckled Pulpit Rock soaring out over the fjord 2,000 feet below.

Guided Hike to Pulpit Rock

Outdoorlife Norway offers guided tours for individuals or small groups. They'll pick you up at your ship and even provide hiking poles. Check out their "Preikestolen Off the Beaten Track Hike" (1,290 NOK, April-Sept, mobile 97 65 87 04, www. outdoorlifenorway.com, booking@outdoorlifenorway.com).

Eating in Stavanger

CASUAL DINING

$$$ XO Mat & Vinhus, in an elegant setting, serves up big portions of traditional Norwegian food and pricier contemporary fare (Mon-Wed 14:30-23:30, Thu 11:00-23:00, Fri-Sat 11:30-late, closed Sun, a block behind main drag along harbor at Skagen 10 ved Prostebakken, mobile 91 00 03 07).

$$ Renaa Xpress, popular with the locals, is inside Stavanger's library and cultural center. It's a cozy café where bakers make their own bread and pastries. In addition to a variety of sandwiches, salads, and soups, they also offer sourdough pizza after 13:00 (Mon-Thu 10:00-22:00, Fri-Sat until 24:00, Sun 12:00-22:00, Sølvberggata 2, mobile 94 00 93 48).

$ Skagen Bageri, in a lovely, leaning wooden building dating to the 1700s, serves baked goods and traditional open-face sandwiches at reasonable prices in a cozy, rustic-elegant setting (Mon-Fri 8:00-15:00, Sat until 16:00, closed Sun; in the blue-and-white building a block off the harborfront at Skagen 18; tel. 51 89 51 71).

Meny is a large supermarket with a good selection and a fine deli for super picnic shopping (Mon-Fri 7:00-20:00, Sat 9:00-18:00, closed Sun, in Straen Senteret shopping mall, Lars Hertervigs Gate 6, tel. 51 50 50 10).

Market Plaza Eateries: The busy square between the cathedral and the harbor is packed with reliable Norwegian chain restaurants. If you're a fan of **Deli de Luca, Dolly Dimple's,** or **Dickens Pub,** you'll find them within a few steps of here.

DINING ALONG THE HARBOR WITH A VIEW

The harborside street of Skansegata is lined with lively restaurants and pubs, and most serve food. Here are a few options:

$$$$ Vågen Spiseri, in the same building as the fish market, serves tasty seafood dishes based on the catch of the day (affordable lunch specials, Mon-Wed 11:00-21:00, Thu-Sat until 24:00, closed Sun, Strandkaien 37, tel. 51 52 73 50, www.fisketorget-stavanger. no).

$$$$ N. B. Sørensen's Dampskibsexpedition consists of a lively pub on the first floor (pasta, fish, meat, and vegetarian dishes; Mon-Wed 16:00-24:00, Sat 11:00-late, Sun 13:00-23:00) and a fine-dining restaurant on the second floor, with tablecloths, view tables overlooking the harbor, and a pricey menu (Mon-Sat 18:00-23:00, closed Sun, Skagenkaien 26, tel. 51 84 38 20, www.

What If I Miss My Ship?

Remember that you can get help from the cruise line's port agent (listed on the destination information sheet distributed on the ship) and the local TI. If the port agent suggests a costly solution (such as a private car with a driver), you may want to consider public transit.

You can catch the bus to **Bergen** (http://kystbussen.no) or the train to **Oslo** (www.nsb.no/en). For **Flåm,** it's probably best to take the bus to Bergen, then a boat or train to the Sognefjord. For any points **outside Norway,** you'll most likely connect through Oslo. To research train schedules, see www.bahn.com.

If you need to catch a **plane** to your next destination, Stavanger's Sola Airport is a nine-mile bus ride outside the city (tel. 67 03 10 00, www.avinor.no).

For more advice on what to do if you miss the boat, see page 130.

herlige-stavanger.no). The restaurant is named after an 1800s company that shipped from this building, among other things, Norwegians heading to the US. Passengers and cargo waited on the first floor, and the manager's office was upstairs. The place is filled with emigrant-era memorabilia.

$$$$ Sjøhuset Skagen, with a woodsy interior, invites diners to its historic building from the late 1700s, which once housed a trading company. Today, you can choose from local seafood specialties with an ethnic flair, as well as plenty of meat options (Mon-Sat 11:30-24:00, Sun from 13:00, Skagenkaien 16, tel. 51 89 51 80, https://skagenrestaurant.no/en).

$$$$ Bølgen og Moi, the restaurant at the Petroleum Museum, has fantastic views over the harbor (good lunch specials, lunch daily 11:00-16:00; Kjeringholmen 748, tel. 51 93 93 53, www.bolgenogmoi.no).

Norwegian Survival Phrases

Norwegian can be pronounced quite differently from region to region. These phrases and phonetics match the mainstream Oslo dialect, but you'll notice variations. Vowels can be tricky: *å* sounds like "oh," *æ* sounds like a bright "ah" (as in "apple"), and *u* sounds like the German *ü* (purse your lips and say u). Certain vowels at the ends of words (such as *d* and *t*) are sometimes barely pronounced (or not at all). In some dialects, the letters *sk* are pronounced "sh." In the phonetics, ī sounds like the long i in "light," and bolded syllables are stressed.

English	Norwegian	Pronunciation
Hello. (formal)	*God dag.*	goo dahg
Hi. / Bye. (informal)	*Hei. / Ha det.*	hī / hah deh
Do you speak English?	*Snakker du engelsk?*	**snahk**-kehr dew **eng**-ehlsk
Yes. / No.	*Ja. / Nei.*	yah / nī
Please.	*Vær så snill.*	vayr soh sneel
Thank you (very much).	*(Tusen) takk.*	**(tew**-sehn) tahk
You're welcome.	*Vær så god.*	vayr soh goo
Can I help you?	*Kan jeg hjelpe deg?*	kahn yī **yehl**-peh dī
Excuse me.	*Unnskyld.*	**ewn**-shuld
(Very) good.	*(Veldig) fint.*	**(vehl**-dee) feent
Goodbye.	*Farvel.*	fahr-**vehl**
zero / one / two	*null / en / to*	newl / ayn / toh
three / four	*tre / fire*	treh / **fee**-reh
five / six	*fem / seks*	fehm / sehks
seven / eight	*syv / åtte*	seev / **oh**-teh
nine / ten	*ni / ti*	nee / tee
hundred	*hundre*	**hewn**-dreh
thousand	*tusen*	**tew**-sehn
How much?	*Hvor mye?*	voor **mee**-yeh
local currency: (Norwegian) crown	*(Norske) kroner*	**(norsk**-keh) **kroh**-nehr
Where is...?	*Hvor er...?*	voor ehr
...the toilet	*...toalettet*	toh-ah-**leh**-teh
men	*menn / herrer*	mehn / **hehr**-rehr
women	*damer*	**dah**-mehr
water / coffee	*vann / kaffe*	vahn / **kah**-feh
beer / wine	*øl / vin*	uhl / veen
Cheers!	*Skål!*	skohl
The bill, please.	*Regningen, takk.*	**rī**-ning-ehn tahk

BERGEN

Norway

Norway Practicalities

Norway (Norge) is stacked with super-latives—it's the most mountainous, most scenic, and most prosperous of all the Scandinavian countries. Perhaps above all, Norway is a land of intense natural beauty, its famously steep mountains and deep fjords carved out and shaped by an ancient ice age. Norway (148,700 square miles—just larger than Montana) is on the western side of the Scandinavian Peninsula, with most of the country sharing a border with Sweden to the east. Rich in resources like timber, oil, and fish, Norway has rejected joining the European Union, mainly to protect its fishing rights. Where the country extends north of the Arctic Circle, the sun never sets at the height of summer and never comes up in the deep of winter. The majority of Norway's 5.3 million people consider themselves Lutheran.

Money: 8 Norwegian kroner (kr, officially NOK) = about $1. An ATM is called a *minibank.* The local VAT (value-added sales tax) rate is 25 percent; the minimum purchase eligible for a VAT refund is 315 kr (for details on refunds, see page 125).

Language: The native language is Norwegian (the two official forms are Bokmål and Nynorsk). For useful phrases, see page 699.

Emergencies: Dial 112 for police, medical, or other emergencies. In case of theft or loss, see page 118.

Time Zone: Norway is on Central European Time (the same as most of the Continent, one hour ahead of Great Britain, and six/nine hours ahead of the East/West Coasts of the US).

Embassies in Oslo: The **US embassy** is at Morgedalsvegen 36 (tel. 21 30 85 58, emergency tel. 21 30 85 40, https://no.usembassy.gov) The **Canadian embassy** is at Wergelandsveien 7 (tel. 22 99 53 00, www.canadainternational.gc.ca/norway-norvege). Call ahead for passport services.

Phoning: With a mobile phone, it's easy to dial: Press and hold zero until you get a + sign, enter the country code (47 for Norway, 1 for the US/Canada), and then the complete phone number (including area code if there is one). When dialing a European phone number, drop an initial zero (except if calling Italy). For more tips, see page 1062.

Tipping: Service is included at sit-down meals, but this goes to the owner, so for great service it's nice to round up your bill about 10 percent. Tip a taxi driver by rounding up the fare (pay 90 kr on an 85-kr fare). For more tips on tipping, see page 129.

Tourist Information: www.goscandinavia.com

BERGEN

Bergen is permanently salted with robust cobbles and a rich sea-trading heritage. Norway's capital in the 13th century, Bergen's wealth and importance came thanks to its membership in the heavyweight medieval trading club of merchant cities called the Hanseatic League. Bergen still wears her rich maritime heritage proudly—nowhere more scenically than the colorful wooden warehouses that make up the picture-perfect Bryggen district along the harbor.

Protected from the open sea by a lone sheltering island, Bergen is a place of refuge from heavy winds for the giant working boats that serve the North Sea oil rigs. (Much of Norway's current affluence is funded by the oil it drills just offshore.) Bergen is also one of the most popular cruise-ship ports in northern Europe, hosting about 300 ships a year and up to five ships a day in peak season. Each morning is rush hour, as cruisers hike past the fortress and into town.

Bergen gets an average of 80 inches of rain annually (compared to 30 inches in Oslo). A good year has 60 days of sunshine. Bring along a light rain jacket.

With 240,000 people, Bergen has big-city parking problems and high prices, but visitors sticking to the old center find it charming. Enjoy Bergen's salty market, then stroll the easy-on-foot old quarter, with cute lanes of delicate old wooden houses. From downtown Bergen, a funicular zips you up little Mount Fløyen for a bird's-eye view of this sailors' town. A foray into the countryside takes you to a variety of nearby experiences: a dramatic cable-car ride to a mountaintop perch (Ulriken643); a scenic stave church

Excursions from Bergen

There's little reason to take an excursion here, as Bergen's top sights are easy to reach and appreciate on your own from the cruise ports. Most **Bergen** excursions include a walking tour around town (including Bryggen), often with tours of Håkon's Hall and Rosenkrantz Tower, and sometimes the funicular trip up Mount Fløyen. Outside town, excursions typically bundle Edvard Grieg's Home at **Troldhaugen** (at Nordås Lake) with **Fantoft Stave Church.** These sights are time-consuming to link by public transportation, so if you're dying to see them, an excursion may be worthwhile. Another excursion covers the ornately decorated, wooden **Villa Lysøen,** the former home of Norwegian violinist Ole Bull (built on its own little island). While interesting, it's about a 30-minute bus ride each way; I'd rather use my time for sights in Bergen itself.

(Fantoft); and the home of Norway's most beloved composer, Edvard Grieg, at Troldhaugen.

PLANNING YOUR TIME

Bergen is compact, with several good sightseeing options that can be visited quickly. With one busy day in Bergen, I'd take the walking tour (including visits to the Bryggens and Hanseatic Museums), ride up to Mount Fløyen, and wrap up my visit with other sights that sound intriguing—or simply poke around Bryggen and the Fish Market. It sounds like a lot, but it's all easily doable.

Bryggen Walking Tour: In summer (June-Aug), plan your day around this excellent 1.5-hour guided tour in English, which leads you through the historic, wooden Bryggen Hanseatic quarter and includes short visits to the top two museums, noted below (daily at 11:00 and 12:00, smart to reserve ahead in July). If the tour's not running when you're in town, you can visit the sights on your own.

Bryggens Museum: This fine archaeological museum focuses on early Bryggen history. Allow one hour.

Hanseatic Museum: Explore the fascinating, still-furnished interior of one of Bryggen's historic wooden houses. Allow one hour.

Fløibanen Funicular: This seven-minute trip takes you to bird's-eye views over town from atop Mount Fløyen. Allow 30-45 minutes round-trip, more if you hike down.

Other Sights in Town: Many of Bergen's lesser attractions—including Håkon's Hall/Rosenkrantz Tower at the fortress, Fortress Museum, Theta Museum, cathedral, and Leprosy Museum—can be seen in 30 minutes each (though the hall and tower at the

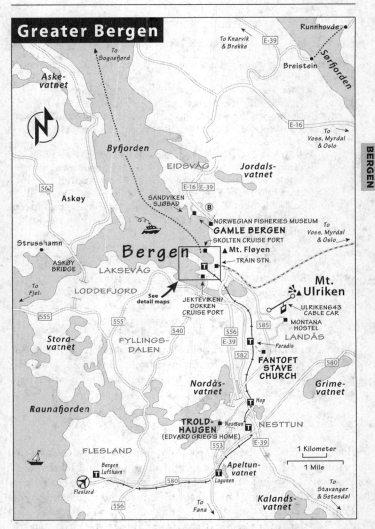

Greater Bergen

Runnhovde.

To Knarvik & Brekke · E-39

Sørfjorden

Breistein

Aske-vatnet

To Sognefjord

Byfjorden

EIDSVÅG

E-16 · E-39 · To Voss, Myrdal & Oslo

Jordals-vatnet

562 · Askøy

SANDVIKEN SJØBAD

Ⓑ

NORWEGIAN FISHERIES MUSEUM

Strusshamn

GAMLE BERGEN

SKOLTEN CRUISE PORT

To Voss, Myrdal & Oslo

Bergen

▲ Mt. Fløyen

ASKØY BRIDGE

LAKSEVÅG

To Fjel:

LODDEFJORD

See detail maps

TRAIN STN.

Mt. Ulriken

JEKTEVIKEN/ DOKKEN CRUISE PORT

ULRIKEN643 CABLE CAR

MONTANA HOSTEL

555

555

540

556

E-39 · Paradis

585

LANDÅS

Stora-vatnet

FYLLINGS-DALEN

582

FANTOFT STAVE CHURCH

580

Nordås-vatnet

Grime-vatnet

Raunafjorden

Hop

TROLD-HAUGEN (EDVARD GRIEG'S HOME)

Nesttun

NESTTUN

FLESLAND

553

E-39

1 Kilometer

1 Mile

Bergen Lufthavn

580 · Lagunen

Apeltun-vatnet

To Stavanger & Setesdal

Fleslard

556

To Fana

Kalands-vatnet

---

fortress are best if you have an hour to spare for the guided tour). The branches of the KODE Art Museum (conveniently located next to where some cruise-line shuttle buses drop off) could keep an art lover busy for hours, but a brief walk through the main collection can take less than an hour. The aquarium and Gamle Bergen (Old Bergen) take longer to reach; I'd skip these unless you have a special interest.

Out-of-Town Sights: If you're feeling adventurous, you can head out to the **Ulriken643 Cable Car,** Edvard Grieg's Home at **Troldhaugen,** or **Fantoft Stave Church**—but each requires a bus

Services in Bergen

Services are virtually nonexistent at the ports. But you'll find what you need downtown.

ATMs: Various ATMs are scattered around the city-center zone near the Fish Market. On your way into town from the Skolten port, the first ATM you'll pass is at the **Windfjord** sweater and souvenir shop, two blocks past the fortress on the harborside road.

Wi-Fi: The TI (near the Fish Market) has good, free Wi-Fi.

Pharmacy: Two handy options are right downtown, near all the sightseeing (both are closed Sun). **Boots Apotek** is just a half-block in front of the funicular station to Mount Fløyen at Vetrlidsallmenningen 11. **Apotek 1** is inside the Galleriet Shopping Mall, facing the Seafarers' Monument on the main square, Torgallmenningen.

or tram ride (figure about an hour each way from downtown Bergen to Troldhaugen or the church, less for the cable car).

Port of Bergen

Arrival at a Glance: It's simple: From the **Skolten** port, you can walk into town in about 10 minutes; from **Jekteviken/Dokken,** ride the free shuttle bus. A taxi into downtown from either port costs about 150-170 NOK.

Port Overview

Bergen has two cruise ports: **Skolten,** just past the fortress on the main harborfront road at the north end of town; and **Jekteviken/ Dokken,** in an industrial zone to the south. If your ship gets in early, you'll be setting up with the fishermen and merchants at the Fish Market.

Tourist Information: There are no TIs at the ports, but it's easy to get downtown to visit Bergen's main TI (right at the Fish Market; see page 668).

GETTING INTO TOWN

First, I'll cover options for getting into town from any port. Then I'll offer specifics on each. To return to your ship, you can generally reverse these directions—I've given suggestions at the end of each section as necessary.

From Either Port

By Taxi: Bergen is easy for cruise passengers, regardless of which of the city's two ports your ship uses. There's little need for a taxi from either port, thanks to their easy proximity to town. But if you do take one, plan on 150-170 NOK to points downtown. If taxis aren't waiting at the port, call 07000 or 08000 to summon one.

From Skolten

By Tour: Hop-on, hop-off **bus tours** meet arriving ships at Skolten (for details, see page 672). But in this compact town, I'd just walk (unless the weather is miserable and you just want a once-over-lightly look at the town).

On Foot: It's a simple and scenic walk into town; figure about 10 minutes to Bryggen, plus five more minutes to the Fish Market and TI. Exiting the port area, follow the busy Skutevikstorget road with the harbor on your right and the fortress/park on your left (follow traffic signs for *Sentrum*). Along road is a **bus** stop (stop name: Bontelabo; buses #3, #4, #5, #6, and #83). All go one stop to Torget, in the town center—but because the walk is simple and takes you past some great sights, there's little point in taking a bus. If you're headed out of town, note that bus #83 continues to stops near Fantoft Stave Church (Paradis stop) and Edvard Grieg's Home at Troldhaugen (Hop stop; 2/hour, about 30 minutes).

Passing the bus stop, continue along the harborfront road, crossing over to the fortress side at the crosswalk. Very shortly you'll pass the side entrance into the fortress complex, which is also the starting point of my self-guided walk.

To head straight downtown, just keep walking, and you'll soon reach the Fish Market, with the TI nearby.

Returning to Skolten: It's an easy walk around the fortress (just walk with the harbor on your left). If you have time to kill before "all aboard," you can browse through Bryggen (which is a quick 10-minute walk from your ship) or tour the fortress sights (even closer).

From Jekteviken/Dokken

This cruise port is in an industrial zone to the south, a bit farther out (about a 20-minute walk).

By Cruise-Line Shuttle: To discourage passengers from walking through all the containers, the port operates a convenient and **free shuttle bus** that zips you into town. It drops you off along the street called Rasmus Meyers Allé (in front of the KODE Art Museums, facing the cute man-made lake called Lille Lungegårdsvannet).

From here, it's a pleasant and easy 10-minute **walk** to the TI, Fish Market, harbor, and most sightseeing: Walk with the lake on your right. At the end of the lake, you'll reach the park called Byparken (where you can meet a hop-on, hop-off bus tour—described on page 672, or take the Bybanen tram to Fantoft Stave Church and Edvard Grieg's Home at Troldhaugen).

Continue through the park, straight past the pretty pavilion, and up the pedestrian mall called Ole Bulls Plass. This is the finishing point of my self-guided walk (consider doing it in reverse from here; or, if you take the walk later, it'll lead you back here and to the bus). Turn right (at the bluish stone slab) up the broad square called Torgallmenningen. At the end of this, you'll pass the blocky Seafarers' Monument. The Fish Market, TI, and Bryggen are just beyond.

Returning to Jekteviken/Dokken: Catch the cruise-line shuttle right where it dropped you, in front of the KODE Art Museums by the little lake along Rasmus Meyers Allé; my self-guided walk leads you there.

Bergen

Bergen clusters around its harbor—nearly everything listed in this chapter is within a few minutes' walk. The busy Torget (the square with the Fish Market) is at the head of the harbor. As you face the sea from here, Bergen's TI is at the left end of the Fish Market. The town's historic Hanseatic Quarter, Bryggen (BRUHY-gun), lines the harbor on the right. Express boats to the Sognefjord (Balestrand and Flåm) dock at the harbor on the left.

Charming cobbled streets surround the harbor and climb the encircling hills. Bergen's popular Fløibanen funicular climbs high above the city to the top of Mount Fløyen for the best view of the town. Surveying the surrounding islands and inlets, it's clear why this city is known as the "Gateway to the Fjords."

Orientation to Bergen

TOURIST INFORMATION
The centrally located TI is upstairs in the long, skinny, modern, Torghallen market building, next to the Fish Market (daily June-Aug 8:30-22:00, May and Sept 9:00-20:00; Oct-April Mon-Sat 9:00-16:00, closed Sun; free Wi-Fi, handy budget eateries downstairs and in Fish Market; tel. 55 55 20 00, www.visitbergen.com).

Pick up this year's edition of the free *Bergen Guide,* which has a fine map and lists sights, hours, and special events. This booklet can answer most of your questions.

Bergen Card: For a short visit, it's not worth buying this card, which covers trams, buses, and most museums (240 NOK/24 hours, sold at TI).

Museum Tours: Many of Bergen's sights are hard to appreciate without a guide. Fortunately, several offer wonderful and intimate guided tours. Make the most of the following sights by taking advantage of their tours: Håkon's Hall and Rosenkrantz Tower, Bryggens Museum, Hanseatic Museum, Leprosy Museum, Gamle Bergen, and Edvard Grieg's Home.

GETTING AROUND BERGEN

Most in-town sights can easily be reached by foot; only the aquarium, the Norwegian Fisheries Museum, and Gamle Bergen (and farther-flung sights such as the Fantoft Stave Church, Edvard Grieg's Home at Troldhaugen, and the Ulriken643 cable car) are more than a 10-minute walk from the TI.

By Bus: City buses cost 60 NOK per ride (pay driver in cash), or 37 NOK per ride if you buy a single-ride ticket from a machine or convenience stores such as Narvesen, 7-Eleven, Rimi, and Deli de Luca. The best buses for a Bergen joyride are #6 (north along the coast) and #11 (into the hills).

By Tram: Bergen's light-rail line (Bybanen) is a convenient way to visit Edvard Grieg's Home and the Fantoft Stave Church. The tram begins next to Byparken (on Kaigaten, between Bergen's little lake and Ole Bulls Plass), then heads to the train station and continues south, ending at the airport. Buy your 37-NOK ticket from the machine before boarding (to use a US credit card, you'll need your PIN, also accepts coins). You can also buy single-ride tickets at Narvesen, 7-Eleven, Rimi, and Deli de Luca stores—you'll get a gray *minikort* pass. Validate the pass when you board by holding it next to the card reader (watch how other passengers do it). Ride it about 20 minutes to the Paradis stop for Fantoft Stave Church (don't get off at the "Fantoft" stop, which is farther from the church); or continue to the next stop, Hop, to hike to Troldhaugen.

By Ferry: The *Beffen,* a little orange ferry, chugs across the harbor (Vågen) every half-hour, from the dock a block south of the Bryggens Museum to the dock—directly opposite the fortress—a block from the Nykirken church (25 NOK, Mon-Fri 7:30-16:00, plus Sat May-Aug 11:00-16:00, fewer on Sun, 4-minute ride). Another *Beffen* ferry runs from the right side of the Fish Market (as you face the water) to the Norwegian Fisheries Museum (for details, see the Hanseatic Museum listing under "Sights in Bergen").

Bergen

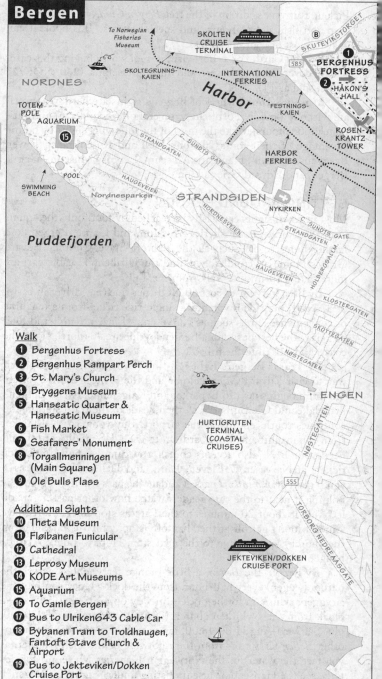

To Norwegian Fisheries Museum

SKOLTEN CRUISE TERMINAL

B

SKUTEVIKSTORGET

585

BERGENHUS FORTRESS ❶

❷ HÅKON'S HALL

SKOLTEGRUNNS-KAIEN

INTERNATIONAL FERRIES

Harbor

NORDNES

FESTNINGS-KAIEN

ROSEN-KRANTZ TOWER

TOTEM POLE

AQUARIUM

❶⑤

STRANDGATEN

C. SUNDTS GATE

HARBOR FERRIES

SWIMMING BEACH

POOL

HAUGEVEIEN

Nordnesparken

STRANDSIDEN

NORDNESVEIEN

NYKIRKEN

C. SUNDTS GATE

STRANDGATEN

Puddefjorden

HAUGEVEIEN

HOLBERGSALM.

KLOSTERGATEN

SKOTTEGATEN

NØSTEGATEN

ENGEN

HURTIGRUTEN TERMINAL (COASTAL CRUISES)

NØSTEGATTEN

555

JEKTEVIKEN/DOKKEN CRUISE PORT

TORBORG NEDREAASGATE

Walk

❶ Bergenhus Fortress
❷ Bergenhus Rampart Perch
❸ St. Mary's Church
❹ Bryggens Museum
❺ Hanseatic Quarter & Hanseatic Museum
❻ Fish Market
❼ Seafarers' Monument
❽ Torgallmenningen (Main Square)
❾ Ole Bulls Plass

Additional Sights

❿ Theta Museum
⓫ Fløibanen Funicular
⓬ Cathedral
⓭ Leprosy Museum
⓮ KODE Art Museums
⓯ Aquarium
⓰ To Gamle Bergen
⓱ Bus to Ulriken643 Cable Car
⓲ Bybanen Tram to Troldhaugen, Fantoft Stave Church & Airport
⓳ Bus to Jekteviken/Dokken Cruise Port

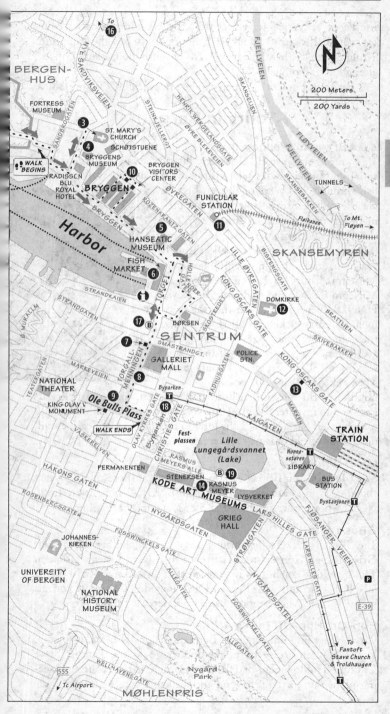

BERGEN

The *Vågen* "Akvariet" ferry runs from the left side of the Fish Market every half-hour to a dock near the aquarium (see the Aquarium listing under "Sights in Bergen"). All of these "poor man's cruises" offer good harbor views.

By Taxi: For a taxi, which can be pricey, call 07000 or 08000.

Tours in Bergen

▲▲▲Bryggen Walking Tour

This tour of the historic Hanseatic district is one of Bergen's best activities. Local guides take visitors on a 1.5-hour walk in English through 900 years of Bergen history via the old Hanseatic town (20 minutes in Bryggens Museum, 20-minute visit to the medieval Hanseatic Assembly Rooms (Schøtstuene), 20-minute walk through Bryggen, and 20 minutes in Hanseatic Museum). Tours leave from the Bryggens Museum (next to the Radisson Blu Royal Hotel). When you consider that the price includes entry tickets to all three sights, the tour more than pays for itself (150 NOK, June-Aug daily at 11:00 and 12:00, maximum 30 in group, no tours Sept-May, tel. 55 30 80 30, post@bymuseet.

no). While the museum visits are a bit rushed, your tour ticket allows you to re-enter the museums for the rest of the day. The 11:00 tour can sell out, especially in July; to be safe, you can call, email, or drop by ahead of time to reserve a spot.

Local Guide

Sue Lindelid is a British expat who has spent more than 25 years showing visitors around Bergen (1,200 NOK/2-hour tour, 1,600 NOK/3-hour tour; mobile 90 78 59 52, suelin@hotmail.no).

▲Bus Tours

The TI sells tickets for various bus tours, including a 2.5-hour Grieg Lunch Concert tour that goes to Edvard Grieg's Home at Troldhaugen—a handy way to reach that distant sight (250 NOK, 50-NOK discount with Bergen Card, includes 30-minute concert but not lunch, May-Sept daily at 11:30, departs from TI).

Hop-On, Hop-Off Buses

City Sightseeing links most of Bergen's major sights and also stops at the Skolten cruise port, but doesn't go to the Fantoft Stave Church, Troldhaugen, or Ulriken643 cable car. If your sightseeing plans don't extend beyond the walkable core of Bergen, skip this (275 NOK/24 hours, early May-late Sept 9:00-16:00, every 30 minutes, also stops in front of Fish Market, mobile 97 78 18 88, www.citysightseeing.no/bergen).

Inflatable Boat Tour

After a scenic cruise along the Bergen harborfront, you'll zip out into the open fjord past islands and rocky skerries aboard a fast and breezy Fjord Tours rigid inflatable boat (RIB). Before heading out you'll don a survival suit and goggles for the thrilling high-speed part of the journey. Tours last 50 minutes and depart from near the round Narvesen kiosk on the Bryggen side of the Fish Market. Get tickets at the TI (595 NOK, meet at dock at 13:10, 1 tour/day, www.fjordtours.com).

Bergen Walk

For a quick self-guided orientation stroll through Bergen, follow this walk from the city's fortress, through its old wooden Hanseatic Quarter and Fish Market, to the modern center of town. This walk is also a handy sightseeing spine, passing most of Bergen's best museums; ideally, you'll get sidetracked and take advantage of their excellent tours along the way. I've pointed out the museums you'll pass en route—all are described in greater detail later, under "Sights in Bergen." To trace the route of this walk, see the Bergen map, earlier.

• *Begin where Bergen did, at its historic fortress. From the harborfront road, 50 yards before the stone tower with the water on your left, veer up the ramp behind the low stone wall on the right, through a gate, and into the fortress complex. Stand before the stony skyscraper.*

❶ Bergenhus Fortress

In the 13th century, Bergen became the Kingdom of Norway's first real capital. (Until then, kings would circulate, staying on royal farms.) This fortress—built in the 1240s and worth ▲—was a garrison, with a tower for the king's residence (Rosenkrantz Tower) and a large hall for his banquets (Håkon's Hall).

Rosenkrantz Tower, the keep of the 13th-century castle, was expanded in the 16th century by the Danish-Norwegian king, who wanted to exercise a little control over the German merchants who dominated his town. He was tired of the Germans making all the money without paying taxes. This tower—with its cannon trained not on external threats but toward Bryggen—while expensive, paid for itself many times over as Germans got the message and paid their taxes.

• *Step through the gate (20 yards to the right of the tower) marked 1728 and into the courtyard of the Bergenhus Fortress. In front of you stands*

Bergen at a Glance

▲▲▲**Bryggen Walking Tour** Wonderful 1.5-hour tour of the historic Hanseatic district that covers 900 years of history and includes short visits to the Bryggens Museum, Hanseatic Assembly Rooms, and Hanseatic Museum, plus a walk through Bryggen. **Hours:** June-Aug daily at 11:00 and 12:00. See page 673.

▲▲**Bryggens Museum** Featuring early bits of Bergen (1050-1500), found in an archaeological dig. **Hours:** Daily 10:00-16:00; Sept-mid-May Mon-Fri 11:00-15:00, Sat-Sun 12:00-16:00. See page 684.

▲▲**Hanseatic Museum and Schøtstuene** Museum highlighting Bryggen's glory days, featuring an old merchant house furnished with artifacts from the time German merchants were tops in trading and a separate building housing assembly rooms—most interesting with included tour. **Hours:** Daily 9:00-17:00, June-Aug until 18:00, Oct-April 11:00-15:00 except Schøtstuene closed Sun. See page 685.

▲▲**Fløibanen Funicular** Zippy lift to top of Mount Fløyen for super views of Bergen, islands, and fjords, with picnic ops, an eatery, playground, and hiking trails. **Hours:** Mon-Fri 7:30-23:00, Sat-Sun from 8:00. See page 687.

▲**Fish Market** Lively market with cheap seafood eateries and free samples. **Hours:** May-Oct daily 8:00-23:00; Nov-Dec Mon-Sat 9:00-21:00, Sun from 11:00-21:00; Jan-April Sat only 9:00-15:00. See page 681.

▲**Bergenhus Fortress: Håkon's Hall and Rosenkrantz Tower** Fortress with a 13th-century medieval banquet hall, a climbable tower offering a history exhibit and views, and a worthwhile guided tour. **Hours:** Hall open daily 10:00-16:00, tower from 9:00; mid-Sept-mid-May hall daily 12:00-15:00, tower Sun only. See page 683.

Håkon's Hall with its stepped gable. Tours for both the hall and the tower leave from the building to the right of Håkon's Hall.

Pop into the museum lobby to enjoy a free exhibit about the massive 1944 explosion of the German ammunition ship in the harbor. For the best view of Håkon's Hall, walk through the gate and around the building to the left. Stand on the rampart between the hall and the harbor.

Håkon's Hall is the largest secular medieval building in Norway. When the pope sent a cardinal to perform Håkon's coronation there was no suitable building in Norway for such a VIP. King Håkon fixed that by having this impressive banqueting hall built in the mid-1200s. When Norway's capital moved to Oslo in 1299,

▲**KODE Art Museums** Collection spread among four neighboring lakeside buildings: KODE 4 (international and Norwegian artists), KODE 3 (Norwegian artists, including Munch), KODE 2 (contemporary art), and KODE 1 (decorative arts). **Hours:** Daily 11:00-17:00 (KODE 3 10:00-18:00), closed Mon mid-Sept-mid-May. See page 689.

▲**St. Mary's Church** Bergen's oldest church, dating to the 12th century. **Hours:** Mon-Fri 9:00-16:00, closed mid-Sept-May. See page 688.

▲**Aquarium** Well-presented sea life, with a walk-through "shark tunnel" and feeding times at the top of most hours in summer. **Hours:** Daily May-Aug 9:00-18:00, shorter hours off-season. See page 690.

▲**Gamle Bergen (Old Bergen)** Quaint gathering of 50 homes and shops dating from 18th-20th century, with guided tours of museum interiors at the top of the hour. **Hours:** Daily 9:00-16:00, closed Sept-mid-May. See page 690.

Near Bergen
▲▲**Edvard Grieg's Home, Troldhaugen** Home of Norway's greatest composer, with artifacts, tours, and concerts. **Hours:** Daily 9:00-18:00, Oct-April 10:00-16:00. See page 691.

▲**Ulriken643 Cable Car** A quick ride up to the summit of Ulriken, Bergen's tallest mountain, with nonstop views, a restaurant, and hiking trails. **Hours:** Daily 9:00-21:00, off-season until 17:00. See page 690.

BERGEN

the hall was abandoned and eventually used for grain storage. For a century it had no roof. In the Romantic 19th century, it was appreciated and restored. It's essentially a giant, grand reception hall used today as it was eight centuries ago: for banquets.

• *Continue walking along the rampart (climbing some steps and going about 100 yards past Håkon's Hall) to the far end of Bergenhus Fortress where you find a statue of a king and a fine harbor view.*

❷ Bergenhus Rampart Perch and Statue of King Håkon VII
The cannon on the ramparts here illustrates how the fort protected

this strategic harbor. The port is busy with both cruise ships and supply ships for the nearby North Sea oil rigs. Long before this modern commerce, this is where the cod fishermen of the north met the traders of Europe. Travelers in the 12th century described how there were so many trading vessels here "you could cross the harbor without getting your feet wet." Beyond the ships is an island protecting Bergen from the open sea.

The statue is of the beloved King Håkon VII (1872-1957), grandfather of today's king. While exiled in London during World War II, King Håkon kept up Norwegian spirits through radio broadcasts. The first king of modern Norway (after the country won its independence from Sweden in 1905), he was a Danish prince married to Queen Victoria's granddaughter—a savvy monarch who knew how to play the royalty game. A few steps behind the statue (just right of tree-lined lane) is the site of Bergen's first cathedral, built in 1070. A hedge grows where its walls once stood. The statue of Mary marks the place of the altar, its pedestal etched with a list of 13th-century kings of Norway crowned and buried here.

These castle grounds (notice the natural amphitheater on the left) host cultural events and music festivals; Elton John, Paul McCartney, and Kygo have all packed this outdoor venue in recent years.

Continuing around Håkon's Hall, follow the linden tree-lined lane. On the left, a massive concrete structure disguised by ivy looms as if evil. It was a German bunker built during the Nazi occupation—easier now to ignore than dismantle.

Twenty yards ahead on the right is a rare set of free public toilets. Notice they come with blue lights to discourage heroin junkies from using these WCs as a place to shoot up. The blue lights make it hard to see veins.

• *You've now returned to the tower and circled the castle grounds. Before leaving, consider taking a guided tour of the hall and tower. Head back down the ramp, out to the main road, and continue with the harbor on your right. (After a block, history buffs could follow Bergenhus signs, up the street to the left, to the free and fascinating **Fortress Museum**—with its collection of Norwegian military history and Nazi occupation exhibits.) Proceed one more block along the harbor until you reach the open, parklike space on your left. Walk 100 yards (just past the handy Rema 1000 supermarket) to the top of this park where you'll see...*

❸ St. Mary's Church (Mariakirken)

Dating from the 12th century, this is Bergen's oldest preserved building. This stately church of the Hanseatic merchants has a dour stone interior, but it's enlivened by a colorful, highly decorated pulpit.

In the park below the church, find the statue of Snorri Stur-

lason. In the 1200s, this Icelandic scribe and scholar wrote down the Viking sagas. Thanks to him, we have a better understanding of this Nordic era. A few steps to the right, look through the window of the big modern building at an archaeological site showing the oldest remains of Bergen—stubs of the 12th-century trading town's streets tumbling to the harbor before land reclamation pushed the harbor farther out.

• *The window is just a sneak peek at the excellent* ❹ *Bryggens Museum, which provides helpful historical context for the Hanseatic Quarter we're about to visit. The museum's outstanding* **Bryggen Walking Tour** *is your best bet for seeing this area (see "Tours in Bergen," earlier). Continue down to the busy harborfront. On the left is the most photographed sight in town, the Bryggen quarter. To get your bearings, first read the "Bryggen's History" sidebar; if it's nice out, cross the street to the wharf and look back for a fine overview of this area. (Or, in the rain, huddle under an awning.)*

❺ Bergen's Hanseatic Quarter (Bryggen)

Bergen's fragile wooden old town is its iconic front door. The long "tenements" (rows of warehouses) hide atmospheric lanes that creak and groan with history.

Remember that while we think of Bergen as "Norwegian," Bryggen was German—the territory of *Deutsch*-speaking merchants and traders. (The most popular surname in Bergen is the German name Hanson—"son of Hans.") From the front of Bryggen, look back at the Rosenkrantz Tower. The little red holes at its top mark where cannons once pointed at the German quarter, installed by Norwegian royalty who wanted a slice of all that taxable trade revenue. Their threat was countered by German grain—without which the Norwegians would've starved.

Notice that the first six houses are perfectly straight; they were built in the 1980s to block the view of a modern hotel behind. The more ramshackle stretch of 11 houses beyond date from the early 1700s. Each front hides a long line of five to ten businesses.

Bryggen's History

Pretty as Bryggen is today, it has a rough-and-tumble history. A horrific plague decimated the population and economy of Norway in 1350, killing about half of its people. A decade later, German merchants arrived and established a Hanseatic trading post, bringing order to that rustic society. For the next four centuries, the port of Bergen was essentially German territory.

Bergen's old German trading center was called "the German wharf" until World War II (and is now just called "the wharf," or "Bryggen"). From 1370 to 1754, German merchants controlled Bergen's trade. In 1550, it was a Germanic city of 1,000 workaholic merchants—surrounded and supported by some 5,000 Norwegians.

The German merchants were very strict and lived in a harsh, all-male world (except for Norwegian prostitutes). This wasn't a military occupation, but a mutually beneficial economic partnership. The Norwegian cod fishermen of the far north shipped their dried cod to Bergen, where the Hanseatic merchants marketed it to Europe. Norwegian cod provided much of Europe with food (a source of easy-to-preserve protein) and cod oil (which lit the lamps until about 1850).

While the city dates from 1070, little survives from before the last big fire in 1702. In its earlier heyday, Bergen was one of the largest wooden cities in Europe. Congested wooden buildings, combined with lots of small fires (to provide heat and light in this cold and dark corner of Europe), spelled disaster for Bergen. Over the centuries, the city suffered countless fires, including 10 devastating ones. Back then, it wasn't a question of *if* there would be a fire, but *when* there would be a fire—with major blazes every 20 or so years. Each time the warehouses burned, the merchants would toss the refuse into the bay and rebuild. Gradually, the land crept

• *To wander into the heart of this woody medieval quarter, head down Bredsgården, the lane a couple of doors before the shop sign featuring the anatomically correct unicorn. We'll make a loop to the right: down this lane nearly all the way, under a passage into a square (with a well, a vibrant outdoor restaurant, and a big wooden cod), and then back to the harbor down a parallel lane. Read the information below, then explore, stopping at the big wooden cod.*

Bit by bit, Bryggen is being restored using medieval techniques and materials. As you explore, you may stumble upon a rebuilding project in action.

Strolling through Bryggen, you feel swallowed up by history.

out, and so did the buildings. (Looking at the Hanseatic Quarter from the harborfront, you can see how the buildings have settled. The foundations, composed of debris from the many fires, settle as they rot.)

After 1702, the city rebuilt using more stone and brick, and suffered fewer fires. But this one small wooden quarter was built after the fire, in the early 1700s. To prevent future blazes, the Germans forbade all fires and candles for light or warmth except in isolated and carefully guarded communal houses behind each tenement. It was in these communal houses that apprentices studied, people dried out their soggy clothes, hot food was cooked, and the men drank and partied. When there was a big banquet, one man always stayed sober—a kind of designated fire watchman.

Flash forward to the 20th century. One of the biggest explosions of World War II occurred in Bergen's harbor on April 20, 1944. An ammunition ship loaded with 120 tons of dynamite blew up just in front of the fortress. The blast leveled entire neighborhoods on either side of the harbor (notice the ugly 1950s construction opposite the fortress) and did serious damage to Håkon's Hall and Rosenkrantz Tower. How big was the blast? There's a hut called "the anchor cabin" a couple of miles away in the mountains. That's where the ship's anchor landed. The blast is considered to be accidental, despite the fact that April 20 happened to be Hitler's 55th birthday and the ship blew up about 100 yards away from the Nazi commander's headquarters (in the fortress).

After World War II, Bryggen was again slated for destruction. Most of the locals wanted it gone—it reminded them of the Germans who had occupied Norway for the miserable war years. Then excavators discovered rune stones indicating that the area predated the Germans. This boosted Bryggen's approval rating, and the quarter was saved. Today this picturesque and historic zone is the undisputed tourist highlight of Bergen.

BERGEN

Long rows of planky buildings (medieval-style double tenements) lean haphazardly across narrow alleys. The last Hanseatic merchant moved out centuries ago, but this is still a place of (touristy) commerce. You'll find artists' galleries, T-shirt boutiques, leather workshops, atmospheric restaurants, fishing tackle shops, sweaters, sweaters, sweaters...and trolls.

Look up at the winch and pulley systems on the buildings. These connected ground-floor workrooms with top-floor storerooms. Notice that the overhanging storerooms upstairs were supported by timbers with an elbow created by a tree trunk and its root—considered the strongest way to make a right angle in con-

struction back then. Turning right at the top of the lane, you enter a lively cobbled square. On the far side is that big wooden cod (next to a well), a reminder that the economic foundation of Bergen—the biggest city in Scandinavia until 1650 and the biggest city in Norway until 1830—was this fish. The stone building behind the carved cod was one of the fireproof cookhouses serving a line of buildings that stretched to the harbor. Today it's the Hetland Gallery, filled with the entertaining work of a popular local artist famous for fun caricatures of the city. Facing the same square is the Bryggen visitors center, worth peeking into.

• *Enjoy the center and the shops. Then return downhill to the harborfront, turn left, and continue the walk.*

Half of Bryggen (the brick-and-stone stretch to your left between the old wooden facades and the head of the bay) was torn down around 1900. Today the stately buildings that replaced it— far less atmospheric than Bryggen's original wooden core—are filled with tacky trinket shops and touristy splurge restaurants. They do make a nice architectural cancan of pointy gables, each with its date of construction indicated near the top. Head to the lone wooden red house at the end of the row, which houses the **Hanseatic Museum.** This highly recommended museum is your best chance to get a peek inside one of those old wooden tenements.

• *The Fish Market is just across the street. Before enjoying that, we'll circle a few blocks inland and around to the right.*

The red-brick building (with frilly white trim, stepped gable, and a Starbucks) is the old **meat market.** It was built in 1877, after the importance of hygiene was recognized and the meat was moved inside from today's Fish Market. At the intersection just beyond, look left (uphill past the meat market) to see the Fløibanen station. Ahead, on the right, is an unusually classy McDonald's in a 1710 building that was originally a bakery.

At the McDonald's, wander the length of the cute lane of 200-year-old buildings. Called Hollendergaten, its name comes from a time when the king organized foreign communities of traders into various neighborhoods; this was where the Dutch lived. The curving street marks the former harborfront—these buildings were originally right on the water.

Hooking left, you reach the end of Hollendergaten. Turn right back toward the harborfront. Ahead is the grand stone **Børsen building** (now Matbørsen, a collection of trendy restaurants), once the stock exchange. Step inside to enjoy its 1920s Art Deco-style murals celebrating Bergen's fishing heritage.

• *Now, cross the street and immerse yourself in Bergen's beloved Fish Market.*

❻ Fish Market (Fisketorget)

A fish market has thrived here since the 1500s, when fishermen rowed in with their catch and haggled with hungry residents. While it's now become a food circus of eateries selling fishy treats to tourists—no local would come here to actually buy fish—this famous market is still worth ▲, offering lots of smelly photo fun and free morsels to taste (May-Oct daily 8:00-23:00, but vendors may close earlier if they're not busy; Nov-Dec Mon-Sat 9:00-21:00, Sun from 11:00; Jan-April Sat only 9:00-15:00).

Many stands sell premade smoked-salmon *(laks)* sandwiches, fish soup, and other snacks ideal for a light lunch (confirm prices before ordering). To try Norwegian jerky, pick up a bag of dried cod snacks *(tørrfisk).*

Watch your wallet: If you're going to get pickpocketed in Bergen, it'll likely be here.

• *When done exploring, with your back to the market, hike a block to the right (note the pointy church spire in the distance and the big blocky stone monument dead ahead) into the modern part of town and a huge wide square. Pause at the intersection just before crossing into the square, about 20 yards before the blocky monument. Look left to see Mount Ulriken with its TV tower. A cable car called **Ulriken643** takes you to its 2,110-foot summit. (Shuttle buses to its station leave from this corner at the top and bottom of the hour; for summit details, see page 690.) Now, walk up to that big square monument and meet some Vikings.*

❼ Seafarers' Monument

Nicknamed "the cube of goat cheese" for its shape, this 1950 monument celebrates Bergen's contact with the sea and remembers those who worked on it and died in it. Study the faces: All social classes are represented. The statues relate to the scenes depicted in the reliefs above. Each side represents a century (start with the Vikings and work clockwise): 10th century—Vikings, with a totem pole in the panel above recalling the pre-Columbian Norwegian discovery of America; 18th century—equipping Europe's ships; 19th century—whaling; 20th century—shipping and war. For the 21st century, see the real people—a cross-section of today's Norway—sitting at the statue's base. Major department stores (Galleriet, Xhibition, and Telegrafen) are all nearby.

• *The monument marks the start of Bergen's main square...*

❽ Torgallmenningen

Allmenningen means "for all the people." Torg means "square." And, while this is the city's main gathering place, it was actually created as a firebreak. The residents of this wood-built city knew fires were inevitable. The street plan was designed with breaks, or open spaces like this square, to help contain the destruction. In 1916, it succeeded in stopping a fire, which is why it has a more modern feel today.

Walk the length of the square to the angled slab of blue stone (quarried in Brazil) at the far end. This is a monument to King Olav V, who died in 1991, and a popular meeting point: Locals like to say, "Meet you at the Blue Stone." It marks the center of a parklike swath known as...

❾ Ole Bulls Plass

This drag leads from the National Theater (above on right) to a little lake (below on left).

Detour a few steps up for a better look at the **National Theater,** built in Art Nouveau style in 1909. Founded by violinist  Ole Bull in 1850, this was the first theater to host plays in the Norwegian language. After 450 years of Danish and Swedish rule, 19th-century Norway enjoyed a cultural awakening, and Bergen became an artistic power. Ole Bull collaborated with the playwright Henrik Ibsen. Ibsen commissioned Edvard Grieg to compose the music for his play *Peer Gynt.* These three lions of Norwegian culture all lived and worked right here in Bergen.

Head downhill on the square to a delightful fountain featuring a **statue of Ole Bull** in the shadow of trees. Ole Bull was an 1800s version of Elvis. A pop idol and heartthrob in his day, Ole Bull's bath water was bottled and sold by hotels, and women fainted when they heard him play violin. Living up to his name, he fathered over 40 children.

From here, the park spills farther downhill to a cast-iron pavilion given to the city by Germans in 1889, and on to the little man-made lake (Lille Lungegårdsvannet), which is circled by an enjoyable path. This green zone is considered a park and is cared for by the local parks department.

• *If you're up for a lakeside stroll, now's your chance. Also notice that alongside the lake (to the right as you face it from here) is a row of buildings housing the enjoyable **KODE Art Museums**. And to the left of the lake are some fine residential streets (including the picturesque, cobbled Marken); within a few minutes' walk is the **Leprosy Museum** and the cathedral.*

Sights in Bergen

Several museums listed here—including the Bryggens Museum, Håkon's Hall, Rosenkrantz Tower, Leprosy Museum, and Gamle Bergen—are part of the Bergen City Museum (Bymuseet) organization. If you buy a ticket to any of them, you'll pay half-price at any of the others simply by showing your ticket.

▲Bergenhus Fortress: Håkon's Hall and Rosenkrantz Tower

The tower and hall, sitting boldly out of place on the harbor just beyond Bryggen, are reminders of Bergen's importance as the first

permanent capital of Norway. Both sights feel vacant and don't really speak for themselves; the guided tours, which provide a serious introduction to Bergen's history, are essential for grasping their significance.

Cost and Hours: Hall and tower—120 NOK for both (or 80 NOK each), half-price with ticket to another Bergen City Museum; hall open daily 10:00-16:00, tower from 9:00; mid-Sept-mid-May hall open daily 12:00-15:00, tower open Sun only; tel. 55 30 80 30, free WC.

Tours: 20 NOK extra for guided tour that includes both buildings (mid-June-Aug tours leave daily at 11:00, 14:00, and 15:00 from the building to the right of Håkon's Hall.

Visiting the Hall and Tower: Dating from the 13th century, **Håkon's Hall** was built as a banqueting hall, and that's essentially what it still is today. It was restored in the early 20th century, but was heavily damaged in World War II when a munitions ship exploded in the harbor, leaving nothing but the walls standing. In the 1950s it was restored again, with the grand wooden ceiling and roof modeled after the medieval roof on a church in northern Norway. Beneath the hall is a whitewashed cellar that is thought to have been used mainly for storage.

Rosenkrantz Tower, the keep of a 13th-century castle, is today a stack of barren rooms connected by tight spiral staircases, with a good history exhibit on the top two floors and a commanding view from its rooftop. In the 16th century, the ruling Danish-Norwegian king enlarged the tower and trained its cannon on the German-merchant district, Bryggen, to remind the merchants of the importance of paying their taxes.

Fortress Museum (Bergenhus Festningmuseum)

This humble museum (which functioned as a prison during the Nazi occupation), set back a couple of blocks from the fortress, will interest historians with its thoughtful exhibits about military history, especially Bergen's WWII experience (look for the Norwegian Nazi flag). You'll learn about the resistance movement in Bergen (including its underground newspapers), the role of women in the Norwegian military, and Norwegian troops who have served with UN forces in overseas conflicts.

Cost and Hours: Free, Tue-Sun 11:00-17:00, ask to borrow a translation of the descriptions, just behind Thon Hotel Orion at Koengen, tel. 55 54 63 87.

▲▲Bryggens Museum

This modern museum explains the 1950s archaeological dig to uncover the earliest bits of Bergen (1050-1500). Brief English explanations are posted. From September through May, when there is no tour, consider buying the good museum guidebook (25 NOK).

Cost and Hours: 80 NOK; in summer, entry included with Bryggen Walking Tour described earlier; daily 10:00-16:00; Sept-mid-May Mon-Fri 11:00-15:00, Sat-Sun 12:00-16:00; inexpensive cafeteria; in big, modern building just beyond the end of Bryggen and the Radisson Blu Royal Hotel, tel. 55 30 80 30, www.bymuseet.no.

Visiting the Museum: The manageable, well-presented permanent exhibit occupies the ground floor. First up are the foundations from original wooden tenements dating back to the 12th century (displayed right where they were excavated) and a giant chunk of the hull of a 100-foot-long, 13th-century ship that was found here. Next, an exhibit (roughly shaped like the long, wooden double-tenements outside) shows off artifacts and explains lifestyles from medieval Bryggen. Behind that is a display of items you might have bought at the medieval market. You'll finish with exhibits about the church in Bergen, the town's role as a royal capital, and its status as a cultural capital. Upstairs are two floors of temporary exhibits.

BERGEN

▲▲Hanseatic Museum and Schøtstuene (Det Hanseatiske Museum og Schøtstuene)

The **Hanseatic Museum** offers the best possible look inside the wooden houses that are Bergen's trademark. Its creaky old rooms—with hundred-year-old cod hanging from the ceiling—offer a time-tunnel experience back to Bryggen's glory days. It's located in an atmospheric old merchant house furnished with dried fish, antique ropes, an old oxtail (used for wringing spilled cod-liver oil back into the bucket), sagging steps, and cupboard beds from the early 1700s—one sporting what some claim is a medieval pinup girl. You'll explore two upstairs levels, fully furnished and with funhouse floors. The place

still feels eerily lived-in; neatly sorted desks with tidy ledgers seem to be waiting for the next workday to begin.

Included with your admission are visits to the **Schøtstuene** (Hanseatic Assembly Rooms) and the Norwegian Fisheries Museum (described later). The Schøtstuene assembly rooms are in a building near St. Mary's Church that's accessed behind Bryggen from Øvregaten. Here, Hanseatic merchants would cook hot meals and gather to feast, hold court, conduct ceremonies, be schooled, and get warm—fires were allowed in this building only because it was separate from the other (highly flammable) Bryggen offices.

Cost: 160 NOK ticket (sold May-mid-Sept) includes all three sights and shuttle bus to Fisheries Museum, 100 NOK Oct-April; 100 NOK after 15:45 for Hanseatic Museum only. (Bryggen Walking Tour entry does not include Fisheries Museum.)

Hours: Daily 9:00-18:00, May and Sept until 17:00, Oct-

The Hanseatic League, Blessed by Cod

Middlemen in trade, the clever German merchants of the Hanseatic League ruled the waves of northern Europe for 500 years (c. 1250-1750). These sea-traders first banded together in a Hanse, or merchant guild, to defend themselves against pirates. As they spread out from Germany, they established trading posts in foreign lands, cut deals with local leaders for trading rights, built boats and wharves, and organized armies to protect ships and ports.

By the 15th century, these merchants had organized more than a hundred cities into the Hanseatic League, a free-trade zone that stretched from London to Russia. The League ran a profitable triangle of trade: Fish from Scandinavia was exchanged for grain from the eastern Baltic and luxury goods from England and Flanders. Everyone benefited, and the German merchants—the middlemen—reaped the profits.

At its peak in the 15th century, the Hanseatic League was the dominant force—economic, military, and political—in northern Europe. This was an age when much of Europe was fragmented into petty kingdoms and dukedoms. Revenue-hungry kings and robber-baron lords levied chaotic and extortionist tolls and duties. Pirates plagued shipments. It was the Hanseatic League, rather than national governments, that brought the stability that allowed trade to flourish.

Bergen's place in this Baltic economy was all about cod—a

April 11:00-15:00 except Schøtstuene closed Sun; Finnegården 1a, tel. 55 54 46 90, www.museumvest.no.

Tours: The Hanseatic Museum has scant English explanations—it's much better if you take the good, included 30-minute guided tour (3/day in English—call to confirm, June-mid-Sept only, times displayed on a monitor). Even if you tour the museum with the Bryggen Walking Tour, you're welcome to revisit (using the same ticket) and take this tour.

Norwegian Fisheries Museum: Just up the coast (along the water just north of Bryggen) is the Norwegian Fisheries Museum, an authentic wharfside warehouse with exhibits about life along and on the sea. Catch the free shuttle bus from the Hanseatic Museum (5-minute ride) or cruise 20 minutes aboard the *Beffen* ferry to the museum (130 NOK round-trip, June-Aug hourly 11:00-17:00, departs from the Bryggen side of the Fish Market).

form of protein that could be dried, preserved, and shipped anywhere. Though cursed by a lack of natural resources, the city was blessed with a good harbor conveniently located between the rich fishing spots of northern Norway and the markets of Europe. Bergen's port shipped dried cod and fish oil southward and imported grain, cloth, beer, wine, and ceramics.

Bryggen was one of four principal Hanseatic trading posts (Kontors), along with London, Bruges, and Novgorod. It was the last Kontor opened (c. 1360), the least profitable, and the final one to close. Bryggen had warehouses, offices, and living quarters. Ships docked here were unloaded by counterpoise cranes. At its peak, as many as a thousand merchants, journeymen, and apprentices lived and worked here.

Bryggen was a self-contained German enclave within the city. The merchants came from Germany, worked a few years here, and retired back in the home country. They spoke German, wore German clothes, and attended their own churches. By law, they were forbidden to intermarry or fraternize with the Bergeners, except on business.

The Hanseatic League peaked around 1500, then slowly declined. Rising nation-states were jealous of the Germans merchants' power and wealth. The Reformation tore apart old alliances. Dutch and English traders broke the Hanseatic monopoly. Cities withdrew from the League and Kontors closed. In 1754, Bergen's Kontor was taken over by the Norwegians. When it closed its doors on December 31, 1899, a sea-trading era was over, but the city of Bergen had become rich...by the grace of cod.

Theta Museum

This small museum highlights Norway's resistance movement. You'll peek into the hidden world of a 10-person cell of courageous students, whose group—called Theta—housed other fighters and communicated with London during the Nazi occupation in World War II. It's housed in Theta's former headquarters—a small upstairs room in a wooden Bryggen building.

Cost and Hours: 50 NOK, June-Aug Tue, Sat, and Sun 14:00-16:00, closed Mon, Wed-Fri, and Sept-May, Enhjørningsgården.

▲▲Fløibanen Funicular

Bergen's popular funicular climbs 1,000 feet in seven minutes to the top of Mount Fløyen for the best view of the town, surrounding islands, and fjords all the way to the west coast. The top is a popular picnic spot. The **$$ Fløien Folkerestaurant,** the white building at the top of the funicular, offers affordable self-service food all day in season. Behind the station, you'll find a playground and a fun giant troll photo op. The top is also the starting point for many peaceful hikes.

You'll buy your funicular ticket at the base of the Fløibanen (notice the photos in the entry hall of the construction of the funicular and its 1918 grand opening).

If you'll want to hike down from the top, ask for the *Fløyen Hiking Map* when you buy your ticket; you'll save 50 percent by purchasing only a one-way ticket up. From the top, walk behind the station and follow the signs to the city center. The top half of the 30-minute hike is a gravelly lane through a forest with fine views. The bottom is a paved lane passing charming you could ride the lift most of the way down and get off at the Promsgate stop to wander through the delightful cobbled and shiplap lanes (note that only the :00 and :30 departures stop at Promsgate).

Cost and Hours: 90 NOK round-trip, 45 NOK one-way, lines can be long if cruise ships are in town—buy tickets online to skip the line; Mon-Fri 7:30-23:00, Sat-Sun from 8:00, departures 4/hour—on the quarter-hour most of the day, runs continuously if busy; tel. 55 33 68 00, www.floyen.no.

▲St. Mary's Church (Mariakirken)

The oldest parish church and preserved building in Bergen dates to between 1130 and 1170, and is said to be one of the best-decorated medieval churches in Norway. For many years, St. Mary's Church was known as the "German Church," as it was used by the German merchants of the Hanseatic League from 1408 to 1766. The last service in German was held in 1906. The stony interior is accented with a golden altarpiece, a Baroque pulpit of Dutch origin partly made from exotic materials (such as turtle skin), and artworks from various time periods.

Cost and Hours: 50 NOK, Mon-Fri 9:00-16:00, closed mid-Sept-May; 25-minute English guided tour (75 NOK, including church entry) runs June-Aug Mon-Fri at 15:30; http://bergendomkirke.no, tel. 55 59 71 75.

Cathedral (Domkirke)

Bergen's main church, dedicated to St. Olav (the patron saint of Norway), dates from 1301. The cathedral may be closed for renovation during your visit, but if it's open, drop in to enjoy its stoic, plain interior with stuccoed stone walls and a giant wooden pulpit. Sit in a hard, straight-backed pew and just try to doze off. Like so many old Norwegian structures, its roof makes you feel like you're huddled under an overturned Viking ship. The church is oddly lop-sided, with just one side aisle. Before leaving, look up to see the gorgeous wood-carved organ over the main entrance. In the entry-way, you'll see portraits of each bishop dating all the way back to the Reformation.

Cost and Hours: Free; Mon-Fri 10:00-16:00, Sun 9:30-13:00, closed Sat; shorter hours mid-Aug-mid-June.

Leprosy Museum (Lepramuseet)

Leprosy is also known as "Hansen's Disease" because in the 1870s a Bergen man named Armauer Hansen did groundbreaking work in understanding the ail-

ment. This unique muse-um is in St. Jørgens Hos-pital, a leprosarium that dates back to about 1700. Up until the 19th century, as much as 3 percent of Norway's population had leprosy. This hospital—once called "a graveyard for the living" (its last patient died in 1946)—has a meager exhibit in a thought-provoking dorm for the dying. It's most worthwhile if you read the translation of the exhibit (borrow a copy at the entry) or take the free tour (at the top of each hour). As you leave, if you're interested, ask if you can see the medicinal herb garden out back.

Cost and Hours: 80 NOK, half-price with ticket to another Bergen City Museum, daily 11:00-15:00, closed Sept-mid-May, between train station and Bryggen at Kong Oscars Gate 59, tel. 55 30 80 30, www.bymuseet.no.

▲KODE Art Museums

If you need to get out of the rain (and you enjoyed the National Gallery in Oslo), check out this collection, filling four neighbor-

ing buildings facing the lake along Rasmus Meyers Allé. The KODE 4 building, on the far left, has an eclectic cross-section of both international and Norwegian artists. The KODE 3 branch specializes in Nor-wegian artists and has an espe-cially good Munch exhibit. The KODE 2 building has installa-tions of contemporary art and a big bookstore on the first floor, while the KODE 1 building has decorative arts and silver crafts from Bergen. Small description sheets in English are in each room.

Cost and Hours: 100 NOK, daily 11:00-17:00 except KODE 3 10:00-18:00, closed Mon mid-Sept-mid-May, Rasmus Meyers Allé 3, tel. 53 00 97 04, www.kodebergen.no.

▲Aquarium (Akvariet)

Small but fun, this aquarium claims to be the second-most-visited sight in Bergen. It's wonderfully laid out and explained in English. Check out the view from inside the "shark tunnel" in the tropical shark exhibit.

Cost and Hours: 270 NOK, kids-185 NOK, daily May-Aug 9:00-18:00, shorter hours off-season, feeding times at the top of most hours in summer, cheery cafeteria with light sandwiches, Nordnesbakken 4, tel. 55 55 71 71, www.akvariet.no.

Getting There: It's at the tip of the peninsula on the south end of the harbor—about a 20-minute walk or short ride on bus #11 from the city center. Or hop on the handy little *Vågen* "Akvariet" ferry that sails from the Fish Market to near the aquarium (50 NOK one-way, 80 NOK round-trip, show ferry ticket for 20 percent off aquarium admission, 2/hour, 10-minute ride, June-Aug 10:00-17:30, off-season until 16:00).

Nearby: The lovely park behind the aquarium has views of the sea and a popular swimming beach.

▲Gamle Bergen (Old Bergen)

This Disney-cute gathering of 50-some 18th- through 20th-century homes and shops was founded in 1934 to save old buildings from destruction as Bergen modernized. Each of the buildings was moved from elsewhere in Bergen and reconstructed here. Together, they create a virtual town that offers a cobbled look at the old life. It's free to wander through the town and park to enjoy the facades of the historic buildings, but to get into the 20 or so museum buildings, you'll have to join a tour (departing on the hour 10:00-16:00).

Cost and Hours: 100 NOK, half-price with ticket to another Bergen City Museum, daily 9:00-16:00, closed Sept-mid-May, tel. 55 39 43 04, www.bymuseet.no.

Getting There: Take any bus heading west from Bryggen (such as #4, #5, or #6, direction: Lønborglien) to Gamle Bergen (stop: Gamle Bergen). You'll get off after the tunnel at a freeway pullout and walk 200 yards, following signs to the museum. Any bus heading back into town takes you to the center (buses come by every few minutes). With the easy bus connection, there's no reason to taxi.

NEAR BERGEN

▲Ulriken643 Cable Car

It's amazingly easy and quick to zip up six minutes to the 643-meter-high (that's 2,110 feet) summit of Ulriken, the tallest mountain near Bergen. Stepping out of the cable car, you enter a different world, with views stretching to the ocean. A chart clearly shows the many well-marked and easy hikes that fan out over the vast, rocky, grassy plateau above the tree line (circular walks of various lengths, a 40-minute hike down, and a 4-hour hike to the top of the Fløibanen funicular). For less exercise, you can simply sunbathe, crack open a picnic, or enjoy the Ulriken restaurant.

Cost and Hours: 110 NOK one-way, 170 NOK round-trip, 8/hour, daily 9:00-21:00, off-season until 17:00, tel. 53 64 36 43, www.ulriken643.no.

Getting There: It's about three miles southeast of Bergen. From the Fish Market, you can take a blue double-decker shuttle bus that includes the cost of the cable-car ride (270 NOK, ticket valid 24 hours, May-Sept daily

9:00-13:00, hourly, departs from the corner of Torgallmenningen and Strandgaten, buy ticket as you board or at TI). Alternatively, public buses #2 and #3 run from Småstrandgaten in the city center and stop 200 yards from the lift station.

▲▲Edvard Grieg's Home, Troldhaugen

Norway's greatest composer spent his last 22 summers here (1885-1907), soaking up inspirational fjord beauty and composing many

of his greatest works. Grieg fused simple Norwegian folk tunes with the bombast of Europe's Romantic style. In a dreamy Victorian setting, Grieg's "Hill of the Trolls" is pleasant for anyone and essential for diehard fans. You can visit his house on your own, but it's more enjoyable if you take the included 20-minute tour. The house and adjacent museum are full of memories and artifacts, including the composer's Steinway. The walls are festooned with photos of the musical and literary superstars of his generation. When the hugely popular Grieg died in 1907, 40,000 mourners attended his funeral. His little studio hut near the water makes you want to sit down and modulate.

Cost and Hours: 100 NOK, includes guided tour in English, daily 9:00-18:00, Oct-April 10:00-16:00, café, tel. 55 92 29 92, www.griegmuseum.no.

Grieg Lunch Concert: Troldhaugen offers a great guided tour/concert package that includes a shuttle bus from the Bergen

TI to the doorstep of Grieg's home on the fjord (departs 11:00), an hour-long tour of the home, a half-hour concert (Grieg's greatest piano hits, at 13:00), and the ride back into town (you're back in the center by 14:25). Your guide will narrate the ride out of town as well as take you around Grieg's house (250 NOK, daily May-Sept). Lunch isn't included, but there is a café on site, or you could bring a sandwich along. While the tour rarely sells out, it's wise to drop by the TI earlier that day to reserve your spot.

Getting to Troldhaugen: It's six miles south of Bergen. The Bybanen tram drops you a long 20-minute walk away from Troldhaugen. Catch the tram in the city center at its terminus near Byparken (between the lake and Ole Bulls Plass), ride it for about 25 minutes, and get off at the stop called Hop. Walk in the direction of Bergen (about 25 yards), cross at the crosswalk, and follow signs to Troldhaugen. Part of the way is on a pedestrian/bike path; you're halfway there when the path crosses over a busy highway. If you want to make the 13:00 lunchtime concert, leave Bergen at 12:00.

To avoid the long walk from the tram stop, consider the Grieg Lunch Concert package (described earlier).

Fantoft Stave Church

This huge, preserved-in-tar stave church burned down in 1992. It was rebuilt and reopened in 1997, but it will never be the same. Situated in a quiet forest next to a mysterious stone cross, this replica of a 12th-century wooden church is bigger, though no better, than others covered in this book. But it's worth a look if you're in the neighborhood, even after-hours, for its atmospheric setting.

Cost and Hours: 60 NOK, mid-May-mid-Sept daily 10:30-18:00, interior closed off-season, no English information, tel. 55 28 07 10, www.fantoftstavkirke.com.

Getting There: It's three miles south of Bergen on E-39 in Paradis. Take the Bybanen tram (from Byparken, between the lake and Ole Bulls Plass) or bus #83 (from Torget, by the Fish Market) to the Paradis stop (not the "Fantoft" stop). From Paradis, walk uphill to the parking lot on the left, and find the steep footpath to the church.

Shopping in Bergen

Most shops are open Monday through Friday 9:00-17:00, Thursday until 19:00, Saturday 9:00-15:00, and closed Sunday. Many of the tourist shops at the harborfront strip along Bryggen are open daily—even during holidays—until 20:00 or 21:00. You'll see the same products offered at different prices, so shopping around can be a good idea.

Ting (Things) offers a fun alternative to troll shopping, with contemporary housewares and quirky gift ideas (daily 9:00-22:30, at Bryggen 13, a block past the Hanseatic Museum, tel. 55 21 54 80).

Nilssen på Bryggen, next to the Hanseatic Museum, is one of the oldest shops in Bergen. You'll find Norwegian yarn for knitting and modern-style Sandnes wool sweaters, along with souvenirs and hand-embroidered Christmas items (Mon-Sat 10:00-18:00, closed Sun, Bryggen 3, tel. 55 31 67 90).

Husfliden is a shop popular for its handmade goodies and reliably Norwegian sweaters (fine variety and quality but expensive, just off Torget, the market square, at Vågsallmenninge 3, tel. 55 54 47 40).

The Galleriet Mall, a shopping center on Torgallmenningen, holds six floors of shops, cafés, and restaurants. You'll find a pharmacy, photo shops, clothing, sporting goods, bookstores, mobile-phone shops, and a basement grocery store (Mon-Fri 9:00-21:00, Sat 9:00-18:00, closed Sun).

Eating in Bergen

Bergen has numerous choices: restaurants with rustic, woody atmosphere, candlelight, and steep prices; trendy pubs and cafés that offer good-value meals; cafeterias, chain restaurants, and ethnic eateries with less ambience where you can get quality food at lower prices; and takeaway sandwich shops, bakeries, and cafés for a light bite.

You can always get a glass or pitcher of water at no charge, and fancy places give you free seconds on potatoes—just ask. Remember, if you get your food to go, it's taxed at a lower rate and you'll save 12 percent.

BERGEN

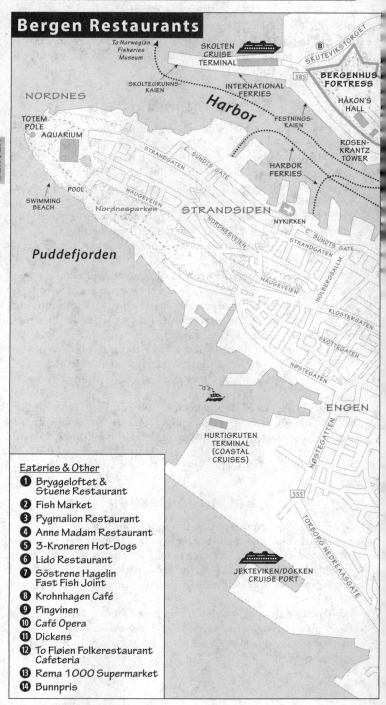

Bergen Restaurants

Eaterie & Other

1. Bryggeloftet & Stuene Restaurant
2. Fish Market
3. Pygmalion Restaurant
4. Anne Madam Restaurant
5. 3-Kroneren Hot-Dogs
6. Lido Restaurant
7. Söstrene Hagelin Fast Fish Joint
8. Krohnhagen Café
9. Pingvinen
10. Café Opera
11. Dickens
12. To Fløien Folkerestaurant Cafeteria
13. Rema 1000 Supermarket
14. Bunnpris

BERGEN

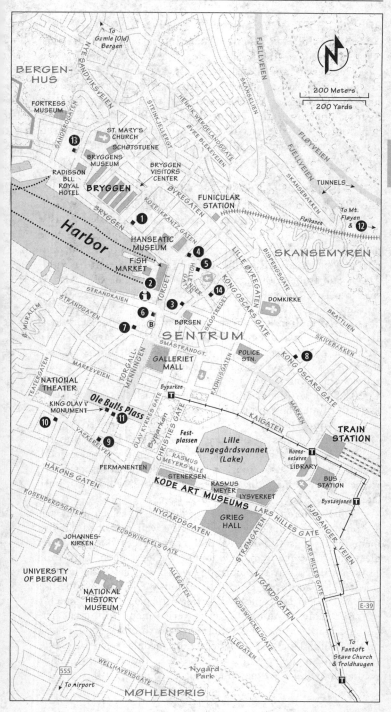

SPLURGE AT BRYGGEN

$$$ Bryggeloftet & Stuene Restaurant, in a brick building just before the wooden stretch of Bryggen, is a vast eatery serving seafood, vegetarian, and traditional meals. You'll pay a premium to eat, but you'll have a memorable meal in a pleasant setting. Upstairs feels more elegant and less touristy than the main floor—if there's a line downstairs, just head on up (Mon-Sat 11:00-23:30, Sun from 13:00, try reserving a view window upstairs—no reservations for outside seating, #11 on Bryggen harborfront, tel. 55 30 20 70).

THE FISH MARKET AND NEARBY

The **Fish Market** has lots of stalls bursting with salmon sandwiches, fresh shrimp, fish-and-chips, and fish cakes. For a tasty, memorable, and inexpensive Bergen meal, assemble a seafood picnic here (ask for prices first; May-Oct daily 8:00-23:00, vendors may close early if they're not busy; Nov-Dec Mon-Sat 9:00-21:00, Sun from 11:00; Jan-April Sat only 9:00-15:00). Also be sure to peruse the places next door on the ground floor of the TI building, Torghallen.

$$ Pygmalion Restaurant has a happy salsa vibe, with local art on the walls and a fun, healthy international menu. It's run with creativity and passion by Sissel. Her burgers are a hit, and there are always good vegetarian options, hearty salads, and pancakes (wraps, burgers, main plates, Mon-Sat 11:00-22:00, Sun 12:00-23:00, two blocks inland from the Fish Market at Nedre Korskirkealmenning 4, tel. 55 31 32 60).

$$ Anne Madam Restaurant serves up well-priced Norwegian-inspired dishes in a laidback atmosphere. It's close to the Fish Market and a good choice if you are up for some seafood, though they also serve traditional Norwegian meat dishes (sandwiches, burgers, main dishes, Sun-Thu 11:00-23:00, Fri-Sat until late, Kong Oscars Gate 2a, tel. 46 52 06 62).

$ 3-Kroneren, your classic hot-dog stand, sells a wide variety of sausages (including reindeer). The well-described English menu makes it easy to order your choice of artery-clogging guilty pleasures (tiny, medium, and jumbo weenies; open daily from 11:00 until 5:00 in the morning—you'll see the little hot-dog shack a block up Kong Oscars Gate from the harbor, Kenneth is the boss). Each dog comes with a free little glass of fruit punch.

$$$ Lido Restaurant offers a varied menu with great harbor and market views and a museum's worth of old-town photos on the walls. Lunch, served until 17:00, includes open-face sandwiches and small plates (Mon-Sat 11:00-22:00, Sun until 23:00; second floor at Torgallmenningen 1a, tel. 55 32 59 12).

$ Söstrene Hagelin Fast Fish Joint is an easygoing eatery that's cheerier than its offerings—a pale extravaganza of Norway's white cuisine: fish soup, fish burgers, fish balls, fish cakes, fish wraps, and even fish pudding (Mon-Fri 9:00-19:00, Sat 10:00-17:00, closed Sun, Strandgaten 3, tel. 55 90 20 13).

$ Krohnhagen Café, a humble community center next to a retirement home, is run by the church and partly staffed by volunteers. While it's designed to give Bergen's poor (and the retired) an inviting place to enjoy, everyone's welcome (it's a favorite of local guides). The dining area is bright and spacious, the staff friendly, and the menu is simple yet tasty (salad, soup, waffles, cheap sandwiches, Mon-Fri 11:00-16:00, closed Sat-Sun, Wi-Fi, Kong Oscars Gate 54, tel. 45 22 07 95).

CHARACTERISTIC PLACES NEAR OLE BULLS PLASS

Bergen's "in" cafés are stylish, cozy, small, and open very late. Around the cinema on Neumannsgate, there are numerous ethnic restaurants, including Italian, Middle Eastern, and Chinese.

$$$ Pingvinen ("The Penguin") is a homey place in a charming neighborhood, serving traditional Norwegian home cooking to an enthusiastic local clientele. The pub has only indoor seating, with a long row of stools at the bar and five charming, living-room-cozy tables—a great setup for solo diners. For Norwegian fare in an untouristy atmosphere, this is a good, affordable option. Their seasonal menu (reindeer in the fall, whale in the spring) is listed on the board (nightly until 22:00, Vaskerelven 14 near the National Theater, tel. 55 60 46 46).

$$$ Café Opera, with a playful-slacker vibe and chessboards for the regulars, is the hip budget choice for its loyal, youthful following. With two floors of seating and tables out front across from the theater, it's a winner (light sandwiches until 16:00, daily 10:00-23:30, Engen 18, tel. 55 23 03 15).

$$$ Dickens is a lively, checkerboard-tiled, turn-of-the-century-feeling place. The window tables in the atrium are great for people-watching, as is the fine outdoor terrace, but you'll pay higher prices for the view (daily 11:00-23:00, Kong Olav V's Plass 4, tel. 55 36 31 30).

ATOP MOUNT FLØYEN

$$ Fløien Folkerestaurant Cafeteria offers meals indoors and out with a panoramic view. It's self-service, with 60-NOK sandwiches and a 139-NOK soup buffet (daily 10:00-22:00, Sept-April Sat-Sun only 12:00-17:00, tel. 55 33 69 99).

What If I Miss My Ship?

Remember that you can get help from the cruise line's port agent (listed on the destination information sheet distributed on the ship) and the local TI (see page 668). If the port agent suggests a costly solution (such as a private car with a driver), you may want to consider public transit.

You can catch the bus to **Stavanger** (tel. 52 70 35 26, http://kystbussen.no). There's also an express boat to **Flåm** (tel. 51 86 87 00, www.norled.no).

Trains work well for other Norwegian destinations. Take the main east-west rail line to **Oslo;** partway along, you can take a bus or train down to the fjord at **Flåm.** For any points **outside Norway,** you're probably best connecting through Oslo. To research train schedules, see www.bahn.com.

If you need to catch a **plane** to your next destination, Bergen's Flesland Airport (tel. 67 03 15 55, www.avinor.no/bergen) is 12 miles south of the city center, connected by airport bus.

For more advice on what to do if you miss the boat, see page 130.

PICNICS AND GROCERIES

The **Rema 1000 supermarket,** just across from the Bryggens Museum and St. Mary's Church, is particularly handy (Mon-Fri 7:00-23:00, Sat 8:00-21:00, closed Sun). For groceries on a Sunday, check out **Bunnpris**—just a short walk inland from the Fish Market, across the street from Korskirken church (Mon-Fri 8:00-22:00, Sat from 9:00, Sun from 10:00, Nedre Korskirkeallmenningen 3a).

Norwegian Survival Phrases

Norwegian can be pronounced quite differently from region to region. These phrases and phonetics match the mainstream Oslo dialect, but you'll notice variations. Vowels can be tricky: *å* sounds like "oh," *æ* sounds like a bright "ah" (as in "apple"), and *u* sounds like the German *ü* (purse your lips and say u). Certain vowels at the ends of words (such as *d* and *t*) are sometimes barely pronounced (or not at all). In some dialects, the letters *sk* are pronounced "sh." In the phonetics, ī sounds like the long i in "light," and bolded syllables are stressed.

BERGEN

English	Norwegian	Pronunciation
Hello. (formal)	*God dag.*	goo dahg
Hi. / Bye. (informal)	*Hei. / Ha det.*	hī / hah deh
Do you speak English?	*Snakker du engelsk?*	snahk-kehr dew **eng**-ehlsk
Yes. / No.	*Ja. / Nei.*	yah / nī
Please.	*Vær så snill.*	vayr soh sneel
Thank you (very much).	*(Tusen) takk.*	(**tew**-sehn) tahk
You're welcome.	*Vær så god.*	vayr soh goo
Can I help you?	*Kan jeg hjelpe deg?*	kahn yī **yehl**-peh dī
Excuse me.	*Unnskyld.*	**ewn**-shuld
(Very) good.	*(Veldig) fint.*	(**vehl**-dee) feent
Goodbye.	*Farvel.*	fahr-**vehl**
zero / one / two	*null / en / to*	newl / ayn / toh
three / four	*tre / fire*	treh / **fee**-reh
five / six	*fem / seks*	fehm / sehks
seven / eight	*syv / åtte*	seev / **oh**-teh
nine / ten	*ni / ti*	nee / tee
hundred	*hundre*	**hewn**-dreh
thousand	*tusen*	**tew**-sehn
How much?	*Hvor mye?*	voor **mee**-yeh
local currency: (Norwegian) crown	*(Norske) kroner*	(**norsh**-keh) **kroh**-nehr
Where is...?	*Hvor er...?*	voor ehr
...the toilet	*...toalettet*	toh-ah-**leh**-teh
men	*menn / herrer*	mehn / **hehr**-rehr
women	*damer*	**dah**-mehr
water / coffee	*vann / kaffe*	vahn / **kah**-feh
beer / wine	*øl / vin*	uhl / veen
Cheers!	*Skål!*	skohl
The bill, please.	*Regningen, takk.*	**rī**-ning-ehn tahk

NORWEGIAN FJORDS

Norway Practicalities

Norway (Norge) is stacked with super-latives—it's the most mountainous, most scenic, and most prosperous of all the Scandinavian countries. Perhaps above all, Norway is a land of intense natural beauty, its famously steep mountains and deep fjords carved out and shaped by an ancient ice age. Norway (148,700 square miles—just larger than Montana) is on the western side of the Scandinavian Peninsula, with most of the country sharing a border with Sweden to the east. Rich in resources like timber, oil, and fish, Norway has rejected joining the European Union, mainly to protect its fishing rights. Where the country extends north of the Arctic Circle, the sun never sets at the height of summer and never comes up in the deep of winter. The majority of Norway's 5.3 million people consider themselves Lutheran.

Money: 8 Norwegian kroner (NOK) = about $1. An ATM is called a *minibank*. The local VAT (value-added sales tax) rate is 25 percent; the minimum purchase eligible for a VAT refund is 315 NOK (for details on refunds, see page 125).

Language: The native language is Norwegian (the two official forms are Bokmål and Nynorsk). For useful phrases, see page 726.

Emergencies: Dial 112 for police, medical, or other emergencies. In case of theft or loss, see page 118.

Time Zone: Norway is on Central European Time (the same as most of the Continent, one hour ahead of Great Britain, and six/nine hours ahead of the East/West Coasts of the US).

Embassies in Oslo: The **US embassy** is at Morgedalsvegen 36 (tel. 21 30 85 58, emergency tel. 21 30 85 40, https://no.usembassy.gov). The **Canadian embassy** is at Wergelandsveien 7 (tel. 22 99 53 00, www.canadainternational.gc.ca/norway-norvege). Call ahead for passport services.

Phoning: With a mobile phone, it's easy to dial: Press and hold zero until you get a + sign, enter the country code (47 for Norway, 1 for the US/Canada), then the complete phone number (including area code if there is one). When dialing a European phone number, drop an initial zero (except if calling Italy). For more tips, see page 1062.

Tipping: Service is included at sit-down meals, but this goes to the owner, so for great service it's nice to round up your bill about 10 percent. Tip a taxi driver by rounding up the fare (pay 90 NOK on an 85-NOK fare). For more tips on tipping, see page 129.

Tourist Information: www.goscandinavia.com

NORWEGIAN FJORDS

Flåm, the Sognefjord, and Norway in a Nutshell • Geirangerfjord

While Oslo and Bergen are fine cities, Norway is first and foremost a place of unforgettable natural beauty—and its greatest claims to scenic fame are its deep, lush fjords. Three million years ago, an ice age made this land as inhabitable as the center of Greenland. As the glaciers advanced and cut their way to the sea, they gouged out long grooves—today's fjords. The entire west coast of the country is slashed by stunning fjords.

Various Norwegian cruise ports offer a taste of fjord scenery (Oslo, Bergen, and Stavanger are all situated on or near fjords), but many cruises also head for two particularly scenic and accessible fjords unencumbered by big cities: the Sognefjord (at the village of Flåm) and the Geirangerfjord. Flåm is the hub for a well-coordinated web of train, boat, and bus connections—appropriately

nicknamed the "Norway in a Nutshell" route—that let you see some of Norway's best scenery efficiently on a tour or on your own. Geirangerfjord, more remote, works best by excursion.

Flåm, the Sognefjord, and Norway in a Nutshell

Among the fjords, the Sognefjord—Norway's longest (120 miles) and deepest (1 mile)—is tops. The seductive Sognefjord has tiny but tough ferries, towering canyons, and isolated farms and villages marinated in the mist of countless waterfalls.

While the port town of Flåm itself has modest charms, with a Norway in a Nutshell day-trip, you'll delve into two offshoots of the Sognefjord, which make an upside-down "U" route: the Aurlandsfjord and the Nærøyfjord. This trip brings you right back to where you started in 6.5-7.5 hours—after cruising Norway's narrowest fjord, riding a bus along an impossibly twisty and waterfall-lined road, taking the train across the mountainous spine of the country, then dropping back down to sea level on yet another super-scenic train. All connections are designed for tourists, explained in English, convenient, and described in this chapter.

This region enjoys mild weather for its latitude, thanks to the warm Gulf Stream. (When it rains in Bergen, it just drizzles here.) But if the weather is bad, don't fret. I've often arrived to gloomy weather, only to enjoy sporadic splashes of brilliant sunshine all day long.

PLANNING YOUR TIME

There's very little to do in Flåm itself. If you're here for a full day, do the Nutshell loop (unless you're on a tight budget or your cruise schedule doesn't allow it, in which case you can still do one or two of the segments). Here are your options:

Norway in a Nutshell Round-Trip: This ultimate boat, bus, and train journey takes 6.5-7.5 hours. You'll enjoy a cruise from Flåm to Gudvangen (including along the stunning Nærøyfjord), ride a bus up from the fjord to join Norway's main train line in the town of Voss, then take a scenic train ride to the mountaintop town of Myrdal, and finally, catch the Flåmsbana mountain line train steeply back down to Flåm. Check your return time carefully.

"Poor Man's Nutshell": If your schedule doesn't allow the full Nutshell, you could cobble together its two best parts in about five hours: the Nærøyfjord cruise and the round-trip on the Flåmsbana train (take the boat to Gudvangen, return to Flåm by a 20-minute bus or shuttle ride, then hop aboard the Flåmsbana). This one-two punch lets you see the best of the Nutshell.

Flåmsbana Mountain Train Only: From Flåm, you can take a round-trip on the Flåmsbana train steeply into the mountains, then back down into the valley. Allow an hour each way on the

Excursions from Flåm

Cruise lines push their own version of the **Norway in a Nutshell** loop, sometimes billed as "Best of Flåm"; you'll likely take some of the same boats, buses, and trains that are available to the public (though some legs may be chartered). Fjords Tours sells the same package online in advance for a much cheaper price. You can also do the Nutshell independently, but you'll have to buy each leg separately.

Other excursion options from Flåm include various individual legs of the Nutshell, such as the **Flåmsbana** mountain train up to Myrdal and back, or a cruise on the **Nærøyfjord**. You may also be offered a **kayak trip** on the Aurlandsfjord (near Flåm). All of these are easy to book yourself. However, a few farther-flung options are more challenging to reach by public transit, and worth considering by excursion, such as a visit to **Borgund Stave Church.**

train, plus time at the top station, Myrdal (not much to see—basically killing time before the return train).

Nærøyfjord Cruise Only: While the first half of this cruise (from Flåm to Gudvangen) is redundant with your cruise ship's sail-away, the second half takes you to the Nærøyfjord, which is too skinny for big ships. From Gudvangen, you can zip back to Flåm on a bus or shuttle (20 minutes), or cruise all the way back (1.5-2 hours). Depending on connections, allow at least 3 hours round-trip if returning by bus or 5 hours if cruising both ways.

Flåm: There's little to do in Flåm other than shopping or dipping into the Railway Museum. Consider renting a boat for a ride on the fjord, taking one of the high-speed boat tours with Fjord-Safari, or going for a hike (the TI hands out a map suggesting local walks).

Outlying Sights: Several intriguing sights lie outside of Flåm, not easily reachable by public transportation. These include **Otternes Farms** and other **fjordside villages** (such as Undredal). While it's possible to reach some of these by renting an electric car, a better option is likely the package tours offered by The Fjords (www.visitflam.com).

The **Borgund Stave Church,** one of Norway's finest, sits 35 miles from Flåm. While visiting the church itself takes an hour or so, the whole excursion by public bus from Flåm takes around three hours round-trip. That's a long way to go just to see a church—but it's one of the best examples anywhere of this uniquely Norwegian church architecture (and includes a museum).

Strategies: In this destination (even more than others), it pays to do some homework and make a plan before you step off the ship. Smart travelers will buy tickets in advance (4-5 weeks), especially for the Nutshell package, the Flåmsbana mountain train (particularly morning trains leaving from Flåm), and the Voss-Myrdal train (if doing the Nutshell on your own). The fjord cruises can also book up on busy days in summer. Without advance tickets, line up early to be one of the first ashore (especially if tendering)—you won't regret it, as those few extra minutes might help you beat the crowds to the TI or visitors center (lines form early). See "Touring the Nutshell," later, for details on where to buy tickets, both locally and online.

Connections are generally coordinated to work efficiently together, but double-check locally to ensure you'll return on time.

Port of Flåm

Arrival at a Glance: From your ship or tender, it's a very short stroll to the train station and boat dock. The key is deciding what you want to do before you get off the ship and getting an early start.

Port Overview

Little Flåm has space for one big cruise ship to **dock** at its pier; stepping off your ship, you'll turn left, go through the port gate, and walk between the water and a row of shops to reach the train station area.

Entering the train station through the door facing the pier, you'll find the TI on your right and the Flåm Visitors Center on your left (both sell various train, boat, and tour tickets—see "Orientation to Flåm," below). The electronic board above the ticket desk notes which, if any, of today's Flåm-Myrdal train departures are sold out. Farther into the station are a gift shop and a cafeteria.

If multiple ships are in town, some will anchor in the harbor and **tender** passengers to the pier right in front of the train station.

Flåm and the Nutshell

Flåm (pronounced "flome")— at the head of the Aurlandsfjord—feels more like a transit junction than a village. But its striking setting, easy transportation connections, and touristy bustle make it a good springboard for the popular Norway in a Nutshell experience, as well as other scenic day trips.

Orientation to Flåm

The train station has most of the town services. The boat dock for fjord cruises is just beyond the end of the tracks. Surrounding the station are a Co-op grocery store and a smattering of hotels, trav-

Services near the Port

Though it's a small town, Flåm has much of what you need. Most of Flåm's services are in a modern cluster of buildings in and around the train station, including the TI, Flåm Visitors Center ticket desk, public WC, cafeteria, an ATM, and souvenir shops.

Grocery Store: The Co-op grocery, near the cruise dock, has a basic pharmacy and post office inside (Mon-Fri 8:00-20:00, Sat-Sun 10:00-18:00, shorter hours off-season).

Pharmacy: There's no real pharmacy in Flåm, but you will find some basics in the **Co-op** grocery store. The nearest pharmacy is in **Lærdal** (just east, through the world's longest car tunnel); if you're doing the Nutshell route, note that there's a pharmacy in **Voss** (Vitus Apotek, a 5-minute walk into town from the train station and a few doors down from the TI, facing the town church at Vangsgatan 22D, closed Sun).

Electric Car Rental: During the summer, eMobility Flåm rents two-person electric cars that come with self-guided tours to viewpoints and nearby attractions (Nedre Fretheim 15, tel. 46 41 17 77, http://emobflam.no).

NORWEGIAN FJORDS

el agencies, and touristy restaurants. Aside from a few scattered farmhouses and some homes lining the road, there's not much of a town here. (The extremely sleepy old town center—where tourists rarely venture, and which you'll pass on the Flåmsbana train—is a few miles up the river, in the valley.)

Tourist Information: Inside the train station you'll find the TI (look for the green-and-white *i* sign) and the Flåm Visitors Center.

The **visitors center** sells tickets for Fjord Tours' packages and The Fjords' ferries to Gudvangen (but not the Flåm-Gudvangen cruises offered by rival Lustrabaatane), the Flåmsbana train, regular train tickets, and other tours in the area (daily 7:00-19:00, shorter hours Sept-April, tel. 57 63 14 00, www.visitflam.com).

At the **TI** you can purchase tickets for the express boat to Bergen, FjordSafari, Njord Seakayak Adventures, and other tours. The TI also hands out schedules for buses, boats, and trains; a diagram of the train-station area, identifying services available in each building; a map of Flåm and the surrounding area, marked with suggested walks and hikes; and information on Bergen or Oslo (daily 8:30-18:00, Oct-March 9:00-15:00, mobile 99 23 15 00, https://en.sognefjord.no).

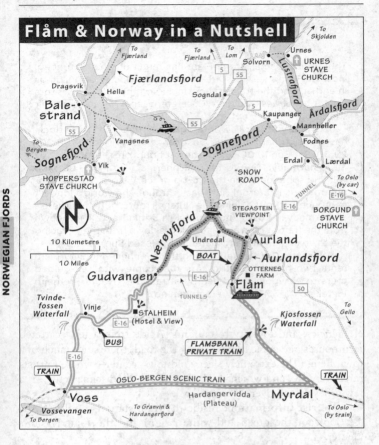

Flåm & Norway in a Nutshell

To Skjolden →

To Fjærland ↑

Urnes
Solvorn
URNES STAVE CHURCH

Lustrafjord

To Fjærland
To Lom

Fjærlandsfjord

Dragsvik   Hella

Bale-strand

Sogndal

5

55

Kaupanger   Årdalsfjord

Vangsnes

Sognefjord

Mannheller
Fodnes

To Bergen

Sognefjord

Vik

Erdal   Lærdal

HOPPERSTAD STAVE CHURCH

"SNOW ROAD"

To Oslo (by car)
E-16

TUNNEL

10 Kilometers

STEGASTEIN VIEWPOINT

E-16

BORGUND STAVE CHURCH

10 Miles

Nærøyfjord

Undredal

Aurland

Gudvangen

BOAT

Aurlandsfjord

OTTERNES FARM

Flåm

TUNNELS

50

Tvinde-fossen Waterfall

Vinje

STALHEIM (Hotel & View)

E-16

Kjosfossen Waterfall

To Geilo →

E-16

BUS

FLAMSBANA PRIVATE TRAIN

TRAIN

OSLO-BERGEN SCENIC TRAIN

TRAIN

Voss

Hardangervidda (Plateau)

Myrdal

Vossevangen
To Bergen

To Granvin & Hardangerfjord

To Oslo (by train)

Norway in a Nutshell Loop

The most exciting single-day trip you could make from Flåm is this circular boat/bus/train jaunt through fjord country.

From Flåm, the basic idea is this: Begin with a cruise on two arms of the Sognefjord (Flåm to Gudvangen), ride a bus up from the fjord to join Norway's main train line (Gudvangen to Voss), and ride that train to catch a different train steeply back down to Flåm and the fjord (Voss to Myrdal and back to Flåm). For cruisers, this loop is only practical if done in this order, counterclockwise. The op-

posite direction (Flåm-Myrdal-Voss-Gudvangen-Flåm) returns to Flåm too late for most cruise ships.

Though it sounds complicated, it's actually quite easy: The connections are carefully coordinated and require almost no walking. In Gudvangen, the bus meets the ferry at the dock; in Voss, the bus drops you at the train station; and at Myrdal, you cross the platform to catch the Flåmsbana mountain train back to Flåm. If any segment of your journey is delayed, the next segment will wait for you. But be sure to leave a cushion between your scheduled return and your cruise departure.

TOURING THE NUTSHELL

To do the whole Nutshell, it's easiest to purchase a package. It's possible to do it on your own, but you'll have to buy each leg separately. You can also do just one or two segments of the Nutshell on your own.

With a Package: The easiest way to purchase Nutshell tickets is to buy a package from Fjord Tours—it will save you time and the trouble of planning your itinerary. Packages start at 1,130 NOK, which covers all of the tickets and reservations you need (price depends on which boat option you choose). The Nutshell ticket by Fjord Tours cannot be purchased in Flåm—your best option is to buy it in advance online and have it printed at the visitor center when you arrive (tel. 81 56 82 22, www.fjordtours.com—select "Norway in a Nutshell" and choose the day trip option starting from Flåm and following the counterclockwise route). If your cruise visits Bergen or Oslo before landing in Flåm, you can purchase the package at the train station or TI in either city. To follow my recommended route, ask for a round-trip from Flåm "starting by fjord-cruise boat."

On Your Own: You may be able to save some money by doing the Nutshell on your own (you may find discounts for the train and can choose the cheapest ferry)—but you'll have to plan your itinerary and buy tickets for each leg of your journey, sometimes at separate ticket offices. Or you may want to do only part of the Nutshell tour. Good options include the Flåmsbana mountain train connecting Flåm with Myrdal (on top of a mountain, with great views); the scenic fjord cruise from Flåm to Gudvangen (return via bus or shuttle); or both (what I call the "Poor Man's Nutshell").

If planning to do any or all of the Nutshell independently, see the "On Your Own" sections (with ticket-buying and schedule information) listed under each leg of my self-guided Nutshell tour, next, and confirm schedules, connections, and prices online (www.kringom.no). It's also smart to check locally with the TI and/or visitors center to ensure you can make all the connections and return to your ship in time.

Ticket Tips: Whether you are doing a package deal or buying tickets on your own, in summer book well in advance—four to five weeks is best. Be aware that certain legs can sell out during busy times, such as the Voss-Myrdal train and the Flåmsbana mountain train (book both ahead at www.nsb.no). The Flåm-Gudvangen ferries are run by two competing companies: The Fjords (more sailings, www.visitflam.com) and Lustrabaatane (cheaper prices, www.lustrabaatane.no); reservations for these boats may be necessary on busy days in summer.

If you wait to buy tickets locally, note that there are two locations (both described earlier, under "Orientation to Flåm").

Eating Tips: Options along the route aren't great—on the Nutshell I'd consider food just as a source of nutrition and forget about fine dining. You can buy some food on the fjord cruises (hot dogs, burgers, and pizza) and the train. Depending on the timing of your layovers, Myrdal, Voss, or Flåm are your best lunch-stop options (the Myrdal and Flåm train stations have decent cafeterias, and other eateries surround the Flåm and Voss stations)—although you won't have a lot of time there if you're making the journey all in one day. Your best bet is to pack picnic meals and munch en route. Or consider discreetly raiding your cruise ship's breakfast buffet. (As this is frowned upon, don't tell them I suggested it.)

⊙ SELF-GUIDED TOUR

Your tour has four segments (boat-bus-train-train) and travels counterclockwise (Flåm-Gudvangen-Voss-Myrdal-Flåm).

▲▲▲Flåm-Gudvangen Fjord Cruise

From Flåm, scenic sightseeing boats ply the fjord's waters around the corner to Gudvangen. With minimal English narration, the boat takes you close to the goats, sheep, waterfalls, and awesome cliffs.

You'll cruise up the lovely **Aurlandsfjord,** motoring by the town of **Aurland,** pass the towns of **Undredal, Dyrdal,** and **Styvi,** and hang a left at the stunning **Nærøyfjord.** The cruise ends at the apex of the Nærøyfjord, in **Gudvangen.**

The trip is breathtaking in any weather. For the last hour, as you sail down the Nærøyfjord, camera-clicking tourists scurry around struggling to get a photo that will catch the magic. Waterfalls turn the black cliffs into bridal veils, and you can nearly reach out and touch the cliffs of the Nærøyfjord. It's the world's narrowest fjord: six miles long and as little as 820 feet wide and 40 feet deep. On a sunny day, the ride is one of those fine times—like when you're high on the tip of an Alp—when a warm camaraderie spontaneously combusts between the strangers who've come together for the experience.

On Your Own: There are two boat companies to choose from—The Fjords (www.visitflam.com) and Lustrabaatane (www.lustrabaatane.com). The Fjords has a Classic option (more than 2 hours; stops at Aurland, Undredal, Dyrdal, and Styvi) and a Premium option on a hybrid catamaran that's faster, silent, and more expensive (1.5 hours, no stops). The cheapest option is the Lustrabaatane ferry (2 hours, similar to the Classic ferry but with no stops). I much prefer the slower boats because the price is lower, you have more time to savor the scenery, and the bus connection in Gudvangen is immediate and reliable. However, these slow boats sail less frequently, so plan your itinerary carefully.

For the whole route, you'll pay 250-645 NOK one-way depending on the ferry (430-705 NOK round-trip). Reservations may

be necessary on busy days in summer. Buy your ticket in Flåm as soon as you know which boat you want or in advance at each boat company's website. Beware: The ticket desk at the Flåm Visitors Center is The Fjords boat desk, and they'll sell you a boat ticket implying it's your only option. Tickets for Lustrabaatane are sold online, from a vendor at the dock, or onboard.

In summer (June-Aug), boats run multiple times daily in both directions—Classic ferry (2/day), Premium ferry (5/day), Lustrabaatane ferry (2/day). Specific departure times can vary, but generally boats leave Flåm starting at 8:00, with a last departure at 19:00. See www.kringom.no for schedules covering both ferry lines.

Returning from Gudvangen to Flåm: To head from Gudvangen directly back to Flåm, you can ride a bus or shuttle that cuts through a tunnel to get there in substantially less time than the return boat. Some buses depart from right in front of the boat dock, with others leaving from a stop out on the main E-16 highway (an easy 5-minute walk from the boat—just walk straight ahead off the boat and up the town's lone road, past its few houses, until you reach the big cross street; the bus stop is just across this road). While the specific schedule is often in flux, a bus usually leaves soon after each boat arrives from Flåm—just ask around for where to catch it, or book the shuttle in advance (50-65 NOK, hourly in summer, 20 minutes, www.visitflam.com).

▲Gudvangen-Voss Bus

Nutshellers get off the boat at Gudvangen and take the 25-mile bus ride to Voss. Gudvangen is little more than a boat dock and giant tourist kiosk. If you want, you can browse through the grass-roofed souvenir stores and walk onto a wooden footbridge—then catch your bus. While some buses—designed for commuters rather than sightseers—take the direct route to Voss, buses tied to the Nutshell schedule take a super-scenic detour via Stalheim. If you're a waterfall junkie, sit on the left.

First the bus takes you up the **Nærøydal** and through a couple of long tunnels. Then you'll take a turnoff to drive past the landmark **Stalheim Hotel** for the first of many spectacular views back into fjord country. Though the hotel dates from 1885, there's been an inn here since about 1700, where the royal mailmen would change horses. The hotel is geared for tour groups (genuine trolls sew the pewter buttons on the sweaters), but the priceless view from the backyard is free.

Leaving the hotel, the bus wends its way down a road called **Stalheimskleiva,** with a corkscrew series of switchbacks flanked by a pair of dramatic waterfalls. With its 18 percent grade, it's the steepest road in Norway.

After winding your way down into the valley, you're back on the same highway. The bus goes through those same tunnels again, then continues straight on the main road through pastoral countryside to Voss. You'll pass a huge lake, then follow a crystal-clear, surging river. Just before Voss, look to the right for the wide **Tvindefossen waterfall,** tumbling down its terraced cliff.

On Your Own: 115 NOK, pay on board, cash only, no rail pass discounts. Reservations are not necessary. Buses meet each ferry, or will show up usually within an hour.

Voss

The Nutshell bus from Gudvangen drops you at the Voss train station. A plain town in a lovely lake-and-mountain setting, Voss lacks the striking fjordside scenery of Flåm, Aurland, or Undredal, and is basically a home base for summer or winter sports (Norway's Winter Olympics teams often practice here). Voss surrounds its fine, 13th-century church with workaday streets—busy with both local shops and souvenir stores—stretching in several directions. Fans of American football may want to see the humble monument to player and coach Knute Rockne, who was born in Voss in 1888; look for the metal memorial plaque on a rock near the train station.

Voss' helpful **TI** is a five-minute walk from the train station—just head toward the church and stay on the right; the TI is down the street past the City Hall signed *Voss Tinghus* (Mon-Sat 9:00-18:00, Sun 10:00-17:00; off-season until 16:00 and closed Sat-Sun; Skulegata 14, mobile 40 61 77 00, www.visitvoss.no).

▲▲Voss-Myrdal Train

Although this super-scenic train line (called "Bergensbanen" by Norwegians) stretches 300 miles all the way from Oslo to Bergen, you'll only do a brief, 40-minute segment right in the middle. Even on this short stretch, you'll see deep woods and lakes, as well as barren, windswept heaths and glaciers.

For the best views, sit on the right-hand side of the train. After passing above sprawling Voss, the train goes through two long tunnels and above canyons. You'll enjoy raging-river-and-waterfalls views, then pass over a lake that's very close to the tree line—vegetation clears out and the landscape looks nearly lunar.

Arriving at Myrdal, hop out of the train and cross the platform for the Flåm-bound train. (If it's not there, it will be shortly.)

On Your Own: The Voss-Myrdal segment costs 130 NOK. You can save money on these fares if you book "minipris" tickets in advance at www.nsb.no. If you have difficulty paying for your ticket with a US credit card online, use PayPal or call 61 05 19 10—press 9 for English, and you'll be given a web link where you can finish your transaction. In peak season, get reservations for this train four to five weeks in advance. Local *(lokaltog)* and intercity trains *(fjern-tog,* all the way from Bergen to Oslo) run from Voss to Myrdal 3-5 times per day. They both cost the same, but the local takes about 10 minutes longer (for a total travel time of 50 minutes).

▲▲Myrdal-Flåm Train (Flåmsbana)

The little 12-mile spur line leaves the Oslo-Bergen line at Myrdal (2,800 feet), which is nothing but a scenic high-altitude train junction with a decent cafeteria. Be-fore boarding, pick up the free, multilingual souvenir pamphlet with lots of info on the trip (or see www.flaamsbana.no). Video screens onboard and sporadic English commentary on the loudspeakers explain points of interest, but there's  not much to say—it's all about the scenery. If you're choosing seats, you'll enjoy slightly more scenery if you sit on the left going down.

From Myrdal, the Flåmsbana train winds down to Flåm (sea level) through 20 tunnels (more than three miles' worth) in 55 thrilling minutes. It's party time on board, and the engineer even stops the train for photos at the best waterfall, Kjosfossen. According to a Norwegian legend, Huldra (a temptress) lives behind these falls and tries to lure men to the rocks with her singing...look out for her—and keep a wary eye on your partner.

The train line is an even more impressive feat of engineering when you realize it's not a cogwheel train—it's held to the tracks only by steel wheels, though it does have five separate braking systems.

On Your Own: 390 NOK one-way, 550 NOK round-trip. You can book one-way tickets on www.nsb.no; the cheapest round-trip tickets are on www.visitflam.com (look for "Flåm Railway").

You also can buy tickets onboard the train or at the visitors center in Flåm. The train departs in each direction nearly hourly.

Round-Trip from Flåm: If you don't want to do the whole Nutshell loop, the Flåmsbana train makes a fine round-trip from Flåm. However, because this is such an easy and fast way to reach grand views from Flåm, many of your fellow passengers head straight for this train, and morning tickets can sell out. In summer, if you want to leave Flåm in the morning, it's best to buy your ticket in advance online; otherwise, try to be at the Flåm visitors center ticket office when it opens. If you can wait to do it later in the day, you'll enjoy fewer crowds. But you should still buy your tickets as early as possible, as even the later trains can sell out on busy days.

Other Sights in Flåm

IN THE VILLAGE

Flåm's village activities are all along or near the pier.

The **Flåm Railway Museum** (Flåmsbana Museet), sprawling through the long old train station alongside the tracks, has surprisingly good exhibits about the history of the train that connects Flåm to the main line up above. You'll find good English explanations, artifacts, re-creations of historic interiors (such as a humble schoolhouse), and an old train car. It's the only real museum in town and a good place to kill time while waiting for your boat or train (free, daily 9:00-17:00, until 20:00 in summer).

The Facts on Fjords

The process that created the majestic Sognefjord began during an ice age about three million years ago. A glacier up to 6,500 feet thick slid downhill at an inch an hour, following a former river valley on its way to the sea. Rocks embedded in the glacier gouged out a steep, U-shaped valley, displacing enough rock material to form a mountain 13 miles high. When the climate warmed up, the ice age came to an end. The melting glaciers retreated and the sea level rose nearly 300 feet, flooding the valley now known as the Sognefjord. The fjord is more than a mile deep, flanked by 3,000-foot mountains—for a total relief of 9,300 feet. Waterfalls spill down the cliffs, fed by runoff from today's glaciers. Powdery sediment tinges the fjords a cloudy green, the distinct color of glacier melt.

Why are there fjords on the west coast of Norway, but not, for instance, on the east coast of Sweden? The creation of a fjord requires a setting of coastal mountains, a good source of moisture, and a climate cold enough for glaciers to form and advance. Due to the earth's rotation, the prevailing winds in higher latitudes blow from west to east, so chances of glaciation are ideal where there is an ocean to the west of land with coastal mountains. When the winds blow east over the water, they pick up a lot of moisture, then bump up against the coastal mountain range, and dump their moisture in the form of snow—which feeds the glaciers that carve valleys down to the sea.

You can find fjords along the northwest coast of Europe—including western Norway and Sweden, Denmark's Faroe Islands, Scotland's Shetland Islands, Iceland, and Greenland; the northwest coast of North America (from Puget Sound in Washington state north to Alaska); the southwest coast of South America (Chile); the west coast of New Zealand's South Island; and on the continent of Antarctica.

As you travel through Scandinavia, bear in mind that, while we English-speakers use the word "fjord" to mean only glacier-cut inlets, Scandinavians often use it in a more general sense to include bays, lakes, and lagoons that weren't formed by glacial action.

A pointless and overpriced **tourist train** does a 45-minute loop around Flåm (130 NOK).

The pleasantly woody **Ægir Bryggeri,** a microbrewery designed to resemble an old Viking longhouse, offers tastes of its five beers (150 NOK).

Consider renting a **boat** to go out on the peaceful waters of the fjord. You can paddle near the walls of the fjord and really get a sense of the immensity of these mountains. You can rent rowboats, motorboats, and paddleboats at the little marina across the harbor. If you'd rather have a kayak, **Njord Seakayak Adventures** does kayak tours, but won't rent you one unless you're certified (mobile 91 32 66 28, www.seakayaknorway.com).

OUTSIDE FLÅM

With a day in Flåm, the best choice is the Norway in a Nutshell trip or just one or two segments of it (all described earlier). Otherwise any of the following are possible—and reachable, to an extent, by public transit. But, as many options are time-consuming, you'll need to be selective.

▲▲▲Nærøyfjord Tours

The most scenic fjord I've seen anywhere in Norway is the Nærøyfjord, about an hour from Flåm (basically the last half of the Flåm-Gudvangen trip). Though your cruise ship passes the mouth of the Nærøyfjord, it doesn't enter it. For a closer look, you can take the sightseeing cruise from Flåm to Gudvangen and get back to Flåm on your own (described earlier, under "Norway in a Nutshell Loop"), or try one of these tours.

The Fjords Tours: This private company runs several trips from Flåm; their most popular is a ferry ride to Gudvangen and a bus ride back to Flåm (430-705 NOK, 4-hour round-trip; departs Flåm at 8:00, 9:00, 11:00, 12:15, 13:30, 14:00, and 16:00; fewer off-season, choose slower Classic ferry for best viewing; other options available including a round-trip ferry ride).

They also do a bus tour up to the Stegastein viewpoint—a concrete-and-wood viewing pier sticking out from a mountainside high above Aurland—for a full panorama view of the fjords (325 NOK, 2 hours, departs 6/day). For details, drop by the Flåm Visitors Center inside the train station, call 57 63 14 00, or see www.visitflam.com.

FjordSafari to Nærøyfjord: FjordSafari takes little groups out onto the fjord in small, open Zodiac-type boats with an English-speaking guide. Participants wear full-body weather suits, furry hats, and spacey goggles (making everyone on the boat look like crash-test dummies). As the boat rockets across the water, you'll be thankful for the gear, no matter what the weather. Their two-hour

NORWEGIAN FJORDS

Flåm-Gudvangen-Flåm tour focuses on the Nærøyfjord, and gets you all the fjord magnificence you can imagine (810 NOK, several departures daily). Their three-hour tour is the same but adds a stop in Undredal, where you can see goat cheese being made, sample it, and wander that sleepy village (910 NOK, one departure daily May-Aug, fewer off-season, kids get discounts, mobile 99 09 08 60, www.fjordsafari.com, Maylene). Skip the 1.5-hour "basic" tour, which just barely touches on the Nærøyfjord.

▲Flåm Valley Bike Ride or Hike

Take the Flåmsbana train to Myrdal, then hike or mountain-bike along the road (half gravel, half paved) back down to Flåm (2-3 hours by bike, gorgeous waterfalls, great mountain scenery, and a cute church with an evocative graveyard, but no fjord views).

Walkers can hike the best two hours from Myrdal to Blomheller, and catch the train from there into the valley. Or, without riding the train, you can simply walk up the valley 2.5 miles to the church and a little farther to a waterfall. Whenever you get tired hiking up or down the valley, you can hop on the next train. Pick up the helpful map with this and other hiking options (ranging from easy to strenuous) at the Flåm TI.

Bikers can rent good mountain bikes from the cabin next to the Flåm train station (180 NOK/2-hour minimum, 350 NOK/day, includes helmet; daily May-June 9:00-18:00, July-Sept 8:00-20:00, closed off-season). It costs 100 NOK to take a bike to Myrdal on the train.

Otternes Farms

This humble but magical cluster of four centuries-old farms is about three miles from Flåm (easy for drivers; a decent walk or bike ride otherwise). It's a ghost village perched high on a ridge, up a twisty

gravel road midway between Flåm and Aurland. These traditional time-warp houses and barns date from the time before emigration decimated the workforce, coinage replaced barter, and industrialized margarine became more popular than butter—all of which left farmers to eke out a living relying only on their goats and the cheese they produced. Until 1919 the only road between Aurland and Flåm passed between this huddle of 27 buildings, high above the fjord. First settled in 1522, farmers lived here until the 1990s.

▲▲Borgund Stave Church

About 16 miles east of Lærdal, in the village of Borgund, is Norway's most-visited and one of its best-preserved stave churches.

Dating from around 1180, the interior features only a few later additions, including a 16th-century pulpit, 17th-century stone altar, painted decorations, and crossbeam reinforcements.

Cost and Hours: 90 NOK, buy tickets in museum across street, daily June-Aug 8:00-20:00, May and Sept 10:00-17:00, closed Oct-April. The museum has a shop and a fine little **$$ cafeteria** serving filling and tasty lunches. Tel. 57 66 81 09, www.stavechurch.com.

Getting There: The bus departs Flåm around midday (direction: Lillehammer) and heads for the church, with a return bus departing Borgund in mid-afternoon (170-NOK round-trip, get ticket from driver, about 1 hour each way with about 1 hour at the church, bus runs daily May-Sept, tell driver you want to get off at the church).

Visiting the Church: Explore the dimly lit interior, illuminated only by the original small, circular windows up high. The oldest and most authentic item in the church is the stone baptismal font. In medieval times, priests conducting baptisms would go outside to shoo away the evil spirits from an infant before bringing it inside the church for the ritual. (If infants died before being baptized, they couldn't be buried in the churchyard, so parents would put their bodies in little coffins and hide them under the church's floorboards to get them as close as possible to God.)

Notice the X-shaped crosses of St. Andrew (the church's patron), carvings of dragons, and medieval runes. Borgund's church also comes with one of this country's best stave-church history museums, which beautifully explains these icons of medieval Norway.

Eating in Flåm

Dining options are expensive and touristy. Don't aim for high cuisine here—go practical. Almost all eateries are clustered near the train station complex. Hours can be unpredictable, flexing with the season, but you can expect these to be open daily in high season.

The **Flåmsbrygga** complex, sprawling through a long building toward the fjord from the station, includes a hotel, the affordable **$$ Furukroa Caféteria** (daily 8:00-20:00 in season, sandwiches, fast-food meals, and pizzas), and the pricey **$$$$ Flåmstova Restaurant** (breakfast and lunch buffet, sit-down dinner service). Next door is their fun, Viking-longhouse-shaped brewpub, **$$$ Ægir Bryggeri** (daily 17:00-22:00, local microbrews, Viking-inspired meals). **$$ Toget Café,** with seating in old train cars, prides itself on using as many locally sourced and organic ingredients as possible. **$$ Bakkastova Kafe,** at the other end of town, feels cozier. Housed in a traditional Norwegian red cabin just above the Fretheim Hotel, with a view terrace, it serves sandwiches, salads, and authentic Norwegian fare (daily 12:00-16:00).

Geirangerfjord

The nine-mile-long, 2,000-foot-deep Geirangerfjord (geh-RAHN-gher-fyord), an offshoot of the long Storfjord, snakes like an S-shaped serpent between the cut-glass peaks of western Norway. Tucked amid cliffs one observer termed "the most preposterous mountains on the entire west coast," the Geirangerfjord is simply stunning. Cruising in—and back out again—you'll drift past steep cliffs and cover-girl waterfalls, such as the famous "Seven Sisters" cascades that tumble 800 feet down a long, craggy swath of gray granite. Facing them is a waterfall dubbed "The Suitor," which sputters endlessly in a futile attempt to impress the seven maidens across the way. (Supposedly the waterfall forms a bottle shape, because perennial rejection has driven the would-be suitor to drink.) And, while any Norwegian fjord waterfall looks like a bridal veil to me, Geirangerfjord actually has one named "The Bridal Veil."

All of this beauty makes Geirangerfjord a magnet for cruise ships, hundreds of which call at the town of Geiranger during their relatively short season. When even just one big ship is in town, the population of this village of about 250 hardy Norwegians can increase more than tenfold...things get very crowded.

While the town tries hard to entertain all those visitors, there's only so much to do in this sleepy corner of the fjord. And, compared with Flåm, Geiranger doesn't have the public-transit con-

Excursions at Geirangerfjord

Of all the ports of call described in this book, Geirangerfjord may be the one where excursions are most worth considering. This is both because of the unique "technical call" arrangement many ships have at Hellesylt (which means paying for an excursion buys you an extra hour or two on land); and because there's relatively little to see in Geiranger town itself, while there's fantastic scenery from up above that's difficult to reach affordably on your own, but easy to reach on an excursion. While Geiranger-based tour operators can get you to many of the worthwhile outlying sights, others—including the fantastic Trollstigen mountain road—are easily accessible only by excursion.

Itineraries starting from **Geiranger town** may include a stop at the Geiranger Fjord Center, the Flydalsjuvet and Dalsnibba viewpoints, and a variety of waterfalls and mountain farms. Some excursions include a guided hike (after a bus ride to the trailhead) up to Storsæter Waterfall, which you can actually walk behind. Other trips head up the Ørnevegen ("Eagle Road") for more views, and some longer trips continue all the way to Trollstigen. You may also be offered kayak tours, RIB (rigid inflatable boat) tours, or mountain-bike trips, all of which can also be booked directly through local agencies (details in this chapter).

If your cruise includes a "technical call" at **Hellesylt,** you'll have the option to pay for an excursion that boards a bus there and drives (gradually) across the mountains to meet your ship in Geiranger, at the far end of the fjord. En route, the tour stops off at Hornindal Lake (Europe's deepest at more than 1,600 feet), the Nordfjord (at the town of Stryn), villages, waterfalls, and more; the final stretch takes you past the Dalsnibba and Flydalsjuvet viewpoints on the way back to your ship. Because it's a one-way journey, this option gives you the maximum Norwegian scenery for your time in this region.

nections that provide an easy and scenic loop trip without your own wheels. No trains or lifts bring you up into the mountains. Instead, to gain some altitude and reach the famous views—which I highly recommend—you'll have to book a tour (either through your cruise line or a local company), hike steeply up, or pay for a very pricey taxi.

About half of the cruises that visit the Geirangerfjord make two stops: First comes a "technical call" in the village of Hellesylt, partway along the fjord; second, an hour or two later, there's a call at the village of Geiranger, at the fjord's endpoint. The "technical call" in Hellesylt means that only passengers who have paid the cruise line for an excursion are allowed off the ship at this point. (While adventurous travelers may be tempted to get off here to

---

Services near the Port of Geiranger

Many of these services are either at the TI (right next to the tender dock) or at the Joker grocery store (facing the marina on a lonesome jetty a quick walk around the harbor to the right as you get off your tender).

ATMs: Geiranger's **ATM** (*minibank*) is outside the front door of the grocery store.

Internet Access: You can get online at the TI, as well as at Café Olé and Hotel Union.

Pharmacy: The grocery store stocks basic pharmacy items; there's no full-service pharmacy in Geiranger town or nearby.

---

poke around, then make their way by public ferry up the fjord to Geiranger, this is typically not permitted.)

PLANNING YOUR TIME

For many cruisers, the best part about the Geirangerfjord is the sail-in and sail-away. If you expect good weather in the morning, it's worth getting up early just to experience your ship plying the fjord's glassy waters when it's relatively quiet (the beauty crescendos about an hour before your call time in Geiranger). If you prefer to sleep in, you'll see the same scenery on the way out—but, as weather here can change on a dime, I'd take advantage of any clearing that you get.

To make the most of your Geiranger visit, consider your options before you arrive. Assuming you don't want to purchase a cruise-line excursion but still want to see some of the area (such as mountain farms and high-altitude viewpoints), your best bet is to book a tour through a local company. It's smart to reserve in advance, as these can fill up quickly (otherwise head straight for the ticket office when you get off your tender).

If you stick around the town of Geiranger, you'll quickly exhaust all of its sightseeing options. The Geiranger Fjord Center, which can be seen in about an hour, is a 30-minute uphill hike from the port (including a few minutes to dip into the church and enjoy the views). After that, it's just strolling, shopping, hiking, or renting a kayak or bike.

If you're fit and adventurous, and have plenty of time, you could ride a sightseeing boat to the fjord below the remote farm called Skageflå. It takes about an hour to hike up, up, up to the farm, after which you can either hike three to four hours all the way back to Geiranger, or walk back down to the fjord and catch a boat to town (be sure to arrange a pickup time in advance with your tour boat company).

Port of Geiranger

Arrival at a Glance: Your tender drops off right in the middle of this tiny town.

Port Overview

Cruise ships tender passengers in to a dock in the harborfront core of town. Stepping off your tender, look right to spot the TI. Nearby are the town bus stop, the boat dock for local ferries, souvenir shops, and eateries. Partway along the harbor to the right is the Joker grocery store, with various services.

Geiranger is basically a one-street town. That street passes the harbor (with the cruise tender dock), then twists up a hill alongside a waterfall, passing the town church, the big Hotel Union, and the Geiranger Fjord Center. Along the waterfront you'll find more hotels, the grocery store, and a campground.

Tourist Information: Geiranger's TI is along the harborfront—look for the green-and-white *i* sign (open long hours daily in summer, Wi-Fi, Internet terminals, WCs, tel. 70 26 30 99, www.visitalesund-geiranger.com). The TI also has a desk for Geiranger Fjordservice (described below).

Taxis: If you need a taxi, ask at the TI or call Geiranger Taxi (tel. 40 00 37 41, www.geirangertaxi.no).

Tours in Geiranger

As public transportation isn't practical for reaching the countryside splendor near the Geirangerfjord, locally based tour operators are your most cost-effective way to enjoy maximum fjord beauty in a limited time. As tours tend to sell out when big ships are in port, it's smartest to book in advance (otherwise head from your tender straight to the ticket office).

Geiranger Fjordservice, the dominant operation (with an office right inside the TI), offers tours and excursions out on the fjord and up into the hills (tel. 70 26 30 07, www.geirangerfjord.no, booking@geirangerfjord.no). They do sightseeing boat trips (with the option of hopping off for a steep hike up to a mountain farm), speedy RIB tours (one-hour ride on a rigid inflatable boat, hourly departures), panoramic bus rides, fishing trips, helicopter rides, bike tours, and more. Their **Mountain Highlight bus tour** to the viewpoints at Dalsnibba and Flydalsjuvet helps you efficiently reach the famous Geiranger views (395 NOK, 2 hours; mid-June-Aug 2/day; fewer in shoulder season). They also offer various "panoramic" tours of the region. For any tour, you can book ahead online, then bring your voucher to their desk in the TI to pick up your boarding pass. They also rent standard cars, electric cars, and ebikes.

Sights on and near Geirangerfjord

IN GEIRANGER
Geiranger Town
This functional little burg, with a waterfall tumbling through its middle, is magnificently set, if not quite "charming." With time to kill in Geiranger, stroll around the harbor, consider a hike into the surrounding hills, and maybe rent a kayak at the campground. To stretch your legs and see the two real "sights" in town, huff steeply up the main street to dip into the small, octagonal town church (with great views from its front yard) and to visit the Geiranger Fjord Center.

Geiranger Fjord Center (Norsk Fjordsenter)
Overlooking Geiranger's rushing waterfall at the top of town, this modern facility has interactive exhibits that illuminate both the geology and the hardscrabble lifestyles of Norway's fjords. You'll see replicas of typical fjordland homes and learn about the traditional steamships that tied fjordside communities together when nothing else did.

Cost and Hours: 120 NOK, daily 10:00-18:00, off-season until 15:00, a 30-minute walk out of town up the main road, across the road and waterfall from the big Hotel Union, tel. 70 26 38 10, www.fjordsenter.com.

Kayaking
Geiranger Fjordservice offers kayak tours, but their base is located at Grande Camping (on a little lip of land nearly two miles out the fjord from Geiranger). They can come pick you up in town for an additional fee or you can email them in advance for a free loaner bike you can pick up at their main office inside the TI (590 NOK, 2-hour tour); see company details and contact info under "Tours in Geiranger," earlier.

Mountain Biking
Geiranger Adventure drops you off at a high mountain road so you can coast back down to the fjord (4/day in summer, tel. 47 37 97 71, www.geiranger-adventure.no). They also rent bikes and ebikes.

Hiking
Ask the TI for advice about various hikes into the countryside around Geiranger (they sell "Rambling Maps"). Given the village's precarious position—on a narrow lip of land surrounded by vertical cliffs—expect a steep walk.

NEAR GEIRANGER

Most of these sights are best seen either with a cruise-ship excursion or on a tour run by a local company (for options, see earlier). While a public ferry does connect Geiranger to Hellesylt in about an hour (departs about every 1.5 hours, www.fjordnorway.com), it's unlikely you'll have time to take it on your short port visit—and it's redundant with your ship's sail-away anyway.

Hellesylt

The best way to see this village, which sits at the opposite end of the Geirangerfjord from Geiranger town—is if you pay for a cruise-line excursion that disembarks here. But even if you don't make it, you're not missing much; aside from the huge waterfall thundering furiously through its middle, Hellesylt is a sleepy village used primarily as a springboard for the grand scenery that stretches to its east.

Viewpoints and Mountain Drives

From Geiranger, highway 63 twists northward up out of the fjord toward Eidsdal. Corkscrewing up 11 switchbacks, this so-called Ørnevegen ("Eagle Road") was built in 1955 to connect remote little Geiranger to the rest of Norway through the frigid winter months. At the highest hairpin (around 2,000 feet), the viewpoint called Ørnesvingen ("Eagle Bend") offers breathtaking Geirangerfjord panoramas. As the road isn't practical by public transit, you're best off reaching it with a tour, an excursion, or a taxi.

To the south, highway 63 scrambles up out of the Geirangerfjord to two other fantastic viewpoints, offering *the* quintessential Geiranger panoramas. The road first passes **Flydalsjuvet** (a modern viewpoint platform, just a few miles out of Geiranger, that stares straight down a 260-foot-deep gorge to the fjord) before summiting at **Dalsnibba** (high above the tree line at nearly 5,000 feet, more distant views of the fjord, accessible only on the three-mile Nibbevegen toll road off of highway 63, www.dalsnibba.no). Various bus tour itineraries combine these two grand viewpoints efficiently.

Yet another popular scenic road, **Trollstigen,** is farther from Geiranger proper but often included in cruise-line excursions. Connecting the fjord to the town of Åndalsnes, to the north, this famous "Troll's Ladder" (highway 63 past the Ørnevegen) traverses 11 switchbacks and provides perhaps the most spectacular scenery in this land of oh-so-spectacular scenery.

Shelf Farms

Because the cliffs rise directly from the deep—leaving precious few patches for fjordside settlements—any relatively flat surface high on the mountain wall seems occupied by a tidy, lonesome, and aptly

What If I Miss My Ship?

You can get help from the cruise line's port agent (listed on the destination information sheet distributed on the ship) and the local TI. If the port agent suggests a costly solution (such as a private car with a driver), consider public transit.

If you get left behind in the well-trafficked Norway in a Nutshell route, it's easy to connect to the main **Oslo-Bergen** train line to reach either of those cities. For **Stavanger,** head to Bergen to catch the bus (http://kystbussen.no)—likely faster— or to Oslo for the train (www.nsb.no). Flåm is also connected to Bergen by express boat (tel. 51 86 87 00, www.norled.no).

If you need to **fly** to your next destination, head to the airport in Oslo (Gardermoen Airport, www.avinor.no/oslo) or Bergen (Flesland Airport, www.avinor.no/bergen).

If you're stuck in the town of Geiranger, you can ride a bus to Oslo (summer only, www.nettbuss.no). To reach Bergen, first take the public ferry to Hellesylt, where you can hop on the main bus line to Bergen (www.kringom.no). The closest airport to Geiranger is about a three-hour bus ride away, in the city of Ålesund (www.avinor.no/alesund).

For more advice on what to do if you miss the boat, see page 130.

named "shelf farm." Most of these, next to impossible to cultivate amid short summers, brutally cold winters, and a constant threat of rockslides, were active well into the 20th century but are now abandoned. A few have been turned into open-air museums that teach visitors about intrepid Norwegian fjord lifestyles. Two popular farms, both perched about 800 feet above the fjord waters, are **Knivsflå** (next to the Seven Sisters falls) and **Skageflå** (directly across the fjord). While visiting these independently is impractical with a short day in port, various local tour companies offer boat rides from Geiranger to the fjord wall, where you get off and hike up to the farms (figure about an hour if you're in shape). When booking your boat ride, be sure to arrange a pickup time for your return to Geiranger. Alternatively, you can hike (about 3-4 hours) from Skageflå back to Geiranger. Guided visits of the farms are sometimes available—check with your tour company.

Norwegian Survival Phrases

Norwegian can be pronounced quite differently from region to region. These phrases and phonetics match the mainstream Oslo dialect, but you'll notice variations. Vowels can be tricky: *å* sounds like "oh," *æ* sounds like a bright "ah" (as in "apple"), and *u* sounds like the German *ü* (purse your lips and say u). Certain vowels at the ends of words (such as *d* and *t*) are sometimes barely pronounced (or not at all). In some dialects, the letters *sk* are pronounced "sh." In the phonetics, ī sounds like the long i in "light," and bolded syllables are stressed.

English	Norwegian	Pronunciation
Hello. (formal)	God dag.	goo dahg
Hi. / Bye. (informal)	Hei. / Ha det.	hī / hah deh
Do you speak English?	Snakker du engelsk?	**snahk**-kehr dew **eng**-ehlsk
Yes. / No.	Ja. / Nei.	yah / nī
Please.	Vær så snill.	vayr soh sneel
Thank you (very much).	(Tusen) takk.	(**tew**-sehn) tahk
You're welcome.	Vær så god.	vayr soh goo
Can I help you?	Kan jeg hjelpe deg?	kahn yī **yehl**-peh dī
Excuse me.	Unnskyld.	**ewn**-shuld
(Very) good.	(Veldig) fint.	(**vehl**-dee) feent
Goodbye.	Farvel.	fahr-**vehl**
zero / one / two	null / en / to	newl / ayn / toh
three / four	tre / fire	treh / **fee**-reh
five / six	fem / seks	fehm / sehks
seven / eight	syv / åtte	seev / **oh**-teh
nine / ten	ni / ti	nee / tee
hundred	hundre	**hewn**-dreh
thousand	tusen	**tew**-sehn
How much?	Hvor mye?	voor **mee**-yeh
local currency: (Norwegian) crown	(Norske) kroner	(**norsh**-keh) **kroh**-nehr
Where is...?	Hvor er...?	voor ehr
...the toilet	...toalettet	toh-ah-**leh**-teh
men	menn / herrer	mehn / **hehr**-rehr
women	damer	**dah**-mehr
water / coffee	vann / kaffe	vahn / **kah**-feh
beer / wine	øl / vin	uhl / veen
Cheers!	Skål!	skohl
The bill, please.	Regningen, takk.	**rī**-ning-ehn tahk

AMSTERDAM

The Netherlands

Netherlands Practicalities

The Netherlands (Nederland)—sometimes referred to by its nickname, "Holland"—is Europe's most densely populated and also one of its wealthiest and best-organized countries. Occupying a delta near the mouth of three large rivers, for centuries the Netherlands has battled the sea, reclaiming low-lying lands and converting marshy estuaries into fertile farmland. The Netherlands has 17 million people: 80 percent are Dutch, and half have no religious affiliation. Despite its small size (16,000 square miles—about twice the size of New Jersey), the Netherlands boasts the planet's 23rd-largest economy. It also has one of Europe's lowest unemployment rates, relying heavily on foreign trade through its port at Rotterdam (Europe's largest).

Money: 1 euro (€) = about $1.20. An ATM is called a *geldautomaat*. The local VAT (value-added sales tax) rate is 21 percent; the minimum purchase eligible for a VAT refund is €50 (for details on refunds, see page 125).

Language: The native language is Dutch. For useful phrases, see page 797.

Emergencies: Dial 112 for police, medical, or other emergencies. In case of theft or loss, see page 118.

Time Zone: The Netherlands is on Central European Time (the same as most of the Continent—one hour ahead of Great Britain, and six/nine hours ahead of the East/West Coasts of the US).

Embassies in the Netherlands: The **US consulate** in Amsterdam is at Museumplein 19 (tel. 020/575-5309, after-hours emergency tel. 070/310-2209, https://nl.usembassy.gov). In The Hague, the **US embassy** is at Lange Voorhout 102 (tel. 070/310-2209), and the **Canadian embassy** is at Sophialaan 7 (tel. 070/311-1600, www.canadainternational.gc.ca/netherlands-pays_bas). Call ahead for passport services.

Phoning: With a mobile phone, it's easy to dial: Press and hold zero until you get a + sign, enter the country code (31 for the Netherlands, 1 for the US/Canada), and then the complete phone number (including area code if there is one). When dialing a European phone number, drop an initial zero (except if calling Italy). For more tips, see page 1062.

Tipping: As service is included at sit-down meals, you don't need to tip further, though it's nice to round up your bill about 5-10 percent for good service. Round up taxi fares a bit (pay €5 on a €4.50 fare). For more tips on tipping, see page 129.

Tourist Information: www.holland.com.

AMSTERDAM

Amsterdam still looks much like it did in the 1600s—the Dutch Golden Age—when it was the world's richest city, an international sea-trading port, and the cradle of capitalism. Wealthy, democratic burghers built a city upon millions of pilings, creating a wonderland of canals lined with trees and townhouses topped with fancy gables. Immigrants, Jews, outcasts, and political rebels were drawn here by its tolerant atmosphere, while painters such as young Rembrandt captured that atmosphere on canvas.

Today's Amsterdam is a progressive place of 820,000 people and almost as many bikes. It's a city of good living, cozy cafés, great art, street-corner jazz, stately history, and a spirit of live and let live.

Amsterdam also offers the Netherlands' best people-watching. The Dutch are unique, and observing them is a sightseeing experience all in itself. They're a handsome and healthy people, and among the world's tallest. They're also open and honest—I think of them as refreshingly blunt—and they like to laugh. As connoisseurs of world culture, they appreciate Rembrandt paintings, Indonesian food, and the latest French film—but with an un-snooty, blue-jeans attitude.

Be warned: Amsterdam, a bold experiment in freedom, may box your Puritan ears. For centuries, the city has taken a tolerant approach to things other places try to forbid. Traditionally, the city attracted sailors and businessmen away from home, so it was profitable to allow them to have a little fun. In the 1960s, Amsterdam became a magnet for Europe's hippies. Since then, it's become a world capital of alternative lifestyles. Stroll through any neighborhood and see things that are commonplace here but rarely found elsewhere. Prostitution is allowed in the Red Light District, while "smartshops" sell psychedelic drugs and marijuana is openly sold and smoked. (The Dutch aren't necessarily more tolerant or decadent than the rest of us—just pragmatic and looking for smart solutions.)

Amsterdam is so touristy that politicians have slashed funds for marketing the city, and are working to reduce the number of cheese shops, chocolate shops, and kitschy tourist attractions that many locals feel are changing the city into a kind of amusement park. But I love Amsterdam even with its crowds. Approach Amsterdam as an ethnologist observing a strange culture. It's a place where carillons chime quaintly from spires towering above coffeeshops where yuppies go to smoke pot. Take it all in, then pause to watch the clouds blow past stately old gables—and see the Golden Age reflected in a quiet canal.

PLANNING YOUR TIME

Although Amsterdam does have a few must-see museums, its best attraction is its own carefree ambience. The city's a joy on foot—and a breezier and faster delight by bike. For sightseers who want to do more than relax, these are the top choices:

Rijksmuseum: You can see the highlights of this world-class collection of Dutch Masters in about an hour and a half.

Van Gogh Museum: The planet's best collection of this beloved Dutch artist's work demands at least an hour to see.

Anne Frank House: This evocative sight, in the actual home where Jewish refugees were hidden from the Nazis, is worth an hour.

Other Museums: Depending on your interests, consider the **Stedelijk Museum** (art since 1945), **Amsterdam Museum** (city history), **Amstelkring Museum** ("Our Lord in the Attic" hidden church), and **Dutch Resistance Museum** (ingenuity of anti-Nazi agitators). Each of these merits an hour. Though not must-sees, the **Netherlands Maritime Museum** and **NEMO** (National Center for Science and Technology) are close to the cruise port and worth a look.

Canal Cruise: A one-hour boat trip offers a fine orientation to the city.

Explore Neighborhoods: Of Amsterdam's many colorful and characteristic neighborhoods, the most popular to explore are the **Jordaan** (an upscale-hipster residential zone at the western edge of downtown) and the **Red Light District** (an in-your-face look at legalized prostitution, southeast of Centraal Station). Allow an hour of strolling apiece.

The two great art museums (Rijks and Van Gogh) cluster near the south end of the town center, so you can tackle things in a geographically logical order: From Centraal Station, zip to the mu-

Excursions from Amsterdam

It's easy to do everything in **Amsterdam** on your own, thanks to the Dutch public transportation system and the fact that everyone here speaks English—even the tram drivers. But for those who want more help, you'll find various excursions offered by your cruise line: bus tours; town walking tours; canal cruises; guided visits to the Van Gogh Museum, Anne Frank House, and Rijksmuseum; diamond-themed tours (including a visit to Gassan Diamonds); and Jewish heritage tours (including a visit to the Jewish Historical Museum and important neighborhoods).

Other cruise excursions focus on small-town and countryside sights that would otherwise be tricky to navigate on your own. If you're here during the flower festival at **Keukenhof** (mid-March–mid-May), it's worth touring the remarkable flower gardens there. Excursion itineraries can link the idyllic **Waterland** towns of Edam, Volendam, Marken, and/or Broek; the open-air museum (with great windmills) of **Zaanse Schans;** and the reclaimed land of **Beemster Polder.** And in this little country, you can even do a "Grand Tour of Holland" in one short day, with brief stops in the charming town of **Delft** and the bustling city of **The Hague.** If you'd like to see a lot of the Netherlands in a little time, these excursions are worth doing for the efficiency they provide.

seums by tram. Then work your way back toward the station (and the cruise terminal), detouring to the Anne Frank House and other sights as time allows.

Reservations: Amsterdam's top sights—the Rijksmuseum, Van Gogh Museum, and Anne Frank House—suffer from long lines. It's essential to purchase tickets ahead of time—especially for the Anne Frank House (for details, see "Advance Tickets and Sightseeing Passes," later). If you book ahead for multiple sights, be sure to leave enough time between reservations to get from sight to sight, enjoy lunch, or explore along the way. For example, if your ship docks at 8:00, you might arrive at the Rijksmuseum around 9:00, book Van Gogh for 11:30, and schedule Anne Frank for 14:00.

Port of Amsterdam

Arrival at a Glance: Amsterdam's cruise terminal is a 3-minute tram ride or 15-minute walk from the central train station, with connections by tram, bus, or boat to anywhere in the city. A few ships dock at one of the Felison terminals in IJmuiden, with bus or shuttle connections to the city.

Port Overview

Passenger Terminal Amsterdam (PTA)—an ultramodern facility with a roof that looks like a glass whale—is just minutes from the center of Amsterdam. Inside the terminal, you'll find an information desk, lockers, an ATM, and shops.

Tourist Information: When ships arrive, the Port of Amsterdam staffs an information desk on the ground floor of the terminal—ask for their map for cruisers. The main Amsterdam TI is in front of the nearby Centraal train station (for details, see "Orientation to Amsterdam," later).

GETTING INTO TOWN

A fleet of **taxis** waits right outside the terminal, but they're expensive (a ride to the Rijksmuseum or Van Gogh Museum costs about €16); meanwhile, **trams** are easy, cheap, and fast. If you're ready to pretend you're an Amsterdammer, there's even a bike-rental facility a few steps away.

From the Cruise Terminal to Centraal Station

By tram or on foot, it's easy to reach Centraal Station, Amsterdam's local transit hub with convenient access to trams, buses, and Metro. The station is packed with shops, eateries (including handy Albert Heijn "to go" supermarkets), ATMs, Wi-Fi, and a pharmacy.

By Tram: Just outside the cruise terminal door, follow the *Town Center* sign and use the crosswalk to cross the busy portside street. You'll see a tram stop with an electric sign reading *Centraal Station* and displaying the arrival time for the next tram. Take tram #26 just one stop to the end of the line, Centraal Station (3-minute ride, runs every 4-8 minutes; when returning to the terminal, ride in direction: IJburg to the Muziekgebouw Bimhuis stop). A one-hour tram ticket costs €3; if you'll be taking more than two transit journeys on your visit, buy a €7.50 one-day transit pass, good for all trams and buses (for either ticket, buy on board with chip-and-PIN card).

On Foot: From the cruise terminal, it's just a 15-minute walk to Centraal Station. As you leave the terminal, follow the *Town Center* sign, turn right at the busy road, and walk past the shops, hotel, and concert hall (Muziekgebouw Bimhuis). Continue walking with the water on your right—you'll see the glass-and-steel arch of the station's roof. You'll end up walking between the station and the water; when you come to a major crosswalk (on your left), follow the crowds crossing the street to enter the lower "back door" level of the train station. Take the main corridor all the way through (crossing under all the platforms) and follow *Centrum* signs to pop out in front.

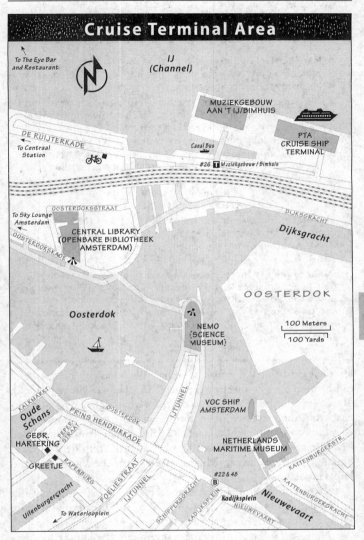

Cruise Terminal Area

To The Eye Bar and Restaurant

N

IJ (Channel)

MUZIEKGEBOUW AAN 'T IJ/BIMHUIS

PTA CRUISE SHIP TERMINAL

DE RUIJTERKADE

To Centraal Station

Canal Bus

#26 [T] Muziekgebouw / Bimhuis

OOSTERDOKSSTRAAT

To Sky Lounge Amsterdam

CENTRAL LIBRARY (OPENBARE BIBLIOTHEEK AMSTERDAM)

OOSTERDOKSKADE

DIJKSGRACHT

Dijksgracht

OOSTERDOK

Oosterdok

NEMO (SCIENCE MUSEUM)

100 Meters
100 Yards

VOC SHIP AMSTERDAM

Kalkmarkt

Oude Schans

PRINS HENDRIKKADE

OOSTERDOK

PEPER STRAAT

IJTUNNEL

NETHERLANDS MARITIME MUSEUM

KATTENBURGERSTR.

GEBR. HARTERING

RAPENBURG

GREETJE

FOELIESTRAAT

IJTUNNEL

#22 & 48

B

KATTENBURGERGRACHT

Uilenburgergracht

To Waterlooplein

SCHIPPERSGRACHT

KADIJKSPLEIN

Kadijksplein

NIEUWEVAART

Nieuwevaart

AMSTERDAM

From Centraal Station to Other Parts of Town

Orient yourself, standing with your back to the station (the Stationsplein plaza in front may be under construction during your visit): Straight ahead, just past the canal, is Damrak street, leading to Dam Square (10-minute walk). To your left are the TI and GVB public-transit offices. Farther to your left is a bike rental place: MacBike (in the station building).

Just beyond the taxis are platforms for the city's blue-and-white **trams,** which come along frequently (buy ticket or pass from conductor with a chip-and-PIN card; if you bought a tram ticket

Services near the Port of Amsterdam

ATMs: The ATM by the revolving door as you leave the cruise terminal may not have the best rates; ideally, wait to use the ATMs inside Centraal Station.

Wi-Fi: There's Wi-Fi at the cruise port and all over town, but the best place for serious surfing is the city's towering **central library,** which has hundreds of fast terminals and Wi-Fi (Openbare Bibliotheek Amsterdam, www.oba.nl). It's very close to the cruise terminal: Turn right when you leave the terminal, walk with the water on your right, turn left at the first bike/pedestrian path that goes under the train tracks, and follow that path to a modern building facing the inner harbor. The library also has a great view and a comfy cafeteria.

Pharmacy: For over-the-counter remedies, try **Hema** on the main floor of Centraal Station. For prescriptions, head for **BENU Apotheek** on Dam Square (Damstraat 2, tel. 020/624-4331).

Other Services: There are pay **lockers** on the cruise terminal's first floor. AmsterBike **bike rentals** is in the parking garage under the Mövenpick Hotel next door; they offer electric bikes and bike tours as well as regular rentals (www.amsterbike.eu; more bike rental options are near Centraal Station—see page 740).

for the ride from the cruise terminal, it's good for an hour and can be used for a connecting tram ride to wherever you're headed). The following trams are most useful for your sightseeing and depart from the west side of Stationsplein (with the station behind you, they're to your right): Trams #2 (direction: Nieuw Sloten) and #12 (direction: A'veen Binnenhof) head south from here to Dam Square, Leidseplein, and Museumplein (with the **Van Gogh** and **Rijks museums**).

To reach the **Anne Frank House,** it's about a 20-minute walk, or you can ride tram #13, #14, or #17 to the Westermarkt stop, about a block south of the museum's entrance.

Note that some of Amsterdam's tram numbers and routes may have changed by the time you visit. Confirm with the conductor before departing.

A variety of **canal boat tours** depart from in front of the station. For details on all of these transit options, see "Getting Around Amsterdam," later.

Alternate Port: From IJmuiden Felison Terminals to Amsterdam

At IJmuiden, about 18 miles from central Amsterdam, there are two terminals set some distance apart. From the older ferry terminal, where only small ships can dock, cruise-line shuttle buses take passengers into town. Larger ships put in at the newer Felison Cruise Terminal, serviced by Connexxion bus #82 to Amsterdam's Sloterdijk train station; cruise lines also offer shuttles for a fee. For more info, see www.felisonterminal.nl.

Amsterdam

Amsterdam's Centraal Station, on the north edge of the city, is your starting point, with the TI, bike rental, and trams branching out to all points. Damrak is the main north-south axis, connecting Centraal Station with Dam Square (people-watching and hangout center) and its Royal Palace. From this main street, the city spreads out like a fan, with 90 islands, hundreds of bridges, and a series of concentric canals that were laid out in the 17th century, Holland's Golden Age. Amsterdam's major sights are all within walking distance of Dam Square (see the color Amsterdam map at the beginning of this book for an overview of the city).

To the east of Damrak is the oldest part of the city (today's Red Light District), and to the west is the newer part, where you'll find the Anne Frank House and the peaceful Jordaan neighborhood. Museums and Leidseplein nightlife cluster at the southern edge of the city center.

Orientation to Amsterdam

TOURIST INFORMATION

The Dutch name for a TI is "VVV," pronounced "fay fay fay." Amsterdam's main TI, located across the street from Centraal Station, is centrally located, but it's crowded and sometimes inefficient, and the free maps are poor quality (Mon-Sat 9:00-17:00, Sun 10:00-16:00, tel. 020/702-6000). The TI sells a good city map (€2.50) and the *A-Mag* entertainment guide (€3.50). A second Centraal Station TI is in the section on the north side. While it's labeled the "I Amsterdam Store," it really is an official TI and is much less crowded (Mon-Sat 8:00-19:00 except Thu-Sat until 20:00, Sun 9:00-18:00).

ADVANCE TICKETS AND SIGHTSEEING PASSES

You can avoid long ticket lines (common from late March-Oct) at Amsterdam's most popular sights—the Rijksmuseum, Van Gogh Museum, and Anne Frank House—by booking tickets in advance or getting a sightseeing pass. (If you're visiting off-season, these strategies are less important, especially if you use my other crowd-beating tips.)

Advance Tickets: It's smart to buy tickets online for the three major museums through each museum's website, generally with no extra booking fee. For the Anne Frank House, online timed-entry tickets go on sale starting two months in advance and sell out quickly. Just print out your ticket and bring it to the ticket-holder's line for a quick entry. You can also buy advance tickets at TIs (though lines there can be long).

Sightseeing Passes: On a brief cruise visit, I'd skip all the passes (and make individual reservations at the sights instead). But if you'll be visiting many museums, a pass could save you money (and time in line).

The €60 **Museumkaart** sightseeing pass covers up to five museums in Amsterdam, but doesn't include public transit. It almost pays for itself if you visit the Rijksmuseum, Van Gogh Museum, Anne Frank House, and Amsterdam Museum (adds up to €56). Tourists can only buy it in person at a covered sight; don't be confused by the Dutch-only website, which doesn't even mention this option (www.museumkaart.nl).

The widely advertised **I Amsterdam Card** covers the Rijksmuseum and the Van Gogh Museum (but not the Anne Frank House), a canal boat ride, and a transportation pass—and lets you skip lines at the Van Gogh Museum (€59/24 hours, €74/48 hours, €87/72 hours, www.iamsterdamcard.com). The **Holland Pass** is not worth it.

Without Advance Tickets or a Pass: If you end up visiting the Anne Frank House without a reservation, trim your time in line by showing up late in the day; this works better in early spring and fall than in summer, when even after-dinner lines can be long. You can visit the Van Gogh Museum until 21:00 on Fridays year-round and on Saturdays in July and August.

HELPFUL HINTS

Theft Alert: Tourists are considered green and rich, and the city has more than its share of hungry thieves—especially in the train station, on trams, in and near crowded museums, at places of drunkenness, and at the many hostels. Wear your money belt. If there's a risk you'll be out late high or drunk, leave all valuables on your cruise ship or in your hotel. Blitzed tourists are easy targets for petty theft.

Street Smarts: When you're on foot, be extremely vigilant for silent but potentially painful bikes, electric mopeds, trams, and crotch-high bollards. Don't walk on tram tracks or pink/maroon bicycle paths. Before you step off a sidewalk, do a double- or triple-check in both directions to make sure all's clear.

Maps: Given the city's maze of streets and canals, I'd definitely get a good city map (€2.50 at Centraal Station TI). I like the *Carto Studio Centrumkaart Amsterdam* map.

Best Views: Although sea-level Amsterdam is notoriously horizontal, there are a few high points where you can get the big picture. My favorite is the rooftop **Sky Lounge Amsterdam,** on the 11th floor of the DoubleTree by Hilton Hotel (daily until very late, 5-minute walk east of train station). Other good choices are from the top-floor view café at the **Central Library,** or nearby, the rooftop terrace—generally open to the public—at the **NEMO science museum.** It's pricey, but the new **A'DAM Tower** has a sky deck and even a swing about 20 stories above the city (€12.50, daily 10:00-22:00, next to the **EYE** Film Institute). The **Westerkerk**—convenient for anyone visiting the Anne Frank House—has a climbable tower with fine views. Another option is the tower of the **Old Church** (Oude Kerk) in the Red Light District.

GETTING AROUND AMSTERDAM

Amsterdam is big, and you'll find the trams handy. The longest walk a tourist would make is an hour from Centraal Station to the Rijksmuseum.

By Tram, Bus, and Metro

Amsterdam's public transit system includes trams, buses, and an underground Metro. Of these, trams are most useful for most tourists.

Tickets and Day Passes: I find a pass to be the simplest option when staying in Amsterdam for a few days. **Passes** good for unlim-

ited transportation are available for 24 hours (€7.50), 48 hours (€12.50), 72 hours (€17.50), and 96 hours (€22.50). Some passes include the train ride to Schiphol Airport (see page 793). Given how expensive single tickets are, think about buying a pass before you buy that first ticket.

Within Amsterdam, a **single transit ticket** costs €3 and is good for one hour on the tram, bus, and Metro, including transfers. Public buses and trams do not accept cash onboard (use credit card with a PIN code, or buy tickets in advance). The full range of tickets and passes are available at Metro-station vending machines, at GVB public-transit offices, at TIs, and at some souvenir shops; for these options you can pay with cash or credit card.

AMSTERDAM

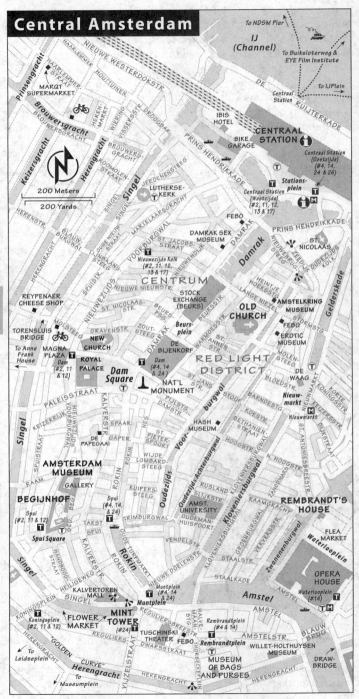

Central Amsterdam

To NDSM Pier

IJ (Channel)

To Buiksloterweg & EYE Film Institute

To IJPlein

NIEUWE WESTERDOKSTR.

HAARLEMMER HOUTTUINEN

HAARLEMMER STRAAT

MARQT SUPERMARKET

Prinsengracht

Brouwersgracht

Keizersgracht

Herengracht

Singel

HERENMARKT

WIERINGENSTR.

VISSERSSTR.

DROOGBAK

BROUWERSGRACHT

KOOMNENSTR.

200 Meters

200 Yards

HERENSTR.

BLAUW BURGWAL

LOUPE NIEUW

SPUISTR.

JEROENSTEEG

LUTHERSE-KERK

MAETELAARSGRACHT

ST. JACOBS-STRAAT

Nieuwezijds Kolk (#2, 11, 12, 13 & 17)

VOORBURGWAL

NIEUWENDIJK

CENTRUM

DE RUIJTERKADE

Centraal Station

IBIS HOTEL

BIKE GARAGE

PRINS HENDRIKKADE

CENTRAAL STATION

Centraal Station (Oostzijde) (#4, 14, 24 & 26)

Stationsplein

Centraal Station (Westzijde) (#2, 11, 12, 13 & 17)

PRINS HENDRIKKADE

FEBO

DAMRAK SEX MUSEUM

Damrak

ST. NICOLAAS

NIEUWEBRUG-STEEG

ZEEDIJK

OUDEZIJDS KOLK

Gelderskade

REYPENAER CHEESE SHOP

HERENGRACHT

MOLSTEEG

BLAUW BURGWAL

NIEUWEZIJDS

ST. NICOLAAS STR.

NIEUWE NIEUWSTR.

GRAVENSTR.

ZOUT-STEEG

Beursplein

STOCK EXCHANGE (BEURS)

BEURSSTR.

BEURS PSG.

Beurs-plein

WARMOESSTR.

OLD CHURCH

HEINTJE HOEKSTEG

LANGE NIEZEL

AMSTELKRING MUSEUM

STORMSTG.

FEBO

EROTIC MUSEUM

MOLENSTEEG

To Anne Frank House

TORENSLUIS BRIDGE

MAGNA PLAZA

NEW CHURCH

ROYAL PALACE

Dam Square

DE BIJENKORF

Dam (#2, 11 & 12)

Dam (#4, 14 & 24)

NAT'L MONUMENT

RED LIGHT DISTRICT

ST. ANNEN STR.

ST. JANS STR.

STOOF

BARNDESTG.

BLOEDSTR.

DE WAAG

Nieuwmarkt

Nieuwmarkt

KORTE KONINGSSTR.

NIEUWMARKT

KEIZERSSTR.

PALEISSTRAAT

KALVERSTR.

KEIZERSRIJK

NIEUWEZIJDS VOORBURGWAL

SPUISTRAAT

Singel

SPAAR-PO

NES

DE PAPEGAAI

ST. PIETERS-POORT

WIJDE LOMBARD-STEEG

ROKIN

PULSTG.

DAMSTR.

HASH MUSEUM

BETHANIEN-STRAAT

KOESTE

HOOGSTR.

ROESTE

N. HOOGSTRAAT

VOOR-burgwal

Oudezijds Achterburgwal

RUSLAND

KLOVENIERSBURGWAL

RAAMGRACHT

N. ANTONIESBREESTR.

REMBRANDT'S HOUSE

AMSTERDAM MUSEUM

GALLERY

BEGIJNHOF

Spui (#2, 11 & 12)

Spui Square

KUIPERS-STEEG

Spui (#4, 14, & 24)

RAAM

SPUISTRAAT

KALVERSTR.

TAKST.

SPUI

ROKIN

OUDE TURFMARKT

GRIMBURGWAL

AMST. UNIVERSITY

OUDEMAN-HUISPOORT

VENDELSTR.

NIEUWE DOELENSTR.

Oudezijds Achterburgwal

GROENBURGWAL

ZANDSTRAAT

VERVERSTR.

Zwanenburgwal

FLEA MARKET

Waterlooplein

OPERA HOUSE

Waterlooplein (#14)

STAALSTR.

STAALKADE

Amstel

AMSTEL

HANDBOOG-STR.

HEILIGEWEG

KALVERTOREN MALL

KALVERSTR.

SINGEL

Koningsplein (#2, 11 & 12)

Koningsplein

"GOLDEN CURVE" Herengracht

To Leidseplein

To Museumplein

FLOWER MARKET

MINT TOWER

Muntplein

Muntplein (#4, 14 & 24)

Mint Tower (#24)

REGULIERSBREESTR.

TUSCHINSKI THEATER

FEBO

Rembrandtplein

Rembrandtplein (#4 & 14)

HALVE MAAN STG.

AMSTELSTR.

AMSTEL

WILLET-HOLTHUYSEN MUSEUM

BLAUW BRUG

DRAW-BRIDGE

YLZELSTRAAT

HERENGRACHT

REGULIERS DWARSSTRAAT

MUSEUM OF BAGS AND PURSES

HERENGRACHT

AMSTERDAM

The entire country's public-transit network operates on a system with a multiple-use **OV-Chipkaart.** But it's not ideal for short-time visitors (it requires a nonrefundable €7.50 deposit plus a €2.50 fee to cash out, and can only be reloaded in person, not online)—on a brief cruise visit, don't bother.

Those staying longer than three or four days or who plan to use Dutch trains as well as trams and buses should consider the **TripKey card** (register in advance from home, then pick it up at the Hertz car rental desk at Schipol Airport or at the Amsterdam Circle Line ticket office in central Amsterdam; see www.tripkey.nl).

Information: For more on riding public transit and a free transit map, visit the helpful GVB public-transit information office in front of Centraal Station (Mon-Fri 7:00-21:00, Sat-Sun from 8:00, www.gvb.nl).

Riding Trams: Board the tram at any entrance that's not marked with a red/white "do not enter" sticker. If you need a ticket or pass, pay the conductor (in a booth at the back, payment by credit card with PIN code only); if there's no conductor, pay the driver in front. You must always "check in" as you board by scanning your ticket or pass at the pink-and-gray scanner, and "check out" by scanning it again when you get off. The scanner will beep and flash a green light after a successful scan. Be careful not to accidentally scan your ticket or pass twice while boarding, or it becomes invalid. Occasionally controllers fine people who don't check in and out. To open the rear door when you reach your stop, press a button on one of the poles near the exit. Don't try to exit through the front door—it's not allowed.

Trams #2 and #12 travel **north-south,** connecting Centraal Station, the Jordaan neighborhood, many of my recommended hotels, and Leidseplein, and continue beyond to the Rijksmuseum, Van Gogh Museum, and Vondelpark. The entire ride takes about 20 minutes, with trams zipping by every few minutes. At Centraal Station, these trams depart from the west side of station's plaza (with the station behind you, they're to your right).

To go **west-east,** use tram #14, which connects Westermarkt near the Anne Frank House and Jordaan neighborhood with Rembrandtplein, Waterlooplein, and Alexanderplein.

Note that some of Amsterdam's tram numbers and routes may have changed by the time you visit. Confirm with the conductor before departing.

If you get lost in Amsterdam, remember that most of the city's trams eventually take you back to Centraal Station, and nearly all drivers speak English.

Buses and Metro: Tickets and passes work on buses and the Metro just as they do on the trams—scan your ticket or pass as you enter and again when you leave. The Metro system is scant—

AMSTERDAM

used mostly for commuting to the suburbs—but it does connect Centraal Station with some sights east of Damrak (Nieuwmarkt-Waterlooplein-Weesperplein).

By Bike

Everyone—bank managers, students, pizza delivery boys, and police—uses this mode of transport. It's by far the smartest way to travel in a city where 40 percent of all traffic rolls on two wheels. You'll get around town by bike faster than you can by taxi. One-speed bikes, with *"brrringing"* bells, rent for about €10 per day.

Rental Shops: Star Bikes Rental has cheap rates, long hours, and inconspicuous black bikes. They're happy to arrange an after-hours drop-off if you give them your credit-card number and prepay (€5/3 hours, €7/day, €9/24 hours, €12/2 days, €17/3 days, Mon-Fri 8:00-19:00, Sat-Sun 9:00-19:00, shorter hours in winter, requires ID but no monetary deposit, 5-minute walk from east end of Centraal Station—walk underneath tracks near DoubleTree by Hilton Hotel and then turn right, De Ruyterkade 143, tel. 020/620-3215, www.starbikesrental.com).

MacBike, with thousands of bikes, is the city's bike-rental powerhouse—you'll see their bright-red bikes all over town (they do stick out a bit). It has a huge and efficient outlet at Centraal Station (€7.50/3 hours, €9.75/24 hours, €6/extra day, more for 3 gears and optional insurance, leave €50 deposit plus a copy of your passport, or provide credit-card number; free helmets, also rents electric bikes, daily 9:00-17:45; at east end of station—on the left as you're leaving; tel. 020/624-8391, www.macbike.nl). They have two smaller satellites at Leidseplein (Weteringschans 2) and Waterlooplein (Nieuwe Uilenburgerstraat 116). Return your bike to the station where you rented it. MacBike sells several €1-2 pamphlets outlining bike tours with a variety of themes in and around Amsterdam.

Frederic Rent-a-Bike, a 10-minute walk from Centraal Station, has quality bikes and a helpful staff (€8/3 hours, €15/24 hours—€10 if returned by 17:30, €25/48 hours, €60/week, 10 percent discount with this book, daily 9:00-17:30, no after-hours drop-off, no deposit but must leave credit-card number, Binnen Wieringerstraat 23, tel. 020/624-5509, www.frederic.nl, Frederic and son Marne).

Lock Your Bike: Bike thieves are bold and brazen. Bikes come with two locks and stern instructions to use both. The wimpy ones go through the spokes, whereas the industrial-strength chains are meant to be wrapped around the actual body of the bike and through the front wheel, and connected to something stronger than any human. (Note the steel bike-hitching racks sticking up all around town, called "staples.") Follow your rental agency's locking directions diligently. If you're sloppy, it's an expensive mistake and one that any "included" theft insurance won't cover.

Biking Tips: As the Dutch believe in fashion over safety, no one here wears a helmet. They do, however, ride cautiously, and so should you: Use arm signals, follow the bike-only traffic signals, stay in the obvious and omnipresent bike lanes, and yield to traffic on the right. Fear oncoming trams and tram tracks. Carefully cross tram tracks at a perpendicular angle to avoid catching your tire in the rut. Warning: Police ticket cyclists just as they do drivers. Obey all traffic signals, and walk your bike through pedestrian zones. Fines for biking through pedestrian zones are reportedly €30-50. Leave texting-while-biking to the locals. A handy bicycle route-planner can be found at www.routecraft.com (select "bikeplanner," then click British flag for English).

By Boat

While the city is great on foot, bike, or tram, you can also get around Amsterdam by hop-on, hop-off boat. **Lovers** boats shuttle tourists on two routes covering different combinations of the city's top sights. Their Green Line, for example, stops near the Hermitage, Rijksmuseum/Van Gogh Museum, and Centraal Station (€25, runs about every 20 minutes, 2 hours). Sales booths in front of Centraal Station (and the boats) offer free brochures listing museum hours and admission prices. Most routes come with recorded narration (departures daily 9:30-18:15, tel. 020/530-1090, www.lovers.nl).

The similar **Stromma** is another hop-on, hop-off boat, offering nine stops on two different boat routes (€24/24-hour pass, online discounts, departures daily 9:30-19:00, until 20:00 July-Aug, leaves near Centraal Station at the Gray Line dock, tel. 020/217-0500, www.stromma.nl).

If you're simply looking for a floating, nonstop tour, the regular canal tour boats (without the stops) give more information, cover more ground, and cost less (see "Tours in Amsterdam," later).

For do-it-yourself canal tours and lots of exercise, Canal Bus also rents "canal bikes" (a.k.a. paddleboats) at several locations: near the Anne Frank House, near the Rijksmuseum, near Leidseplein, and where Leidsestraat meets Keizersgracht (€8/1 hour, €11/1.5

AMSTERDAM

hours, €14/2 hours, prices are per person, daily July-Aug 10:00-21:00, Sept-June 10:00-18:00).

By Taxi and Uber

For short rides, Amsterdam is a bad town for taxis. The city's taxis have a high drop charge (about €7) for the first two kilometers (e.g., from Centraal Station to the Mint Tower), after which it's €2.12 per kilometer. You can wave them down, find a rare taxi stand, or call one (tel. 020/777-7777). All taxis are required to have meters. Uber works in Amsterdam like in the US (€28 from the airport into downtown).

You'll also see **bike taxis,** particularly near Dam Square and Leidseplein. Negotiate a rate for the trip before you board (no meter, estimate €1/3 minutes, no surcharge for baggage or extra weight, sample fare from Leidseplein to Anne Frank House: about €6).

Tours in Amsterdam

🎧 To sightsee on your own, download my free Rick Steves Audio Europe app with **audio tours** that illuminate some of Amsterdam's top neighborhoods, including my Amsterdam City Walk (see sidebar on page 46 for details).

BY BOAT
▲▲Traditional Canal Boat Tours

Long, low, tourist-laden boats leave continually from several docks around town for a relaxing, if uninspiring, one-hour introduction to the city (with recorded headphone commentary). Select a boat tour based on your convenience: your proximity to its starting point, or whether it's included with your I Amsterdam card. Tip: Boats leave only when full, so jump on a full boat to avoid waiting at the dock.

Rederij P. Kooij is cheapest (€11, 3/hour in summer 10:00-22:00, 2/hour in winter 10:00-17:00, boats dock opposite Centraal Station, tel. 020/623-3810, www.rederijkooij.nl).

Blue Boat Company's boats depart from near Leidseplein (€18, €16 if you book online; runs daily 10:00-18:00, every half-hour March-Oct, hourly Nov-Feb 10:00-18:00; 1.25 hours, Stadhouderskade 30, tel. 020/679-1370, www.blueboat.nl). Their evening cruise includes the Red Light District (€21, €19 online, nightly at 20:00, 1.5 hours, March-Oct also at 21:00 and 22:00, reservations required).

Gray Line-Stromma offers a standard one-hour trip and a variety of longer tours from the docks opposite Centraal Station (€18, €15 if you book online; 1-hour "100 Highlights" tour, daily 2-4/hour 9:00-22:00; Prins Hendrikkade 33a, tel. 020/217-0500, www.strcmma.nl).

ON FOOT
Red Light District Tours
If you'd be more comfortable exploring Amsterdam's most infamous neighborhood with a group, **Randy Roy's Red Light Tours** gives fun, casual, yet informative 1.5-hour walks through this fascinating and eye-popping district. Call or email to reserve (€15 includes a drink in a colorful bar at the end, nightly at 20:00, Fri and Sat also at 22:00, no tours Dec-Feb, tours meet in front of Victoria Hotel—in front of Centraal Station, mobile 06-4185-3288, www.randyroysredlighttours.com, kimberley@randyroysredlighttours.com).

Food Tours
Amsterdam has many competing food tours. I enjoyed the **Eating Amsterdam** tour, which takes 6-12 people on an eight-stop, four-hour food tour of the Jordaan neighborhood. You'll sample cheese, cider, pancakes, *bitterballen*, herring, apple pie, and more. They also offer a tour that includes a short boat ride (Jordaan tour-€77, Tue–Sat at 11:00; food tour with canal boat-€101, March-Dec Tue–Sat at 10:30; managed by Camilla Lundberg, tel. 020/808-3099, www.eatingamsterdamours.com).

Free City Walk
New Europe Tours "employs" native, English-speaking students to give irreverent and entertaining three-hour walks. While most guides lack a local's deep understanding of Dutch culture, not to mention professional training, they're certainly high-energy. This long walk covers a lot of the city with an enthusiasm for the contemporary pot-and-prostitution scene (free but tips expected, 5/day, www.neweuropetours.eu). They also offer paid tours (Red Light District-€14, daily at 19:00; coffeeshop scene-€14, daily at 15:00; Amsterdam by bike-€20, includes bike, daily at 12:00). All tours leave from the National Monument on Dam Square.

Private Guides
Larae Malooly and her team of guides offer lively cultural and historic tours, with the option to join a small group or upgrade to a private tour tailored to your interests. Themed walks include World

Amsterdam at a Glance

▲▲▲**Rijksmuseum** Best collection anywhere of the Dutch Masters—Rembrandt, Hals, Vermeer, and Steen—in a spectacular setting. **Hours:** Daily 9:00-17:00. See page 758.

▲▲▲**Van Gogh Museum** More than 200 paintings by the angst-ridden artist. **Hours:** Daily April-Aug 9:00-19:00, Fri until 21:00, Sat until 18:00 (April-June) and 21:00 (July-Aug); Sept-Oct 9:00-18:00, Fri until 21:00; Nov-March 9:00-17:00, Fri until 21:00. See page 763.

▲▲▲**Anne Frank House** Young Anne's hideaway during the Nazi occupation. **Hours:** Daily 9:00-22:00; Nov-March Mon-Fri 9:00-20:00, Sat until 22:00, Sun until 19:00. See page 768.

▲▲**Stedelijk Museum** The Netherlands' top modern-art museum. **Hours:** Daily 10:00-18:00, Fri until 22:00. See page 767.

▲▲**Vondelpark** City park and concert venue. See page 767.

▲▲**Amsterdam Museum** City's growth from fishing village to trading capital to today, including some Rembrandts and a playable carillon. **Hours:** Daily 10:00-17:00. See page 771.

▲▲**Amstelkring Museum** Catholic church hidden in the attic of a 17th-century merchant's house. **Hours:** Mon-Sat 10:00-17:00, Sun 13:00-17:00. See page 772.

▲▲**Red Light District** Women of the world's oldest profession on the job. See page 772.

War II, Jewish heritage, the Red Light District, and Rembrandt (€35 small group tours up to 10 people; €175 private tours, up to four people; www.amsterdamsel.com).

Albert Walet is a knowledgeable local guide who enjoys personalizing tours for Americans interested in knowing his city. Al specializes in history, architecture, and water management, and exudes a passion for Amsterdam (€70/2 hours, €120/4 hours, up to 4 people, on foot or by bike, mobile 06-2069-7882, abwalet@yahoo.com). Al also takes travelers to nearby towns, including Haarlem, Leiden, and Delft.

BY BIKE
Guided Bike Tours
Yellow Bike Guided Tours offers city bike tours of either two hours (€22.50, daily at 10:30, in winter at 13:30) or three hours

▲▲**Netherlands Maritime Museum** Rich seafaring story of the Netherlands, told with vivid artifacts. **Hours:** Daily 9:00-17:00. See page 774

▲▲**Hermitage Amsterdam** Russia's czarist treasures, on loan from St. Petersburg. **Hours:** Daily 10:00-17:00. See page 776.

▲▲**Dutch Resistance Museum** History of the Dutch struggle against the Nazis. **Hours:** Mon-Fri 10:00-17:00, Sat-Sun 11:00-17:00. See page 778.

▲**Museumplein** Square with art museums, street musicians, crafts, and nearby diamond demos. See page 758.

▲**Royal Palace** Lavish City Hall that takes you back to the Golden Age of the 17th century. **Hours:** Daily 10:00-17:00 when not closed for official ceremonies. See page 771.

▲**Rembrandt's House** The master's reconstructed house, displaying his etchings. **Hours:** Daily 10:00-18:00. See page 775.

▲**Jewish Historical Museum and Portuguese Synagogue** Exhibits on Judaism and culture and beloved synagogue that serves today's Jewish community. **Hours:** Daily 11:00-17:00. See page 776.

▲**Dutch Theater** Moving memorial in former Jewish detention center. **Hours:** Daily 11:00-17:00. See page 777.

(€27.50, daily at 13:30), which both include a 20-minute break. All tours leave from Nieuwezijds Kolk 29, three blocks from Centraal Station (reservations smart, tel. 020/620-6940, www.yellowbike. nl). If you'd prefer a private guided bike tour, contact Albert Walet, listed earlier.

Joy Ride Bike Tours pedal through the pastoral polder land in 4.5 hours (€33, April-Sept Sat, Mon, and Thu; meet at 10:15 and depart precisely at 10:30, no kids under 13). They also offer private tours (tours offered April-Nov, €225/4 people plus €25/person after that). Helmets, rain gear, and saddlebags are provided. Private tours must be booked in advance; tours meet behind the Rijksmuseum next to the Cobra Café (mobile 06-4361-1798, www. joyridetours.nl).

Amsterdam City Walk

Take a Dutch sampler walk from one end of the old center to the other, tasting all that Amsterdam has to offer along the way: quintessentially Dutch scenes, hidden churches, surprising shops, thriving happy-hour hangouts, and eight centuries of history. This three-mile walk starts at Centraal Station and ends at Leidseplein, near the Rijksmuseum. Allow three hours.

This information is distilled from the Amsterdam City Walk chapter in *Rick Steves Amsterdam & The Netherlands*, by Rick Steves and Gene Openshaw. You can download a free ∩ Rick Steves audio version of this walk; see page 46.

❶ Centraal Station

Centraal Station sits on reclaimed land at what was once the harbor mouth. With red brick and prickly spires, the station is the first of several Neo-Gothic build-ings we'll see from the late 19th century, the era of Amsterdam's economic revival. One of the station's towers has a clock dial; the other tower's dial is a weath-er vane.

Let's get oriented: *nord, zuid, ost,* and *vest.* Facing the station, you're looking north. On the other side of the station is the IJ (pronounced "eye"), the body of water that gives Amsterdam access to the open sea.

Now turn your back to the station and face the city, looking south. The city spreads out before you like a fan, in a series of con-centric canals. Ahead of you stretches the street called Damrak, which leads—like a red carpet for guests entering Amsterdam—to Dam Square a half-mile away. That's where we're headed.

To the left of Damrak is the city's old *(oude)* town. More re-cently, that historic neighborhood has become the Red Light Dis-trict. Towering above the old part of town is St. Nicholas Church. It was built in the 1880s, when Catholics—after about three centu-ries of oppression—were finally free to worship in public. To your far left is the DoubleTree by Hilton Hotel, with its 11th-floor Sky Lounge Amsterdam offering perhaps the city's best viewpoint.

To the right of Damrak is the new *(nieuwe)* part of town, where you'll find the Anne Frank House and the peaceful Jordaan neighborhood.

On your far right, in front of Ibis Hotel, is a huge, multistory parking garage—for bikes only. Biking in Holland is the way to go—the land is flat, distances are short, and there are designated bike paths everywhere. The bike parking garage is completely free, courtesy of the government, and intended to encourage this green and ultra-efficient mode of transportation.

• *With your back to the station, walk to the head of Damrak.*

Be careful crossing the street—be aware of trams, bikes, and cars. Keep going south straight along the right side of the street, following the crowds on...

❷ Damrak

This street was once a riverbed. It's where the Amstel River flowed north into the IJ, which led to a vast inlet of the North Sea called the Zuiderzee. It's this unique geography that turned Amsterdam into a center of trade. Boats could sail up the Amstel into the interior of Europe, or out to the North Sea, to reach the rest of the world.

As you stroll along Damrak, look left. There's a marina, lined with old brick buildings. Though they aren't terribly historic, the scene still captures a bit of Golden Age Amsterdam. Think of it: Back in the 1600s, this area was the harbor, and those buildings warehoused exotic goods from all over the world.

Today you'll pass a veritable gauntlet of touristy shops. These seem to cover every Dutch cliché. You'll see wooden shoes, which the Dutch used to wear to get around easily in the marshy soil, and all manner of tulips; the real ones come from Holland's famed fresh-flower industry. Heineken fridge magnets advertise one of the world's most popular pilsner beers. There are wheels of cheese, mar-

ijuana-leaf hats, team jerseys for the Ajax football (soccer) club, and memorabilia with the city's "XXX" logo. You'll likely hear a hand-cranked barrel organ and see windmill-shaped saltshakers. And everything seems to be available in bright orange—the official color of the Dutch royal family.

At the **Damrak Sex Museum** at Damrak 18, you'll find the city's most notorious commodity on display. As a port town catering to sailors and businessmen away from home, Amsterdam has always accommodated the sex trade.

Continue up Damrak (noting the **canal boats** on your right) for more touristy delectables. You'll also pass places selling the popular local fast food, *Vlaamse friets* (Flemish fries). The stand at Damrak 41 is a favorite, where plenty of locals stop to dip their

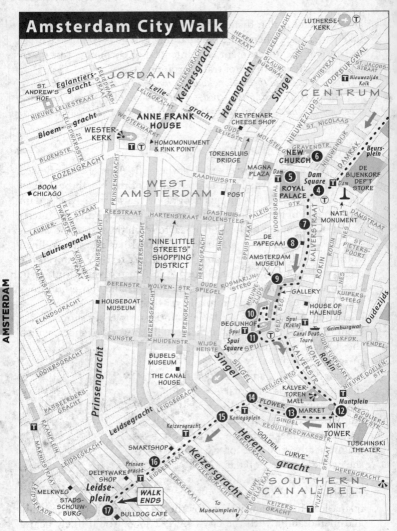

Amsterdam City Walk

fries in mayonnaise (not ketchup). As you pass Damrak's many restaurants, you'll see many offering international cuisine. Rijsttafel, a sampler of assorted Indonesian dishes, is especially popular, thanks to the days when the Dutch East Indies were a colony.

• *The long brick building with the square clock tower, along the left side of Damrak, is the...*

❸ Stock Exchange (Beurs van Berlage)

This impressive structure, a symbol of the city's long tradition as a trading town, was built with nine million bricks. Like so many buildings in this once-marshy city, it was constructed on a founda-

tion of pilings—some 5,000 tree trunks hammered vertically into the soil. When the Beurs opened in 1903, it was one of the world's first modernist buildings, with a geometric, minimal, no-frills style. Emphasizing function over looks, it helped set the architectural tone for many 20th-century buildings.

Make your way to the end of the long, century-old building. Amsterdammers have gathered in this neighborhood to trade since medieval times. Back then, "trading stock" meant buying and selling any kind of goods that could be loaded and unloaded onto a boat—goats, chickens, or kegs of beer. Over time, they began exchanging slips of paper, or "futures," rather than actual goods.

Traders needed moneychangers, who needed bankers, who made money by lending money. By the 1600s, Amsterdam had become one of the world's first great capitalist cities, loaning money to free-spending kings, dukes, and bishops.

• *Continue south along the busy boulevard until it opens into Dam Square. Make your way—carefully—across the street to the cobblestone pavement. Stand in the middle of the square and take it all in.*

❹ Dam Square

The city got its start right here in about the year 1250, when fishermen in this marshy delta settled along the built-up banks of the Amstel River. They built a *damme,* blocking the Amstel River, and creating a small village called "Amstel-damme." To the north was the *damrak* (meaning "outer harbor"), a waterway that eventually led to the sea. That's the street we just walked. To the south was the *rokin* ("inner harbor"), for river traffic—and nowadays also a main street. With access to the sea, fishermen were soon trading with German riverboats traveling downstream and with seafaring boats from Stockholm, Hamburg, and London. Land trade routes converged here as well, and a customs house stood in this spot. Dam Square was the center of it all.

Today, Dam Square is still the center of Dutch life, at least symbolically. The Royal Palace and major department stores face the square. Mimes, jugglers, and human statues mingle with locals and tourists. As Holland's most recognizable place, Dam Square is where political demonstrations begin and end.

Pan the square clockwise, starting with the Royal Palace—the large domed building on the west side. To its right stands the New Church (Nieuwe Kerk); it's located on the pedestrian-only shopping street called Nieuwendijk, which runs parallel to Damrak and stretches all the way to Centraal Station. Panning past Damrak, see the proud old De Bijenkorf ("The Beehive") department store.

Farther right, the Grand Hotel Krasnapolsky has a lovely circa-1900 glass-roofed "winter garden." The white obelisk is the National Monument, honoring WWII casualties. A few blocks behind the hotel is the edge of the Red Light District. To the right of the hotel stretches the street called the Nes, lined with some of Amsterdam's edgy live-theater venues. Panning farther right, find Rokin street—Damrak's southern counterpart, continuing past the square. Next, just to the right of the touristy Madame Tussauds, is

Kalverstraat, a busy pedestrian-only shoppers mall (look for *Rabobank* sign).

❺ Royal Palace (Koninklijk Huis)

Despite the name, this is really the former City Hall—and Amsterdam is one of the cradles of modern democracy. In medieval times,

this was where the city council and mayor met. In about 1650, the old medieval Town Hall was replaced with this one. Its style is appropriately Classical, recalling the democratic Greeks. The triangular pediment features denizens of the sea cavorting with Neptune and his gilded copper trident—all appropriate imagery for sea-trading Amsterdam. The small balcony (just above the entry doors) is where city leaders have long appeared for major speeches, pronouncements, executions, and (these days) for newly married royalty to blow kisses to the crowds. Today, the palace remains one of the four official residences of King Willem-Alexander and is usually open to visitors (for details on visiting, see page 771).

• *A few paces away, to the right as you're facing the Royal Palace, is the...*

❻ New Church (Nieuwe Kerk)

Though called the "New" Church, this building is actually 600 years old—a mere 100 years newer than the "Old" Church in the Red Light District. The sundial above the entrance once served as the city's official timepiece. While it's pricey to enter the church (which offers little besides the temporary exhibits), cheapskates can see much of it for free. Enter through the "Museumshop" door to the left of the main entrance, then climb the stairs to a balcony with a small free

museum and great views of the nave.

Take in the church's main highlights. At the far left end is an organ from 1655, still played for midday concerts. Opposite the entrance, a stained-glass window shows Count William IV giving the city its "XXX" coat of arms. And the window over the entrance portrays the inauguration of Queen Wilhelmina (1880-1962), who became the steadfast center of the Dutch resistance during World War II. The choir, once used by the monks, was, after the Reformation, turned into a mausoleum for a great Dutch admiral.

Leave the shop via the main church entrance. Back outside, look at the **monument** standing tall in the middle of Dam Square, built in 1956 as a WWII memorial. The Nazis occupied Holland from 1940 to 1945; in those years they deported some 60,000 Jewish Amsterdammers, driving many—including young Anne Frank and her family—into hiding. Near the end of the war, the "Hunger Winter" of 1944-1945 killed thousands of Dutch and forced many to survive on little more than tulip bulbs. The national monument both remembers the suffering of that grim time and offers hope for peace.

• *From Dam Square, head south (at the Rabobank sign) on* ❼ *Kalverstraat. This strictly pedestrian-only strip has been a traditional shopping street for centuries. But today it's notorious among locals as a noisy, soulless string of chain stores.*

For smaller and more elegant stores, try the adjacent district called De Negen Straatjes ("The Nine Little Streets"*). About four blocks west of Kalverstraat, it's where 200 or so shops and cafés mingle along tranquil canals.*

About 100 yards along, keep a sharp eye out for the next sight: It's on the right, just before and across from the McDonald's, at #58. Now pop into...

❽ De Papegaai Hidden Church (Petrus en Paulus Kerk)

This Catholic church—with a simple white interior, carved wood, and Stations of the Cross paintings—is an oasis of peace amid crass 21st-century commercialism. It's not exactly a hidden church (after all, you've found it), but it keeps a low profile. That's because it dates from an era when Catholics in Amsterdam were forced to worship in secret. While technically illegal, Catholics could worship so long as they practiced in humble, unadvertised places, like this church. The church gets its nickname from a parrot *(papegaai)* carved over the entrance of the house that formerly stood on this site. Now, a stuffed parrot hangs in the nave to remember that original *papegaai*.

• *Return to Kalverstraat and continue south for about 100 yards. At #92, where Kalverstraat crosses Wijde Kapel Steeg, look to the right at an archway that leads to the entrance and courtyard of the Amsterdam Museum.*

❾ Amsterdam Museum and Amsterdam Gallery

Pause at the entrance to the museum complex to view the archway. On the slumping arch is Amsterdam's coat of arms—a red shield with three Xs and a crown. The X-shaped

crosses represent the crucifixion of St. Andrew, the patron saint of fishermen. They also represent the three virtues of heroism, determination, and mercy—symbolism that was declared by the queen after the Dutch experience in World War II. (Before that, they likely symbolized the three great medieval threats: fire, flood, and plague.) The crown dates from 1489, when Maximilian I—a Habsburg emperor—also ruled the Low Countries. He paid off a big loan with help from Amsterdam's city bankers and, as thanks for the cash, gave the city permission to use his prestigious trademark, the Habsburg crown, atop its shield.

The courtyard leads to the best city history museum in town, the **Amsterdam Museum** (described in "Sights in Amsterdam," later). Next to the museum's entrance is a free, glassed-in passageway lined with paintings. If it's closed, you'll need to backtrack to Kalverstraat to continue our walk (continue south, then turn right on Begijnensteeg, then look for the gate leading to the Begijnhof). Otherwise, step into the **Amsterdam Gallery** (Schuttersgalerij; formerly known as Civic Guard's Gallery).

This hall features group portraits of Amsterdam's citizens from the Golden Age to modern times. Giant statues of Goliath and a knee-high David (from 1650) watch over the whole thing. Civic Guard paintings from the 1600s (featuring men and their weapons) established a tradition of group portraits that continues today. Stroll around and gaze into the eyes of the hardworking men and women who made tiny Holland so prosperous and powerful.

Don't miss the colorful patchwork carpet. Dutch society has long been a melting pot society and this—with a patch representing each country from where Dutch immigrants originated—celebrates today's multicultural reality. (A chart locates the various countries.)

• *The gallery offers a shortcut to our next stop, a hidden and peaceful little courtyard. To get there, exit out the far end of the Amsterdam Gallery. Once in the light of day, continue ahead one block farther south and find the humble gate on the right, which leads to the...*

⑩ Begijnhof

This quiet courtyard, lined with houses around a church, has sheltered women since 1346 (and is worth ▲). For centuries this was

the home of a community of Beguines—pious and simple women who removed themselves from the world at large to dedicate their lives to God. When it was first established, it literally was a "woman's island"—a circle of houses facing a peaceful courtyard, surrounded by water. As you enter, keep in mind that this spot isn't just a tourist attraction; it's also a place where people live. Be considerate.

Begin your visit at the **statue** of one of these charitable sisters, just beyond the church. The Beguines' ranks swelled during the Crusades, when so many men took off, never to return, leaving society with an abundance of single women. Later, women widowed by the hazards of overseas trade lived out their days as Beguines. They spent their days deep in prayer and busy with daily tasks—spinning wool, making lace, teaching, and caring for the sick.

Now turn to the brick-faced **English Reformed church** (Engelse Kerk). The church was built in 1420 to serve the Beguine community. But then, in 1578, Catholicism was outlawed, and the Dutch Reformed Church took over many Catholic monasteries. Still, the Begijnhof survived; in 1607, this church became Anglican. The church served as a refuge for English traders and religious separatists fleeing persecution in England, including the Pilgrims, who prayed here before boarding the Mayflower.

A **Catholic church** faces the English Reformed Church. Because Catholics were being persecuted when it was built, this had to be a low-profile, "hidden" church—notice the painted-out windows on the second and third floors. This church served Amsterdam's oppressed 17th-century Catholics, who refused to worship as Protestants.

The last Beguine died in 1971, but this Begijnhof still thrives, providing subsidized housing to about 100 single women (mostly Catholic seniors). The statue of the Beguine faces a black **wooden house,** at #34. This structure dates from 1528, and is the city's oldest. Originally, the whole city consisted of wooden houses like this one. They were eventually replaced with brick houses, to minimize the fire danger of so many homes packed together.

• *Near the wooden house, find a little corridor leading you back into the modern world. Head up a few steps to emerge into the lively...*

⓫ Spui Square

Lined with cafés and bars, this square is one of the city's more popular spots for nightlife and sunny afternoon people-watching. Its name, Spui (rhymes with "now" and means "spew"), recalls the days when water was moved over dikes to keep the place dry. Head two blocks to the left, crossing busy Kalverstraat, to the bustling street called the **Rokin.** A small black statue of Queen Wilhelmina on the Rokin shows her daintily riding sidesaddle. Remember that in real life, she was the iron-willed inspiration for the Dutch resistance against the Nazis.

Continue south on Kalverstraat. Just before the end of this shopping boulevard, on the right, you'll see modern **Kalvertoren** shopping mall. Enter and go deeper within to find a slanting glass elevator. You can ride this to the recommended top-floor **Blue Amsterdam Restaurant,** where a coffee or light lunch buys you something that's rare in altitude-challenged Amsterdam—a nice view.

• *At the center of the next square stands the...*

⓬ Mint Tower (Munttoren)

This tower marked the limit of the medieval walled city and served as one of its original gates. In the Middle Ages, the city walls were girdled by a moat—the Singel canal. Until about 1500, the area beyond here was nothing but marshy fields and a few farms on reclaimed land. The Mint Tower's steeple was added later—in the year 1620, as you can see written below the clock face. Today, the tower is a favorite within Amsterdam's marijuana culture. Stoners love to take a photo of the clock and its 1620 sign at exactly 4:20 p.m.—the traditional time to quit work and light one up. (On the 24-hour clock, 4:20 p.m. is 16:20... Du-u-u-ude!)

• *Continue past the Mint Tower, first walking a few yards south along busy Vijzelstraat (keep an eye out for trams). Then turn right and walk west along the south bank of the Singel canal. It's lined with the greenhouse shops of the...*

⓭ Flower Market (Bloemenmarkt)

Browse your way along while heading for the end of the block. The Netherlands is by far the largest flower exporter in Europe, and a major flower power worldwide. If you're looking for a

souvenir, note that certain seeds are marked as OK to bring back through customs into the US (the marijuana starter-kit-in-a-can is probably...not).

• *The long Flower Market ends at the next bridge, where you'll see a square named...*

⑭ Koningsplein

This pleasant square, with a popular outdoor *heringhandel* (herring shop), is a great place to choke down a raw herring—a fish that has a special place in every Dutch heart. After all, herring was the commodity that first put Amsterdam on the trading map. Locals eat it chopped up with onions and pickles, using the Dutch-flag toothpick as a utensil.

• *Turn left, heading straight south to Leidseplein along Koningsplein, which changes its name to Leidestraat.*

⑮ Leidsestraat Canals and ⑯ Shops

As you walk along, you'll reach Herengracht, the first of several grand canals. Look left down Herengracht to see the so-called **Golden Curve** of the canal. It's lined with townhouses sporting especially nice gables. Amsterdam has many different types of gable—bell-shaped, step-shaped, and so on. This stretch is best known for its "cornice" gables (straight across); these topped the Classical-looking facades belonging to rich merchants—the *heren*.

Cross over the next canal (Keizersgracht) and find the little **smartshop** on the right-hand corner (at Keisersgracht 508). While "smartshops" like this one are all just as above-board as any other in the city, they sell drugs—some of them quite strong, most of them illegal back home, and not all of them harmless. But since all these products are found in nature, the Dutch government considers them legal. Check out the window displays, or go on in and browse.

Just over the next bridge, where Leidsestraat crosses Prinsengracht, you'll find the **Delftware shop** (to the right, at Prinsengracht 440), which sells the distinctive ceramics known as Delftware. In the early 1600s, Dutch traders brought home blue-

and-white porcelain from China, which became so popular that Dutch potters scrambled to come up with their own version.

• *Follow Leidsestraat down to the big, busy square, called...*

⑰ Leidseplein

This is Amsterdam's liveliest square, worth ▲, filled with outdoor tables under trees; ringed with cafés, theaters, and nightclubs; bus-

tling with tourists, diners, trams, mimes, and fire eaters. Leidseplein's south side is bordered by a gray Neoclassical building that houses a huge Apple Store. Nearby is the city's main serious theater, the **Stadsschouwburg.** The theater company dates back to the 17th-century Golden Age, and the present building is from 1890. Does the building look familiar, with its red brick and fanciful turrets? This building, Centraal Station, and the Rijksmuseum were all built by the same architect, Pierre Cuypers, during the city's late-19th-century revival.

The neighborhood beyond Burger King is Amsterdam's **"Restaurant Row,"** featuring countless Thai, Brazilian, Indian, Italian, Indonesian—and even a few Dutch—eateries. Next, on the east end of Leidseplein, is the flagship **Bulldog Café and Coffeeshop.** (Notice the sign above the door: It once housed the police bureau.) A small green-and-white decal on the window indicates that it's a city-licensed "coffeeshop," where marijuana is sold and smoked legally.

• *Our walk is over. Vondelpark and the Rijksmuseum are one stop away on tram #2 or #12. To return to Centraal Station (or to nearly anyplace along this walk), catch tram #2, #11, or #12 from Leidseplein.*

Sights in Amsterdam

One of Amsterdam's delights is that it has perhaps more small specialty museums than any other city its size. From houseboats to sex, from marijuana to Old Masters, you can find a museum to suit your interests.

For tips on how to save time otherwise spent in the long ticket-buying lines of the big three museums—the Anne Frank House, Van Gogh Museum, and Rijksmuseum—see "Advance Tickets and Sightseeing Passes," earlier. The following sights are arranged by neighborhood for handy sightseeing.

MUSEUMPLEIN

This ▲ parklike square is bordered by the Rijks, Van Gogh, and Stedelijk museums, and is filled with street performers, craft booths, and locals enjoying a park bench. You'll also recognize the climbable "I Amsterdam" letters awaiting the world's selfies.

▲▲▲Rijksmuseum

Built to house the nation's great art, the Rijksmuseum (RIKES-moo-zay-oom, "Rijks" rhymes with "bikes") owns several thousand

paintings, including an incomparable collection of 17th-century Dutch Masters: Rembrandt, Vermeer, Hals, and Steen. Its vast collection also includes interesting artifacts—such as furniture—that help bring the Golden Age to life.

The 17th century saw the Netherlands at the pinnacle of its power. The Dutch had won their independence from Spain, trade and shipping boomed, wealth poured in, the people were understandably proud, and the arts flourished. This era was later dubbed the Dutch Golden Age. With no church bigwigs or royalty around to commission big canvases in the Protestant Dutch Republic, artists had to find different patrons—and they discovered the upper-middle-class businessmen who fueled Holland's capitalist economy. Artists painted their portraits and decorated their homes with pretty still lifes and unpreachy, slice-of-life art.

This delightful museum—recently much improved after a long renovation—offers one of the most exciting and enjoyable art experiences in Europe. As if in homage to Dutch art and history, the Rijksmuseum lets you linger over a vast array of objects and paintings, appreciating the beauty of everyday things.

Cost and Hours: €17.50; daily 9:00-17:00, tram #2 or #12 from Centraal Station to Rijksmuseum stop. The entrance is off the passageway that tunnels right through the center of the building.

Avoiding Crowds/Lines: The museum is most crowded on weekends and holidays, and there's always a midday crush between 11:00 and 14:00. Plan your visit for either first thing in the morning or later in the day (it's least crowded after 15:00). Those with a Museumkaart or advance ticket use a separate entrance and skip the ticket counter.

Information: Info tel. 020/674-7047, www.rijksmuseum.nl.

Tours: Guided tours are often offered at 11:00, 13:00, and 15:00 (€5). A multimedia videoguide (€5) offers both a 45-minute highlights tour and a more in-depth tour. Use the self-guided tour

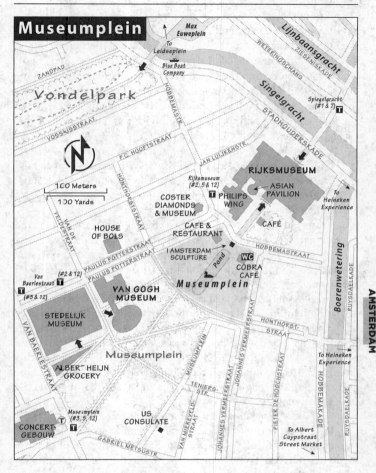

below to hit the highlights, then (if you choose) explore the rest of the collection with the videoguide.

Eating: The Rijksmuseum Café, in the Atrium, is outside the ticket entry, so you don't need a museum ticket to eat here. On the south side of the building, there's a restaurant in the Philips Wing and a pleasant coffee-and-pastry café in the garden to the right. Nearby on Museumplein, you'll find the Cobra Café, a number of takeout stands, and (at the far end, near the Stedelijk Museum), an Albert Heijn grocery. Museumplein and nearby Vondelpark are both perfect for a picnic.

⊘ Self-Guided Tour

Dutch art is meant to be enjoyed, not studied. It's straightforward, meat-and-potatoes art for the common man. The Dutch love the beauty of mundane things painted realistically and with exquisite detail. So set your cerebral cortex on "low" and let this art pass straight from the eyes to the heart, with minimal detours.

Follow the crowds up the stairway to the top (second) floor, where you emerge into the **Great Hall.** With its stained-glass windows, vaulted ceiling, and murals of Golden Age explorers, it feels like a cathedral to Holland's middle-class merchants. Gaze down the long adjoining hall to the far end, with the "altarpiece" of this cathedral—Rembrandt's *The Night Watch.*

• *Follow the flow of the crowds toward it, into the...*

Gallery of Honor: This grand space was purpose-built to hold the Greatest Hits of the Golden Age by the era's biggest rock stars: Hals, Vermeer, Steen, and Rembrandt.

• *In the first alcove to the right is the work of...*

Frans Hals (c. 1582-1666): Hals was the premier Golden Age portrait painter. Merchants hired him the way we'd hire a wedding photographer. With a few quick strokes, Hals captured not only the features, but also the personality. In *A Militiaman Holding a Berkemeyer,* a.k.a. *The Merry Drinker* (c. 1628-1630), you're greeted by a jovial man in a black hat, capturing the earthy, exuberant spirit of the Dutch Golden Age. Notice the details—the happy red face of the man offering us a berkemeyer drinking glass, the sparkle in his eyes, the lacy collar, the decorative belt buckle, and so on. He often painted common people, fishermen, and barflies such as this one. Hals used a stop-action technique, freezing the man in mid-gesture, with the rough brushwork creating a blur that suggests the man is still moving.

• *A little farther along are the small-scale canvases of...*

Johannes Vermeer (1632-1675): Vermeer is the master of tranquility and stillness. He creates a clear and silent pool that is a world in itself. Most of his canvases show interiors of Dutch homes, where Dutch women engage in everyday activities, lit by a side window.

The Rijksmuseum has the best collection of Vermeers in the world—four of them. (There are only some 34 in captivity.) But each is a small jewel worth lingering over. Vermeer's *The Milkmaid* (c. 1660) brings out the beauty in everyday things. The subject is ordinary—a kitchen maid—but you could look for hours at the tiny details and rich color tones. These are everyday objects, but they glow in a diffused light: the crunchy crust, the hanging basket, even the rusty nail in the wall with its tiny shadow.

In paintings such as *Woman Reading a Letter* (c. 1663), notice how Vermeer's placid scenes often have an air of mystery. The woman is reading a letter. From a lover? A father on a two-year business trip to the East Indies? Not even taking time to sit down, she reads intently, with parted lips and a bowed head. It must be important. Again, Vermeer has framed a moment of everyday life. But within this small world are hints of a wider, wilder world—the light coming from the left is obviously from a large window, giving us a whiff of the life going on outside.

• *In an alcove nearby are some rollicking paintings by...*

Jan Steen (c. 1625-1679, pronounced "yahn stain"): Steen was the Norman Rockwell of his day, painting humorous scenes from the lives of the lower classes. As a tavern owner, he observed society firsthand.

Find the painting *The Merry Family* (1668). This family is eating, drinking, and singing like there's no tomorrow. The broken eggshells and scattered cookware symbolize waste and extravagance. The neglected proverb tacked to the fireplace reminds us that children will follow in the footsteps of their parents. Dutch Golden Age families were notoriously lenient with their kids. Even today, the Dutch describe a rowdy family as a "Jan Steen household."

In *Adolf and Catharina Croeser*, a.k.a. *The Burgomaster of Delft and His Daughter* (1655), a well-dressed burgher sits on his front porch, when a poor woman and child approach to beg, putting him squarely between the horns of a moral dilemma. On the one hand, we see his rich home, well-dressed daughter, and a vase of flowers—a symbol that his money came from morally suspect capitalism. On the other hand, there are his poor fellow citizens and the church steeple, reminding him of his Christian duty.

• *You're getting closer to the iconic* Night Watch, *but first you'll find other works by...*

Rembrandt van Rijn (1606-1669): Rembrandt was the greatest of all Dutch painters. Whereas most painters specialized in one field—portraits, landscapes, still lifes—Rembrandt excelled in them all.

The son of a Leiden miller who owned a waterwheel on the Rhine ("van Rijn"), Rembrandt took Amsterdam by storm with his famous painting *The Anatomy Lesson of Dr. Nicolaes Tulp* (1632). Commissions poured in, and he was soon wealthy and married. Holland's war with England (1652-1654) devastated the art market, and Rembrandt's free-spending ways forced him to declare bankruptcy—the ultimate humiliation in success-oriented Amsterdam. His bitter losses added a new wisdom to his work. In his last years, his greatest works were his self-portraits, showing a

AMSTERDAM

tired, wrinkled man stoically enduring life's misfortunes. His death effectively marked the end of the Dutch Golden Age.

At the far end of the Gallery of Honor is the museum's star masterpiece—*The Night Watch*, a.k.a. *The Militia Company of Captain Frans Banninck Cocq* (1642).

This is Rembrandt's most famous—though not necessarily greatest—painting. Created in 1642, when he was 36, it was one of his most important commissions: a group portrait of a company of Amsterdam's Civic Guards to hang in their meeting hall. It's an action shot. With flags waving and drums beating, the guardsmen (who, by the 1640s, were really only an honorary militia of rich bigwigs) spill onto the street from under an arch in the back. These guardsmen on the move epitomize the proud, independent, upwardly mobile Dutch.

Why is *The Night Watch* so famous? Compare it with group portraits nearby, where every face is visible and everyone is well-lit, flat, and flashbulb-perfect. By contrast, Rembrandt rousted the Civic Guards off their fat duffs. By adding movement and depth to an otherwise static scene, he took posers and turned them into warriors. He turned a simple portrait into great art.

Now backtrack a few steps to the Gallery of Honor's last alcove to find Rembrandt's *Self-Portrait as the Apostle Paul* (1661). Rembrandt's many self-portraits show us the evolution of a great painter's style, as well as the progress of a genius's life. For Rembrandt, the two were intertwined. With a lined forehead, a bulbous nose, and messy hair, he peers out from under several coats of glazing, holding old, wrinkled pages. His look is...skeptical? Weary? Resigned to life's misfortunes? Or amused?

This man has seen it all—success, love, money, fatherhood, loss, poverty, death. He took these experiences and wove them into his art. Rembrandt died poor and misunderstood, but he remained very much his own man to the end.

The Rest of the Rijks: The Rijks is dedicated to detailing Dutch history from 1200 until the present, with upward of 8,000 works on display. There's everything from an airplane (third floor, in the 20th-century exhibit) to women's fashion and Delftware (lower level). The Asian Art Pavilion shows off 365 objects from the East Indies—a former Dutch colony—as well as items from India, Japan, Korea, and China. (The bronze Dancing Shiva, in Room 1 of the pavilion, is considered one of the best in the world.)

You might want to seek out the **Van Gogh self-portrait** in Room 1.13 (from the stained-glass Great Hall, go back downstairs the way you came to floor 1 and turn left). The **Philips Wing** hosts temporary exhibits upstairs (with themes that complement the Rijksmuseum's strengths) and a rotating photography collection downstairs (admission covered by Rijksmuseum ticket).

▲▲▲Van Gogh Museum

Near the Rijksmuseum, this remarkable museum features works by the troubled Dutch artist whose art seemed to mirror his life.

Vincent, who killed himself in 1890 at age 37, is best known for sunny, Impressionist canvases that vibrate and pulse with vitality. The museum's 200 paintings—which offer a virtual stroll through the artist's work and life—were owned by Theo, Vincent's younger, art-dealer brother. Highlights include *Sunflowers, The Bedroom, The Potato Eaters,* and many brooding self-portraits. The third floor shows works that influenced Vincent, from Monet and Pissarro to Gauguin, Cézanne, and Toulouse-Lautrec. The worthwhile multimedia guide includes insightful commentaries and quotes from Vincent himself. Temporary exhibits fill the new wing, down the escalator from the ground-floor lobby.

Cost and Hours: €18; daily April-Aug 9:00-19:00, Fri until 21:00, and Sat until 18:00 (April-June) and 21:00 (July-Aug); Sept-Oct 9:00-18:00, Fri until 21:00; Nov-March 9:00-17:00, Fri until 21:00; Paulus Potterstraat 7, tram #2 or #12 from Centraal Station to Van Baerlestraat or Rijksmuseum stop.

Avoiding Lines: To get in without a wait, buy timed-entry tickets online at www.vangoghmuseum.com (tickets go on sale about four months in advance). If you have a Museumkaart or I Amsterdam card, you'll queue up at a shorter line than same-day ticket buyers. During busy times, same-day tickets are often unavailable.

Information: Tel. 020/570-5200, www.vangoghmuseum.nl.

Tours: The €5 multimedia guide gives insightful commentaries about Van Gogh's paintings and his technique, along with related quotations from Vincent himself. There's also a kids' multimedia guide (€3).

Cuisine Art: The museum has a cafeteria-style café.

○ Self-Guided Tour

The collection is laid out roughly chronologically, through the changes in Vincent van Gogh's life (1853-1890). But you'll need to be flexible—the paintings are spread over three floors, and every few months there's a different array of paintings from the museum's large collection. On level 0, self-portraits introduce you to the artist. Level 1 has his early paintings; level 2 focuses on the man and his contemporaries; and level 3 has his final works. The paintings span five periods of Van Gogh's life—spent in the Netherlands, Paris, Arles, St-Rémy, and Auvers-sur-Oise.

You could see Vincent van Gogh's canvases as a series of suicide notes—or as the record of a life full of beauty...perhaps too full of beauty. He attacked life with a passion, experiencing highs and lows more intensely than the average person. The beauty of the world overwhelmed him; its ugliness struck him as only another dimension of beauty. He tried to absorb the full spectrum of experience, good and bad, and channel it onto a canvas. The frustration of this overwhelming task drove him to madness. If all this is a bit overstated—and I guess it is—it's an attempt to show the emotional impact that Van Gogh's works have had on many people, me included.

• *Pass through security and the ticket booth into the glass-pavilion reception hall. Here you'll find an info desk (pick up a free floor plan), bag check, multimedia-guide rental, and WCs. There's also a bookstore (with several good, basic "Vincent" guidebooks and lots of posters with mailing tubes) and an excellent temporary exhibit gallery (generally free).*

Ascend to level 1. Work clockwise around the floor and follow the stages of Vincent's life.

The Netherlands (1880-1885): Start with his stark, dark early work. These dark, gray canvases show us the hard, plain existence of the people and town of Nuenen, in the rural southern Netherlands. The style is crude—Van Gogh couldn't draw very well and would never become a great technician. The paint is laid on thick, as though painted with Nuenen mud. The main subject is almost always dead center, with little or no background, so there's a claustrophobic feeling. We are unable to see anything but the immediate surroundings. For example, *The Potato Eaters* (1885) is set in a dark, cramped room lit only by a dim lamp, where poor workers help themselves to a steaming plate of potatoes. They've earned it. Their hands are gnarly, their faces kind. Vincent deliberately wanted the canvas to be potato-colored.

• *Continue to the room with work he did in...*

Paris (March 1886-Feb 1888): After his father's death, Vincent moved from rural, religious, poor Holland to the City of Light. There his younger brother Theo, an art dealer, provided the financial and emotional support that allowed Vincent to spend the rest of his short life painting.

The sun begins to break through, lighting up everything he paints. His canvases are more colorful and the landscapes more spacious, with plenty of open sky, giving a feeling of exhilaration after the closed, dark world of Nuenen. In the cafés and bars of Paris' bohemian Montmartre district, Vincent met the revolutionary Impressionists. First, Vincent copied from the Impressionist masters. He painted garden scenes like Claude Monet, café snapshots like Edgar Degas, "block prints" like the Japanese masters, and self-portraits like...nobody else.

In his *Self-Portrait as a Painter* (1887-1888), the budding young artist proudly displays his new palette full of bright new colors, try-

ing his hand at the Impressionist technique of building a scene using dabs of different-colored paint. In *Red Cabbages and Onions* (1887), Vincent quickly developed his own style: thicker paint; broad, swirling brushstrokes; and brighter, clashing colors that make even inanimate objects seem to pulsate with life. Despite his new sociability, Vincent never quite fit in with his Impressionist friends. He wanted peace and quiet, a place where he could throw himself into his work completely. He headed for the sunny south of France.

• *Travel to the next room to reach...*

Arles (Feb 1888-May 1889): After the dreary Paris winter, the colors of springtime overwhelmed Vincent. The blossoming trees and colorful fields inspired him to paint canvas after canvas, drenched in sunlight. One fine example is *The Yellow House*, a.k.a. *The Street* (1888). Vincent rented this house with the green shutters. (He ate at the pink café next door.) Look at that blue sky! He painted in a frenzy, working feverishly to try and take it all in. His unique style evolved beyond Impressionism—thicker paint, stronger outlines, brighter colors (often applied right from the paint tube), and swirling brushwork that makes inanimate objects pulse and vibrate with life.

He invited his friend Paul Gauguin to join him, envisioning a sort of artists' colony in Arles. He spent months preparing a room upstairs for Gauguin's arrival. He painted *Sunflowers* (1889) to brighten up the place. At first, Gauguin and Vincent got along great. But then things went sour. They clashed over art, life, and their prickly personalities. On Christmas Eve 1888, Vincent went ballistic. Enraged during an alcohol-fueled argument, he pulled out a razor and waved it in Gauguin's face. Gauguin took the hint and quickly left town. Vincent was horrified at himself. In a fit of remorse and madness, he mutilated his own ear and presented it to a prostitute.

The people of Arles realized they had a madman on their hands. A doctor diagnosed "acute mania with hallucinations," and the local vicar talked Vincent into admitting himself to a mental hospital.

• *Ascend to level 2, where you may see displays about Van Gogh's contemporaries—Gauguin, his brother Theo—as well as more Van Gogh paintings. The visit concludes on level 3, with Vincent's final paintings.*

St-Remy (May 1889-May 1890): In the mental hospital, Vincent continued to paint whenever he was well enough. At St-Remy, we see a change from bright, happy landscapes to more introspective subjects. The colors are less bright and more surreal, the brushwork even more furious. The strong outlines of figures are twisted and tortured, such as in *The Garden of Saint Paul's Hospital,* a.k.a. *Leaf Fall* (1889). A solitary figure (Vincent?) winds along a narrow, snaky path as the wind blows leaves on him. The colors are surreal—blue, green, and red tree trunks with heavy black outlines. A road runs away from us, heading nowhere.

Vincent moved north to Auvers-sur-Oise (May-July 1890), a small town near Paris where he could stay under a doctor-friend's supervision. *Wheat Field with Crows* (1890) is one of the last paintings Vincent finished. We can try to search the wreckage of his life for the black box explaining what happened, but there's not much there. His life was sad and tragic, but the record he left is one not of sadness, but of beauty—intense beauty.

The windblown wheat field is a nest of restless energy. Scenes like this must have overwhelmed Vincent with their incredible beauty—too much, too fast, with no release. The sky is stormy and dark blue, almost nighttime, barely lit by two suns boiling through the deep ocean of blue. The road starts nowhere, leads nowhere, disappearing into the burning wheat field. Above all of this swirling beauty fly the crows, the dark ghosts that had hovered over his life since Nuenen. On July 27, 1890, Vincent left his room, walked out to a nearby field, and put a bullet through his chest. He stumbled back to his room, where he died two days later, with Theo by his side.

Art Beyond Van Gogh: Scattered throughout the museum are works by those who influenced Van Gogh and those who were influenced by him: Academy painters and their smooth-surfaced canvases, Impressionists Claude Monet and Camille Pissarro, and fellow Post-Impressionists Paul Gauguin, Paul Cézanne, and Henri de Toulouse-Lautrec.

Also on Museumplein
▲▲Stedelijk Museum

The Netherlands' top modern-art museum, the Stedelijk (STAYD-eh-lik), is filled with a fun and refreshing collection of 20th-century classics as well as cutting-edge works by Picasso, Chagall, and many more. Before entering, notice the architecture of the modern entrance—aptly nicknamed "the bathtub." Once inside, pick up the map and envision the museum's four main sections: the permanent collection 1850-1950 (ground floor, right half), Dutch design (ground floor, left half), permanent collection 1950-present (first floor), and various temporary exhibits (scattered about, usually some on each floor). Each room comes with thoughtful English descriptions. (And if you're into marijuana, I can't think of a better space than the Stedelijk in which to enjoy its effects.)

Cost and Hours: €15, daily 10:00-18:00, Fri until 22:00, top-notch gift shop, Paulus Potterstraat 13, tram #2 or #12 from Centraal Station to Van Baerlestraat, tel. 020/573-2911, www.stedelijk. nl. The €5 audioguide covers permanent and temporary exhibits.

▲▲Vondelpark

This huge, lively city park is popular with the Dutch—families with little kids, romantic couples, strolling seniors, and hipsters sharing blankets and beers. It's a favored venue for free summer concerts. On a sunny afternoon, it's a hedonistic scene that seems to say, "Parents...

relax." The park's 'T Blauwe Theehuis ("The Blue Tea House") is a delightful spot to nurse a drink and take in the scene; see page 788.

WEST AMSTERDAM
Jordaan District

By the 1600s—Amsterdam's Golden Age—residents needed more land and developed the Jordaan neighborhood. The **Singel canal** was the original moat running around the old walled city. It was served by a new church to the west—the **Westerkerk.** The area still looks much as it might have during the Dutch Golden Age of the 1600s, with houses shoulder-to-shoulder, leaning this way and that.

For me, the bridge over the Egelantiersgracht canal and its surroundings capture the essence of the Jordaan. Take it all in: the bookstores, art galleries, working artists' studios, and small cafés full of rickety tables. The quiet canal is lined with trees and old, narrow buildings with gables—classic Amsterdam. The street called Tweede Egelantiersdwarsstraat is the laid-back Jordaan neighborhood's main shopping-and-people street, where you'll find boutiques, galleries, antique stores, hair salons, and an enticing array of restaurants (see "Eating in Amsterdam," later).

▲▲▲Anne Frank House

A pilgrimage for many, this house offers a fascinating look at the hideaway of young Anne during the Nazi occupation of the Netherlands. Anne, her parents, an older sister, and four others spent a little more than two years in a "Secret Annex" behind her father's business. While in hiding, 13-year-old Anne kept a diary chronicling her extraordinary experience. The thoughtfully designed exhibit offers thorough coverage of the Frank family, the diary, the stories of others who hid, and the Holocaust.

Cost and Hours: €9, €9.50 online, daily 9:00-22:00; Nov-March Mon-Fri 9:00-20:00, Sat until 22:00, Sun until 19:00; best to reserve online two months in advance—only advance-ticket holders are admitted 9:00-15:30, same-day tickets sold only after 15:30 but lines can be up to three hours; cloakroom for coats and small bags, no large bags allowed inside, Prinsengracht 267, near Westerkerk, tel. 020/556-7105, www.annefrank.org.

Advance Reservations: Online timed-entry tickets go on sale starting two months in advance (for example, to visit on Aug 15, you can buy online beginning June 15). From two months until the day you wish to visit, tickets are gradually released—be persistent.

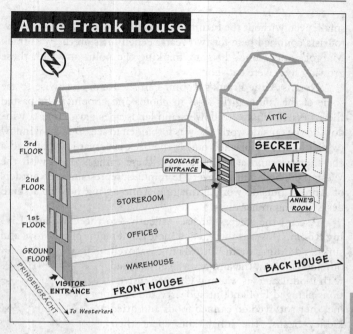

Anne Frank House

ATTIC

SECRET

BOOKCASE
ENTRANCE

ANNEX

3rd FLOOR

2nd FLOOR

STOREROOM

ANNE'S ROOM

1st FLOOR

OFFICES

GROUND FLOOR

WAREHOUSE

BACK HOUSE

PRINSENGRACHT

VISITOR ENTRANCE

FRONT HOUSE

To Westerkerk

Check the website for any changes when reserving; the museum underwent a major renovation in 2018.

Visiting the Museum: Begin in the **first floor** offices, where Otto Frank ran a successful business called Opekta, selling spices and pectin for making jelly. Photos and displays (typewriters, balance sheets) bring to life the business concerns of Otto and his colleagues. During the Nazi occupation, while the Frank family hid in the back of the building, these brave people kept Otto's business running, secretly bringing supplies to the Franks. Upstairs in the second floor **storeroom,** models show the two floors where Anne, her family, and four others lived. All told, eight people lived in a tiny apartment smaller than 1,000 square feet.

In July 1942, the family and four fellow Jews went into hiding. Otto handed over the keys to the business to his "Aryan" colleagues, sent a final postcard to relatives, gave the family cat to a neighbor, spread rumors that they were fleeing to Switzerland, and prepared his family to "dive under" (*onderduik*, as it was called).

At the back of the second floor storeroom is the clever hidden passageway into the **Secret Annex.** Though not exactly a secret (since it's hard to hide an entire building), the annex was a typical back-house *(achterhuis)*, a common feature in Amsterdam buildings, and the Nazis had no reason to suspect anything on the premises of the legitimate Opekta business. Pass through the bookcase entrance into Otto, Edith, and Margot's Room. The room is very small, even without the furniture. Imagine yourself and two fellow tourists confined here for two years. Pencil lines on the wall track Margot's and Anne's heights, marking the point at which these growing lives were cut short.

Next is **Anne Frank's Room.** Pan the room clockwise to see some of the young girl's idols in photos and clippings she pasted there herself. Photos of flowers and landscapes gave Anne a window on the outside world she was forbidden to see. Out the window (which had to be blacked out) is the back courtyard, which had a chestnut tree and a few buildings. These things, along with the Westerkerk bell chiming every 15 minutes, represented the borders of Anne's "outside world." Imagine Anne sitting here at a small desk, writing in her diary.

Ascend the steep staircase—silently—to the **Common Living Room.** This was the kitchen (note the remains of the stove and sink) and dining room. Otto Frank was well off, and early on, the annex was well-stocked with food. Later, as war and German restrictions plunged Holland into poverty and famine, they survived on canned foods and dried kidney beans. The inhabitants spent their days reading and studying in this room. At night, it became sleeping quarters for Hermann and Auguste van Pels.

The next space is **Peter van Pels' Room.** Initially, Anne was cool toward Peter, but after two years together, a courtship developed, and their flirtation culminated in a kiss. The **staircase** (no visitor access) leads up to where the inhabitants stored their food. Anne loved to steal away here for a bit of privacy. At night they'd open a hatch to let in fresh air. From here we leave the Secret Annex, returning to the Opekta storeroom and offices in the front house.

On August 4, 1944, a German policeman accompanied by three Dutch Nazis pulled up in a car, politely entered the Opekta office, and went straight to the bookcase entrance. No one knows who tipped them off. The Franks were sent to Auschwitz, a Nazi extermination camp in Poland. On the platform at Auschwitz, they were "forcibly separated from each other" (as Otto later reported) and sent to different camps. Anne and Margot were sent to Bergen-Belsen. They both died of typhus in March 1945, only weeks before the camp was liberated. The other Secret Annex residents—except Otto—were gassed or died of disease.

The Rest of the Museum: The Otto Frank Room has a 1967 **video** in which Anne's father talks about his reaction as he read the diaries. Downstairs you can see Anne's **diaries.** (You may see one, two, or all three of them, as well as individual pages.) Other exhibits display **memorabilia** of the Franks and their friends.

It was Otto Frank's dream that visitors come away from the Anne Frank House with hope for a better world. He wrote: "The task that Anne entrusted to me continually gives me new strength to strive for reconciliation and for human rights all over the world."

Westerkerk

Located near the Anne Frank House, this landmark Protestant church has an appropriately barren interior, Rembrandt's body buried somewhere under the pews, and Amsterdam's tallest steeple. While the church is free to visit, the Westerkerk tower is climbable only with a guided tour. The English-language, 30-minute tour takes you on a 185-step climb, rewarding you with a look at the carillon and grand city views. Tours are limited to six people; to reserve a spot, come in person on the same day or call.

Cost and Hours: Church entry-free, generally Mon-Fri 10:00-15:00, Sat 11:00-15:00, closed Sun and Oct-March; tower-€7.50 by tour only, Mon-Sat 10:00-20:00, closed Sun and Nov-March, tours leave on the half-hour; Prinsengracht 281, tel. 020/624-7766, www.westerkerk.nl.

CENTRAL AMSTERDAM, NEAR DAM SQUARE

▲Royal Palace (Koninklijk Huis)

This palace was built as a lavish City Hall (1648-1655), when Holland was a proud new republic and Amsterdam was the richest city on the planet—awash in profit from trade. The building became a "Royal Palace" when Napoleon installed his brother Louis as king (1806). After Napoleon's fall, it continued as a royal residence for the Dutch royal family, the House of Orange. Today, it's one of King Willem-Alexander's official residences, with a single impressive floor open to the public. Visitors can gawk at a grand hall and stroll about 20 lavishly decorated rooms full of chandeliers, paintings, statues, and furniture that reflect Amsterdam's former status as the center of global trade. Use my following mini-tour to see the highlights; supplement it with the (free but dry) audioguide.

Cost and Hours: €10, includes audioguide, daily 10:00-17:00 but hours can vary for official business—check website, tel. 020/522-6161, www.paleisamsterdam.nl.

▲▲Amsterdam Museum

Housed in a 500-year-old former orphanage, this creative museum traces the city's growth from fishing village to world trade center to hippie haven. The museum does a good job of making it engaging and fun. Try not to get lost somewhere in the 17th century as you navigate the meandering maze of rooms.

Start with the easy-to-follow "DNA" section, which hits the

historic highlights from 1000-2000. In the first (long) room, you learn how the city was built atop pilings in marshy soil (the museum stands only four feet above sea level). By 1500, they'd built a ring of canals and established the sea trade. As you pass into the next room, the Golden Age (1600s) comes alive in fine paintings of citizens—sometimes even featuring a portrait or two by Rembrandt. Cross the skybridge into rooms covering the last two centuries. The 1800s brought modernization and new technologies like the bicycle. Then, after the gloom of World War II, Amsterdam emerged to become the "Capital of Freedom." The museum's free pedestrian corridor—lined with old-time group portraits—is a powerful teaser.

Cost and Hours: €12.50, includes audioguide, daily 10:00-17:00, pleasant restaurant, next to Begijnhof at Kalverstraat 92, tel. 020/523-1822, www.ahm.nl. This museum is a fine place to buy the Museumkaart.

RED LIGHT DISTRICT
▲▲Amstelkring Museum

Although Amsterdam has long been known for its tolerant attitudes, 16th-century politics forced Dutch Catholics to worship discreetly for a few hundred years. At this museum near Centraal Station, you'll find a fascinating, hidden Catholic church filling the attic of three 17th-century merchants' houses. For two centuries (1578-1795), Catholicism in Amsterdam was illegal but tolerated (similar to marijuana in our generation). When hardline Protestants took power, Catholic churches were vandalized and shut down, priests and monks were rounded up and kicked out of town, and Catholic kids were razzed on their way to school. The city's Catholics were forbidden to worship openly, so they gathered secretly to say Mass in homes and offices. In 1663, a wealthy merchant built Our Lord in the Attic (Ons' Lieve Heer op Solder), one of a handful of places in Amsterdam that served as a secret parish church until Catholics were once again allowed to worship in public.

This one-of-a-kind church provides a rare glimpse inside a historic Amsterdam home straight out of a Vermeer painting. Don't miss the silver collection and other exhibits of daily life from 300 years ago.

Cost and Hours: €10, includes audioguide, Mon-Sat 10:00-17:00, Sun 13:00-17:00, Oudezijds Voorburgwal 38, tel. 020/624-6604, www.opsolder.nl.

▲▲Red Light District Walk

Europe's most popular ladies of the night tease and tempt here, as they have for centuries, in several hundred display-case windows around Oudezijds Achterburgwal and Oudezijds Voorburgwal, surrounding the Old Church (described below). Drunks and druggies make the streets uncomfortable late at night after the gawking tour groups leave (about 22:30), but it's a fascinating walk earlier in the evening.

The neighborhood, one of Amsterdam's oldest, has hosted prostitutes since 1200. Prostitution is entirely legal here, and the prostitutes are generally entrepreneurs, renting space and running their own businesses, as well as filling out tax returns and even paying union dues. Popular prostitutes net about €500 a day (for what's called "S&F" in its abbreviated, printable form, charging €30-50 per customer).

Sex Museums

While visiting one of the Red Light District's sex museums can be called sightseeing, visiting two is harder to explain. Here's a comparison:

The **Erotic Museum** is five floors of uninspired paintings, videos, old photos, and sculpture (€7, daily 11:00-24:00, along the canal at Oudezijds Achterburgwal 54, tel. 020/624-7303, www. erotisch-museum.nl).

Red Light Secrets Museum of Prostitution is a pricey look at the world's oldest profession. If you're wondering what it's like to sit in those red booths, watch the video taken from the prostitute's perspective as "johns" check you out (€10, €8 online, daily 11:00-24:00, Oudezijds Achterburgwal 60, tel. 020/662-5300, www. redlightsecrets.com).

Old Church (Oude Kerk)

This 14th-century landmark—the needle around which the Red Light District spins—has served as a reassuring welcome-home symbol to sailors, a refuge to the downtrodden, an ideological battlefield of the Counter-Reformation, and, today, a tourist sight with a dull interior.

Cost and Hours: €7.50 (credit cards only, no cash), Mon-Sat 10:00-18:00, Sun 13:00-17:30, free carillon concerts Tue and Sat at 16:00, tel. 020/625-8284, www.oudekerk.nl. To climb the 167 steps to the top of the church tower, take a 30-minute tour (€7.50, April-Oct Mon-Sat 12:00-18:00).

Marijuana Sights in the Red Light District

Three related establishments cluster together along a canal in the Red Light District. The **Hash, Marijuana, and Hemp Museum,** worth ▲, is the most worthwhile of the three; it shares a ticket with the less substantial **Hemp Gallery.** Right nearby is **Cannabis College,** a free nonprofit center that's "dedicated to ending the global war against the cannabis plant through public education."

Cost and Hours: Museum and gallery-€9, daily 10:00-

22:00, Oudezijds Achterburgwal 148, tel. 020/624-8926, www. hashmuseum.com. College entry-free, daily 11:00-19:00, Oudezijds Achterburgwal 124, tel. 020/423-4420, www.cannabiscollege. com.

NORTHEAST AMSTERDAM

NEMO (National Center for Science and Technology)

This kid-friendly science museum is a city landmark: Its distinctive copper-green building juts up from the water like a sinking ship.

Several floors feature exhibits that explore topics such as light, sound, and gravity, and play with bubbles, topple giant dominoes, and draw with lasers. Up top is a restaurant with a great city view, as well as a sloping terrace that becomes a popular "beach" in summer, complete with lounge chairs and a lively bar. On the bottom floor is a cafeteria offering €5 sandwiches.

Cost and Hours: €15, daily 10:00-17:30, Sept-May closed Mon, tel. 020/531-3233, www.e-nemo.nl. The roof terrace—open until 19:00 in the summer—is generally free.

Getting There: It's above the entrance to the IJ tunnel at Oosterdok 2. From Centraal Station, you can walk there in 15 minutes, or take bus #22 or #48 to the Kadijksplein stop.

▲▲Netherlands Maritime Museum
(Nederlands Scheepvaartmuseum)

This huge, kid-friendly collection of model ships, maps, and sea-battle paintings fills the 300-year-old Dutch Navy Arsenal (cleverly located a little ways from the city center, as this was where they stored the gunpowder). The Paintings rooms illustrate how ships changed from sail to steam, and how painting styles changed from realistic battle scenes to Romantic seascapes to Impressionism and Cubism.

The Navigational Instruments section has quadrants (a wedge-shaped tool you could line up with the horizon and the stars to determine your location), compasses, and plumb lines. In Ornamentation, admire the busty gals that adorned the prows of ships, and learn of their symbolic meaning for superstitious sailors.

Downstairs on the first floor, see yacht models through the ages, from early warships to today's luxury vessels. The section on atlases shows how human consciousness expanded as knowledge of the earth grew. The finale is a chance to explore below the decks of a replica of the *Amsterdam,* an 18th-century tall-masted cargo ship.

Cost and Hours: €15, includes audioguide, daily 9:00-17:00, bus #22 or #48 from Centraal Station to Kattenburgerplein 1, tel. 020/523-2222, www.scheepvaartmuseum.nl.

SOUTHEAST AMSTERDAM

The following sights are close enough to link by tram, bike, or even on foot. From Centraal Station, take tram #14 to Waterlooplein. On foot from the Mint Tower, it's a 10-minute stroll along the pleasant shopping street called Staalstraat.

▲Rembrandt's House (Museum Het Rembrandthuis)

A middle-aged Rembrandt lived here from 1639 to 1658 after his wife's death, as his popularity and wealth dwindled down to obscurity and bankruptcy. The house is reconstructed and filled with period objects (not his actual belongings). You're not likely to see a single Rembrandt painting in the whole house, but this interesting museum may make you come away wanting to know more about the man and his art. As you enter, ask when the next etching or painting demonstration is scheduled and pick up the excellent audioguide.

Cost and Hours: €12.50, includes audioguide, daily 10:00-18:00, etching and painting demonstrations almost hourly between 11:00 and 15:00, fewer crowds (but fewer demos) early and late in the day, Jodenbreestraat 4, tel. 020/520-0400, www.rembrandthuis.nl.

▲Gassan Diamonds

Many shops in this "city of diamonds" offer tours, followed by a visit to an intimate sales room to see (and perhaps buy) a mighty shiny yet very tiny souvenir.

The handy and professional **Gassan Diamonds** facility fills a huge warehouse one block from Rembrandt's House. A visit here plops you in the big-tour-group fray and you'll have an opportunity to have color and clarity described and illustrated with diamonds ranging in value from $100 to $30,000. Grab a free cup of coffee in the waiting room across the parking lot (daily 9:00-17:00, Nieuwe Uilenburgerstraat 173-175, tel. 020/622-5333, www.gassan.com, handy WC). Another company, **Coster,** also offers diamond demos. They're not as good as Gassan's, but convenient if you're near the Rijksmuseum.

▲▲Hermitage Amsterdam

The famous Hermitage Museum in St. Petersburg, Russia loans art to Amsterdam for a series of rotating, and often exquisitely beautiful, special exhibits in the Amstelhof, a 17th-century former nursing home that takes up a whole city block along the Amstel River.

Cost and Hours: Generally €15, price varies with exhibit; daily 10:00-17:00, come later in the day to avoid crowds, audioguide-€4, mandatory free bag check, café, Nieuwe Herengracht 14, tram #14 from the train station, recorded info tel. 020/530-7488, www.hermitage.nl.

▲Jewish Historical Museum (Joods Historisch Museum) and Portuguese Synagogue

A single ticket admits you to these two sights, located a half-block apart. Start at either one. The Jewish Historical Museum tells the story of the Netherlands' Jews through three centuries, serving as a good introduction to Judaism and Jewish customs and religious traditions. Nearby, the 17th-century Portuguese Synagogue is again in use by a Jewish congregation.

Cost and Hours: €15, includes museum and Portuguese Synagogue, also covers Dutch Theater/National Holocaust Memorial (see next listing), more for special exhibits; museum open daily 11:00-17:00, Portuguese Synagogue open daily 10:00-16:00; free audioguide, English descriptions, children's museum; take tram #14 to Mr. Visserplein, Jonas Daniel Meijerplein 2, tel. 020/531-0310, www.jhm.nl. The museum has a modern, minimalist, kosher **$$** café.

Visiting the Museum: The Jewish Historic Museum joins four historic former synagogues to form the museum's single modern complex. Start in the impressive Great Synagogue. The vast hall would be full for a service—men downstairs, women above in the gallery. On the east wall (the symbolic direction of Jerusalem) is the ark—the alcove where they keep the scrolls of the Torah (the Jewish scriptures, comprising the first five books of the Old Testament of the Bible). Video displays around the room explain Jewish customs, from birth (circumcision) to puberty (the bar/bat mitzvah, celebrating the entry into adulthood) to Passover celebrations to marriage—culminating in the groom stomping on a glass while everyone shouts "Mazel tov!"

The women's gallery exhibits trace the history of Amsterdam's Jews from 1600 to 1900. This was a Golden Age, when Amsterdam and its Jewish population both thrived in relative harmony. Exhibits about Jews in the 20th century are housed in the former New Synagogue.

Visiting the Portuguese Synagogue: This grand structure brings together both old and new—a historic synagogue that today serves a revived Jewish community. It was built in the 1670s (when Catholics were worshipping underground), to house a community of Sephardic (Iberian) Jews who fled persecution. At the time, it was the world's largest.

Inside, the synagogue is majestic in its simplicity—a spacious place of worship with four Ionic columns supporting a wooden roof. There's no electric lighting, only candles and windows. Find the main features: the platform (near the back) where the cantor presides, the wood-columned niche at the far end for the Torah, the two ceremonial sofas for VIPs, the special pew (middle of left wall) for important visitors, the upstairs balconies for the women, the wood canopy (far right corner) where weddings take place...and the sand under your feet, which (may) symbolize the Israelites' sojourn through the desert. Don't miss the downstairs Treasury, containing precious Torah scrolls, ceremonial objects, textiles, and rare books, plus a slideshow on the history of this beloved synagogue, known as the *Esnoga.*

▲Dutch Theater (Hollandsche Schouwburg), a.k.a. National Holocaust Memorial

Once a lively theater in the Jewish neighborhood, and today a moving memorial, this building was used as an assembly hall for local Jews destined for Nazi concentration camps. As you enter, you'll see a wall covered with 6,700 family names, paying tribute to the 107,000 Jews deported and killed by the Nazis. Some 70,000 victims spent time here, awaiting transfer to concentration camps.

Upstairs is a small-but-evocative history exhibit with a model of the ghetto, film footage, and photos. A few reminders of the victims (such as their shoes and letters) puts a human face on the staggering numbers. Back downstairs in the ground-floor courtyard, notice the hopeful messages that visiting school groups attach to the wooden tulips.

Cost and Hours: Donation requested, free with Jewish Historical Museum/Portuguese Synagogue ticket, daily 11:00-17:00,

Plantage Middenlaan 24, take tram #14 to Artis, tel. 020/531-0380, www.hollandscheschouwburg.nl.

▲▲Dutch Resistance Museum (Verzetsmuseum)

This is an impressive look at how the Dutch resisted (or collaborated with) their Nazi occupiers from 1940 to 1945. You'll see propaganda movie clips, study forged ID cards under a magnifying glass, and read about ingenious and courageous efforts—big and small—to hide local Jews from the Germans and undermine the Nazi regime. This museum presents a timeless moral dilemma: Is it better to collaborate with a wicked system to effect small-scale change—or to resist outright, even if your efforts are doomed to fail? You'll learn why some parts of Dutch society opted for the former, and others for the latter.

Cost and Hours: €11, includes audioguide; Mon-Fri 10:00-17:00, Sat-Sun 11:00-17:00, English descriptions, mandatory and free bag check, tram #14 from the train station or Dam Square, Plantage Kerklaan 61, tel. 020/620-2535, www.verzetsmuseum.org.

Shopping in Amsterdam

For shopping information, pick up the TI's *Shopping in Amsterdam* brochure. Street markets (generally 9:30-17:00, closed Sun) include **Waterlooplein** (the flea market), the huge **Albert Cuyp** street market (southeast of the Rijksmuseum), and various flower markets (such as the Singel canal **Flower Market** near the Mint Tower).

Most shops in the center are open 10:00-18:00 (later on Thu—typically until 20:00 or 21:00); many shopkeepers take Sundays and Monday mornings off. Supermarkets are generally open Monday-Saturday 8:00-20:00, with shorter hours on Sunday; Albert Heijn grocery stores are open until 22:00 every day.

Handy stores include **Hema** (at Kalverstraat 212, in the Kalvertoren shopping mall and at Centraal Station) and the **De Bijenkorf** department store, towering high above Dam Square, with a ritzy self-service cafeteria.

Shopping Zones

Amsterdam has four top shopping areas: The **Nine Little Streets** (touristy, tidy, and central); **Haarlemmerstraat/Haarlemmerdijk** (emerging, borderline-edgy neighborhood of creative, unpretentious shops); **Staalstraat** (postcard-cute, short-and-sweet street tucked just away from the tourist crowds); and the **Jordaan** (mellow residential zone with a smattering of fine shops).

The Nine Little Streets (De Negen Straatjes)

Hemmed in by a grid plan between Dam Square and the Jordaan, this zone is home to diverse shops mixing festive, inventive, nostalgic, practical, and artistic items. Walking west from the Amsterdam Museum/Spui Square or south from the Anne Frank House puts you right in the thick of things. For a preview, see www.theninestreets.com.

Haarlemmerstraat/Haarlemmerdijk

The area just west of Centraal Station hosts a thriving and trendy string of shops and eateries. A browse here is a chance to spot new trends and pick up local clothes and goods (vintage and casual young fashions abound). The former dike along what was Amsterdam's harborfront provides the high spine of this neighborhood. From the Singel canal near Centraal Station, this drag leads a half-mile west along a colorful string of lanes, all the way to Haarlem Gate, a triumphal arch built in the 1840s.

Staalstraat

This lively street, boasting more than its share of creative design shops, is tucked in an area just east of the university zone. At #7b is **Droog**—which, despite a name that evokes controlled substances, is actually a "destination" design store. It's half gallery (with cutting-edge installations) and half shop (selling a bumper crop of clever kitchen and household gadgets you never knew you desperately wanted). Nearby is the bustling **Waterlooplein flea market** (at the Waterlooplein Metro station, behind Rembrandt's House), filled with stalls selling cheap clothes, hippie stuff, old records, tourist knickknacks, and garage-sale junk. The somewhat sketchy-feeling streets just north of Waterlooplein—past the colorful tattoo parlors—are fertile breeding grounds for smart young designers; poking around here you'll discover some shops on the cutting edge of Amsterdam's young fashion scene.

The Jordaan

This colorful neighborhood is a wonderland of funky shops. On Mondays, you'll find the busy **Noordermarkt** market at the end of Westerstraat and spilling onto the neighboring street, **Lindengracht. Rozengracht,** the wide street just southwest of the Anne Frank House, has several eclectic shops. **Antiekcentrum Amster-**

dam isn't just an antique mall—it's a sprawling warren of display cases crammed with historic bric-a-brac (including lots of smaller items, easily packed home), and all of it for sale (Mon and Wed-Fri 11:00-18:00, Sat-Sun 11:00-17:00, closed Tue, Elandsgracht 109, tel. 020/624-9038). The cross-street **Hazenstraat** has a fine assortment of art galleries and other shops. **Eerste** and **Tweede Egelantiersdwarsstraat,** both lined with great restaurants, also have some fun shops mixed in.

Eating in Amsterdam

Amsterdam has a thriving and ever-changing restaurant scene. While I've listed options, one good strategy is simply to pick an area and wander. Note that many of my listings are lunch-only (usually termed "café" rather than "restaurant")—good for a handy bite near major sights. Similarly, many top restaurants serve only dinner. Before trekking across town to any of my listings, check the hours.

CENTRAL AMSTERDAM

You'll likely have lunch at some point in the city's core (perhaps at a place listed here), but you'll find a better range of more satisfying choices in the Jordaan area of West Amsterdam. For locations, see the "West/Central Amsterdam Restaurants" map.

On and near Spui

$$$ Restaurant Kantjil en de Tijger is a lively, modern place serving Indonesian food; the waiters are happy to explain your many enticing options. Their four rijsttafels (traditional "rice tables" with about a dozen small courses) are designed for two, but three people can make a meal by getting a rijsttafel for two plus a soup or light dish (daily 12:00-23:00, reservations smart, mostly indoor with a little outdoor seating, Spuistraat 291, tel. 020/620-0994, www.kantjil.nl).

$ Kantjil To Go is a tiny Indonesian takeout bar. Their printed menu explains the mix-and-match plan (daily 12:00-21:00, a half-block off Spui Square at Nieuwezijds Voorburgwal 342, behind the restaurant listed above, tel. 020/620-3074). Split a large box, grab a bench on the charming Spui Square around the corner, and you've got perhaps the best cheap, hot meal in town.

$$$$ Restaurant d'Vijff Vlieghen has a candlelit interior right out of a Rembrandt painting. It's a huge, dressy, and romantic place offering Dutch and international cuisine, professional service, and a multicourse tasting menu with wines (nightly 18:00-22:00, Spuistraat 294, tel. 020/530-4060).

$ Singel 404 Lunch Café, just across the Singel canal from

Restaurant Code

I've assigned each eatery a price category, based on the average cost of a typical main course. Drinks, desserts, and splurge items (steak and seafood) can raise the price considerably.

$$$$ **Splurge:** Most main courses over €20
  $$$ **Pricier:** €15-20
   $$ **Moderate:** €10-15
    $ **Budget:** Under €10

In the Netherlands, a *friets* stand or other takeout spot is **$**; a basic café or sit-down eatery is **$$**; a casual but more upscale restaurant is **$$$**; and a swanky splurge is **$$$$**.

Spui and near the Nine Little Streets, is popular for sandwiches (daily 10:30-18:00, Singel 404, tel. 020/428-0154).

$$$ Café Luxembourg is a venerable old bistro with a tired "grand café" interior and tables (some in a heated veranda) looking right out on Spui Square. The food's basic, but the relaxed atmosphere mixes well with nice Belgian beer on tap. They're famous for their croquettes. If it's a burger you want, try their Luxemburger (daily 9:00-23:00, Spui 24, tel. 020/620-6264).

$$$ The Seafood Bar focuses on fresh and fishy, and is understandably popular—reserve ahead for lunch or dinner (daily 12:00-22:00, Spui 15, tel. 020/233-7452 www.theseafoodbar.nl). Another branch is near the Rijksmuseum (listed later).

Near Rokin

$$ Gartine is a hidden gem, filling a relaxed but borderline-elegant little space tucked just off the tourist-thronged Spui and Rokin zones. It's a calm and classy spot for a good lunch or high tea (Wed-Sun 10:00-18:00, closed Mon-Tue, Taksteeg 7, tel. 020/320-4132).

$$ Pannenkoekenhuis Upstairs is a tight, tiny (just four tables), characteristic perch up some extremely steep stairs, where Arno and Ali cook and serve delicious pancakes. They'll tell you that I discovered this place long before Anthony Bourdain did (Tue-Fri 12:00-19:00, closed Mon, Grimburgwal 2, tel. 020/626-5603).

$ Atrium University Cafeteria feeds students and travelers for great prices (Mon-Fri 11:00-15:00 & 17:00-19:30, closed Sat-Sun; from Spui, walk west down Langebrugsteeg past the recommended Café 't Gasthuys three blocks to Oudezijds Achterburgwal 237, then go through the arched doorway on the right; tel. 020/525-3999).

$$ Van Kerkwijk is tucked away on the narrow street called Nes, running south from Dam Square and paralleling Rokin one

AMSTERDAM

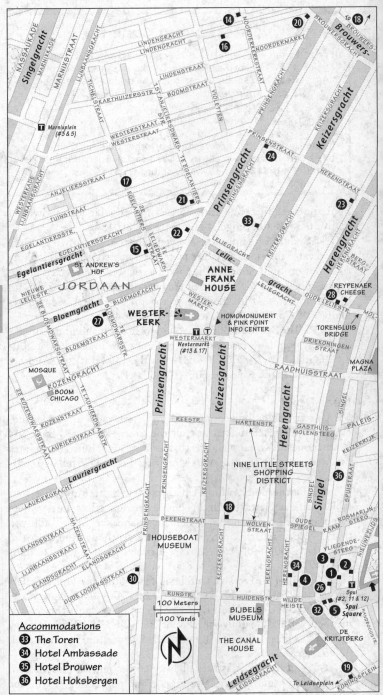

Accommodations

33 The Toren
34 Hotel Ambassade
35 Hotel Brouwer
36 Hotel Hoksbergen

100 Meters

100 Yards

West/Central Amsterdam Hotels & Restaurants

AMSTERDAM

Eateries & Other

1. Restaurant Kantjil en de Tijger
2. Kantjil To Go
3. Restaurant d'Vijff Vlieghen
4. Singel 404 Lunch Café
5. Café Luxembourg
6. The Seafood Bar
7. Gartine
8. Pannenkoekenhuis Upstairs
9. Atrium University Cafeteria
10. Van Kerkwijk
11. De Jaren Café
12. Blue Amsterdam Restaurant
13. Vlemnickx Friets
14. Restaurant Daalder
15. Café Restaurant de Reiger
16. Ristorante Toscanini
17. Jordaan's "Restaurant Row"
18. Marqt Cash-Free Supermarkets (2)
19. Albert Heijn Cash-Only Supermarket (4)

Brown Cafés

20. Café 't Papeneiland
21. Café 't Smalle
22. Café de Prins
23. Proeflokaal Arendsnest
24. Café De II Prinsen
25. Café 't Gasthuys
26. Café Hoppe

Coffeeshops

27. Paradox
28. The Grey Area
29. Siberië
30. La Tertulia
31. The Dampkring
32. 4:20 Coffeeshop

block to the east. This popular, unpretentious eatery has no written menu—your server relays the day's offerings of freshly prepared international dishes. They don't take reservations and there's often a line; pass the time with a drink in the bar (daily 11:00-23:00, Nes 41, tel. 020/620-3316).

Near the Mint Tower

De Jaren Café ("The Years") is chic yet inviting, and clearly a favorite with locals. Upstairs is a minimalist **$$$** restaurant with a top-notch salad bar and canal-view deck (dinners after 17:30, meals include salad bar). Downstairs is a modern **$$** café, great for light lunches (soups, salads, and sandwiches served all day and evening) or just coffee over a newspaper. On a sunny day, the café's canalside patio is a fine spot to savor a drink (daily 9:30-24:00, a long block up from Muntplein at Nieuwe Doelenstraat 20, tel. 020/625-5771).

$$ Blue Amsterdam Restaurant, high above the Kalvertoren shopping mall and across the street from La Place on Kalverstraat, serves light lunches with one of the best views in town (just ride up the slanted elevator, free Wi-Fi, daily 11:00-18:30, tel. 020/427-3901).

Fries: While Amsterdam has no shortage of *Vlaamse friets* ("Flemish fries") stands, locals and in-the-know visitors head for **$ Vlemnickx,** an unpretentious hole-in-the-wall *friets* counter hiding just off the main Kalverstraat shopping street. They sell only fries, with a wide variety of sauces—they call themselves *"de sausmeesters"* (daily 12:00-19:00, Thu until 20:00, Voetboogstraat 31).

WEST AMSTERDAM, IN THE JORDAAN DISTRICT

$$$$ Restaurant Daalder is all about quality, fun, and the chef's surprise. There's no menu. Your waiter will discuss your interests with you and then you must sit back, relax, and dine on a multi-course meal. The dishes are French/Italian/Asian/Dutch and playful, and reservations are a must (options range from €45/4 courses to €68/7 courses, daily 12:00-14:00 & 18:00-22:00, Lindengracht 90, tel. 020/624-8864, http://daalderamsterdam.nl).

$$$ Café Restaurant de Reiger must serve up the best cooking of any *eetcafé* in the Jordaan. Famous for its fresh ingredients, ribs, good beer on tap, and delightful bistro ambience, it's part of the classic Jordaan scene. They're proud of their fresh fish and French-Dutch cuisine. The café, which is crowded late and on weekends, takes no reservations. Come early and have a drink at the bar while you wait (daily 17:00-24:00, Nieuwe Leliestraat 34, tel. 020/624-7426).

$$$ Ristorante Toscanini is an upmarket Italian place that's always packed. With a lively, spacious ambience and great Italian cuisine, this place is a treat—if you can get a seat. Reservations are essentially required. Eating with the dressy, local, in-the-know crowd and the busy open kitchen adds to the fun energy (Mon-Sat 18:00-22:30, closed Sun, deep in the Jordaan at Lindengracht 75, tel. 020/623-2813, http://restauranttoscanini.nl).

On Jordaan's "Restaurant Row": These tempting places are located along the Jordaan's trendiest street, Tweede ("2nd") Egelantiersdwarsstraat, which turns into Tweede Anjeliersdwarsstraat. This is a youthful and exuberant scene, with high-energy eateries that spill out into lively brick-sidewalk seating. Stroll its length from Egelantiers Canal to Westerstraat to survey your options; consider reserving a spot for a return dinner visit.

$ Urker Viswinkel, a classic fish-and-chips joint, is the perfect place to try kibbeling (deep-fried cod bits), herring, or a fish sandwich (Mon-Wed & Sat 11:00-17:00, Thu-Fri 11:00-18:00, closed Sun and sometimes Mon in winter, Tweede Egelantiersdwarsstraat 13, tel. 020/422-3030).

$$ La Perla has a big, busy wood-fired pizza oven surrounded by a few humble tables, with a more formal dining room across the street and—best of all—sidewalk tables on one of the liveliest intersections in the Jordaan (daily 12:00-24:00, locations face each other at Tweede Egelantiersdwarsstraat 14 and 53—take your pick, tel. 020/624-8828).

$$$ Ristorante Hostaria is a tight, steamy Italian place with a fun energy and an open kitchen (Tue-Sun 18:00-22:00, closed Mon, Tweede Egelantiersdwarsstraat 9, tel. 020/626-0028).

Dessert: A popular neighborhood joint, **Monte Pelmo Ice Cream** has delightful ice cream and a helpful staff. It's not surprising there's always a line (daily 13:00-22:00, closes earlier in winter, Tweede Anjeliersdwarsstraat 17).

SOUTHWEST AMSTERDAM

While a few eateries are within just a few steps of the big museums, my less-touristy picks are generally within a 10-minute walk and have better food and service—but none is worth going out of your way for. For locations see the "Southwest Amsterdam Hotels & Restaurants" map.

$$$ The Seafood Bar—modern, slick, and extremely popular—features a tasty array of seafood. The decor is white-subway-tile trendy, and the food focuses on fresh and sustainable dishes with a Burgundian flair. You can try dropping by, but it's best to reserve during mealtimes (daily 12:00-22:00, Van Baerlestraat 5, between the Rijksmuseum and Vondelpark, tel. 020/670-8355, www.theseafoodbar.nl).

$$$ Sama Sebo Indonesian Restaurant is considered one of the best Indonesian restaurants in town. It's a venerable local favor-

AMSTERDAM

AMSTERDAM

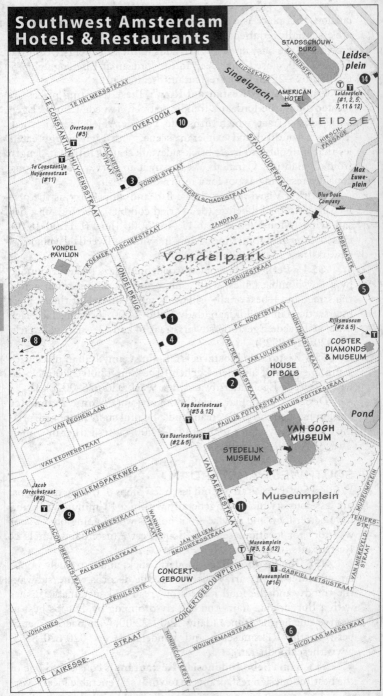

Southwest Amsterdam Hotels & Restaurants

STADSSCHOUW-
BURG

Leidse-
plein

Singelgracht

LEIDSEKADE

MARNIXSTR.

AMERICAN
HOTEL

Leidseplein
(#1, 2, 5,
7, 11 & 12)

LEIDSE

1E HELMERSSTRAAT

1E CONSTANTIJN HUYGENSSTRAAT

Overtoom
(#3)

OVERTOOM

OVERTOOM

HIRSCH-
PASSAGE

1e Constantijn
Huygensstraat
(#11)

PALAMEDES
STRAAT

VONDELSTRAAT

STADHOUDERSKADE

Max
Euwe-
plein

TESSELSCHADESTRAAT

Blue Boat
Company

ROEMER VISSCHERSTRAAT

ZANDPAD

Vondelpark

HOBBEMASTR.

VONDEL
PAVILION

VONDELBRUG

VONDELSTRAAT

VOSSIUSSTRAAT

To

P.C. HOOFTSTRAAT

Rijksmuseum
(#2 & 5)

COSTER
DIAMONDS
& MUSEUM

VAN DE VELDESTRAAT

JAN LUIJKENSTR.

HONTHORSTSTRAAT

HOUSE
OF BOLS

Van Baerlestraat
(#3 & 12)

PAULUS POTTERSTRAAT

PAULUS POTTERSTRAAT

Pond

Van Baerlestraat
(#2 & 5)

VAN GOGH
MUSEUM

VAN EEGHENLAAN

VAN EEGHENSTRAAT

STEDELIJK
MUSEUM

MUSEUMPLEIN

WILLEMSPARKWEG

Jacob
Obrechtstraat
(#2)

VAN BAERLESTRAAT

Museumplein

TENIERS-
STR.

VAN BREESTRAAT

WANNING
STRAAT

Museumplein
(#3, 5 & 12)

VAN MIEREVELD
STRAAT

JACOB OBRECHTSTRAAT

PALESTRINASTRAAT

JAN WILLEM
BROUWERSSTRAAT

CONCERT-
GEBOUW

Museumplein
(#16)

GABRIEL METSUSTRAAT

VERHULSTSTR.

CONCERTGEBOUWPLEIN

JOHANNES

STRAAT

WOUWERMANSTRAAT

NICOLAAS MAESSTRAAT

DE LAIRESSE-

HONDECOETERSTR.

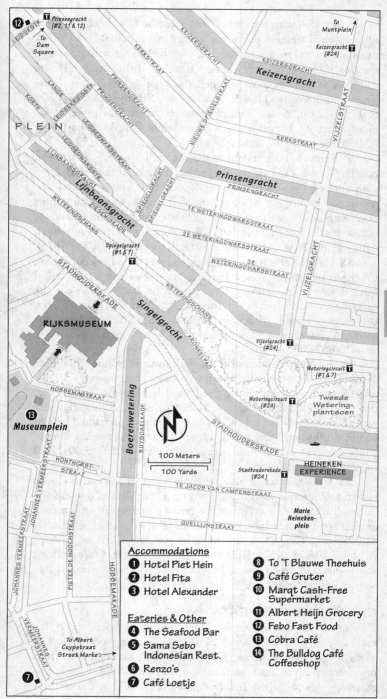

AMSTERDAM

Accommodations

1 Hotel Piet Hein
2 Hotel Fita
3 Hotel Alexander

Eateries & Other

4 The Seafood Bar
5 Sama Sebo Indonesian Rest.
6 Renzo's
7 Café Loetje

8 To 'T Blauwe Theehuis
9 Café Gruter
10 Marqt Cash-Free Supermarket
11 Albert Heijn Grocery
12 Febo Fast Food
13 Cobra Café
14 The Bulldog Café Coffeeshop

ite for rijsttafel, with a waitstaff that seems to have been on board since colonial times. I prefer the energy in the casual "bodega" to the more formal restaurant (and only in the bodega will they serve the smaller lunch plate for dinner). Their 17-dish, classic rijsttafel spread is as good as any. At lunch the *bami goreng* or *nasi goreng* (fried noodles or rice) is a feast of its own (Mon-Sat 12:00-15:00 & 17:00-22:00, closed Sun, reservations smart for dinner, P. C. Hooftstraat 27, between the Rijksmuseum and Vondelpark, tel. 020/662-81460, www.samasebo.nl).

$ Renzo's is a tempting Italian delicatessen, where you can buy good sandwiches or prepared pasta dishes and *antipasti* (priced by weight, can be heated up). Get your food to go, or pay a bit more to sit at one of the tables in the tiny interior, with more seating upstairs (house wine by the glass, or buy a bottle for the takeaway price to enjoy with your meal, daily 11:00-21:00, Van Baerlestraat 67, tel. 020/763-1673).

$$ Café Loetje has a rollicking neighborhood-beer-hall feel. Of the three dining zones, the interior is least interesting; head instead for the glassed-in winter garden (in bad weather) or the sprawling outdoor tables (in good weather). In addition to beer, they slam out good, affordable pub grub (daily 11:00 until late, Johannes Vermeerstraat 52, several blocks southeast of Museumplein, tel. 020/662-8173).

In and Near Vondelpark: $$ 'T Blauwe Theehuis ("The Blue Tea House") is a venerable meeting point where, since the 1930s, all generations have come for drinks and light meals. The setting, deep in Vondelpark, is like a Monet painting. Sandwiches are served at tables outside, inside, and on the rooftop from 11:00 to 16:00, drinks and apple pie are served all day, and pot smoking—while discreet—is as natural here as falling leaves (daily 9:00-22:00 in summer, Vondelpark 5, tel. 020/662-0254).

$$ Café Gruter is just outside Vondelpark. With a classic brown café interior and great seating on a little square, it's a neighborhood hangout—away from the center's tourism in a ritzy residential zone with fashion boutiques and leafy squares (lunch daily 11:00-16:00, also serves dinner, open very late, Willemsparkweg 73, tel. 020/679-6252). Ride tram #2 to the Jacob Obrechtstraat stop—one tram stop beyond the Van Gogh Museum—near a gateway to Vondelpark.

CHEAP AND FAST EATS

To dine cheaply yet memorably alongside the big spenders, grab a meal to go, then find a bench on a lively neighborhood square or along a canal. Sandwiches *(broodjes)* of delicious cheese on fresh bread are cheap at snack bars, delis, and *broodje* shops. Ethnic restaurants—many of them Indonesian or Surinamese, and seemingly all named with varying puns on "Wok"—serve inexpensive, split-table carryout meals. Middle Eastern fast-food stands and diners abound, offering a variety of meats wrapped in pita bread.

Supermarkets: Marqt Cash-Free Supermarket (credit cards only) is the picnicking hipster's dream, with the freshest organic produce and plenty of prepared foods. **Albert Heijn** grocery stores are more traditional, cheaper, take cash, and have great deli sections with picnic-perfect takeaway salads and sandwiches. None of their stores accept US credit cards: Bring cash, and don't get in the checkout lines marked *PIN alleen*.

Dutch Fried Fast Food: $ Febo caters mainly to late-night drinkers looking for greasy fried foods to soak up the booze. A wall of self-service, coin-op windows provides piping-hot fried cheese, burgers, croquettes, and so on (change machine on wall). You'll find branches all over town, including Leidsestraat 94, just north of Leidseplein.

AMSTERDAM'S BROWN CAFÉS

Be sure to experience the Dutch institution of the *bruin* café (brown café)—so called for the typically hardwood decor and nicotine-stained walls. (While smoking was banned several years ago—making these places even more inviting to nonsmokers—the prior pigmentation persists.) Exemplifying the *gezellig* (cozy) quality that the Dutch hold dear, these are convivial hangouts, where you can focus on conversation while slowly nursing a drink (nondrinkers can enjoy a soft drink or coffee). Akin to a British pub, the corner brown café is the neighborhood's living room. See the "West/Central Amsterdam Hotels & Restaurants" map, earlier, for locations.

In the Jordaan: $ Café 't Papeneiland has Delft tiles, an evocative old stove, and a stay-awhile perch overlooking a canal with welcoming benches (daily 10:00-24:00, drinks but almost no food—cheese or liverwurst sandwiches, overlooking northwest end of Prinsengracht at #2, tel. 020/624-1989).

$ Café 't Smalle serves simple meals of soups, salads, and sandwiches from 11:00 to 17:30 (plenty of fine Belgian beers on tap, interesting wines by the glass; at Egelantiersgracht 12—where it hits Prinsengracht, tel. 020/623-9617); **$$ Café de Prins** is a fine spot for *poffertjes*—those beloved tiny Dutch pancakes—as well as bar food, steaks, and fries (daily 10:00-late, Prinsengracht 124, tel. 020/624-9382).

Between Centraal Station and the Jordaan: $ Proeflokaal Arendsnest displays the day's 52 Dutch beers on a big chalkboard. The only food is Dutch bar snacks—local meats and cheeses with crackers—but the place is so inviting (with seating inside and on the canal) that it's tempting to make them into a meal (daily 12:00-24:00, Herengracht 90, tel. 020/421-2057).

$ Café De II Prinsen, dating from 1910, feels more local. It's relaxed and convivial, with a few outdoor tables facing a particularly pretty canal and a lively shopping street (Dutch beers on tap, daily 12:00-24:00, Prinsenstraat 27, tel. 020/428-4488).

Near Rokin: With a lovely secluded back room and peaceful canalside seating, **$$ Café 't Gasthuys** offers a long bar and sometimes slow service. I'd come here to eat outside on a quiet canal in the city center. The busy dumbwaiter cranks out light lunches, sandwiches, and reasonably priced basic dinners (cheeseburgers are a favorite, daily 12:00-16:30 & 17:30-22:00, Grimburgwal 7—from the Rondvaart Kooij boat dock, head down Langebrugsteeg, and it's one block down on the left, tel. 020/624-8230).

On Spui Square: $ Café Hoppe is a classic drinking bar that's as brown as can be. "Hoppe" is their house brew, but there are many beers on tap and a good selection of traditional drinks, sandwiches at lunch, very simple bar food, a packed interior, and fun stools outside to oversee the action on Spui (Mon-Thu 14:00-24:00, Fri-Sun 12:00-24:00, Spui 18, tel. 020/420-4420).

SMOKING IN AMSTERDAM

For tourists from lands where you can do hard time for lighting up, the open use of marijuana here can feel either somewhat disturbing, or exhilaratingly liberating...or maybe just refreshingly sane. Several decades after being decriminalized in the Netherlands, marijuana causes about as much excitement here as a bottle of beer. Throughout Amsterdam, you'll see "coffeeshops"—cafés selling marijuana, with display cases showing various joints or baggies for sale.

Rules and Regulations: The retail sale of marijuana is strictly regulated, and proceeds are taxed. The minimum age for purchase is 18, and coffeeshops can sell up to five grams of marijuana per person per day. It's illegal to advertise marijuana; in fact, in many places you must ask to see the menu.

Shops sell marijuana and hashish both in prerolled joints and in little baggies. Joints are generally sold individually (€4-5, depending on whether it's hash with tobacco, marijuana with tobacco, or pure marijuana), though some places sell only small packs of three or four joints. Baggies generally contain a gram and go for €8-15. The better pot, though costlier, can actually be a better value, as it takes less to get high—and it's a better high. But if you want to take it easy, as a general rule, cheaper is milder.

Smoking Tips: Shops have loaner bongs and inhalers, and dispense rolling papers like toothpicks. While it's good style to ask first, if you're a paying customer (e.g., you buy a cup of coffee), you can generally pop into any coffeeshop and light up, even if you didn't buy your pot there.

Tourists who haven't smoked pot since their college days are famous for overindulging in Amsterdam. Coffeeshop baristas nickname tourists about to pass out "Whitey"—the color their faces turn just before they hit the floor. They warn Americans (who aren't used to the strength of the local stuff) to try a lighter leaf. If you

do overdo it, the key is to eat or drink something sweet to avoid getting sick. Cola is a good fast fix, and coffeeshop staff keep sugar tablets handy. They also recommend trying to walk it off.

Don't ever buy pot on the street in Amsterdam. Well-established coffeeshops are considered much safer, and coffeeshop owners have an interest in keeping their trade safe and healthy. They're also generally very patient in explaining the varieties available.

Coffeeshops

Most of downtown Amsterdam's coffeeshops feel grungy and foreboding to American travelers who aren't part of the youth-hostel crowd. I've listed a few places with a more pub-like ambience for Americans wanting to go local, but within reason. For locations, see the "West/Central Amsterdam Hotels & Restaurants" map, earlier.

Paradox is the most *gezellig* (cozy) coffeeshop—a mellow, graceful place. The managers, Ludo and Wiljan, and their staff

are patient with descriptions and happy to walk you through all your options. This is a rare coffeeshop that serves light meals (daily 10:00-20:00, loaner bongs, games, Wi-Fi, two blocks from Anne Frank House at Eerste Bloemdwarsstraat 2, tel. 020/623-5639).

The Grey Area—a hole-in-the-wall with three tiny tables—is a cool, welcoming, and smoky place appreciated among local aficionados as a perennial winner at Amsterdam's Cannabis Cup Awards. You're welcome to just nurse a bottomless cup of coffee (daily 12:00-20:00, between Dam Square and Anne Frank House at Oude Leliestraat 2, tel. 020/420-4301).

Siberië Coffeeshop is a short walk from Centraal Station,

AMSTERDAM

but feels cozy, with a friendly canalside ambience. Clean, big, and bright, this place has the vibe of a mellow Starbucks, hosts the occasional astrology reading, and is proud that all their pot is "lab tested" (daily 10:00-23:00, Fri-Sat until 24:00, Wi-Fi for customers, helpful staff, English menu, Brouwersgracht 11, tel. 020/623-5909).

La Tertulia is a sweet little mother-and-daughter-run place with pastel decor and a cheery terrarium atmosphere (Tue-Sat 11:00-19:00, closed Sun-Mon, sandwiches, brownies, games, Prinsengracht 312).

The Dampkring is a rough-and-ready constant party. It's a high-profile, busy place, filled with a young clientele and loud music, but the owners still take the time to explain what they offer (daily 10:00-24:00, close to Spui at Handboogstraat 29, tel. 020/638-0705).

4:20 Coffeeshop, conveniently located near Spui Square on Singel canal, has a very casual "brown café" ambience and a mature set of regulars. A couple of tables overlooking the canal are perfect for enjoying the late-afternoon sunshine (daily 12:00-20:00, on the corner of Heisteeg and Singel at Singel 387, tel. 020/624-7624).

The Bulldog Café is the high-profile, leading touristy chain of coffeeshops. These establishments are young but welcoming, with reliable selections. They're comfortable for green tourists wanting to just hang out for a while. The flagship branch, in a former police station right on Leidseplein, is very handy, offering alcohol upstairs, pot downstairs, and fun outdoor seating on a heated patio (daily 10:00-24:00, later on weekends, Leidseplein 17—see the "Southwest Amsterdam Hotels & Restaurants" map, earlier, tel. 020/625-6278). Their original

café still sits on the canal near the Old Church in the Red Light District.

Starting or Ending Your Cruise in Amsterdam

If your cruise begins and/or ends in Amsterdam, you'll want some extra time here; most travelers will want at least one extra day (beyond your cruise departure day) to see the highlights of this grand city. For a longer visit here, pick up my *Rick Steves Amsterdam & the Netherlands* guidebook.

Airport Connections

SCHIPHOL AIRPORT

Schiphol (SKIP-pol) Airport is located about 10 miles southwest of Amsterdam's city center (code: AMS, www.schiphol.nl). Though Schiphol officially has four terminals, it's really just one big building. All terminals have ATMs, banks, shops, bars, and free Wi-Fi.

Baggage-claim areas for all terminals empty into the same arrival zone, officially called Schiphol Plaza but generally signed simply *Arrivals Hall*. Here you'll find a busy **TI** (near Terminal 2, daily 7:00-22:00), a train station, and bus stops for getting into the city.

To get train information or buy a ticket, take advantage of the **"Train Tickets and Services" counter** (Schiphol Plaza ground level, just past Burger King). They have an easy info desk and generally short lines.

Getting Between Schiphol Airport and Downtown or the Cruise Terminal

Direct **trains** to Amsterdam's Centraal Station run frequently from Schiphol Plaza (4-6/hour, 20 minutes, €5.40). The cruise terminal is an easy **tram ride** away: From the plaza in front of the train station, look for the tram stop marked *IJburg* (on the right as you face the station). From here, catch tram #26 and ride one stop to Muziekgebouw Bimhuis, which is right in front of the terminal. If your cruise ends in Amsterdam and you're flying out of Schiphol, just reverse these directions (from the terminal, ride the tram in direction: Centraal Station).

The Connexxion **shuttle bus** departs from lane A7 in front of the airport and takes you directly to most hotels or to the cruise terminal (which is right next to the Mövenpick Hotel Amsterdam City Centre). There are three different routes, so ask the attendant which one works best for you (2/hour, 20 minutes to the first hotel, up to 45 minutes to the last, €17 one-way, pay driver cash, pay inside at Connexxion desk with credit card, or book online, tel. 088-339-4741, www.airporthotelshuttle.nl).

Public Bus #397 (departing from lane B9 in front of the airport) is handy for those going to the Leidseplein district (€5, buy ticket from driver or online, www.connexxion.nl).

By Taxi, allow about €50 to the cruise terminal or downtown Amsterdam. Uber serves the airport for about €28.

Hotels in Amsterdam

**$$$$= Most rooms over €170; $$$= €130-170; $$= €90-130;
$= €50-90 ¢= € Under 50**

If you need a hotel in Amsterdam before or after your cruise, here
are a few to consider.

CANALSIDE HOTELS

For locations, see the "West/Central Amsterdam Hotels & Restaurants" map.

$$$$ The Toren is a smartly renovated, chandeliered mansion with a pleasant canalside setting and a peaceful garden for
guests out back. Run by the Toren family, this super-romantic hotel
is classy yet friendly, with 38 rooms in a great location on a quiet
street two blocks northeast of the Anne Frank House. The capable
staff is a good source of local advice. The gilt-frame, velvet-cur-
tained rooms are an opulent splurge (RS%, breakfast extra, air-con,
elevator, Keizersgracht 164, tel. 020/622-6033, www.thetoren.nl,
info@thetoren.nl).

$$$$ Hotel Ambassade is elegant and fresh, lacing together
57 rooms in a maze of connected houses sitting aristocratically on
Herengracht. The staff is top-notch, and the public areas (including
a library and a breakfast room) are palatial, with antique furnishings and modern art (RS%, breakfast extra, air-con, elevator, Herengracht 341, tel. 020/555-0222, www.ambassade-hotel.nl, info@
ambassade-hotel.nl).

$$$ Hotel Brouwer—woody and old-time homey—has a
tranquil yet central location for its eight rooms with Singel canal
views. With the owner retiring soon, it may have a few rough edges,
but old furniture and soulful throw rugs provide loads of charac-
ter. Stay here before an upgrade turns it into another slick, cookie-
cutter hotel (cash only, small elevator, located between Centraal
Station and Dam Square, near Lijnbaanssteeg at Singel 83, tel.
020/624-6358, www.hotelbrouwer.nl, michelle@hotelbrouwer.nl).

$$ Hotel Hoksbergen is your budget option for a canalside
setting, so expect cramped rooms and a decidedly lived-in feel.
The new owners promise to renovate all 14 rooms eventually—
and the bathrooms are already up to snuff—but there are lots of
steep stairs and ho-hum hallways. Avoid Room 4, which is sold as
a double but should be a single (ask about apartments, fans, Singel 301, tel. 020/626-6043, www.hotelhoksbergen.com, info@
hotelhoksbergen.nl).

AMSTERDAM

SOUTHWEST AMSTERDAM, NEAR VONDELPARK AND MUSEUMPLEIN

These options cluster around Vondelpark in a safe neighborhood. Though they don't have a hint of Old Dutch or romantic canal-side flavor, they're reasonable values and only a short walk from the action. Unless noted, these places have elevators. Many are in a pleasant nook between rollicking Leidseplein and the park, and most are a 5- to 15-minute walk to the Rijks and Van Gogh museums. They are easily connected with Centraal Station by tram #2 or #12. For locations, see the "Southwest Amsterdam Hotels & Restaurants" map.

$$$ Hotel Piet Hein offers 81 stylishly sleek yet comfortable rooms as well as a swanky lounge, good breakfast, and a peaceful garden, all on a quiet street. Be aware that the "economy double" is so tight, you'll have to climb over your partner to get to the other side of the bed (breakfast extra, air-con in some rooms, Vossiusstraat 51, tel. 020/662-7205, www.hotelpiethein.nl, info@hotelpiethein.nl).

$$$ Hotel Fita has 20 bright rooms in a great location—100 yards from the Van Gogh Museum, an even shorter hop from the tram stop, and on a pleasant corner with a grade school's lively recess yard filling a traffic-free street. The style is modern yet rustic, with minimalist plywood furniture and nice extras, including espresso machines in every room. It's well-run by Roel, who offers a friendly welcome and generous advice (air-con on upper floors, elevator, free laundry service, Jan Luijkenstraat 37, tel. 020/679-0976, www.fita.nl, info@fita.nl).

$$ Hotel Alexander is a modern, newly renovated 34-room hotel on a quiet street. Some of the rooms overlook the garden patio out back. If you're looking for a smart, clean, relaxed place, this is it (breakfast extra, tel. 020/589-4020, Vondelstraat 44, www.hotelalexander.nl, info@hotelalexander.nl).

NEAR THE TRAIN STATION AND CRUISE TERMINAL

$$$ Hotel Ibis Amsterdam Centre is a modern, efficient, 363-room place. It offers a central location, comfort, and good value, without a hint of charm (book long in advance—especially for Sept-Oct, air-con, elevators, facing Centraal Station, go left toward multistory bicycle garage to Stationsplein 49; tel. 020/721-9172, www.ibishotel.com, h1556@accor.com).

To sleep right next door to the cruise terminal, consider the **$$$ Mövenpick Hotel Amsterdam City Centre** (www.moevenpick.com)—but keep in mind that this location is less practical for getting to anywhere other than your ship.

AMSTERDAM

What If I Miss My Ship?

Remember that you can get help from the cruise line's port agent (listed on the destination information sheet distributed on the ship) and the local TI. If the port agent suggests a costly solution (such as a private car with a driver), you may want to consider public transit.

Amsterdam is well-connected by train to a variety of cruise ports, including **Zeebrugge** (via Brussels), **Le Havre** (via Paris), **Southampton** and **Dover** (Eurostar via Brussels/London, then train onward to either port), **Copenhagen, Warnemünde** (via Berlin), and beyond.

If you need to catch a **plane** to your next destination, it's an easy train ride from downtown Amsterdam to Schiphol Airport. For more information, see the next section.

For more advice on what to do if you miss the boat, see page 130.

Entertainment in Amsterdam

On summer evenings, people flock to the main squares for drinks at outdoor tables. Leidseplein is the liveliest square, surrounded by theaters, restaurants, and nightclubs. The slightly quieter Rembrandtplein (with adjoining Thorbeckeplein and nearby Reguliersdwarsstraat) is the center of gay clubs and nightlife. Spui features a full city block of bars. And Nieuwmarkt, on the east edge of the Red Light District, is a bit rough, but is probably the least touristy.

The Red Light District (particularly Oudezijds Achterburgwal) is less sleazy in the early evening, and almost carnival-like as the neon lights come on and the streets fill with tour groups. But it starts to feel scuzzy after about 22:30. The **brown cafés** recommended in "Eating in Amsterdam" are ideal after-hours hangouts. Peruse those listings for pre- or post-dinner drink ideas.

For entertainment and nightlife information, the TI's website, www.iamsterdam.com, has good English listings for upcoming events (select "What to do," then "What's on"). Newsstands sell the *A-Mag* entertainment guide and Dutch newspapers (Thu editions generally list events).

Dutch Survival Phrases

Most people speak English, but if you learn the pleasantries and key phrases, you'll connect better with the locals. To pronounce the guttural Dutch "g" (indicated in phonetics by *h*), make a clear-your-throat sound, similar to the "ch" in the Scottish word "loch."

English	Dutch	Pronunciation
Hello.	*Hallo.*	**hah**-loh
Good day.	*Dag.*	da*h*
Good morning.	*Goedemorgen.*	***hoo***-deh-mor-*h*ehn
Good afternoon.	*Goedemiddag.*	***hoo***-deh-mid-da*h*
Good evening.	*Goedenavond.*	***hoo***-dehn-ah-fohnd
Do you speak English?	*Spreekt u Engels?*	shpraykt oo **eng**-ehls
Yes. / No.	*Ja. / Nee.*	yah / nay
I (don't) understand.	*Ik begrijp (het niet).*	ik beh-***h*ripe** (heht neet)
Please. (can also mean "You're welcome")	*Alstublieft.*	**ahl**-stoo-bleeft
Thank you.	*Dank u wel.*	dahnk oo vehl
I'm sorry.	*Het spijt me.*	heht spite meh
Excuse me.	*Pardon.*	**par**-dohn
(No) problem.	*(Geen) probleem.*	(hayn) **proh**-blaym
Good.	*Goede.*	**hoo**-deh
Goodbye.	*Tot ziens.*	toht zeens
one / two	*een / twee*	ayn / t'vay
three / four	*drie / vier*	dree / feer
five / six	*vijf / zes*	fife / zehs
seven / eight	*zeven / acht*	**zay**-fehn / aht
nine / ten	*negen / tien*	**nay**-hehn / teen
What does it cost?	*Wat kost het?*	vaht kohst heht
Is it free?	*Is het vrij?*	is heht fry
Is it included?	*Is het inclusief?*	is heht in-**kloo**-seev
Can you please help me?	*Kunt u alstublieft helpen?*	koont oo **ahl**-stoo-bleeft **hehl**-pehn
Where can I buy / find...?	*Waar kan ik kopen / vinden...?*	var kahn ik **koh**-pehn / **fin**-dehn
I'd like / We'd like...	*Ik wil graag / Wij willen graag...*	ik vil *h*ra*h* / vy **vil**-lehn *h*ra*h*
...a room.	*...een kamer.*	ayn **kah**-mer
...a train / bus ticket to ____.	*...een trein / bus kaartje naar ____.*	ayn trayn / boos **kart**-yeh nar ___
...to rent a bike.	*...een fiets huren.*	ayn feets **hoo**-rehn
Where is...?	*Waar is...?*	var is
...the train / bus station	*...het trein / bus station*	heht trayn / boos **staht**-see-ohn
...the tourist info office	*...de VVV*	deh fay fay fay
...the toilet	*...het toilet*	heht **twah**-leht
men / women	*mannen / vrouwen*	**mah**-nehn / **frow**-ehn
left / right	*links / rechts*	links / reh*h*ts
straight ahead	*rechtdoor*	**reh*h***-dor
What time does it open / close?	*Hoe laat gaat het open / dicht?*	hoo laht *h*aht heht **oh**-pehn / di*h*t
now / soon / later	*nu / straks / later*	noo / strahks / **lah**-ter
today / tomorrow	*vandaag / morgen*	**fahn**-da*h* / **mor**-hehn

BRUGES & BRUSSELS

Belgium

Belgium Practicalities

Travelers are often pleasantly surprised by Belgium—a charming, welcoming, and underrated land that produces some of Europe's best beer, creamiest chocolates, most beloved comic strips, and tastiest French fries. Squeezed between Germany, France, and the Netherlands, Belgium has 11.4 million people packed into nearly 12,000 square miles (similar to Maryland)—making it the second most densely populated country in Europe (after the Netherlands). About three-quarters of the population is Catholic. Belgium is a culturally, linguistically, and politically divided country, with 60 percent of the population speaking Dutch...but an economy dominated by French speakers. The capital city of Brussels is important internationally as the capital of the European Union—more than 25 percent of the people living there are foreigners.

Money: €1 (euro) = about $1.20. The local VAT (value-added sales tax) rate is 21 percent; the minimum purchase eligible for a VAT refund is €50 (for details on refunds, see page 125).

Language: The official languages are Dutch (also called Flemish), French, and German. For useful Dutch phrases, see page 797; for French phrases, see page 1060; and for German phrases, see page 588.

Emergencies: Dial 112 for police, medical, or other emergencies. In case of theft or loss, see page 118.

Time Zone: Belgium is on Central European Time (the same as most of the Continent, one hour ahead of Great Britain, and six/nine hours ahead of the East/West Coasts of the US).

Embassies in Brussels: The **US embassy** is at Boulevard du Régent 27 (tel. 02-811-4300, after-hours emergency tel. 02-811-4000, https://be.usembassy.gov). The **US consulate** is next door to the embassy at Boulevard du Régent 25. The **Canadian embassy** is at Avenue des Arts 58 (tel. 02-741-0611, www.ambassade-canada.be). Call ahead for passport services.

Phoning: With a mobile phone, it's easy to dial: Press and hold zero until you get a + sign, enter the country code (32 for Belgium, 1 for the US/Canada), and then the complete phone number (including area code if there is one). When dialing a European phone number, drop an initial zero (except if calling Italy). For more tips, see page 1062.

Tipping: The bill for sit-down meals already includes a tip, though for good service it's nice to round up about 5-10 percent. Round up taxi fares a bit (pay €3 on a €2.85 fare). For more tips on tipping, see page 129.

Tourist Information: www.visitbelgium.com

BRUGES, BRUSSELS
& the PORT of ZEEBRUGGE

Zeebrugge • Bruges • Brussels • Ghent

Belgium's port of Zeebrugge is the gateway to this entire small country: With several hours in port, you could visit nearly any point within its borders. Most cruisers, however, set their sights on two places: Bruges, a charming, quintessentially medieval town; and Brussels, the bustling capital of Belgium and of Europe.

With pointy, gilded architecture, stay-a-while cafés, vivid time-tunnel art, and dreamy canals dotted with swans, **Bruges** (pronounced "broozh") is a heavyweight sightseeing destination as well as a joy. Where else can you ride a bike along a canal, munch mussels and wash them down with the world's best beer, savor heavenly chocolate, and see Flemish Primitives and a Michelangelo, all within 300 yards of a bell tower that jingles every 15 minutes? And do it all without worrying about a language barrier?

Six hundred years ago, **Brussels** was just a nice place to stop and buy a waffle on the way to Bruges. With no strategic importance, it was allowed to grow as a free trading town. Today it's a city of one million people, the capital of Belgium, the headquarters of NATO, and the seat of the European Union.

If neither of these options fits the bill, consider the midsize city of **Ghent,** which lies halfway between Brussels and Bruges—both geographically and in spirit. This charming university city offers historic, art-packed churches as well as cutting-edge museums.

Cruise lines often advertise their Zeebrugge stop as "Brussels," but I recommend focusing on Bruges instead. Bruges is not only much closer and easier to reach from your ship, but—thanks to its user-friendliness and overall charm—it's all-around the more preferable destination.

PLANNING YOUR TIME

From Zeebrugge, it's a breeze (shuttle bus, or short walk plus 15-minute tram ride to the town of Blankenberge, then 15-minute train ride) to zip into **Bruges.** If you prefer a bigger city, you can continue on the same train to **Ghent** (50 minutes) or **Brussels** (1.5 hours). And for WWI history buffs, the famous **Flanders Fields** are also nearby. With one day in port, you'll need to choose just one of these.

Note: On Mondays, most museums—including major ones in both Bruges (Groeninge, Memling) and Brussels (Royal Museums, BELvue, Musical Instruments, Comic Strip)—are closed.

In Bruges

With a day in Bruges, I'd do the following (ranked here by importance, and in a smart chronological order):

Bruges City Walk: Stroll through town visiting the Markt (Market Square), the Basilica of the Holy Blood, the City Hall's Gothic Room, the Church of Our Lady, and the Begijnhof (allow 2 hours total); if your energy holds up, climb the bell tower on the Markt (add 30-45 minutes).

Groeninge Museum: This fine collection of 15th-century Flemish art takes about an hour to see.

Memling Museum: With a quirky collection of medieval medical trades, plus some paintings by Hans Memling, this deserves an hour.

Canal Cruise: This relaxing and scenic trip takes 30 minutes.

De Halve Maan Brewery Tour: If you have an hour to spare, this tour offers a good taste of Belgian beer.

In Brussels

As a much bigger city, Brussels simply takes more time to get around. But several key sights are in the downtown core. Riding the train to the Central Station, you're within walking distance of these options:

Grand Place: My self-guided tour of Brussels' spectacular main square includes a peek at the famous *Manneken-Pis* statue. Allow two hours.

Royal Museums: For an excellent art collection, head to the Upper Town for the Old Masters, Fin de Siècle, and René Magritte Museums (allow an hour to quickly see the highlights of the Old Masters/Fin de Siècle collections, plus another hour for Magritte).

BELvue Museum: This concise overview of Belgian history, next to the Royal Museums, is worth an hour.

Other Museums: Also consider Brussels' good Musical Instruments Museum or Comic Strip Center (allow an hour apiece).

In Ghent

From Ghent's Sint-Pieters Station, it's a 15-minute tram ride into the heart of town. On a short visit, I'd stroll the historic center, tour the Cathedral of St. Bavo (with its grand Van Eyck altarpiece; allow about an hour), and—depending on your interests—visit the castle or Design Museum (each deserves about an hour).

In Flanders Fields

This spread-out area is best seen on an excursion or with a taxi from the port (Taxi Snel; see page 806). To do it on your own, take the coastal tram to Ostend, rent a car, and tour the WWI battlefields and museums near Ypres. Figure 50 minutes by coastal tram from Zeebrugge to Ostend, then an hour each way to drive between Ostend and Ypres.

Port of Zeebrugge

Arrival at a Glance: From your ship, you'll ride a shuttle bus to the port gate. From here, most cruise lines offer a shuttle to the Blankenberge train station, your jumping-off point for Bruges (15 minutes), Ghent (50 minutes), and Brussels (1.5 hours). Or, you can walk from the port gate to a tram stop, then ride the tram 10-15 minutes to the Blankenberge train station.

Port Overview

Zeebrugge (ZAY-brew-gah), 10 miles north of Bruges, is a little village with a gigantic port (one of Europe's busiest).

The sprawling port zone has two cruise berths: Larger cruise ships use **Swedish Quay** (Zweedse Kaai), which pokes straight up into the main harbor; smaller ships use **Maritime Station** (Zeestation), across the harbor along Leopold II-Dam. From these berths, a free shuttle bus brings you to the port gate or a local tram stop. Cruisers arriving at Swedish Quay will pass through the new **ABC Tower terminal building** located at the port gate. Its services include free Wi-Fi, tourist information, shops, and a view restaurant.

Tourist Information: The Zeebrugge TI—open only in summer—is in a red beachside building three blocks from the Strandwijk tram stop, at the intersection of Sint-Thomas Morusstraat and Zeedijk (daily July-Aug 10:00-13:30 & 14:00-18:00, Zeedijk 25, tel. 050-444-646). Otherwise, the most convenient TI is in Blankenberge, near the train station (daily 9:00-12:00 & 13:30-17:00, until 19:00 July-Aug; closed Sun Feb-March; Koning Leopold III Plein, tel. 050-412-227, www.blankenberge.be).

Sights in Zeebrugge: Zeebrugge is a **beach town** as well as a North Sea port. To just soak up some sun, grab your towel and a

Excursions from Zeebrugge

Just about anything you'd want to see is doable on your own from Zeebrugge using public transportation—with the notable exception of Flanders Fields.

The most popular excursion options are tours to either charming, manageable Bruges or big, bustling Brussels. The Bruges excursion usually includes a walking tour around the Old Town. The Brussels excursion is generally part by bus and part on foot. Given the size and relative ease of reaching Bruges, seeing that city on your own is a no-brainer; for Brussels, less adventurous travelers may want to consider an excursion.

Other popular choices include the pleasant university town of Ghent (halfway between Bruges and Brussels); the big, fashion-oriented port city of Antwerp (including a visit to the Cathedral of Our Lady, decorated with several works by native son Peter Paul Rubens); or a trip to the town of Ypres and the surrounding World War I battlefields known as Flanders Fields. Some cruise lines offer a relaxing canalside bike ride between Bruges and the neighboring hamlet of Damme.

Any of these tours may include a few Belgian clichés: canal boat ride, chocolate workshop, sampling a Belgian waffle, or beer tasting.

swimsuit, and head to the beach—a short tram ride and 10-minute walk away: From the Zeebrugge Kerk tram stop near Swedish Quay (see directions, next page), ride two stops to the Strandwijk stop. Cross the street toward the red-roofed white church, then circle around its front side to walk through an arbor-covered walkway. At the next street, turn left. At the first intersection, turn right to find the sand. A small building has showers, WCs, and a summer-only TI (daily July-Aug 10:00-13:30 & 14:00-18:00). Beach cafés and restaurants are nearby.

GETTING INTO BLANKENBERGE (AND BRUGES, GHENT, OR BRUSSELS)

First, I'll cover how to get from the port to the Blankenberge train station, and then onward to Bruges, Ghent, or Brussels. To return to your ship, you can generally reverse these directions—I've given additional tips where they'll help.

From the Port of Zeebrugge to Blankenberge Train Station

Because Zeebrugge's train stations are inconvenient for cruisers, it's smart to head right for the nearby town of Blankenberge, with frequent, direct trains to Bruges, Ghent, and Brussels. The Blankenberge TI is right behind the train station tram stop in a build-

Services near the Port of Zeebrugge and in Blankenberge

ATMs: Two ATMs are a short distance from the coastal tram's Zeebrugge Kerk stop, about a 15-minute walk from the port gate: Leaving the port area from Swedish Quay, turn right and walk along the coastal road. Once in town, pass the church and tram stop and continue along the tram tracks. At the next major intersection, there's a KBC bank on the left and a BNP Paribas bank on the right. If you're taking the tram to Blankenberge, you'll find ATMs at the train station there.

Wi-Fi: Free Wi-Fi is available around Blankenberge—log in to "Blankenberge Free Wi-Fi"—and at some restaurants.

Pharmacy: The most convenient pharmacy is in Blankenberge. Ride the tram to Blankenberge's train station, cross the large square, and turn right up the pedestrian shopping street called Kerkstraat. You'll see a neon green cross for Apotheek Spaens (closed Wed and Sun, Kerkstraat 83, tel. 050-411-141). In Zeebrugge, Apotheek Havendam is near the beach (closed Sat-Sun, Brusselstraat 34, tel. 050-545-514).

Grocery: To buy a picnic or stock up on snacks, you'll find a Spar grocery store on the main street by the Zeebrugge Kerk tram stop (daily, Kustlaan 94, tel. 050-544-686).

ing facing a large square (Koning Leopold III Plein). You'll also find shops and a pharmacy.

By Cruise-Line Shuttle Bus: Some cruise lines provide a shuttle bus from the dock all the way to Blankenberge's train station (either free or for a fee).

By Taxi: A taxi between the port and the train station in Blankenberge costs about €20.

By Tram: A coastal tram *(kusttram)* runs between Zeebrugge and the Blankenberge train station every 20 minutes (about 14 minutes; direction: Oostende or De Panne, video screen inside tram displays the next stop; ride about 14 minutes to the Blankenberge Station stop, across the street from the train station) and is covered by a €3 ticket (pay driver; good for up to one hour). If you'll be riding the bus in Bruges, it's smart to buy a day pass for €8 (tram info: Toll tel. 070-220-200, www.delijn.be).

To find the tram from **Swedish Quay,** turn right from the port gate and walk 10 minutes along the highway to the Kerk stop (right in front of the church—use the closest platform—don't cross the tracks). From **Maritime Station,** the port shuttle drops you off very near the tram's Strandwijk stop.

Returning to Your Ship: From Blankenberge, ride the tram in direction: Knokke and get off at the Strandwijk (Maritime Station) or Kerk (Swedish Quay) stop.

From Blankenberge Train Station to Bruges, Ghent, and Brussels

Every train leaving Blankenberge goes through Bruges—just take the next train. Most trains leave at :10 past the hour, arriving in **Bruges** in 15 minutes (€3.20 one-way), then continuing on to **Ghent** (€8.90 one-way, 1 hour total, get off at Gent-Sint-Pieters Station), then **Brussels** (€17 one-way, 1.5 hours total, get off at Brussel-Centraal/Bruxelles-Central Station, www.belgianrail.be). To buy tickets, use your US credit card in the ticket machines or visit the station's ticket office.

Getting Around by Taxi

Taxis queue up just outside the port gate. Fares are expensive—most cabs charge at least €50 one-way for a trip to Bruges. It's best to arrange a taxi in advance; try **Taxi Snel,** which has a standard rate of €50 between Zeebrugge and Bruges (tel. 050-363-649, mobile 0478-353-535, www.taxisnel.be). Likely fares for one-way journeys to farther destinations include: Brussels—€300; Ghent—€160; Ypres (Flanders Fields)—€200.

Bruges

Right from the start, Bruges was a trading center. In the 11th century, the city grew wealthy on the cloth trade. By the 14th century, Bruges' population was 35,000, as large as London's. As the middleman in the sea trade between northern and southern Europe, it was one of the biggest cities in the world and an economic powerhouse. In addition, Bruges had become the most important cloth market in northern Europe.

In the 15th century, while England and France were slugging it out in the Hundred Years' War, Bruges was the favored residence of the powerful Dukes of Burgundy—and at peace. Commerce and the arts boomed. The artists Jan van Eyck and Hans Memling had studios here.

But by the 16th century, the harbor had silted up and the economy had collapsed. The Burgundian court left, Belgium became a minor Habsburg possession, and Bruges' Golden Age abruptly ended. For generations, Bruges was known as a mysterious and dead city. In the 19th century, a new port, Zeebrugge, brought renewed vitality to the area. And in the 20th century, tourists discovered the town.

Today, Bruges prospers because of tourism: It's a uniquely well-preserved Gothic city and a handy gateway to Europe. It's no secret, but even with the crowds, it's the kind of place where you don't mind being a tourist.

Orientation to Bruges

The tourist's Bruges is less than one square mile, contained within a canal (the former moat). Nearly everything of interest and importance is within a convenient cobbled swath between the train station and the Markt (Market Square; a 20-minute walk). Most tourists are concentrated in the triangle formed by the Markt, Burg Square, and the Church of Our Lady; outside of that tight zone, the townscape is sleepy and relatively uncrowded.

TOURIST INFORMATION

The main TI, called **In&Uit** ("In and Out"), is in the big, red concert hall on the square called 't Zand (Mon-Sat 10:00-17:00, Sun until 14:00, free Wi-Fi, 't Zand 34, tel. 050-444-646, www. brugge.be, toerisme@brugge.be). Other TI branches include one at the **train station** and one on the **Markt,** sharing a building with the Historium museum (both branches open daily 10:00-17:00).

ARRIVAL AT BRUGES TRAIN STATION

Bruges' train station is situated in a clean, parklike setting, where travelers step out the door and are greeted by a taxi stand and a roundabout with center-bound buses circulating through every couple of minutes. Coming in by train, you'll see the bell tower that marks the main square (Markt, the center of town). Stop by the train station TI to pick up a free map. The station also has ATMs and lockers.

The best way to get to the town center is by **bus.** Bus #12 shuttles between the station and the Markt. Other buses serve the city center, but don't go to the Markt (#1, #6, #11, and #16; all marked *Centrum,* get off at Dijver). Simply hop on, pay €3, and you're there in four minutes.

To return to the train station from the city center, catch any bus at the Stadsschouwburg stop right in front of the City Theater.

A **taxi** from the train station to downtown is about €10-15.

It's a 20-minute **walk** from the station to the center. To walk to the Markt, cross the busy street and canal in front of the station,

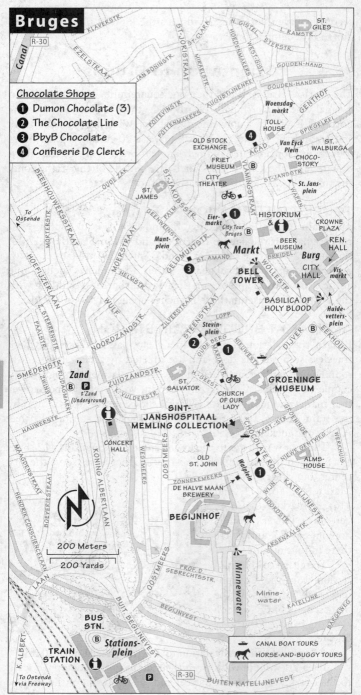

Bruges

Chocolate Shops
1 Dumon Chocolate (3)
2 The Chocolate Line
3 BbyB Chocolate
4 Confiserie De Clerck

head up Oostmeers, and turn right on Zwidzandstraat. You can rent a **bike** at the station, but other bike-rental shops are closer to the center (see "Helpful Hints," next).

HELPFUL HINTS

Sightseeing Tips: The 't Zand TI and city museums sell a "Museumpas" **combo-ticket** for €20 (valid for 3 days at 16 locations). Because the Groeninge and Sint-Janshospitaal museums cost €8 each, you'll save money with this pass if you plan to see at least one other covered sight.

If you're in Bruges on a **Monday,** when several museums are closed, consider the following alternatives: bell-tower climb on the Markt, Begijnhof, De Halve Maan Brewery tour, Basilica of the Holy Blood, City Hall's Gothic Room, Bruges Beer Museum, Historium, chocolate shops and museum, and Church of Our Lady. You can also join a boat, bus, or walking tour, or rent a bike and pedal into the countryside.

For **information** on all of Bruges' art and historical museums, call 050-448-711 or visit www.brugge.be.

Market Days: Bruges hosts markets on Wednesday morning (on the Markt) and Saturday morning ('t Zand). On good-weather Saturdays, Sundays, and public holidays, a flea market hops along Dijver in front of the Groeninge Museum. The Fish Market sells souvenirs daily and seafood Wednesday through Saturday mornings until 13:00.

Bike Rental: Bruges Bike Rental is central and cheap, with friendly service and long hours (€4/hour, €7/2 hours, €10/4 hours, €13/day, show this book to get student rate—€10/day, no deposit required—just ID, daily 10:00-22:00, free city maps and child seats, behind the far-out iron facade at Niklaas Desparsstraat 17, tel. 050-616-108, Bilal). **Fietsen Popelier Bike Rental** is also good (€5/hour, €10/4 hours, €15/day, also has electric bikes, no deposit required, daily 10:00-19:00, sometimes open later in summer, free Damme map, Mariastraat 26, tel. 050-343-262). **Koffieboontje Bike Rental** is

just under the bell tower on the Markt (€5/hour, €15/day, €30/day for tandem, daily 9:00-22:00, free city maps and child seats, Hallestraat 4, tel. 050-338-027). **Fietspunt Brugge** is a big outfit at the train station (7-speed bikes, €10/4 hours, €15/24 hours, Mon-Fri 7:00-19:00, Sat-Sun 9:00-20:00, just outside the station and to the right as you exit in the huge bicycle parking garage, tel. 050-396-826).

Best Town View: The bell tower overlooking the Markt rewards those who climb it with the ultimate Bruges view.

GETTING AROUND BRUGES

Most of the city is easily walkable, but you may want to take the bus or taxi between the train station and the city center at the Markt.

By Bus: Nearly all city buses go directly from the train station to the city center and fan out from there; they then return to the center and go back to the train station. Note that buses returning to the train station from the city center leave from the Stadsschouwburg bus stop, a few blocks off the square on nearby Vlamingstraat (every 5 minutes). Your key: Use buses that say either *Station* or *Centrum*.

A bus **ticket** is €3 and good for an hour (buy as many tickets as you need in advance at Lijnwinkel shop just outside the train station—cash or credit card; can also buy tickets on the bus—exact change only).

By Taxi: You'll find taxi stands at the station and on the Markt (€10-15/first 2 kilometers; to get a cab in the center, call 050-334-444 or 050-333-881).

Tours in Bruges

Boat Tours

The most relaxing and scenic (though not informative) way to see this city of canals is by boat, with the captain narrating. The many companies all offer essentially the same thing: a 30-minute route (roughly 4/hour, daily 10:00-17:00), a price of €8 (cash only), and narration in three or four languages. Let them know you speak English to ensure you'll understand the spiel. Two companies give the group-rate discount to individuals with this book: **Boten Stael** (just over the canal from Sint-Janshospitaal at Katelijnestraat 4, tel. 050-332-771) and **Gruuthuse** (Nieuwstraat 11, opposite Groeninge Museum, tel. 050-333-393).

Bike Tour

QuasiMundo Bike Tours leads daily five-mile English-language bike tours around the city (€28, €2 discount with this book, 2.5 hours, departs March-Oct at 10:00, tel. 050-330-775, www.quasimundo.com).

City Minibus Tour

City Tour Bruges gives a rolling overview of the town in an 18-seat, two-skylight minibus with dial-a-language headsets and video support (€20, 50 minutes, pay driver). The tour leaves every 30 minutes from the Markt (10:00-19:00, until 18:00 in fall, tel. 050-355-024, www.citytour.be). The narration, though clear, is slow-moving and a bit boring. But the tour is a lazy way to cruise past virtually every sight in Bruges.

Walking Tour

The **TI** arranges walks through the core of town (€12.50, 2 hours, daily July-Aug, Sat-Sun only mid-April-June and Sept-Oct, depart from TI on 't Zand Square at 14:30 Mon-Sat, 10:30 on Sun—just drop in a few minutes early and buy tickets at the TI desk). Though earnest, the tours are heavy on history and given in two languages, so they may be less than peppy. Still, to propel you beyond the pretty gables and canal swans of Bruges, they're good medicine.

Local Guides

Daniëlle Janssens gives two-hour walks for €90, three-hour walks for €120, and full-day tours of Bruges and Brussels for €210 (mobile 0476-493-203, www.tourmanagementbelgium.be, info@tmbel. be). You can also hire a guide through the **TI** (typically €70/2-hour tour, reserve at least one week in advance, for contact information see "Tourist Information," earlier).

Horse-and-Buggy Tour

The buggies around town can take you on a clip-clop tour (€50, 35 minutes; price is per carriage, not per person, and seats five; buggies gather in Minnewater, near entrance to Begijnhof, and on the Markt). When divided among four or five people, this can be a good value.

Sights in Bruges

ON OR NEAR THE MARKT

▲Markt (Market Square)

The crossroads of Bruges is one of the most enjoyable town squares in Belgium—and in this country, that's really saying something. In Bruges' heyday as a trading center, a canal came right up to this square. And today it's still the heart of the modern city. The square is ringed by the frilly former post office, enticing restaurant terraces, great old gabled buildings, and the iconic bell tower. Under the bell tower are two great Belgian-style French-fry stands. The streets spoking off this square are lined with tempting eateries and shops.

Bruges at a Glance

▲▲**Bell Tower** Overlooking the Markt—the modern heart of the city—with 366 steps to a fine view and carillon close-up. **Hours:** Daily 9:30-18:00, last entry at 17:15. See page 813.

▲▲**Burg Square** Historic square with sights and impressive architecture. See page 813.

▲▲**Groeninge Museum** Top-notch collection of mainly Flemish art. **Hours:** Tue-Sun 9:30-17:00, closed Mon. See page 814.

▲▲**Church of Our Lady** Tombs and church art, including Michelangelo's *Madonna and Child.* **Hours:** Mon-Sat 9:30-17:00, Sun 13:30-17:00. See page 816.

▲▲**Sint-Janshospitaal Memling Collection** Art by the greatest of the Flemish Primitives. **Hours:** Tue-Sun 9:30-17:00, closed Mon. See page 817.

▲▲**Begijnhof** Peaceful medieval courtyard and Beguine's House museum. **Hours:** Courtyard-daily 6:30-18:30; museum-Mon-Sat 10:00-17:00, closed Sun, shorter hours off-season. See page 820.

▲▲**De Halve Maan Brewery Tour** Fun beer tour. **Hours:** Tours on the hour Sun-Fri 11:00-16:00, Sat until 17:00. See page 821.

▲**Historium** Multimedia exhibit re-creating the sights, sounds, and smells of 1430s Bruges. **Hours:** Daily 10:00-18:00. See page 813.

▲**Basilica of the Holy Blood** Romanesque and Gothic church housing a relic of the blood of Christ. **Hours:** Daily 9:30-12:00 & 14:00-17:00; Nov-March closed on Wed afternoon. See page 813.

▲**City Hall** Beautifully restored Gothic Room from 1400, plus the Renaissance Hall. **Hours:** Daily 9:30-17:00, Renaissance Hall closed 12:30-13:30. See page 814.

▲**Bruges Beer Museum** History of Belgian beer and brewing process, with tastings. **Hours:** Daily 10:00-17:00. See page 821.

▲**Choco-Story: The Chocolate Museum** The delicious story of Belgium's favorite treat. **Hours:** Daily 10:00-17:00. See page 823.

▲▲Bell Tower (Belfort)

Most of this bell tower has presided over the Markt since 1300, serenading passersby with cheery carillon music. The octagonal lantern was added in 1486, making it 290 feet high—that's 366 steps. The view is worth the climb...and probably even the pricey admission. Some mornings and summer evenings, you can sit in the courtyard or out on the square to enjoy a carillon concert.

Cost and Hours: €10, daily 9:30-18:00, 17:15 last-entry time strictly enforced—best to show up before 17:00, pay WC in courtyard; tel. 050/448-743.

▲Historium

I despise the Disneyfication of Europe, but this glitzy sight right on the Markt is actually entertaining—and it takes a genuine interest

in history. It's pricey and cheesy—sort of "Pirates of the Belgian-ean" (or maybe "Hysterium")—but it immerses you in the story of Bruges in a way a textbook cannot.

Cost and Hours: €13.50, includes audioguide, daily 10:00-18:00, last entry one hour before closing, may be too creepy for kids, Markt 1, tel. 050-270-311, www.historium.be.

▲▲Burg Square

This opulent, prickly-spired square is Bruges' civic center, the historic birthplace of Bruges, and the site of the ninth-century castle of the first count of Flanders. It's home to the Basilica of the Holy Blood and City Hall (described next). Today, it's an atmospheric place to take in an outdoor concert while surrounded by six centuries of architecture.

▲Basilica of the Holy Blood

Originally the Chapel of Saint Basil, this church is famous for its relic of the blood of Christ, which, according to tradition, was brought to Bruges in 1150

after the Second Crusade. The lower chapel is dark and solid—a fine example of Romanesque style. The upper chapel (separate entrance, climb the stairs) is decorated Gothic. An interesting treasury museum is next to the upper chapel.

Cost and Hours: Church-free, treasury-€2.50, daily 9:30-12:00 & 14:00-17:00; Nov-March closed on Wed afternoon; Burg Square, tel. 050-336-792, www.holyblood.com.

▲City Hall (Stadhuis)

This complex houses several interesting sights, including a room full of old town maps and paintings, and the highlight—the grand, beautifully restored **Gothic Room** from 1400, starring a painted and carved wooden ceiling adorned with hanging arches. Your ticket also covers the less impressive **Renaissance Hall** (Brugse Vrije), next door and basically just one ornate room with a Renaissance chimney (separate entrance—in corner of square at Burg 11a).

Cost and Hours: €4, includes audioguide; daily 9:30-17:00, Renaissance Hall closed 12:30-13:30; tel. 050-448-711, www.brugge.be.

SOUTH OF THE MARKT

Also in this area is the De Halve Maan Brewery, with an excellent beer tour (described later, under "Experiences in Bruges").

▲▲Groeninge Museum

This museum houses a world-class collection of mostly Flemish art, from Memling to Magritte. While there's plenty of worthwhile modern art, the highlights are the vivid and pristine Flemish Primitives. (In Flanders, "Primitive" simply means "before the Renaissance.") Flemish art is shaped by its love of detail, its merchant patrons' egos, and the power of the Church. Lose yourself in the halls of Groeninge: Gaze across 15th-century canals, into the eyes of reassuring Marys, and through town squares littered with leotards, lace, and lopped-off heads.

Cost and Hours: €8, more for special exhibits; Tue-Sun 9:30-17:00, closed Mon; Dijver 12, tel. 050-448-743, www.brugge.be.

Visiting the Museum: The collection fills 10 rooms on one easy floor, arranged chronologically from the 15th to the 20th century. I'd head right to Rooms 2-4 for the following paintings—the core of the collection.

Virgin and Child with Canon Joris van der Paele (1436): Jan van Eyck (c. 1390-1441) was the world's first and greatest oil painter, and this is his masterpiece—three debatable but defensible assertions. Van Eyck brings Mary and the saints down from heaven and into a typical (rich) Bruges home. He strips off their haloes, banishes all angels, and pulls the plug on heavenly radiance. If this is a religious painting, then where's God?

God's in the details. From the bishop's damask robe and Mary's wispy hair to the folds in Jesus' baby fat and the oriental carpet to "Adonai" (Lord) written on St. George's breastplate, the painting is as complex and beautiful as God's creation.

Portrait of Margareta van Eyck (1439): This simple portrait by Van Eyck is revolutionary—one of history's first individual portraits that wasn't of a saint, a king, a duke, or a pope, and wasn't part of a religious work. It signals the advent of humanism, celebrating the glory of ordinary people. Van Eyck proudly signed the work on the original frame, with his motto saying he painted it *"als ik kan" (ALC IXH KAN)*..."as good as I can."

St. Luke Drawing the Virgin's Portrait (c. 1435): Rogier van der Weyden (c. 1399-1464), the other giant among the Flemish Primitives, adds the human touch to Van Eyck's rather detached precision As Mary prepares to nurse, Baby Jesus can't contain his glee, wiggling his fingers and toes, anticipating lunch. Meanwhile, St. Luke (the patron saint of painters, who was said to have experienced this vision) looks on intently with a sketch pad in his hand, trying to catch the scene. These small gestures, movements, and facial expressions add an element of human emotion that later artists would amplify.

Duke Philip the Good (c. 1450): Tall, lean, and elegant, this charismatic duke transformed Bruges from a commercial powerhouse to a cultural one. In 1425, Philip moved his court to Bruges, making it the de facto capital of a Burgundian empire stretching from Amsterdam to Switzerland. In this portrait by Van der Wyden, he's wearing the gold-chain necklace of the Order of the Golden Fleece, a distinguished knightly honor he gave himself. He inaugurated the Golden Fleece in a lavish ceremony at the Bruges City Hall, complete with parades, jousting, and festive pies that contained live people hiding inside to surprise his guests.

The Moreel Triptych (1484): Hans Memling (c. 1430-1494), though born in Germany, became Bruges' most famous painter. This triptych (three-paneled altarpiece) fuses the detail of Van Eyck with the balanced compositions of (his probable teacher) Rogier van der Weyden, while introducing his own innovations. This is perhaps the art world's first group portrait, and everything about it celebrates  the family of Willem Moreel, the wealthy two-term mayor of Bruges.

The true stars of the triptych are not the saints in the central panel but the earth-bound mortals who paid for it. Moreel (left panel) kneels in devotion along with his five sons (and St. William, who was Willem's patron saint). Barbara (right) kneels with their 13 daughters (and her patron saint, Barbara). Saints and mortals mingle in this unique backdrop that's both down-to-earth (the castle, plants, and St. Barbara's stunning dress) and ethereal (the weird rock formations and unnaturally pristine light). Memling creates a motionless, peaceful world that invites meditation.

Rest of the Museum: Breeze through the final rooms to get a quick once-over of Flemish art after Bruges' Golden Age. As Bruges declined into a cultural backwater, its artists simply copied the trends going on elsewhere: Italian-style Madonnas, British-style aristocrat portraits, French-Realist landscapes, Impressionism, and thick-paint Expressionism. After fast-forwarding through the centuries, pause (in Rooms 9 and 10) to appreciate a couple of Belgium's 20th-century masters—Paul Delvaux and René Magritte.

▲▲Church of Our Lady (Onze-Lieve-Vrouwekerk)

The church stands as a memorial to the power and wealth of Bruges in its heyday. The delicate *Madonna and Child* is said to be the only Michelangelo statue to leave Italy in his lifetime (thanks to the wealth generated by Bruges' cloth trade). If you like tombs and church art, pay to wander through the apse, but note that the church is undergoing a major, years-long renovation, during which different parts of the interior will be closed to visitors. It's supposed to be finished by 2020—but it might take a miracle.

Cost and Hours: The rear of the church is free to the public. To get into the main section costs €4; Mon-Sat 9:30-17:00, Sun 13:30-17:00, Mariastraat, tel. 050-448-711, www.brugge.be.

Visiting the Church: Enter and stand in the back to admire the Church of Our Lady. Its 14th- and 15th-century stained glass was destroyed by iconoclasts, so the church is lit more brightly today than originally. Like most of Belgium, it is Catholic. The medieval-style screen divided the clergy from the commoners who gathered here in the nave. Worshippers are still attended by 12 Gothic-era statues of apostles, each with his symbol and a grandiose Baroque wooden pulpit, with a roof that seems to float in midair. It was from this fancy perch that the priest would interpret the word of God.

Madonna and Child by Michelangelo: Pay and pass through the turnstile, entering first a chapel featuring a small marble Michelangelo statue, bought in Tuscany by a wealthy Bruges businessman who's buried in the same chapel (to the right).

Tombs at the High Altar: The reclining statues mark the

tombs of the last local rulers of Bruges: Mary of Burgundy, and her father, Charles the Bold. The dog and lion at their feet are symbols of fidelity and courage. Underneath the tombs are the actual excavated gravesites with mirrors to help you enjoy the well-lit, centuries-old tomb paintings.

Bruges residents would stand before these tombs and ponder the great decline of their city. In 1482, when 25-year-old Mary of Burgundy tumbled from a horse and died, she left behind a toddler son and a husband who was heir to the Holy Roman Empire. Beside her lies her father, Charles the Bold, who also died prematurely, in war. Their twin deaths meant Bruges belonged to Austria, and would soon be swallowed up by the empire and ruled from Vienna by Habsburgs—who didn't understand or care about its problems. Trade routes shifted, and goods soon flowed through Antwerp, then Amsterdam, as Bruges' North Sea port silted up. The city was eventually mothballed. The sleeping beauty of Flemish towns was later discovered by modern-day tourists to be remarkably well-pickled, which explains its current affluence.

Rest of the Church: The wooden balcony to the left of the painted altarpiece is part of the Gruuthuse mansion next door, providing the noble family with prime seats for Mass. In a side chapel in the apse you'll see excavations that turned up fascinating grave paintings on the tombs below and near the altar. Dating from the 14th and 15th centuries, these show Mary represented as Queen of Heaven (on a throne, carrying a crown and scepter) and Mother of God (with the Baby Jesus on her lap). Since Mary is in charge of advocating with Jesus for your salvation, she's a good person to have painted on the wall of your tomb.

▲▲Sint-Janshospitaal Memling Collection (St. John's Hospital)

The former monastery/hospital complex has a fine collection in what was once the monks' church. It contains several much-loved paintings by the greatest of the Flemish Primitives, Hans Memling. His *St. John Altarpiece* triptych is a highlight, as is the miniature, gilded-oak shrine to St. Ursula. Your ticket also includes entry to the skippable old pharmacy (Apotheek) in a nearby building.

Cost and Hours: €8, Tue-Sun 9:30-17:00, closed Mon, across the street from the Church of Our Lady, Mariastraat 38, tel. 050-448-713, www.brugge.be.

BRUGES & BRUSSELS

❂ **Self-Guided Tour:** After showing your ticket, enter a vast hall. Starting in 1188, this was...

The Hospital: The building is impressive, with stout wood pillars and brick walls. This hall was lined with beds filled with the sick and dying. Nuns served as nurses. At the far end was the high altar, which once displayed Memling's *St. John Altarpiece* (which we'll see). Bedridden patients could gaze on this peaceful, colorful vision and gain a moment's comfort from their agonies.

Browse the hall's displays of medical implements. It's clear that medicine of the day was well-intentioned but very crude. In many ways, this was less a hospital than a hospice, helping the dying make the transition from this world to the next. Religious art (displayed throughout the museum) was therapeutic, addressing the patients' mental and spiritual health.

• Continue through the displays and head through the wooden doorway, turn right into the Memling Collection, and look for a shrine inside a glass case.

St. Ursula Shrine (c. 1489): On October 21, 1489, the mortal remains of St. Ursula were brought here to the church and placed in this gilded oak shrine, built specially for the occasion and decorated with paintings by Memling. Ursula, yet another Christian martyred by the ancient Romans, became a sensation in the Middle Ages when builders in Germany's Cologne unearthed a huge pile of bones believed to belong to her and her 11,000 slaughtered cohorts. The church-shaped shrine, carved of wood and covered with gold, has "stained-glass windows" of

Memling paintings describing Ursula's well-known legend.

• Now continue to the right and find a black-and-white tiled room where Memling's paintings are displayed.

St. John Altarpiece, a.k.a. The Mystical Marriage of St. Catherine (1474): A large triptych (three-paneled altarpiece) dominates the space. Sick and dying patients lay in their beds in the hospital and looked at this colorful, three-part work, which sat atop the hospital/church's high altar. The piece was dedicated to the hospital's patron saints, John the Baptist and John the Evangelist (see the inscription along the bottom of the frame), but Memling broadened the focus to take in a vision of heaven and the end of the world.

In the **central panel**, Mary, with Baby Jesus on her lap, sits in a canopied chair, crowned by hovering blue angels. It's an imagi-

nary gathering of conversing saints *(Sacra Conversazione)*, though nobody in this meditative group is saying a word or even exchanging meaningful eye contact.

The **left panel** shows the beheading of John the Baptist. Even this gruesome scene, with blood still spurting from John's severed neck, becomes serene under Memling's gentle brush. Everyone is solemn, graceful, and emotionless—including both parts of the decapitated John.

In the **right panel** we see John the Evangelist's vision of the Apocalypse. John sits on a high, rocky bluff. Overhead, in a rainbow bubble, God appears on his throne, resting his hand on a sealed book. A lamb steps up to open the seals, unleashing the awful events at the end of time. Standing at the bottom of the rainbow, an angel in green gestures to John and says, "Write this down." John picks up his quill, but he pauses, absolutely transfixed, experiencing the Apocalypse now.

• *In the small adjoining room, find more Memlings.*

Diptych of Martin van Nieuwenhove (1489): Three-dimensional effects—borrowed from the Italian Renaissance style—enliven this two-panel devotional painting. Both Mary and Child and the 23-year-old Martin, though in different panels, inhabit the same space within the painting. If you line up the paintings' horizons (seen in the distance, out the room's windows), you'll see that both panels depict the same room—with two windows at the back and two along the right wall. Want proof? In the convex mirror on the back wall (just to the left of Mary), the scene is reflected back at us, showing Mary and Martin from behind, silhouetted in the two "windows" of the picture frames. Apparently, Mary makes house calls, appearing right in the living room of the young donor Martin.

• *Before leaving this area, take a look to the right.*

Portrait of a Young Woman (1480): Memling's bread-and-butter was portraits created for families of wealthy businessmen (especially visiting Italians and Portuguese). The young woman looks out of the frame as if she were looking out a window. Her hands rest on the "sill," with the fingertips sticking over. Memling accentuates her fashionably pale complexion and gives her a pensive, sober expression, portraying her like a medieval saint. Still, she keeps her personality, with distinct features like her broad nose, neck tendons, and realistic hands. What's she thinking? (My guess: "It's time for a waffle.")

▲▲Begijnhof

Begijnhofs were built to house women of the lay order, called Beguines. Though obedient to a mother superior, they did not have to  take the vows of a nun. They spent their days deep in prayer, spinning wool, making lace, teaching, and caring for the sick. The Beguines' ranks swelled during the Golden Age, when so many women were widowed or unwed due to the hazards of war and overseas trade. The order of Beguines offered such women a dignified place to live and work. When the order died out, many begijnhofs were taken over by towns for subsidized housing. Today, single religious women live in the small homes. Benedictine nuns live in a building on the far side.

Cost and Hours: Courtyard-free, daily 6:30-18:30; museum-€2, Mon-Sat 10:00-17:00, closed Sun, shorter hours off-season, English explanations, museum is left of entry gate; tel. 050-330-011.

Visiting the Begijnhof: Tour the simple **museum** to get a sense of Beguine life. It's a typical Beguine's residence—kitchen, dining room, bedroom—with period furniture (spinning wheel, foot warmer). Don't miss the bedroom out back across the tiny cloister. The "Liturgical Center" is little more than a gift shop.

In the **church,** enjoy the peaceful interior, with its carved pulpit and tombstones on the floor. The altar has corkscrew columns and a painting of the Beguines' patron, St. Elizabeth. On the right wall is an 800-year-old golden statue of Mary. The rope that dangles from the ceiling is yanked by a nun to announce a sung vespers service. The Benedictine nuns gather at 11:55, proceed through the garden, and sing and chant a cappella in the choir of the church. The public is welcome for this service.

Nearby: Just south of the Begijnhof is the waterway called **Minnewater,** an idyllic world of flower boxes, canals, and swans.

BRUGES & BRUSSELS

Experiences in Bruges

While Bruges has some top-notch museums, many of its charms are more experiential.

BEER

Hoisting a glass of beer is a quintessential ▲▲▲ Bruges experience. Much as wine flows through all aspects of French or Italian cuisine, Belgians prize beer above all else. Bruges offers a wide variety of places to sample brews (see listings in the Eating section under "Pubs and Beer Halls," later), one of the most accessible and enjoyable brewery tours in Belgium, and an interesting museum on beer.

▲▲De Halve Maan Brewery Tour

Belgians are Europe's beer connoisseurs, and this handy tour is a great way to pay your respects. The brewery makes the only beers brewed in Bruges: Brugse Zot ("Fool from Bruges") and Straffe Hendrik ("Strong Henry"). The happy gang at this working-family brewery gives entertaining and informative 45-minute tours in two languages (lots of steep steps but a great rooftop panorama). Avoid crowds by visiting at 11:00. Their bistro, where you'll drink your included beer, serves quick, hearty lunch plates daily.

Cost and Hours: €8.50 tour includes a beer; tours run on the hour Sun-Fri 11:00-16:00, Sat until 17:00; smart to book online as tours can fill up—and you get a minor discount; Walplein 26, tel. 050-444-223, www.halvemaan.be.

▲Bruges Beer Museum

With a red-carpet entrance just off the Markt, this ode to beer's frothy history overlooks the square from the top of the former post office.

Head up three flights of steep stairs to the museum's entrance, where you'll get an iPad and headphones to tour the exhibit and learn about the history of beermaking. The most interesting section is on the top floor, where you can run your hands through raw hops, yeast, and barley while getting a step-by-step guide to modern brewing.

When you've had your historical fill, saunter down to the bar and trade the iPad for three tokens good for your choice of tasting-size beers from a rotating list of 15 local drafts. The bar offers Markt views and is also open to the public (ticket not required).

Cost and Hours: €14, ticket includes three tastings, daily 10:00-17:00, Breidelstraat 3, tel. 0479-359-567, www. brugesbeermuseum.com.

CHOCOLATE

Bruggians are connoisseurs of fine chocolate. You'll be tempted by chocolate-filled display windows all over town. While Godiva is the best big-factory/high-price/high-quality brand, there are plenty of smaller family-run places in Bruges that offer exquisite handmade chocolates. The following chocolatiers are proud of their creative varieties and welcome you to assemble a 100-gram assortment of five or six chocolates.

A rule of thumb when buying chocolate: Bruges' informal "chocolate mafia" keeps the price for midrange pralines quite standard, at about €28 per kilogram (or €2.80 for 100 grams). Swankier and "gastronomical" places (like The Chocolate Line or BbyB) charge significantly more, but only aficionados may be able to tell the difference. On the other hand, if a place is priced well *below* this range, be suspicious: Quality may suffer.

If you're looking for value, don't forget to check supermarket shelves. Try Côte d'Or Noir de Noir for a simple bar of pure dark chocolate that won't flatten in your luggage.

▲Chocolate Shops

Katelijnestraat, which runs south from the Church of Our Lady, is "Chocolate Row," with a half-dozen shops within a few steps. For locations, see the map on page 808.

Dumon: Perhaps Bruges' smoothest, creamiest chocolates are at Dumon, just off the Markt (a selection of 5 or 6 chocolates are a deal at €2.80/100 grams).  Nathalie Dumon runs the store with Madame Dumon still dropping by to help make their top-notch chocolate daily and sell it fresh. Try a small mix-and-match box to sample a few out-of-this-world flavors, and come back for more of your favorites. The family runs only the original location just north of the Markt at Eiermarkt 6 (Wed-Mon 10:00-18:00, closed Tue, old chocolate molds on display in basement, tel. 050-346-282). A bigger, glitzier Dumon branch (at Simon Stevinplein 11) has a full coffee-and-hot-chocolate bar (daily 10:00-18:30, tel. 050-333-360). A third, less-interesting branch is farther south, at Walstraat 6.

The Chocolate Line: Locals and tourists alike flock to The Chocolate Line (pricey at €6/100 grams) to taste the *gastronomique* varieties concocted by Dominique Person—the mad scientist of chocolate. His unique creations mix chocolate with various, mostly savory, flavors (be adventurous). The kitchen—busy whipping up 80 varieties—is on display in the back. Enjoy the window display, refreshed monthly (daily 9:30-18:30, between Church of Our Lady and the Markt at Simon Stevinplein 19, tel. 050-341-090).

BbyB: This chichi, top-end chocolate gallery (whose name stands for "Babelutte by Bartholomeus," for the Michelin-starred restaurateur who owns it) lines up its pralines in a minimalist display case like priceless jewels, each type identified by number (about €5 for a 5-flavor sleeve, €10 for a sleek 10-flavor sampler box; Mon-Sat 10:00-18:00 except closed for lunch most days, closed Sun; Sint-Amandsstraat 39, tel. 050-705-760, www.bbyb.be).

Confiserie De Clerck: Third-generation chocolatier Jan sells his handmade chocolates for about €1.50/100 grams, making this one of the best deals in town. Some locals claim his chocolate's just as good as at pricier places, while others insist that any chocolate this cheap must be subpar—taste it and decide for yourself. The time-warp candy shop itself is so delightfully old-school, you'll want to visit one way or the other (Mon-Wed and Fri-Sat 10:00-18:00 except closed for lunch, closed Thu and Sun, Academiestraat 19, tel. 050-345-338).

▲Choco-Story: The Chocolate Museum

With lots of artifacts well-described in English, this kid-friendly museum fills you in on the production of truffles, bonbons, hollow figures, and solid bars of chocolate. Head up the stairs by the gigantic chocolate egg to follow the chronological exhibit, tracing 4,000 years of chocolate history. The finale is downstairs in the "demonstration room," where—after a 10-minute cooking demo—you get a taste.

Cost and Hours: €8, ticket includes chocolate bar; daily 10:00-17:00, last entry 45 minutes before closing; where Wijnzakstraat meets Sint Jansstraat at Sint Jansplein, 3-minute walk from the Markt; tel. 050-612-237, www.choco-story-brugge.be.

Related Sights: The owners of the Chocolate Museum operate two similarly hokey but endearing museums (same hours). Neither is worth its €7 individual admission, but both are cheap add-ons with one of the Chocolate Museum's combo-tickets.

The museum owner's wife got tired of her husband's ancient lamp collection...so the owner opened a **Lamp Museum** next door. While obscure, it's an impressive and well-described collection showing lamps through the ages.

The same folks also run the **Friet Museum,** a few blocks away (at Vlamingstraat 33, www.frietmuseum.be). This fun-loving and kid-friendly place is the only place in the world that enthusiastically tells the story of French fries, which, of course, aren't even French—they're Belgian.

LACE

Lace Center (Kant Centrum)

This lace museum and school lets you learn about lacemaking and then see lace actually being made. Observe as ladies toss bobbins madly while their eyes go bad. They follow mazelike patterns with a forest of pins to help guide their work.

Cost and Hours: €5, Mon-Sat 9:30-16:30, closed Sun, demonstrations usually 14:00-17:00, skip it unless you come when the demonstrations are scheduled, tel. 050-330-072, Balstraat 16, www.kantcentrum.eu.

Nearby: Nearly across the street from the Lace Center is a lace shop with a good reputation, **'t Apostelientje** (Tue 13:15-17:00, Wed-Sat 9:30-12:00 & 13:00-17:00, Sun 10:00-13:00, closed Mon, Balstraat 11, tel. 050-337-860, mobile 0495-562-420).

BIKING

The Dutch word for bike is *fiets* (pronounced "feets"). And though Bruges' sights are close enough for easy walking, the town is a treat for bikers. A bike quickly gets you into dreamy back lanes without a hint of tourism. Take a ride through the town's nooks and crannies and around the outer canal. Ask at the rental shop for maps and ideas (see "Bike Rental," earlier, for more info).

BRUGES & BRUSSELS

Shopping in Bruges

Shops are generally open from 10:00 to 18:00 and closed Sundays.

WHAT TO BUY

Chocolate: A box of Belgian pralines is at the top of most souvenir shoppers' lists; see my recommended chocolate shops under "Experiences in Bruges," earlier.

Beer: Another consumable souvenir is Belgian beer—either a bottle (or three) for later in your trip, or a prized brew checked carefully in your luggage home. In addition to the pubs listed in this chapter—a few of which sell bottles to go—the streets of Bruges are lined with bottle shops. At some, you can buy the glass that's designed to go with each type of beer (it's a fragile item to pack, but purists insist). Options include the touristy souvenir store **2Be** (described below) or **The Bottle Shop,** which sells 600 different beers by the bottle and has a staff that enjoys helping visitors navigate the many choices (daily 10:00-18:30, just south of the Markt at Wollestraat 13, tel. 050-349-980).

Lace: This is a popular item, but very expensive; **'t Apostelientje,** described earlier, is one good option (and conveniently located across the street from the Lace Center).

WHERE TO SHOP

Souvenir shops abound on the streets that fan out from the Markt and the ones heading southwest, toward the Church of Our Lady. **2Be,** in a classic old brick mansion overlooking a canal a block south of the Markt, is huge, obvious, and grotesquely touristy...but well-stocked with a wide variety of tacky and not-so-tacky Belgian souvenirs: Tintin, Smurfs, beer, and chocolates. The "beerwall" at the entrance shows off over a thousand types of Belgian brew; their cellar is filled with a remarkably well-stocked bottle shop; and their pub has several rotating draft beers you can enjoy on a relaxing terrace floating over a perfect canal (daily 10:00-19:00, Wollestraat 53, tel. 050-611-222, www.2-be.biz).

More colorful are the shops a block to the north, along **Geldmuntstraat** (which becomes **Noordzandstraat**). Along this atmospheric drag—with perhaps Bruges' most enjoyable window-shopping—are smaller, more expensive chains and upscale boutiques (including L'Héroïne, highlighting Belgian designers with Antwerp cred at Noordzandstraat 32); housewares shops (such as Cook & Serve, a fun kitchen gadgets shop, at Geldmuntstraat 16); and the popular and recommended Da Vinci gelato shop.

For the highest concentration of tourists (and, consequently, the highest concentration of souvenir, chocolate, lace, and *wafel* shops), head down **Katelijnestraat,** which runs south from the

Church of Our Lady and Memling Museum. While you'll find no great values here, it's convenient for souvenir shopping.

Eating in Bruges

Bruges doesn't really have any specialties all its own, but restaurants here excel at all the predictable Belgian dishes: mussels cooked a variety of ways (one order can feed two), fish dishes, grilled meats, and French fries. The town's famous indigenous beers include the prizewinning Brugse Zot ("Bruges Fool"), a golden ale, and Straffe Hendrik, a potent, bitter triple ale.

RESTAURANTS

$$$$ Rock Fort is a chic spot with a modern, fresh coziness and a high-powered respect for good food. Two young chefs, Peter Laloo and Hermes Vanliefde, give their French cuisine a creative, gourmet twist. At the bar they serve a separate tapas menu (€40 five-tapas special). This place is a winner (Mon-Fri 12:00-14:30 & 18:30-23:00, closed Sat-Sun, reservations recommended, Langestraat 15, tel. 050-334-113, www.rock-fort.be).

$$$ Bistro in den Wittenkop, very Flemish, is a stylishly small, laid-back, old-time place specializing in local favorites, where Lindsey serves while Patrick cooks. It's a classy spot to enjoy hand-cut fries, which go particularly well with Straffe Hendrik beer (Mon-Tue and Thu-Sat 12:00-14:00 & 18:00-21:00, closed Wed and Sun, reserve ahead, terrace in summer, Sint Jakobsstraat 14, tel. 050-332-059, www.indenwittenkop.be).

$$$ Bistro den Amand, with a plain interior and a few outdoor tables, exudes unpretentious quality the moment you step in. In this mussels-free zone, Chef An is enthusiastic about stir-fry and vegetables, as her busy wok and fun salads prove. The creative dishes—some with a hint of Asian influence—are a welcome departure from Bruges' mostly predictable traditional restaurants. It's on a bustling pedestrian lane a half-block off the Markt (Mon-Tue and Thu-Sat 12:00-14:00 & 18:00-21:00, closed Wed and Sun; Sint-Amandstraat 4, tel. 050-340-122, www.denamand.be, An Vissers and Arnout Beyaert).

$$$ Tom's Diner is a trendy, cozy little candlelit bistro in a quiet, cobbled residential area a 10-minute walk from the center. Young chef Tom gives traditional dishes a delightful modern twist, such as his signature Flemish meat loaf with rhubarb sauce. If you want to flee the tourists and experience a popular neighborhood joint, this is it—the locals love it. Reserve before you make the trip (Tue-Sat 12:00-14:00 & 18:00-23:00, closed Sun-Mon, north of the Markt near Sint-Gilliskerk at West-Gistelhof 23, tel. 050-333-382, www.tomsdiner.be).

Restaurant Code

I've assigned each eatery a price category, based on the average cost of a typical main course. Drinks, desserts, and splurge items (steak and seafood) can raise the price considerably.

$$$$ **Splurge:** Most main courses over €20
 $$$ **Pricier:** €15-20
  $$ **Moderate:** €10-15
   $ **Budget:** Under €10

In Belgium, a *frites* stand or other takeout spot is **$**; a basic café or sit-down eatery is **$$**; a casual but more upscale restaurant is **$$**; and a swanky splurge is **$$$$**.

$$$ Bistro Den Huzaar is somewhat touristy but affordable, serving big portions of Belgian classics. The long dining room stretches back on well-worn wooden floors and a few tables are out on the sidewalk. It's dignified but relaxed (Fri-Tue 12:00-14:30 & 18:00-20:30, closed Wed-Thu, 5-minute walk north of the Markt at Vlamingstraat 36, tel. 050-333-797).

$$$ The Flemish Pot is a busy eatery where enthusiastic chefs Mario and Rik cook up a traditional menu of vintage Flemish specialties—from beef and rabbit stew to eel—served in little iron pots and skillets. Seating is tight and cluttered, the tourist-oriented menu can be pricey, and service can be spotty. But you'll enjoy huge portions, refills from the hovering "fries angel," a cozy atmosphere, and a good selection of local beers (Wed-Fri 17:30-21:30, Sat-Sun 12:00-21:30, closed Mon-Tue, reservations smart, just off Geldmuntstraat at Helmstraat 3, tel. 050-340-086, www.devlaamschepot.be).

$$$ De Hobbit, featuring an entertaining menu, is always busy with happy eaters. For a swinging deal, try the all-you-can-eat spareribs with bread and salad. It's nothing fancy, just good, basic food served in a fun, crowded, traditional grill house (daily 18:00-23:00, family-friendly, Kemelstraat 8, reservations smart, tel. 050-335-520, www.hobbitgrill.be).

$$$$ Restaurant de Koetse is handy for central, good-quality, local-style food. The feeling is traditional, a bit formal (stuffy even), and dressy, yet accessible. The cuisine is Belgian and French, with an emphasis on grilled meat, seafood, and mussels (Sat-Wed 12:00-14:30 & 18:00-22:00, closed Thu-Fri, Oude Burg 31, tel. 050-337-680, www.dekoetse-brugge.be, Piet).

$$ Carlito's is a good choice for basic Italian fare. Their informal space, with whitewashed walls and tealight candles, is two blocks from Burg Square (daily 12:00-14:30 & 18:00-22:30, patio seating in back, Hoogstraat 21, tel. 050-490-075).

$$$ Bistro Sint-Anna, on the eastern edge of town, is a

homey little neighborhood place where you can dine on pasta, tapas, steak, or other yummy dishes in a fresh, modern space on two floors (Mon-Tue and Thu-Fri 11:00-15:00 & 18:00-22:00, Sat 18:00-22:00, closed Wed and Sun, St. Annaplein 29, tel. 050-347-800).

$$ L'Estaminet is a youthful, jazz-filled eatery, similar to one of Amsterdam's brown cafés. Don't be intimidated by its lack of tourists. Local students flock here for the Tolkien-chic ambience, hearty spaghetti, and big salads. This is Belgium—it serves more beer than wine. For outdoor dining under an all-weather canopy, enjoy the relaxed patio facing peaceful Astrid Park (Tue-Sun 12:00-24:00, Thu from 17:00, closed Mon, Park 5, tel. 050-330-916).

Restaurants on the Markt: Most tourists seem to be eating on the Markt with the bell tower high overhead and horse carriages clip-clopping by. The square is ringed by tourist traps with aggressive waiters expert at getting you to consume more than you intend. Still, if you order smartly, you can have a memorable meal or drink here on one of the finest squares in Europe at a reasonable price. Consider **$$ Café-Brasserie Craenenburg,** with a straightforward menu, where you can get pasta and beer for €15 and spend all the time you want ogling the magic of Bruges (daily 7:30-23:00, Markt 16, tel. 050-333-402). While it's overpriced for dining, it can be a fine place to savor a before- or after-meal drink with the view.

Cheaper Restaurants Just Off the Markt: For a similar but less expensive array of interchangeable, tourist-focused eateries, head a few steps off the Markt up **Sint-Amandstraat** (through the gap between Café Craenenburg and the clock tower). You'll pop out into a pleasant little square with lots of choices. The best of these is **Bistro den Amand** (recommended earlier), but if that's full or closed, this is a fine place to browse for something else. **$ Medard Brasserie,** also on this square, serves the cheapest hot meal in town—hearty meat spaghetti for only €6.50 (sit inside or out, Mon-Tue and Thu-Sat 12:00-20:00, lunch-only Wed, closed Sun, Sint Amandstraat 18, tel. 050-348-684).

PUBS AND BEER HALLS

My best budget-eating tip for Bruges: Stop into one of the city's bars for a simple meal and a couple of world-class beers with great Bruges ambience.

Just off the Markt: Another good place to gain an appreciation for Belgian beer culture is **De Garre** (deh-HAHR-reh). Rather than a noisy pub scene, it has a dressy, sit-down-and-focus-on-your-friend-and-the-fine-beer vibe. Beer pilgrims flock here, as it's the only place on earth that sells the Tripel van de Garre beer on tap.

Bruges Restaurants & Beer Halls

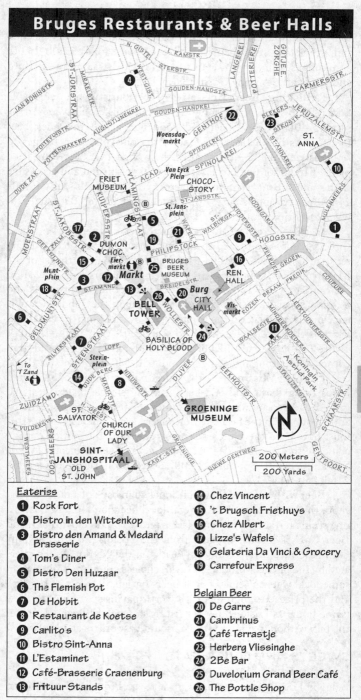

Eateries

1. Rock Fort
2. Bistro in den Wittenkop
3. Bistro den Amand & Medard Brasserie
4. Tom's Diner
5. Bistro Den Huzaar
6. The Flemish Pot
7. De Hobbit
8. Restaurant de Koetse
9. Carlito's
10. Bistro Sint-Anna
11. L'Estaminet
12. Café-Brasserie Craenenburg
13. Frituur Stands

14. Chez Vincent
15. 't Brugsch Friethuys
16. Chez Albert
17. Lizze's Wafels
18. Gelateria Da Vinci & Grocery
19. Carrefour Express

Belgian Beer

20. De Garre
21. Cambrinus
22. Café Terrastje
23. Herberg Vlissinghe
24. 2Be Bar
25. Duvelorium Grand Beer Café
26. The Bottle Shop

As it's 12 percent alcohol, there's a three-Tripel limit...and many tourists find that the narrow alley out front provides much-needed support as they start their stumble back home (daily 12:00-24:00, additional seating up tiny staircase, off Breidelstraat between Burg and the Markt, on tiny Garre alley, tel. 050-341-029).

Rollicking Beer Brasserie: The touristy but enjoyable **$$$ Cambrinus** is a bright, tight, and boisterous *bierbrasserie*, serving 400 types of beer and good pub grub—the thick beer menu looks like a Bible. It's one of the only places in Bruges to try Westvleteren 12—often voted the world's best beer—but it's a pricey €15.50 for one bottle. It's more high-spirited and accessible than some of Bruges' traditional, creaky old beer halls (daily 11:00-23:00, reservations smart, Philipstockstraat 19, tel. 050-332-328, www.cambrinus.eu).

In the Gezellig Quarter, Northeast of the Markt: These three **$$** pubs are tucked in the wonderfully *gezellig* (cozy) quarter that follows the canal past Jan Van Eyckplein, northeast of the Markt. Just walking out here is a treat, as it gets you away from the tourists. **Café Terrastje** is a cozy pub serving light meals and Belgian specialties such as *waterzooi*. Enjoy the subdued ambience inside, or relax on the front terrace overlooking the canal and heart of the *gezellig* district (food served Fri-Mon 12:00-15:00 & 18:00-21:00, open until 23:30; Tue 12:00-18:00; closed Wed-Thu; corner of Genthof and Langerei, tel. 050-330-919, Ian and Patricia). **Herberg Vlissinghe** is the oldest pub in town (1515). Bruno keeps things basic and laid-back, serving simple plates (lasagna, grilled cheese sandwiches, and famous €10 angel-hair spaghetti) and great beer in the best old-time tavern atmosphere in town. This must have been the Dutch Masters' rec room. The garden outside comes with a *boules* court—free for guests to watch or play (Wed-Sat 11:00-22:00, Sun until 19:00, closed Mon-Tue, Blekersstraat 2, tel. 050-343-737).

Beer with a View: Though it's tucked in back of a tacky tourist shop, the bar at **2Be** serves several local beers on tap and boasts a fine scenic terrace over a canal (see page 825). **Duvelorium Grand Beer Café** is located upstairs from the Historium, with a spiny Gothic terrace overlooking the bustle on the Markt. As it's operated by the big beer producer Duvel, choices are more limited than some local watering holes (eight beers on tap, plus lots of bottles), and the prices are high—but it's worth paying extra for the view (same hours as Historium—see listing on page 819, you can enter the pub without paying for the museum, last orders at 19:00).

SWEETS AND QUICK EATS
Belgian Fries

Belgian French fries (*frieten*) are a treat. Proud and traditional

*frituur*s serve tubs of fries and various local-style shish kebabs. Belgians dip their *frieten* in mayonnaise or other flavored sauces, but ketchup is there for the Yankees. I encourage you to skip the ketchup and have a sauce adventure.

For a quick, cheap, and scenic snack on the **Markt,** hit a *frituur* and sit on the steps or benches overlooking the square. Twin takeaway fry carts are at the base of the bell tower (daily 10:00-24:00). I find the cart on the left better quality and more user-friendly.

$ Chez Vincent, with pleasant outdoor tables on a terrace facing St. Salvator's Cathedral along the lively Steenstraat shopping drag, is a cut above. It's understandably popular for using fresh, local ingredients to turn out tasty fries and all manner of other fried and grilled Belgian tasties: burgers, sausages, meatballs, croquettes, and so on. Join the mob at the counter inside to order and pay, then find a table and wait for your pager to buzz (Tue-Fri 11:30-14:30 & 17:30-20:00, Sat-Sun 11:30-20:00, closed Mon, Sint-Salvatorskerkhof 1, tel. 050-684-395).

$$ 't Brugsch Friethuys, a block off the Markt, is handy for fries you can sit down and enjoy, but to sit you must also buy a drink. Its forte is greasy, deep-fried Flemish fast food. The "Big Hunger menu" comes with all the traditional gut bombs (daily 11:00-late, at the corner of Geldmuntstraat and Sint Jakobsstraat, Luc will explain your options).

Picnics

A handy location for groceries is the **Carrefour Express** mini-supermarket, just off the Markt on Vlamingstraat (daily 8:00-19:00); for a slightly wider selection, **Delhaize-Proxy** is just up Geldmuntstraat (Mon-Sat 9:00-19:00, closed Sun, Noordzandstraat 4). For midnight snacks, you'll find Indian-run corner grocery stores scattered around town.

Belgian Waffles and Ice Cream

You'll see waffles sold at restaurants and takeaway stands. One of Bruges' best is also one of its most obvious: **Chez Albert,** on Breidelstraat connecting the Markt and Burg Square, is pricey, but the quality is good and—thanks to the tourist crowds—turnover is quick, so the waffles are fresh (daily 10:00-18:30, at #18, tel. 050-950-009). Another popular spot is **Lizze's Wafels,** which makes them extra-large—try some drizzled in chocolate (Wed-

BRUGES & BRUSSELS

Sun 11:00-17:00, closed Mon-Tue, Sint-Jakobsstraat 16, tel. 050-348-769).

Gelateria Da Vinci, the local favorite for homemade ice cream, has creative flavors and a lively atmosphere. As you approach, you'll see a line of happy lickers. Before ordering, ask to sample the Ferrero Rocher (chocolate, nuts, and crunchy cookie) and plain yogurt (daily 11:00-22:00, later in summer, Geldmuntstraat 34, tel. 050-333-650, run by Sylvia from Austria).

Brussels

The Brussels of today reflects its past. The city enjoyed a Golden Age of peace and prosperity (1400-1550) when many of its signature structures were built. In the late 1800s, Brussels had another growth spurt, fueled by industrialization, wealth taken from the Belgian Congo, and the exhilaration of the country's recent independence (1830). The "Builder King" Leopold II erected grand monuments and palaces. Then, in 1992, 12 countries established the European Union by signing the Treaty of Maastricht, and sleepy Brussels suddenly was thrust into the spotlight as the unofficial capital of the new Europe. It started a frenzy of renovation, infrastructure projects, foreign visitors, and world attention.

In Brussels, people speak French. Bone up on *bonjour* and *s'il vous plaît*. The Bruxellois are cultured and genteel—even a bit snobby compared to their earthier Flemish cousins. The whole feel of the town is urban French, not rural Flemish. And yet Brussels retains an impish sparkle and joie de vivre, as evidenced by the Bruxellois love of comic strips (giant comic-strip panels are painted on buildings all over town) and their civic symbol: a statue of a little boy peeing.

Brussels is the cutting edge of modern Europe, but still clothed in its Old World garments. Stroll the Grand Place, snap a selfie with the *Manneken-Pis,* and watch diplomats at work at the EU assembly halls. Then grab some mussels, fries, and a hearty Belgian beer, and watch the sun set behind the Town Hall's lacy steeple.

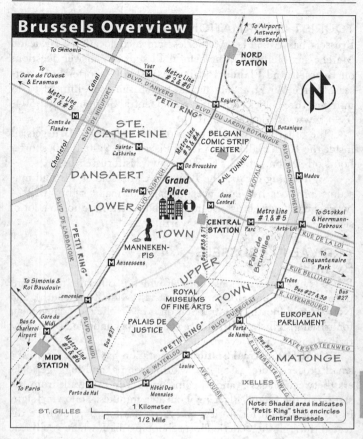

Brussels Overview

Orientation to Brussels

Central Brussels is surrounded by a pentagon-shaped ring of roads, which replaced the old city wall. All the sights I mention are within this ring (romantics think it looks more like a heart than a pentagon). The epicenter (or "petit ring") holds the main square (the Grand Place), the TI, and Central/Centraal station (all within three blocks of one another).

What isn't so apparent from maps is that Brussels is a city divided by altitude. A ridgeline splits the town into the Upper Town (east half, elevation 200 feet) and Lower Town (west, at sea level), with Central Station in between.

Brussels' bilingual street signs give the French name first, then the Dutch. That, combined with the near-complete lack of a regular grid plan, can make navigating the city confusing. It's easy to get turned around. I rely heavily on a good map (such as the TI's €1 map) when exploring this town.

TOURIST INFORMATION

Brussels has two TIs. At the less-crowded location at Rue du Marché aux Herbes 63, the helpful TI staff can answer questions on **Brussels and Flanders** (daily 10:00-18:00, shorter hours off-season; free Wi-Fi, loaner tablets for on-site use—limited to 15 minutes, three blocks downhill from Central Station, tel. 02-504-0390, www.visitflanders.com).

The other TI, which focuses on just the **city of Brussels,** is inside the Town Hall on the Grand Place (daily 9:00-18:00, shorter hours off-season; tel. 02-513-8940, www.visitbrussels.be).

Sightseeing Deals: The **Brussels Card,** sold at TIs and museums, provides free entrance to nearly all major sights (€22/24 hours, http://www.brusselscard.be)—but you'll need to do a lot of sightseeing to get your money's worth.

ARRIVAL IN BRUSSELS
By Train

Brussels has three stations (none of which is officially the "main" train station): Central/Centraal (central), Midi/Zuid (south), and Nord/Noord (north). Central Station is by far the most convenient for arriving sightseers. The three stations are connected by regular trains (leaving every few minutes).

Central/Centraal Station: This station has handy services: a small grocery store, fast food, waiting rooms, and luggage lockers (between tracks 3 and 4, coins only). You can walk from the station to the Grand Place in about five minutes: Following signs inside the station for *Marché aux Herbes/Grasmarkt,* you'll be directed through the Galerie Horta shopping mall, where you'll ride an escalator down, pass a Smurf shop, and pop out 50 yards from the little square nicknamed "Agora." At the far end of this square, turn left to reach the Grand Place, or continue straight ahead to find the big Brussels and Flanders TI on your left.

Hop-on, hop-off tourist buses depart from Central Station—a handy way to get oriented to the city (see "Tours in Brussels," later).

HELPFUL HINTS

Sightseeing Schedules: Brussels' most important museums are closed on Monday. Of course, the city's single best sight—the Grand Place—is always open. You can also enjoy a bus tour any day of the week.

Wi-Fi: It's free at the Brussels and Flanders TI information office (listed earlier), and at many cafés throughout the city.

Bilingual Brussels: Because the city is officially bilingual, Brussels' street signs and maps are in both French and Dutch. In this book—due to space constraints—I've generally given only the French name. Because the languages are so differ-

Brussels at a Glance

▲▲▲**Grand Place** Main square and spirited heart of the Lower Town. See page 839.

▲▲▲**Royal Museums of Fine Arts of Belgium** Include works by the Old Masters and Belgian Surrealist René Magritte. **Hours:** Old Masters and Fin-de-Siècle museums—Tue-Sun 10:00-17:00, closed Mon; Magritte Museum—daily 10:00-17:00. See page 848.

▲▲*Manneken-Pis* World-famous statue of a leaky little boy. **Hours:** Always peeing. See page 847.

▲▲**BELvue Museum** Interesting Belgian history museum with a focus on the popular royal family. **Hours:** Tue-Fri 9:30-17:00, July-Aug until 18:00, Sat-Sun 10:00-18:00, closed Mon. See page 851.

▲**St. Michael's Cathedral** White-stone Gothic church where Belgian royals are married and buried. **Hours:** Mon-Fri 7:00-18:00, Sat-Sun 8:30-18:00. See page 847.

▲**Belgian Comic Strip Center** Homage to hometown heroes including the Smurfs, Tintin, and Lucky Luke. **Hours:** Daily 10:00-18:00. See page 848.

▲**Musical Instruments Museum** Exhibits with more than 1,500 instruments, complete with audio. **Hours:** Tue-Fri 9:30-17:00, Sat-Sun from 10:00, closed Mon. See page 851.

ent, many places have two names that barely resemble each other (for example, Marché aux Herbes/Grasmarkt, or Place Royale/Koningsplein).

GETTING AROUND BRUSSELS

Most of central Brussels' sights can be reached on foot. But public transport is handy for climbing to the Upper Town (buses #38 and #71, from near Central Station).

By Public Transportation: Brussels has an extensive public transport network running the Métro, trams, and buses (www.stib-mivb.be). Transit stops are labeled in both French and Dutch (though sometimes just one name works in both languages). A single-fare €2.10 **ticket** is good for one hour on all public transportation—Métro, buses, trams, and even trains shuttling between the city's train stations. Buy individual tickets in Métro stations (vending machines accept credit cards or coins), machines at many central bus stops, or (for €0.40 extra) from the bus driver.

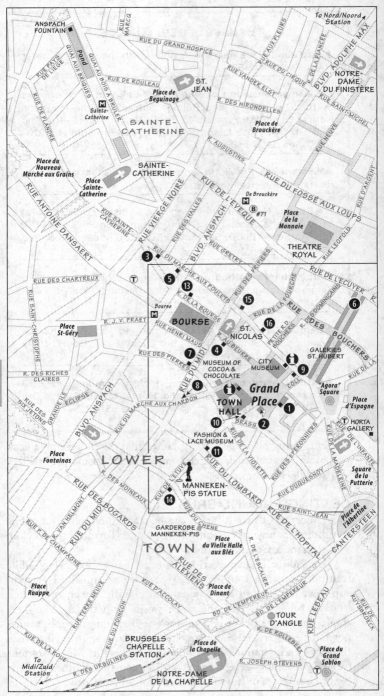

Brussels

Ⓜ *Botanique*

RUE DE LA BLANCHISSERIE

BLVD DU JARDIN BOTANIQUE

RUE DU DAMIER

R. DE L'OMMEGANG

200 Meters

200 Yards

RUE AUX CHOUX

Place des Martyrs

BRUSSELS CONGRÈS STATION

BELGIAN COMIC STRIP CENTER

Place des Barricades

R. DES SABLES

RUE DU MARAIS

RUE DU MEIROOM

BLVD. PACHECO

R. DU GOUVERNMENT PROVISOIRE

RUE DES BOITEUX RUE DES COMÉDIENS

RUE ST. LAURENT

Place du Congrès

RUE DU CONGRÈS

RUE ROYALE

ILOT SACRE

BLVD. DU BERLAIMONT

RUE DE LA BANQUE

RUE DE LIGNE

RUE DE L'ENSEIGNEMENT

RUE DE LA CROIX DE FER

RUE DE LA PRESSE

See Grand Place Walk detail map

RUE D'ASSAUT

Ⓜ 12

ST. MICHAEL'S

RUE DE LOUVAIN

D'ARENBERG

MONTAGNE

Place Sainte Gudule

RUE DE L'IMPERATRICE

RUE DE LOXUM

RUE DES COLONIES

Ⓜ Parc

BELGIAN PARLIAMENT

BD. DE L'IMPERATRICE

Gare Central Ⓜ

RUE DE LA LOI

Carrefour de l'Europe

Ⓑ #38, 71

PUTTERIE

Marché aux Bois

Ⓑ #38, 71

USE-IT

4

CENTRAL STATION ℹ

ISABELLE

RUE RAVENSTEIN

RUE ROYALE

Jardin du Mont des Arts

MUSICAL INSTRUMENTS MUSEUM

BELVUE MUSEUM

MAGRITTE MUSEUM

Ⓑ #38, 71

Place Royale

ROYAL MUSEUMS OF FINE ARTS

COUDENBERG PALACE

ROYAL PALACE

SCULPTURE GARDEN

Ⓑ #27

UPPER TOWN

BRUGES & BRUSSELS

Eateries

❶ L'Estaminet du Kelderke
❷ Brasserie L'Ommegang
❸ Bia Mara & Peck 47
❹ Carrefour Express (2)
❺ AD Delhaize
❻ Arcadi Café & Le Mokafé
❼ La Maison des Crêpes
❽ Yaki
❾ Osteria a l'Ombra
❿ Maison Dandoy
⓫ Waffle Factory

Belgian Beer

⓬ A la Mort Subite Bar
⓭ Le Cirio Café
⓮ Poechenellekelder Estaminet
⓯ A l'Imaige Nostre-Dame & Au Bon Vieux Temps
⓰ De Biertempel

When you enter the Métro, a bus, or a tram, you must validate your ticket by holding it next to the red scanner.

By Taxi or Uber: Cabbies charge a €4 drop fee, then €1.80 per additional kilometer (€2 surcharge after 22:00). Convenient taxi stands near the Grand Place are at Place de Brouckère and at the "Agora" square (Rue du Marché aux Herbes). In the Upper Town, try Place du Grand Sablon. To call a cab, ring **Taxi Bleu** (tel. 02-268-0000) or **Autolux** (tel. 02-512-3123). If you like **Uber,** the ride service (and your app) works in Brussels just like it does in the US (UberX service).

Tours in Brussels

Hop-On, Hop-Off Bus Tour

City Sightseeing Brussels offers two 1.5-hour loops with (mediocre) recorded narration on double-decker buses that go topless on sunny days. The handiest starting point is at Central Station, where you can also transfer between the two loops (€25, ticket valid 24 hours, runs about twice hourly, roughly Mon-Fri 10:00-16:00, an hour or two longer on Sat-Sun, shorter hours in winter; tel. 02-466-1111, www.citysightseeingbrussel.be).

Bus Tour

Brussels City Tour's three-hour guided bus tour (in up to five languages) provides an easy way to get the grand perspective on Brussels. You start with a walk around the Grand Place, then jump on a tour bus (€30, year-round daily at 10:00, meet at their office a block off Grand Place at Rue du Marché aux Herbes 82; buy tickets there or at TIs; tel. 02-513-7744, www.brussels-city-tours.com).

Local Guides

Erwin Liekens and his knowledgeable team at **Taste the City** offer good walks, including tours focused on Belgian food and drink (€180/3 hours, €350/day, mobile 0495-625-215, info@tastethecity.be, www.tastethecity.be). You can also hire a private guide through **Visit Brussels** (€170/3 hours, tel. 02-548-0448, guides@visitbrussels.be; I enjoyed the guiding of Didier Rochette).

Grand Place Walk

Like most European cities, Brussels has a main square, but few are as "Grand" as this one. From its medieval origins as a market for a small village, the Grand Place has grown into a vast public space enclosed by Old World buildings with stately gables. Today, the "Place" is the place to see Europe on parade. Visitors come to bask in the ambience, sample chocolate, and relax with a beer at an outdoor café.

This two-hour walk allows all that, but also goes a bit beyond. We'll take in the spectacular (if heavily touristed) square, browse an elegant shopping arcade, run the frenetic gauntlet of restaurant row (Rue des Bouchers), stand at the center of modern Brussels at the Bourse, and end at the grand finale (he said with a wink): the one-of-a-kind *Manneken-Pis*.

• *Begin this walk standing on...*

❶ The Grand Place

This colorful cobblestone square is the heart—historically and geographically—of heart-shaped Brussels. As the town's market square for 1,000 years, this was where farmers and merchants sold their wares in open-air stalls, enticing travelers from the main east-west highway across Belgium, which ran just north of the square. Today, shops and cafés sell chocolates, *gaufres* (waffles), beer, mussels, fries, *dentelles* (lace), and flowers (for details on cafés and chocolate shops on the Grand Place, see the "Tasty Treats Around the Grand Place" sidebar, later).

Pan the square to get oriented. Face the Town Hall with its skyscraping spire. One TI is on your right, under the Town Hall's arches, while another TI is one block behind you; Rue des Bouchers and its restaurants are another block beyond that. To your right, a block away (downhill), is the Bourse building. The Upper Town is to your left, rising up the hill beyond Central Station. Over your left shoulder a few blocks away is St. Michael's Cathedral. And most important? The *Manneken-Pis* is three blocks ahead, down the street that runs along the left side of the Town Hall.

The **Town Hall** (Hôtel de Ville) dominates the square with its 300-foot-tall tower, topped by a golden statue of St. Michael slay-

ing a devil. Built in the 1400s, this was where the city council met to rule this free trading town. Brussels proudly maintained its self-governing independence while dukes, kings, and clergymen ruled much of Europe. You can step into the Town Hall courtyard for a little peace (but the building's interior is only open by tour—€5, English tours Wed at 14:00; Sun at 11:00, 15:00, and 16:00; get tickets from TI on Grand Place).

Opposite the Town Hall is the impressive, gray **King's House** (Maison du Roi), which now houses the **City Museum**. The structure has gone through several incarnations in its 800-year history. First it was the medieval

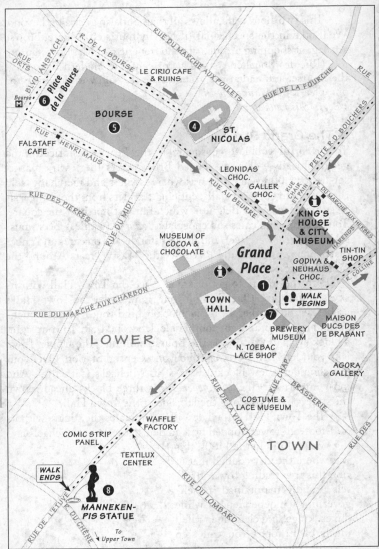

square's bread market, hence the building's Dutch name—Brood-huis. Then (early 1500s) it became the regional office for the vast Habsburg empire of Charles V, hence its French name—Maison du Roi. The lacy, prickly Gothic facade dates from the late 1800s, when it was renovated to be the City Museum (€8, Tue-Sun 10:00-17:00, closed Mon).

The fancy smaller buildings giving the square its uniquely grand medieval character are former **guild halls** (now mostly shops and restaurants), their impressive gabled roofs topped with statues.

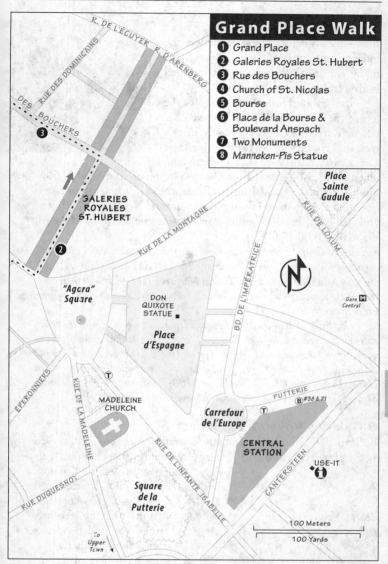

Grand Place Walk

1. Grand Place
2. Galeries Royales St. Hubert
3. Rue des Bouchers
4. Church of St. Nicolas
5. Bourse
6. Place de la Bourse & Boulevard Anspach
7. Two Monuments
8. Manneken-Pis Statue

BRUGES & BRUSSELS

Once the home offices for the town's different professions (brewers, bakers, and *Manneken-Pis* corkscrew makers), they all date from shortly after 1695—the year French king Louis XIV's troops took the high ground east of the city, sighted their cannons on the Town Hall spire, and managed to level everything around it (4,000 mostly wooden buildings) without ever hitting the spire itself. As a matter of pride, these Brussels businessmen rebuilt their offices better than ever, completing everything within seven years. They're in stone, taller, and with ornamented gables and classical statues. While they were all built at about the same time, the many differences in styles reflect the independent spirit of the people and the many cultural influences that converged in this crossroads trading center.

The **Swan House** (#9, just to the left of the Town Hall) once housed a bar where Karl Marx and Friedrich Engels met in February of 1848 to write their *Communist Manifesto*. Later that year, when the treatise sparked socialist revolution around Europe, Belgium exiled Marx and Engels. Today, the once-proletarian bar is one of the city's most expensive restaurants. Next door (#10) was and still is the brewers' guild, now housing the **Brewery Museum** (€5, daily 10:00-17:00).

• *Exit the Grand Place next to Godiva (from the northeast, or uphill, corner of the square), and go north one block on Rue de la Colline. Along the way, you'll pass a popular **Tintin boutique** (at #9). It sells merchandise of the popular Belgian comic-strip hero to both kids and adults who grew up with him.*

Continue to Rue du Marché aux Herbes, which was once the main east-west highway through Belgium. The little parklike square just to your right is nicknamed "Agora" (after the nearby covered shopping area). Looking to the right, notice that it's all uphill from here to the Upper Town, another four blocks (and 200-foot elevation gain) beyond. Straight ahead, you enter the arcaded shopping mall called...

❷ Galeries Royales St. Hubert

Built in 1847, Europe's oldest still-operating shopping mall served as the glass-covered model that inspired many other shopping gal-

leries in Paris, London, and beyond. It celebrated the town's new modern attitude (having recently gained its independence from the Netherlands). Built in an age of expansion and industrialization, the mall demonstrated efficient modern living, with elegant apartments upstairs above trendy shops, theaters, and cafés. Even today, people live in the upstairs apartments.

Looking down the arcade (233 yards long), you'll notice that it bends halfway down, designed to lure shoppers farther. Its iron-and-glass look is still popular, but the decorative columns, cameos,

Tasty Treats Around the Grand Place

Brussels' grand square (and the surrounding area) offers plenty of places to sample Belgium's culinary specialties.

Cafés: Mussels in Brussels, Belgian-style fries, yeasty local beers, waffles...if all you do here is plop down at a café on the square, try some of these specialties, and watch the world go by—hey, that's a great afternoon in Brussels.

The outdoor cafés are casual and come with fair prices (a decent Belgian beer costs €4.50, and a really good one is more like €5-7—with no cover or service charge). Have a seat, and a waiter will serve you. The half-dozen or so cafés on the downhill side of the square are all roughly equal in price and quality for simple drinks and foods—check the posted menus. As they are generally owned by breweries, you won't have a big selection of beers.

Choco-Crawl: The best chocolate shops lie along the north (uphill) side of the square, starting with Godiva at the high end (higher in both altitude and price). The cost goes down slightly as you descend to the other shops. Each shop has a mouthwatering display case of chocolates and sells 100-gram mixes (six or so pieces) for about €5, or individual pieces for about €1.

Godiva is synonymous with fine Belgian chocolate. Now owned by a Turkish company, Godiva still has its management and the original factory (built in 1926) in Belgium. This store, at Grand Place 22, was Godiva's first (est. 1937). The almond and honey goes way beyond Almond Roca.

Neuhaus, a few doors down at #27, has been encouraging local chocoholics since 1857. Their main store is in the Galeries Royales St. Hubert. Neuhaus publishes a good little pamphlet explaining its products. The "caprice" (toffee with vanilla crème) tastes like Easter. Neuhaus claims to be the inventor of the praline.

Galler, just off the square at Rue au Beurre 44, is homier and less famous because it doesn't export. Still family-run, it proudly serves less sugary dark chocolate. The new top-end choice, 85 percent pure chocolate, is called simply "Black 85"—and worth a sample if you like chocolate without the sweetness. Galler's products are well described in English.

Leonidas, four doors down at Rue au Beurre 34, is where cost-conscious Bruxellois get their fix, sacrificing 10 percent in quality to nearly triple their take (machine-made, only €2.20/100 grams). White chocolate is their specialty. If all the chocolate has made you thirsty, wash it down with **250 Beers,** next to Leonidas.

and pastel colors evoke a more elegant time. It's Neo-Renaissance, like a pastel Florentine palace.

• *Midway down the mall, where the two sections bend, turn left and exit the mall onto...*

❸ Rue des Bouchers

Yikes! During meal times, this street is absolutely crawling with tourists browsing through wall-to-wall, low-quality restaurants.

Brussels is known worldwide for its food, serving all kinds of cuisine, but specializing in seafood (particularly mussels). You'll have plenty to choose from along this table-clogged restaurant row, where hustlers will try to draw you into their eateries. Don't count on getting a good value here—better restaurants are just a few steps away (see "Eating in Brussels," later).

The first intersection, with Petite Rue des Bouchers, is the heart of the restaurant quarter, which sprawls for several blocks around. The street names reveal what sorts of shops used to stand here—butchers *(bouchers)*, herbs, chickens, and cheese.

• *At this intersection, turn left onto Petite Rue des Bouchers and walk straight back to the Grand Place. (You'll see the Town Hall tower ahead.) At the Grand Place, turn right (west) on Rue au Beurre. Comparison-shop at the Galler and Leonidas chocolate stores and pass by the little "Is it raining?" fountain. At the intersection with Rue du Midi is the...*

❹ Church of St. Nicolas

Since the 12th century, there's been a church here. The outside has been freshly cleaned, so—like a Hollywood actress—it looks a lot younger than it really is. Inside, along the left aisle, see rough stones in some of the arches from the early church. Outside, notice the barnacle-like shops, such as De Witte Jewelers, built right into the church. The church was rebuilt 300 years ago with money provided by the town's jewelers. As thanks, they were given these shops with apartments upstairs. Close to God, this was prime real estate. And there are still jewelers here.

• *Just beyond the church, you run into the back entrance of a big Neoclassical building.*

❺ The Bourse (Stock Exchange) and Art Nouveau Cafés

The stock exchange was built in the 1870s in the Historicist style—a mix-and-match, Neo-everything architectural movement. Plans are in the works for the former stock exchange to host a big beer museum. The **ruins** under glass on the right side of the Bourse are from a 13th-century convent; there's a small museum inside.

Several **historic cafés** huddle around the Bourse in a new car-free zone. To the right (next to the covered ruins) is the woody **Le Cirio,** with its delightful circa-1900 interior. Around the left side of the Bourse is the **Falstaff Café,** which is worth a peek inside. Some Brussels cafés, like the Falstaff, are still decorated in the early-20th-century Art Nouveau style. Ironwork columns twist and bend like flower stems, and lots of Tiffany-style stained glass and mirrors make them light and spacious. Slender, elegant, willowy Gibson Girls decorate the wallpaper, while waiters in bowties glide by.

• *Circle around to the front of the Bourse, toward Boulevard Anspach.*

❻ Place de la Bourse and Boulevard Anspach

Brussels is the political nerve center of Europe (with as many lobbyists as Washington, DC), and the city sees several hundred dem-

onstrations a year. When the local team wins a soccer match or some political group wants to make a statement, Place de la Bourse is where people flock to wave flags and honk horns. It's also where the old town meets the new. To the right along Boulevard Anspach are two shopping malls and several first-run movie theaters. Rue Neuve, which parallels Anspach, is a bustling pedestrian-only shopping street.

• *Return to the Grand Place.*

BRUGES & BRUSSELS

From the Grand Place to the *Manneken-Pis*

• *Leave the Grand Place kitty-corner, heading south down the street running along the left side of the Town Hall. Rue Charles Buls (which soon changes its name to Stoofstraat). Just five yards off the square, under the arch, are* ❼ *two monuments honoring illustrious Brussels notables.*

The first monument features a beautiful young man—an Art Nouveau allegory of knowledge and science (which brings illumination, as indicated by the Roman oil lamp)—designed by Victor Horta. It honors **Charles Buls,** mayor from 1888 to 1899. If you enjoyed the Grand Place, thank him for saving it. He stopped King Leopold II from blasting a grand esplanade from Grand Place up the hill to the palace.

A few steps farther you'll see tourists and locals rubbing a **brass statue** of a reclining man. This was Alderman Evrard 't Serclaes, who in 1356 bravely refused to surrender the keys of the city to invaders, and so was tortured and killed. Touch him, and his misfortune becomes your good luck. Judging by the reverence with which locals treat this ritual, I figure there must be something to it.

From here, the street serves up a sampler of typical Belgian products. A half-block farther (on the left), the **N. Toebac Lace Shop** shows off some fine lace.

Brussels is perhaps the best-known city for traditional lacemaking, and this shop still sells handmade pieces in the old style: lace clothing, doilies, tablecloths, and ornamental pieces. The shop gives travelers with this book a 15 percent discount.

A block farther down the street is the recommended, always-popular **Waffle Factory,** where a few euros gets you a freshly made takeaway "Belgian" waffle.

Cross busy Rue du Lombard and step into the **Textilux Center** (Rue du Lombard 41, on the left) for a good look at Belgian tapestries—both traditional wall-hangings and modern goods, such as tapestry purses and luggage in traditional designs.

Continuing down the street, notice a **mural** on the wall ahead, depicting that favorite of Belgian comic heroes, Tintin, escaping

down a fire escape. Tintin is known and beloved by virtually all Europeans. His dog is named Snowy, Captain Haddock keeps an eye out for him, and the trio is always getting into misadventures. Dozens of these building-sized comic-strip panels decorate Brussels, celebrating the Belgians' favorite medium.

• *Follow the crowds, noticing the excitement build, because in another block you reach the...*

❽ *Manneken-Pis*

Even with low expectations, this bronze statue is smaller than you'd think—the little squirt's under two feet tall, practically the size of a newborn. Still, the little peeing boy is

an appropriately low-key symbol for the unpretentious Bruxellois. The statue was made in 1619 to provide drinking water for the neighborhood. Notice that the baby, sculpted in Renaissance style, actually has the musculature of a man instead of the pudgy limbs of a child. The statue was knighted by the occupying King Louis XV—so French soldiers had to salute the eternally pissing lad when they passed.

As it's tradition for visiting VIPs to bring the statue an outfit, and he also dresses up for special occasions, you can often see the *Manneken* peeing through a colorful costume. A sign on the fence lists the month's festival days and how he'll be dressed. For example, on January 8, Elvis Presley's birthday, he's an Elvis impersonator; on Prostate Awareness Day, his flow is down to a slow drip. He can also be hooked up to a keg to pee wine or beer.

There are several different legends about the story behind *Manneken*—take your pick: He was a naughty boy who peed inside a witch's house, so she froze him. A rich man lost his son and declared, "Find my son, and we'll make a statue of him doing what he did when

found." Or—the locals' favorite version—the little tyke loved his beer, which came in handy when a fire threatened the wooden city: He bravely put it out. Want the truth? The city commissioned the *Manneken* to show the freedom and joie de vivre of living in Brussels—where happy people eat, drink...and drink...and then pee.

Sights in Brussels

The Grand Place and its attractions may be Brussels' top sight, but the city offers a variety of museums, big and small, to fill your time here.

EAST OF THE GRAND PLACE
▲St. Michael's Cathedral
One of Europe's classic Gothic churches, built between roughly 1200 and 1500, Brussels' cathedral is made from white stone and

topped by twin towers. For nearly 1,000 years, it's been the most important church in this largely Catholic country. (Whereas the Netherlands went in a Protestant direction in the 1500s, Belgium remains 80 percent Catholic—although only about 20 percent attend Mass.)

Cost and Hours: Free, but small fees to visit the underwhelming crypt and treasury, Mon-Fri 7:00-18:00, Sat-Sun 8:30-18:00, www.cathedralisbruxellensis.be.

▲Belgian Comic Strip Center (Centre Belge de la Bande Dessinée)

Belgians are as proud of their comics as they are of their beer, lace, and chocolates. Something about the comic medium resonates

with the wry and artistic-yet-unpretentious Belgian sensibility. Belgium has produced some of the world's most popular comic characters, including the Smurfs, Tintin, and Lucky Luke. You'll find these, and many less famous local comics, at the Comic Strip Center. It's not a wacky, lighthearted place, but a serious museum about a legitimate artistic medium. Most of the cartoons are in French and Dutch, but descriptions are English.

Cost and Hours: €10, daily 10:00-18:00, 10-minute walk from the Grand Place to Rue des Sables 20, tel. 02-219-1980, www.comicscenter.net.

Getting There: From Central Station, walk north along the big boulevard, then turn left down the stairs at the giant comic character (Gaston Lagaffe).

IN THE UPPER TOWN
▲▲▲Royal Museums of Fine Arts of Belgium (Musées Royaux des Beaux-Arts de Belgique)

This sprawling complex houses a trio of museums showing off the country's best all-around art collection. The **Old Masters Museum**—featuring Flemish and Belgian art of the 14th through 18th century—is packed with a dazzling collection of masterpieces by Van der Weyden, Bruegel, Bosch, and Rubens. The **Fin-de-Siècle Museum** covers art of the late 19th and early 20th centuries, including an extensive Art Nouveau collection. The **Magritte Museum** contains more than 200 works by the Surrealist painter René

Magritte. Although you won't see many of Magritte's most famous pieces, you will get an unusually intimate look at the life and work of one of Belgium's top artists.

Cost and Hours: €8 for each museum, €13 combo-ticket covers all three, free first Wed of month after 13:00; Old Masters and Fin-de-Siècle museums—Tue-Sun 10:00-17:00, closed Mon; Magritte Museum—daily 10:00-17:00; audioguides-€4 each, tour booklet-€2.50, pricey cafeteria with salad bar, Rue de la Régence 3, tel. 02-508-3211, www.fine-arts-museum.be or www.musee-magritte-museum.be.

Visiting the Museum: Head into the large entrance hall and get oriented. The Old Masters Museum is on the second floor (in the galleries above you), reached by the staircase directly ahead. The Fin-de-Siècle Museum is through the passageway to the right, down several levels. The Magritte Museum is also to the right, through the same passageway.

• *Go up to the second floor and start with the Flemish masters.*

Old Masters Museum: Art history fans will appreciate this richly creative collection, which encompasses the Flemish Primitives as well as the fertile periods of the Flemish Renaissance and Baroque. Here are just of few of the highlights:

Rogier van der Weyden, *Portrait of Anthony of Burgundy* (c. 1456-1465): Anthony, a member of the Archers Guild, fingers an arrow like a bowstring. From his gold necklace dangles a Golden Fleece, one of Europe's more prestigious knightly honors. Capitalist Flanders in the 1400s was one of the richest, most cultured, and most progressive areas in Europe, rivaling Florence and Venice. Van der Weyden (c. 1399-1464), Brussels' official portrait painter, faithfully rendered life-size, lifelike portraits of wealthy traders, bankers, and craftsmen. Here he captures the wrinkles in Anthony's neck and the faint shadow his chin casts on his Adam's apple.

Hans Memling, *Martyrdom of St. Sebastian* (*Le Martyre de Saint Sébastien,* c. 1475): Serene Sebastian is filled with arrows by a serene firing squad in a serene landscape. Like a *tableau vivant,* the well-dressed archers and saint freeze this moment in the martyrdom so the crowd can applaud the colorful costumes and painted cityscape backdrop. Hans Memling (c. 1430-1494) is clearly a master of detail, and the faces, beautiful textiles, and hazy landscape combine to create a meditative mood appropriate to the church altar in Bruges where this painting was once placed.

Pieter Bruegel I, The Census at Bethlehem (*Le Dénombrement de Bethléem*, 1566): Perched at treetop level, you have a bird's-eye view over a snow-covered village near Brussels. Into the scene rides a woman on a donkey led by a man—it's Mary and husband Joseph hoping to find a room at the inn (or at least a manger), because Mary's going into labor. Bruegel I (c. 1527-1569) was famous for his landscapes filled with crowds of peasants in motion. His religious paintings place the miraculous in everyday settings.

Peter Paul Rubens, The Ascent to Calvary (*La Montée au Calvaire*, c. 1636): Life-size figures scale this 18-foot-tall canvas on the way to Christ's Crucifixion. The scene ripples with motion, from the windblown clothes to steroid-enhanced muscles to billowing flags and a troubled sky. Hiring top-notch assistants, Rubens (1577-1640) could crank out large altarpieces for the area's Catholic churches. This work is from late in Rubens' long and very successful career.

Jacques-Louis David, The Death of Marat (*Marat Assassiné*, 1793): In a scene ripped from the day's headlines, Jean-Paul Marat—a well-known crusading French journalist—has been stabbed to death in his bathtub by Charlotte Corday, a conservative fanatic. With his last strength, he pens a final, patriotic, *"Vive la Révolution"* message to his fellow patriots. Jacques-Louis David (1748-1825), one of Marat's fellow revolutionaries, set to work painting a tribute to his fallen comrade right after the 1793 assassination. David makes it a secular pietà, with the brave writer portrayed as a martyred Christ in a classic dangling-arm pose.

• *To get to the Fin-de-Siècle Museum, return to the ground floor and the large main entrance hall of the Old Masters Museum, where a passageway leads you to the...*

Fin-de-Siècle Museum: Brussels likes to think of itself as the capital of Art Nouveau and the crossroads of Europe, and this space presents a convincing case. Covering the period from the mid-19th century to the early 20th century, it shows the many cultural trends that converged in Brussels to create great art. The collection features a handful of high-powered paintings by notable Impressionists, Post-Impressionists, Realists, and Symbolists (Seurat, Gauguin, Ensor). It also houses a dazzling assemblage of Art Nouveau glassware, jewelry, and furniture.

Don't expect to see this art in chronological order. Galleries are organized thematically, to show the art in context with the period's literature, opera, architecture, and photography.

• *Backtrack along the ground-floor passageway to find the...*

Magritte Museum: René Magritte (1898-1967) is Belgium's most famous 20th-century artist. He trained and worked in Brussels, but also lived for a time in Paris, where he connected with other Surrealist painters. The exhibits take you on a chronological route through Magritte's life and art. The museum divides his life into three sections, with one floor devoted to each. In each section, a detailed timeline (in English) puts the work you'll see in a biographical and historical context.

Magritte had his own private reserve of symbolic images. You'll see clouds, blue sky, windows, the female torso, men in bowler hats, rocks, pipes, sleigh bells, birds, turtles, and castles arranged side by side as if the arrangement means something. He heightens the mystery by making objects unnaturally large or small. People morph into animals or inanimate objects. The juxtaposition short-circuits your brain only when you try to make sense of it. Magritte's works are at once playful and disorienting...and, at times, disturbing.

▲Musical Instruments Museum (Musée des Instruments de Musique)

One of Europe's best music museums (nicknamed "MIM") is housed in one of Brussels' most impressive Art Nouveau buildings, the beautifully renovated Old England department store. This museum has more than 1,500 instruments—from Egyptian harps, to medieval lutes, to groundbreaking harpsichords, to the Brussels-built saxophone. Don't miss the great city views from the corner alcoves on each level.

Cost and Hours: €8, includes audioguide, open Tue-Fri 9:30-17:00, Sat-Sun from 10:00, closed Mon, last entry 45 minutes before closing, mandatory free bag check, Rue Montagne de la Cour 2, just downhill and toward Grand Place from the Royal Museums, tel. 02-545-0130, www.mim.be.

▲▲BELvue Museum

This 21st-century museum is the best introduction to modern Belgian history (1830-2015) that you'll find in Brussels. It's well described in English, organized by modern themes, and spiced up with iPads and interactive technology. But it's also Belgian history—so it is what it is. The museum sits over the (skippable) archaeological remains of the 12th-century Coudenberg Palace. If you do tour

BRUGES & BRUSSELS

the palace ruins, see the BELvue Museum first, because you'll exit the Coudenberg downhill, near the Musical Instruments Museum.

Cost and Hours: €7, Tue-Fri 9:30-17:00, July-Aug until 18:00, Sat-Sun 10:00-18:00, closed Mon; audioguide-€2.50, adjacent to the Royal Palace at Place des Palais 7, tel. 070-220-492, www.belvue.be.

Shopping in Brussels

The obvious temptations—available absolutely everywhere—are chocolate and lace. Other popular Brussels souvenirs include EU gear with the gold circle of stars on a blue background (flags, T-shirts, mugs, bottle openers, hats, pens, and so on) and miniature reproductions of the *Manneken-Pis*. Belgian beers are a fun, imbibable souvenir that you can either enjoy at a picnic while traveling, or pack (carefully) in your checked luggage to take home.

Souvenirs near the Grand Place: The streets immediately surrounding the Grand Place are jammed with Belgium's tackiest souvenir stands, with a few good shops mixed in. In my Grand Place Walk, I've listed some good places to pick up chocolates and to browse for tapestries and lace. **De Biertempel,** facing the TI on the street that runs below the Grand Place, not only stocks hundreds of types of Belgian beer, but an entire wall of beer glasses—each one designed to highlight the qualities of a specific beer (Rue du Marché aux Herbes 56, tel. 02-502-1906).

Fashion on Rue Antoine Dansaert:  While Antwerp is the epicenter of Belgian design, Brussels has worked hard in recent years to catch up. To browse the best selection of Belgian boutiques, start by heading up Rue Antoine Dansaert (from the big Bourse building, cross Boulevard Anspach and continue straight up Rue Auguste Orts, which becomes Rue Antoine Dansaert). You'll see an eclectic array of both Belgian and international apparel. While specific designers seem to come and go, the genteel vibe persists. After Place du Nouveau Marché aux Grains, the high-fashion focus downshifts, and the rest of the street feels like an emerging neighborhood with some funkier, lower-rent shops.

Eating in Brussels

Brussels is known for both its high-quality, French-style cuisine and for multicultural variety. Seafood—fish, eel, shrimp, and oysters—is especially well-prepared here. As in France, if you ask for

the *menù* at a restaurant, you won't get a
list of dishes; you'll get a fixed-price meal
of three or four courses. If you want to
see a printed menu and order individual
items, ask for *la carte*.

When it comes to choosing a restaurant, many tourists congregate on the
Grand Place or at Rue des Bouchers, the
city's restaurant row. While the Grand
Place is undeniably magnificent for enjoying dessert or a drink, go elsewhere
to eat well.

Dining on the Grand Place

My vote for northern Europe's grandest medieval square is lined
with hardworking eateries that serve predictable dishes to tourist
crowds. Of course, you won't get the best quality or prices—but,
after all, it's the Grand Place.

For an atmospheric cellar or a table right on the Grand Place,
two traditional standbys have the same formula, with tables outside
overlooking the action. **$$$$ L'Estaminet du Kelderke**—with its
one steamy vault under the square packed with both natives and
tourists—is a real Brussels fixture. It serves local specialties, including mussels (daily 12:00-24:00, no reservations taken, Grand
Place 15, tel. 02-511-0956). **$$$$ Brasserie L'Ommegang,** with
a fancier restaurant upstairs, offers perhaps the classiest seating and
best food on the square.

Lunches near the Grand Place

The super-central square dubbed the "Agora" (officially Marché
aux Herbes, just between the Grand Place and Central Station)
is lined with low-end eateries—Quick, Subway, Panos sandwich
shop, Exki health-food store—and is especially fun on sunny days.
On the other side of the Grand Place is Rue du Marché aux Fro-
mages, jammed with mostly Greek and gyros places, with diners
sitting elbow-to-elbow at cramped tables out front. For something
fresher and more interesting, stroll a few blocks to one of the following alternatives.

$$ Bia Mara ("Sea Food" in Irish Gaelic) offers five different
styles of fish-and-chips made with sustainable ingredients (plus a
chicken option and a rotating special). The industrial-mod interior
is small, so lines can be long at peak times (daily 12:00-14:30 &
17:30-22:30, Fri-Sun open throughout the day, around the corner
from the Grand Place at Rue du Marché aux Poulets 41, tel. 02-
502-0061).

BRUGES & BRUSSELS

Mussels in Brussels

Mussels *(moules)* are available all over town. Mostly harvested from aqua farms along the North Sea, they are available for most of the year (except from about May through mid-July, when they're brought in from Denmark). The classic Belgian preparation is *à la marinière,* cooked in white wine, onions, celery, parsley, and butter. Or, instead of wine, cooks use light Belgian beer for the stock. For a high-calorie version, try *moules à la crème,* where the stock is thickened with heavy cream.

You order by the kilo (just more than 2 pounds), which is a pretty big bucket. While restaurants don't promote these as splittable, they certainly are. Your mussels come with Belgian fries (what we think of as "French fries"—dip them in mayo).

To accompany your mussels, try a French white wine such as Muscadet or Chablis, or a Belgian blonde ale such as Duvel or La Chouffe.

When eating mussels, you can feel a little more local by nonchalantly using an empty mussel shell as a pincher to pull the meat out of other shells. It actually works quite nicely.

$$ Peck 47 is a mod café with artistic decor and white subway tile. They offer brunch all day and an American dinner menu in the evening with fresh and innovative style—and veggie options. If you have a hankering for eggs Benedict, come here (Mon-Fri 7:30-22:00, Sat-Sun from 9:00, Rue du Marché aux Poulets 47, tel. 02-513-0287).

Picnics: A convenient **Carrefour Express** grocery is along the street between the Grand Place and the Bourse, near a public drinking fountain (long hours daily, Rue au Beurre 27). Another Carrefour is near Central Station on Rue de l'Infante Isabelle. **AD Delhaize,** a major supermarket, is at the intersection of Rue du Marché aux Poulets and Boulevard Anspach (long hours daily, Boulevard Anspach 63).

More Eateries near the Grand Place

$$ Arcadi Café is a delightful little eatery serving daily plates, salads, and a selection of quiche-like tortes for €9.50. The interior comes with a fun, circa-1900 ambience; grab a table there, on the street, or at the end of Galeries St. Hubert (daily 9:00-23:30, 1 Rue d'Arenberg, tel. 02-511-3343).

$$ Le Mokafé is inexpensive but feels splurgy. They dish up light café fare at the quiet end of the elegant Galeries St. Hubert, with great people-watching outdoor tables. This is also a good spot to try a Brussels waffle or to order a *café-filtre*—an old-fashioned method where the coffee drips directly into your cup (daily 7:00-23:00, Galerie du Roi 9, tel. 02-511-7870).

$ La Maison des Crêpes, a little eatery a half-block south of the Bourse, looks underwhelming but serves delicious crêpes (both savory and sweet varieties) and salads. Even though it's just a few steps away from the tourist bustle, it feels laid-back and local (good beers, fresh mint tea, sidewalk seating, daily 12:00-23:00, Rue du Midi 13, mobile 0475-957-368).

$$ Yaki is a tempting Vietnamese and Thai noodle bar in a stately old flatiron building tucked between the Grand Place and the Rue du Marché au Charbon café/nightlife zone. Choose between the tight interior and the outdoor tables (daily 12:00-23:00, Rue du Midi 52, tel. 02-503-3409).

$$$ Osteria a l'Ombra, a true Italian joint, is good for a quality bowl of pasta with a glass of fine Italian wine. A block off the Grand Place, it's pricey, but the woody bistro ambience and tasty food make it a good value. The ground-floor seating on high stools is fine, but also consider sitting upstairs (Mon-Sat 12:00-14:30 & 18:30-23:30, closed Sun, Rue des Harengs 2, tel. 02-511-6710).

Waffles near the Grand Place

Dozens of waffle windows clog the streets surrounding the Grand Place. Most of them are suspiciously cheap (€1)—but the big stack of stale waffles in the window clues you in that these are far from top-quality. Below I've listed a couple of good options.

$ Maison Dandoy, which has been making waffles since the 19th century, is the pricey, elegant choice. You can take the waffles to go or enjoy them at a table in an upscale Parisian atmosphere (Mon-Sat 9:30-19:00, Sun from 10:30, just off the Grand Place at Rue Charles Buls 14, tel. 02-512-6588).

$ Waffle Factory, near the *Manneken-Pis,* is cheaper but still good. While it has an American fast-food ambience, it's efficient and popular—and thanks to the high turnover, you'll usually get a waffle that's grilled while you wait. Get your waffle to go, or sit upstairs to enjoy some peace and quiet (and free Wi-Fi). For a very Belgian taste treat, top your waffle with *speculoos*—a decadent spread of ground-up gingerbread cookies with the consistency of peanut butter (long hours daily, look for green-and-red-striped awning at corner of Rue du Lombard and Rue de l'Etuve).

Sampling Belgian Beer in Brussels

Brussels is full of atmospheric cafés to savor the local brew. The places lining the Grand Place are touristy, but the setting is hard to beat. All varieties of Belgian beer are available, but Brussels' most distinctive beers are *lambic*-based. Look for *lambic doux*, *lambic blanche*, *gueuze* (pronounced "kurrs"), and *faro*, as well as fruit-flavored *lambics*, such as *kriek* (cherry) and *framboise* (raspberry—*frambozen* in Dutch). These beers look and taste more like a dry, somewhat bitter cider. The following places are generally open daily from about 11:00 until late.

A la Mort Subite, a few steps above the top end of the Galeries St. Hubert, is a classic old bar that has retained its 1928 decor...and its loyal customers seem to go back just about as far. The decor is simple, with wood tables, grimy yellow wallpaper, and some-other-era garland trim. A typical lunch or snack here is an omelet with a salad or a *tartine* spread with *fromage blanc* (cream cheese) or pressed meat. Eat it with one of the home-brewed, *lambic*-based beers. This is a good place to  try the *kriek* beer. While their beer list is limited, they do have Chimay on tap (Rue Montagne aux Herbes Potagères 7, tel. 02-513-1318).

Le Cirio, across from the Bourse, feels a bit more upscale, with a faded yet still luxurious gilded-wood interior, booths with velvet padding, and dark tables that bear the skid marks of over a century's worth of beer glasses. The service is jaded—perhaps understandably given its touristy location (Rue de la Bourse 18-20, tel. 02-512-1395).

Poechenellekelder Estaminet is a great bar with lots of real character located right across the street from the *Manneken-Pis*. As the word *estaminet* (tavern) indicates, it's not brewery-owned, so they have a great selection of beers. Inside tables are immersed in *Pis* kitsch and puppets. Outside tables offer some fine people-watching (Rue du Chêne 5, tel. 02-511-9262).

Two tiny and extremely characteristic bars are tucked away down long entry corridors just off Rue du Marché aux Herbes. **A l'Imaige Nostre-Dame** (closed Sun, at #8) and **Au Bon Vieux Temps** (at #12) both treat fine beer with great reverence and seem to have extremely local clientele, whom you're bound to meet if you grab a stool. Au Bon Vieux Temps stocks the legendary Trappist brew Westvleteren 12, which is hard to find outside Belgium.

Ghent

Made terrifically wealthy by the textile trade, medieval Ghent was a powerhouse, and for a time, it was one of the biggest cities in Europe. It erected grand churches and ornate guild houses to celebrate its resident industry. But, like its rival Bruges, eventually Ghent's fortunes fell, leaving it with a well-preserved historic nucleus surrounded by a fairly drab modern shell.

Ghent doesn't ooze with cobbles and charm as Bruges does; this is a living place—home to one of Belgium's biggest universities. Ghent enjoys just the right amount of urban grittiness, with a welcome splash of creative hipster funkiness. It's also a browser's delight, with a wide range of characteristic little shops that aren't aimed squarely at the tourist crowds.

Explore the historic quarter, ogle the breathtaking Van Eyck altarpiece in the massive cathedral, tour impressive art and design museums, stroll picturesque embankments, bask in finely decorated historic gables, and prowl the revitalized Patershol restaurant quarter.

Orientation to Ghent

Although it's a midsized city (pop. 250,000), Ghent's historic core is appealingly compact—you can walk from one end to the other in about 15 minutes. The train station (with several museums nearby) is a 15-minute tram ride south of the center. Its Flemish residents call the town Gent (gutturally: *h*ent), while its French name is Gand (sounds like "gone").

TOURIST INFORMATION

Ghent's TI is in the Old Fish Market (Oude Vismijn) building next to the Castle of the Counts (daily mid-March-mid-Oct 9:30-18:30, off-season until 16:30, tel. 09-266-5660, www.visitgent.be). Pick up a free town map and a pile of brochures (including a good self-guided walk).

ARRIVAL IN GHENT

By Train: Ghent's main train station, Gent-Sint-Pieters, is about a mile and a half south of the city center. As the station is undergoing an extensive renovation (through 2020), it might differ from what's described here. In the main hall, be sure to look up at the meticulously restored frescoes celebrating great Flemish cities and regions.

It's a dull 30-minute **walk** to the city center. Instead, take the **tram:** Buy tickets from the **Lijnwinkel** transportation office (Mon-Fri 7:00-19:00) in the train station, at the ticket machines outside, or on board (€3; on the bus use exact change only). There's also a €6 day pass that must be purchased at the Lijnwinkel office.

Find the stop for tram #1: It's out the front door and 100 yards to the left, under the big, blocky, modern building on stilts. Board tram #1 in the direction of Wondelgem/Evergem (departs about every 10 minutes, 15-minute ride). Get off at the Korenmarkt stop, and continue one block straight ahead to Korenmarkt, where you can see most of the city's landmark towers. Figure €10 for a **taxi** into town.

Sights in Ghent

Ghent is a rewarding town to simply wander and explore. Most visitors focus on the city's historic core, along a gentle bend in the river. You could have an enjoyable day simply strolling the riverbank, crisscrossing the bridges, and lingering in the city's many fine squares (the best are described below). While the city has several fine museums, churches, and other sights, I've listed only those that most warrant your limited time.

▲▲Squares

Of Ghent's many inviting squares, be sure to at least pass through these:

Korenmarkt (Corn Market): The historic square, next to St. Michael's Bridge (one of the town's best viewpoints), is squeezed between the palatial former post office and St. Nicholas' Church. This square flows directly into two others: **Emile-Braunplein** (watched over by a Neo-Gothic belfry) and **St. Bavo's Square** (in front of the namesake cathedral, described later).

Groentenmarkt (Vegetable Market): This tidy and atmospheric square, right on the river, is tucked alongside the medieval Butchers Hall (Groot Vleeshuis, now housing artisanal local foods).

Vrijdagmarkt (Friday Market): Watched over by a statue of local hero Jakob van Artevelde, this fine square is ringed by skinny burghers' mansions and the "House of the People" (Ons Huis), the ornately decorated headquarters for the region's socialist movement.

▲▲St. Bavo's Cathedral (Sint-Baafskathedraal) and Ghent Altarpiece

This cathedral, the main church of Ghent, houses three of the city's art treasures: the exquisite Van Eyck *Adoration of the Mystic Lamb* altarpiece—widely

known as the Ghent Altarpiece; an elaborately carved pulpit; and an altar painting by Rubens depicting the town's patron saint (and the church's namesake).

Cost and Hours: Church free to enter but €4 to see original altarpiece and its facsimile, includes audioguide; April-Oct Mon-Sat 9:30-17:00, Sun 13:00-17:00; Nov-March Mon-Sat 10:30-16:00, Sun 13:00-16:00; Sint-Baafsplein, tel. 09-225-1626, www.sintbaafskathedraal.be.

Church of St. Nicholas (Sint-Niklaaskerk)

This beautiful church, built of Tournai limestone, is a classic of the Scheldt Gothic style. Ghent's merchants started building the Church of St. Nicholas in the 1100s. Among its art treasures is a massive Baroque altar of painted wood.

Cost and Hours: Free, Mon 14:00-17:00, Tue-Sun 10:00-17:00, on Cataloniëstraat at the corner of Korenmarkt, tel. 09-234-2869.

Belfry (Belfort)

This combination watchtower and carillon has been keeping an eye on Ghent since the 1300s. For centuries, this landmark building safeguarded civic documents. Nowadays, the mostly empty interior displays an exhibit of bells, and an elevator whisks visitors up the 300-foot tower to views over the city.

Cost and Hours: €8, daily 10:00-18:00, Sint-Baafsplein, tel. 09-233-3954, www.belfortgent.be.

▲Castle of the Counts (Gravensteen)

Though it dates from 1180, this fortress has morphed over the centuries, and much of it is rebuilt and restored. It's impressive from

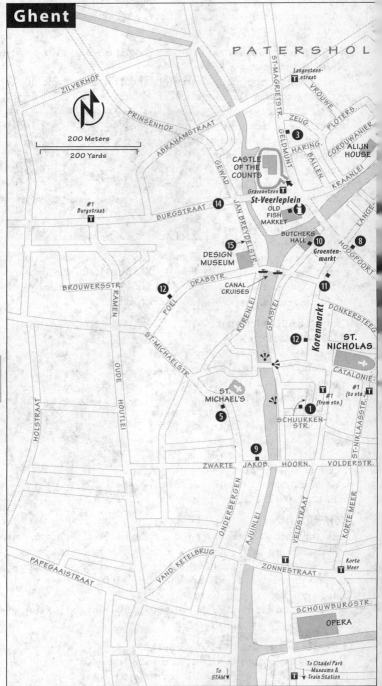

Ghent

PATERSHOL

200 Meters
200 Yards

ZILVERHOF

PRINSENHOF

ABRAHAMSTRAAT

GEWAD

BURGSTRAAT

ST-MAGRIETSTR.

Langesteenstraat

VROUWE

ZEUG.

GELDMUNT

HARING.

BALLEN.

PLOTERS.

CORDUWANIER

ALIJN HOUSE

CASTLE OF THE COUNTS

Gravensteen

St-Veerleplein

OLD FISH MARKET

KRAANLEI

#1 Burgstraat

JAN BREYDELSTR.

BUTCHERS HALL ⑩

Groentenmarkt

LANGE

HOOGPOORT

⑧

⑭

DESIGN MUSEUM ⑮

DRABSTR.

CANAL CRUISES

⑪

BROUWERSSTR.

RAMEN

⑫

POEL

ST-MICHAELSTR.

KORENLEI

GRASLEI

Korenmarkt

⑫

ST. NICHOLAS

DONKERSTEEG.

HOLSTRAAT

OUDE HOUTLEI

ST. MICHAEL'S

⑤

SCHUURKEN-STR.

#1 (from stn.)

①

#1 (to stn.)

CATALONIE

ST-NIKLAASSTR.

⑨

ZWARTE. JAKOB. HOORN. VOLDERSTR.

ONDERBERGEN

AJUINLEI

VELDSTRAAT

KORTE MEER

PAPEGAAISTRAAT

VAND. KETELBRUG

ZONNESTRAAT

Korte Meer

SCHOUWBURGSTR.

OPERA

To STAM ↓

To Citadel Park Museums & Train Station

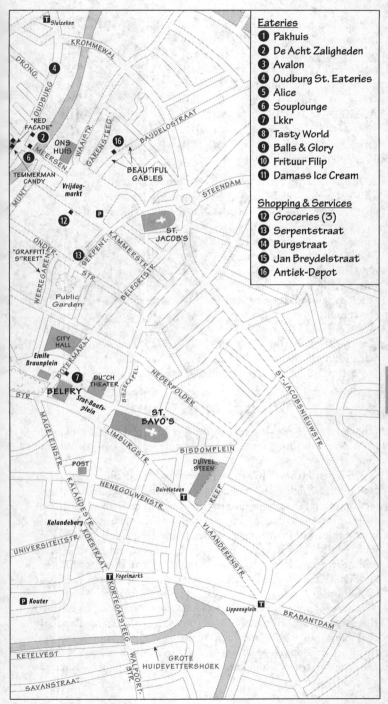

Eateries
1. Pakhuis
2. De Acht Zaligheden
3. Avalon
4. Oudburg St. Eateries
5. Alice
6. Souplounge
7. Lkkr
8. Tasty World
9. Balls & Glory
10. Frituur Filip
11. Damass Ice Cream

Shopping & Services
12. Groceries (3)
13. Serpentstraat
14. Burgstraat
15. Jan Breydelstraat
16. Antiek-Depot

the outside, but mostly bare inside and information is skimpy. Still, it's a fun opportunity to get a feel for the medieval world as you twist through towers and ramble over ramparts.

Cost and Hours: €10, daily April-Oct 10:00-18:00, Nov-March 9:00-17:00, last entry 45 minutes before closing, tel. 09-225-9306, Sint-Veerleplein, www.gravensteengent.be.

▲Ghent Design Museum (Design Museum Gent)

This collection celebrating the Belgian knack for design is enjoyable for everyone, but worth ▲▲▲ for those interested in 17th-

to 21st-century decorative arts. Furniture, glass, ceramics, and jewelry are displayed in a classic old building with a creaky wood interior, with a bright-white, spacious, and glassy new hall in the center.

Cost and Hours: €8, Mon-Tue and Thu-Fri 9:30-17:30, Sat-Sun 10:00-18:00, closed Wed, Jan Breydelstraat 5, tel. 09-267-9999, www.designmuseumgent.be.

Shopping in Ghent

Ghent has an enjoyable real-world feel that makes it a fun place to browse—not for souvenirs, but for interesting, design-oriented items.

Serpentstraat: This little pedestrian street, buried deep between the cathedral and Vrijdagmarkt square, has a fun, funky collection of creative shops. **Roark,** on the corner with Onderstraat at #1B, shows off cutting-edge/retro home decor; next door is the boutique of local clothing designer **Nathalie Engels** (#1A). Zsa, with wildly colorful, smartly designed gadgets and toys (for kids and grown-ups alike), has two branches: **Petit Zsa** for children, at #5, and **Zsa Rogue** at #22. Between them, at #8, sits the **Zoot** shoe shop.

Streets near the Castle of the Counts: The busy, tram-lined **Burgstraat,** just across the bridge from the castle, isn't particularly charming, but it's an enjoyable place to window-shop at several furniture and home-decor shops and art galleries. The side street **Jan Breydelstraat,** which leads to the Ghent Design Museum, has an eclectic array of clothing, linens, jewelry, design, and chocolate shops.

Antiques near Vrijdagmarkt: Antiek-Depot is a sprawling antique mall made for browsing. It sits along a postcard-perfect gabled street just north of Vrijdagmarkt square (closed Tue, Baude-lostraat 15).

Eating in Ghent

CITY CENTER

$$$ Pakhuis is a gorgeously restored, late-19th-century ware-house now filled with a classy, lively brasserie and bar. In this airy, two-story, glassed-in birdhouse of a restaurant, they serve up good traditional Belgian food with an emphasis on locally sourced and organic ingredients. It's tucked down a nondescript brick alley, but worth taking the few steps out of your way (Mon-Sat 12:00-14:30 & 18:30-23:00, closed Sun, Schuurkenstraat 4, tel. 09-223-5555).

$$$ De Acht Zaligheden (The Eight Beatitudes) prides it-self on its regional and seasonal dishes with an always-innovative presentation (Tue-Sun 12:00-14:00 & 18:00-22:00, closed Mon, Oudburg 4, tel. 09-224-3197, www.deachtzaligheden.be).

PATERSHOL

For decades this former sailors' quarter was a derelict and danger-ous no-man's-land, where only fools and thieves dared to tread. But today it's one of Ghent's most inviting—and priciest—neighbor-hoods for dining. Peek into courtyards, many of which hide restau-rant and café tables.

$$ Avalon, up the street from the Castle of the Counts, of-fers tasty vegetarian fare (daily 11:30-14:30, Geldmuntstraat 32, tel. 09-244-3724).

Oudburg street is lined with fun, ethnic, and youthful **$** and **$$** eateries, including a good Turkish place (Ankara, at #44) and the hip, popular, tight, and tasty **Ramen** noodle bar (at #51, open for lunch only, closed Sun-Mon). Continue north beyond the end of Oudburg to find **Sleepstraat,** which is lined with cheap Turkish eateries (locals recommend **Gök,** with three branches along here; **Gök 2** is set in a whimsical 19th-century interior).

QUICK EATS

$ Alice, tucked on a side street near St. Michael's Bridge, serves simple lunches, soups, and sandwiches in a delightful candy-box interior or in the garden (Tue-Sat 8:30-17:30, Sun 9:30-14:30, closed Mon, Onderbergen 6, tel. 09-277-9235).

$ Souplounge is basic, but cheap and good. They offer four daily soups, along with salads. Eat in the mod interior, or at the outdoor tables overlooking one of Ghent's most scenic stretches of canal (daily 10:00-19:00, Zuivelbrugstraat 6, tel. 09-223-6203).

$ Lkkr ("Yum"), behind the belfry, is a small, modern shop selling sandwiches and salads mostly to businesspeople on lunch breaks. Choose between the cozy interior or outdoor tables (Mon-Sat 10:00-18:00, closed Sun, Botermarkt 6, tel. 09-234-1006).

$ Tasty World serves up decent veggie burgers with various toppings, plus a wide range of fresh fruit juices and salads (Mon-Sat 11:00-20:00, until 19:00 in winter, closed Sun, Hoogpoort 1, tel. 09-225-7407).

$$ Balls & Glory, a small Belgian chain that got its start in Ghent, is about a 10-minute walk from Vrijdagmarkt square. They specialize in gigantic meatballs—two flavors per day are noted on the chalkboard menu. Get yours to go or pay a few euros more to eat in their hip dining room at shared stainless-steel tables. Your meal includes water and fruit (Mon-Sat 10:00-21:00, closed Sun, Jakobijnenstraat 6, mobile 0486-678-776).

$ Frituur Filip, a fry shack attached to the Meat Hall on the Pensmarkt, serves real Belgian *frites* cooked twice in ox fat. Try them with Filip's homemade *stoofvleessaus*—the sauce skimmed off his Flemish stew (Thu-Tue 11:30-22:00, closed Wed).

Dessert: Damass is a popular ice cream place where you can hang out and enjoy people-watching or get a cone to stroll with (at the north end of Korenmarkt, #2-C, closed Tue).

Grocery Stores: You'll find a well-supplied **Albert Heijn** below the former post office on Korenmarkt (Mon 12:00-20:00, Tue-Sun 8:00-20:00, Korenmarkt 16). On Vrijdagmarkt, **Carrefour Express** is handy for picnic supplies and basic toiletries (daily 8:30-19:30 except Sun until 14:30, Mon from 14:30, at #54). Two blocks behind the Ghent Design Museum is a **Spar** (Mon-Sat 7:30-19:30, closed Sun, Poel 22).

What If I Miss My Ship?

Remember that you can get help from the cruise line's port agent (listed on the destination information sheet distributed on the ship) and the local TI. If the port agent suggests a costly solution (such as a private car with a driver), you may want to consider public transit.

From the Blankenberge station, you can connect through Brussels or Antwerp by train to reach **Le Havre** (via Paris), London (with connections to **Southampton** and **Dover**), Amsterdam, Copenhagen, Warnemünde (via Berlin), and beyond.

If you need to catch a plane to your next destination, you have two options: the main Brussels Airport (sometimes called "Zaventem," www.brusselsairport.be), and Brussels South Charleroi Airport, used primarily by discount airlines and located about 30 miles from downtown Brussels (www.charleroi-airport.com).

For more advice on what to do if you miss the boat, see page 130.

Dutch Survival Phrases

Northern Belgium speaks Dutch, but for cultural and historical reasons, the language is often called Flemish. Most people speak English, but if you learn the pleasantries and key phrases, you'll connect better with the locals. To pronounce the guttural Dutch "g" (indicated in phonetics by *h*), make a clear-your-throat sound, similar to the "ch" in the Scottish word "loch."

English	Dutch	Pronunciation
Hello.	*Hallo.*	**hah**-loh
Good day.	*Dag.*	da*h*
Good morning.	*Goedemorgen.*	**hoo**-deh-mor-*h*ehn
Good afternoon.	*Goedemiddag.*	**hoo**-deh-mid-da*h*
Good evening.	*Goedenavond.*	**hoo**-dehn-ah-fohnd
Do you speak English?	*Spreekt u Engels?*	shpraykt oo **eng**-ehls
Yes. / No.	*Ja. / Nee.*	yah / nay
I (don't) understand.	*Ik begrijp (het niet).*	ik beh-*h***ripe** (heht neet)
Please. (can also mean "You're welcome")	*Alstublieft.*	**ahl**-stoo-bleeft
Thank you.	*Dank u wel.*	dahnk oo vehl
I'm sorry.	*Het spijt me.*	heht spite meh
Excuse me.	*Pardon.*	**par**-dohn
(No) problem.	*(Geen) probleem.*	(*h*ayn) **proh**-blaym
Good.	*Goede.*	**hoo**-deh
Goodbye.	*Tot ziens.*	toht zeens
one / two	*een / twee*	ayn / t'vay
three / four	*drie / vier*	dree / feer
five / six	*vijf / zes*	fife / zehs
seven / eight	*zeven / acht*	**zay**-fehn / aht
nine / ten	*negen / tien*	**nay**-*h*ehn / teen
What does it cost?	*Wat kost het?*	vaht kohst heht
Is it free?	*Is het vrij?*	is heht fry
Is it included?	*Is het inclusief?*	is heht in-**kloo**-seev
Can you please help me?	*Kunt u alstublieft helpen?*	koont oo **ahl**-stoo-bleeft **hehl**-pehn
Where can I buy / find...?	*Waar kan ik kopen / vinden...?*	var kahn ik **koh**-pehn / **fin**-dehn
I'd like / We'd like...	*Ik wil graag / Wij willen graag...*	ik vil *h*rah / vy **vil**-lehn *h*rah
...a room.	*...een kamer.*	ayn **kah**-mer
...a train / bus ticket to ____.	*...een trein / bus kaartje naar ____.*	ayn trayn / boos **kart**-yeh nar ____
...to rent a bike.	*...een fiets huren.*	ayn feets **hoo**-rehn
Where is...?	*Waar is...?*	var is
...the train / bus station	*...het trein / bus station*	heht trayn / boos **staht**-see-ohn
...the tourist info office	*...de VVV*	deh fay fay fay
...the toilet	*...het toilet*	heht **twah**-leht
men / women	*mannen / vrouwen*	**mah**-nehn / **frow**-ehn
left / right	*links / rechts*	links / re*h*ts
straight ahead	*rechtdoor*	**re*h*t**-dor
What time does it open / close?	*Hoe laat gaat het open / dicht?*	hoo laht *h*aht heht **oh**-pehn / di*h*t
now / soon / later	*nu / straks / later*	noo / strahks / **lah**-ter
today / tomorrow	*vandaag / morgen*	**fahn**-da*h* / **mor**-*h*ehn

LONDON

Great Britain

Great Britain Practicalities

The island of Great Britain contains the countries of England, Wales, and Scotland. Hilly England—which contains all of the places in this chapter—occupies the lower two-thirds of the isle. The size of Louisiana (about 50,000 square miles), England's population is just over 55 million. England's ethnic diversity sets it apart from its fellow UK countries: Nearly one in three citizens is not associated with the Christian faith. The cradle of the Industrial Revolution, today's Britain has little heavy industry—its economic drivers are banking, insurance, and business services, plus energy production and agriculture. For the tourist, England offers a little of everything associated with Britain: castles, cathedrals, royalty, theater, and tea.

Money: 1 British pound (£1) = about $1.40. An ATM is called a cashpoint. The local VAT (value-added sales tax) rate is 20 percent; the minimum purchase eligible for a VAT refund is £30 (for details on refunds, see page 125).

Language: The native language is English.

Emergencies: Dial 112 for police, medical, or other emergencies. In case of theft or loss, see page 118.

Time Zone: Great Britain is one hour earlier than most of continental Europe, and five/eight hours ahead of the East/West Coasts of the US.

Embassies in London: The **US embassy** is at 33 Nine Elms Lane (tel. 020/7499-9000, https://uk.usembassy.gov,). The **High Commission of Canada** is at Trafalgar Square (tel. 020/7004-6000, www.unitedkingdom.gc.ca). Call ahead for passport services.

Phoning: With a mobile phone, it's easy to dial: Press and hold zero until you get a + sign, enter the country code (44 for Britain, 1 for the US/Canada), and then the complete phone number (including area code if there is one). When dialing a European phone number, drop an initial zero (except if calling Italy). For more tips, see page 1062.

Tipping: Tipping in Britain isn't as automatic as it is in the US; always check your menu or bill to see if gratuity is included. If not, tip about 10-12 percent. To tip a cabbie, round up a bit (if the fare is £4.50, give £5). For more tips on tipping, see page 129.

Tourist Information: www.visitbritain.com

LONDON & the PORTS of SOUTHAMPTON and DOVER

Southampton • Portsmouth • Dover • Canterbury • London

Many cruises begin, end, or call at English ports with easy access to London. Cruise lines favor two in particular: Southampton, 80 miles southwest of London; and Dover, 80 miles southeast of London (each about a 1.5-hour drive or train ride into the city).

From Southampton and Dover, most people choose to head into **London**—and for good reason. London is more than its museums and landmarks. It's the LA, DC, and NYC of Britain—a living, breathing, thriving organism...a coral reef of humanity. Those beginning or ending their cruise in one of these ports will want to allocate ample extra time to experience London. But if your cruise only stops here for the day—even if it's a long day—you'll be very limited in what you can see in London. For this reason, some people choose to skip the trip into the big city and visit towns closer to their port, which offer an enticing taste of English culture.

In **Southampton** there's little to see there beyond its fine SeaCity Museum. However, it's a short train ride from here to **Portsmouth,** a gentrified city with a wide array of maritime and nautical-themed sights.

Dover has a castle that's well worth touring, famous White Cliffs (visible from the cruise dock)...and not much else. But it's a quick train trip to **Canterbury,** an exceptionally pleasant town with one of England's biggest and best cathedrals.

All of these destinations—Southampton, Portsmouth, Dover, Canterbury, and, of course, London—are covered individually in this chapter, with "Planning Your Time" suggestions for each.

Port of Southampton

Arrival at a Glance: From the Ocean Cruise Terminal, QEII Cruise Terminal, or City Cruise Terminal, you can walk into town or hop a bus to the train station; from the Mayflower Cruise Terminal, spring for a taxi. Trains go to London (1.5 hours, 2/hour) and Portsmouth (50 minutes, hourly).

Port Overview

Southampton has two port areas: the **Eastern Docks** and the **Western Docks.** The Eastern Docks (Ocean Cruise and QEII Cruise terminals) consist of long piers jabbing straight out from Southampton; the **Western Docks** (City Cruise and Mayflower Cruise terminals) hug Southampton's coastline west of downtown. For details, see www.cruisesouthampton.com.

Terminal Services: Each terminal has similar services, including WCs, a rack of tourist brochures and maps, a basic café, and a taxi stand out front (but no ATMs).

Tourist Information: Neither the terminals nor the town has a TI. Your best bet for visitor information is www.discoversouthampton.co.uk.

GETTING INTO SOUTHAMPTON
(AND TO THE TRAIN STATION)

Southampton is a sprawling port town with a relatively compact downtown core. The train station—with convenient connections to London, Portsmouth, and more—sits northwest of the port zone; it's walkable, but far enough away that a taxi or bus is worth considering.

First, I'll cover transportation options that work from any port. Then I'll offer specifics on each port. To **return to your ship,** you can generally reverse these directions; I've given additional tips where they'll help.

From Any Port

Cruise-Line Shuttle: If your cruise line offers an affordable shuttle bus to downtown or the train station, consider taking it.

By Taxi: Depending on where you arrive, I'd consider the simplicity of a taxi. For rides within Southampton city limits, drivers are required to use the meter. It should cost about £6-8 from any cruise terminal to either the train station or the town center. Look for cabs with a Hackney Coach license hanging from the bumper, ask for an estimate up front, and make sure they use the meter (it's required within the city).

Excursions from Southampton and Dover

Cruise-line excursions from both ports feature visits to London, as well as local destinations.

Excursions to London: There are plenty of ways to skin this cat, but most begin with an orientation **bus tour** around town; you'll zip by (and possibly have a photo-op stop) at such landmarks as the Houses of Parliament (Big Ben), Westminster Abbey, Buckingham Palace, London Eye, and the Tower of London. Some also feature a guided sightseeing visit; popular options include the **Tower of London** and a guided tour of the interior of **Buckingham Palace. Shopping tours** ("West End shopping" at Harrods and other famous department stores) are also offered. A **"London On Your Own"** excursion—a round-trip bus ride to Piccadilly Circus and free time in the city with no guide—runs about $100 (compared to about $55 round-trip by train from Southampton, or about $50 from Dover).

Other Excursions from Southampton: A side-trip to **Stonehenge and Salisbury** is perhaps the best choice, as it shows you Britain's iconic, mysterious, and ancient stone circle as well as a lovely midsize market town with a grand cathedral. A tour of **Windsor Castle,** the primary residence of the royal family, is another good choice. Other options are a scenic drive through the **Dorset County Countryside** (often with a stop at the dramatic ruins of **Corfe Castle**); the stately **Palace of Beaulieu,** with its nearby National Motor Museum (250 historic automobiles); and a shopping-oriented visit to the town of **Winchester,** with yet another giant cathedral.

Other Excursions from Dover: The nearby town of **Canterbury** combines charm, history, and one of England's most important cathedrals—making it the best choice here. (Canterbury is also easy to do on your own, using the information in this chapter.) Other options include a boat trip for a closer look at Dover's famous **White Cliffs;** the adorable village of **Rye** and a scenic drive through the Kent countryside; the stout, ninth-century **Leeds Castle;** the 15th-century, timber-framed **Great Dixter** house and its delightful gardens; Henry VIII's heavily fortified **Walmer Castle,** generally combined with the enchanting village of **Sandwich;** and the village of **Chilham** (a popular filming location).

If leaving Southampton, you can either use the meter or negotiate a fixed price. Here are some ballpark one-way figures for trips farther afield: Central London: £160-180; Heathrow Airport: £130-145; Gatwick Airport: £130-150; Salisbury: £60; Portsmouth: £45-50; Southampton Airport: £20-25.

To call a taxi, try West Quay Cars (tel. 023/8099-9999, www. westquaycars.com).

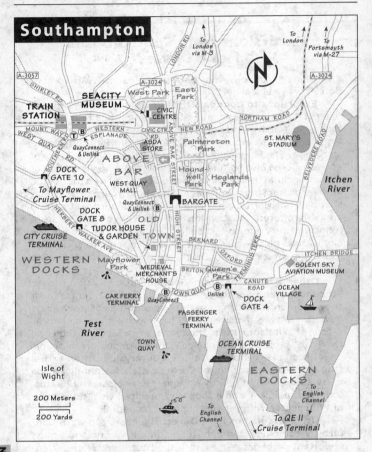

Southampton

(map labels)

To London RD · To London via M-3 · To London · To Portsmouth via M-27

A-3057 · A-3024 · A-3024

SHIRLEY RD.

SEACITY MUSEUM · West Park · East Park

TRAIN STATION · CIVIC CENTRE · NORTHAM ROAD

MOUNT WAY · WESTERN ESPLANADE · CIVIC CTR. RD. · NEW ROAD · ST. MARY'S STADIUM

WEST QUAY · QuayConnect & Unilink · ASDA STORE · Palmerston Park

SOUTHERN RD. · ABOVE BAR · Hound-well Park · Hoglands Park · BELVEDERE ROAD · Itchen River

DOCK GATE 10 · WEST QUAY MALL

To Mayflower Cruise Terminal · QuayConnect & Unilink · BARGATE

DOCK GATE 8 · HIGH STREET · OLD

HERBERT WALKER AVE. · TUDOR HOUSE & GARDEN · TOWN

CITY CRUISE TERMINAL · BERNARD · ITCHEN BRIDGE

WESTERN DOCKS · Mayflower Park · OXFORD · TERMINUS TERR. · SOLENT SKY AVIATION MUSEUM

MEDIEVAL MERCHANT'S HOUSE · Briton · Queen's Park · CANUTE ROAD · OCEAN VILLAGE

CAR FERRY TERMINAL · TOWN QUAY · QuayConnect · Unilink · DOCK GATE 4

PASSENGER FERRY TERMINAL

Test River · TOWN QUAY · OCEAN CRUISE TERMINAL · EASTERN DOCKS

Isle of Wight · To English Channel

200 Meters · 200 Yards · To English Channel · To QE II Cruise Terminal

From the Eastern Docks

There are two cruise terminals at the Eastern Docks: **Ocean Cruise Terminal** at the near end (Berth 46/47), and **QEII Cruise Terminal** at the tip (Berth 38/39). Access to this area is through Dock Gate 4, a 10-20-minute walk from the terminals on this very long pier. The bus and walking directions below work from either terminal.

By Bus: The city's **Unilink bus #U1A/#U1C** connects the Eastern Docks with the train station, Civic Centre, and town center (£2, £3.50 all-day ticket; #U1A runs from the Eastern Docks to the train station, direction: Airport; #U1C runs from the train station to the Eastern Docks, direction: NOCS, City Centre, or Dock Gate 4—get off at Platform Tavern stop; www.unilinkbus. co.uk). You can walk to the bus stop in 10 to 20 minutes, depending on which terminal your boat uses: From the dock exit, turn left onto the busy road, and after two long blocks you'll see a stop for the Unilink #U1A bus on the left.

On Foot: If you feel like walking, go left from the port gate and continue along the main road until you reach Town Quay.

Turn right up High Street, which leads in about 15 minutes up through the town center to the Civic Centre area. Halfway up the main drag, you reach Bargate, one of the original town wall's towers. Beyond that, the street becomes "Above Bar." After a few short blocks, turn left on Civic Centre Road and you'll see a big, stately building with a lighthouse tower on your right—this is the Civic Centre, with the SeaCity Museum next door. To reach the train station, continue on Civic Centre Road across the busy intersection and down Western Esplanade, following the *Station* signposts to the station in about 10 minutes.

From the Western Docks

Shuffled between the endless parking lots and container shipping berths of the Western Docks are the **City Cruise Terminal,** close to the town center (Berth 101); and the farther-out **Mayflower Cruise Terminal** (Berth 106). Access to this port area is through Dock Gate 8 (closer to downtown) or Dock Gate 10 (just south of the train station).

Mayflower Cruise Terminal

This terminal is far enough out that a **taxi** is your best bet (the taxi stand is to the left as you exit the terminal).

City Cruise Terminal

This terminal is conveniently situated at the near end of the Western Docks.

By Bus: Southampton's **QuayConnect bus** is the closest bus option for passengers arriving at this terminal. It runs through the city every 30 minutes and connects the public ferry dock—called Town Quay—with the town center and train station for just £2 (ticket good all day; www.bluestarbus.co.uk).

To reach the bus stop (a 15-minute walk), exit the terminal area at Dock Gate 8. Continue straight along the street (keeping the port on your right) until you reach Town Quay (at the base of the pier that juts out at the end of Southampton's High Street).

Services in Southampton

Few services are available at the cruise terminals. For most, you'll need to head into town (or wait for London).

ATMs: Your best bet is either in downtown Southampton (several banks with ATMs line High Street, the main drag) or in London (Waterloo Station, where you'll arrive, has several). Most taxi drivers take credit cards (ask before you hop in), and you can buy train **tickets** with credit cards—so it's relatively easy to get into London cash-free.

Wi-Fi: There is no Wi-Fi at the terminals. Wi-Fi is available at one of the many ubiquitous Costa Coffee shops (including one on High Street), or at Starbucks (at Town Quay or Above Bar).

Pharmacy: The biggest and handiest is Boots, on Above Bar just past Bargate (open daily).

Board the bus at the stop in front of the Red Funnel ticket office. The bus arrives at the train station in about 10-15 minutes. To visit the **SeaCity Museum,** ask if the driver will let you off at the Asda supermarket (between West Quay and the train station, a short walk from the Civic Centre).

On Foot: It's a dreary 20-minute walk to the train station (turn left out of the terminal, hike through the port area to Dock Gate 10—at the roundabout, turn right to exit through the gate, continue straight up Southern Road, then turn right after the second cross-street, following the *Station* signs, and cut through the park to the station.

GETTING TO LONDON (AND ELSEWHERE)
By Shuttle Bus
Many cruise lines offer a "London On Your Own" excursion, providing an unguided, round-trip bus transfer to Piccadilly Circus in London. Most lines charge about $100 for this trip—almost twice the price of a round-trip train ticket, but very convenient.

By Train
Southampton Central Station is small and manageable, with ticket windows and ticket machines just inside the door. You can enter or exit the station from either side, but most people come and go from the southern entrance, which is also the location of the bus stops to Town Quay (Western Docks) and Platform Tavern (Eastern Docks). A walkway over the tracks connects this entrance to tracks 1 and 2, used by London-bound trains.

Trains depart at least every 30 minutes from Southampton to **London's Waterloo Station** (about 1.5 hours; additional departures require a change in Basingstoke; slower trains go to London's Victoria Station in 2.5 hours). A same-day off-peak return (round-trip) ticket to London costs about £45; a one-way ticket costs about £42.

For a closer and more manageable side-trip, consider **Portsmouth.** Trains leave Southampton about hourly (typically at :05 past the hour) and head directly to Portsmouth Harbour Station, within easy walking distance of the sights (50 minutes; £10.40 "single"/one-way, £11.20 "day return"/same-day round-trip). Additional connections with a change in Fareham or Havant take longer (60-70 minutes).

Returning to Southampton and Your Ship: From **London,** first take the train from London's Waterloo Station (or Portsmouth Harbour Station) to Southampton Central Station (don't get off at Southampton Airport Parkway). Exiting the station, you'll see a taxi stand (figure around £6-8 to your ship), and stops for the QuayConnect and Unilink buses (remember that they won't take you all the way to your ship—you'll have to walk 10-20 minutes from the bus stop). QuayConnect works best for the City Cruise Terminal; the Unilink #U1C bus serves the Ocean Cruise and QEII Cruise Terminals—look for buses marked *NOCS, City Centre,* or *Dock Gate 4.* Take a cab to the Mayflower Cruise Terminal.

From **Portsmouth,** direct trains depart for Southampton about hourly.

Southampton

An important English port city for centuries, Southampton is best known for three ships that set sail from here and gained fame for very different reasons: the *Mayflower* in 1620, the *Titanic* in 1912, and in 1936, the *Queen Mary*—the luxurious great-grandma of the ship you arrived on. Like many port cities, Southampton was badly damaged by WWII bombs, obliterating whatever cobbled charm it once had. Today Southampton has one excellent museum (the state-of-the-art SeaCity Museum), but otherwise disappoints sightseers with a gloomy urban core, a few fragments of old city walls and towers, and an "Old Town" halfheartedly rebuilt to vaguely resemble a long-gone salty sailor's town.

PLANNING YOUR TIME

Upon arrival in Southampton, most people will want to get out. London is a 1.5-hour train ride away, and Portsmouth (with a variety of great maritime exhibits; see page 877) is just 50 minutes away. However, for those who want to stay in Southampton, there are a few ways to occupy your times.

SeaCity Museum: This well-presented museum thoughtfully

tells the story of Southampton and the *Titanic*. It could occupy an attentive sightseer for two hours or longer.

Tudor House and Gardens: Worth about 30 minutes, this modest museum peels back the layers of history of an old house in the town center.

There's little else to do in Southampton. The town center is nondescript, and the so-called "Old Town" near the Tudor House and Gardens is tiny and disappointing.

Sights in Southampton

▲▲SeaCity Museum

This state-of-the-art facility, designed to consolidate and update various crusty old museums, features one of the best exhibits anywhere on the *Titanic*. It also has a good local history collection and well-presented temporary exhibits.

Cost and Hours: £8.50, £12 combo-ticket with Tudor House and Gardens, daily 10:00-17:00, last entry one hour before closing, Havelock Road, tel. 023/8083-3007, www.seacitymuseum.co.uk.

Visiting the Museum: From the ground-floor entrance level (with a gift shop, cafeteria, and temporary exhibits), head upstairs to the Grand Hall. From here, you can enter the two permanent collections.

The highlight, called **Southampton's *Titanic* Story,** explores every facet of the ill-fated ocean liner that set sail from here on April 10, 1912, and sank in the North Atlantic a few days later. Three-quarters of the *Titanic*'s 897 crew members lived in Southampton—making the global disaster a very local matter. With a smart multimedia approach, this outstanding exhibit invites you to linger over each detail.

Across the Grand Hall is the other permanent exhibit, **Southampton: Gateway to the World,** which traces the history of this shipping settlement from prehistoric and Anglo Saxon times until today. The museum's prized possession is its 23-foot-long model of the *Queen Mary*, which made its maiden voyage from Southampton in 1936.

Tudor House and Gardens

A rare surviving 525-year-old home tucked in Southampton's underwhelming and mostly reconstructed Old Town, this house offers a step back in time. Your visit begins with a 10-minute, semi-hokey audio-visual show of "ghosts" telling the building's history. Then

you'll explore the various rooms, with exhibits and videos explaining how restorers have peeled back the historical layers of the place: Tudor, Georgian, Victorian, and even a WWII-era bunker. The experience is worthwhile for those with an interest in historical architecture (or anyone wanting to kill some time). But anyone can enjoy the pleasant garden (free to enter) and fine café.

Cost and Hours: £5, includes audioguide, £12 combo-ticket with SeaCity Museum, Tue-Fri 10:00-5:00, Sat-Sun 10:00-17:00, closed Mon, Bugle Street, tel. 023/8083-4242, www.tudorhouseandgarden.com.

Portsmouth

Portsmouth, the age-old home of the Royal Navy and Britain's second-busiest ferry port after Dover, is best known for its Historic Dockyard and many

nautical sights. For centuries, Britain, a maritime superpower, relied on the fleets based in Portsmouth to expand and maintain its vast empire and guard against invaders. When sea power was needed, British leaders—from Henry VIII to Winston Churchill to Margaret Thatcher—have called upon Portsmouth to ready the ships. But an impressive gentrification is under way here. As the navy shrinks, tourism is moving in. Efforts to rejuvenate tourism have included refurbishing Old Portsmouth, building a sprawling new waterfront shopping complex, and adding a sail-like monolith to the skyline.

Visiting landlubbers can tour the HMS *Victory,* which played a key role in Britain's battles with Napoleon's navy, and see the *Mary Rose,* a 16th-century warship that was a favorite of Henry VIII.

PLANNING YOUR TIME

On a visit from nearby Southampton, Portsmouth can easily fill a day. Focus your time on the Historic Dockyards (allow 2-3 hours to tour all the museums and ships). With more time, explore Old Portsmouth or ascend Spinnaker Tower.

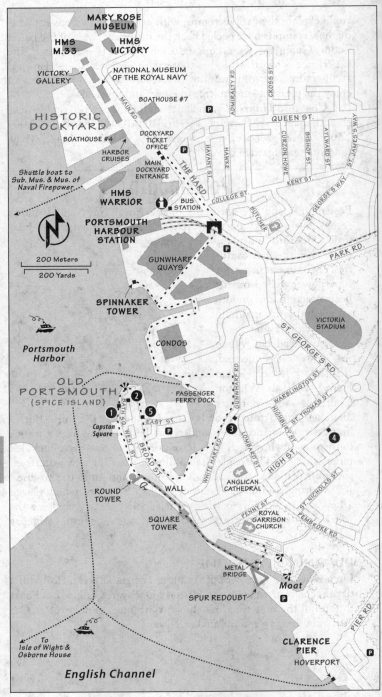

MARY ROSE MUSEUM

HMS M.33

HMS VICTORY

VICTORY GALLERY

NATIONAL MUSEUM OF THE ROYAL NAVY

BOATHOUSE #7

HISTORIC DOCKYARD

BOATHOUSE #4

HARBOR CRUISES

DOCKYARD TICKET OFFICE

MAIN DOCKYARD ENTRANCE

Shuttle boat to Sub. Mus. & Mus. of Naval Firepower

HMS WARRIOR

BUS STATION

PORTSMOUTH HARBOUR STATION

GUNWHARF QUAYS

200 Meters

200 Yards

SPINNAKER TOWER

Portsmouth Harbor

CONDOS

OLD PORTSMOUTH (SPICE ISLAND)

PASSENGER FERRY DOCK

BATH SQ.

WEST ST.

EAST ST.

Capstan Square

BROAD ST.

ROUND TOWER

WALL

SQUARE TOWER

WHITE HART RD.

GUNWHARF RD.

ANGLICAN CATHEDRAL

PENNY ST.

ROYAL GARRISON CHURCH

METAL BRIDGE

SPUR REDOUBT

Moat

To Isle of Wight & Osborne House

English Channel

ADMIRALTY RD.

CROSS ST.

QUEEN ST.

HAVANT ST.

HAWKE

CURZON HOWE

BISHOP ST.

AYLWARD ST.

ST. JAMES'S WAY

KENT ST.

COLLEGE ST.

BUTCHER

ST. GEORGE'S WAY

PARK RD.

VICTORIA STADIUM

ST. GEORGE'S RD.

WARBLINGTON ST.

ST. THOMAS ST.

HIGHBURY ST.

LOMBARD ST.

HIGH ST.

ST. NICHOLAS ST.

PEMBROKE RD.

PIER RD.

CLARENCE PIER

HOVERPORT

LONDON

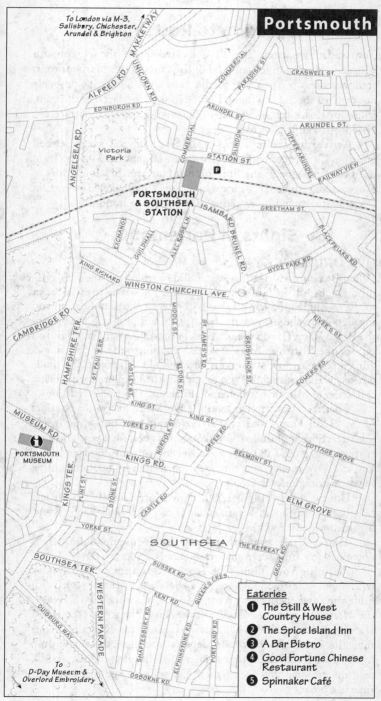

Portsmouth

To London via M-3,
Salisbury, Chichester,
Arundel & Brighton

MARKETWAY

ALFRED RD.
UNICORN RD.
ED'NBURGH RD.
ANGELSEA RD.
Victoria Park

COMMERCIAL
PARADISE ST.
CRASWELL ST.
ARUNDEL ST.
UPPER ARUNDEL
ARUNDEL ST.
RAILWAY VIEW

STATION ST.

P

PORTSMOUTH & SOUTHSEA STATION

ISAMBARD BRUNEL RD.
GREETHAM ST.
BLACKFRIARS RD.
EXCHANGE
GUILDHALL
ALEC ROBE LN.
HYDE PARK RD.
KING RICHARD

WINSTON CHURCHILL AVE.

CAMBRIDGE RD.
HAMPSHIRE TER.
ST. PAUL'S RD.
ST. PAUL'S RD.
MIDDLE ST.
ST. JAMES'S RD.
GROSVENOR ST.
RIVERS ST.
SOMERS RD.
ELDON ST.

KING ST.
KING ST.
YORKE ST.
NORFOLK ST.
GREEN RD.
COTTAGE GROVE

MUSEUM RD.

ⓘ

PORTSMOUTH MUSEUM

KINGS TER.
KINGS RD.
BELMONT ST.
ELM GROVE
FLINT ST.
STONE ST.
CASTLE RD.
YORKE ST.

SOUTHSEA
THE RETREAT
GROVE RD.

SOUTHSEA TER.
SUSSEX RD.
WESTERN PARADE
DUISBURG WAY
KENT RD.
SHAFTESBURY RD.
ELPHINSTONE RD.
QUEEN'S CRES.
PORTLAND RD.
OSBORNE RD.

To
D-Day Museum &
Overlord Embroidery

Eateries
❶ The Still & West Country House
❷ The Spice Island Inn
❸ A Bar Bistro
❹ Good Fortune Chinese Restaurant
❺ Spinnaker Café

LONDON

Orientation to Portsmouth

Tourist Information: The TI is located inside the Portsmouth Museum, about a mile southeast of the Portsmouth Harbour train station; unless you're going to the museum anyway, it's probably not worth a special trip (daily 10:00-17:00, Oct-March until 16:30, Museum Road, tel. 023/9282-6722, www.visitportsmouth.co.uk, vis@portsmouthcc.gov.uk).

Arrival by Train: Trains from Southampton are described on page 874. Portsmouth has two train stations. Stay on the train until the final stop at the **Portsmouth Harbour Station.** Most of Portsmouth's sights (Historic Dockyards, Spinnaker Tower, Old Portsmouth) are within walking distance of the station.

Sights in Portsmouth

HISTORIC DOCKYARD

When Britannia ruled the waves, it did so from Portsmouth's Historic Dockyard. Britain's great warships, known as the "Wooden Walls of England," were all that lay between the island nation and invaders from the Continent. Today, this harbor is still the base of the Royal Navy. (If you sneak a peek beyond the guard stations, you can see the British military at work.) The shipyard offers visitors a glimpse of maritime attractions new and old. Marvel at the modern-day warships anchored on the docks, then explore the fantastic collection of historic naval memorabilia and well-preserved ships.

Cost: You can stroll around the Dockyard to see the exteriors of the HMS *Victory* and HMS *Warrior* for free, but going inside the attractions requires a £35 ticket that is good for a year and covers everything (an £18 ticket gives you entry to any one attraction). You can save money and time waiting in line by booking online (www.historicdockyard.co.uk/tickets).

Hours: Daily 10:00-17:30, Nov-March until 17:00 (last tickets sold 1.5 hours before closing, tel. 023/9283-9766, www. historicdockyard.co.uk).

Tours: A free app with a Mary Rose Museum audio tour is downloadable from www.maryrose.org.

Planning Your Time: The Dockyard is a sprawling complex with about 10 attractions (several a shuttle-boat ride away). With finite time and energy, save most of your visit for the HMS *Victory,* the *Mary Rose,* and the Museum of the Royal Navy. Visit the HMS *Warrior* and the HMS *M.33* briefly. If you have extra time, consider the included harbor tour (departs from near the entry; drop by the dock to check on times and availability first). Upon arrival, pick up the map and locate these priorities to see things in the smartest order.

▲▲▲HMS *Victory*

This grand historic warship changed the course of world history. At the turn of the 19th century, Napoleon's forces were terrorizing the Continent. In 1805, Napoleon amassed a fleet of French and Spanish ships for the purpose of invading England. The Royal Navy managed to blockade the fleets, but some French ships broke through. Admiral Nelson, commander of the British fleet, pursued the ships aboard the HMS *Victory,* cornering them at Cape Trafalgar, off the coast of Spain. Wounded in battle, Nelson died aboard this ship, gasping his final words: "Thank God, I have done my duty." Today, the dry-docked HMS *Victory* is so well-preserved that it feels ready to haul anchor and pull out of the harbor at any moment. Visitors follow a one-way route that spirals up and down through the ship's six decks, taking at least an hour (possibly longer if you linger with the free audioguide).

▲▲*Mary Rose* Museum

The dark, rounded building next to the *Victory* is the home of the warship *Mary Rose*—King Henry VIII's favorite—that sank in 1545 and was raised in 1982.

This £35 million museum—shaped like an oval jewel box—was built to reunite the preserved hull with thousands of its previously unseen contents. All sorts of Tudor-era items were found inside the wreck, such as

clothes, dishes, weapons, a backgammon board, and an oboe-like instrument. There's even the skeleton of Hatch, the ship's dog. It's a fascinating look at everyday shipboard life from almost 500 years ago.

▲National Museum of the Royal Navy

This museum, situated in three buildings, is packed with model ships, paintings, uniforms, and lots more Nelson hero-worship. The *Victory* Gallery includes a corny but informative 15-minute *Trafalgar Experience* multimedia show (a blow-by-blow account of the Battle of Trafalgar) and culminates with a viewing of a panoramic painting of the battle (*Panorama of the Battle of Trafalgar,* by W. L. Wyllie, 1931). If you want to see this, sign up for a time as you enter.

More Dockyard Sights

With more time, dip into the **HMS** *Warrior* (the first ironclad warship, built in 1860) or the **HMS** *M.33* (the last surviving WWI ship of the bloody Gallipoli Campaign), visit **Boathouse #4** (displays of historic boats in a re-created boatyard), and consider a 50-minute **harbor cruise** (departs about hourly during the summer).

OTHER SIGHTS IN PORTSMOUTH

Gunwharf Quays

Part of the major (and successful) makeover of Portsmouth, the bustling Gunwharf Quays (pronounced "keys") is an American-style outdoor shopping center on steroids, with restaurants, shops, and entertainment.

Hours: Shops generally open daily 10:00-20:00, until 18:00 on Sun, www.gunwharf-quays.com.

Spinnaker Tower

Out at the far end of the shopping zone is this can't-miss-it 560-foot-tall tower, evocative of the billowing ships' sails that have played such a key role in the history of this city and country. You can ride to the 330-foot-high view deck for a panorama of the port and sea beyond, or court acrophobia with a stroll across "Europe's biggest glass floor."

Cost and Hours: £10.50, discounts available online or through TI, daily 10:00-18:00, book ahead in midsummer, booking tel. 023/9285-7520, www.spinnakertower.co.uk).

Old Portsmouth

Portsmouth's historic district—once known as "Spice Island" after the ships' precious cargo—is surprisingly quiet. For a long time, the old sea village was dilapidated and virtually empty. But successful revitalization efforts have brought a few inviting pubs and B&Bs. It's a pleasant place to stroll around and imagine how different this district was in the old days, when it was filled with salty fishermen and sailors who told tall tales and sang sea shanties in rough-and-tumble pubs.

▲D-Day Museum and Overlord Embroidery

This museum was built to commemorate the 40th anniversary of the D-Day invasions, and its centerpiece is the 272-foot-long Overlord Embroidery (named for the invasion's code name). The 34 appliquéd panels—stitched together over five years by a team of seamstresses—were inspired by the Bayeux Tapestry that recorded William the Conqueror's battles during the Norman invasion of England a thousand years earlier. The panels chronologically trace the years from 1940 to 1944, from the first British men receiving their call-up papers in the mail to the successful implementation of D-Day. It celebrates everyone from famous WWII figures to unsung heroes of the home front.

Cost and Hours: £10, daily 10:00-17:30, Oct-March until 17:00, café on site—closed in off-season, tel. 023/9282-7261, www.ddaymuseum.co.uk.

Getting There: The museum is on the waterfront about two miles south of the Spinnaker Tower, on the Clarence Esplanade in Southsea. From Portsmouth's Hard Interchange bus station (it's next to the train station), take First Bus Company's bus #16 or #1, or Stagecoach bus #23.

Eating in Portsmouth

AT THE HISTORIC DOCKYARD

The Historic Dockyard has an acceptable **cafeteria,** called **$ Boathouse No. 7,** with a play area that kids enjoy (daily 10:00-17:00). There is also a fancier eatery with water views at **$$$ Boathouse No. 4** (near HMS *Warrior,* daily 10:00-16:00) as well as a **$ café** at the *Mary Rose* (daily 10:00-17:00).

IN OLD PORTSMOUTH

$$ The Still & West Country House pub has dining in two appealing zones, both offering the same menu. Eat in the more casual main floor, or outside on the picnic benches with fantastic views of the harbor. Or head upstairs to the dining room with a gorgeous glassed-in conservatory that offers sea views and lovely window seats—especially enticing in cold weather (dining room open Mon-Sat 12:00-21:00, Sun 12:00-20:00, longer hours in the bar, 2 Bath Square, tel. 023/9282-1567).

$$ The Spice Island Inn, at the tip of the Old Portsmouth peninsula, has terrific outdoor seating, a family-friendly dining room upstairs, and many vegetarian offerings. This eatery is more down-and-dirty and less expensive (food served daily 11:00-22:00, bar open longer, 1 Bath Square, tel. 023/9287-0543). Their crowd spills into "the Point," the harborside square.

$$$ A Bar Bistro is a classy but relaxed seafood-and-wine kind of place (daily 12:00-24:00, 58 White Hart Road, tel. 023/9281-1585).

$$ Good Fortune Chinese Restaurant, across the street from the Duke of Buckingham pub, is favored by locals (daily 12:00-15:00 & 17:30-23:00, 21 High Street, tel. 023/9286-3293).

LONDON

$ Spinnaker Café is great for a lunch or snack if you're in Old Portsmouth before dinner (breakfast served all day, daily 8:00-16:00, 96 Broad Street, mobile 0777-295-3143).

Port of Dover

Arrival at a Glance: As it's a long walk into town (30 minutes or more), take an affordable shuttle bus or a taxi into downtown or up to the castle. From downtown, it's an easy 15-minute walk to the train station for trains to London (1.5 hours) or Canterbury (20-30 minutes).

Port Overview

Little Dover has a huge port, and cruises put in at its far western edge—at the **Western Docks,** along the extremely long Admiralty Pier. Near the port gate at the base of the pier, Terminal 1 is a converted old railway station; farther out at the tip, Terminal 2 is a modern facility. For more info, see www.doverport.co.uk.

Tourist Information: There's no TI at the cruise terminal, but the shuttle bus drops you near one that is inside the Dover Museum.

GETTING INTO TOWN
(AND THE TRAIN STATION)

Since the walk into Dover is long and dull, I'd spring for a taxi or reasonably priced shuttle bus into town or to the castle. To reach the train station, you'll either take the shuttle downtown, then walk 15 minutes; or take a taxi straight there. To **return to your ship,** just reverse the directions given below.

To Dover

By Taxi: In this small town, taxis are reasonable (about £8 to Market Square, the train station, or the castle). Most taxis take credit cards, as well as British pounds and US dollars. Taxis are standing by, or you can call Unity Cars (01304/204-040), Dover Club Travel (01304/204-420), or Longleys (for Canterbury or airports only, book at 01227/710-777).

The hourly rate is about £30. Expect to pay the following rates (one-way): To downtown London or Heathrow Airport–£180; Gatwick Airport–£150; Canterbury–£30-40.

LONDON

Services in Dover

There aren't many services at the port itself, but if you make your way to Market Square, you'll find the following:

ATMs: Several ATMs are on or near Market Square and Cannon Street/Biggin Street.

Wi-Fi: Eateries and cafés in town (Costa Coffee, McDonald's) have Wi-Fi.

Pharmacy: The most convenient is Boots, next door to Costa Coffee, two blocks up Cannon Street/Biggin Street from Market Square (Mon-Sat 8:00-17:30, Sun 10:00-16:00).

By Shuttle Bus: When cruise ships are in port, YMS Travel runs a blue shuttle bus into town from the terminals (10-minute trip). There are three stops: first at Market Square (in the heart of town, next to the TI and a 15-minute walk from the train station); and then up at the castle and the White Cliffs of Dover Visitor Centre. If you don't have British pounds, you can pay in dollars or euros (£5/€7/$8 one-way into town; add £1/€1/$2 to continue up to the castle and cliffs; tel. 01227/456-331, www.ymstravel.co.uk).

From the **Market Square** bus stop, walk straight ahead a few steps and curl around to the left into the square. The TI and Dover Museum are just to your left. The main drag, Cannon Street—which becomes Biggin Street—begins across the square from the TI.

To Canterbury or London by Train

The **Dover Priory** train station is about a 15-minute walk from Market Square. First, head up Cannon Street (directly across from the TI), and follow it for three blocks. Just after passing Costa Coffee and Boots pharmacy, and just before the street becomes cobbled and traffic-free, turn left onto Priory Street. After a short block, you'll come to a big roundabout; circle around the right and use the crosswalks to go more or less straight through it. On the far side of the roundabout, continue slightly uphill on Folkestone Road; a half-block after the gas station, watch for *Dover Priory* signs on the right marking the station.

Trains depart for **Canterbury** twice hourly; some are direct (16 minutes), while others make a few stops en route (27 minutes; for either, fares are £8.30 "single"/one-way, £8.50 "day return"/same-day round trip). These trains stop at the Canterbury East Station.

To reach **London,** choose between the high-speed train to St. Pancras Station (2/hour, 1.5 hours, change at Ashford; £40.50 one-way or off-peak same-day return, £74 anytime return) or the slower train direct to Victoria Station or Charing Cross Station (1-2/hour, 2 hours; around £36 one-way or off-peak same-day return). When choosing which train to take, consider this: St. Pancras and Victoria stations are both well-connected to any point in the city by Tube (subway) or bus (and St. Pancras is right next to the British Library), while Charing Cross is within easy walking distance of Trafalgar Square, National Gallery, West End, Whitehall, and Houses of Parliament—so the extra time spent on that train could save you some time commuting to your sightseeing in London.

Returning to Your Ship: There's no direct public-transit option to the ship from Dover Priory station. Either take a taxi, or walk to Market Square and catch the cruise shuttle bus (described earlier).

Dover

Dover—like much of southern England—sits on a foundation of chalk. Miles of cliffs stand at attention above the beaches; the most famous are the White Cliffs of Dover. Sitting above those cliffs is the impressive Dover Castle, England's primary defensive stronghold from Roman through modern times. From the nearby port, ferries, hydrofoils, and hovercrafts shuttle people and goods back and forth across the English Channel. France is only 23 miles away—on a sunny day, you can see it off in the distance.

PLANNING YOUR TIME

Dover's run-down town center isn't worth a second look. But you can fill the better part of a day in Dover if you linger at the castle or cliffs. Better yet, for a busy but satisfying day, make a quick trip up to Dover Castle, then ride the train just 20-30 minutes to pleasant Canterbury for the afternoon (see the Canterbury section, later in this chapter). The **TI** is inside the Dover Museum, on Market Square (Mon-Sat 9:30-17:00, Sun 10:00-15:00 except closed Sun Oct-March, tel. 01304/201-066, www.whitecliffscountry.org.uk).

Dover Castle: If you do both of the guided tours at the Secret Wartime Tunnels, as well as touring the Great Tower and hiking around the battlements, this could easily take 4-5 hours; if you're in a rush, do only the Operation Dynamo tour and sprint through the tower (allow 2 hours).

White Cliffs: There are a number of ways to get a good look at these famous cliffs, from an easy walk out the Prince of Wales Pier, to a harbor cruise (allow an hour for either), to a trip to a viewpoint farther from town (allow 2-3 hours).

Sights in Dover

▲▲DOVER CASTLE

Strategically located Dover Castle—considered "the key to England" by would-be invaders—perches grandly atop the White

Cliffs of Dover. English troops were garrisoned within the castle's medieval walls for almost 900 years, protecting the coast from European invaders. With a medieval Great Tower as its centerpiece and battlements that survey 360 degrees of windswept coast, Dover Castle has undeniable majesty. While the historic parts of the castle are unexceptional, the exhibits in the WWII-era Secret Wartime Tunnels are unique and engaging—particularly the powerful, well-presented tour that tells the story of Operation Dynamo, the harrowing WWII rescue operation that saved the British Army at Dunkirk.

Cost and Hours: £20, £51 family ticket; April-Sept daily 10:00-18:00, from 9:30 in Aug; Oct daily until 17:00; Nov-March Sat-Sun until 16:00, closed Mon-Fri; last entry and last tour departures one hour before closing.

Information: Tel. 01304/211-067, www.english-heritage.org.uk/dovercastle.

Getting There: The easiest way to the castle is by taxi or shuttle bus from the cruise port (both options explained earlier).

Entrances: Two entry gates have kiosks where you can buy your ticket and pick up a helpful map. The Canons Gate is closer to the Secret Wartime Tunnels, at the lower end of the castle, while the Constable's Gate is near the Great Tower, at the top of the castle.

Crowd Alert: Summer weekends and holidays can be very crowded (especially around late morning). But the biggest potential headaches are lines for the two tours of the Secret Wartime Tunnels: the Operation Dynamo exhibit (with the worst wait) and the Underground Hospital. When you buy your ticket, get advice on timing your tunnel visits smartly.

Planning Your Time: The key is timing the two Secret Wartime Tunnels tours—Operation Dynamo (often with a longer wait) and Underground Hospital. Each tour allows 30 people to enter at a time, with departures every 10-15 minutes. The two tours are next to each other. You'll see a line outside each door.

If you're early on a busy day, go directly to the Operation Dynamo tour. It makes sense to do this tour first: It's a better tour and

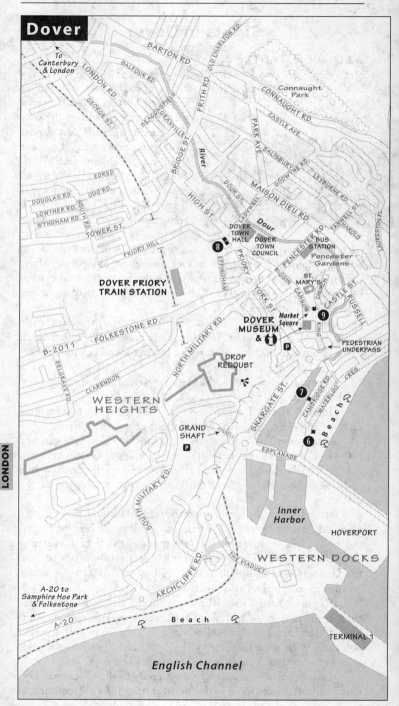

Dover

To Canterbury & London

BARTON RD

LONDON RD

GEORGE ST

BALFOUR RD

BEACONSFIELD

GRANVILLE ST

BRIDGE ST

FRITH RD

OLD CHARLTON RD

Connaught Park

CONNAUGHT RD

CASTLE AVE

PARK AVE

SALISBURY RD

GODWYNE RD

LEYBURNE RD

TASWELL ST

EDRED

DOUGLAS RD

LOWTHER RD

ODO RD

SOUTH RD

WYNDHAM RD

TOWER ST.

River

HIGH ST

DOUR ST.

LADYWELL

Dour

MAISON DIEU RD.

PRIORY HILL

EFFINGHAM

PENCESTER RD.

BUS STATION

Pencester Gardens

LAURESTON PL

DOVER PRIORY TRAIN STATION

DOVER TOWN HALL

DOVER TOWN COUNCIL

PRIORY

YORK ST

BIGGIN

CANNON

ST. MARY'S CH.

CHURCH

CASTLE ST.

RUSSELL ST

8

FOLKESTONE RD.

B-2011

NORTH MILITARY RD.

DOVER MUSEUM & ℹ

Market Square

KING

9

PEDESTRIAN UNDERPASS

BELGRAVE RD

CLARENDON

DROP REDOUBT

P

CAMBRIDGE RD.

WATERLOO CRES.

WESTERN HEIGHTS

SNARGATE ST.

7

Beach

GRAND SHAFT

P

ESPLANADE

6

SOUTH MILITARY RD.

Inner Harbor

HOVERPORT

A-20 to Samphire Hoe Park & Folkestone

ARCHCLIFFE RD.

THE VIADUCT

WESTERN DOCKS

A-20

Beach

TERMINAL 1

English Channel

LONDON

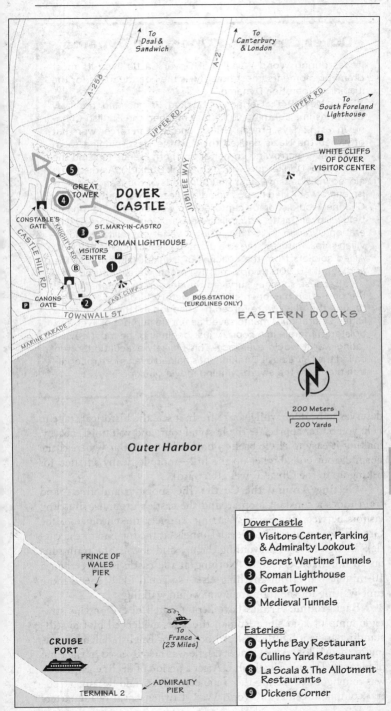

Dover Castle and Operation Dynamo

It was during World War II that Dover Castle lived its most dramatic moments, most notably as the headquarters for the inspiring Operation Dynamo.

In May 1940, Germany attacked France and the Low Countries in a lightning strike that reached the English Channel in just 12 days. French, British, and Belgian forces were cut off when the Nazis flanked them to the west, pinning them into an ever-narrowing corner of northern France (around the port city of Dunkerque, which Brits call Dunkirk). As the Nazis closed in, it became clear that hundreds of thousands of British and other Allied troops being squeezed against the English Channel would soon be captured—or worse. From the tunnels below Dover Castle, Admiral Sir Bertram Ramsay oversaw Operation Dynamo. In 10 days, using a variety of military and civilian ships, Ramsay staged a dramatic evacuation of 338,000 Allied soldiers from the beaches of Dunkirk (although at the end about 40,000 troops, mostly French, were captured).

Because so many survived the desperate circumstances, the operation has been called a "victory in defeat." And although the Allies were forced to abandon northern France to Hitler, Operation Dynamo saved an untold number of lives and bolstered morale in a country just beginning the most devastating war it would ever face. This unlikely evacuation, often called the "Miracle at Dunkirk," has gained even more recognition thanks to the award-winning movie *Dunkirk*.

---

deserves to be done while you're fresh; it sets the historical stage to help you better appreciate the hospital tour; and you finish nearby, making it easy to circle back to do the hospital tour (whereas the hospital tour ends higher up the hill—more logically situated for hiking up to the Great Tower afterward).

Getting Around the Castle: The sporadic and free "land train" does a constant loop around the castle's grounds, shuttling visitors between the Secret Wartime Tunnels, the entrance to the Great Tower, and the Medieval Tunnels (at the top end of the castle). Though handy for avoiding the ups and downs, the train runs on an unreliable schedule. Nothing at the castle is more than a 10-minute walk from anything else—so you'll likely spend more time waiting for the train than you would walking.

Background: Armies have kept a watchful eye on this strategic lump of land since Roman times (as evidenced by the still-standing ancient lighthouse). A linchpin for English defense starting in the Middle Ages, Dover Castle was heavily used in the time of Henry VIII and Elizabeth I. After a period of decline, the castle was reinvigorated during the Napoleonic Wars and became a central command center in World War II (when naval headquarters were buried deep in the cliffside). The tunnels were also used as a hospital and triage station for injured troops. After the war, in the 1960s, the tunnels were converted into a dramatic Cold War bunker—one of 12 designated sites in the UK that would house government officials and a BBC studio in the event of nuclear war. When it became clear that even the stout cliffs of Dover couldn't be guaranteed to stand up to a nuclear attack, Dover Castle was retired from active duty in 1984.

OTHER SIGHTS IN DOVER

▲Dover Museum

This museum, at the TI on Dover's main square, houses an amazing artifact: a large and well-preserved 3,500-year-old Bronze Age

boat unearthed near Dover's shoreline. It's displayed on the top floor along with other finds from the archaeological site, an exhibit on boat construction techniques, and a brief film. Nearby, an exhibit in one big room (the Dover History Gallery) tells the story of how this small but strategically located town has shaped history—from Tudor times to the Napoleonic era to World War II. The ground floor has exhibits covering the Roman and Anglo-Saxon periods.

Cost and Hours: Free, Mon-Sat 9:30-17:00, Sun 10:00-15:00 except closed Sun in Oct-March; tel. 01304/201-066, www.dovermuseum.co.uk.

Prince of Wales Pier

If it's a sunny day and you want a nice view of the cliffs and castle without heading out of town, stroll to the western end of the beachfront promenade (to the right, as you face the water), then hike out along the Prince of Wales Pier for perfect panoramas back toward the city.

Cost and Hours: Free, daily 8:00-dusk.

Boat Tours

The famous White Cliffs of Dover are almost impossible to appreciate from town. A 1.5-hour White Cliffs and Beyond boat tour around the bay gives you all the photo ops you need. You'll ride in a rigid inflatable boat that leaves from the Dover Sea Sports Centre (beach side), on the western end of the waterfront promenade.

Cost and Hours: £35, two or more tours per day—smart to book ahead (max 12 people/boat), tel. 01304/212-880, www.doverseasafari.co.uk.

Eating in Dover

My first two listings are on or near the beachfront promenade. The castle's two cafés work fine for lunch.

$$$ Hythe Bay Restaurant is your best yacht club-style fish restaurant. It's literally built over the beach with a modern dining room, nice views, and a reputation for the best fish in town—including award-winning fish-and-chips (daily 12:00-21:30, The Esplanade, tel. 01304/207-740, www.hythebay.co.uk/dover.htm—if reserving, ask for window seat with a view).

$$$ Cullins Yard Restaurant is a quirky, family-friendly microbrewery with a playful, international menu ranging from pasta, salads, and *panini* to fish-and-chips. Choose between picnic tables on the harbor or the shipwreck interior (daily 11:00-21:30, 11 Cambridge Road, tel. 01304/211-666).

$$$ La Scala is tiny, romantic, and serves a good variety of Italian dishes (Mon-Sat 12:00-14:00 & 18:00-22:00, closed Sun, 19 High Street, tel. 01304/208-044).

$$ The Allotment is trying to bring class to this ruddy town, with an emphasis on locally sourced ingredients (in Brit-speak, an "allotment" is like a community garden). The rustic-chic interior feels a bit like an upscale deli, and there's a charming patio out back. They serve a traditional afternoon tea on vintage crockery (Tue-Sat 9:00-21:30, Sun 12:00-16:00, closed Mon, 9 High Street, tel. 01304/214-467).

$ Dickens Corner, on the main square, is a folksy diner with a tearoom above the ground floor. Note that dining upstairs gets you the same menu and prices but with table service and a great view overlooking the square (yummy "jacket potatoes," Mon-Sat 8:00-16:45, closed Sun, 7 Market Square, tel. 01304/206-692).

Canterbury

Canterbury—an easy train ride from Dover (less than 30 minutes away)—is one of England's most important religious destinations. For centuries, it has welcomed hordes of pilgrims to its grand cathedral and abbey. Pleasant, walkable Canterbury, like many cities in southern England, was originally founded by the pagan Romans. Later, as Christianity became more established in England, Canterbury became its center, and the Archbishop of Canterbury emerged as one of the country's most powerful men. The

famous pilgrimages to Canterbury increased in the 12th century, after the assassination of Archbishop Thomas Becket by followers of King Henry II (with whom Becket had been in a long feud). Becket was canonized as a martyr, rumors of miracles at the cathedral spread, and flocks of pilgrims showed up at its doorstep. Today, much of the medieval city—heavily bombed during World War II—exists only in fragments. Miraculously, the cathedral and surrounding streets are fairly well-preserved. Thanks to its huge student population and thriving pedestrian-and-shopper-friendly zone in the center, Canterbury is an exceptionally livable and fun-to-visit town.

PLANNING YOUR TIME

On a quick visit to Canterbury, head straight for the cathedral and then consider doing my Canterbury Walk. Afterward, spend any extra time you might have strolling the town's pleasant pedestrian core. Allow 4-5 hours, including the round-trip train ride.

Orientation to Canterbury

With about 40,000 people (plus 30,000 when its four universities are in session), Canterbury is big enough to be lively but small enough to be manageable. The walkable town center is enclosed by the old city walls and cut in two by its main drag, High Street (called St. Peter's Street at one end and St. George's Street at the other). During the day, the action is on High Street and in the knot of medieval lanes surrounding the cathedral.

Tourist Information: The TI, housed in the atrium of the Beaney House of Art and Knowledge, assists modern-day pilgrims. Pick up the free *Visitors Guide* with a map and buy a ticket for the walking tour, described later (Mon-Sat 9:00-17:00, Thu until 19:00, Sun 10:00-17:00, on High Street, free Wi-Fi, second entrance past the pasty shop on Best Lane, tel. 01227/862-162, www.canterbury.co.uk).

Arrival in Canterbury: Trains from Dover arrive at Canterbury's East Station, about a 10-minute walk or £5 taxi ride from the center.

Guided Walk: Canterbury Tourist Guides offer a 1.5-hour walk departing from Buttermarket, the square opposite the cathedral entrance (£7.50, buy ticket at TI; daily at 11:00, April-Sept also at 14:00, www.canterburyguidedtours.com, tel. 01227/459-779).

Shopping: A **Marks & Spencer** department store, with a supermarket at the back on the ground floor, is located near the east end of High Street (Mon-Sat 8:00-19:00, Sun 11:00-17:00, tel. 01227/462-281). Sprawling behind it is the vast **Whitefriars**

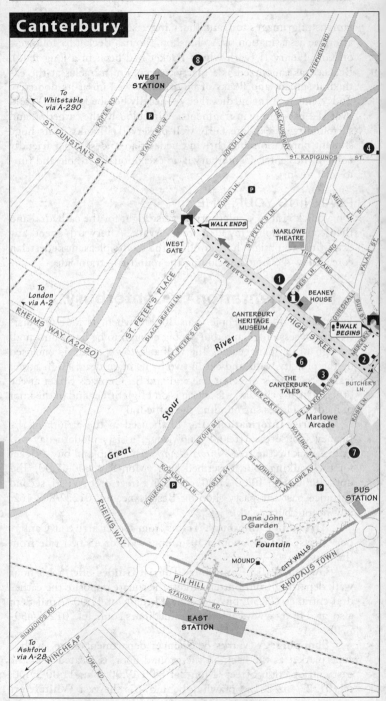

Canterbury

To Whitstable via A-290

WEST STATION

8

ST. STEPHEN'S RD.

THE CAUSEWAY

ST. RADIGUNDS ST.

4

ROPER RD.

STATION RD. V.

ST. DUNSTAN'S ST.

NORTH LN.

POUND LN.

MILL LN.

ST. PETER'S LN.

P

P

WALK ENDS

WEST GATE

MARLOWE THEATRE

THE FRIARS

KING ST.

PALACE ST.

ST. PETER'S ST.

BEST LN.

GUILDHALL ST.

SUN ST.

1

Beaney House

WALK BEGINS

To London via A-2

ST. PETER'S PLACE

BLACK GRIFFIN LN.

ST. PETER'S GR.

CANTERBURY HERITAGE MUSEUM

HIGH STREET

MERCERY LN.

RHEIMS WAY (A2050)

River

Stour

6

3

THE CANTERBURY TALES

ST. MARGARET'S ST.

2

BUTCHERY LN.

ROSE LN.

Great

BEER CART LN.

STOUR ST.

Marlowe Arcade

WATLING ST.

7

ROSEMARY LN.

CHURCH LN.

CASTLE ST.

ST. JOHN'S ST.

MARLOWE AV.

P

BUS STATION

RHEIMS WAY

Dane John Garden

Fountain

MOUND

CITY WALLS

RHODAUS TOWN

PIN HILL

STATION RD. E.

EAST STATION

SIMMONDS RD.

To Ashford via A-28

WINCHEAP

YORK RD.

LONDON

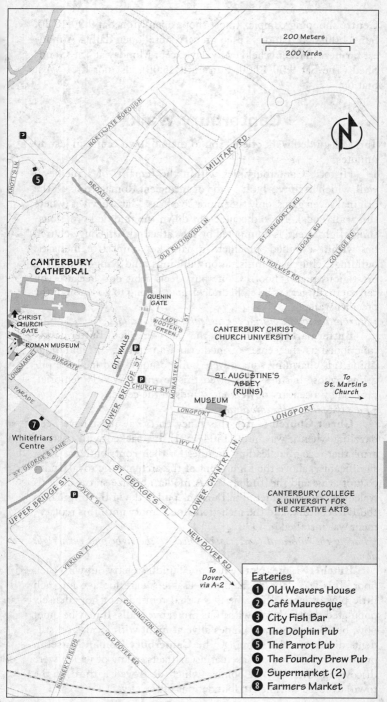

200 Meters
200 Yards

N

NORTHGATE BOROUGH

MILITARY RD.

KNOTT'S LN.

BROAD ST.

OLD RUTTINGTON LN.

ST. GREGORY'S RD.

EDGAR RD.

COLLEGE RD.

N. HOLMES RD.

CANTERBURY
CATHEDRAL

QUENIN
GATE

LADY
WOOTEN'S
GREEN

CANTERBURY CHRIST
CHURCH UNIVERSITY

CHRIST
CHURCH
GATE

ROMAN MUSEUM

CITY WALLS

BURGATE

LONGMARKET

PARADE

CHURCH ST.

LOWER BRIDGE ST.

MONASTERY ST.

ST. AUGUSTINE'S
ABBEY
(RUINS)

MUSEUM

LONGPORT

LONGPORT

To
St. Martin's
Church

IVY LN.

Whitefriars
Centre

ST. GEORGE'S LANE

ST. GEORGE'S PL.

LOWER CHANTRY LN.

CANTERBURY COLLEGE
& UNIVERSITY FOR
THE CREATIVE ARTS

UPPER BRIDGE ST.

LOVER ST.

VERNON PL.

NEW DOVER RD.

COSSINGTON RD.

OLD DOVER RD.

NUNNERY FIELDS

To
Dover
via A-2

Eateries

1 Old Weavers House
2 Café Mauresque
3 City Fish Bar
4 The Dolphin Pub
5 The Parrot Pub
6 The Foundry Brew Pub
7 Supermarket (2)
8 Farmers Market

LONDON

Centre shopping complex (most shops open Mon-Sat 9:00-18:30, Sun 11:00-17:00) and a **Tesco** grocery store (open daily). A modest **farmers market** is held every day except Monday at The Goods Shed (Tue-Sat 9:00-19:00, Sun until 16:00), just north of West Station.

Canterbury Walk

This self-guided walk orients you to the old town center in just 30 minutes.

Historic Canterbury lies within the remains of a medieval wall, which itself was built on top of an ancient Roman wall. Of the original seven gates, only the impressive West Gate survives (where this walk ends). The old center, cut down the middle by the bustling High Street, is dominated by the cathedral. This huge church lies within a walled "precinct," a parklike complex of monastic buildings, church administration buildings, and King's School (a prestigious prep school). Canterbury feels a bit odd because you can't actually get to the cathedral without paying to go through the precinct wall.

• *Start at the square outside the cathedral grounds called...*

Buttermarket: Originally the dairy market, Buttermarket functioned as the center of medieval Canterbury. The buildings lining this charming square were built to house and feed the pilgrims, whose business supported this town. A WWI memorial, ravaged by a century of weather, stands in the center.

• *Face the entry to the cathedral grounds.*

Christ Church Gate: This fancy entryway must have been dazzling when it was built (1504-1521). It's packed with coats of arms that recognize leading families for their contributions. Most significantly, above the high point of the arch are the royal Tudor coat of arms and the Tudor rose. A modern bronze statue of Jesus welcomes all who enter. The Puritans pulled down the original in the 17th century, and the niche remained empty until this replacement was installed in 1990.

• *Facing the cathedral gate, walk a block to the right and turn right down...*

Butchery Lane: Notice how the buildings jetty out with each floor. This was done to maximize usable square footage for each little plot of land. This lane is a visual reminder of how densely populated the town was within its protective walls. It may be quiet now, but Butchery Lane comes alive at night with locals and students dining and barhopping. The **Canterbury Roman Museum** on this street shows off fascinating artifacts, many of which were discovered after WWII bombs (which destroyed a third of the town) exposed the ancient foundations of the city.

• *When Butchery Lane ends at the next street, turn right onto...*

High Street: This street has a fun energy that could rob your attention and dominate your day. To the left, modern architecture provides a reminder that Canterbury was bombed in World War II. If you stroll the length of High Street, you'll eventually reach the stony West Gate. It's amazing to think that, until the 1960s, the A-2 highway ran through the center of town, bringing all the Dover-London traffic right down today's delightfully pedestrianized High Street.

As you cross a narrow alley called Mercery Lane, you can see that it leads back to Christ Church Gate. The street names hearken back to a time when each street was the site of a special market—similar to departments in today's department stores. Mercery would have been where fine cloth was sold.

Farther down you come to the TI, students hawking their boat tours (both punting and big rowboats that go up and down the River Stour), the Pilgrims' Hospital (at #25, a 12th-century inn built to house pilgrims), and the Old Weavery (with its big windows for looms upstairs and its romantic setting over the River Stour). Your walk ends at the medieval West Gate.

Sights in Canterbury

▲▲▲CANTERBURY CATHEDRAL

One of the most important churches in England, this cathedral is the headquarters of the Anglican Church (something like the English Vatican). There's been a church here ever since St. Augustine, the cathedral's first archbishop, broke ground in 597. In the 12th century, the cathedral's archbishop, Thomas Becket, was murdered in front of the altar. Three years later he became a saint, and Canterbury became a prime destination for religious pilgrims. When Henry VIII broke with the Roman Catholic Church 400 years later, this cathedral became the Anglican version of St. Peter's Basilica. A visit here leaves you impressed by the resilience of this spot—so holy to so many for so long.

Cost and Hours: £12; Easter-Oct Mon-Sat 9:00-17:30, Sun 12:30-14:30; slightly shorter hours Nov-Easter.

Information: Tel. 01227/762-862, www.canterbury-cathedral.org.

Tours: Knowledgeable guides wearing golden sashes are post-

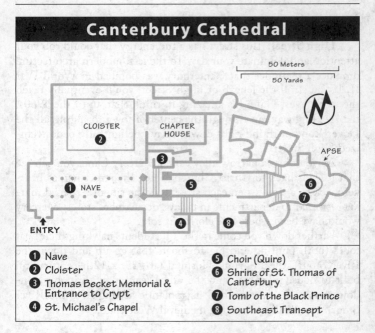

Canterbury Cathedral

50 Meters

50 Yards

CLOISTER ❷

CHAPTER HOUSE

❸

APSE

❶ NAVE

❺

❻

❼

ENTRY

❹

❽

❶ Nave
❷ Cloister
❸ Thomas Becket Memorial & Entrance to Crypt
❹ St. Michael's Chapel

❺ Choir (Quire)
❻ Shrine of St. Thomas of Canterbury
❼ Tomb of the Black Prince
❽ Southeast Transept

ed throughout the cathedral to answer your questions. Guided £5 tours are offered Mon-Sat at 10:30, 12:00, and 14:30 (14:00 in winter); no tours Sun. At the shop inside the cathedral, you can rent an informative £4 audioguide. They also have a handy little brochure called "An American Trail" describing points that are interesting to Americans visiting the cathedral.

❍ **Self-Guided Tour:** It's simple just to wander through the cathedral on your own, using this tour for the basics. There is much to see and learn as you go (take advantage of the volunteer guides).
• *Go through the gate (where you'll buy your ticket) and walk into the courtyard that surrounds this massive church. An information booth (with free maps) is to your right. A small café is just beyond that.*

Cathedral Exterior: Notice that the cathedral seems to be built in two parts—the west is Gothic and the east is in the older Romanesque or Norman style. While it was built in fits and starts, most of what you see was constructed between 1100 and 1400. For me, the interior is far more impressive than the exterior.
• *Enter the church and take a seat at the back of the nave.*

❶ **Nave:** In the year 597, missionaries from Rome converted the king of Kent (this part of England) to Christianity. This was the king's seat of power; since they had his protection, the missionaries established Canterbury as the leading Christian church here in England. Its importance grew as Christianity spread, but the church really boomed after the murder of Thomas Becket in 1170 put it on the pilgrimage trail. To accommodate the steady stream of pilgrims (so important to Canterbury's medieval economy), the church grew bigger and bigger.

When Henry VIII broke with the Catholic Church during the Protestant Reformation, he destroyed the Becket relics, and pilgrims stopped coming. But Henry made this cathedral the leading church of his independent Church of England. Today Canterbury Cathedral is the mother church of the worldwide Anglican Communion, and it remains the seat of its leading bishop, the Archbishop of Canterbury.

Today the church feels like two churches—the Gothic half (where you're sitting), which was for the common people, and the older Romanesque half (beyond the stone "screen," where you find the choir—or "quire" in British English), reserved exclusively for the community of Benedictine monks and church VIPs who ran the place.

The nave was once slathered in Catholic ornamentation—lots of ornate chapels, painted walls, and more stained glass. But with Henry VIII and the Reformation, the church's many chapels dedicated to various saints and wealthy families were cleared out. And then, after England's Civil War in the 1640s, came the more extreme Puritans. The Puritans made the building even more stern—whitewashing the paintings and purging the interior of its Gothic finery.

Behind you, notice the fine **West Window** portraying 13 of Christ's ancestors. The bottom two rows are mostly original, 12th-century stained glass. Looking ahead on the left side of the nave, notice also the **Victorian pulpit** carved and painted in the Gothic Revival style (1898). At the top of each hour a priest recites a welcome and a prayer from here, reminding all visitors that this place of worship is holy and alive.

All of this could have been lost during World War II. The city was heavily bombed on several occasions, but heroic "fire-watchers" with long-handled shovels kept German incendiary bombs from destroying the building (like their counterparts on the rooftop of St. Paul's in London). A round **plaque** in the floor (center rear of nave) remembers these heroic men.

• *Exit the nave through the large wooden door to your left, and turn right into the...*

❷ **Cloister:** Although Henry VIII ended the Benedictine order in England in 1540, you can still get a good sense of the old monastery complex by strolling through the cloister. Notice the ceiling, speckled with 800 family crests. Just as today we put names on bricks to recognize private contributions to a building project, these shields thanked wealthy medieval families for helping fund this amazing edifice.

• *Return to the nave and follow the route laid out by the map you picked up when you entered. Head up the left aisle. When you get to the choir (marked by a beautifully carved stone screen in the center of the nave), go down the stairs to your left (signs point to The Martyrdom). Immediately to your right is the...*

❸ **Thomas Becket Memorial:** This is where, in 1170, Thomas Becket was martyred. You'll see a humble plaque in the floor below a dramatic sculpture of two swords pointing to the place where he died (the shadows make it look like there are two more swords—fitting since there were four murderers). In 1982, Pope John Paul II knelt at the place of Becket's murder and prayed with the Archbishop of Canterbury—the first visit ever by a pope to England. Notice the tunnel to your right. Built in the 15th century, this allowed for the steady flow of pilgrims to go under the altar to visit the site of the martyrdom without disturbing the worship service above.

• *Continue down the stairs between the memorial and the tunnel to enter the...*

Crypt: Notice the heavy stone arches. This lower section was started by the Normans, who probably built on top of St. Augustine's original wooden church from about A.D. 600. (If the door is open on the left, a ramp leads to a garden surrounded by the remains of the Benedictine monastic community and the sprawling green of King's School—a private boarding school across the way.)

The far end of the crypt is newer; it's Gothic rather than Romanesque and therefore has higher ceilings and more light. Hanging from the ceiling is a modern statue—a body made of rusty nails from the church's rooftop. Becket's tomb rested in the crypt from 1170 until 1220, and the spot became famous as a place of many miracles.

• *Continuing clockwise, circle back toward the stairway leading out of the crypt. On the left is a small chapel marked Église Protestante Française.*

Huguenot Chapel: This space is literally a church within a church. For 300 years this chapel has been used by the French (Huguenot) Protestant community, who fled persecution in their homeland for the more welcoming atmosphere in Protestant England. There's a service in French every Sunday at 15:00. The plaque

Thomas Becket and Canterbury Cathedral

In the 12th century, Canterbury Cathedral had already been a Christian church for more than 500 years. The king at the time, Henry II, was looking for a new archbishop, someone who would act as a yes-man and allow him to gain control of the Church (and its followers). He found a candidate in his drinking buddy and royal chancellor: Thomas Becket (also called Thomas à Becket). In 1162, the king had his friend made a priest one day and consecrated as archbishop the next.

But Becket respected his holy office—surprising the king, and maybe even himself. Inspired by his new position—and wanting to be a true religious leader to his vast flock—he cleaned up his act, became dedicated to the religious tenets of the Church (dressing as a monk), and refused to bow to the king's wishes. As tensions grew, Henry wondered aloud, "Will no one rid me of this turbulent priest?" Four knights took his words seriously, and assassinated Becket with their swords during vespers in the cathedral. The act shocked the medieval world. King Henry later submitted to walking barefoot through town and to being flogged by priests as an act of pious penitence.

Not long after Becket's death in 1170, word spread that miracles were occurring in the cathedral, prompting the pope to canonize Becket. Soon the pilgrims came, hoping some of St. Thomas Becket's steadfast goodness would rub off (perhaps they also wanted to see the world—just like travelers today).

declares that providing refuge against religious oppression and tyranny is just as important in the 21st century as it was 300 years ago.

• *Facing this chapel, turn right, walk to the end of the crypt, and climb up the stairs. Turn left to find...*

❹ **St. Michael's Chapel:** Also known as the Warrior's Chapel, this was built by Lady Margaret Holland to house family tombs. (She died in 1439 and lies in the middle between two of her husbands.) The chapel is also associated with the Royal East Kent Regiment ("The Buffs"). Notice the fragile old military flags adorning the walls.

• *Turning to the center of the church, climb the seven steps ahead of you and stand directly under the bell tower.*

Bell Harry Tower: Built in 1503, this tower reaches 190 feet high. (It's named for the church's biggest bell, cast in the early 1600s.) Bend back and look way, way up at the fine fan vaulting at the highest point. The white cross in the center is called a "hatch." Five hundred years ago, above that hatch, was a human-powered treadmill used for hoisting stones during construction. Do a 360-degree spin and appreciate all the fine stonework here. Imagine the effort needed to build this. Even though it was made of bricks rather than heavier stone, the columns supporting it weren't strong enough. Around you are several "strainer arches" retrofitted to give the tower extra support.

❺ **Choir:** Facing east, enjoy the impressive 15th-century **choir screen**—the finely carved wall that separated the public part of the church (behind you) from the

monks' zone (the intimate central choir, through the arched doorway). Statues of six kings decorate the screen. Flanking the door are King Ethelbert (left) with the church in his hand—a reminder that he gave the land for this church in 597, and Edward the Confessor (right)—who was both a saint and an English king. The stone chair to the right was for a guard who made sure the public stayed out of the monastic half.

If the chair's empty, step into the choir and the vast, older half of the church. Opening before you is the monk's world. (You can sit in these venerable chairs to enjoy a musical evensong service.)

This part of the church is mostly Romanesque on the outside, but because a fire gutted the interior, the decoration you see is mostly Gothic. **St. Augustine's Chair,** which sits like a throne beyond the high altar, dates from the 13th century. It's a reminder that this church is the seat of the bishop—in fact, the leading bishop of all Anglican bishops.

• *Walk toward the high altar. Leave the choir through a gate on the left and turn right, passing photos of WWII damage to the town. Continue up the stairs to the far end (apse) behind the high altar, where you'll see a candle in the center of the floor. This was the site of the...*

❻ **Shrine of St. Thomas of Canterbury:** Beginning in the 12th century, hundreds of thousands of pilgrims came to worship the relics of Becket and to leave offerings. Originally his tomb was in the crypt, but it was moved here in 1220 to improve access for the countless pilgrims. Imagine this site in the Middle Ages. You're surrounded by humble, devout travelers who've trudged miles upon miles to reach this spot. Now that they've finally arrived, they're hoping to soak up just a bit of the miraculous power that's supposed to reside here.

Then came King Henry VIII, who broke away from the pope so he could run his affairs without the Church's meddling. In 1538, he destroyed the original shrine. Dictatorial Henry VIII—no fan of a priest so loved for standing up to a king—had Thomas Becket's body removed. Legend says that to end the pilgrim traffic here, Henry had Becket's bones burned and the ashes scattered. It worked.

The chapel at the far east end of the church once held another Becket relic—his head. It's now dedicated to "saints and martyrs of our own time"—people who have given their lives for their Christian faith. Page through the binders on either side of the entrance to review the stories of these inspirational pillars of faith. If so moved, light a candle.

• *Enjoy the 800-year-old windows—the best in the church—all around you. Then follow the curve of the apse about 20 steps to a fancy tomb with a fancy set of armor.*

❼ **Tomb of the Black Prince:** Marked by a famous sculpture on his tomb, this is the final resting place of the Black Prince, Edward of Woodstock (d. 1376). The Prince of Wales and the eldest son of Edward III, the Black Prince was famous for his cunning in battle and his chivalry—the original "knight in shining armor." Look for a nearby glass case on the wall containing his actual armor used in the 1376 funeral procession.

• *Head downstairs and make your way to the...*

❽ **Southeast Transept:** The stained-glass windows in the transept are refreshingly modern, created by Hungarian-born artist and refugee Ervin Bossányi, who was commissioned by the Dean of Canterbury to replace earlier windows damaged by WWII bombs. The themes are "Salvation" (left) and "Peace Among the Nations" (with Jesus blessing all different races, on the right).

Our tour is finished. As you leave the cathedral, consider this: Even with all their power, wealth, and influence, two English kings were unable to successfully eradicate Thomas Becket's influence. A man of conscience—who once stood up to the most powerful ruler in England—continues to inspire visitors, nearly a thousand years after his death.

Eating in Canterbury

As a student town, Canterbury is packed with eateries—especially along the pedestrianized shopping zone and around the cathedral.

$$$ Old Weavers House serves solid English food in a pleasant, historic building next to the river. Sit inside beneath sunny walls and creaky beams, or outside on their riverside patio under a leafy canopy. This is the most atmospheric of my listings, but it can feel touristy and be very busy (daily 12:00-23:00, 1 St. Peter's Street, tel. 01227/464-660).

$$$ Café Mauresque is a tasty alternative to the pub scene. It offers a variety of Spanish and Moroccan tapas, platters, and *tagines* in an inviting setting with authentic Moroccan decor. If the place looks full, ask about additional seating upstairs (daily 12:00-21:30, reservations smart on weekends, 8 Butchery Lane, tel. 01227/464-300, www.cafemauresque.co.uk).

$ City Fish Bar is your quintessential British "chippy," serving several kinds of fried fish. Get yours for takeaway or grab a sidewalk table on this charming pedestrian street (Mon-Sat 10:00-19:00, Sun until 16:00, 30 St. Margaret's Street, tel. 01227/760-873).

$$ The Dolphin Pub, a local favorite, is a homey 1930s pub with carefully chosen ales. The food is a cut above typical pub grub and burgers, with quality local ingredients and daily specials. Sit in the main bar, in the sunroom, or—in nice weather—at a picnic table in the grassy garden. It's easy to imagine local professors hanging out here (food served daily 12:00-14:00 & 18:00-21:00, Thu-Sat until 22:00, bar open later; 17 St. Radigunds Street, tel. 01227/455-963).

$$$ The Parrot Pub claims to be the oldest pub in town. It feels it, with a creaky ground floor and a kingly dining hall upstairs under lumbering timbers (same menu and cost). Perhaps less intimate and more formulaic than its neighbors, the food is highly regarded. Their specialties: hearty burgers and fajita-like "sizzlers" (daily 12:00-21:30, 1 Church Lane, tel. 01227/454-170).

$$ The Foundry Brew Pub offers up to 16 home brews on tap and serves beer-inspired dishes like steak-and-ale pie and BBQ beer ribs. Bartenders happily pour generous samples for curious customers (with the intent of selling you a pint) and explain the inspiration behind the name of their signature draft, Torpedo. This cozy beer lovers' hangout offers a fun sampler of three small meat pies and three small beers for only £12 (food served daily 12:00-18:00, Wed-Sat until 20:00, bar open later, White Horse Lane, tel. 01227/455-899).

London

London, which has long attracted tourists, seems perpetually at your service, with an impressive slate of sights, entertainment, and eateries, all linked by a great transit system. With just a few hours here, you'll get no more than a quick splash in this teeming human tidal pool. But with a good orientation, you'll find London manageable and fun.

Blow through the city on a double-decker bus or take a pinch-me-I'm-in-London walk through the West End. Gawk at the crown jewels at the Tower of London, gaze up at Big Ben, or see the Houses of Parliament in action. Cruise the Thames River, or take a spin on the London Eye. Hobnob with poets' tombstones in Westminster Abbey, or visit with Leonardo, Botticelli, and Rembrandt in the National Gallery. Whisper across the dome of St. Paul's Cathedral, or rummage through our civilization's attic at the British Museum. Sip your tea with pinky raised and clotted cream dribbling down your scone.

PLANNING YOUR TIME

The sights of London alone could easily fill a trip to Great Britain. But you may only have a few hours...so you'll need to be very selective. I've clustered sights geographically and listed them roughly in the order of priority for a first-time visitor who just wants a taste.

With limited time, it may be folly to focus too tightly on any particular sight. Consider instead a **hop-on, hop-off bus tour** to get your bearings in this grand and sprawling metropolis. For suggested companies, see page 916.

Westminster: For the best single-day visit to London, focus on the big, famous sights on and near Whitehall. Begin by dipping into **Westminster Abbey** (allow an hour) and consider visiting the **Houses of Parliament.** Follow my self-guided **Westminster Walk** up Whitehall (30 minutes)—possibly poking into the **Churchill War Rooms** (history buffs will want at least an hour)—to reach Trafalgar Square. Here you can pop in to the **National Gallery** and/or the **National Portrait Gallery** (allow an hour each). Or, to get a look at nonmuseum London, stroll behind the National Gallery to explore London's famously trendy and lively **"West End"** (allow an hour or more just to wander here). With time to spare, you could hook around to see the exterior of **Buckingham Palace.** The options noted here will more than eat up your London time—pick and choose your museum and church visits carefully.

If you'd rather focus on other parts of the city, consider the next few options.

London Eye: While famous and relatively close to the West-

London's Neighborhoods

minster sights, this gigantic observation wheel is very expensive and can be time-consuming (allow 30 minutes for the ride, plus time waiting in lines).

British Museum: One of the world's best collections of antiquities— from Egyptian mummies to the Rosetta Stone to the Parthenon Frieze—but inconveniently located relative to other places listed here (worth at least two hours).

British Library: This succinct collection of great works of literature can be seen in an hour and is conveniently located next door to St. Pancras Station (with trains to Dover).

St. Paul's Cathedral: It takes about an hour to tour London's biggest church and Christopher Wren's masterpiece (add another hour to climb the dome).

Tower of London: London's original fortress takes about two hours to see (including an entertaining Beefeater tour).

Orientation to London

To grasp London more comfortably, see it as the old town in the city center without the modern, congested sprawl. (Even from that perspective, it's still huge.) The Thames River (pronounced "tems") runs roughly west to east through the city, with most of the visitor's sights on the North Bank.

Central London: This area contains Westminster and what Londoners call the West End. The Westminster district includes Big Ben, Parliament, Westminster Abbey, and Buckingham Palace—the grand government buildings from which Britain is ruled. Trafalgar Square, London's gathering place, has many major museums. The West End is the center of London's cultural life, with bustling squares: Piccadilly Circus and Leicester Square host cinemas, tourist traps, and nighttime glitz. Soho and Covent Garden are thriving people zones with theaters, restaurants, pubs, and boutiques. And Regent and Oxford streets are the city's main shopping zones.

North London: Neighborhoods in this part of town contain such major sights as the British Museum and the overhyped Madame Tussauds Waxworks.

The City: In today's modern financial district, gleaming skyscrapers are interspersed with historical landmarks such as St. Paul's Cathedral. The Tower of London and Tower Bridge lie at The City's eastern border.

East London: Just east of The City is the East End—the former stomping ground of Cockney ragamuffins and Jack the Ripper, and now an increasingly gentrified neighborhood of hipsters, "pop-up" shops, and an emerging food scene.

The South Bank: The South Bank of the Thames River offers major sights (Tate Modern, Shakespeare's Globe, London Eye, Imperial War Museum) linked by a riverside walkway.

West London: This huge area is home to London's wealthy and has many trendy shops and enticing restaurants. Here you'll find a range of museums (Victoria and Albert Museum, Tate Britain, and more), lively Victoria Station, and the vast green expanses of Hyde Park and Kensington Gardens.

TOURIST INFORMATION

You'll see "Tourist Information" offices everywhere, but most are private agencies that make a big profit selling tours and advance sightseeing and/or theater tickets; others are run by Transport for London (TFL) and are primarily focused on providing public-transit advice.

The **City of London Information Centre** next to St. Paul's Cathedral (just outside the church entrance) is the city's only publicly funded—and impartial—"real" TI. It sells Oyster cards, London Passes, and advance "Fast Track" sightseeing tickets, and stocks various free publications, such as the *London Planner* events guide (Mon-Sat 9:30-17:30, Sun 10:00-16:00; Tube: St. Paul's, tel. 020/7332-1456, www.visitthecity.co.uk).

Visit London, which serves the greater London area, doesn't have an office you can visit in person—but does have an info-packed website (www.visitlondon.com).

London Pass: This pass, which covers many big sights and lets you skip some lines, is expensive but potentially worth the investment for extremely busy sightseers. Think through your sightseeing plans, study their website to see what's covered, and do the math before you buy (£69/1 day, £94/2 days; also sold at major train stations and airports, tel. 020/7293-0972, www.londonpass.com).

ARRIVAL IN LONDON

By Train from Southampton: You'll ride to London's **Waterloo Station** (for details, see the "Airport Connections" section at the end of this chapter). The Jubilee Promenade along the South Bank and London Eye are both a short walk from the station. Or you can hop on the Tube to get anywhere in town: As you exit the train, with the tracks to your back, the stop for the Jubilee line is to the right, and the stop for the Northern/Waterloo and Bakerloo lines are to the left.

By Train from Dover: If arriving at **St. Pancras Station,** head down the escalator and go toward the big, glass, modern entryway nearby; you'll find an Underground (Tube) station just inside the door. Alternatively, to reach the British Library or buses, first follow signs for *Euston Station,* then turn left and head all the way down the long main hall, and follow signs for *Way Out* and *Euston Road.* You'll pop out the station's front door along busy Euston Road. Public bus stops are on the road in front of you, and the British Library is a block to your right.

If arriving at **Charing Cross Station,** simply exit the station, turn left along the busy street called The Strand, and you're a short walk from Trafalgar Square—right in the heart of town.

From **Victoria Station,** hop on the Tube; the Circle or District line zips you in two stops to Westminster, where you can exit the Tube station and peer up at Big Ben.

By Shuttle Bus: If you take a **"London On Your Own"** shuttle bus excursion into London from your ship, it will likely drop you off at Piccadilly Circus, in the center of London's bustling West End. From this point, it's an easy 10-minute walk to Trafalgar Square, with the National Gallery and National Portrait Gallery. You can also hop on the Tube; the Piccadilly Circus Tube stop serves the Bakerloo line and the Piccadilly line.

Returning to Southampton or Dover: To make it back to your ship, follow the instructions under "Getting from Central London to the Cruise Ports," on page 966.

HELPFUL HINTS

Theft Alert: Wear your money belt. The Artful Dodger is alive and well in London. Be on guard, particularly on public transportation and in places crowded with tourists, who, considered naive and rich, are targeted. The Changing of the Guard scene is a favorite for thieves. And more than 7,500 purses are stolen annually at Covent Garden alone.

Pedestrian Safety: Cars drive on the left side of the road—which can be as confusing for foreign pedestrians as for foreign drivers. Before crossing a street, I always look right, look left, then look right again just to be sure. Most crosswalks are even painted with instructions, reminding foreign guests to "Look right" or "Look left."

Wi-Fi: Many major museums, sights, and even entire boroughs offer free Wi-Fi access. **O2 Wifi** hotspots let you connect for free in Trafalgar Square, Leicester Square, and Piccadilly (www.o2wifi.co.uk). Or get a free account with **The Cloud,** a Wi-Fi service found in most London train stations and many museums, coffee shops, cafés, and shopping centers. When you sign up at www.skywifi.cloud, you'll be asked to enter a street address and postal code; it doesn't matter which one (use the Queen's: Buckingham Palace, SW1A 1AA). Then use the **Sky WiFi app** to locate hotspots.

Useful Apps: Mapway's free **Tube Map London Underground** and **Bus Times London** (www.mapway.com) apps show the easiest way to connect tube stations and provide bus stops and route information. The handy **Citymapper** app for London covers every mode of public transit in the city. **City Maps 2Go** lets you download searchable offline maps. And **Time Out London**'s free app has reviews and listings for theater, museums, and movies.

GETTING AROUND LONDON

In London, you're never more than a 10-minute walk from a stop on the Underground (the Tube). Buses are also convenient, and taxis are everywhere. For public transit info, see www.tfl.gov.uk.

Tickets and Cards

While London's transit system has nine zones, almost all tourist sights are within Zones 1 and 2, so those are the prices I've listed. For more information, visit www.tfl.gov.uk/tickets. A few odd special passes are available, but for nearly every tourist, the answer is simple: Get the Oyster card and use it.

Individual Tickets: Individual paper tickets for the Tube are ridiculously expensive (£5 per Tube ride). Tickets are sold at any Tube station, either at (often-crowded) ticket windows or at easy-to-use self-service machines (hit "Adult Single" and enter your destination). Tickets are valid only on the day of purchase. But un-

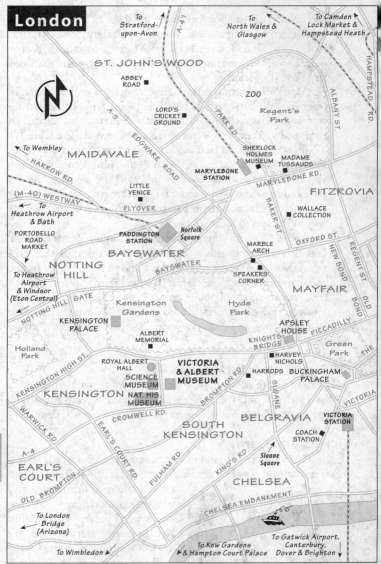

London

To Stratford-upon-Avon

To North Wales & Glasgow

To Camden Lock Market & Hampstead Heath

A-41

HAMPSTEAD RD.

ST. JOHN'S WOOD

ABBEY ROAD

ZOO

Regent's Park

ALBANY ST.

LORD'S CRICKET GROUND

PARK RD.

A-5

EDGWARE ROAD

To Wembley

MAIDAVALE

HARROW RD.

SHERLOCK HOLMES MUSEUM

MADAME TUSSAUDS

MARYLEBONE STATION

MARYLEBONE RD.

FITZROVIA

(M-40) WESTWAY

LITTLE VENICE

BAKER ST.

WALLACE COLLECTION

OXFORD ST.

To Heathrow Airport & Bath

FLYOVER

PADDINGTON STATION

Norfolk Square

MARBLE ARCH

NEW BOND

REGENT ST.

OLD BOND

PORTOBELLO ROAD MARKET

BAYSWATER

BAYSWATER

SPEAKERS CORNER

MAYFAIR

NOTTING HILL

NOTTING HILL GATE

To Heathrow Airport & Windsor (Eton Central)

Kensington Gardens

Hyde Park

APSLEY HOUSE

PICCADILLY

Green Park

THE

Holland Park

KENSINGTON PALACE

ALBERT MEMORIAL

KNIGHTS BRIDGE

HARVEY NICHOLS

ROYAL ALBERT HALL

VICTORIA & ALBERT MUSEUM

HARRODS

BUCKINGHAM PALACE

KENSINGTON HIGH ST.

SCIENCE MUSEUM

NAT. HIS. MUSEUM

BROMPTON RD.

SLOANE

VICTORIA

WARWICK RD.

EARL'S COURT RD.

CROMWELL RD.

SOUTH KENSINGTON

BELGRAVIA

VICTORIA STATION

COACH STATION

A-4

EARL'S COURT

OLD BROMPTON

FULHAM RD.

KING'S RD.

Sloane Square

CHELSEA

To London Bridge (Arizona)

CHELSEA EMBANKMENT

To Wimbledon

To Kew Gardens & Hampton Court Palace

To Gatwick Airport, Canterbury, Dover & Brighton

less you're literally taking only one Tube ride your entire visit, you'll save money (and time) with an Oyster card.

Oyster Card: A pay-as-you-go Oyster card (a plastic card embedded with a microchip) allows you to ride the Tube, buses, and suburban trains for about half the rate of individual tickets. To use it, simply touch the card against the yellow card reader at the turnstile or entrance. It flashes green and the fare is automatically

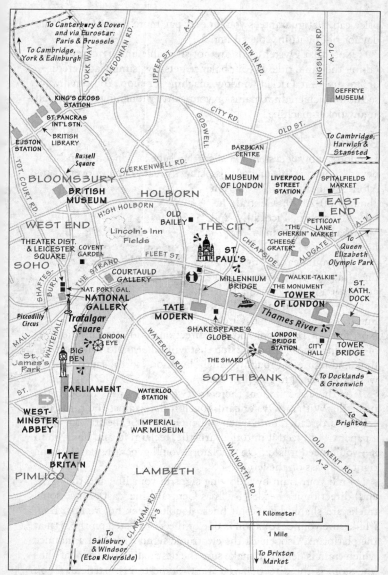

deducted. (You must also tap your card again to "touch out" as you exit the Tube, but not buses.)

Buy the card at any Tube station ticket window, or look for nearby shops displaying the Oyster logo, where you can purchase a card or add credit without the wait. You'll pay a £5 refundable deposit up front, then load it with as much credit as you'll need. One ride in Zones 1 and 2 during peak time costs £2.90; off-peak is a little cheaper (£2.40/ride). The system comes with an automatic price cap that guarantees you'll never pay more than £6.80 in one day for rides within Zones 1 and 2.

Note that Oyster cards are not shareable among companions taking the same ride. If your balance gets low, simply add credit—or "top up"—at a ticket window, machine, or shop. You can always see how much credit remains on your card by touching it to the pad at any ticket machine.

By Tube

London's subway system is called the Tube or Underground (but never "subway"). It's one of this planet's great people-movers (runs Mon-Sat about 5:00-24:00, Sun about 7:00-23:00; Central, Jubilee, Northern, Piccadilly, and Victoria lines also run Fri-Sat 24 hours).

Get your bearings by studying a map of the system, free at any station (or download a transit app—described earlier). Each line has a name (such as Circle, Northern, or Bakerloo) and two directions (indicated by the end-of-the-line stops). Find the line that will take you to your destination, and figure out roughly which direction (north, south, east, or west) you'll need to go to get there.

At the Tube station, there are two ways to pass through the turnstile. With an Oyster card, touch it flat against the turnstile's yellow card reader, both when you enter and exit the station. With a paper ticket, feed it into the turnstile, reclaim it, and hang on to it—you'll need it later. On escalators, you'll generally stand on the right and pass on the left.

Find your train by following signs to your line and the (general) direction it's headed (such as Central Line: east). Since some tracks are shared by several lines, double-check before boarding: Make sure your destination is one of the stops listed on the sign at the platform. Also, check the electronic signboards that announce which train is next, and make sure the destination (the end-of-the-line stop) is the direction you want. Some trains, particularly on the Circle and District lines, split off for other directions, but each train has its final destination marked above its windshield.

When you leave the system, "touch out" with your Oyster card at the electronic reader on the turnstile, or feed your paper ticket into the turnstile (it will eat your now-expired ticket). Check maps and signs for the most convenient exit.

If you get confused, ask advice from a local, a blue-vested staffer, or at the information window located before the turnstile entry. Online, get help from the "Plan a Journey" feature at www. tfl.gov.uk, which is accessible (via free Wi-Fi) on any mobile device within most Tube stations before you go underground.

By Bus

Get in the habit of hopping buses for quick little straight shots, even just to get to a Tube stop. However, during bump-and-grind rush hours (8:00-10:00 and 16:00-19:00), you'll usually go faster by Tube.

You can't buy single-trip tickets for buses, and you can't use cash to pay when boarding. Instead, you must have an Oyster card or a one-day Bus & Tram Pass (£5, can buy on day of travel only—not beforehand, from ticket machine in any Tube station). If you're using your Oyster card, any bus ride in downtown London costs £1.50 (capped at £4.50/day).

When your bus approaches, hold your arm out to let the driver know you want on. Hop on and confirm your destination with the driver (often friendly and helpful). As you board, touch your Oyster card to the card reader, or show your Bus & Tram Pass to the driver. Unlike on the Tube, there's no need to show or tap your card when you hop off. On the older heritage "Routemaster" buses without card-readers (used on the #15 route), you simply take a seat, and the conductor comes around to check cards and passes. To get off, press one of the red buttons (on the poles between the seats) before your stop.

By Taxi

London is the best taxi town in Europe. Big, black cabs are everywhere, and there's no meter-cheating. They know every nook and cranny in town. I've never met a crabby London cabbie.

If a cab's top light is on, just wave it down—even if it's going the opposite way—or find the nearest taxi stand. Telephoning a cab will get you one in minutes, but costs a few more pounds (tel. 0871-871-8710).

Rides start at £2.60. All extra charges are explained in writing on the cab wall. Tip a cabbie by rounding up (maximum 10 percent).

A typical daytime trip—from the Tower of London to St. Paul's—costs about £8-10. All cabs can carry five passengers, and some take six, for the same cost as a single traveler. So for a short

Handy Bus Routes

The best views are upstairs on a double-decker. Here are some of the most useful routes:

Route #9: High Street Kensington to Knightsbridge (Harrods) to Hyde Park Corner to Trafalgar Square to Somerset House.

Route #11: Victoria Station to Westminster Abbey to Trafalgar Square to St. Paul's and Liverpool Street Station and the East End.

Route #15: Trafalgar Square to St. Paul's to Tower of London (sometimes with heritage "Routemaster" old-style double-decker buses).

Routes #23 and #159: Paddington Station (#159 begins at Marble Arch) to Oxford Circus to Piccadilly Circus to Trafalgar Square; from there, #23 heads east to St. Paul's and Liverpool Street Station, while #159 heads to Westminster and the Imperial War Museum. In addition, several buses (including #6, #12, and #139) also make the corridor run between Marble Arch, Oxford Circus, Piccadilly Circus, and Trafalgar Square.

Route #24: Pimlico to Victoria Station to Westminster Abbey to Trafalgar Square to Euston Square, then all the way north to Cam-

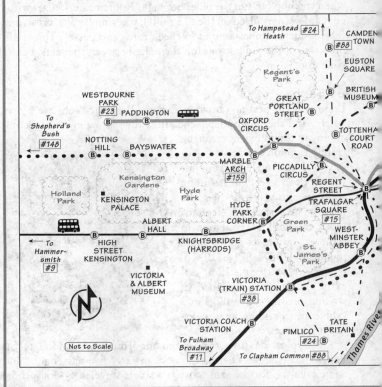

den Town (Camden Lock Market).

Route #38: Victoria Station to Hyde Park Corner to Piccadilly Circus to British Museum.

Route #88: Tate Britain to Westminster Abbey to Trafalgar Square to Piccadilly Circus to Oxford Circus to Great Portland Street Station (Regent's Park), then north to Camden Town.

Route #148: Westminster Abbey to Victoria Station to Notting Hill and Bayswater (by way of the east end of Hyde Park and Marble Arch).

Route #RV1 (a scenic South Bank joyride): Tower of London to Tower Bridge to Southwark Street (five-minute walk behind Tate Modern/Shakespeare's Globe) to London Eye/Waterloo Station, then over Waterloo Bridge to Somerset House and Covent Garden.

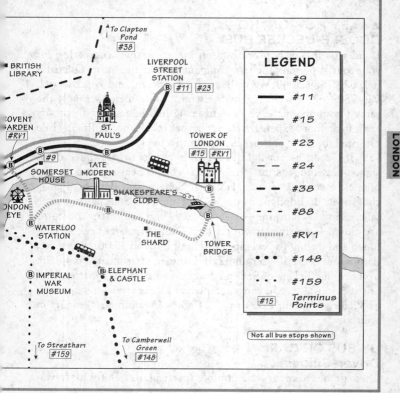

LONDON

ride, three adults in a cab travel at close to Tube prices. Avoid cabs when traffic is bad—they're slow and expensive, because the meter keeps running even at a standstill.

By Uber

Uber faces legal challenges in London and may not be operating when you visit. If Uber is running, it can be much cheaper than a taxi and is a handy alternative if there's a long line for a taxi or if no cabs are available. However, Uber drivers generally don't know the city as well as regular cabbies, and they don't have the access to some fast lanes that taxis do.

Tours in London

🎧 To sightsee on your own, download my free Rick Steves Audio Europe app with **audio tours** that illuminate some of London's top sights and neighborhoods, including my Westminster Walk, Historic London: The City Walk, and tours of the British Museum, British Library, and St. Paul's Cathedral (see sidebar on page 46 for details).

▲▲▲BY HOP-ON, HOP-OFF DOUBLE-DECKER BUS

London is full of hop-on, hop-off bus companies competing for your tourist pound. The two companies I like the most: **Original** (tel. 020/7389-5040, www.theoriginaltour.com) and **Big Bus** (tel. 020/7808-6753, www.bigbustours.com). Both offer essentially the same two tours of the city's sightseeing highlights. Big Bus tours are a little more expensive (£35, cheaper in advance online), while Original tours are cheaper (£26 with this book).

These once-over-lightly bus tours drive by all the famous sights, providing a stress-free way to get your bearings and see the biggies: Piccadilly Circus, Trafalgar Square, Big Ben, St. Paul's, the Tower of London, Marble Arch, Victoria Station, and elsewhere. Sunday morning—when traffic is light and many museums are closed—is a fine time for a tour. Traffic is at its peak around lunch and during the evening rush hour (around 17:00). Buses run daily about every 10-15 minutes in summer, starting at about 8:30. You can buy tickets online in advance, from drivers, or from staff at street kiosks (credit cards accepted at kiosks at major stops such as Victoria Station, ticket valid 24 hours in summer, 48 hours in winter).

BY BUS OR CAR
Driver-Guides

These guides have cars or a minibus (particularly helpful for travel-

Combining a London Bus Tour and the Changing of the Guard

For a grand and efficient intro to London, consider catching an 8:30 departure of a hop-on, hop-off overview bus tour, riding most of the loop (which takes just over 1.5 hours, depending on traffic). Hop off just before 10:00 at Trafalgar Square (Cockspur Street, stop "S") and walk briskly to Buckingham Palace to find a spot to watch the Changing of the Guard ceremony at 11:00.

ers with limited mobility), and also do walking-only tours: **Janine Barton** (£390/half-day, £560/day, tel. 020/7402-4600, http:// seeitinstyle.synthasite.com, jbsiis@aol.com); cousins **Hugh Dickson** and **Mike Dickson** (£345/half-day, £535/day, overnights also possible, both registered Blue Badge guides; Hugh's mobile 07771/602-069, hughdickson@hotmail.com; Mike's mobile 07769/905-811, michael.dickson5@btinternet.com); and **David Stubbs** (£225/half-day, £330/day, about £50 more for groups of 4-6 people, also does tours to the Cotswolds, Stonehenge, and Stratford, mobile 07775-888-534, www.londoncountrytours. co.uk, info@londoncountrytours.co.uk).

▲▲ON FOOT

Top-notch local guides lead (sometimes big) groups on walking tours through specific slices of London's past. Look for brochures at TIs or ask at hotels. *Time Out*, the weekly entertainment guide, lists some, but not all, scheduled walks. Check with the various tour companies by phone or online to get their full picture. To take a walking tour, simply show up at the announced location and pay the guide.

London Walks

This leading company lists its extensive and creative daily schedule online, as well as in a beefy *London Walks* brochure (available at hotels and in racks all over town). Their two-hour walks, led by top-quality professional guides (ranging from archaeologists to actors), cost £10 (cash only, walks offered year-round, private tours for groups-£140, tel. 020/7624-3978 for a live person, tel. 020/7624-9255 for a recording of today's or tomorrow's walks and the Tube station they depart from, www.walks.com).

Jack the Ripper Walks

Each walking tour company seems to make most of its money with "haunted" and Jack the Ripper tours. Two reliably good two-hour tours start every night at the Tower Hill Tube station exit. **London**

LONDON

London at a Glance

▲▲▲**Westminster Abbey** Britain's finest church and the site of royal coronations and burials since 1066. **Hours:** Mon-Fri 9:30-16:30, Wed until 19:00, Sat 9:00-16:00 (Sept-April until 14:00), closed Sun to sightseers except for worship. Diamond Jubilee Galleries—Mon-Fri 10:00-16:00, Sat 9:30-15:30, closed Sun. See page 923.

▲▲▲**Churchill War Rooms** Underground WWII headquarters of Churchill's war effort. **Hours:** Daily 9:30-18:00. See page 928.

▲▲▲**National Gallery** Remarkable collection of European paintings (1250-1900), including Leonardo, Botticelli, Velázquez, Rembrandt, Turner, Van Gogh, and the Impressionists. **Hours:** Daily 10:00-18:00, Fri until 21:00. See page 929.

▲▲▲**British Museum** The world's greatest collection of artifacts of Western civilization, including the Rosetta Stone and the Parthenon's Elgin Marbles. **Hours:** Daily 10:00-17:30, Fri until 20:30 (selected galleries only). See page 936.

▲▲▲**British Library** Fascinating collection of important literary treasures of the Western world. **Hours:** Mon-Fri 9:30-18:00, Tue-Thu until 20:00, Sat until 17:00, Sun 11:00-17:00. See page 940.

▲▲▲**St. Paul's Cathedral** The main cathedral of the Anglican Church, designed by Christopher Wren, with a climbable dome and daily evensong services. **Hours:** Mon-Sat 8:30-16:30, closed Sun except for worship. See page 942.

▲▲▲**Tower of London** Historic castle, palace, and prison housing the crown jewels and a witty band of Beefeaters. **Hours:** Tue-Sat 9:00-17:30, Sun-Mon from 10:00; Nov-Feb closes one hour earlier. See page 945.

▲▲**Houses of Parliament** London landmark famous for Big Ben and occupied by the Houses of Lords and Commons. **Hours:** When Parliament is in session, generally open Oct-late July Mon-Thu, closed Fri-Sun and during recess late July-Sept. Guided

Walks leaves nightly at 19:30 (£10, pay at the start, tel. 020/7624-3978, recorded info tel. 020/7624-9255, www.jacktheripperwalk.com). **Ripping Yarns,** which leaves earlier, is guided by off-duty Yeoman Warders—the Tower of London "Beefeaters" (£8, pay at end, nightly at 18:30, mobile 07813-559-301, www.jack-the-ripper-tours.com).

tours offered year-round on Sat and most weekdays during recess. See page 927.

▲▲**Trafalgar Square** The heart of London, where Westminster, The City, and the West End meet. **Hours:** Always open. See page 929.

▲▲**National Portrait Gallery** A *Who's Who* of British history, featuring portraits of this nation's most important historical figures. **Hours:** Daily 10:00-18:00, Fri until 21:00, first and second floors open Mon at 11:00. See page 932.

▲▲**Covent Garden** Vibrant people-watching zone with shops, cafés, street musicians, and an iron-and-glass arcade that once hosted a produce market. See page 933.

▲▲**Changing of the Guard at Buckingham Palace** Hour-long spectacle at Britain's royal residence. **Hours:** May-July daily at 11:00, Aug-April Sun, Mon, Wed, and Fri. See page 934.

▲▲**London Eye** Enormous observation wheel, dominating—and offering commanding views over—London's skyline. **Hours:** Daily June-Aug 10:00-20:30 or later, Sept-May 11:00-18:00. See page 949.

▲▲**Imperial War Museum** Exhibits examining military conflicts from the early 20th century to today. **Hours:** Daily 10:00-18:00. See page 950.

▲▲**Tate Modern** Works by Monet, Matisse, Dalí, Picasso, and Warhol displayed in a converted powerhouse complex. **Hours:** Daily 10:00-18:00, Fri-Sat until 22:00. See page 950.

▲▲**Shakespeare's Globe** Timbered, thatched-roofed reconstruction of the Bard's original "wooden O." **Hours:** Theater complex, museum, and actor-led tours generally daily 9:00-17:30; April-Oct generally morning theater tours only. Plays are also staged here. See page 951.

Private Walks with Local Guides

Standard rates for London's registered Blue Badge guides are about £160-200 for four hours and £260 or more for nine hours (tel. 020/7611-2545, www.guidelondon.org.uk or www.britainsbestguides.org). I know and like these fine local guides: **Sean Kelleher,** an engaging storyteller who knows his history (tel. 020/8673-1624, mobile 07764-612-770, sean@seanlondonguide.

com); **Britt Lonsdale** (great with families, tel. 020/7386-9907, mobile 07813-278-077, brittl@btinternet.com); and **Joel Reid,** an imaginative guide who specializes in off-the-beaten-track London (mobile 07887-955-720, joelyreid@gmail.com).

BY BIKE

Many of London's best sights can be laced together with a pleasant pedal through its parks. Confirm schedules in advance.

London Bicycle Tour Company

Three tours covering London are offered daily from their base at Gabriel's Wharf on the South Bank of the Thames. Sunday is the best, as there is less car traffic (£25-28.50, office open daily April-Oct 9:30-18:00, west of Blackfriars Bridge on the South Bank, 1 Gabriel's Wharf, tel. 020/7928-6838, www.londonbicycle.com). They also rent bikes (£3.50/hour, £20/day).

Fat Tire Bike Tours

Nearly daily bike tours cover the highlights of downtown London, on two different itineraries (£22 and up, £2 discount with this book). Their guiding style mixes history with humor (mobile 078-8233-8779, www.fattirebiketourslondon.com).

▲▲BY CRUISE BOAT

London offers many made-for-tourist cruises, most on slow-moving, open-top boats accompanied by entertaining commentary about passing sights. Generally speaking, you can either do a **short city center cruise** by riding a boat 30 minutes from Westminster Pier to Tower Pier (particularly handy if you're interested in visiting the Tower of London anyway), or take a **longer cruise** that includes a peek at the East End, riding from Westminster all the way to Greenwich (save time by taking the Tube back). A one-way trip within the city center costs about £10; going all the way to Greenwich costs about £2.50 more. Most companies charge around £4 more for a round-trip ticket.

The three dominant companies are **City Cruises** (handy 45-minute cruise from Westminster Pier to Tower Pier; www.citycruises.com), **Thames River Services** (fewer stops, classic boats, friendlier and more old-fashioned feel; www.thamesriverservices.co.uk), and **Circular Cruise** (full cruise takes about an hour, operated by Crown River Services, www.circularcruise.london).

To compare all of your options in one spot, head to Westminster Pier at the base of Big Ben, which has a row of kiosks for all of the big outfits.

Westminster Walk

Just about every visitor to London strolls along historic Whitehall from Big Ben to Trafalgar Square. This self-guided walk gives meaning to that touristy ramble (most of the sights you'll see are described in more detail later). Under London's modern traffic and big-city bustle lie 2,000 fascinating years of history. You'll get a whirlwind tour as well as a practical orientation to London.

This information is distilled from the "Westminster Walk" chapter in *Rick Steves London*, by Rick Steves and Gene Openshaw. You can download a free ⌂ Rick Steves audio version of this walk; see page 46.

Start halfway across ❶ **Westminster Bridge** for that "Wow, I'm really in London!" feeling. Get a close-up view of the **Houses of Parliament** and **Big Ben** (floodlit at night). Downstream you'll see the **London Eye,** the city's giant Ferris wheel. Down the stairs to Westminster Pier are boats to the Tower of London and Greenwich (downstream) or Kew Gardens (upstream).

En route to Parliament Square, you'll pass a ❷ **statue of Boadicea,** the Celtic queen who unsuccessfully resisted Roman invaders in A.D. 60. Julius Caesar was the first Roman general to cross the Channel, but even he was weirded out by the island's strange inhabitants, who worshipped trees, sacrificed virgins, and went to war painted blue. Later, Romans subdued and civilized them, building roads and making this spot on the Thames—"Londinium"—a major urban center.

You'll find four red phone booths lining the north side of ❸ **Parliament Square** along Great George Street—great for a phone-box-and-Big-Ben photo op.

Wave hello to Winston Churchill and Nelson Mandela in Parliament Square. To Churchill's right is the historic **Westminster Abbey,** with its two stubby, elegant towers. The white building (flying the Union Jack) at the far end of the square houses Britain's **Supreme Court.**

Head north up Parliament Street, which turns into ❹ **Whitehall,** and walk toward Trafalgar Square. You'll see the thought-provoking ❺ **Cenotaph** in the middle of the boulevard, reminding passersby of the many Brits who died in the last century's world wars. To visit the **Churchill War Rooms,** take a left before the Cenotaph, on King Charles Street.

Continuing on Whitehall, stop at the barricaded and guarded ❻ **#10 Downing Street** to see the British "White House," the traditional home of the prime minister since the position was created in the early 18th century. Break the bobby's boredom and ask him a question. The huge building across Whitehall from Downing Street is the **Ministry of Defence** (MOD), the "British Pentagon."

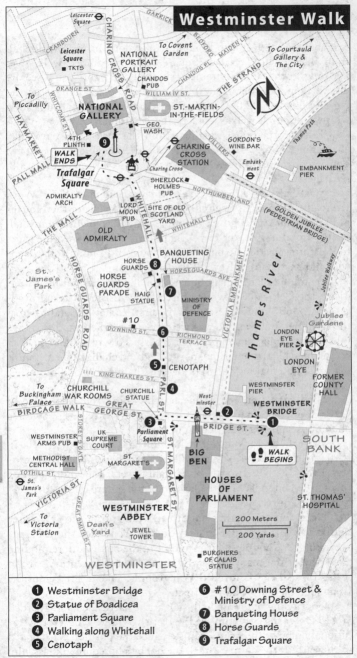

Westminster Walk

LONDON

- ❶ Westminster Bridge
- ❷ Statue of Boadicea
- ❸ Parliament Square
- ❹ Walking along Whitehall
- ❺ Cenotaph
- ❻ #10 Downing Street & Ministry of Defence
- ❼ Banqueting House
- ❽ Horse Guards
- ❾ Trafalgar Square

Nearing Trafalgar Square, look for the 17th-century ❼ **Banqueting House** across the street, which is just about all that remains of what was once the biggest palace in Europe—Whitehall Palace. If you visit, you can enjoy its ceiling paintings by Peter Paul Rubens, and the exquisite hall itself. Also take a look at the ❽ **Horse Guards** behind the gated fence. For 200 years, soldiers in cavalry uniforms have guarded this arched entrance that leads to Buckingham Palace. These elite troops constitute the Queen's personal bodyguard.

The column topped by Lord Nelson marks ❾ **Trafalgar Square,** London's central meeting point. The stately domed building on the far side of the square is the **National Gallery,** which is filled with the national collection of European paintings, and has a classy café in the Sainsbury wing. To the right of the National Gallery is the 1722 **St. Martin-in-the-Fields Church** and its Café in the Crypt.

To get to Piccadilly from Trafalgar Square, walk up Cockspur Street to Haymarket, then take a short left on Coventry Street to colorful **Piccadilly Circus.** Near Piccadilly, you'll find several theaters. **Leicester Square** (with its half-price TKTS booth for plays—see page 970) thrives just a few blocks away. From Piccadilly or Oxford Circus, you can take a taxi, bus, or the Tube home.

Sights in London

WESTMINSTER

These sights are listed in roughly geographical order from Westminster Abbey to Trafalgar Square, and are linked in my self-guided Westminster Walk (earlier) and my 🎧 free Westminster Walk audio tour.

▲▲▲Westminster Abbey

The greatest church in the English-speaking world, Westminster Abbey is where the nation's royalty has been wedded, crowned, and buried since 1066. Indeed, the histories of Westminster Abbey and England are almost the same. A thousand years of English history—3,000 tombs, the remains of 29 kings and queens, and hundreds of memorials to poets, politicians, scientists, and warriors—lie within its stained-glass splendor and under its stone slabs.

Cost and Hours: £22, £45 family ticket (covers 2 adults and 2

children), includes cloister and audioguide; Mon-Fri 9:30-16:30, Wed until 19:00 (main church only), Sat 9:00-16:00 (Sept-April until 14:00), last entry one hour before closing, closed Sun to sightseers but open for services, guided tours available; cloister-daily 8:00-18:00; Tube: Westminster or St. James's Park, tel. 020/7222-5152, www.westminster-abbey.org.

Diamond Jubilee Galleries: Timed-entry tickets, available on the Abbey's website, are required to see this new exhibit (Mon-Fri 10:00-16:00, Sat 9:30-15:30, closed Sun, ticket includes entry to the Abbey).

When to Go: The place is most crowded every day at mid-morning and all day Saturdays and Mondays. Visit early, during lunch, or late to avoid tourist hordes. Weekdays after 14:30—especially Wed—are less congested. The main entrance, on the Parliament Square side, often has a sizable line. You can skip it by booking tickets in advance via the Abbey's website, then show your ticket to the marshal at the entrance.

Tours: The included **audioguide** is excellent. The Westminster Abbey Official Tour **app** includes an audio tour narrated by Jeremy Irons. Or, you can take an entertaining **guided tour** from a verger—the church equivalent of a museum docent (£5, schedule posted outside and inside entry, up to 6/day in summer, 1.5 hours).

⊘ Self-Guided Tour: You'll have no choice but to follow the steady flow of tourists through the church, along the route laid out for the audioguide. My tour covers the Abbey's top stops.

• *Walk straight through the north transept. Follow the crowd flow to the right and enter the spacious...*

Nave: Look down the long and narrow center aisle of the church. Lined with the praying hands of the Gothic arches, glowing with light from the stained glass, this is more than a museum. With saints in stained glass, heroes in carved stone, and the bodies of England's greatest citizens under the floor stones, Westminster Abbey is the religious heart of England.

The king who built the Abbey was Edward the Confessor. Find him in the stained-glass windows on the left side of the nave (as you face the altar). He's in the third bay from the end (marked *S: Edwardus rex...*), with his crown, scepter, and ring. The Abbey's 10-story nave is the tallest in England. The chandeliers, 10 feet tall, look small in comparison (16 were given to the Abbey by the Guinness family).

On the floor near the west entrance of the Abbey is the flower-lined Grave of the Unknown Warrior, one ordinary WWI soldier buried in soil from France with lettering made from melted-down weapons from that war. Take time to contemplate the million-man army from the British Empire, and all those who gave their lives. Their memory is so revered that, when Kate Middleton walked up the aisle on her wedding day, by tradition she had to step around the tomb (and her wedding bouquet was later placed atop this tomb, also in accordance with tradition).

• *Walk up the nave toward the altar. This is the same route every future monarch walks on the way to being crowned. Midway up the nave, you pass through the colorful screen of an enclosure known as the...*

Choir: These elaborately carved wood-and-gilt seats are where monks once chanted their services in the "quire"—as it's known in British churchspeak. Today, it's where the Abbey boys' choir sings the evensong. The "high" (main) altar (which usually has a cross and candlesticks atop it) sits on the platform up the five stairs in front of you.

• *It's on this platform that the monarch is crowned.*

Coronation Spot: The area immediately before the high altar is where every English coronation since 1066 has taken place. Royalty are also given funerals here. Princess Diana's coffin was carried to this spot for her funeral service in 1997. The "Queen Mum" (mother of Elizabeth II) had her funeral here in 2002. This is also where most of the last century's royal weddings have taken place, including the unions of Queen Elizabeth II and Prince Philip (1947), Prince Andrew and Sarah Ferguson (1986), and Prince William and Kate Middleton (2011).

• *Veer left and follow the crowd. Pause at the wooden staircase on your right.*

Shrine of Edward the Confessor: Step back and peek over the dark coffin of Edward I to see the tippy-top of the green-and-gold wedding-cake tomb of King Edward the Confessor—the man who built Westminster Abbey.

God had told pious Edward to visit St. Peter's Basilica in Rome. But with the Normans thinking conquest, it was too dangerous for him to leave England. Instead, he built this grand church and dedicated it to St. Peter. It was finished just in time to bury Edward and to crown his foreign successor, William the Conqueror, in 1066. After Edward's death, people prayed at his tomb, and, after getting good results, Pope Alexander III canonized him. This elevated, central tomb—which lost some of its luster when Henry VIII melted down the gold coffin-case—is surrounded by the tombs of eight kings and queens.

• *At the top of the stone staircase, veer left into the private burial chapel of Queen Elizabeth I.*

Tomb of Queens Elizabeth I and Mary I: Although only one effigy is on the tomb (Elizabeth's), there are actually two queens buried beneath it, both daughters of Henry VIII (by different mothers). Bloody Mary—meek, pious, sickly, and Catholic—enforced Catholicism during her short reign (1553-1558) by burning "heretics" at the stake.

Elizabeth—strong, clever, and Protestant—steered England

on an Anglican course. She holds a royal orb symbolizing that she's queen of the whole globe. When 26-year-old Elizabeth was crowned in the Abbey, her right to rule was questioned (especially by her Catholic subjects) because she was considered the bastard seed of Henry VIII's unsanctioned marriage to Anne Boleyn. But Elizabeth's long reign (1559-1603) was one of the greatest in English history, a time when England ruled the seas and Shakespeare explored human emotions. When she died, thousands turned out for her funeral in the Abbey. Elizabeth's face on the tomb, modeled after her death mask, is considered a very accurate take on this hook-nosed, imperious "Virgin Queen" (she never married).

• *Continue into the ornate, flag-draped room up a few more stairs, directly behind the main altar.*

Chapel of King Henry VII (The Lady Chapel): The light from the stained-glass windows; the colorful banners overhead; and the elaborate tracery in stone, wood, and glass give this room the festive air of a medieval tournament. The prestigious Knights of the Bath meet here, under the magnificent ceiling studded with gold pendants. The ceiling—of carved stone, not plaster (1519)—is the finest English Perpendicular Gothic and fan vaulting you'll see (unless you're going to King's College Chapel in Cambridge). The ceiling was sculpted on the floor in pieces, then jigsaw-puzzled into place. It capped the Gothic period and signaled the vitality of the coming Renaissance.

• *Go to the far end of the chapel and stand at the banister in front of the modern set of stained-glass windows.*

Royal Air Force Chapel: Saints in robes and halos mingle with pilots in parachutes and bomber jackets. This tribute to WWII flyers is for those who earned their angel wings in the Battle of Britain (July-Oct 1940). A bit of bomb damage has been preserved—look for the little glassed-over hole in the wall below the windows in the lower left-hand corner.

• *Exit the Chapel of Henry VII. Turn left into a side chapel with the tomb (the central one of three in the chapel).*

Tomb of Mary, Queen of Scots: The beautiful, French-educated queen (1542-1587) was held under house arrest for 19 years by Queen Elizabeth I, who considered her a threat to her sovereignty. Elizabeth got wind of an assassination plot, suspected Mary was behind it, and had her first cousin (once removed) beheaded. When Elizabeth died childless, Mary's son—James VI, King of Scots—also became King James I of England and Ireland. James buried his mum here (with her head sewn back on) in the Abbey's most sumptuous tomb.

• *Exit Mary's chapel. Continue on, until you emerge in the south transept. Look for the doorway that leads to a stairway and elevator to the...*

Queen's Diamond Jubilee Galleries: In the summer of 2018, the Abbey opened a space that had been closed off for 700 years—an internal gallery 70 feet above the main floor known as the triforium. This balcony houses the new Queen's Diamond Jubilee Galleries, a small museum where you'll see exhibits covering royal coronations, funerals, and much more from the Abbey's 1,000-year history, including the coronation chair of Queen Mary II and Prince William and Kate's marriage license. There are also stunning views of the nave straight down to the Great West Door. Because of limited space, a timed-entry ticket is required (see page 924).

• *After touring the Queen's Galleries, return to the main floor. You're in...*

Poets' Corner: England's greatest artistic contributions are in the written word. Here the masters of arguably the world's most

complex and expressive language are remembered: Geoffrey Chaucer *(Canterbury Tales)*, Lord Byron, Dylan Thomas, W. H. Auden, Lewis Carroll *(Alice's Adventures in Wonderland)*, T. S. Eliot *(The Waste Land)*, Alfred Tennyson, Robert Browning, and Charles Dickens. Many writers are honored with plaques and monuments; relatively few are actually buried here. Shakespeare is commemorated by a fine statue that stands near the end of the transept, overlooking the others.

• *Exit the church (temporarily) at the south door, which leads to the...*

Great Cloister: The buildings that adjoin the church housed the monks. Cloistered courtyards gave them a place to meditate on God's creations.

• *Go back into the church for the last stop.*

Coronation Chair: A gold-painted oak chair waits here under a regal canopy for the next coronation. For every English coronation since 1308 (except two), it's been moved to its spot before the high altar to receive the royal buttocks. The chair's legs rest on lions, England's symbol.

▲▲Houses of Parliament (Palace of Westminster)

This Neo-Gothic icon of London, the site of the royal residence from 1042 to 1547, is now the meeting place of the legislative branch of government. You can view parliamentary sessions in either the bickering House of Commons or the sleepy House of Lords. Or you can simply wander on your own (through a few closely monitored rooms) to appreciate the historic building itself.

The Palace of Westminster has been the center of political power in England for nearly a thousand years. In 1834, a horrendous fire gutted the Palace. It was rebuilt in a retro, Neo-Gothic style that recalled England's medieval Christian roots—pointed arches, stained-glass windows, spires, and saint-like statues. At the same time, Britain was also retooling its government. Democracy was on the rise, the queen became a constitutional monarch, and Parliament emerged as the nation's ruling body. The Palace of Westminster became a symbol—a kind of cathedral—of democracy. A visit here offers a chance to tour a piece of living history and see the British government in action.

Cost and Hours: Free when Parliament is in session, otherwise must visit with a paid tour (see below); hours for nonticketed entry to House of Commons—Oct-late July Mon 14:30-22:30, Tue-Wed 11:30-19:30, Thu 9:30-17:30; for House of Lords—Oct-late July Mon-Tue 14:30-22:00, Wed 15:00-22:00, Thu 11:00-19:30; last entry depends on debates; exact schedule at www.parliament.uk.

Tours: Audioguide-£20.50, guided tour-£28, cheaper online, Sat year-round 9:00-16:30 and most weekdays during recess (late July-Sept), 1.5 hours. Confirm the tour schedule and book ahead at www.parliament.uk or by calling 020/7219-4114.

Nearby: Big Ben, the 315-foot-high clock tower at the north end of the Palace of Westminster, is named for its 13-ton bell, Ben. The light above the clock is lit when Parliament is in session. The face of the clock is huge—you can actually see the minute hand moving. For a good view of it, walk halfway over Westminster Bridge.

▲▲▲Churchill War Rooms

This excellent sight offers a fascinating walk through the underground headquarters of the British government's WWII fight against the Nazis in the darkest days of the Battle of Britain. It has two parts: the war rooms themselves, and a

top-notch museum dedicated to the man who steered the war from here, Winston Churchill. For details on all the blood, sweat, toil, and tears, pick up the excellent, essential, and included audioguide at the entry, and dive in. Allow 1-2 hours for your visit.

Cost and Hours: £21, includes audioguide, daily 9:30-18:00, last entry one hour before closing; on King Charles Street, 200 yards off Whitehall—follow signs, Tube: Westminster; tel. 020/7930-6961, www.iwm.org.uk/churchill-war-rooms. The museum's gift shop is great for anyone nostalgic for the 1940s.

Avoiding Lines: Purchasing a timed-entry ticket online in advance is smart to avoid long ticket-buying lines. You may still have to wait up to 30 minutes in the security line.

ON TRAFALGAR SQUARE

Trafalgar Square, London's central square worth ▲▲, is at the intersection of Westminster, The City, and the West End. It's the

climax of most marches and demonstrations, and is a thrilling place to simply hang out. A remodeling of the square has rerouted car traffic, helping reclaim the area for London's citizens. At the top of Trafalgar Square (north) sits the domed National Gallery with its grand staircase, and to the right, the steeple of St. Martin-in-the-

Fields, built in 1722, inspiring the steeple-over-the-entrance style of many town churches in New England. In the center of the square, Lord Nelson stands atop his 185-foot-tall fluted granite column, gazing out toward Trafalgar, where he lost his life but defeated the French fleet. Part of this 1842 memorial is made from his victims' melted-down cannons. He's surrounded by spraying fountains, giant lions, hordes of people, and—until recently—even more pigeons. A former London mayor decided that London's "flying rats" were a public nuisance and evicted Trafalgar Square's venerable seed salesmen (Tube: Charing Cross).

▲▲▲National Gallery

Displaying an unsurpassed collection of European paintings from 1250 to 1900—including works by Leonardo, Botticelli, Velázquez, Rembrandt, Turner, Van Gogh, and the Impressionists—this is one of Europe's great galleries. You'll peruse 700 years of art—from gold-backed Madonnas to Cubist bathers.

Cost and Hours: Free, £5 suggested donation, special exhibits extra, daily 10:00-18:00, Fri until 21:00, last entry to special exhib-

its 45 minutes before closing, on Trafalgar Square, Tube: Charing Cross or Leicester Square.

Info: Tel. 020/7747-2885, www.nationalgallery.org.uk.

Tours: Free one-hour overview tours leave from Sainsbury Wing info desk daily at 11:30 and 14:30, plus Fri at 19:00; excellent £5 audioguides—choose from one-hour highlights tour, several theme tours, or an option that lets you dial up info on any painting in the museum.

Eating: Consider splitting afternoon tea at the excellent-but-pricey National Dining Rooms, on the first floor of the Sainsbury Wing. The National Café, located near the Getty Entrance, has a table-service restaurant and a café. Seek out the Espresso Bar, near the Portico and Getty entrances, for sandwiches, pastries, and soft couches.

◗ Self-Guided Tour: Enter through the Sainsbury Entrance (in the smaller building to the left of the main entrance) and approach the collection chronologically.

Medieval and Early Renaissance: In the first rooms, you see shiny paintings of saints, angels, Madonnas, and crucifixions floating in an ethereal gold never-never land. Art in the Middle Ages was religious, dominated by the Church.

After leaving this gold-leaf peace, you'll stumble into Uccello's *Battle of San Romano* and Van Eyck's *The Arnolfini Portrait*, called by some "The Shotgun Wedding."

This painting—a masterpiece of down-to-earth details—was once thought to depict a wedding ceremony forced by the lady's swelling belly. Today it's understood as a portrait of a solemn, well-dressed, well-heeled couple, the Arnolfinis of Bruges, Belgium (she likely was not pregnant—the fashion of the day was to gather up the folds of one's extremely full-skirted dress).

Italian Renaissance: In painting, the Renaissance meant realism. Artists rediscovered the beauty of nature and the human body, expressing the optimism and confidence of this new age. Look for Botticelli's *Venus and Mars*, Michelangelo's *The Entombment*, and Raphael's *Pope Julius II*.

In Leonardo's *The Virgin of the Rocks*, Mary plays with her son Jesus and little Johnny the Baptist (with cross, at left) while an androgynous angel looks on. Leonardo brings this holy scene right down to earth by setting it among rocks, stalactites, water, and flowering plants. But looking closer, we see that Leonardo has deliberately posed his people into a pyramid shape, with Mary's head at the peak, creating an oasis of maternal stability and serenity amid the hard rock of the earth.

In *The Origin of the Milky Way* by Venetian Renaissance painter Tintoretto, the god Jupiter places his illegitimate son, baby Hercules, at his wife's breast. Juno says, "Wait a minute. That's not my baby!" Her milk spurts upward, becoming the Milky Way.

Northern Protestant: While Italy had wealthy aristocrats and the powerful Catholic Church to purchase art, the North's patrons were middle-class, hardworking, Protestant merchants. Greek gods and Virgin Marys are out, and hometown folks and hometown places are in.

Highlights include Vermeer's *A Young Woman Standing at a Virginal* and Rembrandt's *Belshazzar's Feast.* Rembrandt painted

his *Self-Portrait* at the age of 63 in the year he would die. He throws the light of truth on...himself. He was bankrupt, his mistress had just passed away, and he had also buried several of his children. We see a disillusioned, well-worn, but proud old genius.

Baroque: The museum's outstanding Baroque collection includes Van Dyck's *Equestrian Portrait of Charles I* and Caravaggio's *The Supper at Emmaus.* In Velázquez's *The Rokeby Venus,* Venus lounges diagonally across the canvas, admiring herself, with flaring red, white, and gray fabrics to highlight her rosy white skin and inflame our passion. This work by the king's personal court painter is a rare Spanish nude from that ultra-Catholic country.

British: The reserved British were more comfortable cavorting with nature than with the lofty gods, as seen in Constable's *The Hay Wain.* But Constable's landscape was about to be paved over by the Industrial Revolution, as Turner's *The Fighting Téméraire* shows. Turner's messy, colorful style influenced the Impressionists and gives us our first glimpse into the modern art world.

Impressionism: At the end of the 19th century, a new breed of artists burst out of the stuffy confines of the studio. They donned scarves and berets and set up their canvases in farmers' fields or carried their notebooks into crowded cafés, dashing off quick sketches in order to catch a momentary...impression. Check out Impressionist and Post-Impressionist masterpieces such as Monet's *Gare St.*

LONDON

Lazare and *The Water-Lily Pond,* Renoir's *The Skiff,* Seurat's *Bathers at Asnières,* and Van Gogh's *Sunflowers.*

Cézanne's *Bathers* are arranged in strict triangles. Cézanne uses the Impressionist technique of building a figure with dabs of paint (though his "dabs" are often larger-sized "cube" shapes) to make solid, 3-D geometrical figures in the style of the Renaissance. In the process, his cube shapes helped inspire a radical new style—Cubism—bringing art into the 20th century.

▲▲National Portrait Gallery

Put off by halls of 19th-century characters who meant nothing to me, I used to call this museum "as interesting as someone else's yearbook." But a selective walk through this 500-year-long *Who's Who* of British history is quick and free, and puts faces on the story of England. The collection is well-described, not huge, and in historical sequence, from the 16th century on the second floor to today's royal family, usually housed on the ground floor.

Highlights include Henry VIII and wives; portraits of the "Virgin Queen" Elizabeth I, Sir Francis Drake, and Sir Walter Raleigh; the only real-life portrait of William Shakespeare; Oliver Cromwell and Charles I with his head on; portraits by Gainsborough and Reynolds; the Romantics (William Blake, Lord Byron, William Wordsworth, and company); Queen Victoria and her era; and the present royal family, including the late Princess Diana and the current Duchess of Cambridge—Kate.

Cost and Hours: Free, £5 suggested donation, special exhibits extra; daily 10:00-18:00, Fri until 21:00, first and second floors open Mon at 11:00, last entry to special exhibits one hour before closing; excellent audioguide-£3, floor plan-£1; entry 100 yards off Trafalgar Square (around the corner from National Gallery, opposite Church of St. Martin-in-the-Fields), Tube: Charing Cross or Leicester Square, tel. 020/7306-0055, recorded info tel. 020/7312-2463, www.npg.org.uk.

▲St. Martin-in-the-Fields

The church, built in the 1720s with a Gothic spire atop a Greek-type temple, is an oasis of peace on wild and noisy Trafalgar Square. St. Martin cared for the poor. "In the fields" was where the first church stood on this spot (in the 13th century), between Westminster and The City. Stepping inside, you still feel a compassion for the needs of the people in this neighborhood—the church serves the homeless and houses a Chinese community center. A freestanding glass pavilion to the left of the church serves as the entrance to the church's underground areas. There you'll find the concert ticket office, a gift shop, brass-rubbing center, and the recommended support-the-church Café in the Crypt.

Cost and Hours: Free, donations welcome; hours vary but generally Mon-Fri 8:30-13:00 & 14:00-18:00, Sat 9:30-18:00, Sun 15:30-17:00; services listed at entrance; Tube: Charing Cross, tel. 020/7766-1100, www.stmartin-in-the-fields.org.

THE WEST END AND NEARBY
▲Piccadilly Circus

Although this square is slathered with neon billboards and tacky attractions (think of it as the Times Square of London), the surrounding streets are packed with great shopping opportunities and swimming with youth on the rampage.

Nearby Shaftesbury Avenue and Leicester Square teem with fun-seekers, theaters, Chinese restaurants, and street singers. To the northeast is London's Chinatown and, beyond that, the funky Soho neighborhood. And curling to the northwest from Piccadilly Circus is genteel Regent Street, lined with exclusive shops.

▲Soho

North of Piccadilly, once-seedy Soho has become trendy—with many recommended restaurants—and is well worth a gawk. It's the epicenter of London's thriving, colorful youth scene, a fun and funky *Sesame Street* of urban diversity. Soho is also London's red light district (especially near Brewer and Berwick Streets), where "friendly models" wait in tiny rooms up dreary stairways, voluptuous con artists sell strip shows, and eager male tourists are frequently ripped off.

▲▲Covent Garden

The square's centerpiece is a covered marketplace. A market has been here since medieval times, when it was the "convent" garden owned by Westminster Abbey. A tourist market thrives here today.

The "Actors' Church" of St. Paul and the Royal Opera House border the square, and theaters are nearby. The

LONDON

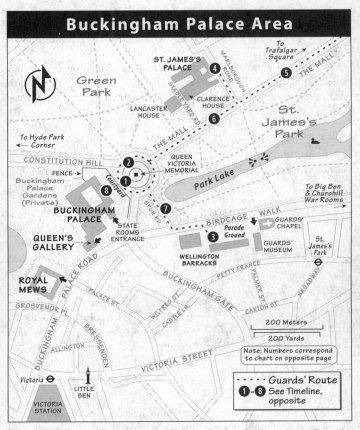

Buckingham Palace Area

area is a people-watcher's delight, with cigarette eaters, Punch-and-Judy acts, food that's good for you (but not your wallet), trendy crafts, and row after row of boutique shops and market stalls. For better Covent Garden lunch deals, walk a block or two away from the eye of this touristic hurricane (check out the places north of the Tube station, along Endell and Neal Streets).

BUCKINGHAM PALACE AREA

While it's possible to enter various sights related to the palace, on a brief visit I'd just take a quick look at its famous facade. Planning your day around the Changing of the Guard leaves little time for other options; because you'll need to fight the crowds to secure a suitable vantage point, this is more time-consuming than it sounds.

▲▲Changing of the Guard at Buckingham Palace

This is the spectacle every visitor to London has to see at least once: stone-faced, red-coated (or in winter, gray-coated), bearskin-hatted guards changing posts with much fanfare, in an hour-long ceremo-

Changing of the Guard Timeline

When	What
10:00	Tourists begin to gather. Arrive now for a spot front and center by the ❶ fence outside Buckingham Palace in anticipation of the most famous event—when the"Queen's Guard" does its shift change at 11:00.
10:30	❷ By now, the Victoria Memorial in front of the palace—the best all-purpose viewing spot—is crowded.
10:30-10:45	Meanwhile, at the nearby ❸ Wellington Barracks, the "New Guard" gathers for inspection and the "Old Guard" gathers for inspection at ❹ St. James's Palace.
10:30 (9:30 Sun)	Farther away, along Whitehall, the Horse Guard also changes guard, and begins parading down ❺ the Mall.
10:43	Relieved of duty, the tired St. James's Palace guards march down ❻ the Mall, heading for Buckingham Palace.
10:57	Fresh replacement troops (led by a marching band) head in a grand parade from Wellington Barracks down ❼ Spur Road to Buckingham Palace.
11:00	All guards gradually converge around the Victoria Memorial in front of the palace. The ceremony approaches its climax.
11:00-11:30	Now, the famous Changing of the Guard ceremony takes place ❽ inside the fenced courtyard of Buckingham Palace. Everyone parades around, the guard changes, and they pass the regimental flag (or "colour")—all with much shouting. The band plays a happy little concert, and then marches out.
11:40	The tired "Old Guard" (led by a band) heads up Spur Road for Wellington Barracks. The fresh "New Guard" heads up the Mall for St. James's Palace.
11:45	As the fresh "New Guard" takes over at St. James's Palace, there's a smaller changing of the guard ceremony. And with that—"Tourists...d-i-i-s missed!"

LONDON

ny accompanied by a brass band. The most famous part takes place right in front of Buckingham Palace at 11:00. But there actually are several different guard-changing ceremonies and parades going on simultaneously, at different locations within a few hundred yards of the palace. All of these spectacles converge around Buckingham Palace in a perfect storm of red-coated pageantry.

To plan your sightseeing strategy (and understand what's going on), see the blow-by-blow account in the "Changing of the Guard Timeline."

Cost and Hours: Free, May-July daily at 11:00, Aug-April Sun, Mon, Wed, and Fri, no ceremony in very wet weather; exact schedule subject to change—call 020/7766-7300 for the day's plan, or check www.householddivision.org.uk (search "Changing the Guard"); Buckingham Palace, Tube: Victoria, St. James's Park, or Green Park. Or hop into a big black taxi and say, "Buck House, please."

Sightseeing Strategies: Most tourists just show up and get lost in the crowds, but those who anticipate the action and know where to perch will enjoy the event more. The action takes place in stages over the course of an hour, at multiple locations; see the map. There are several ways to experience the pageantry. Get out your map (or download the official app at www.royalcollection.org.uk) and strategize. Here are a few options to consider:

Watch near the Palace: The main event is in the forecourt right in front of Buckingham Palace (between the palace and the fence) from 11:00 to 11:30. You'll need to get here as close to 10:00 as possible to get a place front and center, next to the fence. The key to good viewing is to get either right up front along the road or fence, or find some raised surface to stand or sit on—a balustrade or a curb—so you can see over people's heads.

Watch near the Victoria Memorial: The high ground on the circular Victoria Memorial provides the best overall view (come before 10:30 to get a place). From a high spot on the memorial, you have good (if more distant) views of the palace as well as the arriving and departing parades along The Mall and Spur Road.

Watch near St. James's Palace: If you don't feel like jostling for a view, stroll down to St. James's Palace and wait near the corner for a great photo-op. At about 11:45, the parade marches up The Mall to the palace and performs a smaller changing ceremony—with almost no crowds. Afterward, stroll through nearby St. James's Park.

NORTH LONDON
▲▲▲British Museum

Simply put, this is the greatest chronicle of civilization...anywhere. A visit here is like taking a long hike through *Encyclopedia Britannica* National Park. The vast British Museum wraps around its Great Court (the huge entrance hall), with the most popular sections filling the ground floor: Egyptian, Assyrian, and ancient

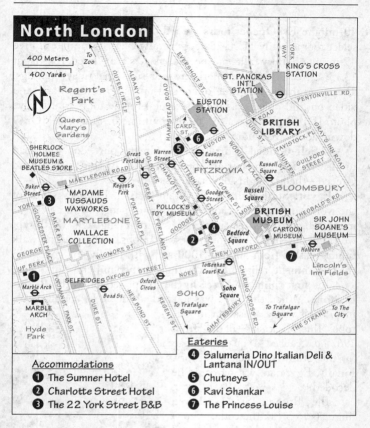

North London

400 Meters
400 Yards

To Zoo

Regent's Park

Queen Mary's Gardens

SHERLOCK HOLMES MUSEUM & BEATLES STORE

Baker Street

MADAME TUSSAUDS WAXWORKS

Regent's Park

MARYLEBONE

WALLACE COLLECTION

GEORGE ST.

UP. BERK.

Marble Arch

MARBLE ARCH

Hyde Park

SELFRIDGES

Bond St.

OXFORD STREET

Oxford Circus

SOHO

To Trafalgar Square

EVERSHOLT ST.

HAMPSTEAD ROAD

ST. PANCRAS INT'L STATION

KING'S CROSS STATION

YORK WAY

PENTONVILLE RD.

EUSTON STATION

CARD. ST.

EUSTON ROAD

JUDD ST.

BRITISH LIBRARY

GRAY'S INN ROAD

Warren Street

Euston Square

WOBURN PLACE

TAVISTOCK PL.

HUNTER

GUILFORD STREET

Great Portland Street

FITZROVIA

Russell Square

BLOOMSBURY

Goodge Street

Russell Square

THEOBALD'S RD.

POLLOCK'S TOY MUSEUM

GOODGE

BATH PL.

Bedford Square

BRITISH MUSEUM

CARTOON MUSEUM

SIR JOHN SOANE'S MUSEUM

Holborn

NEW OXFORD

Tottenham Court Rd.

CHARING CROSS RD.

Lincoln's Inn Fields

NOEL

Soho Square

SHAFTESBURY

To Trafalgar Square

THE STRAND

To The City

Eateries
4 Salumeria Dino Italian Deli & Lantana IN/OUT

Accommodations
1 The Sumner Hotel
2 Charlotte Street Hotel
3 The 22 York Street B&B

5 Chutneys
6 Ravi Shankar
7 The Princess Louise

Greek, with the famous frieze sculptures from the Parthenon in Athens. The museum's stately Reading Room—famous as the place where Karl Marx hung out while formulating his ideas on communism and writing *Das Kapital*—sometimes hosts special exhibits.

Cost and Hours: Free, £5 donation requested, special exhibits usually extra (and with timed ticket); daily 10:00-17:30, Fri until 20:30 (selected galleries only), least crowded late on weekday afternoons, especially Fri; Great Russell Street, Tube: Tottenham Court Road, ticket desk tel. 020/7323-8181, www.britishmuseum.org.

Visitor Information and Tours: Info desks offer a basic map (£2 donation), but it's not essential; the *Visitor's Guide* (£6) offers 15 different tours and skimpy text. Free 30- to

40-minute **EyeOpener tours** are led by volunteers who focus on select rooms (daily 11:00-15:45, generally every 15 minutes). Free 45-minute **gallery talks** on specific subjects are offered Tue-Sat at 13:15; a free 20-minute **spotlight** tour runs on Friday evenings. The £7 **multimedia guide** offers dial-up audio commentary and video on 200 objects, as well as several theme tours (must leave photo ID). There's also a fun family multimedia guide (£6). Or 🎧 download my free audio tour.

🠖 **Self-Guided Tour:** From the Great Court, doorways lead to all wings. To the left are the exhibits on Egypt, Assyria, and Greece—the highlights of your visit.

Egypt: Start with the Egyptian section. Egypt was one of the world's first "civilizations"—a group of people with a government, religion, art, free time, and a written language. The Egypt we think of—pyramids, mummies, pharaohs, and guys who walk funny—lasted from 3000 to 1000 B.C. with hardly any change in the government, religion, or arts. Imagine two millennia of Nixon.

The first thing you'll see in the Egypt section is the **Rosetta Stone.** When this rock was unearthed in the Egyptian desert in 1799, it was a sensation in Europe. This black slab, dating from 196 B.C., caused a quantum leap in the study of ancient history. Finally, Egyptian writing could be decoded.

The Rosetta Stone allowed linguists to break the code. It contains a single inscription repeated in three languages. The bottom third is plain old Greek, while the middle is medieval Egyptian. By comparing the two known languages with the one they didn't know, translators figured out the hieroglyphics.

Next, wander past the many **statues,** including a seven-ton Ramesses, with the traditional features of a pharaoh (goatee, cloth headdress, and cobra diadem on his forehead). When Moses told the king of Egypt, "Let my people go!" this was the stony-faced look he got. You'll also see the Egyptian gods as animals—these include Amun, king of the gods, as a ram, and Horus, the god of the living, as a falcon.

At the end of the hall, climb the stairs or take the elevator to **mummy** land. To mummify a body is much like following a recipe. First, disembowel it (but leave the heart inside), then pack the cavities with pitch, and dry it with natron, a natural form of sodium carbonate (and, I believe, the active ingredient in Twinkies). Then carefully bandage it head to toe with hundreds of yards of linen strips. Let it sit 2,000 years, and...*voilà!* The mummy was placed in a wooden coffin, which was put in a stone coffin, which was placed in a tomb. The result is that we now have Egyptian bodies that are as well preserved as Larry King.

Many of the mummies here are from the time of the Roman occupation, when fine memorial portraits painted in wax became popular. X-ray photos in the display cases tell us more about these people.

Assyria: Long before Saddam Hussein, Iraq was home to other palace-building, iron-fisted rulers—the Assyrians, who conquered their southern neighbors and dominated the Middle East for 300 years (c. 900-600 B.C.).

Their strength came from a superb army (chariots, mounted cavalry, and siege engines), a policy of terrorism against enemies ("I tied their heads to tree trunks all around the city," reads a royal inscription), ethnic cleansing and mass deportations of the vanquished, and efficient administration (roads and express postal service). They have been called the "Romans of the East."

Standing guard over the Assyrian exhibit halls are two human-headed **winged lions.** These stone lions guarded an Assyrian palace (11th-8th century B.C.). With the strength of a lion, the wings of an eagle, the brain of a man, and the beard of ZZ Top, they protected the king from evil spirits and scared the heck out of foreign ambassadors and left-wing newspaper reporters. (What has five legs and flies? Take a close look. These winged quintupeds, which appear complete from both the front and the side, could guard both directions at once.)

Carved into the stone between the bearded lions' loins, you can see one of civilization's most impressive achievements—writing. This wedge-shaped **(cuneiform)** script is the world's first written language, invented 5,000 years ago by the Sumerians (of southern Iraq) and passed down to their less-civilized descendants, the Assyrians.

The **Nimrud Gallery** is a mini version of the throne room and royal apartments of King Ashurnasirpal II's Northwest Palace at Nimrud (9th century B.C.). It's filled with royal propaganda reliefs, 30-ton marble bulls, and panels depicting wounded lions (lion-hunting was Assyria's sport of kings).

Greece: During their civilization's Golden Age (500-430 B.C.), the ancient Greeks set the tone for all of Western civilization to follow. Democracy, theater, literature, mathematics, philosophy, science, gyros, art, and architecture as we know them, were virtually all invented by a single generation of Greeks in a small town of maybe 80,000 citizens.

Your walk through Greek art history starts with pottery, usually painted red and black and a popular export product for the sea-trading Greeks. The earliest featured geometric patterns (eighth century B.C.), then a painted black silhouette on the natural orange clay, then a red figure on a black background. Later, painted vases show a culture really into partying.

The highlight is the **Parthenon Sculptures**—taken from the temple dedicated to Athena—the crowning glory of an enormous urban-renewal plan during Greece's Golden Age. While the build-ing itself remains in Athens, many of the Parthenon's best sculptures are right here in the British Museum. The sculptures are also called the Elgin Marbles, named for the shrewd British ambassador who had his men hammer, chisel, and saw them off the Parthenon in the early 1800s. Though the Greek government complains about losing its marbles, the Brits feel they rescued and preserved the sculptures.

These much-wrangled-over bits of the Parthenon (from about 450 B.C.) are indeed impressive. The marble panels you see lining the walls of this large hall are part of the frieze that originally ran around the exterior of the Parthenon, under the eaves. The statues at either end of the hall once filled the Parthenon's triangular-shaped pediments and showed the birth of Athena. The relief panels known as metopes tell the story of the struggle between the forces of human civilization and animal-like barbarism.

The Rest of the Museum: Be sure to venture upstairs to see artifacts from **Roman Britain** that surpass anything you'll see at Hadrian's Wall or elsewhere in the country. Also look for the Sutton Hoo Ship Burial artifacts from a seventh-century royal burial on the east coast of England (Room 41). A rare Michelangelo cartoon (preliminary sketch) is in Room 90 (level 4).

▲▲▲British Library

Here, in just two rooms, are the literary treasures of Western civilization, from early Bibles to Shakespeare's *Hamlet* to Lewis Carroll's *Alice's Adventures in Wonderland* to the *Magna Carta*. You'll see the Lindisfarne Gospels transcribed on an illuminated manuscript, Beatles lyrics scrawled on the back of a greeting card, and Leonardo da Vinci's genius sketched into his notebooks. The British Empire built its greatest monuments out of paper; it's through literature that England made her most lasting and significant contribution to civilization and the arts. Entering the library courtyard, you'll see a big statue of a naked Isaac Newton bending forward with a compass to measure the universe. The statue symbolizes the library's purpose: to gather all knowledge and promote humanity's endless search for truth. Note that exhibits change often, and many

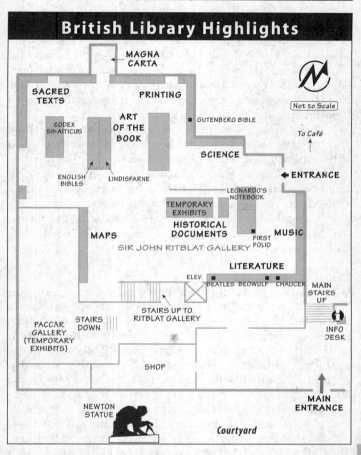

British Library Highlights

MAGNA CARTA

SACRED TEXTS

PRINTING

ART OF THE BOOK

CODEX SINAITICUS

■ GUTENBERG BIBLE

Not to Scale

To Café

SCIENCE

ENGLISH BIBLES

LINDISFARNE

◄ ENTRANCE

LEONARDO'S NOTEBOOK

TEMPORARY EXHIBITS

HISTORICAL DOCUMENTS

MAPS

MUSIC

■ FIRST FOLIO

SIR JOHN RITBLAT GALLERY

LITERATURE

ELEV.

■ BEATLES   ■ BEOWULF   ■ CHAUCER

MAIN STAIRS UP

STAIRS UP TO RITBLAT GALLERY

INFO DESK

PACCAR GALLERY (TEMPORARY EXHIBITS)

STAIRS DOWN

SHOP

NEWTON STATUE

MAIN ENTRANCE

Courtyard

of the museum's old, fragile manuscripts need to "rest" periodically in order to stay well-preserved.

Cost and Hours: Free, £5 suggested donation, admission charged for special exhibits; Mon-Fri 9:30-18:00, Tue-Thu until 20:00, Sat until 17:00, Sun 11:00-17:00; 96 Euston Road, Tube: King's Cross St. Pancras or Euston, tel. 019/3754-6060 or 020/7412-7676, www.bl.uk.

Tours: There are no guided tours or audioguides for the permanent collection, but you can 🎧 download my free British Library audio tour. There are guided tours of the building itself—the archives and reading rooms. Touch-screen computers in the permanent collection let you page virtually through some of the rare books.

▲Madame Tussauds Waxworks

This waxtravaganza is gimmicky, crass, and crazily expensive, but dang fun...a hit with the kind of tourists who skip the British Museum. The original Madame Tussaud did wax casts of heads lopped off during the French Revolution (such as Marie-Antoinette's). Now it's all about singing with Lady Gaga, partying with Benedict Cumberbatch, and hanging with the Beatles.

Cost: £35, kids-£30 (free for kids under 5), up to 25 percent discount and shorter lines if you buy tickets in advance on their website; combo-deal with the London Eye.

Hours: Roughly July-Aug and school holidays daily 8:30-18:00, Sept-June Mon-Fri 10:00-16:00, Sat-Sun 9:00-17:00, these are last entry times—it stays open roughly two hours later; check website for the latest times as hours vary widely depending on season, Marylebone Road, Tube: Baker Street, tel. 0871-894-3000, www.madametussauds.com.

THE CITY

When Londoners say "The City," they mean the one-square-mile business center in East London that 2,000 years ago was Roman Londinium. The outline of the Roman city walls can still be seen in the arc of roads from Blackfriars Bridge to Tower Bridge. Within The City are 23 churches designed by Sir Christopher Wren, mostly just ornamentation around St. Paul's Cathedral. Today, while home to only 10,000 residents, The City thrives with around 400,000 office workers coming and going daily. It's a fascinating district to wander on weekdays, but since almost nobody actually lives there, it's dull in the evening and on Saturday and Sunday.

For a walking tour, you can 🎧 download my free audio tour of The City, which peels back the many layers of history in this oldest part of London.

▲▲▲St. Paul's Cathedral

Sir Christopher Wren's most famous church is the great St. Paul's, its elaborate interior capped by a 365-foot dome. There's been a church on this spot since 604. After the Great Fire of 1666 destroyed the old cathedral, Wren created this Baroque masterpiece. And since World War II, St. Paul's has been Britain's symbol of resilience. Despite 57 nights of bombing, the Nazis failed to destroy the cathedral,

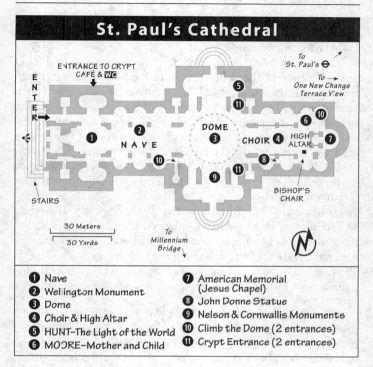

St. Paul's Cathedral

ENTRANCE TO CRYPT
CAFÉ & **WC**

ENTER

NAVE

DOME

CHOIR

HIGH ALTAR

STAIRS

To St. Paul's ⊖

To One New Change Terrace View

BISHOP'S CHAIR

30 Meters

30 Yards

To Millennium Bridge

1 Nave
2 Wellington Monument
3 Dome
4 Choir & High Altar
5 HUNT—The Light of the World
6 MOORE—Mother and Child
7 American Memorial (Jesus Chapel)
8 John Donne Statue
9 Nelson & Cornwallis Monuments
10 Climb the Dome (2 entrances)
11 Crypt Entrance (2 entrances)

thanks to St. Paul's volunteer fire watchmen, who stayed on the dome.

Cost and Hours: £18, £16 in advance online, includes church entry, dome climb, crypt, tour, and audio/videoguide; Mon-Sat 8:30-16:30 (dome opens at 9:30), closed Sun except for worship; book ahead online to skip the line, 15-30-minute wait at busy times; Tube: St. Paul's; recorded info tel. 020/7246-8348, reception tel. 020/7246-8350, www.stpauls.co.uk.

Tours: Admission includes an **audioguide** (with video clips), as well as a 1.5-hour guided **tour** (Mon-Sat at 10:00, 11:00, 13:00, and 14:00; call 020/7246-8357 to confirm or ask at church). Free 20-minute **introductory talks** are offered throughout the day. You can also ⌂ download my free St. Paul's Cathedral **audio tour.**

⊘ Self-Guided Tour: Even now, as skyscrapers encroach, the 365-foot-high dome of St. Paul's rises majestically above the rooftops of the neighborhood. The tall dome is set on classical columns, capped with a lantern, topped by a six-foot ball, and iced with a cross. As the first Anglican cathedral built in London after the Reformation, it is Baroque: St. Peter's in Rome filtered through clear-eyed English reason. Though often the site of historic funerals (Queen Victoria and Winston Churchill), St. Paul's most famous ceremony was a wedding—when Prince Charles married Lady Diana Spencer in 1981.

Enter, buy your ticket, pick up the free visitor's map, and stand at the far back of the ❶ **nave,** behind the font. This big church feels big. At 515 feet long and 250 feet wide, it's Europe's fourth largest, after those in Rome (St. Peter's), Sevilla, and Milan. The spaciousness is accentuated by the relative lack of decoration. The simple, cream-colored ceiling and the clear glass in the windows light everything evenly. Wren wanted this: a simple, open church with nothing to hide. Unfortunately, only this entrance area keeps his original vision—the rest was encrusted with 19th-century Victorian ornamentation.

Ahead and on the left is the towering, black-and-white ❷ **Wellington Monument.** Wren would have been appalled, but his church has become so central to England's soul that many national heroes are buried here (in the basement crypt). General Wellington, Napoleon's conqueror at Waterloo (1815) and the embodiment of British stiff-upper-lippedness, was honored here in a funeral packed with 13,000 fans.

The ❸ **dome** you see from here, painted with scenes from the life of St. Paul, is only the innermost of three. From the painted interior of the first dome, look up through the opening to see the light-filled lantern of the second dome. Finally, the whole thing is covered on the outside by the third and final dome, the shell of lead-covered wood that you see from the street. Wren's ingenious three-in-one design was psychological as well as functional—he wanted a low, shallow inner dome so worshippers wouldn't feel diminished. The ❹ **choir** area blocks your way, but you can see the altar at the far end under a golden canopy.

Do a quick clockwise spin around the church. In the north transept (to your left as you face the altar), find the big painting ❺ *The Light of the World* (1904), by the Pre-Raphaelite William Holman Hunt. Inspired by Hunt's own experience of finding Christ during a moment of spiritual crisis, the crowd-pleasing work was criticized by art highbrows for being "syrupy" and "simple"— even as it became the most famous painting in Victorian England.

Along the left side of the choir is the modern statue ❻ *Mother and Child,* by the great modern sculptor Henry Moore. Typical of Moore's work, this Mary and Baby Jesus—inspired by the sight of British moms nursing babies in WWII bomb shelters—renders a traditional subject in an abstract, minimalist way.

The area behind the altar, with three bright and modern stained-glass windows, is the ❼ **American Memorial Chapel**— honoring the Americans who sacrificed their lives to save Britain in World War II. In colored panes that arch around the big windows, spot the American eagle (center window, to the left of

Christ), George Washington (right window, upper-right corner), and symbols of all 50 states (find your state seal). In the carved wood beneath the windows, you'll see birds and foliage native to the US. The Roll of Honor (a 500-page book under glass immediately behind the altar) lists the names of 28,000 US servicemen and women based in Britain who gave their lives during the war.

Around the other side of the choir is a shrouded statue honoring ❽ **John Donne** (1621–1631), a passionate preacher in old St. Paul's, as well as a great poet ("never wonder for whom the bell tolls—it tolls for thee"). In the south transept are monuments to military greats ❾ **Horatio Nelson,** who fought Napoleon, and **Charles Cornwallis,** who was finished off by George Washington at Yorktown.

Climbing the Dome: You can climb 528 steps to reach the dome and great city views. Along the way, have some fun in the **Whispering Gallery** (257 steps up). Whisper sweet nothings into the wall, and your partner (and anyone else) standing far away can hear you. A long, tight metal staircase takes you to the very top of the cupola, the **Golden Gallery.** Once at the top, you emerge to stunning, unobstructed views of the city.

Visiting the Crypt: The crypt is a world of historic bones and interesting cathedral models. Many legends are buried here— Horatio Nelson, who wore down Napoleon; the Duke of Wellington, who finished Napoleon off; and even Wren himself. Wren's actual tomb is marked by a simple black slab with no statue, though he considered this church to be his legacy. Back up in the nave, on the floor directly under the dome, is Christopher Wren's name and epitaph (written in Latin): "Reader, if you seek his monument, look around you."

▲▲▲Tower of London

The Tower has served as a castle in wartime, a king's residence in peacetime, and, most notoriously, as the prison and execution site of rebels. You can see the crown jewels, take a witty Beefeater tour, and ponder the executioner's block that dispensed with Anne Boleyn, Sir Thomas More, and troublesome heirs to the throne. You'll find more bloody history per square inch in this original tower of power than anywhere else in Britain.

Cost and Hours: £29.50, family-£75, entry fee includes Beefeater tour (described later), Tue-Sat 9:00-17:30, Sun-Mon from 10:00, Nov-Feb until 16:30, skippable audioguide-£4; Tube: Tower Hill, tel. 0844-482-7788, www.hrp.org.uk.

Advance Tickets: To avoid the long ticket-buying lines, and save a few pounds off the gate price, buy a **voucher** or ticket in advance. You can purchase vouchers at the Trader's Gate gift shop, located down the steps from the Tower Hill Tube stop—look for the blue awning (pick it up on your way to the Tower). Vouchers can be used any day but they must be exchanged for tickets at the Tower's group ticket office (see map). You can also buy tickets in advance on the Tower's website (£24, family-£59; only valid for the date selected).

You can also try buying tickets, with credit card only, at the Tower Welcome Centre to the left of the normal ticket lines—though on busy days they may turn you away. Tickets are also sold by phone (tel. 0844-482-7788 within UK or tel. 011-44-20-3166-6000 from the US; £2 fee, pick up your tickets at the Tower's group ticket office).

More Crowd-Beating Tips: For fewer crowds, arrive before 10:00 and go straight for the jewels. Alternatively, arrive in the afternoon, tour the rest of the Tower first, and see the jewels an hour before closing time, when crowds die down.

Yeoman Warder (Beefeater) Tours: Today, while the Tower's military purpose is history, it's still home to the Beefeaters—the 35 Yeoman Warders and their families. (The original duty of the Yeoman Warders was to guard the Tower, its prisoners, and the jewels.) Free, worthwhile, one-hour Beefeater tours leave every 30 minutes from just inside the entrance gate (first tour Tue-Sat at 10:00, Sun-Mon at 10:30, last one at 15:30—or 14:30 in Nov-Feb). The boisterous Beefeaters are great entertainers, whose historical talks include lots of bloody anecdotes and corny jokes.

◑ Self-Guided Tour: Even an army the size of the ticket line couldn't storm this castle. The **entrance gate** where you'll show your ticket was just part of two concentric rings of complete defenses. As you go in, consult the daily event schedule, and consider catching the Beefeater tour.

When you're all set, go 50 yards straight ahead to the **traitors' gate.** This was the boat entrance to the Tower from the Thames. Many English leaders who fell from grace entered through here—only a lucky few walked back out.

Turn left to pass under the archway into the inner courtyard. The big William I, still getting used to his new title of "the Conqueror," built the stone **"White Tower"** (1077-1097) in the middle to keep the Londoners in line. Standing high above the rest of old London, the White Tower provided a gleaming reminder of the

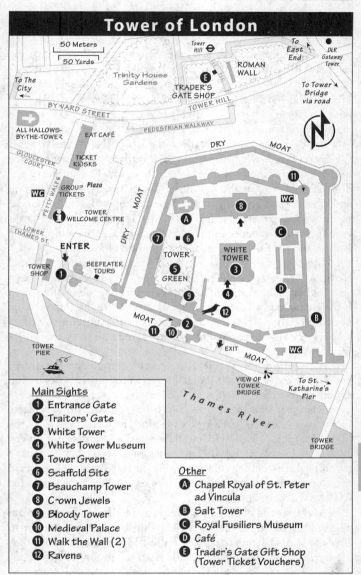

Tower of London

Main Sights
1. Entrance Gate
2. Traitors' Gate
3. White Tower
4. White Tower Museum
5. Tower Green
6. Scaffold Site
7. Beauchamp Tower
8. Crown Jewels
9. Bloody Tower
10. Medieval Palace
11. Walk the Wall (2)
12. Ravens

Other
A. Chapel Royal of St. Peter ad Vincula
B. Salt Tower
C. Royal Fusiliers Museum
D. Café
E. Trader's Gate Gift Shop (Tower Ticket Vouchers)

monarch's absolute power over subjects. The Tower also served as an effective lookout for seeing invaders coming up the Thames.

This square, 90-foot-tall tower was the original structure that gave this castle complex of 20 towers its name. William's successors enlarged the complex to its present 18-acre size. Because of the security it provided, the Tower of London served over the centuries as a royal residence, the Royal Mint, the Royal Jewel House, and, most famously, as the prison and execution site of those who dared oppose the Crown.

Inside the White Tower is a **museum** with exhibits re-creating medieval life and chronicling the torture and executions that took place here. In the Royal Armory, you'll see some suits of armor of Henry VIII—slender in his youth (c. 1515), heavyset by 1540—with his bigger-is-better codpiece. On the top floor, see the Tower's actual execution ax and chopping block.

Back outside, the courtyard to the left of the White Tower is the **Tower Green.** In medieval times, this spacious courtyard within the walls was the "town square" for those who lived in the castle. The **scaffold site,** in the middle of Tower Green, looks pleasant enough today. A modern sculpture encourages visitors to ponder those who died here. Henry VIII axed a couple of his ex-wives here (divorced readers can insert their own joke), including Anne Boleyn and his fifth wife, teenage Catherine Howard.

The north side of the Green is bordered by the stone **Chapel Royal of St. Peter ad Vincula** ("in Chains"), where Anne Boleyn and Catherine Howard are buried. Overlooking the scaffold sight is the **Beauchamp Tower,** one of several places in the complex that housed Very Important Prisoners. You can climb upstairs to a room where the walls are covered by graffiti carved into the stone by despondent inmates.

Across from the White Tower is the entrance to the **crown jewels.** Here you'll pass through a series of rooms with videos and exhibits showing the actual coronation items in the order they're used whenever a new king or queen is crowned. The Imperial State Crown is what the Queen wears for official functions such as the State Opening of Parliament. Among its 3,733 jewels are Queen Elizabeth I's former earrings (the hanging pearls, top center), a stunning 13th-century ruby look-alike in the center, and Edward the Confessor's ring (the blue sapphire on top, in the center of the Maltese cross of diamonds).

At the far end of the Tower Green is the **Bloody Tower** (where 13-year-old King Edward V and his kid brother are thought to have died) and beyond that, the **Medieval Palace,** built in 1240 by Henry III. From the medieval palace's throne room you can continue up the stairs to **walk the walls.** The Tower was defended by state-of-the-art walls and fortifications in the 13th century. Walking along them offers a good look at the walls, along with a fine view of the famous Tower Bridge, with its twin towers and blue spans.

Between the White Tower and the Thames are cages housing **ravens:** According to tradition, the Tower and the British throne are only safe as long as ravens are present here. Other sights at the

Tower include the Salt Tower and the Royal Fusiliers Regimental Museum.

Nearby: The iconic **Tower Bridge** (often mistakenly called London Bridge) was built in 1894 to accommodate the growing East End. While fully modern and hydraulically powered, the drawbridge was designed with a retro Neo-Gothic look.

SOUTH BANK

The South Bank of the Thames is a thriving arts and cultural center, tied together by the riverfront Jubilee Walkway that offers grand views of the Houses of Parliament and St. Paul's.

▲▲London Eye

This giant 443-foot-high Ferris wheel, towering above London opposite Big Ben, is one of the world's highest observational wheels and London's answer to the Eiffel Tower. Riding it is a memorable experience, even though London doesn't have much of a skyline, and the price is borderline outrageous. Whether you ride or not, the wheel is a sight to behold.

Designed like a giant bicycle wheel, it's a pan-European undertaking: British steel and Dutch engineering, with Czech, German, French, and Italian mechanical parts. It's also very "green," running extremely efficiently and virtually silently. Twenty-eight people ride in each of its 32 air-conditioned capsules (representing the boroughs of London) for the 30-minute rotation (you go around only once).

Cost: £27, about 10 percent cheaper if bought online. Combo-tickets save money if you plan on visiting Madame Tussauds. Buy tickets in advance at www.londoneye.com or try in person at the box office (in the corner of the County Hall building nearest the Eye), though day-of tickets are often sold out.

Hours: Daily June-Aug 10:00-20:30 or later, Sept-May generally 11:00-18:00, check website for latest schedule, these are last-ascent times, closed Dec 25 and a few days in Jan for maintenance, Tube: Waterloo or Westminster. Thames boats come and go from London Eye Pier at the foot of the wheel.

Crowd-Beating Tips: The London Eye is busiest between 11:00 and 17:00, especially on weekends year-round and every day in July and August. You may wait up to 30 minutes to buy your ticket, then another 30-45 minutes to board your capsule—it's best to prebook your ticket during these times. Print your advance ticket at home, retrieve it from an onsite ticket machine (bring your payment card and confirmation code), or stand in the "Ticket Collection" line.

▲▲Imperial War Museum

This impressive museum covers the wars and conflicts of the 20th and 21st centuries—from World War I biplanes, to the London Blitz and World War II, the Holocaust, the Cold War, the Cuban Missile Crisis, the Troubles in Northern Ireland, the wars in Iraq and Afghanistan, and terrorism. Rather than glorify war, the museum encourages an understanding of the history of modern warfare and the wartime experience, including the effect it has on the everyday lives of people back home. The museum's coverage never neglects the human side of one of civilization's more uncivilized, persistent traits. Allow plenty of time, as this powerful museum—with lots of artifacts and video clips—can be engrossing.

Cost and Hours: Free, £5 suggested donation, special exhibits extra, daily 10:00-18:00, last entry one hour before closing, Tube: Lambeth North or Elephant and Castle; buses #3, #12, and #159 from Westminster area; tel. 020/7416-5000, www.iwm.org.uk.

▲▲Tate Modern

This striking museum fills a derelict old power station across the river from St. Paul's Cathedral. Its powerhouse collection includes Dalí, Picasso, Warhol, and much more. The permanent collection is generally on levels 2 through 4 of the Boiler House. Paintings are arranged according to theme—such as "Poetry and Dream"—not chronologically or by artist. Paintings by Picasso, for example, are scattered all over the building. Don't just come to see the Old Masters  of modernism. Push your mental envelope with more recent works by Miró, Bacon, Picabia, Beuys, Twombly, and others.

Of equal interest are the many temporary exhibits of cutting-edge art. Each year, the main hall features a different monumental installation by a prominent artist—always one of the highlights of the art world. The Tate recently opened a wing to the south: This new Blavatnik Building (Switch House) gave the Tate an extra quarter-million square feet of display space.

Cost and Hours: Free, £4 donation appreciated, fee for special exhibits; open daily 10:00-18:00, Fri-Sat until 22:00, last entry to special exhibits 45 minutes before closing, especially crowded on weekend days (crowds thin out Fri and Sat evenings); view restaurant on top floor; tel. 020/7887-8888, www.tate.org.uk.

Tours: Multimedia guide-£4.75, free 45-minute guided tours at 11:00, 12:00, 14:00, and 15:00.

Getting There: Cross the Millennium Bridge from St. Paul's; take the Tube to Southwark, London Bridge, St. Paul's, Mansion House, or Blackfriars and walk 10-15 minutes; or catch Thames Clippers' Tate Boat ferry from the Tate Britain (Millbank Pier) for a 15-minute crossing (£8 one-way, every 40 minutes Mon-Fri 10:00-16:00, Sat-Sun 9:15-18:40, www.tate.org.uk/visit/tate-boat).

▲▲Shakespeare's Globe

This replica of the original Globe Theatre was built, half-timbered and thatched, as it was in Shakespeare's time. (This is the first

thatched roof constructed in London since they were outlawed after the Great Fire of 1666.) The Globe originally accommodated 2,200 seated and another 1,000 standing. Today, slightly smaller and leaving space for reasonable aisles, the theater holds 800 seated and 600 groundlings.

Its promoters brag that the theater melds "the three A's"—actors, audience, and architecture—with each contributing to the play. The working theater hosts authentic performances of Shakespeare's plays with actors in period costumes, modern interpretations of his works, and some works by other playwrights. For details on attending a play, see page 970.

The Globe complex has four parts: the Globe theater itself, the box office, a museum (called the Exhibition), and the Sam Wanamaker Playhouse (an indoor Jacobean theater around back). The Playhouse, which hosts performances through the winter, is horseshoe-shaped, intimate (seating fewer than 350), and sometimes uses authentic candle-lighting for period performances.

Cost: £17 for adults, £10 for kids 5-15, free for kids 5 and under, family ticket available; ticket includes Exhibition, audioguide, and 40-minute tour of the Globe; when theater is in use, you can tour the Exhibition only for £6.

Hours: The complex is open daily 9:00-17:30. Tours start every 30 minutes; during Globe theater season (late April-mid-Oct) last tour Mon at 17:00, Tue-Sat at 12:30, Sun at 11:30—it's safest to arrive for a tour before noon; located on the South Bank over the Millennium Bridge from St. Paul's, Tube: Mansion House or London Bridge plus a 10-minute walk; tel. 020/7902-1400, box office tel. 020/7401-9919, www.shakespearesglobe.com.

Eating: The **$$$$ Swan at the Globe** café offers a sit-down restaurant (for lunch and dinner, reservations recommended, tel. 020/7928-9444), a drinks-and-plates bar, and a sandwich-and-coffee cart (Mon-Fri 8:00-closing, depends on performance times, Sat-Sun from 10:00).

OUTSIDE LONDON

Those starting or ending their cruise in London can consider a day-trip to Stonehenge.

▲▲▲Stonehenge

As old as the pyramids, and far older than the Acropolis and the Colosseum, this iconic stone circle amazed medieval Europeans, who figured it was built by a race of giants. And it still impresses visitors today. As one of Europe's most famous sights, Stonehenge does a valiant job of retaining an air of mystery and majesty (partly because cordons, which keep hordes of tourists from trampling all over it, foster the illusion that it stands alone in a

field). Most of its almost one million annual visitors agree that it's well worth the trip. Adjacent to the site, an excellent, state-of-the-art exhibit uses an artful combination of multimedia displays and actual artifacts to provide context for the stones. Start by touring the visitors center, then take a shuttle (or walk) to the stone circle.

Cost: £17.50, includes shuttle-bus ride to stone circle, best to buy in advance online.

Hours: Daily June-Aug 9:00-20:00, April-May and Sept-mid-Oct 9:30-19:00, mid-Oct-March 9:30-17:00. Note that the last ticket is sold two hours before closing. Expect shorter hours and possible closures June 20-22 due to huge, raucous solstice crowds.

Advance Tickets and Crowd-Beating Tips: You can avoid the long ticket-buying line by prebooking at least 24 hours in advance at www.english-heritage.org.uk/stonehenge. Either print out an e-ticket or bring the booking number from your confirmation email to the designated window at the entrance. For a less crowded, more mystical experience, come to Stonehenge early or late. Things are pretty quiet before 10:30 (head out to the stones first) and just before the "last ticket" time (two hours before closing).

Information: Tel. 0870-333-1181, www.english-heritage.org. uk/stonehenge.

Getting There: Several companies offer **big-bus day trips** to Stonehenge from London. These generally cost about £45-85 (including Stonehenge admission), last 8-12 hours, and pack a 45-seat bus. Well-known companies are **Evan Evans** (www. evanevanstours.co.uk) and **Golden Tours** (www.goldentours.com). **International Friends** runs pricier but smaller 16-person tours that include Windsor and Bath (www.internationalfriends.co.uk).

London Walks offers a guided "Stonehenge and Salisbury Tour" from London by train and bus on Tuesdays from May through October (£78, cash only, www.walks.com).

To go on your own on **public transport,** catch a train (2/hour, 1.5 hours) from London's Waterloo Station to Salisbury (www. southwesttrains.co.uk or www.nationalrail.co.uk). From Salisbury, you can get to Stonehenge by taxi (£40-50) or take the **Stonehenge Tour bus** (£15, £29 with Stonehenge admission; daily June-Aug 10:00-18:00, 2/hour, 30 minutes, fewer departures off-season, timetable at www.thestonehengetour.info).

Tours: Worthwhile audioguides are available behind the ticket counter (£3). Or you can use the visitors center's free Wi-Fi to download the free "Stonehenge Audio Tour" app.

Eating: There's a large **$ café** within the visitors center.

Shopping in London

Most stores are open Monday through Saturday from roughly 9:00 or 10:00 until 17:00 or 18:00, with a late night on Wednesday or Thursday (usually until 19:00 or 20:00). Many close on Sundays. Large department stores stay open later during the week (until about 21:00 Mon-Sat) with shorter hours on Sundays. If you're looking for bargains, visit one of the city's many street markets.

Shopping Streets

London is famous for its shopping. The best and most convenient shopping streets are in the West End and West London (roughly between Soho and Hyde Park). You'll find midrange shops along **Oxford Street** (running

east from Tube: Marble Arch), and fancier shops along **Regent Street** (stretching south from Tube: Oxford Circus to Piccadilly Circus) and **Knightsbridge** (where you'll find Harrods and Harvey Nichols; Tube: Knightsbridge). Other streets are more specialized, such as **Jermyn Street** for old-fashioned men's clothing (just south of Piccadilly Street) and **Charing Cross Road** for books. **Floral Street,** connecting Leicester Square to Covent Garden, is lined with fashion boutiques.

Fancy Department Stores

Harrods is London's most famous and touristy department store. With more than four acres of retail space covering seven floors, it's a place where some shoppers could spend all day. Big yet classy, Harrods has everything from elephants to toothbrushes (Mon-Sat 10:00-21:00, Sun 11:30-18:00; Brompton Road, Tube: Knightsbridge, tel. 020/7730-1234, www.harrods.com).

Once Princess Diana's favorite and later Duchess Kate's, **Harvey Nichols** remains the department store *du jour* (Mon-Sat 10:00-20:00, Sun 11:30-18:00, near Harrods, 109 Knightsbridge, Tube: Knightsbridge, tel. 020/7235-5000, www.harveynichols.com). Want to pick up a £20 scarf? You won't do it here, where they're more like £200.

The official department store of the Queen, **Fortnum & Mason** embodies old-fashioned, British upper-class taste. With rich displays and deep red carpet, it feels classier and more relaxed than Harrods (Mon-Sat 10:00-21:00, Sun 11:30-18:00, elegant tea served in their Diamond Jubilee Tea Salon, 181 Piccadilly, Tube: Green Park, tel. 020/7734-8040, www.fortnumandmason.com).

Street Markets

The best markets—which combine lively stalls and a colorful neighborhood with cute and characteristic shops of their own—are Portobello Road and Camden Lock Market. Hagglers will enjoy the no-holds-barred bargaining encouraged in London's street markets. Be warned: Markets attract two kinds of people—tourists and pickpockets.

Portobello Road Market (Notting Hill): Portobello Road stretches for several blocks through the delightful, colorful, funky-yet-quaint Notting Hill neighborhood. Already-charming streets lined with pastel-painted houses and offbeat antique shops are enlivened on Fridays and Saturdays with 2,000 additional stalls (9:00-19:00), plus food, live music, and more. (Tube: Notting Hill Gate, tel. 020/7727-7684, www.portobelloroad.co.uk).

Camden Lock Market (Camden Town): This huge, trendy arts-and-crafts festival is divided into three areas, each with its own vibe. You'll find boutique crafts, artisanal foods, cheap ethnic food stalls, lots of canalside seating, punk crafts, cheap clothes, junk jewelry, and loud music (daily 10:00-19:00, busiest on week-ends, tel. 020/3763-9999, www.camdenmarket.com).

Covent Garden Market: Originally the convent garden for Westminster Abbey, the iron-and-glass market hall now offers a mix of fun shops, eateries, and markets. Yesteryear's produce stalls are open daily 10:30-18:00, and on Thursdays, a food market brightens up the square (Tube: Covent Garden, tel. 020/7395-1350, www.coventgardenlondonuk.com).

Eating in London

Whether it's dining well with the upper crust, sharing hearty pub fare with the blokes, or joining young professionals at the sushi bar, eating out has become an essential part of the London experience. The sheer variety of foods—from every corner of Britain's former empire and beyond—is astonishing.

I've listed places by neighbor-hood—handy to your sightseeing. Pub grub (at one of London's 7,000 pubs) and ethnic restaurants (especially In-dian and Chinese) are good low-cost options. Of course, picnicking is the fastest and cheapest way to go. Good grocery stores and sandwich shops, fine park benches, and polite pigeons abound in Britain's most expensive city.

CENTRAL LONDON

I've arranged these options by neighborhood, but they're all within about a 15-minute walk of each other. Survey your options before settling on a place.

Soho and Nearby

London has a trendy scene that many Beefeater seekers miss. Food-ies who want to eat well head to Soho. These restaurants are scat-tered throughout a chic, creative, and once-seedy zone that teems with hipsters, theatergoers, and London's gay community.

On and near Wardour Street

$$ Princi is a vast, bright, efficient, wildly popular Italian deli/bakery with Milanese flair. Along one wall is a long counter with display cases offering a tempting array of *pizza rustica*, *panini* sand-wiches, focaccia, pasta dishes, and desserts. Order your food at the counter, then find a space to share at a long table; or get it to go.

Central London

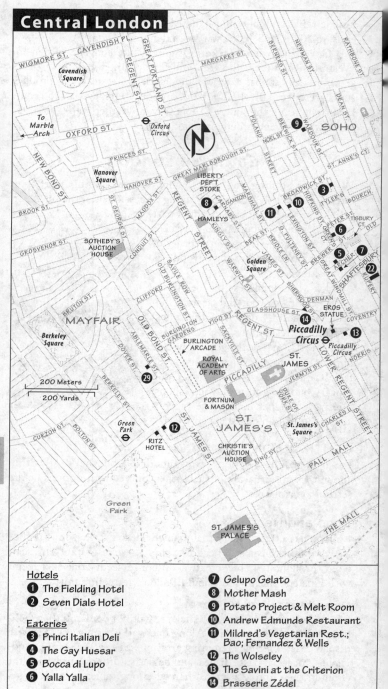

Hotels
1. The Fielding Hotel
2. Seven Dials Hotel

Eateries
3. Princi Italian Deli
4. The Gay Hussar
5. Bocca di Lupo
6. Yalla Yalla
7. Gelupo Gelato
8. Mother Mash
9. Potato Project & Melt Room
10. Andrew Edmunds Restaurant
11. Mildred's Vegetarian Rest.; Bao; Fernandez & Wells
12. The Wolseley
13. The Savini at the Criterion
14. Brasserie Zédel

LONDON

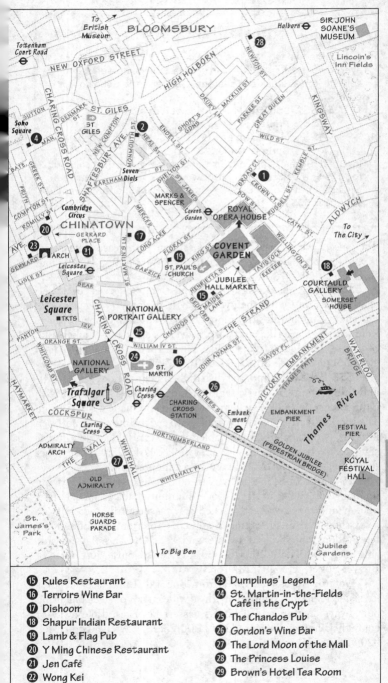

15 Rules Restaurant
16 Terroirs Wine Bar
17 Dishoom
18 Shapur Indian Restaurant
19 Lamb & Flag Pub
20 Y Ming Chinese Restaurant
21 Jen Café
22 Wong Kei

23 Dumplings' Legend
24 St. Martin-in-the-Fields Café in the Crypt
25 The Chandos Pub
26 Gordon's Wine Bar
27 The Lord Moon of the Mall
28 The Princess Louise
29 Brown's Hotel Tea Room

Restaurant Code

I've assigned each eatery a price category, based on the average cost of a typical main course. Drinks, desserts, and splurge items (steak and seafood) can raise the price considerably.

$$$$	**Splurge:** Most main courses over £20
$$$	**Pricier:** £15-20
$$	**Moderate:** £10-15
$	**Budget:** Under £10

In Great Britain, carryout fish-and-chips and other takeout food is **$**; a basic pub or sit-down eatery is **$$**; a gastropub or casual but more upscale restaurant is **$$$**; and a swanky splurge is **$$$$**.

They also have a classy restaurant section with reasonable prices if you'd rather have table service (daily 8:00-24:00, 135 Wardour Street, tel. 020/7478-8888).

$$$ The Gay Hussar, dressy and tight, squeezes several elegant tables into what the owners say is the only Hungarian restaurant in England. It's traditional Hungarian fare: cabbage, sauerkraut, sausage, paprika, and pork, as well as duck and chicken and, of course, Hungarian wine (Mon-Sat 12:15-14:30 & 17:30-22:45, closed Sun, 2 Greek Street, tel. 020/7437-0973).

$$$ Bocca di Lupo, a stylish and popular option, serves half-and full portions of classic regional Italian food. Dressy but with a fun energy, it's a place where you're glad you made a reservation. The counter seating, on cushy stools with a view into the lively open kitchen, is particularly memorable, or you can take a table in the snug, casual back end (daily 12:30-15:00 & 17:15-23:00, 12 Archer Street, tel. 020/7734-2223, www.boccadilupo.com).

$$ Yalla Yalla is a bohemian-chic hole-in-the-wall serving up high-quality Beirut street food—hummus, baba ghanoush, tabbouleh, and *shawarmas*. It's tucked down a seedy alley across from a sex shop. Eat in the cramped and cozy interior or at one of the few outdoor tables (£4 sandwiches and *meze*, £8 *mezes* platter available until 17:00, daily 10:00-24:00, 1 Green's Court—just north of Brewer Street, tel. 020/7287-7663).

Gelato: Across the street from Bocca di Lupo (see above) is its sister *gelateria*, **Gelupo,** with a wide array of ever-changing but always creative and delicious dessert favorites. Take away or enjoy their homey interior (daily 11:00-23:00, 7 Archer Street, tel. 020/7287-5555).

Cheap Eats near Carnaby Street

The area south of Oxford Circus between Regent Street and Soho Gardens entices hungry shoppers with attention-grabbing, gimmicky restaurants that fill the niche between chains and upscale eateries. Stroll along Ganton, Carnaby, or Great Marlborough streets for something that fits your budget and appetite, or try one of these: **$$ Mother Mash** is a bangers-and-mash version of a fish-and-chips shop (daily 10:00-22:00, 26 Ganton Street, tel. 020/7494-9644). **$ Potato Project** features imaginative fillings that turn baked "jacket" potatoes into gourmet creations (Mon-Fri 10:00-18:00, closed Sat-Sun, 27 Noel Street, tel. 020/3620-1585). Next door, **$ Melt Room** crafts anything-but-Kraft grilled cheese masterpieces (Mon-Fri 8:00-20:00, Sat-Sun 11:00-18:00, 26 Noel Street, tel. 020/7096-2002).

Lexington Street, in the Heart of Soho

$$$ Andrew Edmunds Restaurant is a tiny candlelit space where you'll want to hide your camera and guidebook and not act like a tourist. This little place—with a jealous and loyal clientele—is the closest I've found to Parisian quality in a cozy restaurant in London (daily 12:30-15:30 & 17:30-22:45, these are last-order times, come early or call ahead, request ground floor rather than basement, 46 Lexington Street, tel. 020/7437-5708, www.andrewedmunds.com).

$$ Mildred's Vegetarian Restaurant, across from Andrew Edmunds, has a creative, fun menu and a tight, high-energy interior filled with happy herbivores (Mon-Sat 12:00-23:00, closed Sun, vegan options, 45 Lexington Street, tel. 020/7494-1634).

$$$ Bao is a tight, minimalist eatery selling top-quality Taiwanese cuisine, specializing in delicate and delectable steamed-bun sandwiches. While it's pricey (portions are small), it's a great experience and worth the splurge (Mon-Sat 12:00-15:00 & 17:30-22:00, closed Sun, 53 Lexington Street).

$$ Fernandez & Wells is a cozy, convivial, delightfully simple little wine, cheese, and ham bar. Grab a stool as you belly up to the big wooden bar. Share a plate of tapas, top-quality cheeses, and/or Spanish, Italian, or French hams with fine bread and oil, all while sipping a nice glass of wine (Mon-Sat 11:00-23:00, Sun until 18:00, quality sandwiches at lunch, 43 Lexington Street, tel. 020/7734-1546).

Swanky Splurges

$$$$ The Wolseley is the grand 1920s showroom of a long-defunct British car. The last Wolseley drove out with the Great Depression, but today this old-time bistro bustles with formal waiters serving traditional Austrian and French dishes in an elegant black-marble-and-chandeliers setting fit for its location next to the Ritz. Reservations are a must (cheaper soup, salad, and sandwich "café menu" available in all areas of restaurant, daily 7:00-24:00, 160 Piccadilly, tel. 020/7499-6996, www.thewolseley.com). They're popular for their fancy cream tea or afternoon tea 963).

$$$$ The Savini at the Criterion is a palatial dining hall offering an Italian menu in a dreamy neo-Byzantine setting from the 1870s. It's right on Piccadilly Circus but a world away from the punk junk, with fairly normal food served in an unforgettable Great Gatsby space. It's a deal if you order the £29-36 fixed-price meal or £16 cream tea (daily 12:00-23:30, 224 Piccadilly, tel. 020/7930-1459, www.saviniatcriterion.co.uk).

$$$ Brasserie Zédel is the former dining hall of the old Regent Palace Hotel, the biggest hotel in the world when built in 1915. Climbing down the stairs from street level, you're surprised by a gilded grand hall that feels like a circa 1920 cruise ship, filled with a boisterous crowd enjoying big, rich French food—old-fashioned brasserie dishes (daily 11:30-23:00, 20 Sherwood Street, tel. 020/7734-4888).

$$$$ Rules Restaurant, established in 1798, is as traditional as can be—extremely British, classy yet comfortable. It's a big, borderline-stuffy place, where you'll eat in a plush Edwardian atmosphere with formal service and plenty of game on the menu. This is the place to dress up and splurge for classic English dishes (daily 12:00-23:00, between the Strand and Covent Garden at 34 Maiden Lane, tel. 020/7836-5314, www.rules.co.uk).

Near Covent Garden

Covent Garden bustles with people and touristy eateries. The area feels overrun, but if you must eat around here, you have some good choices.

$$$ Terroirs Wine Bar is an enticing place with a casual but classy ambience that exudes happiness. It's a few steps below street level, with a long zinc bar that has a kitchen view and two levels of tables. The fun menu is mostly Mediterranean and designed to share (Mon-Sat 12:00-15:00 & 17:30-23:00, closed Sun, reservations smart, just two blocks from Trafalgar Square but tucked away from the tourist crowds at 5 William IV Street, tel. 020/7036-0660, www.terroirswinebar.com).

$$$ Dishoom is London's hotspot for upscale Indian cuisine, with top-quality ingredients and carefully executed recipes. The dishes seem familiar, but the flavors are a revelation. People line up early (starting around 17:30) for a seat, either on the bright, rollicking, brasserie-like ground floor or in the less appealing basement (daily 8:00-23:00, 12 Upper St. Martin's Lane, tel. 020/7420-9320).

$$$ Shapur Indian Restaurant is a well-respected place serving classic Indian dishes from many regions, fine fish, and a tasty £19 vegetarian *thali* (combo platter). It's small, low energy, and dressy with good service (Mon-Fri 12:00-14:30 & 17:30-23:30, Sat 15:00-23:30, closed Sun, next to Somerset House at 149 Strand, tel. 020/7836-3730, Syed Khan).

$$ Lamb and Flag Pub is a survivor—a spit-and-sawdust pub serving traditional grub (like meat pies) two blocks off Covent Garden, yet seemingly a world away. Here since 1772, this pub was a favorite of Charles Dickens and is now a hit with local workers. At lunch, it's all food. In the evening, the ground floor is for drinking and the food service is upstairs (long hours daily, 33 Rose Street, across from Stanfords bookstore entrance on Floral Street, tel. 020/7497-9504).

Chinatown and Good Chinese Nearby

The main drag of Chinatown (Gerrard Street, with the ornamental archways) is lined with touristy, interchangeable Chinese joints—but these places seem to have an edge.

$$ Y Ming Chinese Restaurant—across Shaftesbury Avenue from the ornate gates, clatter, and dim sum of Chinatown—has dressy, porcelain-blue European decor, serious but helpful service, and authentic Northern Chinese cooking (good £15 meal deal offered 12:00-18:00, open Mon-Sat 12:00-23:30, closed Sun, 35 Greek Street, tel. 020/7734-2721, run for 22 years by William).

$ Jen Café, across the little square called Newport Place, is a humble Chinese corner eatery much loved for its homemade dumplings. It's just stools and simple seating, with fast service, a fun and inexpensive menu, and a devoted following (Mon-Wed 11:00-20:30, Thu-Sun until 21:30, cash only, 4 Newport Place, tel. 020/7287-9708).

$$ Wong Kei Chinese restaurant, at the Wardour Street (west) end of the Chinatown drag, offers a bewildering variety of dishes served by notoriously brusque waiters in a setting that feels like a hospital cafeteria. Londoners put up with the abuse and lack of ambience to enjoy one of the satisfying BBQ rice dishes or hot pots (£10-15 chef special combos, daily 11:30-23:30, cash only, 41 Wardour Street, tel. 020/7437-8408).

$$S Dumplings' Legend is a cut above Wong Kei if you'd like to spend a bit more. They serve a standard Chinese menu with full dim sum only until 18:00 (open daily for lunch and dinner, no reservations, on pedestrian main drag, 15 Gerrard Street, tel. 020/7494-1200).

Pubs and Crypts near Trafalgar Square

These places, all of which provide a more "jolly olde" experience than high cuisine, are within about 100 yards of Trafalgar Square.

$$ St. Martin-in-the-Fields Café in the Crypt is just right for a tasty meal on a monk's budget—maybe even on a monk's tomb. You'll dine sitting on somebody's gravestone in an ancient crypt. Their enticing buffet line is kept stocked all day, serving breakfast, lunch, and dinner (hearty traditional desserts, free jugs of water). They also serve a restful £10 afternoon tea (daily 12:00-18:00). You'll find the café directly under St. Martin-in-the-Fields, facing Trafalgar Square—enter through the glass pavilion next to the church (generally about 8:00-20:00 daily, profits go to the church, Tube: Charing Cross, tel. 020/7766-1158).

$$ The Chandos Pub's Opera Room floats amazingly apart from the tacky crush of tourism around Trafalgar Square. Look for it opposite the National Portrait Gallery (corner of William IV Street and St. Martin's Lane) and climb the stairs—to the left or right of the pub entrance—to the Opera Room. This is a fine Trafalgar rendezvous point and wonderfully local pub (kitchen open daily 11:30-21:00, Fri until 18:00, order and pay at the bar, 29 St. Martin's Lane, Tube: Leicester Square, tel. 020/7836-1401).

$$ Gordon's Wine Bar is a candlelit 15th-century wine cellar filled with dusty old bottles, faded British memorabilia, and nine-to-fivers. At the "English rustic" buffet, choose a hot meal or cold meat dish with a salad (figure around £11/dish); the £12 cheese plate comes with two big hunks of cheese (from your choice of 20), bread, and a pickle. Then step up to the wine bar and consider the many varieties of wine and port available by the glass (daily 11:00-23:00, 2 blocks from Trafalgar Square, bottom of Villiers Street at #47—the door is locked but it's just around the corner to the right, Tube: Embankment, tel. 020/7930-1408, manager Gerard Menan).

$ The Lord Moon of the Mall Pub is a sloppy old eating pub, actually filling a former bank, right at the top of Whitehall. While nothing extraordinary, it's a very handy location and cranks out cheap, simple pub grub and fish-and-chips all day (long hours daily, 16 Whitehall, Tube: Charing Cross, tel. 020/7839-7701).

Near the British Museum

For locations, see the "North London" map on page 937.

$ Salumeria Dino serves up hearty £5 sandwiches, pasta, and Italian coffee. Dino, a native of Naples, has run his little shop for more than 30 years and has managed to create a classic-feeling Italian deli (cheap takeaway cappuccinos, Mon-Fri 9:00-18:00, closed Sat-Sun, 15 Charlotte Place, tel. 020/7580-3938).

$ Lantana OUT, next door to Salumeria Dino, is an Australian coffee shop that sells modern soups, sandwiches, and salads at their takeaway window (£8 daily hot dish). **Lantana IN** is an adjacent sit-down café that serves pricier meals (both open long hours daily, 13 Charlotte Place, tel. 020/7637-3347).

$$ Indian Food near the British Library: Drummond Street (running just west of Euston Station) is famous for cheap and good Indian vegetarian food. For a good, moderately priced *thali* (combo platter) consider **Chutneys** (124 Drummond, tel. 020/7388-0604) and **Ravi Shankar** (135 Drummond, tel. 020/7388-6458, both open long hours daily).

$$ Princess Louise, a lovingly restored Victorian pub dating from 1897, serves good beer and grub (daily midday until 23:00, lunch and dinner served Mon-Sat 12:00-21:00 in less atmospheric upstairs lounge, no food Sun, 208 High Holborn, Tube: Holborn, tel. 020/7405-8816).

TAKING TEA IN LONDON

While visiting London, consider partaking in this most British of traditions. The cheapest "tea" on the menu is generally a "cream tea"; the most expensive is the "champagne tea." **Cream tea** is simply a pot of tea and a homemade scone or two with jam and thick clotted cream. (For maximum pinkie-waving taste per calorie, slice your scone thin like a miniature loaf of bread.) **Afternoon tea**—what many Americans would call "high tea"—generally is a cream tea plus a tier of three plates holding small finger foods (such as cucumber sandwiches) and an assortment of small pastries. **Champagne tea** includes all of the goodies, plus a glass of bubbly.

Most tearooms are usually open for lunch and close about 17:00. At all the places listed below, it's perfectly acceptable for two people to order one afternoon tea and one cream tea and share the afternoon tea's goodies.

Traditional Tea Experiences

$$$ The Wolseley serves a good afternoon tea between their meal service. Split one with your companion and enjoy two light meals at a great price in classic elegance (£13 cream tea, £30 afternoon tea, £40 champagne tea, generally served 15:00-18:30 daily, see full listing earlier in this section).

$$$$ Fortnum & Mason department store offers tea at several different restaurants within its walls. You can "Take Tea in the Parlour" for £22 (including ice cream and scones; Mon-Sat 10:00-19:30, Sun 11:30-17:00). The *pièce de résistance* is their Diamond Jubilee Tea Salon, named in honor of the Queen's 60th year on the throne (and, no doubt, to remind visitors of Her Majesty's visit for tea here in 2012 with Camilla and Kate). At these royal prices, consider it dinner (£48, Mon-Sat 12:00-19:00, Sun until 18:00, dress up a bit—no shorts, 181 Piccadilly, smart to reserve at least a week in advance, tel. 020/7734-8040, www.fortnumandmason.com).

$$$$ Brown's Hotel in Mayfair serves a fancy £55 afternoon tea (you're welcome to ask for second helpings of your favorite scones and sandwiches) in its English tearoom. Said to be the inspiration for Agatha Christie's *At Bertram's Hotel*, the wood-paneled walls and inviting fire set a scene that's more contemporary-cozy than pinky-raising classy (daily 12:00-18:00, reservations smart, no casual clothing, 33 Albemarle Street—see map on page 956, Tube: Green Park, tel. 020/7518-4155, www.roccofortehotels.com).

Starting or Ending Your Cruise in London

If your cruise begins and/or ends in London, you'll want plenty of extra time here; for most travelers, two days is a bare minimum. For a longer visit here, pick up my *Rick Steves London* guidebook; for other destinations in the country, see *Rick Steves England* or *Rick Steves Great Britain*.

Airport Connections

London has six airports. Most tourists arrive at **Heathrow** or **Gatwick** airport, although flights from elsewhere in Europe may land at **Stansted, Luton, Southend,** or **London City** airport.

To get from any airport to your cruise port (or vice versa), you'll connect through London. I've given specific directions for each airport below, followed by tips for continuing on to Southampton or Dover. For a list of hotels in London, see the end of this chapter.

Some cruise lines offer convenient **shuttle bus service** directly from the airport to the cruise port; check with your cruise line for details.

HEATHROW AIRPORT

Heathrow Airport is one of the world's busiest airports. For Heathrow's airport, flight, and transfer information, call the switchboard at 0844-335-1801, or visit the helpful website www.heathrow.com (airport code: LHR).

Heathrow's terminals are numbered T-1 through T-5, though T-1 is now closed. You can walk between T-2 and T-3. From this central hub (called "Heathrow Central"), T-4 and T-5 split off in opposite directions (and are not walkable). The easiest way to travel between the T-2/T-3 cluster and either T-4 or T-5 is by Heathrow Express train (free to transfer between terminals, departs every

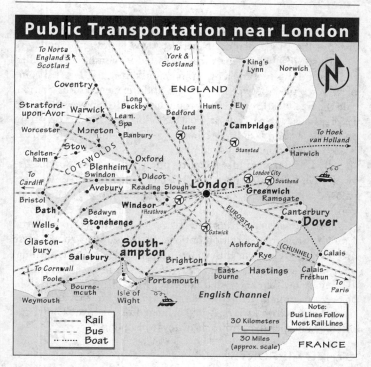

Public Transportation near London

15-20 minutes). You can also take a shuttle bus (free, serves all terminals), or the Tube (requires a ticket, serves all terminals).

Getting from Heathrow to London

To get between Heathrow and London (14 miles away), you have several options:

Taxi: The one-hour trip costs £45-75 to west and central London, for up to four people. Just get in the queue outside the terminal. If running, Uber also offers London airport pickup and drop-off.

Tube (Underground): For £6, the Tube takes you from any Heathrow terminal to downtown London in 50-60 minutes on the Piccadilly Line (6/hour). If you plan to use the Tube for transport in London, consider buying a pay-as-you-go Oyster card.

Train: The **Heathrow Express** is fast and runs frequently, but it's pricey (£22-25 one-way, price depends on time of day, £37 round-trip; 4/hour, Mon-Sat 5:00-24:00, Sun 6:00-24:00, 15 minutes to downtown from Heathrow Central Station serving T-2/T-3, 21 minutes from T-5; for T-4 take free transfer to Heathrow Central, tel. 0345-600-1515, www.heathrowexpress.co.uk). A cheaper alternative to the Heathrow Express—the new **Crossrail**

LONDON

Elizabeth line—may be operational by the time you visit (not as cheap as the Tube, but much faster; see www.tfl.gov.uk for updates).

Bus: Most buses depart from the outdoor common area called the Central Bus Station, a five-minute walk from the T-2/T-3 complex. To connect between T-4 or T-5 and the Central Bus Station, ride the free Heathrow Express train or the shuttle buses. **National Express** buses go to Victoria Coach Station near the Victoria train and Tube station (£8-10, 1-2/hour, 45-75 minutes, tel. 0871-781-8181, www.nationalexpress.com).

By Car Service: Just Airports offers a private car service between five London airports and the city center (from £32/car, see website for price quote, tel. 020/8900-1666, www.justairports.com).

From London to Heathrow: To get to Heathrow from central London, your transportation options are the same as above. Here are a few tips: Confirm with your airline in advance which terminal your flight will use, to avoid having to transfer between terminals. If arriving by Tube, note that not every Piccadilly Line train stops at every terminal. Before boarding, make sure your train is going to the terminal you want. A taxi arranged through your hotel can often be cheaper than from Heathrow to London.

OTHER AIRPORTS

Gatwick is London's second-biggest airport (airport code: LGW, tel. 0844-892-0322, www.gatwickairport.com). To get from Gatwick into London, **Gatwick Express trains** shuttle conveniently to Victoria Station (£20 one-way, £35 round-trip, Oyster card accepted, 4/hour, 30 minutes, tel. 0845-850-1530, www.gatwickexpress.com).

London's other, lesser airports are **Stansted Airport** (airport code: STN, tel. 0844-335-1803, www.stanstedairport.com), **Luton Airport** (airport code: LTN, tel. 01582/405-100, www.london-luton.co.uk), **London City Airport** (airport code: LCY, tel. 020/7646-0088, www.londoncityairport.com), and **Southend Airport** (airport code: SEN, tel. 01702/608-100, www.southendairport.com).

GETTING FROM CENTRAL LONDON TO THE CRUISE PORTS

Even if you're coming directly from any of London's airports, you'll need to transfer through London to reach either Southampton or Dover (unless your cruise line offers **shuttle service** from the airport to your ship). For either port, also ask your cruise line whether they're offering a shuttle from the train station in Southampton or Dover to your ship.

To Southampton

To reach Southampton's cruise ports, go by bus, Tube, or taxi to London **Waterloo** train station, where trains depart to Southampton Central (about £42 "single"/one-way, 2-3/hour, 1.5 hours; a few more options with a change in Basingstoke; a few slow trains go from London Victoria in 2.5 hours). Don't get off at "Southampton Airport Parkway"—stay on until "Southampton Central."

Exiting the station in Southampton, you'll find a row of **taxis** ready to take you to your ship. Figure around £6-8 (£1 extra on Sun)—ask for an estimate first, then insist on the meter.

If you're packing light and feeling thrifty and energetic, you could take advantage of the **QuayConnect** or **Unilink buses** that depart from the curb just outside the station; however, note that they do not take you all the way to your ship—you'll still have to walk between 5 and 20 minutes, depending on where your ship is. For the Mayflower Cruise Terminal, take a taxi. For details on these buses, see page 872.

To Dover

Trains head to Dover from various London stations. The fastest connection is on the high-speed train from **St. Pancras Station** (£40.50 "single"/one-way, 2/hour, 1.5 hours). Slower trains to Dover leave from **Victoria** or **Charing Cross Stations** (for either: around £36 "single"/one-way, 1-2/hour, 2 hours).

If you're staying near Victoria or Charing Cross Stations, you might as well take the train from there; but all other things being equal, I'd take the faster connection from St. Pancras Station.

Arriving at Dover Priory Station, your best bet is to pay £8 for a **taxi** to your ship. While it's possible to walk 15 minutes to Market Square to catch a **shuttle bus** to your ship, two people can take a taxi for about the same price. There's no public bus from the station to the cruise port.

Hotels in London

$$$$= Most rooms over £160; $$$= £120-160; $$= £80-120; $= £40-80; ¢= Under £40

London is an expensive city for lodging. Cheaper rooms are relatively dumpy. Don't expect £160 cheeriness in an £80 room. For £100, you'll get a basic, reasonably cheery double with worn carpet and a private bath in a usually cramped, somewhat outdated, cracked-plaster building, or a soulless but comfortable room without breakfast in a huge Motel 6-type place. My London splurges, at £160-300, are spacious, thoughtfully appointed places good for entertaining or romancing.

VICTORIA STATION NEIGHBORHOOD

The streets behind Victoria Station teem with little, moderately-priced-for-London B&Bs. It's a safe, surprisingly tidy, and decent area without a hint of the trashy, touristy glitz of the streets in front of the station.

$$$$ Lime Tree Hotel, enthusiastically run by Charlotte and Matt, is a gem, with 28 spacious, stylish, comfortable, thoughtfully decorated rooms, a helpful staff, and a fun-loving breakfast room (small lounge opens onto quiet garden, 135 Ebury Street, tel. 020/7730-8191, www.limetreehotel.co.uk, info@limetreehotel.co.uk, Laura manages the office).

$$$ Luna Simone Hotel rents 36 fresh, spacious, remodeled rooms with modern bathrooms. It's a smartly managed place, run for more than 40 years by twins Peter and Bernard—and Bernard's son Mark—and they still seem to enjoy their work (RS%, family rooms, 47 Belgrave Road near the corner of Charlwood Street, handy bus #24 stops out front, tel. 020/7834-5897, www.lunasimonehotel.com, stay@lunasimonehotel.com).

$ Cherry Court Hotel, run by the friendly and industrious Patel family, rents 12 very small but bright and well-designed rooms with firm mattresses in a central location. Considering London's sky-high prices, this is a fine budget choice (family rooms, fruit-basket breakfast in room, air-con, laundry, 23 Hugh Street, tel. 020/7828-2840, www.cherrycourthotel.co.uk, info@cherrycourthotel.co.uk, daughter Neha answers emails and offers informed restaurant advice).

IN NORTH AND CENTRAL LONDON

$$$$ The Sumner Hotel rents 19 rooms in a 19th-century Georgian townhouse sporting large contemporary rooms and a lounge with fancy modern Italian furniture. This swanky place packs in all the amenities and is conveniently located close to Selfridges and a Marks & Spencer (RS%, air-con, elevator, 54 Upper Berkeley Street, a block and a half off Edgware Road, Tube: Marble Arch—see map on page 937, tel. 020/7723-2244, www.thesumner.com, reservations@thesumner.com).

$$$$ Charlotte Street Hotel has 52 rooms with a bright countryside English garden motif, and inviting public spaces in the up-and-coming Fitzrovia neighborhood close to the British Museum. Their rooms start at twice the cost of my favorite London B&Bs—but are worth considering if you want to splurge (connecting family rooms, air-con, elevator, 15 Charlotte Street, Tube: Tottenham Court Road—see map on page 937, tel. 020/7806-2000, www.charlottestreethotel.com, reservations@charlottestreethotel.com).

$$$$ The Fielding Hotel is a simple and slightly more affordable place lodged in the center of all the action—just steps from Covent Garden—on a quiet lane. They rent 25 basic rooms, serve no breakfast, and have almost no public spaces. Grace, the manager, sticks with straight pricing (family rooms, air-con, 4 Broad Court off Bow Street, Tube: Covent Garden—see map on page 956, tel. 020/7836-8305, www.thefieldinghotel.co.uk, reservations@thefieldinghotel.co.uk).

$$$ The 22 York Street B&B offers a casual alternative in the city center, with an inviting lounge and 10 traditional, hardwood, comfortable rooms, each named for a notable London landmark (near Marylebone/Baker Street: From Baker Street Tube station, walk 2 blocks down Baker Street and take a right to 22 York Street—no sign, just look for #22; see map on page 937; tel. 020/7224-2990, www.22yorkstreet.co.uk, mc@22yorkstreet.co.uk, energetically run by Liz and Michael Callis).

$$ Seven Dials Hotel's 18 no-nonsense rooms are plain and fairly tight, but they're also clean, reasonably priced, and incredibly well located. Since doubles here all cost the same, request a larger room when you book (family rooms, 7 Monmouth Street, Tube: Leicester Square or Covent Garden—see map on page 956, tel. 020/240-0823, www.sevendialshotel.co.uk, info@sevendialshotel.co.uk, run by friendly and hardworking Hanna).

BIG, GOOD-VALUE, MODERN HOTELS

If you can score a double for £90-100 (or less—often possible with promotional rates) and don't mind a modern, impersonal, American-style hotel, one of these can be a decent value. **$$ Premier Inn** has more than 70 hotels in greater London (www.premierinn.com, tel. 0871-527-9222; from North America, dial 011-44-1582-567-890), as does **$$ Travelodge** (www.travelodge.co.uk). **$$ Ibis,** the budget branch of the AccorHotels group, has a few dozen options across the city, with a handful of locations convenient to London's center, (www.ibishotel.com)

Entertainment in London

For the best list of what's happening and a look at the latest London scene, check www.timeout.com/london. Also, the free monthly *London Planner* guide covers sights, events, and plays, though generally not as well as the Time Out website.

LONDON

Theater (a.k.a. "Theatre")

London's theater scene rivals Broadway's in quality and sometimes beats it in price. You'll see the latest offerings advertised all over the Tube and elsewhere. The free *Official London Theatre Guide*, updated weekly, is a handy tool (find it at hotels, box offices, the City of London TI, and online at www.officiallondontheatre.co.uk). You can check reviews at www.timeout.com/london.

Tickets range from about £25 to £120 for the best seats at big shows. Matinees are generally cheaper and rarely sell out. It's generally cheapest to buy your tickets directly from the theater, either through its website or by calling the theater box office. You'll pay with a credit card, and generally be charged a per-ticket booking fee (around £3).

The famous **TKTS booth** at Leicester Square sells discounted tickets (25-50 percent off) for many shows (£3/ticket service charge included, open Mon-Sat 10:00-19:00, Sun 11:00-16:30). The list of shows and prices is posted outside the booth and updated throughout the day. The same info is available on their constantly refreshed website (www.tkts.co.uk). For the best choice and prices, come early in the day.

Shakespeare's Globe

At this round, thatch-roofed, open-air theater, the Bard's plays are performed much as he intended—under the sky, with no amplification. The play's the thing from late April through early October (usually Tue-Sat 14:00 and 19:30, Sun either 13:00 and/or 18:30, tickets can be sold out months in advance). You'll pay £5 to stand and £20-45 to sit, usually on a backless bench (no extra charge to book by phone, tel. 020/7401-9919). You can also reserve online (www.shakespearesglobe.com, £2.50 booking fee). The theater is on the South Bank, directly across the Thames over the Millennium Bridge from St. Paul's Cathedral (see listing in "Sights in London," earlier).

LONDON

What If I Miss My Ship?

Remember that you can get help from the cruise line's port agent (listed on the destination information sheet distributed on the ship) and the local TI. If the port agent suggests a costly solution (such as a private car with a driver), you may want to consider public transit.

You'll very likely find that your best option is to **fly.** London has several airports, and many low-cost, no-frills carriers are based here, offering frequent and cheap flights to just about anywhere. Check www.skyscanner.com for options. For information on London's airports, see "Airport Connections."

Overland, it could be more complicated to reach your next destination. The fast option is to head back to London and hop the speedy Eurostar train under the English Channel to Paris (then 2 hours by train to **Le Havre**), Brussels (then 1.5 hours by train to **Zeebrugge**), or **Amsterdam.** For points west or north (such as **Copenhagen** or **Berlin/Warnemünde**), you'll probably find it's best to Chunnel to Brussels or Amsterdam and connect from there.

To reach **Le Havre,** you could consider the ferry connections across the English Channel from Portsmouth, such as those offered by Brittany Ferries (www.brittany-ferries.co.uk).

For more advice on what to do if you miss the ship, see page 130.

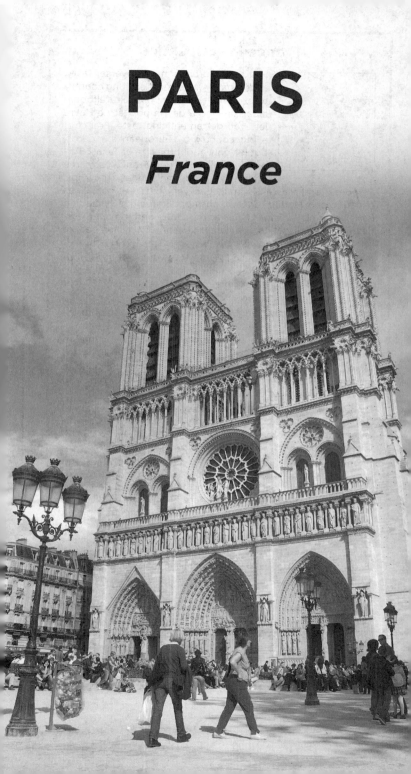

PARIS

France

France Practicalities

France is Europe's most diverse, tasty, and, in many ways, most exciting country to explore. It's a complex cultural bouillabaisse—and a day in port at Le Havre lets you get an enticing taste. France is a big country by European standards, but it's only about the size of Texas. Bordering eight countries, France has three impressive mountain ranges (the Alps, Pyrenees, and Massif Central), two very different coastlines (Atlantic and Mediterranean), cosmopolitan cities (including Paris), charming villages (such as Honfleur), and romantic castles. The majority of its population of nearly 67 million people is Roman Catholic, and virtually everyone speaks French.

Money: 1 euro (€) = about $1.20. An ATM is called a *distributeur*. The local VAT (value-added sales tax) rate is 20 percent; the minimum purchase eligible for a VAT refund is €175 (for details on refunds, see page 125).

Language: The native language is French. For useful phrases, see page 1060.

Emergencies: In case of any emergency, dial 112; to summon an ambulance, dial 15. In case of theft or loss, see page 118.

Time Zone: France is on Central European Time (the same as most of the Continent, one hour ahead of Great Britain, and six/nine hours ahead of the East/West Coasts of the US).

Embassies in Paris: The **US embassy** is at 2 Avenue Gabriel (tel. 01 43 12 22 22, https://fr.usembassy.gov/). The **Canadian embassy** is at 35 Avenue Montaigne (tel. 01 44 43 29 00, www.amb-canada.fr). Call ahead for passport services.

Phoning: With a mobile phone, it's easy to dial: Press and hold zero until you get a + sign, enter the country code (33 for France, 1 for the US/Canada), and then the complete phone number (including area code if there is one). When dialing a European phone number, drop an initial zero (except if calling Italy). For more tips, see page 1062.

Tipping: Restaurant prices already include a tip, and most French people never leave anything extra, but for special service, it's kind to tip up to 5 percent. To tip a cabbie, round up a bit (if the fare is €13, pay €14). For more tips on tipping, see page 129.

Tourist Information: http://us.rendezvousenfrance.com

PARIS
& the PORT of LE HAVRE

Le Havre • Honfleur • D-Day Beaches • Rouen • Paris

Ships call at the Port of Le Havre, on France's northwestern coast. From here you can access **Paris**—the City of Light—with its sweeping boulevards, chatty crêpe stands, chic boutiques, and world-class art galleries. Sip decaf with deconstructionists at a sidewalk café, then step into an Impressionist painting in a tree-lined park. Climb Notre-Dame and rub shoulders with the gargoyles. Cruise the Seine, zip to the top of the Eiffel Tower, or saunter down Avenue des Champs-Elysées. Master the Louvre and Orsay museums.

This chapter covers detailed directions for getting from Le Havre's cruise port to Paris—and explains how to make the most of your limited time in the city. For those who'd rather focus on sights nearer to Le Havre, there are excellent alternatives: the adorable harbor town of **Honfleur;** the historic **D-Day beaches;** and the vibrant small city of **Rouen.**

PLANNING YOUR TIME

While Paris is the big draw for most cruisers, several other options lie closer to Le Havre. Listed in order of distance from the port, the most likely choices are the charming seafront town of Honfleur, the WWII D-Day beaches of Normandy, and—about halfway to Paris—the fine cathedral at Rouen.

Honfleur: This magical little port is an easy day trip (30 minutes by bus over the impressive Pont de Normandie Bridge, 6/day). This lively, colorful town that inspired the Impressionists can fill much of a relaxed day.

D-Day Beaches: The historic beaches of the WWII Allied invasion, west of Le Havre, are best visited with an excursion, or a guide who can transport you from the cruise terminal (1.5 hours to the beaches).

Rouen: Just an hour from Le Havre on the main Paris-bound train line (frequent departures), this city (with a cobbled old town and historic ties to Joan of Arc) is a good choice if you want a dose of a smaller yet lively French city.

More Normandy: With a driver or on a cruise-line excursion, you can reach **Caen,** with its top-notch D-Day Museum, or **Bayeux,** home to a historic tapestry. A popular choice for art and garden lovers is **Giverny,** whose water lily ponds inspired Monet. (For details on these, see the "Excursions from Le Havre" sidebar.)

Paris: To reach Paris from Le Havre, it's about a 2.5-hour train ride each way (plus travel time from the port terminal to the train station—10 minutes by taxi or 40 minutes on foot). The trip is time-consuming, but hard to resist if this is your one chance to experience the City of Light. With just a few hours in Paris, you'll need to be selective. For guidance in planning your day, see page 1007.

Port of Le Havre

Arrival at a Glance: Ride a cruise-line shuttle bus or take a taxi from the port to the train/bus station; from there, connect to Honfleur (30 minutes by bus), Rouen (1 hour by train), or Paris (2.5 hours by train).

Port Overview

Le Havre's cruise port is located at Pointe de Floride, which is flanked by two piers: Roger Meunier Pier and Pierre Callet Pier. Both feed into a spacious, modern terminal building with Wi-Fi, car rental, bike rental, a gift shop, and WCs. Port information: www.cruiselehavre.com.

Tourist Information: There's a TI right at the cruise terminal. Pick up a map of the city, info on local and regional sights, and current train and bus schedules. The main TI is in Le Havre (described later).

GETTING INTO LE HAVRE
(AND TO THE TRAIN/BUS STATION)

Le Havre's cruise port is about 1.5 miles from the train station (to the northeast) or downtown (due north). First I'll cover your options for getting from the port to Le Havre's train/bus station. Then I'll offer specifics for getting to Honfleur, Rouen, and Paris. To return to your ship, you can generally reverse these directions—I've given suggestions at the end of each section as necessary.

Excursions from Le Havre

Because it's hard to efficiently link this region's destinations (especially the D-Day beaches) using public transportation, a guided excursion or a privately arranged guide can be a smart choice.

In Normandy: Le Havre itself may be offered as a tour, but you can see it on your own using the tips in this chapter. Adorable **Honfleur,** with its colorful harbor and historic ties to Impressionist painters such as Boudin and Monet, is the nearest attraction to Le Havre (just a 30-minute drive; also doable by public bus). Trips to the so-called **Alabaster Coast** north of Le Havre (including the chalky cliffs at Etrétat—which inspired several Impressionists, and the salty fishing harbor of Fécamp) are pretty but lack the impact of other options.

Excursions to the **D-Day beaches,** where the Allies came ashore on June 6, 1944, often include some beaches, the **American Cemetery, Arromanches** (the tiny seafront town that became the staging area for the invasion), and the **Longues-sur-Mer** gun battery. The city of **Caen** has the definitive museum about Operation Overlord.

A few more-distant sights eat up lots of transit time, and are only occasionally offered as excursions. Bayeux, just beyond the D-Day beaches, houses the famous **Bayeux Tapestry,** a remarkable, intricately woven medieval masterwork detailing another invasion—the 1066 Battle of Hastings. The famous and touristy abbey at **Mont St-Michel is** at the very southwest edge of the Normandy region.

Between Normandy and Paris: The city of **Rouen** has a half-timbered old town, terrific Gothic architecture, a church honoring Joan of Arc, and a cathedral that was famously painted 30 different times by Claude Monet; excursions to the city may include a stop at the enchanting lily-pad gardens at **Giverny** built by Monet.

Paris: The basic excursion option is a **bus-and-riverboat tour** of the city, with fleeting glimpses of the Arc de Triomphe, Champs-Elysées, Opéra Garnier, Louvre, Ile de la Cité with Notre-Dame Cathedral, Latin Quarter, and Hôtel des Invalides. Some tours include a guided tour of the **Louvre;** on others, you'll get about three hours of free time. For more independence, the cruise lines' **"Paris On Your Own"** excursion—a round-trip bus ride with no guiding—is pricier than a round-trip train ticket but saves you the stress of getting there and back.

Near Paris: The sumptuous **Palace of Versailles** (with its sprawling gardens and famously opulent Hall of Mirrors) is best seen by cruise-ship excursion, as the public-transit connection from Le Havre to Versailles is a hassle.

PARIS

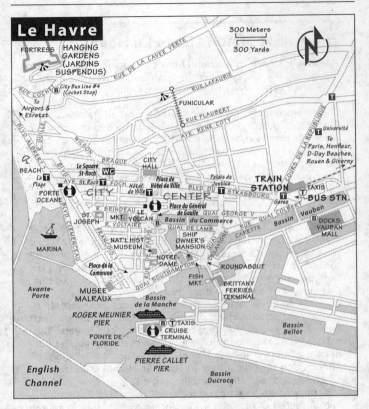

Le Havre

FORTRESS
HANGING GARDENS (JARDINS SUSPENDUS)

RUE DE LA CAVEE VERTE

300 Meters
300 Yards

N

City Bus Line #4 (Cochet Stop)

RUE COCHET
To Airport & Etretat

RUE LAFAURIE

FUNICULAR

RUE FLAUBERT

AVE. RENE COTY

Université
To Paris, Honfleur, D-Day Beaches, Rouen & Giverny

COURS DE LA REPUBLIQUE

BLVD ALBERT 1ER

BLVD. FOCH

WILSON

BRAQUE

Le Square St-Roch

WC

CITY HALL

BEACH
La Plage

AVE. St.Roch

PORTE OCEANE

CITY

ST. JOSEPH

R. BRINDEAU

R. VOLTAIRE

Place de Hôtel de Ville

Hôtel de Ville

CITY CENTER

Palais du Justice

BLVD DU STRASBOURG

TRAIN STATION

TAXIS

BUS STN.

Gares

Place du Général de Gaulle

LE MKT. VOLCAN

Bassin du Commerce

QUAI GEORGE V

RUE COLBERT

Bassin Vauban

DOCKS VAUBAN MALL

BLVD. FRANCOIS 1ER

NAT'L HIST MUSEUM

QUAI DE LAMB.

SHIP OWNER'S MANSION

QUAI DE LAVIGNE

QUAI CARETTE

MARINA

Place de la Commune

NOTRE-DAME

QUAI SOUTHAMPTON

RUE DE

FISH MKT.

ROUNDABOUT

BRITTANY FERRIES TERMINAL

BLVD CLEMENCEAU

Avante-Porte

MUSEE MALRAUX

ROGER MEUNIER PIER

Bassin de la Manche

TAXIS

CRUISE TERMINAL

Bassin Bellot

POINTE DE FLORIDE

PIERRE CALLET PIER

English Channel

Bassin Ducrocq

From the Cruise Port to Downtown Le Havre

To make the short trip from your ship to downtown Le Havre, you can either take a shuttle bus or taxi, or walk.

By Shuttle Bus: The port runs a shuttle bus connecting the cruise terminal with Place Général de Gaulle and the Docks Vauban mall (2-3/hour, €4 ticket includes all-day access to Le Havre's trams and buses). Cruise lines sometimes run their own shuttle (drop-off points vary by company), in which case the port shuttles don't operate.

For the train/bus station, get off at the **Docks Vauban shopping mall** and walk five minutes: Cross the harbor canal on the skinny Passerelle Hubert Raoul Duval footbridge, continue straight through a few crosswalks, and you'll arrive on the bus side of the station.

For in-town sightseeing, get off at **Place Général de Gaulle.** Most sightseeing is south and west of here; the **market** is just one block west on Rue Voltaire. This square itself is graced by the solemn Monument aux Morts (erected in 1924 to honor WWI casualties). Across the street, you'll see the big, white, tub-shaped Le

Services near the Port of Le Havre

ATMs: While there are no ATMs at the terminal, you'll find one inside the train/bus station and others at banks in the vicinity of the main TI. Just ask for *"un distributeur des billets."*

Wi-Fi: There's Wi-Fi in the terminal.

Pharmacy: The nearest pharmacy is at 27 Rue du Général Faidherbe, one block up from the first roundabout as you leave the port area (toward downtown). Several more are downtown (including on Rue de Paris, across from Notre-Dame Cathedral). French pharmacies generally close at lunch, on Saturday afternoons, and on Sundays.

Car Rental: The terminal's **Rent-A-Car** agency often runs out of cars by midmorning, making it smart to book ahead (www.rentacar.fr, le_havre@rentacar.fr). **Sixt** (www.sixt.fr) and others also have locations near the port.

Tramway: Le Havre's sleek tram zips silently through the city center (from the train station west to City Hall, the inviting Square St-Roch, and Porte Océane near the TI and beach). While it's not useful for getting into town from the port, the tram can be handy for sightseers who stick around Le Havre. For details, ask at the TI or see www.transports-lia.fr.

Volcan, dubbed *le pot de yaourt* ("the yogurt pot") by locals. It's the city's cultural center for music, theater, dance, and cinema.

By Taxi: Taxis wait to the right as you exit the cruise terminal. A ride to anywhere in the Le Havre city center (including the train/bus station) costs about €8-10.

On Foot: Walking into town takes about 40 minutes (25 minutes to the roundabout at the port's edge, another 15 minutes to the town center or train/bus station): From the terminal follow the small pedestrian signs to *centre-ville* (green pedestrian-area stripes also help guide you along the length of the pier). Continue following signs for *centre-ville* (passing the Brittany Lines ferry terminal on your right), after which you'll reach a roundabout; from here, important places around town are well marked. To get to the **city center,** bear left through the roundabout.

To reach the **train/bus station** (Gare du Havre), bear right onto Quai Casimir Delavigne, staying on the right (along the water). Keep following the water, veering right onto Quai Colbert and following signs for *Les Gares*, *Gare SNCF*, and *Les Docks*. The train station is on the left, across Quai Colbert from the Docks Vauban mall.

From Le Havre to Honfleur, Rouen, Paris, and Other Points

From the train/bus station, you can make your way to anywhere

PARIS

in northern France. The train station *(gare)* and bus station *(gare routière)* are conveniently located side by side.

By Train to Paris or Rouen

For regional trips (to Rouen, for example), you may be able to buy tickets from the yellow machines (may accept American credit cards). To buy a ticket to destinations farther afield—such as Paris—or if you prefer speaking with a human or paying cash, you can buy tickets at the *guichets* (ticket windows). Before boarding the train, validate your ticket at the slender yellow ticket puncher near the doors leading to the train tracks.

Trains leave about every 1-2 hours for **Paris** (arriving at St. Lazare station, 2.5 hours); these all stop in **Rouen** (station called "Rouen-Rive-Droite," 1 hour). A few Paris connections require a change in Rouen, and fast TGV trains require a reservation (possible anytime up to departure if seats available). Be aware that on weekends there are fewer trains. For schedules, see the French rail website at www.sncf.com.

Returning to Your Ship by Train: Return trains to Le Havre from **Rouen** depart about hourly and take around an hour. To reach the train station from downtown Rouen, head straight up Rue Jeanne d'Arc from Rue du Gros Horloge (the main shopping street). For a quicker return, take the subway in direction: Boulingrin and get off at Gare-Rue Verte.

When returning from **Paris** to Le Havre, be sure to allow plenty of time. Trains leave Paris from the St. Lazare Station for Le Havre about every two hours and take about 2.5 hours (double-check the departure time of your return train before you head out), plus the time it takes to get back to your ship from the Le Havre station.

To get to St. Lazare from central Paris, hop a taxi, ride the Métro (line 14/purple stops near Notre-Dame, but several other lines also serve the station), or take bus #24 (from Notre-Dame, the Orsay, and Place de la Concorde); either way, get off at the stop called "Gare Saint-Lazare."

By Bus to Honfleur

From Le Havre's bus station, buses #20, #39, and #50 go over the Normandy Bridge to **Honfleur** (6/day Mon-Sat, 2/day Sun, 30 minutes, www.busverts.fr).

Returning to Your Ship by Bus: Since buses back to Le Havre are relatively infrequent, it's smart to confirm your departure time when you arrive at the Honfleur station.

By Regional Taxi Tour

Taxis waiting at the cruise port or train station offer "discovery tours," with some commentary en route, for the following round-trip rates (these are approximate prices for up to 4 people): Etrétat (3 hours)—€125; Honfleur (3 hours)—€125; Rouen (6 hours)—€280; Giverny (6 hours)—€340; Normandy (8 hours)—€320; Versailles (8 hours)—€395; D-Day Beaches (8 hours)—€450; Mont St-Michel (10 hours)—€460; Paris (10 hours)—€460.

While most cabbies speak a bit of English, some are more fluent than others; if you're paying for a tour, feel free to chat with several drivers to assess their language abilities before choosing. Note: These cabbies may provide information, but they're not trained guides. Most drivers belong to **Radio Taxi Le Havre** (tel. 02 35 25 81 00, www.radiotaxi-lehavre.com, check website for latest rates).

By Cruise-Line Excursion to Paris

Most cruise lines offer a "Paris On Your Own" excursion, which consists of an unnarrated bus ride to a designated point in Paris (generally near Place de la Concorde, between the Champs-Elysées and the Louvre), then back again at an appointed time. While the price is higher than taking the train, some cruisers appreciate the efficiency and lack of stress about making it back to the ship on time. For tips on arriving via shuttle bus in Paris, see page 1010.

By Tour with a Private Guide

The Le Havre TI can help you arrange a private guide in town. **Normandy Sightseeing Tours** can pick you up at the ship, and offers a variety of tours, including Paris, Bayeux/Caen, Mont St-Michel, various D-Day itineraries, Monet-themed tours, and more (tel. 02 31 51 70 52, www.normandy-sightseeing-tours.com). For other tour options, see the D-Day Beaches section, later.

Le Havre

A city of 175,000, Le Havre is France's second-biggest port (after Marseille), and the primary French port on the Atlantic. Its name (pronounced "luh ahv") means, simply, "The Port." Situated at the mouth of the Seine River, Le Havre faces the English Channel and the British Isles. Its sprawling port area—harboring industrial, leisure, and cruise ships—stretches along the northern bank of the Seine.

Le Havre is proud of its connection to the Impressionist painters who found inspiration in this part of France, and panels scattered around town show Impressionist depictions of real-world locations. Fittingly, the city's best sight is the fine Impressionist collection at the Malraux Museum. Le Havre was bombed to bits in World War II and rebuilt in a charmless old-meets-modern style, but it is a useful springboard for northern France and Paris.

PARIS

Le Havre Experiences for Cruisers

To experience the city like a local, stop by **Les Halles Centrales** indoor market, featuring stalls selling fresh produce, deli foods, baked goods, regional specialties, and more (one block west of Place Général de Gaulle on Rue Voltaire, Mon-Sat 8:30-19:30, Sun 9:00-13:00). On Sunday mornings, Les Halles Centrales' parking lot hosts a sprawling farmers market.

Bring your freshly purchased picnic on a 10-minute walk north to **Le Square St-Roch** (at the corner of Avenue Foch and Rue Raoul Dufy)—a serene oasis in the middle of the city—where you can park yourself on a bench or a patch of grass, enjoy your lunch, and watch the world go by. This park is dappled with wistful willows that tickle a petite pond, flamboyant flowers, humble statues, and play areas for children. WCs are available on the east end, not far from the entrance.

For a more competitive experience, try a taste of *pétanque,* the French cousin to American horseshoes and Italian *bocce.* The best place to watch a round or two is at the small, gravelly square called **Place de la Commune** (near the Malraux Museum, on the corner of Boulevard François I and Rue Jeanne d'Arc). In the afternoons, you'll often find crusty old fishermen and their not-yet-crusty descendants playing this traditional French game.

PLANNING YOUR TIME

A full day in port allows you to fully experience Le Havre at a relaxed pace. Visit the Malraux Museum, dip into your choice of other museums, drop by St. Joseph Church, browse the market, consider a stroll through the Hanging Gardens, or relax at the beach. Any of these activities can take as little or as long as you like.

TOURIST INFORMATION

The cruise terminal's TI is most convenient, but there are also **TIs** in town (both open daily from 9:00 or 10:00 until 19:00, shorter hours off-season, www.le-havre-tourism.com): the **main** TI is at the marina at the western edge of town, near the city beach (186 Boulevard Clemenceau, tel. 02 32 74 04 04,), but the **downtown** location, near the Place Général de Gaulle shuttle drop-off point, is closer in (181 Rue de Paris, adjacent to Place de l'Hôtel de Ville—the park in front of City Hall, tel. 02 35 22 31 22).

Sights in Le Havre

While none of Le Havre's sights can match the thrills of Paris, here are some ideas to fill your time.

▲André Malraux Museum of Modern Art
(Musée d'Art Moderne André Malraux, a.k.a. "MuMa")

Named for the former Minister of Culture André Malraux, this delightfully airy and modern space is home to a superb collection of works by Impressionist biggies who lived and worked in Normandy: Monet, Renoir, Degas, Manet, Courbet, Cézanne, Camille Corot, and others. It also boasts the world's largest collection of works by Eugène Boudin, Monet's mentor. While it may not quite live up to its billing as the "finest Impressionist collection in France outside Paris," it's a wonderful opportunity to get up close and personal with quality examples of late-19th- and early-20th-century artwork. Beyond the Impressionists, the collection spans five centuries, from the 16th century up to modern works by Matisse and Pierre Bonnard. Take a break and enjoy sea views in their restaurant or tearoom.

Cost and Hours: €10, Tue-Sun 11:00-18:00, Sat-Sun until 19:00, closed Mon, 2 Boulevard Clemenceau, tel. 02 35 19 62 62, www.muma-lehavre.fr.

St. Joseph Church (Eglise St-Joseph)

Built in the 1950s, this church serves as a memorial to the 5,000 Le Havre civilians who died during World War II. Its 350-foot-tall octagonal tower (which resembles a Chicago skyscraper more than a steeple) is *the* dominant structure on Le Havre's skyline. The stark, somber, Neo-Gothic interior is worth a quick visit to appreciate its Greek-cross floor plan and to peer up inside the tower. On a sunny day, the whimsical play of light through its 13,000 panels of stained glass is delightful.

Cost and Hours: Free, daily 9:00-17:30 except during services, at corner of Boulevard François I and Rue Louis Brindeau.

Ship Owner's Mansion (Maison de l'Armateur)

This historic building offers a glimpse into the 18th-century lifestyle of a wealthy Le Havre citizen. Five stories of furnishings, artwork, and collectibles evoke life in this port city from 1750 to 1870.

Cost and Hours: €7, includes obligatory guided tour in French (English pamphlet provided); Wed-Mon 10:00-12:30 & 13:45-18:00, closed Tue; 3 Quai de l'Ile, tel. 02 35 19 09 85.

PARIS

▲Hanging Gardens (Jardins Suspendus)

For nature enthusiasts who need a break from shipboard life or a place to picnic, this fine park—about two miles north of the port—is the place. The grass-topped walls of a former fortress enclose a massive complex, with splendid city and beach views that invite you to wander and explore. Inside the fort are more gardens, along with extensive greenhouses that feature plants from five continents.

Cost and Hours: Free, €1 to enter greenhouses, April-Sept daily 10:30-20:00, shorter hours off-season, Rue du Fort, tel. 02 35 19 45 45.

Getting There: It's easiest by taxi (€8-10 each way from the port), but prearrange a pickup to avoid getting stranded. You can also take bus #3 (to Cochet or A. Copieux).

Beach

On a sunny day, relax at Le Havre's pebbly beach (at the western edge of town, just north of the main TI). Bring your flip-flops (better than going barefoot on pebbles) and find your own patch of beach (the tempting cabanas are usually rented monthly or yearly). While working on your tan, enjoy the view of dozens of sailboats gliding across the water. The boardwalk offers all types of tasty treats, plus activities and services including bike rentals, water equipment rentals, volleyball, *pétanque*, WCs, and showers (most open April-Sept). You can get there by taxi or tram.

Honfleur

Gazing at its cozy harbor lined with skinny, soaring houses, it's easy to overlook the historic importance of Honfleur (ohn-flur).

For more than a thousand years, sailors have enjoyed this port's ideal location, where the Seine River greets the English Channel. The town was also a favorite of 19th-century Impressionists who were captivated by Honfleur's unusual light—the result of its river-meets-sea setting. The 19th-century artist Eugène Boudin lived and painted in Honfleur, attracting Monet and other creative types from Paris. In some ways, modern art was born in the fine light of idyllic little Honfleur.

Honfleur escaped the bombs of World War II, and today offers a romantic port enclosed on three sides by sprawling outdoor cafés. Long eclipsed by the gargantuan port of Le Havre just across the Seine, Honfleur happily uses its past as a bar stool...and sits on it.

Orientation to Honfleur

All of Honfleur's appealing lanes and activities are within a short stroll of its old port, the Vieux Bassin. The Seine River flows just east of the center, the hills of the Côte de Grâce form its western limit, and Rue de la République slices north-south through the center to the port. Honfleur has two can't-miss sights—the harbor and St. Catherine Church—and a handful of other intriguing monuments. But really, the town itself is its best sight.

TOURIST INFORMATION

The TI is in the glassy public library *(Mediathéque)* on Quai le Paulmier, two blocks from the Vieux Bassin (Mon-Sat 9:30-19:00, Sun 10:00-17:00; Sept-June Mon-Sat until 18:30 and closed daily for lunch 12:30-14:00; closed Sun afternoon Nov-Easter; free WCs, tel. 02 31 89 23 30, www.ot-honfleur.fr).

ARRIVAL IN HONFLEUR

By Bus: Get off at the small bus station *(gare routière)*, and confirm your departure at the information counter. To reach the TI and old town, turn right as you exit the station and walk five minutes up Quai le Paulmier.

HELPFUL HINTS

Museum Pass: The €11-13 museum pass, sold at participating museums, covers the Eugène Boudin Museum, Maisons Satie, and the Museum of Ethnography and Norman Popular Arts (www.musees-honfleur.fr).

Grocery Store: There's one with long hours near the TI (daily July-Aug, closed Mon off-season, 16 Quai le Paulmier).

Regional Products with Panache: Visit **Produits Regionaux Gribouille** for any Norman delicacy you can dream up. Ask about tastings (16 Rue de l'Homme de Bois, tel. 02 31 89 29 54).

Wi-Fi: Free Wi-Fi is available at the port and at several cafés.

Taxi: Call mobile 06 08 60 17 98.

Sights in Honfleur

▲▲Vieux Bassin (Old Port)

Stand near the water facing Honfleur's square harbor, with the merry-go-round across the lock to your left, and survey the town.

The word "Honfleur" is Scandinavian, meaning the shelter *(fleur)* of Hon (a Viking warlord). This town has been sheltering residents for about a thousand years. During the Hundred Years' War (14th century), the entire harbor was fortified by a big wall with twin gatehouses (the one surviving gatehouse, La

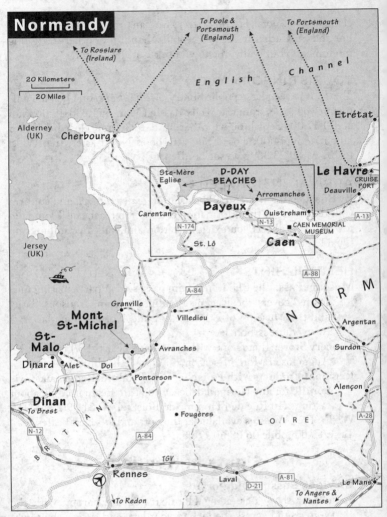

Normandy

To Rosslare (Ireland)

To Poole & Portsmouth (England)

To Portsmouth (England)

English Channel

20 Kilometers
20 Miles

Alderney (UK)

Cherbourg

Etrétat

Ste-Mère Eglise

D-DAY BEACHES

Le Havre

CRUISE PORT

Arromanches

Deauville

Carentan

Bayeux

Ouistreham

A-13

Jersey (UK)

N-174

N-13

CAEN MEMORIAL MUSEUM

St. Lô

Caen

N O R M

A-88

A-84

Granville

Villedieu

Argentan

Mont St-Michel

St-Malo

Avranches

Surdon

Dinard

Alet

Dol

Pontorson

Alençon

Dinan

To Brest

B R I T T A N Y

Fougères

L O I R E

A-28

N-12

A-84

TGV

Rennes

Laval

A-81

Le Mans

To Redon

D-21

To Angers & Nantes

Lieutenance, is on your right). A narrow channel allowing boats to pass was protected by a heavy chain.

After the walls were demolished around 1700, those skinny houses on the right side were built for the town's fishermen. How about a room on the top floor, with no elevator? Imagine moving a piano or a refrigerator into one of these units today. The spire halfway up the left side of the port belongs to Honfleur's oldest church. The port, once crammed with fishing boats, now harbors sleek sailboats.

Walk toward the Lieutenance gatehouse. In front of the barrel-vaulted arch (once the entry to the town), you can see a bronze bust of Samuel de Champlain—the explorer who, 400 years ago,

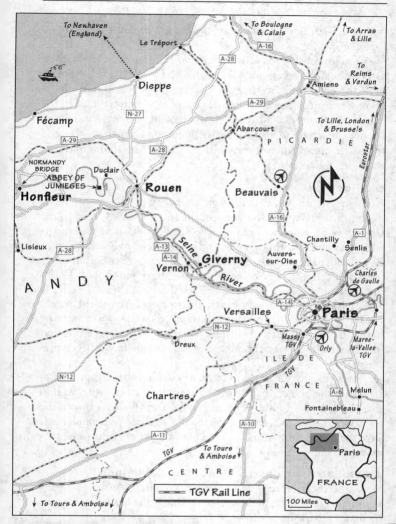

sailed with an Honfleur crew to make his discoveries in the New World. Champlain is acknowledged as the founder of the Canadian city of Quebec—which remains French-speaking to this day.

Turn around to see various tour and fishing boats and the masts of the high-flying Normandy Bridge in the distance. Fisherfolk catch flatfish, scallops, and tiny shrimp daily to bring to the Marché au Poisson, located 100 yards to your right (look for white metal structures with blue lettering). Thursday through Sunday, you may see fishermen's wives selling *crevettes* (shrimp). You can buy them *cuites* (cooked) or *vivantes* (alive and wiggly). They are happy to let you sample one (rip off the cute little head and tail, and pop what's left into your mouth—*délicieuse!*), or buy a cupful to go for a few euros.

You'll probably see artists sitting at easels around the harbor, as Boudin and Monet did. Many consider Honfleur the birthplace of 19th-century Impressionism, thanks to the unusual luminosity of the region. And with the advent of new railway lines in the late 1800s, artists could travel to the best light like never before. Monet came here to visit the artist Boudin, a hometown boy, and the battle cry of the Impressionists—"Out of the studio and into the light!"—was born.

Old Honfleur

A chance to study the Lego-style timber-frame houses of Honfleur awaits just off the harbor. On the southern quay, next to the Church of St. Etienne, head up Rue de la Prison (past the worthwhile Museum of Ethnography) and bend around to Rue des Petites Boucheries for some prime examples. The beams of these buildings were numbered so they could be disassembled and moved. Walking through a slate-sided passage, you'll pop out onto Rue de la Ville with more historic Norman architecture. Across the way is one of three huge 17th-century salt warehouses. It's worth entering to see the huge stone hall with its remarkable wooden ceiling and imagine the importance of salt as a preservative before refrigeration existed.

Strategically positioned Honfleur guarded Paris from a naval attack up the Seine. That's why the king fortified it with a wall in the 1300s. In the 1600s, when England was no longer a threat, the walls were torn down, leaving the town with some wide boulevards (like the one in front of the TI) and plenty of stones (like those that made the salt warehouse).

▲▲St. Catherine Church (Eglise Ste. Catherine)

St. Catherine's replaced an earlier stone church, destroyed in the Hundred Years' War. In those chaotic times, the town's money was spent to fortify its walls, leaving only enough funds to erect a wooden church. The unusual wood-shingled exterior suggests that this church has a different story to tell than most. In the last months of World War II, a bomb fell through the church's roof—but didn't explode—leaving this unique church intact for you to visit today.

Cost and Hours: Free, daily 9:00-18:30, Sept-June until 17:15, Place Ste-Catherine.

Visiting the Church: Walk inside. You'd swear that if it were turned over, the building would float—the legacy of a community of sailors and fishermen, with loads of talented boat-builders (and no church architect). When workers put up the first (left) nave in 1466, it soon became apparent that more space was needed—so a second was built in 1497 (on the right). Because it felt too much like a market hall, they added side aisles.

The oak columns were prepared as if the wood was meant for a ship—soaked in seawater for seven years and then dried for seven years. Notice some pillars are full-length and others are supported by stone bases. Trees come in different sizes, yet each pillar had to be the same length.

The pipe organ (from 1772, rebuilt in 1953) behind you is popular for concerts, and half of the modern pews are designed to flip so that you can face the music.

▲Eugène Boudin Museum

This pleasing little museum opened in 1869 and has several interesting floors with many paintings of Honfleur and the surrounding countryside, giving you a feel for Honfleur in the 1800s.

Cost and Hours: €8 in summer, €6 off-season, covered by museum pass; Wed-Mon 10:00-12:00 & 14:00-18:00, closed Tue, shorter hours Oct-April; audioguide-€2 (good but skippable), elevator, Rue de l'Homme de Bois, tel. 02 31 89 54 00, www.musees-honfleur.fr.

▲Maisons Satie

If Honfleur is over-the-top cute, this museum, housed in composer Erik Satie's birthplace, is a burst of witty charm—just like the musical genius it honors. If you like Satie's music, this is a delight—a 1920s "Yellow Submarine." If not, it can be a ho-hum experience. Allow an hour for your visit.

Cost and Hours: €6.30, includes audioguide, covered by museum pass; May-Sept Wed-Mon 10:00-19:00, off-season 11:00-18:00, closed Jan-mid-Feb and Tue year-round; last entry one hour before closing, 5-minute walk from harbor at 67 Boulevard Charles V, tel. 02 31 89 11 11, www.musees-honfleur.fr.

▲Museum of Ethnography and Norman Popular Arts (Musée d'Ethnographie et d'Art Populaire Normand)

Honfleur's engaging little Museum of Ethnography and Norman Popular Arts (pick up English translation at the desk) is located in the old prison and courthouse a short block off the harbor in the heart of Old Honfleur. It re-creates typical rooms from Honfleur's past and crams them with objects of daily life—costumes, furniture, looms, and an antique printing press. The museum paints a

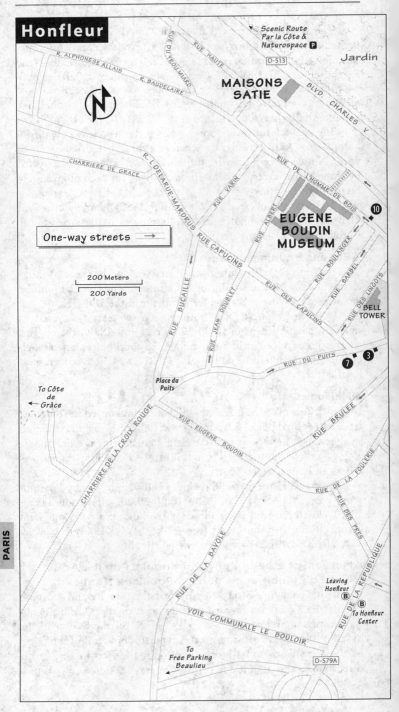

Honfleur

PARIS

Scenic Route
Par la Côte &
Naturospace 🅿

D-513

Jardin

R. ALPHONESE ALLAIS

RUE DU TROUMARD

RUE HAUTE

R. BAUDELAIRE

**MAISONS
SATIE**

BLVD. CHARLES V

CHARRIERE DE GRACE

R. L DELARUE-MARDRUS

RUE DE L'HOMME DE BOIS

RUE YARIN

RUE CAPUCINS

RUE ALBERT I

**EUGENE
BOUDIN
MUSEUM**

RUE BOULANGER

RUE BARBEL

RUE DES LINGOTS

⑩

One-way streets ⟶

200 Meters

200 Yards

RUE BUCAILLE

RUE JEAN DOUBLET

RUE DES CAPUCINS

**BELL
TOWER**

RUE DU PUITS

⑦ ③

To Côte
de
Grâce ←

Place du
Puits

CHARRIERE DE LA CROIX ROUGE

RUE EUGENE BOUDIN

RUE BRULEE

RUE DE LA FOULERIE

RUE DES PRES

RUE DE LA BAVOLE

Leaving
Honfleur
Ⓑ

RUE DE LA REPUBLIQUE

Ⓑ
To Honfleur
Center

VOIE COMMUNALE LE BOULOIR

To
Free Parking
Beaulieu

D-579A

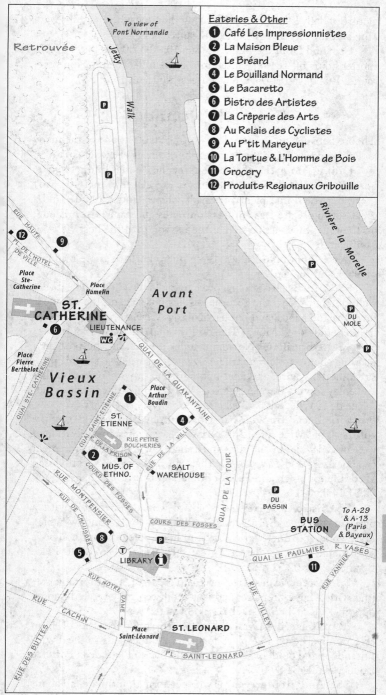

Eateries & Other

1. Café Les Impressionnistes
2. La Maison Bleue
3. Le Bréard
4. Le Bouilland Normand
5. Le Bacaretto
6. Bistro des Artistes
7. La Crêperie des Arts
8. Au Relais des Cyclistes
9. Au P'tit Mareyeur
10. La Tortue & L'Homme de Bois
11. Grocery
12. Produits Regionaux Gribouille

picture of daily life in Honfleur during the time when its ships were king and the city had global significance.

Cost and Hours: €4.20, Tue-Sun 10:00-12:00 & 14:00-18:30, shorter hours off-season, closed mid-Nov–mid-Feb and Mon year-round, Rue de la Prison, www.musees-honfleur.fr.

Eating in Honfleur

Choose between an irresistible waterfront table at one of the many lookalike places lining the harbor or finer dining elsewhere in town.

Dining Along the Harbor: Survey the eateries lining the harbor (all open Wed when other places are closed). The food isn't great, but you'll find plenty of salads, crêpes, and seafood—and a great setting. **Café Les Impressionnistes** and **La Maison Bleue,** on the Quai St. Etienne side of the harbor, own the best views of Honfleur.

Better Food, No Views: These finer alternatives are a couple of blocks off the harbor.

$$$$ Le Bréard is a fine place to dial it up a little and eat very well for a fair price. The decor is low key but elegant, the cuisine is inventive, delicious, and not particularly *Normand,* and the service is excellent (closed Mon, 7 Rue du Puits, tel. 02 31 89 53 40).

$$ Le Bouilland Normand hides a block off the port on a pleasing square and offers true *Normand* cuisine at reasonable prices. Annette, Claire, and chef-hubby Bruno provide quality dishes and enjoy serving travelers (closed Wed and Sun, dine inside or out, 7 Rue de la Ville, tel. 02 31 89 02 41).

$ Le Bacaretto wine bar-café is run by laid-back Hervé, the antithesis of a wine snob. This relaxed place offers a fine selection of well-priced wines by the glass and a small but appealing assortment of appetizers and *plats du jour* that can make a full meal (closed Wed-Thu for lunch and Sun for dinner, 44 Rue de la Chaussée, tel. 02 31 14 83 11).

$$ Bistro des Artistes is a two-woman operation with a pleasant 10-table dining room (call ahead for a window table). Hardworking Anne-Marie cooks up huge portions; one course is plenty...and maybe a dessert (great salads, closed Wed, 30 Place Berthelot, tel. 02 31 89 95 90).

$ La Crêperie des Arts serves up crêpes in a comfortable setting with a huge fireplace, and is a good, centrally located budget option (13 Rue du Puits, tel. 02 31 89 14 02).

$ Au Relais des Cyclistes, on a busy street near the TI, is an eclectic, lively, pub-like place for a simple, inexpensive meal with fun indoor and outdoor seating (closed Thu, 10 Place de la Porte de Rouen, tel. 02 31 89 09 76).

$$$ Au P'tit Mareyeur is whisper-formal, intimate, all about seafood, and a good value. The ground floor and upstairs rooms offer equal comfort and ambience (famous €38 Bouillabaisse Honfleuraise, closed Tue-Wed and Jan, 4 Rue Haute, tel. 02 31 98 84 23, Julie speaks some English).

At **$$ La Tortue,** the owner/chef prepares tasty cuisine, including good vegetarian dishes, and serves it in a pleasing setting (open daily in summer, closed Tue-Wed rest of year, tel. 02 31 81 24 60, 36 Rue de l'Homme de Bois).

$$ L'Homme de Bois combines cozy ambience with authentic *Normand* cuisine that is loved by locals, so book a day ahead. Fish is their forte (daily, a few outside tables, skip the upstairs room, 30 Rue de l'Homme de Bois, tel. 02 31 89 75 27).

D-Day Beaches

The 54 miles of Atlantic coast north of Bayeux—stretching from Utah Beach in the west to Sword Beach in the east—are littered with WWII museums, monuments, cemeteries, and battle remains left in tribute to the courage of the British, Canadian, and American armies that successfully carried out the largest military operation in history: D-Day. (It's called *Jour J* in French.) It was on these serene beaches, at the crack of dawn on June 6, 1944, that the Allies (roughly one-third Americans and two-thirds British and Canadians) finally gained a foothold in France. From this moment, Nazi Europe was destined to crumble.

The most famous D-Day sights lie significantly west of Le Havre; for example, Omaha Beach is about a 1.5-hour drive from your cruise port (in good traffic). Many of the best D-Day guides are based closer to the beaches, making it a long journey for them to come meet your ship, then take you back later. This makes visiting the D-Day beaches more expensive and less efficient than it could be. But if you don't mind splurging on a guide or an excursion to efficiently see this historic sliver of French coastline, a D-Day side-trip is worth considering.

PLANNING YOUR TIME
The D-Day sights are best seen with a guided tour. With one day, you'll only have time to visit a few D-Day locations. From Le Havre, it takes longer to reach the American sector, which is west of Arromanches, with sights scattered between Omaha and Utah beaches. The British and Canadian sectors (east of Arromanches) are closer to Le Havre, but have been overbuilt with resorts, making it harder to envision the events of June 1944. For more information on visiting the D-Day beaches, www.normandie-tourisme.fr is a useful resource.

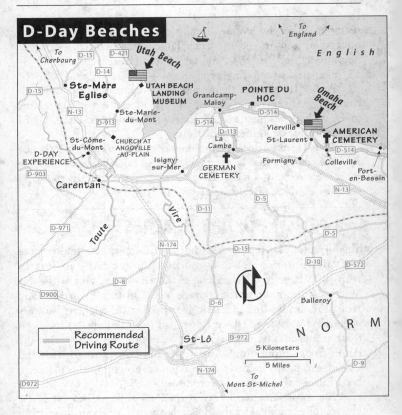

Recommended Driving Route

GETTING AROUND THE D-DAY BEACHES
By Guided Tour

An army of small companies and private guides offers all-day visits to the D-Day beaches. The tour companies and guides listed here are people I trust to take your time seriously. Most deliver riveting commentary about these moving sites. To land one of these guides, book your tour (3-6 months is best during peak periods).

Tours in a Shared Minivan

Figure about €110/person for a day and €65/person for a half-day. These companies also run private tours.

Bayeux Shuttle is well-run and user-friendly for individuals. Their vans have monitors explaining what's out the window, and they offer several all-day and half-day tours with well-trained guides (tel. 09 70 44 49 89, www.bayeuxshuttle.com).

Normandy Sightseeing Tours delivers a French perspective with capable guides and will pick you up anywhere you like—for a price (tel. 02 31 51 70 52, www.normandy-sightseeing-tours.com).

Overlord Tours is another good choice (www.overlordtour.com).

Tours with a Private Guide

Private groups should expect to pay €500-650 for up to eight people for an all-day tour and €250-330 for a half-day. Most private guides levy a surcharge for a Le Havre pickup. Consider **Sylvain Kast** (mobile 06 17 44 04 46, www.d-day-experience-tours.com), **Mathias Leclere** (www.ddayguidedtours.com), or **Magali Desquesne** (mobile 06 88 75 86 17, www.dday4you.com).

On Your Own

Though the tours listed above teach important history lessons, **renting a car** can be a less expensive way to visit the beaches, particularly for three or more people (for rental suggestions in Le Havre, see page 979). Consider hiring a guide to join you, and leave yourself plenty of time to make it back to Le Havre, drop your car, and return to your ship.

D-Day Sights

West of Arromanches

The small town of **Arromanches** was ground zero for the D-Day invasion. Almost overnight, it sprouted the immense harbor, Port Winston, which gave the Allies a foothold in Normandy, allowing them to begin their victorious push to Berlin and end World War II. You'll find a view over the site of that gigantic makeshift harbor, a good museum, an evocative beach and bluff, and a touristy-but-fun little town that offers a pleasant cocktail of war memories, cotton candy, and beachfront trinket shops. From here, you can choose among the following sights (listed roughly from east to west):

Longues-sur-Mer Gun Battery: Four German casemates (three with guns intact)—built to guard against seaborne attacks—hunker down at the end of a country road. This battery—with the only original coastal artillery guns remaining in place in the D-Day region—was a critical link in Hitler's Atlantic Wall defense, which consisted of more than 15,000 structures stretching from Norway to the Pyrenees. Today visitors can see the bunkers at this strategic site.

WWII Normandy American Cemetery and Memorial: Crowning a bluff just above Omaha Beach and the eye of the D-Day storm, 9,387 brilliant white-marble crosses and Stars of David glow in memory of Americans who gave their lives to free Europe on the beaches below.

Vierville-sur-Mer and Omaha Beach: Omaha Beach witnessed by far the most intense battles of any along the D-Day beaches. The hills above were heavily fortified, and a single German machine gun could fire 1,200 rounds a minute. The highest casualty rates in Normandy occurred at Omaha Beach, nicknamed "Bloody Omaha." Here you'll find a museum and a chance to walk on the beach where anywhere from 2,500 to 4,800 Americans were killed and wounded, making way for some 34,000 to land on the beach by day's end.

Pointe du Hoc: The intense bombing of the beaches by Allied forces is best experienced here, where US Army Rangers scaled impossibly steep cliffs to disable a German gun battery. Pointe du Hoc's bomb-cratered, lunar-like landscape and remaining bunkers make it one of the most evocative of the D-Day sites.

German Military Cemetery at La Cambe: To ponder German losses, visit this somber, thought-provoking resting place of 21,000 German soldiers. Compared to the American Cemetery, which symbolizes hope and victory, this one is a clear symbol of defeat and despair. A small visitors center gives more information on this and other German war cemeteries.

Utah Beach Landing Museum: Built around the remains of

a concrete German bunker, this museum—the best one located on the D-Day beaches—nestles in the sand dunes on Utah Beach. For the Allied landings to succeed, many coordinated tasks had to be accomplished: Paratroopers had to be dropped inland, the resistance had to disable bridges and cut communications, bombers had to deliver payloads on target and on time, the infantry had to land safely on the beaches, and supplies had to follow the infantry closely. This thorough yet manageable museum pieces those many parts together in a series of fascinating exhibits and displays.

Church at Angoville-au-Plain: At this simple Romanesque church, two American medics (Kenneth Moore and Robert Wright) treated German and American wounded while battles raged only steps away.

Ste-Mère Eglise: This celebrated village lies 15 minutes west of Utah Beach and was the first village to be liberated by the Americans. The area around Ste-Mère Eglise was the center of action for American paratroopers, whose objective was to land behind enemy lines before dawn on D-Day and wreak havoc in support of the Americans landing at Utah Beach that day.

East of Arromanches

Juno Beach Centre: Located on the beachfront in the Canadian sector, this facility is dedicated to teaching travelers about the vital role Canadian forces played in the invasion.

Canadian Cemetery at Bény-sur-Mer: This small, touching cemetery hides a few miles above the Juno Beach Centre. Surrounded by pastoral farmland with distant views to  the beaches, you'll find 2,000 graves marked with maple leaves.

Caen Memorial Museum: Caen, the modern capital of lower Normandy, has the most thorough WWII museum in France. Located at the site of an important German headquarters during World War II, its official name is "The Caen Memorial: Center for the History for Peace" *(Le Mémorial de Caen: La Cité de l'Histoire pour la Paix).* With video presentations and numerous exhibits on the lead-up to World War II, coverage of the war in both Europe and the Pacific, accounts of the Holocaust and Nazi-occupied France, the Cold War aftermath, and more, it effectively puts the Battle of Normandy into a broader context.

Rouen

This 2,000-year-old city mixes Gothic architecture, half-timbered houses, and contemporary bustle like no other place in France. Busy Rouen (roo-ahn) is France's fifth-largest port and Europe's biggest food exporter (mostly wheat and grain). Its cobbled old town is a delight to wander.

Rouen was a regional capital during Roman times, and France's second-largest city in medieval times (with 40,000 residents—only Paris had more). In the ninth century, the Normans made the town their capital. William the Conqueror called it home before moving to England. Rouen walked a political tightrope between England and France for centuries and was an English base during the Hundred Years' War. Joan of Arc was burned here (in 1431).

Rouen's historic wealth was built on its wool industry and trade—for centuries, it was the last bridge across the Seine River before the Atlantic. In April 1944, as America and Britain weakened German control of Normandy prior to the D-Day landings, Allied bombers destroyed 50 percent of Rouen. Although the industrial suburbs were devastated, most of the historic core survived, keeping Rouen a pedestrian haven.

Orientation to Rouen

Although Paris embraces the Seine, Rouen ignores it. The area we're most interested in is bounded by the river to the south, the Museum of Fine Arts (Esplanade Marcel Duchamp) to the north, Rue de la République to the east, and Place du Vieux Marché to the west. It's a 20-minute walk from the train station to the Notre-Dame Cathedral, and everything else of interest is within a 10-minute walk of the cathedral.

TOURIST INFORMATION

The TI faces the cathedral and rents €5 audioguides covering the cathedral, Rouen's historic center, and the history of Joan of Arc in Rouen—though this book's self-guided walk is plenty for most (Mon-Sat 9:00-19:00, Sun 9:30-12:30 & 14:00-18:00; Oct-April Mon-Sat 9:30-12:30 & 14:00-18:00, closed Sun; 25 Place de la Cathédrale, tel. 02 32 08 32 40, www.rouentourisme.com).

ARRIVAL IN ROUEN

Rue Jeanne d'Arc cuts straight from Rouen's **train station** through the town center to the Seine River. Day-trippers can **walk** from the station down Rue Jeanne d'Arc toward Rue du Gros Horloge—a busy pedestrian mall in the medieval center and near the starting point of my self-guided walk.

Rouen's **subway** (Métrobus) whisks travelers from under the train station to the Palais de Justice in one stop (€1.70 for 1 hour; buy tickets from machines one level underground, then validate ticket on subway two levels down; subway direction: Technopôle or Georges Braque).

Taxis (to the right as you exit station) will take you to various points in town for about €10.

HELPFUL HINTS

Closed Days: Many Rouen sights are closed midday (12:00-14:00), and most museums are closed on Tuesdays. The cathedral doesn't open until 14:00 on Monday, and the Joan of Arc Church is closed Friday and Sunday mornings.

Supermarket: A big **Monoprix** is on Rue du Gros Horloge (groceries at the back, Mon-Sat 8:30-21:00, Sun 9:00-13:00).

Wi-Fi: You'll find Wi-Fi at several cafés within a few blocks of the train station on Rue Jeanne d'Arc.

Taxi: Call **Les Taxi Blancs** at 02 35 61 20 50.

Rouen Walk

On this 1.5-hour self-guided walk, you'll see the essential Rouen sights (all but the Joan of Arc Museum and Bell Tower Panorama are free) and experience the city's pedestrian-friendly streets.

We'll stroll the length of Rue du Gros Horloge to Notre-Dame Cathedral, visit the plague cemetery (Aître St. Maclou), pass the church of St. Ouen, and end at the Museum of Fine Arts, a short walk back to the train station. The map in this section highlights our route.

• *From the train station, walk down Rue Jeanne d'Arc and turn right on Rue du Guillaume le Conquérant (notice the Gothic Palace of Justice building across Rue Jeanne d'Arc—we'll get to that later). This takes you to the back door of our starting point...*

▲Place du Vieux Marché

Stand in the small garden near the entrance of the Joan of Arc Church. Find a spot above the tall aluminum cross for striking views of the church. Surrounded by half-timbered buildings, this old market square houses a cute, covered produce-and-fish market, a park commemorating Joan of Arc's burning, and a modern

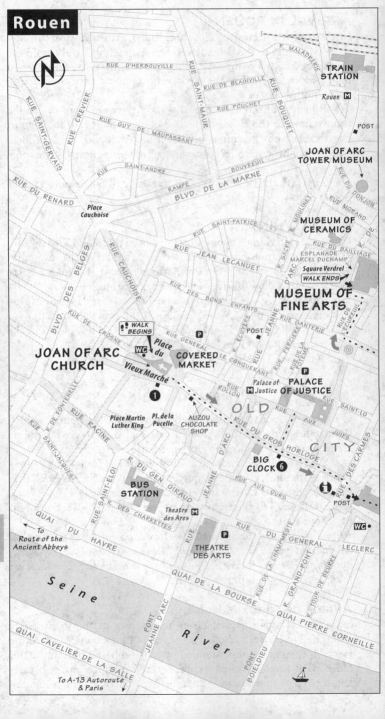

Rouen

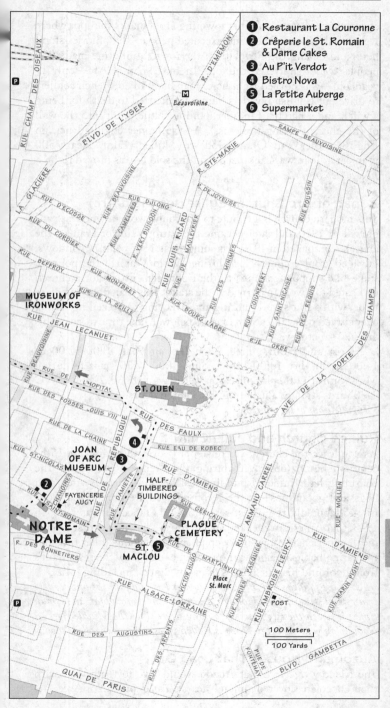

1 Restaurant La Couronne
2 Crêperie le St. Romain & Dame Cakes
3 Au P'it Verdot
4 Bistro Nova
5 La Petite Auberge
6 Supermarket

PARIS

church named after her. That towering cross marks the spot where Rouen publicly punished and executed people. The pillories stood here, and during the Revolution, the town's guillotine made 800 people "a foot shorter at the top." In 1431, Joan of Arc—only 19 years old—was burned right here. Joan had rallied French soldiers to drive out English invaders but was sentenced to death for being a witch and a heretic. Find her flaming statue (built into the wall of the church, facing the cross). As the flames engulfed her, an English soldier said, "Oh my God, we've killed a saint." Nearly 500 years later, Joan was canonized, and the soldier was proved right.

• *Now step inside...*

▲Joan of Arc Church (Eglise Jeanne d'Arc)

This modern church is a tribute to the young woman who was canonized in 1920 and later became the patron saint of France. The church, completed in 1979, has sumptuous 16th-century windows, salvaged from a church lost during World War II. The pointed, stake-like support columns to the right seem fitting for a church dedicated to a woman burned at the stake. This is an uplifting place to be, with a ship's-hull vaulting and sweeping wood ceiling sailing over curved pews and a wall of glass below. Make time to savor this unusual sanctuary.

Cost and Hours: Free, Mon-Thu and Sat 10:00-12:00 & 14:00-18:00, Fri 10:00-12:00, Sun 14:00-17:30, closed during Mass (Sun at 11:00 plus offseason weekdays at 18:30. A public WC is 30 yards straight ahead from the church doors.

• *Turn left out of the church.*

Ruined Church and Julia Child

As you leave the church, you're stepping over the ruins of a 15th-century church (destroyed during the French Revolution). The charming half-timbered building just beyond—overflowing with flags and geraniums—is the recommended Restaurant La Couronne, reputedly the oldest restaurant in France. It was here, in 1948, that American chef and author Julia Child ate her first French meal, experiencing a culinary epiphany that changed her life (and the eating habits of a generation of Americans). By the restaurant's front door find historic photos of happy diners, including Julia.

• *Leave the square with the church on your left and join the busy pedestrian street, Rue du Gros Horloge. An important thoroughfare in Roman times, it's been the city's main shopping street since the Middle Ages. A block up on your right (at #163) is Rouen's most famous chocolate shop.*

Auzou and Houses That Lean Out

The friendly *chocolatiers* at Auzou would love to tempt you with their chocolate-covered almond "tears *(larmes)* of Joan of Arc." Although you must resist touching the chocolate fountain, you are welcome to taste a tear (delicious). Before moving on, notice the architecture. The higher floors of the Auzou house lean out, evidence that the building dates from before 1520, when such street-crowding construction was prohibited. (People feared that houses leaning over the street like this would block breezes and make the city more susceptible to disease.) Look around the corner and down the lane behind the Auzou building to see a fine line of half-timbered Gothic façades.

• *Your route continues past a medieval McDonald's to busy **Rue Jeanne d'Arc**. Cross the street and continue straight to the...*

▲Great Clock (Gros Horloge)

This impressive, circa-1528 Renaissance clock, the Gros Horloge (groh or-lohzh), decorates the former City Hall. Originally, the clock had only an hour hand but no minute hand. In the 16th century, an hour hand offered sufficient precision; minute hands became necessary only in a later, faster-paced age (forget second hands). The silver orb above the clock makes one revolution in 29 days. (The cycle of the moon let people know the tides—of practical value here as Rouen was a seaport.) The town medallion (sculpted into the stone below the clock) features a sacrificial lamb, which has both religious meaning (Jesus is the Lamb of God) and commercial significance (wool was the source of Rouen's wealth). The clock's artistic highlight fills the underside of the arch (walk underneath and stretch your back), with the "Good Shepherd" and loads of sheep.

Bell Tower Panorama: To see the inner workings of the clock and an extraordinary panorama over Rouen and its cathedral, climb the clock tower's 100 steps. Don't miss the 360-degree view outside from the very top (€7, includes audioguide, Tue-Sun 10:00-13:00 & 14:00-19:00, shorter hours off-season, closed Mon year-round).

• *Walk under the Gros Horloge and continue straight a half-block, then take a one-block detour left (up Rue Thouret) to see the...*

Palace of Justice (Palais de Justice)

Rouen is the capital of Normandy, and this impressive building is its parliament. The section on the left is the oldest, in Flamboyant Gothic style dating from 1550. Normandy was an independent little country from 911 to 1204, and since then, while a part of France, it's had an independent spirit and has enjoyed a bit of autonomy.

• *Double back and continue up Rue du Gros Horloge. In a block, high on the left, you'll see a stone plaque dedicated to hometown hero **Cavelier de la Salle**, who explored the mouth of the Mississippi River, claimed the* *state of Louisiana for France, and was assassinated in Texas in 1687. Soon you'll reach...*

▲▲Notre-Dame Cathedral (Cathédrale Notre-Dame)

There's been a church on this site for more than a thousand years. Charlemagne honored it with a visit in the eighth century before

the Vikings sacked it a hundred years later. The building you see today was constructed between the 12th and 14th centuries, though lightning strikes, wars (the cathedral was devastated in WWII fighting), and other destructive forces meant constant rebuilding.

This cathedral is a landmark of art history. You're seeing essentially what Claude Monet saw as he painted 30 different studies of this frilly Gothic facade at various times of day. Using the physical building only as a rack upon which to hang light, mist, dusk, and shadows, Monet was capturing "impressions." One of these paintings is in Rouen's Museum of Fine Arts; others are at the Orsay Museum in Paris. Find the plaque showing one of the paintings (in the corner of the square, about 30 paces to your right if exiting the TI).

Cost and Hours: Free, Tue-Sun 9:00-19:00 (Nov-March closed 12:00-14:00), Mon 14:00-19:00.

• *To learn more about Rouen's most famous figure, consider touring the...*

▲Joan of Arc Museum (Historial Jeanne d'Arc)

Rouen's Archbishop's Palace, where in 1431 Joan of Arc was tried and sentenced to death, now hosts a multimedia experience that tells her story. Equipped with headphones, you'll walk for 75 minutes through a series of rooms, each with a brief video presentation that tries very hard to teach and entertain. Your tour ends in the Officialité—the room where the trial took place.

Cost and Hours: €9.50, required tours depart on the quarter-hour Tue-Sun from 10:00, last tour generally at 17:15, closed 12:00-13:00 and Mon year-round, 7 Rue St. Romain, tel. 02 35 52 48 00, www.historial-jeannedarc.fr.

• *From the museum, continue down atmospheric Rue St. Romain. At #26, find the shop marked...*

Fayencerie Augy

Monsieur Augy and his family welcome shoppers to browse his studio/gallery/shop and see Rouen's earthenware "china" being made in the traditional faience style (Mon-Sat 10:00-19:00, closed

Sun, shipping available, 26 Rue St. Romain, www.fayencerie-augy.
com). First, the clay is molded and fired. Then it's dipped in white
enamel, dried, lovingly hand painted, and fired a second time.
Rouen was the first city in France to make this colorfully glazed faience earthenware. In the 1700s, the town had 18 factories churn-
ing out the popular product.

• *Peer down Rue des Chanoines (next to Augy) for a skinny example of
the higgledy-piggledy streets common in medieval Rouen. Back on Rue
St. Romain, walk along the massive Archbishop's Palace, which (after
crossing Rue de la République) leads to the fancy...*

St. Maclou Church (Eglise St. Maclou)

This church's unique, bowed facade is textbook Flamboyant Gothic. Notice the flame-like tracery decorating its gable. Because this
was built at the very end of the Gothic age—and construction took
many years—the carved wooden doors are from the next age: the
Renaissance (c. 1550). The bright and airy interior is worth a quick
peek.

• *Leaving the church, turn right, and then take another right (giving
the little boys on the corner wall a wide berth). Wander past a fine wall
of half-timbered buildings fronting Rue Martainville, to the back end of
St. Maclou Church.*

Half-Timbered Buildings

Half-timbered buildings became a Rouen specialty from the 14th
through 19th century. There are still 2,000 half-timbered buildings in town; about 100 date from before 1520. Cantilevered floors
were standard until the early 1500s. These top-heavy designs made
sense: City land was limited, property taxes were based on ground-
floor square footage, and the cantilevering minimized unsupported
spans on upper floors. The oak beams provided the structural skeleton of the building, which was then filled in with a mix of clay,
straw, or whatever was available.

• *A block after the church, on the left at 186 Rue Martainville, a short
lane leads to the...*

▲Plague Cemetery (Aître St. Maclou)

During the great plagues of the Middle Ages, as many as two-
thirds of the people in this parish died. For the decimated community, dealing with the corpses was an overwhelming task. This half-
timbered courtyard (c. 1520, free to enter, daily 9:00-18:00) was a
mass grave, an ossuary where the bodies were "processed." Bodies
were dumped into the grave (an open pit where the well is now) and
drenched in liquid lime to help speed decomposition. Later, the
bones were stacked in alcoves above the once-open arcades that line
this courtyard. Notice the colonnades with their ghoulish carvings

of gravediggers' tools, skulls, crossbones, and characters doing the "dance of death." In this *danse macabre*, Death, the great equalizer, grabs people of all social classes.

Nearby: Farther down Rue Martainville, at Place St. Marc, a colorful market is lively Sunday until about 13:30 and all day Tuesday, Friday, and Saturday.

• *Our tour is over. To return to the* **train station** *or reach the* ▲ **Museum of Fine Arts** *(free admission and worth a short visit for its Old Master and Impressionist paintings, www.musees-rouen-normandie.fr), turn right from the boneyard, then right again at the little boys (onto Rue Damiette), and hike up a pleasing antique row to the vertical St. Ouen Church (a seventh-century abbey turned 15th-century church; fine park behind). Turn left when you see St. Ouen Church and continue down traffic-free Rue de l'Hôpital (which becomes Rue Ganterie). Turn right on Rue de l'Ecureuil to find the museum directly ahead. To continue to the train station, turn left onto Rue Jean-Lecanuet, then right onto Rue Jeanne d'Arc.*

Eating in Rouen

To find the best eating action, prowl the streets between the St. Maclou and St. Ouen churches (Rues Martainville and Damiette) for *crêperies*, wine bars, international cuisine, and traditional restaurants.

$$$$ Restaurant La Couronne is a venerable and cozy place to dine very well. Reserve ahead to experience the same cuisine that Julia Child tasted when she ate here in 1948 (31 Place du Vieux Marché, tel. 02 35 71 40 90, www.lacouronne.com.fr).

$ Crêperie le St. Romain, between the cathedral and St. Maclou Church, is an excellent budget option. Gentle Mr. Pegis serves filling crêpes with small salads in a warm setting (tables in the rear are best). The hearty *gatiflette*—a crêpe with scalloped potatoes—is delicious (lunch Tue-Sat, dinner Thu-Sat, 52 Rue St. Romain, tel. 02 35 88 90 36).

$$ Dame Cakes is ideal if it's lunchtime or teatime and you need a Jane Austen fix. The decor is from a more precious era, and the baked goods are out of this world. Locals adore the tables in the back garden, while tourists eat up the cathedral view from the first-floor room (Mon-Sat 10:30-19:00, closed Sun, 70 Rue St. Romain, tel. 02 35 07 49 31).

$ Au P'it Verdot is a lively wine bar-café where locals gather for a glass of wine and meat-and-cheese plates in the thick of restaurant row (appetizers only, Tue-Sat 18:00-24:00, closed Sun-Mon, 13 Rue Père Adam, tel. 02 35 36 34 43).

$ Bistro Nova is a nifty place to eat well in a warm, friendly setting at good prices. The menu changes daily, but one meat, one fish, and one veggie *plat* are always available (excellent wine list, lunch and dinner, closed Sun-Mon, 2 Place du Lieutenant Aubert, tel. 02 35 70 20 25).

$$ La Petite Auberge, a block off Rue Damiette, is the most traditional place I list. It has an Old World interior, a nice terrace, and good prices—and it's open Sundays (good escargot and *entrecôte* with Camembert, reservations smart, closed Mon, 164 Rue Martainville, tel. 02 35 70 80 18).

Paris

Paris—the City of Light—has been a beacon of culture for centuries. As a world capital of art, fashion, food, literature, and ideas, it stands as a symbol of all the fine things human civilization can offer. Come prepared to celebrate this, rather than judge our cultural differences, and you'll capture the romance and joie de vivre that this city exudes.

Paris is magnificent, but it's also super-sized, crowded, and fast-paced. Take a deep breath, then use this orientation to the City of Light to help illuminate your trip.

PLANNING YOUR TIME

Of course, "seeing" Paris in just a few hours is in-Seine. On a brief visit, you'll need to be very selective. Choose just two or three options, and take geography and public-transit connections into account to be as efficient as possible. The best first-time plan may be to do my Historic Paris Walk, followed by a visit to the Louvre or Orsay.

Historic Paris Walk: My self-guided stroll orients you to the city's core (Ile de la Cité, Notre-Dame, Latin Quarter, Sainte-Chapelle) in about four hours.

Louvre: While art lovers could spend all day at one of the world's great museums, a targeted visit can take two hours. You can tack on a visit to the nearby **Orangerie** (a misty world of Monet's water lilies) in about an hour.

Orsay: This sumptuous collection of Impressionist art can be seen succinctly in two hours.

Eiffel Tower: If you reserve ahead to avoid the long line, you can zip to the top of Paris' most iconic structure, and back down, in two hours; to save time, do only the first level.

Arc de Triomphe and Champs-Elysées: On a quick visit, you can stroll down Paris' finest boulevard in about an hour (or even less, if you only do the more interesting upper half, to Rond Point). Add an hour to ascend to the top of the Arc de Triomphe.

PARIS

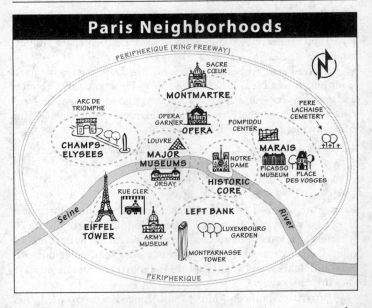

Paris Neighborhoods

Other Museums and Sights: With a special interest, consider Paris' other excellent museums, including Rodin, Picasso, Army Museum/Napoleon's Tomb, Marmottan Museum, Cluny Museum, and more. Any of these destinations can take at least an hour or two.

Orientation to Paris

Central Paris (population 2.3 million) is circled by a ring road and split in half by the Seine River, which runs east-west. As you look downstream, the Right Bank (Rive Droite) is on your right, and the Left Bank (Rive Gauche) on your left. The bull's-eye on your map is Notre-Dame, on an island in the middle of the Seine and ground zero in Paris.

Historic Core: This area centers on the Ile de la Cité ("Island of the City"), located in the middle of the Seine. On the Ile de la Cité, you'll find Paris' oldest sights, from Roman ruins to the medieval Notre-Dame and Sainte-Chapelle churches.

Major Museums Neighborhood: Located just west of the historic core, this is where you'll find the Louvre, Orsay, Orangerie, and Tuileries Garden.

Champs-Elysées: The greatest of the many grand, 19th-century boulevards on the Right Bank, the Champs-Elysées runs northwest from Place de la Concorde to the Arc de Triomphe.

Eiffel Tower Neighborhood: Dominated by the Eiffel Tower, this area also boasts the colorful Rue Cler, the Army Museum and Napoleon's Tomb, and the Rodin Museum.

Opéra Neighborhood: Surrounding the Opéra Garnier, this classy area on the Right Bank is home to a series of grand boulevards and monuments, as well as high-end shopping.

Left Bank: The Left Bank is home to...the Left Bank. Anchored by the large Luxembourg Garden, the Left Bank is the traditional neighborhood of Paris' intellectual, artistic, and café life.

Marais: Stretching eastward to Bastille along Rue de Rivoli/ Rue St. Antoine, this neighborhood has lots of restaurants, shops, and artistic sights such as the Pompidou Center and Picasso Museum.

Montmartre: This hill, topped by the bulbous white domes of the Sacré-Cœur basilica, hovers on the northern fringes of your Paris map.

TOURIST INFORMATION

Paris' TIs can provide useful information and sell Museum Passes but may have long lines (www.parisinfo.com).

Paris has several TI locations, including **Pyramides** (daily May-Oct 9:00-19:00, Nov-April from 10:00, free Wi-Fi, 25 Rue des Pyramides—at Pyramides Métro stop between the Louvre and Opéra), and **Hôtel de Ville-Paris Rendez-Vous** (Mon-Sat 10:00-19:00, closed Sun, 29 Rue de Rivoli—located on the north side of the Hôtel de Ville City Hall). In summer, TI kiosks may pop up in the squares in front of Notre-Dame and Hôtel de Ville.

ARRIVAL IN PARIS
By Train at St. Lazare Station (Gare St. Lazare)

All trains from Le Havre arrive and depart at this compact station, about a mile north of the river. Trains are one floor above street level. Trains to and from Le Havre use tracks 23-27; from here, it's a long, well-signed walk from the tracks to the Métro. The ticket office is near track 27; train information offices *(accueil)* are scattered about the station.

To head straight to Notre-Dame to begin my self-guided Historic Paris Walk, your best bet is to either take the Métro (faster, but a longer walk to Notre-Dame) or the bus (which drops you closer to the cathedral). Take **Métro** line 14 (purple) south (direction: Olympiades), and ride three stops to Châtelet; this stop is three short blocks north of the river and Ile de la Cité. **Bus #24** departs from in front of the station and goes to Madeleine, Place de la Concorde, the Orsay, the Louvre, St. Michel, Notre-Dame, and beyond.

By Shuttle Bus, on or near Place de la Concorde

If you arrive in Paris via an "On Your Own" shuttle-bus excursion, the bus will likely drop you off on or near the square called Place de la Concorde (between the Louvre and the bottom of the grand Champs-Elysées boulevard). From here, it's an easy 15- to 20-minute **walk** to either the Louvre or (just across the river) the Orsay. From the nearby Concorde **Métro** stop, line 1 (yellow) makes things easier: Ride it in direction: Château de Vincennes, and hop off at the second stop, Palais Royal-Musée du Louvre, for the Louvre's entrance; a few stops later, Châtelet and Hôtel de Ville are a short walk north of the river and Notre-Dame. If you ride this Métro line in the opposite direction, toward La Défense, you can get off at Charles de Gaulle-Etoile for the Arc de Triomphe, at the start of the Champs-Elysées. **Bus #24,** described earlier, stops at Place de la Concorde.

HELPFUL HINTS

Theft Alert: Paris is safe, but filled with thieves and scammers who target tourists. Wherever there are crowds, pickpockets work busy lines (e.g., at ticket windows at train stations). It's smart to wear a money belt, put your wallet in your front pocket, loop your day bag over your shoulders, and keep a tight hold on your purse or shopping bag.

Wi-Fi: You'll find free hotspots at many cafés and in many public areas (look for the Paris Wi-Fi logo to find a network). The Orange network also has many hotspots and offers a free two-hour pass.

Public WCs: Many public toilets are free, but you get what you pay for. Bold travelers can walk into any sidewalk café like they own the place and find the toilet downstairs or in the back.

Tobacco Stands *(Tabacs):* These little kiosks—usually just a counter inside a café—are handy and very local. Most sell public-transit tickets, cards for parking meters, postage stamps (though not all sell international postage), and...oh yeah, cigarettes. To find a kiosk, just look for a *Tabac* sign and the red cylinder-shaped symbol above certain cafés.

GETTING AROUND PARIS

Paris is easy to navigate. Your basic choices are Métro (in-city subway), suburban train (formerly called RER, rapid transit tied into the Métro system), public bus, tram, Uber, and taxi. Also consider the hop-on, hop-off bus and boat tours (see "Tours in Paris," later).

You can buy tickets and passes at Métro stations and at many *tabacs*. Some machines accept only credit cards and coins, though key stations always have machines that take small bills of €20 or less and chip-and-PIN cards (some American cards are accepted—

try). These machines work logically with easy-to-follow instructions in English; for single tickets or a *carnet* of 10 tickets, choose the first (top) option on the screen.

Public-Transit Tickets: The Métro, suburban trains (lines A-K), trams, and buses all work on the same tickets. You can make as many transfers as you need on a single ticket, except when transferring between the bus or tram systems and the Métro/suburban train system (an additional ticket is required). A **single ticket** costs €1.90. If planning to use multiple tickets, buy a *carnet* (kar-nay) of 10 tickets for €14.50. *Carnets* can be shared among travelers.

By Métro

In Paris, you're never more than a 10-minute walk from a Métro station. Europe's best subway system allows you to hop from sight to sight quickly and cheaply (runs 5:30-1:00 in the morning, Fri-Sat until 2:00 in the morning, www.ratp.fr). Learn to use it.

Using the Métro System: To get to your destination, determine the closest "Mo" stop and which line *(ligne)* or lines will get

you there. The lines are color-coded and numbered. You can tell their direction by the end-of-the-line stops. For example, the La Défense/Château de Vincennes line, also known as line 1 (yellow), runs between La Défense, on its west end, and Vincennes on its east end. Once in the Métro station, you'll see the color-coded line numbers and/or blue-and-white signs directing you to the train going in your direction (e.g., *direction: La Défense*). Insert your ticket in the turnstile, reclaim your ticket, pass through, and keep it until you exit the system (some stations require you to pass your ticket through a turnstile to exit).

Transfers are free and can be made wherever lines cross, provided you do so within 1.5 hours and don't exit the station. When you transfer, follow the appropriately colored line number and end-of-the-line stop to find your next train, or look for *correspondance* (connection) signs that lead to your next line.

When you reach your destination, blue-and-white *sortie* signs point you to the exit. Before leaving the station, check the helpful *plan du quartier* (map of the neighborhood) to get your bearings. At stops with several *sorties*, you can save time by choosing the best exit.

Métro Resources: For an **interactive map** of Paris' sights and Métro lines, with a trip-planning feature and information about

PARIS

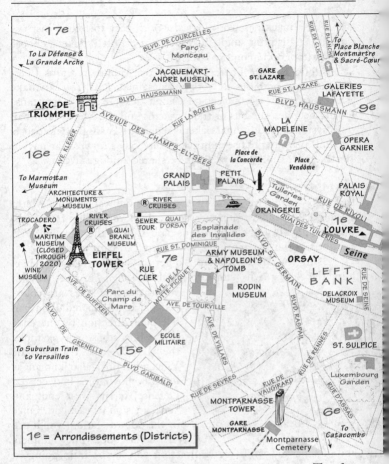

1e = Arrondissements (Districts)

each sight and station's history, see www.metro.paris. The free **RATP mobile app** can estimate Métro travel times, help you locate the best station exit, and tell you when the next bus will arrive, among other things.

Beware of Pickpockets: Thieves dig public transit. You'll hear regular announcements in the Métro to beware of *les pickpockets*. Any jostling or commotion—especially when boarding or leaving trains—is likely the sign of a thief or a team of thieves in action.

By Suburban Train

The suburban train, formerly called the RER, is an arm of the Métro, serving outlying destinations such as Versailles, Disneyland Paris, and airports. These routes are indicated by thick lines on your Métro map and identified by the letters A-K (travelers may still see the name "RER" on some signage and maps).

Within the city center, the suburban train works like the

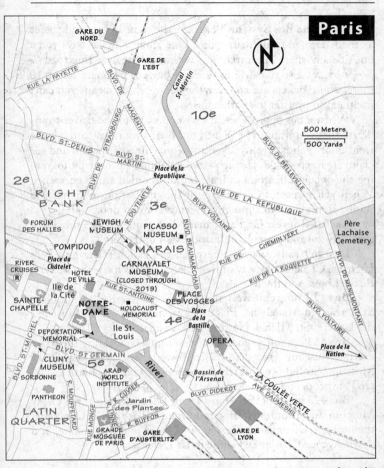

Métro and can be speedier if it serves your destination directly, because it makes fewer stops. Métro tickets are good on the suburban train; you can transfer between the Métro and suburban train systems with the same ticket.

By City Bus

Paris' excellent bus system is worth figuring out (www.ratp.fr). Buses require less walking and fewer stairways than the Métro, and you can see Paris unfold as you travel.

Bus Stops: Stops are everywhere, and most come with all the information you need. This includes a good city bus map, route maps for each bus that stops there, a frequency chart and schedule, live screens showing the time the next two buses will arrive, and a *plan du quartier* map of the immediate neighborhood. Bus-system maps are also available in any Métro station (and in the *Paris Pratique par Arrondissement* booklet sold at newsstands).

Using the Bus System: Buses use the same tickets and passes as the Métro and suburban trains. One Zone 1 ticket buys you a bus ride anywhere in central Paris within the freeway ring road *(le périphérique)*. Use your Métro ticket or buy one on board for €0.10 more. These tickets are *sans correspondance*, which means you can't use them to transfer to another bus.

When a bus approaches, it's wise to wave to the driver to indicate that you want to be picked up. Board your bus through the front door. Validate your ticket in the machine (stripe up) and reclaim it. Keep track of which stop is coming up next by following the onboard diagram or listening to recorded announcements. When you're ready to get off, push the red button to signal you want a stop, then exit through the central or rear door.

Useful Routes: Of Paris' many bus routes, these provide a great, cheap, and convenient introduction to the city.

Bus #69 runs east-west between the Eiffel Tower and Père Lachaise Cemetery by way of Rue Cler, Quai d'Orsay, the Louvre, Ile St. Louis, and the Marais.

Bus #24 runs east-west along the Seine riverbank from Gare St. Lazare to Madeleine, Place de la Concorde, Orsay Museum, the Louvre, St. Michel, Notre-Dame, and Jardin des Plantes.

Bus #63 is another good east-west route, connecting the Marmottan Museum, Trocadéro (Eiffel Tower), Pont de l'Alma, Orsay Museum, St. Sulpice Church, Luxembourg Garden, Latin Quarter/Panthéon, and Gare de Lyon.

Bus #73 is one of Paris' most scenic lines, starting at the Orsay Museum and running westbound around Place de la Concorde, then up the Champs-Elysées, around the Arc de Triomphe, and down Avenue Charles de Gaulle to La Défense.

By Uber

Uber works in Paris like it does at home (as long as you have a data plan or access to Wi-Fi), and in general works better than taxis in Paris (www.uber.com). Uber drivers can pick you up anywhere so you don't have to track down a taxi stand, and you can text them if you don't see the car. There's no language problem giving directions, as you can type your destination into the app.

By Taxi

Parisian taxis are reasonable, especially for couples and families. The meters are tamper-proof. Fares and supplements (described in English on the rear windows) are straightforward and tightly regulated.

Cabbies are legally required to accept four passengers, though they don't always like it. If you have five in your group, you can book a larger taxi in advance, or try your luck at a taxi stand.

PARIS

Rates: All Parisian taxis start with €2.60 on the meter and have a minimum charge of €7. A 20-minute ride (such as Bastille to the Eiffel Tower) costs about €25. Taxi drivers charge higher rates at rush hour, at night, all day Sunday, and for extra passengers. To tip, round up to the next euro (at least €0.50). The A, B, or C lights on a taxi's rooftop sign correspond to hourly rates, which vary with the time of day and day of the week. Tired travelers need not bother with the subtle differences in fares—if you need a cab, take it.

How to Catch *un Taxi*: You can try waving down a taxi, but it's often easier to ask someone for the nearest taxi stand (*"Où est une station de taxi?"*; oo ay ewn stah-see-ohn duh tahk-see). Taxi stands are indicated by a circled "T" on good city maps and on many maps in this chapter.

Tours in Paris

🎧 To sightsee on your own, download my free Rick Steves Audio Europe app with **audio tours** that illuminate some of Paris' top sights and neighborhoods, including my Historic Paris Walk and tours of the Louvre and Orsay museums (see sidebar on page 46 for details).

BY BUS OR PETIT TRAIN
Hop-On, Hop-Off Bus Tours
Double-decker buses connect Paris' main sights, giving you an easy once-over of the city with a basic recorded commentary, punctuated with music. You can hop off at any stop, tour a sight, then hop on a later bus. Because of traffic and stops, these buses can be slow. (Busy sightseers will do better using the Métro to connect sights.) Buses normally run from about 9:30-17:45. Look up the various routes and stops either on their website or by picking up a brochure (available at any TI or on one of their bright yellow-and-green buses). Buy tickets from the driver or online.

L'OpenTour has the most options with reasonably frequent service on four routes covering central Paris (transfers between routes are OK). Their Paris Grand Tour (green route) offers by far the best introduction and most frequent buses (every 10 minutes). You can catch the bus at just about any major sight—look for the Open Bus icon on public transit bus shelters and signs (1 day-€33, allow 2 hours to complete a route with stops to visit a sight, tel. 01 42 66 56 56, www.paris.opentour.com).

Big Bus Paris runs a fleet of buses around Paris on two routes with just 11 stops and recorded narration—or use their even better free app for sight descriptions (1 day-€34, tel. 01 53 95 39 53, www.bigbustours.com).

City Sightseeing Tours' red buses run along one long route with 36 stops (1 day-€29, 3 buses/hour, 9 Avenue de l'Opèra, www.citysightseeing.com).

Petit Train Tour

For a relaxing cultural overview of Paris that requires no walking, **Another Paris** offers tours on their blue *petit train* with huge view windows. Listening to simple yet informative audio commentary, passengers enjoy a leisurely ride through streets that large buses can't access. See their website for itinerary and departure details (€13-19, daily, 1.5 hours, disabled access, reservations required, mobile 06 31 99 29 38, www.another-paris.com, contact@another-paris.com).

BY BOAT
Seine Cruises

Several companies run one-hour boat cruises on the Seine. A typical cruise loops back and forth between the Eiffel Tower and the Pont d'Austerlitz, and drops you off where you started.

Bateaux-Mouches departs from Pont de l'Alma's right bank and has the biggest open-top, double-decker boats (higher up means better views). But this company caters to tour groups, making their boats jammed and noisy (€13.50, kids 4-12-€6, tel. 01 42 25 96 10, www.bateaux-mouches.fr).

Bateaux Parisiens has smaller covered boats with audio-guides, fewer crowds, and only one deck. I'd pass on this cruise, as you're stuck inside the boat. It leaves from right in front of the Eiffel Tower (€15, kids 3-12-€7, tel. 01 76 64 14 45, www.bateauxparisiens.com).

Vedettes du Pont Neuf starts and ends at Pont Neuf. The boats feature a live guide whose delivery (in English and French) is as stiff as a recorded narration—and as hard to understand, given the quality of their sound system (€14, €12 with this book if you book directly, kids 4-12-€7, tip requested, nearly 2/hour, daily 10:30-22:30, tel. 01 46 33 98 38, www.vedettesdupontneuf.com).

Hop-On, Hop-Off Boat Tour

Batobus allows you to get on and off at eight popular stops along the Seine: Eiffel Tower, Orsay Museum, St. Germain-des-Prés, Notre-Dame, Jardin des Plantes, Hôtel de Ville, the Louvre, and Pont Alexandre III, near the Champs-Elysées (1 day-€17, every 20 minutes 10:00-21:30, Sept-March every 25 minutes until 19:00,

45 minutes one-way, 1.5-hour round-trip, www.batobus.com). It's worthwhile as a scenic, floating alternative to the Métro, but if you just want a guided boat tour, the Seine cruises described earlier are a better choice.

ON FOOT
Walking Tours
Paris Walks offers a variety of thoughtful and entertaining two-hour walks, led by British and American guides (€15-20, generally 2/day—morning and afternoon, private tours available, family-friendly and Louvre tours are a specialty, best to check current offerings on their website, tel. 01 48 09 21 40, www.paris-walks. com, paris@paris-walks.com). Reservations aren't necessary for most tours.

Context Travel offers "intellectual by design" walking tours geared for serious learners. The tours are led by well-versed do-cents (historians, architects, and academics) and cover both museums and specific neighborhoods. It's best to book in advance—groups are limited to six participants and can fill up fast (about €100/person, admission to sights extra, generally 3 hours, tel. 09 75 18 04 15, US tel. 800-691-6036, www.contexttravel.com, info@ contexttravel.com).

Fat Tire Tours offers high-on-fun, casual walking tours. Their two-hour Classic Paris Walking Tour covers most major sights and has an option that includes a "Skip the Line" Louvre ticket (usually Mon, Wed, and Fri at 10:00 or 15:00). Other "Skip the Line" tours of major sights include Notre-Dame Tower, Catacombs, Eiffel Tower, Sainte-Chapelle, and Versailles. Reservations are required (€20-40/person for walking tours, €40-90/person for "Skip the Line" tours, €2 discount per person with this book—two-discount maximum per book; 36 Avenue de la Bourdonnais, Mo: Ecole Militaire, tel. 01 82 88 80 96, www.fattiretours.com/paris).

Local Guides
For many, Paris merits hiring a Parisian as a personal guide. All charge €200-230 for half-day. **Thierry Gauduchon** is a terrific guide and a gifted teacher (mobile 06 19 07 30 77, tgauduchon@ gmail.com). **Sylvie Moreau** also leads good tours in Paris (tel. 01 74 30 27 46, mobile 06 87 02 80 67, sylvie.ja.moreau@gmail.com). **Arnaud Servignat** is a top guide who has taught me much about Paris (also does minivan tours of the countryside around Paris for more, mobile 06 68 80 29 05, www.french-guide.com, arnotour@ me.com). **Elisabeth Van Hest** is another likable and very capable guide (tel. 01 43 41 47 31, mobile 06 77 80 19 89, elisa.guide@ gmail.com). **Sylviane Ceneray** is gentle and knowledgeable (mobile 06 84 48 02 44, www.paris-asyoulikeit.com).

PARIS

Paris at a Glance

▲▲▲**Notre-Dame Cathedral** Paris' most beloved church, with towers and gargoyles. **Hours:** Cathedral-Mon-Sat 7:45-18:45, Sun 7:15-19:15; Tower-daily April-Sept 10:00-18:30, Fri-Sat until 23:00 in July-Aug, Oct-March 10:00-17:30; Treasury-Mon-Fri 9:30-18:00, Sat 9:30-18:30, Sun 13:30-18:40. See page 1020.

▲▲▲**Sainte-Chapelle** Gothic cathedral with peerless stained glass. **Hours:** Daily 9:00-19:00, Oct-March until 17:00. See page 1027.

▲▲▲**Louvre** Europe's oldest and greatest museum, starring *Mona Lisa* and *Venus de Milo*. **Hours:** Wed-Mon 9:00-18:00, Wed and Fri until 21:45, closed Tue. See page 1031.

▲▲▲**Orsay Museum** Nineteenth-century art, including Europe's greatest Impressionist collection. **Hours:** Tue-Sun 9:30-18:00, Thu until 21:45, closed Mon. See page 1037.

▲▲▲**Eiffel Tower** Paris' soaring exclamation point. **Hours:** Daily mid-June-Aug 9:00-24:45, Sept-mid-June 9:30-23:45. See page 1043.

▲▲▲**Champs-Elysées** Paris' grand boulevard. See page 1048.

▲▲**Orangerie Museum** Monet's water lilies and modernist classics in a lovely setting. **Hours:** Wed-Mon 9:00-18:00, closed Tue. See page 1042.

▲▲**Rue Cler** Ultimate Parisian market street. **Hours:** Stores open Tue-Sat plus Sun morning, dead on Mon. See page 1045.

Sightseeing Strategies

For most sightseers, the best single way to avoid long lines is to buy a Paris Museum Pass. If you decide to forego the pass—or for sights not covered by the pass—you have other options. Note, though, that because of heightened terrorism concerns, there are likely to be slow security checks at most tourist-heavy sights.

Paris Museum Pass: This pass admits you to many of Paris' most popular sights, and allows you to skip to the front of most lines (except security lines), which can save hours of waiting, especially in summer. Another benefit is that you can pop into lesser sights that otherwise might not be worth the expense. For more info, visit www.parismuseumpass.com (2 days-€48, 4 days-€62, 6 days-€74, no youth or senior discounts). It's sold at participating

▲▲**Army Museum and Napoleon's Tomb** The emperor's imposing tomb, flanked by museums of France's wars. **Hours:** Daily 10:00-18:00, Nov-March until 17:00; tomb also open July-Aug until 19:00 and April-Sept Tue until 21:00; museum (except for tomb) closed first Mon of month Oct-June; Charles de Gaulle exhibit closed Mon year-round. See page 1046.

▲▲**Rodin Museum** Works by the greatest sculptor since Michelangelo, with many statues in a peaceful garden. **Hours:** Tue-Sun 10:00-17:45, closed Mon. See page 1046.

▲▲**Marmottan Museum** Art museum focusing on Monet. **Hours:** Tue-Sun 10:00-18:00, Thu until 21:00, closed Mon. See page 1047.

▲▲**Cluny Museum** Medieval art with unicorn tapestries. **Hours:** Wed-Mon 9:15-17:45, closed Tue. See page 1047.

▲▲**Arc de Triomphe** Triumphal arch marking start of Champs-Elysées. **Hours:** Always viewable; interior daily 10:00-23:00, Oct-March until 22:30. See page 1048.

▲▲**Picasso Museum** World's largest collection of Picasso's works. **Hours:** Tue-Fri 10:30-18:00, Sat-Sun 9:30-18:00, closed Mon. See page 1049.

▲▲**Pompidou Center** Modern art in colorful building with city views. **Hours:** Permanent collection open Wed-Mon 11:00-21:00, closed Tue. See page 1050.

museums, monuments, TIs, and at some souvenir stores located near major sights.

Avoiding Lines Without a Pass: For some sights, you can buy **advance tickets** either at the official website or through a third party (for a fee). Some tickets require you to choose a specific entry time, like at the line-plagued Eiffel Tower.

TIs, FNAC department stores, and travel-services companies such as Fat Tire Tours (see www.fattiretours.com/paris) sell individual *"coupe-file"* tickets (pronounced "koop feel") for some sights, which allow you to use the Museum Pass entrance (worth the extra cost and trouble only for sights where lines are longest). TIs sell these tickets for a small fee, but elsewhere you can expect a surcharge of 10-20 percent. FNAC stores are in many locations (www.fnactickets.com), even on the Champs-Elysées.

At certain sights, including the Louvre and Orsay, **nearby shops** sell tickets, allowing you to avoid the main ticket lines (for details, see the Louvre and Orsay listings).

Historic Paris Walk

Allow four hours to do justice to this three-mile self-guided walk, beginning at Notre-Dame Cathedral and ending at Pont Neuf; just follow the dotted line on the "Historic Paris Walk" map.

This information is distilled from the Historic Paris Walk chapter in *Rick Steves Paris,* by Rick Steves, Steve Smith, and Gene Openshaw. You can download a free 🎧 Rick Steves audio version of this walk; see page 46.

• *Start where the city did—on the Ile de la Cité, the island in the Seine River and the physical and historic bull's-eye of your Paris map. The closest Métro stops are Cité, Hôtel de Ville, and St. Michel, each a short walk away.*

❶ Notre-Dame Cathedral

For centuries, the main figure in the Christian pantheon has been Mary, the mother of Jesus. Catholics petition her in times of trouble to gain comfort, and to ask her to convince God to be compassionate with them. This church, worth ▲▲▲, is dedicated to "Our Lady" (Notre-Dame), and there she is, cradling God, right in the heart of the facade, surrounded by the halo of the rose window.

Imagine the faith of the people who built this cathedral. They broke ground in 1163 with the hope that someday their great-great-great-great-great-great grandchildren might attend the dedication Mass, which finally took place two centuries later, in 1345. Look up the 200-foot-tall bell towers and imagine a tiny medieval community mustering the money and energy for construction. Master masons supervised, but the people did much of the grunt work themselves for free—hauling the huge stones from distant quarries, digging a 30-foot-deep trench to lay the foundation, and treading like rats on a wheel designed to lift the stones up, one by one. This kind of backbreaking, arduous manual labor created the real hunchbacks of Notre-Dame.

Cost and Hours: Cathedral-free, Mon-Sat 7:45-18:45, Sun 7:15-19:15; treasury-€5, not covered by Museum Pass, Mon-Fri 9:30-18:00, Sat 9:30-18:30, Sun 13:30-18:40; audioguide-€5, free

English tours normally Mon, Tue, and Sat at 14:30, Wed and Thu at 14:00. Modest dress is required—no shorts or bare shoulders (Mo: Cité, Hôtel de Ville, or St. Michel; tel. 01 42 34 56 10, www. notredamedeparis.fr).

Tower Climb: The entrance for Notre-Dame's tower climb is outside the cathedral, along the left side. To climb the tower, you must reserve a time in advance, even with a Museum Pass. Reservations can be made same-day only (starting at 7:30) with the JeFile app or at ticket machines on-site (€10, covered by Museum Pass but no bypass line; daily April-Sept 10:00-18:30, Fri-Sat until 23:00 in July-Aug, Oct-March 10:00-17:30, last entry 45 minutes before closing; tel. 01 53 40 60 80, www.tours-notre-dame-de-paris.fr).

● Self-Guided Tour

"Walk this way" toward the front of the cathedral, and view it from the bronze plaque on the ground marked **"Point Zero"** (30 yards from the central doorway). You're standing at the center of France, the point from which all distances are measured.

Facade: Look at the left doorway, and to the left of the door, find the statue with his head in his hands. The man with the misplaced head is **St. Denis,** the city's first bishop and patron saint. He stands among statues of other early Christians who helped turn pagan Paris into Christian Paris. Sometime in the third century, Denis came here from Italy to convert the Parisii. He settled here on the Ile de la Cité, back when there was a Roman temple on this spot and Christianity was suspect. Denis proved so successful at winning converts that the Romans' pagan priests got worried. Denis was beheaded as a warning to those forsaking the Roman gods. But those early Christians were hard to keep down. The man who would become St. Denis got up, tucked his head under his arm, and headed north.

Notre-Dame Interior: Enter the church at the right doorway (the line moves quickly) and find a spot where you can view the long, high central aisle. (Be careful: Pickpockets attend church here religiously.)

Notre-Dame has the typical basilica floor plan shared by so many Catholic churches: a long central nave lined with columns and flanked by side aisles. It's designed in the shape of a cross, with the altar placed where the crossbeam intersects. The church can

PARIS

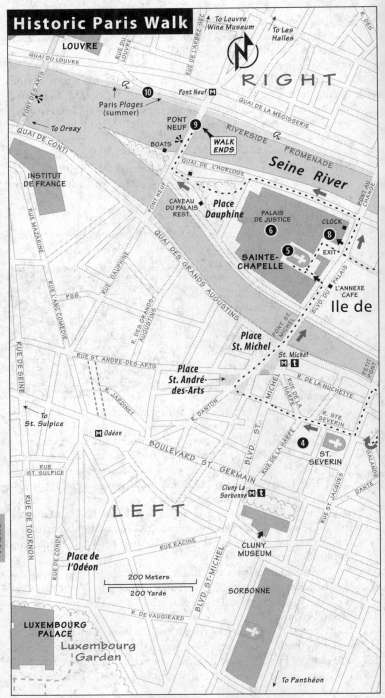

Historic Paris Walk

LOUVRE

QUAI DU LOUVRE

R. DU LOUVRE

R. DE L'ARBRE-SEC

R. DES

To Louvre
Wine Museum

To Les Halles

RIGHT

Pont Neuf M

QUAI DE LA MEGISSERIE

Paris Plages
(summer) **10**

PONT
NEUF **9**

RIVERSIDE

Seine River

WALK
ENDS

PROMENADE

To Orsay

QUAI DE CONTI

BOATS

PONT NEUF

QUAI DE L'HORLOGE

QUAI AU CHANGE

INSTITUT
DE FRANCE

CAVEAU
DU PALAIS
REST.

Place
Dauphine

PALAIS
DE JUSTICE

6

CLOCK

8

RUE MAZARINE

QUAI DES GRANDS AUGUSTINS

5

SAINTE-
CHAPELLE

EXIT

BLVD. DU PALAIS

L'ANNEXE
CAFE

RUE DAUPHINE

RUE ANC. COMEDIE

PSG.

R. DES GRANDS
AUGUSTINS

Ile de

PONT ST.
MICHEL

RUE DE SEINE

RUE ST. ANDRE-DES-ARTS

Place
St. Michel

Place
St. André-
des-Arts

St. Michel
M t

PETIT
PONT

R. JARDINET

R. DANTON

MICHEL

ST.

RUE DE LA HARPE

RUE DE LA HUCHETTE

R. STE.
SEVERIN

To St. Sulpice

M Odéon

BOULEVARD ST. GERMAIN

BLVD.

RUE DE LA HARPE

4

ST.
SEVERIN

R. STE.
SEVERIN

GALANDE

RUE
ST. SULPICE

Cluny La
Sorbonne M t

RUE ST. JACQUES

DANTE

RUE DE TOURNON

RUE DE CONDE

LEFT

CLUNY
MUSEUM

Place de
l'Odéon

RUE RACINE

200 Meters

200 Yards

BLVD. ST.-MICHEL

SORBONNE

LUXEMBOURG
PALACE

R. DE VAUGIRARD

Luxembourg
Garden

To Panthéon

PARIS

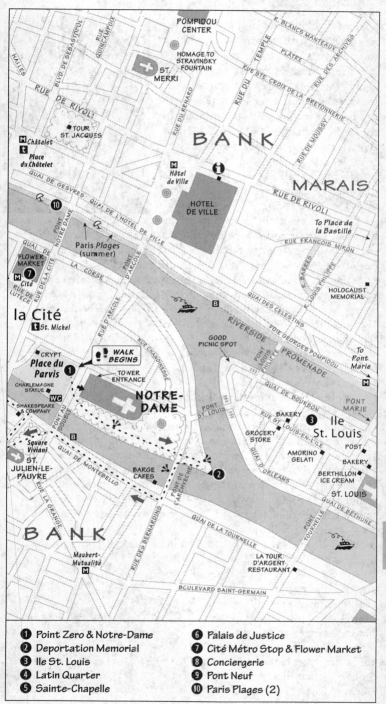

PARIS

1. Point Zero & Notre-Dame
2. Deportation Memorial
3. Ile St. Louis
4. Latin Quarter
5. Sainte-Chapelle
6. Palais de Justice
7. Cité Métro Stop & Flower Market
8. Conciergerie
9. Pont Neuf
10. Paris Plages (2)

hold up to 10,000 faithful, and it's probably buzzing with visitors now, just as it
was 600 years ago.

Just past the altar is the so-called
choir, the area enclosed with carved-
wood walls, where more intimate services
can be held in this spacious building. In
the right transept, a statue of **Joan of
Arc** (Jeanne d'Arc, 1412-1431), dressed
in armor and praying, honors the French
teenager who rallied her country's soldiers to try to drive English invaders from
Paris.

Join the statue in gazing up to the
blue-and-purple, **rose-shaped window** in the opposite transept—
with teeny green Mary and Baby Jesus in the center—the only one
of the three rose windows still with its original medieval glass.

The back side of the choir walls feature **scenes of the resurrected Jesus** (c. 1350) appearing to his followers, starting with
Mary Magdalene. Their starry robes still gleam, thanks to a
19th-century renovation. The niches below these carvings mark
the tombs of centuries of archbishops. Just ahead on the right is
the **Treasury.** It contains lavish robes, golden reliquaries, and the
humble tunic of King (and St.) Louis IX, but it probably isn't worth
the entry fee.

Notre-Dame Side View: Back outside, alongside the church
you'll notice many of the elements of Gothic: pointed arches, the
lacy stone tracery of the windows, pinnacles, statues on rooftops,
a lead roof, and a pointed steeple covered with the prickly "flames"
(Flamboyant Gothic) of the Holy Spirit. Most distinctive of all are
the flying buttresses. These 50-foot stone "beams" that stick out of
the church were the key to the complex Gothic architecture. The
pointed arches we saw inside cause the weight of the roof to push
outward rather than downward. The "flying" buttresses support the
roof by pushing back inward.

Picture Quasimodo (the fictional hunchback) limping around

along the railed balcony at the
base of the roof among the "gargoyles." These grotesque beasts
sticking out from pillars and
buttresses represent souls caught
between heaven and earth. They
also function as rainspouts (from
the same French root word as
"gargle") when there are no evil
spirits to battle.

• *Behind Notre-Dame, cross the street and enter through the iron gate into the park at the tip of the island. (If this gate is closed, you can still enter the park 30 yards to the left.) Look for the stairs and head down to reach the...*

❷ Deportation Memorial (Mémorial de la Déportation)

This ▲ memorial to the 200,000 French victims of the Nazi concentration camps (1940-1945) draws you into their experience. France was quickly overrun by Nazi Germany, and Paris spent the war years under Nazi occupation. Jews and dissidents were rounded up and deported—many never returned.

Cost and Hours: Free, Tue-Sun 10:00-19:00, Oct-March until 17:00, closed Mon year-round, may randomly close at other times, free 40-minute audioguide, Mo: Cité, tel. 01 46 33 87 56.

Visiting the Memorial: Inside, the circular plaque in the floor reads, "They went to the end of the earth and did not return." The hallway stretching in front of you is lined with 200,000 lighted crystals, one for each French citizen who died. Flickering at the far end is the eternal flame of hope. The tomb of the unknown deportee lies at your feet. The side rooms are filled with triangles—reminiscent of the identification patches inmates were forced to wear—each bearing the name of a concentration camp. Above the exit as you leave is the message you'll find at many other Holocaust sites: "Forgive, but never forget."

• *To exit, climb the same stairs you descended. Before leaving the memorial park, look across the river (north) to the island called...*

❸ Ile St. Louis

If Ile de la Cité is a tugboat laden with the history of Paris, it's towing this classy little residential dinghy, laden only with high-rent apartments, boutiques, characteristic restaurants, and famous ice-cream shops. Ile St. Louis wasn't developed until much later than Ile de la Cité (17th century). What was a swampy mess is now harmonious Parisian architecture and one of Paris' most exclusive neighborhoods. If you won't have time to come back, consider taking a brief detour across the pedestrian bridge, Pont St. Louis, to explore this little island.

• *From the Deportation Memorial, cross the bridge to the Left Bank. Turn right and walk along the river, toward the front end of Notre-*

Dame and to the next bridge. Stairs detour down to the riverbank if you need a place to picnic.

After passing the Pont au Double (the bridge leading to the facade of Notre-Dame), veer left across the street and find a small park called Square Viviani. Angling across the square, you'll find the small rough-stone church of St. Julien-le-Pauvre. Leave the park, walking past the church, to tiny Rue Galande.

Medieval Paris

Picture Paris in 1250, when the church of St. Julien-le-Pauvre was still new. Notre-Dame was nearly done (so they thought), Sainte-Chapelle had just opened, the university was expanding human knowledge, and Paris was fast becoming a prosperous industrial and commercial center. The area around the church and along Rue Galande gives you some of the medieval feel of ramshackle architecture and old houses leaning every which way as they scrambled for this prime real estate near the main commercial artery of the day—the Seine. The smell of fish competed with the smell of neighbors in this knot of humanity.

• *Now, return toward the river, walking past the church and park on the cobbled lane. Turn left on Rue de la Bûcherie and watch on your left for Shakespeare and Company, an atmospheric reincarnation of the original 1920s bookshop and a good spot to page through books (37 Rue de la Bûcherie). Walk a block behind Shakespeare and Company, and take a spin through...*

❹ The Latin Quarter

This area's touristy fame relates to its intriguing, artsy, bohemian character. This was perhaps Europe's leading university district in the Middle Ages, when Latin was the language of higher education. The neighborhood's main boulevards (St. Michel and St. Germain) are lined with cafés—once the haunts of great poets and philosophers, now the hangouts of tired tourists. Exploring a few blocks up or downriver from here gives you a better chance of feeling the pulse of what survives of Paris' classic Left Bank.

Although it may look more like the Greek Quarter today (cheap gyros abound), this area is the Latin Quarter, worth ▲ and named for the language you'd have heard on these streets if you walked them in the Middle Ages. The University of Paris (founded 1215), one of the leading educational institutions of medieval Europe, was (and still is) nearby. Walking along Rue St. Séverin, you can still see the shadow of the medieval sewer system. The street slopes into a central channel of bricks. In the days before plumbing and toilets, when people still went to the river or neighborhood wells for their water, flushing meant throwing it out the window. At certain times of day, maids on the fourth floor would holler,

"Garde de l'eau!" ("Watch out for the water!") and heave it into the streets, where it would eventually wash down into the Seine.

Don't miss **Place St. Michel.** This square (facing Pont St. Michel) is the traditional core of the Left Bank's artsy, liberal, hippie, bohemian district of poets, philosophers, winos, and *baba cool*s (neo-hippies). In less commercial times, Place St. Michel was a gathering point for the city's malcontents and misfits. In 1830, 1848, and again in 1871, the citizens took the streets from the government troops, set up barricades *Les Miz*-style, and fought against royalist oppression. During World War II, the locals rose up against their Nazi oppressors (read the plaques under the dragons at the foot of the St. Michel fountain). Even today, whenever there's a student demonstration, it starts here.

• *From Place St. Michel, look across the river and find the prickly steeple of the Sainte-Chapelle church. Head toward it. Cross the river on Pont St. Michel and continue north along the Boulevard du Palais. On your left, you'll see the doorway to Sainte-Chapelle (usually with a line of people).*

❺ Sainte-Chapelle

This ▲▲▲ triumph of Gothic church architecture is a cathedral of glass like no other. It was speedily built between 1242 and 1248

for King Louis IX—the only French king who is now a saint—to house the supposed Crown of Thorns. Its architectural harmony is due to the fact that it was completed under the direction of one architect and in only six years—unheard of in Gothic times. By contrast, Notre-Dame took more than 200 years.

Cost and Hours: €10, €15 combo-ticket with Conciergerie, free for those under age 18, covered by Museum Pass; daily 9:00-19:00, Oct-March until 17:00; audioguide-€3, 4 Boulevard du Palais, Mo: Cité, tel. 01 53 40 60 80, www.sainte-chapelle.fr.

Getting In: Expect long lines. Security lines are shortest if you come first thing (be in line by 9:00, or arrive at 10:00 after the early rush subsides). It may be worth rearranging the order of the walk: See Sainte-Chapelle first thing, then walk over to Notre-Dame (5 minutes away) to begin this walk; or, see Sainte-Chapelle last.

Visiting the Church: Though the inside is beautiful, the exterior is basically functional. The muscular buttresses hold up the stone roof, so the walls are essentially there to display stained glass. The lacy spire is Neo-Gothic—added in the 19th century. Inside, the layout clearly shows an *ancien régime* approach to worship. The

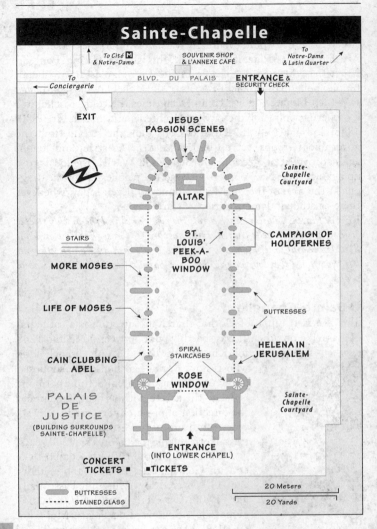

Sainte-Chapelle

To Cité M & Notre-Dame

SOUVENIR SHOP & L'ANNEXE CAFÉ

To Notre-Dame & Latin Quarter

To Conciergerie

BLVD. DU PALAIS

ENTRANCE & SECURITY CHECK

EXIT

JESUS' PASSION SCENES

ALTAR

Sainte-Chapelle Courtyard

STAIRS

ST. LOUIS' PEEK-A-BOO WINDOW

CAMPAIGN OF HOLOFERNES

MORE MOSES

LIFE OF MOSES

BUTTRESSES

CAIN CLUBBING ABEL

SPIRAL STAIRCASES

HELENA IN JERUSALEM

ROSE WINDOW

PALAIS DE JUSTICE
(BUILDING SURROUNDS SAINTE-CHAPELLE)

Sainte-Chapelle Courtyard

ENTRANCE (INTO LOWER CHAPEL)

CONCERT TICKETS ■

■TICKETS

20 Meters

20 Yards

■ BUTTRESSES
---- STAINED GLASS

PARIS

low-ceilinged basement was for staff and other common folks—worshipping under a sky filled with painted fleurs-de-lis, a symbol of the king. Royal Christians worshipped upstairs. The paint job, a 19th-century restoration, helps you imagine how grand this small, painted, jeweled chapel was. (Imagine Notre-Dame painted like this...) Each capital is playfully carved with a different plant's leaves.

Climb the spiral staircase to the Chapelle Haute. Fill the place with choral music, crank up the sunshine, face the top of the altar, and really believe that the Crown of Thorns is there, and this becomes one awesome space.

Fiat lux. "Let there be light." From the first page of the Bible, it's clear. Light is divine. Light shines through stained glass like God's grace shining down to earth. Gothic architects used their new technology to turn dark stone buildings into lanterns of light. The glory of Gothic shines brighter here than in any other church.

There are 15 separate panels of stained glass (6,500 square feet—two-thirds of it 13th-century original), with more than 1,100 different scenes, mostly from the Bible. These cover the entire Christian history of the world, from the Creation in Genesis (first window on the left, as you face the altar), to the coming of Christ (over the altar), to the end of the world (the round "rose"-shaped window at the rear

of the church. Each individual scene is interesting, and the whole effect is overwhelming. Allow yourself a few minutes to bask in the glow of the colored light.

The **altar** was raised up high to better display the Crown of Thorns, which cost King Louis more than three times as much as this church. Today, the relic is kept by the Notre-Dame Treasury (though it's occasionally brought out for display).

• *Next door to Sainte-Chapelle is the...*

❻ Palais de Justice

Sainte-Chapelle sits within a huge complex of buildings that has housed the local government since ancient Roman times. It was the

site of the original Gothic palace of the early kings of France. The only surviving medieval parts are Sainte-Chapelle and the Conciergerie prison.

Most of the site is now covered by the giant Palais de Justice, built in 1776, home of the French Supreme Court. The motto *Liberté, Egalité, Fraternité*

over the doors is a reminder that this was also the headquarters of the Revolutionary government. Here they doled out justice, condemning many to imprisonment in the Conciergerie downstairs—or to the guillotine.

• *Now pass through the big iron gate to the noisy Boulevard du Palais. Cross the street to the wide, pedestrian-only Rue de Lutèce and walk about halfway down.*

❼ Cité "Metropolitain" Métro Stop

Of the 141 original early-20th-century subway entrances, this is one of only a few survivors—now preserved as a national art treasure. (New York's Museum of Modern Art even exhibits one.) It marks Paris at its peak in 1900—on the cutting edge of Modernism, but with an eye for beauty. The curvy, plantlike ironwork is a textbook example of Art Nouveau, the style that rebelled against the erector-set squareness of the Industrial Age.

The flower and plant market on Place Louis Lépine is a pleasant detour. On Sundays this square flutters with a busy bird market.

• *Double back to the Palais de Justice, turn right onto Boulevard du Palais, and enter the Conciergerie (free with Museum Pass).*

❽ Conciergerie

Though pretty barren inside, this former prison echoes with history. Positioned next to the courthouse, the Conciergerie was the

gloomy prison famous as the last stop for 2,780 victims of the guillotine, including France's last *ancien régime* queen, Marie-Antoinette. Before then, kings had used the building to torture and execute failed assassins. (One of its towers along the river was called "The Babbler," named for the pain-induced sounds that leaked from it.) When the Revolution (1789) toppled the king, the building kept its same function, but without torture. The progressive Revolutionaries proudly unveiled a modern and more humane way to execute people—the guillotine. The Conciergerie was the epicenter of the Reign of Terror—the year-long period of the Revolution (1793-94) during which Revolutionary fervor spiraled out of control and thousands were killed. It was here at the Conciergerie that "enemies of the Revolution" were imprisoned, tried, sentenced, and marched off to Place de la Concorde for decapitation. It was here that on October 16, 1793, Marie-Antoinette was awakened at 4:00 in the morning and led away.

Cost and Hours: €9, €15 combo-ticket with Sainte-Chapelle, covered by Museum Pass, daily 9:30-18:00, 2 Boulevard du Palais, Mo: Cité, tel. 01 53 40 60 80, www.paris-conciergerie.fr.

• *Back outside, turn left on Boulevard du Palais. On the corner is the city's oldest public clock. The mechanism of the present clock is from 1334, and even though the case is Baroque, it keeps on ticking.*

Turn left onto Quai de l'Horloge and walk along the river. The bridge up ahead is the Pont Neuf, where we'll end this walk. At the first corner, veer left into a sleepy triangular square called Place Dauphine. It's amazing to find such coziness in the heart of Paris. From the equestrian statue of Henry IV, turn right onto Pont Neuf. Pause at the little nook halfway across.

❾ Pont Neuf and the Seine

This "new bridge" is now Paris' oldest. Built during Henry IV's reign (about 1600), its arches span the widest part of the river. Unlike other bridges, this one never had houses or buildings growing on it. The turrets were originally for vendors and street entertainers. In the days of Henry IV, who promised his peasants "a chicken in every pot every Sunday," this would have been a lively scene. From the bridge, look downstream (west) to see the next bridge, the pedestrian-only Pont des Arts. Ahead on the Right Bank is the long Louvre museum. Beyond that, on the Left Bank, is the Orsay. And what's that tall black tower in the distance?

• *Our walk is finished. From here, you can tour the Seine by boat (the departure point for Seine River cruises offered by Vedettes du Pont Neuf is through the park at the end of the island), continue to the Louvre, or head to the riverside promenades along the banks of the river—each summer, the Paris city government trucks in potted palm trees, hammocks, and lounge chairs to create colorful urban beaches (❿ "Paris Plages").*

Sights in Paris

Some of the city's premier historical sights—Notre-Dame, Sainte-Chapelle, the Latin Quarter—are covered in detail in my "Historic Paris Walk," earlier. A 🎧 means the sight is covered by a free audio tour (via my Rick Steves Audio Europe app).

MAJOR MUSEUMS NEIGHBORHOOD

Paris' grandest park, the Tuileries Garden, was once the private property of kings and queens. Today it links the Louvre, Orangerie, and Orsay museums.

▲▲▲Louvre (Musée du Louvre)

This is Europe's oldest, biggest, greatest, and second-most-crowded museum (after the Vatican). Housed in a U-shaped, 16th-century palace (accentuated by a 20th-century glass pyramid), the Lou-

Major Museums Neighborhood

US EMBASSY
HOTEL CRILLON
LADUREE
RITZ HOTEL
RIGHT BANK
RUE ST. AUGUSTIN
Bourse
R. ROYALE
RUE ST. FLORENTIN
RUE CAMBON
WH SMITH
Place Vendôme
AVE DE L'OPERA
RUE DE LA PAIX
RUE DES PETITS CHAMPS
GALLERIE VIVIENNE
RUE VIVIENNE
Concorde
RUE DE RIVOLI
RUE DE CASTIGLIONE
RUE ST. HONORE
RUE DU MARCHE
RUE ST. ROCH
RUE DE RICHELIEU
Pyramides
Jardin du Palais Royal
BANQUE DE FRANCE
CHAMPS ELYSEES
Place de la Concorde
WC
KIDS PLAY AREA
Tuileries
RUE DES PYRAMIDES
Place du Palais Royal
PALAIS ROYAL
To Petit Palais
ORANGERIE
Tuileries Garden
QUAI DES TUILERIES
TOY SAILBOAT RENTAL
ARC DU CARROUSEL
Palais Royal-Musée du Louvre
To Pompidou Center
Seine River
RIVERSIDE PROMENADE
QUAI ANATOLE FRANCE
PONT DE LA CONC.
PONT ROYAL
Canauxrama Boat Dock
Place du Carrousel
Louvre-Rivoli
FRENCH NATIONAL ASSEMBLY
Assemblée Nationale
Musée d'Orsay
B
ORSAY MUSEUM
LOUVRE
RUE DE L'AMIRAL DE COLIGNY
Solférino
RUE DE LILLE
RUE DE L'UNIVERSITE
QUAI VOLTAIRE
PONT DU CARR.
PONT DES ARTS
QUAI MALAQUAIS
RIVERSIDE PROMENADE
Ile de la Cité
To Eiffel Tower
RUE DE BELLECHASSE
BLVD ST. GERMAIN
LEFT BANK
R. DES STS-PERES
R. DE SEINE
To Rodin Museum & Army Museum
Rue du Bac
To Left Bank Walk
N
300 Meters
300 Yards
· · · · · Bike Route
❶ Bus #69 eastbound
❷ Bus #69 westbound

vre is Paris' top museum and one of its key landmarks. It's home to *Mona Lisa, Venus de Milo,* and hall after hall of Greek and Roman masterpieces, medieval jewels, Michelangelo statues, and paintings by the greatest artists from the Renaissance to the Romantics. Touring the Louvre can be overwhelming, so be selective.

Cost and Hours: €15, includes special exhibits, free on first Sun of month Oct-March, covered by Museum Pass, tickets good all day, re-entry allowed; open Wed-Mon 9:00-18:00, Wed and Fri until 21:45 (except on holidays), closed Tue, galleries start shutting 30 minutes before closing, last entry 45 minutes before closing; several cafés.

Information: Tel. 01 40 20 53 17, recorded info tel. 01 40 20 51 51, www.louvre.fr.

When to Go: Crowds can be miserable on Sun, Mon (the worst day), Wed, and in the morning (arrive 30 minutes before opening to secure a good place in line).

PARIS

Buying Tickets: Self-serve ticket machines located under the pyramid may be faster to use than the ticket windows (machines accept euro bills, coins, and chip-and-PIN Visa cards). A handy shop in the underground mall sells tickets to the Louvre, Orsay, and Versailles, plus Museum Passes, for no extra charge (cash only). Timed-entry tickets are available online—see the Louvre website for details Skip-the-line tickets (extra fee) are sold at FNAC stores and by Paris tour companies; see "Sightseeing Strategies," earlier.

Getting There: Métro stop Palais Royal-Musée du Louvre is the closest. Eastbound bus #69 stops along the Seine River; the best stop is labeled Quai François Mitterrand. Westbound #69 stops in front of the pyramid. You'll find a taxi stand on Rue de Rivoli, next to the Palais Royal-Musée du Louvre Métro station.

Getting In: There is no grander entry than through the **main entrance** at the pyramid in the central courtyard. But the security line here can be very long.

Anyone can enter the Louvre from its less crowded **underground entrance,** accessed through the Carrousel du Louvre shopping mall. Enter the mall at 99 Rue de Rivoli (the door with the red awning) or directly from the Métro stop Palais Royal-Musée du Louvre (stepping off the train, take the exit to *Musée du Louvre-Le Carrousel du Louvre*). Once inside the underground mall, continue toward the inverted pyramid next to the Louvre's security entrance.

Tours: Ninety-minute English-language **guided tours** leave twice daily (except the first Sun of the month Oct-March) from the *Accueil des Groupes* area, under the pyramid (normally at 11:00 and 14:00, possibly more often in summer; €12 plus admission, tour tel. 01 40 20 52 63). **Videoguides** (€5) provide commentary on about 700 masterpieces.

🎧 Download my free Louvre Museum **audio tour.**

Baggage Check: You can store bags for free in the Louvre's slick self-service lockers (look for the *Vestiaires* sign).

Services: WCs are located under the pyramid, behind the escalators to the Denon and Richelieu wings. Once you're in the galleries, WCs are scarce.

Eating Near the Louvre: Try venerable, Art Deco **$$ Café le Nemours** or **$$$ Le Fumoir,** which has a good-value two-course lunch *menu.* For a **picnic** in the adjacent Palais Royal gardens (enter

PARIS

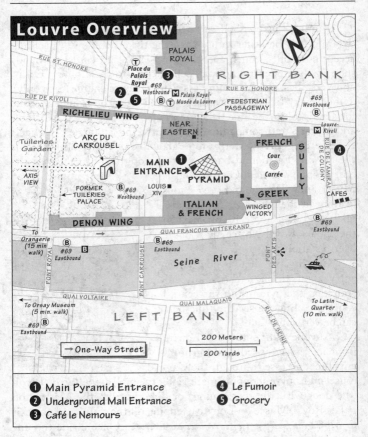

Louvre Overview

PALAIS ROYAL

RIGHT BANK

RUE ST. HONORE

Place du Palais Royal

#69 Westbound

Palais Royal–Musée du Louvre

PEDESTRIAN PASSAGEWAY

#69 Westbound

Louvre-Rivoli

RICHELIEU WING

NEAR EASTERN

FRENCH

SULLY

RUE DE L'AMIRAL DE COLIGNY

Tuileries Garden

ARC DU CARROUSEL

MAIN ENTRANCE → PYRAMID

Cour Carrée

AXIS VIEW

FORMER TUILERIES PALACE

#69 Westbound

LOUIS XIV

ITALIAN & FRENCH

GREEK

WINGED VICTORY

CAFES

DENON WING

QUAI FRANCOIS MITTERRAND

#69 Eastbound

To Orangerie (15 min. walk)

#69 Eastbound

#69 Eastbound

PONT ROYAL

PONT CARROUSEL

Seine River

PONT DES ARTS

QUAI VOLTAIRE

QUAI MALAQUAIS

To Orsay Museum (5 min. walk)

LEFT BANK

RUE DE SEINE

To Latin Quarter (10 min. walk)

#69 Eastbound

→ One-Way Street

200 Meters

200 Yards

1 Main Pyramid Entrance
2 Underground Mall Entrance
3 Café le Nemours
4 Le Fumoir
5 Grocery

from Place du Palais Royal), get supplies at the Franprix market on Rue St-Honoré.

⊘ Self-Guided Tour

With more than 30,000 works of art, the Louvre is a full inventory of Western civilization. To cover it all in one visit is impossible. Let's focus on the Louvre's specialties—Greek sculpture, Italian painting, and French painting. Start in the Denon Wing and visit the highlights, in the following order.

Begin with the pre-classical **Greek statues,** then look for the famous *Venus de Milo (Aphrodite).* You'll find her not far from another famous statue, the *Winged Victory of Samothrace.* This goddess of love (late 2nd century B.C.) created a sensation when she was discovered in 1820 on the Greek island of Melos. Most "Greek" statues are actually later Roman copies, but *Venus* is a rare Greek original. She, like Golden Age Greeks, epitomizes stability, beauty, and balance.

After viewing *Venus,* wander through Room 6 to see the **Par-**

thenon friezes (stone fragments that once decorated the exterior of the greatest Athenian temple, dating from the mid-5th century B.C.). A left turn into Room 22 takes you on a detour through some **Roman works,** including mosaics from the ancient city of Antioch, Etruscan sarcophagi, and Roman portrait busts.

Later Greek art was Hellenistic, adding motion and drama. For a good example, see the exciting **Winged Victory of Samothrace** (*Victoire de Samothrace,* c. 190 B.C., on the landing). This statue of a woman with wings, poised on the prow of a ship, once stood on a hilltop to commemorate a naval victory. This is the *Venus de Milo* gone Hellenistic.

The Italian collection—including the *Mona Lisa*—is scattered throughout the rooms of the long Grand Gallery (to the right of *Winged Victory;* look for **two Botticelli frescoes** as you enter). In painting, the Renaissance (1400-1600) meant realism, and for the Italians, realism was spelled "3-D." Painters were inspired by the realism and balanced beauty of Greek sculpture. Painting a 3-D world on a 2-D surface is tough, and after a millennium of Dark Ages, artists were rusty. Living in a religious age, they painted mostly altarpieces full of saints, angels, Madonnas-and-bambinos, and crucifixes floating in an ethereal gold-leaf heaven. Gradually, though, they brought these otherworldly scenes down to earth.

Two masters of the Italian High Renaissance (1500-1600) were **Raphael** (see his *La Belle Jardinière,* showing the Madonna, Child, and John the Baptist) and **Leonardo da Vinci.** The Louvre has the greatest collection of Leonardos in the world—five of them, including the exquisite *Virgin and Child with St. Anne;* the neighboring *Virgin of the Rocks;* and the androgynous *John the Baptist.*

But his most famous, of course, is the **Mona Lisa** (located in Room 6 a few steps away from the black statue of Diana). Leonardo was already an old man when François

I invited him to France. Determined to pack light, he took only a few paintings with him. One was a portrait of Lisa del Giocondo, the wife of a wealthy Florentine merchant. When Leonardo arrived, François immediately fell in love with the painting, making it the centerpiece of the small collection of Italian masterpieces that would, in three centuries, become the Louvre museum. He called it *La Gioconda* (*La Joconde* in French)—a play on both her last name and the Italian word for "happiness." We know her as the *Mona Lisa*—a contraction of the Italian for "my lady Lisa." Warning: François was impressed, but *Mona* may surprise you.

She's smaller than you'd expect, darker, engulfed in a huge room, and hidden behind a glaring pane of glass.

The huge canvas opposite *Mona* is Paolo Veronese's ***The Marriage at Cana***, showing the Renaissance love of beautiful things gone hog-wild. Venetian artists like Veronese painted the good life of rich, happy-go-lucky Venetian merchants.

Now for something **Neoclassical.** Exit behind *Mona Lisa* and turn right into Room 75 to find ***The Coronation of Emperor Napoleon*** by Jacques-Louis David. Neoclassicism, once the rage in France (1780-1850), usually features Greek subjects, patriotic sentiment, and a clean, simple style. After Napoleon quickly conquered most of Europe, he insisted on being made emperor (not merely king) of this "New Rome." He staged an elaborate coronation ceremony in Paris, and rather than let the pope crown him, he crowned himself. The setting was Notre-Dame Cathedral, with Greek columns and Roman arches thrown in for effect. Napoleon's mom was also added, since she couldn't make it to the ceremony. A key on the frame describes who's who in the picture.

The **Romantic** collection, displayed here and in Room 77, has works by Théodore Géricault (*The Raft of the Medusa*—one of my favorites) and Eugène Delacroix ***(Liberty Leading the People).*** Romanticism, with an emphasis on motion and emotion, is the flip side of cool, balanced Neoclassicism, though they both flourished in the early 1800s. Delacroix's *Liberty*, commemorating the stirrings of democracy in France, is also an appropriate tribute to the Louvre, the first museum ever opened to the common rabble of humanity. The good things in life don't belong only to a small, wealthy part of society, but to everyone. The motto of France is *Liberté, Egalité, Fraternité*—liberty, equality, and the brotherhood of all.

Exit the room at the far end (past Café Mollien) and go downstairs, where you'll bump into the bum of a large, twisting male nude looking like he's just waking up after a thousand-year nap. The two *Slaves* (1513-1515) by Michelangelo are a fitting end to this museum—works that bridge the ancient and modern worlds. Michelangelo, like his fellow Renaissance artists, learned from the Greeks. The perfect anatomy, twisting poses, and idealized faces appear as if they could have been created 2,000 years earlier. Michelangelo said that his purpose was to carve away the marble to reveal the figures God put inside. The *Rebellious Slave*, fighting against his bondage, shows the agony of that process and the ecstasy of the result.

Although this makes for a good first tour, there's so much more. After a break (or on a second visit), consider a stroll through a few rooms of the Richelieu wing, which contain some of the Louvre's most ancient pieces.

▲▲▲Orsay Museum (Musée d'Orsay)

The Musée d'Orsay (mew-zay dor-say) houses French art of the 1800s and early 1900s (specifically, 1848-1914), picking up where the Louvre's art collection leaves off. For us, that means Impressionism, the art of sun-dappled fields, bright colors, and crowded Parisian cafés. The Orsay houses the best general collection anywhere of Manet, Monet, Renoir, Degas, Van Gogh, Cézanne, and Gauguin.

Cost and Hours: €12, €9.50 Tue-Wed and Fri-Sun after 16:30 and Thu after 18:00, free on first Sun of month, covered by Museum Pass, combo-ticket with Orangerie Museum (€16) or Rodin Museum (€18). Museum open Tue-Sun 9:30-18:00, Thu until 21:45, closed Mon, last entry one hour before closing (45 minutes before on Thu), Impressionist galleries start shutting 45 minutes before closing.

Information: Tel. 01 40 49 48 14, www.musee-orsay.fr.

Avoiding Lines: You can skip long ticket-buying lines by using a Museum Pass, a combo-ticket, or purchasing tickets in advance (available online—see the Orsay website for details); any of these entitle you to use a separate entrance. You can also buy tickets and Museum Passes (no mark-up; tickets valid 3 months) at the newspaper kiosk just outside the Orsay entrance (along Rue de la Légion d'Honneur). If you're planning to get a combo-ticket with either the Orangerie or the Rodin Museum, consider starting at one of those museums instead, as they have shorter lines.

Getting There: The museum, at 1 Rue de la Légion d'Honneur, sits above the Train-C Musée d'Orsay stop; the nearest Métro stop is Solférino, three blocks southeast of the Orsay. Bus #69 also stops at the Orsay. From the Louvre, it's a lovely 15-minute walk through the Tuileries Garden and across the pedestrian bridge to the Orsay.

Getting In: As you face the entrance, pass holders and ticket holders enter on the right (Entrance C). Ticket purchasers enter on the left (Entrance A). Security checks slow down all entrances.

Tours: Audioguides cost €5. English **guided tours** usually run daily at 11:30 (€6/1.5 hours, none on Sun, tours may also run at 14:30—inquire when you arrive).

🎧 Download my free Orsay Museum **audio tour.**

Cuisine Art: The snazzy $$ **Le Restaurant** is on the second floor, with affordable tea and coffee served daily. A simple sandwich-and-salad $ **café** is on the main floor (far end), and a convenient-if-pricier one is on the fifth floor beyond the Impressionist galleries. Outside, behind the museum, several classy eateries line Rue du Bac.

❍ Self-Guided Tour

This former train station, the Gare d'Orsay, barely escaped the wrecking ball in the 1970s, when the French realized it'd be a great place to house the enormous collections of 19th-century art scattered throughout the city.

The ground floor (level 0) houses early-19th-century art, mainly conservative art of the Academy and Salon, plus Realism. On the top floor (not visible from here) is the core of the collection—the Impressionist rooms. If you're pressed for time, go directly there. Remember that the museum rotates its large collection often, so find the latest arrangement on your current Orsay map, and be ready to go with the flow.

Conservative Art

In the Orsay's first few rooms, you're surrounded by visions of idealized beauty—nude women in languid poses, Greek mythological figures, and anatomically perfect statues. This was the art adored by 19th-century French academics and the middle-class *(bourgeois)* public.

Jean-Auguste-Dominique **Ingres'** *The Source* (1856) is virtually a Greek statue on canvas. Like *Venus de Milo*, she's a balance of opposite motions. Alexandre **Cabanel** lays Ingres' *The Source* on her back. His *Birth of Venus* (1863) is a perfect fantasy, an orgasm of beauty.

Realism

The French Realists rejected idealized classicism and began painting what they saw in the world around them. For Honoré **Daumier,** that meant looking at the stuffy bourgeois establishment that controlled the Academy and the Salon. In the 36 bustlets of *Celebrities of the Happy Medium* (1835), Daumier, trained as a political cartoonist, exaggerates each subject's most distinct characteristic to capture with vicious precision the pomposity and self-righteousness of these self-appointed arbiters of taste.

Jean-François **Millet**'s *The Gleaners* (1867) shows us three gleaners, the poor women who pick up the meager leftovers after a field has already been harvested for the wealthy. Here he captures the innate dignity of these stocky, tanned women who bend their backs quietly in a large field for their small reward. This is "Realism" in two senses. It's painted "realistically," not prettified. And it's the "real" world—not the fantasy world of Greek myth, but the harsh life of the working poor.

For a Realist's take on the traditional Venus, find Edouard **Manet**'s *Olympia* (1863). Compare this uncompromising nude with Cabanel's idealized, pastel, Vaseline-on-the-lens beauty in *The Birth of Venus*. In *Olympia*, the sharp outlines and harsh, contrasting colors are new and shocking. Manet replaced soft-core porn with hard-core art.

Gustave **Courbet**'s *The Painter's Studio* (1855) takes us backstage, showing us the gritty reality behind the creation of pretty pictures. We see Courbet himself in his studio, working diligently on a Realistic landscape, oblivious to the confusion around him. Milling around are ordinary citizens, not Greek heroes.

At the far end of the gallery, you'll find the **Opéra Exhibit**— a glass floor over a model of Paris with the 19th-century, green-domed Opéra Garnier at the center. The Opéra, which opened in 1875, was the symbol of the belle époque, or "beautiful age," when Paris was a global center of prosperity, new technology, opera, ballet, painting, and joie de vivre.

Toulouse-Lautrec Detour

The Henri **Toulouse-Lautrec** paintings, near the Opéra Exhibit (Room 10), rightly belong with the Post-Impressionist works on level 2, but since you're already here, enjoy his paintings incarnating the artist's love of nightlife and show business. Every night, Toulouse-Lautrec put on his bowler hat and visited the Moulin Rouge to draw the crowds, the can-can dancers, and the backstage action. He worked quickly, creating sketches in paint that serve as snapshots of a golden era. In *Jane Avril Dancing* (1891), he depicts the slim, graceful, elegant, and melancholy dancer who stood out above the rabble. Her legs keep dancing while her mind is far away.

Impressionism

The Impressionist collection is scattered randomly through Rooms 29-36 on the top floor. In Edouard **Manet**'s *Luncheon on the Grass* (*Le Déjeuner sur l'Herbe*, 1863), you can see that a new revolutionary movement was starting to bud—Impressionism. Notice the background: the messy brushwork of trees and leaves, the play of light on the pond, and the light that filters through the trees onto the woman who stoops in the haze. Also note the strong contrast of colors (white skin, black clothes, green grass). Let the Impressionist revolution begin!

Edgar **Degas** blends classical lines and Realist subjects with Impressionist color, spontaneity, and everyday scenes from urban Paris. He loved the unposed "snapshot" effect, catching his models off guard. Dance students, women at work, and café scenes are approached from odd angles that aren't always ideal but make the scenes seem more real. He gives us the backstage view of life. For instance, a dance rehearsal let Degas capture a behind-the-scenes look at bored, tired, restless dancers (*The Dance Class, La Classe de Danse*, c. 1873-1875). In the painting *In a Café* (*Dans un Café*, 1875-1876), a weary lady of the evening meets morning with a last, lonely, nail-in-the-coffin drink in the glaring light of a four-in-the-morning café.

Next up is Claude **Monet** (mo-nay), the father of Impressionism. In the 1860s, Monet (along with Renoir) began painting landscapes in the open air. He studied optics and pigments to know just the right colors he needed to reproduce the shimmering quality of reflected light. The key was to work quickly—at that "golden hour" (to use a modern photographer's term), when the light was just right. Then he'd create a fleeting "impression" of the scene. In fact, that was the title of one of Monet's canvases (now hanging in Paris' Marmottan museum); it gave the movement its name.

One of Monet's favorite places to paint was the garden he landscaped at his home in Giverny, west of Paris. The Japanese bridge and the water lilies floating in the pond were his two favorite subjects. As Monet aged and his eyesight failed, he made bigger canvases of smaller subjects. The final water lilies are monumental smudges of thick paint surrounded by paint-splotched clouds that are reflected on the surface of the pond.

Pierre-Auguste **Renoir** (ren-wah) started out as a painter of landscapes, along with Monet, but later veered from the Impressionist's philosophy and painted images that were unabashedly "pretty." His best-known work is *Dance at the Moulin de la Galette* (*Bal du Moulin de la Galette*, 1876). On Sunday afternoons, working-class folk would dress up and head for the fields on Butte Montmartre (near Sacré-Cœur basilica) to dance, drink, and eat little crêpes (galettes) till dark.

Renoir liked to go there to paint the common Parisians living and loving in the afternoon sun. The sunlight filtering through the trees creates a kaleidoscope of colors, like the 19th-century equivalent of a mirror ball throwing darts of light onto the dancers. Like a photographer who uses a slow shutter speed to show motion, Renoir paints a waltzing blur.

Post-Impressionism

Post-Impressionism—the style that employs Impressionism's bright colors while branching out in new directions—is scattered all around the museum. You'll get a taste of the style with Paul Cézanne on the top floor, with much more on level 2.

Paul **Cézanne** brought Impressionism into the 20th century. After the color of Monet and the warmth of Renoir, Cézanne's rather impersonal canvases can be difficult to appreciate (see *The Card Players, Les Joueurs de Cartes,* 1890-1895). Where the Impressionists built a figure out of a mosaic of individual brushstrokes, Cézanne used blocks of paint to create a more solid, geometrical shape. These chunks are like little "cubes." It's no coincidence that his experiments in reducing forms to their geometric basics inspired the...Cubists. Because of his style (not the content), he is often called the first modern painter.

Like Michelangelo, Beethoven, and a select handful of others, Vincent **van Gogh** put so much of himself into his work that art and life became one. In the Orsay's collection of paintings (level 2), you'll see both Van Gogh's painting style and his life unfold.

Encouraged by his art-dealer brother, Van Gogh moved to Paris. He met Monet, drank with Gauguin and Toulouse-Lautrec, and soaked up the Impressionist style. But the social life of Paris became too much for the solitary Van Gogh, and he moved to the south of France. But being alone in a strange country began to wear on him. In crazed despair, Van Gogh cut off a piece of his own ear. Vincent sought help at a mental hospital. The paintings he finished in the peace of the hospital are more meditative—there are fewer bright landscapes and more closed-in scenes with deeper, almost surreal colors.

His final self-portrait shows a man engulfed in a confused background of brushstrokes that swirl and rave (*Self-Portrait, Portrait de l'Artiste,* 1889). But in the midst of this rippling sea of mystery floats a still, detached island of a face. Perhaps his troubled eyes know that in only a few months, he'll take a pistol and put a bullet through his chest.

Nearby are the paintings of Paul **Gauguin,** who got the travel bug early in childhood and grew up wanting to be a sailor. Instead, he became a stockbroker. At the age of 35, he got fed up with it all, quit his job, abandoned his wife (her stern portrait bust may be nearby) and family, and took refuge in his art.

Gauguin traveled to the South Seas in search of the exotic, finally settling on Tahiti. There he found his Garden of Eden. Gauguin's best-known works capture an idyllic Tahitian landscape peopled by exotic women engaged in simple tasks and making music (*Arearea*, 1892). The native girls lounge placidly in unself-conscious innocence. The style is intentionally "primitive," collapsing the three-dimensional landscape into a two-dimensional pattern of bright colors. Gauguin intended that this simple style carry a deep undercurrent of symbolic meaning. He wanted to communicate to his "civilized" colleagues back home that he'd found the paradise he'd always envisioned.

French Sculpture

The open-air mezzanine of level 2 is lined with statues. Stroll the mezzanine, enjoying the work of great French sculptors, including Auguste **Rodin.** Born of working-class roots and largely self-taught, Rodin combined classical solidity with Impressionist surfaces to become one of the greatest sculptors since the Renaissance. His sculptures capture the groundbreaking spirit of much of the art in the Orsay Museum. With a stable base of 19th-century stone, he launched art into the 20th century.

▲▲Orangerie Museum (Musée de l'Orangerie)

Located a 10-minute walk from the Orsay Museum in the Tuileries Garden and drenched by natural light from skylights, the

Orangerie (oh-rahn-zhuh-ree) is the closest you'll ever come to stepping right into an Impressionist painting. Start with the museum's claim to fame: Monet's *Water Lilies*. Then head downstairs to enjoy the manageable collection of select works by Utrillo, Cézanne, Renoir, Matisse, and Picasso.

Cost and Hours: €9, €6.50 after 17:00, free for those under age 18, €16 combo-ticket with Orsay Museum, €18.50 combo-ticket with Monet's Garden and House at Giverny, covered by Museum Pass; Wed-Mon 9:00-18:00, closed Tue; audioguide-€5, English guided tours usually Mon and Thu at 14:30 and Sat at 11:00, located in Tuileries Garden near Place de la Concorde (Mo: Concorde or scenic bus #24), 15-minute stroll from the Orsay, tel. 01 44 77 80 07, www.musee-orangerie.fr.

PARIS

EIFFEL TOWER AND NEARBY
▲▲▲Eiffel Tower (La Tour Eiffel)

Built on the 100th anniversary of the French Revolution (and in the spirit of the Industrial Revolution), the tower was the center-

piece of a World Expo designed simply to show off what people could build in 1889. For decades it was the tallest structure the world had ever known, and though it's since been eclipsed, it's still the most visited monument. Ride the elevators to the top of its 1,063 feet for expansive views that stretch 40 miles. Then descend to the two lower levels, where the views are arguably even better, since the monuments are more recognizable.

Cost and Hours: €25 to ride all the way to the top, €16 for just the two lower levels, €10 to climb the stairs to the first or second level, not covered by Museum Pass; daily mid-June-Aug 9:00-00:45; Sept-mid-June 9:30-23:45; cafés and great view restaurants, Mo: Bir-Hakeim or Trocadéro, Train-C: Champ de Mars-Tour Eiffel (all stops about a 10-minute walk away).

Information: Recorded information tel. 08 92 70 12 39, www.toureiffel.paris.

Reservations: Since long waits are common, it's wise to make a reservation well in advance of your visit. At www.toureiffel.paris, you can book a time slot to begin your ascent; this allows you to skip the long initial entry line.

Time slots can fill up months in advance (especially from April through September). Online ticket sales open up about three months before any given date (at 8:30 Paris time). Be sure of your date, as reservations are nonrefundable. When you "Choose a ticket," make sure you select "Lift entrance ticket with access to the summit" to go all the way to the top. You must create an account, with your 10-digit mobile phone number as your log-in. After paying with a credit card, print your tickets or have the ticket text-messaged to your phone. You must have a ticket showing the bar code (print-out or phone version).

If no reservation slots are available, try buying a "Lift entrance ticket with access to 2nd floor" only—you can upgrade once inside. Or, try the website again about a week before your visit—last-minute spots occasionally open up.

Other Tips for Avoiding Lines: You can bypass some (but not all) lines if you have a reservation at either of the tower's view restaurants (Le Jules Verne or 58 Tour Eiffel). Or you can take a

Eiffel Tower & Nearby

Eateries
1. Rue Cler Eateries
2. Café le Bosquet
3. La Terrasse du 7ème
4. Café de Mars
5. Ristorante Gusto

guided tour that gets you to the second level (€46, 1.5 hours) or the tower's summit (€64, 2 hours) through Fat Tire Tours (both tours usually have space available most days; see "Sightseeing Strategies," earlier).

Getting In: If you have a reservation, arrive at the tower 10 minutes before your entry time and look for either of the two entrances marked *Visiteurs avec Reservation* (Visitors with Reservation). If you don't have a reservation, follow signs for *Individuels* or *Visiteurs sans Tickets* (avoid lines selling tickets only for *Groupes*). The stairs entrance (usually a shorter line) is at the south pillar (next to Le Jules Verne restaurant entrance). When you buy tickets onsite, all members of your party must be with you. To get reduced fares for kids, bring ID.

Pickpockets: Beware. Street thieves plunder awestruck visitors gawking below the tower. And tourists in crowded elevators are like fish in a barrel for predatory pickpockets. *En garde.* A police station is at the Jules Verne pillar.

Security Check: Bags larger than 19" × 8" × 12" are not allowed, but there is no baggage check. All bags are subject to a security search. No knives, glass bottles, or cans are permitted.

Services: The Eiffel Tower information office is at the west pillar. Free WCs are at the base of the tower, behind the east pillar. Inside the tower itself, WCs are on all levels.

Visiting the Tower: There are three observation platforms, at roughly 200, 400, and 900 feet. If you want to see the entire tower, from top to bottom, then see it...from top to bottom.

There isn't a single elevator straight to the top *(le sommet)*. To get there, you'll first ride an elevator to the second level. (For the hardy, there are 360 stairs to the first level and another 360 to the second.) Once on the second level, immediately line up for the next elevator, to the top. Enjoy the views from the "summit," then ride back down to the second level. When you're ready, head to the first level via the stairs (no line and can take as little as five minutes) or take the elevator down. Explore the shops and exhibits on the first level. To leave, you can line up for the elevator, but it's quickest and most memorable to take the stairs back down to earth.

Back on the Ground: Nearby, you can catch the Bateaux Parisiens boat for a Seine cruise or hop on bus #69 for a tour of the city. The Trocadero viewpoint, which looks "right there," is a 20-minute walk away. The entertaining riverbank promenade starts on the south side of the river near here and stretches to the Orsay Museum. Also nearby are the Rue Cler area, Army Museum and Napoleon's Tomb, and Rodin Museum.

▲▲Rue Cler

Paris is changing quickly, but a stroll down this market street introduces you to a thriving, traditional Parisian neighborhood and offers insights into the local culture. Although this is a wealthy district, Rue Cler retains the workaday charm still found in most neighborhoods throughout Paris. The shops lining the street are filled with the freshest produce, the stinkiest cheese, the tastiest chocolate, and the

finest wines (markets generally open Tue-Sat 8:30-13:00 & 15:00-19:30, Sun 8:30-12:00, dead on Mon). I'm still far from a gourmet eater, but my time spent tasting my way along Rue Cler has substantially bumped up my appreciation of good cuisine (as well as the French knack for good living).

For a self-guided walk, download my free 🎧 Rue Cler audio tour.

▲▲Army Museum and Napoleon's Tomb (Musée de l'Armée)

Napoleon's tomb rests beneath the golden dome of Les Invalides church. In addition to the tomb, the complex of Les Invalides— a former veterans' hospital built by Louis XIV—has various military collections, together called the Army Museum, Europe's greatest military museum. Visiting the different sections, you can watch the art of war unfold from stone axes to Axis powers.

Cost and Hours: €11, €9 after 17:00 (16:00 Nov-March), free for military personnel in uniform, free for kids but they must wait in line for ticket, covered by Museum Pass, special exhibits are extra; open daily 10:00-18:00, Nov-March until 17:00; tomb also open July-Aug until 19:00 and April-Sept Tue until 21:00; museum (except for tomb) closed first Mon of month Oct-June; Charles de Gaulle exhibit closed Mon year-round; videoguide-€6, cafeteria, tel. 08 10 11 33 99, www.musee-armee.fr.

Getting There: The Hôtel des Invalides is at 129 Rue de Grenelle, a 10-minute walk from Rue Cler (Mo: La Tour Maubourg, Varenne, or Invalides). You can also take bus #69 (from the Marais and Rue Cler), bus #87 (from Rue Cler and Luxembourg Garden area), or bus #63 from the St. Germain-des-Prés area.

▲▲Rodin Museum (Musée Rodin)

This user-friendly museum and its gardens are filled with passionate works by Auguste Rodin (1840-1917), the greatest sculptor since Michelangelo. You'll see *The Kiss, The Thinker, The Gates of Hell,* and many more, well displayed in the mansion where the sculptor lived and worked.

Cost and Hours: €10, free for those under age 18, free on first Sun of the month Oct-March, €4 for just the garden (with several important works on display), €18 combo-ticket with Orsay Museum, both museum and garden covered by Museum Pass; Tue-Sun 10:00-17:45, closed

Mon; gardens close at 18:00, Oct-March at 17:00; audioguide-€6, mandatory baggage check, self-service café in garden, 77 Rue de Varenne, Mo: Varenne, tel. 01 44 18 61 10, www.musee-rodin.fr.

▲▲Marmottan Museum (Musée Marmottan Monet)

In this private, intimate, and untouristy museum, you'll find the best collection anywhere of works by Impressionist headliner Claude Monet. Follow Monet's life through more than a hundred works, from simple sketches to the *Impression: Sunrise* painting that gave his artistic movement its start—and a name. The museum also displays some of the enjoyable large-scale canvases featuring the water lilies from his garden at Giverny.

Cost and Hours: €11, not covered by Museum Pass, Tue-Sun 10:00-18:00, Thu until 21:00, closed Mon; audioguide-€3, 2 Rue Louis-Boilly, Mo: La Muette, tel. 01 44 96 50 33, www.marmottan.fr.

LEFT BANK

Opposite Notre-Dame, on the left bank of the Seine, is the Latin Quarter. (For more about this neighborhood, see my Historic Paris Walk, earlier).

▲▲Cluny Museum (Musée National du Moyen Age)

The Cluny is a treasure trove of Middle Ages (Moyen Age) art. Located on the side of a Roman bathhouse, it offers close-up looks

at stained glass, Notre-Dame carvings, fine goldsmithing and jewelry, and rooms of tapestries. The highlights are several original stained-glass windows from Sainte-Chapelle and the exquisite series of six Lady and the Unicorn tapestries: A delicate, as-medieval-as-can-be noble lady introduces a delighted unicorn to the senses of taste, hearing, sight, smell, and touch. The museum is undergoing a multiyear renovation. Expect changes and some room closures when you visit.

Cost and Hours: €8, includes audioguide, free on first Sun of month, covered by Museum Pass (though pass holders pay €1 for audioguide); Wed-Mon 9:15-17:45, closed Tue; near corner of Boulevards St. Michel and St. Germain at 6 Place Paul Painlevé; Mo: Cluny-La Sorbonne, St. Michel, or Odéon; tel. 01 53 73 78 16, www.musee-moyenage.fr.

CHAMPS-ELYSEES AND NEARBY
▲▲▲Champs-Elysées

This famous boulevard is Paris' backbone, with its greatest concentration of traffic (although it's delightfully traffic-free on the first Sunday of each month). From

the Arc de Triomphe down Avenue des Champs-Elysées, all of France seems to converge on Place de la Concorde, the city's largest square. And though the Champs-Elysées has become as international as it is Parisian, a walk down the two-mile boulevard is still a must.

Start at the Arc de Triomphe (Mo: Charles de Gaulle-Etoile; if you're planning to tour the Arc, do it before starting this walk) and head downhill on the left-hand side. The arrival of McDonald's (at #140) was an unthinkable horror, but these days dining chez MacDo has become typically Parisian, and this branch is the most profitable McDonald's in the world.

Fancy car showrooms abound, including Peugeot (#136). The Lido (#116) is Paris' largest burlesque-type cabaret (and a multiplex cinema). Across the boulevard is the flagship store of leather-bag makers Louis Vuitton (#101). Fouquet's café (#99) is a popular spot for French celebrities, especially movie stars—note the names in the sidewalk in front. Enter if you dare for a €10 espresso. Ladurée café (#75) is also classy but has a welcoming and affordable takeout bakery.

Continuing on, you pass international-brand stores, such as Sephora, Nike, Disney, and the Gap. Car buffs should park themselves at the sleek café in the Renault store (#53, open until midnight). The car exhibits change regularly, but the great tables looking down onto the Champs-Elysées are permanent.

You can end your walk at the round Rond Point intersection (Mo: Franklin D. Roosevelt) or continue to obelisk-studded Place de la Concorde, Paris' largest square.

▲▲Arc de Triomphe

Napoleon had the magnificent Arc de Triomphe commissioned to commemorate his victory at the 1805 battle of Austerlitz. The foot of the arch is a stage on which the last two centuries of Parisian history have played out—from the funeral of Napoleon to the goose-stepping arrival of the Nazis to the triumphant return of Charles de Gaulle after the Allied liberation. Examine the carvings on the pillars, featuring a mighty Napoleon and excitable Lady

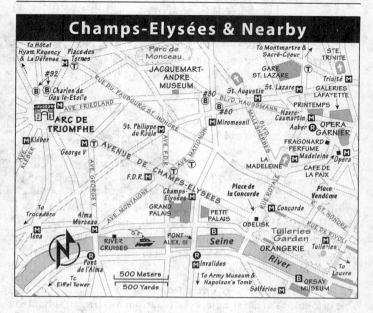

Champs-Elysées & Nearby

Liberty. Pay your respects at the Tomb of the Unknown Soldier. Then climb the 284 steps to the observation deck up top, with sweeping skyline panoramas and a mesmerizing view down onto the traffic that swirls around the arch.

Cost and Hours: You can tour much of the base of the Arc for free, steps to rooftop-€12, free for those under age 18, free on first Sun of month Oct-March, covered by Museum Pass; daily 10:00-23:00, Oct-March until 22:30, last entry 45 minutes before closing; Place Charles de Gaulle, use underpass to reach arch, Mo: Charles de Gaulle-Etoile, tel. 01 55 37 73 77, www. paris-arc-de-triomphe.fr.

MARAIS NEIGHBORHOOD AND NEARBY

The Marais extends along the Right Bank of the Seine, from the Bastille to the Pompidou Center.

▲▲Picasso Museum (Musée Picasso)

Whatever you think about Picasso the man, as an artist he was unmatched in the 20th century for his daring and productivity. The Picasso Museum has the world's largest collection of his work—

some 400 paintings, sculptures, sketches, and ceramics—spread across five levels of this mansion in the Marais. A visit here walks you through the full range of this complex man's life and art. The museum's fine audioguide is updated with each change to the exhibit and expertly describes exactly what you'll see.

Cost and Hours: €12.50, covered by Museum Pass, free on first Sun of month and for those under age 18 with ID; open Tue-Fri 10:30-18:00, Sat-Sun 9:30-18:00, closed Mon, last entry 45 minutes before closing; audioguide-€5, 5 Rue de Thorigny, Mo: St. Sébastien-Froissart, St-Paul, or Chemin Vert, tel. 01 42 71 25 21, www.musee-picasso.fr.

▲▲Pompidou Center (Centre Pompidou)

One of Europe's greatest collections of far-out modern art is housed in the Musée National d'Art Moderne, on the fourth and fifth

floors of this colorful exoskeletal building. Created ahead of its time, the modern and contemporary art in this collection is still waiting for the world to catch up. The Pompidou Center and the square that fronts it are lively, with lots of people, street theater, and activity inside and out—a perpetual street fair. Kids of any age enjoy the fun, colorful fountain (an homage to composer Igor Stravinsky) next to the Pompidou Center.

Cost and Hours: €14, free on first Sun of month, Museum Pass covers permanent collection and escalators to sixth-floor panoramic views (plus occasional special exhibits); permanent collection open Wed-Mon 11:00-21:00, closed Tue; free "Pompidou Centre" app, café on mezzanine, pricey view restaurant on level 6, Mo: Rambuteau or Hôtel de Ville, tel. 01 44 78 12 33, www.centrepompidou.fr.

Shopping in Paris

Shopping in chic Paris is altogether tempting—even reluctant shoppers can find good reasons to indulge. Even if you don't intend to

buy anything, budget some time for window shopping, or, as the French call it, *faire du lèche-vitrines* ("window licking").

Before you enter a Parisian store, remember the following points: In small stores, always say, *"Bonjour, Madame* or *Mademoiselle* or *Monsieur"* when

entering. And remember to say *"Au revoir, Madame* or *Mademoiselle* or *Monsieur"* when leaving.

Except in department stores, it's not normal for the customer to handle clothing. Ask first before you pick up an item: *"Je peux?"* (zhuh puh), meaning, "Can I?"

By law the price of items in a window display must be visible, often written on a slip of paper set on the floor or framed on the wall. This gives you an idea of how expensive or affordable the shop is before venturing inside.

Stores are generally closed on Sunday. Exceptions include the Galeries Lafayette store near the Opéra Garnier, the Carrousel du Louvre (underground shopping mall at the Louvre with a Printemps department store), and some shops near Sèvres-Babylone, along the Champs-Elysées, and in the Marais.

Don't feel obliged to buy. If a shopkeeper offers assistance, just say, *"Je regarde, merci."*

Department Stores (Les Grands Magasins)

Helpful information desks are usually located at the main entrances near the perfume section (with floor plans in English). Stores generally have affordable restaurants (some with view terraces) and a good selection of fairly priced souvenirs and toys. Shop at these great Parisian department stores: **Galeries Lafayette** (Mo: Chaussée d'Antin–La Fayette, Havre-Caumartin, or Opéra), **Printemps** (next door to Galeries Lafayette), and **Bon Marché** (Mo: Sèvres-Babylone). Opening hours are customarily Monday through Saturday from 10:00 to 19:00. The Galeries Lafayette main store and the Printemps store in the Carrousel du Louvre are open daily.

PARIS

Boutique Strolls
Place de la Madeleine to Place de l'Opéra

The ritzy streets connecting several high-priced squares—Place de la Madeleine, Place de la Concorde, Place Vendôme, and Place de l'Opéra—form a miracle mile of gourmet food shops, glittering jewelry stores, five-star hotels, exclusive clothing boutiques, and people who spend more on clothes in one day than I do in a year.

Start at Eglise de la Madeleine (Mo: Madeleine). In the northeast corner at #24 is the black-and-white awning of **Fauchon.** Founded on this location in 1886, this bastion of over-the-top edibles became famous around the world, catering to the refined tastes of the rich and famous. **Hédiard** (#21, northwest corner of the square) is older than Fauchon, and it's weathered the tourist mobs a bit better. Hédiard's small red containers—of mustards, jams, coffee, candies, and tea—make great souvenirs.

Step inside tiny **La Maison des Truffe** (#19) to get a whiff of the product—truffles, those prized, dank, and dirty cousins of mushrooms. Check out the tiny jars in the display case. Ponder how something so ugly, smelly, and deformed can cost so much. The venerable **Mariage Frères** (#17) shop demonstrates how good tea can smell and how beautifully it can be displayed. At **Caviar Kaspia** (#16), you can add caviar, eel, and vodka to your truffle collection.

Continue along, past **Marquise de Sévigné chocolates** (#11) and Fauchon's new razzle-dazzle hotel, then cross to the island in the middle of **Boulevard Malesherbes.** When the street officially opened in 1863, it ushered in the Golden Age of this neighborhood. Continue across Boulevard Malesherbes. Straight ahead is **Patrick Roger Chocolates** (#3), famous for its chocolates, and even more so for M. Roger's huge, whimsical, 150-pound chocolate sculptures of animals and fanciful creatures.

Turn right down **Rue Royale.** There's Dior, Chanel, and Gucci. At Rue St. Honoré, turn left and cross Rue Royale, pausing in the middle for a great view both ways. Check out **Ladurée** (#16) for an out-of-this-world pastry break in the busy 19th-century tea salon, or to just pick up some world-famous macarons. Continue east down **Rue St. Honoré.** The street is a three-block parade of chic boutiques. Looking for a €1,000 handbag? This is your spot.

Turn left on Rue de Castiglione to reach **Place Vendôme.** This octagonal square is *très* elegant—enclosed by symmetrical Mansart buildings around a 150-foot column. On the left side is the original Hôtel Ritz, opened in 1898. The square is also known for its upper-crust jewelry and designer stores—Van Cleef & Arpels, Dior, Chanel, Cartier, and others (if you have to ask how much...).

Sèvres-Babylone to St. Sulpice

This Left Bank shopping area lets you sample smart clothing boutiques and clever window displays—and be tempted by tasty treats—while enjoying one of Paris' more attractive neighborhoods.

Start at the Sèvres-Babylone Métro stop (take the Métro or bus #87). You'll find **Bon Marché,** Paris' oldest department store. Continue along Rue de Sèvres, working your way to Place St. Sulpice and making detours left and right as the spirit moves you. You'll pass some of Paris' smartest boutiques and coolest cafés, such as **La Maison du Chocolat** at #19 and **Hermès** (a few doors down, at #17). Make a short detour up Rue du Cherche-Midi and find Paris' most celebrated bread—beautiful round loaves with designer crust—at the low-key **Poilâne** at #8. At the end of your walk, spill into Place St. Sulpice, with its big, twin-tower church.

Eating in Paris

I've focused my recommendations on eateries convenient to your sightseeing—near the Eiffel Tower and in the historic core around Notre-Dame. These places are (mostly) authentically local, but—for the most part—fast and functional rather than haute cuisine.

You'll also find good eateries at or near many museums, including the Louvre and Orsay. Another alternative is to head into the Latin Quarter, where the dense streets are loaded with touristy but quick *crêperies* and falafel joints. To save piles of euros, go to a bakery for takeout.

NEAR THE EIFFEL TOWER

For locations, see "Eiffel Tower & Nearby" map, earlier. The Ecole Militaire Métro is your best bet for these spots.

On Rue Cler

The Rue Cler neighborhood caters to its residents. Its eateries, while not destination places, have an intimate charm.

$$ Le Petit Cler is an adorable and popular little bistro with long leather booths, a vintage interior, tight ranks of tiny and cramped tables—indoors and out, and simple, tasty, inexpensive dishes. Eating outside here with a view of the Rue Cler action can be marvelous (delicious *pots de crème,* daily, opens early for dinner, arrive early or call in advance, 29 Rue Cler, tel. 01 45 50 17 50).

$ Café le Roussillon offers a younger, pub-meets-café ambience with good-value food. You'll find hearty hamburgers, salads, design-your-own omelets, fajitas, and easygoing waiters (daily, serves nonstop from lunch until late, indoor seating only, corner of Rue de Grenelle and Rue Cler, tel. 01 45 51 47 53).

$ Brasserie Aux PTT, a simple traditional café delivering

Restaurant Code

I've assigned each eatery a price category, based on the average cost of a typical main course. Drinks, desserts, and splurge items (steak and seafood) can raise the price considerably.

$$$$ **Splurge:** Most main courses over €25
$$$ **Pricier:** €20-25
$$ **Moderate:** €15-20
$ **Budget:** Under €15

In France, a crêpe stand or other takeout spot is **$**; a sit-down brasserie, café, or bistro with affordable *plats du jour* is **$$**; a casual but more upscale restaurant is **$$$**; and a swanky splurge is **$$$$**.

fair-value fare, reminds Parisians of the old days on Rue Cler (good *salade niçoise*, cheap wine, closed Sun, opposite 53 Rue Cler, tel. 01 45 51 94 96).

Close to Ecole Militaire

$$ Café le Bosquet is a contemporary Parisian brasserie where you'll dine for a decent price inside or outside on a broad sidewalk. Come here for standard café fare—salad, French onion soup, *steak-frites*, or a *plat du jour* (serves nonstop, closed Sun, corner of Rue du Champ de Mars at 46 Avenue Bosquet, tel. 01 45 51 38 13, www.bosquetparis.com).

$$$ La Terrasse du 7ème is a sprawling, happening café with grand outdoor seating and a living room-like interior with comfy love seats. Located on a corner, it overlooks a busy intersection with a constant parade of people and traffic. A meal here is like dinner theater—and the show is slice-of-life Paris (good *salades*, French onion soup, and foie gras, nonstop service daily until at least 24:00, 2 Place de l'Ecole Militaire, tel. 01 45 55 00 02).

$$ Café de Mars is a relaxed place for a reasonably priced and delicious meal of classic French dishes prepared with a creative twist. With its simple setting and quality cuisine, it feels more designed for neighbors than tourists (closed Sun, 11 Rue Augereau, tel. 01 45 50 10 90, www.cafedemars.com).

Affordable Italian: For reasonably priced Italian cuisine, try **Ristorante Gusto** (199 Rue de Grenelle, tel. 01 45 55 00 43).

IN THE HISTORIC CORE

Eating options abound as you spiral out from the center of Paris. The lively, colorful Marais is just northeast of Notre-Dame, across the river. I've focused on two parts of this neighborhood: the heart of the Marais and the area near Hôtel de Ville (a bit closer to Notre-Dame). Another option is the peaceful island of Ile St. Louis, just a few minutes behind Notre-Dame (across the bridge).

In the Heart of the Marais

These are closest to the St-Paul Métro stop.

$$ On Place du Marché Ste. Catherine: This small, romantic square, just off Rue St. Antoine, is cloaked in extremely Parisian, leafy-square ambience. It feels like the Latin Quarter but classier. You'll find three French bistros with similar features and menus: **Le Marché, Chez Joséphine,** and **Le Bistrot de la Place** (all open daily).

$$ Les Bougresses, just off the charming square, offers less romance but more taste for the same price (inside seating only, daily from 18:30, 6 Rue de Jarente, tel. 01 48 87 71 21).

In the Jewish Quarter, Rue des Rosiers

The closest Métro stops are St-Paul or Hôtel de Ville.

$$ Chez Marianne is a neighborhood fixture that serves tasty Jewish cuisine in a fun atmosphere with Parisian *élan*. Vegetarians will find great options (takeaway falafel sandwiches, long hours daily, corner of Rue des Rosiers and Rue des Hospitalières-St-Gervais, tel. 01 42 72 18 86).

$$ Le Loir dans la Théière ("The Dormouse in the Teapot"—think Alice in Wonderland) is a cozy, mellow teahouse offering a welcoming ambience for tired travelers. It's ideal for lunch and popular on weekends. They offer a daily assortment of creatively filled quiches and bake up an impressive array of homemade desserts that are proudly displayed in the dining room (daily 9:00-19:00 but only dessert-type items offered after 15:00, 3 Rue des Rosiers, tel. 01 42 72 90 61).

$ "Falafel Row" is a series of inexpensive joints serving filling falafel sandwiches (and other Jewish dishes to go or to eat in) that line Rue des Rosiers between Rue des Ecouffes and Rue Vieille du Temple (long hours most days, most are closed Fri evening and all day Sat).

$ La Droguerie, a hole-in-the-wall crêpe stand on Rue des Rosiers near Rue Vieille du Temple, is a good budget option if falafels don't work for you but cheap does (daily 12:00-22:00, 56 Rue des Rosiers).

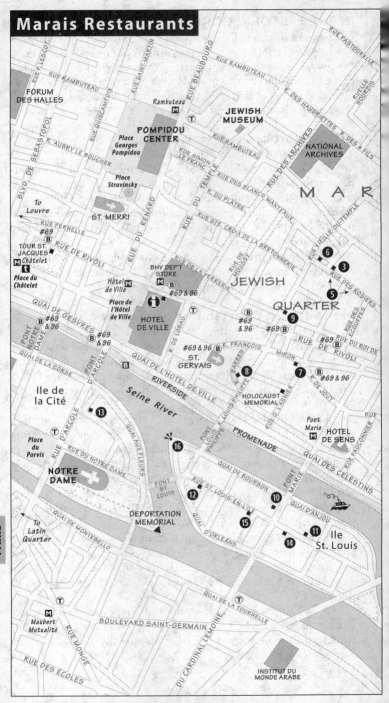

Marais Restaurants

FORUM DES HALLES

RUE PLESCOT

RUE RAMBUTEAU

RUE SAINT-MARTIN

RUE QUINCAMPOIX

RUE BEAUBOURG

RUE RAMBUTEAU

RUE PASTOURELLE

RUELLE SOURDIS

R. DES HAUDRIETTES

R. DES 4 FILS

Rambuteau Ⓜ Ⓣ

POMPIDOU CENTER

JEWISH MUSEUM

NATIONAL ARCHIVES

Place Georges Pompidou

RUE SIMON LE FRANC

RUE RAMBUTEAU

R. AUBRY LE BOUCHER

RUE DES ARCHIVES

M A R

Place Stravinsky

RUE DES BLANCS MANTEAUX

RUE DU TEMPLE

R. DU PLATRE

RUE STE. CROIX DE LA BRETONNERIE

To Louvre

RUE PERNELLE #69 Ⓑ

ST. MERRI

RUE DU RENARD

RUE VIEILLE-DU-TEMPLE

RUE DE MOUSSY

Ⓑ 6

3

TOUR ST. JACQUES

Ⓜ Châtelet Ⓣ

Place du Châtelet

RUE DE RIVOLI

Hôtel de Ville

BHV DEP'T STORE

Ⓜ

#69 & 96

RUE DE LA VERRERIE

JEWISH

RUE DES ROSIERS

5

QUAI DE GESVRES

Place de l'Hôtel de Ville

Ⓘ

QUARTER

Ⓑ 9

RUE DES ECOUFFES

#69 & 96 Ⓑ #69 Ⓑ

Ⓑ #69 & 96

PONT NOTRE DAME

Ⓑ #69 & 96

HOTEL DE VILLE

R. DE LOBAU

#69 & 96 R. FRANÇOIS

MIRON

#69 Ⓑ

RUE DU ROI DE SICILE

RUE DE RIVOLI

QUAI DE LA CORSE

ST. GERVAIS

BARRES

8

7

R. DE JOUY

Ⓑ #69 & 96

Ⓑ

QUAI DE L'HÔTEL DE VILLE

R. GEOFFROY L'ASNIER

RIVERSIDE

Ile de la Cité

PONT D'ARCOLE

Seine River

13

HOLOCAUST MEMORIAL

R. LOUIS PHILIPPE

PROMENADE

Pont Marie Ⓜ

HOTEL DE SENS

RUE FAUCONNIER

Place du Parvis

Ⓣ

RUE D'ARCOLE

RUE DU NOTRE DAME

16

QUAI AUX FLEURS

QUAI DE BOURBON

QUAI DES CELESTINS

NOTRE DAME

PONT ST. LOUIS

12

RUE ST. LOUIS-EN-L'ILE

10

QUAI D'ANJOU

PONT MARIE

To Latin Quarter

QUAI DE MONTEBELLO

DEPORTATION MEMORIAL

15

QUAI D'ORLEANS

14

11 Ile St. Louis

Ⓣ

Maubert Mutualité Ⓜ

RUE MONGE

BOULEVARD SAINT-GERMAIN

QUAI DE LA TOURNELLE

Ⓣ

RUE DES ECOLES

DU CARDINAL LEMOINE

INSTITUT DU MONDE ARABE

PARIS

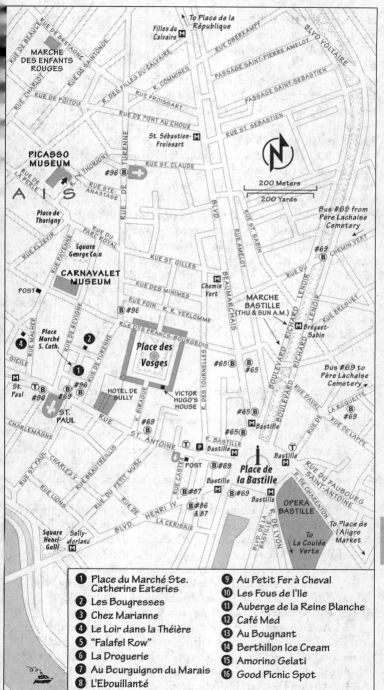

1. Place du Marché Ste. Catherine Eateries
2. Les Bougresses
3. Chez Marianne
4. Le Loir dans la Théière
5. "Falafel Row"
6. La Droguerie
7. Au Bourguignon du Marais
8. L'Ebouillanté
9. Au Petit Fer à Cheval
10. Les Fous de l'Ile
11. Auberge de la Reine Blanche
12. Café Med
13. Au Bougnant
14. Berthillon Ice Cream
15. Amorino Gelati
16. Good Picnic Spot

PARIS

Near Hôtel de Ville

Use the Hôtel de Ville Métro for these eateries.

$$$$ Au Bourguignon du Marais is a dressy wine bar/bistro for Burgundy lovers, where excellent wines blend with a good selection of well-designed dishes and efficient service. The *œufs en meurette* are mouthwatering, the *bœuf bourguignon* could feed two, and the hamburger *à l'Epoisses* is a hit (daily, pleasing indoor and outdoor seating on a perfect Marais corner, 52 Rue François Miron, tel. 01 48 87 15 40).

$$ L'Ebouillanté is a breezy café, romantically situated near the river on a broad, cobbled pedestrian lane behind a church. With great outdoor seating on flimsy chairs and an artsy interior, it's good for an inexpensive and relaxing tea, snack, or lunch. Their €15 *bricks*—paper-thin, Tunisian-inspired pancakes stuffed with what you would typically find in an omelet—come with a small salad (daily 12:00-21:30, closes earlier in winter, a block off the river at 6 Rue des Barres, tel. 01 42 74 70 57).

$$ Au Petit Fer à Cheval delivers classic seating ideal for admiring the Marais' active scene. The horseshoe-shaped zinc bar carbonates rich conversation—and the rear room is Old World adorable, but the few outdoor tables are street-theater perfect. The food is fairly priced, standard café fare (daily, 30 Rue Vieille du Temple, tel. 01 42 72 47 47).

On Ile St. Louis

These recommended spots line the island's main drag, Rue St. Louis-en-l'Ile. To get here, use the Pont Marie Métro stop. If you're picnicking, there's a good place at the tip of the island near the Pont St. Louis.

$$ Les Fous de l'Ile is a tasty, lighthearted mash-up of a collector's haunt, art gallery, and bistro. It's a fun place to eat bistro fare with gourmet touches for a good price (daily, serves nonstop, 33 Rue des Deux Ponts, tel. 01 43 25 76 67).

$$ Auberge de la Reine Blanche—woodsy, cozy, and tight— welcomes diners willing to rub elbows with their neighbors. Earnest owner Michel serves basic French cuisine at reasonable prices (closed Wed, 30 Rue St. Louis-en-l'Ile, tel. 01 46 33 07 87).

$ Café Med, near the pedestrian bridge to Notre-Dame, is a tiny, cheery *crêperie* with good-value salads, crêpes, pasta, and several meat dishes (daily, 77 Rue St. Louis-en-l'Ile, tel. 01 43 29 73 17). Two similar *crêperies* are just across the street.

$$ Au Bougnat, a block north of Notre-Dame on nearby Ile de la Cité, is a picturesque place with good tables inside and out. It's where local cops and workers get sandwiches, coffee, and reasonably priced *menus* (daily, 26 Rue Chanoinesse, tel. 01 43 54 50 74).

Ice-Cream Dessert: Half the people strolling Ile St. Louis are

What If I Miss My Ship?

Remember that you can get help from the cruise line's port agent (listed on the destination information sheet distributed on the ship) and the local TI. If the port agent suggests a costly solution (such as a private car with a driver), you may want to consider public transit.

For destinations on the Continent, your best bet is to ride the train to Paris, where you can connect to **Zeebrugge** (via Brussels), **Amsterdam, Warnemünde** (via Berlin), **Copenhagen,** and beyond.

To reach the ports for **London** (Southampton or Dover), consider an overnight ferry, several of which leave from Normandy. From Caen, Brittany Ferries runs to Portsmouth (www.brittany-ferries.co.uk). And from Dieppe, DFDS Seaways goes to Newhaven (www.dfdsseaways.co.uk).

If you need to catch a **plane** to your next destination, your best bet is to head to one of Paris' two main airports: Charles de Gaulle or Orly (these share a website: www.adp.fr). Slightly closer to Le Havre, at the northern edge of Paris, is Beauvais Airport, used predominantly by budget carriers (www.aeroportbeauvais.com).

For more advice on what to do if you miss the boat, see page 130.

licking an ice-cream cone of the famous *les glaces Berthillon* (made here on Ile St. Louis). The original **Berthillon** shop, at 31 Rue St. Louis-en-l'Ile, is marked by the line of salivating customers (closed Mon-Tue). For a less famous but satisfying treat, the Italian gelato a block away at **Amorino Gelati** is giving Berthillon competition (47 Rue St. Louis-en-l'Ile, tel. 01 44 07 48 08).

French Survival Phrases

When using the phonetics, try to nasalize the n sound.

English	French	Pronunciation
Good day.	Bonjour.	bohn-zhoor
Mrs. / Mr.	Madame / Monsieur	mah-dahm / muhs-yuh
Do you speak English?	Parlez-vous anglais?	par-lay-voo ahn-glay
Yes. / No.	Oui. / Non.	wee / nohn
I understand.	Je comprends.	zhuh kohn-prahn
I don't understand.	Je ne comprends pas.	zhuh nuh kohn-prahn pah
Please.	S'il vous plaît.	see voo play
Thank you.	Merci.	mehr-see
I'm sorry.	Désolé.	day-zoh-lay
Excuse me.	Pardon.	par-dohn
(No) problem.	(Pas de) problème.	(pah duh) proh-blehm
It's good.	C'est bon.	say bohn
Goodbye.	Au revoir.	oh ruh-vwahr
one / two	un / deux	uhn / duh
three / four	trois / quatre	trwah / kah-truh
five / six	cinq / six	sank / sees
seven / eight	sept / huit	seht / weet
nine / ten	neuf / dix	nuhf / dees
How much is it?	Combien?	kohn-bee-an
Write it?	Ecrivez?	ay-kree-vay
Is it free?	C'est gratuit?	say grah-twee
Included?	Inclus?	an-klew
Where can I buy / find...?	Où puis-je acheter / trouver...?	oo pwee-zhuh ah-shuh-tay / troo-vay
I'd like / We'd like...	Je voudrais / Nous voudrions...	zhuh voo-dray / noo voo-dree-ohn
...a room.	...une chambre.	ewn shahn-bruh
...a ticket to ___.	...un billet pour ___.	uhn bee-yay poor ___
Is it possible?	C'est possible?	say poh-see-bluh
Where is...?	Où est...?	oo ay
...the train station	...la gare	lah gar
...the bus station	...la gare routière	lah gar root-yehr
...tourist information	...l'office du tourisme	loh-fees dew too-reez-muh
Where are the toilets?	Où sont les toilettes?	oo sohn lay twah-leht
men	hommes	ohm
women	dames	dahm
left / right	à gauche / à droite	ah gohsh / ah drwaht
straight	tout droit	too drwah
When does this open / close?	Ça ouvre / ferme à quelle heure?	sah oo-vruh / fehrm ah kehl ur
At what time?	À quelle heure?	ah kehl ur
Just a moment.	Un moment.	uhn moh-mahn
now / soon / later	maintenant / bientôt / plus tard	man-tuh-nahn / bee-an-toh / plew tar
today / tomorrow	aujourd'hui / demain	oh-zhoor-dwee / duh-man

APPENDIX

Tourist Information

Before your trip, scan the websites of national tourist offices for the countries you'll be visiting, or contact them to briefly describe your trip and request information. You can often download brochures. For websites, see the **Practicalities** section that precedes each port destination.

In Europe, a good first stop is generally the tourist information office (abbreviated **TI** in this book). TIs are in business to help you enjoy spending money in their town, but even so, I still make a point to swing by the local TI upon arrival in a new town.

Staying Connected

One of the most common questions I hear from travelers is, "How can I stay connected in Europe?" The short answer is: more easily and cheaply than you might think.

The simplest solution is to bring your own device—mobile phone, tablet, or laptop—and use it to get tourist information, reserve restaurants, confirm tour times, and phone home. For the

How to Dial

Here's how to make an international call. For the dialing instructions below, use the complete phone number, including the area code (if there is one).* I've used the telephone number of one of my recommended Copenhagen hotels as an example (tel. 33 13 19 13).

From a Mobile Phone

It's easy to dial with a mobile phone. Whether calling from the US to Europe, country to country within Europe, or from Europe to the US—it's all the same.

Press zero until you get a + sign, enter the country code (45 for Denmark), then dial the phone number.

▶ To call the Copenhagen hotel from any location, dial +45 33 13 19 13.

From a US Landline to Europe

Dial 011 (US/Canada access code), country code (45 for Denmark), and phone number.

▶ To call the Copenhagen hotel from home, dial 011 45 33 13 19 13.

From a European Landline to the US or Europe

Dial 00 (Europe access code), country code (1 for the US, 45 for Denmark), and phone number.

▶ To call my US office from Denmark, dial 00 1 425 771 8303.
▶ To call the Copenhagen hotel from Germany, dial 00 45 33 13 19 13.

For more phoning help, see www.howtocallabroad.com.

details on your options—both from a cruise ship and in port—see page 81.

For emergency telephone numbers and dialing advice, see the Practicalities sections earlier in this book. For more in-depth information on dialing, see www.ricksteves.com/phoning.

Transportation

While in port, you're likely to use public transportation to get around (and, in some cases, to get to) the cities you're here to see.

TAXIS AND UBER

Taxis are underrated, scenic time-savers that zip you effortlessly from the cruise terminal to any sight in town, or between sights. Especially for couples and small groups who value their time, a taxi ride can be a good investment. Unfortunately, many predatory taxi drivers exploit cruisers who are in town just for the day by charging them inflated fares for short rides. Prepare yourself by reading the "Taxi Tips" on page 116.

European Country Codes		Ireland & N. Ireland	353 / 44
Austria	43	Italy	39
Belgium	32	Latvia	371
Bosnia-Herzegovina	387	Montenegro	382
Croatia	385	Morocco	212
Czech Republic	420	Netherlands	31
Denmark	45	Norway	47
Estonia	372	Poland	48
Finland	358	Portugal	351
France	33	Russia	7
Germany	49	Slovakia	421
Gibraltar	350	Slovenia	386
Great Britain	44	Spain	34
Greece	30	Sweden	46
Hungary	36	Switzerland	41
Iceland	354	Turkey	90

*Drop an initial zero, if present, when dialing a European phone number—
except when calling Italy.

Uber is available in several cities covered in this book—including Berlin, Amsterdam, and Paris—and rides can be cheaper than taxis. Like at home, you request a car via the Uber app on your mobile device, and the fare automatically gets charged to your credit card. You'll need an Internet connection to request a car, so it's best to do it when you're on Wi-Fi (unless you have a data roaming plan).

CITY TRANSIT

Shrink and tame big cities by mastering their subway, bus, and tram systems. Europe's public-transit systems are so good that many Europeans go through life never learning to drive. With a map, anyone can decipher the code to cheap and easy urban transportation.

Subway Basics

Most of Europe's big cities are blessed with excellent subway systems, often linked effortlessly with suburban trains. Learning a city's network of underground trains is a key to efficient sightseeing. European subways go by many names, but "Metro" is the most common term. In Scandinavia, these systems often start with "T" (*T-bane* in Oslo and *T-bana* in Stockholm, for example). In some cities—such as Copenhagen and Berlin—the network also includes suburban trains, often marked with "S."

Plan your route. Figure out your route before you enter the station so you can march confidently to the correct train. Get a good subway map (often included on free city maps, or ask for one at the station) and consult it often. In the stations, maps are usually posted prominently. Individual lines are color-coded, numbered, and/or lettered; their end points are also indicated. These end points—while probably places you will never go—are important, since they tell you which direction the train is moving and appear (usually) as the name listed on the front of the train. Figure out the line you need, the end point of the direction you want to go, and (if necessary) where to transfer to another line.

Validate your ticket. You may need to insert your ticket into a slot in the turnstile (then retrieve it) in order to validate it. If you have an all-day or multiday ticket, you may only need to validate it the first time you use it, or not at all (ask when you buy it).

Get off at the right place. Once on the train, follow along with each stop on your map. Most cars have an electronic screen showing the next station. Sometimes the driver or an automated voice announces the upcoming stop—but don't count on this cue, as a foreign name spoken by a native speaker over a crackly loudspeaker can be difficult to understand. As you pull into each station, its name will be posted on the platform or along the wall.

Transfer. Changing from one subway line to another can be as easy as walking a few steps away to an adjacent platform—or a bewildering wander via a labyrinth of stairs and long passageways. Fortunately, most subway systems are clearly signed—just follow along (or ask a local for help).

Exit the station. When you arrive at your destination station, follow exit signs up toward street level, keeping an eye out for posted maps of the surrounding neighborhood to help you get your bearings. Bigger stations have multiple exits, signposted by street name or nearby landmarks. Choosing the right exit will help you avoid extra walking and having to cross busy streets.

Bus and Tram Basics

Getting around town on the city bus or tram system has some advantages over subways. Buses or trams are often a better bet for shorter distances. Some buses go where the subway can't. Since you're not underground, it's easier to stay oriented and get the lay of the land.

Plan your route. Tourist maps often indicate bus and tram lines and stops. If yours doesn't, ask for a specific bus map at the TI.

Many bus and tram stops have timetables and route maps posted, and some have electronic signs noting how many minutes until the next bus or tram arrives.

Validate your ticket. Tickets are checked on European buses and trams in a variety of ways. Usually you enter at the front of the bus or tram and show your ticket to the driver, or validate it by sticking it in a time-stamp box. In some cases, you buy your ticket directly from the driver; other times, you'll buy your ticket at a kiosk or machine near the stop. Observe and imitate locals.

TRAINS

If you venture beyond your port city, European trains generally go where you need them to go and are fast, frequent, and affordable. "Point-to-point" or buy-as-you-go tickets can be your best bet for short travel distances anywhere. (If you're doing a substantial amount of pre- or post-cruise travel on your own, a rail pass can be a good value.) You can buy train tickets either from home, or once you get to Europe. If your travel plans are set, and you don't want to risk a specific train journey selling out, it can be smart to get your tickets before your trip. For details on buying tickets on European websites and complete rail pass information, see www.ricksteves.com/rail. To study schedules before your trip, check www.bahn.com (Germany's excellent Europe-wide timetable).

If you want to be more flexible, you can buy tickets in Europe. Nearly every station has old-fashioned ticket windows staffed by human beings, usually marked by long lines. Bridge any communication gap by writing out your plan: destination city, date (European-style: day/month), time (if you want to reserve a specific train), number of people, and first or second class.

To get tickets faster, savvy travelers figure out how to use ticket machines: Choose English, follow the step-by-step instructions, and insert your credit card (though you may need to know your PIN, and some machines don't accept American cards—see page 122). Some machines accept cash. It's often possible to buy tickets on board the train, but expect to pay an additional fee for the convenience. Be sure to have enough cash in case the conductor can't use your American credit card.

Seat reservations guarantee you a place to sit on the train, and can be optional or required depending on the route and train. Reservations are required for any train marked with an "R" in the schedule. Note that seat reservations are already included with many tickets, especially for the fastest trains (such as France's TGV). But for many trains (local, regional, interregional, and many EuroCity and InterCity trains), reservations are not necessary and not worth the trouble and expense unless you're traveling during a busy holiday period.

Be aware that many cities have more than one train station. Ask for help and pay attention. Making your way through stations and onto trains is largely a matter of asking questions, letting people help you, and assuming things are logical. I always ask someone on the platform if the train is going where I think it is (point to the train or track and ask, *"Pah-ree?"*).

BUSES

In most countries, trains are faster, more comfortable, and have more extensive schedules than buses. Bus trips are usually less expensive than trains, but often take longer. Use buses mainly to pick up where Europe's great train system leaves off.

Resources

Begin Your Trip at RickSteves.com

My mobile-friendly **website** is *the* place to explore Europe in preparation for your trip. You'll find thousands of fun articles, videos, and radio interviews; a wealth of money-saving tips for planning your dream trip; travel news dispatches; a video library of my travel talks; my travel blog; my latest guidebook updates (www.ricksteves.com/update); and my free Rick Steves Audio Europe app. You can also follow me on Facebook and Twitter.

Our **Travel Forum** is a well-groomed collection of message boards, where our travel-savvy community answers questions and shares their personal travel experiences—and our well-traveled staff chimes in when they can be helpful (www.ricksteves.com/forums).

Our **online Travel Store** offers bags and accessories that I've designed to help you travel smarter and lighter. These include my popular carry-on bags (which I live out of four months a year), money belts, totes, toiletries kits, adapters, guidebooks, and planning maps (www.ricksteves.com/shop).

Our website can also help you find the perfect rail pass for your itinerary and your budget, with easy, one-stop shopping for rail passes, seat reservations, and point-to-point tickets (www.ricksteves.com/rail).

Rick Steves' Tours, Guidebooks, TV Shows, and More

Small Group Tours: Want to travel with greater efficiency and less stress? We offer more than 40 itineraries reaching the best destinations in this book...and beyond. Each year about 25,000 travelers join us on about 1,000 Rick Steves bus tours. You'll enjoy great guides and a fun bunch of travel partners (with small groups of 24 to 28 travelers). You'll find European adventures to fit every vacation length. For all the details, and to get our tour catalog, visit www.ricksteves.com/tours or call us at 425/608-4217.

Books: *Rick Steves Scandinavian & Northern Cruise Port*s is just one of many books in my series on European travel, which includes country and city guidebooks, Snapshots (excerpted chapters from bigger guides), Pocket guides (full-color little books on big cities), "Best Of" guidebooks (condensed, full-color country guides), and my budget-travel skills handbook, *Rick Steves Europe Through the Back Door*. A more complete list of my titles—including *Rick Steves Mediterranean Cruise Ports*, phrase books, and more—appears near the end of this book.

TV Shows and Travel Talks: My public television series, *Rick Steves' Europe*, covers Europe from top to bottom with over 100 half-hour episodes—and we're working on new shows every year (watch full episodes at my website for free). Look for new episodes about cruise travel, including one devoted to travel skills for cruisers. Or, to raise your travel I.Q., check out the video versions of our popular classes (covering most European countries as well as travel skills, packing smart, cruising, tech for travelers, European art, and travel as a political act—www.ricksteves.com/travel-talks).

Radio: My weekly public radio show, *Travel with Rick Steves,* features interviews with travel experts from around the world. It airs on 400 public radio stations across the US, or you can hear it as a podcast. A complete archive of programs is available at www.ricksteves.com/radio.

Audio Tours on My Free App: I've produced dozens of free, self-guided audio tours of the top sights in Europe. For those tours and other audio content, get my free Rick Steves Audio Europe app, an extensive online library organized by destination. For more on my app, see page 46.

MORE RESOURCES

If you're like most travelers, this book is all you need, though there's a staggering array of websites, guidebooks, and other useful resources for people interested in cruising. For a summary of good websites to peruse to help you choose your cruise, and for reviews of various cruise lines and ships, refer to page 16.

Beyond the guidebook format, look for the well-written history of the cruise industry, *Devils on the Deep Blue Sea* (by Kristoffer Garin). A variety of tell-all type books offer behind-the-scenes intrigue from a life working on cruise ships. More titillating than well-written, these are good vacation reads to enjoy poolside. They include *Cruise Confidential* (by Brian David Bruns) and *The Truth about Cruise Ships* (by Jay Herring).

Holidays

This list includes national holidays observed throughout Europe that might coincide with your day in port. While holidays can close sights and banks and bring crowds, they can also occasion festivals, parades, and merrymaking. Your best source for general information is the TI in each town—it's worth a quick look at their websites to turn up possible holiday closures and/or special events. You can also check my "Upcoming Holidays and Festivals" web pages at www.ricksteves.com.

Jan 1	New Year's Day
Jan 6	Epiphany
March/April	Easter weekend (Good Friday-Easter Monday): April 19-21, 2019; April 10-12, 2020
May 1	Labor Day
May	Ascension: May 30, 2019; May 21, 2020
May/June	Pentecost and Whitmonday: June 9-10, 2019; May 31-June 1, 2020
May/June	Corpus Christi: June 20, 2019; June 11, 2020
Aug 15	Assumption
Nov 1	All Saint's Day
Nov 11	Armistice Day/St. Martin's Day
Dec 25	Christmas Day
Dec 26	Boxing Day
Dec 31	New Year's Eve

Note that many of the above holidays are Catholic and Protestant dates; in Orthodox countries (such as Russia and certain communities in Estonia, Latvia, and Finland), the dates for these holidays can differ.

Conversions and Climate

NUMBERS AND STUMBLERS

- Europeans write a few of their numbers differently than we do. 1 =1, 4 =4, 7 =7.
- In Europe, dates appear as day/month/year, so Christmas 2020 is 25/12/20.
- Commas are decimal points and decimals are commas. A dollar and a half is $1,50, one thousand is 1.000, and there are 5.280 feet in a mile.
- When counting with fingers, start with your thumb. If you hold up your first finger to request one item, you'll probably get two.
- What Americans call the second floor of a building is the first floor in some parts of Europe (not in Scandinavia).
- On escalators and moving sidewalks, Europeans keep the left "lane" open for passing. Keep to the right.

METRIC CONVERSIONS

A **kilogram** equals 1,000 grams (about 2.2 pounds). One hundred **grams** (a common unit at markets) is about a quarter-pound. One **liter** is about a quart, or almost four to a gallon.

A **kilometer** is six-tenths of a mile. To convert kilometers to miles, cut the kilometers in half and add back 10 percent of the original (120 km: 60 + 12 = 72 miles). One **meter** is 39 inches—just over a yard.

1 foot = 0.3 meter	1 square yard = 0.8 square meter
1 yard = 0.9 meter	1 square mile = 2.6 square kilometers
1 mile = 1.6 kilometers	1 ounce = 28 grams
1 centimeter = 0.4 inch	1 quart = 0.95 liter
1 meter = 39.4 inches	1 kilogram = 2.2 pounds
1 kilometer = 0.62 mile	32°F = 0°C

IMPERIAL WEIGHTS AND MEASURES

Britain hasn't completely gone metric. Driving distances and speed limits are measured in miles. Beer is sold as pints (though milk can be measured in pints or liters), and a person's weight is measured in stone (a 168-pound person weighs 12 stone).

1 stone = 14 pounds
1 British pint = 1.2 US pints
1 imperial gallon = 1.2 US gallons or about 4.5 liters

CLOTHING SIZES

For US-to-European clothing size conversions, see page 125.

CLIMATE

First line, average daily high; second line, average daily low; third line, average days without rain. For more detailed weather statistics for European destinations (and the rest of the world), check www.wunderground.com.

	J	F	M	A	M	J	J	A	S	O	N	D

DENMARK
Copenhagen

J	F	M	A	M	J	J	A	S	O	N	D
37°	37°	42°	51°	60°	66°	70°	69°	64°	55°	46°	41°
29°	28°	31°	37°	45°	51°	56°	56°	51°	44°	38°	33°
14	15	19	18	20	18	17	16	14	14	11	12

SWEDEN
Stockholm

J	F	M	A	M	J	J	A	S	O	N	D
30°	30°	37°	47°	58°	67°	71°	68°	60°	49°	40°	35°
26°	25°	29°	37°	45°	53°	57°	56°	50°	43°	37°	32°
15	14	21	19	20	17	18	17	16	16	14	14

FINLAND
Helsinki

J	F	M	A	M	J	J	A	S	O	N	D
26°	25°	32°	44°	56°	66°	71°	68°	59°	47°	37°	31°
17°	15°	20°	30°	40°	49°	55°	53°	46°	37°	30°	23°
11	10	17	17	19	17	17	16	16	13	11	11

RUSSIA
St. Petersburg

J	F	M	A	M	J	J	A	S	O	N	D
29°	28°	37°	50°	60°	69°	74°	71°	60°	48°	35°	30°
18°	15°	22°	32°	40°	49°	55°	52°	44°	36°	26°	20°
10	11	15	15	16	13	15	15	14	09	10	11

ESTONIA
Tallinn

J	F	M	A	M	J	J	A	S	O	N	D
25°	25°	32°	45°	57°	66°	68°	66°	59°	50°	37°	30°
14°	12°	19°	32°	41°	50°	54°	52°	48°	39°	30°	19°
12	12	18	19	19	20	18	16	14	14	12	12

LATVIA
Rīga

J	F	M	A	M	J	J	A	S	O	N	D
33°	33°	40°	53°	62°	69°	74°	72°	62°	51°	39°	33°
26°	24°	28°	36°	44°	51°	56°	56°	47°	40°	32°	26°
12	12	15	16	17	15	16	15	15	12	11	12

	J	F	M	A	M	J	J	A	S	O	N	D

POLAND
Gdańsk

35°	36°	42°	52°	62°	67°	71°	71°	62°	53°	41°	35°
27°	27°	30°	35°	43°	49°	54°	54°	47°	41°	33°	28°
30	27	30	29	30	30	30	30	29	29	29	29

GERMANY
Berlin

35°	37°	46°	56°	66°	72°	75°	74°	68°	56°	45°	38°
26°	26°	31°	39°	47°	53°	57°	56°	50°	42°	36°	29°
14	13	19	17	19	17	17	17	18	17	14	16

NORWAY
Oslo

28°	30°	39°	50°	61°	68°	72°	70°	60°	48°	38°	32°
19°	19°	25°	34°	43°	50°	55°	53°	46°	38°	31°	25°
16	16	22	19	21	17	16	17	16	17	14	14

THE NETHERLANDS
Amsterdam

41°	42°	49°	55°	64°	70°	72°	71°	66°	56°	48°	41°
30°	31°	35°	40°	45°	52°	55°	55°	51°	43°	37°	33°
8	9	16	14	16	16	14	12	11	11	10	9

BELGIUM
Brussels

41°	44°	51°	58°	65°	71°	73°	72°	69°	60°	48°	42°
30°	32°	34°	40°	45°	53°	55°	55°	52°	45°	38°	32°
9	11	14	12	15	15	13	12	15	13	10	11

GREAT BRITAIN
London

43°	44°	50°	56°	62°	69°	71°	71°	65°	58°	50°	45°
36°	36°	38°	42°	47°	53°	56°	56°	52°	46°	42°	38°
16	15	20	18	19	19	19	20	17	18	15	16

FRANCE
Paris

43°	45°	54°	60°	68°	73°	76°	75°	70°	60°	50°	44°
34°	34°	39°	43°	49°	55°	58°	58°	53°	46°	40°	36°
14	14	19	17	19	18	19	18	17	18	15	15

Fahrenheit and Celsius Conversion

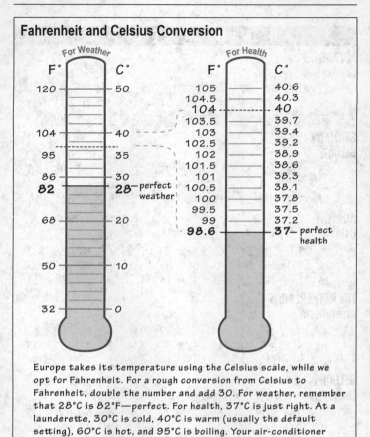

Europe takes its temperature using the Celsius scale, while we opt for Fahrenheit. For a rough conversion from Celsius to Fahrenheit, double the number and add 30. For weather, remember that 28°C is 82°F—perfect. For health, 37°C is just right. At a launderette, 30°C is cold, 40°C is warm (usually the default setting), 60°C is hot, and 95°C is boiling. Your air-conditioner should be set at about 20°C.

INDEX

INDEX

INDEX

INDEX

MAP INDEX

Explore Europe

At ricksteves.com you can browse through thousands of articles, videos, photos and radio interviews, plus find a wealth of money-saving travel tips for planning your dream trip. And with our mobile-friendly website, you can easily access all this great travel information anywhere you go.

TV Shows

Preview the places you'll visit by watching entire half-hour episodes of Rick Steves' Europe (choose from all 100 shows) on-demand, for free.

ricksteves.com

your travel dreams into affordable reality

Radio Interviews

Enjoy ready access to Rick's vast library of radio interviews covering travel

tips and cultural insights that relate specifically to your Europe travel plans.

Travel Forums

Learn, ask, share! Our online community of savvy travelers is a great resource for first-time travelers to Europe, as well as seasoned pros. You'll find forums on each country, plus travel tips and restaurant/hotel reviews. You can even ask one of our well-traveled staff to chime in with an opinion.

Travel News

Subscribe to our free Travel News e-newsletter, and get monthly updates from Rick on what's happening in Europe.

Audio Europe™

Rick's Free Travel App

Get your FREE **Rick Steves Audio Europe**™ app to enjoy...

- Dozens of self-guided tours of Europe's top museums, sights and historic walks
- Hundreds of tracks filled with cultural insights and sightseeing tips from Rick's radio interviews
- All organized into handy geographic playlists
- For Apple and Android

With Rick whispering in your ear, Europe gets even better.

Find out more at ricksteves.com

Pack Light and Right

Gear up for your next adventure at ricksteves.com

Light Luggage

Pack light and right with Rick Steves' affordable, custom-designed rolling carry-on bags, backpacks, day packs and shoulder bags.

Accessories

From packing cubes to moneybelts and beyond, Rick has personally selected the travel goodies that will help your trip go smoother.

Experience maximum Europe

Save time and energy

This guidebook is your independent-travel toolkit. But for all it delivers, it's still up to you to devote the time and energy it takes to manage the preparation and logistics that are essential for a happy trip. If that's a hassle, there's a solution.

Rick Steves Tours

A Rick Steves tour takes you to Europe's most interesting places with great

great tours, too!

with minimum stress

guides and small groups of 28 or less. We follow Rick's favorite itineraries, ride in comfy buses, stay in family-run hotels, and bring you intimately close to the Europe you've traveled so far to see. Most importantly, we take away the logistical headaches so you can focus on the fun.

travelers—nearly half of them repeat customers—along with us on four dozen different itineraries, from Ireland to Italy to Athens. Is a Rick Steves tour the

right fit for your travel dreams? Find out at ricksteves.com, where you can also request Rick's latest tour catalog. Europe is best

Join the fun

This year we'll take thousands of free-spirited

experienced with happy travel partners. We hope you can join us.

See our itineraries at ricksteves.com

A Guide for Every Trip

BEST OF GUIDES

Full color easy-to-scan format, focusing on Europe's most popular destinations and sights.

Best of England
Best of Europe
Best of France
Best of Germany
Best of Ireland
Best of Italy
Best of Spain

COMPREHENSIVE GUIDES

City, country, and regional guides with detailed coverage for a multi-week trip exploring the most iconic sights and venturing off the beaten track.

Amsterdam & the Netherlands
Barcelona
Belgium: Bruges, Brussels, Antwerp & Ghent
Berlin
Budapest
Croatia & Slovenia
Eastern Europe
England
Florence & Tuscany
France
Germany
Great Britain
Greece: Athens & the Peloponnese
Iceland
Ireland
Istanbul
Italy
London
Paris
Portugal
Prague & the Czech Republic
Provence & the French Riviera
Rome
Scandinavia
Scotland
Spain
Switzerland
Venice
Vienna, Salzburg & Tirol

THE BEST OF ROME

Rome, Italy's capital, is studded with Roman remnants and floodlit-fountain squares. From the Vatican to the Colosseum, with crazy traffic in between, Rome wonderful, huge, and exhausting. The owds, the heat, and the weighty history

of the Eternal City where Caesars walked can make tourists wilt. Recharge by taking siestas, gelato breaks, and after-dark walks, strolling from one atmospheric square to another in the refreshing evening air.

nired **Pantheon**—which argest dome until the nearly 2,000 years old a day over 1,500).

ool of Athens in the Vat-
me another; entertaining
nbodies the humanistic
sance.

m, gladiators fought
ne another; entertaining
00.

this Rome **ristorante.**

uards at **St. Peter's**
ork seriously.

tain, toss in a coin

Rick Steves guidebooks are published by Avalon Travel, an imprint of Perseus Books, a Hachette Book Group company.

POCKET GUIDES

Compact, full color city guides with the essentials for shorter trips

Amsterdam
Athens
Barcelona
Florence
Italy's Cinque Terre
London
Munich & Salzburg

Paris
Prague
Rome
Venice
Vienna

SNAPSHOT GUIDES

Focused single-destination coverage.

Basque Country: Spain & France
Copenhagen & the Best of Denmark
Dublin
Dubrovnik
Edinburgh
Hill Towns of Central Italy
Krakow, Warsaw & Gdansk
Lisbon
Loire Valley
Madrid & Toledo
Milan & the Italian Lakes District
Naples & the Amalfi Coast
Normandy
Northern Ireland
Norway
Reykjavík
Sevilla, Granada & Southern Spain
St. Petersburg, Helsinki & Tallinn
Stockholm

CRUISE PORTS GUIDES

Reference for cruise ports of call.

Mediterranean Cruise Ports
Scandinavian & Northern European
Cruise Ports

Complete your library with...

TRAVEL SKILLS & CULTURE

Study up on travel skills and gain insight on history and culture.

Europe 101
Europe Through the Back Door
European Christmas
European Easter
European Festivals
Postcards from Europe
Travel as a Political Act

PHRASE BOOKS & DICTIONARIES

French
French, Italian & German
German
Italian
Portuguese
Spanish

PLANNING MAPS

Britain, Ireland & London
Europe
France & Paris
Germany, Austria & Switzerland
Ireland
Italy
Spain & Portugal

Rick Steves books are available from your favorite bookseller.
Many guides are available as ebooks.

Credits

RESEARCHERS
To help update this book, Rick relied on...

Glenn Eriksen
A solo backpacking trip across Europe and Scandinavia back in the '70s turned out to be Glenn's first step on the road to Rick Steves' Europe. Today, as a guidebook editor and researcher, he indulges his love for the Old Country while helping Rick's readers "keep on travelin'." When not on the road, Glenn lives in Seattle with his wife, Kathy, and enjoys hiking, photography, and keeping in touch with his Norwegian roots.

Pål Bjarne Johansen
A tour guide and guidebook researcher for Rick Steves' Europe covering Scandinavia and Spain, Pål grew up in the Norwegian countryside near the Swedish border and has family ties in Denmark. He discovered his passion for travel and adventure at a young age, and has backpacked much of the world since graduating high school. When Pål's not working for Rick Steves, you'll find him skiing the Norwegian woods in the winter, and sailing the seven seas in the summer.

Suzanne Kotz
Suzanne, an editor with Rick Steves' Europe, began her travel career riding in a station wagon with her six siblings from Michigan to Florida for spring break. Since then, she's broadened her destinations to include much of Europe and parts of Asia. A librarian by training and a longtime editor of art publications, she's happiest with a good book in her hands. She lives in Seattle with her husband and son.

Steve Smith

Steve Smith has lived in France on several occasions starting when he was very young. He restored a farmhouse on the Burgundy canal, and he still hangs his beret there in research season. Steve has managed guides for Rick Steves' Europe's tour programs and researched guidebooks with Rick for more than two decades. He now focuses his time on guidebooks and exploring every corner of his favorite country. Karen Lewis Smith—an expert on French cuisine and wine—provides invaluable contributions to his books.

Robyn Stencil

Robyn credits the origin of her love affair with London to the Thames, supporting her motto "where there's a river, there's a run." Her ideal English adventure involves the call of gulls, plenty of flat whites, and friendly people from rocky coastline to green hills. When she's not researching, trapezing, or pursuing the perfect burger, Robyn calls Everett, Washington home and works as a tour product manager for Rick Steves' Europe.

CONTRIBUTOR

Gene Openshaw

Gene is the co-author of a dozen Rick Steves books. For this book, he wrote material on Europe's art, history, and contemporary culture. When not traveling, Gene enjoys composing music, recovering from his 1973 trip to Europe with Rick, and living everyday life with his daughter.

ACKNOWLEDGMENTS

This book would not have been possible without the help of our cruising friends. Special thanks to Todd and Carla Hoover, cruisers extraordinaire, and to Sheri Smith at Elizabeth Holmes Travel (www. elizabethholmes.com). Applause for Vanessa Bloy at Windstar Cruises, Paul Allen and John Primeau at Holland America Line, Courtney Recht at Norwegian Cruise Line, and Melissa Rubin at Oceania Cruises. And high fives for Ben Curtis, Sheryl Harris, Paul and Bev Hoerlein, Lauren Mills, Jenn Schutte, Lisa Friend, and Noelle Kenney.